Official WNBA
Guide and Register
2004 Edition

Editors

John Maxwell

Jay Moore

Jeanne Tang

John Gardella

Sporting News Contributors:
Kathy Sheldon, Chad Painter, Keith Camden, Darin Kelkhoff, Frank Gallion

Copyright ©2004 WNBA Enterprises, LLC. All rights reserved.
Published by the Sporting News, a division of Vulcan Sports Media, 10176 Corporate Square Drive, Suite 200, St. Louis, MO 63132. Printed in the USA.

ISBN: 0-89204-736-4

10 9 8 7 6 5 4 3 2 1

CONTENTS

2004 SEASON

Team Information

REVIEW

RECORDS

OFFICIAL WNBA RULES

WNBA PLAYER PROFILES

WNBA DIRECTORY
LEAGUE OFFICE

NEW YORK OFFICE
Women's National Basketball Association
Olympic Tower, 645 Fifth Avenue
New York, NY 10022
Main Number: 212-688-WNBA (9622)
Main Fax Number: 212-750-WNBA (9622)
www.wnba.com

NEW JERSEY OFFICE
WNBA Enterprises, LLC
450 Harmon Meadow Boulevard
Secaucus, NJ 07094
Main Number: 201-865-7700
Fax Number: 201-974-1143

President ....Valerie B. Ackerman
Chief Operating Officer ....Ann Sarnoff
Vice President, Player Personnel ....Reneé Brown
Vice President, Programming and Marketing ....Teri Schindler
Vice President, Marketing Partnerships ....Mary Reiling Spencer
General Counsel ....Jamin S. Dershowitz
Senior Director, Business Operations ....Tatia Mays-Russell
Senior Director, WNBA Communications.....................................Sharon Robustelli
Senior Director, Editorial ....Jeanne Tang
Director, Basketball Operations ....Tracy Ellis-Ward
Director, Basketball Communications...John Maxwell
Senior Manager, Business Operations ....Maureen Brown
Senior Manager, Security ....Kelley Hardwick
Senior Manager, Player Personnel ....Angela Taylor
Senior Manager, Broadcasting and Programming...................................Robin Zisson
Manager, Community Relations ....Jason Guy
Manager, Public Relations ....Dina Pappas
Editor, WNBA.com...Matthew Wurst
Coordinator, Basketball Operations ....Thomas Tedesco
Coordinator, Player Programs ....Monique Thompson
Administrative Assistant to the President ....Joan Ferris
Senior Assistant ....Sylvia Harris
Assistant, Communications ....Jay Moore
Staff Assistant, Player Personnel ....Rose Davis
Staff Assistant, Business Operations ....Denise Doucet
Associate, Basketball Operations ....Antonio Williams
Associate, Communications..Nicole Dye-Anderson
Supervisor of Officials ....Patty Broderick
Director of Referee Development..Dee Kantner
Special Advisor ....Rebecca Lobo
Team Business Development .... Paula Hanson, Jerry Murphy

6

Val Ackerman — President

Val Ackerman was named President of the Women's National Basketball Association in August 1996. A former collegiate basketball standout, she spent eight years as an executive at the NBA prior to her appointment to the WNBA.

A native of Pennington, N.J., Ackerman was absorbed in all things basketball from a very early age and developed a passion for the game from her family—her father and grandfather played and coached several sports and were high school athletic directors—and from watching her heroes on TV. She played small forward and was a four-year starter for the women's basketball team at the University of Virginia, where she was named a two-time CoSIDA Academic All-American. After racking up more than 1,300 points in college, Ackerman played one season of professional basketball in France before entering UCLA Law School.

She served as NBA Staff Attorney, Special Assistant to Commissioner David Stern, Director of Business Affairs and Vice President of Business Affairs before being named to head the WNBA.

At the NBA, Ackerman managed the NBA's relationships with a variety of basketball organizations, including USA Basketball, the Continental Basketball Association, the Basketball Hall of Fame and FIBA (the International Basketball Federation). She supported various women's basketball initiatives and the effort to create a women's league in the NBA for years and spearheaded many committees on that behalf.

As a member of the Board of Directors of USA Basketball, Ackerman was a driving force behind the creation of the 1995-96 USA Basketball Women's National Team, which compiled a 60-0 record during a year-long tour against college and international opponents that culminated with the gold medal at the 1996 Summer Olympics in Atlanta. She currently serves on the board of USA Basketball, the Executive Committee of the Naismith Memorial Basketball Hall of Fame, the National Board of Trustees for the March of Dimes and the National Board of Directors for Girls Incorporated.

Ackerman resides in New York City with her husband, Charlie Rappaport, and their daughters, Emily and Sally.

Ann Sarnoff — Chief Operating Officer

As Chief Operating Officer, Ann Sarnoff oversees the business functions of the league, including its advertising, broadcasting, marketing, merchandising, player programs and communications activities.

Sarnoff joined the WNBA in February 2004 from Viacom, where she served as Chief Operating Officer for both VH1 and Country Music Television. Her responsibilities there included strategic planning and business development for both channels, together with oversight of the digital television networks, program enterprises businesses and the research, legal, financial and human resource functions.

Prior to her role at VH1 and CMT, Sarnoff served as Executive Vice President of Consumer Products and Business Development for Nickelodeon, where she launched Rugrats and Blues Clues products into the market and built Nickelodeon's merchandising division into a sizable business. She began her career at Nickelodeon in 1994 as Vice President of Business Development and was later responsible for developing the business plans of TV Land and Noggin, Nick's successful spinoff channels. Before joining Viacom, Sarnoff was a strategic consultant for Marakon Associates, where she assisted Fortune 50 companies in developing strategies and improving their operations.

Sarnoff graduated cum laude from Georgetown University with a B.S. in marketing and received an M.B.A. from the Harvard Business School. She is a member of the Board of the Georgetown University McDonough School of Business and lives in New York City with her husband, Richard, and their two children.

Reneé Brown   Vice President, Player Personnel

Reneé Brown, WNBA Vice President of Player Personnel, oversees all player scouting and acquisition for the league as well as the administration of player-related policies and programs. Brown joined the WNBA in September 1996 as Director of Player Personnel and was promoted to Senior Director in October 1999. She was named Vice President in March 2000.

During the 1995-96 season, Brown served as an assistant coach to Tara VanDerveer for the gold medal-winning USA Basketball Women's National Team in Colorado Springs, Colo., where she helped with game preparation, player conditioning and scouting. She currently serves on the Executive Committee for USA Basketball as the Vice President for the Senior Women's Programs for 2000-2004.

Brown, a 1978 graduate of the University of Nevada-Las Vegas, also was an assistant coach for the women's basketball teams at the University of Kansas, Stanford University and San Jose State University. During her tenure at Kansas, she helped guide the Jayhawks to an 88-31 record, four trips to the NCAA tournament and a Big Eight Conference title. Her Stanford team won the NCAA tournament in 1990 and earned a trip to the Final Four in 1991.

Teri Schindler   Vice President, Programming & Marketing

As Vice President, Programming and Marketing, NBA Entertainment, Teri Schindler oversees WNBA broadcasting, production, programming as well as the marketing activities for the league.

Schindler joined NBA Entertainment in April 1997 as Director, Broadcasting and was promoted to her current position in January 2004. She has previously worked as a producer at NBC, CBS, ESPN and HBO Sports and served as Executive Producer of Connecticut Women's basketball for Connecticut Public Television. A graduate of the University of Notre Dame, Schindler made All-America honors on the swim team and was awarded the Rotary Scholarship to study film in France after graduating in 1983.

Mary Reiling Spencer Vice President, Marketing Partnerships

Mary Reiling Spencer was named Vice President, Marketing Partnerships for NBA Entertainment in March 2000. Spencer was formerly Vice President and Managing Director, NBA Asia Pacific, based in Hong Kong. In her current position, Spencer is responsible for overseeing all of the Marketing Partnership programs as well as New Business Development for the WNBA.

In Asia, Spencer was responsible for directing the activities for all NBA business including Sponsorship and Promotions, Television, Consumer Products, Events and Basketball Programs and Public Relations throughout the Asia Pacific Region. Prior to working in Hong Kong, she served as the Managing Director of NBA Australia, where she held similar responsibilities. Spencer started with the NBA in January 1994 as Director and Group Manager in the Marketing and Media Group in New York, where she was responsible for managing corporate sponsorship relationships for several multi-national companies.

Prior to joining the NBA, Spencer served as the National Director of Sponsorship and Promotions at AT&T and was responsible for directing the selection and negotiation of sponsorship properties, development of advertising, promotion and public relations programs and strategic planning. Spencer, 45, graduated from Southeast Missouri State University.

Jamin Dershowitz — General Counsel

As the WNBA's General Counsel, Jamin Dershowitz is responsible for overseeing the legal affairs of the league and for administering the salary cap. He has been with the WNBA since its inception and has been a member of the NBA Legal Department since 1993.

A graduate of Yale Law School in 1988, Dershowitz began his legal career as a law clerk for Judge Joseph Tauro of the United States District Court for the District of Massachusetts. He then worked for the New York Legal Aid Society, representing indigent people accused of crimes. At the NBA, Dershowitz has worked on a variety of legal matters, including salary cap administration, collective bargaining, Internet and new technologies and the NBA's relationship with USA Basketball.

Tatia R. Mays-Russell — Senior Dir., Business Operations

As Senior Director, Collective Bargaining Agreement, for the WNBA, Tatia Mays-Russell leads the WNBA's league and team financial and operational processes, ensures financial compliance with the Collective Bargaining Agreement and oversees administrative and planning functions.

Mays-Russell came to the NBA in 1998 as Director, Financial Planning & Analysis. She was responsible for supporting the NBA's financial reporting, business planning and budgeting processes, as well as providing financial planning and analysis support to the WNBA.
Prior to joining the NBA, Mays-Russell worked as a Financial Analyst for Pfizer, a pharmaceutical company. While there, she focused on evaluating the company's financial and operational performance, as well as analyzing the impact of acquisitions/dispositions on operations.

Mays-Russell also has experience working as a Senior Consultant for The Deloitte & Touche Management Consulting Group, a general management consulting firm.

Mays-Russell graduated from Cornell University in 1988 with a B.S. in materials science engineering and received an MBA from The Wharton School in 1993.

Sharon Robustelli — Senior Dir., WNBA Communications

As Senior Director, WNBA Communications, Sharon Robustelli is responsible for all sports, marketing, corporate and non-sports communications strategies and programs at large for the league. She was named to the position in April 2004.

Prior to joining the WNBA, Robustelli spent five years as Vice President at Marina Maher Communications (MMC), a New York City-based public relations agency that specializes in marketing to women. While at MMC Robustelli developed and led consumer programs for companies including Procter and Gamble, Johnson and Johnson and BBC Worldwide.

Previously, she held supervisory roles at GCI Group, Inc. and Ruder-Finn where she managed communications plans for clients including the New York State Lottery, JP Morgan Chase Inc. and Aetna.

In addition to her consumer marketing work, Robustelli spent seven years in entertainment public relations and counts such high-profile personalities and events as Mick Fleetwood, Eartha Kitt, The Grammy Awards and the MTV Music Video Awards among her former clients. Robustelli is an accomplished writer who has written speeches for prominent public figures including Vice President Al Gore and is also a published poet and poetry "slam" champion.

Robustelli graduated with a B.A. in Communications from Mansfield University of Pennsylvania.

Tracy Ellis-Ward   Director of Basketball Operations

As WNBA Director of Basketball Operations, Tracy Ellis-Ward oversees scheduling, game conduct, playing rules, draft camps and medical policies for the league. She joined the WNBA in January 2000 as Manager of Basketball Operations and was promoted to her current post in November 2002.

Prior to the WNBA, Ellis-Ward served as an assistant athletics director at Michigan State University, where she oversaw event management for 20 sports, summer sports camps, the departmental internship program, NCAA and Big Ten championships and diversity training, in addition to serving as the sport administrator for swimming & diving, track & field, tennis, women's crew and women's field hockey. Ellis-Ward previously worked as an admissions representative in the Office of High School and Transfer Relations at the University of Missouri-Columbia.

Ellis-Ward graduated from the University of Missouri-Columbia in 1989, where she served as captain of the women's basketball team and earned All-Big Eight and District V All-America honors. She received an advanced degree in sports administration from Ohio University in 1992, where she served as a graduate assistant coach for women's basketball and interned in the area of compliance and marketing. She also spent a year as an intern at the NCAA as one of six individuals selected annually for career development and was the recipient of an NCAA postgraduate scholarship.

Ellis-Ward currently resides in Tarrytown, N.Y., with her husband, Michael, and their two children, Gabrielle and Langston.

John Maxwell   Director, Basketball Communications

As Director of WNBA Basketball Communications, John Maxwell oversees the WNBA's sports public relations efforts, serving as the primary league contact for all sports and general media, as well as the WNBA team public relations departments. Prior to joining the league office, Maxwell spent five seasons with the Charlotte Sting. He was named Director of Public Relations prior to the 1999 season after serving for one year as the team's media relations assistant. With the Sting, Maxwell was responsible for publicizing all of the team's on- and off-court exploits, facilitating local and national media and maintaining the team's online presence.

Before joining the Sting, Maxwell worked at the Salisbury (N.C.) Post after owning and operating his own graphic design company, Shoreline Graphic Design, from 1995-97. Prior to that, Maxwell served as the assistant sports information director and director of athletics publications at Davidson College. He joined the Sports Information Department as an intern in 1990 after graduating from Davidson with a degree in history.

Patty Broderick — Supervisor of Officials

As WNBA Director of Officials, Patty Broderick is responsible for recruiting, training and supervising officials and assisting in rules development for the league. A 30-year basketball officiating veteran, Broderick served as an official in the WNBA for six years, beginning with the league's inaugural season in 1997.

Broderick has been a collegiate officiating supervisor since 1986 and currently serves as the supervisor for the Women's Basketball Officiating Consortium (WBOC), a partnership of five conferences, including the Big Ten, Conference USA, the Horizon League, the Mid-Continent Conference and the Great Lakes Valley Conference.

The inaugural winner of the Naismith Female Basketball Official of the Year Award in 1988, Broderick has reached many milestones throughout her career. She became the first woman to officiate women's basketball at the Pan American Games in 1987, served as one of two U.S. basketball officials at the 1988 Seoul Olympics and worked as an NCAA Women's Basketball Tournament official from 1986-1992, including five Women's Final Four appearances.

Broderick attended Indiana University-Purdue University at Indianapolis. She currently resides in Indianapolis. Her daughter, Jamie, 27, graduated from Denver University, where she was a member of the women's basketball team.

Dee Kantner — Director of Referee Development

As Director of Referee Development for the WNBA, Dee Kantner assists in the recruitment and training of WNBA referees. She served as the league's WNBA Supervisor of Officials in 1997 and 1998.

Kanter continues to officiate a full schedule of women's collegiate games and previously served as an NBA referee for five seasons. She has officiated six women's NCAA Final Fours, including four national championships, and was named the Naismith Award winner as the 1997 Official of the Year as well as the 1996 Atlantic Coast Conference Women's Official of the Year. Kantner has extensive FIBA officiating experience, including the 1995 and 1998 Women's World Championship and the 2000 Olympics, and spent two seasons as a referee in the CBA.

Kantner graduated from the University of Pittsburgh, where she was a four-year member of the women's field hockey team and participated in one season of basketball and track. She resides in Charlotte, N.C.

2004 WNBA SCHEDULE

Date	Road Team	at	Home Team	Eastern Time
Thursday, May 20	San Antonio	at	Houston	8:30
Thursday, May 20	Sacramento	at	Phoenix	10:00
Thursday, May 20	Minnesota	at	Seattle	10:00
Friday, May 21	Houston	at	Charlotte	7:00
Friday, May 21	New York	at	Indiana	8:00
Saturday, May 22	Phoenix	at	Connecticut	4:00
Saturday, May 22	Charlotte	at	Washington	6:00
Saturday, May 22	Detroit	at	San Antonio	8:00
Saturday, May 22	Minnesota	at	Sacramento	10:00
Saturday, May 22	Los Angeles	at	Seattle	10:00
Sunday, May 23	Houston	at	New York	4:00
Sunday, May 23	Washington	at	Indiana	8:00
Tuesday, May 25	Houston	at	Connecticut	7:00
Tuesday, May 25	Los Angeles	at	Washington	7:00
Wednesday, May 26	Detroit	at	New York	7:30
Wednesday, May 26	Minnesota	at	San Antonio	8:00
Thursday, May 27	Los Angeles	at	Connecticut	7:00
Friday, May 28	Indiana	at	Charlotte	7:00
Friday, May 28	Washington	at	Minnesota	8:00
Friday, May 28	Sacramento	at	San Antonio	8:00
Friday, May 28	Seattle	at	Phoenix	10:00
Saturday, May 29	Los Angeles	at	Detroit	4:00
Sunday, May 30	Sacramento	at	Houston	4:00
Sunday, May 30	New York	at	Minnesota	6:00
Tuesday, June 1	New York	at	Charlotte	7:00
Tuesday, June 1	Indiana	at	San Antonio	8:00
Tuesday, June 1	Houston	at	Phoenix	10:00
Tuesday, June 1	Seattle	at	Los Angeles	10:30
Wednesday, June 2	Washington	at	Detroit	11:30
Thursday, June 3	Charlotte	at	Connecticut	7:00
Thursday, June 3	San Antonio	at	Minnesota	8:00
Thursday, June 3	New York	at	Houston	8:30
Thursday, June 3	Los Angeles	at	Sacramento	10:00
Thursday, June 3	Phoenix	at	Seattle	10:30
Friday, June 4	Connecticut	at	Washington	7:00
Saturday, June 5	Los Angeles	at	Houston	4:00
Saturday, June 5	Charlotte	at	Indiana	8:00
Saturday, June 5	Phoenix	at	Minnesota	8:00
Saturday, June 5	New York	at	San Antonio	8:00
Saturday, June 5	Seattle	at	Sacramento	10:00
Sunday, June 6	Detroit	at	Connecticut	4:00
Wednesday, June 9	Connecticut	at	Phoenix	3:00
Wednesday, June 9	Detroit	at	Indiana	8:00
Wednesday, June 9	San Antonio	at	Houston	8:30
Wednesday, June 9	Charlotte	at	Los Angeles	10:30
Friday, June 11	Detroit	at	Washington	7:00
Friday, June 11	Indiana	at	New York	7:30
Friday, June 11	Charlotte	at	Phoenix	10:00
Friday, June 11	Connecticut	at	Seattle	10:00
Friday, June 11	Minnesota	at	Los Angeles	10:30
Saturday, June 12	Indiana	at	Detroit	7:30
Saturday, June 12	Houston	at	San Antonio	8:00
Saturday, June 12	Connecticut	at	Sacramento	10:00
Sunday, June 13	New York	at	Washington^	2:00
Monday, June 14	Connecticut	at	Los Angeles	10:30

Tuesday, June 15	San Antonio	at	Charlotte	7:00
Tuesday, June 15	Seattle	at	New York	7:30
Wednesday, June 16	Sacramento	at	Indiana	8:00
Thursday, June 17	San Antonio	at	Washington	8:00
Thursday, June 17	Sacramento	at	Minnesota	8:00
Friday, June 18	Charlotte	at	Connecticut	7:00
Friday, June 18	Seattle	at	Houston	8:30
Friday, June 18	Los Angeles	at	Phoenix	10:00
Saturday, June 19	Detroit	at	Sacramento	4:00
Saturday, June 19	New York	at	Indiana	8:00
Saturday, June 19	Houston	at	Minnesota	8:00
Saturday, June 19	Seattle	at	San Antonio	8:00
Sunday, June 20	Washington	at	Connecticut	4:00
Sunday, June 20	Los Angeles	at	Charlotte	4:00
Tuesday, June 22	Los Angeles	at	New York	7:30
Tuesday, June 22	Washington	at	Detroit	7:30
Tuesday, June 22	Connecticut	at	Indiana	8:00
Tuesday, June 22	Minnesota	at	Phoenix	10:00
Tuesday, June 22	Houston	at	Seattle	10:00
Wednesday, June 23	Detroit	at	Charlotte	7:00
Thursday, June 24	Minnesota	at	San Antonio	8:00
Thursday, June 24	New York	at	Phoenix	10:00
Friday, June 25	Detroit	at	Connecticut	7:00
Friday, June 25	Los Angeles	at	Indiana	8:00
Friday, June 25	Houston	at	Sacramento	10:00
Saturday, June 26	Indiana	at	Charlotte	6:00
Saturday, June 26	San Antonio	at	Phoenix	10:00
Saturday, June 26	New York	at	Seattle *	10:00
Sunday, June 27	Washington	at	Houston	4:00
Sunday, June 27	Connecticut	at	Detroit	6:00
Sunday, June 27	Los Angeles	at	Minnesota	6:00
Sunday, June 27	Phoenix	at	Sacramento	10:00
Tuesday, June 29	Indiana	at	Detroit	7:30
Tuesday, June 29	Phoenix	at	San Antonio	8:00
Tuesday, June 29	New York	at	Los Angeles	10:30
Wednesday, June 30	Washington	at	Connecticut	7:00
Wednesday, June 30	Houston	at	Minnesota	8:00
Thursday, July 1	Phoenix	at	Charlotte	7:00
Thursday, July 1	Indiana	at	Washington	8:00
Thursday, July 1	New York	at	Sacramento	10:00
Thursday, July 1	San Antonio	at	Seattle	10:00
Friday, July 2	San Antonio	at	Los Angeles	10:30
Saturday, July 3	Phoenix	at	Indiana	8:00
Saturday, July 3	Detroit	at	Minnesota	8:00
Saturday, July 3	Charlotte	at	Houston	8:30
Saturday, July 3	Sacramento	at	Seattle	10:00
Tuesday, July 6	Indiana	at	Connecticut	7:00
Tuesday, July 6	Sacramento	at	New York	7:30
Tuesday, July 6	Houston	at	Detroit	7:30
Wednesday, July 7	Seattle	at	Washington	7:00
Wednesday, July 7	Phoenix	at	Los Angeles	10:30
Thursday, July 8	Seattle	at	Charlotte	7:00
Thursday, July 8	Washington	at	New York	8:00
Thursday, July 8	Minnesota	at	Indiana	8:00
Friday, July 9	Sacramento	at	Connecticut	7:00
Friday, July 9	Phoenix	at	Minnesota	8:00
Friday, July 9	Los Angeles	at	San Antonio	8:00
Saturday, July 10	Seattle	at	Detroit	4:00

Saturday, July 10	Washington	at	Charlotte	6:00
Saturday, July 10	Los Angeles	at	Houston	9:00
Sunday, July 11	Phoenix	at	New York	4:00
Sunday, July 11	Sacramento	at	Minnesota	7:00
Sunday, July 11	Connecticut	at	Indiana	6:00
Monday, July 12	Sacramento	at	Detroit	7:30
Monday, July 12	San Antonio	at	Seattle	10:00
Wednesday, July 14	Houston	at	Indiana	2:00
Wednesday, July 14	Connecticut	at	Minnesota	1:00
Thursday, July 15	Charlotte	at	Washington	11:30 AM
Thursday, July 15	Seattle	at	Sacramento	2:30
Thursday, July 15	Minnesota	at	New York	7:30
Thursday, July 15	Detroit	at	Houston	8:00
Thursday, July 15	Connecticut	at	San Antonio	8:00
Friday, July 16	Detroit	at	Indiana	8:00
Saturday, July 17	Connecticut	at	Houston	8:30
Saturday, July 17	Washington	at	Seattle	10:00
Saturday, July 17	Sacramento	at	Los Angeles	10:30
Sunday, July 18	San Antonio	at	Detroit	12:00
Sunday, July 18	Charlotte	at	New York	4:00
Sunday, July 18	Minnesota	at	Phoenix	9:00
Sunday, July 18	Washington	at	Sacramento	10:00
Monday, July 19	Indiana	at	Los Angeles	10:30
Tuesday, July 20	New York	at	Charlotte	12:00
Wednesday, July 21	Connecticut	at	Detroit	11:30 AM
Wednesday, July 21	San Antonio	at	Phoenix	3:00
Wednesday, July 21	Washington	at	Los Angeles	3:30
Thursday, July 22	Indiana	at	Seattle	3:00
Thursday, July 22	Minnesota	at	Connecticut	8:00
Thursday, July 22	Phoenix	at	Sacramento	10:00
Friday, July 23	Minnesota	at	Washington	7:00
Friday, July 23	Charlotte	at	Detroit	7:30
Friday, July 23	Houston	at	Los Angeles	10:30
Saturday, July 24	San Antonio	at	Connecticut	12:00
Saturday, July 24	Washington	at	Charlotte	6:00
Saturday, July 24	Detroit	at	New York #	7:30
Saturday, July 24	Indiana	at	Phoenix	10:00
Saturday, July 24	Houston	at	Seattle	10:00
Sunday, July 25	Indiana	at	Sacramento	10:00
Tuesday, July 27	Seattle	at	Houston	8:30
Wednesday, July 28	Detroit	at	Washington	7:00
Wednesday, July 28	Charlotte	at	Indiana	8:00
Wednesday, July 28	San Antonio	at	Minnesota	8:00
Thursday, July 29	Los Angeles	at	Sacramento	10:00
Friday, July 30	Connecticut	at	Washington	7:00
Friday, July 30	New York	at	Detroit	7:30
Friday, July 30	Seattle	at	Minnesota	8:00
Friday, July 30	Phoenix	at	San Antonio	8:00
Saturday, July 31	Indiana	at	Houston	4:00
Saturday, July 31	Connecticut	at	New York #	7:30
Saturday, July 31	Los Angeles	at	San Antonio	8:00
Saturday, July 31	Charlotte	at	Sacramento	10:00
Sunday, August 1	Phoenix	at	Washington	12:00
Sunday, August 1	Minnesota	at	Detroit	6:00
Sunday, August 1	Charlotte	at	Seattle	9:00
Thursday, August 5	WNBA vs. USA Basketball: The Game at Radio City			7:00
Wednesday, September 1	Indiana	at	Washington	7:00
Wednesday, September 1	Connecticut	at	Charlotte	7:00

Wednesday, September 1	Phoenix	at	Detroit	7:30
Wednesday, September 1	Minnesota	at	Houston	8:30
Wednesday, September 1	Sacramento	at	Seattle	10:30
Wednesday, September 1	San Antonio	at	Los Angeles	10:30
Thursday, September 2	Charlotte	at	New York #	7:30
Thursday, September 2	San Antonio	at	Sacramento	10:00
Friday, September 3	New York	at	Connecticut	7:00
Friday, September 3	Indiana	at	Minnesota	8:00
Friday, September 3	Phoenix	at	Houston	8:30
Friday, September 3	Seattle	at	Los Angeles	10:30
Saturday, September 4	Detroit	at	Charlotte	6:00
Saturday, September 4	Washington	at	Indiana	8:00
Saturday, September 4	Sacramento	at	San Antonio	8:00
Saturday, September 4	Seattle	at	Phoenix	10:00
Tuesday, September 7	Sacramento	at	Washington	7:00
Wednesday, September 8	Charlotte	at	Minnesota	8:00
Wednesday, September 8	Los Angeles	at	Phoenix	10:00
Wednesday, September 8	Detroit	at	Seattle	10:00
Thursday, September 9	New York	at	Washington	7:00
Thursday, September 9	Sacramento	at	Charlotte	7:00
Thursday, September 9	Houston	at	San Antonio	8:00
Thursday, September 9	Detroit	at	Los Angeles	10:30
Friday, September 10	Connecticut	at	New York #	7:30
Friday, September 10	San Antonio	at	Indiana	8:00
Friday, September 10	Seattle	at	Minnesota	8:00
Saturday, September 11	Minnesota	at	Charlotte	6:00
Saturday, September 11	Detroit	at	Phoenix	10:00
Sunday, September 12	Houston	at	Washington	12:00
Sunday, September 12	Seattle	at	Connecticut	2:00
Sunday, September 12	San Antonio	at	New York #	4:00
Sunday, September 12	Sacramento	at	Los Angeles	4:00
Monday, September 13	Seattle	at	Indiana	8:00
Tuesday, September 14	New York	at	Detroit	7:30
Tuesday, September 14	Minnesota	at	Houston	8:30
Tuesday, September 14	Phoenix	at	Los Angeles	10:30
Wednesday, September 15	Connecticut	at	Charlotte	7:00
Wednesday, September 15	Washington	at	San Antonio	8:00
Wednesday, September 15	Phoenix	at	Seattle	10:00
Thursday, September 16	Indiana	at	New York #	7:30
Thursday, September 16	Sacramento	at	Houston	8:00
Friday, September 17	New York	at	Connecticut	7:00
Friday, September 17	Charlotte	at	San Antonio	8:00
Friday, September 17	Washington	at	Phoenix	10:00
Friday, September 17	Minnesota	at	Los Angeles	10:30
Saturday, September 18	Houston	at	Sacramento	10:00
Saturday, September 18	Los Angeles	at	Seattle	10:00
Sunday, September 19	Indiana	at	Connecticut	12:00
Sunday, September 19	Charlotte	at	Detroit	2:00
Sunday, September 19	Washington	at	New York	4:00
Sunday, September 19	Houston	at	Phoenix	9:00
Sunday, September 19	Minnesota	at	Sacramento	10:00

* Denotes game to be played at Spokane Arena, Spokane, Wash.
\# Denotes game to be played at Radio City Music Hall, New York, N.Y.
^ Denotes game to be played at Comcast Center, College Park, Md.

2004 WNBA TELEVISION SCHEDULE

(Eastern starting times shown)

ABC SCHEDULE

Saturday, May 22	Phoenix	at	Connecticut	4:00 PM
Saturday, May 29	Los Angeles	at	Detroit	4:00 PM
Saturday, June 5	Los Angeles	at	Houston	4:00 PM
Saturday, June 19	Detroit	at	Sacramento	4:00 PM
Saturday, July 10	Seattle	at	Detroit	4:00 PM
Saturday, July 31	Indiana	at	Houston	4:00 PM
Sunday, September 12	Sacramento	at	Los Angeles	4:00 PM

ESPN2 SCHEDULE

Thursday, June 3	Phoenix	at	Seattle	10:30 PM
Thursday, June 17	San Antonio	at	Washington	8:00 PM
Thursday, July 1	Indiana	at	Washington	8:00 PM
Saturday, July 3	Sacramento	at	Seattle	10:00 PM
Thursday, July 8	Washington	at	New York	8:00 PM
Saturday, July 10	Los Angeles	at	Houston	9:00 PM
Thursday, July 15	Detroit	at	Houston	8:00 PM
Thursday, July 22	Minnesota	at	Connecticut	8:00 PM
Thursday, July 29	Los Angeles	at	Sacramento	10:00 PM
Thursday, August 5	WNBA vs. USA Basketball: The Game at Radio City			7:00 PM (ESPN)
Thursday, September 9	Detroit	at	Los Angeles	10:30 PM
Sunday, September 12	Seattle	at	Connecticut	2:00 PM
Thursday, September 16	Sacramento	at	Houston	8:00 PM
Thursday, September 19	Charlotte	at	Detroit	2:00 PM

OXYGEN SCHEDULE

Sunday, July 18	San Antonio	at	Detroit	12:00 PM
Saturday, July 24	San Antonio	at	Connecticut	12:00 PM
Sunday, August 1	Phoenix	at	Washington	12:00 PM
Sunday, September 12	Houston	at	Washington	12:00 PM
Sunday, September 19	Indiana	at	Connecticut	12:00 PM

PLAYOFFS SCHEDULE

FIRST ROUND

Friday, September 24:	One East/One West — Game #1
Saturday, September 25:	One East/One West — Game #1
Sunday, September 26:	One East/One West —Game #2
Monday, September 27:	One East/One West — Game #2
Tuesday, September 28:	One East/One West — Game #3*
Wednesday, September 29:	One East/One West — Game #3*

CONFERENCE FINALS

Friday, October 1:	Game #1 – Eastern Conf./Western Conf.
Sunday, October 3:	Game #2 – Eastern Conf. / Western Conf.
Tuesday, October 5:	Game #3 – Eastern Conf. / Western Conf.*

FINALS

Friday, October 8:	Game #1
Sunday, October 10:	Game #2
Tuesday, October 12:	Game #3*

* - if necessary
Playoff broadcast schedule TBD.

TEAM DIRECTORIES

- Team Personnel

- Game Schedule

- 2004 Rosters

- 2003 Results

CHARLOTTE STING
EASTERN CONFERENCE

129 W. Trade St.
Suite 700
Charlotte, NC 28202
Telephone: (704) 420-4120
Fax: (704) 333-2340

Ticket Information: (704) 424-WNBA
www.charlottesting.com
Arena: Charlotte Coliseum (10,637)
Radio: WNMX Mix 106
TV: WJZY UPN 46

2004 SEASON
TEAM DIRECTORY

Owner and President ....Robert L. Johnson
Executive Vice President/Chief Operating Officer ....Ed Tapscott
Chief Financial Officer..Peter Smul
General Manager and Head Coach ....Trudi Lacey
Assistant Coaches...Cheryl Reeve, Fred Williams
Coordinator of Sports Medicine ....Michelle T. Leget
Head Athletic Trainer ....Samantha Hicks
Strength and Conditioning Coach..Jodi Hopkins
Equipment Manager ....James McCullough
Training Facility/Basketball Operations Manager ....Tim Burke
Executive Assistant, Basketball Operations ....Tairee Wilson
Team Physicians ....Dr. Jerry Barron, Dr. Glenn Perry
Vice President of Business Operations ....Kelly Chopus
Senior Vice President of Ticket Sales and Service.........................Steve Swetoha
Vice President of Corporate Partnerships ....Tod Rosensweig
Vice President of Game Operations and Broadcasting ....John Guagliano
Director of Public Relations ....Karen Kase
Director of Ticket Operations...Jamie Hall
Director of Ticket Sales ....Chris Gargani
Corporate Partnerships Manager..Heidi Coleman
Marketing Manager ....Deanna Evans
Game Operations Coordinators ....John Woodman, Yaa Obeng
Public Relations Assistant ....Malinda Murray
Administrative Assistant ....Sheneika Bowen
Team Photographer ....Kent Smith
Radio/TV Announcer ....Sam Smith

Ed Tapscott

Trudi Lacey

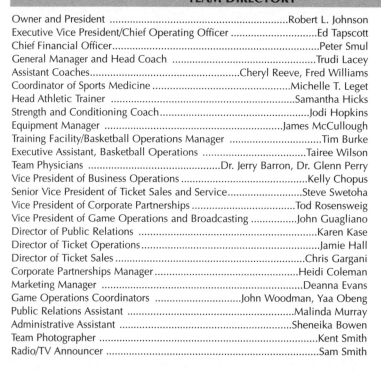

May

S	M	T	W	T	F	S
						1
2	3	4	5	6	7	8
9	10	11	12	13	14	15
16	17	18	19	20	21 Hou	22 Was
23	24	25	26	27	28 Ind	29

June

S	M	T	W	T	F	S
		1	2 NY	3	4 Con	5 Ind
6	7	8	9 LA	10	11 Pho	12
13	14	15 SA	16	17	18 Con	19
20	21	22	23 Det	24	25	26 Ind
27	28	29	30			

July

S	M	T	W	T	F	S
				1	2 Pho	3 Hou
4	5	6	7	8 Sea	9	10 Was
11	12	13	14	15 Was	16	17
18	19	20 NY	21	22	23 Det	24 Was
25	26	27	28 Ind	29	30	31 Sac

August

Sea 1	2	3	4	★5

September

S	M	T	W	T	F	S
			1 † 2 Con	3 NY		4 Det
5	6	7	8 Min	9 Sac	10	11 Min
12	13	14	15 Con	16	17	18
19	20	21	22 SA	23	24	25
26 Det	27	28	29	30		

■ = Home ☐ = Away ★ WNBA vs. USA Basketball: The Game at Radio City
† - Denotes game to be played at Radio City Music Hall, New York, N.Y.

2004 ROSTER

No.	Player	Pos.	Ht./Wt.	Metric	Born	College/Country
23	Mery Andrade	F	6-0/169	1,83/ 76,7	12-31-75	Old Dominion
	Jenni Benningfield	F	6-3/185	1,91/ 83,9	10-6-81	Vanderbilt
25	Marla Brumfield	G	5-8/133	1,73/ 60,3	6-6-78	Rice
11	Erin Buescher	G	6-2/181	1,88/ 82,1	6-5-79	The Master's College
21	Allison Feaster	F	5-11/168	1,80/ 76,2	2-11-76	Harvard
20	Tynesha Lewis	G-F	5-10/150	1,78/ 68,0	5-8-79	North Carolina State
	Kelly Mazzante	G	5-11/162	1,80/ 73,5	2-2-82	Penn State
33	Teana McKiver	C	6-3/203	1,91/ 92,1	10-5-80	Tulane
	Jia Perkins	G	5-9	1,75/	2-23-82	Texas Tech
	Nicole Powell	G-F	6-1/172	1,85/ 78,0	6-22-82	Stanford
10	Telisha Quarles	G	5-8/135	1,73/ 61,2	6-20-80	Virginia
0	Olympia Scott-Richardson	C-F	6-2/175	1,88/ 79,4	8-5-76	Stanford
32	Andrea Stinson	G	5-10/158	1,78/ 71,7	11-25-67	North Carolina State
55	Tammy Sutton-Brown	C	6-4/199	1,93/ 90,3	1-27-78	Rutgers
52	Kara Wolters	C	6-7/227	2,01/103,0	8-15-75	Connecticut

Head Coach - Trudi Lacey
Assistant Coaches - Cheryl Reeve, Fred Williams
Trainer - Samantha Hicks

2003 REVIEW

RESULTS

May
23—Washington *70-74 0-1
29—Indiana 66-57 1-1
31—At Detroit 70-67 2-1

June
4—San Antonio 67-52 3-1
6—Houston 69-58 4-1
7—At Cleveland *57-67 4-2
12—At Phoenix 58-50 5-2
14—At San Antonio *52-62 5-3
17—At Indiana *60-71 5-4
20—Minnesota 76-72 6-4
22—At New York *57-69 6-5

25—Cleveland 61-50 7-5
28—Connecticut 69-55 8-5
30—Seattle *71-83 8-6

July
3—At Detroit 92-79 9-6
5—Sacramento 67-65 10-6
7—At Washington 62-56 11-6
10—Detroit 65-58 12-6
17—At Washington *60-68 12-7
18—At New York *48-56 12-8
20—Cleveland *57-59 12-9
24—Detroit 67-61 13-9
26—At Connecticut *70-74 13-10

31—At Seattle *54-69 13-11

August
2—At Los Angeles 84-73 14-11
3—At Sacramento *60-76 14-12
7—New York 65-54 15-12
9—Connecticut 69-68 16-12
14—Washington *69-76 16-13
16—At Indiana *63-69 16-14
20—Indiana 80-50 17-14
22—At Connecticut *55-63 17-15
2—New York 61-59 18-15
25—At Cleveland *66-75 18-16
*Loss. † Single overtime.

TEAM LEADERS

Points: Allison Feaster (422).
Field goals made: Andrea Stinson (147).
Free throws made: Tammy Sutton-Brown (90).
Three-pointers made: Allison Feaster (72).
Rebounds: Tammy Sutton-Brown (201).
Assists: Dawn Staley (174).
Steals: Allison Feaster (52).
Blocks: Tammy Sutton-Brown (50).

TEAM-BY-TEAM RESULTS

vs. Cleveland: 1-3
vs. Connecticut: 2-2
vs. Detroit: 4-0
vs. Houston: 1-0
vs. Indiana: 2-2
vs. Los Angeles: 1-0
vs. Minnesota: 1-0
vs. New York: 2-2
vs. Phoenix: 1-0
vs. Sacramento: 1-1
vs. San Antonio: 1-1
vs. Seattle: 0-2
vs. Washington: 1-3

CONNECTICUT SUN
EASTERN CONFERENCE

1 Mohegan Sun Boulevard
Uncasville, CT 06382
Tel: (860) 862-4000
Fax: (860) 862-4006, 862-4010
Ticket Information: (877) 786-8499

www.connecticutsun.com
Arena: Mohegan Sun Arena (9,341)
Training Facility: Charles B. Luce Field House
Radio: Connecticut Radio Network
TV: WB 20

2004 SEASON
TEAM DIRECTORY

Governor...Mitchell Etess
Alternate Governor ....Jeffrey Hartmann
President..Paul Munick
General Manager ....Chris Sienko
Head Coach...Michael Thibault
Assistant Coaches ....Bernadette Mattox, Scott Hawk
Head Athletic Trainer...Georgia Fischer
Strength & Conditioning Coach ....Lisa Ciaravella
Director of Marketing ....Stacey Dengler
Consumer Sales Manager ....Todd McDonald
Business Manager ....Dave Martinelli
Community Relations Manager ....Tina James
Media Relations Manager ....Bill Tavares
Consumer Sales Representatives ....Mike Winkler, Mike Reynolds,
....Annmarie Gengo, Dan Kowal
Consumer Sales Assistant ....Rachel Manke
Basketball Operations Coordinator...Bill Tinnel
Office Coordinator ....Wanita Richards
Play-by-Play Announcer ....Bob Heussler
Color Analyst ....Leah Secondo

Paul Munick

Chris Sienko

Mike Thibault

May

S	M	T	W	T	F	S
						1
2	3	4	5	6	7	8
9	10	11	12	13	14	15
16	17	18	19	20	21	22 Pho
23	24	25 Hou	26	27 LA	28	29

June

S	M	T	W	T	F	S
		1	2	3 Cha	4 Was	5
6 Det	7	8	9	10	11 Sea	12 Sac
13	14 LA	15	16	17	18 Cha	19
20 Was	21	22 Ind	23	24	25 Det	26
27 Det	28	29	30 Was			

July

S	M	T	W	T	F	S
				1	2	3
4	5	6	7	8	9 Sac	10
11 Ind	12	13	14 Min	15 SA	16	17 Hou
18	19	20	21 Det	22 Min	23	24 SA
25	26	27	28	29	30 Was †31 NY	

September

S	M	T	W	T	F	S
			1	2 Cha	3	4 NY
5	6	7	8	9 †10 NY		11
12 Sea	13	14	15 Cha	16	17 NY	18
19 Ind	20	21	22	23	24	25
26	27	28	29	30		

August

	1	2	3	4	★5	

■ = Home □ = Away ★ WNBA vs. USA Basketball: The Game at Radio City

† - Denotes game to be played at Radio City Music Hall, New York, N.Y.

2004 ROSTER

No.	Player	Pos.	Ht./Wt.	Metric	Born	College/Country
22	Jessica Brungo	F	6-1/165	1,85/ 74,8	4-16-82	Penn State
50	Courtney Coleman	C	6-0/170	1,83/ 77,1	4-11-81	Ohio State
32	Katie Douglas	G-F	6-0/165	1,83/ 74,8	5-7-79	Purdue
12	Candace Futrell	G	5-10/154	1,78/ 69,9	7-10-82	Duquesne
15	Asjha Jones	F	6-2/198	1,88/ 89,8	8-1-80	Connecticut
10	Anastasia Kostaki	G-F	5-7/137	1,70/ 62,1	3-26-78	From - Greece
35	Ugo Oha	C	6-4/185	1,93/ 83,9	7-18-82	George Washington
42	Nykesha Sales	F-G	6-0/184	1,83/ 83,5	5-10-76	Connecticut
2	Brianne Stepherson	G	5-8/155	1,73/ 70,3	2-23-80	Boston College
13	Lindsay Whalen	G	5-8/150	1,73/ 68,0	5-9-82	Minnesota
21	Brooke Wyckoff	F	6-1/183	1,85/ 83,0	3-30-80	Florida State
8	Anna Zimerle	G	5-7/134	1,70/ 60,8	8-28-76	From - Italy

Coach - Mike Thibault
Assistant Coach - Bernadette Mattox, Scott Hawk
Trainer - Georgia Fischer

2003 REVIEW

RESULTS

May
24—Los Angeles *73-82 0-1
30—At Houston 91-83 1-1
June
1—At San Antonio 83-64 2-1
5—At Detroit *89-103 2-2
7—Houston 65-58 3-2
13—Washington 84-70 4-2
14—At Cleveland *56-84 4-3
18—Cleveland 70-57 5-3
20—At Indiana *74-84 5-4
22—Detroit *73-82 †5-5
24—At Washington 65-63 6-5
26—Indiana *90-94 ‡6-6

28—At Charlotte *55-69 6-7
July
1—At New York *64-90 6-8
2—Cleveland 64-57 7-8
4—Sacramento 69-67 8-8
6—New York 62-58 9-8
8—At Detroit *50-66 9-9
10—At Minnesota *75-83 9-10
17—Seattle *65-67 9-11
19—At Phoenix 75-67 10-11
20—At Los Angeles 76-73 11-11
23—Minnesota 84-70 12-11
26—Charlotte 74-70 13-11

August
1—Washington *45-48 13-12
3—Indiana 66-55 14-12
5—Detroit *61-78 14-13
9—At Charlotte *68-69 14-14
12—New York *73-74 14-15
16—At New York 84-71 15-15
19—At Cleveland *52-69 15-16
22—Charlotte 63-55 16-16
23—At Washington 74-67 17-16
25—At Indiana 72-62 18-16
*Loss. † Single overtime.
‡ Double overtime.

TEAM LEADERS

Points: Nykesha Sales (548).
Field goals made: Nykesha Sales (194).
Free throws made: Shannon Johnson (125).
Three-pointers made: Katie Douglas (47).
Rebounds: Taj McWilliams-Franklin (227).
Assists: Shannon Johnson (196).
Steals: Nykesha Sales (46).
Blocks: Taj McWilliams-Franklin (33).

TEAM-BY-TEAM RESULTS

vs. Charlotte: 2-2
vs. Cleveland: 2-2
vs. Detroit: 0-4
vs. Houston: 2-0
vs. Indiana: 2-2
vs. Los Angeles: 1-1
vs. Minnesota: 1-1
vs. New York: 2-2
vs. Phoenix: 1-0
vs. Sacramento: 1-0
vs. San Antonio: 1-0
vs. Seattle: 0-1
vs. Washington: 3-1

DETROIT SHOCK
EASTERN CONFERENCE

Three Championship Drive
Auburn Hills, MI 48326-1752
Phone: (248) 377-0100
Fax: (248) 377-3260
Ticket Information: (248) 377-0100

www.detroitshock.com
Arena: The Palace of Auburn Hills (11,268)
Radio: Fox Sports Radio AM 1310 The X
TV: TBD

2004 SEASON
TEAM DIRECTORY

Managing Partner ....William Davidson
Legal Counsel ....Oscar H. Feldman
President and CEO...Tom Wilson
Chief Operating Officer ....Alan Ostfield
Head Coach ....Bill Laimbeer
Assistant Coach ....Laurie Byrd
Assistant Coach ....Korie Hlede
Athletic Trainer...Laura Ramus
Team Manager..Jamie Fichera
Vice President of Shock Operations ....Kristin Bernert
Director of Media Relations..Paul Hickey
Director of Business Operations ....Dennis Sampier
Market Development Manager ....Alicia Valdez
Business Operations Coordinator ....Rachael Dobberstein
Shock Assistant ....Rachel Sutton
Media Relations Seasonal Assistant ....Cletus Lewis, Jr.
Television/Radio Broadcaster ....Matt Shepard
Team Physician ....Dr. Ben Paolucci
Team Photographer ....Allen Einstein

Tom Wilson

Kristin Bernert

Bill Laimbeer

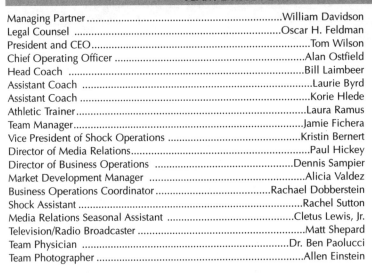

= Home   = Away   ★ WNBA vs. USA Basketball: The Game at Radio City

† - Denotes game to be played at Radio City Music Hall, New York, N.Y.

2004 ROSTER

No.	Player	Pos.	Ht./Wt.	Metric	Born	College/Country
32	Swin Cash	F	6-2/162	1,88/ 73,5	9-22-79	Connecticut
6	Jae Cross	G	5-9/148	1,75/ 67,1	1-20-76	Australia
13	Allison Curtin	G	5-11/151	1,80/ 68,5	3-31-80	Tulsa
54	Barbara Farris	F-C	6-3/195	1,91/ 88,5	9-10-76	Tulane
35	Cheryl Ford	F	6-3/215	1,91/ 97,5	6-6-81	Louisiana Tech
2	Chandi Jones	G-F	5-11/154	1,80/ 69,9	3-25-82	Houston
25	Merlakia Jones	G	5-10/147	1,78/ 66,7	6-21-73	Florida
14	Deanna Nolan	G-F	6-0/160	1,83/ 72,6	8-25-79	Georgia
00	Ruth Riley	C	6-5/195	1,96/ 88,5	8-28-79	Notre Dame
3	Isabel Sanchez	G	5-10/152	1,78/ 68,9	11-28-76	Spain
45	Jennifer Smith	C	6-3	1,91/	4-10-82	Michigan
9	Stacey Thomas	F	5-10/154	1,78/ 69,9	8-29-78	Michigan
33	Iciss Tillis	C-F	6-5/165	1,96/ 74,8	12-6-81	Duke
55	Petra Ujhelyi	C	6-4/200	1,93/ 90,7	12-17-80	South Carolina

Coach - Bill Laimbeer
Assistant Coaches - Laurie Byrd, Korie Hlede
Trainer - Laura Ramus

2003 REVIEW

RESULTS

May
31—Charlotte	*67-70	0-1

June
5—Connecticut	103-89	1-1
7—At San Antonio	74-55	2-1
14—At Washington	93-56	3-1
17—Los Angeles	87-78	†4-1
2—New York	88-83	5-1
22—At Connecticut	82-73	†6-1
24—Indiana	68-60	7-1
27—At New York	75-69	8-1
28—Phoenix	*65-68	8-2

July
1—San Antonio	99-88	9-2
3—Charlotte	*79-92	9-3
6—At Indiana	*54-85	9-4
8—Connecticut	66-50	10-4
10—At Charlotte	*58-65	10-5
16—At Indiana	70-68	11-5
18—Seattle	74-61	12-5
19—At Cleveland	58-57	13-5
22—Cleveland	74-71	14-5
24—At Charlotte	*61-67	14-6
27—Washington	81-71	15-6
29—At Cleveland	77-65	16-6

August
1—At New York	62-60	17-6
2—Indiana	72-58	18-6
5—At Connecticut	78-61	19-6
6—At Washington	*81-92	19-7
8—Houston	*56-66	19-8
10—New York	90-87	†20-8
13—At Phoenix	78-76	21-8
15—At Sacramento	*63-75	21-9
17—At Seattle	95-86	22-9
21—Cleveland	71-56	23-9
23—At Minnesota	86-77	†24-9
25—Washington	68-60	25-9

*Loss. † Single overtime.

TEAM LEADERS

Points: Swin Cash (548).
Field goals made: Swin Cash (195).
Free throws made: Swin Cash (146).
Three-pointers made: Kedra Holland-Corn (50).
Rebounds: Cheryl Ford (334).
Assists: Elaine Powell (129).
Steals: Elaine Powell (45).
Blocks: Ruth Riley (58).

TEAM-BY-TEAM RESULTS

vs. Charlotte: 0-4
vs. Cleveland: 4-0
vs. Connecticut: 4-0
vs. Houston: 0-1
vs. Indiana: 3-1
vs. Los Angeles: 1-0
vs. Minnesota: 1-0
vs. New York: 4-0
vs. Phoenix: 1-1
vs. Sacramento: 0-1
vs. San Antonio: 2-0
vs. Seattle: 2-0
vs. Washington: 3-1

HOUSTON COMETS
WESTERN CONFERENCE

1510 Polk Street
Houston, TX 77002
Tel: (713) 758-7200
Fax: (713) 758-7339
Ticket Information: (713) 627-WNBA

www.houstoncomets.com
Arena: Toyota Center (17,974)
Radio Station: SportsRadio 610
TV Station: KNWS TV51

2004 SEASON
TEAM DIRECTORY

Owner ....Leslie L. Alexander
President & Chief Executive Officer ....George N. Postolos
Chief Financial Officer ....Marcus Jolibois
Vice President & General Counsel ....Mark Biskamp
Senior Vice President of Corporate Development.....................Thaddeus Brown
Vice President of Business Development ....David Carlock
Vice President of Marketing ....Tim McDougall
Vice President of Ticket Sales & Services ....Mark Norelli
Executive Vice President of Basketball ....Carroll Dawson
Head Coach & General Manager ....Van Chancellor
Assistant Coaches ....Alisa Scott, Kevin Cook
Head Athletic Trainer..Michelle T. Leget
Video Coordinator ....Harold Liggans
Strength & Conditioning Coach ....Wendy Dutch
Equipment Manager ....Anthony Nila
Basketball Operations Executive Assistant ....Sandie Largent
Director of Broadcasting & Promotions..Joel Blank
Director of Finance ....David Jackson
Director of Community Services...Sarah Joseph
Director of Human Resources...Vivian Leflore
Director of Ticket Operations ....Josh Logan
Manager of Comets Tickets Sales & Services ....April Sanders
Media Relations Manager ....Bob Schranz
Business & Travel Coordinator ....Tricia Santopinto
Comets Broadcasters.....................Jeff Hagedorn, Craig Ackerman, Matt Bullard

Leslie Alexander

Van Chancellor

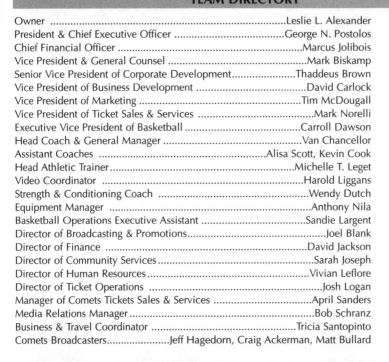

May

S	M	T	W	T	F	S
						1
2	3	4	5	6	7	8
9	10	11	12	13	14	15
16	17	18	19	20 SA	21 Cha	22
NY 23 30 Sac	24 Con	25	26	27	28	29

June

S	M	T	W	T	F	S
		1	2 Pho	3	4 NY	5 LA
6	7	8	9 SA	10	11	12 SA
13	14	15	16	17	18 Sea	19 Min
20	21	22 Sea	23	24	25 Sac	26
27 Was	28	29	30 Min			

July

S	M	T	W	T	F	S
				1	2	3 Cha
4	5	6 Det	7	8	9	10 LA
11	12	13	14 Ind	15 Det	16	17 Con
18	19	20	21	22	23 LA	24 Sea
25	26	27 Sea	28	29	30	31 Ind

September

S	M	T	W	T	F	S
			1	2 Min	3 Pho	4
5	6	7	8	9 SA	10	11
12 Was	13	14	15	16 Sac	17	18 Sac
19 Pho	20	21	22	23	24	25
26	27	28	29	30		

August

1	2	3	4 Sea	★ 5

■ = Home   □ = Away   ★ WNBA vs. USA Basketball: The Game at Radio City

24

2004 ROSTER

No.	Player	Pos.	Ht./Wt.	Metric	Born	College/Country
31	Octavia Blue	F	6-1/163	1,85/ 73,9	4-18-76	Miami
3	Kelley Gibson	F-G	5-9/137	1,75/ 62,1	11-7-76	Maryland
6	Gordana Grubin	G	5-11/165	1,80/ 74,8	8-20-72	Serbia-Montenegro
11	Kedra Holland-Corn	G	5-8/136	1,73/ 61,7	11-5-74	Georgia
12	Nicky McCrimmon	G	5-8/125	1,73/ 56,7	3-22-72	USC
34	Felicia Ragland	G	5-7/133	1,70/ 60,3	2-3-80	Oregon State
2	Michelle Snow	C	6-5/158	1,96/ 71,7	3-20-80	Tennessee
15	Stacy Stephens	C	6-4/205	1,93/ 93,0	1-21-82	Texas
45	Tora Suber	G	5-7/137	1,70/ 62,1	11-23-74	Virginia
22	Sheryl Swoopes	F	6-0/145	1,83/ 65,8	3-25-71	Texas Tech
7	Tina Thompson	F	6-2/178	1,88/ 80,7	2-10-75	USC
30	Mfon Udoka	F	6-0/187	1,83/ 84,8	6-16-76	DePaul
5	Maria Villarroel	G	5-8/135	1,73/ 61,2	12-3-78	Oklahoma

Coach - Van Chancellor
Assistant Coaches - Kevin Cook, Alisa Scott
Trainer - Michelle T. Leget

2003 REVIEW

RESULTS

May		
22—Seattle	75-64	1-0
24—At Phoenix	69-62	2-0
30—Connecticut	*83-91	2-1

June		
1—At Minnesota	*64-68	†2-2
3—Phoenix	66-51	3-2
6—At Charlotte	*58-69	3-3
7—At Connecticut	*58-65	3-4
10—Sacramento	71-66	4-4
14—At Phoenix	*61-76	4-5
17—At Minnesota	77-68	5-5
20—At San Antonio	*69-76	5-6
21—Cleveland	63-62	6-6

24—Los Angeles	*62-71	6-7
28—San Antonio	64-49	7-7

July		
1—Minnesota	71-69	8-7
5—Washington	76-54	9-7
8—Indiana	60-56	10-7
15—At Seattle	*55-69	10-8
18—At Los Angeles	79-74	11-8
19—At Sacramento	74-71	12-8
26—New York	61-53	13-8
29—Minnesota	73-58	14-8

August		
1—At San Antonio	*53-63	14-9
2—San Antonio	64-55	15-9

5—Sacramento	74-47	16-9
7—At Indiana	68-55	17-9
8—At Detroit	66-56	18-9
10—Phoenix	69-46	19-9
16—Los Angeles	*63-64	19-10
18—At New York	*64-67	19-11
19—Seattle	52-47	20-11
21—At Sacramento	*54-62	20-12
23—At Seattle	*64-71	20-13
25—At Los Angeles	*64-67	20-14

*Loss. † Single overtime.

TEAM LEADERS

Points: Sheryl Swoopes (484).
Field goals made: Tina Thompson (176).
Free throws made: Sheryl Swoopes (110).
Three-pointers made: Tina Thompson (39).
Rebounds: Michelle Snow (263).
Assists: Sheryl Swoopes (121).
Steals: Sheryl Swoopes (77).
Blocks: Michelle Snow (62).

TEAM-BY-TEAM RESULTS

vs. Charlotte: 0-1
vs. Cleveland: 1-0
vs. Connecticut: 0-2
vs. Detroit: 1-0
vs. Indiana: 2-0
vs. Los Angeles: 1-3
vs. Minnesota: 3-1
vs. New York: 1-1
vs. Phoenix: 3-1
vs. Sacramento: 3-1
vs. San Antonio: 2-2
vs. Seattle: 2-2
vs. Washington: 1-0

INDIANA FEVER
EASTERN CONFERENCE

125 S. Pennsylvania Street
Indianapolis, IN 46204
Tel: (317) 917-2500
Fax: (317) 917-2899
Ticket Information: (317) 917-2500

www.wnba.com/fever
Arena: Conseco Fieldhouse (18,345)
Radio Station: WIBC 1070 AM
TV Station: FOX Sports Midwest, WB4

2004 SEASON
TEAM DIRECTORY

Pacers Sports & Entertainment Ownership ....Herb Simon, Melvin Simon
President, Pacers Sports & Entertainment ....Donnie Walsh
Senior VP/Chief Operating Officer ....Kelly Krauskopf
Executive Senior VP/Exec. Director of Conseco Fieldhouse...............Rick Fuson
Senior VP/Chief Financial Officer ....Kevin Bower
Senior VP/Marketing ....Larry Mago
Senior VP/Basketball Administration ....David Morway
Head Coach ....Brian Winters
Assistant Coaches ....Julie Plank, Lin Dunn
Trainer ....Holly Heitzman-Allison
Strength Coach ....Greg Moore
Operations Coordinator ....Elizabeth Dewhirst
Video Coordinator ....Rob Cleveland
Administrative Assistant...Michelle Cassaday
Team Physician...David Harsha, M.D.
Team Orthopedist ....Scott A. Lintner, M.D.
Director of Business Development...Lori Satterfield
Director of Game Operations/Promotions ....Jeff Scalf
Director of Group Ticket Sales ....Rob Robinson
Director of Media Relations ....Kevin Messenger
Director of Sponsorship Sales..Mike McClure
Manager of Community Relations ....Dan Gaines
Manager of Ticket Sales ....Julie Southworth
Game Operations Manager..Doug Morgan
Media Relations Assistant ....Tim Edwards
Promotions Managers...Karen Atkeson, Dean Heaviland
Sponsorship Service Coordinator ....Ramona Christen
Dance Teams Coordinator/Choreographer ....Stacey Austin
Radio/TV Play-by-Play...Chris Denari, Kevin Lee
Radio/TV Analysts.............................Debbie Antonelli (TV), Jane Schott (Radio)
Public Address Announcer ....Kevin Cole
Team Photographer ....Frank McGrath

Donnie Walsh

Kelly Krauskopf

Brian Winters

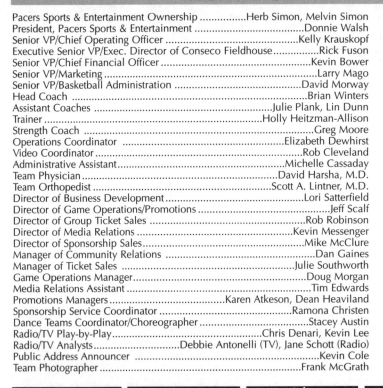

= Home   = Away   ★ WNBA vs. USA Basketball: The Game at Radio City

† - Denotes game to be played at Radio City Music Hall, New York, N.Y.

2004 ROSTER

No.	Player	Pos.	Ht./Wt.	Metric	Born	College/Country
2	Leigh Aziz	F	6-3/177	1,91/ 80,3	2-28-79	Syracuse
14	Coretta Brown	G	5-9/150	1,75/ 68,0	10-21-80	North Carolina
24	Tamika Catchings	F	6-1/167	1,85/ 75,7	7-21-79	Tennessee
34	Ebony Hoffman	C	6-2/210	1,88/ 95,3	8-27-82	USC
33	Niele Ivey	G	5-7/149	1,70/ 67,6	9-24-77	Notre Dame
5	Deanna Jackson	F	6-2/159	1,88/ 72,1	12-15-79	Alabama-Birmingham
41	Ieva Kublina	F-C	6-4/190	1,93/ 86,2	7-8-82	Virginia Tech
8	Kelly Miller	G	5-10/140	1,78/ 63,5	9-6-78	Georgia
44	Astou Ndiaye-Diatta	F-C	6-3/182	1,91/ 82,6	11-5-73	Southern Nazarene
52	Kristen Rasmussen	F	6-2/172	1,88/ 78,0	11-1-78	Michigan State
11	Kelly Schumacher	C	6-4/189	1,93/ 85,7	10-14-77	Connecticut
30	Kate Starbird	F-G	6-1/153	1,85/ 69,4	7-30-75	Stanford
22	Stephanie White	G-F	5-9/155	1,75/ 70,3	6-20-77	Purdue
12	Natalie Williams	F	6-2/210	1,88/ 95,3	11-30-70	UCLA

Coach - Brian Winters
Assistant Coaches - Julie Plank, Lin Dunn
Trainer - Holly Heitzman-Allison

2003 REVIEW

RESULTS

May
29—At Charlotte   *57-66   0-1
31—Washington   71-60   1-1

June
7—New York   86-66   2-1
10—At Seattle   *51-78   2-2
12—At Los Angeles   *66-74   2-3
14—At Sacramento   79-67   3-3
17—Charlotte   71-60   4-3
20—Connecticut   84-74   5-3
21—At Minnesota   *58-66   5-4
24—At Detroit   *60-68   5-5
26—At Connecticut   94-90   ‡6-5
28—Seattle   79-70   7-5

29—At Cleveland   *53-66   7-6

July
2—Phoenix   79-68   8-6
6—Detroit   85-54   9-6
8—At Houston   *56-60   9-7
10—New York   76-69   10-7
16—Detroit   *68-70   10-8
20—At New York   *65-73   10-9
23—San Antonio   81-47   11-9
24—At Washington   80-75   12-9
26—Minnesota   *65-70   12-10
29—At Washington   92-91†13-10

August
2—At Detroit   *58-72   13-11

3—At Connecticut   *55-66   13-12
7—Houston   *55-68   13-13
9—Cleveland   *62-66   13-14
10—At Cleveland   *67-71   13-15
12—Washington   *80-84   13-16
16—Charlotte   69-63   14-16
20—At Charlotte   *50-80   14-17
22—At New York   64-51   15-17
23—Cleveland   59-46   16-17
25—Connecticut   *62-72   16-18

*Loss. † Single overtime.
‡ Double overtime.

TEAM LEADERS

Points: Tamika Catchings (671).
Field goals made: Tamika Catchings (221).
Free throws made: Tamika Catchings (155).
Three-pointers made: Tamika Catchings (74).
Rebounds: Tamika Catchings (272).
Assists: Tamika Catchings (114).
Steals: Tamika Catchings (72).
Blocks: Tamika Catchings (35).

TEAM-BY-TEAM RESULTS

vs. Charlotte: 2-2
vs. Cleveland: 1-3
vs. Connecticut: 2-2
vs. Detroit: 1-3
vs. Houston: 0-2
vs. Los Angeles: 0-1
vs. Minnesota: 0-2
vs. New York: 3-1
vs. Phoenix: 1-0
vs. Sacramento: 1-0
vs. San Antonio: 1-0
vs. Seattle: 1-1
vs. Washington: 3-1

LOS ANGELES SPARKS
WESTERN CONFERENCE

2151 E. Grand Avenue
El Segundo, CA 90245
Tel: (310) 341-1000
Fax: (310) 341-1029
Ticket Information: (877) 44-SPARKS

www.lasparks.com
Arena: STAPLES Center (13,141)
Radio: KLAC Radio 570 and KWKU Radio 1220
TV: Fox Sports West, FSW 2

2004 SEASON
TEAM DIRECTORY

Chairman..Dr. Jerry Buss
President...Johnny Buss
Chief Financial Officer ....Joe McCormack
General Counsel...Jim Perzik
General Manager ....Penny Toler
Assistant, General Manager ....Rondre Jackson
Senior Assistant to the President..Brandi Bratcher
Executive Assistant to the President ....Christine Rackohn
Head Coach ....Michael Cooper
Assistant Coach(s) ....Karleen Thompson, Ryan Weisenberg
Team Physicians...Dr. John Moe, Dr. Stephen Lombardo
Head Athletic Trainer...Sandee Teruya
Assistant Trainer..Tiffany Matson
Team Manager ....Thomas Archie
Assistant Manager..Specelle Williams
Video Coordinator..TBD
Exec. Dir. Corporate Sponsorship.............................Eva Campbell, Ron Rockoff
Exec. Dir. Multimedia Marketing ....Keith Harris
Director, Advertising ....Michael Harris
Director, Business Development and Entertainment....................Stacey Stewart
BD&E Assistant(s) ....TBD
Director, Communications ....Kristal Shipp
Communications Manager(s) ....Octavia Dosier, Abby Morycz
Director, Community Relations ....Cindy Jarvis
Community Relations Assistant ....Tenecia Cassey
Director, Corporate Marketing ....Robin McLaughlin
Director, Event Production and Game Operations ....Ian Levitt
Director, Strategic Marketing ....Heather LaBella
Director, Ticket Operations ....Veronica Lawlor
Assistant Director(s), Ticket Operations ....Jim Bakken, Charles Bingham
Account Executives, Ticket Operations ....Joe Bucz, Tomika Hawkins
....Cindy Iwami, Patricia Pilot, Erica Woods
Radio ....Larry Burnett
Television ....Larry Burnett, Ann Meyers-Drysdale

Johnny Buss

Penny Toler

Michael Cooper

May

S	M	T	W	T	F	S
						1
2	3	4	5	6	7	8
9	10	11	12	13	14	15
16	17	18	19	20	21	22 Sea
23	24	25 Was	26	27 Con	28	29 Det

June

S	M	T	W	T	F	S
		1	2	3 Sea	4 Sac	5 Hou
6	7	8	9 Cha	10	11 Min	12
13	14 Con	15	16	17	18 Pho	19
20 Cha	21	22 NY	23	24	25 Ind	26
27 Min	28	29 NY	30			

July

S	M	T	W	T	F	S
				1	2 SA	3
4	5	6	7 Pho	8	9 SA	10 Hou
11	12	13	14	15	16	17 Sac
18 Ind	19	20	21 Was	22	23 Hou	24
25	26	27	28	29 Sac	30	31 SA

August
| 1 | 2 | 3 | 4 | ★5 |

September

S	M	T	W	T	F	S
			1	2 SA	3 Sea	4
5	6	7	8 Pho	9 Det	10	11
12 Sac	13	14	15	16 Pho	17 Min	18 Sea
19	20	21	22	23	24	25
26	27	28	29	30		

■ = Home ☐ = Away ★ WNBA vs. USA Basketball: The Game at Radio City

2004 ROSTER

No.	Player	Pos.	Ht./Wt.	Metric	Born	College/Country
	Monique Coker	F-C	6-2/180	1,88/ 81,6	11-28-82	Old Dominion
	Maria Conlon	G	5-9	1,75/	11-20-82	Connecticut
34	Danielle Crockrom	F	6-1/158	1,85/ 71,7	2-11-81	Baylor
21	Tamecka Dixon	G	5-9/148	1,75/ 67,1	12-14-75	Kansas
13	Isabelle Fijalkowski	C-F	6-5/200	1,96/ 90,7	5-23-72	Colorado
10	Doneeka Hodges	G	5-9/160	1,75/ 72,6	7-19-82	Louisiana State
9	Lisa Leslie	C	6-5/170	1,96/ 77,1	7-7-72	USC
4	Mwadi Mabika	F	5-11/165	1,80/ 74,8	7-27-76	Congo
	Laura Macchi	F	6-1	1,85/	5-24-79	
	Raffaella Masciadri	F	6-0	1,83/	9-30-80	
8	DeLisha Milton-Jones	F	6-1/172	1,85/ 78,0	9-11-74	Florida
4	Tamara Stocks	F-C	6-2/165	1,88/ 74,8	1-29-79	Florida
	Candice Sutton	C	6-4/200	1,93/ 90,7	9-27-82	North Carolina
42	Nikki Teasley	G	6-0/169	1,83/ 76,7	3-22-79	North Carolina
32	Christi Thomas	F	6-3/185	1,91/ 83,9	8-14-82	Georgia
11	Teresa Weatherspoon	G	5-8/161	1,73/ 73,0	12-8-65	Louisiana Tech
20	Shaquala Williams	G	5-6/135	1,68/ 61,2	4-14-80	Oregon

Coach - Michael Cooper
Assistant Coaches - Karleen Thompson, Ryan Weisenberg
Trainer - Sandee Teruya

2003 REVIEW

RESULTS

May

24—At Connecticut	82-73	1-0
27—At Cleveland	79-71	2-0
28—At Minnesota	83-80	3-0
30—At Seattle	77-74	†4-0

June

5—Sacramento	63-61	5-0
7—At Sacramento	79-61	6-0
10—Minnesota	76-75	7-0
12—Indiana	74-66	8-0
14—At New York	67-60	9-0
17—At Detroit	*78-87	†9-1
19—Seattle	*67-69	9-2
21—At Phoenix	54-48	10-2
24—At Houston	71-62	11-2
26—At San Antonio	67-58	12-2
28—Sacramento	*60-69	12-3

July

5—Seattle	84-75	13-3
7—Cleveland	81-75	14-3
9—At Washington	97-91	15-3
15—Phoenix	80-77	‡16-3
18—Houston	*74-79	16-4
20—Connecticut	*73-76	16-5
22—Washington	77-73	17-5
24—Phoenix	82-65	18-5
30—San Antonio	*62-70	18-6
31—At Sacramento	*75-83	18-7

August

2—Charlotte	*73-84	18-8
6—At Seattle	*56-92	18-9
8—At Phoenix	67-64	19-9
9—At San Antonio	*52-69	19-10
14—At Minnesota	87-83	20-10
16—At Houston	64-63	21-10
21—Minnesota	88-65	22-10
23—San Antonio	83-70	23-10
25—Houston	67-64	24-10

*Loss. † Single overtime.
‡ Double overtime.

TEAM LEADERS

Points: Mwadi Mabika (441).
Field goals made: Lisa Leslie (165).
Free throws made: DeLisha Milton-Jones (115).
Three-pointers made: Nikki Teasley (70).
Rebounds: Lisa Leslie (231).
Assists: Nikki Teasley (214).
Steals: DeLisha Milton-Jones (49).
Blocks: Lisa Leslie (63).

TEAM-BY-TEAM RESULTS

vs. Charlotte: 0-1
vs. Cleveland: 2-0
vs. Connecticut: 1-1
vs. Detroit: 0-1
vs. Houston: 3-1
vs. Indiana: 1-0
vs. Minnesota: 4-0
vs. New York: 1-0
vs. Phoenix: 4-0
vs. Sacramento: 2-2
vs. San Antonio: 2-2
vs. Seattle: 2-2
vs. Washington: 2-0

MINNESOTA LYNX
WESTERN CONFERENCE

Target Center
600 First Avenue North
Minneapolis, MN 55403
Tel: (612) 673-1600
Fax: (612) 673-8367

Ticket Information: (612) 673-8400
www.lynxbasketball.com
Arena: Target Center (11,380)
Radio: KLBB-AM 1400/1470
TV: Fox Sports Net

2004 SEASON
TEAM DIRECTORY

Owner ....Glen Taylor
Chief Operating Officer...Roger Griffith
Sr. Vice President and Chief Marketing Officer ....Chris Wright
Head Coach ....Suzie McConnell Serio
Assistant Coaches ....Nancy Darsch, Carolyn Jenkins
Trainer...Alisha Hvistendahl
Operations Manager..Megan Murphy
Public Relations Coordinator...................................Courtney Lawson
Public Relations Manager ....Michael Cristaldi
Director of Communications ....Ted Johnson
Director of Marketing ....Jason LaFrenz
Director of Ticket Sales..Bryant Pfeiffer
Vice President of Corporate Sales ....Conrad Smith
Executive Director of Fan Relations & Guest Services ....Jeff Munneke
Community Relations Manager ....Terrell Battle
Box Office Manager ....Molly Tomczak

Roger Griffith

Suzie McConnell Serio

May
S	M	T	W	T	F	S
						1
2	3	4	5	6	7	8
9	10	11	12	13	14	15
16	17	18	19	20 Sea	21	22 Sac
23	24	25	26	27 SA	28 Was	29
30 NY						

June
S	M	T	W	T	F	S
		1	2	3 SA	4	5 Pho
6	7	8	9	10	11 LA	12
13	14	15	16	17 Sac	18	19 Hou
20	21	22 Pho	23	24 SA	25	26
27 LA	28	29	30 Hou			

July
S	M	T	W	T	F	S
				1	2	3 Det
4	5	6	7	8 Ind	9 Pho	10
11 Sac	12	13	14 Con	15 NY	16	17
18 Pho	19	20	21	22 Con	23 Was	24
25	26	27	28 SA	29	30 Sea	31

August: 1 Det | 2 | 3 | 4 | ★5

September
S	M	T	W	T	F	S
			1 Hou	2	3 Ind	4
5	6	7	8 Cha	9	10 Sea	11 Cha
12	13	14 Hou	15	16	17 LA	18
19 Sac	20	21	22	23	24	25
26	27	28	29	30		

■ = Home □ = Away ★ WNBA vs. USA Basketball: The Game at Radio City

2004 ROSTER

No.	Player	Pos.	Ht./Wt.	Metric	Born	College/Country
25	Svetlana Abrosimova	F	6-2/169	1,88/ 76,7	7-9-80	Connecticut
40	Jordan Adams	F	6-3/180	1,91/ 81,6	5-24-81	New Mexico
42	Kate Bulger	G	5-11/155	1,80/ 70,3	3-27-82	West Virginia
1	Tasha Butts	F	5-11/155	1,80/ 70,3	3-10-82	Tennessee
12	Helen Darling	G	5-6/164	1,68/ 74,4	8-29-78	Penn State
4	Teresa Edwards	G	5-11/155	1,80/ 70,3	7-19-64	Georgia
32	Shaunzinski Gortman	G	6-1/156	1,85/ 70,8	12-7-79	South Carolina
55	Vanessa Hayden	C	6-4/224	1,93/101,6	6-5-82	Florida
23	Amber Jacobs	G	5-8/147	1,73/ 66,7	6-29-82	Boston College
24	Amanda Lassiter	F	6-1/143	1,85/ 64,9	6-9-79	Missouri
3	Nicole Ohlde	F-C	6-4/180	1,93/ 81,6	3-12-82	Kansas State
22	Georgia Schweitzer	G-F	6-0/160	1,83/ 72,6	1-31-79	Duke
30	Katie Smith	G	5-11/175	1,80/ 79,4	6-4-74	Ohio State
20	Tamika Williams	C	6-2/205	1,88/ 93,0	4-12-80	Connecticut

Coach - Suzie McConnell Serio
Assistant Coaches - Nancy Darsch, Carolyn Jenkins
Trainer - Alisha Hvistendahl

2003 REVIEW

RESULTS

May

24—Sacramento	72-71	1-0
28—Los Angeles	*80-83	1-1
30—At San Antonio	75-65	2-1

June

1—Houston	68-64	†3-1
6—New York	*60-70	3-2
10—At Los Angeles	*75-76	3-3
12—At Sacramento	*55-68	3-4
14—At Seattle	77-72	4-4
17—Houston	*68-77	4-5
20—At Charlotte	*72-76	4-6
21—Indiana	66-58	5-6

27—Phoenix	67-59	6-6
29—At Washington	59-50	7-6

July

1—At Houston	*69-71	7-7
5—Cleveland	*71-79	7-8
8—Sacramento	77-59	8-8
10—Connecticut	83-75	9-8
16—San Antonio	85-78	10-8
17—At Cleveland	*61-70	10-9
20—Seattle	69-58	11-9
23—At Connecticut	*70-84	11-10
25—San Antonio	81-54	12-10
26—At Indiana	70-65	13-10

29—At Houston	*58-73	13-11

August

2—Seattle	73-71	14-11
4—Phoenix	61-56	15-11
6—At Phoenix	*49-56	15-12
8—At Seattle	*65-68	15-13
9—At Sacramento	77-73	16-13
14—Los Angeles	*83-87	16-14
16—At San Antonio	73-64	17-14
20—At Phoenix	69-66	18-14
21—At Los Angeles	*65-88	18-15
23—Detroit	*77-86	†18-16

*Loss. † Single overtime.

TEAM LEADERS

Points: Katie Smith (620).
Field goals made: Katie Smith (208).
Free throws made: Katie Smith (126).
Three-pointers made: Katie Smith (78).
Rebounds: Tamika Williams (209).
Assists: Teresa Edwards (148).
Steals: Svetlana Abrosimova (44).
Blocks: Janell Burse (28).

TEAM-BY-TEAM RESULTS

vs. Charlotte: 0-1
vs. Cleveland: 0-2
vs. Connecticut: 1-1
vs. Detroit: 0-1
vs. Houston: 1-3
vs. Indiana: 2-0
vs. Los Angeles: 0-4
vs. New York: 0-1
vs. Phoenix: 3-1
vs. Sacramento: 3-1
vs. San Antonio: 4-0
vs. Seattle: 3-1
vs. Washington: 1-0

NEW YORK LIBERTY
EASTERN CONFERENCE

Madison Square Garden
Two Pennsylvania Plaza
New York, NY 10121-0091
Phone: (212) 465-6256
www.nyliberty.com

Arena: Madison Square Garden (19,763)
Radio City Music Hall (5,901)
Radio: WWRL (1600 AM)
TV: MSG Network (cable)

2004 SEASON
TEAM DIRECTORY

President and Chief Executive Officer, Cablevision Systems Corporation;
    Chairman, Madison Square Garden ....James L. Dolan
President and Chief Operating Officer, MSG Sports...........................Steve Mills
Senior Vice President & General Manager ....Carol Blazejowski
Vice President, Marketing and Communications ....Amy Scheer
Head Coach ....Richie Adubato
Assistant Coaches ....Pat Coyle, Jeff House
Assistant Coach/Video Coordinator..Jeff House
Head Athletic Trainer/Manager of Basketball Operations ....Lisa White
Manager, Communications..Larry Torres
Assistant, Communications ....Camille Currie
TV Announcers ....Gus Johnson, Doris Burke
Radio Announcers ....Bob Wischusen, Vera Jones

Carol Blazejowski

Richie Adubato

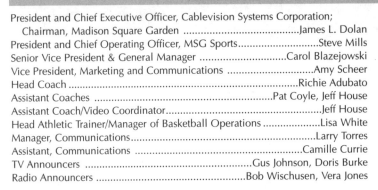

	May					
S	M	T	W	T	F	S
						1
2	3	4	5	6	7	8
9	10	11	12	13	14	15
16	17	18	19	20	21 Ind	22
Hou 23 / 30	24 Min	25	26 Det	27	28	29

	June					
S	M	T	W	T	F	S
		1	2	3	4 Hou	5 SA
6	7	8 Cha	9	10	11 Ind	12
§13 Was	14	15 Sea	16	17	18	19 Ind
20	21	22 LA	23	24 Pho	25 ‡26 Sea	
27	28	29 LA	30		August	

	July					
S	M	T	W	T	F	S
				1	2 Sac	3
4	5	6 Sac	7	8 Was	9	10
11 Pho	12	13	14	15 Min	16	17
18 Cha	19	20 Cha	21	22	23 †24 Det	
25	26	27	28	29	30 †31 Det Con	
1	2	3	4	★5		

	September					
S	M	T	W	T	F	S
			1	†2 Cha	3 Con	4
5	6	7	8	9 Was	†10 Con	11
†12 SA	13	14 Det	15	†16 Ind	17 Con	18
19 Was	20	21	22	23	24	25
26	27	28	29	30		

[shaded] = Home   [blank] = Away   ★ WNBA vs. USA Basketball: The Game at Radio City

† - Denotes game to be played at Radio City Music Hall, New York, N.Y.

‡ - Denotes game to be played at Spokane Arena, Spokane, Wash.

§ - Denotes game to be played at Comcast Center, College Park, Md.

2004 ROSTER

No.	Player	Pos.	Ht./Wt.	Metric	Born	College/Country
21	Amisha Carter	F	6-2/179	1,88/ 81,2	6-21-82	Louisiana Tech
20	Shameka Christon	G-F	6-1/175	1,85/ 79,4	2-15-82	Arkansas
33	Katie Cronin	G	6-0/155	1,83/ 70,3	9-8-77	Colorado State
41	Bethany Donaphin	F-C	6-2/195	1,88/ 88,5	8-27-80	Stanford
25	Becky Hammon	G	5-6/136	1,68/ 61,7	3-11-77	Colorado State
1	Cathy Joens	G-F	5-11/165	1,80/ 74,8	2-12-81	George Washington
55	Vickie Johnson	G-F	5-9/150	1,75/ 68,0	4-15-72	Louisiana Tech
	April McDivitt	G	5-7	1,70/	12-9-80	California-Santa Barbara
	Ndeye Ndiaye	C	6-3	1,91/		Southern Nazarene
52	Tasha Pointer	G	5-6/159	1,68/ 72,1	6-27-79	Rutgers
3	Crystal Robinson	F	5-11/155	1,80/ 70,3	1-22-74	SE Oklahoma State
32	K.B. Sharp	G	5-9/149	1,75/ 67,6	4-18-81	Cincinnati
5	Erin Thorn	G	5-10/150	1,78/ 68,0	5-19-81	Brigham Young
12	Ann Wauters	C	6-4/193	1,93/ 87,5	10-12-80	Belgium
23	DeTrina White	F	5-11/183	1,80/ 83,0	4-3-80	Louisiana State
22	Lindsey Yamasaki	G-F	6-1/185	1,85/ 83,9	6-2-80	Stanford

Coach - Richie Adubato
Assistant Coaches - Pat Coyle, Jeff House
Trainer - Lisa White

2003 REVIEW

RESULTS

May

31—At Cleveland	*50-74	0-1

June

1—Washington	70-57	1-1
6—At Minnesota	70-60	2-1
7—At Indiana	*66-86	2-2
10—Cleveland	73-65	3-2
14—Los Angeles	*60-67	3-3
17—Sacramento	70-61	4-3
20—At Detroit	*83-88	4-4
22—Charlotte	69-57	5-4
25—Phoenix	70-64	6-4
27—Detroit	*69-75	6-5

July

1—Connecticut	90-64	7-5
6—At Connecticut	*58-62	7-6
10—At Indiana	*69-76	7-7
15—Washington	*64-77	7-8
18—Charlotte	56-48	8-8
20—Indiana	73-65	9-8
23—At Seattle	*65-75	9-9
24—At Sacramento	*53-67	9-10
26—At Houston	*53-61	9-11
29—At Phoenix	*59-66	9-12

August

1—Detroit	*60-62	9-13

3—Cleveland	60-48	10-13
5—San Antonio	69-60	11-13
7—At Charlotte	*54-65	11-14
9—At Washington	65-56	12-14
10—At Detroit	*87-90	†12-15
12—At Connecticut	74-73	13-15
16—Connecticut	*71-84	13-16
17—At Cleveland	71-54	14-16
18—Houston	67-64	15-16
21—At Washington	65-60	16-16
22—Indiana	*51-64	16-17
24—At Charlotte	*59-61	†16-18

*Loss. † Single overtime.

TEAM LEADERS

Points: Vickie Johnson (430).
Field goals made: Vickie Johnson (158).
Free throws made: Tari Phillips (87).
Three-pointers made: Crystal Robinson (62).
Rebounds: Tari Phillips (280).
Assists: Teresa Weatherspoon (149).
Steals: Tari Phillips (56).
Blocks: Elena Baranova (43).

TEAM-BY-TEAM RESULTS

vs. Charlotte: 2-2
vs. Cleveland: 3-1
vs. Connecticut: 2-2
vs. Detroit: 0-4
vs. Houston: 1-1
vs. Indiana: 1-3
vs. Los Angeles: 0-1
vs. Minnesota: 1-0
vs. Phoenix: 1-1
vs. Sacramento: 1-1
vs. San Antonio: 1-0
vs. Seattle: 0-1
vs. Washington: 3-1

PHOENIX MERCURY
WESTERN CONFERENCE

201 East Jefferson
Phoenix, AZ 85004
Tel: (602) 514-8333
Fax: (602) 514-8303
Ticket Information: (602) 379-7878

www.phoenixmercury.com
Arena: America West Arena (10,746)
Radio: ESPN Radio 860 AM
TV: AZ TV

2004 SEASON
TEAM DIRECTORY

Chairman and CEO ....Jerry Colangelo
Minority Owners...Anne Mariucci, Kathy Munro
President, Business..Rick Welts
President, Basketball...Bryan Colangelo
Vice President/General Manager ....Seth Sulka
Vice President, Corporate Sales ....Lynn Agnello
Chief Operating Officer ....Jay Parry
Director of Sales ....Chris Montgomery
Head Coach ....Carrie Graf
Assistant Coaches ....TBD
Trainer ....Carolyn Griffiths
Director of Communications...Tami Nealy
Communications Manager..Jo Marie Garber
Communications Assistant ....Justin Molina
Director of Youth Programs...Ilene Hauser
Director of Game Operations ....Kip Helt
Season Ticket Manager ....Jeff Marcussen

Rick Welts

Seth Sulka

Carrie Graf

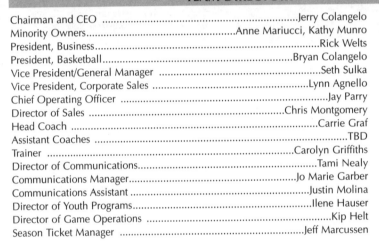

May						
S	M	T	W	T	F	S
						1
2	3	4	5	6	7	8
9	10	11	12	13	14	15
16	17	18	19	20 Sac	21	22
23	24	25	26	27	28 Sea	29

June						
S	M	T	W	T	F	S
		1	2	3 Hou	4	5
6	7	8 Con	9	10	11 Cha	12
13	14	15	16	17	18 LA	19
20	21	22 Min	23	24 NY	25	26 SA
27 Sac	28	29 SA	30			

July						
S	M	T	W	T	F	S
				1	2 Cha	3 Ind
4	5	6	7 LA	8	9 Min	10
11 NY	12	13	14	15	16	17
18 Min	19	20	21 SA	22 Sac	23	24 Ind
25	26	27	28	29	30 SA	31

September						
S	M	T	W	T	F	S
			1	2 Det	3 Hou	4 Sea
5	6	7	8 LA	9	10	11 Det
12	13	14	15 LA	16 Sea	17	18 Was
19 Hou	20	21	22	23	24	25
26	27	28	29	30		

August: 1 Was | 2 | 3 | 4 | ★ 5

= Home   = Away   ★ WNBA vs. USA Basketball: The Game at Radio City

2004 ROSTER

No.	Player	Pos.	Ht./Wt.	Metric	Born	College/Country
24	Edwina Brown	G-F	5-9/163	1,75/73,9	7-1-78	Texas
18	Iziane Castro Marques	G	6-0/140	1,83/63,5	3-13-82	Brazil
20	Kayte Christensen	F	6-3/171	1,91/77,6	11-16-80	California-Santa Barbara
1	Edniesha Curry	G	5-4/138	1,63/62,6	7-9-79	Oregon
30	Anna DeForge	G	5-10/160	1,78/72,6	4-14-76	Nebraska
31	Linda Frohlich	F-C	6-2/185	1,88/83,9	6-23-79	Nevada-Las Vegas
24	Lisa Harrison	F	6-0/164	1,83/74,4	1-2-71	Tennessee
	Nikki McCray	G	5-11/158	1,80/75,0	12-17-71	Tennessee
45	Michaela Pavlickova	F	6-3/175	1,91/79,4	11-27-77	Denver
54	Plenette Pierson	F-C	6-2/170	1,88/77,1	8-31-81	Texas Tech
43	Ashley Robinson	C	6-4/180	1,93/81,6	8-12-82	Tennessee
12	Gergana Slavtcheva	G	6-1/163	1,85/73,9	10-20-79	Florida International
3	Diana Taurasi	G	5-11/172	1,80/78,0	6-11-82	Connecticut
44	Lindsay Taylor	C	6-8/200	2,03/90,7	5-20-81	California-Santa Barbara
13	Penny Taylor	F	6-1/168	1,85/76,2	5-24-81	Australia
14	Slobodanka Tuvic	C	6-4/194	1,93/88,0	9-19-77	Serbia-Montenegro
15	Erika Valek	G	5-6/146	1,68/66,2	4-9-82	Purdue
33	Adrian Williams	C-F	6-4/170	1,93/77,1	2-15-77	USC
50	Shereka Wright	F	5-10/155	1,78/70,3	9-21-81	Purdue

Coach - Carrie Graf
Assistant Coaches - TBD
Trainer - Carolyn Griffiths

2003 REVIEW

RESULTS

May

22—Sacramento	*56-65	0-1
24—Houston	*62-69	0-2
28—San Antonio	51-50	1-2
30—At Sacramento	*49-69	1-3

June

3—At Houston	*51-66	1-4
5—At San Antonio	*55-70	1-5
7—At Seattle	*57-66	1-6
12—Charlotte	*50-58	1-7
14—Houston	76-61	2-7
17—Seattle	*60-61	2-8
21—Los Angeles	*48-54	2-9
25—At New York	*64-70	2-10

27—At Minnesota	*59-67	2-11
28—At Detroit	68-65	3-11

July

2—At Indiana	*68-79	3-12
5—At San Antonio	*70-81	3-13
10—Cleveland	*67-68	3-14
15—At Los Angeles	*77-80	‡3-15
19—Connecticut	*67-75	3-16
24—At Los Angeles	*65-82	3-17
25—At Seattle	*53-82	3-18
29—New York	66-59	4-18

August

1—At Cleveland	*56-73	4-19
3—At Washington	70-69	‡5-19

4—At Minnesota	*56-61	5-20
6—Minnesota	56-49	6-20
8—Los Angeles	*64-67	6-21
10—At Houston	*46-69	6-22
13—Detroit	*76-78	6-23
15—Seattle	64-50	7-23
16—Sacramento	*61-65	†7-24
20—Minnesota	*66-69	7-25
22—San Antonio	89-62	8-25
23—At Sacramento	*54-61	8-26

*Loss. † Single overtime.
‡ Double overtime.

TEAM LEADERS

Points: Anna DeForge (405).
Field goals made: Anna DeForge (147).
Free throws made: Plenette Pierson (64).
Three-pointers made: Anna DeForge (61).
Rebounds: Adrian Williams (252).
Assists: Tamicha Jackson (146).
Steals: Adrian Williams (57).
Blocks: Adrian Williams (19).

TEAM-BY-TEAM RESULTS

vs. Charlotte: 0-1
vs. Cleveland: 0-2
vs. Connecticut: 0-1
vs. Detroit: 1-1
vs. Houston: 1-3
vs. Indiana: 0-1
vs. Los Angeles: 0-4
vs. Minnesota: 1-3
vs. New York: 1-1
vs. Sacramento: 0-4
vs. San Antonio: 2-2
vs. Seattle: 1-3
vs. Washington: 1-0

SACRAMENTO MONARCHS
WESTERN CONFERENCE

ARCO Arena
One Sports Parkway
Sacramento, CA 95834
Tel: (916) 928-0000
Fax: (916) 928-0727

Ticket Information: (916) 419-WNBA
www.sacramentomonarchs.com
Arena: ARCO Arena (17,317)
Radio Station: KHTK Sports 1140 AM
TV Station: KXTV, News10

2004 SEASON
TEAM DIRECTORY

Ownership ....Maloof Family
President ....John Thomas
Head Coach/General Manager ....John Whisenant
Assistant Coaches ....Tom Abatemarco, Steve Shuman, Monique Ambers
Trainer ....Jill Jackson
Strength and Conditioning Coach..Al Biancani
Equipment Coordinator ....Marcella Muniz
Radio/Television Play-by-Play ....Jim Kozimor
Radio/Television Analyst ....Krista Blunk
Vice President, Arena Services ....Mark Stone
Vice President, Arena Programming ....Mike Duncan
Vice President, Finance ....John Rinehart
Vice President, Human Resources ....Donna Ruiz
Vice President, Service and Development ....Tom Peterson
Vice President, Strategic Alliances ....Blake Edwards
Vice President, Ticket Sales and Services.....................................Orin Anderson
Senior Director, Public Relations ....Sonja Brown
Senior Director, Marketing & Monarchs Business Operations ..Danette Leighton
Manager, Basketball Operations ....Pam Kay
Manager, Media Relations ....Kimberly Williams
Media Relations Coordinator..Rebecca Brutlag

John Whisenant

May

S	M	T	W	T	F	S
						1
2	3	4	5	6	7	8
9	10	11	12	13	14	15
16	17	18	19	20 Pho	21	22 Min
23	24	25	26	27	28 SA	29
30 Hou						

June

S	M	T	W	T	F	S
		1	2	3 LA	4	5 Sea
6	7	8	9	10	11	12 Con
13	14	15	16 Ind	17 Min	18	19 Det
20	21	22	23	24	25 Hou	26
27 Pho	28	29	30			

July

S	M	T	W	T	F	S
				1	2 NY	3
4	5	6	7 NY	8	9	10 Sea
11 Min	12 Det	13	14	15 Sea	16	17 LA
18 Was	19	20	21	22 Pho	23	24
25 Ind	26	27	28	29 LA	30	31 Cha

August

1	2	3	4	★5

September

S	M	T	W	T	F	S
		1	2 Sea	3 SA	4	
5	6	7 Was	8	9 Cha	10	11
12 LA	13	14	15	16 Hou	17	18 Hou
19 Min	20	21	22	23	24	25
26	27	28	29	30		

■ = Home   □ = Away   ★ WNBA vs. USA Basketball: The Game at Radio City

2004 ROSTER

No.	Player	Pos.	Ht./Wt.	Metric	Born	College/Country
7	Chantelle Anderson	C	6-6/192	1,98/ 87,1	1-22-81	Vanderbilt
32	Rebekkah Brunson	F	6-3/175	1,91/ 79,4	12-11-81	Georgetown
30	Chelsea Grear	F-G	5-10	1,78/		New Mexico
33	Yolanda Griffith	C-F	6-4/175	1,93/ 79,4	3-1-70	Florida Atlantic
27	Lady Grooms	F	5-10/160	1,78/ 72,6	9-12-70	Georgia
34	Valerie King	G	5-10/152	1,78/ 68,9	2-23-82	Cincinnati
20	Kara Lawson	G	5-8/160	1,73/ 72,6	2-14-81	Tennessee
11	Nuria Martinez	G	5-9	1,75/	2-29-84	Spain
21	Ticha Penicheiro	G	5-11/158	1,80/ 71,7	9-18-74	Old Dominion
50	Tangela Smith	F-C	6-4/160	1,93/ 72,6	4-1-77	Iowa
22	DeMya Walker	F	6-4/168	1,93/ 76,2	11-28-77	Virginia

Coach - John Whisenant
Assistant Coaches - Tom Abatemarco, Monique Ambers, Steve Shuman
Trainer - Jill Jackson

2003 REVIEW

RESULTS

May

22—At Phoenix	65-56	1-0
24—At Minnesota	*71-72	1-1
30—Phoenix	69-49	2-1

June

3—At Seattle	*56-70	2-2
5—At Los Angeles	*61-63	2-3
7—Los Angeles	*61-79	2-4
10—At Houston	*66-71	2-5
12—Minnesota	68-55	3-5
14—Indiana	*67-79	3-6
17—At New York	*61-70	3-7
18—At Washington	69-61	4-7
21—Seattle	69-64	5-7
24—San Antonio	*57-60	5-8
28—At Los Angeles	69-60	6-8

July

2—Washington	83-62	7-8
4—At Connecticut	*67-69	7-9
5—At Charlotte	*65-67	7-10
8—At Minnesota	*59-77	7-11
10—San Antonio	89-76	8-11
15—At Cleveland	66-57	9-11
17—At San Antonio	62-60	10-11
19—Houston	*71-74	10-12
24—New York	67-53	11-12
26—Seattle	76-63	12-12
31—Los Angeles	83-75	13-12

August

3—Charlotte	76-60	14-12
5—At Houston	*47-74	14-13
7—At San Antonio	86-61	15-13
9—Minnesota	*73-77	15-14
15—Detroit	75-63	16-14
16—At Phoenix	65-61	†17-14
21—Houston	62-54	18-14
23—Phoenix	61-54	19-14
25—At Seattle	*57-70	19-15

*Loss. † Single overtime.

TEAM LEADERS

Points: Yolanda Griffith (469).
Field goals made: Tangela Smith (188).
Free throws made: Yolanda Griffith (147).
Three-pointers made: Kara Lawson (54).
Rebounds: Yolanda Griffith (248).
Assists: Ticha Penicheiro (229).
Steals: Ticha Penicheiro (61).
Blocks: Yolanda Griffith (39).

TEAM-BY-TEAM RESULTS

vs. Charlotte: 1-1
vs. Cleveland: 1-0
vs. Connecticut: 0-1
vs. Detroit: 1-0
vs. Houston: 1-3
vs. Indiana: 0-1
vs. Los Angeles: 2-2
vs. Minnesota: 1-3
vs. New York: 1-1
vs. Phoenix: 4-0
vs. San Antonio: 3-1
vs. Seattle: 2-2
vs. Washington: 2-0

SAN ANTONIO SILVER STARS
WESTERN CONFERENCE

SBC Center
One SBC Center
San Antonio, TX 78219
Phone: (210) 444-5000
Fax: (210) 444-5003

Ticket Info: (210) 444-5050
www.sasilverstars.com
Arena: SBC Center (9,877 / 18,797)
Radio: KSJL 810 AM, KSJL 92.5 FM
TV: KRRT WB-35

2004 SEASON
TEAM DIRECTORY

Owner Spurs Sports & Entertainment Chairman & CEO ....Peter Holt
Exec. Vice President/Business Operations, Governor........................Russ Bookbinder
Executive Vice President/Finance and Corporate Development ....Rick Pych
Chief Operating Officer, Alternate Governor ....Clarissa Davis-Wrightsil
Silver Stars Assistant ....Adrienne Thompson
Senior Vice President/Broadcasting ....Lawrence Payne
Vice President/Marketing ....Bruce Guthrie
Vice President/Ticket Sales and Services...Joe Clark
Vice President/Community Relations ....Alison Fox
Vice President/Finance...Lori Warren
Vice President/Human Resources ....Paula Winslow
Vice President and GM/SBC Center ....Steve Zito
Head Coach ....Dee Brown
Assistant Coach ....Shell Dailey
Assistant Coach ....Vonn Read
Video/Travel Coordinator ....Jefferson Sweeney
Strength & Conditioning Coach ....Patrice Arnold
Athletic Trainer ....Kevin Semans
Equipment Manager...Carissa Raucci
Team Physicians ....David R. Schmidt, Timothy S. Palomera
Media Service Manager ....Kris Davis
Game Operations Manager...Chris Garcia
Game Operations Coordinator ....Brian Ricketts
Ticket Manager ....Arthur Serna

Clarissa
Davis-Wrightsil

Dee Brown

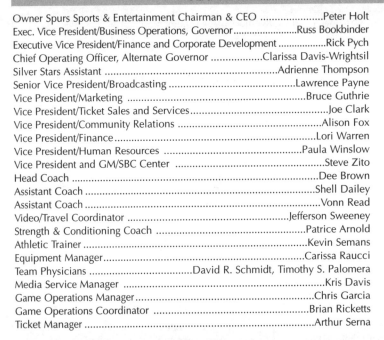

= Home   = Away   ★ WNBA vs. USA Basketball: The Game at Radio City

† - Denotes game to be played at Radio City Music Hall, New York, N.Y.

38

2004 ROSTER

No.	Player	Pos.	Ht./Wt.	Metric	Born	College/Country
22	Erin Batth	F-C	6-4/189	1,93/ 85,7	10-22-78	Clemson
10	Agnieszka Bibrzycka	G-F	6-2	1,88/	10-21-82	Poland
25	Juana Brown	G	5-10/151	1,78/ 68,5	4-29-79	North Carolina
00	Sylvia Crawley	F	6-5/187	1,96/ 84,8	9-27-72	North Carolina
55	Cindy Dallas	F	6-2	1,88/	1-17-80	Illinois
9	Tai Dillard	G	5-9/146	1,75/ 66,2	5-6-81	Texas
12	Margo Dydek	C	7-2/223	2,18/101,2	4-28-74	Poland
3	Marie Ferdinand	G	5-9/145	1,75/ 65,8	10-13-78	LSU
15	Adrienne Goodson	F	6-0/163	1,83/ 73,9	10-19-66	Old Dominion
7	Jessie Hicks	C-F	6-4/188	1,93/ 85,3	12-2-71	Maryland
40	Kym Hope	F-C	6-2/165	1,88/ 74,8	11-23-77	Miami
13	Gwen Jackson	F	6-2/184	1,88/ 83,5	10-23-80	Tennessee
23	LaTonya Johnson	F	6-1/150	1,85/ 68,0	8-17-75	Memphis
14	Shannon Johnson	G	5-7/144	1,70/ 65,3	8-18-74	South Carolina
18	Vanessa Nygaard	F	6-1/175	1,85/ 79,4	3-13-75	Stanford
33	LaQuanda Quick	G-F	5-10/156	1,78/ 70,8	10-3-79	North Carolina
21	Semeka Randall	G	5-8/168	1,73/ 76,2	2-7-79	Tennessee
	Mandisa Stevenson	C	6-3	1,91/	2-4-82	Auburn
32	LaToya Thomas	F	6-2/170	1,88/ 77,1	7-6-81	Mississippi State
1	Toccara Williams	G	5-9/145	1,75/ 65,8	1-11-82	Texas A&M

Coach - Dee Brown
Assistant Coaches - Shell Dailey, Vonn Read
Trainer - Kevin Semans

2003 REVIEW

RESULTS

May

24—Seattle	65-56	1-0
28—At Phoenix	*50-51	1-1
30—Minnesota	*65-75	1-2

June

1—Connecticut	*64-83	1-3
4—At Charlotte	*52-67	1-4
5—Phoenix	70-55	2-4
7—Detroit	*55-74	2-5
10—At Washington	*72-79	2-6
14—Charlotte	62-52	3-6
20—Houston	76-69	4-6
22—At Seattle	*53-93	4-7

24—At Sacramento	60-57	5-7
26—Los Angeles	*58-67	5-8
28—At Houston	*49-64	5-9

July

1—At Detroit	*88-99	5-10
5—Phoenix	81-70	6-10
10—At Sacramento	*76-89	6-11
16—At Minnesota	*78-85	6-12
17—Sacramento	*60-62	6-13
19—Washington	*77-85	6-14
23—At Indiana	*47-81	6-15
25—At Minnesota	*54-81	6-16
27—Cleveland	64-55	7-16

30—At Los Angeles	70-62	8-16

August

1—Houston	63-53	9-16
2—At Houston	*55-64	9-17
5—At New York	*60-69	9-18
7—Sacramento	*61-86	9-19
9—Los Angeles	69-52	10-19
12—At Seattle	87-77	11-19
16—Minnesota	*64-73	11-20
20—Seattle	78-70	†12-20
22—At Phoenix	*62-89	12-21
23—At Los Angeles	*70-83	12-22

*Loss. † Single overtime

TEAM LEADERS

Points: Marie Ferdinand (470).
Field goals made: Margo Dydek (156).
Free throws made: Marie Ferdinand (176).
Three-pointers made: Jennifer Azzi (39).
Rebounds: Margo Dydek (251).
Assists: Jennifer Azzi (111).
Steals: Marie Ferdinand (58).
Blocks: Margo Dydek (100).

TEAM-BY-TEAM RESULTS

vs. Charlotte: 1-1
vs. Cleveland: 1-0
vs. Connecticut: 0-1
vs. Detroit: 0-2
vs. Houston: 2-2
vs. Indiana: 0-1
vs. Los Angeles: 2-2
vs. Minnesota: 0-4
vs. New York: 0-1
vs. Phoenix: 2-2
vs. Sacramento: 1-3
vs. Seattle: 3-1
vs. Washington: 0-2

SEATTLE STORM
WESTERN CONFERENCE

351 Elliott Ave. W., Suite 500
Seattle, WA 98119
Tel: (206) 281-5800
Fax: (206) 281-5839
Ticket Information: (206) 217-WNBA (9622)

www.storm.wnba.com
Arena: KeyArena at Seattle Center (9,686)
Radio: SportsRadio KJR 950 AM
TV: Fox Sports Net (FSN)

2004 SEASON
TEAM DIRECTORY

Chairman ....Howard Schultz
President and CEO ....Wally Walker
Chief Operating Officer ....Karen Bryant
Head Coach & Director of Player Personnel...............................Anne Donovan
Assistant Coaches ....Jenny Boucek, Jessie Kenlaw
Director of Basketball Operations ....Missy Bequette
Head Athletic Trainer ....Annmarie Henkel
Strength & Conditioning Coach ....Greg Fahrendorf
Vice President, Marketing ....Rob Martin
Vice President, Corporate Sponsorship & Entertainment....................John Croley
Senior Director of Public Relations ....Valerie O'Neil
Director of Broadcasting ....Bridget Billig Backschies
Director of Marketing..Shelli Blank
Marketing Manager ....Sam Maccarrone
Community Relations Coordinator ....Sarah Childs
Corporate Sales Manager..Anthony O'Neil
Assistant Director of Public Relations ....Liam O'Mahony
Equipment Manager ....TBD
Video Coordinator ....Ayana Clinton
Public Relations Coodinator ....Jennifer Carroll
Sales Development Representatives ....Amy Burdick, Susie Jarosch,
                                                          Michele Swartz-Ireland
Play-By-Play Announcer ....David Locke
Color Analyst ....Elise Woodward

Karen Bryant

Anne Donovan

| May | | | | | | |
S	M	T	W	T	F	S
						1
2	3	4	5	6	7	8
9	10	11	12	13	14	15
16	17	18	19	20 Min	21	22 LA
23	24	25	26	27	28 Pho	29

| June | | | | | | |
S	M	T	W	T	F	S
		1	2	3 Pho	4	5 Sac
6	7	8	9	10	11 Con	12
13	14	15 NY	16	17	18 Hou	19 SA
20	21	22 Hou	23	24	25	‡26 NY
27	28	29	30			

| July | | | | | | |
S	M	T	W	T	F	S
				1	2 SA	3 Sac
4	5	6	7 Was	8 Cha	9	10 Det
11	12 SA	13	14	15 Sac	16	17 Was
18	19	20	21	22 Ind	23	24 Hou
25	26	27 Hou	28	29	30 Min	31

| September | | | | | | |
S	M	T	W	T	F	S
			1	2 Sac	3 LA	4 Pho
5	6	7	8 Det	9	10 Min	11
12 Con	13 Ind	14	15 Pho	16	17	18 LA
19	20	21	22	23	24	25
26	27	28	29	30		

August				
1 Cha	2	3	4 ★	5

▨ = **Home**   ☐ = **Away**   ★ WNBA vs. USA Basketball: The Game at Radio City

‡ - Denotes game to be played at Spokane Arena, Spokane, Wash.

2004 ROSTER

No.	Player	Pos.	Ht./Wt.	Metric	Born	College/Country
10	Sue Bird	G	5-9/150	1,75/ 68,0	10-16-80	Connecticut
6	Sandy Brondello	G	5-7/136	1,70/ 61,7	8-20-68	Australia
33	Janell Burse	C	6-5/199	1,96/ 90,3	5-19-79	Tulane
4	Simone Edwards	C	6-4/164	1,93/ 74,4	11-17-73	Iowa
50	Trina Frierson	F	6-2/186	1,88/ 84,4	10-13-80	Louisiana Tech
15	Lauren Jackson	F-C	6-5/187	1,96/ 84,8	5-11-81	Australia
17	Sun-Min Jung	C	6-1/168	1,85/ 76,2	10-12-74	Korea
22	Betty Lennox	G	5-8/143	1,73/ 64,9	12-4-76	Louisiana Tech
12	LaTonya Massaline	G-F	5-11/160	1,80/ 72,6	12-30-77	Florida
55	Sheri Sam	F-G	6-0/160	1,83/ 72,6	5-5-74	Vanderbilt
6	Alicia Thompson	F	6-1/180	1,85/ 81,6	6-30-76	Texas Tech
7	Kamila Vodichkova	C-F	6-4/185	1,93/ 83,9	12-19-72	Czech Republic
54	Maren Walseth	F	6-2/184	1,88/ 83,5	10-28-78	Penn State

Coach - Anne Donovan
Assistant Coaches - Jenny Boucek, Jessie Kenlaw
Trainer - Annmarie Henkel

2003 REVIEW

RESULTS

May

22—At Houston	*64-75	0-1
24—At San Antonio	*56-65	0-2
30—Los Angeles	*74-77	†0-3

June

3—Sacramento	70-56	1-3
7—Phoenix	66-57	2-3
10—Indiana	78-51	3-3
14—Minnesota	*72-77	3-4
17—At Phoenix	61-60	4-4
19—At Los Angeles	69-67	5-4
21—At Sacramento	*64-69	5-5
22—San Antonio	93-53	6-5

27—At Cleveland	71-59	7-5
28—At Indiana	*70-79	7-6
30—At Charlotte	83-71	8-6

July

3—Washington	76-72	9-6
5—At Los Angeles	*75-84	9-7
15—Houston	69-55	10-7
17—At Connecticut	67-65	11-7
18—At Detroit	*61-74	11-8
20—At Minnesota	*58-69	11-9
23—New York	75-65	12-9
25—Phoenix	82-53	13-9
26—At Sacramento	*63-76	13-10

31—Charlotte	69-54	14-10

August

2—At Minnesota	*71-73	14-11
6—Los Angeles	92-56	15-11
8—Minnesota	68-65	16-11
12—San Antonio	*77-87	16-12
15—At Phoenix	*50-64	16-13
17—Detroit	*86-95	16-14
19—At Houston	*47-52	16-15
20—At San Antonio	*70-78	†16-16
23—Houston	71-64	17-16
25—Sacramento	70-57	18-16

*Loss. † Single overtime.

TEAM LEADERS

Points: Lauren Jackson (698).
Field goals made: Lauren Jackson (254).
Free throws made: Lauren Jackson (151).
Three-pointers made: Sue Bird (49).
Rebounds: Lauren Jackson (307).
Assists: Sue Bird (221).
Steals: Sue Bird (48).
Blocks: Lauren Jackson (64).

TEAM-BY-TEAM RESULTS

vs. Charlotte: 2-0
vs. Cleveland: 1-0
vs. Connecticut: 1-0
vs. Detroit: 0-2
vs. Houston: 2-2
vs. Indiana: 1-1
vs. Los Angeles: 2-2
vs. Minnesota: 1-3
vs. New York: 1-0
vs. Phoenix: 3-1
vs. Sacramento: 2-2
vs. San Antonio: 1-3
vs. Washington: 1-0

WASHINGTON MYSTICS
EASTERN CONFERENCE

MCI Center
601 F Street, N.W.
Washington, DC 20004
Tel: (202) 661-5000
Fax: (202) 661-5108

Ticket Information: (202) 661-5050
www.washingtonmystics.com
Arena: MCI Center (20,173)
Radio: Sportstalk 1260
TV: Comcast Sports Net

2004 SEASON
TEAM DIRECTORY

Chairman ....Abe Pollin
President ....Susan O'Malley
Senior Vice President, Sponsorship ....Rick Moreland
Senior Vice President, Communications ....Matt Williams
Sr. VP, Mystics Business and Basketball Operations ....Judy Holland Burton
Vice President, Customer Service ....Rhonda Ballute
Vice President, Marketing...Ann Nicolaides
Vice President, Ticket Sales ....Mark Schiponi
Player Personnel Consultant ....Pat Summitt
Head Coach...Michael Adams
Assistant Coaches ....Linda Hargrove, Stephanie Ready, Ledell Eackles
Head Trainer ....Annemarie Francis
Director of the Mystics...Dyani Gordon
Senior Director, Community Relations..Sashia Jones
Assistant Director, Community Relations ....Tracy Ward
Assistant Director, Customer Service ....Greg Hall
Assistant Director, Public Relations..Ketsia Colimon
Public Relations Assistant ....Nicole Boden
Director, Game Operations ....Ken Bradford
Assistant Director, Game Operations ....Damian Bass

Abe Pollin

Susan O'Malley

Michael Adams

May								June								July								September						
S	M	T	W	T	F	S		S	M	T	W	T	F	S		S	M	T	W	T	F	S		S	M	T	W	T	F	S
						1				1	2	3 Det	4 Con	5						1 Ind	2	3					1	2	3 Ind	4 Ind
2	3	4	5	6	7	8		6	7	8	9	10 Det	11 Con	12		4	5	6	7 Sea	8 NY	9	10 Cha		5	6 Sac	7	8	9 NY	10	11
9	10	11	12	13	14	15		§13 NY	14	15	16	17 SA	18	19		11	12	13	14	15 Cha	16	17 Sea		12 Hou	13	14	15 SA	16	17 Pho	18
16	17	18	19	20	21	22 Cha		20 Con	21	22 Det	23	24	25	26		18 Sac	19	20	21 LA	22	23 Min	24 Cha		19 NY	20	21	22	23	24	25
23 Ind	24	25 LA	26	27	28	29 Min		27	28 Hou	29	30 Con					25	26	27	28 Det	29	30 Con	31		26	27	28	29	30		

August | 1 Pho | 2 | 3 | 4 | ★5 |

 = Home   = Away   ★ WNBA vs. USA Basketball: The Game at Radio City

§ - Denotes game to be played at Comcast Center, College Park, Md.

2004 ROSTER

No.	Player	Pos.	Ht./Wt.	Metric	Born	College/Country
	Alana Beard	G-F	5-11/160	1,80/ 72,6	5-14-82	Duke
00	Tamara Bowie	F	6-0/165	1,83/ 74,8	6-3-81	Ball State
5	Annie Burgess	G	5-7/141	1,70/ 64,0	4-10-69	Australia
	Kaayla Chones	C	6-3/180	1,91/ 81,6	1-11-81	North Carolina State
21	Stacey Dales-Schuman	F	6-0/155	1,83/ 70,3	9-6-79	Oklahoma
1	Chamique Holdsclaw	F	6-2/172	1,88/ 78,0	8-9-77	Tennessee
35	Tamicha Jackson	G	5-6/120	1,68/ 54,4	4-22-78	Louisiana Tech
25	Helen Luz	G	5-8/144	1,73/ 65,3	11-23-72	Brazil
44	Chasity Melvin	C-F	6-3/185	1,91/ 83,9	5-3-76	North Carolina State
9	Coco Miller	G	5-9/140	1,75/ 63,5	9-6-78	Georgia
10	Murriel Page	C	6-2/160	1,88/ 72,6	9-18-75	Florida
45	Jocelyn Penn	F	6-0	1,83/	9-10-79	South Carolina
43	Nakia Sanford	F-C	6-4/200	1,93/ 90,7	5-10-76	Kansas
31	Aiysha Smith	F	6-2/173	1,88/ 78,5	7-18-80	Louisiana State
	Evan Unrau	F	6-1/165	1,85/ 74,8	1-21-82	Missouri

Coach - Michael Adams
Assistant Coaches - Linda Hargrove, Stephanie Ready, Ledell Eackles
Trainer - Annemarie Francis

2003 REVIEW

RESULTS

May
23—At Charlotte 74-70 1-0
31—At Indiana *60-71 1-1
June
1—At New York *57-70 1-2
6—Cleveland *53-63 1-3
10—San Antonio 79-72 2-3
13—At Connecticut *70-84 2-4
14—Detroit *56-93 2-5
18—Sacramento *61-69 2-6
20—At Cleveland *74-79 2-7
24—Connecticut *63-65 2-8
29—Minnesota *50-59 2-9
July
2—At Sacramento *62-83 2-10

3—At Seattle *72-76 2-11
5—At Houston *54-76 2-12
7—Charlotte *56-62 2-13
9—Los Angeles *91-97 2-14
15—At New York 77-64 3-14
17—Charlotte 68-60 4-14
19—At San Antonio 85-77 5-14
22—At Los Angeles *73-77 5-15
24—Indiana *75-80 5-16
26—At Cleveland *78-89 5-17
27—At Detroit *71-81 5-18
29—Indiana *91-92 †5-19
August
1—At Connecticut 48-45 6-19
3—Phoenix *69-70 ‡6-20

6—Detroit 92-81 7-20
9—New York *56-65 7-21
12—At Indiana 84-80 8-21
14—At Charlotte 76-69 9-21
16—Cleveland *68-72 9-22
21—New York *60-65 9-23
23—Connecticut *67-74 9-24
25—At Detroit *60-68 9-25
*Loss. † Single overtime. ‡ Double overtime.

TEAM LEADERS

Points: Chamique Holdsclaw (554).
Field goals made: Chamique Holdsclaw (204).
Free throws made: Chamique Holdsclaw (140).
Three-pointers made: Stacey Dales-Schuman (57).
Rebounds: Chamique Holdsclaw (294).
Assists: Stacey Dales-Schuman (114).
Steals: Coco Miller (39).
Blocks: Asjha Jones (25).

TEAM-BY-TEAM RESULTS

vs. Charlotte: 3-1
vs. Cleveland: 0-4
vs. Connecticut: 1-3
vs. Detroit: 1-3
vs. Houston: 0-1
vs. Indiana: 1-3
vs. Los Angeles: 0-2
vs. Minnesota: 0-1
vs. New York: 1-3
vs. Phoenix: 0-1
vs. Sacramento: 0-2
vs. San Antonio: 2-0
vs. Seattle: 0-1

DETROIT SHOCK, 2003 WNBA CHAMPIONS

Front Row (l. to r.) – Sheila Lambert, Assistant Coach Korie Hlede, Assistant Coach Pamela McGee, Head Coach Bill Laimbeer, Assistant Coach Laurie Byrd, Elaine Powell, Kedra Holland-Corn.
Back Row (l. to r.) – Allison Curtin, Swin Cash, Stacey Thomas, Barbara Farris, Ayana Walker, Ruth Riley, Petra Ujhelyi, Cheryl Ford, Astou Ndiaye-Diatta, Deanna Nolan, Team Trainer Laura Ramus.

FINAL STANDINGS

EASTERN CONFERENCE

TEAM	W	L	PCT	GB	HOME	ROAD	LAST-10	STREAK
Detroit	25	9	.735	-	13-4	12-5	7-3	Won 4
Charlotte	18	16	.529	7	13-4	5-12	5-5	Lost 1
Connecticut	18	16	.529	7	10-7	8-9	5-5	Won 3
Cleveland	17	17	.500	8	11-6	6-11	6-4	Won 1
Indiana	16	18	.471	9	11-6	5-12	3-7	Lost 1
New York	16	18	.471	9	11-6	5-12	5-5	Lost 2
Washington	9	25	.265	16	3-14	6-11	4-6	Lost 4

WESTERN CONFERENCE

TEAM	W	L	PCT	GB	HOME	ROAD	LAST-10	STREAK
Los Angeles	24	10	.706	-	11-6	13-4	6-4	Won 5
Houston	20	14	.588	4	14-3	6-11	5-5	Lost 3
Sacramento	19	15	.559	5	12-5	7-10	7-3	Lost 1
Minnesota	18	16	.529	6	11-6	7-10	5-5	Lost 2
Seattle	18	16	.529	6	13-4	5-12	4-6	Won 2
San Antonio	12	22	.353	12	9-8	3-14	4-6	Lost 2
Phoenix	8	26	.235	16	6-11	2-15	3-7	Lost 1

TEAM STANDINGS

OFFENSIVE

TEAM	G	FG	FGA	PCT	FG3	FG3A	PCT	FT	FTA	PCT	OFF	DEF	REB	AST	PF	DQ	STL	TO	BLK	PTS	AVG
Det.	34	902	2004	.450	125	323	.387	624	882	.707	379	851	1230	545	605	3	263	608	158	2553	75.1
L.A.	34	894	2140	.418	174	528	.330	537	678	.792	336	813	1149	587	682	12	242	470	161	2499	73.5
Sea.	34	890	2045	.435	166	500	.332	442	567	.780	342	732	1074	548	644	8	232	465	138	2388	70.2
Conn.	34	864	2102	.411	177	549	.322	479	646	.741	333	762	1095	520	663	5	270	434	111	2384	70.1
Minn.	34	875	1978	.442	180	524	.344	450	624	.721	361	718	1079	580	634	6	242	558	101	2380	70.0
Ind.	34	839	2011	.417	210	600	.350	449	563	.798	334	654	988	539	668	5	299	474	121	2337	68.7
Wash.	34	896	2191	.409	157	505	.311	381	507	.751	382	703	1085	568	676	5	213	462	99	2330	68.5
Sac.	34	862	2107	.409	150	473	.317	425	626	.679	349	718	1067	568	641	7	297	461	122	2299	67.6
Hou.	34	828	1916	.432	115	344	.334	473	600	.788	266	764	1030	465	490	2	231	450	129	2244	66.0
N.Y.	34	825	1923	.429	181	500	.362	412	537	.767	271	686	957	527	587	5	262	470	128	2243	66.0
Clev.	34	815	1975	.413	135	425	.318	464	643	.722	349	720	1069	517	639	4	226	466	86	2229	65.6
Cha.	34	787	1881	.418	187	517	.362	456	590	.773	342	629	971	499	697	3	279	497	115	2217	65.2
S.A.	34	792	2068	.383	93	315	.295	538	736	.731	350	795	1145	428	728	8	187	513	167	2215	65.1
Phoe.	34	801	2095	.382	116	349	.332	379	556	.682	357	643	1000	461	664	8	310	479	111	2097	61.7

DEFENSIVE

Team	FG	FGA	PCT	FG3	FG3A	PCT	FT	FTA	PCT	OFF	DEF	REB	AST	PF	DQ	STL	TO	BLK	PTS	AVG	DIFF
Hou.	824	2030	.406	169	500	.338	325	448	.725	298	708	1006	516	634	2	227	430	122	2142	63.0	+3.0
Cha.	790	1902	.415	138	407	.339	477	667	.715	386	621	1007	491	606	2	264	469	104	2195	64.6	+0.6
Clev.	809	1927	.420	127	355	.358	465	607	.766	300	704	1004	510	659	9	223	467	135	2210	65.0	+0.6
Sac.	816	1991	.410	149	467	.319	435	597	.729	345	751	1096	516	640	9	224	576	141	2216	65.2	+2.4
N.Y.	821	1959	.419	155	467	.332	459	581	.790	326	736	1062	506	614	5	269	480	96	2256	66.4	-0.4
Phoe.	834	1867	.447	136	371	.367	466	626	.744	303	811	1114	509	667	4	275	610	146	2270	66.8	-5.1
Sea.	844	2039	.414	145	437	.332	441	591	.746	352	689	1041	456	570	9	245	459	104	2274	66.9	+3.4
Ind.	837	1908	.439	157	421	.373	490	638	.768	309	677	986	570	631	4	227	512	170	2321	68.3	+0.5
Minn.	878	2067	.425	141	446	.316	473	633	.747	337	652	989	528	666	10	271	471	126	2370	69.7	+0.3
Det.	911	2286	.399	161	541	.298	412	556	.741	390	674	1064	504	774	5	309	497	129	2395	70.4	+4.6
Conn.	864	2104	.411	172	536	.321	509	673	.756	366	812	1178	553	669	8	252	476	88	2409	70.9	-0.7
S.A.	867	2176	.398	149	482	.309	544	745	.730	389	783	1172	530	669	8	275	424	140	2427	71.4	-6.2
L.A.	866	2147	.403	196	540	.363	504	702	.718	316	789	1105	572	654	6	241	468	127	2432	71.5	+2.0
Wash.	909	2033	.447	171	482	.355	509	691	.737	334	781	1115	591	565	0	251	468	119	2498	73.5	-4.9
AVG.'S	848	2031	.417	155	461	.336	465	625	.743	339	728	1067	525	644	6	254	486	125	2315	68.1	---
	11870	28436	---	2166	6452	---	6509	8755	---	4751	10188	14939	7352	9018	81	3553	6807	1747	32415	---	---

TEAM COMPARISONS

TEAM	Points Per Game		Field Goal Percentage		Turnovers Per Game		Rebound Percentages			Below 70 Pts.		Overtime Games		3 PTS or Less		10 PTS or More	
	OWN	OPP	OWN	OPP	OWN	OPP	OFF	DEF	TOT	OWN	OPP	W	L	W	L	W	L
Charlotte	65.2	64.6	.418	.415	14.6	13.8	.355	.620	.487	26	24	1	1	4	1	8	7
Cleveland	65.6	65.0	.413	.420	13.7	13.7	.331	.706	.519	21	22	1	0	2	3	8	8
Connecticut	70.1	70.9	.411	.411	12.8*	14.0	.291	.676	.483	16	18	0	2	3	4	7	8
Detroit	75.1*	70.4	.450*	.399	17.9	14.6	.360*	.686	.523*	12	18	4	0	6	2	11	5
Houston	66.0	63.0*	.432	.406	13.2	12.6	.273	.719	.496	24	27	0	1	3	3	9	4
Indiana	68.7	68.3	.417	.439	13.9	15.1	.330	.679	.505	20	19	2	0	1	1	10	7
Los Angeles	73.5	71.5	.418	.403	13.8	13.8	.299	.720*	.509	12	15	2	1	8	2	4	3
Minnesota	70.0	69.7	.442	.425	16.4	13.9	.356	.681	.518	16	15	1	1	3	4	4	5
New York	66.0	66.4	.429	.419	13.8	14.1	.269	.678	.473	22	24	0	2	2	3	6	8
Phoenix	61.7	66.8	.382	.447	14.1	17.9*	.306	.680	.493	28	24	1	2	3	6	3	9
Sacramento	67.6	65.2	.409	.410	13.6	16.9	.317	.675	.496	24	21	1	0	1	6	9	6
San Antonio	65.1	71.4	.383	.398*	15.1	12.5	.309	.671	.490	22	16	1	0	1	2	6	13
Seattle	70.2	66.9	.435	.414	13.7	13.5	.332	.675	.503	15	21	0	2	4	2	11	6
Washington	68.5	73.5	.409	.447	13.6	13.8	.328	.678	.503	18	12	0	2	1	3	2	9
COMPOSITE; 238 games																	
	68.1		.417		14.3		.318	.682		276	276	14		42		98	

* - League Leader

REBOUND PERCENTAGES

OFF. - Percentage of a given team's missed shots which that team rebounds.

DEF. - Percentage of opponents' missed shots which a given team rebounds.

TOT. - Average of offensive and defensive rebound percentages.

SCORING AVERAGE

	G	FG	FT	PTS	AVG
Jackson, Sea.	33	254	151	698	21.2
Holdsclaw, Was.	27	204	140	554	20.5
Catchings, Ind.	34	221	155	671	19.7
Leslie, L.A.	23	165	82	424	18.4
Smith, Min.	34	208	126	620	18.2
Thompson, Hou.	28	176	81	472	16.9
Cash, Det.	33	195	146	548	16.6
Sales, Ct.	34	194	116	548	16.1
Swoopes, Hou.	31	175	110	484	15.6
Ferdinand, S.A.	34	139	176	470	13.8
Griffith, Sac.	34	161	147	469	13.8
Mabika, L.A.	32	158	97	441	13.8
Dixon, L.A.	30	159	83	412	13.7
Williams, Ind.	34	176	105	457	13.4
Johnson, N.Y.	32	158	79	430	13.4
Milton, L.A.	31	139	115	416	13.4
Melvin, Cle.	34	159	123	444	13.1
Smith, Sac.	34	188	41	430	12.6
Miller, Was.	33	172	37	413	12.5
Feaster, Cha.	34	142	66	422	12.4

REBOUNDS PER GAME

	G	OFF	DEF	TOT	AVG
Holdsclaw, Was.	27	72	222	294	10.9
Ford, Det.	32	99	235	334	10.4
Leslie, L.A.	23	76	155	231	10.0
Jackson, Sea.	33	82	225	307	9.3
Phillips, N.Y.	33	99	181	280	8.5
Catchings, Ind.	34	82	190	272	8.0
Snow, Hou.	34	76	187	263	7.7
Williams, Ind.	34	109	146	255	7.5
Williams, Pho.	34	68	184	252	7.4
Dydek, S.A.	34	45	206	251	7.4
Griffith, Sac.	34	92	156	248	7.3
Milton, L.A.	31	59	161	220	7.1
McWilliams-Franklin, Ct.	34	78	149	227	6.7
Melvin, Cle.	34	82	133	215	6.3
Jackson, S.A.	33	86	119	205	6.2
Williams, Min.	34	92	117	209	6.1
Riley, Det.	34	59	142	201	5.9
Sutton-Brown, Cha.	34	73	128	201	5.9
Thompson, Hou.	28	39	126	165	5.9
Cash, Det.	33	65	128	193	5.8

ASSISTS PER GAME

	G	AST	AVG
Penicheiro, Sac.	34	229	6.7
Bird, Sea.	34	221	6.5
Teasley, L.A.	34	214	6.3
S. Johnson, Ct.	34	196	5.8
Staley, Cha.	34	174	5.1
Weatherspoon, N.Y.	34	149	4.4
Edwards, Min.	34	148	4.4
Jackson, Pho.	34	146	4.3
Powell, Det.	33	129	3.9
Swoopes, Hou.	31	121	3.9
Darling, Cle.	34	128	3.8
Cash, Det.	33	119	3.6
Catchings, Ind.	34	114	3.4
Dales-Schuman, Was.	34	114	3.4
Holdsclaw, Was.	27	89	3.3
Burgess, Was.	34	112	3.3
Azzi, S.A.	34	111	3.3
Dixon, L.A.	30	89	3.0
Stinson, Cha.	34	97	2.9
Abrosimova, Min.	30	82	2.7

FIELD GOAL PCT.

	FG	FGA	PCT
Williams, Min.	129	193	.668
Snow, Hou.	126	253	.498
Riley, Det.	115	231	.498
Griffith, Sac.	161	332	.485
Williams, Ind.	176	363	.485
Jackson, Sea.	254	526	.483
Melvin, Cle.	159	333	.477
Vodichkova, Sea.	101	213	.474
Ford, Det.	128	270	.474
Rasmussen, Ind.	94	200	.470

3-PT FIELD GOAL PCT.

	3FG	3GA	PCT
Hammon, N.Y.	23	49	.469
Brondello, Sea.	21	48	.437
Teasley, L.A.	70	165	.424
Miller, Cha.	22	52	.423
Nolan, Det.	48	114	.421
Enis, Cha.	26	62	.419
Campbell, Sac.	46	111	.414
Jackson, Cle.	29	70	.414
DeForge, Pho.	61	148	.412
Holland-Corn, Det.	50	124	.403

FREE THROW PCT.

	FT	FTA	PCT
Hammon, N.Y.	39	41	.951
White, Ind.	45	48	.937
Holdsclaw, Was.	140	155	.903
Swoopes, Hou.	110	124	.887
Bird, Sea.	61	69	.884
Dixon, L.A.	83	94	.883
Smith, Min.	126	143	.881
Teasley, L.A.	98	112	.875
Mabika, L.A.	97	112	.866
Johnson, N.Y.	79	92	.859

STEALS PER GAME

	G	STL	AVG
Swoopes, Hou.	31	77	2.48
Catchings, Ind.	34	72	2.12
Penicheiro, Sac.	34	61	1.79
Ferdinand, S.A.	34	58	1.71
Phillips, N.Y.	33	56	1.70
Griffith, Sac.	34	57	1.68
Williams, Pho.	34	57	1.68
Milton, L.A.	31	49	1.58
Feaster, Cha.	34	52	1.53
Jackson, Pho.	34	52	1.53

BLOCKS PER GAME

	G	BLK	AVG
Dydek, S.A.	34	100	2.94
Leslie, L.A.	23	63	2.74
Jackson, Sea.	33	64	1.94
Snow, Hou.	34	62	1.82
Riley, Det.	34	58	1.71
Sutton-Brown, Cha.	34	50	1.47
Milton, L.A.	31	41	1.32
Baranova, N.Y.	33	43	1.30
Griffith, Sac.	34	39	1.15
Catchings, Ind.	34	35	1.03

MINUTES PER GAME

	G	MIN	AVG
Catchings, Ind.	34	1210	35.6
Holdsclaw, Was.	27	948	35.1
Milton, L.A.	31	1086	35.0
Teasley, L.A.	34	1189	35.0
Swoopes, Hou.	31	1084	35.0
Smith, Min.	34	1185	34.9
Thompson, Hou.	28	974	34.8
Dixon, L.A.	30	1042	34.7
Leslie, L.A.	23	792	34.4
Jackson, Sea.	33	1109	33.6

CHARLOTTE STING

Player	G	Min	FGM	FGA	Pct	FTM	FTA	Pct	Off	Def	Tot	Ast	PF	Dq	Stl	TO	Blk	Pts	Avg	Hi
Allison Feaster............34		1096	142	378	.376	66	78	.846	37	76	113	73	75	0	52	72	9	422	12.4	23
Andrea Stinson...........34		1000	147	321	.458	60	79	.759	28	112	140	97	70	0	48	75	5	377	11.1	23
Shalonda Enis.............29		613	82	188	.436	62	77	.805	62	63	125	16	63	0	29	41	2	252	8.7	29
Tammy Sutton-Brown..34		864	98	233	.421	90	131	.687	73	128	201	15	132	2	19	59	50	286	8.4	21
Dawn Staley................34		1086	90	216	.417	61	73	.836	14	44	58	174	76	0	49	78	4	269	7.9	20
Kelly Miller 34		523	68	167	.407	31	40	.775	20	33	53	47	44	0	18	35	2	189	5.6	14
Rushia Brown.............34		483	53	116	.457	19	23	.826	34	49	83	16	88	1	29	35	10	125	3.7	14
Charlotte Smith-Tayl....27		443	31	98	.316	24	36	.667	23	37	60	18	54	0	10	24	2	95	3.5	10
Teana McKiver 31		341	41	78	.526	23	31	.742	37	54	91	6	58	0	14	27	24	105	3.4	15
Tynesha Lewis 23		234	26	62	.419	11	12	.917	11	22	33	20	18	0	10	16	6	70	3.0	13
Marla Brumfield 25		123	6	16	.375	6	6	1.000	1	9	10	14	13	0	1	6	1	18	0.7	6
Erin Buescher 14		44	3	8	.375	3	4	.750	2	2	4	3	6	0	0	2	0	9	0.6	3
Charlotte 34		6850	787	1881	.418	456	590	.773	342	629	971	499	697	3	279	497	115	2217	65.2	92
Opponents 34		6850	790	1902	.415	477	667	.715	386	621	1007	491	606	2	264	469	104	2195	64.6	83

3-pt. FG: Charlotte 187-517 (.362)
Feaster 72-205 (.351); Stinson 23-75 (.307); Enis 26-62 (.419); Staley 28-72 (.389); Miller 22-52 (.423); Brown 0-2 (.000)
Smith-Taylor 9-32 (.281); McKiver 0-1 (.000); Lewis 7-13 (.538); Brumfield 0-3 (.000); Opponents 138-407 (.339)

CLEVELAND ROCKERS

Player	G	Min	FGM	FGA	Pct	FTM	FTA	Pct	Off	Def	Tot	Ast	PF	Dq	Stl	TO	Blk	Pts	Avg	Hi
Chasity Melvin 34		1061	159	333	.477	123	176	.699	82	133	215	52	108	0	28	67	22	444	13.1	22
Penny Taylor 34		898	143	340	.421	78	95	.821	44	104	148	80	53	0	38	60	10	398	11.7	33
LaToya Thomas 32		852	137	296	.463	71	90	.789	63	101	164	37	62	1	28	42	13	345	10.8	23
Betty Lennox 34		560	100	269	.372	26	36	.722	19	70	89	32	77	0	14	58	4	258	7.6	23
Deanna Jackson 34		763	83	198	.419	50	70	.714	37	52	89	51	92	1	20	33	13	245	7.2	30
Merlakia Jones 34		672	66	196	.337	28	39	.718	18	79	97	44	59	0	22	36	3	164	4.8	14
Helen Darling 34		832	44	143	.308	30	41	.732	25	62	87	128	87	2	39	74	6	141	4.1	10
Lucienne Berthieu 22		201	27	52	.519	30	46	.652	20	22	42	6	38	0	10	22	4	84	3.8	15
Pollyanna Johns Kimb 30		416	35	63	.556	19	34	.559	31	51	82	19	35	0	12	19	10	89	3.0	13
Jennifer Rizzotti 33		525	20	72	.278	9	16	.563	4	38	42	65	22	0	14	35	0	59	1.8	8
Tracy Henderson 11		45	1	13	.077	0	0	---	6	8	14	3	6	0	1	4	1	2	0.2	2
Cleveland...................34		6825	815	1975	.413	464	643	.722	349	720	1069	517	639	4	226	466	86	2229	65.6	89
Opponents 34		6825	809	1927	.420	465	607	.766	300	704	1004	510	659	9	223	467	135	2210	65.0	81

3-pt. FG: Cleveland 135-425 (.318)
Melvin 3-11 (.273); Taylor 34-99 (.343); Thomas 0-6 (.000); Lennox 32-103 (.311); Jackson 29-70 (.414); Jones 4-13 (.308)
Darling 23-71 (.324); Berthieu 0-1 (.000); Rizzotti 10-51 (.196); Opponents 127-355 (.358)

CONNECTICUT SUN

Player	G	Min	FGM	FGA	Pct	FTM	FTA	Pct	Off	Def	Tot	Ast	PF	Dq	Stl	TO	Blk	Pts	Avg	Hi
Nykesha Sales 34		1106	194	468	.415	116	144	.806	27	118	145	92	107	3	46	73	13	548	16.1	31
Shannon Johnson 34		1107	138	319	.433	125	171	.731	39	95	134	196	77	0	44	107	3	420	12.4	31
Katie Douglas 28		843	120	274	.438	49	68	.721	33	73	106	56	38	0	31	28	11	336	12.0	28
Taj McWilliams-Frank 34		983	133	301	.442	76	102	.745	78	149	227	49	103	1	43	54	33	354	10.4	28
Adrienne Johnson.......34		584	69	195	.354	18	24	.750	23	35	58	18	36	0	17	21	1	173	5.1	15
Wendy Palmer 32		433	58	147	.395	23	28	.821	29	77	106	16	62	0	11	35	3	149	4.7	20
Brooke Wyckoff 34		755	55	142	.387	26	36	.722	48	98	146	35	109	1	33	39	19	156	4.6	17
Jessie Hicks 27		253	37	80	.463	24	25	.960	23	25	48	6	47	0	11	26	9	98	3.6	12
Rebecca Lobo 25		297	25	88	.284	2	9	.222	9	43	52	5	33	0	6	14	15	59	2.4	12
Courtney Coleman 20		141	11	20	.550	14	30	.467	8	14	22	1	18	0	8	13	2	36	1.8	6
Debbie Black 34		373	24	68	.353	6	9	.667	16	35	51	46	33	0	20	18	2	55	1.6	8
Connecticut 34		6875	864	2102	.411	479	646	.741	333	762	1095	520	663	5	270	434	111	2384	70.1	91
Opponents 34		6875	864	2104	.411	509	673	.756	366	812	1178	553	669	8	252	476	88	2409	70.9	103

3-pt. FG: Connecticut 177-549 (.322)
Sales 44-114 (.386); S. Johnson 19-73 (.260); Douglas 47-123 (.382); McWilliams-Frank 12-43 (.279); A. Johnson 17-49 (.347)
Palmer 10-46 (.217); Wyckoff 20-70 (.286); Lobo 7-28 (.250); Black 1-3 (.333); Opponents 172-536 (.321)

DETROIT SHOCK

Player	G	Min	FGM	FGA	Pct	FTM	FTA	Pct	Off	Def	Tot	Ast	PF	Dq	Stl	TO	Blk	Pts	Avg	Hi
Swin Cash 33		1097	195	430	.453	146	214	.682	65	128	193	119	76	0	43	108	23	548	16.6	26
Deanna Nolan 32		954	136	312	.436	76	96	.792	12	95	107	83	65	0	41	69	14	396	12.4	27
Cheryl Ford 32		956	128	270	.474	88	129	.682	99	235	334	27	109	1	32	79	31	344	10.8	20
Ruth Riley 34		995	115	231	.498	97	127	.764	59	142	201	64	128	2	25	82	58	327	9.6	19
Kedra Holland-Corn....34		694	107	232	.461	48	63	.762	12	45	57	63	26	0	36	59	3	312	9.2	23
Elaine Powell 33		938	105	233	.451	79	106	.745	43	63	106	129	65	0	45	79	9	296	9.0	16

47

Player	G	Min	FGM	FGA	Pct	FTM	FTA	Pct	REBOUNDS			Ast	PF	Dq	Stl	TO	Blk	SCORING		
									Off	Def	Tot							Pts	Avg	Hi
Barbara Farris..............34	522	43	99	.434	41	63	.651	29	53	82	23	62	0	10	41	4	127	3.7	14
Sheila Lambert 27	187	24	66	.364	32	41	.780	10	18	28	14	15	0	5	29	0	87	3.2	14
Stacey Thomas(*) 11	82	5	16	.313	4	11	.364	5	11	16	5	10	0	9	6	1	15	1.4	6
Stacey Thomas(!) 30	269	20	62	.323	14	27	.519	15	28	43	15	24	0	20	16	9	61	2.0	9
Astou Ndiaye-Diatta 11	70	10	21	.476	0	2	.000	5	9	14	1	3	0	3	9	1	20	1.8	10
Ayana Walker...............34	271	24	70	.343	8	21	.381	34	37	71	10	33	0	10	19	11	56	1.6	14
Tamara Moore(>) 15	66	8	16	.500	5	6	.833	3	6	9	4	5	0	4	6	2	21	1.4	5
Petra Ujhelyi...............14	68	2	8	.250	0	3	.000	3	9	12	3	8	0	0	10	1	4	0.3	2
Detroit 34	6900	902	2004	.450	624	882	.707	379	851	1230	545	605	3	263	608	158	2553	75.1	103
Opponents 34	6900	911	2286	.399	412	556	.741	390	674	1064	504	774	5	309	497	129	2395	70.4	92

3-pt. FG: Detroit 125-323 (.387).

Cash 12-40 (.300); Nolan 48-114 (.421); Holland-Corn 50-124 (.403); Powell 7-20 (.350); Lambert 7-16 (.438); Thomas(*) 1-5 (.200)
Thomas(!) 7-27 (.259); Moore(>) 0-4 (.000); Opponents 161-541 (.298)

HOUSTON COMETS

Player	G	Min	FGM	FGA	Pct	FTM	FTA	Pct	REBOUNDS			Ast	PF	Dq	Stl	TO	Blk	SCORING		
									Off	Def	Tot							Pts	Avg	Hi
Tina Thompson 28	974	176	426	.413	81	104	.779	39	126	165	47	65	0	18	69	23	472	16.9	30
Cynthia Cooper 4	144	16	38	.421	25	28	.893	2	8	10	22	9	0	4	14	1	64	16.0	22
Sheryl Swoopes 31	1084	175	434	.403	110	124	.887	32	111	143	121	48	0	77	73	26	484	15.6	29
Janeth Arcain 34	1136	151	324	.466	94	112	.840	24	112	136	67	64	0	41	50	1	390	11.5	20
Michelle Snow 34	1025	126	253	.498	62	85	.729	76	187	263	42	120	2	35	68	62	314	9.2	19
Dominique Canty.......32	648	55	145	.379	62	93	.667	36	64	100	56	62	0	22	49	1	172	5.4	14
Ukari Figgs.................34	952	52	124	.419	19	22	.864	11	70	81	82	33	0	26	59	1	149	4.4	13
Tiffani Johnson 22	359	30	62	.484	17	23	.739	19	44	63	13	33	0	3	20	7	77	3.5	8
Mfon Udoka.................25	251	32	64	.500	16	23	.696	22	29	51	4	38	0	4	21	2	80	3.2	12
Kelley Gibson..............26	209	14	42	.333	0	0	---	4	12	16	8	14	0	1	9	5	38	1.5	9
Octavia Blue 16	37	1	4	.250	2	4	.500	1	1	2	2	3	0	0	2	0	4	0.3	2
Itoro Umoh-Coleman ...3	6	0	0	---	0	0	---	0	0	0	1	1	0	0	1	0	0	0.0	0
Houston.....................34	6825	828	1916	.432	473	600	.788	266	764	1030	465	490	2	231	450	129	2244	66.0	83
Opponents 34	6825	824	2030	.406	325	448	.725	298	708	1006	516	634	2	227	430	122	2142	63.0	91

3-pt. FG: Houston 115-344 (.334).

Thompson 39-114 (.342); Cooper 7-18 (.389); Swoopes 24-79 (.304); Arcain 9-37 (.243); Snow 0-1 (.000); Canty 0-1 (.000)
Figgs 26-69 (.377); Udoka 0-1 (.000); Gibson 10-24 (.417); Opponents 169-500 (.338)

INDIANA FEVER

Player	G	Min	FGM	FGA	Pct	FTM	FTA	Pct	REBOUNDS			Ast	PF	Dq	Stl	TO	Blk	SCORING		
									Off	Def	Tot							Pts	Avg	Hi
Tamika Catchings........34	1210	221	512	.432	155	183	.847	82	190	272	114	122	2	72	102	35	671	19.7	32
Natalie Williams 34	1054	176	363	.485	105	148	.709	109	146	255	46	138	2	43	70	21	457	13.4	24
Stephanie White..........28	577	60	173	.347	45	48	.938	14	27	41	58	60	0	34	37	6	194	6.9	16
Kristen Rasmussen 33	814	94	200	.470	31	39	.795	44	71	115	64	65	0	24	48	15	226	6.8	16
Coretta Brown 30	522	61	164	.372	28	33	.848	11	30	41	31	30	0	21	36	4	186	6.2	26
Kelly Schumacher 34	480	81	169	.479	23	27	.852	40	59	99	20	63	0	7	32	24	189	5.6	22
Niele Ivey...................27	651	45	116	.388	12	17	.706	5	27	32	71	40	0	29	28	7	135	5.0	14
Nikki McCray..............34	734	52	138	.377	20	24	.833	18	33	51	49	67	1	37	44	2	131	3.9	11
Coquese Washington ...20	348	19	67	.284	11	13	.846	2	27	29	48	32	0	14	30	2	63	3.2	18
Zuzi Klimesova 1	3	0	1	.000	2	2	1.000	0	0	0	0	1	0	0	0	0	2	2.0	2
Bridget Pettis 31	148	15	52	.288	13	17	.765	5	14	19	8	17	0	4	8	1	49	1.6	9
Leigh Aziz 7	44	4	14	.286	2	4	.500	2	7	9	1	5	0	0	3	4	10	1.4	4
Sonja Henning(*) 23	290	11	42	.262	2	8	.250	2	23	25	29	28	0	14	13	0	24	1.0	6
Sonja Henning(!) 24	295	11	43	.256	2	8	.250	2	23	25	29	28	0	15	13	0	24	1.0	6
Indiana......................34	6875	839	2011	.417	449	563	.798	334	654	988	539	668	5	299	474	121	2337	68.7	94
Opponents 34	6875	837	1908	.439	490	638	.768	309	677	986	570	631	4	227	512	170	2321	68.3	91

3-pt. FG: Indiana 210-600 (.350)

Catchings 74-191 (.387); Williams 0-1 (.000); White 29-84 (.345); Rasmussen 7-15 (.467); Brown 36-100 (.360); Ivey 33-84 (.393)
Schumacher 4-9 (.444); McCray 7-32 (.219); Washington 14-48 (.292); Pettis 6-27 (.222); Henning(*) 0-9 (.000)
Henning(!) 0-9 (.000); Opponents 157-421 (.373)

LOS ANGELES SPARKS

Player	G	Min	FGM	FGA	Pct	FTM	FTA	Pct	REBOUNDS			Ast	PF	Dq	Stl	TO	Blk	SCORING		
									Off	Def	Tot							Pts	Avg	Hi
Lisa Leslie...................23	792	165	373	.442	82	133	.617	76	155	231	46	93	3	31	65	63	424	18.4	31
Mwadi Mabika...........32	1042	158	388	.407	97	112	.866	34	107	141	82	105	3	30	74	18	441	13.8	28
Tamecka Dixon 30	1042	159	364	.437	83	94	.883	41	85	126	89	83	0	35	69	10	412	13.7	28
DeLisha Milton-Jones ..31	1086	139	328	.424	115	143	.804	59	161	220	64	109	3	49	79	41	416	13.4	23
Nikki Teasley 34	1189	112	288	.389	98	112	.875	30	145	175	214	68	0	39	108	15	392	11.5	23
Latasha Byears 5	72	10	25	.400	8	11	.727	12	9	21	2	12	0	0	2	2	28	5.6	7
Vanessa Nygaard 11	168	16	36	.444	3	4	.750	11	8	19	5	22	1	3	4	0	41	3.7	14
Jennifer Gillom............33	397	40	97	.412	16	21	.762	18	37	55	21	65	1	16	9	3	103	3.1	12
Rhonda Mapp 24	255	30	60	.500	2	4	.500	26	42	68	6	45	0	7	12	6	62	2.6	12
Sophia Witherspoon ...23	235	17	53	.321	12	14	.857	6	13	19	4	17	0	7	7	0	56	2.4	10

Player	G	Min	FGM	FGA	Pct	FTM	FTA	Pct	Off	Def	Tot	Ast	PF	Dq	Stl	TO	Blk	Pts	Avg	Hi
Nicky McCrimmon.....33		299	28	63	.444	7	8	.875	7	22	29	32	20	0	19	17	1	68	2.1	12
Shaquala Williams 25		229	19	53	.358	10	14	.714	11	21	32	19	25	0	6	7	0	49	2.0	13
Lynn Pride(*) 4		28	0	5	.000	1	4	.250	3	3	6	0	9	1	0	3	0	1	0.3	1
Lynn Pride(!)................17		94	7	19	.368	4	8	.500	11	12	23	1	20	1	3	11	1	18	1.1	6
Chandra Johnson 8		45	1	5	.200	3	4	.750	2	4	6	3	6	0	0	4	1	6	0.8	4
Jenny Mowe.................1		21	0	2	.000	0	0	---	0	1	1	0	3	0	0	1	1	0	0.0	0
Los Angeles 34		6900	894	2140	.418	537	678	.792	336	813	1149	587	682	12	242	470	161	2499	73.5	97
Opponents 34		6900	866	2147	.403	504	702	.718	316	789	1105	572	654	6	241	468	127	2432	71.5	92

3-pt. FG: Los Angeles 174-528 (.330)
Leslie 12-37 (.324); Mabika 28-106 (.264); Dixon 11-52 (.212); Milton-Jones 23-61 (.377); Teasley 70-165 (.424); Byears 0-1 (.000)
Nygaard 6-17 (.353); Gillom 7-26 (.269); Mapp 0-1 (.000); Witherspoon 10-29 (.345); McCrimmon 5-12 (.417); Williams 1-16 (.063)
Johnson 1-5 (.200); Opponents 196-540 (.363)

MINNESOTA LYNX

Player	G	Min	FGM	FGA	Pct	FTM	FTA	Pct	Off	Def	Tot	Ast	PF	Dq	Stl	TO	Blk	Pts	Avg	Hi
Katie Smith..................34		1185	208	455	.457	126	143	.881	40	98	138	84	112	2	25	67	6	620	18.2	34
Sheri Sam....................34		953	138	360	.383	74	105	.705	46	96	142	88	70	0	38	48	6	374	11.0	20
Svetlana Abrosimova ..30		792	112	285	.393	69	98	.704	44	97	141	82	79	0	44	90	11	318	10.6	23
Tamika Williams..........34		1121	129	193	.668	45	93	.484	92	117	209	44	78	0	34	58	10	303	8.9	16
Janell Burse 29		438	76	155	.490	54	70	.771	40	68	108	19	81	2	13	42	28	206	7.1	21
Michele Van Gorp.......31		528	70	162	.432	35	52	.673	32	75	107	17	87	2	10	56	20	175	5.6	17
Teresa Edwards...........34		854	63	168	.375	31	40	.775	24	81	105	148	60	0	41	92	11	181	5.3	15
Jordan Adams..............10		96	13	33	.394	2	2	1.000	10	13	23	4	10	0	2	10	3	33	3.3	13
Kristi Harrower............31		499	32	87	.368	8	13	.615	9	30	39	72	15	0	18	39	3	88	2.8	10
Shaunzinski Gortman...25		200	21	49	.429	3	4	.750	9	23	32	14	25	0	11	20	1	50	2.0	11
Lynn Pride(>) 13		66	7	14	.500	3	4	.750	8	9	17	1	11	0	3	8	1	17	1.3	6
Georgia Schweitzer 16		118	6	17	.353	0	0	---	7	11	18	7	6	0	3	8	1	15	0.9	5
Minnesota 34		6850	875	1978	.442	450	624	.721	361	718	1079	580	634	6	242	558	101	2380	70.0	85
Opponents 34		6850	878	2067	.425	473	633	.747	337	652	989	528	666	10	271	471	126	2370	69.7	88

3-pt. FG: Minnesota 180-524 (.344)
Smith 78-200 (.390); Sam 24-73 (.329); Abrosimova 25-82 (.305); Williams 0-2 (.000); Burse 0-2 (.000); Van Gorp 0-1 (.000)
Edwards 24-80 (.300); Adams 5-12 (.417); Harrower 16-43 (.372); Gortman 5-20 (.250); Schweitzer 3-9 (.333)
Opponents 141-446 (.316)

NEW YORK LIBERTY

Player	G	Min	FGM	FGA	Pct	FTM	FTA	Pct	Off	Def	Tot	Ast	PF	Dq	Stl	TO	Blk	Pts	Avg	Hi
Becky Hammon 11		257	50	87	.575	39	41	.951	1	20	21	18	13	0	10	27	1	162	14.7	33
Vickie Johnson 32		1042	158	345	.458	79	92	.859	30	65	95	75	65	0	29	55	7	430	13.4	27
Crystal Robinson 33		1078	143	326	.439	47	56	.839	13	57	70	63	94	0	40	43	13	395	12.0	22
Tari Phillips 33		1033	142	358	.397	87	134	.649	99	181	280	56	118	3	56	92	28	372	11.3	20
Elena Baranova 33		850	107	257	.416	31	35	.886	45	136	181	64	69	0	36	62	43	278	8.4	20
Tamika Whitmore.......33		823	110	242	.455	50	76	.658	38	84	122	25	100	1	35	57	22	271	8.2	21
Linda Frohlich 26		214	31	72	.431	14	22	.636	11	25	36	15	26	0	6	14	8	83	3.2	12
K.B. Sharp 30		398	28	71	.394	31	39	.795	11	21	32	37	15	0	14	26	0	94	3.1	14
Teresa Weatherspoon ..34		824	37	96	.385	24	32	.750	19	78	97	149	60	0	28	62	5	98	2.9	13
Erin Thorn 23		181	13	42	.310	10	10	1.000	3	8	11	16	8	0	4	13	1	44	1.9	12
Lindsey Yamasaki 24		148	6	27	.222	0	0	---	1	11	12	9	19	1	4	5	0	16	0.7	3
Bethany Donaphin 1		2	0	0	---	0	0	---	0	0	0	0	0	0	0	0	0	0	0.0	0
New York 34		6850	825	1923	.429	412	537	.767	271	686	957	527	587	5	262	470	128	2243	66.0	90
Opponents 34		6850	821	1959	.419	459	581	.790	326	736	1062	506	614	5	269	480	96	2256	66.4	90

3-pt. FG: New York 181-500 (.362)
Hammon 23-49 (.469); Johnson 35-96 (.365); Robinson 62-168 (.369); Phillips 1-5 (.200); Baranova 33-91 (.363); Whitmore 1-3 (.333)
Frohlich 7-13 (.538); Sharp 7-24 (.292); Weatherspoon 0-4 (.000); Thorn 8-33 (.242); Yamasaki 4-14 (.286)
Opponents 155-467 (.332)

PHOENIX MERCURY

Player	G	Min	FGM	FGA	Pct	FTM	FTA	Pct	Off	Def	Tot	Ast	PF	Dq	Stl	TO	Blk	Pts	Avg	Hi
Anna DeForge 34		1065	147	357	.412	50	69	.725	32	73	105	72	61	0	51	53	12	405	11.9	24
Adrian Williams 34		985	141	351	.402	52	85	.612	68	184	252	31	95	1	57	73	19	334	9.8	20
Tamicha Jackson 34		958	124	361	.343	17	21	.810	24	58	82	146	62	0	52	76	4	300	8.8	20
Slobodanka Tuvic.......37		365	45	116	.388	37	46	.804	31	36	67	12	61	2	10	32	15	127	7.5	17
Kayte Christensen......30		659	78	161	.484	50	83	.602	61	65	126	16	104	4	25	39	16	206	6.9	16
Plenette Pierson 33		602	67	177	.379	64	101	.634	37	43	80	22	87	1	19	42	13	198	6.0	26
Lisa Harrison 33		838	74	179	.413	35	51	.686	42	76	118	36	58	0	29	34	6	183	5.5	16
Iziane Castro Marque..16		178	25	71	.352	11	18	.611	6	6	12	9	11	0	6	10	1	69	4.3	12
Edwina Brown 34		524	41	152	.270	36	44	.818	29	42	71	62	44	0	30	47	7	118	3.5	15
Nevriye Yilmaz............5		34	7	15	.467	0	0	.000	3	0	3	2	7	0	0	4	0	14	2.8	10

Player	G	Min	FGM	FGA	Pct	FTM	FTA	Pct	REBOUNDS Off	Def	Tot	Ast	PF	Dq	Stl	TO	Blk	SCORING Pts	Avg	Hi
Stacey Thomas(>)	19	187	15	46	.326	10	16	.625	10	17	27	10	14	0	11	10	8	46	2.4	9
Tamara Moore(*)	11	110	11	26	.423	11	13	.846	3	16	19	8	9	0	5	10	4	33	3.0	8
Tamara Moore(!)	26	176	19	42	.452	16	19	.842	6	22	28	12	14	0	9	16	6	54	2.1	8
Sonja Mallory	6	44	4	9	.444	2	2	1.000	4	6	10	0	7	0	1	6	4	10	1.7	4
Felicia Ragland	3	39	1	12	.083	2	2	1.000	0	2	2	2	4	0	2	3	0	5	1.7	5
Edniesha Curry	20	205	13	35	.371	2	3	.667	1	10	11	24	25	0	9	15	0	33	1.7	8
Dalma Ivanyi	4	34	3	8	.375	0	0	---	2	2	4	2	4	0	0	2	1	6	1.5	2
Tracy Reid	2	12	1	3	.333	0	0	---	1	0	1	1	4	0	2	1	0	2	1.0	2
Michaela Pavlickova	8	29	3	7	.429	0	0	---	1	3	4	1	1	0	1	2	0	6	0.8	2
Grace Daley	3	28	1	5	.200	0	0	---	1	1	2	3	2	0	3	1	2	2	0.7	2
Gergana Slavtcheva	2	12	0	2	.000	0	0	---	0	0	0	1	2	0	1	0	0	0	0.0	0
Charmin Smith	4	17	0	2	.000	0	0	---	1	3	4	1	2	0	0	0	0	0	0.0	0
Phoenix	34	6925	801	2095	.382	379	556	.682	357	643	1000	461	664	8	310	479	111	2097	61.7	89
Opponents	34	6925	834	1867	.447	466	626	.744	303	811	1114	509	667	4	275	610	146	2270	66.8	82

3-pt. FG: Phoenix 116-349 (.332).
DeForge 61-148 (.412); Williams 0-1 (.000); Jackson 35-99 (.354); Tuvic 0-4 (.000); Pierson 0-2 (.000); Harrison 0-3 (.000)
Castro Marques 8-27 (.296); Brown 0-3 (.000); Thomas(>) 6-22 (.273); Moore(*) 0-5 (.000); Moore(!) 0-9 (.000); Ragland 1-5 (.200)
Curry 5-22 (.227); Ivanyi 0-2 (.000); Daley 0-2 (.000); Slavtcheva 0-2 (.000); Smith 0-2 (.000); Opponents 136-371 (.367)

SACRAMENTO MONARCHS

Player	G	Min	FGM	FGA	Pct	FTM	FTA	Pct	REBOUNDS Off	Def	Tot	Ast	PF	Dq	Stl	TO	Blk	SCORING Pts	Avg	Hi
Yolanda Griffith	34	1015	161	332	.485	147	190	.774	92	156	248	46	125	3	57	75	39	469	13.8	27
Tangela Smith	34	986	188	427	.440	41	58	.707	61	126	187	52	103	2	43	56	32	430	12.6	24
DeMya Walker	34	740	111	242	.459	83	143	.580	61	88	149	47	95	0	25	69	23	307	9.0	21
Edna Campbell	34	724	98	244	.402	25	33	.758	17	53	70	43	42	0	21	43	5	267	7.9	15
Kara Lawson	34	769	89	227	.392	31	40	.775	30	77	107	56	45	0	15	42	5	263	7.7	24
Ticha Penicheiro	34	1089	62	205	.302	44	76	.579	29	90	119	229	76	1	61	81	1	183	5.4	16
Ruthie Bolton	33	521	55	175	.314	20	26	.769	15	42	57	35	52	0	33	21	2	149	4.5	13
Lady Grooms	34	470	45	112	.402	21	26	.808	15	31	46	29	27	0	17	21	5	111	3.3	13
Tanty Maiga	22	190	17	52	.327	8	20	.400	13	24	37	14	27	0	18	14	2	42	1.9	6
Chantelle Anderson	26	171	19	44	.432	4	12	.333	7	17	24	5	33	1	5	17	5	42	1.6	8
La'Keshia Frett	24	150	17	47	.362	1	2	.500	9	14	23	12	16	0	2	10	3	36	1.5	7
Sacramento	34	6825	862	2107	.409	425	626	.679	349	718	1067	568	641	7	297	461	122	2299	67.6	89
Opponents	34	6825	816	1991	.410	435	597	.729	345	751	1096	516	640	9	224	576	141	2216	65.2	79

3-pt. FG: Sacramento 150-473 (.317).
Griffith 0-2 (.000); Smith 13-49 (.265); Walker 2-15 (.133); Campbell 46-111 (.414); Lawson 54-135 (.400); Penicheiro 15-60 (.250)
Bolton 19-98 (.194); Grooms 0-1 (.000); Frett 1-2 (.500); Opponents 149-467 (.319)

SAN ANTONIO SILVER STARS

Player	G	Min	FGM	FGA	Pct	FTM	FTA	Pct	REBOUNDS Off	Def	Tot	Ast	PF	Dq	Stl	TO	Blk	SCORING Pts	Avg	Hi
Marie Ferdinand	34	1116	139	384	.362	176	223	.789	28	99	127	90	87	0	58	85	6	470	13.8	26
Margo Dydek	34	926	156	346	.451	94	130	.723	45	206	251	58	113	1	19	80	100	406	11.9	27
Adrienne Goodson	33	969	141	357	.395	81	102	.794	74	111	185	71	96	2	24	85	6	371	11.2	26
Gwen Jackson	33	975	114	286	.399	56	88	.636	86	119	205	20	85	1	15	46	17	289	8.8	16
Jennifer Azzi	34	1136	85	211	.403	51	65	.785	10	81	91	111	98	2	27	61	9	260	7.6	18
Sylvia Crawley	33	564	50	130	.385	15	22	.682	39	66	105	19	76	1	18	40	19	115	3.5	13
Semeka Randall	33	339	32	90	.356	24	45	.533	25	28	53	23	41	0	11	44	0	88	2.7	14
LaQuanda Quick	26	168	21	79	.266	2	2	1.000	8	25	33	5	21	0	1	10	3	59	2.3	22
Tausha Mills	29	185	20	49	.408	18	31	.581	27	28	55	7	58	1	4	23	2	58	2.0	7
LaTonya Johnson	31	279	18	71	.254	16	22	.727	7	18	25	9	31	0	3	14	1	58	1.9	7
Tai Dillard	24	168	16	65	.246	5	6	.833	1	14	15	15	22	0	7	14	4	41	1.7	9
San Antonio	34	6825	792	2068	.383	538	736	.731	350	795	1145	428	728	8	187	513	167	2215	65.1	88
Opponents	34	6825	867	2176	.398	544	745	.730	389	783	1172	530	669	8	275	424	140	2427	71.4	99

3-pt. FG: San Antonio 93-315 (.295).
Ferdinand 16-52 (.308); Dydek 0-1 (.000); Goodson 8-36 (.222); Jackson 5-30 (.167); Azzi 39-97 (.402); Randall 0-1 (.000)
Quick 15-52 (.288); Johnson 6-23 (.261); Dillard 4-23 (.174); Opponents 149-482 (.309)

SEATTLE STORM

Player	G	Min	FGM	FGA	Pct	FTM	FTA	Pct	REBOUNDS Off	Def	Tot	Ast	PF	Dq	Stl	TO	Blk	SCORING Pts	Avg	Hi
Lauren Jackson	33	1109	254	526	.483	151	183	.825	82	225	307	62	106	1	38	69	64	698	21.2	34
Sue Bird	34	1136	155	368	.421	61	69	.884	22	91	113	221	47	0	48	110	1	420	12.4	27
Kamila Vodichkova	28	709	101	213	.474	82	101	.812	55	88	143	31	101	4	20	53	21	284	10.1	18
Sandy Brondello	34	975	117	282	.415	25	31	.806	19	37	56	69	58	0	31	37	2	280	8.2	21
Adia Barnes	16	396	32	84	.381	12	21	.571	26	39	65	23	36	1	11	18	7	88	5.5	12
Amanda Lassiter	32	733	60	156	.385	19	30	.633	33	79	112	42	92	2	27	42	26	163	5.1	16
Simone Edwards	34	577	61	134	.455	35	56	.625	54	79	133	16	55	0	10	31	9	157	4.6	15
Alisa Burras	27	270	35	75	.467	19	27	.704	27	34	61	5	58	0	5	25	5	89	3.3	12

									REBOUNDS									SCORING		
Player	G	Min	FGM	FGA	Pct	FTM	FTA	Pct	Off	Def	Tot	Ast	PF	Dq	Stl	TO	Blk	Pts	Avg	Hi
Rita Williams 32		381	28	75	.373	11	15	.733	3	19	22	41	34	0	14	27	0	78	2.4	9
LaTonya Massaline(*) ..11		121	13	33	.394	5	5	1.000	7	4	11	5	8	0	4	5	0	33	3.0	9
LaTonya Massaline(!) ..24		222	20	63	.317	7	7	1.000	12	9	21	8	12	0	5	10	0	53	2.2	15
Tully Bevilaqua...........31		252	17	51	.333	16	21	.762	9	17	26	32	30	0	14	20	1	58	1.9	14
Sun-Min Jung 17		118	13	32	.406	4	4	1.000	1	9	10	1	13	0	5	5	0	30	1.8	10
Mactabene Amachree ..7		47	3	10	.300	2	4	.500	4	10	14	0	3	0	5	9	2	8	1.1	4
Danielle McCulley 7		26	1	6	.167	0	0	---	0	1	1	0	3	0	0	4	0	2	0.3	2
Seattle 34		6850	890	2045	.435	442	567	.780	342	732	1074	548	644	8	232	465	138	2388	70.2	93
Opponents 34		6850	844	2039	.414	441	591	.746	352	689	1041	456	570	9	245	459	104	2274	66.9	95

3-pt. FG: Seattle 166-500 (.332)

Jackson 39-123 (.317); Bird 49-140 (.350); Vodichkova 0-5 (.000); Brondello 21-48 (.438); Barnes 12-31 (.387); Jung 0-7 (.000)
Lassiter 24-73 (.329); Williams 11-43 (.256); Massaline(*) 2-8 (.250); Massaline(!) 6-20 (.300); Bevilaqua 8-21 (.381)
McCulley 0-1 (.000); Opponents 145-437 (.332)

WASHINGTON MYSTICS

									REBOUNDS									SCORING		
Player	G	Min	FGM	FGA	Pct	FTM	FTA	Pct	Off	Def	Tot	Ast	PF	Dq	Stl	TO	Blk	Pts	Avg	Hi
Chamique Holdsclaw..27		948	204	480	.425	140	155	.903	72	222	294	89	74	0	34	72	15	554	20.5	34
Coco Miller 33		1076	172	382	.450	37	53	.698	55	72	127	86	95	1	39	53	7	413	12.5	23
Stacey Dales-Schuman 34		998	122	298	.409	39	55	.709	44	57	101	114	97	2	29	72	12	340	10.0	20
Asjha Jones................34		748	121	279	.434	41	55	.745	62	73	135	52	109	1	16	63	25	290	8.5	21
Murriel Page...............34		850	83	220	.377	42	56	.750	62	90	152	35	101	0	18	41	24	213	6.3	19
Annie Burgess 34		841	50	134	.373	15	25	.600	24	55	79	112	47	1	27	52	1	131	3.9	15
Aiysha Smith 31		422	41	120	.342	17	34	.500	21	44	65	10	44	0	11	26	9	104	3.4	10
Helen Luz 20		165	19	53	.358	9	10	.900	2	8	10	21	16	0	6	11	2	59	3.0	9
Nakia Sanford 17		134	20	40	.500	9	20	.450	10	16	26	1	35	0	3	14	2	49	2.9	10
Jocelyn Penn 30		288	31	78	.397	22	33	.667	19	33	52	16	28	0	15	20	1	86	2.9	13
Kiesha Brown.............27		269	24	72	.333	2	3	.667	6	26	32	28	23	0	13	22	1	60	2.2	9
Zuzana Zirkova 6		30	2	4	.500	6	6	1.000	0	2	2	1	3	0	0	2	0	11	1.8	5
LaTonya Massaline(>)..13		101	7	30	.233	2	2	1.000	5	5	10	3	4	0	1	5	0	20	1.5	15
Sonja Henning(>) 1		5	0	1	.000	0	0	---	0	0	0	0	0	0	0	0	0	0	0.0	0
Washington 34		6875	896	2191	.409	381	507	.751	382	703	1085	568	676	5	213	462	99	2330	68.5	92
Opponents 34		6875	909	2033	.447	509	691	.737	334	781	1115	591	565	0	251	468	119	2498	73.5	97

3-pt. FG: Washington 157-505 (.311)

Holdsclaw 6-35 (.171); Miller 32-89 (.360); Dales-Schuman 57-160 (.356); Jones 7-17 (.412); Page 5-12 (.417); Burgess 16-58 (.276)
Smith 5-34 (.147); Luz 12-40 (.300); Penn 2-13 (.154); Brown 10-33 (.303); Zirkova 1-2 (.500); Massaline(>) 4-12 (.333)
Opponents 171-482 (.355)

(*) Statistics with this team only
(!) Totals with all teams
(>) Continued season with another team

PLAYOFF RESULTS

FIRST ROUND

Los Angeles defeats Minnesota, 2-1

August 28	Minnesota 74, Los Angeles 72
August 30	Los Angeles 80, Minnesota 69
September 1	Los Angeles 74, Minnesota 64

Sacramento defeats Houston, 2-1

August 29	Sacramento 65, Houston 59
August 31	Houston 69, Sacramento 48
September 2	Sacramento 70, Houston 68

Detroit defeats Cleveland, 2-1

August 29	Detroit 76, Cleveland 74
August 31	Cleveland 66, Detroit 59
September 2	Detroit 77, Cleveland 63

Connecticut defeats Charlotte, 2-0

August 28	Connecticut 68, Charlotte 66
August 30	Connecticut 68, Charlotte 62

CONFERENCE FINALS

Detroit defeats Connecticut, 2-0

September 5	Detroit 73, Connecticut 63
September 7	Detroit 79, Connecticut 73

Los Angeles defeats Sacramento, 2-1

September 5	Sacramento 77, Los Angeles 69
September 7	Los Angeles 79, Sacramento 54
September 9	Los Angeles 66, Sacramento 63

FINALS

Detroit defeats Los Angeles, 2-1

September 12	Los Angeles 75, Detroit 63
September 14	Detroit 62, Los Angeles 61
September 16	Detroit 83, Los Angeles 78

TEAM STANDINGS

OFFENSIVE

TEAM	G	FG	FGA	PCT	FG3	FG3A	PCT	FT	FTA	PCT	OFF	DEF	REB	AST	PF	DQ	STL	TO	BLK	PTS	AVG
L.A.	9	246	564	.436	40	123	.325	122	154	.792	80	197	277	177	182	2	76	116	48	654	72.7
Det.	8	202	516	.391	41	103	.398	127	160	.794	87	195	282	139	141	0	53	109	38	572	71.5
Minn.	3	69	175	.394	14	44	.318	55	72	.764	25	58	83	53	56	0	29	47	8	207	69.0
Conn.	4	103	221	.466	12	48	.250	54	67	.806	26	83	109	65	75	0	26	38	13	272	68.0
Clev.	3	67	173	.387	10	35	.286	59	77	.766	22	74	96	42	67	0	22	39	12	203	67.7
Hou.	3	71	184	.386	10	37	.270	44	54	.815	33	68	101	39	50	0	22	34	12	196	65.3
Cha.	2	44	112	.393	13	31	.419	27	34	.794	21	31	52	28	40	1	12	22	7	128	64.0
Sac.	6	141	347	.406	21	75	.280	74	96	.771	51	137	188	84	106	0	24	82	19	377	62.8

DEFENSIVE

Team	FG	FGA	PCT	FG3	FG3A	PCT	FT	FTA	PCT	OFF	DEF	REB	AST	PF	DQ	STL	TO	BLK	PTS	AVG	DIFF
Hou.	71	174	.408	11	41	.268	30	40	.750	25	75	100	38	56	0	9	42	11	183	61.0	+4.3
L.A.	213	543	.392	38	114	.333	145	181	.801	83	191	274	151	150	0	63	125	35	609	67.7	+5.0
Cha.	51	103	.495	5	16	.313	29	38	.763	14	40	54	34	36	0	13	18	6	136	68.0	-4.0
Sac.	154	368	.418	24	77	.312	78	102	.765	58	130	188	104	110	0	49	72	29	410	68.3	-5.5
Det.	195	491	.397	35	120	.292	128	157	.815	64	193	257	124	163	1	57	90	35	553	69.1	+2.4
Conn.	98	238	.412	27	57	.474	57	76	.750	48	78	126	64	71	1	24	49	10	280	70.0	-2.0
Clev.	74	195	.379	13	41	.317	51	65	.785	28	77	105	51	66	0	22	44	16	212	70.7	-3.0
Minn.	87	180	.483	8	30	.267	44	55	.800	25	59	84	61	65	1	27	47	15	226	75.3	-6.3
Averages	118	287	.411	20	62	.325	70	89	.787	43	105	149	78	90	0	33	61	20	326	68.7	---
Totals	943	2292	---	161	406	---	562	714	---	345	843	1188	627	717	3	264	487	157	2609	---	---

TEAM COMPARISONS

	Points Per Game		Field Goal Percentage		Turnovers Per Game		Rebound Percentages			Below 70 Pts.		Overtime Games		3 PTS or Less		10 PTS or More	
TEAM	OWN	OPP	OWN	OPP	OWN	OPP	OFF	DEF	TOT	OWN	OPP	W	L	W	L	W	L
Charlotte	64.0	68.0	.393	.495	11.0	9.0	.344*	.689	.517	2	2	0	0	0	1	0	0
Cleveland	67.7	70.7	.387	.379*	13.0	14.7	.222	.725	.474	2	1	0	0	0	1	0	1
Connecticut	68.0	70.0	.466*	.412	9.5*	12.3	.250	.634	.442	3	2	0	0	1	0	0	1
Detroit	71.5	69.1	.391	.397	13.6	11.3	.311	.753*	.532*	3	4	0	0	2	0	2	1
Houston	65.3	61.0*	.386	.408	11.3	14.0	.306	.731	.518	3	2	0	0	0	1	1	0
Los Angeles	72.7*	67.7	.436	.392	12.9	13.9	.295	.704	.499	3	6	0	0	1	2	4	0
Minnesota	69.0	75.3	.394	.483	15.7	15.7*	.298	.699	.498	2	0	0	0	1	0	0	2
Sacramento	62.8	68.3	.406	.418	13.7	12.0	.282	.703	.492	4	5	0	0	1	1	0	2
COMPOSITE; 19 games	68.7	---	.411	---	12.8	---	.290	.710	---	22	22	0	---	6	---	7	---

* - League Leader
REBOUND PERCENTAGES
OFF. - Percentage of a given team's missed shots which that team rebounds.
DEF. - Percentage of opponents' missed shots which a given team rebounds.
TOT. - Average of offensive and defensive rebound percentages.

INDIVIDUAL PLAYOFF STATISTICS, TEAM BY TEAM

CHARLOTTE STING

Player	G	Min	FGM	FGA	Pct	FTM	FTA	Pct	REBOUNDS Off	Def	Tot	Ast	PF	Dq	Stl	TO	Blk	SCORING Pts	Avg	Hi
Andrea Stinson	2	64	12	28	.429	9	9	1.000	4	5	9	7	4	0	2	4	0	36	18.0	25
Allison Feaster	2	63	7	20	.350	3	4	.750	2	3	5	1	5	0	2	0	0	21	10.5	12
Dawn Staley	2	58	6	17	.353	2	5	.400	1	4	5	7	6	0	4	4	0	18	9.0	15
Shalonda Enis	2	58	4	10	.400	6	6	1.000	5	7	12	1	9	1	2	6	2	15	7.5	11
Tynesha Lewis	2	29	4	8	.500	5	6	.833	2	1	3	4	2	0	0	0	1	14	7.0	9
Kelly Miller	2	23	4	10	.400	0	0	---	0	1	1	2	2	0	0	1	0	8	4.0	6
Rushia Brown	2	46	3	7	.429	1	2	.500	3	5	8	4	4	0	2	4	0	7	3.5	6
Tammy Sutton-Brown	2	32	2	7	.286	0	0	---	1	5	6	0	5	0	0	2	3	4	2.0	4
Marla Brumfield	2	7	1	2	.500	1	2	.500	0	0	0	1	1	0	0	1	0	3	1.5	3
Charlotte Smith-Tayl	2	7	1	1	1.000	0	0	---	1	0	1	0	0	0	0	0	0	2	1.0	2
Teana McKiver	2	13	0	2	.000	0	0	---	2	0	2	0	2	0	0	0	1	0	0.0	0
Charlotte	2	400	44	112	.393	27	34	.794	21	31	52	28	40	1	12	22	7	128	64.0	66
Opponents	2	400	51	103	.495	29	38	.763	14	40	54	34	36	0	13	18	6	136	68.0	68

3-pt. FG: Charlotte 13-31 (.419)
Stinson 3-7 (.429); Feaster 4-10 (.400); Staley 4-8 (.500); Enis 1-3 (.333); Lewis 1-1 (1.000); Miller 0-2 (.000)
Opponents 5-16 (.313)

CONNECTICUT SUN

Player	G	Min	FGM	FGA	Pct	FTM	FTA	Pct	Off	Def	Tot	Ast	PF	Dq	Stl	TO	Blk	Pts	Avg	Hi
Taj McWilliams-Frank ..4		122	24	47	.511	16	17	.941	9	21	30	5	10	0	6	6	2	65	16.3	20
Nykesha Sales 4		131	17	40	.425	13	18	.722	1	12	13	9	12	0	5	7	3	47	11.8	22
Shannon Johnson 4		131	13	29	.448	14	18	.778	3	9	12	19	11	0	7	11	1	45	11.3	16
Katie Douglas..............4		126	10	30	.333	6	7	.857	2	8	10	12	9	0	3	1	1	29	7.3	13
Wendy Palmer 4		64	13	22	.591	2	3	.667	1	11	12	3	9	0	0	7	0	29	7.3	13
Rebecca Lobo 2		38	4	10	.400	0	0	---	3	5	8	5	4	0	0	2	4	9	4.5	9
Brooke Wyckoff 4		89	7	16	.438	3	4	.750	3	9	12	5	11	0	2	2	1	18	4.5	9
Adrienne Johnson.........3		43	6	9	.667	0	0	---	0	4	4	4	2	0	1	0	0	12	4.0	10
Jessie Hicks 4		27	5	8	.625	0	0	---	3	3	6	1	5	0	0	2	1	10	2.5	4
Debbie Black 4		29	4	10	.400	0	0	---	1	1	2	2	2	0	2	0	0	8	2.0	6
Connecticut 4		800	103	221	.466	54	67	.806	26	83	109	65	75	0	26	38	13	272	68.0	73
Opponents 4		800	98	238	.412	57	76	.750	48	78	126	64	71	1	24	49	10	280	70.0	79

3-pt. FG: Connecticut 12-48 (.250)
McWilliams-Frank 1-5 (.200); Sales 0-6 (.000); S. Johnson 5-10 (.500); Douglas 3-12 (.250); Palmer 1-4 (.250); Lobo 1-4 (.250)
Wyckoff 1-6 (.167); A. Johnson 0-1 (.000); Opponents 27-57 (.474)

CLEVELAND ROCKERS

Player	G	Min	FGM	FGA	Pct	FTM	FTA	Pct	Off	Def	Tot	Ast	PF	Dq	Stl	TO	Blk	Pts	Avg	Hi
Chasity Melvin 3		104	12	31	.387	26	34	.765	3	10	13	5	10	0	2	8	4	50	16.7	21
Penny Taylor 3		99	16	36	.444	10	12	.833	1	12	13	3	10	0	6	6	1	45	15.0	17
LaToya Thomas 3		100	14	32	.438	13	17	.765	6	17	23	4	11	0	1	6	4	41	13.7	17
Betty Lennox 3		45	9	19	.474	1	2	.500	1	6	7	3	7	0	3	4	0	21	7.0	14
Deanna Jackson 3		60	4	20	.200	4	6	.667	2	10	12	2	7	0	2	0	0	12	4.0	6
Jennifer Rizzotti 3		36	4	6	.667	0	0	---	0	2	2	8	2	0	0	1	0	12	4.0	9
Helen Darling 3		83	2	13	.154	4	4	1.000	4	8	12	13	11	0	6	10	0	9	3.0	5
Tracy Henderson 1		3	1	1	1.000	0	0	---	0	1	1	0	1	0	0	0	0	2	2.0	2
Merlakia Jones 3		37	2	5	.400	1	2	.500	3	2	5	0	2	0	0	2	0	5	1.7	3
Lucienne Berthieu 3		13	2	9	.222	0	0	---	2	2	4	1	5	0	1	2	1	4	1.3	4
Pollyanna Johns Kimb ..3		20	1	1	1.000	0	0	---	0	4	4	3	1	0	1	0	2	2	0.7	2
Cleveland......................3		600	67	173	.387	59	77	.766	22	74	96	42	67	0	22	39	12	203	67.7	74
Opponents 3		600	74	195	.379	51	65	.785	28	77	105	51	66	0	22	44	16	212	70.7	77

3-pt. FG: Cleveland 10-35 (.286)
Melvin 0-1 (.000); Taylor 3-10 (.300); Thomas 0-2 (.000); Lennox 2-5 (.400); Jackson 0-2 (.000); Rizzotti 4-6 (.667)
Darling 1-8 (.125); Jones 0-1 (.000); Opponents 13-41 (.317)

DETROIT SHOCK

Player	G	Min	FGM	FGA	Pct	FTM	FTA	Pct	Off	Def	Tot	Ast	PF	Dq	Stl	TO	Blk	Pts	Avg	Hi
Swin Cash 8		289	43	104	.413	42	52	.808	24	27	51	35	21	0	4	28	5	130	16.3	26
Deanna Nolan 8		257	44	96	.458	15	16	.938	4	25	29	21	21	0	10	13	2	124	15.5	26
Ruth Riley 8		258	41	106	.387	21	26	.808	15	34	49	20	26	0	5	13	20	103	12.9	27
Cheryl Ford 8		232	24	74	.324	19	23	.826	25	55	80	4	30	0	11	10	6	67	8.4	17
Kedra Holland-Corn......8		155	21	53	.396	8	10	.800	2	10	12	15	7	0	10	12	0	65	8.1	16
Elaine Powell 8		219	16	46	.348	7	11	.636	6	24	30	38	17	0	7	13	4	41	5.1	9
Barbara Farris...............8		133	10	25	.400	11	17	.647	8	12	20	4	14	0	1	10	0	31	3.9	6
Ayana Walker 4		24	1	5	.200	3	3	1.000	3	3	6	0	0	0	4	1	1	5	1.3	3
Sheila Lambert 7		14	2	6	.333	0	0	---	0	2	2	1	3	0	0	4	0	5	0.7	3
Astou Ndiaye-Diatta.....2		6	0	0	---	1	2	.500	0	0	0	1	1	0	0	0	0	1	0.5	1
Stacey Thomas.............4		13	0	1	.000	0	0	---	0	3	3	0	1	0	1	1	0	0	0.0	0
Detroit 8		1600	202	516	.391	127	160	.794	87	195	282	139	141	0	53	109	38	572	71.5	83
Opponents 8		1600	195	491	.397	128	157	.815	64	193	257	124	163	1	57	90	35	553	69.1	78

3-pt. FG: Detroit 41-103 (.398)
Cash 2-10 (.200); Nolan 21-47 (.447); Holland-Corn 15-32 (.469); Powell 2-10 (.200); Farris 0-1 (.000); Lambert 1-3 (.333)
Opponents 35-120 (.292)

HOUSTON COMETS

Player	G	Min	FGM	FGA	Pct	FTM	FTA	Pct	Off	Def	Tot	Ast	PF	Dq	Stl	TO	Blk	Pts	Avg	Hi
Sheryl Swoopes 3		110	20	46	.435	15	16	.938	2	17	19	13	8	0	4	5	2	56	18.7	27
Tina Thompson 3		106	18	46	.391	6	7	.857	3	11	14	5	9	0	2	6	6	45	15.0	21
Janeth Arcain 3		107	12	31	.387	12	13	.923	6	8	14	3	5	0	8	7	0	37	12.3	13
Michelle Snow 3		89	10	25	.400	5	8	.625	12	17	29	5	10	0	4	5	4	25	8.3	16
Ukari Figgs..................3		81	6	15	.400	0	0	---	1	5	6	7	4	0	1	3	0	17	5.7	8
Dominique Canty.........3		48	3	9	.333	5	8	.625	7	4	11	5	7	0	1	3	0	11	3.7	6
Kelley Gibson...............2		18	2	5	.400	0	0	---	0	1	1	0	1	0	0	0	0	4	2.0	4
Mfon Udoka.................1		6	0	0	---	1	2	.500	0	1	1	0	2	0	0	2	0	1	1.0	1
Octavia Blue 1		4	0	1	.000	0	0	---	0	0	0	1	0	0	0	2	0	0	0.0	0
Tiffani Johnson 3		31	0	6	.000	0	0	---	2	4	6	0	4	0	2	1	0	0	0.0	0
Houston 3		600	71	184	.386	44	54	.815	33	68	101	39	50	0	22	34	12	196	65.3	69
Opponents 3		600	71	174	.408	30	40	.750	25	75	100	38	56	0	9	42	11	183	61.0	70

3-pt. FG: Houston 10-37 (.270)
Swoopes 1-10 (.100); Thompson 3-13 (.231); Arcain 1-5 (.200); Figgs 5-7 (.714); Gibson 0-2 (.000); Opponents 11-41 (.268)

LOS ANGELES SPARKS

Player	G	Min	FGM	FGA	Pct	FTM	FTA	Pct	REBOUNDS			Ast	PF	Dq	Stl	TO	Blk	SCORING		
									Off	Def	Tot							Pts	Avg	Hi
Lisa Leslie	9	327	74	137	.540	38	54	.704	22	58	80	23	39	1	12	24	28	187	20.8	26
DeLisha Milton-Jones	9	338	47	106	.443	27	35	.771	20	37	57	25	40	1	17	20	13	131	14.6	20
Mwadi Mabika	9	344	53	121	.438	11	13	.846	10	40	50	21	29	0	14	20	2	129	14.3	29
Tamecka Dixon	9	316	40	94	.426	26	27	.963	8	21	29	29	27	0	14	11	2	110	12.2	18
Nikki Teasley	9	312	22	67	.328	16	20	.800	11	29	40	71	23	0	12	27	0	70	7.8	13
Vanessa Nygaard	5	24	3	5	.600	0	0	---	3	2	5	0	1	0	1	1	1	8	1.6	3
Nicky McCrimmon	7	54	4	18	.222	0	0	---	0	4	4	7	5	0	2	4	0	9	1.3	3
Sophia Witherspoon	5	14	1	5	.200	3	4	.750	0	2	2	0	1	0	1	2	0	5	1.0	5
Lynn Pride	6	36	2	6	.333	1	1	1.000	6	3	9	1	10	0	2	3	1	5	0.8	3
Jennifer Gillom	6	22	0	5	.000	0	0	---	0	1	1	0	5	0	1	0	1	0	0.0	0
Shaquala Williams	4	13	0	0	---	0	0	---	0	0	0	2	0	0	0	0	0	0	0.0	0
Los Angeles	9	1800	246	564	.436	122	154	.792	80	197	277	177	182	2	76	116	48	654	72.7	80
Opponents	9	1800	213	543	.392	145	181	.801	83	191	274	151	150	0	63	125	35	609	67.7	83

3-pt. FG: Los Angeles 40-123 (.325)
Leslie 1-3 (.333); Milton-Jones 10-18 (.556); Mabika 12-34 (.353); Dixon 4-12 (.333); Teasley 10-45 (.222); Nygaard 2-2 (1.000)
McCrimmon 1-6 (.167); Witherspoon 0-3 (.000); Opponents 38-114 (.333)

MINNESOTA LYNX

Player	G	Min	FGM	FGA	Pct	FTM	FTA	Pct	REBOUNDS			Ast	PF	Dq	Stl	TO	Blk	SCORING		
									Off	Def	Tot							Pts	Avg	Hi
Katie Smith	3	120	18	42	.429	11	12	.917	3	10	13	9	11	0	1	8	0	52	17.3	23
Tamika Williams	3	116	17	28	.607	16	24	.667	12	10	22	3	5	0	7	4	1	50	16.7	17
Sheri Sam	3	74	10	28	.357	6	8	.750	5	11	16	8	6	0	6	8	0	26	8.7	11
Svetlana Abrosimova	3	69	6	22	.273	8	8	1.000	1	4	5	4	8	0	4	8	1	23	7.7	10
Teresa Edwards	3	83	6	19	.316	4	4	1.000	1	9	10	19	6	0	5	8	1	20	6.7	8
Janell Burse	3	42	6	18	.333	4	6	.667	2	7	9	2	3	0	4	3	2	16	5.3	6
Kristi Harrower	3	65	4	11	.364	1	2	.500	1	6	7	5	6	0	1	3	0	11	3.7	6
Michele Van Gorp	3	31	2	7	.286	5	8	.625	0	1	1	3	11	0	1	4	3	9	3.0	5
Minnesota	3	600	69	175	.394	55	72	.764	25	58	83	53	56	0	29	47	8	207	69.0	74
Opponents	3	600	87	180	.483	44	55	.800	25	59	84	61	65	1	27	47	15	226	75.3	80

3-pt. FG: Minnesota 14-44 (.318)
Smith 5-14 (.357); Sam 0-4 (.000); Abrosimova 3-7 (.429); Edwards 4-12 (.333); Harrower 2-7 (.286); Opponents 8-30 (.267)

SACRAMENTO MONARCHS

Player	G	Min	FGM	FGA	Pct	FTM	FTA	Pct	REBOUNDS			Ast	PF	Dq	Stl	TO	Blk	SCORING		
									Off	Def	Tot							Pts	Avg	Hi
Yolanda Griffith	6	200	36	67	.537	31	34	.912	19	34	53	7	16	0	7	12	6	103	17.2	27
Tangela Smith	6	176	29	73	.397	14	20	.700	9	37	46	11	17	0	5	11	3	77	12.8	17
DeMya Walker	6	170	24	55	.436	11	20	.550	14	13	27	10	17	0	1	21	3	59	9.8	16
Edna Campbell	6	148	17	36	.472	2	2	1.000	1	3	4	11	11	0	1	8	0	40	6.7	12
Kara Lawson	6	154	9	42	.214	7	8	.875	2	21	23	16	8	0	1	4	2	32	5.3	12
Ticha Penicheiro	6	143	8	24	.333	7	8	.875	1	13	14	18	12	0	6	7	3	25	4.2	16
Ruthie Bolton	6	91	6	28	.214	0	0	---	2	8	10	6	10	0	2	5	0	15	2.5	6
Lady Grooms	6	65	7	12	.583	1	2	.500	2	3	5	3	3	0	1	1	0	15	2.5	6
La'Keshia Frett	1	9	1	2	.500	0	0	---	0	0	0	0	1	0	0	1	0	2	2.0	2
Chantelle Anderson	5	29	3	5	.600	1	2	.500	0	3	3	0	7	0	0	4	2	7	1.4	3
Tanty Maiga	4	15	1	3	.333	0	0	---	1	2	3	2	4	0	0	5	0	2	0.5	2
Sacramento	6	1200	141	347	.406	74	96	.771	51	137	188	84	106	0	24	82	19	377	62.8	77
Opponents	6	1200	154	368	.418	78	102	.765	58	130	188	104	110	0	49	72	29	410	68.3	79

3-pt. FG: Sacramento 21-75 (.280)
Smith 5-15 (.333); Campbell 4-16 (.250); Lawson 7-23 (.304); Penicheiro 2-8 (.250); Bolton 3-12 (.250); Frett 0-1 (.000)
Opponents 24-77 (.312)
(*) Statistics with this team only
(!) Totals with all teams
(>) Continued season with another team

INDIVIDUAL FINALS STATISTICS, TEAM BY TEAM

DETROIT SHOCK

Player	G	Min	FGM	FGA	Pct	FTM	FTA	Pct	REBOUNDS			Ast	PF	Dq	Stl	TO	Blk	SCORING		
									Off	Def	Tot							Pts	Avg	Hi
Deanna Nolan	3	92	15	35	.429	10	10	1.000	2	6	8	9	7	0	5	6	1	46	15.3	17
Ruth Riley	3	97	18	43	.419	8	10	.800	5	10	15	9	10	0	0	5	10	44	14.7	27
Swin Cash	3	116	14	41	.341	10	13	.769	8	14	22	16	4	0	0	6	1	38	12.7	16
Cheryl Ford	3	99	10	30	.333	9	10	.900	11	19	30	2	10	0	5	4	5	29	9.7	11
Kedra Holland-Corn	3	56	9	21	.429	4	4	1.000	1	4	5	4	1	0	5	7	0	29	9.7	16
Elaine Powell	3	84	5	15	.333	1	2	.500	3	11	14	9	7	0	4	3	2	11	3.7	7
Barbara Farris	3	42	2	7	.286	4	4	1.000	2	5	7	3	4	0	0	5	0	8	2.7	4
Sheila Lambert	2	8	1	3	.333	0	0	---	0	1	1	0	1	0	0	1	0	3	1.5	1
Stacey Thomas	2	5	0	0	---	0	0	---	0	1	1	0	0	0	0	0	0	0	0.0	0
Ayana Walker	1	1	0	0	---	0	0	---	0	0	0	0	0	0	0	0	0	0	0.0	0
Detroit	3	600	74	195	.379	46	53	.868	32	71	103	52	44	0	19	38	19	208	69.3	83
Opponents	3	600	76	200	.380	44	51	.863	30	76	106	51	57	1	22	31	16	214	71.3	78

3-pt. FG: Detroit 14-36 (.389) Nolan 6-16 (.375); Cash 0-3 (.000); Holland-Corn 7-12 (.583); Powell 0-3 (.000); Lambert 1-2 (.500); Opponents 18-53 (.340)

LOS ANGELES SPARKS

Player	G	Min	FGM	FGA	Pct	FTM	FTA	Pct	Off	Def	Tot	Ast	PF	Dq	Stl	TO	Blk	Pts	Avg	Hi
DeLisha Milton-Jones	3	115	18	47	.383	14	16	.875	7	12	19	7	12	0	7	7	5	56	18.7	19
Lisa Leslie	3	119	21	50	.420	12	16	.750	10	28	38	7	13	1	6	9	7	54	18.0	23
Mwadi Mabika	3	118	16	42	.381	7	7	1.000	3	16	19	7	6	0	4	6	1	42	14.0	29
Tamecka Dixon	3	106	13	31	.419	9	9	1.000	2	6	8	6	11	0	2	3	2	37	12.3	15
Nikki Teasley	3	111	6	22	.273	2	3	.667	4	11	15	24	9	0	3	4	0	19	6.3	10
Vanessa Nygaard	1	4	1	1	1.000	0	0	---	1	1	2	0	0	0	0	0	0	3	3.0	3
Nicky McCrimmon	2	5	1	3	.333	0	0	---	0	0	0	0	1	0	0	0	0	3	1.5	3
Jennifer Gillom	1	1	0	0	---	0	0	---	0	0	0	0	1	0	0	0	0	0	0.0	0
Lynn Pride	3	13	0	1	.000	0	0	---	3	0	3	0	4	0	0	1	1	0	0.0	0
Sophia Witherspoon	2	8	0	3	.000	0	0	---	0	2	2	0	0	0	0	1	0	0	0.0	0
Los Angeles	3	600	76	200	.380	44	51	.863	30	76	106	51	57	1	22	31	16	214	71.3	78
Opponents	3	600	74	195	.379	46	53	.868	32	71	103	52	44	0	19	38	19	208	69.3	83

3-pt. FG: Los Angeles 18-53 (.340)
Milton-Jones 6-9 (.667); Leslie 0-1 (.000); Mabika 3-10 (.300); Dixon 2-7 (.286); Teasley 5-19 (.263); Nygaard 1-1 (1.000)
McCrimmon 1-3 (.333); Witherspoon 0-3 (.000); Opponents 14-36 (.389)
(*) Statistics with this team only
(!) Totals with all teams
(>) Continued season with another team

FINALS BOX SCORES
GAME 1
At STAPLES Center, September 12, 2003

OFFICIALS: Lisa Mattingly. Bob Trammell, June Courteau.   **TIME OF GAME:** 1:54. **ATTENDANCE:** 10,264

SCORE BY PERIODS	1	2	FINAL
Detroit	21	42	63
Los Angeles	42	33	75

VISITORS: Detroit: 4-2. **Head Coach:** Bill Laimbeer

No Player	MIN	FG	FGA	3P	3PA	FT	FTA	OR	DR	TOT	A	PF	ST	TO	TEC	PTS
32 Swin Cash, F	40	5	15	0	0	6	6	4	3	7	4	1	0	1	0	16
35 Cheryl Ford, F	37	3	14	0	0	5	6	7	5	12	0	2	2	2	0	11
00 Ruth Riley, C	32	2	10	0	0	2	2	1	5	6	1	5	0	3	0	6
14 Deanna Nolan, G	36	6	13	1	5	2	2	1	4	5	2	1	1	2	0	15
5 Elaine Powell, G	19	1	5	0	1	0	0	1	4	5	3	1	1	1	0	2
11 Kedra Holland-Corn	17	2	8	2	5	2	2	1	0	1	1	0	3	4	0	8
54 Barbara Farris	12	0	2	0	0	2	2	1	3	4	3	1	0	2	0	2
31 Sheila Lambert	7	1	3	1	2	0	0	0	1	1	0	1	0	0	0	3
44 Ndiaye-Diatta		DNP														
9 Stacey Thomas		DNP														
12 Ayana Walker		DNP														
TOTALS	200	20	70	4	13	19	20	16	25	41	14	12	7	15	0	63
PERCENTAGES		28.6	30.8	95.0												

TM REB: 9. **TOT TO:** 15 (24 PTS)

HOME: Los Angeles: 5-2.   **Head Coach:** Michael Cooper

No Player	MIN	FG	FGA	3P	3PA	FT	FTA	OR	DR	TOT	A	PF	ST	TO	TEC	PTS
8 Milton-Jones, F	39	6	16	2	3	5	6	2	7	9	3	5	2	1	1	19
4 Mwadi Mabika, F	39	4	11	1	5	0	0	1	4	5	4	2	2	3	1	9
9 Lisa Leslie, C	40	10	18	0	0	3	4	2	10	12	3	5	1	4	1	23
42 Nikki Teasley, G	40	2	11	1	10	1	1	2	5	7	11	4	1	1	0	6
21 Tamecka Dixon, G	34	4	11	2	4	5	5	1	2	3	1	4	1	2	0	15
31 Vanessa Nygaard	4	1	1	1	1	0	0	1	1	2	0	0	0	0	0	3
34 Lynn Pride	3	0	1	0	0	0	0	1	0	1	0	1	0	0	0	0
12 Nicky McCrimmon	1	0	0	0	0	0	0	0	0	0	0	0	0	0	0	0
22 Jennifer Gillom		DNP														
20 Shaquala Williams		DNP														
13 Sophia Witherspoon		DNP														
TOTALS	200	27	69	7	23	14	16	10	29	39	22	21	7	11	3	75
PERCENTAGES		39.1	30.4	87.5												

TM REB: 6. **TOT TO:** 11 (9 PTS)

BLOCKED SHOTS: Shock 7:Cash1,Ford3,Riley3. Sparks 6: Milton-Jones2, Leslie3,Dixon1.
TECHNICAL FOULS: Shock 0. Sparks 3: Milton-Jones1,Mabika 1,Leslie 1.

	ILL	PTO	FBP	PIP	2PT
DET	0	9	7	20	10
LA	0	24	3	18	13

FLAGRANT FOUL
None.

GAME 2

At The Palace of Auburn Hills, September 14, 2003

OFFICIALS: Matthew Boland, Sally Bell, Roy Gulbeyan.   **TIME OF GAME:** 1:54. **ATTENDANCE:** 17,846

SCORE BY PERIODS	1	2	FINAL
Los Angeles	22	39	61
Detroit	38	24	62

VISITORS: Los Angeles: 5-3. **Head Coach:** Michael Cooper

No Player	MIN	FG	FGA	3P	3PA	FT	FTA	OR	DR	TOT	A	PF	ST	TO	TEC	PTS
4 Mwadi Mabika, F	39	1	11	0	2	2	2	0	5	5	1	1	1	1	0	4
8 Milton-Jones, F	36	6	18	2	3	4	4	2	1	3	3	3	3	3	0	18
9 Lisa Leslie, C	40	6	13	0	1	6	8	4	11	15	1	2	3	3	0	8
21 Tamecka Dixon, G	36	4	9	0	0	0	0	0	2	2	1	2	0	1	0	8
42 Nikki Teasley, G	36	3	5	3	5	1	2	1	4	5	6	2	1	1	0	10
34 Lynn Pride	4	0	0	0	0	0	0	1	0	1	0	0	0	1	0	0
12 Nicky McCrimmon	4	1	3	1	3	0	0	0	0	0	0	1	0	0	0	3
13 Sophia Witherspoon	4	0	1	0	1	0	0	0	2	2	0	0	0	1	0	0
22 Jennifer Gillom	1	0	0	0	0	0	0	0	0	0	1	0	0	0	0	0
31 Vanessa Nygaard		DNP														
20 Shaquala Williams		DNP														
TOTALS	200	21	60	6	15	13	16	8	25	33	12	12	8	11	0	61
PERCENTAGES	35.0	40.0	81.3													

TM REB: 8. **TOT TO:** 11 (9 PTS)

HOME: Detroit: 5-2. **Head Coach:** Bill Laimbeer

No Player	MIN	FG	FGA	3P	3PA	FT	FTA	OR	DR	TOT	A	PF	ST	TO	TEC	PTS
32 Swin Cash, F	36	4	12	0	2	1	1	1	2	3	3	1	0	2	0	9
35 Cheryl Ford, F	33	4	9	0	0	0	0	2	5	7	2	4	2	1	0	8
00 Ruth Riley, C	31	5	14	0	0	1	2	0	3	3	5	2	0	2	0	11
14 Deanna Nolan, G	30	5	11	2	5	2	2	0	2	2	3	2	3	3	0	14
5 Elaine Powell, G	29	1	4	0	0	0	0	2	6	8	1	3	1	0	0	2
11 Kedra Holland-Corn	22	6	11	4	5	0	0	0	4	4	3	0	1	1	0	16
54 Barbara Farris	14	1	2	0	0	0	0	0	2	2	0	2	0	2	0	2
9 Stacey Thomas	4	0	0	0	0	0	0	0	1	1	0	0	0	0	0	0
12 Ayana Walker	1	0	0	0	0	0	0	0	0	0	0	0	0	0	0	0
31 Sheila Lambert		DNP														
44 Ndiaye-Diatta		DNP														
TOTALS	200	26	63	6	12	4	5	5	25	30	17	14	7	11	0	62
PERCENTAGES	41.3	50.0	80.0													

TM REB: 9. **TOT TO:** 12 (14 PTS)
BLOCKED SHOTS: Sparks 5: Milton-Jones, Mabika 1, Leslie 2, Dixon. Shock 6: Ford 1, Riley 4, Powell 1.
TECHNICAL FOULS: None

	ILL	PTO	FBP	PIP	2PT
LA	0	14	6	20	7
DET	0	9	6	22	8

FLAGRANT FOUL: None

GAME 3

At The Palace of Auburn Hills, September 16, 2003

OFFICIALS: June Courteau, Lisa Mattingly, Michael Price. **TIME OF GAME:** 2:02. **ATTENDANCE:** 22,076

SCORE BY PERIODS	1	2	FINAL
Los Angeles	37	41	78
Detroit	42	41	83

VISITORS: Los Angeles 5-4. **Head Coach:** Michael Cooper

No Player	MIN	FG	FGA	3P	3PA	FT	FTA	OR	DR	TOT	A	PF	ST	TO	TEC	PTS
8 Milton-Jones, F	40	6	13	2	3	5	6	3	4	7	1	4	2	3	0	19
4 Mwadi Mabika, F	40	11	20	2	3	5	5	2	7	9	2	3	1	2	0	29
9 Lisa Leslie, C	39	5	19	0	0	3	4	4	7	11	3	6	2	2	0	13
21 Tamecka Dixon, G	36	5	11	0	3	4	4	1	2	3	4	5	1	0	0	14
42 Nikki Teasley, G	35	1	6	1	4	0	0	1	2	3	7	3	1	2	0	3
34 Lynn Pride	6	0	0	0	0	0	0	1	0	1	0	3	0	0	0	0
13 Sophia Witherspoon	4	0	2	0	2	0	0	0	0	0	0	0	0	0	0	0
31 Vanessa Nygaard		DNP														
20 Shaquala Williams		DNP														
22 Jennifer Gillom		DNP														
12 Nicky McCrimmon		DNP														
TOTALS	200	28	71	5	15	17	19	12	22	34	17	24	7	9	0	78
PERCENTAGES	39.4	33.3	89.5													

TM REB: 8. **TOT TO:** 9 (11 PTS)

HOME: Detroit 6-2. **Head Coach:** Bill Laimbeer

No Player	MIN	FG	FGA	3P	3PA	FT	FTA	OR	DR	TOT	A	PF	ST	TO	TEC	PTS
32 Swin Cash, F	40	5	14	0	1	3	6	3	9	12	9	2	0	3	0	13
35 Cheryl Ford, F	29	3	7	0	0	4	4	2 –	9	11	0	4	1	1	0	10
00 Ruth Riley, C	34	11	19	0	0	5	6	4	2	6	3	3	0	0	0	27
5 Elaine Powell, G	36	3	6	0	2	1	2	0	1	1	5	3	2	2	0	7
14 Deanna Nolan, G	26	4	11	3	6	6	6	1	0	1	4	4	1	1	0	17
11 Kedra Holland-Corn	17	1	2	1	2	2	2	0	0	0	0	1	1	2	0	5
54 Barbara Farris	16	1	3	0	0	2	2	1	0	1	0	1	0	1	0	4
31 Sheila Lambert	1	0	0	0	0	0	0	0	0	0	0	0	0	1	0	0
9 Stacey Thomas	1	0	0	0	0	0	0	0	0	0	0	0	0	0	0	0
44 Ndiaye-Diatta		DNP														
12 Ayana Walker		DNP														
TOTALS	200	28	62	4	11	23	28	11	21	32	21	18	5	11	0	83
PERCENTAGES	45.2	36.4	82.1													

TM REB: 10. **TOT TO:** 11 (12 PTS)
BLOCKED SHOTS: Sparks 5: Milton-Jones 2, Leslie 2, Pride 1. Shock 6: Ford 1, Riley 3, Powell 1, Nolan 1.
TECHNICAL FOULS: None.

	ILL	PTO	FBP	PIP	2PT
LA	0	12	9	34	12
DET	0	11	7	32	8

FLAGRANT FOUL: None.

ALL-STAR GAME BOX SCORE

At Madison Square Garden, July 12, 2003

OFFICIALS: Roy Gulbeyan, Sue Blauch, Lamont Simpson. **TIME OF GAME:** 2:05. **ATTENDANCE:** 18,610.

SCORE BY PERIODS   1   2   FINAL
West ... 38   46   84
East ... 46   29   75

VISITORS: West

No Player	MIN	FG	FGA	3P	3PA	FT	FTA	OR	DR	TOT	A	PF	ST	TO	TEC	PTS
22 Sheryl Swoopes, F	21	1	4	0	1	2	4	0	4	4	4	1	1	2	0	4
9 Lisa Leslie, F	16	7	10	1	2	2	2	1	2	3	0	2	1	2	0	17
15 Lauren Jackson, C	19	3	7	1	2	2	3	1	3	4	0	0	0	0	0	9
10 Sue Bird, G	21	3	8	1	4	4	5	1	3	4	2	1	0	2	0	11
21 Tamecka Dixon, G	14	0	2	0	0	0	0	1	2	3	1	0	0	2	0	0
33 Yolanda Griffith	25	6	8	0	0	2	3	2	5	7	1	3	2	6	0	14
42 Nikki Teasley	24	2	6	2	5	4	4	0	6	6	6	0	5	0	0	10
33 Adrian Williams	19	4	6	0	0	1	2	1	5	6	0	1	2	1	0	9
3 Marie Ferdinand	19	3	7	0	1	0	0	0	0	0	1	4	2	3	0	6
30 Katie Smith	15	1	4	0	0	0	0	0	0	0	0	1	0	1	0	2
12 Margo Dydek	7	1	3	0	0	0	0	1	1	2	0	0	1	1	0	2
7 Tina Thompson		DNP														
14 Cynthia Cooper		DNP														
TOTALS	200	31	65	5	15	17	23	8	31	39	15	13	14	20	0	84
PERCENTAGES	47.7	33.3	73.9													

TM REB: 6. **TOT TO:** 20 (21 PTS)

HOME: East

No Player	MIN	FG	FGA	3P	3PA	FT	FTA	OR	DR	TOT	A	PF	ST	TO	TEC	PTS
24 Tamika Catchings, F	30	6	15	4	6	1	2	2	2	4	2	4	2	5	0	17
1 Chamique Holdsclaw, F	15	3	8	0	1	0	0	0	1	1	0	0	1	0	0	6
24 Tari Phillips, C	20	6	12	0	0	1	1	2	5	7	1	4	2	1	0	13
5 Dawn Staley, G	24	1	6	1	4	2	2	0	4	4	7	1	0	4	0	5
11 Weatherspoon, G	16	0	1	0	0	0	2	1	2	3	2	0	0	3	0	0
14 Deanna Nolan	22	5	10	3	7	2	3	2	4	6	1	1	1	0	0	15
12 Natalie Williams	22	3	5	0	0	0	0	7	4	11	1	1	3	1	0	6
32 Swin Cash	19	3	13	0	4	0	0	1	1	2	1	1	2	1	0	6
14 Shannon Johnson	2	0	5	0	1	0	0	0	1	1	2	1	0	1	0	0
42 Nykesha Sales	11	3	6	1	3	0	0	0	1	1	0	1	1	1	0	7
35 Cheryl Ford	9	0	2	0	0	0	0	0	1	1	0	2	0	2	0	0
25 Becky Hammon		DNP														
TOTALS	200	30	83	9	26	6	10	15	26	41	17	16	12	19	0	75
PERCENTAGES	36.1	34.6	60.0													

TM REB: 11. **TOT TO:** 20 (30 PTS)
BLOCKED SHOTS: West 5: Jackson 3, Griffith 2. East 4: Holdsclaw 1, Phillips 2, Ford 1.
TECHNICAL FOULS: None.

	ILL	PTO	FBP	PIP	2PT
West	0	30	16	50	8
East	0	21	4	28	10

FLAGRANT FOUL: None.

Front Row (l. to r.) - Marlies Askamp, M. Nikki Teasley, DeLisha Milton, President Johnny Buss, Lisa Leslie, Vedrana Grgin-Fonseca, Erika DeSouza. Back Row (l. to r.) - Head Coach Michael Cooper, Assistant Coach Glenn McDonald, General Manager Penny Toler, Assistant Coach Karleen Thompson, Latasha Byears, Nicky McCrimmon, Tamecka Dixon, Mwadi Mabika, Sophia Witherspoon, Team Trainer Sandee Teruya, Team Manager Thomas Archie, Assistant to the General Manager Rondre Jackson, Video Coordinator Ryan Weisenberg.

FINAL STANDINGS

EASTERN CONFERENCE

TEAM	W	L	PCT	GB	HOME	ROAD	LAST-10	STREAK
New York	18	14	.562	-	10-6	8-8	5-5	Lost 2
Charlotte	18	14	.562	-	11-5	7-9	5-5	Won 4
Washington	17	15	.531	1	9-7	8-8	2-8	Lost 1
Indiana	16	16	.500	2	10-6	6-10	7-3	Won 2
Orlando	16	16	.500	2	10-6	6-10	6-4	Won 2
Miami	15	17	.469	3	9-7	6-10	5-5	Won 1
Cleveland	10	22	.312	8	4-12	6-10	2-8	Lost 6
Detroit	9	23	.281	9	7-9	2-14	5-5	Lost 2

WESTERN CONFERENCE

TEAM	W	L	PCT	GB	HOME	ROAD	LAST-10	STREAK
Los Angeles	25	7	.781	-	12-4	13-3	7-3	Won 3
Houston	24	8	.750	1	14-2	10-6	8-2	Won 1
Utah	20	12	.625	5	12-4	8-8	5-5	Won 1
Seattle	17	15	.531	8	10-6	7-9	7-3	Lost 1
Portland	16	16	.500	9	9-7	7-9	3-7	Lost 4
Sacramento	14	18	.437	11	10-6	4-12	8-2	Won 1
Phoenix	11	21	.344	14	10-6	1-15	3-7	Lost 1
Minnesota	10	22	.312	15	7-9	3-13	3-7	Lost 3

TEAM STANDINGS

OFFENSIVE

TEAM	G	FG	FGA	PCT	FG3	FG3A	PCT	FT	FTA	PCT	OFF	DEF	REB	AST	PF	DQ	STL	TO	BLK	PTS	AVG
L.A.	32	891	2002	.445	194	515	.377	476	645	.738	329	814	1143	583	664	18	257	517	161	2452	76.6
Utah	32	843	1911	.441	89	247	.360	643	844	.762	347	721	1068	478	665	7	228	522	178	2418	75.6
Orl.	32	808	1914	.422	145	461	.315	493	646	.763	320	595	915	446	669	6	295	456	113	2254	70.4
Cha.	32	770	1790	.430	211	527	.400	490	663	.739	302	653	955	496	647	9	241	408	105	2241	70.0
Port.	32	829	1951	.425	127	391	.325	410	564	.727	307	641	948	492	623	1	239	493	120	2195	68.6
Sea.	32	794	1948	.408	182	506	.360	418	543	.770	362	633	995	514	623	5	282	477	151	2188	68.4
Sac.	32	780	1945	.401	112	395	.284	494	653	.757	301	648	949	500	675	8	247	456	109	2166	67.7
Wash.	32	806	1910	.422	164	443	.370	359	478	.751	330	708	1038	516	583	3	221	455	94	2135	66.7
Det.	32	766	1919	.399	110	364	.302	472	651	.725	360	719	1079	478	609	1	201	541	132	2114	66.1
Ind.	32	731	1825	.401	180	543	.331	455	580	.784	315	633	948	447	559	6	268	438	100	2097	65.5
Phoe.	32	793	1889	.420	100	328	.305	405	538	.753	292	626	918	427	623	1	267	501	94	2091	65.3
N.Y.	32	772	1740	.444	145	400	.363	400	567	.705	260	610	870	496	638	5	261	458	100	2089	65.3
Hou.	32	755	1778	.425	109	332	.328	453	585	.774	299	702	1001	450	467	1	260	455	126	2072	64.8
Clev.	32	760	1820	.418	121	374	.324	430	553	.778	295	674	969	480	567	8	221	451	83	2071	64.7
Miami	32	774	1856	.417	129	389	.332	369	529	.698	296	573	869	476	643	4	274	435	96	2046	63.9
Minn.	32	727	1775	.410	166	500	.332	383	578	.663	309	650	959	466	617	7	226	529	102	2003	62.6

DEFENSIVE

Team	FG	FGA	PCT	FG3	FG3A	PCT	FT	FTA	PCT	OFF	DEF	REB	AST	PF	DQ	STL	TO	BLK	PTS	AVG	DIFF
Hou.	705	1880	.375	151	489	.309	331	452	.732	309	664	973	446	606	7	262	464	71	1892	59.1	+5.6
N.Y.	691	1733	.399	149	434	.343	484	645	.750	312	649	961	410	597	2	228	478	88	2015	63.0	+2.3
Miami	745	1722	.433	129	382	.338	469	614	.764	278	693	971	446	588	4	222	515	104	2088	65.3	-1.3
Sea.	783	1818	.431	102	342	.298	435	587	.741	307	662	969	488	563	5	254	531	125	2103	65.7	+2.7
Minn.	747	1807	.413	141	389	.362	469	613	.765	302	612	914	495	618	4	273	465	117	2104	65.8	-3.2
Wash.	786	1903	.413	147	446	.330	397	538	.738	309	680	989	442	570	3	237	441	101	2116	66.1	+0.6
Ind.	804	1817	.442	162	464	.349	359	503	.714	288	644	932	507	647	9	226	470	145	2129	66.5	-1.0
Cha.	778	1807	.431	133	372	.358	444	598	.742	295	620	915	489	600	2	208	424	103	2133	66.7	+3.4
Clev.	797	1834	.435	149	441	.338	397	521	.762	278	640	918	530	613	5	242	428	109	2140	66.9	-2.2
Port.	819	1885	.434	126	348	.362	463	647	.716	334	678	1012	486	616	6	272	508	139	2227	69.6	-1.0
L.A.	796	2040	.390	163	521	.313	480	649	.740	314	645	959	508	623	6	275	453	111	2235	69.8	+6.8
Orl.	804	1862	.432	156	422	.370	491	668	.735	362	684	1046	519	637	9	251	541	108	2255	70.5	-0.0
Det.	828	1984	.417	146	447	.327	464	605	.767	314	669	983	465	637	4	277	443	139	2266	70.8	-4.8
Phoe.	850	1870	.455	155	388	.399	436	608	.717	309	692	1001	532	600	6	268	491	127	2291	71.6	-6.3
Sac.	815	1944	.419	149	453	.329	515	681	.756	352	723	1075	493	633	8	233	496	128	2294	71.7	-4.0
Utah	851	2067	.412	126	377	.334	516	688	.750	361	645	1006	489	724	10	260	444	149	2344	73.3	+2.3
Avg	787	1873	.420	143	420	.340	447	601	.743	314	663	977	484	617	6	249	475	117	2165	67.6	—
Totals	12599			2284			7150			5024	15624		9872	3988			1864				
	29973			6715			9617			10600			7745		90		7592		34632		

TEAM COMPARISONS

TEAM	Points Per Game OWN	OPP	Field Goal Percentage OWN	OPP	Turnovers Per Game OWN	OPP	Rebound Percentages OFF	DEF	TOT	Below 70 Pts. OWN	OPP	Overtime Games W	L	3 PTS or Less W	L	10 PTS or More W	L
Charlotte	70.0	66.7	.430	.431	12.8*	13.3	.328	.689	.508	14	23	2	0	1	6	11	5
Cleveland	64.7	66.9	.418	.435	14.1	13.4	.316	.708	.512	24	22	0	4	1	2	7	8
Detroit	66.1	70.8	.399	.417	16.9	13.8	.350	.696	.523	22	14	0	2	3	3	4	12
Houston	64.8	59.1*	.425	.375*	14.2	14.5	.310	.694	.502	24	29	1	0	5	1	13	3
Indiana	65.5	66.5	.401	.442	13.7	14.7	.328	.687	.508	21	19	0	1	2	1	6	9
Los Angeles	76.6*	69.8	.445*	.390	16.2	14.2	.338	.722*	.530*	9	17	2	1	0	2	13	2
Miami	63.9	65.3	.417	.433	13.6	16.1	.299	.673	.486	26	21	2	1	1	2	3	7
Minnesota	62.6	65.8	.410	.413	16.5	14.5	.336	.683	.509	24	20	1	2	3	6	3	10
New York	65.3	63.0	.444	.399	14.3	14.9	.286	.662	.474	19	23	0	1	3	3	9	5
Orlando	70.4	70.5	.422	.432	14.3	16.9*	.319	.622	.470	14	17	3	0	4	3	6	5
Phoenix	65.3	71.6	.420	.455	15.7	15.3	.297	.670	.483	18	14	0	0	4	4	2	12
Portland	68.6	69.6	.425	.434	15.4	15.9	.312	.657	.485	15	16	0	2	3	4	7	7
Sacramento	67.7	71.7	.401	.419	14.3	15.5	.294	.648	.471	18	11	2	2	6	3	4	12
Seattle	68.4	65.7	.408	.431	14.9	16.6	.354*	.673	.513	18	19	1	1	2	2	9	5
Utah	75.6	73.3	.441	.412	16.3	13.9	.350	.666	.508	9	12	2	0	3	1	9	5
Washington	66.7	66.1	.422	.413	14.2	13.8	.327	.696	.511	23	21	1	0	3	1	6	5
COMPOSITE; 256 games	67.6		.420		14.8		.322	.678		298		17		44		112	

* - League Leader

REBOUND PERCENTAGES — OFF. - Percentage of a given team's missed shots which that team rebounds. DEF. - Percentage of opponents' missed shots which a given team rebounds. TOT. - Average of offensive and defensive rebound percentages.

SCORING AVERAGE

	G	FG	FT	PTS	AVG
Holdsclaw, Was.	20	149	88	397	19.9
Catchings, Ind.	32	184	150	594	18.6
Swoopes, Hou.	32	221	127	592	18.5
Jackson, Sea.	28	186	68	482	17.2
Leslie, L.A.	31	189	133	523	16.9
Mabika, L.A.	32	188	99	539	16.8
Thompson, Hou.	29	176	93	485	16.7
Smith, Min.	31	162	126	512	16.5
S. Johnson, Orl.	31	157	164	499	16.1
Goodson, Utah	32	189	117	503	15.7
Ferdinand, Utah	32	176	132	489	15.3
Gillom, Pho.	31	166	105	473	15.3
Cash, Det.	32	144	173	474	14.8
Smith, Sac.	32	184	86	469	14.7
Sam, Mia.	32	191	55	463	14.5
Bird, Sea.	32	151	102	461	14.4
Phillips, N.Y.	32	183	85	451	14.1
Sales, Orl.	32	155	84	431	13.5
Dydek, Utah	30	139	114	394	13.1
Taylor, Cle.	30	133	87	391	13.0

REBOUNDS PER GAME

	G	OFF	DEF	TOT	AVG
Holdsclaw, Was.	20	54	178	232	11.6
Leslie, L.A.	31	78	244	322	10.4
Dydek, Utah	30	52	210	262	8.7
Catchings, Ind.	32	92	184	276	8.6
Williams, Utah	31	105	150	255	8.2
Thompson, Hou.	29	67	150	217	7.5
Williams, Min.	31	96	133	229	7.4
Phillips, N.Y.	32	69	154	223	7.0
Cash, Det.	32	77	145	222	6.9
Williams, Pho.	32	64	156	220	6.9
Scott-Richardson, Ind.	31	80	131	211	6.8
Jackson, Sea.	28	66	124	190	6.8
Milton, L.A.	32	65	146	211	6.6
Melvin, Cle.	32	84	110	194	6.1
Sutton-Brown, Cha.	32	76	115	191	6.0
Palmer, Det.-Orl.	32	47	142	189	5.9
Smith, Sac.	32	56	132	188	5.9
Bullett, Was.	32	46	140	186	5.8
Goodson, Utah	32	91	90	181	5.7
Stinson, Cha.	32	37	140	177	5.5

ASSISTS PER GAME

	G	AST	AVG
Penicheiro, Sac.	24	192	8.0
Bird, Sea.	32	191	6.0
Weatherspoon, N.Y.	32	181	5.7
S. Johnson, Orl.	31	163	5.3
Staley, Cha.	32	164	5.1
Azzi, Utah	32	158	4.9
Teasley, L.A.	32	140	4.4
Black, Mia.	32	137	4.3
Dixon, L.A.	30	119	4.0
Catchings, Ind.	32	118	3.7
Burgess, Was.	26	93	3.6
Figgs, Por.	31	104	3.4
Swoopes, Hou.	32	107	3.3
Rizzotti, Cle.	26	85	3.3
Grubin, Pho.	32	104	3.3
Nagy, Sac.	24	73	3.0
Powell, Orl.-Det.	30	90	3.0
Jackson, Por.	32	95	3.0
Canty, Det.	28	83	3.0
Mabika, L.A.	32	92	2.9

FIELD GOAL PCT.

	FG	FGA	PCT
Burras, Por.	117	186	.629
Williams, Min.	124	221	.561
Wauters, Cle.	120	217	.553
Sutton-Brown, Cha.	129	243	.531
Griffith, Sac.	93	179	.520
Harrison, Pho.	120	242	.496
Phillips, N.Y.	183	373	.491
Milton, L.A.	132	271	.487
Scott-Richardson, Ind.	113	232	.487
Walker, Por.	139	287	.484

3-PT FIELD GOAL PCT.

	3FG	3GA	PCT
Miller, Cha.	24	51	.471
Azzi, Utah	41	92	.446
Washington, Hou.-Ind.	22	52	.423
Johnson, N.Y.	32	76	.421
Milton, L.A.	21	50	.420
Feaster, Cha.	79	189	.418
Witherspoon, L.A.	28	67	.418
Stinson, Cha.	29	70	.414
Bird, Sea.	57	142	.401
2 tied			.400

FREE THROW PCT.

	FT	FTA	PCT
Bird, Sea.	102	112	.911
Figgs, Por.	59	65	.908
Arcain, Hou.	98	111	.883
Douglas, Orl.	58	67	.866
Moore, Mia.-Min.	54	63	.857
Grooms, Sac.	71	83	.855
Taylor, Cle.	87	102	.853
Smith, Sac.	86	101	.851
Wauters, Cle.	74	87	.851
Rasmussen, Mia.	39	46	.848

STEALS PER GAME

	G	STL	AVG
Catchings, Ind.	32	94	2.94
Swoopes, Hou.	32	88	2.75
Penicheiro, Sac.	24	64	2.67
Sam, Mia.	32	69	2.16
Sales, Orl.	32	60	1.88
Black, Mia.	32	59	1.84
Phillips, N.Y.	32	58	1.81
Bird, Sea.	32	55	1.72
Jackson, Por.	32	55	1.72
Bullett, Was.	32	54	1.69

BLOCKS PER GAME

	G	BLK	AVG
Dydek, Utah	30	107	3.57
Leslie, L.A.	31	90	2.90
Jackson, Sea.	28	81	2.89
Riley, Mia.	26	41	1.58
Smith, Sac.	32	46	1.44
Catchings, Ind.	32	43	1.34
Whitmore, N.Y.	32	43	1.34
Bullett, Was.	32	37	1.16
Crawley, Por.	32	37	1.16
Sutton-Brown, Cha.	32	36	1.13

MINUTES PER GAME

	G	MIN	AVG		G	MIN	AVG
Smith, Min.	31	1138	36.7	S. Johnson, Orl.	31	1110	35.8
Catchings, Ind.	32	1167	36.5	Penicheiro, Sac.	24	853	35.5
Thompson, Hou.	29	1052	36.3	Bird, Sea.	32	1121	35.0
Swoopes, Hou.	32	1154	36.1	Arcain, Hou.	32	1116	34.9
Azzi, Utah	32	1151	36.0	Goodson, Utah	32	1101	34.4

INDIVIDUAL STATISTICS, TEAM BY TEAM

CHARLOTTE STING

Player	G	Min	FGM	FGA	Pct	FTM	FTA	Pct	Off	Def	Tot	Ast	PF	Dq	Stl	TO	Blk	Pts	Avg	Hi
Andrea Stinson	32	950	159	349	.456	64	93	.688	37	140	177	91	56	0	37	52	9	411	12.8	27
Tammy Sutton-Brown	32	885	129	243	.531	124	174	.713	76	115	191	15	125	3	29	49	36	382	11.9	22
Allison Feaster	32	956	115	292	.394	70	85	.824	37	81	118	61	79	0	39	40	12	379	11.8	24
Dawn Staley	32	1061	84	231	.364	77	101	.762	8	48	56	164	67	0	48	80	0	278	8.7	19
Charlotte Smith-Tayl	32	890	91	222	.410	40	54	.741	39	82	121	53	113	3	21	60	17	256	8.0	14
Kelly Miller	32	554	79	177	.446	29	38	.763	31	37	68	49	39	0	22	27	1	211	6.6	23
Shalonda Enis	4	59	5	18	.278	9	9	1.000	6	3	9	3	4	0	1	1	2	19	4.8	11
Tonya Edwards	29	303	36	99	.364	33	46	.717	11	30	41	24	28	0	16	17	2	112	3.9	14
Erin Buescher	29	392	33	82	.402	25	36	.694	32	59	91	18	61	1	13	27	15	95	3.3	11
Summer Erb	31	342	35	62	.565	18	25	.720	20	51	71	10	70	2	13	35	11	88	2.8	11
Keisha Anderson	7	31	3	12	.250	0	0	—	2	4	6	5	4	0	3	0	1	7	1.0	5
Elena Shakirova	1	5	0	0	—	1	2	.500	1	0	1	0	0	0	1	0	0	1	1.0	1
Sheila Lambert	3	16	1	3	.333	0	0	—	2	1	3	3	1	0	1	2	0	2	0.7	2
Shantia Owens	2	6	0	0	—	0	0	—	0	2	2	0	0	0	0	0	0	0	0.0	0
Charlotte	32	6450	770	1790	.430	490	663	.739	302	653	955	496	647	9	241	408	105	2241	70.0	94
Opponents	32	6450	778	1807	.431	444	598	.742	295	620	915	489	600	2	208	424	103	2133	66.7	87

3-pt. FG: Charlotte 211-527 (.400) Stinson 29-70 (.414); Feaster 79-189 (.418); Staley 33-83 (.398); Smith-Taylor 34-91 (.374); Miller 24-51 (.471); Enis 0-3 (.000) Edwards 7-25 (.280); Buescher 4-11 (.364); Anderson 1-4 (.250); Opponents 133-372 (.358)

CLEVELAND ROCKERS

Player	G	Min	FGM	FGA	Pct	FTM	FTA	Pct	Off	Def	Tot	Ast	PF	Dq	Stl	TO	Blk	Pts	Avg	Hi
Penny Taylor	30	908	133	320	.416	87	102	.853	51	107	158	68	66	0	37	58	11	391	13.0	27
Chasity Melvin	32	1055	153	330	.464	90	131	.687	84	110	194	57	104	2	28	74	18	399	12.5	30
Merlakia Jones	32	1094	157	393	.399	62	79	.785	33	143	176	72	60	0	44	55	4	391	12.2	27
Ann Wauters	28	802	120	217	.553	74	87	.851	45	95	140	39	74	0	16	59	21	314	11.2	20
Jennifer Rizzotti	26	695	54	135	.400	32	40	.800	5	65	70	85	53	3	23	45	3	178	6.8	16
Rushia Brown	28	468	42	105	.400	28	38	.737	29	46	75	27	54	0	21	39	8	112	4.0	11
Deanna Jackson	18	143	19	46	.413	17	24	.708	10	17	27	6	11	0	2	9	1	55	3.1	14
Mery Andrade	32	665	34	111	.306	18	23	.783	17	39	56	67	82	2	29	41	6	91	2.8	11
Brandi McCain	31	392	25	86	.291	12	16	.750	4	22	26	41	29	0	11	34	3	83	2.7	9
Lucienne Berthieu	5	16	3	7	.429	2	4	.500	3	1	4	0	5	0	0	0	0	8	1.6	5
Tracy Henderson	23	173	16	41	.390	3	3	1.000	12	22	34	3	26	1	3	18	7	35	1.5	5
Tricia Bader Binford	18	132	4	26	.154	5	6	.833	1	6	7	15	3	0	6	7	1	14	0.8	5
Paige Sauer	1	7	0	3	.000	0	0	—	1	1	2	0	0	0	1	1	0	0	0.0	0
Cleveland	32	6550	760	1820	.418	430	553	.778	295	674	969	480	567	8	221	451	83	2071	64.7	99
Opponents	32	6550	797	1834	.435	397	521	.762	278	640	918	530	613	5	242	428	109	2140	66.9	103

3-pt. FG: Cleveland 121-374 (.324) Taylor 38-111 (.342); Melvin 3-6 (.500); Jones 15-54 (.278); Wauters 0-1 (.000); Rizzotti 38-99 (.384); Brown 0-1 (.000) Jackson 0-3 (.000); Andrade 5-26 (.192); McCain 21-58 (.362); Berthieu 0-1 (.000); Bader Binford 1-14 (.071) Opponents 149-441 (.338)

DETROIT SHOCK

Player	G	Min	FGM	FGA	Pct	FTM	FTA	Pct	Off	Def	Tot	Ast	PF	Dq	Stl	TO	Blk	Pts	Avg	Hi
Swin Cash	32	1079	144	353	.408	173	227	.762	77	145	222	86	85	0	37	100	31	474	14.8	25
Wendy Palmer(‡)	16	464	65	153	.425	35	53	.660	27	69	96	20	44	0	13	34	2	184	11.5	20
Deanna Nolan	32	804	103	248	.415	29	36	.806	17	70	87	62	74	1	27	61	12	277	8.7	18
Astou Ndiaye-Diatta	32	776	126	270	.467	23	39	.590	44	118	162	39	65	0	17	58	12	275	8.6	15
Elaine Powell(*)	15	397	54	121	.446	34	40	.850	26	37	63	60	19	0	23	41	8	148	9.9	18
Elaine Powell(†)	30	705	89	220	.405	50	66	.758	33	62	95	90	50	0	43	71	12	236	7.9	18
Dominique Canty	28	625	52	154	.338	55	76	.724	24	45	69	83	59	0	21	56	4	160	5.7	17
Ayana Walker	32	548	63	167	.377	34	49	.694	56	62	118	17	56	0	12	29	34	162	5.1	16
Barbara Farris	32	564	49	117	.419	45	61	.738	29	65	94	16	62	0	12	38	9	143	4.5	14
Edwina Brown	28	549	43	131	.328	23	32	.719	29	53	82	58	73	0	25	60	7	115	4.1	12
Kelly Santos	12	169	16	42	.381	12	20	.600	12	20	32	7	20	0	3	14	9	44	3.7	9
Lenae Williams	27	177	30	101	.297	0	5	.000	7	12	19	4	15	0	4	14	0	73	2.7	8

Player	G	Min	FGM	FGA	Pct	FTM	FTA	Pct	REBOUNDS Off	Def	Tot	Ast	PF	Dq	Stl	TO	Blk	SCORING Pts	Avg	Hi
Stacy Clinesmith..........12	105	8	21	.381	5	6	.833	1	4	5	17	6	0	1	6	1	27	2.3	8
Jill Chapman-Daily......19	119	10	27	.370	2	3	.667	11	15	26	0	20	0	3	8	2	22	1.2	4
Begona Garcia 8	64	2	11	.182	2	4	.500	0	4	4	9	8	0	3	11	0	8	1.0	6
O. Zakaluzhnaya(‡) 3	10	1	3	.333	0	0	—	0	0	0	0	3	0	0	0	1	2	0.7	2
Detroit 32	6450	766	1919	.399	472	651	.725	360	719	1079	478	609	1	201	541	132	2114	66.1	91
Opponents 32	6450	828	1984	.417	464	605	.767	314	669	983	465	637	4	277	443	139	2266	70.8	94

3-pt. FG: Detroit 110-364 (.302) Cash 13-63 (.206); Palmer(‡) 19-60 (.317); Nolan 42-114 (.368); Ndiaye-Diatta 0-2 (.000); Powell(*) 6-22 (.273); Canty 1-5 (.200) Powell(†) 8-33 (.242); Walker 2-9 (.222); Farris 0-1 (.000); Brown 6-12 (.500); Williams 13-54 (.241); Clinesmith 6-15 (.400) Chapman-Daily 0-1 (.000); Garcia 2-6 (.333); Opponents 146-447 (.327)

HOUSTON COMETS

Player	G	Min	FGM	FGA	Pct	FTM	FTA	Pct	REBOUNDS Off	Def	Tot	Ast	PF	Dq	Stl	TO	Blk	SCORING Pts	Avg	Hi
Sheryl Swoopes 32	1154	221	509	.434	127	154	.825	30	128	158	107	50	0	88	87	23	592	18.5	32
Tina Thompson 29	1052	176	408	.431	93	113	.823	67	150	217	62	76	0	25	92	20	485	16.7	31
Janeth Arcain 32	1116	128	302	.424	98	111	.883	42	84	126	86	49	0	51	71	6	364	11.4	23
Tiffani Johnson 32	815	77	178	.433	47	58	.810	73	100	173	39	67	0	17	38	24	201	6.3	13
Rita Williams(*) 9	85	5	11	.455	7	10	.700	0	6	6	7	11	0	11	10	0	19	2.1	15
Rita Williams(†) 29	569	44	146	.301	32	44	.727	10	33	43	50	45	0	32	39	2	139	4.8	17
Michelle Snow 32	480	45	96	.469	34	57	.596	31	88	119	13	59	0	12	22	26	125	3.9	16
Grace Daley................23	185	16	37	.432	29	47	.617	13	10	23	16	15	0	3	17	1	63	2.7	19
Coquese Washington(‡)21	349	17	50	.340	2	2	1.000	7	34	41	31	38	1	13	20	0	44	2.1	6
Kelley Gibson...........29	276	21	55	.382	4	6	.667	3	17	20	14	21	0	8	21	7	60	2.1	13
Sonja Henning(*) 23	521	18	52	.346	5	11	.455	10	48	58	51	42	0	23	36	6	44	1.9	8
Sonja Henning(†) 31	728	26	74	.351	7	15	.467	18	66	84	66	57	0	32	43	7	62	2.0	8
Tynesha Lewis 17	145	13	30	.433	5	8	.625	6	12	18	9	18	0	9	9	3	34	2.0	12
Rebecca Lobo 21	132	15	32	.469	1	4	.250	9	14	23	12	10	0	1	11	5	34	1.6	9
Tammy Jackson 5	69	3	8	.375	0	2	.000	7	6	13	1	7	0	3	6	3	6	1.2	2
Amanda Lassiter(‡)........6	46	0	10	.000	1	2	.500	1	5	6	2	4	0	2	2	1	1	0.2	1
Houston 32	6425	755	1778	.425	453	585	.774	299	702	1001	450	467	1	260	455	126	2072	64.8	89
Opponents 32	6425	705	1880	.375	331	452	.732	309	664	973	446	606	7	262	464	71	1892	59.1	75

3-pt. FG: Houston 109-332 (.328) Swoopes 23-80 (.288); Thompson 40-108 (.370); Arcain 10-37 (.270); Johnson 0-2 (.000); Williams(*) 2-6 (.333); Snow 1-2 (.500) Williams(†) 19-73 (.260); Daley 2-8 (.250); Washington(‡) 8-21 (.381); Gibson 14-36 (.389); Henning(*) 3-12 (.250) Henning(†) 3-16 (.188); Lewis 3-8 (.375); Lobo 3-7 (.429); Lassiter(‡) 0-5 (.000); Opponents 151-489 (.309)

INDIANA FEVER

Player	G	Min	FGM	FGA	Pct	FTM	FTA	Pct	REBOUNDS Off	Def	Tot	Ast	PF	Dq	Stl	TO	Blk	SCORING Pts	Avg	Hi
Tamika Catchings........32	1167	184	439	.419	150	184	.815	92	184	276	118	105	2	94	82	43	594	18.6	35
Nikki McCray..............32	1058	132	318	.415	84	103	.816	29	68	97	70	73	2	28	82	3	369	11.5	30
Olympia Scott-Richar..31	975	113	232	.487	66	82	.805	80	131	211	52	127	2	38	69	13	292	9.4	31
Rita Williams(‡) 20	484	39	135	.289	25	34	.735	10	27	37	43	34	0	21	29	2	120	6.0	17
Alicia Thompson 18	314	39	109	.358	12	17	.706	12	30	42	14	20	0	7	18	2	97	5.4	16
Nadine Malcolm 29	599	58	158	.367	28	37	.757	22	39	61	21	42	0	13	34	3	156	5.4	19
Coquese Washington(*)11	325	26	70	.371	14	20	.700	7	26	33	48	22	0	23	24	2	80	7.3	14
Coquese Washington(†)32	674	43	120	.358	16	22	.727	14	60	74	79	60	1	36	44	2	124	3.9	14
Bridget Pettis 32	375	38	107	.355	28	39	.718	17	22	39	17	22	0	8	24	0	113	3.5	15
Kelly Schumacher 31	352	45	89	.506	18	26	.692	18	41	59	13	49	0	7	21	23	108	3.5	15
Niele Ivey..................31	439	25	71	.352	17	21	.810	6	22	28	39	31	0	16	22	3	86	2.8	9
Jackie Moore 18	128	16	38	.421	10	14	.714	9	20	29	3	16	0	5	14	1	42	2.3	13
Monica Maxwell 18	170	14	47	.298	2	2	1.000	12	19	31	7	16	0	7	6	4	35	1.9	6
Zuzi Klimesova...........11	39	2	12	.167	1	1	1.000	1	4	5	2	2	0	1	2	1	5	0.5	5
Indiana......................32	6425	731	1825	.401	455	580	.784	315	633	948	447	559	6	268	438	100	2097	65.5	81
Opponents 32	6425	804	1817	.442	359	503	.714	288	644	932	507	647	9	226	470	145	2129	66.5	89

3-pt. FG: Indiana 180-543 (.331) Catchings 76-193 (.394); McCray 21-66 (.318); Scott-Richardson 0-4 (.000); Williams(‡) 17-67 (.254); Thompson 7-29 (.241) Malcolm 12-41 (.293); Washington(*) 14-31 (.452); Washington(†) 22-52 (.423); Pettis 9-43 (.209); Schumacher 0-1 (.000) Ivey 19-50 (.380); Moore 0-1 (.000); Maxwell 5-17 (.294); Opponents 162-464 (.349)

LOS ANGELES SPARKS

Player	G	Min	FGM	FGA	Pct	FTM	FTA	Pct	REBOUNDS Off	Def	Tot	Ast	PF	Dq	Stl	TO	Blk	SCORING Pts	Avg	Hi
Lisa Leslie...................31	1060	189	406	.466	133	183	.727	78	244	322	83	123	7	46	108	90	523	16.9	30
Mwadi Mabika...........32	1050	188	444	.423	99	118	.839	32	135	167	92	90	1	38	62	9	539	16.8	32
DeLisha Milton...........32	966	132	271	.487	77	104	.740	65	146	211	45	122	3	50	94	35	362	11.3	23
Tamecka Dixon 30	958	125	320	.391	49	59	.831	18	74	92	119	74	2	28	82	5	319	10.6	20
Latasha Byears 26	486	76	123	.618	30	53	.566	65	76	141	13	89	4	19	20	4	182	7.0	15
Nikki Teasley 32	882	67	166	.404	30	40	.750	17	67	84	140	63	1	25	68	9	204	6.4	18

Player	G	Min	FGM	FGA	Pct	FTM	FTA	Pct	Off	Def	Tot	Ast	PF	Dq	Stl	TO	Blk	Pts	Avg	Hi
Sophia Witherspoon....31		358	49	118	.415	35	46	.761	9	20	29	29	27	0	13	22	2	161	5.2	19
Marlies Askamp(*) 20		215	26	55	.473	9	14	.643	24	25	49	4	25	0	11	11	4	61	3.1	12
Marlies Askamp(†) 26		287	30	65	.462	12	25	.480	30	30	60	7	34	0	12	12	5	72	2.8	12
Vedrana Grgin-Fonsec 12		79	12	31	.387	2	3	.667	3	5	8	1	11	0	1	8	0	31	2.6	8
Vicki Hall....................3		19	2	4	.500	3	4	.750	1	1	2	1	2	0	1	1	0	7	2.3	4
Nicky McCrimmon......32		356	20	49	.408	7	11	.636	9	14	23	53	22	0	22	24	3	51	1.6	7
Erika Desouza 11		41	5	14	.357	2	10	.200	8	6	14	2	14	0	3	6	0	12	1.1	4
Katryna Gaither(‡) 1		5	0	1	.000	0	0	—	0	1	1	1	2	0	0	1	0	0	0.0	0
Los Angeles 32		6475	891	2002	.445	476	645	.738	329	814	1143	583	664	18	257	517	161	2452	76.6	102
Opponents 32		6475	796	2040	.390	480	649	.740	314	645	959	508	623	6	275	453	111	2235	69.8	94

3-pt. FG: Los Angeles 194-515 (.377) Leslie 12-37 (.324); Mabika 64-175 (.366); Milton 21-50 (.420); Dixon 20-57 (.351); Teasley 40-100 (.400); Askamp(*) 0-1 (.000) Witherspoon 28-67 (.418); Askamp(†) 0-1 (.000); Grgin-Fonseca 5-12 (.417); Hall 0-1 (.000); McCrimmon 4-15 (.267) Opponents 163-521 (.313)

MIAMI SOL

Player	G	Min	FGM	FGA	Pct	FTM	FTA	Pct	Off	Def	Tot	Ast	PF	Dq	Stl	TO	Blk	Pts	Avg	Hi
Sheri Sam....................32		1073	191	440	.434	55	89	.618	58	97	155	83	83	0	69	71	6	463	14.5	27
Betty Lennox(*)............26		581	119	307	.388	44	58	.759	18	55	73	47	79	2	25	62	5	310	11.9	24
Betty Lennox(†) 31		719	120	355	.338	50	68	.735	20	69	89	63	102	3	30	82	5	341	11.0	24
Sandy Brondello..........30		763	97	266	.365	55	67	.821	7	34	41	46	40	0	26	40	4	263	8.8	23
Pollyanna Johns Kimb 31		801	78	149	.523	61	97	.629	58	82	140	32	75	0	27	53	15	217	7.0	16
Ruth Riley 26		519	60	129	.465	28	46	.609	24	66	90	25	87	1	11	49	41	148	5.7	14
Tamara Moore(‡) 5		83	8	25	.320	10	10	1.000	3	4	7	10	16	0	7	11	0	28	5.6	22
Kristen Rasmussen 31		674	64	116	.552	39	46	.848	41	76	117	41	63	0	18	37	16	170	5.5	19
Debbie Black 32		899	64	160	.400	25	33	.758	41	82	123	137	75	1	59	32	5	153	4.8	14
Vanessa Nygaard 29		443	43	101	.426	10	13	.769	27	40	67	9	49	0	11	13	1	120	4.1	11
Iziane Castro Marque ..19		182	24	72	.333	17	25	.680	7	10	17	7	22	0	7	18	0	66	3.5	11
Lindsey Yamasaki 15		147	19	43	.442	5	10	.500	3	12	15	9	20	0	4	10	1	52	3.5	12
Claudia Neves 20		194	11	31	.355	11	16	.688	0	7	7	25	18	0	8	13	0	37	1.9	9
Marlies Askamp(‡) 6		72	4	10	.400	3	11	.273	6	5	11	3	9	0	1	1	1	11	1.8	4
Trisha Stafford-Odom 6		38	1	6	.167	6	8	.750	3	3	6	2	5	0	1	6	0	8	1.3	4
Carolyn Moos...............2		6	0	1	.000	0	0	—	0	0	0	0	2	0	0	0	1	0	0.0	0
Miami 32		6475	774	1856	.417	369	529	.698	296	573	869	476	643	4	274	435	96	2046	63.9	86
Opponents 32		6475	745	1722	.433	469	614	.764	278	693	971	446	588	4	222	515	104	2088	65.3	91

3-pt. FG: Miami 129-389 (.332) Sam 26-76 (.342); Lennox(*) 46-131 (.351); Lennox(†) 51-154 (.331); Brondello 14-44 (.318); Moore(‡) 2-9 (.222); Black 0-3 (.000) Rasmussen 3-7 (.429); Nygaard 24-64 (.375); Castro Marques 1-17 (.059); Yamasaki 9-17 (.529); Neves 4-21 (.190) Opponents 129-382 (.338)

MINNESOTA LYNX

Player	G	Min	FGM	FGA	Pct	FTM	FTA	Pct	Off	Def	Tot	Ast	PF	Dq	Stl	TO	Blk	Pts	Avg	Hi
Katie Smith..................31		1138	162	401	.404	126	153	.824	24	68	92	79	87	2	32	70	7	512	16.5	28
Svetlana Abrosimova ...27		805	119	316	.377	56	116	.483	45	101	146	60	73	0	42	92	10	314	11.6	26
Tamika Williams..........31		1023	124	221	.561	63	108	.583	96	133	229	51	57	0	44	74	13	314	10.1	19
Tamara Moore(*) 26		653	63	172	.366	44	53	.830	20	56	76	78	65	0	23	74	9	196	7.5	19
Tamara Moore(†) 31		736	71	197	.360	54	63	.857	23	60	83	88	81	0	30	85	9	224	7.2	22
Betty Lennox(‡) 5		138	10	48	.208	6	10	.600	2	14	16	16	23	1	5	20	0	31	6.2	13
Michele Van Gorp 22		352	41	90	.456	16	22	.727	29	35	64	14	53	2	6	20	11	100	4.5	18
Georgia Schweitzer 30		509	42	87	.483	26	30	.867	7	44	51	37	47	1	15	27	5	124	4.1	17
Lynn Pride 31		589	57	148	.385	8	17	.471	25	78	103	43	73	1	25	47	25	123	4.0	9
Kristi Harrower............27		481	39	95	.384	4	10	.400	9	37	46	54	24	0	12	28	0	96	3.6	9
Shaunzinski Gortman ..29		369	35	97	.361	7	9	.778	16	45	61	21	42	0	13	25	6	91	3.1	14
Janell Burse 31		344	31	83	.373	21	36	.583	29	31	60	7	60	0	7	18	13	83	2.7	10
Val Whiting-Raymond ..6		52	4	13	.308	5	12	.417	3	6	9	5	10	0	2	4	2	13	2.2	6
Shanele Stires..............9		25	2	4	.500	1	2	.500	4	2	6	1	3	0	0	2	1	6	0.7	5
Minnesota 32		6475	727	1775	.410	383	578	.663	309	650	959	466	617	7	226	529	102	2003	62.6	85
Opponents 32		6475	747	1807	.413	469	613	.765	302	612	914	495	618	4	273	465	117	2104	65.8	87

3-pt. FG: Minnesota 166-500 (.332) Smith 62-188 (.330); Abrosimova 20-60 (.333); Williams 3-11 (.273); Moore(*) 26-68 (.382); Moore(†) 28-77 (.364); Burse 0-1 (.000) Lennox(‡) 5-23 (.217); Van Gorp 2-7 (.286); Schweitzer 14-33 (.424); Pride 1-10 (.100); Harrower 18-54 (.333); Stires 1-2 (.500) Gortman 14-43 (.326); Opponents 141-389 (.362)

NEW YORK LIBERTY

Player	G	Min	FGM	FGA	Pct	FTM	FTA	Pct	Off	Def	Tot	Ast	PF	Dq	Stl	TO	Blk	Pts	Avg	Hi
Tari Phillips 32		1009	183	373	.491	85	126	.675	69	154	223	41	113	2	58	93	14	451	14.1	23
Tamika Whitmore........32		977	148	310	.477	110	150	.733	43	98	141	23	102	1	27	49	43	406	12.7	28
Crystal Robinson 32		1068	126	302	.417	59	72	.819	22	70	92	81	101	0	48	52	12	378	11.8	24

Player	G	Min	FGM	FGA	Pct	FTM	FTA	Pct	Off	Def	Tot	Ast	PF	Dq	Stl	TO	Blk	Pts	Avg	Hi
Vickie Johnson 31		1028	139	305	.456	49	61	.803	42	67	109	86	60	0	27	45	4	359	11.6	21
Becky Hammon 32		659	87	197	.442	38	56	.679	18	50	68	54	49	0	25	55	0	256	8.0	22
Teresa Weatherspoon ..32		954	39	114	.342	28	54	.519	23	63	86	181	88	2	42	78	3	108	3.4	10
Sue Wicks 30		428	24	70	.343	18	27	.667	30	71	101	14	60	0	22	30	15	66	2.2	8
Korie Hlede 16		129	11	26	.423	4	9	.444	4	12	16	12	24	0	6	21	2	26	1.6	6
Camille Cooper 23		119	11	28	.393	5	8	.625	5	11	16	3	28	0	4	10	5	27	1.2	5
Bernadette Ngoyisa 7		12	3	5	.600	0	0	—	1	4	5	0	2	0	0	2	6	0.9	2
Linda Frohlich 16		67	1	10	.100	4	4	1.000	3	10	13	1	11	0	2	4	0	6	0.4	2
New York 32		6450	772	1740	.444	400	567	.705	260	610	870	496	638	5	261	458	100	2089	65.3	84
Opponents 32		6450	691	1733	.399	484	645	.750	312	649	961	410	597	2	228	478	88	2015	63.0	80

3-pt. FG: New York 145-400 (.363) Phillips 0-2 (.000); Whitmore 0-1 (.000); Robinson 67-181 (.370); Johnson 32-76 (.421); Hammon 44-114 (.386); Wicks 0-1 (.000) Weatherspoon 2-20 (.100); Hlede 0-1 (.000); Frohlich 0-4 (.000); Opponents 149-434 (.343)

ORLANDO MIRACLE

Player	G	Min	FGM	FGA	Pct	FTM	FTA	Pct	Off	Def	Tot	Ast	PF	Dq	Stl	TO	Blk	Pts	Avg	Hi
Shannon Johnson 31		1110	157	389	.404	164	214	.766	49	80	129	163	78	1	51	98	7	499	16.1	35
Nykesha Sales 32		1042	155	376	.412	84	106	.792	36	84	120	60	97	0	60	71	7	431	13.5	29
Wendy Palmer(*) 16		501	65	148	.439	27	39	.692	20	73	93	21	46	0	22	23	6	180	11.3	17
Wendy Palmer(†) 32		965	130	301	.432	62	92	.674	47	142	189	41	90	0	35	57	8	364	11.4	20
Katie Douglas 32		830	92	205	.449	58	67	.866	41	94	135	53	66	1	49	42	13	271	8.5	19
Taj McWilliams-Frank 13		383	41	82	.500	27	31	.871	21	42	63	13	40	1	19	22	14	110	8.5	17
Jessie Hicks 31		471	73	153	.477	44	63	.698	60	42	102	23	77	1	19	51	25	190	6.1	18
Elaine Powell(‡) 15		308	35	99	.354	16	26	.615	7	25	32	30	31	0	20	30	4	88	5.9	13
Adrienne Johnson 32		602	68	181	.376	12	17	.706	14	32	46	22	40	0	15	26	2	166	5.2	12
Clarisse Machanguana 29		428	61	114	.535	16	25	.640	26	38	64	17	61	0	12	33	4	138	4.8	14
Cintia dos Santos 26		260	26	53	.491	36	46	.783	15	20	35	10	48	1	4	20	13	88	3.4	18
Brooke Wyckoff 32		514	31	95	.326	5	7	.714	28	62	90	32	71	1	19	30	18	81	2.5	13
Carla McGhee 2		4	2	4	.500	1	1	1.000	1	0	1	0	0	0	0	0	0	5	2.5	3
Tiffany McCain...........16		51	2	10	.200	3	4	.750	1	2	3	2	9	0	3	3	0	7	0.4	3
Davalyn Cunningham ..6		21	0	5	.000	0	0	—	1	1	2	0	5	0	2	1	0	0	0.0	0
Orlando 32		6525	808	1914	.422	493	646	.763	320	595	915	446	660	6	295	456	113	2254	70.4	103
Opponents 32		6525	804	1862	.432	491	668	.735	362	684	1046	519	637	9	251	541	108	2255	70.5	99

3-pt. FG: Orlando 145-461 (.315); S. Johnson 21-77 (.273); Sales 37-115 (.322); Palmer(*) 23-60 (.383); Palmer(†) 42-120 (.350); Douglas 29-79 (.367) McWilliams-Frank 1-3 (.333); Powell(‡) 2-11 (.182); A. Johnson 18-61 (.295); dos Santos 0-1 (.000); Wyckoff 14-50 (.280) McCain 0-4 (.000); Opponents 156-422 (.370)

PHOENIX MERCURY

Player	G	Min	FGM	FGA	Pct	FTM	FTA	Pct	Off	Def	Tot	Ast	PF	Dq	Stl	TO	Blk	Pts	Avg	Hi
JJennifer Gillom 31		874	166	400	.415	105	131	.802	36	80	116	37	90	0	29	61	21	473	15.3	26
Gordana Grubin.........32		859	114	297	.384	60	79	.759	16	48	64	104	59	0	36	58	3	317	9.9	23
Lisa Harrison 32		899	120	242	.496	20	23	.870	43	83	126	40	62	0	31	45	3	262	8.2	22
Brandy Reed.................5		85	15	41	.366	8	11	.727	1	3	4	4	8	0	2	8	3	38	7.6	20
Adrain Williams 32		878	79	169	.467	42	60	.700	64	156	220	35	88	0	48	63	29	200	6.3	15
Adriana Moises Pinto ..32		619	63	164	.384	48	60	.800	15	45	60	79	53	0	30	72	3	193	6.0	20
Susanna Bonfiglio......22		306	43	89	.483	19	25	.760	16	21	37	23	35	0	12	18	0	105	4.8	12
Tracy Reid 24		421	48	117	.410	17	28	.607	33	44	77	14	29	0	22	36	2	113	4.7	16
Kayte Christensen.......30		413	48	95	.505	24	35	.686	39	41	80	15	73	1	24	32	13	120	4.0	11
Jaynetta Saunders........27		302	39	103	.379	21	32	.656	10	28	38	23	23	0	9	20	4	99	3.7	12
Slobodanka Tuvic.......26		320	30	77	.390	25	32	.781	11	52	63	11	53	0	9	31	9	86	3.3	11
Kristen Veal 23		361	24	79	.304	10	13	.769	6	21	27	41	41	0	14	42	2	71	3.1	9
Shea Mahoney 3		13	2	3	.667	1	1	1.000	2	0	2	1	4	0	0	1	0	5	1.7	5
Quacy Barnes...............2		13	0	7	.000	3	4	.750	0	1	1	0	1	0	1	0	2	3	1.5	3
Oksana Zakaluzhnaya(*)5		37	2	6	.333	2	4	.500	0	3	3	0	4	0	0	4	0	6	1.2	3
Oksana Zakaluzhnaya(†)8		47	3	9	.333	2	4	.500	0	3	3	0	7	0	0	4	1	8	1.0	3
Phoenix 32		6400	793	1889	.420	405	538	.753	292	626	918	427	623	1	267	501	94	2091	65.3	82
Opponents 32		6400	850	1870	.455	436	608	.717	309	692	1001	532	600	6	268	491	127	2291	71.6	91

3-pt. FG: Phoenix 100-328 (.305) Gillom 36-93 (.387); Grubin 29-92 (.315); Harrison 2-6 (.333); Reed 0-5 (.000); Moises Pinto 19-66 (.288); Bonfiglio 0-6 (.000) Reid 0-1 (.000); Christensen 0-1 (.000); Saunders 0-4 (.000); Tuvic 1-6 (.167); Veal 13-47 (.277); Mahoney 0-1 (.000) Opponents 155-388 (.399)

PORTLAND FIRE

Player	G	Min	FGM	FGA	Pct	FTM	FTA	Pct	Off	Def	Tot	Ast	PF	Dq	Stl	TO	Blk	Pts	Avg	Hi
DeMya Walker............31		848	139	287	.484	59	95	.621	55	99	154	51	97	1	26	90	33	339	10.9	21
Tamicha Jackson 32		692	122	291	.419	46	66	.697	20	39	59	95	59	0	55	64	1	314	9.8	21

Player	G	Min	FGM	FGA	Pct	FTM	FTA	Pct	Off	Def	Tot	Ast	PF	Dq	Stl	TO	Blk	Pts	Avg	Hi
LaQuanda Barksdale ..17		285	36	101	.356	23	26	.885	18	22	40	12	31	0	8	23	7	100	5.9	13
Sylvia Crawley 32		819	114	284	.401	44	63	.698	46	88	134	47	90	0	18	62	37	279	8.7	18
Alisa Burras 32		633	117	186	.629	44	52	.846	52	95	147	7	58	0	10	49	7	278	8.7	19
Ukari Figgs 31		866	83	233	.356	59	65	.908	13	67	80	104	50	0	25	44	2	264	8.5	22
Jackie Stiles 21		382	43	135	.319	24	30	.800	7	11	18	20	38	0	4	21	0	125	6.0	18
Kristin Folkl 32		602	62	126	.492	31	35	.886	41	107	148	32	56	0	18	32	17	155	4.8	13
Stacey Thomas 32		621	51	148	.345	31	61	.508	34	60	94	67	62	0	42	36	12	143	4.5	12
Carolyn Young 19		186	26	74	.351	21	24	.875	5	9	14	12	18	0	4	18	0	83	4.4	11
Tully Bevilaqua.......27		421	25	61	.410	19	29	.655	7	26	33	44	49	0	22	27	3	84	3.1	8
Amber Hall 20		104	11	24	.458	8	16	.500	8	18	26	1	12	0	7	12	1	30	1.5	6
Jenny Mowe.............5		16	0	1	.000	1	2	.500	1	0	1	0	3	0	0	1	0	1	0.2	1
Portland 32		6475	829	1951	.425	410	564	.727	307	641	948	492	623	0	239	493	120	2195	68.6	87
Opponents 32		6475	819	1885	.434	463	647	.716	334	678	1012	486	616	6	272	508	139	2227	69.6	89

3-pt. FG: Portland 127-391 (.325) Walker 2-12 (.167); Jackson 24-76 (.316); Crawley 7-17 (.412); Figgs 39-120 (.325); Stiles 15-44 (.341); Barksdale 5-22 (.227) Folkl 0-3 (.000); Thomas 10-39 (.256); Young 10-22 (.455); Bevilaqua 15-36 (.417); Opponents 126-348 (.362).

SACRAMENTO MONARCHS

Player	G	Min	FGM	FGA	Pct	FTM	FTA	Pct	Off	Def	Tot	Ast	PF	Dq	Stl	TO	Blk	Pts	Avg	Hi
Yolanda Griffith 17		577	93	179	.520	102	127	.803	66	82	148	19	70	0	16	45	13	288	16.9	28
Tangela Smith.............32		1063	184	435	.423	86	101	.851	56	132	188	40	126	4	27	59	46	469	14.7	27
Ruthie Bolton 32		737	125	316	.396	56	77	.727	31	63	94	37	74	0	45	35	2	349	10.9	21
Kedra Holland-Corn 32		902	102	299	.341	54	72	.750	28	62	90	63	74	1	41	81	5	296	9.3	28
Ticha Penicheiro 24		853	60	159	.377	75	103	.728	7	95	102	192	49	0	64	69	1	203	8.5	23
Lady Grooms 32		850	78	181	.431	71	83	.855	38	61	99	39	69	0	21	46	8	227	7.1	15
La'Keshia Frett 32		648	84	187	.449	14	17	.824	30	65	95	23	70	2	5	27	19	187	5.8	15
Edna Campbell.............1		12	2	5	.400	0	0	—	0	1	1	0	0	0	1	0	0	4	4.0	4
Hamchetou Maiga 23		197	13	53	.245	14	30	.467	18	19	37	9	37	0	15	23	3	40	1.7	6
Cass Bauer-Bilodeau...25		233	17	57	.298	9	15	.600	14	27	41	1	34	0	2	25	5	43	1.7	6
Kara Wolters 14		78	9	28	.321	6	10	.600	8	15	23	3	18	0	0	6	3	24	1.7	9
Andrea Nagy 24		409	12	44	.273	7	16	.438	3	26	29	73	51	1	10	31	4	34	1.4	9
Stacey Ford 5		12	1	2	.500	0	2	.000	2	0	2	1	1	0	0	1	0	2	0.4	2
Monique Ambers 2		4	0	0	—	0	0	—	0	0	0	0	2	0	0	0	0	0	0.0	0
Sacramento 32		6575	780	1945	.401	494	653	.757	301	648	949	500	675	8	247	456	109	2166	67.7	86
Opponents 32		6575	815	1944	.419	515	681	.756	352	723	1075	493	633	8	233	496	128	2294	71.7	87

3-pt. FG: Sacramento 112-395 (.284) Smith 15-42 (.357); Bolton 43-132 (.326); Holland-Corn 38-157 (.242); Penicheiro 8-32 (.250); Grooms 0-1 (.000); Frett 5-15 (.333) Campbell 0-2 (.000); Nagy 3-14 (.214); Opponents 149-453 (.329).

SEATTLE STORM

Player	G	Min	FGM	FGA	Pct	FTM	FTA	Pct	Off	Def	Tot	Ast	PF	Dq	Stl	TO	Blk	Pts	Avg	Hi
Lauren Jackson...........28		882	186	462	.403	68	90	.756	66	124	190	41	95	1	30	47	81	482	17.2	27
Sue Bird 32		1121	151	375	.403	102	112	.911	17	66	83	191	48	0	55	109	3	461	14.4	33
Kamila Vodichkova 32		817	114	245	.465	54	67	.806	61	115	176	47	96	1	36	55	18	295	9.2	20
Simone Edwards.........32		694	84	158	.532	54	73	.740	46	95	141	19	66	0	21	44	12	223	7.0	18
Semeka Randall(‡) 21		458	47	133	.353	36	51	.706	38	30	68	29	33	0	20	36	1	134	6.4	21
Jamie Redd 10		112	17	34	.500	9	12	.750	8	5	13	7	17	0	2	7	0	52	5.2	14
Felicia Ragland...........31		432	48	125	.384	23	28	.821	27	21	48	23	44	0	27	29	1	141	4.5	19
Amanda Lassiter(*) 24		554	47	130	.362	12	17	.706	23	40	63	55	58	1	27	49	19	126	5.3	14
Amanda Lassiter(†) 30		600	47	140	.336	13	19	.684	24	45	69	57	62	1	29	51	21	127	4.2	14
Adia Barnes 26		493	37	111	.333	15	29	.517	45	57	102	28	64	1	32	25	9	90	3.5	12
Kate Starbird(*) 9		186	20	44	.455	8	9	.889	3	16	19	12	19	0	6	11	4	53	5.9	13
Kate Starbird(†) 24		274	30	69	.435	12	16	.750	3	23	26	19	35	0	15	13	8	79	3.3	13
Michelle Marciniak 23		280	24	68	.353	22	29	.759	8	20	28	38	33	0	11	25	2	72	3.1	18
Sonja Henning(‡) 8		207	8	22	.364	2	4	.500	8	18	26	15	15	0	9	7	1	18	2.3	8
Takeisha Lewis 14		57	4	10	.400	10	18	.556	7	17	24	3	12	0	2	7	0	18	1.3	7
Kate Paye 19		114	7	19	.368	1	2	.500	2	5	7	5	18	1	3	8	0	21	1.1	11
Danielle McCulley 4		43	0	12	.000	2	2	1.000	3	4	7	1	5	0	1	2	0	2	0.5	2
Seattle 32		6450	794	1948	.408	418	543	.770	362	633	995	514	623	5	282	477	151	2188	68.4	90
Opponents 32		6450	783	1818	.431	435	587	.741	307	662	969	488	563	5	254	531	125	2103	65.7	82

3-pt. FG: Seattle 182-506 (.360) Jackson 42-120 (.350); Bird 57-142 (.401); Vodichkova 13-38 (.342); Edwards 1-1 (1.000); Randall(‡) 4-19 (.211); Redd 9-18 (.500) Ragland 22-55 (.400); Lassiter(*) 20-66 (.303); Lassiter(†) 20-71 (.282); Barnes 1-4 (.250); Starbird(*) 5-11 (.455) Starbird(†) 7-19 (.368); Marciniak 2-8 (.250); Henning(‡) 0-4 (.000); Lewis 0-1 (.000); Paye 6-16 (.375); McCulley 0-3 (.000) Opponents 102-342 (.298).

UTAH STARZZ

Player	G	Min	FGM	FGA	Pct	FTM	FTA	Pct	REBOUNDS			Ast	PF	Dq	Stl	TO	Blk	SCORING		
									Off	Def	Tot							Pts	Avg	Hi
Adrienne Goodson	32	1101	189	419	.451	117	157	.745	91	90	181	67	92	0	45	102	6	503	15.7	30
Marie Ferdinand	32	1065	176	371	.474	132	171	.772	19	88	107	91	86	0	51	89	7	489	15.3	27
Margo Dydek	30	876	139	319	.436	114	135	.844	52	210	262	71	99	2	25	96	107	351	13.1	27
Natalie Williams	31	1008	124	285	.435	98	132	.742	105	150	255	38	122	4	38	72	16	351	11.3	22
Jennifer Azzi	32	1151	91	198	.460	83	104	.798	15	54	69	158	102	0	27	67	14	306	9.6	19
Semeka Randall(*)	8	135	18	40	.450	22	29	.759	4	17	21	8	16	0	4	10	1	58	7.3	16
Semeka Randall(†)	29	593	65	173	.376	58	80	.725	42	47	89	37	49	0	24	46	2	192	6.6	21
LaTonya Johnson	28	269	25	76	.329	15	20	.750	8	11	19	10	36	1	7	15	2	75	2.7	10
Amy Herrig	28	269	23	53	.434	22	30	.733	15	42	57	4	35	0	9	21	14	68	2.4	11
LaNeishea Caufield	8	65	6	15	.400	2	2	1.000	3	2	5	1	13	0	7	8	0	19	2.4	8
Andrea Gardner-Combs	30	198	18	49	.367	21	38	.553	29	32	61	5	35	0	3	13	3	57	1.9	14
Kate Starbird(‡)	15	88	10	25	.400	4	7	.571	0	7	7	7	16	0	9	2	4	26	1.7	5
Danielle Crockrom	18	84	10	28	.357	9	12	.750	6	7	13	2	8	0	0	3	2	29	1.6	6
Elisa Aguilar	28	141	14	33	.424	4	7	.571	0	11	11	16	5	0	3	11	2	43	1.5	7
Utah	32	6450	843	1911	.441	643	844	.762	347	721	1068	478	665	7	228	522	178	2418	75.6	94
Opponents	32	6450	851	2067	.412	516	688	.750	361	645	1006	489	724	10	260	444	149	2344	73.3	102

3-pt. FG: Utah 89-247 (.360) Goodson 8-28 (.286); Ferdinand 5-34 (.147); Dydek 2-8 (.250); Williams 5-12 (.417); Azzi 41-92 (.446); Randall(*) 0-2 (.000) Randall(†) 4-21 (.190); Johnson 10-32 (.313); Caufield 5-9 (.556); Starbird(‡) 2-8 (.250); Crockrom 0-1 (.000) Aguilar 11-21 (.524); Opponents 126-377 (.334).

WASHINGTON MYSTICS

Player	G	Min	FGM	FGA	Pct	FTM	FTA	Pct	REBOUNDS			Ast	PF	Dq	Stl	TO	Blk	SCORING		
									Off	Def	Tot							Pts	Avg	Hi
Chamique Holdsclaw	20	634	149	330	.452	88	106	.830	54	178	232	45	50	0	20	45	6	397	19.9	32
Stacey Dales-Schuman	31	805	93	230	.404	74	100	.740	26	55	81	84	79	1	16	68	4	303	9.8	26
Coco Miller	32	904	114	263	.433	46	56	.821	44	72	116	82	84	0	33	59	2	298	9.3	22
Vicky Bullett	32	953	109	236	.462	34	41	.829	46	140	186	53	84	0	54	56	37	271	8.5	23
Asjha Jones	32	612	93	233	.399	20	33	.606	39	50	89	28	88	2	13	39	17	208	6.5	16
Murriel Page	32	750	88	195	.451	30	53	.566	55	100	155	37	79	0	14	45	15	208	6.5	20
Helen Luz	32	474	65	148	.439	15	19	.789	9	23	32	48	40	0	18	43	5	187	5.8	15
Annie Burgess	26	632	39	101	.386	35	45	.778	16	46	62	93	39	0	34	41	4	125	4.8	15
Tonya Washington	25	291	28	86	.326	11	13	.846	27	11	38	15	6	0	3	16	2	73	2.9	9
Audrey Sauret	15	165	10	24	.417	3	5	.600	3	8	11	18	12	0	8	15	2	24	1.6	6
Kiesha Brown	18	108	12	35	.343	3	3	1.000	4	8	12	6	10	0	5	5	0	28	1.6	8
Maren Walseth	18	104	6	25	.240	0	2	.000	7	14	21	7	8	0	2	9	0	13	0.7	4
Katryna Gaither(*)	1	1	0	0	—	0	0	—	0	0	0	0	1	0	0	0	0	0	0.0	0
Katryna Gaither(†)	2	6	0	1	.000	0	0	—	0	1	1	1	3	0	0	1	0	0	0.0	0
Tausha Mills	4	17	0	4	.000	0	2	.000	0	3	3	0	3	0	1	2	0	0	0.0	0
Washington	32	6450	806	1910	.422	359	478	.751	330	708	1038	516	583	3	221	455	94	2135	66.7	97
Opponents	32	6450	786	1903	.413	397	538	.738	309	680	989	442	570	3	237	441	101	2116	66.1	89

3-pt. FG: Washington 164-443 (.370) Holdsclaw 11-28 (.393); Dales-Schuman 43-109 (.394); Miller 24-64 (.375); Bullett 19-48 (.396); Jones 2-10 (.200); Page 2-4 (.500) Luz 42-106 (.396); Burgess 12-33 (.364); Washington 6-18 (.333); Sauret 1-5 (.200); Brown 1-11 (.091); Walseth 1-7 (.143) Opponents 147-446 (.330).

(*) Statistics with this team only

(†) Totals with all teams

(‡) Continued season with another team

2002 PLAYOFFS RESULTS

FIRST ROUND

New York defeats Indiana, 2-1

August 16	Indiana 73, New York 55
August 18	New York 84, Indiana 65
August 20	New York 75, Indiana 60

Washington defeats Charlotte, 2-0

| August 15 | Washington 74, Charlotte 62 |
| August 17 | Washington 62, Charlotte 59 |

Los Angeles defeats Seattle, 2-0

| August 15 | Los Angeles 78, Seattle 61 |
| August 17 | Los Angeles 69, Seattle 59 |

Utah defeats Houston, 2-1

August 16	Utah 66, Houston 59
August 18	Houston 83, Utah 77 (2ot)
August 20	Utah 75, Houston 72

CONFERENCE FINALS

New York defeats Washington, 2-1

August 22	Washington 79, New York 74
August 24	New York 96, Washington 79
August 25	New York 64, Washington 57

Los Angeles defeats Utah, 2-0

| August 22 | Los Angeles 75, Utah 67 |
| August 24 | Los Angeles 103, Utah 77 |

FINALS

Los Angeles defeats New York, 2-0

| August 29 | Los Angeles 71, New York 63 |
| August 31 | Los Angeles 69, New York 66 |

OFFENSIVE

TEAM	G	FG	FGA	PCT	FG3	FG3A	PCT	FT	FTA	PCT	OFF	DEF	REB	AST	PF	DQ	STL	TO	BLK	PTS	AVG
L.A. 6		170	372	.457	34	88	.386	91	119	.765	53	148	201	119	128	2	62	78	29	465	77.5
Utah 5		133	307	.433	16	49	.327	80	111	.721	46	128	174	83	98	1	28	81	31	362	72.4
N.Y..........8		214	443	.483	42	108	.389	107	143	.748	60	154	214	132	130	0	45	87	14	577	72.1
Hou. 3		78	213	.366	15	48	.313	43	53	.811	38	65	103	41	57	0	27	30	14	214	71.3
Wash. 5		133	294	.452	26	72	.361	59	77	.766	44	89	133	94	85	0	32	47	14	351	70.2
Ind. 3		75	170	.441	19	54	.352	29	40	.725	34	58	92	46	52	1	11	46	4	198	66.0
Cha. 2		49	122	.402	12	43	.279	11	23	.478	20	43	63	28	34	0	14	27	5	121	60.5
Sea...........2		39	112	.348	10	37	.270	32	37	.865	15	34	49	28	35	0	20	36	8	120	60.0

DEFENSIVE

Team	FG	FGA	PCT	FG3	FG3A	PCT	FT	FTA	PCT	OFF	DEF	REB	AST	PF	DQ	STL	TO	BLK	PTS	AVG	DIFF
L.A......137	355	.386	29	97	.299	90	116	.776	51	118	169	85	115	0	36	97	25	393	65.5	+12.0
Cha. 51	115	.443	10	30	.333	24	31	.774	17	42	59	38	26	0	19	22	4	136	68.0	-7.5
N.Y. 207	460	.450	44	122	.361	95	129	.736	80	156	236	138	155	2	38	98	24	553	69.1	+3.0
Wash. ...133	279	.477	30	82	.366	59	84	.702	41	104	145	76	78	0	29	59	11	355	71.0	-0.8
Ind.........86	170	.506	12	34	.353	30	42	.714	22	55	77	59	49	0	21	33	3	214	71.3	-5.3
Hou. 79	180	.439	9	24	.375	51	72	.708	27	82	109	51	55	1	21	42	19	218	72.7	-1.3
Sea. 58	119	.487	8	23	.348	23	25	.920	11	53	64	38	41	1	23	33	5	147	73.5	-13.5
Utah 140	355	.394	32	87	.368	80	104	.769	61	109	170	86	100	0	52	48	28	392	78.4	-6.0
Averages111	254	.438	22	62	.349	57	75	.750	39	90	129	71	77	1	30	54	15	301	70.8	—
Totals ..891	2033	—	174	499	—	452	603	—	310	719	1029	571	619	4	239	432	119	2408	—	—

TEAM COMPARISONS

TEAM	Points Per Game OWN	OPP	Field Goal Percentage OWN	OPP	Turnovers Per Game OWN	OPP	Rebound Percentages OFF	DEF	TOT	Below 70 Pts. OWN	OPP	Overtime Games W	L	3 PTS or Less W	L	10 PTS or More W	L
Charlotte 60.5		68.0	.402	.443	13.5	11.0	.323	.717	.520	2	1	0	0	1	0	0	1
Houston..............71.3		72.7	.366	.439	10.0	14.0	.317	.707	.512	1	1	1	0	0	1	0	0
Indiana 66.0		71.3	.441	.506	15.3	11.0	.382*	.725	.554*	2	1	0	0	0	0	1	2
Los Angeles 77.5*		65.5*	.457	.386*	13.0	16.2	.310	.744	.527	2	5	0	1	0	1	3	0
New York 72.1		69.1	.483*	.450	10.9	12.3	.278	.658	.464	4	4	0	0	1	3	1
Seattle 60.0		73.5	.348	.487	18.0	16.5*	.221	.756*	.488	2	1	0	0	0	0	0	2
Utah 72.4		78.4	.433	.394	16.2	9.6	.297	.677	.487	2	1	0	1	1	0	0	1
Washington 70.2		71.0	.452	.477	9.4*	11.8	.297	.685	.491	2	3	0	0	1	0	1	1
COMPOSITE; 17 games																	
...........................70.8			.438		12.7		.301	.699		17	1		3		8		

* - League Leader

REBOUND PERCENTAGES — OFF. - Percentage of a given team's missed shots which that team rebounds. DEF. - Percentage of opponents' missed shots which a given team rebounds. TOT. - Average of offensive and defensive rebound percentages.

INDIVIDUAL PLAYOFFS STATISTICS, TEAM BY TEAM

CHARLOTTE STING

Player	G	Min	FGM	FGA	Pct	FTM	FTA	Pct	REBOUNDS Off	Def	Tot	Ast	PF	Dq	Stl	TO	Blk	SCORING Pts	Avg	Hi
Andrea Stinson 2		65	12	25	.480	2	2	1.000	7	4	11	9	4	0	7	4	0	30	15.0	16
Erin Buescher 2		31	7	8	.875	2	4	.500	2	5	7	1	6	0	0	3	1	17	8.5	11
Dawn Staley 2		78	6	21	.286	3	6	.500	2	3	5	10	2	0	3	4	0	17	8.5	9
Allison Feaster 2		65	6	20	.300	0	0	—	3	12	15	7	1	0	2	4	0	15	7.5	15
Tammy Sutton-Brown 2		56	7	14	.500	1	6	.167	4	8	12	0	6	0	1	7	1	15	7.5	9
Charlotte Smith-Tayl......2		53	5	17	.294	2	2	1.000	0	7	7	0	7	0	1	2	2	12	6.0	10
Summer Erb 2		17	3	5	.600	1	1	1.000	0	1	1	0	3	0	0	0	1	7	3.5	5
Kelly Miller 2		13	2	4	.500	0	0	—	0	2	2	0	3	0	0	1	0	5	2.5	3
Tonya Edwards 2		19	1	5	.200	0	2	.000	0	1	1	1	2	0	0	1	0	3	1.5	3
Shalonda Enis...............1		3	0	3	.000	0	0	—	2	0	2	0	0	0	0	0	0	0	0.0	0
Charlotte	2	400	49	122	.402	11	23	.478	20	43	63	28	34	0	14	27	5	121	60.5	62
Opponents	2	400	51	115	.443	24	31	.774	17	42	59	38	26	0	19	22	4	136	68.0	74

3-pt. FG: Charlotte 12-43 (.279) Stinson 4-7 (.571); Buescher 1-1 (1.000); Staley 2-10 (.200); Feaster 3-13 (.231); Smith-Taylor 0-7 (.000); Miller 1-1 (1.000) Edwards 1-3 (.333); Enis 0-1 (.000); Opponents 10-30 (.333).

HOUSTON COMETS

Player	G	Min	FGM	FGA	Pct	FTM	FTA	Pct	Off	Def	Tot	Ast	PF	Dq	Stl	TO	Blk	Pts	Avg	Hi
Sheryl Swoopes 3	127	25	63	.397	20	25	.800	10	12	22	17	7	0	12	8	2	73	24.3	28
Tina Thompson 3	128	16	44	.364	7	10	.700	9	15	24	4	12	0	6	2	3	43	14.3	18
Janeth Arcain 3	119	15	35	.429	7	8	.875	2	9	11	4	11	0	5	5	1	39	13.0	17
Rita Williams 3	69	8	25	.320	0	0	—	3	3	6	7	5	0	3	1	0	20	6.7	9
Michelle Snow 3	79	6	18	.333	7	8	.875	6	15	21	4	9	0	0	5	2	19	6.3	12
Kelley Gibson................2	22	4	8	.500	0	0	—	3	1	4	0	3	0	0	1	0	10	5.0	7
Tiffani Johnson 3	51	4	9	.444	0	0	—	2	7	9	1	8	0	0	4	6	8	2.7	4
Grace Daley..................1	7	0	2	.000	2	2	1.000	2	0	2	0	0	0	0	1	0	2	2.0	2
Sonja Henning 3	48	0	9	.000	0	0	—	1	3	4	4	2	0	1	2	0	0	0.0	0
Houston 3	650	78	213	.366	43	53	.811	38	65	103	41	57	0	27	30	14	214	71.3	83
Opponents 3	650	79	180	.439	51	72	.708	27	82	109	51	55	1	21	42	19	218	72.7	77

3-pt. FG: Houston 15-48 (.313) Swoopes 3-9 (.333); Thompson 4-12 (.333); Arcain 2-7 (.286); Williams 4-14 (.286); Snow 0-1 (.000); Gibson 2-3 (.667) Henning 0-2 (.000); Opponents 9-24 (.375)

INDIANA FEVER

Player	G	Min	FGM	FGA	Pct	FTM	FTA	Pct	Off	Def	Tot	Ast	PF	Dq	Stl	TO	Blk	Pts	Avg	Hi
Tamika Catchings 3	103	22	45	.489	9	11	.818	12	20	32	7	7	0	4	11	1	61	20.3	29
Kelly Schumacher 3	52	13	20	.650	4	8	.500	6	3	9	3	6	0	0	2	2	32	10.7	17
Coquese Washington 3	110	9	27	.333	1	1	1.000	1	5	6	14	10	0	3	6	0	25	8.3	13
Nikki McCray................3	99	10	27	.370	3	5	.600	1	3	4	11	4	0	1	5	0	24	8.0	14
Olympia Scott-Richar....3	99	8	16	.500	5	5	1.000	7	17	24	5	11	0	1	14	1	21	7.0	10
Nadine Malcolm 3	69	7	13	.538	2	3	.667	1	5	6	0	9	1	0	2	0	17	5.7	8
Bridget Pettis 3	43	5	15	.333	5	7	.714	6	3	9	2	0	0	0	4	0	16	5.3	6
Alicia Thompson 1	2	1	1	1.000	0	0	—	0	0	0	0	0	0	0	0	0	2	2.0	2
Niele Ivey.....................3	9	0	1	.000	0	0	—	0	1	1	3	2	0	1	0	0	0	0.0	0
Monica Maxwell 2	8	0	3	.000	0	0	—	0	0	0	1	0	0	0	0	0	0	0.0	0
Jackie Moore 2	6	0	2	.000	0	0	—	0	1	1	0	3	0	1	0	0	0	0.0	0
Indiana 3	600	75	170	.441	29	40	.725	34	58	92	46	52	1	11	46	4	198	66.0	73
Opponents 3	600	86	170	.506	30	42	.714	22	55	77	59	49	0	21	33	3	214	71.3	84

3-pt. FG: Indiana 19-54 (.352) Catchings 8-21 (.381); Schumacher 2-2 (1.000); Washington 6-16 (.375); McCray 1-6 (.167); Malcolm 1-4 (.250); Pettis 1-3 (.333) Ivey 0-1 (.000); Maxwell 0-1 (.000); Opponents 12-34 (.353)

LOS ANGELES SPARKS

Player	G	Min	FGM	FGA	Pct	FTM	FTA	Pct	Off	Def	Tot	Ast	PF	Dq	Stl	TO	Blk	Pts	Avg	Hi
Lisa Leslie.....................6	232	46	86	.535	19	26	.731	10	37	47	11	22	0	11	8	17	116	19.3	25
Mwadi Mabika 6	212	31	82	.378	18	26	.692	11	30	41	25	19	0	8	10	1	88	14.7	23
DeLisha Milton 6	204	27	60	.450	15	16	.938	9	32	41	8	22	0	10	11	9	78	13.0	19
Tamecka Dixon 5	147	25	44	.568	9	10	.900	2	18	20	17	15	1	12	13	0	61	12.2	15
Nikki Teasley 6	184	14	42	.333	16	19	.842	3	10	13	47	22	1	9	22	1	49	8.2	11
Latasha Byears 6	128	19	30	.633	4	11	.364	15	14	29	5	19	0	9	10	1	42	7.0	10
Erika Desouza 1	3	0	1	.000	3	4	.750	1	0	1	0	0	0	0	0	0	3	3.0	3
Sophia Witherspoon.....6	39	5	14	.357	4	4	1.000	1	4	5	2	3	0	1	1	0	18	3.0	6
Nicky McCrimmon.......5	22	3	7	.429	1	1	1.000	0	1	1	2	2	0	2	1	0	8	1.6	3
Marlies Askamp 4	24	0	5	.000	2	2	1.000	1	2	3	0	4	0	0	0	0	2	0.5	2
Vedrana Grgin-Fonsec ..1	5	0	1	.000	0	0	—	0	0	0	2	0	0	0	0	0	0	0.0	0
Los Angeles 6	1200	170	372	.457	91	119	.765	53	148	201	119	128	2	62	78	29	465	77.5	103
Opponents 6	1200	137	355	.386	90	116	.776	51	118	169	85	115	0	36	97	25	393	65.5	77

3-pt. FG: Los Angeles 34-88 (.386) Leslie 5-8 (.625); Mabika 8-25 (.320); Milton 9-16 (.563); Dixon 2-4 (.500); Teasley 5-22 (.227); Witherspoon 4-11 (.364) McCrimmon 1-2 (.500); Opponents 29-97 (.299)

NEW YORK LIBERTY

Player	G	Min	FGM	FGA	Pct	FTM	FTA	Pct	Off	Def	Tot	Ast	PF	Dq	Stl	TO	Blk	Pts	Avg	Hi
Tamika Whitmore..........8	271	51	93	.548	26	37	.703	8	28	36	10	20	0	3	9	4	129	16.1	24
Tari Phillips 8	249	45	91	.495	25	35	.714	16	31	47	10	26	0	9	19	4	115	14.4	23
Vickie Johnson 8	244	36	75	.480	12	16	.750	8	22	30	24	10	0	7	11	0	98	12.3	19
Becky Hammon 8	183	29	54	.537	7	8	.875	2	15	17	16	12	0	5	11	0	79	9.9	18
Crystal Robinson 8	259	23	65	.354	9	9	1.000	8	16	24	14	17	0	8	5	2	67	8.4	20
Teresa Weatherspoon 8	241	19	40	.475	15	18	.833	8	27	35	53	18	0	8	14	0	53	6.6	11
Bernadette Ngoyisa 3	10	3	5	.600	2	5	.400	1	2	3	0	2	0	0	1	0	8	2.7	5

Player	G	Min	FGM	FGA	Pct	FTM	FTA	Pct	REBOUNDS Off	Def	Tot	Ast	PF	Dq	Stl	TO	Blk	SCORING Pts	Avg	Hi
Sue Wicks	8	96	7	14	.500	6	7	.857	6	6	12	2	19	0	1	6	4	21	2.6	5
Korie Hlede	2	12	0	1	.000	3	4	.750	2	1	3	1	1	0	1	2	0	3	1.5	3
Camille Cooper	3	15	1	2	.500	1	2	.500	1	1	2	0	3	0	2	2	0	3	1.0	2
Linda Frohlich	3	20	0	3	.000	1	2	.500	0	5	5	2	2	0	1	3	0	1	0.3	1
New York	8	1600	214	443	.483	107	143	.748	60	154	214	132	130	0	45	87	14	577	72.1	96
Opponents	8	1600	207	460	.450	95	129	.736	80	156	236	138	155	2	38	98	24	553	69.1	79

3-pt. FG: New York 42-108 (.389) Whitmore 1-3 (.333); Phillips 0-3 (.000); Johnson 14-27 (.519); Hammon 14-33 (.424); Robinson 12-39 (.308); Wicks 1-1 (1.000) Weatherspoon 0-2 (.000); Opponents 44-122 (.361).

SEATTLE STORM

Player	G	Min	FGM	FGA	Pct	FTM	FTA	Pct	REBOUNDS Off	Def	Tot	Ast	PF	Dq	Stl	TO	Blk	SCORING Pts	Avg	Hi
Sue Bird	2	73	9	22	.409	7	7	1.000	0	0	0	12	6	0	5	5	0	28	14.0	17
Kamila Vodichkova	2	61	7	16	.438	10	11	.909	2	8	10	3	3	0	2	2	0	25	12.5	17
Lauren Jackson	2	68	9	26	.346	5	7	.714	5	5	10	3	9	0	3	4	6	23	11.5	19
Adia Barnes	2	50	4	9	.444	0	0	—	3	5	8	3	4	0	3	7	0	10	5.0	5
Amanda Lassiter	2	46	4	15	.267	0	0	—	0	7	7	4	4	0	3	5	1	10	5.0	6
Michelle Marciniak	2	29	1	5	.200	6	6	1.000	0	2	2	1	3	0	3	4	0	8	4.0	6
Felicia Ragland	2	19	3	9	.333	0	0	—	2	4	6	1	0	0	0	2	0	7	3.5	7
Kate Starbird	2	23	1	2	.500	2	2	1.000	1	2	3	1	2	0	1	4	1	5	2.5	3
Simone Edwards	2	31	1	8	.125	2	4	.500	2	1	3	0	4	0	0	2	0	4	2.0	3
Seattle	2	400	39	112	.348	32	37	.865	15	34	49	28	35	0	20	36	8	120	60.0	61
Opponents	2	400	58	119	.487	23	25	.920	11	53	64	38	41	1	23	33	5	147	73.5	78

3-pt. FG: Seattle 10-37 (.270) Bird 3-11 (.273); Vodichkova 1-2 (.500); Jackson 0-6 (.000); Barnes 2-4 (.500); Lassiter 2-9 (.222); Marciniak 0-1 (.000) Ragland 1-3 (.333); Starbird 1-1 (1.000); Opponents 8-23 (.348).

UTAH STARZZ

Player	G	Min	FGM	FGA	Pct	FTM	FTA	Pct	REBOUNDS Off	Def	Tot	Ast	PF	Dq	Stl	TO	Blk	SCORING Pts	Avg	Hi
Marie Ferdinand	5	186	25	56	.446	23	34	.676	4	18	22	13	16	0	10	20	0	74	14.8	22
Adrienne Goodson	5	190	29	74	.392	12	17	.706	9	18	27	8	11	0	7	21	0	72	14.4	20
Natalie Williams	5	186	25	47	.532	19	28	.679	21	25	46	7	16	1	5	8	7	70	14.0	25
Margo Dydek	5	171	22	55	.400	13	15	.867	3	41	44	12	17	0	1	16	17	60	12.0	16
Jennifer Azzi	5	186	13	33	.394	7	8	.875	2	11	13	34	20	0	4	8	5	40	8.0	16
Semeka Randall	5	62	8	22	.364	4	5	.800	3	9	12	5	9	0	1	3	0	20	4.0	8
LaTonya Johnson	5	40	7	14	.500	1	2	.500	2	2	4	2	2	0	0	1	0	17	3.4	9
Danielle Crockrom	1	2	1	2	.500	0	0	—	0	0	0	0	0	0	0	0	0	2	2.0	2
Andrea Gardner-Combs	3	14	2	3	.667	1	2	.500	1	3	4	0	5	0	0	1	1	5	1.7	3
Amy Herrig	2	9	1	1	1.000	0	0	—	1	1	2	0	1	0	0	1	0	2	1.0	2
Elisa Aguilar	2	4	0	0	—	0	0	—	0	0	0	2	1	0	0	0	0	0	0.0	0
Utah	5	1050	133	307	.433	80	111	.721	46	128	174	83	98	1	28	81	31	362	72.4	77
Opponents	5	1050	140	355	.394	80	104	.769	61	109	170	86	100	0	52	48	28	392	78.4	103

3-pt. FG: Utah 16-49 (.327) Ferdinand 1-5 (.200); Goodson 2-7 (.286); Williams 1-4 (.250); Dydek 3-5 (.600); Azzi 7-19 (.368); Johnson 2-9 (.222) Opponents 32-87 (.368).

WASHINGTON MYSTICS

Player	G	Min	FGM	FGA	Pct	FTM	FTA	Pct	REBOUNDS Off	Def	Tot	Ast	PF	Dq	Stl	TO	Blk	SCORING Pts	Avg	Hi
Chamique Holdsclaw	5	173	35	78	.449	22	30	.733	10	33	43	16	14	0	10	10	3	94	18.8	26
Coco Miller	5	163	21	50	.420	6	10	.600	7	8	15	12	13	0	2	7	0	54	10.8	21
Murriel Page	5	113	17	27	.630	14	15	.933	6	16	22	4	12	0	1	3	4	48	9.6	17
Stacey Dales-Schuman	5	98	13	30	.433	4	4	1.000	5	3	8	16	8	0	2	5	0	38	7.6	12
Annie Burgess	5	160	11	29	.379	6	9	.667	7	8	15	27	4	0	2	10	0	30	6.0	9
Vicky Bullett	5	110	11	27	.407	2	2	1.000	5	10	15	4	11	0	8	6	5	25	5.0	12
Tonya Washington	4	52	7	14	.500	4	5	.800	1	2	3	2	4	0	3	1	0	20	5.0	11
Helen Luz	4	46	7	12	.583	0	0	—	0	3	3	8	2	0	2	3	0	18	4.5	16
Asjha Jones	5	63	8	19	.421	1	2	.500	3	5	8	3	13	0	0	1	1	18	3.6	6
Kiesha Brown	2	15	3	6	.500	0	0	—	0	1	1	1	3	0	2	0	0	6	3.0	4
Maren Walseth	1	7	0	2	.000	0	0	—	0	0	0	1	1	0	0	1	1	0	0.0	0
Washington	5	1000	133	294	.452	59	77	.766	44	89	133	94	85	0	32	47	14	351	70.2	79
Opponents	5	1000	133	279	.477	59	84	.702	41	104	145	76	78	0	29	59	11	355	71.0	96

3-pt. FG: Washington 26-72 (.361) Holdsclaw 2-11 (.182); Miller 6-11 (.545); Dales-Schuman 8-18 (.444); Burgess 2-8 (.250); Bullett 1-7 (.143); Luz 4-8 (.500) Washington 2-5 (.400); Jones 1-2 (.500); Brown 0-2 (.000); Opponents 30-82 (.366).

(*) Statistics with this team only

LOS ANGELES SPARKS

Player	G	Min	FGM	FGA	Pct	FTM	FTA	Pct	Off	Def	Tot	Ast	PF	Dq	Stl	TO	Blk	Pts	Avg	Hi
									REBOUNDS									SCORING		
Lisa Leslie......................2		80	12	24	.500	7	10	.700	2	14	16	3	8	0	1	3	4	32	16.0	17
Mwadi Mabika...............2		76	9	27	.333	10	13	.769	4	9	13	7	5	0	2	4	0	32	16.0	20
DeLisha Milton..............2		73	10	19	.526	4	5	.800	2	9	11	2	9	0	3	2	5	25	12.5	17
Nikki Teasley 2		76	6	18	.333	6	8	.750	1	4	5	22	6	0	3	11	0	19	9.5	11
Latasha Byears 2		65	7	14	.500	2	5	.400	10	12	22	1	8	0	3	2	1	16	8.0	10
Tamecka Dixon...............1		14	3	3	1.000	0	0	—	0	2	2	1	6	1	2	4	0	6	6.0	6
Sophia Witherspoon......2		14	2	4	.500	2	2	1.000	0	1	1	0	1	0	0	0	0	8	4.0	5
Nicky McCrimmon.......1		2	1	2	.500	0	0	—	0	0	0	0	1	0	0	0	0	2	2.0	2
Los Angeles 2		400	50	111	.450	31	43	.721	19	51	70	36	44	1	14	27	10	140	70.0	71
Opponents 2		400	44	116	.379	29	40	.725	17	38	55	25	37	0	9	22	5	129	64.5	66

3-pt. FG: Los Angeles 9-26 (.346) Leslie 1-2 (.500); Mabika 4-10 (.400); Milton 1-3 (.333); Teasley 1-8 (.125); Witherspoon 2-3 (.667); Opponents 12-35 (.343)

NEW YORK LIBERTY

Player	G	Min	FGM	FGA	Pct	FTM	FTA	Pct	Off	Def	Tot	Ast	PF	Dq	Stl	TO	Blk	Pts	Avg	Hi
									REBOUNDS									SCORING		
Becky Hammon 2		49	10	18	.556	2	2	1.000	1	4	5	4	5	0	1	2	0	27	13.5	18
Vickie Johnson 2		65	9	19	.474	3	5	.600	2	6	8	5	5	0	1	3	0	24	12.0	17
Tari Phillips 2		65	7	22	.318	10	14	.714	5	7	12	3	7	0	2	6	3	24	12.0	12
Tamika Whitmore.........2		73	7	22	.318	8	11	.727	0	10	10	2	6	0	0	5	0	22	11.0	17
Crystal Robinson 2		62	5	18	.278	0	0	—	4	1	5	2	4	0	1	3	2	13	6.5	13
Teresa Weatherspoon 2		62	3	10	.300	6	8	.750	2	8	10	8	6	0	3	1	0	12	6.0	9
Sue Wicks 2		24	3	7	.429	0	0	—	3	2	5	1	4	0	1	1	0	7	3.5	5
New York 2		400	44	116	.379	29	40	.725	17	38	55	25	37	0	9	22	5	129	64.5	66
Opponents 2		400	50	111	.450	31	43	.721	19	51	70	36	44	1	14	27	10	140	70.0	71

3-pt. FG: New York 12-35 (.343) Hammon 5-12 (.417); Johnson 3-7 (.429); Phillips 0-2 (.000); Whitmore 0-1 (.000); Robinson 3-10 (.300); Weatherspoon 0-2 (.000) Wicks 1-1 (1.000); Opponents 9-26 (.346)

(*) Statistics with this team only

2002 FINALS BOX SCORES

GAME 1

At Madison Square Garden, August 29, 2002

OFFICIALS: Patty Broderick, Bob Trammell, Matthew Boland. TIME OF GAME: 2:02. ATTENDANCE: 17,666

SCORE BY PERIODS	1	2	FINAL
Los Angeles 35		36	71
New York 35		28	63

VISITORS: Los Angeles   5-0   Head Coach: Michael Cooper

No Player	MIN	FG	FGA	3P	3PA	FT	FTA	OR	DR	TOT	A	PF	ST	TO	TEC	PTS
8 DeLisha Milton 40		7	11	0	1	3	3	2	4	6	0	4	2	0	0	17
4 Mwadi Mabika 40		6	18	3	7	5	7	4	4	8	5	3	1	0	0	20
9 Lisa Leslie 40		6	12	1	1	2	2	1	8	9	2	4	1	2	0	15
42 Nikki Teasley.....................38		2	7	0	3	4	6	1	1	2	11	3	2	7	0	8
00 Latasha Byears 34		2	8	0	0	2	3	5	6	11	0	3	3	1	0	6
13 Sophia Witherspoon 6		1	3	1	2	0	0	0	1	1	0	1	0	0	0	3
10 Nicky McCrimmon 2		1	2	0	0	0	0	0	0	0	0	1	0	0	0	2
41 Marlies Askamp...................						Did not play.										
14 Erika Desouza						Did not play.										
21 Tamecka Dixon						Did not play.										
17 Grgin-Fonseca....................						Did not play.										
TOTALS 200		25	61	5	14	16	21	13	24	37	18	19	9	10	0	71

PERCENTAGES: 41.0 35.7 76.2   TM REB: 6   TOT TO: 11 (15 PTS)

HOME: New York   4-3   Head Coach: Richie Adubato

No Player	MIN	FG	FGA	3P	3PA	FT	FTA	OR	DR	TOT	A	PF	ST	TO	TEC	PTS
44 Tamika Whitmore.............38		2	9	0	0	1	2	0	6	6	2	2	0	2	0	5
3 Crystal Robinson 36		5	12	3	7	0	0	2	0	2	1	3	0	3	0	13
24 Tari Phillips 35		4	13	0	2	4	6	1	3	4	3	3	0	3	0	12
55 Vickie Johnson 30		3	7	1	3	0	0	1	3	4	3	2	1	2	0	7

70

No Player	MIN	FG	FGA	3P	3PA	FT	FTA	OR	DR	TOT	A	PF	ST	TO	TEC	PTS
11 Weatherspoon 29		0	4	0	0	3	4	0	7	7	3	3	1	1	0	3
25 Becky Hammon 23		7	9	4	6	0	0	0	1	1	2	3	0	1	0	18
23 Sue Wicks 9		2	3	1	1	0	0	1	0	1	1	1	0	1	0	5
42 Camille Cooper.................						Did not play.										
31 Linda Frohlich...................						Did not play.										
7 Korie Hlede......................						Did not play.										
50 Bernadette Ngoyisa						Did not play.										
TOTALS 200		23	57	9	19	8	12	5	20	25	15	17	2	13	0	63
PERCENTAGES: 40.4 47.4 66.7				TM REB: 11			TOT TO: 13 (16 PTS)									

BLOCKED SHOTS: Sparks 6: Milton 3, Leslie 3. Liberty 4: Robinson 2, Phillips 2.
TECHNICAL FOULS: None.

	ILL	PTO	FBP	PIP	2PT
LA 0		16	2	24	18
NY 0		15	2	20	8

Flagrant Fouls: None.

GAME 2
At Staples Center, August 31, 2002

OFFICIALS: Roy Gulbeyan, June Courteau, Lisa Mattingly. TIME OF GAME: 2:07. ATTENDANCE: 13,493

SCORE BY PERIODS	1	2	FINAL
New York 24		42	66
Los Angeles 31		38	69

VISITORS: New York 4-4   Head Coach: Richie Adubato

No Player	MIN	FG	FGA	3P	3PA	FT	FTA	OR	DR	TOT	A	PF	ST	TO	TEC	PTS
44 Tamika Whitmore 35		5	13	0	1	7	9	0	4	4	0	4	0	3	0	17
3 Crystal Robinson 26		0	6	0	3	0	0	2	1	3	1	1	1	0	0	0
24 Tari Phillips 30		3	9	0	0	6	8	4	4	8	0	4	2	3	1	12
55 Vickie Johnson 35		6	12	4	3	5	1	3	4	2	3	0	1	0	17	
11 Weatherspoon 33		3	6	0	2	3	4	2	1	3	5	3	2	0	0	9
25 Becky Hammon 26		3	9	1	6	2	2	1	3	4	2	2	1	1	0	9
23 Sue Wicks 15		1	4	0	0	0	0	2	2	4	0	3	1	0	0	2
42 Camille Cooper.................						Did not play.										
31 Linda Frohlich...................						Did not play.										
7 Korie Hlede......................						Did not play.										
50 Bernadette Ngoyisa						Did not play.										
TOTALS 200		21	59	3	16	21	28	12	18	30	10	20	7	8	2	66
PERCENTAGES: 35.6 18.8 75.0				TM REB: 8			TOT TO: 9 (3 PTS)									

HOME: Los Angeles 6-0   Head Coach: Michael Cooper

No Player	MIN	FG	FGA	3P	3PA	FT	FTA	OR	DR	TOT	A	PF	ST	TO	TEC	PTS
8 DeLisha Milton 33		3	8	1	2	1	2	0	5	5	2	5	1	2	0	8
00 Latasha Byears 31		5	6	0	0	0	2	5	6	11	1	5	0	1	0	10
9 Lisa Leslie 40		6	12	0	1	5	8	1	6	7	1	4	0	1	1	17
42 Nikki Teasley..................38		4	11	1	5	2	2	0	3	3	11	3	1	4	0	11
4 Mwadi Mabika 36		3	9	1	3	5	6	0	5	5	2	2	1	4	0	12
21 Tamecka Dixon 14		3	3	0	0	0	0	0	2	2	1	6	2	4	0	6
13 Sophia Witherspoon 8		1	1	1	1	2	2	0	0	0	0	0	0	0	0	5
41 Marlies Askamp.................						Did not play.										
14 Erika Desouza						Did not play.										
17 Grgin-Fonseca...................						Did not play.										
10 Nicky McCrimmon						Did not play.										
TOTALS 200		25	50	4	12	15	22	6	27	33	18	25	5	16	1	69
PERCENTAGES: 50.0 33.3 68.2				TM REB: 6			TOT TO: 16 (23 PTS)									

BLOCKED SHOTS: Liberty 1. Phillips 1. Sparks 4. Milton 2, Adubato 1, Leslie 1.
TECHNICAL FOULS: Liberty 2. Byears 1, Leslie 1. Sparks 1. Phillips 1

	ILL	PTO	FBP	PIP	2PT
NY 0		23	2	28	13
LA 0		3	9	34	12

Flagrant Fouls: None.

2002 ALL-STAR GAME BOX SCORE

At MCI Center, July 15, 2002

OFFICIALS: Teresa Dahlem, Tony Brown, Bob Trammell. TIME OF GAME: 1:58. ATTENDANCE: 19,487

SCORE BY PERIODS	1	2	FINAL
West...................................40	41	81	
East 40	36	76	

VISITORS: West 1-0   Head Coach: Michael Cooper

No Player	MIN	FG	FGA	3P	3PA	FT	FTA	OR	DR	TOT	A	PF	ST	TO	TEC	PTS
7 Tina Thompson	28	7	16	1	3	5	6	3	4	7	0	2	2	2	0	20
22 Sheryl Swoopes	23	4	12	0	1	3	4	5	1	6	3	1	2	2	0	11
9 Lisa Leslie	28	6	13	0	1	6	10	3	11	14	0	2	1	4	0	18
21 Ticha Penicheiro	22	1	1	0	0	0	0	0	1	1	2	2	2	2	0	2
10 Sue Bird	21	1	8	0	5	0	0	4	1	5	7	0	1	1	0	2
15 Lauren Jackson	20	6	11	2	3	1	1	2	4	6	0	4	1	0	0	15
4 Mwadi Mabika	16	1	5	0	3	0	0	1	5	6	1	1	0	1	0	2
21 Tamecka Dixon	13	2	6	1	3	0	0	0	1	1	0	0	0	2	0	5
30 Katie Smith	11	2	4	0	2	0	0	0	3	3	4	1	0	2	0	4
15 Adrienne Goodson	9	0	2	0	1	0	0	0	1	1	0	0	0	0	0	0
3 Marie Ferdinand	9	1	3	0	0	0	0	0	0	0	1	0	0	1	0	2
TOTALS	200	31	81	4	22	15	21	18	32	50	18	13	9	17	0	81

PERCENTAGES: 38.3 18.2 71.4   TM REB: 14   TOT TO: 17 (18 PTS)

HOME: East 0-1   Head Coach: Anne Donovan

No Player	MIN	FG	FGA	3P	3PA	FT	FTA	OR	DR	TOT	A	PF	ST	TO	TEC	PTS
24 Tamika Catchings	21	4	12	2	5	2	2	3	6	9	1	3	1	1	0	12
32 Andrea Stinson	20	3	10	1	4	2	2	0	1	1	2	3	1	1	0	9
24 Tari Phillips	22	1	9	0	0	2	2	5	5	10	0	6	0	5	0	4
11 Weatherspoon	21	2	3	0	1	0	0	0	2	2	2	1	2	4	0	4
5 Dawn Staley	18	2	5	0	0	0	0	1	3	4	5	0	1	1	0	4
14 Shannon Johnson	20	2	7	2	6	0	0	2	0	2	3	3	1	0	0	6
55 Sheri Sam	19	3	9	1	4	0	0	2	3	5	2	1	1	0	0	7
55 Tammy Sutton-Brown	17	3	5	0	0	3	4	1	3	4	1	1	0	0	0	9
14 Penny Taylor	17	4	8	0	2	1	1	1	2	3	0	0	2	0	0	9
42 Nykesha Sales	14	3	11	0	2	3	3	1	0	1	0	2	2	2	0	9
21 Dales-Schuman	11	1	5	1	3	0	0	1	2	3	0	0	0	0	0	3
1 Chamique Holdsclaw						Did not play.										
TOTALS	200	28	84	7	27	13	14	17	27	44	16	20	11	14	0	76

PERCENTAGES: 33.3 25.9 92.9   TM REB: 5   TOT TO: 14 (14 PTS)

BLOCKED SHOTS: Sparks: 7. Thompson 1, Leslie 4, Penicheiro 1, Jackson 1. Sting: 8. Catchings 4, Weatherspoon 1, Sutton-Brown 3.
TECHNICAL FOULS: None.

	ILL	PTO	FBP	PIP	2PT
West.....................................0		14	14	28	18
East 0		18	11	32	15

Flagrant Fouls: None.

MVP-West, Lisa Leslie (2nd consecutive, third overall)

Chamique Holdsclaw (Washington) was elected to start, bue replaced due to injury.

72

Front Row (l. to r.)—Latasha Byears, Vedrana Grgin Fonseca, Lisa Leslie, President Johnny Buss, DeLisha Milton, Mwadi Mabika, Rhonda Mapp. Back Row (l. to r.)—Head Coach Michael Cooper, Coaches Assistant Rondre Jackson, Team Manager Karleen Thompson, Tamecka Dixon, Nicky McCrimmon, Wendi Willits, Nicole Levandusky, Ukari Figgs, Team Trainer Sandee Teruya, General Manager Penny Toler, Assistant Coach Glenn McDonald.

FINAL STANDINGS
EASTERN CONFERENCE

TEAM	W	L	PCT	GB	HOME	ROAD	LAST-10	STREAK
Cleveland	22	10	.687	-	14-2	8-8	5-5	Lost 3
New York	21	11	.656	1	13-3	8-8	5-5	Won 1
Miami	20	12	.625	2	10-6	10-6	7-3	Lost 1
Charlotte	18	14	.562	4	11-5	7-9	9-1	Won 7
Orlando	13	19	.406	9	10-6	3-13	4-6	Won 1
Detroit	10	22	.312	12	6-10	4-12	4-6	Won 1
Indiana	10	22	.312	12	7-9	3-13	3-7	Lost 1
Washington	10	22	.312	12	8-8	2-14	4-6	Lost 1

WESTERN CONFERENCE

TEAM	W	L	PCT	GB	HOME	ROAD	LAST-10	STREAK
Los Angeles	28	4	.875	-	16-0	12-4	9-1	Won 1
Sacramento	20	12	.625	8	12-4	8-8	7-3	Won 4
Utah	19	13	.594	9	9-7	10-6	8-2	Won 1
Houston	19	13	.594	9	11-5	8-8	4-6	Lost 1
Phoenix	13	19	.406	15	10-6	3-13	3-7	Won 2
Minnesota	12	20	.375	16	6-10	6-10	5-5	Lost 1
Portland	11	21	.344	17	6-10	5-11	0-10	Lost 10
Seattle	10	22	.312	18	5-11	5-11	2-8	Lost 3

TEAM STANDINGS

OFFENSIVE

TEAM	G	FG	FGA	PCT	FG3	FG3A	PCT	FT	FTA	PCT	OFF	DEF	REB	AST	PF	DQ	STL	TO	BLK	PTS	AVG
L.A.	32	916	2031	.451	160	436	.367	449	594	.756	350	755	1105	596	616	9	281	438	138	2441	76.3
Sac.	32	837	1974	.424	163	423	.385	457	618	.739	374	723	1097	558	588	4	276	494	158	2294	71.7
Utah	32	811	1849	.439	78	244	.320	507	675	.751	295	775	1070	524	622	7	202	493	156	2207	69.0
N.Y.	32	833	1828	.456	160	421	.380	326	500	.672	255	660	915	553	616	6	265	437	82	2162	67.6
Ind.	32	762	1822	.418	157	446	.352	472	591	.799	286	649	935	458	600	5	242	491	118	2153	67.3
Orl.	32	768	1914	.401	174	532	.327	430	587	.733	356	614	970	452	643	3	320	532	125	2140	66.9
Det.	32	774	1914	.404	143	405	.353	412	542	.760	324	621	945	469	602	3	225	498	82	2103	65.7
Port.	32	733	1891	.388	172	519	.331	450	612	.735	300	696	996	451	633	3	244	500	106	2088	65.3
Minn.	32	671	1810	.371	176	552	.319	559	727	.769	308	693	1001	437	695	9	210	507	127	2077	64.9
Phoe.	32	767	1894	.405	101	313	.323	429	587	.731	300	642	942	514	625	6	292	519	138	2064	64.5
Cha.	32	746	1780	.419	153	428	.357	410	528	.777	309	639	948	467	605	5	217	474	114	2055	64.2
Hou.	32	747	1908	.392	138	435	.317	415	539	.770	348	710	1058	426	509	2	251	436	95	2047	64.0
Clev.	32	763	1770	.431	106	335	.316	372	505	.737	297	662	959	503	532	1	267	444	83	2004	62.6
Miami	32	754	1826	.413	93	295	.315	356	469	.759	292	651	943	467	602	5	300	448	153	1957	61.2
Wash.	32	739	1915	.386	117	418	.280	333	504	.661	356	699	1055	424	537	3	257	495	127	1928	60.3
Sea.	32	689	1821	.378	128	412	.311	415	606	.685	306	585	891	412	605	6	273	431	127	1921	60.0

DEFENSIVE

Team	FG	FGA	PCT	FG3	FG3A	PCT	FT	FTA	PCT	OFF	DEF	REB	AST	PF	DQ	STL	TO	BLK	PTS	AVG	DIFF
Clev.	664	1745	.381	132	417	.317	328	444	.739	297	594	891	434	597	3	225	496	127	1788	55.9	+6.8
Miami	679	1725	.394	120	395	.304	420	588	.714	301	667	968	388	538	3	259	512	87	1898	59.3	+1.8
Hou.	740	1883	.393	152	456	.333	362	504	.718	297	685	982	452	561	3	248	433	120	1994	62.3	+1.7
Cha.	732	1846	.397	114	369	.309	431	562	.767	344	567	911	443	579	1	257	447	124	2009	62.8	+1.4
Sea.	756	1750	.430	125	325	.385	417	559	.746	296	756	1052	492	588	3	228	519	127	2048	64.0	-4.0
Wash.	791	1945	.407	146	408	.358	347	467	.743	331	737	1068	487	543	4	261	454	103	2075	64.8	-4.6
N.Y.	744	1759	.423	133	394	.338	461	640	.720	304	679	983	430	600	4	223	496	76	2082	65.1	+2.5
Sac.	804	2003	.401	116	400	.290	415	578	.718	343	662	1005	496	616	5	261	481	143	2139	66.8	+4.8
Minn.	752	1927	.390	153	472	.324	499	624	.800	328	688	1016	511	719	7	259	470	126	2156	67.4	-2.5
L.A.	779	1985	.392	192	603	.318	416	547	.761	294	627	921	538	591	8	234	453	114	2166	67.7	+8.6
Phoe.	785	1892	.415	137	391	.350	462	584	.791	333	698	1031	524	603	4	283	517	127	2169	67.8	-3.3
Utah	789	1976	.399	125	429	.291	489	660	.741	344	630	974	478	645	13	275	390	148	2192	68.5	+0.5
Port.	791	1944	.407	159	410	.388	461	656	.703	343	763	1106	501	643	6	293	474	144	2202	68.8	-3.6
Orl.	806	1831	.440	157	438	.358	436	605	.721	316	659	975	534	600	2	298	546	114	2205	68.9	-2.0
Ind.	853	1899	.449	131	367	.357	412	583	.707	306	660	966	565	616	6	256	466	140	2249	70.3	-3.0
Det.	848	1837	.462	127	340	.374	446	583	.765	279	702	981	438	591	5	262	483	109	2269	70.9	-5.2
Avg.	769	1872	.411	139	413	.336	425	574	.741	316	673	989	482	602	5	258	477	121	2103	65.7	—
Totals	12310			2219			6802			5056		15830	9630				4122		1929		
	29947			6614			9184			10774			7711		77		7637		33641	

TEAM COMPARISONS

TEAM	Points Per Game		Field Goal Percentage		Turnovers Per Game		Rebound Percentages			Below 70 Pts.		Overtime Games		3 PTS or Less		10 PTS or More	
	OWN	OPP	OWN	OPP	OWN	OPP	OFF	DEF	TOT	OWN	OPP	W	L	W	L	W	L
Charlotte	64.2	62.8	.419	.397	14.8	14.0	.353	.650	.501	22	22	0	3	3	3	6	5
Cleveland	62.6	55.9*	.431	.381*	13.9	15.5	.333	.690	.512	27	26	1	0	1	2	12	1
Detroit	65.7	70.9	.404	.462	15.6	15.1	.316	.690	.503	22	16	3	2	4	4	3	9
Houston	64.0	62.3	.392	.393	13.6	13.5	.337	.705	.521	20	26	0	1	3	3	9	6
Indiana	67.3	70.3	.418	.449	15.3	14.6	.302	.680	.491	21	15	1	2	1	4	3	8
Los Angeles	76.3*	67.7	.451	.392	13.7	14.2	.358	.720*	.539*	10	22	2	1	3	1	14	1
Miami	61.2	59.3	.413	.394	14.0	16.0	.304	.684	.494	24	29	3	4	3	2	10	5
Minnesota	64.9	67.4	.371	.390	15.8	14.7	.309	.679	.494	24	20	1	2	1	4	5	6
New York	67.6	65.1	.456*	.423	13.7	15.5	.273	.685	.479	19	25	0	5	5	0	11	7
Orlando	66.9	68.9	.401	.440	16.6	17.1*	.351	.660	.505	21	16	0	2	2	3	3	9
Phoenix	64.5	67.8	.405	.415	16.2	16.2	.301	.658	.480	22	19	0	2	3	3	6	11
Portland	65.3	68.8	.388	.407	15.6	14.8	.282	.670	.476	23	17	4	1	3	4	3	9
Sacramento	71.7	66.8	.424	.401	15.4	15.0	.361*	.678	.520	14	21	2	2	3	3	13	5
Seattle	60.0	64.0	.378	.430	13.5*	16.2	.288	.664	.476	25	23	2	1	2	4	3	11
Utah	69.0	68.5	.439	.399	15.4	12.2	.319	.693	.506	18	20	3	0	4	1	5	7
Washington	60.3	64.8	.386	.407	15.5	14.2	.326	.679	.502	27	22	1	0	3	3	4	10
COMPOSITE; 256 games	65.7		.411		14.9		.319	.681		339	23			44		110	

* - League Leader

REBOUND PERCENTAGES — OFF. - Percentage of a given team's missed shots which that team rebounds. DEF. - Percentage of opponents' missed shots which a given team rebounds. TOT. - Average of offensive and defensive rebound percentages.

SCORING AVERAGE

	G	FG	FT	PTS	AVG
Smith, Min.	32	204	246	739	23.1
Leslie, L.A.	31	221	142	606	19.5
Thompson, Hou.	30	199	137	579	19.3
Arcain, Hou.	32	217	135	591	18.5
Holdsclaw, Was.	29	187	101	486	16.8
Griffith, Sac.	32	192	134	518	16.2
Phillips, N.Y.	32	208	73	489	15.3
Jackson, Sea.	29	149	104	442	15.2
Stiles, Por.	32	156	116	478	14.9
Williams, Utah	31	171	97	439	14.2
Stinson, Cha.	32	179	63	450	14.1
Sam, Mia.	32	180	57	444	13.9
Sales, Orl.	32	166	58	433	13.5
Jones, Cle.	30	165	65	404	13.5
Abrosimova, Min.	26	114	96	343	13.2
Brondello, Mia.	29	142	57	367	12.7
McWilliams-Frank, Orl.	32	157	87	403	12.6
Gillom, Pho.	32	150	71	395	12.3
Goodson, Utah	28	138	62	343	12.3
Witherspoon, Por.	31	113	90	373	12.0

REBOUNDS PER GAME

	G	OFF	DEF	TOT	AVG
Griffith, Sac.	32	162	195	357	11.2
Williams, Utah	31	111	197	308	9.9
Leslie, L.A.	31	88	210	298	9.6
Holdsclaw, Was.	29	72	184	256	8.8
Phillips, N.Y.	32	89	168	257	8.0
Thompson, Hou.	30	84	149	233	7.8
Folkl, Por.	32	49	196	245	7.7
Dydek, Utah	32	29	214	243	7.6
McWilliams-Frank, Orl	32	114	129	243	7.6
Bullett, Was.	32	65	166	231	7.2
Palmer, Det.	22	38	116	154	7.0
Abrosimova, Min.	26	43	131	174	6.7
Jackson, Sea.	29	57	136	193	6.7
Crawley, Por.	32	63	140	203	6.3
Stepanova, Pho.	32	66	135	201	6.3
Baranova, Mia.	32	40	151	191	6.0
Byears, L.A.	32	80	103	183	5.7
Melvin, Cle.	27	66	88	154	5.7
Smith, Sac.	32	48	131	179	5.6
Page, Was.	32	74	103	177	5.5

ASSISTS PER GAME

	G	AST	AVG
Penicheiro, Sac.	23	172	7.5
Weatherspoon, N.Y.	32	203	6.3
Staley, Cha.	32	179	5.6
Azzi, Utah	32	171	5.3
Veal, Pho.	29	125	4.3
Timms, Pho.	21	87	4.1
Figgs, L.A.	32	126	3.9
Dixon, L.A.	29	114	3.9
Black, Mia.	32	123	3.8
Washington, Hou.	32	122	3.8
R. Williams, Ind.	32	114	3.6
Darling, Cle.	32	109	3.4
Bevilaqua, Por.	31	103	3.3
Andrade, Cle.	32	100	3.1
Mabika, L.A.	28	87	3.1
Powell, Orl.	32	98	3.1
Paye, Min.	32	97	3.0
Arcain, Hou.	32	94	2.9
Henning, Sea.	32	93	2.9
Burgess, Was.	31	88	2.8

FIELD GOAL PCT.

	FG	FGA	PCT
Byears, L.A.	133	221	.602
Wauters, Cle.	87	153	.569
Griffith, Sac.	192	368	.522
Brown, Cle.	101	195	.518
Phillips, N.Y.	208	410	.507
Stepanova, Pho.	143	282	.507
Ferdinand, Utah	143	290	.493
Fallon, Pho.	127	259	.490
Williams, Utah	171	349	.490
Stinson, Cha.	179	370	.484

3-PT FIELD GOAL PCT.

	3FG	3GA	PCT
Azzi, Utah	38	74	.514
Figgs, L.A.	54	117	.462
Campbell, Sac.	43	94	.457
Tornikidou, Det.	22	49	.449
Stinson, Cha.	29	65	.446
Stiles, Por.	50	116	.431
Robinson, N.Y.	70	168	.417
Malcolm, Ind.	23	56	.411
McCarty, Ind.	23	57	.404
Brondello, Mia.	26	66	.394

FREE THROW PCT.

	FT	FTA	PCT
Baranova, Mia.	66	71	.930
Feaster, Cha.	58	63	.921
Azzi, Utah	88	96	.917
Arcain, Hou.	135	150	.900
Staley, Cha.	51	57	.895
Smith, Min.	246	275	.895
Tornikidou, Det.	63	71	.887
Malcolm, Ind.	54	62	.871
Harrison, Pho.	51	59	.864
Vodichkova, Sea.	38	44	.864

REVIEW 2001 Regular Season

STEALS PER GAME

	G	STL	AVG
Black, Mia.	32	82	2.56
R. Williams, Ind.	32	72	2.25
Sales, Orl.	32	70	2.19
Washington, Hou.	32	69	2.16
Griffith, Sac.	32	63	1.97
Bevilaqua, Por.	31	59	1.90
Arcain, Hou.	32	60	1.88
Jackson, Sea.	29	54	1.86
Holland-Corn, Sac.	32	56	1.75
Penicheiro, Sac.	23	40	1.74

BLOCKS PER GAME

	G	BLK	AVG
Dydek, Utah	32	113	3.53
Leslie, L.A.	31	71	2.29
Jackson, Sea.	29	64	2.21
Stepanova, Pho.	32	64	2.00
Bullett, Was.	32	58	1.81
Baranova, Mia.	32	57	1.78
Smith, Sac.	32	55	1.72
McWilliams-Frank, Orl.	32	50	1.56
Riley, Mia.	32	46	1.44
Sutton-Brown, Cha.	29	39	1.34

MINUTES PER GAME

	G	MIN	AVG
Smith, Min.	32	1234	38.6
Azzi, Utah	32	1205	37.7
Thompson, Hou.	30	1102	36.7
Arcain, Hou.	32	1154	36.1
Staley, Cha.	32	1152	36.0
Jackson, Sea.	29	1001	34.5
Sam, Mia.	32	1100	34.4
Williams, Utah	31	1064	34.3
Griffith, Sac.	32	1077	33.7
Holdsclaw, Was.	29	975	33.6

INDIVIDUAL STATISTICS, TEAM BY TEAM

CHARLOTTE STING

Player	G	Min	FGM	FGA	Pct	FTM	FTA	Pct	Off	Def	Tot	Ast	PF	Dq	Stl	TO	Blk	Pts	Avg	Hi
Andrea Stinson	32	1006	179	370	.484	63	79	.797	39	98	137	88	59	0	43	70	19	450	14.1	25
Allison Feaster	32	1007	126	336	.375	58	63	.921	55	98	153	46	86	1	29	59	10	365	11.4	23
Dawn Staley	32	1152	107	281	.381	51	57	.895	11	60	71	179	54	0	52	100	1	298	9.3	18
Tammy Sutton-Brown	29	602	72	147	.490	52	72	.722	51	78	129	11	84	1	21	40	39	196	6.8	20
Tonya Edwards(*)	22	372	34	100	.340	27	37	.730	11	32	43	30	49	0	14	40	6	100	4.5	16
Tonya Edwards(†)	32	580	60	171	.351	64	84	.762	16	46	62	48	79	1	19	62	7	194	6.1	17
Shalonda Enis	32	623	66	158	.418	45	63	.714	48	65	113	14	60	0	10	36	5	191	6.0	18
Charlotte Smith	30	678	57	146	.390	47	64	.734	36	65	101	50	73	1	16	41	13	171	5.7	13
Clarisse Machanguana	30	580	63	126	.500	37	57	.649	34	87	121	17	95	2	16	41	16	163	5.4	14
Summer Erb	18	148	18	42	.429	18	21	.857	8	27	35	4	23	0	1	10	5	54	3.0	16
Kelly Miller	26	225	22	57	.386	4	5	.800	11	17	28	14	14	0	9	9	0	55	2.1	7
Keisha Anderson	18	102	2	16	.125	8	10	.800	3	12	15	14	8	0	6	17	0	12	0.7	10
Reshea Bristol	1	5	0	1	.000	0	0	—	2	0	2	0	0	0	0	1	0	0	0.0	0
Charlotte	32	6500	746	1780	.419	410	528	.777	309	639	948	467	605	5	217	474	114	2055	64.2	86
Opponents	32	6500	732	1846	.397	431	562	.767	344	567	911	443	579	1	257	447	124	2009	62.8	85

3-pt. FG: Charlotte 153-428 (.357) Stinson 29-65 (.446); Feaster 55-168 (.327); Staley 33-89 (.371); Edwards(*) 5-22 (.227); Edwards(!) 10-36 (.278) Enis 14-31 (.452); Smith 10-32 (.313); Miller 7-19 (.368); Anderson 0-2 (.000); Opponents 114-369 (.309)

CLEVELAND ROCKERS

Player	G	Min	FGM	FGA	Pct	FTM	FTA	Pct	Off	Def	Tot	Ast	PF	Dq	Stl	TO	Blk	Pts	Avg	Hi
Merlakia Jones	30	998	165	377	.438	65	82	.793	43	121	164	45	59	0	29	53	4	404	13.5	26
Chasity Melvin	27	754	102	215	.474	60	86	.698	66	88	154	50	81	0	24	45	16	266	9.9	22
Ann Wauters	24	622	87	153	.569	60	75	.800	35	79	114	35	55	0	17	50	13	234	9.8	19
Rushia Brown	30	760	101	195	.518	46	63	.730	49	83	132	37	73	1	44	37	10	249	8.3	20
Penny Taylor	32	561	86	225	.382	36	46	.783	36	76	112	44	46	0	35	38	11	230	7.2	21
Helen Darling	32	778	59	166	.355	55	72	.764	18	58	76	109	59	0	34	70	4	196	6.1	18
Mery Andrade	32	893	58	171	.339	30	45	.667	21	66	87	100	77	0	51	61	10	152	4.8	13
Vicki Hall(‡)	14	225	27	66	.409	4	8	.500	10	23	33	9	22	0	1	11	5	65	4.6	9
Eva Nemcova	8	113	13	38	.342	5	8	.625	1	9	10	8	9	0	2	6	5	34	4.3	10
Jennifer Rizzotti	32	476	42	110	.382	7	11	.636	2	28	30	51	30	0	25	41	2	119	3.7	9
Angelina Wolvert	1	5	1	3	.333	0	0	—	1	0	1	0	1	0	0	0	0	2	2.0	2
P. Johns Kimbrough	18	119	12	27	.444	4	9	.444	12	19	31	4	12	0	0	10	2	28	1.6	8
Tricia Bader Binford	19	114	8	20	.400	0	0	—	2	10	12	11	7	0	5	8	0	21	1.1	6
Paige Sauer	2	4	1	3	.333	0	0	—	1	1	2	0	1	0	0	1	1	2	1.0	2
Adia Barnes	3	3	1	1	1.000	0	0	—	0	1	1	0	0	0	0	0	0	2	0.7	2
Cleveland	32	6425	763	1770	.431	372	505	.737	297	662	959	503	532	1	267	444	83	2004	62.6	86
Opponents	32	6425	664	1745	.381	328	444	.739	297	594	891	434	597	3	225	496	127	1788	55.9	76

3-pt. FG: Cleveland 106-335 (.316) Jones 9-34 (.265); Melvin 2-2 (1.000); Wauters 0-2 (.000); Brown 1-1 (1.000); Taylor 22-73 (.301); Darling 23-70 (.329) Andrade 6-30 (.200); Hall(>) 7-22 (.318); Nemcova 3-15 (.200); Rizzotti 28-73 (.384); Bader Binford 5-13 (.385) Opponents 132-417 (.317)

DETROIT SHOCK

Player	G	Min	FGM	FGA	Pct	FTM	FTA	Pct	Off	Def	Tot	Ast	PF	Dq	Stl	TO	Blk	Pts	Avg	Hi
Astou Ndiaye-Diatta....32		913	156	341	.457	59	76	.776	60	111	171	49	82	1	22	73	28	376	11.8	27
Wendy Palmer 22		651	91	215	.423	40	59	.678	38	116	154	23	64	0	23	48	4	233	10.6	17
Elena Tornikidou 32		777	111	249	.446	63	71	.887	28	49	77	56	59	0	19	59	14	307	9.6	22
Edwina Brown 32		800	85	232	.366	47	60	.783	31	70	101	87	83	1	33	68	7	237	7.4	19
Deanna Nolan 27		545	64	194	.330	43	53	.811	16	37	53	30	43	0	17	35	6	192	7.1	15
Dominique Canty.......32		625	70	193	.363	56	74	.757	45	38	83	70	69	0	31	55	1	197	6.2	20
Jae Kingi.....................29		625	55	142	.387	26	36	.722	20	43	63	74	42	0	31	53	8	169	5.8	25
Claudia M. das Neves 22		407	34	94	.362	8	8	1.000	3	26	29	34	21	0	21	28	0	95	4.3	16
Barbara Farris..............31		559	46	98	.469	37	58	.638	41	68	109	16	68	1	7	30	5	129	4.2	12
Kelly Santos 14		153	20	42	.476	12	18	.667	11	16	27	5	23	0	3	12	3	52	3.7	11
Carla Boyd 21		230	23	67	.343	18	20	.900	10	16	26	14	32	0	11	16	2	75	3.6	14
Rachael Sporn 23		265	19	47	.404	3	9	.333	21	31	52	11	16	0	7	13	4	41	1.8	9
Detroit 32		6550	774	1914	.404	412	542	.760	324	621	945	469	602	3	225	498	82	2103	65.7	89
Opponents 32		6550	848	1837	.462	446	583	.765	279	702	981	438	591	5	262	483	109	2269	70.9	98

3-pt. FG: Detroit 143-405 (.353) Ndiaye-Diatta 5-15 (.333); Palmer 11-33 (.333); Tornikidou 22-49 (.449); Brown 20-53 (.377); Nolan 21-73 (.288); Canty 1-5 (.200) Kingi 33-88 (.375); das Neves 19-52 (.365); Santos 1-0 (1.000); Boyd 11-36 (.306); Opponents 127-340 (.374)

HOUSTON COMETS

Player	G	Min	FGM	FGA	Pct	FTM	FTA	Pct	Off	Def	Tot	Ast	PF	Dq	Stl	TO	Blk	Pts	Avg	Hi
Tina Thompson 30		1102	199	528	.377	137	163	.840	84	149	233	58	74	0	29	87	22	579	19.3	29
Janeth Arcain 32		1154	217	509	.426	135	150	.900	49	87	136	94	82	1	60	83	3	591	18.5	29
Coquese Washington ..32		1013	63	177	.356	14	22	.636	20	98	118	122	63	1	69	57	9	169	5.3	12
Tiffani Johnson 32		672	62	138	.449	24	28	.857	44	94	138	22	67	0	12	42	15	148	4.6	14
Amanda Lassiter..........32		613	51	139	.367	10	15	.667	27	83	110	34	66	0	16	35	21	138	4.3	15
Trisha Stafford-Odom ..30		365	39	106	.368	35	52	.673	37	48	85	16	42	0	12	26	2	113	3.8	11
Tynesha Lewis 29		419	39	92	.424	11	17	.647	21	41	62	15	26	0	11	26	4	97	3.3	11
Tammy Jackson 32		442	43	86	.500	18	40	.450	40	51	91	21	53	0	22	29	11	104	3.3	18
Kelley Gibson 28		288	13	57	.228	15	22	.682	6	23	29	13	20	0	8	15	6	44	1.6	10
Elena Shakirova 26		203	12	38	.316	14	23	.609	15	20	35	9	11	0	6	9	2	38	1.5	6
Nekeshia Henderson ..23		179	9	38	.237	2	7	.286	5	16	21	22	5	0	6	16	0	26	1.1	11
Houston 32		6450	747	1908	.392	415	539	.770	348	710	1058	426	509	2	251	436	95	2047	64.0	87
Opponents 32		6450	740	1883	.393	362	504	.718	297	685	982	452	561	3	248	433	120	1994	62.3	78

3-pt. FG: Houston 138-435 (.317) Thompson 44-150 (.293); Arcain 22-66 (.333); Washington 29-81 (.358); Lassiter 26-67 (.388); Stafford-Odom 0-1 (.000) Lewis 8-20 (.400); Gibson 3-21 (.143); Shakirova 0-7 (.000); Henderson 6-22 (.273); Opponents 152-456 (.333)

INDIANA FEVER

Player	G	Min	FGM	FGA	Pct	FTM	FTA	Pct	Off	Def	Tot	Ast	PF	Dq	Stl	TO	Blk	Pts	Avg	Hi
Rita Williams 32		1042	115	293	.392	109	130	.838	25	79	104	114	71	0	72	100	11	380	11.9	21
Jurgita Streimikyte....27		707	99	207	.478	48	57	.842	45	94	139	52	81	2	37	52	19	246	9.1	21
O. Scott-Richardson ..32		775	99	217	.456	82	111	.739	52	109	161	40	108	1	22	72	12	280	8.8	19
Alicia Thompson 22		381	76	174	.437	17	23	.739	21	42	63	25	24	0	9	22	7	186	8.5	17
Nadine Malcolm 31		705	90	212	.425	54	62	.871	31	60	91	26	75	2	13	48	3	257	8.3	25
Gordana Grubin.........27		481	62	167	.371	29	39	.744	18	31	49	33	30	0	7	34	0	170	6.3	23
Stephanie McCarty 30		504	52	137	.380	42	55	.764	13	42	55	58	50	0	26	38	14	169	5.6	20
Angie Braziel 23		341	50	115	.435	27	35	.771	21	56	77	7	27	0	9	20	13	127	5.5	14
Kelly Schumacher 28		380	46	93	.495	17	20	.850	23	47	70	10	41	0	5	21	29	112	4.0	10
Vicki Hall(*) 13		123	14	34	.412	8	14	.571	5	11	16	4	11	0	4	7	0	36	2.8	8
Vicki Hall(t) 27		348	41	100	.410	12	22	.545	15	34	49	13	33	0	5	18	5	101	3.7	9
Niele Ivey...................32		708	38	102	.373	14	15	.933	16	39	55	70	51	0	33	35	5	115	3.6	13
Danielle McCulley 8		90	5	18	.278	17	18	.944	4	13	17	5	12	0	0	7	2	28	3.5	12
Monica Maxwell 15		238	16	53	.302	8	12	.667	12	26	38	14	19	0	5	22	3	47	3.1	11
Indiana.......................32		6475	762	1822	.418	472	591	.799	286	649	935	458	600	5	242	491	118	2153	67.3	86
Opponents 32		6475	853	1899	.449	412	583	.707	306	660	966	565	616	6	256	466	140	2249	70.3	86

3-pt. FG: Indiana 157-446 (.352) R. Williams 41-109 (.376); Streimikyte 0-9 (.000); Scott-Richardson 0-2 (.000); Thompson 17-43 (.395); Malcolm 23-56 (.411) Grubin 17-58 (.293); McCarty 23-57 (.404); Braziel 0-1 (.000); Schumacher 3-5 (.600); Hall(*) 0-3 (.000); Hall(!) 7-25 (.280) Ivey 25-70 (.357); McCulley 1-2 (.500); Maxwell 7-31 (.226); Opponents 131-367 (.357)

LOS ANGELES SPARKS

Player	G	Min	FGM	FGA	Pct	FTM	FTA	Pct	Off	Def	Tot	Ast	PF	Dq	Stl	TO	Blk	Pts	Avg	Hi
Lisa Leslie....................	31	1033	221	467	.473	142	193	.736	88	210	298	73	132	3	34	98	71	606	19.5	32
Tamecka Dixon	29	925	133	319	.417	68	86	.791	19	66	85	114	52	2	27	71	2	340	11.7	24
Mwadi Mabika..........	28	828	99	256	.387	68	79	.861	22	108	130	87	74	0	39	44	11	313	11.2	23
DeLisha Milton...........	32	938	134	296	.453	50	63	.794	71	98	169	68	101	0	49	58	29	330	10.3	20
Latasha Byears	32	739	133	221	.602	30	52	.577	80	103	183	29	112	4	42	38	13	297	9.3	17
Ukari Figgs..................	32	930	76	179	.425	51	63	.810	14	86	100	126	42	0	43	55	4	257	8.0	17
Rhonda Mapp	30	395	51	123	.415	24	32	.750	34	45	79	14	60	0	16	25	6	126	4.2	12
Vedrana Grgin Fonsec	24	223	28	65	.431	9	14	.643	13	22	35	12	21	0	4	15	1	71	3.0	12
Nicky McCrimmon......	28	350	28	63	.444	3	7	.429	3	9	12	63	19	0	21	22	0	64	2.3	11
Nicole Levandusky......	13	67	7	22	.318	1	1	1.000	5	4	9	7	3	0	5	5	1	20	1.5	6
Wendi Willits	13	47	6	20	.300	3	4	.750	1	4	5	3	0	0	1	2	0	17	1.3	5
Los Angeles	32	6475	916	2031	.451	449	594	.756	350	755	1105	596	616	9	281	438	138	2441	76.3	100
Opponents	32	6475	779	1985	.392	416	547	.761	294	627	921	538	591	8	234	453	114	2166	67.7	95

3-pt. FG: Los Angeles 160-436 (.367) Leslie 22-60 (.367); Dixon 6-34 (.176); Mabika 47-123 (.382); Milton 12-35 (.343); Byears 1-3 (.333); Figgs 54-117 (.462) Mapp 0-3 (.000); Grgin Fonseca 6-19 (.316); McCrimmon 5-12 (.417); Levandusky 5-17 (.294); Willits 2-13 (.154) Opponents 192-603 (.318)

MIAMI SOL

Player	G	Min	FGM	FGA	Pct	FTM	FTA	Pct	Off	Def	Tot	Ast	PF	Dq	Stl	TO	Blk	Pts	Avg	Hi
Sheri Sam....................	32	1100	180	417	.432	57	76	.750	41	96	137	88	67	0	55	87	8	444	13.9	26
Sandy Brondello.........	29	850	142	344	.413	57	70	.814	10	40	50	63	61	0	28	36	4	367	12.7	23
Elena Baranova	32	984	141	330	.427	66	71	.930	40	151	191	63	81	2	33	62	57	378	11.8	22
Ruth Riley....................	32	799	77	162	.475	64	83	.771	51	79	130	26	107	3	25	63	46	218	6.8	16
Debbie Black	32	946	70	187	.374	37	48	.771	43	83	126	123	69	0	82	51	2	180	5.6	15
Tracy Reid	21	278	32	63	.508	16	26	.615	10	27	37	13	28	0	15	25	5	80	3.8	12
Kristen Rasmussen	28	416	31	86	.360	12	16	.750	33	55	88	16	48	0	11	31	14	75	2.7	11
Marlies Askamp	30	431	28	58	.483	18	32	.563	35	52	87	15	62	0	12	19	11	74	2.5	6
Kisha Ford	30	395	26	80	.325	18	32	.563	19	46	65	21	43	0	17	18	5	71	2.4	7
Katrina Colleton	14	121	10	39	.256	6	10	.600	2	5	7	7	9	0	2	7	1	26	1.9	5
Marla Brumfield	27	247	17	60	.283	5	5	1.000	8	17	25	32	27	0	20	24	0	44	1.6	12
Levys Torres	2	8	0	0	—	0	0	—	0	0	0	0	0	0	0	2	0	0	0.0	0
Miami	32	6575	754	1826	.413	356	469	.759	292	651	943	467	602	5	300	448	153	1957	61.2	75
Opponents	32	6575	679	1725	.394	420	588	.714	301	667	968	388	538	3	259	512	87	1898	59.3	86

3-pt. FG: Miami 93-295 (.315) Sam 27-98 (.276); Brondello 26-66 (.394); Baranova 30-80 (.375); Black 3-20 (.150); Rasmussen 1-4 (.250); Ford 1-11 (.091) Colleton 0-1 (.000); Brumfield 5-15 (.333); Opponents 120-395 (.304)

MINNESOTA LYNX

Player	G	Min	FGM	FGA	Pct	FTM	FTA	Pct	Off	Def	Tot	Ast	PF	Dq	Stl	TO	Blk	Pts	Avg	Hi
Katie Smith..................	32	1234	204	519	.393	246	275	.895	40	82	122	70	94	0	23	87	5	739	23.1	46
Svetlana Abrosimova ..26	26	846	114	293	.389	96	132	.727	43	131	174	53	70	2	42	85	9	343	13.2	27
Betty Lennox	11	241	41	110	.373	19	20	.950	13	41	54	16	29	0	10	25	4	121	11.0	18
Erin Buescher.............	32	725	64	184	.348	47	76	.618	42	76	118	62	101	2	27	65	29	183	5.7	16
Lynn Pride	32	713	68	174	.391	33	55	.600	47	99	146	28	77	2	28	46	20	170	5.3	13
Kristi Harrower.............	4	72	7	15	.467	4	4	1.000	1	3	4	11	4	0	3	3	0	21	5.3	13
Georgia Schweitzer 24	24	423	33	103	.320	13	17	.765	15	35	50	34	34	1	11	17	6	87	3.6	14
Val Whiting-Raymond	26	462	24	90	.267	40	54	.741	25	58	83	16	62	0	15	34	14	88	3.4	13
Maylana Martin	31	494	35	103	.340	19	31	.613	27	59	86	19	87	2	17	37	15	95	3.1	14
Kate Paye	32	652	30	78	.385	11	16	.688	7	54	61	97	55	0	21	46	0	91	2.8	11
Shanele Stires.............	18	201	20	53	.377	5	7	.714	10	17	27	14	26	0	8	19	4	51	2.8	9
Janell Burse	20	169	16	48	.333	15	20	.750	23	19	42	5	20	0	2	20	15	47	2.4	12
Michele VanGorp.......	22	243	15	40	.375	11	20	.550	15	19	34	12	36	0	3	18	6	41	1.9	8
Minnesota	32	6475	671	1810	.371	559	727	.769	308	693	1001	437	695	9	210	507	127	2077	64.9	95
Opponents	32	6475	752	1927	.390	499	624	.800	328	688	1016	511	719	7	259	470	126	2156	67.4	100

3-pt. FG: Minnesota 176-552 (.319) Smith 85-240 (.354); Abrosimova 19-76 (.250); Lennox 20-52 (.385); Buescher 8-29 (.276); Pride 1-4 (.250); Harrower 3-6 (.500) Schweitzer 8-43 (.186); Whiting-Raymond 0-1 (.000); Martin 6-18 (.333); Paye 20-56 (.357); Stires 6-25 (.240); Burse 0-1 (.000) VanGorp 0-1 (.000); Opponents 153-472 (.324)

NEW YORK LIBERTY

Player	G	Min	FGM	FGA	Pct	FTM	FTA	Pct	Off	Def	Tot	Ast	PF	Dq	Stl	TO	Blk	Pts	Avg	Hi
Tari Phillips	32	1049	208	410	.507	73	125	.584	89	168	257	34	110	0	48	84	17	489	15.3	27
Vickie Johnson	32	939	135	326	.414	53	70	.757	23	84	107	87	62	1	35	52	4	353	11.0	23
Crystal Robinson	32	980	123	267	.461	26	29	.897	23	69	92	83	86	1	32	28	8	342	10.7	18
Becky Hammon	32	619	90	197	.457	40	51	.784	10	42	52	51	46	0	27	48	1	262	8.2	21
Tamika Whitmore	32	752	96	222	.432	33	58	.569	29	68	97	19	70	0	17	33	10	226	7.1	23
Camille Cooper	4	51	8	12	.667	10	13	.769	7	4	11	1	6	0	0	3	2	26	6.5	10
Teresa Weatherspoon	32	974	72	167	.431	53	79	.671	29	89	118	203	83	1	55	81	4	207	6.5	16
Sue Wicks	30	602	61	130	.469	35	52	.673	36	102	138	37	86	2	36	43	30	157	5.2	14
Katarina Lazic	8	55	8	20	.400	1	2	.500	2	4	6	3	9	0	3	10	0	17	2.1	8
Stacey Ford	1	3	1	1	1.000	0	0	—	0	1	1	0	0	0	0	0	0	2	2.0	2
Grace Daley	15	66	10	21	.476	5	9	.556	3	5	8	10	12	0	8	7	1	25	1.7	7
Andrea Nagy	23	213	13	31	.419	2	4	.500	0	9	9	24	25	1	2	23	3	34	1.5	7
Rebecca Lobo	16	85	7	22	.318	2	4	.500	2	12	14	1	16	0	2	7	0	17	1.1	9
Hajdana Radunovic	4	9	1	2	.500	2	2	1.000	1	3	4	0	3	0	2	1	1	4	1.0	2
Mactabene Amachree	2	3	0	0	—	1	2	.500	1	0	1	0	2	0	0	1	1	1	0.5	1
New York	32	6400	833	1828	.456	336	500	.672	255	660	915	553	616	6	265	437	82	2162	67.6	95
Opponents	32	6400	744	1759	.423	461	640	.720	304	679	983	430	600	4	223	496	76	2082	65.1	86

3-pt. FG: New York 160-421 (.380) Phillips 0-4 (.000); Johnson 30-82 (.366); Robinson 70-168 (.417); Hammon 42-111 (.378); Whitmore 1-2 (.500); Wicks 0-7 (.000) Weatherspoon 10-26 (.385); Lazic 0-2 (.000); Daley 0-5 (.000); Nagy 6-12 (.500); Lobo 1-2 (.500); Opponents 133-394 (.338)

ORLANDO MIRACLE

Player	G	Min	FGM	FGA	Pct	FTM	FTA	Pct	Off	Def	Tot	Ast	PF	Dq	Stl	TO	Blk	Pts	Avg	Hi
Nykesha Sales	32	1039	166	379	.438	58	74	.784	57	115	172	58	109	0	70	72	6	433	13.5	21
T. McWilliams-Franklin	32	1059	157	331	.474	87	117	.744	114	129	243	69	74	1	52	80	50	403	12.6	23
Shannon Johnson	26	785	90	245	.367	84	111	.757	15	62	77	68	66	0	34	54	6	302	11.6	25
Elaine Powell	32	1055	119	296	.402	80	106	.755	32	66	98	98	64	0	49	79	7	357	11.2	20
Katie Douglas	22	439	51	141	.362	34	47	.723	16	35	51	39	34	0	37	44	7	154	7.0	18
Jessie Hicks	32	456	63	162	.389	43	66	.652	38	54	92	22	85	0	23	53	17	169	5.3	16
Brooke Wyckoff	32	648	41	125	.328	20	28	.714	48	74	122	37	91	2	26	50	15	108	3.4	8
Tiffany McCain	32	442	35	109	.321	6	9	.667	7	31	38	36	52	0	10	34	8	97	3.0	13
Jaclyn Johnson	17	139	14	25	.560	4	5	.800	10	13	23	9	21	0	4	17	3	35	2.1	11
Cintia dos Santos	10	65	7	19	.368	5	6	.833	1	5	6	2	18	0	3	7	5	19	1.9	8
Tawona Alhaleem	26	252	19	58	.328	7	14	.500	15	23	38	14	20	0	11	28	0	49	1.9	10
Carla McGhee	17	71	6	24	.250	2	4	.500	3	7	10	0	9	0	1	6	1	14	0.8	6
Orlando	32	6450	768	1914	.401	430	587	.733	356	614	970	452	643	3	320	532	125	2140	66.9	92
Opponents	32	6450	806	1831	.440	436	605	.721	316	659	975	534	600	2	298	546	114	2205	68.9	86

3-pt. FG: Orlando 174-532 (.327) Sales 43-137 (.314); McWilliams-Frank 2-10 (.200); S. Johnson 38-104 (.365); Powell 39-102 (.382); Douglas 18-57 (.316) Wyckoff 6-37 (.162); McCain 21-67 (.313); J. Johnson 3-7 (.429); Alhaleem 4-11 (.364); Opponents 157-438 (.358)

PHOENIX MERCURY

Player	G	Min	FGM	FGA	Pct	FTM	FTA	Pct	Off	Def	Tot	Ast	PF	Dq	Stl	TO	Blk	Pts	Avg	Hi
Jennifer Gillom	32	858	150	355	.423	71	96	.740	36	91	127	35	91	1	31	71	19	395	12.3	25
Maria Stepanova	32	815	143	282	.507	48	78	.615	66	135	201	41	110	3	43	50	64	334	10.4	20
Trisha Fallon	31	841	127	259	.490	53	65	.815	35	42	77	33	43	0	35	47	12	322	10.4	24
Tonya Edwards(‡)	10	208	26	71	.366	37	47	.787	5	14	19	18	30	1	5	22	1	94	9.4	17
Lisa Harrison	32	915	96	223	.430	51	59	.864	39	100	139	52	58	0	39	49	1	246	7.7	15
Adriana Moises Pinto	7	123	14	36	.389	9	12	.750	4	12	16	17	11	0	6	16	0	41	5.9	13
Bridget Pettis	32	497	53	159	.333	46	56	.821	30	30	60	50	47	1	28	38	4	172	5.4	26
Michele Timms	21	408	38	110	.345	8	10	.800	11	34	45	87	42	0	21	42	2	98	4.7	14
Kristen Veal	29	658	35	125	.280	32	42	.762	14	46	60	125	58	0	33	82	4	116	4.0	16
Adrain Williams	25	375	38	113	.336	20	28	.714	21	54	75	11	43	0	15	34	5	96	3.8	12
Brandy Reed	1	13	1	8	.125	1	1	1.000	0	3	3	0	0	0	0	0	0	3	3.0	3
Jaynetta Saunders	28	253	25	77	.325	17	25	.680	13	27	40	7	28	0	10	14	8	68	2.4	12
Slobodanka Tuvic	30	325	13	42	.310	28	59	.475	18	45	63	17	49	0	16	28	17	54	1.8	8
Ilona Korstine	12	75	7	25	.280	6	7	.857	6	5	11	5	4	0	3	9	0	21	1.8	8
Nicole Kubik	3	21	1	4	.250	0	0	—	0	2	2	5	7	0	4	3	0	2	0.7	2

Player	G	Min	FGM	FGA	Pct	FTM	FTA	Pct	Off	Def	Tot	Ast	PF	Dq	Stl	TO	Blk	Pts	Avg	Hi
									REBOUNDS									**SCORING**		
Michelle Cleary 4	4	49	0	3	.000	2	2	1.000	2	1	3	9	2	0	2	3	0	2	0.5	2
E.C. Hill 3	3	8	0	1	.000	0	0	—	0	0	0	1	2	0	1	0	0	0	0.0	0
Pat Luckey 1	1	8	0	1	.000	0	0	—	0	1	1	1	0	0	0	0	1	0	0.0	0
Phoenix 32	32	6450	767	1894	.405	429	587	.731	300	642	942	514	625	6	292	519	138	2064	64.5	89
Opponents 32	32	6450	785	1892	.415	462	584	.791	333	698	1031	524	603	4	283	517	127	2169	67.8	95

3-pt. FG: Phoenix 101-313 (.323) Gillom 24-70 (.343); Stepanova 0-2 (.000); Fallon 15-37 (.405); Edwards(>) 5-14 (.357); Harrison 3-9 (.333); Pettis 20-63 (.317) Moises Pinto 4-12 (.333); Timms 14-46 (.304); Veal 14-50 (.280); Saunders 1-3 (.333); Korstine 1-3 (.333); Kubik 0-1 (.000) Cleary 0-2 (.000); Hill 0-1 (.000); Opponents 137-391 (.350)

PORTLAND FIRE

Player	G	Min	FGM	FGA	Pct	FTM	FTA	Pct	Off	Def	Tot	Ast	PF	Dq	Stl	TO	Blk	Pts	Avg	Hi
									REBOUNDS									**SCORING**		
Jackie Stiles 32	32	1023	156	385	.405	116	149	.779	24	53	77	55	75	0	24	68	3	478	14.9	32
Sophia Witherspoon....31	31	862	113	358	.316	90	106	.849	20	54	74	54	59	0	30	72	8	373	12.0	26
Sylvia Crawley 32	32	921	120	267	.449	59	77	.766	63	140	203	54	85	3	19	61	26	299	9.3	19
Kristin Folkl 32	32	862	71	166	.428	33	40	.825	49	196	245	45	56	0	20	39	34	180	5.6	13
DeMya Walker...........21	21	297	44	100	.440	23	40	.575	29	29	58	10	51	0	7	35	12	113	5.4	12
Tully Bevilaqua...........31	31	788	39	119	.328	52	71	.732	27	61	88	103	102	0	59	52	6	153	4.9	13
Carolyn Young 23	23	279	37	99	.374	27	37	.730	10	24	34	15	27	0	14	27	1	111	4.8	13
Tamicha Jackson........32	32	497	55	169	.325	16	23	.696	10	34	44	50	35	0	28	45	0	132	4.1	12
Alisa Burras 26	26	272	44	83	.530	18	31	.581	22	37	59	10	30	0	5	30	3	106	4.1	18
Vanessa Nygaard 31	31	259	28	72	.389	1	3	.333	13	22	35	10	48	0	6	14	2	76	2.5	8
Stacey Thomas...........32	32	413	22	60	.367	15	35	.429	31	39	70	41	57	0	30	40	10	59	1.8	8
LaQuanda Barksdale 5	5	35	1	10	.100	0	0	—	1	5	6	4	3	0	2	1	0	2	0.4	2
Jenny Mowe.................5	5	17	3	3	1.000	0	0	—	1	2	3	0	5	0	0	2	1	6	1.2	2
Portland 32	32	6525	733	1891	.388	450	612	.735	300	696	996	451	633	3	244	500	106	2088	65.3	86
Opponents 32	32	6525	791	1944	.407	461	656	.703	343	763	1106	501	643	6	293	474	144	2202	68.8	90

3-pt. FG: Portland 172-519 (.331) Stiles 50-116 (.431); Witherspoon 57-182 (.313); Crawley 0-1 (.000); Folkl 5-12 (.417); Walker 2-3 (.667); Bevilaqua 23-73 (.315) Young 10-34 (.294); Jackson 6-39 (.154); Nygaard 19-49 (.388); Thomas 0-7 (.000); Barksdale 0-3 (.000); Opponents 159-410 (.388)

SACRAMENTO MONARCHS

Player	G	Min	FGM	FGA	Pct	FTM	FTA	Pct	Off	Def	Tot	Ast	PF	Dq	Stl	TO	Blk	Pts	Avg	Hi
									REBOUNDS									**SCORING**		
Yolanda Griffith 32	32	1077	192	368	.522	134	186	.720	162	195	357	54	114	1	63	75	37	518	16.2	30
Tangela Smith.............32	32	912	148	352	.420	62	85	.729	48	131	179	41	106	2	34	66	55	358	11.2	27
Kedra Holland-Corn....32	32	874	111	251	.442	41	60	.683	33	42	75	69	62	0	56	66	5	322	10.1	26
Edna Campbell...........32	32	854	92	244	.377	33	43	.767	11	74	85	74	45	0	19	64	9	260	8.1	21
Ruthie Bolton 31	31	582	73	216	.338	36	52	.692	34	59	93	55	55	0	28	39	1	222	7.2	21
Ticha Penicheiro 23	23	744	42	124	.339	49	64	.766	6	80	86	172	58	1	40	64	8	144	6.3	17
Kara Wolters 31	31	378	63	134	.470	25	31	.806	21	53	74	17	55	0	4	33	25	151	4.9	18
Lady Grooms 31	31	543	49	114	.430	43	58	.741	32	46	78	38	43	0	15	25	10	141	4.5	13
La'Keshia Frett 30	30	403	49	126	.389	30	35	.857	23	32	55	18	30	0	10	32	6	128	4.3	18
Cindy Blodgett 11	11	72	13	29	.448	0	0	—	1	8	9	6	6	0	6	11	1	34	3.1	19
Dana Wynne 1	1	3	0	0	—	2	2	1.000	1	0	1	0	2	0	0	1	2	2	2.0	2
Maren Walseth.............4	4	8	1	2	.500	2	2	1.000	2	0	2	0	2	0	0	2	0	4	1.0	4
Stacy Clinesmith........16	16	75	4	14	.286	0	0	—	0	3	3	14	10	0	1	6	0	10	0.6	3
Sacramento 32	32	6525	837	1974	.424	457	618	.739	374	723	1097	558	588	4	276	494	158	2294	71.7	91
Opponents 32	32	6525	804	2003	.401	415	578	.718	343	662	1005	496	616	5	261	481	143	2139	66.8	83

3-pt. FG: Sacramento 163-423 (.385) Smith 0-2 (.000); Holland-Corn 59-150 (.393); Campbell 43-94 (.457); Bolton 40-110 (.364); Penicheiro 11-42 (.262) Blodgett 8-15 (.533); Clinesmith 2-10 (.200); Opponents 116-400 (.290)

SEATTLE STORM

Player	G	Min	FGM	FGA	Pct	FTM	FTA	Pct	Off	Def	Tot	Ast	PF	Dq	Stl	TO	Blk	Pts	Avg	Hi
									REBOUNDS									**SCORING**		
Lauren Jackson...........29	29	1001	149	406	.367	104	143	.727	57	136	193	44	97	3	54	53	64	442	15.2	26
Semeka Randall 32	32	884	117	315	.371	66	100	.660	32	73	105	44	45	0	29	73	4	300	9.4	28
Simone Edwards.........32	32	810	91	190	.479	55	83	.663	67	90	157	26	54	0	24	37	20	237	7.4	19
Jamie Redd.................32	32	659	82	216	.380	45	66	.682	29	53	82	48	101	0	17	48	3	231	7.2	24
Kamila Vodichkova 29	29	405	51	122	.418	38	44	.864	25	46	71	23	56	0	16	34	7	150	5.2	14
Michelle Marciniak 27	27	392	51	139	.367	20	37	.541	17	21	38	47	49	0	30	30	2	132	4.9	15

Player	G	Min	FGM	FGA	Pct	FTM	FTA	Pct	Off	Def	Tot	Ast	PF	Dq	Stl	TO	Blk	Pts	Avg	Hi
Katy Steding	26	393	35	94	.372	16	20	.800	9	26	35	24	23	1	16	22	9	102	3.9	16
Stacey Lovelace	22	211	27	71	.380	12	17	.706	14	18	32	9	23	0	8	18	5	76	3.5	14
Quacy Barnes	20	229	23	59	.390	21	27	.778	14	20	34	11	29	0	9	16	6	68	3.4	10
Sonja Henning	32	902	41	129	.318	18	35	.514	14	57	71	93	62	2	52	43	6	108	3.4	13
Charmin Smith	32	589	17	63	.270	13	21	.619	18	37	55	39	52	0	17	26	1	58	1.8	8
Michelle Edwards	3	13	1	3	.333	2	2	1.000	0	2	2	4	2	0	1	3	0	4	1.3	2
Alessandra Santos de ..	10	62	4	14	.286	5	11	.455	0	16	16	0	12	0	0	3	0	13	1.3	5
Seattle	32	6550	689	1821	.378	415	606	.685	306	585	891	412	605	6	273	431	127	1921	60.0	83
Opponents	32	6550	753	1750	.430	417	559	.746	296	756	1052	492	588	3	228	519	127	2048	64.0	85

3-pt. FG: Seattle 128-412 (.311); Jackson 40-129 (.310); Randall 0-4 (.000); Redd 22-77 (.286); Vodichkova 10-25 (.400); Marciniak 10-33 (.303); Barnes 1-1 (1.000) Steding 16-35 (.457); Lovelace 10-26 (.385); Henning 8-44 (.182); Smith 11-38 (.289); Opponents 125-325 (.385)

UTAH STARZZ

Player	G	Min	FGM	FGA	Pct	FTM	FTA	Pct	Off	Def	Tot	Ast	PF	Dq	Stl	TO	Blk	Pts	Avg	Hi
Natalie Williams	31	1064	171	349	.490	97	133	.729	111	197	308	55	128	4	41	70	10	439	14.2	26
Adrienne Goodson	28	854	138	319	.433	62	89	.697	66	86	152	58	64	0	27	75	0	343	12.3	21
Marie Ferdinand	32	864	143	290	.493	69	113	.611	23	63	86	79	70	1	40	63	4	366	11.4	19
Margo Dydek	32	970	128	291	.440	87	109	.798	29	214	243	64	108	1	25	90	113	349	10.9	24
Jennifer Azzi	32	1205	75	184	.408	88	96	.917	10	88	98	171	89	1	22	69	10	276	8.6	19
Korie Hlede	27	455	55	141	.390	33	38	.868	15	25	40	43	56	0	25	42	1	151	5.6	20
Kate Starbird	23	310	41	110	.373	22	27	.815	13	17	30	21	30	0	8	15	1	109	4.7	21
Amy Herrig	32	448	43	93	.462	35	46	.761	23	58	81	14	47	0	8	35	14	121	3.8	11
LaTonya Johnson	26	228	17	65	.262	11	14	.786	4	15	19	7	26	0	2	13	1	50	1.9	7
Cara Consuegra	15	50	0	5	.000	2	4	.500	1	5	6	10	4	0	4	11	0	2	0.1	1
Michaela Pavlickova	10	21	0	2	.000	1	2	.500	0	6	6	1	0	0	0	1	2	1	0.1	1
Keitha Dickerson	4	6	0	0	—	0	4	.000	0	1	1	1	0	0	0	0	0	0	0.0	0
Utah	32	6475	811	1849	.439	507	675	.751	295	775	1070	524	622	7	202	493	156	2207	69.0	87
Opponents	32	6475	789	1976	.399	489	660	.743	304	974		478	645	13	275	390	148	2192	68.5	87

3-pt. FG: Utah 78-244 (.320) Williams 0-4 (.000); Goodson 5-31 (.161); Ferdinand 11-42 (.262); Dydek 6-15 (.400); Azzi 38-74 (.514); Hlede 8-23 (.348) Starbird 5-23 (.217); Johnson 5-30 (.167); Consuegra 0-2 (.000); Opponents 125-429 (.291)

WASHINGTON MYSTICS

Player	G	Min	FGM	FGA	Pct	FTM	FTA	Pct	Off	Def	Tot	Ast	PF	Dq	Stl	TO	Blk	Pts	Avg	Hi
Chamique Holdsclaw	29	975	187	467	.400	101	148	.682	72	184	256	66	49	0	44	94	14	486	16.8	31
Nikki McCray	32	828	119	290	.410	91	128	.711	22	34	56	47	68	1	26	73	0	351	11.0	25
Vicky Bullett	32	1073	112	286	.392	35	48	.729	65	166	231	41	86	0	53	53	58	278	8.7	24
Murriel Page	32	989	100	231	.433	21	36	.583	74	103	177	55	88	2	30	60	36	225	7.0	14
Helen Luz	32	489	55	136	.404	22	25	.880	10	27	37	55	47	0	28	43	5	164	5.1	15
Annie Burgess	31	731	47	141	.333	16	27	.593	27	49	76	88	45	0	26	60	2	124	4.0	13
Tonya Washington	30	336	41	114	.360	9	11	.818	19	24	43	10	5	0	4	14	2	101	3.4	12
Audrey Sauret	25	455	33	111	.297	7	24	.292	11	31	42	43	39	0	24	41	4	76	3.0	12
Tausha Mills	30	319	23	69	.333	18	31	.581	40	65	105	6	72	0	14	25	4	64	2.1	6
Coco Miller	20	137	13	40	.325	6	11	.545	5	4	9	8	10	0	6	13	0	34	1.7	6
Markita Aldridge	5	35	3	9	.333	1	1	1.000	2	0	2	2	5	0	0	4	0	7	1.4	4
Cass Bauer-Bilodeau	15	102	5	17	.294	5	10	.500	8	10	18	3	12	0	2	6	1	15	1.0	3
Tamara Stocks	3	11	1	3	.333	1	2	.500	0	2	2	0	3	0	0	0	0	3	1.0	3
Jennifer Whittle	4	20	0	1	.000	0	2	.000	1	0	1	0	8	0	0	3	1	0	0.0	0
Washington	32	6500	739	1915	.386	333	504	.661	356	699	1055	424	537	3	257	495	127	1928	60.3	80
Opponents	32	6500	791	1945	.407	347	467	.743	331	737	1068	487	543	4	261	454	103	2075	64.8	86

3-pt. FG: Washington 117-418 (.280) Holdsclaw 11-46 (.239); McCray 22-95 (.232); Bullett 19-64 (.297); Page 4-17 (.235); Luz 32-82 (.390); Burgess 14-47 (.298) Washington 10-29 (.345); Sauret 3-26 (.115); Mills 0-1 (.000); Miller 2-6 (.333); Aldridge 0-3 (.000); Bauer-Bilodeau 0-1 (.000) Whittle 0-1 (.000); Opponents 146-408 (.358)

(*) Statistics with this team only

(†) Totals with all teams

(‡) Continued season with another team

FIRST ROUND

Charlotte defeats Cleveland, 2-1
August 16   Charlotte 53, Cleveland 46
August 18   Cleveland 69, Charlotte 51
August 20   Charlotte 72, Cleveland 64

New York defeats Miami, 2-1
August 17   New York 62, Miami 46
August 19   Miami 53, New York 50
August 21   New York 72, Miami 61

Los Angeles defeats Houston, 2-0
August 18   Los Angeles 64, Houston 59
August 20   Los Angeles 70, Houston 58

Sacramento defeats Utah, 2-0
August 17   Sacramento 89, Utah 65
August 19   Sacramento 71, Utah 66

CONFERENCE FINALS

Charlotte defeats New York, 2-1
August 24   New York 61, Charlotte 57
August 26   Charlotte 62, New York 53
August 27   Charlotte 48, New York 44

Los Angeles defeats Sacramento, 2-1
August 24   Los Angeles 74, Sacramento 73
August 26   Sacramento 80, Los Angeles 60
August 27   Los Angeles 93, Sacramento 62

FINALS

Los Angeles defeats Charlotte, 2-0
August 30   Los Angeles 75, Charlotte 66
September 1   Los Angeles 82, Charlotte 54

TEAM STANDINGS

OFFENSIVE

TEAM	G	FG	FGA	PCT	FG3	FG3A	PCT	FT	FTA	PCT	OFF	DEF	REB	AST	PF	DQ	STL	TO	BLK	PTS	AVG
Sac.	5	125	324	.386	34	80	.425	91	112	.813	49	101	150	79	89	0	35	53	20	375	75.0
L.A.	7	195	439	.444	33	110	.300	95	130	.731	71	178	249	140	119	0	47	86	57	518	74.0
Utah	2	45	110	.409	2	19	.105	39	50	.780	18	46	64	25	47	2	13	30	13	131	65.5
Clev.	3	68	162	.420	9	33	.273	34	41	.829	36	48	84	53	54	0	24	35	12	179	59.7
Hou.	2	45	120	.375	9	36	.250	18	26	.692	17	50	67	23	33	0	9	26	9	117	58.5
Cha.	8	177	429	.413	39	103	.379	70	90	.778	67	146	213	112	143	0	49	112	31	463	57.9
N.Y.	6	134	323	.415	24	74	.324	50	75	.667	56	116	172	88	96	1	44	76	21	342	57.0
Miami	3	57	154	.370	11	34	.324	35	57	.614	30	55	85	35	50	1	18	38	7	160	53.3

DEFENSIVE

Team	FG	FGA	PCT	FG3	FG3A	PCT	FT	FTA	PCT	OFF	DEF	REB	AST	PF	DQ	STL	TO	BLK	PTS	AVG	DIFF
N.Y.	116	302	.384	28	72	.389	67	94	.713	52	115	167	74	100	1	39	83	18	327	54.5	+2.5
Clev.	67	159	.421	16	40	.400	26	36	.722	30	49	79	44	50	0	17	39	9	176	58.7	+1.0
Miami	72	167	.431	12	37	.324	28	45	.622	33	64	97	47	54	1	19	36	6	184	61.3	-8.0
Cha.	186	435	.428	28	96	.292	94	120	.783	77	144	221	137	131	0	61	96	43	494	61.8	-3.9
L.A.	172	446	.386	40	121	.331	68	90	.756	58	142	200	107	126	0	41	87	34	452	64.6	+9.4
Hou.	50	125	.400	8	31	.258	26	34	.765	21	54	75	33	28	0	15	20	10	134	67.0	-8.5
Sac.	134	307	.436	20	72	.278	70	97	.722	50	126	176	89	103	2	33	75	44	358	71.6	+3.4
Utah	49	120	.408	9	20	.450	53	65	.815	23	46	69	24	39	0	14	20	6	160	80.0	-14.5
Avg	106	258	.410	20	61	.329	54	73	.744	43	93	136	69	79	1	30	57	21	286	63.5	—
Totals	846	2061		161	489		432	581		344	740	1084	555	631	4	239	456	170	2285		

TEAM COMPARISONS

TEAM	Points Per Game		Field Goal Percentage		Turnovers Per Game		Rebound Percentages			Below 70 Pts.		Overtime Games		3 PTS or Less		10 PTS or More	
	OWN	OPP	OWN	OPP	OWN	OPP	OFF	DEF	TOT	OWN	OPP	W	L	W	L	W	L
Charlotte	57.9	61.8	.413	.428	14.0	12.0	.318	.655	.486	7	6	0	0	0	0	0	2
Cleveland	59.7	58.7	.420	.421	11.7	13.0	.424*	.615	.519	3	2	0	0	0	0	1	0
Houston	58.5	67.0	.375	.400	13.0	10.0	.239	.704	.472	2	1	0	0	0	0	0	1
Los Angeles	74.0	64.6	.444*	.386	12.3	12.4	.333	.754*	.544*	2	5	0	0	1	0	3	1
Miami	53.3	61.3	.370	.431	12.7	12.0	.319	.625	.472	3	2	0	0	1	0	0	2
New York	57.0	54.5*	.415	.384*	12.7	13.8	.327	.690	.509	5	6	0	0	0	1	2	0
Sacramento	75.0*	71.6	.386	.436	10.6*	15.0*	.280	.669	.474	1	3	0	0	0	1	2	1
Utah	65.5	80.0	.409	.408	15.0	10.0	.281	.667	.474	2	0	0	0	0	0	0	1
COMPOSITE; 18 games																	
	63.5		.410		12.7		.317	.683		25	0		2			8	

* - League Leader

REBOUND PERCENTAGES — OFF. - Percentage of a given team's missed shots which that team rebounds. DEF. - Percentage of opponents' missed shots which a given team rebounds. TOT. - Average of offensive and defensive rebound percentages.

REVIEW 2001 Playoffs

CHARLOTTE STING

Player	G	Min	FGM	FGA	Pct	FTM	FTA	Pct	REBOUNDS			Ast	PF	Dq	Stl	TO	Blk	SCORING		
									Off	Def	Tot							Pts	Avg	Hi
Andrea Stinson	8	278	37	95	.389	17	21	.810	12	37	49	26	18	0	13	18	2	96	12.0	18
Dawn Staley	8	301	32	77	.416	17	21	.810	3	15	18	35	19	0	9	34	2	94	11.8	18
Allison Feaster	8	248	26	74	.351	1	1	1.000	8	26	34	14	18	0	9	9	4	64	8.0	14
Tammy Sutton-Brown	8	167	25	46	.543	10	14	.714	10	16	26	4	25	0	1	8	11	60	7.5	12
Charlotte Smith	8	224	16	54	.296	10	11	.909	13	19	32	14	24	0	6	7	8	47	5.9	10
Clarisse Machanguana	8	132	17	32	.531	4	6	.667	7	12	19	2	11	0	3	6	3	38	4.8	10
Shalonda Enis	8	101	11	22	.500	9	12	.750	6	9	15	4	16	0	2	7	1	34	4.3	12
Tonya Edwards	8	119	9	21	.429	2	2	1.000	6	10	16	12	8	0	5	11	0	22	2.8	15
Summer Erb	4	15	4	5	.800	0	0	—	2	2	4	0	3	0	0	3	0	8	2.0	6
Keisha Anderson	2	7	0	1	.000	0	0	—	0	0	0	1	1	0	1	1	0	0	0.0	0
Kelly Miller	2	8	0	2	.000	0	2	.000	0	0	0	0	0	0	0	0	0	0	0.0	0
Charlotte	8	1600	177	429	.413	70	90	.778	67	146	213	112	143	0	49	112	31	463	57.9	72
Opponents	8	1600	186	435	.428	94	120	.783	77	144	221	137	131	0	61	96	43	494	61.8	82

3-pt. FG: Charlotte 39-103 (.379) Stinson 5-13 (.385); Staley 13-26 (.500); Feaster 11-35 (.314); Smith 5-20 (.250); Enis 3-4 (.750); Edwards 2-4 (.500) Anderson 0-1 (.000); Opponents 28-96 (.292)

CLEVELAND ROCKERS

Player	G	Min	FGM	FGA	Pct	FTM	FTA	Pct	REBOUNDS			Ast	PF	Dq	Stl	TO	Blk	SCORING		
									Off	Def	Tot							Pts	Avg	Hi
Merlakia Jones	3	103	15	32	.469	5	5	1.000	8	10	18	9	5	0	1	3	1	36	12.0	19
Ann Wauters	3	86	13	19	.684	8	9	.889	6	4	10	2	10	0	2	4	3	34	11.3	12
Rushia Brown	3	62	10	15	.667	5	6	.833	2	6	8	5	9	0	4	3	2	25	8.3	14
Chasity Melvin	3	81	8	16	.500	8	11	.727	6	6	12	6	5	0	2	6	2	24	8.0	11
Penny Taylor	3	59	8	25	.320	3	4	.750	2	7	9	3	4	0	6	5	1	21	7.0	10
Helen Darling	3	80	5	27	.185	5	6	.833	5	6	11	19	9	0	7	5	1	18	6.0	12
Mery Andrade	3	72	6	17	.353	0	0	—	5	4	9	1	9	0	2	7	2	13	4.3	7
Jennifer Rizzotti	3	45	2	6	.333	0	0	—	0	3	3	7	2	0	0	0	0	6	2.0	3
Paige Sauer	1	4	1	3	.333	0	0	—	0	1	1	0	0	0	0	1	0	2	2.0	2
Tricia Bader Binford	1	4	0	2	.000	0	0	—	1	0	1	0	0	0	0	0	0	0	0.0	0
P Johns Kimbrough	1	4	0	0	—	0	0	—	1	1	2	1	1	0	1	1	0	0	0.0	0
Cleveland	3	600	68	162	.420	34	41	.829	36	48	84	53	54	0	24	35	12	179	59.7	69
Opponents	3	600	67	159	.421	26	36	.722	30	49	79	44	50	0	17	39	9	176	58.7	72

3-pt. FG: Cleveland 9-33 (.273) Jones 1-3 (.333); Taylor 2-11 (.182); Darling 3-9 (.333); Andrade 1-2 (.500); Rizzotti 2-6 (.333); Bader Binford 0-2 (.000) Opponents 16-40 (.400)

HOUSTON COMETS

Player	G	Min	FGM	FGA	Pct	FTM	FTA	Pct	REBOUNDS			Ast	PF	Dq	Stl	TO	Blk	SCORING		
									Off	Def	Tot							Pts	Avg	Hi
Janeth Arcain	2	71	13	34	.382	2	2	1.000	2	9	11	5	5	0	2	5	0	29	14.5	18
Tina Thompson	2	68	11	20	.550	4	5	.800	4	8	12	7	5	0	1	10	0	29	14.5	16
Amanda Lassiter	2	54	7	16	.438	2	2	1.000	1	8	9	0	4	0	0	2	3	19	9.5	17
Tiffani Johnson	2	71	7	17	.412	4	7	.571	4	13	17	3	5	0	0	4	3	18	9.0	13
Tammy Jackson	1	15	0	3	.000	4	6	.667	2	1	3	0	4	0	1	1	1	4	4.0	4
Kelley Gibson	2	23	3	7	.429	0	0	—	0	3	3	0	1	0	1	2	0	7	3.5	5
Coquese Washington	2	74	3	17	.176	0	0	—	2	7	9	5	5	0	2	2	0	7	3.5	7
Trisha Stafford-Odom	2	16	1	5	.200	2	4	.500	2	1	3	1	3	0	2	0	2	4	2.0	4
Nekeshia Henderson	1	1	0	0	—	0	0	—	0	0	0	0	0	0	0	0	0	0	0.0	0
Tynesha Lewis	2	6	0	1	.000	0	0	—	0	0	0	2	1	0	0	0	0	0	0.0	0
Elena Shakirova	1	1	0	0	—	0	0	—	0	0	0	0	0	0	0	0	0	0	0.0	0
Houston	2	400	45	120	.375	18	26	.692	17	50	67	23	33	0	9	26	9	117	58.5	59
Opponents	2	400	50	125	.400	26	34	.765	21	54	75	33	28	0	15	20	10	134	67.0	70

3-pt. FG: Houston 9-36 (.250) Arcain 1-8 (.125); Thompson 3-5 (.600); Lassiter 3-9 (.333); Jackson 0-1 (.000); Gibson 1-3 (.333); Washington 1-10 (.100) Opponents 8-31 (.258)

LOS ANGELES SPARKS

Player	G	Min	FGM	FGA	Pct	FTM	FTA	Pct	Off	Def	Tot	Ast	PF	Dq	Stl	TO	Blk	Pts	Avg	Hi
Lisa Leslie.................7		260	58	118	.492	37	50	.740	28	58	86	21	22	0	12	26	31	156	22.3	35
Tamecka Dixon 7		253	40	83	.482	9	11	.818	5	12	17	29	14	0	9	20	2	95	13.6	19
DeLisha Milton.............7		226	35	64	.547	13	19	.684	12	32	44	20	22	0	7	11	10	86	12.3	19
Mwadi Mabika.............7		231	21	66	.318	11	14	.786	6	40	46	17	21	0	7	10	6	63	9.0	15
Ukari Figgs.................7		239	18	53	.340	12	16	.750	3	12	15	41	14	0	4	6	4	58	8.3	12
Latasha Byears 7		102	18	36	.500	9	14	.643	15	13	28	2	16	0	3	5	4	45	6.4	9
Rhonda Mapp 5		27	3	9	.333	0	0	—	1	6	7	3	5	0	0	2	0	6	1.2	4
Vedrana Grgin Fonsec ..4		7	1	3	.333	2	2	1.000	0	1	1	0	0	0	0	0	0	4	1.0	4
Nicky McCrimmon.......7		41	1	2	.500	2	4	.500	0	4	4	6	5	0	5	4	0	5	0.7	3
Nicole Levandusky........3		5	0	3	.000	0	0	—	0	0	0	0	0	0	0	0	0	0	0.0	0
Wendi Willits 4		9	0	2	.000	0	0	—	1	0	1	1	0	0	0	1	0	0	0.0	0
Los Angeles 7		1400	195	439	.444	95	130	.731	71	178	249	140	119	0	47	86	57	518	74.0	93
Opponents 7		1400	172	446	.386	68	90	.756	58	142	200	107	126	0	41	87	34	452	64.6	80

3-pt. FG: Los Angeles 33-110 (.300) Leslie 3-7 (.429); Dixon 6-13 (.462); Milton 3-8 (.375); Mabika 10-40 (.250); Figgs 10-36 (.278); Grgin Fonseca 0-1 (.000) McCrimmon 1-1 (1.000); Levandusky 0-2 (.000); Willits 0-2 (.000); Opponents 40-121 (.331)

MIAMI SOL

Player	G	Min	FGM	FGA	Pct	FTM	FTA	Pct	Off	Def	Tot	Ast	PF	Dq	Stl	TO	Blk	Pts	Avg	Hi
Elena Baranova 3		105	15	33	.455	8	11	.727	7	11	18	7	9	0	2	9	2	44	14.7	18
Sandy Brondello...........3		107	13	36	.361	5	6	.833	1	9	10	7	5	0	2	3	0	34	11.3	18
Sheri Sam.....................3		109	10	31	.323	9	11	.818	4	6	10	4	11	1	5	8	0	31	10.3	17
Ruth Riley 3		110	8	19	.421	8	19	.421	5	11	16	3	12	0	1	3	4	24	8.0	12
Debbie Black 3		95	7	18	.389	0	0	—	7	9	16	11	7	0	5	4	1	14	4.7	6
Tracy Reid 3		21	2	5	.400	0	4	.000	1	4	5	1	1	0	1	2	0	4	1.3	2
Marla Brumfield 2		4	1	2	.500	0	0	—	0	0	0	0	0	0	1	0	0	2	1.0	2
Katrina Colleton 2		3	0	0	—	2	2	1.000	1	0	1	0	1	0	0	0	0	2	1.0	2
Levys Torres 2		3	0	0	—	2	2	1.000	0	2	2	0	0	0	0	1	0	2	1.0	2
Kisha Ford 3		20	1	5	.200	0	0	—	1	0	1	2	3	0	0	1	0	2	0.7	2
Kristen Rasmussen 3		23	0	5	.000	1	2	.500	3	3	6	0	1	0	1	6	0	1	0.3	1
Miami 3		600	57	154	.370	35	57	.614	30	55	85	35	50	1	18	38	7	160	53.3	61
Opponents 3		600	72	167	.431	28	45	.622	33	64	97	47	54	1	19	36	6	184	61.3	72

3-pt. FG: Miami 11-34 (.324) Baranova 6-11 (.545); Brondello 3-10 (.300); Sam 2-9 (.222); Black 0-3 (.000); Brumfield 0-1 (.000); Opponents 12-37 (.324)

NEW YORK LIBERTY

Player	G	Min	FGM	FGA	Pct	FTM	FTA	Pct	Off	Def	Tot	Ast	PF	Dq	Stl	TO	Blk	Pts	Avg	Hi
Vickie Johnson 6		218	34	75	.453	15	15	1.000	7	20	27	28	11	0	13	14	2	89	14.8	22
Crystal Robinson 6		223	27	54	.500	3	4	.750	7	16	23	8	15	0	8	14	2	69	11.5	16
Tari Phillips 6		202	26	62	.419	16	34	.471	15	34	49	10	17	1	9	17	6	68	11.3	16
Tamika Whitmore.........6		152	18	44	.409	6	10	.600	10	12	22	4	13	0	4	7	4	42	7.0	12
Sue Wicks 6		118	12	27	.444	4	5	.800	10	10	20	5	17	0	2	8	6	28	4.7	9
Teresa Weatherspoon 6		198	8	38	.211	4	4	1.000	7	15	22	28	16	0	7	5	0	23	3.8	10
Becky Hammon 6		48	6	17	.353	0	0	—	0	3	3	2	3	0	1	3	0	15	2.5	6
Andrea Nagy 4		30	3	4	.750	2	3	.667	0	4	4	3	2	0	0	3	1	8	2.0	3
Camille Cooper 3		8	0	2	.000	0	0	—	0	1	1	0	2	0	0	0	0	0	0.0	0
Grace Daley.................1		1	0	0	—	0	0	—	0	0	0	0	0	0	0	1	0	0	0.0	0
Katarina Lazic 2		2	0	0	—	0	0	—	0	1	1	0	0	0	0	1	0	0	0.0	0
New York......................6		1200	134	323	.415	50	75	.667	56	116	172	88	96	1	44	76	21	342	57.0	72
Opponents 6		1200	116	302	.384	67	94	.713	52	115	167	74	100	1	39	83	18	327	54.5	62

3-pt. FG: New York 24-74 (.324) Johnson 6-22 (.273); Robinson 12-29 (.414); Phillips 0-1 (.000); Whitmore 0-1 (.000); Weatherspoon 3-11 (.273); Hammon 3-10 (.300) Opponents 28-72 (.389)

SACRAMENTO MONARCHS

Player	G	Min	FGM	FGA	Pct	FTM	FTA	Pct	REBOUNDS Off	Def	Tot	Ast	PF	Dq	Stl	TO	Blk	SCORING Pts	Avg	Hi
Yolanda Griffith 5		181	32	67	.478	42	55	.764	18	26	44	7	18	0	8	11	6	106	21.2	30
Kedra Holland-Corn 5		160	21	48	.438	14	16	.875	2	16	18	7	10	0	8	7	2	69	13.8	17
Ruthie Bolton 5		121	17	44	.386	12	13	.923	10	12	22	9	11	0	4	10	0	55	11.0	17
Tangela Smith...............5		164	23	60	.383	9	11	.818	8	16	24	8	16	0	5	4	5	55	11.0	17
Ticha Penicheiro 5		163	10	40	.250	4	4	1.000	3	16	19	33	9	0	3	9	4	31	6.2	19
Edna Campbell.............5		115	11	31	.355	2	3	.667	4	7	11	11	9	0	5	5	1	28	5.6	15
Cindy Blodgett 2		7	2	4	.500	1	2	.500	0	2	2	1	1	0	0	1	0	6	3.0	4
Kara Wolters.................4		37	5	14	.357	0	0	—	1	3	4	1	10	0	2	1	2	10	2.5	6
Lady Grooms 5		31	2	7	.286	5	6	.833	1	3	4	1	3	0	0	3	0	9	1.8	7
Dana Wynne 2		3	1	1	1.000	0	0	—	0	0	0	0	0	0	0	0	0	2	1.0	2
La'Keshia Frett 5		18	1	8	.125	2	2	1.000	2	0	2	1	2	0	0	1	0	4	0.8	4
Sacramento 5		1000	125	324	.386	91	112	.813	49	101	150	79	89	0	35	53	20	375	75.0	89
Opponents 5		1000	134	307	.436	70	97	.722	50	126	176	89	103	2	33	75	44	358	71.6	93

3-pt. FG: Sacramento 34-80 (.425) Holland-Corn 13-27 (.481); Bolton 9-23 (.391); Penicheiro 7-19 (.368); Campbell 4-9 (.444); Blodgett 1-2 (.500) Opponents 20-72 (.278)

UTAH STARZZ

Player	G	Min	FGM	FGA	Pct	FTM	FTA	Pct	REBOUNDS Off	Def	Tot	Ast	PF	Dq	Stl	TO	Blk	SCORING Pts	Avg	Hi
Adrienne Goodson........2		71	13	29	.448	5	9	.556	6	10	16	3	7	0	3	4	2	31	15.5	18
Marie Ferdinand...........2		69	7	16	.438	15	18	.833	2	6	8	7	4	0	3	2	0	29	14.5	15
Margo Dydek 2		69	9	21	.429	10	13	.769	1	13	14	3	10	1	1	4	7	28	14.0	15
Natalie Williams 2		57	8	16	.500	5	6	.833	7	9	16	0	10	1	3	5	1	21	10.5	17
Jennifer Azzi.................2		75	3	12	.250	1	1	1.000	0	3	3	10	7	0	1	5	1	9	4.5	8
Cara Consuegra 1		2	1	1	1.000	1	1	1.000	0	1	1	0	0	0	1	1	0	3	3.0	3
Korie Hlede 2		17	2	5	.400	0	0	—	1	2	3	1	1	0	1	3	0	4	2.0	2
LaTonya Johnson 2		15	1	4	.250	2	2	1.000	0	1	1	0	4	0	0	3	1	4	2.0	4
Amy Herrig 2		21	1	5	.200	0	0	—	1	1	2	1	4	0	0	1	1	2	1.0	2
Michaela Pavlickova 1		2	0	0	—	0	0	—	0	0	0	0	0	0	0	0	0	0	0.0	0
Kate Starbird.................1		2	0	1	.000	0	0	—	0	0	0	0	0	0	0	0	0	0	0.0	0
Utah..............................2		400	45	110	.409	39	50	.780	18	46	64	25	47	2	13	30	13	131	65.5	66
Opponents 2		400	49	120	.408	53	65	.815	23	46	69	24	39	0	14	20	6	160	80.0	89

3-pt. FG: Utah 2-19 (.105) Goodson 0-4 (.000); Ferdinand 0-2 (.000); Azzi 2-7 (.286); Hlede 0-2 (.000); Johnson 0-3 (.000); Starbird 0-1 (.000) Opponents 9-20 (.450)

(*) Statistics with this team only

(†) Totals with all teams

(‡) Continued season with another team

INDIVIDUAL FINALS STATISTICS, TEAM BY TEAM

CHARLOTTE STING

Player	G	Min	FGM	FGA	Pct	FTM	FTA	Pct	REBOUNDS Off	Def	Tot	Ast	PF	Dq	Stl	TO	Blk	SCORING Pts	Avg	Hi
Andrea Stinson.............2		69	11	29	.379	2	4	.500	1	8	9	7	7	0	2	4	1	24	12.0	18
Dawn Staley..................2		73	7	18	.389	4	5	.800	1	3	4	7	8	0	1	8	0	19	9.5	10
Allison Feaster 2		64	8	21	.381	0	0	—	1	7	8	6	3	0	6	3	3	18	9.0	11
Charlotte Smith 2		59	7	19	.368	1	2	.500	5	5	10	3	10	0	0	1	3	18	9.0	10
Tammy Sutton-Brown....2		37	5	13	.385	4	5	.800	3	3	6	1	5	0	0	2	4	14	7.0	12
Clarisse Machanguana ..2		34	6	7	.857	0	0	—	0	3	3	0	3	0	0	1	0	12	6.0	10
Tonya Edwards.............2		28	3	6	.500	1	1	1.000	3	5	8	4	2	0	2	3	0	7	3.5	5
Summer Erb 2		9	3	4	.750	0	0	—	1	1	2	0	2	0	0	3	0	6	3.0	6
Shalonda Enis...............2		21	1	2	.500	0	0	—	0	2	2	1	3	0	0	1	0	2	1.0	2

| | | | | | | | | REBOUNDS | | | | | | | | | SCORING | | |
Player	G	Min	FGM	FGA	Pct	FTM	FTA	Pct	Off	Def	Tot	Ast	PF	Dq	Stl	TO	Blk	Pts	Avg	Hi
Keisha Anderson 1		3	0	1	.000	0	0	—	0	0	0	0	0	0	0	1	0	0	0.0	0
Kelly Miller 1		3	0	2	.000	0	0	—	0	0	0	0	0	0	0	0	0	0	0.0	0
Charlotte 2		400	51	122	.418	12	17	.706	15	37	52	29	43	0	11	28	11	120	60.0	66
Opponents 2		400	56	117	.479	38	49	.776	18	44	62	43	35	0	12	21	16	157	78.5	82

3-pt. FG: Charlotte 6-25 (.240) Stinson 0-1 (.000); Staley 1-4 (.250); Feaster 2-9 (.222); Smith 3-10 (.300); Anderson 0-1 (.000); Opponents 7-26 (.269)

LOS ANGELES SPARKS

| | | | | | | | | REBOUNDS | | | | | | | | | SCORING | | |
Player	G	Min	FGM	FGA	Pct	FTM	FTA	Pct	Off	Def	Tot	Ast	PF	Dq	Stl	TO	Blk	Pts	Avg	Hi
Lisa Leslie......................2		76	16	35	.457	15	19	.789	6	15	21	10	5	0	2	7	9	48	24.0	24
DeLisha Milton..............2		69	13	18	.722	7	10	.700	6	10	16	8	7	0	3	3	2	34	17.0	19
Tamecka Dixon 2		71	10	22	.455	4	4	1.000	0	2	2	10	6	0	2	5	2	25	12.5	13
Latasha Byears 2		23	7	12	.583	3	4	.750	3	0	3	1	2	0	0	1	2	17	8.5	9
Ukari Figgs 2		67	5	10	.500	2	4	.500	1	5	6	6	6	0	1	0	0	14	7.0	9
Mwadi Mabika...............2		59	3	15	.200	6	6	1.000	1	9	10	5	6	0	2	4	1	14	7.0	12
Rhonda Mapp 1		11	2	4	.500	0	0	—	1	1	2	0	2	0	0	0	0	4	4.0	4
Nicky McCrimmon.......2		16	0	0	—	1	2	.500	0	1	1	2	1	0	2	1	0	1	0.5	1
Vedrana Grgin Fonsec ..1		3	0	0	—	0	0	—	0	1	1	0	0	0	0	0	0	0	0.0	0
Nicole Levandusky.......1		2	0	1	.000	0	0	—	0	0	0	0	0	0	0	0	0	0	0.0	0
Wendi Willits 1		3	0	0	—	0	0	—	0	0	0	1	0	0	0	0	0	0	0.0	0
Los Angeles 2		400	56	117	.479	38	49	.776	18	44	62	43	35	0	12	21	16	157	78.5	82
Opponents 2		400	51	122	.418	12	17	.706	15	37	52	29	43	0	11	28	11	120	60.0	66

3-pt. FG: Los Angeles 7-26 (.269) Leslie 1-3 (.333); Milton 1-2 (.500); Dixon 1-3 (.333); Figgs 2-7 (.286); Mabika 2-10 (.200); Levandusky 0-1 (.000) Opponents 6-25 (.240)

(*) Statistics with this team only
(†) Totals with all teams
(‡) Continued season with another team

FINALS BOX SCORES
GAME 1
At Charlotte Coliseum, August 30, 2001

OFFICIALS: Melissa Barlow, Gary Zielinski, Michael Price. TIME OF GAME: 2:00. ATTENDANCE: 16,132

SCORE BY PERIODS	2	4	FINAL
Los Angeles	35	40	75
Charlotte	39	27	66

VISITORS: Los Angeles   Head Coach: Michael Cooper

No Player	MIN	FG	FGA	3P	3PA	FT	FTA	OR	DR	TOT	A	PF	ST	TO	TEC	PTS
8 DeLisha Milton 40		7	9	1	2	4	5	4	4	8	5	5	2	3	0	19
4 Mwadi Mabika 26		1	6	0	4	0	0	0	4	4	1	5	1	2	0	2
9 Lisa Leslie 39		9	16	0	0	6	9	1	7	8	4	2	1	4	0	24
21 Tamecka Dixon 34		5	12	0	0	2	2	0	1	1	3	4	0	3	0	12
5 Ukari Figgs 33		3	5	1	3	2	4	0	2	2	4	2	1	0	0	9
00 Latasha Byears 18		4	9	0	0	0	0	2	0	2	1	2	0	1	0	8
10 Nicky McCrimmon 10		0	0	0	0	1	2	0	1	1	1	1	2	0	0	1
51 Rhonda Mapp						Did not play.										
17 Vedrana Grgin Fonseca						Did not play.										
40 Nicole Levandusky						Did not play.										
20 Wendi Willits						Did not play.										
TOTALS 200		29	57	2	9	15	22	7	19	26	19	21	7	13	0	75

PERCENTAGES: ....50.9   22.268.2   TM REB: 9   TOT TO: 13 (19 PTS)

HOME: Charlotte   Head Coach: Anne Donovan

No Player	MIN	FG	FGA	3P	3PA	FT	FTA	OR	DR	TOT	A	PF	ST	TO	TEC	PTS
21 Allison Feaster................33		5	10	1	4	0	0	1	4	5	3	1	3	2	0	11
23 Charlotte Smith 31		3	8	3	6	1	2	0	2	2	1	5	0	0	0	10
55 Tammy Sutton-Brown 16		0	4	0	0	2	2	2	2	4	1	3	0	0	0	2

No Player	MIN	FG	FGA	3P	3PA	FT	FTA	OR	DR	TOT	A	PF	ST	TO	TEC	PTS
5 Dawn Staley	39	3	9	1	3	3	4	1	2	3	2	5	0	6	0	10
32 Andrea Stinson	35	8	17	0	1	2	4	1	3	4	5	4	2	3	0	18
33 Machanguana	22	5	6	0	0	0	0	0	3	3	0	1	0	0	0	10
13 Tonya Edwards	13	2	3	0	0	1	1	2	0	2	2	0	1	2	0	5
7 Shalonda Enis	9	0	0	0	0	0	0	0	1	1	1	2	0	0	0	0
3 Summer Erb	2	0	1	0	0	0	0	0	0	0	0	1	0	0	0	0
20 Keisha Anderson						Did not play.										
8 Kelly Miller						Did not play.										
TOTALS	200	26	58	5	14	9	13	7	17	24	15	22	6	14	0	66
PERCENTAGES:	44.8	35.7	69.2			TM REB: 12		TOT TO: 14 (15 PTS)								

BLOCKED SHOTS: Sparks: 6. Milton 1, Mabika 1, Leslie 2, Byears: 2. Sting: 5. Feaster 3, Smith 2.
TECHNICAL FOULS: None.

	ILL	PTO	FBP	PIP	2PT
LA	0	15	10	38	9
CHA	0	19	9	26	11

Flagrant Fouls: None.

GAME 2
At STAPLES Center, September 1, 2001

OFFICIALS: Patty Broderick, June Courteau, Bob Trammell. TIME OF GAME: 1:55. ATTENDANCE: 13,141

SCORE BY PERIODS	1	2	FINAL
Charlotte	30	24	54
Los Angeles	38	44	82

VISITORS: Charlotte   Head Coach: Anne Donovan

No Player	MIN	FG	FGA	3P	3PA	FT	FTA	OR	DR	TOT	A	PF	ST	TO	TEC	PTS
21 Allison Feaster	31	3	11	1	5	0	0	0	3	3	3	2	3	1	0	7
23 Charlotte Smith	28	4	11	0	4	0	0	5	3	8	2	5	0	1	0	8
55 Tammy Sutton-Brown	21	5	9	0	0	2	3	1	1	2	0	2	0	2	0	12
5 Dawn Staley	34	4	9	0	1	1	1	0	1	1	5	3	1	2	0	9
32 Andrea Stinson	34	3	12	0	0	0	0	0	5	5	2	3	0	1	0	6
13 Tonya Edwards	15	1	3	0	0	0	0	1	5	6	2	2	1	1	0	2
7 Shalonda Enis	12	1	2	0	0	0	0	0	1	1	0	1	0	1	0	2
33 Machanguana	12	1	1	0	0	0	0	0	0	0	2	0	1	0	0	2
3 Summer Erb	7	3	3	0	0	0	0	1	1	2	0	1	0	3	0	6
20 Keisha Anderson	3	0	1	0	1	0	0	0	0	0	0	0	0	1	0	0
8 Kelly Miller	3	0	2	0	0	0	0	0	0	0	0	0	0	0	0	0
TOTALS	200	25	64	1	11	3	4	8	20	28	14	21	5	14	0	54
PERCENTAGES:	39.1	9.1	75.0			TM REB: 8		TOT TO: 14 (17 PTS)								

HOME: Los Angeles   Head Coach: Michael Cooper

No Player	MIN	FG	FGA	3P	3PA	FT	FTA	OR	DR	TOT	A	PF	ST	TO	TEC	PTS
4 Mwadi Mabika	33	2	9	2	6	6	6	1	5	6	4	1	1	2	0	12
8 DeLisha Milton	29	6	9	0	0	3	5	2	6	8	3	2	1	0	0	15
9 Lisa Leslie	37	7	19	1	3	9	10	5	8	13	6	3	1	3	0	24
21 Tamecka Dixon	37	5	10	1	3	2	2	0	1	1	7	2	2	2	0	13
5 Ukari Figgs	34	2	5	1	4	0	0	1	3	4	2	4	0	0	0	5
51 Rhonda Mapp	11	2	4	0	0	0	0	1	1	2	0	2	0	0	0	4
10 Nicky McCrimmon	6	0	0	0	0	0	0	0	0	0	1	0	0	1	0	0
00 Latasha Byears	5	3	3	0	0	3	4	1	0	1	0	0	0	0	0	9
17 Grgin Fonseca	3	0	0	0	0	0	0	0	1	1	0	0	0	0	0	0
20 Wendi Willits	3	0	0	0	0	0	0	0	0	0	1	0	0	0	0	0
40 Nicole Levandusky	2	0	1	0	1	0	0	0	0	0	0	0	0	0	0	0
TOTALS	200	27	60	5	17	23	27	11	25	36	24	14	5	8	0	82
PERCENTAGES:	45.0	29.4	85.2													

TM REB: 5   TOT TO: 8 (8 PTS)

BLOCKED SHOTS: Sting: 6. Smith 1, Sutton-Brown 4, Stinson 1. Sparks: 10. Milton 1, Leslie 7, Dixon 2.
TECHNICAL FOULS: None.

	ILL	PTO	FBP	PIP	2PT
CHA	0	8	6	42	8
LA	0	17	21	32	10

Flagrant Fouls: None.

ALL-STAR GAME BOX SCORE

At TD Waterhouse Centre, July 16, 2001

OFFICIALS: Michael Price, Bonita Spence, Melissa Barlow. TIME OF GAME: 1:59. ATTENDANCE: 16,906

SCORE BY PERIODS	1	2	FINAL
West	40	40	80
East	30	42	72

VISITORS: West   Head Coach: Van Chancellor

No Player	MIN	FG	FGA	3P	3PA	FT	FTA	OR	DR	TOT	A	PF	ST	TO	TEC	PTS
6 Ruthie Bolton	20	3	8	0	3	0	0	0	4	4	3	2	6	1	0	6
7 Tina Thompson	19	2	12	0	2	0	0	1	2	3	0	5	3	3	0	4
33 Yolanda Griffith	18	7	8	0	0	3	4	3	4	7	0	2	2	2	0	17
21 Ticha Penicheiro	21	0	2	0	0	1	2	0	3	3	5	1	2	5	0	1
9 Janeth Arcain	20	2	7	1	2	2	2	1	0	1	0	0	0	2	0	7
9 Lisa Leslie	23	8	14	1	2	3	4	3	6	9	1	4	1	3	0	20
30 Katie Smith	20	1	5	0	3	0	0	0	2	2	0	1	1	1	0	2
10 Jackie Stiles	20	0	3	0	0	4	4	0	2	2	0	3	0	0	0	4
21 Tamecka Dixon	20	4	7	0	1	0	0	0	2	2	4	0	0	1	0	8
15 Lauren Jackson	19	4	9	2	4	1	1	2	1	3	1	3	3	1	0	11
24 Natalie Williams								Did not play.								
TOTALS	200	31	75	4	17	14	17	10	26	36	14	21	18	19	0	80
PERCENTAGES:		41.3	23.5	82.4												

TM REB: 12   TOT TO: 19 (14 PTS)

HOME: East   Head Coach: Richie Adubato

No Player	MIN	FG	FGA	3P	3PA	FT	FTA	OR	DR	TOT	A	PF	ST	TO	TEC	PTS
11 McWilliams-Franklin	26	4	7	0	0	2	4	2	2	4	1	3	2	1	0	10
55 Vickie Johnson	19	2	8	2	5	2	2	0	3	3	1	0	0	3	0	8
24 Tari Phillips	24	4	8	0	0	1	6	4	5	9	0	1	1	7	0	9
15 Nikki McCray	22	2	7	0	0	1	2	0	0	0	2	1	0	1	0	5
11 Weatherspoon	15	0	1	0	0	0	0	0	1	1	2	0	3	3	0	0
28 Elena Baranova	25	4	8	1	2	1	2	0	7	7	2	2	1	2	0	10
25 Merlakia Jones	18	4	8	0	1	4	6	1	5	6	1	3	1	1	0	12
32 Andrea Stinson	17	2	9	0	3	0	0	2	3	5	1	2	0	1	0	4
5 Dawn Staley	15	2	3	0	0	0	0	0	0	0	3	2	4	0	0	4
42 Nykesha Sales	10	4	8	1	3	1	2	0	1	1	0	1	0	1	0	10
23 Rita Williams	9	0	2	0	2	0	0	0	0	0	1	0	0	0	0	0
44 Chasity Melvin								Did not play.								
23 Chamique Holdsclaw								Did not play.								
TOTALS	200	28	69	4	16	12	24	9	27	36	14	15	12	21	0	72
PERCENTAGES:		40.6	25.0	50.0												

TM REB: 16   TOT TO: 21 (25 PTS)

BLOCKED SHOTS: West: 5. Griffith 1, Leslie 3, Smith 1. East: 5. McWilliams-Franklin 1, Baranova 4
TECHNICAL FOULS: None.

	ILL	PTO	FBP	PIP	2PT
West	0	25	6	50	18
East	0	14	18	34	14

FLAGRANT FOUL: None.

Holdsclaw was voted to the starting lineup but replaced due to injury
Melvin was named to the team but replaced due to injury

REVIEW 2001 Finals

2000 SEASON IN REVIEW

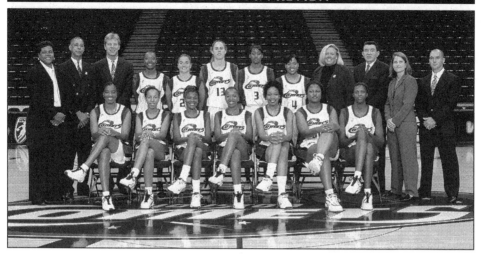

Front Row (l. to r.) - Tammy Jackson, Janeth Arcain, Sheryl Swoopes, Cynthia Cooper, Tina Thompson, Tiffani Johnson, Monica Lamb. Back Row (l. to r.) - Assistant Coach Alisa Scott, Video Coordinator Harold Liggans, Assistant Coach Kevin Cook, Nekeshia Henderson, Jennifer Rizzotti, Amaya Valdemoro, Kelley Gibson, Coquese Washington, Equipment Manager Jennie Vance, Head Coach & General Manager Van Chancellor, Trainer Michelle T. Leget, Strength & Conditioning Coach Anthony Falsone.

FINAL STANDINGS

EASTERN CONFERENCE

	CHA	CLE	DET	HOU	IND	LA	MIA	MIN	NY	ORL	PHO	POR	SAC	SEA	UTA	WAS	W	L	PCT	GB	Last-10	Streak
NY 3	2	1	1	3	0	2	1	--	2	1	1	0	1	1	1	20	12	.625	-	7-3	Lost 1
CLE....3	--	2	0	2	0	1	0	1	2	1	0	1	1	1	2	17	15	.531	3	4-6	Lost 2
ORL ..3	1	3	0	2	0	2	0	1	--	0	0	1	1	1	1	16	16	.500	4	2-8	Lost 1
DET ..2	1	--	0	3	0	2	0	2	0	0	0	1	2	1	0	14	18	.438	6	4-6	Won 2
WAS..1	1	3	0	2	0	2	0	2	2	0	0	0	1	0	--	14	18	.438	6	4-6	Won 1
MIA ..2	2	1	0	1	0	--	0	1	1	0	1	0	2	1	1	13	19	.406	7	5-5	Won 3
IND ..2	1	0	0	--	0	2	0	0	1	0	1	0	1	0	1	9	23	.281	11	3-7	Won 1
CHA..--	0	1	0	1	0	1	0	0	0	0	2	0	0	1	2	8	24	.250	12	3-7	Lost 2

WESTERN CONFERENCE

	CHA	CLE	DET	HOU	IND	LA	MIA	MIN	NY	ORL	PHO	POR	SAC	SEA	UTA	WAS	W	L	PCT	GB	Last-10	Streak
LA......1	1	2	3	1	--	1	3	2	1	3	2	2	2	2	2	28	4	.875	-	9-1	Lost 1
HOU 2	1	1	--	1	0	1	3	1	1	2	3	3	3	2	2	27	5	.844	1	8-2	Won 5
SAC ..1	0	1	0	1	1	1	3	1	1	2	3	--	3	1	2	21	11	.656	7	8-2	Won 1
PHO..1	1	1	1	2	0	1	2	1	1	--	3	1	3	1	1	20	12	.625	8	6-4	Won 1
UTA ..1	1	0	0	1	1	0	2	0	1	2	3	2	3	--	1	18	14	.563	10	6-4	Won 2
MIN ..1	2	1	0	1	0	2	--	0	2	1	2	0	1	1	1	15	17	.469	13	5-5	Lost 1
POR ..0	1	1	0	1	1	1	1	0	1	0	--	0	2	0	1	10	22	.313	18	3-7	Lost 4
SEA....1	0	0	0	1	1	0	2	0	0	0	1	0	--	0	0	6	26	.188	22	3-7	Lost 2

TEAM STANDINGS
OFFENSIVE

TEAM	G	FG	FGA	PCT	FG3	FG3A	PCT	FT	FTA	PCT	OFF	DEF	REB	AST	PF	DQ	STL	TO	BLK	PTS	AVG
Hou.	32	891	1894	.470	172	491	.350	521	634	.822	273	724	997	494	554	2	284	440	104	2475	77.3
L.A.	32	861	1956	.440	150	452	.332	545	693	.786	308	783	1091	586	704	13	271	466	156	2417	75.5
Utah	32	858	1896	.453	88	262	.336	609	790	.771	348	732	1080	522	698	6	214	544	157	2413	75.4
Sac.	32	876	1993	.440	142	459	.309	449	650	.691	388	650	1038	567	571	5	332	458	157	2343	73.2
Det.	32	868	1981	.438	76	273	.278	519	699	.742	341	644	985	503	701	4	260	530	88	2331	72.8
Phoe.	32	803	1800	.446	124	394	.315	513	661	.776	275	619	894	465	630	5	285	429	91	2243	70.1
Ind.	32	796	1838	.433	193	521	.370	428	569	.752	285	647	932	501	642	9	271	518	126	2213	69.2
Orl.	32	833	1911	.436	145	424	.342	397	546	.727	319	606	925	473	583	5	255	486	130	2208	69.0
Minn.	32	770	1831	.421	204	571	.357	449	592	.758	258	612	870	495	690	11	237	497	63	2193	68.5
Cha.	32	812	1903	.427	131	386	.339	431	577	.747	305	630	935	551	713	8	222	496	90	2186	68.3
Clev.	32	809	1828	.443	141	407	.346	426	570	.747	331	603	934	539	647	7	259	538	91	2185	68.3
Wash.	32	832	1813	.459	109	335	.325	403	578	.697	300	646	946	521	597	3	245	506	126	2176	68.0
Port.	32	761	1828	.416	145	433	.335	488	697	.700	309	627	936	480	761	11	265	593	93	2155	67.3
N.Y.	32	792	1815	.436	135	396	.341	429	567	.757	288	652	940	477	617	7	246	474	102	2148	67.1
Miami	32	647	1774	.365	85	310	.274	452	664	.681	365	595	960	415	707	5	272	524	88	1831	57.2
Sea.	32	667	1741	.383	109	364	.299	379	561	.676	256	537	793	390	648	4	255	525	93	1822	56.9

DEFENSIVE

Team	FG	FGA	PCT	FG3	FG3A	PCT	FT	FTA	PCT	OFF	DEF	REB	AST	PF	DQ	STL	TO	BLK	PTS	AVG	DIFF
Miami	.715	1676	.427	117	315	.371	454	627	.724	275	648	923	416	661	10	247	528	118	2001	62.5	-5.3
N.Y.	741	1822	.407	116	420	.276	437	590	.741	320	647	967	462	645	5	223	479	94	2035	63.6	+3.5
Hou.	786	1939	.405	124	418	.297	370	508	.728	290	612	902	473	648	3	233	480	85	2066	64.6	+12.8
Phoe.	773	1828	.423	135	416	.325	421	574	.733	334	635	969	486	698	8	224	531	91	2102	65.7	+4.4
Clev.	774	1761	.440	119	368	.323	455	583	.780	277	596	873	540	693	8	305	552	95	2122	66.3	+2.0
L.A.	776	1963	.395	122	413	.295	495	692	.715	300	678	978	445	650	12	243	485	105	2169	67.8	+7.8
Sea.	778	1721	.452	117	334	.350	498	654	.761	288	721	1009	506	618	9	284	529	123	2171	67.8	-10.9
Sac.	811	1918	.423	144	418	.344	410	544	.754	320	631	951	503	600	2	226	524	116	2176	68.0	+5.2
Minn.	755	1758	.429	164	481	.341	514	702	.732	300	677	977	472	707	8	275	547	130	2188	68.4	+0.2
Wash.	845	1875	.451	149	397	.375	382	555	.688	299	612	911	513	595	4	261	456	102	2221	69.4	-1.4
Orl.	851	1964	.433	153	450	.340	378	495	.764	348	669	1017	536	637	2	264	500	108	2233	69.8	-0.8
Ind.	839	1868	.449	109	358	.304	503	669	.752	321	633	954	528	612	5	267	476	75	2290	71.6	-2.4
Port.	788	1847	.427	150	447	.336	577	766	.753	307	646	953	487	729	8	277	531	130	2303	72.0	-4.6
Utah	860	1964	.438	156	448	.348	531	721	.736	313	598	911	503	702	11	301	437	112	2407	75.2	+0.2
Det.	905	1968	.460	136	372	.366	480	652	.736	331	640	971	513	672	9	284	543	148	2426	75.8	-3.0
Cha.	879	1930	.455	138	423	.326	533	716	.744	326	640	990	596	596	1	259	426	123	2429	75.9	-7.6
Avg.	805	1863	.432	134	405	.332	465	628	.740	309	644	954	499	654	7	261	502	110	2209	69.0	---
12876				2149			7438			4949	15256		10463	4173		1755					
29802				6478			10048			10307		7979		105		8024		35339			

TEAM COMPARISONS

TEAM	Points Per Game		Field Goal Percentage		Turnovers Per Game		Rebound Percentages			Below 70 Pts.		Overtime Games		3 PTS or Less		10 PTS or More	
	OWN	OPP	OWN	OPP	OWN	OPP	OFF	DEF	TOT	OWN	OPP	W	L	W	L	W	L
Charlotte	68.3	75.9	.427	.455	15.5	13.3	.315	.659	.487	17	8	2	1	3	5	1	14
Cleveland	66.3	66.3	.443	.440	16.8	17.3*	.357	.685	.521	16	18	3	1	4	2	11	10
Detroit	72.8	75.8	.438	.460	16.6	17.0	.348	.661	.504	15	9	0	1	4	2	5	12
Houston	77.3*	64.6	.470*	.405	13.8	15.0	.308	.714	.511	5	23	2	0	2	0	22	2
Indiana	69.2	71.6	.433	.449	16.2	14.9	.310	.668	.489	15	13	0	1	1	3	8	9
Los Angeles	75.5	67.8	.440	.395*	14.6	15.2	.312	.723*	.511	7	20	1	1	3	1	12	2
Miami	57.2	62.5*	.365	.427	16.4	16.5	.360	.684	.522	28	24	2	0	3	2	7	13
Minnesota	68.5	68.4	.421	.429	15.5	17.1	.276	.671	.473	18	17	1	0	2	1	8	9
New York	67.1	63.6	.436	.407	14.8	15.0	.308	.671	.489	20	23	0	1	1	4	12	6
Orlando	69.0	69.8	.436	.433	15.2	15.6	.323	.635	.479	20	15	0	3	4	3	6	7
Phoenix	70.1	65.7	.446	.423	13.4*	16.6	.302	.650	.476	19	21	1	0	3	3	12	6
Portland	67.3	72.0	.416	.427	18.5	16.6	.324	.671	.497	18	14	0	4	1	4	5	9
Sacramento	73.2	68.0	.440	.423	14.3	16.4	.381*	.670	.525	10	17	0	0	3	1	13	4
Seattle	56.9	67.8	.383	.452	16.4	16.5	.262	.651	.456	31	20	2	1	0	2	1	18
Utah	75.4	75.2	.453	.438	17.0	13.7	.368	.700	.534*	9	11	0	0	5	3	6	8
Washington	68.0	69.4	.459	.451	15.8	14.3	.329	.684	.506	18	13	0	0	2	5	8	6
COMPOSITE;256 games																	
	69.0		.432		15.7		.324	.676		266	14			41		137	

* - League Leader

REBOUND PERCENTAGES — OFF. - Percentage of a given team's missed shots which that team rebounds. DEF. - Percentage of opponents' missed shots which a given team rebounds. TOT. - Average of offensive and defensive rebound percentages.

SCORING AVERAGE

	G	FG	FT	PTS	AVG
Swoopes, Hou.	31	245	119	643	20.7
Smith, Min.	32	203	152	646	20.2
Reed, Pho.	32	231	128	608	19.0
Williams, Utah	29	179	182	543	18.7
Leslie, L.A.	32	197	169	570	17.8
Cooper, Hou.	31	180	147	550	17.7
Stinson, Cha.	32	214	99	565	17.7
Holdsclaw, Was.	32	232	87	561	17.5
Goodson, Utah	29	199	92	498	17.2
Lennox, Min.	32	201	84	541	16.9
Thompson, Hou.	32	191	103	540	16.9
Witherspoon, Por.	32	175	128	538	16.8
Griffith, Sac.	32	193	137	523	16.3
McCray, Was.	32	167	113	497	15.5
Palmer, Det.	32	167	95	441	13.8
Phillips, Por.-N.Y.	31	170	85	427	13.8
McWilliams-Franklin, Orl.	32	173	87	438	13.7
A. Johnson, Orl.	32	175	34	436	13.6
Sales, Orl.	32	170	43	430	13.4
Bolton-Holifield, Sac.	29	133	64	380	13.1

REBOUNDS PER GAME

	G	OFF	DEF	TOT	AVG
Williams, Utah	29	132	204	336	11.6
Griffith, Sac.	32	148	183	331	10.3
Leslie, L.A.	32	75	231	306	9.6
Phillips, Por.-N.Y.	31	86	161	247	8.0
Thompson, Hou.	32	68	177	245	7.7
McWilliams-Franklin, Orl.	32	90	154	244	7.6
Holdsclaw, Was.	32	57	183	240	7.5
Askamp, Mia.	32	96	135	231	7.2
Palmer, Det.	32	67	152	219	6.8
Mapp, Cha.	30	60	145	205	6.8
Page, Was.	32	79	129	208	6.5
Swoopes, Hou.	31	40	155	195	6.3
Milton, L.A.	32	55	139	194	6.1
Crawley, Por.	31	64	121	185	6.0
Ndiaye-Diatta, Det.	32	65	122	187	5.8
Reed, Pho.	32	59	128	187	5.8
Bullett, Was.	32	61	122	183	5.7
Goodson, Utah	29	69	95	164	5.7
Mabika, L.A.	32	45	134	179	5.6
Lennox, Min.	32	53	125	178	5.6

ASSISTS PER GAME

	G	AST	AVG
Penicheiro, Sac.	30	236	7.9
Weatherspoon, N.Y.	32	205	6.4
Staley, Cha.	32	190	5.9
S. Johnson, Orl.	32	169	5.3
Nagy, Was.	23	118	5.1
Cooper, Hou.	31	156	5.0

Figgs, L.A.	32	127	4.0
Swoopes, Hou.	31	119	3.8
Stinson, Cha.	32	121	3.8
McConnell Serio, Cle.	32	119	3.7
Cleary, Pho.	24	77	3.2
Thomas, Por.	32	101	3.2
R. Williams, Ind.	32	101	3.2
Dixon, L.A.	31	96	3.1
Black, Mia.	32	98	3.1
Mabika, L.A.	32	98	3.1
Hlede, Utah	31	92	3.0
Canty, Det.	28	82	2.9
Smith, Min.	32	90	2.8
Bevilaqua, Por.	32	89	2.8

FIELD GOAL PCT.

	FG	FGA	PCT
Page, Was.	131	222	.590
Wolters, Ind.	148	264	.561
Griffith, Sac.	193	361	.535
McWilliams-Franklin, Orl.	173	330	.524
Thompson, Ind.	131	255	.514
Milton, L.A.	150	293	.512
Reed, Pho.	231	456	.507
Tornikidou, Det.	122	241	.506
Swoopes, Hou.	245	484	.506
Brown, Cle.	93	187	.497

3-PT FIELD GOAL PCT.

	3FG	3GA	PCT
Hlede, Utah	25	58	.431
Thompson, Hou.	55	132	.417
Nemcova, Cle.	29	71	.408
Maxwell, Ind.	62	156	.397
Lennox, Min.	55	139	.396
Sales, Orl.	47	119	.395
McConnell Serio, Cle	38	97	.392
McCarty, Ind.	27	70	.386
Mabika, L.A.	61	159	.384
Johnson, N.Y.	27	71	.380

FREE THROW PCT.

	FT	FTA	PCT
Azzi, Utah	40	43	.930
Tornikidou, Det.	85	93	.914
Reed, Pho.	128	142	.901
Hammon, N.Y.	61	69	.884
Johnson, N.Y.	67	76	.882
Staley, Cha.	65	74	.878
Cooper, Hou.	147	168	.875
Witherspoon, Por.	128	147	.871
Smith, Min.	152	175	.869
Maxwell, Ind.	50	58	.862

REVIEW 2000 Regular Season

STEALS PER GAME

	G	STL	AVG
Swoopes, Hou.	31	87	2.81
Griffith, Sac.	32	83	2.59
R. Williams, Ind.	32	76	2.38
Penicheiro, Sac.	30	70	2.33
Reed, Pho.	32	66	2.06
Weatherspoon, N.Y.	32	65	2.03
Bullett, Was.	32	64	2.00
Henning, Sea.	32	61	1.91
Phillips, Por.-N.Y.	31	59	1.90
McWilliams-Franklin, Orl.	32	59	1.84

BLOCKS PER GAME

	G	BLK	AVG
Dydek, Utah	32	96	3.00
Leslie, L.A.	32	74	2.31
Smith, Sac.	32	64	2.00
dos Santos, Orl.	32	63	1.97

	G		AVG
Griffith, Sac.	32	61	1.91
Wolters, Ind.	31	49	1.58
Bullett, Was.	32	47	1.47
Wicks, N.Y.	32	39	1.22
Barnes, Sea.	31	33	1.06
Swoopes, Hou.	31	33	1.06

MINUTES PER GAME

	G	MIN	AVG
Smith, Min.	32	1193	37.3
Azzi, Utah	15	559	37.3
Williams, Utah	29	1039	35.8
Holdsclaw, Was.	32	1131	35.3
S. Johnson, Orl.	32	1126	35.2
Swoopes, Hou.	31	1090	35.2
Stinson, Cha.	32	1123	35.1
Cooper, Hou.	31	1085	35.0
A. Johnson, Orl.	32	1100	34.4
Staley, Cha.	32	1099	34.3

INDIVIDUAL STATISTICS, TEAM BY TEAM

CHARLOTTE STING

Player	G	Min	FGM	FGA	Pct	FTM	FTA	Pct	Off	Def	Tot	Ast	PF	Dq	Stl	TO	Blk	Pts	Avg	Hi
Andrea Stinson	32	1123	214	463	.462	99	134	.739	35	101	136	121	77	0	55	86	23	565	17.7	33
Rhonda Mapp	30	856	138	300	.460	73	88	.830	60	145	205	64	112	3	30	59	24	357	11.9	25
Shalonda Enis	12	323	41	104	.394	46	60	.767	21	24	45	10	30	0	10	16	1	139	11.6	20
Dawn Staley	32	1099	94	253	.372	65	74	.878	21	56	77	190	80	1	37	91	1	282	8.8	19
Tracy Reid	29	620	86	180	.478	39	72	.542	45	55	100	29	47	1	14	51	9	211	7.3	21
Tiffany Travis	32	574	70	158	.443	21	28	.750	24	57	81	26	74	0	31	32	4	173	5.4	16
Charlotte Smith	30	659	56	159	.352	20	25	.800	29	77	106	55	88	2	15	48	17	156	5.2	17
Niesa Johnson	6	78	9	17	.529	6	6	1.000	0	4	4	11	3	0	4	9	0	26	4.3	10
Summer Erb	29	275	32	73	.438	28	43	.651	26	37	63	10	68	0	8	17	6	92	3.2	21
Cass Bauer	29	398	29	72	.403	18	21	.857	20	36	56	14	72	1	8	28	3	76	2.6	9
Angie Braziel	22	203	19	49	.388	13	19	.684	16	18	34	5	24	0	5	17	0	51	2.3	10
Larecha Jones	9	54	8	19	.421	1	2	.500	0	5	5	2	5	0	0	4	1	19	2.1	8
E.C. Hill	26	213	16	56	.286	2	5	.400	8	15	23	14	33	0	5	25	1	39	1.5	8
Charlotte	32	6475	812	1903	.427	431	577	.747	305	630	935	551	713	8	222	496	90	2186	68.3	87
Opponents	32	6475	879	1930	.455	533	716	.744	326	664	990	596	596	1	259	426	123	2429	75.9	96

3-pt. FG: Charlotte 131-386 (.339) Stinson 38-106 (.358); Mapp 8-22 (.364); Enis 11-32 (.344); Staley 29-88 (.330); Reid 0-2 (.000); Travis 12-25 (.480) Smith 24-76 (.316); Johnson 2-5 (.400); Erb 0-1 (.000); Bauer 0-1 (.000); Jones 2-6 (.333); Hill 5-22 (.227) Opponents 138-423 (.326)

CLEVELAND ROCKERS

Player	G	Min	FGM	FGA	Pct	FTM	FTA	Pct	Off	Def	Tot	Ast	PF	Dq	Stl	TO	Blk	Pts	Avg	Hi
Eva Nemcova	14	443	67	164	.409	22	24	.917	9	32	41	23	29	0	15	27	8	185	13.2	23
Chasity Melvin	32	904	136	289	.471	100	137	.730	69	103	172	61	113	4	29	62	18	373	11.7	28
Merlakia Jones	32	948	153	323	.474	32	47	.681	52	87	139	63	86	2	29	60	2	352	11.0	21
Rushia Brown	30	679	93	187	.497	66	78	.846	54	70	124	44	81	0	38	59	13	253	8.4	24
Mery Andrade	32	797	89	195	.456	60	80	.750	32	63	95	75	91	1	41	65	10	265	8.3	18
Ann Wauters	32	598	78	149	.523	43	58	.741	47	82	129	37	75	0	21	63	24	199	6.2	17
Suzie McConnell Seri..	32	705	58	140	.414	19	25	.760	9	41	50	119	30	0	15	69	1	173	5.4	12
Helen Darling	32	556	47	150	.313	48	65	.738	24	39	63	65	52	0	37	67	5	155	4.8	17
Vicki Hall	32	577	59	158	.373	22	34	.647	24	68	92	24	60	0	17	25	8	150	4.7	19
Michelle Edwards(‡)	3	17	4	10	.400	0	0	---	0	2	2	1	3	0	0	4	0	8	2.7	6
Tricia Bader Binford	25	201	17	48	.354	5	6	.833	2	9	11	21	16	0	17	18	1	47	1.9	8
Adia Barnes	5	18	3	5	.600	2	4	.500	2	0	2	4	2	0	0	2	0	8	1.6	7

| | | | REBOUNDS | | | | | | | | | | | | | | | | SCORING | |
Player	G	Min	FGM	FGA	Pct	FTM	FTA	Pct	Off	Def	Tot	Ast	PF	Dq	Stl	TO	Blk	Pts	Avg	Hi
P. Johns kimbrough 12	57	5	10	.500	7	12	.583	7	7	14	2	9	0	0	8	1	17	1.4	4
Cleveland................32	6500	809	1828	.443	426	570	.747	331	603	934	539	647	7	259	538	91	2185	68.3	83
Opponents 32	6500	774	1761	.440	455	583	.780	277	596	873	540	693	8	305	552	95	2122	66.3	93

3-pt. FG: Cleveland 141-407 (.346) Nemcova 29-71 (.408); Melvin 1-7 (.143); Jones 14-45 (.311); Brown 1-2 (.500); Andrade 27-75 (.360); Wauters 0-2 (.000) McConnell Serio 38-97 (.392); Darling 13-38 (.342); Hall 10-42 (.238); Edwards(‡) 0-3 (.000); Bader Binford 8-24 (.333) Barnes 0-1 (.000); Opponents 119-368 (.323)

DETROIT SHOCK

| | | | | | | REBOUNDS | | | | | | | | | | | | | SCORING | |
Player	G	Min	FGM	FGA	Pct	FTM	FTA	Pct	Off	Def	Tot	Ast	PF	Dq	Stl	TO	Blk	Pts	Avg	Hi
Wendy Palmer 32	914	167	374	.447	95	135	.704	67	152	219	39	112	2	20	65	10	441	13.8	32
Astou Ndiaye-Diatta....32	868	158	333	.474	29	51	.569	65	122	187	40	87	0	23	64	22	346	10.8	19
Elena Tornikidou 32	869	122	241	.506	85	93	.914	41	69	110	82	73	0	29	68	13	330	10.3	25
Dominique Canty........28	784	83	203	.409	91	131	.695	31	39	70	82	64	0	49	51	5	257	9.2	22
Tamicha Jackson 17	267	41	106	.387	26	35	.743	8	17	25	36	30	0	22	21	0	116	6.8	14
Claudia Maria das Ne 30	636	63	166	.380	25	30	.833	8	27	35	59	30	0	31	55	1	179	6.0	19
Edwina Brown 32	619	60	168	.357	67	80	.838	36	52	88	72	77	0	24	68	5	188	5.9	17
Anna DeForge 27	433	51	126	.405	25	32	.781	9	38	47	47	34	0	27	33	4	145	5.4	13
Oksana Zakaluzhnaya 23	258	38	73	.521	10	11	.909	15	31	46	2	45	0	5	19	13	89	3.9	15
Olympia Scott-Richar..28	369	37	89	.416	26	40	.650	28	52	80	28	83	2	12	45	10	100	3.6	16
Barbara Farris 14	130	15	30	.500	15	27	.556	16	16	32	2	30	0	6	14	1	45	3.2	9
Joy Holmes-Harris 29	271	33	70	.471	21	30	.700	17	28	45	14	36	0	11	16	4	91	3.1	11
Madinah Slaise.............3	7	0	2	.000	4	4	1.000	0	1	1	0	0	0	1	0	0	4	1.3	4
Detroit 32	6425	868	1981	.438	519	699	.742	341	644	985	503	701	4	260	530	88	2331	72.8	111
Opponents 32	6425	905	1968	.460	480	652	.736	331	640	971	513	672	9	284	543	148	2426	75.8	108

3-pt. FG: Detroit 76-273 (.278) Palmer 12-48 (.250); Ndiaye-Diatta 1-6 (.167); Tornikidou 1-8 (.125); Canty 0-5 (.000); Jackson 8-32 (.250); Brown 1-4 (.250) das Neves 28-92 (.304); DeForge 18-56 (.321); Zakaluzhnaya 3-7 (.429); Scott-Richardson 0-2 (.000); Farris 0-1 (.000) Holmes-Harris 4-11 (.364); Slaise 0-1 (.000); Opponents 136-372 (.366)

HOUSTON COMETS

| | | | | | | REBOUNDS | | | | | | | | | | | | | SCORING | |
Player	G	Min	FGM	FGA	Pct	FTM	FTA	Pct	Off	Def	Tot	Ast	PF	Dq	Stl	TO	Blk	Pts	Avg	Hi
Sheryl Swoopes 31	1090	245	484	.506	119	145	.821	40	155	195	119	67	0	87	82	33	643	20.7	31
Cynthia Cooper 31	1085	180	392	.459	147	168	.875	17	68	85	156	61	0	39	99	6	550	17.7	28
Tina Thompson 32	1087	191	407	.469	103	123	.837	68	177	245	48	88	0	47	84	25	540	16.9	28
Janeth Arcain 32	977	109	233	.468	41	49	.837	36	83	119	60	66	1	42	53	3	268	8.4	18
Tiffani Johnson 31	687	48	100	.480	35	50	.700	59	88	147	10	86	1	10	17	16	131	4.2	10
Elen Chakirova............14	150	13	30	.433	29	33	.879	14	17	31	4	12	0	5	7	2	57	4.1	11
Tammy Jackson 29	339	35	61	.574	6	11	.545	18	43	61	11	62	0	12	24	9	76	2.6	8
Amaya Valdemoro 22	171	20	60	.333	6	6	1.000	3	18	21	13	21	0	8	13	4	57	2.6	10
Monica Lamb..............13	140	10	20	.500	6	12	.500	5	21	26	3	23	0	2	4	4	26	2.0	5
Jennifer Rizzotti 32	437	21	55	.382	6	9	.667	6	30	36	44	38	0	15	26	2	60	1.9	10
Coquese Washington ...25	236	12	33	.364	16	20	.800	3	16	19	24	19	0	16	19	0	43	1.7	7
Jawann Kelley-Gibson 17	76	7	19	.368	7	8	.875	4	8	12	2	11	0	1	4	0	24	1.4	6
Houston 32	6475	891	1894	.470	521	634	.822	273	724	997	494	554	2	284	440	104	2475	77.3	107
Opponents 32	6475	786	1939	.405	370	508	.728	290	612	902	473	648	3	233	480	85	2066	64.6	90

3-pt. FG: Houston 172-491 (.350) Swoopes 34-91 (.374); Cooper 43-121 (.355); Thompson 55-132 (.417); Arcain 9-45 (.200); Chakirova 2-12 (.167) Valdemoro 11-29 (.379); Rizzotti 12-39 (.308); Washington 3-15 (.200); Kelley-Gibson 3-7 (.429); Opponents 124-418 (.297)

INDIANA FEVER

| | | | | | | REBOUNDS | | | | | | | | | | | | | SCORING | |
Player	G	Min	FGM	FGA	Pct	FTM	FTA	Pct	Off	Def	Tot	Ast	PF	Dq	Stl	TO	Blk	Pts	Avg	Hi
Kara Wolters...............31	793	148	264	.561	74	100	.740	46	118	164	39	99	2	12	73	49	370	11.9	24
Rita Williams 32	1014	112	274	.409	79	108	.731	22	73	95	101	69	1	76	69	3	352	11.0	21
Monica Maxwell 32	1029	110	285	.386	50	58	.862	40	120	160	63	92	0	49	64	16	332	10.4	29
Alicia Thompson 31	792	131	255	.514	30	42	.714	48	109	157	41	85	4	24	53	4	310	10.0	22
Gordana Grubin..........29	720	90	239	.377	31	40	.775	20	56	76	63	47	0	31	60	0	239	8.2	19
Stephanie McCarty 32	635	66	166	.398	71	86	.826	14	46	60	57	49	0	31	47	6	230	7.2	20
Danielle McCulley 29	456	63	153	.412	46	63	.730	45	37	82	19	63	1	16	37	22	175	6.0	17
Jurgita Streimikyte 27	424	46	117	.393	27	35	.771	25	46	71	44	67	1	16	32	23	121	4.5	15

Player	G	Min	FGM	FGA	Pct	FTM	FTA	Pct	Off	Def	Tot	Ast	PF	Dq	Stl	TO	Blk	Pts	Avg	Hi
Chantel Tremitiere 25		318	18	51	.353	10	16	.625	6	25	31	51	30	0	10	30	1	50	2.0	12
Katryna Gaither(*) 6		24	3	8	.375	0	0	---	1	2	3	1	2	0	0	1	1	6	1.0	4
Katryna Gaither(†) 15		78	5	15	.333	10	10	1.000	8	12	20	5	10	0	4	5	1	20	1.3	4
Donna Harrington 8		67	1	6	.167	6	10	.600	4	5	9	5	16	0	2	11	1	8	1.0	2
Alessandra Santos de 3		11	1	1	1.000	1	6	.167	0	3	3	0	3	0	0	2	0	3	1.0	2
Texlin Quinney............17		118	6	14	.429	3	5	.600	11	5	16	15	12	0	4	10	0	15	0.9	2
Usha Gilmore................4		21	1	5	.200	0	0	---	3	2	5	2	6	0	0	4	0	2	0.5	2
Beverly Williams 1		3	0	0	---	0	0	---	0	0	0	0	2	0	0	0	0	0	0.0	0
Indiana 32		6425	796	1838	.433	428	569	.752	285	647	932	501	642	9	271	518	126	2213	69.2	87
Opponents 32		6425	839	1868	.449	503	669	.752	321	633	954	528	612	5	267	476	75	2290	71.6	111

3-pt. FG: Indiana 193-521 (.370) R. Williams 49-131 (.374); Maxwell 62-156 (.397); Thompson 18-40 (.450); Grubin 28-91 (.308); McCarty 27-70 (.386) McCulley 3-17 (.176); Streimikyte 2-6 (.333); Tremitiere 4-9 (.444); Gilmore 0-1 (.000); Opponents 109-358 (.304)

LOS ANGELES SPARKS

Player	G	Min	FGM	FGA	Pct	FTM	FTA	Pct	Off	Def	Tot	Ast	PF	Dq	Stl	TO	Blk	Pts	Avg	Hi
Lisa Leslie....................32		1028	197	430	.458	169	205	.824	75	231	306	60	134	7	31	103	74	570	17.8	30
Mwadi Mabika............32		940	130	335	.388	73	89	.820	45	134	179	98	117	2	58	51	18	394	12.3	26
DeLisha Milton...........32		983	150	293	.512	76	102	.745	55	139	194	68	124	3	44	67	29	378	11.8	20
Tamecka Dixon 31		882	132	291	.454	62	77	.805	34	71	105	96	86	0	40	60	10	338	10.9	24
Ukari Figgs..................32		803	66	153	.431	54	65	.831	14	41	55	127	53	0	21	43	3	215	6.7	15
Allison Feaster 32		469	60	167	.359	60	72	.833	36	49	85	33	46	0	23	35	2	202	6.3	18
Clarisse Machanguana 31		421	48	83	.578	14	25	.560	20	52	72	18	66	1	13	19	4	110	3.5	10
Nicky McCrimmon......32		488	39	77	.506	7	14	.500	9	23	32	65	41	0	29	48	8	101	3.2	9
Vedrana Grgin Fonseca 18		183	17	62	.274	14	23	.609	9	14	23	12	17	0	3	14	1	49	2.7	8
Paige Sauer 12		66	8	14	.571	4	5	.800	3	13	16	3	10	0	2	6	1	20	1.7	7
La'Keshia Frett 25		187	14	51	.275	12	16	.750	8	16	24	6	10	0	7	13	6	40	1.6	6
Los Angeles 32		6450	861	1956	.440	545	693	.786	308	783	1091	586	704	13	271	466	156	2417	75.5	94
Opponents 32		6450	776	1963	.395	495	692	.715	300	678	978	445	650	12	243	485	105	2169	67.8	89

3-pt. FG: Los Angeles 150-452 (.332) Leslie 7-32 (.219); Mabika 61-159 (.384); Milton 2-8 (.250); Dixon 12-34 (.353); Figgs 29-82 (.354); Feaster 22-85 (.259) Machanguana 0-1 (.000); McCrimmon 16-33 (.485); Grgin Fonseca 1-17 (.059); Frett 0-1 (.000); Opponents 122-413 (.295)

MIAMI SOL

Player	G	Min	FGM	FGA	Pct	FTM	FTA	Pct	Off	Def	Tot	Ast	PF	Dq	Stl	TO	Blk	Pts	Avg	Hi
Sheri Sam 31		904	147	380	.387	67	100	.670	38	94	132	66	67	0	35	74	5	396	12.8	26
Katrina Colleton 32		873	103	293	.352	53	70	.757	15	48	63	50	65	0	27	65	7	264	8.3	19
Marlies Askamp 32		869	85	209	.407	80	117	.684	96	135	231	29	95	0	17	49	21	251	7.8	21
Kristen Rasmussen(*) ..25		454	35	100	.350	54	64	.844	44	52	96	27	47	0	24	29	14	126	5.0	17
Kristen Rasmussen(†) ..26		463	35	100	.350	54	64	.844	45	53	98	28	49	0	25	30	14	126	4.8	17
Debbie Black 32		820	57	150	.380	29	42	.690	23	69	92	98	86	0	58	50	1	152	4.8	13
Sharon Manning..........24		403	44	92	.478	14	26	.538	41	59	100	17	59	1	23	39	4	103	4.3	13
Shantia Owens............31		605	51	131	.389	29	54	.537	47	50	97	21	95	3	11	54	26	131	4.2	12
Kisha Ford 28		424	33	108	.306	37	63	.587	32	30	62	21	65	1	32	27	1	104	3.7	14
Milena Flores 32		474	34	112	.304	26	42	.619	6	17	23	49	36	0	23	48	3	112	3.5	10
Jamie Cassidy..............22		175	20	55	.364	30	43	.698	7	16	23	9	17	0	5	13	2	74	3.4	13
Umeki Webb 13		195	10	40	.250	21	25	.840	3	11	14	14	29	0	7	23	4	43	3.3	10
Jameka Jones 21		233	25	95	.263	11	16	.688	10	12	22	10	40	0	8	25	0	68	3.2	10
Tanja Kostic 5		46	3	9	.333	1	2	.500	3	2	5	4	6	0	2	7	0	7	1.4	4
Miami 32		6475	647	1774	.365	452	664	.681	365	595	960	415	707	5	272	524	88	1831	57.2	76
Opponents 32		6475	715	1676	.427	454	627	.724	275	648	923	416	661	10	247	528	118	2001	62.5	80

3-pt. FG: Miami 85-310 (.274) Sam 35-120 (.292); Colleton 5-21 (.238); Askamp 1-2 (.500); Rasmussen(*) 2-7 (.286); Rasmussen(†) 2-7 (.286); Black 9-42 (.214); Manning 1-2 (.500); K. Ford 1-4 (.250); Flores 18-61 (.295); Cassidy 4-8 (.500); Webb 2-8 (.250); Jones 7-35 (.200) Opponents 117-315 (.371)

MINNESOTA LYNX

Player	G	Min	FGM	FGA	Pct	FTM	FTA	Pct	Off	Def	Tot	Ast	PF	Dq	Stl	TO	Blk	Pts	Avg	Hi
									REBOUNDS									SCORING		
Katie Smith	32	1193	203	482	.421	152	175	.869	28	65	93	90	71	0	44	76	7	646	20.2	34
Betty Lennox	32	984	201	471	.427	84	105	.800	53	125	178	82	112	4	53	97	9	541	16.9	31
Kristin Folkl	32	845	86	191	.450	66	94	.702	38	116	154	67	80	1	23	50	22	242	7.6	20
Grace Daley	30	577	57	147	.388	42	65	.646	32	40	72	57	49	0	12	50	0	173	5.8	17
Andrea Lloyd Curry	14	333	26	68	.382	12	17	.706	14	29	43	22	32	0	12	24	2	75	5.4	11
Keitha Dickerson	32	791	54	142	.380	34	45	.756	31	110	141	59	107	4	37	70	2	142	4.4	15
Maylana Martin	30	456	54	118	.458	19	32	.594	25	42	67	21	81	1	17	29	13	132	4.4	14
Marla Brumfield	32	613	47	101	.465	29	42	.690	22	38	60	42	70	1	22	40	2	124	3.9	14
Sonja Tate	8	94	10	22	.455	1	2	.500	6	7	13	5	13	0	3	7	0	27	3.4	13
Kate Paye	28	408	19	58	.328	6	9	.667	3	27	30	38	49	0	8	28	6	56	2.0	9
Shanele Stires	21	117	13	29	.448	4	6	.667	6	8	14	7	22	0	6	14	0	35	1.7	9
Angela Aycock(*)	3	6	0	0	---	0	0	---	0	3	3	4	1	0	0	0	0	0	0.0	0
Angela Aycock(†)	4	13	0	3	.000	0	0	---	1	4	5	4	3	0	0	0	0	0	0.0	0
Angie Potthoff	3	8	0	2	.000	0	0	---	0	2	2	1	3	0	0	0	0	0	0.0	0
Minnesota	32	6425	770	1831	.421	449	592	.758	258	612	870	495	690	11	237	497	63	2193	68.5	88
Opponents	32	6425	755	1758	.429	514	702	.732	300	677	977	472	707	8	275	547	130	2188	68.4	85

3-pt. FG: Minnesota 204-571 (.357) Smith 88-232 (.379); Lennox 55-139 (.396); Folkl 4-19 (.211); Daley 17-56 (.304); Lloyd Curry 11-32 (.344); Dickerson 0-2 (.000) Martin 5-19 (.263); Brumfield 1-9 (.111); Tate 6-11 (.545); Paye 12-41 (.293); Stires 5-10 (.500); Aycock(†) 0-2 (.000) Potthoff 0-1 (.000); Opponents 164-481 (.341)

NEW YORK LIBERTY

Player	G	Min	FGM	FGA	Pct	FTM	FTA	Pct	Off	Def	Tot	Ast	PF	Dq	Stl	TO	Blk	Pts	Avg	Hi
									REBOUNDS									SCORING		
Tari Phillips	31	978	170	364	.467	85	130	.654	86	161	247	28	110	5	59	85	21	427	13.8	30
Vickie Johnson	31	1023	143	324	.441	67	76	.882	40	97	137	77	48	0	22	57	5	380	12.3	22
Becky Hammon	32	835	119	252	.472	61	69	.884	19	45	64	58	55	0	29	62	1	351	11.0	23
Crystal Robinson	27	722	86	201	.428	30	33	.909	26	42	68	48	74	0	23	33	10	238	8.8	19
Tamika Whitmore	32	689	109	253	.431	59	84	.702	34	71	105	20	102	1	17	53	17	277	8.7	17
Teresa Weatherspoon	32	1078	67	153	.438	60	81	.741	16	93	109	205	85	0	65	86	5	205	6.4	14
Sue Wicks	32	680	55	143	.385	45	62	.726	49	100	149	21	78	1	26	50	39	156	4.9	14
Venus Lacy	2	18	2	5	.400	2	4	.500	1	4	5	0	0	0	0	2	0	6	3.0	6
Marina Ferragut	23	154	23	53	.434	1	2	.500	4	13	17	4	34	0	0	11	2	50	2.2	10
Shea Mahoney	15	158	11	38	.289	4	8	.500	10	20	30	4	14	0	2	5	1	27	1.8	9
Olga Firsova	9	19	4	10	.400	4	5	.800	0	4	4	1	8	0	0	2	1	12	1.3	3
Jessica Bibby	17	69	3	18	.167	11	13	.846	3	2	5	11	9	0	3	12	0	19	1.1	7
Desiree Francis	1	2	0	1	.000	0	0	---	0	0	0	0	0	0	0	0	0	0	0.0	0
New York	32	6425	792	1815	.436	429	567	.757	288	652	940	477	617	7	246	474	102	2148	67.1	87
Opponents	32	6425	741	1822	.407	437	590	.741	320	647	967	462	645	5	223	479	94	2035	63.6	84

3-pt. FG: New York 135-396 (.341) Phillips 2-8 (.250); Johnson 27-71 (.380); Hammon 52-141 (.369); Robinson 36-102 (.353); Whitmore 0-3 (.000); Wicks 1-5 (.200) Weatherspoon 11-44 (.250); Ferragut 3-10 (.300); Mahoney 1-5 (.200); Firsova 0-1 (.000); Bibby 2-6 (.333) Opponents 116-420 (.276)

ORLANDO MIRACLE

Player	G	Min	FGM	FGA	Pct	FTM	FTA	Pct	Off	Def	Tot	Ast	PF	Dq	Stl	TO	Blk	Pts	Avg	Hi
									REBOUNDS									SCORING		
Taj McWilliams-Frank	32	1098	173	330	.524	87	122	.713	90	154	244	54	86	0	59	83	31	438	13.7	23
Adrienne Johnson	32	1100	175	393	.445	34	38	.895	30	60	90	54	59	1	24	56	3	436	13.6	25
Nykesha Sales	32	995	170	383	.444	43	62	.694	43	96	139	69	92	2	47	67	12	430	13.4	25
Shannon Johnson	32	1126	122	309	.395	107	144	.743	53	102	155	169	83	0	58	102	7	381	11.9	23
Cintia dos Santos	32	820	94	222	.423	40	57	.702	35	89	124	38	111	2	16	54	63	228	7.1	17
Elaine Powell	20	347	26	66	.394	17	22	.773	17	33	50	42	21	0	12	30	1	72	3.6	9
Carla McGhee	32	408	30	83	.361	27	39	.692	27	37	64	23	58	0	21	31	5	87	2.7	9
Tiffany McCain	25	214	15	49	.306	16	18	.889	2	9	11	5	18	0	3	9	1	51	2.0	8

Player	G	Min	FGM	FGA	Pct	FTM	FTA	Pct	Off	Def	Tot	Ast	PF	Dq	Stl	TO	Blk	Pts	Avg	Hi
									REBOUNDS									**SCORING**		
LaCharlotte Smith..........3	12	2	3	.667	1	1	1.000	1	1	2	1	2	0	2	2	0	5	1.7	5
Jannon Roland 21	173	13	37	.351	4	8	.500	7	10	17	8	16	0	6	19	0	33	1.6	9
Jessie Hicks 26	157	10	23	.435	18	29	.621	13	13	26	4	33	0	2	17	7	38	1.5	5
Cornelia Gayden 3	7	1	2	.500	0	0	---	0	0	0	1	0	0	0	0	0	2	0.7	2
Romana Hamzova 15	43	2	11	.182	3	6	.500	1	2	3	5	4	0	5	4	0	7	0.5	2
Orlando 32	6500	833	1911	.436	397	546	.727	319	606	925	473	583	5	255	486	130	2208	69.0	92
Opponents 32	6500	851	1964	.433	378	495	.764	348	669	1017	536	637	2	264	500	108	2233	69.8	92

3-pt. FG: Orlando 145-424 (.342); McWilliams-Frank 5-17 (.294); A. Johnson 52-148 (.351); Sales 47-119 (.395); S. Johnson 30-90 (.333); dos Santos 0-1 (.000); Powell 3-9 (.333); McGhee 0-3 (.000); McCain 5-22 (.227); Smith 0-1 (.000); Roland 3-10 (.300); Gayden 0-1 (.000); Hamzova 0-3 (.000); Opponents 153-450 (.340)

PHOENIX MERCURY

Player	G	Min	FGM	FGA	Pct	FTM	FTA	Pct	Off	Def	Tot	Ast	PF	Dq	Stl	TO	Blk	Pts	Avg	Hi
									REBOUNDS									**SCORING**		
Brandy Reed................32	1090	231	456	.507	128	142	.901	59	128	187	86	52	0	66	90	21	608	19.0	32
Jennifer Gillom............30	826	139	316	.440	79	106	.745	31	85	116	45	91	1	21	59	29	376	12.5	28
Tonya Edwards 32	926	112	298	.376	79	101	.782	19	57	76	58	80	0	36	63	9	338	10.6	19
Michelle Brogan..........28	725	70	137	.511	63	79	.797	40	71	111	49	88	2	30	36	6	211	7.5	18
Lisa Harrison 31	750	81	154	.526	30	37	.811	38	83	121	36	62	0	30	22	4	200	6.5	22
Bridget Pettis 32	583	60	168	.357	49	61	.803	19	41	60	46	62	1	31	39	4	189	5.9	22
Maria Stepanova 15	170	24	54	.444	9	15	.600	15	33	48	8	42	1	4	22	9	57	3.8	9
Michele Timms..............8	176	11	30	.367	4	4	1.000	2	14	16	18	22	0	15	18	2	30	3.8	11
Rankica Sarenac..........20	142	23	44	.523	17	27	.630	11	19	30	8	30	0	0	17	1	64	3.2	15
Adrain Williams 28	351	29	72	.403	20	38	.526	24	47	71	16	42	0	14	29	4	78	2.8	12
Michelle Cleary 24	509	14	45	.311	19	27	.704	12	25	37	77	36	0	34	14	2	57	2.4	12
Dena Head.................17	149	8	22	.364	10	16	.625	5	13	18	15	17	0	4	11	0	27	1.6	6
Nicole Kubik 4	19	1	3	.333	4	4	1.000	0	2	2	2	4	0	0	3	0	6	1.5	4
Amanda Wilson 3	9	0	1	.000	2	4	.500	0	1	1	1	2	0	0	0	0	2	0.7	2
Phoenix 32	6425	803	1800	.446	513	661	.776	275	619	894	465	630	5	285	429	91	2243	70.1	90
Opponents 32	6425	773	1828	.423	421	574	.733	334	635	969	486	698	8	224	531	91	2102	65.7	87

3-pt. FG: Phoenix 124-394 (.315); Reed 18-43 (.419); Gillom 19-69 (.275); Edwards 35-114 (.307); Brogan 8-25 (.320); Harrison 8-12 (.667); Pettis 20-75 (.267); Timms 4-17 (.235); Sarenac 1-1 (1.000); Cleary 10-30 (.333); Head 1-7 (.143); Kubik 0-1 (.000); Opponents 135-416 (.325)

PORTLAND FIRE

Player	G	Min	FGM	FGA	Pct	FTM	FTA	Pct	Off	Def	Tot	Ast	PF	Dq	Stl	TO	Blk	Pts	Avg	Hi
									REBOUNDS									**SCORING**		
Sophia Witherspoon....32	1061	175	456	.384	128	147	.871	23	82	105	68	72	1	38	88	8	538	16.8	31
Sylvia Crawley 31	930	143	298	.480	71	102	.696	64	121	185	34	96	2	29	88	24	357	11.5	25
Vanessa Nygaard 32	843	91	209	.435	41	54	.759	50	71	121	30	98	2	17	38	5	253	7.9	18
Alisa Burras 21	314	64	109	.587	31	41	.756	20	54	74	6	36	0	3	36	7	159	7.6	22
Michelle Marciniak 32	537	58	154	.377	43	75	.573	11	48	59	73	79	2	37	67	6	177	5.5	13
Stacey Thomas 32	863	58	163	.356	44	74	.595	48	78	126	101	93	1	54	68	15	163	5.1	14
Tully Bevilaqua...........32	796	40	112	.357	56	72	.778	19	76	95	89	93	1	41	66	6	153	4.8	11
Lynn Pride 32	462	41	118	.347	29	42	.690	22	39	61	40	59	1	16	33	9	114	3.6	9
Tara Williams 26	174	31	69	.449	4	8	.500	5	12	17	13	26	0	8	10	2	80	3.1	15
DeMya Walker...........30	311	35	88	.398	22	47	.468	29	18	47	19	69	1	17	35	7	92	3.1	12
Michele VanGorp.......28	199	25	50	.500	19	35	.543	16	26	42	5	37	0	3	30	4	69	2.5	16
Jamila Wideman..........5	35	0	2	.000	0	0	---	2	2	4	2	3	0	2	6	0	0	0.0	0
Portland 32	6525	761	1828	.416	488	697	.700	309	627	936	480	761	11	265	593	93	2155	67.3	89
Opponents 32	6525	788	1847	.427	577	766	.753	307	646	953	487	729	8	277	531	130	2303	72.0	94

3-pt. FG: Portland 145-433 (.335); Witherspoon 60-163 (.368); Crawley 0-2 (.000); Nygaard 30-90 (.333); Marciniak 18-54 (.333); Thomas 3-12 (.250); Pride 3-9 (.333); Bevilaqua 17-60 (.283); Williams 14-41 (.341); Walker 0-2 (.000); Opponents 150-447 (.336)

SACRAMENTO MONARCHS

Player	G	Min	FGM	FGA	Pct	FTM	FTA	Pct	Off	Def	Tot	Ast	PF	Dq	Stl	TO	Blk	Pts	Avg	Hi
									REBOUNDS									SCORING		
Yolanda Griffith 32	32	1026	193	361	.535	137	194	.706	148	183	331	47	110	1	83	82	61	523	16.3	30
Ruthie Bolton 29	29	868	133	368	.361	64	84	.762	42	64	106	57	60	0	34	45	1	380	13.1	28
Tangela Smith...............32	32	925	176	371	.474	36	46	.783	61	117	178	43	107	1	30	60	64	388	12.1	22
Kedra Holland-Corn...32	32	934	111	253	.439	46	66	.697	28	42	70	81	63	1	43	74	5	312	9.8	23
Ticha Penicheiro 30	30	936	68	185	.368	62	107	.579	12	77	89	236	71	1	70	71	6	208	6.9	17
Latasha Byears 32	32	521	75	143	.524	30	49	.612	42	80	122	21	72	1	30	35	5	181	5.7	17
Lady Grooms 30	30	401	39	88	.443	46	61	.754	27	17	44	13	27	0	10	21	3	124	4.1	16
Katy Steding 29	29	309	36	95	.379	2	7	.286	11	28	39	14	22	0	11	17	10	91	3.1	12
Cindy Blodgett 20	20	133	20	50	.400	4	6	.667	1	8	9	3	9	0	8	13	1	52	2.6	9
Stacy Clinesmith.........26	26	285	20	57	.351	14	17	.824	7	23	30	49	19	0	12	25	1	66	2.5	10
Linda Burgess..............5	5	41	3	15	.200	6	9	.667	7	10	17	2	8	0	1	4	0	12	2.4	6
Rhonda Banchero.........9	9	21	2	7	.286	2	4	.500	2	1	3	1	3	0	0	2	0	6	0.7	2
Sacramento 32	32	6400	876	1993	.440	449	650	.691	388	650	1038	567	571	5	332	458	157	2343	73.2	108
Opponents 32	32	6400	811	1918	.423	410	544	.754	320	631	951	503	600	2	226	524	116	2176	68.0	96

3-pt. FG: Sacramento 142-459 (.309); Bolton-Holifield 50-160 (.313); Holland-Corn 44-122 (.361); Penicheiro 10-50 (.200); Byears 1-2 (.500); Hardmon 0-1 (.000); Steding 17-53 (.321); Blodgett 8-28 (.286); Clinesmith 12-41 (.293); Banchero 0-2 (.000); Opponents 144-418 (.344)

SEATTLE STORM

Player	G	Min	FGM	FGA	Pct	FTM	FTA	Pct	Off	Def	Tot	Ast	PF	Dq	Stl	TO	Blk	Pts	Avg	Hi
									REBOUNDS									SCORING		
Edna Campbell...........16	16	510	84	215	.391	41	58	.707	8	26	34	37	35	0	19	40	4	222	13.9	22
Kamila Vodichkova 23	23	489	68	171	.398	60	78	.769	28	69	97	22	63	0	13	57	12	200	8.7	22
Robin Threatt 20	20	377	60	158	.380	23	35	.657	10	22	32	18	36	1	13	30	3	155	7.8	24
Simone Edwards..........29	29	645	83	182	.456	50	80	.625	38	69	107	22	57	0	16	45	10	216	7.4	18
Quacy Barnes..............31	31	705	89	213	.418	30	56	.536	27	57	84	33	103	2	19	62	33	209	6.7	17
Michelle Edwards(*)...20	20	455	51	143	.357	23	35	.657	7	27	34	40	29	0	14	38	5	131	6.6	20
Michelle Edwards(†)....23	23	472	55	153	.359	23	35	.657	7	29	36	41	32	0	14	42	5	139	6.0	20
Jamie Redd.................26	26	387	49	125	.392	24	34	.706	18	27	45	16	53	0	19	35	1	140	5.4	17
Sonja Henning 32	32	980	53	151	.351	37	61	.607	22	64	86	79	73	1	61	54	3	168	5.3	19
Stacey Lovelace 23	23	324	36	103	.350	25	31	.806	19	38	57	16	42	0	13	35	2	99	4.3	13
Charisse Sampson 21	21	280	22	47	.468	25	28	.893	14	27	41	11	37	0	18	14	6	78	3.7	13
Andrea Garner 32	32	560	37	115	.322	24	38	.632	42	55	97	25	44	0	27	43	10	99	3.1	10
Katrina Hibbert...........20	20	240	19	59	.322	7	9	.778	8	22	30	18	22	0	7	17	1	53	2.7	17
Charmin Smith 32	32	516	16	56	.286	10	18	.556	14	33	47	53	52	0	16	32	3	52	1.6	10
Angela Aycock(‡) 1	1	7	0	3	.000	0	0	---	1	1	2	0	2	0	0	0	0	0	0.0	0
Seattle 32	32	6475	667	1741	.383	379	561	.676	256	537	793	390	648	4	255	525	93	1822	56.9	78
Opponents 32	32	6475	778	1721	.452	498	654	.761	288	721	1009	506	618	9	284	529	123	2171	67.8	85

3-pt. FG: Seattle 109-364 (.299); Campbell 13-49 (.265); Vodichkova 4-20 (.200); Threatt 12-37 (.324); Barnes 1-9 (.111); M. Edwards(*) 6-32 (.188); M. Edwards(†) 6-35 (.171); Redd 18-52 (.346); Henning 25-66 (.379); Lovelace 2-9 (.222); Sampson 9-23 (.391); Garner 1-2 (.500); Hibbert 8-31 (.258); Smith 10-32 (.313); Aycock(‡) 0-2 (.000); Opponents 117-334 (.350).

UTAH STARZZ

Player	G	Min	FGM	FGA	Pct	FTM	FTA	Pct	Off	Def	Tot	Ast	PF	Dq	Stl	TO	Blk	Pts	Avg	Hi
									REBOUNDS									SCORING		
Natalie Williams 29	29	1039	179	365	.490	182	228	.798	132	204	336	51	124	3	35	79	18	543	18.7	30
Adrienne Goodson......29	29	929	199	415	.480	92	134	.687	69	95	164	69	67	0	41	81	7	498	17.2	29
Korie Hlede 31	31	867	118	260	.454	51	70	.729	25	68	93	92	84	1	38	76	4	312	10.1	20
Jennifer Azzi...............15	15	559	47	104	.452	40	43	.930	5	36	41	92	43	0	12	28	5	144	9.6	20
Margo Dydek 32	32	775	105	236	.445	82	103	.796	29	146	175	51	114	1	18	82	96	294	9.2	19
LaTonya Johnson 29	29	481	52	129	.403	28	43	.651	14	38	52	26	65	0	12	34	2	144	5.0	14
Naomi Mulitauaopele 22	22	291	41	69	.594	15	20	.750	12	22	34	6	37	0	4	30	6	99	4.5	10
Kate Starbird...............29	29	340	39	109	.358	34	42	.810	12	21	33	30	32	0	13	29	11	117	4.0	17

Player	G	Min	FGM	FGA	Pct	FTM	FTA	Pct	REBOUNDS Off	Def	Tot	Ast	PF	Dq	Stl	TO	Blk	SCORING Pts	Avg	Hi
Amy Herrig	25	341	36	75	.480	19	31	.613	26	33	59	20	41	1	7	29	5	91	3.6	14
Dalma Ivanyi	27	489	30	96	.313	21	28	.750	12	42	54	63	67	0	25	50	3	93	3.4	9
Stacy Frese	21	222	10	30	.333	33	36	.917	4	14	18	17	14	0	4	14	0	62	3.0	11
Katryna Gaither(‡)	9	54	2	7	.286	10	10	1.000	7	10	17	4	8	0	4	4	0	14	1.6	4
Kym Hope	3	4	0	1	.000	2	2	1.000	0	2	2	0	0	0	0	1	0	2	0.7	2
Kristen Rasmussen(‡)	1	9	0	0	---	0	0	---	1	1	2	1	2	0	1	1	0	0	0.0	0
Utah	32	6400	858	1896	.453	609	790	.771	348	732	1080	522	698	6	214	544	157	2413	75.4	96
Opponents	32	6400	860	1964	.438	531	721	.736	313	598	911	503	702	11	301	437	112	2407	75.2	107

3-pt. FG: Utah 88-262 (.336); Williams 3-5 (.600); Goodson 8-29 (.276); Hlede 25-58 (.431); Azzi 10-24 (.417); Dydek 2-14 (.143); Johnson 12-36 (.333); Mulitauaopele 2-3 (.667); Starbird 5-23 (.217); Herrig 0-1 (.000); Ivanyi 12-43 (.279); Frese 9-26 (.346); Opponents 156-448 (.348)

WASHINGTON MYSTICS

Player	G	Min	FGM	FGA	Pct	FTM	FTA	Pct	REBOUNDS Off	Def	Tot	Ast	PF	Dq	Stl	TO	Blk	SCORING Pts	Avg	Hi
Chamique Holdsclaw	32	1131	232	499	.465	87	128	.680	57	183	240	80	74	0	47	93	18	561	17.5	30
Nikki McCray	32	1046	167	385	.434	113	147	.769	22	34	56	85	79	0	45	89	5	497	15.5	26
Vicky Bullett	32	1094	143	294	.486	45	63	.714	61	122	183	42	88	0	64	58	47	342	10.7	22
Murriel Page	32	1046	131	222	.590	52	92	.565	79	129	208	64	103	2	23	63	32	314	9.8	20
Andrea Nagy	23	694	31	79	.392	21	26	.808	10	53	63	118	55	0	17	55	8	97	4.2	10
Tausha Mills	31	295	46	105	.438	38	51	.745	39	41	80	9	71	1	10	37	8	130	4.2	17
Beth Cunningham	21	198	17	68	.250	16	19	.842	4	17	21	12	23	0	2	12	0	59	2.8	10
Keisha Anderson	30	434	29	68	.426	14	18	.778	12	34	46	75	53	0	25	47	3	75	2.5	13
Markita Aldridge	29	272	25	54	.463	7	22	.318	8	16	24	28	30	0	9	27	4	63	2.2	9
Renee Robinson	2	5	0	1	.000	4	4	1.000	0	0	0	0	3	0	1	1	0	4	2.0	4
Tonya Washington	19	103	8	29	.276	4	6	.667	6	8	14	5	4	0	2	4	0	26	1.4	6
Michelle Campbell	5	22	2	5	.400	2	2	1.000	0	2	2	1	2	0	0	3	1	6	1.2	4
Heather Owen	11	60	1	4	.250	0	0	---	2	7	9	2	12	0	0	3	0	2	0.2	2
Washington	32	6400	832	1813	.459	403	578	.697	300	646	946	521	597	3	245	506	126	2176	68.0	96
Opponents	32	6400	845	1875	.451	382	555	.688	299	612	911	513	595	4	261	456	102	2221	69.4	87

3-pt. FG: Washington 109-335 (.325); Holdsclaw 10-39 (.256); McCray 50-151 (.331); Bullett 11-34 (.324); Nagy 14-39 (.359); Cunningham 9-37 (.243); Anderson 3-8 (.375); Aldridge 6-12 (.500); Robinson 0-1 (.000); Washington 6-14 (.429); Opponents 149-397 (.375)

(*) Statistics with this team only

(†) Totals with all teams

(‡) Continued season with another team

PLAYOFFS RESULTS

FIRST ROUND

Cleveland defeats Orlando, 2-1
August 11 Orlando 62, Cleveland 55
August 13 Cleveland 63, Orlando 54
August 15 Cleveland 72, Orlando 43

New York defeats Washington, 2-0
August 12 New York 72, Washington 63
August 14 New York 78, Washington 57

Los Angeles defeats Phoenix, 2-0
August 11 Los Angeles 86, Phoenix 71
August 13 Los Angeles 101, Phoenix 76

Houston defeats Sacramento, 2-0
August 12 Houston 72, Sacramento 64
August 14 Houston 75, Sacramento 70

CONFERENCE FINALS

Houston defeats Los Angeles, 2-0
August 17 Houston 77, Los Angeles 56
August 20 Houston 74, Los Angeles 69

New York defeats Cleveland, 2-1
August 17 Cleveland 56, New York 43
August 20 New York 51, Cleveland 45
August 21 New York 81, Cleveland 67

CHAMPIONSHIP

Houston defeats New York, 2-0
August 24 Houston 59, New York 52
August 26 Houston 79, New York 73 (OT)

OFFENSIVE

TEAM	G	FG	FGA	PCT	FG3	FG3A	PCT	FT	FTA	PCT	OFF	DEF	REB	AST	PF	DQ	STL	TO	BLK	PTS	AVG
L.A.	4	112	250	.448	30	74	.405	58	72	.806	49	93	142	73	84	1	23	63	13	312	78.0
Phoe.	2	53	119	.445	11	40	.275	30	42	.714	12	36	48	34	45	1	11	23	10	147	73.5
Hou.	6	155	365	.425	34	90	.378	92	105	.876	63	122	185	70	83	0	54	74	13	436	72.7
Sac.	2	48	118	.407	11	32	.344	27	32	.844	19	44	63	31	34	1	15	24	4	134	67.0
N.Y.	7	171	390	.438	27	76	.355	81	100	.810	62	134	196	113	130	2	68	103	25	450	64.3
Wash.	2	47	101	.465	6	22	.273	20	32	.625	14	30	44	30	30	0	13	32	6	120	60.0
Clev.	6	136	340	.400	23	91	.253	63	89	.708	72	133	205	97	90	0	52	85	13	358	59.7
Orl.	3	64	169	.379	10	39	.256	21	30	.700	22	53	75	37	49	0	18	39	14	159	53.0

DEFENSIVE

Team	FG	FGA	PCT	FG3	FG3A	PCT	FT	FTA	PCT	OFF	DEF	REB	AST	PF	DQ	STL	TO	BLK	PTS	AVG	DIFF
Clev.	135	329	.410	20	72	.278	44	63	.698	41	113	154	90	105	0	50	85	27	334	55.7	+4.0
N.Y.	157	388	.405	27	95	.284	85	111	.766	75	136	211	97	112	0	59	107	21	426	60.9	+3.4
Orl.	76	179	.425	12	47	.255	26	42	.619	36	70	106	54	45	0	21	38	4	190	63.3	-10.3
Hou.	134	357	.375	34	101	.337	82	93	.882	66	122	188	89	117	4	41	93	18	384	64.0	+8.7
Sac.	51	115	.443	13	33	.394	32	36	.889	17	42	59	21	25	0	14	23	3	147	73.5	-6.5
L.A.	107	243	.440	22	68	.324	62	79	.785	33	73	106	59	66	1	36	46	14	298	74.5	+3.5
Wash.	58	114	.509	10	21	.476	24	28	.857	23	36	59	33	32	0	22	28	5	150	75.0	-15.0
Phoe.	68	127	.535	14	27	.519	37	50	.740	22	53	75	42	43	0	11	23	6	187	93.5	-20.0
Avg.	98	232	.424	19	58	.328	49	63	.781	39	81	120	61	68	1	32	55	12	265	66.1	---
	786	1852		152	464		392	502		313	645	958	485	545	5	254	443	98	2116		

TEAM COMPARISONS

TEAM	Points Per Game		Field Goal Percentage		Turnovers Per Game		Rebound Percentages			Below 70 Pts.		Overtime Games		3 PTS or Less		10 PTS or More	
	OWN	OPP	OWN	OPP	OWN	OPP	OFF	DEF	TOT	OWN	OPP	W	L	W	L	W	L
Cleveland	59.7	55.7*	.400	.410	14.2	14.2	.389	.764*	.577*	5	5	0	0	0	0	2	1
Houston	72.7	64.0	.425	.375*	12.3	15.5*	.341	.649	.495	1	4	1	0	0	0	1	0
Los Angeles	78.0*	74.5	.448	.440	15.8	11.5	.402*	.738	.570	2	0	0	0	0	0	2	1
New York	64.3	60.9	.438	.405	14.7	15.3	.313	.641	.477	3	6	0	1	0	0	2	1
Orlando	53.0	63.3	.379	.425	13.0	12.7	.239	.596	.417	3	2	0	0	0	0	0	1
Phoenix	73.5	93.5	.445	.535	11.5*	11.5	.185	.621	.403	0	0	0	0	0	0	0	2
Sacramento	67.0	73.5	.407	.443	12.0	11.5	.311	.721	.516	1	0	0	0	0	0	0	0
Washington	60.0	75.0	.465*	.509	16.0	14.0	.280	.566	.423	2	0	0	0	0	0	0	1
COMPOSITE;16 games	66.1		.424		13.8		.327	.673		17	1	0		7			

* - League Leader

REBOUND PERCENTAGES — OFF. - Percentage of a given team's missed shots which that team rebounds. DEF. - Percentage of opponents' missed shots which a given team rebounds. TOT. - Average of offensive and defensive rebound percentages.

INDIVIDUAL PLAYOFFS STATISTICS, TEAM BY TEAM

CLEVELAND ROCKERS

Player	G	Min	FGM	FGA	Pct	FTM	FTA	Pct	REBOUNDS Off	Def	Tot	Ast	PF	Dq	Stl	TO	Blk	SCORING Pts	Avg	Hi
Merlakia Jones	6	207	34	86	.395	9	12	.750	11	32	43	11	14	0	7	8	0	83	13.8	18
Rushia Brown	6	167	21	45	.467	21	24	.875	19	15	34	10	17	0	17	17	2	63	10.5	18
Chasity Melvin	6	183	20	38	.526	13	18	.722	16	24	40	11	20	0	5	11	3	53	8.8	14
Suzie McConnell Serio	6	147	14	45	.311	2	2	1.000	3	11	14	25	5	0	5	16	1	39	6.5	13
Helen Darling	6	106	9	28	.321	10	14	.714	7	13	20	13	5	0	7	6	0	33	5.5	15
Ann Wauters	6	107	13	27	.481	2	6	.333	5	13	18	5	7	0	3	8	3	28	4.7	12
Mery Andrade	6	166	8	33	.242	5	9	.556	5	12	17	14	17	0	6	11	3	21	3.5	7
Vicki Hall	6	69	10	24	.417	0	1	.000	5	10	15	4	4	0	0	2	1	21	3.5	8
P. Johns Kimbrough	4	6	3	3	1.000	1	2	.500	1	1	2	1	0	0	0	0	0	7	1.8	7
Tricia Bader Binford	5	36	3	9	.333	0	1	.000	0	1	1	1	1	0	2	1	0	8	1.6	8
Adia Barnes	4	6	1	2	.500	0	0	---	0	1	1	2	0	0	0	1	0	2	0.5	2
Cleveland	6	1200	136	340	.400	63	89	.708	72	133	205	97	90	0	52	85	13	358	59.7	72
Opponents	6	1200	135	329	.410	44	63	.698	41	113	154	90	105	0	50	85	27	334	55.7	81

3-pt. FG: Cleveland 23-91 (.253) Jones 6-20 (.300); Brown 0-1 (.000); Melvin 0-1 (.000); McConnell Serio 9-36 (.250); Darling 5-13 (.385); Wauters 0-2 (.000); Andrade 0-9 (.000); Hall 1-5 (.200); Bader Binford 2-3 (.667); Barnes 0-1 (.000); Opponents 20-72 (.278)

HOUSTON COMETS

Player	G	Min	FGM	FGA	Pct	FTM	FTA	Pct	Off	Def	Tot	Ast	PF	Dq	Stl	TO	Blk	Pts	Avg	Hi
Cynthia Cooper 6		228	45	119	.378	35	39	.897	5	10	15	22	11	0	9	18	1	136	22.7	29
Sheryl Swoopes 6		220	41	87	.471	23	29	.793	9	25	34	19	11	0	17	12	0	113	18.8	31
Tina Thompson 6		233	25	62	.403	17	18	.944	17	31	48	10	19	0	5	10	5	76	12.7	21
Janeth Arcain 6		201	21	47	.447	6	7	.857	6	21	27	12	14	0	10	16	0	50	8.3	16
Tiffani Johnson 6		135	10	20	.500	2	2	1.000	12	17	29	1	15	0	3	7	2	22	3.7	6
Amaya Valdemoro 3		16	2	5	.400	4	4	1.000	1	3	4	0	0	0	1	0	0	9	3.0	6
Tammy Jackson 6		94	8	14	.571	0	0	---	9	8	17	0	9	0	4	2	4	16	2.7	12
Coquese Washington 6		92	3	9	.333	5	6	.833	4	7	11	6	4	0	5	8	1	14	2.3	6
Jawann Kelley-Gibson ..1		3	0	1	.000	0	0	---	0	0	0	0	0	0	0	0	0	0	0.0	0
Jennifer Rizzotti 1		3	0	1	.000	0	0	---	0	0	0	0	0	0	0	0	0	0	0.0	0
Houston 6		1225	155	365	.425	92	105	.876	63	122	185	70	83	0	54	74	13	436	72.7	79
Opponents 6		1225	134	357	.375	82	93	.882	66	122	188	89	117	4	41	93	18	384	64.0	73

3-pt. FG: Houston 34-90 (.378) Cooper 11-32 (.344); Swoopes 8-17 (.471); Thompson 9-23 (.391); Arcain 2-7 (.286); Valdemoro 1-3 (.333); Washington 3-7 (.429); Rizzotti 0-1 (.000); Opponents 34-101 (.337).

LOS ANGELES SPARKS

Player	G	Min	FGM	FGA	Pct	FTM	FTA	Pct	Off	Def	Tot	Ast	PF	Dq	Stl	TO	Blk	Pts	Avg	Hi
Lisa Leslie......................4		139	28	57	.491	19	23	.826	10	31	41	8	14	0	1	13	5	75	18.8	29
Mwadi Mabika...............4		136	25	46	.543	3	4	.750	6	15	21	4	14	0	6	5	4	70	17.5	21
DeLisha Milton..............4		136	20	37	.541	10	12	.833	11	11	22	12	14	1	6	10	2	50	12.5	19
Tamecka Dixon 4		127	17	46	.370	8	9	.889	4	7	11	16	12	0	3	8	0	47	11.8	17
Ukari Figgs....................4		106	7	23	.304	6	6	1.000	6	10	16	19	10	0	2	11	0	24	6.0	9
Allison Feaster 4		44	5	16	.313	2	2	1.000	3	6	9	3	11	0	2	5	1	15	3.8	8
Clarisse Machanguana ..4		47	4	8	.500	4	6	.667	6	5	11	0	6	0	1	1	1	12	3.0	10
Nicky McCrimmon 4		49	3	12	.250	3	4	.750	3	4	7	10	2	0	1	5	0	10	2.5	7
La'Keshia Frett 3		7	2	3	.667	3	4	.750	0	0	0	0	0	0	0	0	0	7	2.3	5
Vedrana Grgin Fonseca 3		7	1	2	.500	0	2	.000	0	3	3	1	0	0	1	2	0	2	0.7	2
Paige Sauer 1		2	0	0	---	0	0	---	0	1	1	0	1	0	0	0	0	0	0.0	0
Los Angeles 4		800	112	250	.448	58	72	.806	49	93	142	73	84	1	23	63	13	312	78.0	101
Opponents 4		800	107	243	.440	62	79	.785	33	73	106	59	66	1	36	46	14	298	74.5	77

3-pt. FG: Los Angeles 30-74 (.405) Leslie 0-3 (.000); Mabika 17-32 (.531); Dixon 5-10 (.500); Figgs 4-11 (.364); Feaster 3-13 (.231); McCrimmon 1-4 (.250); Grgin Fonseca 0-1 (.000); Opponents 22-68 (.324).

NEW YORK LIBERTY

Player	G	Min	FGM	FGA	Pct	FTM	FTA	Pct	Off	Def	Tot	Ast	PF	Dq	Stl	TO	Blk	Pts	Avg	Hi
Tari Phillips 7		222	48	95	.505	18	23	.783	16	37	53	8	26	1	12	16	6	114	16.3	24
Tamika Whitmore..........7		196	31	65	.477	18	24	.750	9	18	27	6	22	0	3	15	9	81	11.6	19
Vickie Johnson 7		237	27	71	.380	12	14	.857	10	25	35	24	14	0	8	13	0	72	10.3	20
Becky Hammon 7		206	21	49	.429	17	19	.895	5	5	10	15	10	0	9	17	0	66	9.4	19
Crystal Robinson 7		150	16	39	.410	5	5	1.000	7	13	20	5	12	0	9	10	1	46	6.6	13
Teresa Weatherspoon 7		253	12	34	.353	7	11	.636	2	17	19	49	20	1	19	20	0	32	4.6	7
Sue Wicks 7		131	9	26	.346	4	4	1.000	11	16	27	3	21	0	7	5	9	23	3.3	7
Marina Ferragut 3		12	2	3	.667	0	0	---	0	3	3	1	4	0	1	0	0	6	2.0	3
Olga Firsova.................3		6	3	4	.750	0	0	---	1	0	1	0	1	0	0	0	0	6	2.0	4
Jessica Bibby 3		8	2	2	1.000	0	0	---	0	0	0	2	0	0	2	0	0	4	1.3	2
Desiree Francis.............2		4	0	2	.000	0	0	---	1	0	1	0	0	0	0	0	0	0	0.0	0
New York 7		1425	171	390	.438	81	100	.810	62	134	196	113	130	2	68	103	25	450	64.3	81
Opponents 7		1425	157	388	.405	85	111	.766	75	136	211	97	112	0	59	107	21	426	60.9	79

3-pt. FG: New York 27-76 (.355) Phillips 0-1 (.000); Whitmore 1-2 (.500); Johnson 6-22 (.273); Hammon 7-23 (.304); Robinson 9-19 (.474); Weatherspoon 1-5 (.200); Wicks 1-1 (1.000); Ferragut 2-2 (1.000); Francis 0-1 (.000); Opponents 27-95 (.284).

ORLANDO MIRACLE

Player	G	Min	FGM	FGA	Pct	FTM	FTA	Pct	Off	Def	Tot	Ast	PF	Dq	Stl	TO	Blk	Pts	Avg	Hi
Taj McWilliams-Frank ..3		107	18	38	.474	7	9	.778	6	17	23	5	8	0	2	5	3	43	14.3	16
Adrienne Johnson..........3		111	14	42	.333	3	4	.750	3	1	4	8	7	0	1	7	1	34	11.3	17
Nykesha Sales 3		106	15	31	.484	0	2	.000	1	8	9	4	9	0	3	9	0	33	11.0	15

Player	G	Min	FGM	FGA	Pct	FTM	FTA	Pct	Off	Def	Tot	Ast	PF	Dq	Stl	TO	Blk	Pts	Avg	Hi
Cintia dos Santos	3	82	8	16	.500	2	2	1.000	3	5	8	3	9	0	2	5	7	18	6.0	12
Shannon Johnson 3		119	6	27	.222	4	8	.500	4	17	21	14	9	0	5	7	2	18	6.0	7
Tiffany McCain..............2		11	2	3	.667	0	0	---	0	1	1	1	4	0	0	1	0	6	3.0	3
Carla McGhee 3		37	1	7	.143	3	3	1.000	4	1	5	1	3	0	4	3	0	5	1.7	3
Jannon Roland 3		26	0	5	.000	2	2	1.000	1	3	4	1	0	0	1	0	1	2	0.7	2
LaCharlotte Smith..........1		1	0	0	---	0	0	---	0	0	0	0	0	0	0	0	0	0	0.0	0
Orlando 3		600	64	169	.379	21	30	.700	22	53	75	37	49	0	18	39	14	159	53.0	62
Opponents 3		600	76	179	.425	26	42	.619	36	70	106	54	45	0	21	38	4	190	63.3	72

3-pt. FG: Orlando 10-39 (.256) McWilliams-Frank 0-2 (.000); A. Johnson 3-10 (.300); Sales 3-10 (.300); S. Johnson 2-13 (.154); McCain 2-3 (.667); Roland 0-1 (.000); Opponents 12-47 (.255)

PHOENIX MERCURY

Player	G	Min	FGM	FGA	Pct	FTM	FTA	Pct	Off	Def	Tot	Ast	PF	Dq	Stl	TO	Blk	Pts	Avg	Hi
Brandy Reed.................2		73	12	22	.545	3	4	.750	2	5	7	8	5	0	0	5	1	28	14.0	17
Jennifer Gillom..............2		64	10	20	.500	5	10	.500	1	3	4	2	10	0	1	4	5	26	13.0	16
Lisa Harrison 2		68	12	17	.706	2	2	1.000	4	7	11	10	5	0	3	3	0	26	13.0	16
Michelle Brogan...........2		52	5	13	.385	11	14	.786	0	9	9	1	5	0	1	3	1	22	11.0	13
Bridget Pettis 2		41	7	18	.389	2	2	1.000	1	4	5	6	7	0	1	3	0	21	10.5	14
Tonya Edwards 2		61	5	20	.250	4	6	.667	1	5	6	5	8	1	4	2	0	17	8.5	12
Adrain Williams 2		30	2	4	.500	1	2	.500	1	3	4	1	3	0	0	1	2	5	2.5	3
Nicole Kubik 2		5	0	2	.000	2	2	1.000	0	0	0	0	2	0	0	1	0	2	1.0	2
Dena Head...................1		6	0	3	.000	0	0	---	2	0	2	1	0	0	1	1	1	0	0.0	0
Phoenix 2		400	53	119	.445	30	42	.714	12	36	48	34	45	1	11	23	10	147	73.5	76
Opponents 2		400	68	127	.535	37	50	.740	22	53	75	42	43	0	11	23	6	187	93.5	101

3-pt. FG: Phoenix 11-40 (.275) Reed 1-4 (.250); Gillom 1-5 (.200); Harrison 0-2 (.000); Brogan 1-4 (.250); Pettis 5-11 (.455); Edwards 3-13 (.231); Head 0-1 (.000); Opponents 14-27 (.519)

SACRAMENTO MONARCHS

Player	G	Min	FGM	FGA	Pct	FTM	FTA	Pct	Off	Def	Tot	Ast	PF	Dq	Stl	TO	Blk	Pts	Avg	Hi
R. Bolton-Holifield 2		70	13	34	.382	9	9	1.000	4	5	9	7	6	0	4	5	0	39	19.5	23
Yolanda Griffith 2		78	12	23	.522	5	8	.625	6	18	24	2	4	0	1	4	1	29	14.5	18
Tangela Smith...............2		59	9	22	.409	3	4	.750	0	8	8	1	5	0	2	2	1	21	10.5	13
Kedra Holland-Corn......2		60	7	16	.438	2	2	1.000	3	5	8	6	3	0	3	1	0	19	9.5	10
Ticha Penicheiro 2		77	4	16	.250	5	6	.833	2	5	7	14	10	1	4	6	0	16	8.0	12
Linda Burgess 1		8	1	1	1.000	2	2	1.000	1	1	2	0	1	0	0	1	2	4	4.0	4
Stacy Clinesmith............2		3	1	1	1.000	0	0	---	0	0	0	0	2	0	0	0	0	3	1.5	3
Lady Grooms 2		23	1	2	.500	1	1	1.000	2	0	2	0	3	0	0	1	0	3	1.5	3
Latasha Byears 2		12	0	1	.000	0	0	---	0	2	2	0	1	0	1	0	0	0	0.0	0
Katy Steding 2		10	0	2	.000	0	0	---	1	0	1	1	0	0	0	2	0	0	0.0	0
Sacramento 2		400	48	118	.407	27	32	.844	19	44	63	31	34	1	15	24	4	134	67.0	70
Opponents 2		400	51	115	.443	32	36	.889	17	42	59	21	25	0	14	23	3	147	73.5	75

3-pt. FG: Sacramento 11-32 (.344) Bolton-Holifield 4-14 (.286); Holland-Corn 3-9 (.333); Penicheiro 3-6 (.500); Clinesmith 1-1 (1.000); Steding 0-2 (.000); Opponents 13-33 (.394)

WASHINGTON MYSTICS

Player	G	Min	FGM	FGA	Pct	FTM	FTA	Pct	Off	Def	Tot	Ast	PF	Dq	Stl	TO	Blk	Pts	Avg	Hi
Vicky Bullett.................2		69	10	20	.500	6	6	1.000	2	7	9	3	5	0	5	2	5	30	15.0	22
Chamique Holdsclaw....2		75	13	29	.448	4	4	1.000	3	8	11	1	2	0	3	6	1	30	15.0	18
Nikki McCray 2		70	7	16	.438	0	0	---	2	4	6	13	6	0	1	10	0	15	7.5	15
Markita Aldridge 2		49	5	11	.455	4	8	.500	1	3	4	7	3	0	1	1	0	14	7.0	12
Tausha Mills 2		21	4	7	.571	3	8	.375	2	1	3	0	7	0	0	3	0	11	5.5	9
Murriel Page................2		69	4	9	.444	3	4	.750	2	4	6	1	5	0	2	4	0	11	5.5	7
Beth Cunningham 2		13	3	6	.500	0	0	---	0	0	0	0	0	0	1	1	0	7	3.5	7
Keisha Anderson 2		30	1	3	.333	0	2	.000	2	3	5	5	1	0	0	4	0	2	1.0	2
Tonya Washington 1		4	0	0	---	0	0	---	0	0	0	0	1	0	0	1	0	0	0.0	0
Washington 2		400	47	101	.465	20	32	.625	14	30	44	30	30	0	13	32	6	120	60.0	63
Opponents 2		400	58	114	.509	24	28	.857	23	36	59	33	32	0	22	28	5	150	75.0	78

3-pt. FG: Washington 6-22 (.273) Bullett 4-7 (.571); Holdsclaw 0-1 (.000); McCray 1-7 (.143); Aldridge 0-3 (.000); Cunningham 1-4 (.250); Opponents 10-21 (.476)

(*) Statistics with this team only

HOUSTON COMETS

Player	G	Min	FGM	FGA	Pct	FTM	FTA	Pct	Off	Def	Tot	Ast	PF	Dq	Stl	TO	Blk	Pts	Avg	Hi
									REBOUNDS									SCORING		
Cynthia Cooper 2		82	15	44	.341	12	13	.923	3	4	7	12	4	0	3	6	1	45	22.5	25
Sheryl Swoopes 2		78	15	30	.500	10	13	.769	4	10	14	3	3	0	3	3	0	43	21.5	31
Tina Thompson 2		81	9	26	.346	4	4	1.000	5	11	16	3	6	0	3	4	3	26	13.0	15
Janeth Arcain 2		67	5	14	.357	0	0	---	4	7	11	5	8	0	2	8	0	10	5.0	8
Tiffani Johnson 2		47	4	7	.571	0	0	---	5	6	11	0	7	0	1	1	0	8	4.0	6
Tammy Jackson 2		41	2	4	.500	0	0	---	4	4	8	0	5	0	1	0	2	4	2.0	2
Coquese Washington 2		29	0	1	.000	2	2	1.000	0	1	1	1	4	0	2	6	0	2	1.0	2
Houston 2		425	50	126	.397	28	32	.875	25	43	68	24	37	0	15	28	6	138	69.0	79
Opponents 2		425	42	116	.362	34	39	.872	20	38	58	27	42	2	14	29	7	125	62.5	73

3-pt. FG: Houston 10-29 (.345) Cooper 3-10 (.300); Swoopes 3-6 (.500); Thompson 4-11 (.364); Arcain 0-1 (.000); Washington 0-1 (.000); Opponents 7-22 (.318)

NEW YORK LIBERTY

Player	G	Min	FGM	FGA	Pct	FTM	FTA	Pct	Off	Def	Tot	Ast	PF	Dq	Stl	TO	Blk	Pts	Avg	Hi
									REBOUNDS									SCORING		
Tari Phillips 2		74	17	38	.447	10	11	.909	6	16	22	1	9	1	4	8	3	44	22.0	24
Tamika Whitmore..........2		59	5	18	.278	11	14	.786	0	5	5	2	8	0	1	4	1	22	11.0	15
Crystal Robinson 2		56	6	14	.429	3	3	1.000	2	3	5	2	4	0	4	5	1	18	9.0	13
Vickie Johnson 2		76	5	20	.250	6	6	1.000	6	6	12	5	4	0	1	5	0	17	8.5	11
Teresa Weatherspoon 2		79	5	11	.455	2	3	.667	1	5	6	13	9	1	3	2	0	13	6.5	7
Sue Wicks 2		37	3	8	.375	0	0	---	4	3	7	0	5	0	1	2	2	7	3.5	7
Becky Hammon 2		44	1	7	.143	2	2	1.000	1	0	1	4	3	0	0	2	0	4	2.0	4
New York 2		425	42	116	.362	34	39	.872	20	38	58	27	42	2	14	29	7	125	62.5	73
Opponents 2		425	50	126	.397	28	32	.875	25	43	68	24	37	0	15	28	6	138	69.0	79

3-pt. FG: New York 7-22 (.318) Whitmore 1-2 (.500); Robinson 3-8 (.375); Johnson 1-6 (.167); Weatherspoon 1-2 (.500); Wicks 1-1 (1.000); Hammon 0-3 (.000); Opponents 10-29 (.345)

(*) Statistics with this team only

FINALS BOX SCORES

GAME 1
At Madison Square Garden, August 24, 2000

OFFICIALS: Gary Zielinski, Sally Bell, Dennis DeMayo. TIME OF GAME: 2:00. ATTENDANCE: 19,563

SCORE BY PERIODS	1	2	FINAL
Houston 29		30	59
New York 22		30	52

VISITORS: Houston. Head Coach: Van Chancellor.

No Player	MIN	FG	FGA	3P	3PA	FT	FTA	OR	DR	TOT	A	PF	ST	TO	TEC	PTS
7 Tina Thompson 38		5	12	3	6	2	2	1	7	8	2	3	2	1	0	15
22 Sheryl Swoopes 38		4	12	0	2	4	6	2	6	8	2	2	2	2	0	12
00 Tiffani Johnson 16		1	4	0	0	0	0	2	3	5	0	4	1	0	0	2
14 Cynthia Cooper 38		7	23	2	6	4	5	3	0	3	5	1	0	2	0	20
9 Janeth Arcain 35		4	8	0	0	0	0	2	5	7	4	3	2	5	0	8
23 Tammy Jackson 25		1	2	0	0	0	0	2	2	4	0	2	0	0	0	2
4 Coquese Washington 10		0	1	0	1	0	0	0	0	0	0	3	1	2	0	0
3 Jawann Kelley-Gibson						Did not play.										
40 Monica Lamb..................						Did not play.										
21 Jennifer Rizzotti						Did not play.										
13 Amaya Valdemoro						Did not play.										
TOTALS 200		22	62	5	15	10	13	12	23	35	13	18	8	12	0	59

FG pct.: .355. 3PT pct.: .333. FT pct.: .769. Team Rebounds: 10. Total Turnovers: 12 (6 PTS).

HOME: New York. Head Coach: Richie Adubato.

No Player	MIN	FG	FGA	3P	3PA	FT	FTA	OR	DR	TOT	A	PF	ST	TO	TEC	PTS
55 Vickie Johnson 35		2	7	0	1	2	2	4	2	6	2	3	1	1	0	6
44 Tamika Whitmore..........32		1	11	0	0	5	6	0	4	4	1	4	1	1	0	7

No Player	MIN	FG	FGA	3P	3PA	FT	FTA	OR	DR	TOT	A	PF	ST	TO	TEC	PTS
24 Tari Phillips 37		10	19	0	0	4	4	4	11	15	0	3	1	6	0	24
11 Teresa Weatherspoon 37		2	5	0	1	2	3	1	2	3	5	3	2	0	0	6
25 Becky Hammon 26		1	5	0	2	2	2	0	0	0	2	2	0	1	0	4
3 Crystal Robinson 22		2	8	0	4	1	1	1	3	4	0	1	2	3	0	5
23 Sue Wicks.....................11		0	1	0	0	0	0	1	1	2	0	2	0	0	0	0
42 Desiree Francis.................						Did not play.										
00 Olga Firsova.....................						Did not play.										
22 Jessica Bibby						Did not play.										
13 Marina Ferragut						Did not play.										
TOTALS 200		18	56	0	8	16	18	11	23	34	10	18	7	13	0	52

FG pct.: .321. 3PT pct.: .000. FT pct. .889. Team Rebounds: 4. Total Turnovers: 13 (14 PTS).
Blocked Shots: Comets 3: Thompson 1, Cooper 1, Jackson 1. Liberty 2; Phillips 1, Robinson 1.
Technical Fouls: None.
Flagrant Fouls: None.
Points off Turnovers: Houston 14, New York 6.
Fast Break Points: Houston 4, New York 2.
Points in Paint: Houston 24, New York 22.
Second Chance Points: Houston 9, New York 10.

GAME 2
At Compaq Center, August 26, 2000

OFFICIALS: June Courteau, Michael Price, Courtney Kirkland. TIME OF GAME: 2:20. ATTENDANCE: 16,285.

SCORE BY PERIODS	1	2	FINAL	OT
New York 25		39	9	73
Houston 27		37	15	79

VISITORS: New York. Head Coach: Richie Adubato

No Player	MIN	FG	FGA	3P	3PA	FT	FTA	OR	DR	TOT	A	PF	ST	TO	TEC	PTS
55 Vickie Johnson 41		3	13	1	5	4	4	2	4	6	3	1	0	4	0	11
44 Tamika Whitmore 27		4	7	1	2	6	8	0	1	1	1	4	0	3	0	15
24 Tari Phillips 37		7	19	0	0	6	7	2	5	7	1	6	3	2	0	20
11 Teresa Weatherspoon.....42		3	6	1	1	0	0	0	3	3	8	6	1	2	0	7
25 Becky Hammon 18		0	2	0	1	0	0	1	0	1	2	1	0	1	0	0
3 Crystal Robinson 34		4	6	3	4	2	2	1	0	1	2	3	2	2	0	13
23 Sue Wicks 26		3	7	1	1	0	0	3	2	5	0	3	1	2	0	7
42 Desiree Francis						Did not play.										
00 Olga Firsova						Did not play.										
22 Jessica Bibby						Did not play.										
13 Marina Ferragut.................						Did not play.										
TOTALS 225		24	60	7	14	18	21	9	15	24	17	24	7	16	0	73

FG pct.: .400. 3PT pct.: .500. FT pct.: .857. Team Rebounds: 12. Total Turnovers: 16 (14 PTS).

HOME: Houston. Head Coach: Van Chancellor.

No Player	MIN	FG	FGA	3P	3PA	FT	FTA	OR	DR	TOT	A	PF	ST	TO	TEC	PTS
7 Tina Thompson 43		4	14	1	5	2	2	4	4	8	1	3	1	3	0	11
22 Sheryl Swoopes.............40		11	18	3	4	6	7	2	4	6	1	1	1	1	0	31
00 Tiffani Johnson 31		3	3	0	0	0	0	3	3	6	0	3	0	1	0	6
14 Cynthia Cooper.............44		8	21	1	4	8	8	0	4	4	7	3	3	4	0	25
9 Janeth Arcain.................32		1	6	0	1	0	0	2	2	4	1	5	0	3	0	2
4 Coquese Washington 19		0	0	0	0	2	2	0	1	1	1	1	1	4	0	2
23 Tammy Jackson 16		1	2	0	0	0	0	2	2	4	0	3	1	0	0	2
3 Jawann Kelley-Gibson........						Did not play.										
40 Monica Lamb						Did not play.										
21 Jennifer Rizzotti.................						Did not play.										
13 Amaya Valdemoro.............						Did not play.										
TOTALS 225		28	64	5	14	18	19	13	20	33	11	19	7	16	0	79

FG pct.: .438. 3PT pct.: .357. FT pct. .947. Team Rebounds: 7. Total Turnovers: 16 (23 PTS).
Blocked Shots: Liberty 5: Whitmore 1, Phillips 2, Wicks 2. Comets 3: Thompson 2, Jackson 1.
Technical Fouls: None. Flagrant Fouls: None.
Points off Turnovers: New York 23, Houston 14.
Fast Break Points: New York 0, Houston 6.
Points in Paint: New York 22, Houston 38.
Second Chance Points: New York 15, Houston 17.

ALL-STAR GAME BOX SCORE

At America West Arena, July 17, 2000

OFFICIALS: Barb Smith, Lisa Mattingly, Bill Stokes. TIME OF GAME: 1:57. ATTENDANCE: 17,717

SCORE BY PERIODS	1	2	FINAL
East	33	28	61
West	40	33	73

VISITORS: East. Head Coach: Richie Adubato.

No Player	MIN	FG	FGA	3P	3PA	FT	FTA	OR	DR	TOT	A	PF	ST	TO	TEC	PTS
23 Chamique Holdsclaw	25	4	11	0	0	1	2	1	3	4	1	0	0	1	0	9
23 Sue Wicks	16	1	6	0	0	0	0	0	3	3	0	0	0	0	0	2
11 Taj McWilliams-Frank	24	4	8	0	0	2	2	7	2	9	0	2	2	0	0	10
11 Teresa Weatherspoon	20	1	4	0	1	0	0	1	2	3	3	3	3	4	0	2
15 Nikki McCray	19	1	11	1	6	2	2	0	0	0	1	0	3	3	0	5
24 Tari Phillips	22	5	14	0	2	0	3	8	1	9	1	4	0	2	0	10
14 Shannon Johnson	20	2	6	0	4	2	2	0	3	3	2	4	3	1	0	6
25 Merlakia Jones	14	3	8	0	0	0	0	1	1	2	0	1	0	1	0	6
3 Wendy Palmer	14	1	6	0	2	1	2	0	2	2	0	1	0	0	0	3
32 Andrea Stinson	13	1	6	0	1	1	1	1	1	2	2	0	1	3	0	3
42 Nykesha Sales	13	2	5	1	3	0	0	3	0	3	1	1	2	0	0	5
TOTALS	200	25	85	2	19	9	14	22	18	40	11	16	14	15	0	61

FG pct.: .294. 3PT pct.: .105. FT pct.: .643. Team Rebounds: 12 Total Turnovers: 15 (18 PTS).

HOME: West. Head Coach: Van Chancellor.

No Player	MIN	FG	FGA	3P	3PA	FT	FTA	OR	DR	TOT	A	PF	ST	TO	TEC	PTS
7 Tina Thompson	23	5	14	1	4	2	2	6	5	11	1	1	3	4	0	13
22 Sheryl Swoopes	21	3	7	0	1	0	0	1	5	6	3	1	0	2	0	6
9 Lisa Leslie	21	8	15	0	0	0	0	4	2	6	0	0	0	0	0	16
21 Ticha Penicheiro	25	1	2	0	1	1	2	0	2	2	4	0	1	7	0	3
30 Katie Smith	18	0	2	0	2	0	0	0	1	1	2	0	2	0	0	0
24 Natalie Williams	17	2	6	0	0	1	2	4	6	10	0	3	1	0	0	5
33 Yolanda Griffith	16	3	8	0	0	4	6	5	5	10	0	0	0	2	0	10
4 Mwadi Mabika	16	3	7	2	3	2	2	0	1	1	2	1	1	1	0	10
8 DeLisha Milton	16	2	2	0	0	0	0	3	1	4	3	0	0	0	0	4
23 Brandy Reed	14	1	11	0	2	1	2	0	4	4	0	1	2	3	0	3
22 Betty Lennox	13	1	3	1	2	0	0	2	3	5	1	1	0	4	0	3
14 Cynthia Cooper								Did not play.								
TOTALS	200	29	77	4	15	11	16	25	35	60	16	8	10	23	0	73

FG pct.: .377. 3PT pct.: .267. FT pct.: .688. Team Rebounds: 6. Total Turnovers: 23 (13 PTS).

Blocked Shots: East 5: Wicks 1, Phillips 3, S. Johnson 1. West 3: Thompson, Leslie, Griffith.

Technical Fouls: None.

Flagrant Fouls: None.

Points off Turnovers: East 13, West 18.

Fast Break Points: East 4, West 10.

Points in Paint: East 28, West 46.

Second Chance Points: East 12, West 25.

MVP: Tina Thompson.

Front Row (l. to r.) - Janeth Arcain, Tina Thompson, Sheryl Swoopes, Owner/President Leslie L. Alexander, Cynthia Cooper, Polina Tzekova, Sonja Henning. Back Row (l. to r.) - Assistant Coach Kevin Cook, Head Coach Van Chancellor, Assistant Coach Alisa Scott, Jennifer Rizzotti, Tammy Jackson, Kara Wolters, Mila Nikolich, Amaya Valdemoro, Video Coordinator Harold Liggans, Trainer Michelle T. Leget, Manager of Operations Shelly Patterson.

FINAL STANDINGS

EASTERN CONFERENCE

Team	CHA	CLE	DET	HOU	LA	MIN	NY	ORL	PHO	SAC	UTA	WAS	W	L	PCT	GB	Last-10	Streak
NY	2	3	2	1	1	0	—	4	1	1	2	1	18	14	.563	—	6-4	Lost 1
CHA	—	3	2	0	0	1	2	3	1	0	1	2	15	17	.469	3	3-7	Lost 5
DET	2	3	—	0	1	1	2	3	0	0	1	2	15	17	.469	3	5-5	Won 2
ORL	1	4	1	1	1	1	0	—	1	1	1	3	15	17	.469	3	6-4	Lost 1
WAS	2	2	2	0	1	1	3	1	0	0	0	—	12	20	.375	6	6-4	Lost 3
CLE	1	—	1	0	0	1	1	0	1	0	0	2	7	25	.219	11	2-8	Won 1

WESTERN CONFERENCE

Team	CHA	CLE	DET	HOU	LA	MIN	NY	ORL	PHO	SAC	UTA	WAS	W	L	PCT	GB	Last-10	Streak
HOU	2	2	2	—	2	4	1	1	3	3	4	2	26	6	.813	—	8-2	Won 1
LA	2	2	1	2	—	3	1	1	3	2	2	1	20	12	.625	6	4-6	Lost 1
SAC	2	2	2	1	2	2	1	1	3	—	1	2	19	13	.594	7	5-5	Lost 3
MIN	1	1	1	0	1	—	2	1	2	2	3	1	15	17	.469	11	3-7	Won 1
PHO	1	1	2	1	1	2	1	1	—	1	2	2	15	17	.469	11	5-5	Lost 2
UTA	1	2	1	0	2	1	0	1	2	3	—	2	15	17	.469	11	7-3	Won 2

TEAM STANDINGS
OFFENSIVE

TEAM	G	FG	FGA	PCT	FG3	FG3A	PCT	FT	FTA	PCT	OFF	DEF	REB	AST	PF	DQ	STL	TO	BLK	PTS	AVG
L.A.	32	890	2044	.435	163	476	.342	506	676	.749	342	725	1067	581	693	6	237	484	124	2449	76.5
Sac.	32	849	2006	.423	126	421	.299	568	847	.671	412	700	1112	500	614	4	329	508	123	2392	74.8
Utah	32	845	1949	.434	107	362	.296	570	742	.768	344	717	1061	552	740	5	240	560	158	2367	74.0
Hou.	32	841	1912	.440	176	547	.322	509	622	.818	303	682	985	499	586	4	272	452	139	2367	74.0
Det.	32	791	1972	.401	121	336	.360	536	764	.702	321	675	996	464	728	14	238	483	96	2239	70.0
Orl.	32	793	1869	.424	155	461	.336	465	672	.692	329	637	966	467	648	10	297	521	93	2206	68.9
Phoe.	32	762	1910	.399	134	456	.294	519	695	.747	343	659	1002	510	652	8	229	460	121	2177	68.0
N.Y.	32	800	1914	.418	175	473	.370	394	529	.745	319	625	944	522	700	9	297	482	91	2169	67.8
Cha.	32	793	1805	.439	108	369	.293	410	535	.766	268	685	953	568	560	3	233	469	97	2104	65.8
Wash.	32	759	1794	.423	100	345	.290	482	679	.710	312	701	1013	461	646	7	203	574	87	2100	65.6
Minn.	32	748	1925	.389	200	603	.332	339	470	.721	298	608	906	525	670	11	204	437	78	2035	63.6
Clev.	32	766	1852	.414	88	309	.285	394	545	.723	289	688	977	489	627	3	235	547	116	2014	62.9

DEFENSIVE

Team	FG	FGA	PCT	FG3	FG3A	PCT	FT	FTA	PCT	OFF	DEF	REB	AST	PF	DQ	STL	TO	BLK	PTS	AVG	DIFF
Hou.	763	1954	.390	125	442	.283	419	566	.740	350	621	971	459	633	3	216	491	78	2070	64.7	+9.3
N.Y.	720	1747	.412	109	405	.269	540	723	.747	299	682	981	451	584	3	252	557	89	2089	65.3	+2.5
Minn.	749	1763	.425	137	458	.299	476	641	.743	296	732	1028	507	614	3	194	492	92	2111	66.0	-2.4
Cha.	814	1920	.424	136	428	.318	378	522	.724	318	626	944	506	597	6	221	440	99	2142	66.9	-1.2
Phoe.	794	1911	.415	119	395	.301	475	637	.746	334	678	1012	494	676	15	234	479	108	2182	68.2	-0.2
Orl.	812	1892	.429	161	438	.368	431	608	.709	340	664	1004	537	660	9	257	534	124	2216	69.3	-0.3
Clev.	823	1939	.424	137	445	.308	434	616	.705	335	672	1007	536	608	3	314	477	113	2217	69.3	-6.3
Wash.	825	1986	.415	127	403	.315	469	650	.722	359	636	995	518	663	9	304	436	119	2246	70.2	-4.6
Sac.	829	1981	.418	161	474	.340	439	590	.744	310	665	975	535	718	8	226	569	152	2258	70.6	+4.2
Det.	830	1901	.437	114	338	.337	529	736	.719	293	769	1062	514	723	11	262	532	133	2303	72.0	-2.0
L.A.	818	1993	.410	147	445	.330	535	721	.742	335	696	1031	511	681	6	250	493	99	2318	72.4	+4.1
Utah	860	1965	.438	180	487	.370	567	766	.740	311	661	972	570	707	8	284	477	117	2467	77.1	-3.1
Avg	803	1913	.420	138	430	.320	474	648	.732	323	675	999	512	655	7	251	498	110	2218	69.3	---
Totals	9637			1653			5692			3880		11982	7864				3014	1323			
	22952			5158			7776			8102		6138			84		5977		26619	

TEAM COMPARISONS

TEAM	Points Per Game		Field Goal Percentage		Turnovers Per Game		Rebound Percentages			Below 70 Pts.		Overtime Games		3 PTS or Less		10 PTS or More	
	OWN	OPP	OWN	OPP	OWN	OPP	OFF	DEF	TOT	OWN	OPP	W	L	W	L	W	L
Charlotte	65.8	66.9	.439	.424	14.7	13.8	.300	.683	.491	23	20	1	0	1	3	6	8
Cleveland	62.9	69.3	.414	.424	17.1	14.9	.301	.673	.487	24	13	0	0	1	5	6	12
Detroit	70.0	72.0	.401	.437	15.1	16.6	.294	.697	.496	15	17	0	2	3	1	4	11
Houston	74.0	*64.7	*.440	*.390	14.1	15.3	.328	.661	.494	9	22	1	0	2	2	15	3
Los Angeles	*76.5	72.4	.435	.410	15.1	15.4	.329	.684	.507	6	13	2	0	3	3	12	4
Minnesota	63.6	66.0	.389	.425	*13.7	15.4	.289	.673	.481	20	20	0	2	4	2	6	10
New York	67.8	65.3	.418	.412	15.1	17.4	.319	.676	.498	18	22	2	3	2	4	10	6
Orlando	68.9	69.3	.424	.429	16.3	16.7	.331	.652	.492	18	14	1	1	4	0	4	4
Phoenix	68.0	68.2	.399	.415	14.4	15.0	.336	.664	.500	18	16	0	0	1	2	9	9
Sacramento	74.8	70.6	.423	.418	15.9	*17.8	*.383	.693	*.538	9	14	0	0	1	2	14	4
Utah	74.0	77.1	.434	.438	17.5	14.9	.342	*.697	.520	11	10	1	2	2	1	6	10
Washington	65.6	70.2	.423	.415	17.9	13.6	.329	.661	.495	22	12	2	0	4	3	2	13
COMPOSITE; 192 games																	
	69.3		.420		15.6		.324	.676		193	10			28		94	

* - League Leader

REBOUND PERCENTAGES

OFF. - Percentage of a given team's missed shots which that team rebounds.

DEF. - Percentage of opponents' missed shots which a given team rebounds.

TOT. - Average of offensive and defensive rebound percentages.

SCORING AVERAGE

	G	FG	FT	PTS	AVG
Cooper, Hou.	31	212	204	686	22.1
Griffith, Sac.	29	200	145	545	18.8
Swoopes, Hou.	32	226	100	585	18.3
Williams, Utah	28	180	144	504	18.0
McCray, Was.	32	193	129	561	17.5
Holdsclaw, Was.	31	202	116	525	16.9
Reed, Min.	25	168	53	402	16.1
Leslie, L.A.	32	182	114	500	15.6
Gillom, Pho.	32	163	141	485	15.2
Goodson, Utah	32	182	99	476	14.9
Edwards, Min.	32	165	79	475	14.8
S. Johnson, Orl.	32	151	105	447	14.0
Sales, Orl.	32	153	95	437	13.7
Bolton-Holifield, Sac.	31	143	75	421	13.6
Stinson, Cha.	32	174	65	434	13.6
Johnson, N.Y.	32	165	72	427	13.3
Brondello, Det.	32	152	83	424	13.3
McWilliams, Orl.	32	153	94	420	13.1
Dydek, Utah	32	141	114	403	12.6
Thompson, Hou.	32	142	68	391	12.2

REBOUNDS PER GAME

	G	OFF	DEF	TOT	AVG
Griffith, Sac.	29	141	188	329	11.3
Williams, Utah	28	109	148	257	9.2
Holdsclaw, Was.	31	74	172	246	7.9
Leslie, L.A.	32	72	176	248	7.8
McWilliams, Orl.	32	81	158	239	7.5
Askamp, Pho.	30	92	123	215	7.2
Wicks, N.Y.	32	76	147	223	7.0
Bullett, Cha.	32	60	159	219	6.8
Whiting, Det.	31	66	141	207	6.7
Page, Was.	32	68	145	213	6.7
Thompson, Hou.	32	67	139	206	6.4
Mapp, Cha.	30	48	145	193	6.4
Dydek, Utah	32	38	166	204	6.4
Swoopes, Hou.	32	48	154	202	6.3
Palmer, Utah-Det.	31	50	138	188	6.1
Reed, Min.	25	55	96	151	6.0
Gillom, Pho.	32	53	131	184	5.8
Hampton, N.Y.	32	61	118	179	5.6
Milton, L.A.	32	60	116	176	5.5
Enis, Was.	29	53	104	157	5.4

ASSISTS PER GAME

	G	AST	AVG
Penicheiro, Sac.	32	226	7.1
Weatherspoon, N.Y.	32	205	6.4
Staley, Cha.	32	177	5.5
Cooper, Hou.	31	162	5.2
Timms, Pho.	30	151	5.0
Black, Utah	32	161	5.0
Nagy, Was.	32	146	4.6

S. Johnson, Orl.	32	141	4.4
Swoopes, Hou.	32	127	4.0
Azzi, Det.	28	106	3.8
Mabika, L.A.	32	112	3.5
Johnson, N.Y.	32	106	3.3
Tate, Min.	32	100	3.1
Harrower, Pho.	32	96	3.0
Stinson, Cha.	32	93	2.9
Lloyd Curry, Min.	32	91	2.8
Sales, Orl.	32	91	2.8
Grubin, L.A.	32	90	2.8
Goodson, Utah	32	87	2.7
Edwards, Cle.	31	82	2.6

FIELD GOAL PCT.

	FG	FGA	PCT
Page, Was.	105	183	.574
Griffith, Sac.	200	370	.541
Burras, Cle.	103	191	.539
Byears, Sac.	130	242	.537
Milton, L.A.	125	236	.530
Williams, Utah	180	347	.519
Azzi, Det.	93	181	.514
Mapp, Cha.	118	236	.500
Dydek, Utah	141	283	.498
Bullett, Cha.	142	292	.486

3-PT FIELD GOAL PCT

.	3FG	3GA	PCT
Azzi, Det.	30	58	.517
Brondello, Det.	37	76	.487
McWilliams, Orl.	20	45	.444
Robinson, N.Y.	76	174	.437
Grubin, L.A.	40	93	.430
Leslie, L.A.	22	52	.423
Baranova, Utah	20	48	.417
Hlede, Det.-Utah	21	53	.396
K. Smith, Min.	52	136	.382
Weatherspoon, N.Y.	31	82	.378

FREE THROW PCT.

	FT	FTA	PCT
Nemcova, Cle.	62	63	.984
Staley, Cha.	85	91	.934
Cooper, Hou.	204	229	.891
Hlede, Det.-Utah	72	82	.878
Toler, L.A.	39	45	.867
Dydek, Utah	114	133	.857
Brondello, Det.	83	98	.847
Robinson, N.Y.	49	58	.845
Johnson, N.Y.	72	86	.837
Congreaves, Orl.	44	53	.830

STEALS PER GAME

	G	STL	AVG
Griffith, Sac.	29	73	2.52
Weatherspoon, N.Y.	32	78	2.44

REVIEW 1999 Regular Season

	G		AVG			G		AVG
Black, Utah	32	77	2.41	Wicks, N.Y.	32	43	1.34
Swoopes, Hou.	32	76	2.38	Smith, Sac.	31	38	1.23
Sales, Orl.	32	69	2.16	McWilliams, Orl.	32	38	1.19
Penicheiro, Sac.	32	67	2.09	Whiting, Det.	31	31	1.00
Holland-Corn, Sac.	32	63	1.97				
Bullett, Cha.	32	62	1.94				
McWilliams, Orl.	32	57	1.78				
S. Johnson, Orl.	32	54	1.69				

MINUTES PER GAME

	G	MIN	AVG
S. Johnson, Orl.	32	1147	35.8
Cooper, Hou.	31	1101	35.5
Penicheiro, Sac.	32	1120	35.0
Swoopes, Hou.	32	1100	34.4
Holdsclaw, Was.	31	1061	34.2
Gillom, Pho.	32	1095	34.2
Williams, Utah	28	954	34.1
Sam, Orl.	32	1088	34.0
Weatherspoon, N.Y.	32	1086	33.9
Johnson, N.Y.	32	1082	33.8

BLOCKS PER GAME

	G	BLK	AVG
Dydek, Utah	32	77	2.41
Stepanova, Pho.	32	62	1.94
Griffith, Sac.	29	54	1.86
Leslie, L.A.	32	49	1.53
Swoopes, Hou.	32	46	1.44
Bullett, Cha.	32	45	1.41

INDIVIDUAL STATISTICS, TEAM BY TEAM

CHARLOTTE STING

Player	G	Min	FGM	FGA	Pct	FTM	FTA	Pct	Off	Def	Tot	Ast	PF	Dq	Stl	TO	Blk	Pts	Avg	Hi
Andrea Stinson	32	1041	174	378	.460	65	88	.739	32	81	113	93	56	0	32	67	18	434	13.6	27
Vicky Bullett	32	1008	142	292	.486	75	97	.773	60	159	219	50	77	1	62	60	45	369	11.5	24
Dawn Staley	32	1065	125	301	.415	85	91	.934	12	60	72	177	71	0	38	90	3	368	11.5	23
Rhonda Mapp	30	790	118	236	.500	49	68	.721	48	145	193	56	102	0	25	60	13	286	9.5	22
Charlotte Smith	32	746	62	188	.330	41	58	.707	46	69	115	58	87	1	10	50	7	173	5.4	12
Stephanie McCarty	30	563	53	130	.408	30	33	.909	16	33	49	52	47	1	19	38	2	159	5.3	18
Tracy Reid	10	154	21	49	.429	6	14	.429	7	16	23	9	12	0	1	17	2	48	4.8	15
Sharon Manning	32	521	57	113	.504	24	46	.522	37	77	114	17	51	0	28	27	4	139	4.3	12
Angie Braziel	7	41	7	14	.500	10	12	.833	1	10	11	3	6	0	2	2	0	24	3.4	8
Christy Smith	4	19	3	4	.750	5	6	.833	0	1	1	1	3	0	1	1	0	13	3.3	10
Niesa Johnson	31	296	15	50	.300	11	12	.917	3	15	18	43	19	0	10	27	2	47	1.5	6
Cass Bauer	25	123	13	34	.382	7	8	.875	4	16	20	4	20	0	1	13	1	33	1.3	6
Sonia Chase	13	58	3	16	.188	2	2	1.000	2	3	5	5	9	0	4	2	0	11	0.8	6
Charlotte	32	6425	793	1805	.439	410	535	.766	268	685	953	568	560	3	233	469	97	2104	65.8	88
Opponents	32	6425	814	1920	.424	378	522	.724	318	626	944	506	597	6	221	440	99	2142	66.9	82

3-pt. FG: Charlotte 108-369 (.293) Stinson 21-68 (.309); Bullett 10-27 (.370); Staley 33-104 (.317); Mapp 1-9 (.111); Cha. Smith 8-56 (.143); McCarty 23-65 (.354) Reid 0-1 (.000); Manning 1-1 (1.000); Chr. Smith 2-3 (.667); Johnson 6-23 (.261); Bauer 0-1 (.000); Chase 3-11 (.273) Opponents 136-428 (.318)

CLEVELAND ROCKERS

Player	G	Min	FGM	FGA	Pct	FTM	FTA	Pct	Off	Def	Tot	Ast	PF	Dq	Stl	TO	Blk	Pts	Avg	Hi
Eva Nemcova	31	925	124	296	.419	62	63	.984	27	87	114	50	50	0	31	81	22	344	11.1	20
Merlakia Jones	32	853	141	325	.434	60	78	.769	47	75	122	51	81	1	41	66	5	347	10.8	27
Chasity Melvin	32	709	95	218	.436	68	98	.694	53	74	127	38	93	1	20	42	22	259	8.1	16
Michelle Edwards	31	745	88	245	.359	45	65	.692	6	66	72	82	58	0	26	72	8	236	7.6	17
Alisa Burras	31	563	103	191	.539	26	47	.553	40	84	124	17	47	0	17	38	10	232	7.5	20
S. McConnell Serio	18	511	36	98	.367	16	19	.842	4	39	43	76	31	0	10	54	2	108	6.0	15
Janice Braxton	26	476	52	113	.460	46	66	.697	26	85	111	33	53	0	19	34	13	151	5.8	12
Rushia Brown	30	434	53	124	.427	25	37	.676	31	56	87	20	60	1	19	34	10	131	4.4	13
Tracy Henderson	27	308	27	87	.310	17	29	.586	28	51	79	9	45	0	9	25	20	71	2.6	8
Mery Andrade	32	364	23	59	.390	18	26	.692	15	35	50	49	73	0	18	40	4	71	2.2	11
Jamila Wideman	26	401	21	77	.273	11	17	.647	8	26	34	51	22	0	20	40	0	56	2.2	9
Vanessa Nygaard	4	20	1	2	.500	0	0	---	1	2	3	1	4	0	2	2	0	3	0.8	3
Tricia Bader(*)	9	72	2	13	.154	0	0	---	3	8	11	11	8	0	3	3	0	5	0.6	3

Player	G	Min	FGM	FGA	Pct	FTM	FTA	Pct	REBOUNDS Off	Def	Tot	Ast	PF	Dq	Stl	TO	Blk	SCORING Pts	Avg	Hi
Tricia Bader(†)	16	106	2	16	.125	2	2	1.000	3	10	13	12	20	0	6	7	1	7	0.4	3
Jennifer Howard	4	15	0	4	.000	0	0	---	0	0	0	0	2	0	0	3	0	0	0.0	0
Kellie Jolly Harper	1	4	0	0	---	0	0	---	0	0	0	1	0	0	0	2	0	0	0.0	0
Cleveland	32	6400	766	1852	.414	394	545	.723	289	688	977	489	627	3	235	547	116	2014	62.9	85
Opponents	32	6400	823	1939	.424	434	616	.705	335	672	1007	536	608	3	314	477	113	2217	69.3	87

3-pt. FG: Cleveland 88-309 (.285) Nemcova 34-93 (.366); Jones 5-18 (.278); Melvin 1-1 (1.000); Edwards 15-69 (.217); McConnell Serio 20-60 (.333); Brown 0-1 (.000) Braxton 1-8 (.125); Andrade 7-24 (.292); Wideman 3-22 (.136); Nygaard 1-2 (.500); Bader(*) 1-8 (.125); Bader(†) 1-10 (.100) Howard 0-3 (.000); Opponents 137-445 (.308).

DETROIT SHOCK

Player	G	Min	FGM	FGA	Pct	FTM	FTA	Pct	REBOUNDS Off	Def	Tot	Ast	PF	Dq	Stl	TO	Blk	SCORING Pts	Avg	Hi
Sandy Brondello	32	1002	152	347	.438	83	98	.847	29	37	66	73	81	4	25	75	5	424	13.3	33
Jennifer Azzi	28	838	93	181	.514	86	104	.827	5	56	61	106	103	3	24	56	4	302	10.8	27
Wendy Palmer(*)	11	295	47	100	.470	42	55	.764	27	78	105	12	44	2	6	26	4	140	12.7	27
Wendy Palmer(†)	31	741	104	241	.432	86	123	.699	50	138	188	42	101	3	9	58	12	307	9.9	27
Dominique Canty	26	646	76	229	.332	94	136	.691	35	45	80	38	57	1	26	45	1	249	9.6	18
Korie Hlede(‡)	21	408	67	172	.390	42	49	.857	24	31	55	25	49	1	22	32	2	184	8.8	22
Cindy Brown(‡)	21	490	46	146	.315	45	65	.692	35	78	113	22	45	0	25	35	12	144	6.9	18
Val Whiting	31	764	76	200	.380	50	110	.455	66	141	207	49	84	1	40	46	31	202	6.5	12
Rachael Sporn	18	340	44	94	.468	18	28	.643	26	33	59	27	45	0	15	16	4	106	5.9	14
Carla Porter	32	694	69	174	.397	17	27	.630	25	47	72	51	84	2	24	54	8	172	5.4	14
Astou Ndiaye	31	438	70	160	.438	24	39	.615	25	74	99	17	51	0	11	32	18	164	5.3	14
C. Maria das Neves	30	306	25	95	.263	12	19	.632	8	15	23	29	32	0	16	23	0	76	2.5	11
O. Scott-Richardson(*)	8	52	6	18	.333	4	6	.667	3	9	12	3	14	0	0	5	3	16	2.0	6
O. Scott-Richardson(†)	12	88	9	28	.321	7	12	.583	8	12	20	5	21	0	1	8	3	25	2.1	9
Wanda Guyton	11	98	4	17	.235	13	16	.813	8	18	26	2	21	0	2	10	2	21	1.9	7
Elena Tornikidou	11	86	9	23	.391	2	6	.333	3	6	9	8	8	0	1	11	1	20	1.8	8
Lesley Brown	13	43	7	16	.438	4	6	.667	2	7	9	2	10	0	1	6	1	19	1.5	9
Detroit	32	6500	791	1972	.401	536	764	.702	321	675	996	464	728	14	238	483	96	2239	70.0	94
Opponents	32	6500	828	1901	.437	529	736	.719	293	769	1062	514	723	11	262	532	133	2303	72.0	104

3-pt. FG: Detroit 121-336 (.360) Brondello 37-76 (.487); Azzi 30-58 (.517); Palmer(*) 4-16 (.250); Palmer(†) 13-46 (.283); Canty 3-17 (.176); Hlede(‡) 8-24 (.333) C. Brown(‡) 7-30 (.233); Sporn 0-1 (.000); Porter 17-51 (.333); Ndiaye 0-1 (.000); das Neves 14-60 (.233); L. Brown 1-2 (.500) Opponents 114-338 (.337).

HOUSTON COMETS

Player	G	Min	FGM	FGA	Pct	FTM	FTA	Pct	REBOUNDS Off	Def	Tot	Ast	PF	Dq	Stl	TO	Blk	SCORING Pts	Avg	Hi
Cynthia Cooper	31	1101	212	458	.463	204	229	.891	17	70	87	162	61	0	43	104	11	686	22.1	42
Sheryl Swoopes	32	1100	226	489	.462	100	122	.820	48	154	202	127	57	0	76	83	46	585	18.3	33
Tina Thompson	32	1074	142	339	.419	68	87	.782	67	139	206	28	95	0	31	72	31	391	12.2	26
Polina Tzekova	32	778	76	177	.429	31	40	.775	54	109	163	32	118	4	13	52	19	194	6.1	15
Janeth Arcain	32	735	71	164	.433	34	41	.829	32	59	91	38	63	0	30	39	2	187	5.8	13
Monica Lamb	3	36	4	10	.400	5	6	.833	3	3	6	0	6	0	0	1	2	13	4.3	6
Sonja Henning	32	798	52	117	.444	11	18	.611	22	58	80	74	60	0	34	29	7	128	4.0	14
Tammy Jackson	28	382	24	58	.414	25	35	.714	45	46	91	7	75	0	15	26	20	74	2.6	8
Amaya Valdemoro	17	92	13	35	.371	12	16	.750	4	9	13	9	16	0	11	12	0	40	2.4	12
Jennifer Rizzotti	25	242	14	40	.350	7	12	.583	2	25	27	19	21	0	18	16	1	42	1.7	9
Kara Wolters	10	41	3	13	.231	10	12	.833	5	7	12	2	11	0	1	3	0	16	1.6	4
Mila Nikolich	7	29	4	11	.364	1	2	.500	3	2	5	1	3	0	0	3	0	10	1.4	4
Nyree Roberts(‡)	4	17	0	1	.000	1	2	.500	1	1	2	0	0	0	1	1	0	1	0.3	1
Houston	32	6425	841	1912	.440	509	622	.818	303	682	985	499	586	4	272	452	139	2367	74.0	93
Opponents	32	6425	763	1954	.390	419	566	.740	350	621	971	459	633	3	216	491	78	2070	64.7	84

3-pt. FG: Houston 176-547 (.322) Cooper 58-173 (.335); Swoopes 33-98 (.337); Thompson 39-111 (.351); Tzekova 11-44 (.250); Arcain 11-44 (.250); Jackson 1-1 (1.000) Henning 13-41 (.317); Valdemoro 2-5 (.400); Rizzotti 7-26 (.269); Nikolich 1-4 (.250); Opponents 125-442 (.283).

LOS ANGELES SPARKS

Player	G	Min	FGM	FGA	Pct	FTM	FTA	Pct	REBOUNDS Off	Def	Tot	Ast	PF	Dq	Stl	TO	Blk	SCORING Pts	Avg	Hi
Lisa Leslie	32	930	182	389	.468	114	156	.731	72	176	248	56	136	4	36	94	49	500	15.6	30
Mwadi Mabika	32	938	125	336	.372	56	78	.718	42	111	153	112	100	1	44	58	15	347	10.8	20

Player	G	Min	FGM	FGA	Pct	FTM	FTA	Pct	Off	Def	Tot	Ast	PF	Dq	Stl	TO	Blk	Pts	Avg	Hi
DeLisha Milton	32	835	125	236	.530	68	86	.791	60	116	176	50	112	0	47	71	17	318	9.9	20
Gordana Grubin	32	708	96	238	.403	52	68	.765	18	54	72	90	53	1	24	53	2	284	8.9	20
Tamecka Dixon	32	563	77	199	.387	48	65	.738	17	49	66	53	42	0	17	39	4	217	6.8	14
La'Keshia Frett	31	658	77	162	.475	34	43	.791	48	46	94	63	42	0	9	26	5	188	6.1	15
Allison Feaster	32	410	51	103	.495	39	57	.684	28	30	58	32	51	0	15	28	7	162	5.1	16
Penny Toler	30	427	51	150	.340	39	45	.867	12	31	43	66	36	0	13	40	0	143	4.8	21
Nina Bjedov	27	431	52	100	.520	9	18	.500	21	49	70	17	60	0	9	25	22	121	4.5	17
Ukari Figgs	22	330	30	82	.366	21	24	.875	8	27	35	33	27	0	15	31	0	95	4.3	15
C. Machanguana	28	245	24	49	.490	26	36	.722	16	36	52	9	34	0	8	14	3	74	2.6	8
Los Angeles	32	6475	890	2044	.435	506	676	.749	342	725	1067	513	693	6	237	484	124	2449	76.5	102
Opponents	32	6475	818	1993	.410	535	721	.742	335	696	1031	511	681	6	250	493	99	2318	72.4	89

3-pt. FG: Los Angeles 163-476 (.342) Leslie 22-52 (.423); Mabika 41-146 (.281); Milton 0-1 (.000); Grubin 40-93 (.430); Dixon 15-48 (.313); Feaster 21-57 (.368) Toler 2-13 (.154); Bjedov 8-19 (.421); Figgs 14-47 (.298); Opponents 147-445 (.330)

MINNESOTA LYNX

Player	G	Min	FGM	FGA	Pct	FTM	FTA	Pct	REBOUNDS Off	Def	Tot	Ast	PF	Dq	Stl	TO	Blk	SCORING Pts	Avg	Hi
Brandy Reed	25	757	168	366	.459	53	70	.757	55	96	151	64	57	0	29	63	17	402	16.1	28
Tonya Edwards	32	1031	165	462	.357	79	98	.806	15	97	112	84	104	6	27	68	13	475	14.8	25
Katie Smith	30	971	113	292	.387	72	94	.766	42	46	88	60	106	3	19	55	10	350	11.7	27
A. Lloyd Curry	32	899	75	200	.375	34	45	.756	38	100	138	91	92	1	30	62	12	214	6.7	17
Kristin Folkl	32	518	67	140	.479	21	39	.538	41	75	116	23	68	0	14	23	12	157	4.9	21
Sonja Tate	32	828	52	147	.354	23	30	.767	48	79	127	100	84	0	36	65	3	143	4.5	19
Angela Potthoff	32	710	53	140	.379	18	33	.545	26	59	85	37	84	0	24	35	5	127	4.0	13
Trisha Fallon	26	281	24	80	.300	23	31	.742	9	13	22	22	30	1	11	16	6	77	3.0	13
Annie LaFleur	25	333	23	66	.348	2	8	.250	14	24	38	36	19	0	8	20	0	59	2.4	9
Adia Barnes	19	91	7	23	.304	6	12	.500	8	12	20	6	16	0	5	8	0	21	1.1	9
Charmin Smith	13	56	1	9	.111	8	10	.800	2	7	9	2	10	0	1	5	0	10	0.8	4
Minnesota	32	6475	748	1925	.389	339	470	.721	298	608	906	525	670	11	204	437	78	2035	63.6	86
Opponents	32	6475	749	1763	.425	476	641	.743	296	732	1028	507	614	3	194	492	92	2111	66.0	86

3-pt. FG: Minnesota 200-603 (.332) Reed 13-38 (.342); Edwards 66-192 (.344); K. Smith 52-136 (.382); Lloyd-Curry 30-90 (.333); Folkl 2-14 (.143); Tate 16-67 (.239) Potthoff 3-18 (.167); Fallon 6-17 (.353); LaFleur 11-24 (.458); Barnes 1-3 (.333); C. Smith 0-4 (.000); Opponents 137-458 (.299)

NEW YORK LIBERTY

Player	G	Min	FGM	FGA	Pct	FTM	FTA	Pct	REBOUNDS Off	Def	Tot	Ast	PF	Dq	Stl	TO	Blk	SCORING Pts	Avg	Hi
Vickie Johnson	32	1082	165	394	.419	72	86	.837	43	99	142	106	77	0	44	66	1	427	13.3	26
Crystal Robinson	32	901	125	285	.439	49	58	.845	38	51	89	49	78	1	44	46	11	375	11.7	27
Kym Hampton	32	856	112	260	.431	68	91	.747	61	118	179	22	110	1	22	51	18	293	9.2	21
S. Witherspoon	32	581	97	245	.396	49	69	.710	20	27	47	37	54	0	33	48	2	271	8.5	22
Tamika Whitmore	27	573	80	184	.435	53	78	.679	43	53	96	18	78	1	16	56	6	214	7.9	20
T. Weatherspoon	32	1086	80	190	.421	38	56	.679	22	82	104	205	91	1	78	80	3	229	7.2	16
Sue Wicks	32	938	91	226	.403	32	52	.615	76	147	223	45	123	5	41	63	43	216	6.8	16
R. Hammon	30	202	27	64	.422	15	17	.882	2	17	19	17	27	0	6	24	0	80	2.7	16
Venus Lacy	17	111	10	24	.417	12	15	.800	7	13	20	1	24	0	3	14	4	32	1.9	8
Michele VanGorp	21	117	8	24	.333	4	5	.800	5	12	17	7	23	0	1	3	3	20	1.0	5
C. Washington	19	77	5	18	.278	2	2	1.000	1	6	7	15	15	0	9	13	0	12	0.6	4
Rebecca Lobo	1	1	0	0	---	0	0	---	1	0	1	0	0	0	0	1	0	0	0.0	0
New York	32	6525	800	1914	.418	394	529	.745	319	625	944	522	700	9	297	482	91	2169	67.8	88
Opponents	32	6525	720	1747	.412	540	723	.747	299	682	981	451	584	3	252	557	89	2089	65.3	91

3-pt. FG: New York 175-473 (.370) Johnson 25-71 (.352); Robinson 76-174 (.437); Hampton 1-2 (.500); Witherspoon 28-78 (.359); Whitmore 1-8 (.125); Wicks 2-15 (.133) Weatherspoon 31-82 (.378); Hammon 11-38 (.289); Washington 0-5 (.000); Opponents 109-405 (.269)

ORLANDO MIRACLE

Player	G	Min	FGM	FGA	Pct	FTM	FTA	Pct	REBOUNDS Off	Def	Tot	Ast	PF	Dq	Stl	TO	Blk	SCORING Pts	Avg	Hi
Shannon Johnson	32	1147	151	338	.447	105	153	.686	44	106	150	141	79	0	54	121	12	447	14.0	31
Nykesha Sales	32	1039	153	397	.385	95	118	.805	44	91	135	91	97	2	69	69	8	437	13.7	29

Player	G	Min	FGM	FGA	Pct	FTM	FTA	Pct	Off	Def	Tot	Ast	PF	Dq	Stl	TO	Blk	Pts	Avg	Hi
Taj McWilliams	32	1042	153	319	.480	94	141	.667	81	158	239	51	96	3	57	80	38	420	13.1	24
Sheri Sam	32	1088	134	345	.388	55	80	.688	39	107	146	77	112	4	41	64	9	364	11.4	22
A. Congreaves	32	812	75	150	.500	44	53	.830	40	61	101	34	84	1	24	49	7	209	6.5	16
Tari Phillips	32	335	52	128	.406	26	54	.481	26	40	66	9	54	0	19	48	8	130	4.1	8
Elaine Powell	18	256	17	33	.515	12	22	.545	9	14	23	32	22	0	9	19	4	47	2.6	9
Adrienne Johnson	29	224	25	62	.403	6	9	.667	12	16	28	14	21	0	5	14	2	57	2.0	8
Carla McGhee	30	234	15	47	.319	15	18	.833	22	24	46	8	38	0	8	22	3	45	1.5	5
Yolanda Moore	23	114	10	21	.476	6	12	.500	4	9	13	1	21	0	4	13	0	26	1.1	5
Tora Suber	25	114	7	24	.292	5	10	.500	4	9	13	9	14	0	5	10	0	20	0.8	4
Kisha Ford	8	45	1	5	.200	2	2	1.000	4	2	6	0	10	0	2	1	2	4	0.5	2
Orlando	32	6450	793	1869	.424	465	672	.692	329	637	966	467	648	10	297	521	93	2206	68.9	93
Opponents	32	6450	812	1892	.429	431	608	.709	340	664	1004	537	660	9	257	534	124	2216	69.3	86

3-pt. FG: Orlando 155-461 (.336) S. Johnson 40-110 (.364); Sales 36-109 (.330); McWilliams 20-45 (.444); Sam 41-125 (.328); Congreaves 15-41 (.366) Phillips 0-3 (.000); Powell 1-9 (.111); A. Johnson 1-8 (.125); Moore 0-1 (.000); Suber 1-9 (.111); Ford 0-1 (.000) Opponents 161-438 (.368)

PHOENIX MERCURY

Player	G	Min	FGM	FGA	Pct	FTM	FTA	Pct	Off	Def	Tot	Ast	PF	Dq	Stl	TO	Blk	Pts	Avg	Hi
Jennifer Gillom	32	1095	163	428	.381	141	177	.797	53	131	184	54	105	2	37	87	7	485	15.2	29
Edna Campbell	28	750	95	261	.364	40	56	.714	11	42	53	37	53	0	25	48	10	268	9.6	22
Marlies Askamp	30	781	95	197	.482	93	114	.816	92	123	215	25	98	1	22	37	18	283	9.4	23
C. Davis-Wrightsil	14	259	52	120	.433	16	24	.667	15	23	38	20	39	2	12	22	4	130	9.3	23
Maria Stepanova	32	554	96	198	.485	55	88	.625	62	102	164	24	86	1	13	43	62	248	7.8	19
Michele Timms	30	804	68	192	.354	38	49	.776	17	62	79	151	87	0	43	89	7	205	6.8	22
Lisa Harrison	32	828	81	170	.476	30	44	.682	47	83	130	52	65	1	23	35	5	193	6.0	21
Bridget Pettis	32	541	65	214	.304	29	47	.617	29	30	59	45	57	1	26	30	2	181	5.7	16
Kristi Harrower	32	666	36	99	.364	59	73	.808	9	54	63	96	45	0	25	45	4	143	4.5	20
Toni Foster	10	42	7	12	.583	11	16	.688	4	4	8	1	6	0	0	4	1	25	2.5	5
Amanda Wilson	12	34	4	12	.333	3	3	1.000	4	2	6	2	3	0	1	2	1	12	1.0	6
Angela Aycock	8	30	0	4	.000	4	4	1.000	0	1	1	3	5	0	2	6	0	4	0.5	4
Andrea Kuklova	5	13	0	3	.000	0	0	---	0	0	0	0	2	0	1	0	0	0	0.0	0
M. Lange-Harris	1	3	0	0	---	0	0	---	0	2	2	0	1	0	0	0	0	0	0.0	0
Phoenix	32	6400	762	1910	.399	519	695	.747	343	659	1002	510	652	8	229	460	121	2177	68.0	86
Opponents	32	6400	794	1911	.415	475	637	.746	334	678	1012	494	676	15	234	479	108	2182	68.2	96

3-pt. FG: Phoenix 134-456 (.294) Gillom 18-72 (.250); Campbell 38-101 (.376); Askamp 0-2 (.000); Davis-Wrightsil 10-33 (.303); Stepanova 1-1 (1.000) Timms 31-89 (.348); Harrison 1-9 (.111); Pettis 22-98 (.224); Harrower 12-43 (.279); Wilson 1-5 (.200); Aycock 0-3 (.000) Opponents 119-395 (.301)

SACRAMENTO MONARCHS

Player	G	Min	FGM	FGA	Pct	FTM	FTA	Pct	Off	Def	Tot	Ast	PF	Dq	Stl	TO	Blk	Pts	Avg	Hi
Yolanda Griffith	29	979	200	370	.541	145	235	.617	141	188	329	45	91	0	73	66	54	545	18.8	31
R. Bolton-Holifield	31	970	143	393	.364	75	94	.798	46	86	132	73	68	0	31	44	0	421	13.6	34
K. Holland-Corn	32	1034	123	321	.383	76	108	.704	24	44	68	51	100	2	63	72	10	379	11.8	22
Latasha Byears	32	705	130	242	.537	35	62	.565	77	94	171	31	101	1	36	60	6	295	9.2	19
Tangela Smith	31	632	104	235	.443	47	72	.653	46	73	119	17	72	0	26	38	38	256	8.3	28
Ticha Penicheiro	32	1120	71	222	.320	87	131	.664	29	126	155	226	87	1	67	135	5	235	7.3	27
Linda Burgess	27	233	33	76	.434	31	41	.756	17	38	55	3	42	0	6	20	2	97	3.6	10
Lady Grooms	32	450	27	72	.375	44	63	.698	23	31	54	39	21	0	11	36	2	98	3.1	11
Kate Starbird	24	215	12	55	.218	22	27	.815	9	14	23	14	23	0	13	17	4	48	2.0	5
Cindy Blodgett	12	34	3	13	.231	5	9	.556	0	1	1	1	4	0	1	5	0	11	0.9	5
Heather Quella	13	28	3	7	.429	1	5	.200	0	5	5	0	5	0	2	5	2	7	0.5	4
Sacramento	32	6400	849	2006	.423	568	847	.671	412	700	1112	500	614	4	329	508	123	2392	74.8	107
Opponents	32	6400	829	1981	.418	439	590	.744	310	665	975	535	718	8	226	569	152	2258	70.6	100

3-pt. FG: Sacramento 126-421 (.299) Griffith 0-1 (.000); Bolton-Holifield 60-187 (.321); Holland-Corn 57-167 (.341); Byears 0-1 (.000); Smith 1-2 (.500) Penicheiro 6-38 (.158); Burgess 0-1 (.000); Hardmon 0-2 (.000); Starbird 2-15 (.133); Blodgett 0-7 (.000) Opponents 161-474 (.340)

UTAH STARZZ

Player	G	Min	FGM	FGA	Pct	FTM	FTA	Pct	Off	Def	Tot	Ast	PF	Dq	Stl	TO	Blk	Pts	Avg	Hi
									REBOUNDS									SCORING		
Natalie Williams 28		954	180	347	.519	144	191	.754	109	148	257	25	108	2	38	68	22	504	18.0	31
Adrienne Goodson 32		1068	182	427	.426	99	129	.767	71	67	138	87	76	0	27	98	8	476	14.9	25
Malgorzata Dydek 32		733	141	283	.498	114	133	.857	38	166	204	59	112	1	13	91	77	403	12.6	25
Korie Hlede(*) 11		277	44	95	.463	30	33	.909	7	23	30	28	34	0	8	22	1	131	11.9	21
Korie Hlede(†) 32		685	111	267	.416	72	82	.878	31	54	85	53	83	1	30	54	3	315	9.8	22
Wendy Palmer(‡) 20		446	57	141	.404	44	68	.647	23	60	83	30	57	1	3	32	8	167	8.4	22
LaTonya Johnson 31		718	66	181	.365	47	58	.810	14	40	54	50	65	1	21	40	8	203	6.5	19
Elena Baranova 29		572	60	148	.405	33	41	.805	25	73	98	45	58	0	20	44	23	173	6.0	20
Cindy Brown(*) 9		156	11	32	.344	11	16	.688	14	19	33	10	16	0	9	12	2	34	3.8	11
Cindy Brown(†) 30		646	57	178	.320	56	81	.691	49	97	146	32	61	0	34	47	14	178	5.9	18
Debbie Black 32		1014	62	163	.380	31	50	.620	31	80	111	161	116	0	77	67	6	163	5.1	10
Krystyna Lara 25		204	23	68	.338	6	6	1.000	1	12	13	23	29	0	10	36	2	62	2.5	17
O. Scott-Richardson(‡) ..4		36	3	10	.300	3	6	.500	5	3	8	2	7	0	1	3	0	9	2.3	9
Chantel Tremitiere 20		191	9	29	.310	1	1	1.000	3	16	19	22	28	0	6	13	0	21	1.1	4
Michelle Campbell........8		30	3	10	.300	2	4	.500	0	6	6	2	4	0	0	4	0	8	1.0	4
Dalma Ivanyi 14		67	4	12	.333	3	4	.750	3	2	5	7	18	0	4	11	0	11	0.8	4
Tricia Bader(‡) 7		34	0	3	.000	2	2	1.000	0	2	2	1	12	0	3	4	1	2	0.3	2
Utah...........................32		6500	845	1949	.434	570	742	.768	344	717	1061	552	740	5	240	560	158	2367	74.0	104
Opponents 32		6500	860	1965	.438	567	766	.740	311	661	972	570	707	8	284	477	117	2467	77.1	107

3-pt. FG: Utah 107-362 (.296) Williams 0-2 (.000); Goodson 13-53 (.245); Dydek 7-20 (.350); Hlede(*) 1-10 (.100); Hlede(†) 21-53 (.396); Palmer(‡) 9-30 (.300) Johnson 24-82 (.293); Baranova 20-48 (.417); Brown(*) 1-10 (.100); Brown(†) 8-40 (.200); Black 8-40 (.200); Lara 10-33 (.303) Tremitiere 2-8 (.250); Campbell 0-1 (.000); Ivanyi 0-4 (.000); Bader(‡) 0-2 (.000); Opponents 180-487 (.370).

WASHINGTON MYSTICS

Player	G	Min	FGM	FGA	Pct	FTM	FTA	Pct	Off	Def	Tot	Ast	PF	Dq	Stl	TO	Blk	Pts	Avg	Hi
									REBOUNDS									SCORING		
Nikki McCray..............32		1043	193	455	.424	129	160	.806	35	51	86	78	86	1	34	107	1	561	17.5	26
C. Holdsclaw 31		1061	202	462	.437	116	150	.773	74	172	246	74	67	0	37	108	27	525	16.9	24
Murriel Page...............32		916	105	183	.574	71	104	.683	68	145	213	28	103	4	24	49	30	281	8.8	19
Shalonda Enis..............29		844	83	228	.364	39	57	.684	53	104	157	47	82	0	23	60	4	216	7.4	18
Andrea Nagy 32		947	54	132	.409	45	59	.763	11	67	78	146	111	2	31	83	3	162	5.1	12
A. Santos de Oliveira ..13		216	22	39	.564	7	22	.318	19	23	42	1	25	0	1	16	2	51	3.9	16
Rita Williams 31		312	31	62	.500	23	36	.639	7	30	37	30	41	0	21	26	1	104	3.4	10
Markita Aldridge 31		379	29	94	.309	20	33	.606	12	25	37	33	35	0	15	41	7	81	2.6	10
Heather Owen 17		235	10	25	.400	16	23	.696	11	27	38	7	42	0	2	15	4	36	2.1	6
Monica Maxwell 20		141	11	50	.220	5	9	.556	3	19	22	10	9	0	5	11	1	34	1.7	9
Nyree Roberts(*).........8		62	6	10	.600	4	7	.571	2	8	10	1	5	0	5	10	1	16	2.0	6
Nyree Roberts(†).........12		79	6	11	.545	5	9	.556	3	9	12	1	5	0	5	11	1	17	1.4	6
Valerie Still 23		282	12	49	.245	7	19	.368	16	27	43	6	38	0	4	20	4	31	1.3	6
Penny Moore 4		19	1	3	.333	0	0	---	1	0	1	0	1	0	0	4	1	2	0.5	2
Jennifer Whittle 3		18	0	2	.000	0	0	---	0	3	3	0	1	0	1	5	1	0	0.0	0
Washington 32		6475	759	1794	.423	482	679	.710	312	701	1013	461	646	7	203	574	87	2100	65.6	83
Opponents 32		6475	825	1986	.415	469	650	.722	359	636	995	518	663	9	304	436	119	2246	70.2	88

3-pt. FG: Washington 100-345 (.290) McCray 46-153 (.301); Holdsclaw 5-29 (.172); Enis 11-40 (.275); Nagy 9-33 (.273); Williams 19-34 (.559); Aldridge 3-20 (.150) Maxwell 7-33 (.212); Still 0-3 (.000); Opponents 127-403 (.315).

(*) Statistics with this team only
(†) Totals with all teams
(‡) Continued season with another team

PLAYOFFS RESULTS

FIRST ROUND

| August 24 | Charlotte 60, Detroit 54 at Detroit |
| August 24 | Los Angeles 71, Sacramento 58 at Los Angeles |

New York defeats Charlotte, 2-1

August 27	Charlotte 78, New York 67 at Charlotte
August 29	New York 74, Charlotte 70 at New York
August 30	New York 69, Charlotte 54 at New York

CONFERENCE FINALS

Houston defeats Los Angeles, 2-1

August 26	Los Angeles 75, Houston 60 at Los Angeles
August 29	Houston 83, Los Angeles 55 at Houston
August 30	Houston 72, Los Angeles 62 at Houston

CHAMPIONSHIP

Houston defeats New York, 2-1

September 2	Houston 73, New York 60 at New York
September 4	New York 68, Houston 67 at Houston
September 5	Houston 59, New York 47 at Houston

TEAM STATISTICS

OFFENSIVE

TEAM	G	FG	FGA	PCT	FG3	FG3A	PCT	FT	FTA	PCT	OFF	DEF	REB	AST	PF	DQ	STL	TO	BLK	PTS	AVG
Hou.	6	129	327	.394	30	94	.319	126	157	.803	55	127	182	73	92	1	52	74	28	414	69.0
L.A.	4	109	268	.407	13	56	.232	32	45	.711	44	88	132	76	77	3	38	51	17	263	65.8
Cha.	4	98	232	.422	14	46	.304	52	71	.732	39	85	124	65	59	0	32	41	11	262	65.5
N.Y.	6	147	339	.434	34	93	.366	57	86	.663	57	115	172	107	121	1	30	81	19	385	64.2
Sac.	1	23	66	.348	2	10	.200	10	16	.625	11	25	36	10	14	0	13	21	4	58	58.0
Det.	1	21	63	.333	3	17	.176	9	12	.750	13	23	36	10	18	0	8	13	5	54	54.0

DEFENSIVE

Team	FG	FGA	PCT	FG3	FG3A	PCT	FT	FTA	PCT	OFF	DEF	REB	AST	PF	DQ	STL	TO	BLK	PTS	AVG	DIFF
Det.	22	61	.361	1	9	.111	15	19	.789	12	29	41	16	14	0	10	13	5	60	60.0	-6.0
Hou.	142	364	.390	28	90	.311	55	80	.688	66	122	188	96	135	4	38	86	17	367	61.2	+7.8
Cha.	105	232	.453	19	61	.311	35	52	.673	38	77	115	74	67	0	23	44	13	264	66.0	-0.5
N.Y.	128	323	.396	26	79	.329	119	155	.768	58	117	175	79	91	0	55	64	16	401	66.8	-2.7
L.A.	100	241	.415	19	62	.306	54	70	.771	35	91	126	53	60	1	32	59	22	273	68.3	-2.5
Sac.	30	74	.405	3	15	.200	8	11	.727	10	27	37	23	14	0	15	15	11	71	71.0	-13.0
AVG.'S	88	216	.407	16	53	.304	48	65	.739	37	77	114	57	64	1	29	47	14	239	65.3	---
	527	1295		96	316		286	387		219	463	682	341	381	5	173	281	84	1436		

TEAM COMPARISONS

TEAM	Points Per Game OWN	OPP	Field Goal Percentage OWN	OPP	Turnovers Per Game OWN	OPP	Rebound Percentages OFF	DEF	TOT	Below 70 Pts. OWN	OPP	Overtime Games W	L	3 PTS or Less W	L	10 PTS or More W	L
Charlotte	65.5	66.0	.422	.453	10.3*	11.0	.336*	.691	.514	2	3	0	0	0	0	1	1
Detroit	54.0	60.0*	.333	.361*	13.0	13.0	.310	.657	.483	1	1	0	0	0	0	0	0
Houston	69.0*	61.2	.394	.390	12.3	14.3	.311	.658	.484	3	5	0	0	0	1	4	1
Los Angeles	65.8	68.3	.407	.415	12.8	14.8	.326	.715*	.521*	2	2	0	0	0	0	2	2
New York	64.2	66.8	.434*	.396	13.5	10.7	.328	.665	.496	5	3	0	0	1	0	1	3
Sacramento	58.0	71.0	.348	.405	21.0	15.0*	.289	.714	.502	1	0	0	0	0	0	0	1
COMPOSITE; 11 games	65.3	65.3	.407	.407	12.8	12.8	.321	.679		14		0	0	1	1	8	8

* - League Leader

REBOUND PERCENTAGES

OFF. - Percentage of a given team's missed shots which that team rebounds.

DEF. - Percentage of opponents' missed shots which a given team rebounds.

TOT. - Average of offensive and defensive rebound percentages.

INDIVIDUAL PLAYOFFS STATISTICS, TEAM BY TEAM

CHARLOTTE STING

Player	G	Min	FGM	FGA	Pct	FTM	FTA	Pct	REBOUNDS Off	Def	Tot	Ast	PF	Dq	Stl	TO	Blk	SCORING Pts	Avg	Hi
Andrea Stinson	4	153	32	64	.500	15	19	.789	6	24	30	17	8	0	11	5	1	83	20.8	27
Dawn Staley	4	157	13	40	.325	15	18	.833	2	3	5	23	7	0	3	11	0	48	12.0	16
Rhonda Mapp	4	121	17	32	.531	7	13	.538	9	19	28	4	14	0	1	8	0	42	10.5	16
Charlotte Smith	4	106	14	31	.419	9	11	.818	8	10	18	3	11	0	4	7	0	36	9.0	10
Vicky Bullett	4	121	13	32	.406	2	4	.500	5	21	26	8	10	0	7	8	9	29	7.3	11
Sharon Manning	4	59	4	13	.308	3	4	.750	5	4	9	2	6	0	1	0	0	11	2.8	6
Angie Braziel	4	19	4	10	.400	1	2	.500	2	1	3	0	1	0	0	0	1	9	2.3	4
Tracy Reid	3	7	1	2	.500	0	0	---	1	0	1	0	0	0	1	1	0	2	0.7	2
Niesa Johnson	4	57	1	8	.125	0	0	---	1	3	4	8	2	0	4	1	0	2	0.5	2
Charlotte	4	800	98	232	.422	52	71	.732	39	85	124	65	59	0	32	41	11	262	65.5	78
Opponents	4	800	105	232	.453	35	52	.673	38	77	115	74	67	0	23	44	13	264	66.0	74

3-pt. FG: Charlotte 14-46 (.304) Stinson 4-14 (.286); Staley 7-16 (.438); Mapp 1-3 (.333); Cha. Smith 1-6 (.167); Bullett 1-3 (.333); Johnson 0-4 (.000) Opponents 19-61 (.311)

DETROIT SHOCK

Player	G	Min	FGM	FGA	Pct	FTM	FTA	Pct	Off	Def	Tot	Ast	PF	Dq	Stl	TO	Blk	Pts	Avg	Hi
Wendy Palmer 1		37	4	11	.364	2	3	.667	4	5	9	2	3	0	1	1	1	10	10.0	10
Sandy Brondello...........1		29	4	12	.333	0	0	---	2	1	3	0	2	0	2	1	1	9	9.0	9
Astou Ndiaye 1		16	4	5	.800	0	0	---	3	3	6	0	2	0	1	3	0	8	8.0	8
Val Whiting 1		27	2	7	.286	3	5	.600	3	3	6	1	4	0	2	2	1	7	7.0	7
Dominique Canty..........1		21	2	6	.333	2	2	1.000	1	2	3	1	3	0	1	2	0	6	6.0	6
Jennifer Azzi.................1		40	2	13	.154	0	0	---	0	5	5	3	3	0	0	2	1	5	5.0	5
Carla Porter 1		19	2	5	.400	0	0	---	0	2	2	2	1	0	0	2	1	5	5.0	5
C. Maria das Neves 1		11	1	4	.250	2	2	1.000	0	2	2	1	0	0	1	0	0	4	4.0	4
Detroit 1		200	21	63	.333	9	12	.750	13	23	36	10	18	0	8	13	5	54	54.0	54
Opponents 1		200	22	61	.361	15	19	.789	12	29	41	16	14	0	10	13	5	60	60.0	60

3-pt. FG: Detroit 3-17 (.176) Palmer 0-2 (.000); Brondello 1-4 (.250); Azzi 1-6 (.167); Porter 1-3 (.333); das Neves 0-2 (.000); Opponents 1-9 (.111).

HOUSTON COMETS

Player	G	Min	FGM	FGA	Pct	FTM	FTA	Pct	Off	Def	Tot	Ast	PF	Dq	Stl	TO	Blk	Pts	Avg	Hi
Cynthia Cooper 6		220	33	85	.388	45	52	.865	5	21	26	41	14	0	9	20	6	122	20.3	29
Sheryl Swoopes 6		216	29	81	.358	26	28	.929	7	15	22	7	9	0	14	12	3	88	14.7	23
Tina Thompson 6		208	21	57	.368	16	21	.762	6	24	30	4	24	1	5	13	7	67	11.2	15
Janeth Arcain 6		156	13	29	.448	10	16	.625	4	14	18	6	7	0	6	2	1	38	6.3	11
Tammy Jackson 6		115	13	24	.542	11	16	.688	18	24	42	1	15	0	7	7	7	37	6.2	11
Polina Tzekova 6		130	10	25	.400	10	12	.833	7	16	23	2	17	0	4	5	3	32	5.3	11
Sonja Henning 6		136	8	23	.348	2	6	.333	7	11	18	11	5	0	7	7	1	19	3.2	8
Amaya Valdemoro 2		4	1	1	1.000	2	2	1.000	0	0	0	0	1	0	0	1	0	5	2.5	5
Kara Wolters.................2		5	1	1	1.000	2	2	1.000	1	0	1	0	0	0	0	1	0	4	2.0	4
Mila Nikolich 2		5	0	0	---	2	2	1.000	0	1	1	0	0	0	0	1	0	2	1.0	2
Jennifer Rizzotti 2		5	0	1	.000	0	0	---	0	1	1	1	0	0	0	0	0	0	0.0	0
Houston 6		1200	129	327	.394	126	157	.803	55	127	182	73	92	1	52	74	28	414	69.0	83
Opponents 6		1200	142	364	.390	55	80	.688	66	122	188	96	135	4	38	86	17	367	61.2	75

3-pt. FG: Houston 30-94 (.319) Cooper 11-34 (.324); Swoopes 4-13 (.308); Thompson 9-24 (.375); Arcain 2-9 (.222); Tzekova 2-3 (.667); Henning 1-9 (.111) Valdemoro 1-1 (1.000); Rizzotti 0-1 (.000); Opponents 28-90 (.311).

LOS ANGELES SPARKS

Player	G	Min	FGM	FGA	Pct	FTM	FTA	Pct	Off	Def	Tot	Ast	PF	Dq	Stl	TO	Blk	Pts	Avg	Hi
Lisa Leslie.....................4		145	29	60	.483	14	18	.778	6	28	34	11	12	0	4	14	6	76	19.0	23
DeLisha Milton.............4		127	18	40	.450	3	7	.429	6	15	21	10	12	1	7	5	6	39	9.8	16
Mwadi Mabika..............4		127	17	45	.378	0	1	.000	7	11	18	11	22	2	13	10	1	37	9.3	14
Gordana Grubin...........4		119	13	37	.351	1	2	.500	3	9	12	23	9	0	5	8	0	31	7.8	13
La'Keshia Frett 4		121	11	30	.367	6	7	.857	12	9	21	13	6	0	2	3	2	28	7.0	11
C. Machanguana 1		7	2	3	.667	0	0	---	1	1	2	0	1	0	0	0	0	4	4.0	4
Tamecka Dixon 4		42	7	20	.350	1	1	1.000	4	4	8	5	4	0	3	5	0	15	3.8	6
Allison Feaster 4		32	4	15	.267	5	5	1.000	1	1	2	1	3	0	1	1	0	14	3.5	7
Penny Toler 4		42	4	12	.333	2	4	.500	1	5	6	2	4	0	2	3	0	10	2.5	4
Nina Bjedov 4		34	4	5	.800	0	0	---	2	5	7	0	4	0	1	2	2	9	2.3	7
Ukari Figgs 1		4	0	1	.000	0	0	---	1	0	1	0	0	0	0	0	0	0	0.0	0
Los Angeles 4		800	109	268	.407	32	45	.711	44	88	132	76	77	3	38	51	17	263	65.8	75
Opponents 4		800	100	241	.415	54	70	.771	35	91	126	53	60	1	32	59	22	273	68.3	83

3-pt. FG: Los Angeles 13-56 (.232) Leslie 4-13 (.308); Mabika 3-17 (.176); Grubin 4-16 (.250); Dixon 0-1 (.000); Feaster 1-5 (.200); Toler 0-1 (.000) Bjedov 1-2 (.500); Figgs 0-1 (.000); Opponents 19-62 (.306).

NEW YORK LIBERTY

Player	G	Min	FGM	FGA	Pct	FTM	FTA	Pct	Off	Def	Tot	Ast	PF	Dq	Stl	TO	Blk	Pts	Avg	Hi
Crystal Robinson 6		205	32	64	.500	7	7	1.000	7	11	18	13	20	1	6	10	2	86	14.3	21
Vickie Johnson 6		185	24	57	.421	9	14	.643	4	17	21	18	15	0	2	15	2	61	10.2	16
Kym Hampton 6		181	21	49	.429	11	17	.647	16	31	47	11	15	0	2	11	7	53	8.8	14
Teresa Weatherspoon 6		203	19	42	.452	6	8	.750	4	17	21	45	23	0	6	12	0	51	8.5	19
Sophia Witherspoon......6		86	17	38	.447	7	11	.636	7	6	13	2	13	0	4	8	0	45	7.5	18
Sue Wicks	6	174	17	46	.370	6	9	.667	14	27	41	10	17	0	6	4	6	42	7.0	11
Tamika Whitmore..........6		114	15	31	.484	5	14	.357	5	5	10	3	14	0	4	10	2	35	5.8	11

Player	G	Min	FGM	FGA	Pct	FTM	FTA	Pct	Off	Def	Tot	Ast	PF	Dq	Stl	TO	Blk	Pts	Avg	Hi
									REBOUNDS									SCORING		
Rebecca Hammon	6	50	2	12	.167	6	6	1.000	0	1	1	5	3	0	0	6	0	12	2.0	10
Venus Lacy...................	1	2	0	0	---	0	0	---	0	0	0	0	1	0	0	1	0	0	0.0	0
New York	6	1200	147	339	.434	57	86	.663	57	115	172	107	121	1	30	81	19	385	64.2	74
Opponents	6	1200	128	323	.396	119	155	.768	58	117	175	79	91	0	55	64	16	401	66.8	78

3-pt. FG: New York 34-93 (.366) Robinson 15-39 (.385); Johnson 4-10 (.400); Hampton 0-1 (.000); Weatherspoon 7-19 (.368); Witherspoon 4-10 (.400) Wicks 2-5 (.400); Hammon 2-9 (.222); Opponents 26-79 (.329)

SACRAMENTO MONARCHS

Player	G	Min	FGM	FGA	Pct	FTM	FTA	Pct	Off	Def	Tot	Ast	PF	Dq	Stl	TO	Blk	Pts	Avg	Hi
									REBOUNDS									SCORING		
R. Bolton-Holifield	1	32	6	15	.400	2	2	1.000	1	0	1	4	1	0	1	2	0	15	15.0	15
Tangela Smith...............	1	38	6	16	.375	2	6	.333	1	1	2	0	4	0	3	1	1	14	14.0	14
Linda Burgess	1	14	3	6	.500	2	2	1.000	1	3	4	0	2	0	2	2	0	8	8.0	8
Lady Grooms	1	25	3	7	.429	0	0	---	1	4	5	1	0	0	1	2	0	6	6.0	6
Ticha Penicheiro	1	20	1	5	.200	2	2	1.000	0	4	4	3	1	0	1	2	0	4	4.0	4
Cindy Blodgett	1	6	1	1	1.000	0	0	---	0	1	1	1	1	0	2	2	2	3	3.0	3
Heather Quella	1	4	1	2	.500	1	2	.500	0	2	2	0	1	0	0	1	0	3	3.0	3
Kedra Holland-Corn	1	21	1	5	.200	0	0	---	2	3	5	1	2	0	2	4	0	2	2.0	2
Kate Starbird.................	1	16	1	5	.200	0	0	---	0	2	2	0	0	0	0	2	1	2	2.0	2
Latasha Byears	1	24	0	4	.000	1	2	.500	5	5	10	0	2	0	1	3	0	1	1.0	1
Sacramento	1	200	23	66	.348	10	16	.625	11	25	36	10	14	0	13	21	4	58	58.0	58
Opponents	1	200	30	74	.405	8	11	.727	10	27	37	23	14	0	15	15	11	71	71.0	71

3-pt. FG: Sacramento 2-10 (.200) Bolton-Holifield 1-6 (.167); Burgess 0-1 (.000); Blodgett 1-1 (1.000); Holland-Corn 0-1 (.000); Starbird 0-1 (.000) Opponents 3-15 (.200)

(*) Statistics with this team only

(†) Totals with all teams

(‡) Continued season with another team

INDIVIDUAL FINALS STATISTICS, TEAM BY TEAM

HOUSTON COMETS

Player	G	Min	FGM	FGA	Pct	FTM	FTA	Pct	Off	Def	Tot	Ast	PF	Dq	Stl	TO	Blk	Pts	Avg	Hi
									REBOUNDS									SCORING		
Cynthia Cooper	3	109	14	38	.368	33	37	.892	4	9	13	13	7	0	8	12	0	65	21.7	29
Sheryl Swoopes	3	112	11	37	.297	16	17	.941	5	6	11	4	5	0	6	5	1	40	13.3	15
Tina Thompson	3	109	11	29	.379	12	15	.800	4	14	18	4	10	0	2	6	2	39	13.0	15
Janeth Arcain	3	78	5	12	.417	7	10	.700	3	7	10	5	4	0	4	2	1	17	5.7	10
Tammy Jackson	3	65	6	16	.375	4	8	.500	9	14	23	1	6	0	6	3	6	16	5.3	7
Polina Tzekova.............	3	60	2	9	.222	8	10	.800	2	6	8	0	10	0	2	0	0	13	4.3	11
Sonja Henning	3	67	3	11	.273	2	6	.333	4	5	9	3	4	0	5	4	0	9	3.0	8
Houston	3	600	52	152	.342	82	103	.796	31	61	92	30	46	0	33	36	10	199	66.3	73
Opponents	3	600	63	170	.371	31	46	.674	32	61	93	43	72	1	15	50	11	175	58.3	68

3-pt. FG: Houston 13-42 (.310) Cooper 4-13 (.308); Swoopes 2-7 (.286); Thompson 5-13 (.385); Arcain 0-2 (.000); Tzekova 1-1 (1.000); Henning 1-6 (.167) Opponents 18-49 (.367)

NEW YORK LIBERTY

Player	G	Min	FGM	FGA	Pct	FTM	FTA	Pct	Off	Def	Tot	Ast	PF	Dq	Stl	TO	Blk	Pts	Avg	Hi
									REBOUNDS									SCORING		
Crystal Robinson	3	99	12	31	.387	7	7	1.000	1	4	5	9	13	1	3	7	2	38	12.7	21
Vickie Johnson	3	88	13	27	.481	1	4	.250	3	9	12	5	10	0	2	11	2	29	9.7	16
Sophia Witherspoon......	3	50	10	24	.417	6	9	.667	5	3	8	1	8	0	1	5	0	28	9.3	18
Sue Wicks	3	90	9	28	.321	3	4	.750	11	17	28	3	12	0	4	4	3	22	7.3	11
Teresa Weatherspoon	3	100	8	18	.444	1	1	1.000	2	10	12	17	11	0	3	8	0	21	7.0	8
Kym Hampton	3	89	7	24	.292	6	9	.667	8	14	22	6	8	0	1	5	3	20	6.7	10
Rebecca Hammon	3	32	2	7	.286	6	6	1.000	0	1	1	2	2	0	0	3	0	12	4.0	10
Tamika Whitmore..........	3	52	2	11	.182	1	6	.167	2	3	5	0	8	0	1	3	1	5	1.7	4
New York	3	600	63	170	.371	31	46	.674	32	61	93	43	72	1	15	50	11	175	58.3	68
Opponents	3	600	52	152	.342	82	103	.796	31	61	92	30	46	0	33	36	10	199	66.3	73

3-pt. FG: New York 18-49 (.367) Robinson 7-23 (.304); Johnson 2-6 (.333); Witherspoon 2-5 (.400); Wicks 1-2 (.500); Weatherspoon 4-9 (.444); Hammon 2-4 (.500) Opponents 13-42 (.310)

FINALS BOX SCORES

GAME 1

At Madison Square Garden, September 2, 1999

OFFICIALS: Derek Collins, Gary Zielinski, Sally Bell. TIME OF GAME: 1:56. ATTENDANCE: 17,113.

SCORE BY PERIODS	1	2	FINAL
Houston	29	44	73
New York	20	40	60

VISITORS: Houston. Head Coach: Van Chancellor.

No Player	MIN	FG	FGA	3P	3PA	FT	FTA	OR	DR	TOT	A	PF	ST	TO	TEC	PTS
22 Sheryl Swoopes	37	5	13	0	2	5	5	0	2	2	1	2	1	2	0	15
7 Tina Thompson	36	3	6	2	4	3	4	0	7	7	3	3	1	2	0	11
15 Polina Tzekova	20	0	0	0	0	2	4	1	0	1	0	2	1	0	0	2
14 Cynthia Cooper	38	8	16	3	5	10	10	1	2	3	6	2	4	1	0	29
34 Sonja Henning	21	3	6	1	3	1	2	1	2	3	0	1	1	3	0	8
9 Janeth Arcain	26	1	3	0	1	1	2	2	2	4	4	0	2	1	0	3
23 Tammy Jackson	22	2	6	0	0	1	2	3	5	8	0	3	0	3	0	5
24 Mila Nikolich							Did not play.									
21 Jennifer Rizzotti							Did not play.									
13 Valdemoro Madari							Did not play.									
52 Kara Wolters							Did not play.									
TOTALS	200	22	50	6	15	23	29	8	20	28	14	13	10	13	0	73

FG pct.: .440. 3PT pct.: .400. FT pct.: .793. Team Rebounds: 7. Total Turnovers: 13 (13 PTS).

HOME: New York. Head Coach: Richie Adubato.

No Player	MIN	FG	FGA	3P	3PA	FT	FTA	OR	DR	TOT	A	PF	ST	TO	TEC	PTS
55 Vickie Johnson	28	7	12	1	4	1	4	1	0	1	1	1	1	3	0	16
23 Sue Wicks	26	1	7	0	1	1	2	4	7	11	1	4	4	0	0	3
34 Kym Hampton	27	1	8	0	0	0	0	3	4	7	3	1	1	1	0	2
11 Weatherspoon	38	2	5	0	1	1	1	0	4	4	10	3	0	2	0	5
3 Crystal Robinson	34	4	10	2	7	2	2	1	2	3	3	6	1	3	0	12
44 Tamika Whitmore	23	2	3	0	0	0	2	1	2	3	0	2	1	2	0	4
13 Sophia Witherspoon	21	7	13	2	4	2	4	1	1	2	0	1	0	2	0	18
25 Rebecca Hammon	3	0	1	0	1	0	0	0	0	0	0	0	0	0	0	0
5 Venus Lacy							Did not play.									
31 Michele VanGorp							Did not play.									
4 Coquese Washington							Did not play.									
TOTALS	200	24	59	5	18	7	15	11	20	31	18	18	8	16	1	60

FG pct.: .407. 3PT pct.: .278. FT pct. .467. Team Rebounds: 11. Total Turnovers: 16 (19 PTS).
Blocked Shots: Houston 1: Jackson. New York 2: Johnson, Wicks. Technical Fouls: New York: Adubato. Flagrant Fouls: None.
Points off Turnovers: Houston 19, New York 13. Fast Break Points: Houston 11, New York 12. Points in Paint: Houston 24, New York 30. Second Chance Points: Houston 6, New York 7

GAME 2

At Compaq Center, September 4, 1999

OFFICIALS: June Courteau, Patty Broderick. Jason Phillips. TIME OF GAME: 2:14. ATTENDANCE: 16,285.

SCORE BY PERIODS	1	2	FINAL
New York	23	45	68
Houston	37	30	67

VISITORS: New York. Head Coach: Richie Adubato.

No Player	MIN	FG	FGA	3P	3PA	FT	FTA	OR	DR	TOT	A	PF	ST	TO	TEC	PTS
23 Sue Wicks	29	3	9	0	0	2	2	2	6	8	1	4	0	3	0	8
55 Vickie Johnson	24	2	8	0	1	0	0	2	3	5	3	5	1	4	0	4
34 Kym Hampton	33	4	10	0	0	2	4	4	5	9	1	3	0	2	0	10
3 Crystal Robinson	33	6	11	4	9	5	5	0	0	0	3	3	0	1	0	21
11 Weatherspoon	32	3	5	2	3	0	0	2	4	6	5	3	2	3	0	8
44 Tamika Whitmore	17	0	4	0	0	1	4	1	1	2	0	4	0	0	0	1
13 Sophia Witherspoon	17	2	5	0	0	2	3	2	1	3	1	3	1	1	0	6

116

No	Player	MIN	FG	FGA	3P	3PA	FT	FTA	OR	DR	TOT	A	PF	ST	TO	TEC	PTS
25	Rebecca Hammon	15	2	4	2	3	4	4	0	1	1	1	1	0	3	0	10
5	Venus Lacy						Did not play.										
31	Michele VanGorp						Did not play.										
4	Coquese Washington						Did not play.										
	TOTALS	200	22	56	8	16	16	22	13	21	34	15	26	4	18	0	68

FG pct.: .393. 3PT pct.: .500. FT pct.: .727. Team Rebounds: 10. Total Turnovers: 18 (14 PTS).

HOME: Houston. Head Coach: Van Chancellor.

No	Player	MIN	FG	FGA	3P	3PA	FT	FTA	OR	DR	TOT	A	PF	ST	TO	TEC	PTS
22	Sheryl Swoopes	38	3	12	1	2	7	8	3	3	6	3	3	4	3	0	14
7	Tina Thompson	35	4	9	3	4	4	6	2	3	5	0	3	0	2	0	15
15	Polina Tzekova	28	2	7	1	1	6	6	1	5	6	0	5	1	0	0	11
14	Cynthia Cooper	37	1	10	0	4	10	12	1	3	4	6	1	1	5	0	12
34	Sonja Henning	13	0	1	0	0	1	4	0	1	1	1	0	2	0	0	1
9	Janeth Arcain	32	3	6	0	1	4	4	1	1	2	0	4	1	0	0	10
23	Tammy Jackson	17	2	5	0	0	0	2	1	3	4	0	2	3	0	0	4
24	Mila Nikolich						Did not play.										
21	Jennifer Rizzotti						Did not play.										
13	Valdemoro Madari						Did not play.										
52	Kara Wolters						Did not play.										
	TOTALS	200	15	50	5	12	32	42	9	19	28	10	18	12	11	0	67

FG pct.: .300. 3PT pct.: .417. FT pct.: .762. Team Rebounds: 13. Total Turnovers: 11 (10 PTS).
Blocked Shots: New York 8:Hampton 3, Wicks 2, Robinson 2, Johnson. Houston: 4 Jackson 2, Swoopes, Thompson. Technical Fouls: None. Flagrant Fouls: None. Points off Turnovers: New York 10, Houston 14. Fast Break Points: New York 5, Houston 0. Points in Paint: New York 18, Houston 16. Second Chance Points: New York 8, Houston 10

GAME 3
At Compaq Center, September 5, 1999

OFFICIALS: Sally Bell, Michael Price, Stan Gaxiola. TIME OF GAME: 2:00. ATTENDANCE: 16,285.

SCORE BY PERIODS	1	2	FINAL
New York	25	22	47
Houston	33	26	59

VISITORS: New York. Head Coach: Richie Adubato.

No	Player	MIN	FG	FGA	3P	3PA	FT	FTA	OR	DR	TOT	A	PF	ST	TO	TEC	PTS
55	Vickie Johnson	36	4	7	1	1	0	0	0	6	6	1	4	0	4	0	9
23	Sue Wicks	35	5	12	1	1	0	0	5	4	9	1	4	0	1	0	11
34	Kym Hampton	29	2	6	0	0	4	5	1	5	6	2	4	0	2	0	8
3	Crystal Robinson	32	2	10	1	7	0	0	0	2	2	3	4	2	3	0	5
11	Weatherspoon	30	3	8	2	5	0	0	0	2	2	2	5	1	3	0	8
25	Rebecca Hammon	14	0	2	0	0	2	2	0	0	0	1	1	0	0	0	2
44	Tamika Whitmore	12	0	4	0	0	0	0	0	0	0	0	2	0	1	0	0
13	Sophia Witherspoon	12	1	6	0	1	2	2	2	1	3	0	4	0	2	0	4
4	Coquese Washington						Did not play.										
5	Venus Lacy						Did not play.										
31	Michele VanGorp						Did not play.										
	TOTALS	200	17	55	5	15	8	9	8	20	28	10	28	3	16	0	47

FG pct.: .309. 3PT pct.: .333. FT pct.: .889. Team Rebounds: 8. Total Turnovers: 16 (7 PTS).

HOME: Houston. Head Coach: Van Chancellor.

No	Player	MIN	FG	FGA	3P	3PA	FT	FTA	OR	DR	TOT	A	PF	ST	TO	TEC	PTS
7	Tina Thompson	38	4	14	0	5	5	5	2	4	6	1	4	1	2	0	13
22	Sheryl Swoopes	37	3	12	1	3	4	4	2	1	3	0	0	1	0	0	11
15	Polina Tzekova	12	0	2	0	0	0	0	0	1	1	0	3	0	0	0	0
14	Cynthia Cooper	34	5	12	1	4	13	15	2	4	6	1	4	3	6	0	24
34	Sonja Henning	33	0	4	0	3	0	0	3	2	5	2	3	2	1	0	0
23	Tammy Jackson	26	2	5	0	0	3	4	5	6	11	1	1	3	0	0	7
9	Janeth Arcain	20	1	3	0	0	2	4	0	4	4	1	0	1	1	0	4

No	Player	MIN	FG	FGA	3P	3PA	FT	FTA	OR	DR	TOT	A	PF	ST	TO	TEC	PTS
24	Mila Nikolich						Did not play.										

117

21	Jennifer Rizzotti	....								Did not play.
13	Valdemoro Madari	....								Did not play.
52	Kara Wolters	....								Did not play.

TOTALS 200 15 52 2 15 27 32 14 22 36 6 15 11 12 0 59

FG pct.: .288. 3PT pct.: .133. FT pct.: .844. Team Rebounds:9. Total Turnovers: 12 (6 PTS).

Blocked Shots: New York 1: Whitmore. Houston 5: Jackson 3, Thompson, Arcain. Technical Fouls: None. Flagrant Fouls: None. Points off Turnovers: New York 6, Houston 7. Fast Break Points: New York 2, Houston 12. Points in Paint: New York 22, Houston 24. Second Chance Points: New York 8, Houston 9.

ALL-STAR GAME BOX SCORE

At Madison Square Garden, July 14, 1999

OFFICIALS: Sally Bell, Patty Broderick, June Courteau. TIME OF GAME: 1:49. ATTENDANCE: 18,649.

SCORE BY PERIODS	1	2	FINAL
West	43	36	79
East	29	32	61

VISITORS: West. Head Coach: Van Chancellor.

No Player	MIN	FG	FGA	3P	3PA	FT	FTA	OR	DR	TOT	A	PF	ST	TO	TEC	PTS
22 Sheryl Swoopes 19		4	7	0	0	0	0	1	7	8	0	2	3	2	0	8
7 Tina Thompson 14		4	8	0	0	0	0	0	5	5	0	0	0	2	0	8
9 Lisa Leslie......................17		5	11	0	1	3	4	3	2	5	1	2	1	0	0	13
7 Michele Timms..............18		1	1	1	1	0	0	0	4	4	4	1	1	3	0	3
14 Cynthia Cooper 18		3	5	0	2	1	1	0	4	4	4	0	2	1	0	7
24 Natalie Williams............21		3	4	0	0	8	10	4	4	8	3	0	1	1	0	14
33 Yolanda Griffith 21		5	10	0	0	0	0	2	3	5	1	2	1	3	0	10
6 Bolton-Holifield 20		1	7	0	4	0	0	1	2	3	1	0	1	0	0	2
21 Ticha Penicheiro 19		0	3	0	1	1	2	0	0	0	3	2	0	3	0	1
22 Jennifer Gillom..............18		2	6	0	1	2	2	0	5	5	1	0	1	0	0	6
13 Tonya Edwards 15		3	8	1	4	0	0	0	1	1	1	1	0	2	0	7
TOTALS 200		31	70	2	14	15	19	11	37	48	19	10	11	17	0	79

FG pct.: .443. 3PT pct.: .143. FT pct.: .789. Team Rebounds: 6 Total Turnovers: 17 (0 PTS).

HOME: East. Head Coach: Linda Hill-MacDonald.

No Player	MIN	FG	FGA	3P	3PA	FT	FTA	OR	DR	TOT	A	PF	ST	TO	TEC	PTS
23 Vicky Bullett..................25		2	6	0	1	0	0	1	4	5	1	5	0	2	0	4
23 Chamique Holdsclaw 11		2	6	0	0	1	1	0	5	5	0	0	0	2	0	5
34 Kym Hampton 21		2	6	0	0	1	2	1	2	3	0	2	2	0	0	5
11 Weatherspoon 17		1	6	1	2	0	0	0	2	2	4	2	1	3	0	3
15 Nikki McCray.................16		2	11	0	2	0	0	0	2	2	0	1	3	0	0	4
11 Taj McWilliams..............31		2	5	1	1	3	4	2	5	7	1	2	2	2	0	8
14 Shannon Johnson 23		3	6	2	5	0	0	2	2	4	2	2	3	2	0	8
42 Nykesha Sales 17		3	8	0	3	0	2	0	0	0	1	1	0	2	0	6
55 Vickie Johnson 15		3	8	0	3	0	0	0	2	2	3	0	0	2	0	6
25 Merlakia Jones 13		2	4	0	0	0	0	1	2	3	3	0	0	0	0	4
6 Sandy Brondello............11		4	8	0	1	0	0	2	1	3	1	0	0	0	0	8
50 Rebecca Lobo								Did not play.								
TOTALS 200		26	74	4	18	5	9	9	27	36	16	15	11	15	0	61

FG pct.: .351. 3PT pct.: .222. FT pct.: .556. Team Rebounds: 5. Total Turnovers: 15 (0 PTS).

Blocked Shots: West 3: Swoopes, Leslie, Griffith. East 4: Bullett 2, McWilliams, S. Johnson. Technical Fouls: None. Flagrant Fouls: None. Fast Break Points: West 25, East 4. Points in Paint: West 50, East 22. Second Chance Points: West 14, East 3.

REVIEW 1999 Finals

Front Row (l. to r.) Sheryl Swoopes, Tina Thompson, Kim Perrot, Coach Van Chancellor, Cynthia Cooper, Janeth Arcain, Monica Lamb. Back Row (l. to r.) Trainer Michelle T. Leget, Assistant Coach Alisa Scott, Tammy Jackson, Wanda Guyton, Tiffany Woosley, Amaya Valdemoro, Yolanda Moore, Nyree Roberts, Equipment Manager Stacey Johnson, Assistant Coach Kevin Cook.

FINAL STANDINGS

EASTERN CONFERENCE

Team	CHA	CLE	DET	HOU	LA	NY	PHO	SAC	UTA	WAS	W	L	PCT	GB	Last-10	Streak
CLE	3	—	2	1	1	3	0	3	3	4	20	10	.667	—	8-2	Won 4
CHA	—	1	3	0	1	3	2	2	2	4	18	12	.600	2	4-6	Won 1
NY	1	1	2	1	2	—	3	3	1	4	18	12	.600	2	7-3	Lost 2
DET	1	2	—	0	3	2	0	3	3	3	17	13	.567	3	6-4	Won 2
WAS	0	0	1	0	1	0	0	0	1	—	3	27	.100	17	1-9	Lost 5

WESTERN CONFERENCE

Team	CHA	CLE	DET	HOU	LA	NY	PHO	SAC	UTA	WAS	W	L	PCT	GB	Last-10	Streak
HOU	3	2	2	—	4	2	3	4	4	3	27	3	.900	—	8-2	Won 2
PHO	0	3	3	1	2	0	—	4	3	3	19	11	.633	8	7-3	Won 4
LA	2	1	0	0	—	1	2	1	3	2	12	18	.400	15	5-5	Lost 2
SAC	1	0	0	0	3	0	0	—	2	2	8	22	.267	19	2-8	Lost 2
UTA	1	0	0	0	1	1	1	2	—	2	8	22	.267	19	1-9	Lost 3

TEAM STATISTICS

OFFENSIVE

TEAM	G	FG	FGA	PCT	FG3	FG3A	PCT	FT	FTA	PCT	OFF	DEF	REB	AST	PF	DQ	STL	TO	BLK	PTS	AVG
Hou.	30	795	1824	.436	177	523	.338	518	646	.802	297	630	927	428	510	3	332	435	81	2285	76.2
Phoe.	30	787	1856	.424	130	405	.321	513	709	.724	327	614	941	543	595	3	288	483	86	2217	73.9
Clev.	30	804	1719	.468	106	279	.380	483	631	.765	227	649	876	575	600	4	270	528	99	2197	73.2
L.A.	30	797	1914	.416	111	335	.331	443	609	.727	337	683	1020	472	675	7	229	511	148	2148	71.6
Cha.	30	798	1855	.430	105	377	.279	442	624	.708	304	677	981	512	507	4	273	457	96	2143	71.4
Utah	30	777	1837	.423	113	346	.327	426	608	.701	302	699	1001	481	638	9	221	543	170	2093	69.8
Det.	30	771	1875	.411	97	300	.323	448	638	.702	345	732	1077	432	602	3	197	490	81	2087	69.6
N.Y.	30	758	1784	.425	92	281	.327	450	629	.715	320	624	944	513	630	3	291	501	84	2058	68.6
Wash.	30	720	1821	.395	114	432	.264	400	620	.645	325	599	924	397	692	9	266	625	91	1954	65.1
Sac.	30	734	1802	.407	72	277	.260	376	560	.671	326	619	945	463	633	7	263	533	107	1916	63.9

DEFENSIVE

Team	FG	FGA	PCT	FG3	FG3A	PCT	FT	FTA	PCT	OFF	DEF	REB	AST	PF	DQ	STL	TO	BLK	PTS	AVG	DIFF
Hou.	729	1803	.404	110	369	.298	340	470	.723	324	630	954	450	637	6	206	560	102	1908	63.6	+12.6
N.Y.	709	1693	.419	103	325	.317	445	625	.712	272	620	892	420	610	4	261	538	81	1966	65.5	+3.1
Phoe.	758	1747	.434	77	244	.316	432	601	.719	298	643	941	406	664	9	242	581	96	2025	67.5	+6.4
Cha.	780	1878	.415	113	381	.297	378	529	.715	305	663	968	470	601	5	242	501	108	2051	68.4	+3.1
Det.	768	1869	.411	113	375	.301	429	602	.713	282	667	949	445	635	8	249	447	114	2078	69.3	+0.3
Sac.	733	1752	.418	107	366	.292	509	674	.755	307	646	953	493	556	5	239	500	134	2082	69.4	-5.5
Clev.	776	1835	.423	128	395	.324	430	625	.688	327	596	923	523	620	3	309	546	101	2110	70.3	+2.9
L.A.	780	1898	.411	119	372	.320	490	693	.707	337	663	1000	522	603	4	244	481	109	2169	72.3	-0.7
Utah	832	1942	.428	135	410	.329	495	680	.728	336	685	1021	539	559	7	304	441	94	2294	76.5	-6.7
Wash.	876	1870	.468	112	318	.352	551	775	.711	322	713	1035	548	597	1	334	511	104	2415	80.5	-15.4
AVG.'S	.774	1829	.423	112	356	.314	450	627	.717	311	653	964	482	608	5	263	511	104	2110	70.3	---
	7741	18287		1117	3555		4499	6274		3110	6526	9636	4816	6082	52	2630	5106	1043	21098		

TEAM COMPARISONS

TEAM	Points Per Game		Field Goal Percentage		Turnovers Per Game		Rebound Percentages			Below 70 Pts.		Overtime Games		3 PTS or Less		10 PTS or More	
	OWN	OPP	OWN	OPP	OWN	OPP	OFF	DEF	TOT	OWN	OPP	W	L	W	L	W	L
Charlotte	71.4	68.4	.430	.415	15.2	16.7	.314	.689	.502	13	20	0	0	3	2	6	6
Cleveland	73.2	70.3	.468*	.423	17.6	18.2	.276	.665	.470	12	14	1	1	3	2	12	8
Detroit	69.6	69.3	.411	.411	16.3	14.9	.341*	.722*	.531*	15	15	0	0	3	4	9	6
Washington	65.1	80.5	.395	.468	20.8	17.0	.313	.650	.482	21	4	0	1	1	2	1	23
Houston	76.2*	63.6*	.436	.404*	14.5*	18.7	.320	.660	.490	5	25	1	1	3	2	19	1
Los Angeles	71.6	72.3	.416	.411	17.0	16.0	.337	.670	.503	13	10	1	0	2	5	5	8
New York	68.6	65.5	.425	.419	16.7	17.9	.340	.696	.518	18	18	2	0	5	1	11	6
Phoenix	73.9	67.5	.424	.434	16.1	19.4*	.337	.673	.505	11	19	1	1	4	6	13	4
Sacramento	63.9	69.4	.407	.418	17.8	16.7	.335	.668	.502	19	14	0	1	1	3	3	11
Utah	69.8	76.5	.423	.428	18.1	14.7	.306	.675	.491	19	7	0	1	3	1	4	10
COMPOSITE; 150 games																	
	70.3	70.3	.423	.423	17.0	17.0	.323	.677			146	6	6	28	28	83	83

* - League Leader

REBOUND PERCENTAGES

OFF. - Percentage of a given team's missed shots which that team rebounds.

DEF. - Percentage of opponents' missed shots which a given team rebounds.

TOT. - Average of offensive and defensive rebound percentages.

SCORING AVERAGE

	G	FG	FT	PTS	AVG
Cooper, Hou.	30	203	210	680	22.7
Gillom, Pho.	30	228	137	624	20.8
Leslie, L.A.	28	202	136	549	19.6
McCray, Was.	29	191	107	512	17.7
Dixon, L.A.	22	124	88	357	16.2
Swoopes, Hou.	29	173	71	453	15.6
Stinson, Cha.	30	173	75	450	15.0
Byears, Sac.	30	181	61	427	14.2
Brondello, Det.	30	157	96	426	14.2
Hlede, Det.	27	135	83	382	14.1
Reid, Cha.	30	151	111	413	13.8
Witherspoon, N.Y.	30	144	92	413	13.8
Fijalkowski, Cle.	28	146	87	383	13.7
Palmer, Utah	28	145	81	377	13.5
Bullett, Cha.	30	162	71	399	13.3
Baranova, Utah	20	92	59	258	12.9
Dydek, Utah	30	146	93	386	12.9
Thompson, Hou.	27	121	63	342	12.7
Johnson, N.Y.	30	146	63	376	12.5
Toler, L.A.	30	145	55	370	12.3

REBOUNDS PER GAME

	G	OFF	DEF	TOT	AVG
Leslie, L.A.	28	77	208	285	10.2
Brown, Det.	30	70	231	301	10.0
Baranova, Utah	20	61	125	186	9.3
Dydek, Utah	30	41	186	227	7.6
Gillom, Pho.	30	62	157	219	7.3
Thompson, Hou.	27	65	127	192	7.1
Page, Was.	30	81	127	208	6.9
Lobo, N.Y.	30	70	137	207	6.9
Fijalkowski, Cle.	28	59	133	192	6.9
Palmer, Utah	28	70	116	186	6.6
Byears, Sac.	30	85	114	199	6.6
Bullett, Cha.	30	62	132	194	6.5
Hampton, N.Y.	30	53	128	181	6.0
Braxton, Cle.	30	37	131	168	5.6
Manning, Cha.	30	60	106	166	5.5
Reid, Cha.	30	60	97	157	5.2
Hlede, Det.	27	39	102	141	5.2
Swoopes, Hou.	29	39	110	149	5.1
Mujanovic, Det.	30	54	100	154	5.1
Burgess, Sac.	30	53	93	146	4.9

ASSISTS PER GAME

	G	AST	AVG
Penicheiro, Sac.	30	224	7.5
Weatherspoon, N.Y.	30	191	6.4
McConnell Serio, Cle.	28	178	6.4
Timms, Pho.	30	158	5.3
Toler, L.A.	30	143	4.8
Perrot, Hou.	30	142	4.7
Stinson, Cha.	30	134	4.5
Cooper, Hou.	30	131	4.4
Tremitiere, Utah	28	102	3.6
Baranova, Utah	20	70	3.5
Brondello, Det.	30	98	3.3
McCray, Was.	29	90	3.1
Webb, Pho.	30	92	3.1
Chr. Smith, Cha.	24	71	3.0
Suber, Cha.	30	86	2.9
Edwards, Cle.	23	65	2.8
Hlede, Det.	27	73	2.7
Leslie, L.A.	28	70	2.5
Braxton, Cle.	30	74	2.5
Johnson, N.Y.	30	74	2.5

FIELD GOAL PCT.

	FG	FGA	PCT
Fijalkowski, Cle.	146	267	.547
Mujanovic, Det.	106	204	.520
Griffiths, Pho.	93	184	.505
Braxton, Cle.	108	218	.495
Reid, Cha.	151	310	.487
Lobo, N.Y.	136	281	.484
Dydek, Utah	146	303	.482
Page, Was.	104	217	.479
Leslie, L.A.	202	423	.478
Burgess, Sac.	90	189	.476

3-PT FIELD GOAL PCT.

	3FG	3GA	PCT
Nemcova, Cle.	28	62	.452
Toler, L.A.	25	60	.417
McConnell Serio, Cle.	29	71	.408
Cooper, Hou.	64	160	.400
Hlede, Det.	29	74	.392
Gillom, Pho.	31	82	.378
Johnson, N.Y.	21	56	.375
Swoopes, Hou.	36	100	.360
Thompson, Hou.	37	103	.359
Price, Sac.	28	78	.359

FREE THROW PCT.

	FT	FTA	PCT
Brondello, Det.	96	104	.923
Nemcova, Cle.	67	75	.893
Pettis, Pho.	77	89	.865
Cooper, Hou.	210	246	.854
Thompson, Hou.	63	74	.851
Baranova, Utah	59	71	.831
Bullett, Cha.	71	86	.826
Swoopes, Hou.	71	86	.826
Fijalkowski, Cle.	87	106	.821
Hlede, Det.	83	103	.806

STEALS PER GAME

	G	STL	AVG
Weatherspoon, N.Y.	30	100	3.33
Perrot, Hou.	30	84	2.80

	G		AVG
Swoopes, Hou.	29	72	2.48
Penicheiro, Sac.	30	67	2.23
Bullett, Cha.	30	66	2.20
Williams, Was.	30	63	2.10
Stinson, Cha.	30	54	1.80
McConnell Serio, Cle	28	49	1.75
Braxton, Cle.	30	51	1.70
Brown, Det.	30	51	1.70

BLOCKS PER GAME

	G	BLK	AVG
Dydek, Utah	30	114	3.80
Leslie, L.A.	28	60	2.14
Smith, Sac.	28	46	1.64
Bullett, Cha.	30	46	1.53
Baranova, Utah	20	30	1.50
Lobo, N.Y.	30	33	1.10

	G		AVG
Fijalkowski, Cle	28	27	0.96
Thompson, Hou.	27	25	0.93
Brown, Was.	22	20	0.91
Rycraw, L.A.	20	18	0.90

MINUTES PER GAME

	G	MIN	AVG
Penicheiro, Sac.	30	1080	36.0
Cooper, Hou.	30	1051	35.0
Stinson, Cha.	30	1046	34.9
Hlede, Det.	27	912	33.8
Baranova, Utah	20	671	33.6
McCray, Was.	29	969	33.4
Weatherspoon, N.Y.	30	1002	33.4
Brondello, Det.	30	993	33.1
Perrot, Hou.	30	986	32.9
Nemcova, Cle.	30	972	32.4

INDIVIDUAL STATISTICS, TEAM BY TEAM

CHARLOTTE STING

Player	G	Min	FGM	FGA	Pct	FTM	FTA	Pct	Off	Def	Tot	Ast	PF	Dq	Stl	TO	Blk	Pts	Avg	Hi
Andrea Stinson	30	1046	173	414	.418	75	100	.750	29	109	138	134	72	0	54	77	15	450	15.0	25
Tracy Reid	30	966	151	310	.487	111	181	.613	60	97	157	46	59	1	40	71	12	413	13.8	22
Vicky Bullett	30	947	162	367	.441	71	86	.826	62	132	194	46	88	2	66	64	46	399	13.3	22
Rhonda Mapp	21	456	83	164	.506	45	60	.750	35	54	89	33	60	0	13	39	8	212	10.1	20
Tora Suber	30	682	58	185	.314	29	46	.630	12	41	53	86	55	1	30	44	1	181	6.0	14
Sharon Manning	30	575	59	134	.440	44	66	.667	60	106	166	30	62	0	32	43	7	162	5.4	14
Andrea Congreaves	24	372	35	81	.432	19	21	.905	18	53	71	36	37	0	11	23	5	104	4.3	23
Christy Smith	24	448	27	75	.360	17	20	.850	3	31	34	71	34	0	10	48	0	89	3.7	14
P. Johns Kimbrough	24	180	22	45	.489	18	28	.643	14	23	37	6	9	0	3	9	2	62	2.6	7
Sonia Chase	23	166	14	28	.500	6	6	1.000	5	9	14	13	16	0	5	13	0	34	1.5	8
Tia Paschal	20	110	11	37	.297	4	6	.667	4	11	15	9	12	0	8	11	0	27	1.4	5
Kelly Boucher	9	52	3	15	.200	3	4	.750	2	11	13	2	3	0	1	3	0	10	1.1	5
Charlotte	30	6000	798	1855	.430	442	624	.708	304	677	981	512	507	4	273	457	96	2143	71.4	105
Opponents	30	6000	780	1878	.415	378	529	.715	305	663	968	470	601	5	242	501	108	2051	68.4	86

3-pt. FG: Charlotte 105-377 (.279); Stinson 29-103 (.282); Reid 0-2 (.000); Bullett 4-26 (.154); Mapp 1-10 (.100); Suber 36-116 (.310); Manning 0-2 (.000); Congreaves 15-51 (.294); Chr. Smith 18-57 (.316); Paschal 1-4 (.250); Boucher 1-6 (.167); Opponents 113-381 (.297).

CLEVELAND ROCKERS

Player	G	Min	FGM	FGA	Pct	FTM	FTA	Pct	Off	Def	Tot	Ast	PF	Dq	Stl	TO	Blk	Pts	Avg	Hi
Isabelle Fijalkowski	28	806	146	267	.547	87	106	.821	59	133	192	58	115	3	17	81	27	383	13.7	25
Eva Nemcova	30	972	132	282	.468	67	75	.893	28	83	111	67	77	0	33	64	21	359	12.0	19
Janice Braxton	30	840	108	218	.495	77	102	.755	37	131	168	74	77	0	51	67	15	295	9.8	18
Merlakia Jones	30	683	109	235	.464	61	81	.753	28	67	95	39	69	0	32	52	3	286	9.5	19
S. McConnell Serio	28	882	80	176	.455	51	70	.729	8	54	62	178	48	0	49	104	5	240	8.6	19
Michelle Edwards	23	533	68	163	.417	31	50	.620	6	46	52	65	42	0	23	46	1	178	7.7	24
Rushia Brown	30	522	64	139	.460	66	85	.776	34	59	93	28	79	1	34	49	16	194	6.5	15
Adrienne Johnson	29	330	53	116	.457	13	18	.722	17	31	48	15	35	0	7	24	4	133	4.6	9
Cindy Blodgett	22	184	19	66	.288	15	24	.625	2	12	14	18	18	0	9	12	0	63	2.9	12
Tully Bevilaqua	12	126	9	16	.563	4	6	.667	2	8	10	24	14	0	12	9	2	23	1.9	7
Raegan Scott	22	167	14	38	.368	10	12	.833	5	24	29	7	24	0	3	9	5	38	1.7	10
Tanja Kostic	5	30	2	3	.667	1	2	.500	1	1	2	2	2	0	0	3	0	5	1.0	5
Cleveland	30	6075	804	1719	.468	483	631	.765	227	649	876	575	600	4	270	528	99	2197	73.2	96
Opponents	30	6075	776	1835	.423	430	625	.688	327	596	923	523	620	3	309	546	101	2110	70.3	87

REVIEW 1998 Regular Season

3-pt. FG: Cleveland 106-279 (.380); Fijalkowski 4-10 (.400); Nemcova 28-62 (.452); Braxton 2-6 (.333); Jones 7-20 (.350); McConnell Serio 29-71 (.408); Edwards 11-34 (.324); Brown 0-1 (.000); Johnson 14-33 (.424); Blodgett 10-37 (.270); Bevilaqua 1-3 (.333); Scott 0-2 (.000); Opponents 128-395 (.324)

DETROIT SHOCK

Player	G	Min	FGM	FGA	Pct	FTM	FTA	Pct	Off	Def	Tot	Ast	PF	Dq	Stl	TO	Blk	Pts	Avg	Hi
									REBOUNDS									SCORING		
Sandy Brondello	30	993	157	367	.428	96	104	.923	18	69	87	98	58	0	38	64	1	426	14.2	24
Korie Hlede	27	912	135	345	.391	83	103	.806	39	102	141	73	66	0	21	88	1	382	14.1	23
Cindy Brown	30	965	126	268	.470	82	114	.719	70	231	301	53	105	1	51	67	22	354	11.8	22
Razija Brcaninovic	30	695	106	204	.520	60	90	.667	54	100	154	29	86	1	9	64	26	272	9.1	25
Carla Porter	30	817	89	260	.342	48	76	.632	51	67	118	68	88	1	27	52	10	245	8.2	19
Rachael Sporn	30	535	60	147	.408	16	34	.471	51	57	108	38	58	0	8	34	12	136	4.5	12
Lynette Woodard	27	383	36	93	.387	23	40	.575	31	35	66	22	33	0	22	31	3	95	3.5	18
Gergana Branzova	26	204	29	65	.446	11	20	.550	13	29	42	7	42	0	3	21	4	69	2.7	11
Rhonda Blades	29	340	20	78	.256	14	29	.483	5	27	32	41	47	0	12	41	1	66	2.3	11
Tajama Abraham	12	44	5	14	.357	8	15	.533	2	5	7	0	8	0	2	5	1	18	1.5	5
Aneta Kausaite	10	58	5	20	.250	4	7	.571	8	3	11	1	4	0	3	3	0	14	1.4	5
Mfon Udoka	3	25	1	6	.167	2	4	.500	1	2	3	0	3	0	0	1	0	4	1.3	4
Angie Hamblin	6	29	2	8	.250	1	2	.500	2	5	7	2	4	0	1	7	0	6	1.0	3
Detroit	30	6000	771	1875	.411	448	638	.702	345	732	1077	432	602	3	197	490	81	2087	69.6	85
Opponents	30	6000	768	1869	.411	429	602	.713	282	667	949	445	635	8	249	447	114	2078	69.3	96

3-pt. FG: Detroit 97-300 (.323); Brondello 16-44 (.364); Hlede 29-74 (.392); Brown 20-61 (.328); Porter 19-63 (.302); Branzova 0-4 (.000); Blades 12-50 (.240); Kausaite 0-2 (.000); Hamblin 1-2 (.500); Opponents 113-375 (.301)

HOUSTON COMETS

Player	G	Min	FGM	FGA	Pct	FTM	FTA	Pct	Off	Def	Tot	Ast	PF	Dq	Stl	TO	Blk	Pts	Avg	Hi
									REBOUNDS									SCORING		
Cynthia Cooper	30	1051	203	455	.446	210	246	.854	25	85	110	131	65	0	48	95	11	680	22.7	34
Sheryl Swoopes	29	937	173	405	.427	71	86	.826	39	110	149	62	42	0	72	58	14	453	15.6	28
Tina Thompson	27	874	121	289	.419	63	74	.851	65	127	192	24	89	0	31	47	25	342	12.7	23
Kim Perrot	30	986	88	218	.404	49	70	.700	17	75	92	142	70	0	84	82	0	254	8.5	22
Janeth Arcain	30	657	83	195	.426	34	45	.756	43	65	108	26	48	0	25	38	3	205	6.8	14
Monica Lamb	30	649	66	122	.541	29	42	.690	62	80	142	9	87	3	24	27	21	161	5.4	16
Yolanda Moore	30	533	32	71	.451	33	41	.805	32	54	86	10	54	0	26	20	0	98	3.3	10
Amaya Valdemoro	16	61	8	16	.500	12	17	.706	2	8	10	7	8	0	7	17	1	30	1.9	10
Tammy Jackson(*)	19	160	8	21	.381	8	11	.727	6	15	21	6	31	0	4	14	5	24	1.3	6
Tammy Jackson(†)	21	174	10	24	.417	8	13	.615	7	18	25	6	34	0	4	14	5	28	1.3	6
Tiffany Woosley	18	96	7	23	.304	5	7	.714	3	4	7	9	9	0	8	13	0	22	1.2	8
Nyree Roberts	14	55	6	7	.857	4	7	.571	3	7	10	2	3	0	1	4	0	16	1.1	9
Karen Booker	1	2	0	1	.000	0	0	---	0	0	0	0	0	0	1	0	0	0	0.0	0
Wanda Guyton	1	14	0	1	.000	0	0	---	0	0	0	0	4	0	1	2	1	0	0.0	0
Houston	30	6075	795	1824	.436	518	646	.802	297	630	927	428	510	3	332	435	81	2285	76.2	110
Opponents	30	6075	729	1803	.404	340	470	.723	324	630	954	450	637	6	206	560	102	1908	63.6	74

3-pt. FG: Houston 177-523 (.338); Cooper 64-160 (.400); Swoopes 36-100 (.360); Thompson 37-103 (.359); Perrot 29-108 (.269); Arcain 5-33 (.152); Moore 1-2 (.500); Valdemoro 2-5 (.400); Woosley 3-12 (.250); Opponents 110-369 (.298)

LOS ANGELES SPARKS

Player	G	Min	FGM	FGA	Pct	FTM	FTA	Pct	Off	Def	Tot	Ast	PF	Dq	Stl	TO	Blk	Pts	Avg	Hi
									REBOUNDS									SCORING		
Lisa Leslie	28	898	202	423	.478	136	177	.768	77	208	285	70	121	3	42	102	60	549	19.6	30
Tamecka Dixon	22	710	124	283	.438	88	113	.779	13	43	56	54	67	2	24	57	8	357	16.2	26
Penny Toler	30	945	145	349	.415	55	74	.743	37	69	106	143	77	2	32	101	3	370	12.3	22
Mwadi Mabika	29	710	87	257	.339	30	43	.698	29	98	127	44	73	0	30	37	9	237	8.2	17
Haixia Zheng	6	98	20	32	.625	5	7	.714	8	18	26	3	11	0	0	6	1	45	7.5	19
Pamela McGee	30	570	80	183	.437	43	70	.614	62	83	145	13	104	0	23	54	24	203	6.8	18

REVIEW 1998 Regular Season

Player	G	Min	FGM	FGA	Pct	FTM	FTA	Pct	Off	Def	Tot	Ast	PF	Dq	Stl	TO	Blk	Pts	Avg	Hi
A.a VanEmbricqs	28	470	43	89	.483	8	16	.500	34	41	75	16	57	0	24	19	9	94	3.4	9
Allison Feaster	3	41	3	14	.214	2	2	1.000	1	1	2	3	10	0	2	4	0	10	3.3	5
Erin Alexander(‡)	8	73	7	22	.318	2	2	1.000	8	7	15	6	11	0	2	7	0	22	2.8	10
Katrina Colleton	30	575	30	99	.303	15	18	.833	25	26	51	47	44	0	18	29	11	80	2.7	14
Octavia Blue	30	331	26	77	.338	15	24	.625	19	30	49	10	41	0	13	27	3	73	2.4	13
Eugenia Rycraw	20	226	15	32	.469	16	22	.727	17	33	50	4	27	0	7	14	18	46	2.3	8
Jamila Wideman	25	329	12	43	.279	21	29	.724	5	17	22	57	28	0	10	34	1	48	1.9	9
Michelle Reed	9	49	3	11	.273	7	12	.583	2	9	11	2	4	0	2	6	1	14	1.6	7
Los Angeles	30	6025	797	1914	.416	443	609	.727	337	683	1020	472	675	7	229	511	148	2148	71.6	89
Opponents	30	6025	780	1898	.411	490	693	.707	337	663	1000	522	603	4	244	481	109	2169	72.3	92

3-pt. FG: Los Angeles 111-335 (.331); Leslie 9-23 (.391); Dixon 21-59 (.356); Toler 25-60 (.417); Mabika 33-107 (.308); McGee 0-4 (.000); Feaster 2-10 (.200); Alexander(‡) 6-16 (.375); Colleton 5-19 (.263); Blue 6-21 (.286); Wideman 3-12 (.250); Reed 1-4 (.250); Opponents 119-372 (.320)

NEW YORK LIBERTY

Player	G	Min	FGM	FGA	Pct	FTM	FTA	Pct	Off	Def	Tot	Ast	PF	Dq	Stl	TO	Blk	Pts	Avg	Hi
Sophia Witherspoon	30	898	144	359	.401	92	117	.786	33	58	91	57	54	0	40	73	4	413	13.8	26
Vickie Johnson	30	905	146	327	.446	63	82	.768	44	70	114	74	70	1	31	45	7	376	12.5	27
Rebecca Lobo	30	875	136	281	.484	66	93	.710	70	137	207	44	98	1	17	67	33	350	11.7	22
Kym Hampton	30	745	98	217	.452	78	109	.716	53	128	181	26	90	1	33	62	15	274	9.1	22
T. Weatherspoon	30	1002	73	188	.388	42	69	.609	20	100	120	191	85	0	100	96	0	204	6.8	15
Kisha Ford	30	471	60	138	.435	25	40	.625	23	14	37	23	68	0	32	16	2	147	4.9	19
Sue Wicks	30	444	46	107	.430	36	45	.800	40	43	83	36	66	0	16	48	10	128	4.3	12
Trena Trice	10	77	7	17	.412	7	11	.636	7	11	18	1	12	0	0	7	3	21	2.1	5
Albena Branzova	11	94	9	25	.360	3	4	.750	6	10	16	5	12	0	3	12	1	23	2.1	5
Coquese Washington	28	226	15	51	.294	18	26	.692	5	21	26	44	31	0	17	37	0	53	1.9	7
Elisabeth Cebrian	22	187	15	35	.429	8	14	.571	12	15	27	8	32	0	1	20	7	38	1.7	6
Alicia Thompson	19	126	9	39	.231	12	19	.632	7	17	24	4	12	0	1	8	2	31	1.6	7
New York	30	6050	758	1784	.425	450	629	.715	320	624	944	513	630	3	291	501	84	2058	68.6	92
Opponents	30	6050	709	1693	.419	445	625	.712	272	620	892	420	610	4	261	538	81	1966	65.5	82

3-pt. FG: New York 92-281 (.327); Witherspoon 33-96 (.344); Johnson 21-56 (.375); Lobo 12-39 (.308); Hampton 0-1 (.000); Weatherspoon 16-49 (.327); Ford 2-11 (.182); Wicks 0-3 (.000); Branzova 2-4 (.500); Washington 5-21 (.238); Thompson 1-1 (1.000); Opponents 103-325 (.317)

PHOENIX MERCURY

Player	G	Min	FGM	FGA	Pct	FTM	FTA	Pct	Off	Def	Tot	Ast	PF	Dq	Stl	TO	Blk	Pts	Avg	Hi
Jennifer Gillom	30	962	228	492	.463	137	195	.703	62	157	219	42	94	1	50	89	10	624	20.8	36
Bridget Pettis	30	849	113	300	.377	77	89	.865	34	69	103	62	75	0	29	62	9	338	11.3	23
Michelle Griffiths	30	779	93	184	.505	78	98	.796	45	88	133	41	48	0	44	52	5	275	9.2	18
Michele Timms	30	934	71	223	.318	34	49	.694	18	56	74	158	76	0	38	69	4	207	6.9	15
Umeki Webb	30	846	59	161	.366	39	59	.661	47	69	116	92	105	2	47	41	21	161	5.4	15
Marlies Askamp	26	319	49	104	.471	41	62	.661	36	49	85	12	45	0	12	22	7	139	5.3	13
Brandy Reed	24	254	50	95	.526	22	31	.710	36	42	78	20	30	0	18	33	7	124	5.2	13
Toni Foster	16	218	28	60	.467	23	30	.767	10	20	30	19	20	0	14	15	5	79	4.9	14
Andrea Kuklova	29	340	38	95	.400	20	36	.556	19	18	37	31	40	0	18	40	4	97	3.3	10
Maria Stepanova	20	130	26	61	.426	14	22	.636	17	21	38	7	29	0	3	9	11	66	3.3	15
Pauline Jordan(‡)	6	30	5	8	.625	5	7	.714	1	4	5	4	4	0	0	1	0	15	2.5	9
Kristi Harrower	30	355	19	52	.365	21	28	.750	2	19	21	52	25	0	15	31	3	70	2.3	7
Mikiko Hagiwara	10	59	8	21	.381	2	3	.667	0	2	2	3	4	0	0	5	0	22	2.2	8
Tiffani Johnson(*)	0	0	0	0	---	0	0	---	0	0	0	0	0	0	0	0	0	0	---	--
Tiffani Johnson(†)	6	32	0	6	.000	2	4	.500	3	7	10	0	5	0	2	3	0	2	0.3	1
Phoenix	30	6075	787	1856	.424	513	709	.724	327	614	941	543	595	3	288	483	86	2217	73.9	96
Opponents	30	6075	758	1747	.434	432	601	.719	298	643	941	406	664	9	242	581	96	2025	67.5	90

3-pt. FG: Phoenix 130-405 (.321); Gillom 31-82 (.378); Pettis 35-123 (.285); Griffiths 11-23 (.478); Timms 31-104 (.298); Webb 4-14 (.286); Reed 2-8 (.250); Kuklova 1-7 (.143); Harrower 11-32 (.344); Hagiwara 4-12 (.333); Opponents 77-244 (.316)

SACRAMENTO MONARCHS

Player	G	Min	FGM	FGA	Pct	FTM	FTA	Pct	REBOUNDS Off	Def	Tot	Ast	PF	Dq	Stl	TO	Blk	SCORING Pts	Avg	Hi
Latasha Byears 30	30	828	181	400	.453	61	92	.663	85	114	199	29	121	4	43	71	13	427	14.2	28
R. Bolton-Holifield 5	5	133	17	58	.293	17	28	.607	5	6	11	6	12	0	6	7	0	55	11.0	17
Tangela Smith.............28	28	707	113	279	.405	40	54	.741	45	84	129	31	78	0	17	46	46	271	9.7	26
Adia Barnes 29	29	619	88	223	.395	29	39	.744	35	49	84	22	70	1	14	53	10	219	7.6	24
Linda Burgess.............30	30	692	90	189	.476	45	59	.763	53	93	146	28	81	0	42	61	11	226	7.5	33
Lady Grooms 30	30	792	75	154	.487	63	94	.670	37	43	80	48	35	0	20	52	3	214	7.1	16
Ticha Penicheiro 30	30	1080	55	165	.333	70	109	.642	13	128	141	224	90	1	67	116	3	190	6.3	14
Franthea Price 26	26	379	43	115	.374	13	18	.722	7	37	44	35	29	0	20	32	2	127	4.9	14
Rehema Stephens.........8	8	81	11	41	.268	2	4	.500	7	3	10	4	8	0	2	11	0	26	3.3	7
Pauline Jordan(*) 18	18	247	21	61	.344	17	28	.607	14	30	44	16	44	1	14	24	12	59	3.3	8
Pauline Jordan(†) 24	24	277	26	69	.377	22	35	.629	15	34	49	20	48	1	14	25	12	74	3.1	9
Nadine Domond 9	9	92	10	33	.303	4	4	1.000	6	3	9	9	13	0	7	11	1	27	3.0	7
Bridgette Gordon 22	22	253	24	63	.381	9	16	.563	11	19	30	9	27	0	8	30	0	57	2.6	12
Quacy Barnes.............17	17	90	6	15	.400	4	11	.364	5	3	8	2	20	0	1	9	6	16	0.9	4
Tiffani Johnson(‡) 6	6	32	0	6	.000	2	4	.500	3	7	10	0	5	0	2	3	0	2	0.3	1
Sacramento 30	30	6025	734	1802	.407	376	560	.671	326	619	945	463	633	7	263	533	107	1916	63.9	82
Opponents 30	30	6025	733	1752	.418	509	674	.755	307	646	953	493	556	5	239	500	134	2082	69.4	88

3-pt. FG: Sacramento 72-277 (.260); Byears 4-18 (.222); Bolton-Holifield 4-26 (.154); Smith 5-14 (.357); A. Barnes 14-47 (.298); Burgess 1-8 (.125); Gordon 0-8 (.000); Hardmon 1-6 (.167); Penicheiro 10-43 (.233); Price 28-78 (.359); Stephens 2-12 (.167); Jordan(*) 0-1 (.000); Jordan(†) 0-1 (.000); Domond 3-16 (.188); Opponents 107-366 (.292)

UTAH STARZZ

Player	G	Min	FGM	FGA	Pct	FTM	FTA	Pct	REBOUNDS Off	Def	Tot	Ast	PF	Dq	Stl	TO	Blk	SCORING Pts	Avg	Hi
Wendy Palmer 28	28	761	145	307	.472	81	124	.653	70	116	186	30	75	1	18	56	5	377	13.5	31
Elena Baranova 20	20	671	92	219	.420	59	71	.831	61	125	186	70	44	1	21	55	30	258	12.9	22
Malgorzata Dydek 30	30	839	146	303	.482	93	127	.732	41	186	227	53	126	3	14	108	114	386	12.9	27
Kim Williams 30	30	543	91	223	.408	36	49	.735	24	34	58	46	74	1	43	66	6	227	7.6	19
Tammi Reiss 22	22	477	54	134	.403	19	29	.655	14	25	39	48	32	0	11	25	1	143	6.5	17
Chantel Tremitiere 28	28	709	48	132	.364	41	54	.759	13	49	62	102	53	0	22	42	2	155	5.5	16
LaTonya Johnson 28	28	490	58	145	.400	21	34	.618	14	40	54	20	42	0	11	42	1	151	5.4	15
O. Scott-Richardson 29	29	466	58	135	.430	37	65	.569	37	48	85	22	78	2	24	49	10	154	5.3	15
Fran Harris 18	18	353	28	79	.354	10	12	.833	14	25	39	30	33	0	13	17	1	71	3.9	10
Dena Head.................30	30	467	36	85	.424	23	33	.697	14	38	52	37	40	0	30	44	0	108	3.6	13
Tricia Bader 22	22	206	16	53	.302	4	8	.500	0	10	10	20	34	1	13	26	0	46	2.1	10
Erin Alexander(*) 12	12	68	5	22	.227	2	2	1.000	0	3	3	3	7	0	1	5	0	17	1.4	6
Erin Alexander(†) 20	20	141	12	44	.273	4	4	1.000	8	10	18	9	18	0	3	12	0	39	2.0	10
Utah...........................30	30	6050	777	1837	.423	426	608	.701	302	699	1001	481	638	9	221	543	170	2093	69.8	99
Opponents 30	30	6050	832	1942	.428	495	680	.728	336	685	1021	539	559	7	304	441	94	2294	76.5	96

3-pt. FG: Utah 113-346 (.327); Palmer 6-17 (.353); Baranova 15-48 (.313); Dydek 1-7 (.143); Williams 9-28 (.321); Reiss 16-54 (.296); Tremitiere 18-49 (.367); Johnson 14-49 (.286); Scott-Richardson 1-5 (.200); Harris 5-16 (.313); Head 13-27 (.481); Bader 10-27 (.370); Alexander(*) 5-19 (.263); Alexander(†) 11-35 (.314); Opponents 135-410 (.329)

WASHINGTON MYSTICS

Player	G	Min	FGM	FGA	Pct	FTM	FTA	Pct	REBOUNDS Off	Def	Tot	Ast	PF	Dq	Stl	TO	Blk	SCORING Pts	Avg	Hi
Nikki McCray...............29	29	969	191	457	.418	107	143	.748	34	51	85	90	81	2	43	125	2	512	17.7	29
A. Santos de Oliveira ..16	16	481	63	122	.516	50	108	.463	60	69	129	1	45	1	12	55	7	176	11.0	19
Murriel Page...............30	30	955	104	217	.479	41	65	.631	81	127	208	40	97	1	19	57	13	249	8.3	19
Penny Moore 29	29	756	93	271	.343	33	46	.717	35	73	108	46	58	0	44	61	20	238	8.2	18
Heidi Burge 30	30	501	81	159	.509	37	62	.597	31	69	100	26	93	2	16	73	15	201	6.7	19
Marie Chaconas..........30	30	397	44	148	.297	33	42	.788	7	17	24	38	52	2	13	49	0	144	4.8	17

125

REVIEW 1998 Regular Season

									REBOUNDS									SCORING		
Player	G	Min	FGM	FGA	Pct	FTM	FTA	Pct	Off	Def	Tot	Ast	PF	Dq	Stl	TO	Blk	Pts	Avg	Hi
Rita Williams	30	712	41	127	.323	38	60	.633	13	55	68	69	51	0	63	69	2	132	4.4	11
Deborah Carter	29	434	39	144	.271	21	26	.808	20	45	65	23	57	0	16	40	4	111	3.8	12
Adrienne Shuler	25	363	31	84	.369	14	17	.824	12	40	52	48	52	0	23	41	3	89	3.6	14
Tammy Jackson(‡)	2	14	2	3	.667	0	2	.000	1	3	4	0	3	0	0	0	0	4	2.0	2
La'Shawn Brown	22	272	13	37	.351	17	33	.515	17	36	53	8	62	1	10	24	20	43	2.0	4
Margo Graham	10	49	8	19	.421	3	6	.500	8	5	13	1	14	0	1	8	1	19	1.9	10
Leila Sobral	14	71	6	25	.240	9	13	.692	3	7	10	6	14	0	5	9	2	24	1.7	6
Angela Jackson	6	36	3	6	.500	4	6	.667	3	1	4	0	7	0	1	0	2	10	1.7	4
Leslie Johnson	7	15	1	2	.500	0	0	---	0	1	1	1	6	0	0	4	0	2	0.3	2
Washington	30	6025	720	1821	.395	400	620	.645	325	599	924	692	397	9	266	625	91	1954	65.1	88
Opponents	30	6025	876	1870	.468	551	775	.711	322	713	1035	548	597	1	334	511	104	2415	80.5	110

3-pt. FG: Washington 114-432 (.264); McCray 23-73 (.315); Page 0-2 (.000); Moore 19-92 (.207); Burge 2-7 (.286); Chaconas 30-105 (.286); Williams 12-55 (.218); Carter 12-49 (.245); Shuler 13-38 (.342); Sobral 3-11 (.273); Opponents 112-318 (.352)

(*) Statistics with this team only
(†) Totals with all teams
(‡) Continued season with another team

PLAYOFFS RESULTS

SEMIFINALS

Houston defeats Charlotte, 2-0

| August 22 | Houston 85, Charlotte 71 at Charlotte |
| August 24 | Houston 77, Charlotte 61 at Houston |

Phoenix defeats Cleveland, 2-1

August 22	Phoenix 78, Cleveland 68 at Phoenix
August 24	Cleveland 67, Phoenix 66 at Cleveland
August 25	Phoenix 71, Cleveland 60 at Cleveland

CHAMPIONSHIP

Houston defeats Phoenix, 2-1

August 27	Phoenix 54, Houston 51 at Phoenix
August 29	Houston 74, Phoenix 69 (overtime) at Houston
September 1	Houston 80, Phoenix 71 at Houston

TEAM STATISTICS

OFFENSIVE

TEAM	G	FG	FGA	PCT	FG3	FG3A	PCT	FT	FTA	PCT	OFF	DEF	REB	AST	PF	DQ	STL	TO	BLK	PTS	AVG
Hou.	5	136	301	.452	25	84	.298	70	89	.787	40	125	165	83	77	0	41	71	21	367	73.4
Phoe.	6	156	369	.423	26	73	.356	71	92	.772	58	136	194	100	116	2	44	84	19	409	68.2
Cha.	2	55	131	.420	5	27	.185	17	30	.567	18	36	54	34	38	0	18	26	6	132	66.0
Clev.	3	72	186	.387	6	24	.250	45	55	.818	38	59	97	50	59	0	26	45	6	195	65.0

DEFENSIVE

Team	FG	FGA	PCT	FG3	FG3A	PCT	FT	FTA	PCT	OFF	DEF	REB	AST	PF	DQ	STL	TO	BLK	PTS	AVG	DIFF
Hou.	130	318	.409	18	68	.265	48	74	.649	46	106	152	77	94	1	37	68	20	326	65.2	+8.2
Phoe.	149	370	.403	19	67	.284	83	104	.798	61	128	189	98	104	0	52	84	19	400	66.7	+1.5
Clev.	81	182	.445	13	32	.406	40	48	.833	30	66	96	57	60	1	25	42	5	215	71.7	-6.7
Cha.	59	117	.504	12	41	.293	32	40	.800	17	56	73	35	32	0	15	32	8	162	81.0	-15.0
AVG.'S	105	247	.425	16	52	.298	51	67	.763	39	89	128	67	73	1	32	57	13	276	68.9	---
	419	987		62	208		203	266			154	356	510	267	290	2	129	226	52	1103		

TEAM COMPARISONS

TEAM	Points		Field Goal		Turnovers		Rebound			Below		Overtime		3 PTS		10 PTS	
	Per Game		Percentage		Per Game		Percentages			70 Pts.		Games		or Less		or More	
	OWN	OPP	OWN	OPP	OWN	OPP	OFF	DEF	TOT	OWN	OPP	W	L	W	L	W	L
Charlotte	66.0	81.0	.420	.504	13.0*	16.0*	.243	.679	.461	1	0	0	0	0	0	0	2

Cleveland 65.0	71.7	.387	.445	15.0	14.0	.365*	.663	.514*	3	1	0	0	1	0	0	2		
Houston 73.4*	65.2*	.452*	.409	14.2	13.6	.274	.731*	.502	1	3	1	0	0	1	2	0		
Phoenix 68.2	66.7	.423	.403*	14.0	14.0	.312	.690	.501	3	4	0	1	1	1	2	0		
COMPOSITE; 8 games																		
.........................68.9	68.9	.425	.425	14.1	14.1	.302	.698			8	1	1	2	2	4	4		

* - League Leader
REBOUND PERCENTAGES
OFF. - Percentage of a given team's missed shots which that team rebounds.
DEF. - Percentage of opponents' missed shots which a given team rebounds.
TOT. - Average of offensive and defensive rebound percentages.

INDIVIDUAL PLAYOFFS STATISTICS, TEAM BY TEAM

CHARLOTTE STING

								REBOUNDS									SCORING		
Player	G	Min	FGM	FGA	Pct	FTM	FTA	Pct	Off	Def	Tot	Ast	PF	Dq	Stl	TO	Blk	Pts	Avg	Hi
Tracy Reid 2	74	14	25	.560	4	11	.364	5	5	10	0	2	0	2	5	1	32	16.0	18
Andrea Stinson.............2	71	12	27	.444	3	5	.600	2	8	10	13	9	0	4	6	0	29	14.5	16
Rhonda Mapp 2	65	12	21	.571	3	3	1.000	5	9	14	2	10	0	0	2	1	27	13.5	16
Tora Suber 2	74	9	23	.391	2	3	.667	1	1	2	10	5	0	5	7	0	23	11.5	15
Vicky Bullett.................2	69	6	24	.250	4	4	1.000	5	7	12	8	6	0	6	1	3	16	8.0	10
Christy Smith 2	19	1	6	.167	1	4	.250	0	1	1	1	4	0	0	0	0	3	1.5	2
Sharon Manning...........2	22	1	4	.250	0	0	---	0	4	4	0	2	0	1	3	0	2	1.0	2
Andrea Congreaves 1	6	0	1	.000	0	0	---	0	1	1	0	0	0	0	2	1	0	0.0	0
Charlotte 2	400	55	131	.420	17	30	.567	18	36	54	34	38	0	18	26	6	132	66.0	71
Opponents 2	400	59	117	.504	32	40	.800	17	56	73	35	32	0	15	32	8	162	81.0	85

3-pt. FG: Charlotte 5-27 (.185); Stinson 2-7 (.286); Mapp 0-1 (.000); Suber 3-12 (.250); Bullett 0-2 (.000); Chr. Smith 0-4 (.000); Congreaves 0-1 (.000); Opponents 12-41 (.293)

CLEVELAND ROCKERS

								REBOUNDS									SCORING		
Player	G	Min	FGM	FGA	Pct	FTM	FTA	Pct	Off	Def	Tot	Ast	PF	Dq	Stl	TO	Blk	Pts	Avg	Hi
Isabelle Fijalkowski 3	107	17	40	.425	19	22	.864	6	21	27	4	13	0	2	5	2	53	17.7	20
Janice Braxton 3	83	10	26	.385	12	14	.857	9	10	19	6	9	0	2	7	0	32	10.7	18
Michelle Edwards.........3	95	12	33	.364	4	7	.571	4	6	10	10	5	0	6	8	0	29	9.7	18
Merlakia Jones 3	65	11	24	.458	4	4	1.000	5	7	12	1	7	0	0	3	0	27	9.0	10
Eva Nemcova................3	92	9	28	.321	2	2	1.000	4	5	9	14	10	0	2	8	2	21	7.0	9
S. McConnell Serio 3	99	7	14	.500	2	3	.667	3	4	7	15	9	0	8	9	1	19	6.3	8
Raegan Scott 3	26	4	12	.333	1	1	1.000	3	4	7	0	4	0	0	0	1	9	3.0	5
Rushia Brown................3	21	2	6	.333	1	2	.500	3	0	3	0	2	0	5	5	0	5	1.7	3
Adrienne Johnson........2	12	0	3	.000	0	0	---	1	2	3	0	0	0	1	0	0	0	0.0	0
Cleveland.....................3	600	72	186	.387	45	55	.818	38	59	97	50	59	0	26	45	6	195	65.0	68
Opponents 3	600	81	182	.445	40	48	.833	30	66	96	57	60	1	25	42	5	215	71.7	78

3-pt. FG: Cleveland 6-24 (.250); Fijalkowski 0-1 (.000); Braxton 0-1 (.000); Edwards 1-6 (.167); Jones 1-2 (.500); Nemcova 1-5 (.200); McConnell Serio 3-7 (.429); Johnson 0-2 (.000); Opponents 13-32 (.406)

HOUSTON COMETS

								REBOUNDS									SCORING		
Player	G	Min	FGM	FGA	Pct	FTM	FTA	Pct	Off	Def	Tot	Ast	PF	Dq	Stl	TO	Blk	Pts	Avg	Hi
Cynthia Cooper 5	198	42	93	.452	38	45	.844	4	12	16	22	10	0	9	15	5	129	25.8	29
Sheryl Swoopes 5	188	27	61	.443	14	15	.933	7	43	50	26	10	0	9	16	7	73	14.6	18
Tina Thompson 5	186	20	49	.408	11	12	.917	12	34	46	6	19	0	7	8	4	58	11.6	18
Kim Perrot 5	182	15	40	.375	5	12	.417	5	11	16	25	8	0	8	17	0	41	8.2	13
Monica Lamb................5	107	14	25	.560	1	2	.500	5	13	18	0	16	0	2	8	4	29	5.8	12
Yolanda Moore.............5	61	10	15	.667	1	3	.333	6	3	9	0	9	0	4	1	0	21	4.2	10
Janeth Arcain 5	92	8	18	.444	0	0	---	1	7	8	4	5	0	2	3	1	16	3.2	6
Tammy Jackson 3	11	0	0	---	0	0	---	0	2	2	0	0	0	0	0	0	0	0.0	0
Houston 5	1025	136	301	.452	70	89	.787	40	125	165	83	77	0	41	71	21	367	73.4	85
Opponents 5	1025	130	318	.409	48	74	.649	46	106	152	77	94	1	37	68	20	326	65.2	71

3-pt. FG: Houston 25-84 (.298); Cooper 7-28 (.250); Swoopes 5-18 (.278); Thompson 7-20 (.350); Perrot 6-16 (.375); Arcain 0-2 (.000); Opponents 18-68 (.265)

PHOENIX MERCURY

Player	G	Min	FGM	FGA	Pct	FTM	FTA	Pct	Off	Def	Tot	Ast	PF	Dq	Stl	TO	Blk	Pts	Avg	Hi
Jennifer Gillom	6	214	36	95	.379	22	26	.846	8	39	47	2	18	0	8	17	7	102	17.0	27
Bridget Pettis	6	183	30	60	.500	15	19	.789	10	12	22	13	11	0	11	11	2	77	12.8	27
Michelle Griffiths	6	171	28	56	.500	13	20	.650	14	25	39	14	14	0	4	10	2	74	12.3	24
Michele Timms	6	208	19	54	.352	10	10	1.000	2	18	20	31	20	1	5	21	0	54	9.0	21
Kristi Harrower	6	78	12	20	.600	0	0	---	1	5	6	7	4	0	5	4	1	27	4.5	12
Brandy Reed	6	62	9	25	.360	2	2	1.000	7	10	17	5	6	0	2	6	1	20	3.3	8
Maria Stepanova	4	22	5	11	.455	1	2	.500	3	3	6	1	8	1	1	1	1	11	2.8	6
Umeki Webb	6	158	6	21	.286	3	5	.600	6	9	15	18	23	0	1	9	2	16	2.7	7
Andrea Kuklova	4	43	4	7	.571	0	0	---	1	1	2	3	2	0	3	0	2	9	2.3	7
Marlies Askamp	5	36	4	10	.400	1	4	.250	3	9	12	1	6	0	0	3	1	9	1.8	6
Toni Foster	6	50	3	10	.300	4	4	1.000	3	5	8	5	4	0	4	2	0	10	1.7	6
Phoenix	6	1225	156	369	.423	71	92	.772	58	136	194	100	116	2	44	84	19	409	68.2	78
Opponents	6	1225	149	370	.403	83	104	.798	61	128	189	98	104	0	52	84	19	400	66.7	80

3-pt. FG: Phoenix 26-73 (.356); Gillom 8-16 (.500); Pettis 2-10 (.200); Griffiths 5-11 (.455); Timms 6-22 (.273); Harrower 3-7 (.429); Reed 0-1 (.000); Webb 1-5 (.200); Kuklova 1-1 (1.000); Opponents 19-67 (.284)

INDIVIDUAL FINALS STATISTICS, TEAM BY TEAM

HOUSTON COMETS

Player	G	Min	FGM	FGA	Pct	FTM	FTA	Pct	Off	Def	Tot	Ast	PF	Dq	Stl	TO	Blk	Pts	Avg	Hi
Cynthia Cooper	3	123	27	62	.435	21	27	.778	2	6	8	13	6	0	5	11	3	79	26.3	29
Sheryl Swoopes	3	117	13	37	.351	10	11	.909	4	25	29	17	3	0	6	10	5	38	12.7	16
Tina Thompson	3	109	13	31	.419	4	4	1.000	8	14	22	1	12	0	5	3	1	34	11.3	18
Monica Lamb	3	65	10	16	.625	0	0	---	3	8	11	0	10	0	1	3	3	20	6.7	12
Kim Perrot	3	109	6	24	.250	3	6	.500	4	8	12	14	4	0	4	9	0	18	6.0	13
Janeth Arcain	3	68	6	11	.545	0	0	---	1	6	7	3	5	0	2	1	1	12	4.0	6
Yolanda Moore	3	27	2	3	.667	0	1	.000	1	0	1	0	5	0	3	1	0	4	1.3	2
Tammy Jackson	2	7	0	0	---	0	0	---	0	2	2	0	0	0	0	0	0	0	0.0	0
Houston	3	625	77	184	.418	38	49	.776	23	69	92	48	45	0	26	39	13	205	68.3	80
Opponents	3	625	75	187	.401	31	44	.705	28	70	98	43	56	1	19	42	14	194	64.7	71

3-pt. FG: Houston 13-43 (.302); Cooper 4-14 (.286); Swoopes 2-9 (.222); Thompson 4-11 (.364); Perrot 3-9 (.333); Opponents 13-41 (.317)

PHOENIX MERCURY

Player	G	Min	FGM	FGA	Pct	FTM	FTA	Pct	Off	Def	Tot	Ast	PF	Dq	Stl	TO	Blk	Pts	Avg	Hi
Jennifer Gillom	3	109	14	47	.298	12	15	.800	5	20	25	1	6	0	4	8	6	43	14.3	20
Michelle Griffiths	3	99	14	28	.500	9	14	.643	7	17	24	6	7	0	3	6	1	39	13.0	24
Michele Timms	3	109	12	34	.353	5	5	1.000	2	12	14	14	11	1	1	13	0	32	10.7	21
Bridget Pettis	3	86	12	25	.480	2	5	.400	3	5	8	4	7	0	5	6	1	26	8.7	13
Kristi Harrower	3	56	10	16	.625	0	0	---	1	3	4	2	4	0	3	3	1	23	7.7	12
Umeki Webb	3	65	4	13	.308	2	3	.667	4	5	9	6	14	0	0	2	1	11	3.7	7
Andrea Kuklova	3	39	4	6	.667	0	0	---	1	1	2	3	2	0	2	0	2	9	3.0	7
Maria Stepanova	3	13	2	6	.333	1	2	.500	2	2	4	0	2	0	0	1	0	5	1.7	3
Toni Foster	3	25	2	5	.400	0	0	---	1	3	4	5	1	0	0	0	0	4	1.3	2
Brandy Reed	3	17	1	6	.167	0	0	---	2	0	2	2	1	0	1	2	1	2	0.7	2
Marlies Askamp	2	7	0	1	.000	0	0	---	0	2	2	0	1	0	0	1	1	0	0.0	0
Phoenix	3	625	75	187	.401	31	44	.705	28	70	98	43	56	1	19	42	14	194	64.7	71
Opponents	3	625	77	184	.418	38	49	.776	23	69	92	48	45	0	26	39	13	205	68.3	80

3-pt. FG: Phoenix 13-41 (.317); Gillom 3-8 (.375); Griffiths 2-6 (.333); Timms 3-15 (.200); Pettis 0-2 (.000); Harrower 3-6 (.500); Webb 1-3 (.333); Kuklova 1-1 (1.000); Opponents 13-43 (.302)

Front Row (l. to. r.) - Fran Harris, Kim Perrot, Tina Thompson, Wanda Guyton, Cynthia Cooper, Janeth Arcain, Sheryl Swoopes. Back Row (l. to r.) - Assistant Coach Kevin Cook, Equipment Manager Stacey Johnson, Assistant Coach Peggie Gillom, Nykeshia Henderson, Racquel Spurlock, Tammy Jackson, Catarina Pollini, Yolanda Moore, Pietra Gay, Tiffany Woosley, Trainer Michelle T. Leget, Head Coach Van Chancellor.

FINAL STANDINGS

EASTERN CONFERENCE

Team	CHA	CLE	HOU	LA	NY	PHO	SAC	UTA	W	L	PCT	GB	Last-10	Streak
HOU	3	2	--	3	1	3	3	3	18	10	.643	-	7-3	Lost 2
NY	2	3	3	2	--	2	3	2	17	11	.607	1	3-7	Won 1
CHA	--	2	1	3	2	2	2	3	15	13	.536	3	5-5	Won 1
CLE	2	--	2	2	1	2	2	4	15	13	.536	3	5-5	Lost 1

WESTERN CONFERENCE

Team	CHA	CLE	HOU	LA	NY	PHO	SAC	UTA	W	L	PCT	GB	Last-10	Streak
PHO	2	2	1	2	2	--	4	3	16	12	.571	-	7-3	Won 3
LA	1	2	1	--	2	2	3	3	14	14	.500	2	6-4	Lost 1
SAC	2	2	1	1	1	0	--	3	10	18	.357	6	5-5	Won 1
UTA	1	0	1	1	2	1	1	--	7	21	.250	9	2-8	Lost 2

TEAM STATISTICS
OFFENSIVE

TEAM	G	FG	FGA	PCT	FG3	FG3A	PCT	FT	FTA	PCT	OFF	DEF	REB	AST	PF	DQ	STL	TO	BLK	PTS	AVG
L.A.	28	794	1782	.446	65	242	.269	419	620	.676	290	683	973	495	601	6	259	528	138	2072	74.0
Hou.	28	700	1660	.422	169	485	.348	441	592	.745	.316	543	859	389	535	1	311	492	67	2010	71.8
Clev.	28	725	1633	.444	65	177	.367	450	623	.722	267	624	891	456	514	8	256	526	86	1965	70.2
Phoe.	28	660	1768	.373	134	436	.307	484	634	.763	322	599	921	437	570	4	343	475	80	1938	69.2
N.Y.	28	707	1715	.412	93	339	.274	404	607	.666	320	600	920	484	556	4	289	536	116	1911	68.3
Sac.	28	704	1732	.406	101	345	.293	393	536	.733	341	538	879	404	593	14	263	562	60	1902	67.9
Cha.	28	719	1651	.435	110	321	.343	337	487	.692	279	635	914	485	465	0	219	496	116	1885	67.3
Utah	28	666	1781	.374	106	349	.304	371	528	.703	339	612	951	425	567	4	252	520	123	1809	64.6

DEFENSIVE

Team	FG	FGA	PCT	FG3	FG3A	PCT	FT	FTA	PCT	OFF	DEF	REB	AST	PF	DQ	STL	TO	BLK	PTS	AVG	DIFF
Phoe.	670	1622	.413	89	313	.284	397	589	.674	275	649	924	408	598	11	243	599	114	1826	65.2	+4.0
Hou.	679	1630	.417	91	305	.298	384	545	.705	296	557	853	405	558	4	237	537	102	1833	65.5	+6.3
N.Y.	661	1690	.391	106	320	.331	416	564	.738	327	604	931	397	563	3	278	570	87	1844	65.9	+2.4
Cha.	686	1707	.402	118	366	.322	359	513	.700	288	597	885	432	488	4	276	464	72	1849	66.0	+1.3
Clev.	709	1715	.413	122	356	.343	375	533	.704	306	563	869	464	599	6	303	494	96	1915	68.4	+1.8
L.A.	719	1812	.397	95	343	.277	477	649	.735	323	597	920	457	575	3	287	505	82	2010	71.8	+2.2
Utah	776	1808	.429	115	376	.306	436	606	.719	328	680	1008	498	501	6	278	458	119	2103	75.1	-10.5
Sac.	775	1738	.446	107	315	.340	455	628	.725	331	587	918	514	519	4	290	508	114	2112	75.4	-7.5
AVG.'S	709	1715	.414	105	337	.313	412	578	.713	309	604	914	447	550	5	274	517	98	1937	69.2	---
....	5675	13722		843	2694		3299	4627		2474	4834	7308	3575	4401	41	2192	4135	7861	5492		

TEAM COMPARISONS

TEAM	Points Per Game		Field Goal Percentage		Turnovers Per Game		Rebound Percentages			Below 70 Pts.		Overtime Games		3 PTS or Less		10 PTS or More	
	OWN	OPP	OWN	OPP	OWN	OPP	OFF	DEF	TOT	OWN	OPP	W	L	W	L	W	L
Charlotte	67.3	66.0	.435	.402	17.7	16.6	.318	.688*	.503	16	16	0	0	2	2	11	9
Cleveland	70.2	68.4	.444	.413	18.8	17.6	.322	.671	.496	11	15	0	2	2	2	11	7
Houston	71.8	65.5	.422	.417	17.6	19.2	.362	.647	.505	8	19	1	1	1	3	13	3
Los Angeles	74.0*	71.8	.446*	.397	18.9	18.0	.327	.679	.503	9	12	2	2	3	2	9	7
New York	68.3	65.9	.412	.391*	19.1	20.4	.346	.647	.497	16	18	3	0	3	3	9	5
Phoenix	69.2	65.2*	.373	.413	17.0*	21.4*	.332	.685	.508*	15	19	2	1	1	3	10	4
Sacramento	67.9	75.4	.406	.446	20.1	18.1	.367*	.619	.493	16	8	0	2	1	0	5	16
Utah	64.6	75.1	.374	.429	18.6	16.4	.333	.651	.492	21	5	1	1	2	0	2	19
COMPOSITE; 112 games																	
	69.2	69.2	.414	.414	18.5	18.5	.339	.661			112	9	9	15	15	70	70

* - League Leader

REBOUND PERCENTAGES

OFF. - Percentage of a given team's missed shots which that team rebounds.

DEF. - Percentage of opponents' missed shots which a given team rebounds.

TOT. - Average of offensive and defensive rebound percentages.

SCORING AVERAGE

	G	FG	FT	PTS	AVG
Cooper, Hou.	28	191	172	621	22.2
Bolton-Holifield, Sac.	23	164	53	447	19.4
Leslie, L.A.	28	160	113	445	15.9
Palmer, Utah	28	157	117	443	15.8
Gillom, Pho.	28	163	94	440	15.7
Stinson, Cha.	28	177	60	439	15.7
Witherspoon, N.Y.	28	140	83	407	14.5
Nemcova, Cle.	28	138	71	384	13.7
Thompson, Hou.	28	133	67	370	13.2
Toler, L.A.	28	144	73	368	13.1
Gordon, Sac.	28	135	84	365	13.0
Bullett, Cha.	28	145	62	359	12.8
Pettis, Pho.	28	107	97	352	12.6
Lobo, N.Y.	28	133	64	348	12.4
Baranova, Utah	28	129	43	341	12.2
Timms, Pho.	27	99	79	326	12.1
Fijalkowski, Cle.	28	125	81	332	11.9
Dixon, L.A.	27	115	68	320	11.9
Mapp, Cha.	28	120	82	326	11.6
Braxton, Cle.	25	88	106	287	11.5

REBOUNDS PER GAME

	G	OFF	DEF	TOT	AVG
Leslie, L.A.	28	63	203	266	9.5
Palmer, Utah	28	76	149	225	8.0
Braxton, Cle.	25	38	151	189	7.6
Baranova, Utah	28	56	151	207	7.4
Lobo, N.Y.	28	62	141	203	7.3
Byears, Sac.	28	87	106	193	6.9
Thompson, Hou.	28	67	117	184	6.6
Bullett, Cha.	28	66	112	178	6.4
Foster, Pho.	28	64	108	172	6.1
Bolton-Holifield, Sac	23..31	103	134		5.8
Hampton, N.Y.	28	52	111	163	5.8
Fijalkowski, Cle.	28	62	94	156	5.6
Stinson, Cha.	28	48	107	155	5.5
Mapp, Cha.	28	53	101	154	5.5
Guyton, Hou.	25	76	60	136	5.4
Gillom, Pho.	28	45	106	151	5.4
Askamp, Pho.	28	66	80	146	5.2
Gordon, Sac.	28	67	68	135	4.8
Congreaves, Cha.	28	40	93	133	4.8
McGee, Sac.	27	54	66	120	4.4

ASSISTS PER GAME

	G	AST	AVG
Weatherspoon, N.Y.	28	172	6.1
Toler, L.A.	28	143	5.1
Timms, Pho.	27	137	5.1
Tremitiere, Sac.	28	135	4.8
Cooper, Hou.	28	131	4.7

Edwards, Cle.	20	89	4.5
Stinson, Cha.	28	124	4.4
Wideman, L.A.	28	103	3.7
Perrot, Hou.	28	88	3.1
Reiss, Utah	28	87	3.1
Gordon, Sac.	28	78	2.8
Pettis, Pho.	28	78	2.8
Levesque, Cha.	27	75	2.8
Leslie, L.A.	28	74	2.6
Bolton-Holifield, Sac.	23	59	2.6
Johnson, N.Y.	26	66	2.5
Fijalkowski, Cle.	28	68	2.4
Webb, Pho.	28	68	2.4
3 tied			2.4

FIELD GOAL PCT.

	FG	FGA	PCT
Zheng, L.A.	110	178	.618
Fijalkowski, Cle.	125	246	.508
Mapp, Cha.	120	244	.492
Nemcova, Cle.	138	292	.473
Hampton, N.Y.	99	210	.471
Cooper, Hou.	191	406	.470
Foster, Pho.	94	201	.468
McGee, Sac.	102	222	.459
Byears, Sac.	96	209	.459
Dixon, L.A.	115	252	.456

3-PT FIELD GOAL PCT.

	3FG	3GA	PCT
Nemcova, Cle.	37	85	.435
Dixon, L.A.	22	52	.423
Cooper, Hou.	67	162	.414
Suber, Cha.	23	58	.397
Baranova, Utah	40	106	.377
Thompson, Hou.	37	100	.370
Witherspoon, N.Y.	44	126	.349
Levesque, Cha.	23	66	.348
Timms, Pho.	49	142	.345
Bolton-Holifield, Sa	66	192	.344

FREE THROW PCT.

	FT	FTA	PCT
Pettis, Pho.	97	108	.898
Arcain, Hou.	76	85	.894
Cooper, Hou.	172	199	.864
Nemcova, Cle.	71	83	.855
Head, Utah	38	45	.844
Toler, L.A.	73	87	.839
Thompson, Hou.	67	80	.838
Fijalkowski, Cle.	81	103	.786
Gordon, Sac.	84	107	.785
Gillom, Pho.	94	121	.777

REVIEW 1997 Regular Season

STEALS PER GAME

	G	STL	AVG
Weatherspoon, N.Y.	28	85	3.04
Timms, Pho.	27	71	2.63
Perrot, Hou.	28	69	2.46
Webb, Pho.	28	68	2.43
Bolton-Holifield, Sa	23	54	2.35
Cooper, Hou.	28	59	2.11
Bullett, Cha.	28	54	1.93
Tremitiere, Sac.	28	54	1.93
Foster, Pho.	28	53	1.89
Dixon, L.A.	27	49	1.81

BLOCKS PER GAME

	G	BLK	AVG
Baranova, Utah	28	63	2.25
Leslie, L.A.	28	59	2.11
Bullett, Cha.	28	55	1.96
Lobo, N.Y.	28	51	1.82

	G		
Braxton, Cle.	25	28	1.12
Thompson, Hou.	28	28	1.00
Foster, Pho.	28	21	0.75
Stinson, Cha.	28	21	0.75
Zheng, L.A.	28	20	0.71
Hampton, N.Y.	28	19	0.68

MINUTES PER GAME

	G	MIN	AVG
Tremitiere, Sac.	28	1051	37.5
Stinson, Cha.	28	1011	36.1
Timms, Pho.	27	966	35.8
Bolton-Holifield, Sac.	23	813	35.3
Cooper, Hou.	28	982	35.1
Gordon, Sac.	28	981	35.0
Nemcova, Cle.	28	944	33.7
Lobo, N.Y.	28	939	33.5
Palmer, Utah	28	936	33.4
Weatherspoon, N.Y.	28	924	33.0

INDIVIDUAL STATISTICS, TEAM BY TEAM

CHARLOTTE STING

Player	G	Min	FGM	FGA	Pct	FTM	FTA	Pct	REBOUNDS Off	Def	Tot	Ast	PF	Dq	Stl	TO	Blk	SCORING Pts	Avg	Hi
Andrea Stinson	28	1011	177	396	.447	60	89	.674	48	107	155	124	55	0	43	99	21	439	15.7	29
Vicky Bullett	28	875	145	324	.448	62	80	.775	66	112	178	65	84	0	54	68	55	359	12.8	24
Rhonda Mapp	28	710	120	244	.492	82	106	.774	53	101	154	64	104	0	21	68	12	326	11.6	21
Andrea Congreaves	28	658	63	126	.500	43	56	.768	40	93	133	41	52	0	16	31	5	187	6.7	15
Sharon Manning	28	438	58	125	.464	21	50	.420	42	56	98	13	31	0	25	29	5	137	4.9	11
Penny Moore	28	539	57	159	.358	16	31	.516	15	57	72	28	35	0	16	44	11	135	4.8	13
Tora Suber	28	475	40	108	.370	28	41	.683	5	37	42	56	32	0	13	51	3	131	4.7	13
Nicole Levesque	27	622	36	98	.367	14	15	.933	5	42	47	75	47	0	21	71	3	109	4.0	12
Milica Vukadinovic	1	14	1	1	1.000	0	0	---	0	1	1	1	0	0	1	3	0	3	3.0	3
Debra Williams	10	116	11	43	.256	1	2	.500	3	10	13	9	9	0	2	6	0	27	2.7	5
S. Hopson-Shelton	6	29	7	11	.636	2	2	1.000	1	4	5	1	3	0	1	2	0	16	2.7	8
Katasha Artis	20	113	4	16	.250	8	15	.533	1	15	16	8	13	0	6	12	1	16	0.8	5
Charlotte	28	5600	719	1651	.435	337	487	.692	279	635	914	485	465	0	219	496	116	1885	67.3	87
Opponents	28	5600	686	1707	.402	359	513	.700	288	597	885	432	488	4	276	464	72	1849	66.0	81

3-pt. FG: Charlotte 110-321 (.343); Stinson 25-77 (.325); Bullett 7-23 (.304); Mapp 4-8 (.500); Congreaves 18-44 (.409); Moore 5-25 (.200); Suber 23-58 (.397); Levesque 23-66 (.348); Vukadinovic 1-1 (1.000); Williams 4-18 (.222); Artis 0-1 (.000); Opponents 118-366 (.322)

CLEVELAND ROCKERS

Player	G	Min	FGM	FGA	Pct	FTM	FTA	Pct	REBOUNDS Off	Def	Tot	Ast	PF	Dq	Stl	TO	Blk	SCORING Pts	Avg	Hi
Eva Nemcova	28	944	138	292	.473	71	83	.855	23	87	110	67	53	0	39	78	8	384	13.7	23
Isabelle Fijalkowski	28	803	125	246	.508	81	103	.786	62	94	156	68	129	7	17	73	18	332	11.9	24
Janice Braxton	25	822	88	211	.417	106	138	.768	38	151	189	49	64	0	36	53	28	287	11.5	21
Michelle Edwards	20	622	76	170	.447	45	86	.523	13	57	70	89	40	1	34	77	3	203	10.2	17
Merlakia Jones	28	589	92	229	.402	40	56	.714	31	51	82	25	55	0	23	54	3	229	8.2	19
Lynette Woodard	28	712	87	218	.399	43	64	.672	37	79	116	67	44	0	46	69	10	217	7.8	20
Rushia Brown	28	511	64	123	.520	47	64	.734	48	65	113	20	72	0	34	27	14	175	6.3	17
Adrienne Johnson	25	194	22	59	.373	7	9	.778	8	14	22	9	12	0	5	27	1	53	2.1	11
Anita Maxwell	9	63	8	24	.333	3	8	.375	2	10	12	8	5	0	4	6	0	19	2.1	7

Player	G	Min	FGM	FGA	Pct	FTM	FTA	Pct	Off	Def	Tot	Ast	PF	Dq	Stl	TO	Blk	Pts	Avg	Hi
Tina Nicholson...........24		273	18	44	.409	3	5	.600	2	8	10	42	28	0	10	28	1	48	2.0	9
Jenny Boucek 10		112	7	15	.467	4	7	.571	3	7	10	9	10	0	6	22	0	18	1.8	6
Marcie Alberts 5		30	0	2	.000	0	0	---	0	1	1	3	2	0	2	3	0	0	0.0	0
Cleveland..................28		5675	725	1633	.444	450	623	.722	267	624	891	456	514	8	256	526	86	1965	70.2	95
Opponents 28		5675	709	1715	.413	375	533	.704	306	563	869	464	599	6	303	494	96	1915	68.4	87

3-pt. FG: Cleveland 65-177 (.367); Nemcova 37-85 (.435); Fijalkowski 1-4 (.250); Braxton 5-10 (.500); Edwards 6-26 (.231); Jones 5-12 (.417); Woodard 0-7 (.000); Johnson 2-4 (.500); Nicholson 9-24 (.375); Boucek 0-3 (.000); Alberts 0-2 (.000); Opponents 122-356 (.343).

HOUSTON COMETS

Player	G	Min	FGM	FGA	Pct	FTM	FTA	Pct	Off	Def	Tot	Ast	PF	Dq	Stl	TO	Blk	Pts	Avg	Hi
Cynthia Cooper 28		982	191	406	.470	172	199	.864	33	78	111	131	68	0	59	109	6	621	22.2	44
Tina Thompson 28		885	133	318	.418	67	80	.838	67	117	184	32	107	1	21	62	28	370	13.2	24
Janeth Arcain 28		784	110	250	.440	76	85	.894	41	69	110	45	56	0	43	67	4	305	10.9	23
Sheryl Swoopes 9		129	25	53	.472	10	14	.714	6	9	15	7	5	0	7	4	4	64	7.1	20
Wanda Guyton.............25		668	57	122	.467	38	68	.559	76	60	136	12	83	0	26	43	8	152	6.1	17
Kim Perrot 28		692	59	162	.364	15	37	.405	18	57	75	88	53	0	69	65	2	161	5.8	19
Fran Harris 25		369	37	107	.346	22	31	.710	16	40	56	25	27	0	17	29	3	104	4.2	13
Tammy Jackson 28		545	45	110	.409	25	41	.610	42	74	116	12	84	0	45	49	10	115	4.1	14
Tiffany Woosley 26		397	29	88	.330	2	8	.250	8	20	28	29	19	0	18	30	1	76	2.9	9
Catarina Pollini 13		94	8	22	.364	6	12	.500	3	9	12	5	21	0	4	8	1	22	1.7	4
Yolanda Moore...........13		93	5	20	.250	6	12	.500	6	7	13	1	9	0	1	7	0	16	1.2	4
Pietra Gay 5		12	1	2	.500	2	5	.400	0	3	3	2	3	0	1	4	0	4	0.8	2
Houston 28		5650	700	1660	.422	441	592	.745	316	543	859	389	535	1	311	492	67	2010	71.8	89
Opponents 28		5650	679	1630	.417	384	545	.705	296	557	853	405	558	4	237	537	102	1833	65.5	80

3-pt. FG: Houston 169-485 (.348); Cooper 67-162 (.414); Thompson 37-100 (.370); Arcain 9-33 (.273); Swoopes 2-16 (.250); Perrot 28-99 (.283); Harris 8-24 (.333); Jackson 0-1 (.000); Woosley 16-50 (.320); Opponents 91-305 (.298).

LOS ANGELES SPARKS

Player	G	Min	FGM	FGA	Pct	FTM	FTA	Pct	Off	Def	Tot	Ast	PF	Dq	Stl	TO	Blk	Pts	Avg	Hi
Lisa Leslie....................28		902	160	371	.431	113	189	.598	63	203	266	74	99	1	39	109	59	445	15.9	28
Penny Toler 28		907	144	338	.426	73	87	.839	25	69	94	143	66	3	36	107	3	368	13.1	19
Tamecka Dixon 27		715	115	252	.456	68	88	.773	22	59	81	55	76	0	49	58	5	320	11.9	25
Haixia Zheng 28		557	110	178	.618	39	59	.661	32	91	123	17	77	0	11	46	20	259	9.3	28
Linda Burgess..............28		492	73	135	.541	36	49	.735	46	71	117	9	46	0	20	47	13	183	6.5	20
Mwadi Mabika............21		325	53	136	.390	13	24	.542	22	32	54	22	48	0	23	27	6	126	6.0	12
Katrina Colleton 28		613	55	126	.437	17	30	.567	25	35	60	45	46	1	35	35	9	136	4.9	9
Heidi Burge 22		282	32	72	.444	23	45	.511	23	46	69	15	52	1	12	25	12	87	4.0	14
Jamila Wideman..........28		633	25	106	.236	27	34	.794	16	41	57	103	44	0	24	51	1	84	3.0	16
Daedra Charles 28		282	27	67	.403	10	15	.667	16	32	48	12	41	0	10	14	10	64	2.3	8
Travesa Gant 2		13	0	1	.000	0	0	---	0	3	3	0	4	0	0	2	0	0	0.0	0
Kim Gessig...................1		4	0	0	---	0	0	---	0	1	1	0	2	0	0	1	0	0	0.0	0
Los Angeles 28		5725	794	1782	.446	419	620	.676	290	683	973	495	601	6	259	528	138	2072	74.0	93
Opponents 28		5725	719	1812	.397	477	649	.735	323	597	920	457	575	3	287	505	82	2010	71.8	102

3-pt. FG: Los Angeles 65-242 (.269); Leslie 12-46 (.261); Toler 7-38 (.184); Dixon 22-52 (.423); Burgess 1-2 (.500); Mabika 7-38 (.184); Colleton 9-25 (.360); Burge 0-4 (.000); Wideman 7-36 (.194); Charles 0-1 (.000); Opponents 95-343 (.277).

NEW YORK LIBERTY

Player	G	Min	FGM	FGA	Pct	FTM	FTA	Pct	Off	Def	Tot	Ast	PF	Dq	Stl	TO	Blk	Pts	Avg	Hi
Sophia Witherspoon....28		867	140	345	.406	83	111	.748	30	54	84	64	62	0	49	77	7	407	14.5	27
Rebecca Lobo 28		939	133	354	.376	64	105	.610	62	141	203	53	73	1	26	88	51	348	12.4	27
Kym Hampton 28		663	99	210	.471	73	114	.640	52	111	163	38	68	1	39	49	19	271	9.7	21
Vickie Johnson 26		789	108	269	.401	27	35	.771	46	64	110	66	52	0	19	49	4	247	9.5	20

Player	G	Min	FGM	FGA	Pct	FTM	FTA	Pct	Off	Def	Tot	Ast	PF	Dq	Stl	TO	Blk	Pts	Avg	Hi
									REBOUNDS									SCORING		
T. Weatherspoon 28		924	64	137	.467	65	100	.650	25	91	116	172	72	0	85	94	2	196	7.0	19
Trena Trice 28		340	51	92	.554	30	45	.667	32	36	68	2	65	0	9	40	9	134	4.8	17
Kisha Ford 28		473	43	114	.377	27	44	.614	28	20	48	25	56	1	28	38	5	116	4.1	11
Sue Wicks 28		332	38	107	.355	22	33	.667	36	58	94	29	52	0	17	46	18	100	3.6	9
Rhonda Blades 28		290	25	70	.357	13	20	.650	6	15	21	30	55	1	14	39	1	80	2.9	8
Jasmina Perazic-Gipe 9		47	5	13	.385	0	0	---	2	9	11	4	1	0	3	7	0	10	1.1	2
C. Crumpton-Moorer 2		11	1	4	.250	0	0	---	1	1	2	1	0	0	0	1	0	2	1.0	2
New York 28		5675	707	1715	.412	404	607	.666	320	600	920	484	556	4	289	536	116	1911	68.3	80
Opponents 28		5675	661	1690	.391	416	564	.738	327	604	931	397	563	3	278	570	87	1844	65.9	87

3-pt. FG: New York 93-339 (.274); Witherspoon 44-126 (.349); Lobo 18-63 (.286); Hampton 0-1 (.000); Johnson 4-21 (.190); Weatherspoon 3-35 (.086); Trice 2-8 (.250) Ford 3-20 (.150); Wicks 2-7 (.286); Blades 17-54 (.315); Perazic-Gipe 0-3 (.000); Crumpton-Moorer 0-1 (.000); Opponents 106-320 (.331)

PHOENIX MERCURY

Player	G	Min	FGM	FGA	Pct	FTM	FTA	Pct	Off	Def	Tot	Ast	PF	Dq	Stl	TO	Blk	Pts	Avg	Hi
									REBOUNDS									SCORING		
Jennifer Gillom...........28		874	163	376	.434	94	121	.777	45	106	151	21	93	0	37	58	15	440	15.7	29
Bridget Pettis 28		842	107	321	.333	97	108	.898	36	71	107	78	57	1	49	82	12	352	12.6	27
Michele Timms...........27		966	99	295	.336	79	104	.760	23	76	99	137	95	0	71	80	3	326	12.1	24
Toni Foster 28		736	94	201	.468	57	81	.704	64	108	172	27	77	1	53	53	21	246	8.8	16
Marlies Askamp 28		517	70	178	.393	71	93	.763	66	80	146	23	59	0	21	46	9	211	7.5	16
Umeki Webb 28		775	47	158	.297	46	67	.687	42	75	117	68	92	2	68	55	8	141	5.0	9
Tara Williams 12		84	16	39	.410	0	0	---	1	7	8	3	9	0	3	4	0	37	3.1	9
Mikiko Hagiwara(*) 12		186	10	39	.256	5	10	.500	5	9	14	10	10	0	2	7	0	33	2.8	7
Mikiko Hagiwara(†) 26		360	25	86	.291	9	16	.563	7	16	23	20	16	0	4	16	2	76	2.9	9
Tia Jackson 26		320	25	73	.342	21	25	.840	24	31	55	26	31	0	23	37	8	74	2.8	11
N. Lieberman-Cline 25		279	25	77	.325	8	10	.800	6	26	32	40	34	0	15	39	1	64	2.6	9
Monique Ambers 19		85	4	9	.444	6	15	.400	10	10	20	4	13	0	0	7	2	14	0.7	4
Ryneldi Becenti 1		8	0	0	---	0	0	---	0	0	0	0	0	0	1	1	0	0	0.0	0
Molly Tuter...................3		3	0	2	.000	0	0	---	0	0	0	0	0	0	0	0	0	0	0.0	0
Phoenix 28		5675	660	1768	.373	484	634	.763	322	599	921	437	570	4	343	475	80	1938	69.2	84
Opponents 28		5675	670	1622	.413	397	589	.674	275	649	924	408	598	11	243	599	114	1826	65.2	86

3-pt. FG: Phoenix 134-436 (.307); Gillom 20-65 (.308); Pettis 41-134 (.306); Timms 49-142 (.345); Foster 1-6 (.167); Askamp 0-1 (.000); Webb 1-15 (.067); Williams 5-11 (.455); Hagiwara(*) 8-28 (.286); Hagiwara(†) 17-61 (.279); Jackson 3-8 (.375); Lieberman-Cline 6-26 (.231); Opponents 89-313 (.284)

SACRAMENTO MONARCHS

Player	G	Min	FGM	FGA	Pct	FTM	FTA	Pct	Off	Def	Tot	Ast	PF	Dq	Stl	TO	Blk	Pts	Avg	Hi
									REBOUNDS									SCORING		
R. Bolton-Holifield 23		813	164	408	.402	53	69	.768	31	103	134	59	71	3	54	58	1	447	19.4	34
Bridgette Gordon 28		981	135	312	.433	84	107	.785	67	68	135	78	58	0	39	83	9	365	13.0	23
Pamela McGee............27		691	102	222	.459	79	112	.705	54	66	120	20	113	5	27	73	14	285	10.6	23
Latasha Byears 28		656	96	209	.459	51	69	.739	87	106	193	48	98	4	39	67	8	244	8.7	23
Chantel Tremitiere 28		1051	69	196	.352	67	90	.744	25	89	114	135	80	2	54	122	1	212	7.6	16
Judy Mosley-McAfee ...12		265	22	48	.458	11	11	1.000	24	23	47	10	30	0	8	25	2	55	4.6	10
Tajama Abraham 28		422	48	126	.381	26	38	.684	32	35	67	13	70	0	12	49	12	122	4.4	13
Mikiko Hagiwara(‡) 14		174	15	47	.319	4	6	.667	2	7	9	10	6	0	2	9	2	43	3.1	9
Yvette Angel 5		90	7	16	.438	0	3	.000	2	7	9	11	6	0	4	8	1	14	2.8	6
Corissa Yasen 19		188	23	57	.404	6	12	.500	12	8	20	6	17	0	18	16	2	52	2.7	10
Laure Savasta 14		157	11	45	.244	7	9	.778	1	5	6	12	14	0	4	21	1	33	2.4	8
Margold Clark 5		46	3	8	.375	1	2	.500	0	6	6	1	10	0	1	2	1	7	1.4	2
Danielle Viglione 7		30	3	11	.273	0	0	---	1	3	4	1	5	0	1	0	0	7	1.0	3
Denique Graves..........22		86	6	27	.222	4	8	.500	3	12	15	0	15	0	0	12	6	16	0.7	4
Sacramento 28		5650	704	1732	.406	393	536	.733	341	538	879	404	593	14	263	562	60	1902	67.9	93
Opponents 28		5650	775	1738	.446	455	628	.725	331	587	918	514	519	4	290	508	114	2112	75.4	93

3-pt. FG: Sacramento 101-345 (.293); Bolton-Holifield 66-192 (.344); Gordon 11-40 (.275); McGee 2-7 (.286); Byears 1-5 (.200); Tremitiere 7-37 (.189); Angel 0-5 (.000); Hagiwara(‡) 9-33 (.273); Yasen 0-1 (.000); Savasta 4-20 (.200); Clark 0-1 (.000); Viglione 1-4 (.250); Opponents 107-315 (.340)

UTAH STARZZ

Player	G	Min	FGM	FGA	Pct	FTM	FTA	Pct	Off	Def	Tot	Ast	PF	Dq	Stl	TO	Blk	Pts	Avg	Hi
									REBOUNDS									SCORING		
Wendy Palmer	28	936	157	420	.374	117	173	.676	76	149	225	48	86	0	47	71	6	443	15.8	28
Elena Baranova	28	913	129	331	.390	43	62	.694	56	151	207	62	82	0	43	82	63	341	12.2	26
Kim Williams	28	608	88	229	.384	41	53	.774	34	47	81	60	83	2	38	57	7	226	8.1	17
Tammi Reiss	28	831	72	231	.312	42	55	.764	29	48	77	87	57	0	23	61	2	216	7.7	17
Dena Head	27	471	53	136	.390	38	45	.844	22	41	63	46	45	0	14	61	8	154	5.7	15
Lady Grooms	28	691	58	167	.347	36	55	.655	33	51	84	67	39	0	23	79	2	153	5.5	14
Deborah Carter	19	286	32	82	.390	10	14	.714	22	31	53	8	34	0	13	17	1	76	4.0	16
Greta Koss	13	268	15	29	.517	12	16	.750	12	25	37	10	15	0	9	18	4	44	3.4	12
Jessie Hicks	26	263	37	80	.463	9	16	.563	17	19	36	10	57	1	13	12	11	83	3.2	13
Karen Booker	26	321	20	60	.333	21	37	.568	34	46	80	24	62	1	24	49	15	61	2.3	8
Raegan Scott	8	43	5	13	.385	2	2	1.000	4	3	7	1	3	0	1	0	3	12	1.5	6
Megan Compain	4	19	0	3	.000	0	0	---	0	1	1	2	4	0	4	3	1	0	0.0	0
Utah	28	5650	666	1781	.374	371	528	.703	339	612	951	425	567	4	252	520	123	1809	64.6	102
Opponents	28	5650	776	1808	.429	436	606	.719	328	680	1008	498	501	6	278	458	119	2103	75.1	95

3-pt. FG: Utah 106-349 (.304); Palmer 12-48 (.250); Baranova 40-106 (.377); Williams 9-34 (.265); Reiss 30-101 (.297); Head 10-32 (.313); Hardmon 1-10 (.100); Carter 2-9 (.222); Koss 2-3 (.667); Hicks 0-1 (.000); Booker 0-3 (.000); Compain 0-2 (.000); Opponents 115-376 (.306)

(*) Statistics with this team only

(†) Totals with all teams

(‡) Continued season with another team

PLAYOFF RESULTS

SEMIFINALS

| August 28 | Houston 70, Charlotte 54 at Houston |
| August 28 | New York 59, Phoenix 41 at Phoenix |

FINAL

| August 30 | Houston 65, New York 51 at Houston |

TEAM STATISTICS

OFFENSIVE

TEAM	G	FG	FGA	PCT	FG3	FG3A	PCT	FT	FTA	PCT	OFF	DEF	REB	AST	PF	DQ	STL	TO	BLK	PTS	AVG
Hou.	2	45	115	.391	10	34	.294	35	49	.714	25	48	73	17	30	0	16	24	4	135	67.5
N.Y.	2	46	110	.418	2	12	.167	16	27	.593	20	57	77	28	42	0	14	34	10	110	55.0
Cha.	1	21	55	.382	3	12	.250	9	12	.750	4	18	22	13	20	0	8	13	4	54	54.0
Phoe.	1	15	67	.224	1	11	.091	10	14	.714	14	18	32	9	17	0	11	13	3	41	41.0

DEFENSIVE

Team	FG	FGA	PCT	FG3	FG3A	PCT	FT	FTA	PCT	OFF	DEF	REB	AST	PF	DQ	STL	TO	BLK	PTS	AVG	DIFF
Hou.	44	115	.383	4	20	.200	13	22	.591	17	41	58	26	43	0	15	28	6	105	52.5	+15.0
N.Y.	37	121	.306	5	25	.200	27	39	.692	23	40	63	15	31	0	19	23	6	106	53.0	+2.0
Phoe.	23	50	.460	1	4	.250	12	17	.706	7	34	41	15	19	0	7	19	8	59	59.0	-18.0
Cha.	23	61	.377	6	20	.300	18	24	.750	16	26	42	11	16	0	8	14	1	70	70.0	-16.0
AVG.'S	32	87	.366	4	17	.232	18	26	.686	16	35	51	17	27	0	12	21	5	85	56.7	---
	127	347		16	69		70	102		63	141	204	67	109	0	49	84	21	340		

135

TEAM COMPARISONS

TEAM	Points Per Game		Field Goal Percentage		Turnovers Per Game		Rebound Percentages			Below 70 Pts.		Overtime Games		3 PTS or Less		10 PTS or More	
	OWN	OPP	OWN	OPP	OWN	OPP	OFF	DEF	TOT	OWN	OPP	W	L	W	L	W	L
Charlotte	65.5	66.0	.422	.453	10.3*	11.0	.336*	.691	.514	2	3	0	0	0	0	1	1
Detroit	54.0	60.0*	.333	.361*	13.0	13.0	.310	.657	.483	1	1	0	0	0	0	0	0
Houston	69.0*	61.2	.394	.390	12.3	14.3	.311	.658	.484	3	5	0	0	0	1	4	1
Los Angeles	65.8	68.3	.407	.415	12.8	14.8	.326	.715*	.521*	2	2	0	0	0	0	2	2
New York	64.2	66.8	.434*	.396	13.5	10.7	.328	.665	.496	5	3	0	0	1	0	1	3
Sacramento	58.0	71.0	.348	.405	21.0	15.0*	.289	.714	.502	1	0	0	0	0	0	0	1
COMPOSITE; 11 games																	
....	65.3	65.3	.407	.407	12.8	12.8	.321	.679		14	0	0	0	1	1	8	8

* - League Leader

REBOUND PERCENTAGES

OFF. - Percentage of a given team's missed shots which that team rebounds.

DEF. - Percentage of opponents' missed shots which a given team rebounds.

TOT. - Average of offensive and defensive rebound percentages.

INDIVIDUAL PLAYOFFS STATISTICS, TEAM BY TEAM

CHARLOTTE STING

Player	G	Min	FGM	FGA	Pct	FTM	FTA	Pct	REBOUNDS Off	Def	Tot	Ast	PF	Dq	Stl	TO	Blk	SCORING Pts	Avg	Hi
Andrea Congreaves 1		32	4	7	.571	2	4	.500	0	3	3	1	3	0	1	1	0	12	12.0	12
Rhonda Mapp 1		36	4	12	.333	4	4	1.000	1	6	7	3	5	0	1	2	0	12	12.0	12
Vicky Bullett.................1		40	5	12	.417	0	0	---	2	7	9	2	3	0	3	3	4	10	10.0	10
Andrea Stinson 1		34	3	11	.273	2	2	1.000	0	0	0	3	4	0	0	3	0	8	8.0	8
Penny Moore 1		17	3	8	.375	1	2	.500	1	1	2	0	3	0	2	1	0	7	7.0	7
Nicole Levesque............1		30	1	2	.500	0	0	---	0	1	1	3	0	0	0	2	0	3	3.0	3
Sharon Manning...........1		4	1	2	.500	0	0	---	0	0	0	0	0	0	1	0	0	2	2.0	2
Tora Suber 1		7	0	1	.000	0	0	---	0	0	0	1	2	0	1	0	0	0	0.0	0
Charlotte 1		200	21	55	.382	9	12	.750	4	18	22	13	20	0	8	13	4	54	54.0	54
Opponents 1		200	23	61	.377	18	24	.750	16	26	42	11	16	0	8	14	1	70	70.0	70

3-pt. FG: Charlotte 3-12 (.250); Congreaves 2-3 (.667); Bullett 0-1 (.000); Stinson 0-2 (.000); Moore 0-4 (.000); Levesque 1-2 (.500); Opponents 6-20 (.300).

HOUSTON COMETS

Player	G	Min	FGM	FGA	Pct	FTM	FTA	Pct	REBOUNDS Off	Def	Tot	Ast	PF	Dq	Stl	TO	Blk	SCORING Pts	Avg	Hi
Cynthia Cooper 2		77	16	30	.533	20	27	.741	1	8	9	9	3	0	3	7	1	56	28.0	31
Tina Thompson 2		74	9	21	.429	6	10	.600	8	10	18	3	5	0	2	6	1	26	13.0	18
Janeth Arcain 2		70	9	27	.333	2	2	1.000	7	8	15	1	4	0	1	1	0	21	10.5	15
Kim Perrot 2		76	5	22	.227	3	4	.750	2	7	9	4	5	0	6	9	0	16	8.0	9
Tammy Jackson 2		60	5	8	.625	4	6	.667	4	11	15	0	7	0	4	0	1	14	7.0	7
Wanda Guyton..............1		23	1	2	.500	0	0	---	2	2	4	0	4	0	0	0	0	2	2.0	2
Yolanda Moore..............1		3	0	0	---	0	0	---	0	0	0	0	1	0	0	0	0	0	0.0	0
Sheryl Swoopes 2		14	0	5	.000	0	0	---	1	2	3	0	1	0	0	0	1	0	0.0	0
Tiffany Woosley 1		3	0	0	---	0	0	---	0	0	0	0	0	0	0	1	0	0	0.0	0
Houston 2		400	45	115	.391	35	49	.714	25	48	73	17	30	0	16	24	4	135	67.5	70
Opponents 2		400	44	115	.383	13	22	.591	17	41	58	26	43	0	15	28	6	105	52.5	54

3-pt. FG: Houston 10-34 (.294); Cooper 4-10 (.400); Thompson 2-5 (.400); Arcain 1-3 (.333); Perrot 3-14 (.214); Swoopes 0-2 (.000); Opponents 4-20 (.200).

NEW YORK LIBERTY

Player	G	Min	FGM	FGA	Pct	FTM	FTA	Pct	REBOUNDS Off	Def	Tot	Ast	PF	Dq	Stl	TO	Blk	SCORING Pts	Avg	Hi
Kym Hampton 2		65	10	19	.526	7	10	.700	5	22	27	1	2	0	1	3	1	27	13.5	14
Rebecca Lobo 2		68	9	21	.429	7	12	.583	5	13	18	4	8	0	0	5	4	25	12.5	16
Vickie Johnson 2		68	11	26	.423	1	2	.500	5	7	12	4	6	0	2	2	1	23	11.5	12
Sophia Witherspoon	2	65	5	18	.278	0	0	---	2	8	10	5	7	0	3	5	2	12	6.0	7
Teresa Weatherspoon 2		75	5	10	.500	0	2	.000	1	2	3	10	6	0	4	12	0	10	5.0	6
Trena Trice 2		16	4	5	.800	1	1	1.000	1	1	2	0	5	0	1	2	1	9	4.5	6

Player	G	Min	FGM	FGA	Pct	FTM	FTA	Pct	Off	Def	Tot	Ast	PF	Dq	Stl	TO	Blk	Pts	Avg	Hi
Sue Wicks	2	11	2	6	.333	0	0	---	0	4	4	1	4	0	1	3	1	4	2.0	2
Rhonda Blades	1	13	0	0	---	0	0	---	0	0	0	2	1	0	0	2	0	0	0.0	0
Kisha Ford	2	19	0	5	.000	0	0	---	1	0	1	1	3	0	2	0	0	0	0.0	0
New York	2	400	46	110	.418	16	27	.593	20	57	77	28	42	0	14	34	10	110	55.0	59
Opponents	2	400	37	121	.306	27	39	.692	23	40	63	15	31	0	19	23	6	106	53.0	65

3-pt. FG: New York 2-12 (.167); Lobo 0-3 (.000); Johnson 0-1 (.000); Witherspoon 2-5 (.400); Weatherspoon 0-2 (.000); Ford 0-1 (.000); Opponents 5-25 (.200)

PHOENIX MERCURY

Player	G	Min	FGM	FGA	Pct	FTM	FTA	Pct	Off	Def	Tot	Ast	PF	Dq	Stl	TO	Blk	Pts	Avg	Hi
Marlies Askamp 1	19	2	6	.333	5	5	1.000	1	1	2	1	3	0	0	0	1	9	9.0	9
Jennifer Gillom 1	31	4	11	.364	0	0	---	2	5	7	1	2	0	2	2	0	9	9.0	9
Toni Foster 1	29	3	9	.333	1	2	.500	2	3	5	1	2	0	3	1	0	7	7.0	7
Michele Timms 1	40	1	11	.091	3	5	.600	1	3	4	1	5	0	4	2	0	5	5.0	5
Umeki Webb 1	33	2	9	.222	1	2	.500	3	3	6	2	4	0	0	1	0	5	5.0	5
Bridget Pettis 1	27	2	15	.133	0	0	---	3	3	6	2	1	0	2	2	0	4	4.0	4
Mikiko Hagiwara 1	11	1	2	.500	0	0	---	0	0	0	0	0	0	0	3	1	2	2.0	2
Tia Jackson 1	8	0	4	.000	0	0	---	2	0	2	1	0	0	0	0	0	0	0.0	0
N. Lieberman-Cline 1	1	0	0	---	0	0	---	0	0	0	0	0	0	0	0	1	0	0.0	0
Tara Williams 1	1	0	0	---	0	0	---	0	0	0	0	0	0	0	0	0	0	0.0	0
Phoenix 1	200	15	67	.224	10	14	.714	14	18	32	9	17	0	11	13	3	41	41.0	41
Opponents 1	200	23	50	.460	12	17	.706	7	34	41	15	19	0	7	19	8	59	59.0	59

3-pt. FG: Phoenix 1-11 (.091)
Gillom 1-3 (.333); Timms 0-2 (.000); Pettis 0-5 (.000); Hagiwara 0-1 (.000); Opponents 1-4 (.250)

INDIVIDUAL FINALS STATISTICS, TEAM BY TEAM

HOUSTON COMETS

Player	G	Min	FGM	FGA	Pct	FTM	FTA	Pct	Off	Def	Tot	Ast	PF	Dq	Stl	TO	Blk	Pts	Avg	Hi
Cynthia Cooper 1	40	7	13	.538	11	15	.733	0	4	4	4	1	0	2	1	1	25	25.0	25
Tina Thompson 1	40	6	10	.600	5	8	.625	3	3	6	1	1	0	0	3	1	18	18.0	18
Kim Perrot 1	38	3	13	.231	0	0	---	2	3	5	0	3	0	3	5	0	9	9.0	9
Tammy Jackson 1	37	3	6	.500	1	2	.500	3	8	11	0	5	0	2	0	1	7	7.0	7
Janeth Arcain 1	37	3	11	.273	0	0	---	1	4	5	1	3	0	1	1	0	6	6.0	6
Yolanda Moore 1	3	0	0	---	0	0	---	0	0	0	0	1	0	0	0	0	0	0.0	0
Sheryl Swoopes 1	5	0	1	.000	0	0	---	0	0	0	0	0	0	0	0	0	0	0.0	0
Houston 1	200	22	54	.407	17	25	.680	9	22	31	6	14	0	8	10	3	65	65.0	65
Opponents 1	200	23	60	.383	4	10	.400	13	23	36	13	23	0	7	15	2	51	51.0	51

3-pt. FG: Houston 4-14 (.286); Cooper 0-2 (.000); Thompson 1-2 (.500); Perrot 3-9 (.333); Arcain 0-1 (.000); Opponents 1-8 (.125)

NEW YORK LIBERTY

Player	G	Min	FGM	FGA	Pct	FTM	FTA	Pct	Off	Def	Tot	Ast	PF	Dq	Stl	TO	Blk	Pts	Avg	Hi
Kym Hampton 1	30	6	13	.462	1	4	.250	3	10	13	0	1	0	1	2	0	13	13.0	13
Vickie Johnson 1	34	6	16	.375	0	0	---	5	0	5	2	5	0	1	1	0	12	12.0	12
Rebecca Lobo 1	34	3	8	.375	3	4	.750	1	8	9	0	3	0	0	1	1	9	9.0	9
Trena Trice 1	11	3	4	.750	0	0	---	1	0	1	0	2	0	0	1	1	6	6.0	6
Sophia Witherspoon 1	29	2	8	.250	0	0	---	1	2	3	3	4	0	0	2	0	5	5.0	5
Teresa Weatherspoon 1	35	2	6	.333	0	2	.000	1	1	2	5	4	0	4	5	0	4	4.0	4
Sue Wicks 1	5	1	3	.333	0	0	---	0	2	2	0	2	0	1	1	0	2	2.0	2
Rhonda Blades 1	13	0	0	---	0	0	---	0	0	0	2	1	0	0	2	0	0	0.0	0
Kisha Ford 1	9	0	2	.000	0	0	---	1	0	1	1	1	0	0	0	0	0	0.0	0
New York 1	200	23	60	.383	4	10	.400	13	23	36	13	23	0	7	15	2	51	51.0	51
Opponents 1	200	22	54	.407	17	25	.680	9	22	31	6	14	0	8	10	3	65	65.0	65

3-pt. FG: New York 1-8 (.125); Johnson 0-1 (.000); Lobo 0-1 (.000); Witherspoon 1-4 (.250); Weatherspoon 0-2 (.000); Opponents 4-14 (.286)

2004 PLAYER ACQUISITION SUMMARIES
JANUARY 6, 2004 – DISPERSAL DRAFT — CLEVELAND

1. Phoenix Mercury ....Penny Taylor
2. Washington Mystics ....Chasity Melvin
3. San Antonio Silver Stars ....LaToya Thomas
4. New York Liberty ....Ann Wauters
5. Indiana Fever ....Deanna Jackson
6. Seattle Storm ....Betty Lennox
7. Minnesota Lynx ....Helen Darling
8. Houston Comets (from Connecticut).....................Pollyanna Johns Kimbrough
9. Charlotte Sting ....Mery Andrade
10. Sacramento Monarchs ....Jennifer Butler
11. Houston Comets...Lucienne Berthieu
12. Los Angeles Sparks...Isabelle Fijalkowski
13. Detroit Shock ....Jennifer Rizzotti

APRIL 17, 2004 - WNBA DRAFT

FIRST ROUND

1. Phoenix Mercury ....Diana Taurasi
2. Washington Mystics ....Alana Beard
3. Charlotte Sting (from Indiana) ....Nicole Powell
4. Connecticut Sun (from San Antonio).....................Lindsay Whalen
5. New York Liberty ....Shameka Christon
6. Minnesota Lynx (from Seattle)...............................Nicole Ohlde
7. Minnesota Lynx ....Vanessa Hayden
8. Phoenix Mercury (from Connecticut) ....Chandi Jones**
9. Indiana Fever (from Charlotte) ....Ebony Hoffman
10. Sacramento Monarchs ....Rebekkah Brunson
11. Detroit Shock (from Houston)...............................Iciss Tillis
12. Los Angeles Sparks...Christi Thomas
13. Detroit Shock ....Shereka Wright**

SECOND ROUND

14. Phoenix Mercury ....Ashley Robinson
15. Washington Mystics ....Kaayla Chones
16. Connecticut Sun (from San Antonio).....................Jessica Brungo
17. New York Liberty ....Amisha Carter
18. Charlotte Sting (from Indiana) ....Kelly Mazzante
19. Seattle Storm ....Catrina Frierson
20. Minnesota Lynx ....Tasha Butts
21. San Antonio Silver Stars (from Connecticut) ....Cindy Dallas
22. Charlotte Sting ....Jenni Benningfield
23. Detroit Shock (from Sacramento) ....Erika Valek**
24. Connecticut Sun (from Houston) ....Ugo Oha
25. Los Angeles Sparks...Doneeka Hodges
26. Houston Comets (from Detroit).............................Lindsay Taylor*

THIRD ROUND

27. Phoenix Mercury ....Maria Villarroel*
28. Washington Mystics ....Evan Unrau

29. Connecticut Sun (from San Antonio)......................Candace Futrell
30. New York Liberty ....Cathy Joens
31. Indiana Fever ....Ieva Kublina
32. Detroit Shock (from Houston from Seattle) ....Jennifer Smith
33. Minnesota Lynx ....Amber Jacobs
34. San Antonio Silver Stars (from Connecticut) ....Toccara Williams
35. Charlotte Sting ....Jia Perkins
36. Sacramento Monarchs ....Nuria Martinez
37. Houston Comets...Stacy Stephens
38. Minnesota Lynx (from Detroit) ....Kate Bulger

*Houston traded the draft rights of Lindsay Taylor to Phoenix in exchange for the draft rights of Maria Villarroel.

**Detroit traded the draft rights of Shereka Wright and Erika Valek and Sheila Lambert to Phoenix in exchange for the draft rights to Chandi Jones.

2003 PLAYER ACQUISITION SUMMARIES
APRIL 24, 2003 - DISPERSAL DRAFT — MIAMI AND PORTLAND

1. Detroit Shock ....Ruth Riley (Miami)
2. Minnesota Lynx ....Sheri Sam (Miami)
3. Cleveland Rockers ....Betty Lennox (Miami)
4. Phoenix Mercury ....Tamicha Jackson (Portland)
5. Sacramento Monarchs ....DeMya Walker (Portland)
6. Connecticut Sun..Debbie Black (Miami)
7. Indiana Fever ....Sylvia Crawley (Portland)
8. Washington Mystics ....Jenny Mowe (Portland)
9. Seattle Storm ....Alisa Burras (Portland)
10. Charlotte Sting ....Pollyana Johns Kimbrough (Miami)
11. New York Liberty ....Elena Baranova (Miami)
12. San Antonio Silver Stars ....LaQuanda Quick (Portland)
13. Houston Comets..Ukari Figgs (Portland)
14. Los Angeles Sparks ....Jackie Stiles (Portland)

APRIL 25, 2003 - WNBA DRAFT

FIRST ROUND
1. Cleveland Rockers ....LaToya Thomas
2. Sacramento Monarchs ....Chantelle Anderson
3. Detroit Shock ....Cheryl Ford
4. Phoenix Mercury ....Plenette Pierson
5. Detroit Shock (from Connecticut) ....Kara Lawson
6. Indiana Fever ....Gwen Jackson
7. Washington Mystics ....Aiysha Smith
8. Seattle Storm ....Jung Sun-min
9. Charlotte Sting ....Jocelyn Penn
10. New York Liberty ....Molly Creamer
11. San Antonio Silver Stars ....Coretta Brown
12. Houston Comets..Allison Curtin

SECOND ROUND
13. Connecticut Sun (from Detroit)..............................Courtney Coleman
14. Minnesota Lynx ....Teresa Edwards
15. Cleveland Rockers ....Jennifer Butler
16. Phoenix Mercury ....Petra Ujhelyi
17. New York Liberty (from Sacramento) ....Erin Thorn
18. Minnesota Lynx (from Miami)................................Jordan Adams

19. Houston Comets (from Connecticut)......................Lori Nero
20. Indiana Fever ....DeTrina White
21. Washington Mystics ....Zuzana Zirkova
22. Seattle Storm ....Suzy Batkovic
23. Charlotte Sting ....Dana Cherry
24. New York Liberty ....Sonja Mallory
25. San Antonio Silver Stars ....Ke-Ke Tardy
26. New York Liberty (from Houston) .........................K.B. Sharp
27. Los Angeles Sparks ....Schuye LaRue

THIRD ROUND
28. Detroit Shock ....Syreeta Bromfield
29. Minnesota Lynx ....Carla Bennett
30. Cleveland Rockers ....Shaquala Williams
31. Phoenix Mercury ....Telisha Quarles
32. Washington Mystics (from Sacramento) ....Trish Juhline
33. Phoenix Mercury (from Miami).............................Marion Jones
34. Connecticut Sun..Lindsey Wilson
35. Indiana Fever ....Ashley McElhiney
36. Washington Mystics ....Tamara Bowie
37. Seattle Storm ....Chrissy Floyd
38. Houston Comets (from Charlotte) ....Constance Jinks
39. New York Liberty ....Nicole Kaczmarski
40. San Antonio Silver Stars ....Brooke Armistead
41. Houston Comets..Oksana Rakhmatulina
42. Los Angeles Sparks ....Mary Jo Noon

2002 PLAYER ACQUISITION SUMMARIES
APRIL 19, 2002 - WNBA DRAFT

FIRST ROUND
1. Seattle Storm ....Sue Bird
2. Detroit Shock ....Swin Cash
3. Washington Mystics ....Stacey Dales-Schuman
4. Washington Mystics ....Asjha Jones
5. Portland Fire..Nikki Teasley*
6. Minnesota Lynx ....Tamika Williams
7. Charlotte Sting ....Sheila Lambert
8. Cleveland Rockers ....Deanna Jackson
9. Charlotte Sting ....Shaunzinski Gortman[+]
10. Houston Comets..Michelle Snow
11. Utah Starzz..Danielle Crockrom
12. Sacramento Monarchs ....Hamchétou Maïga
13. Indiana Fever ....Tawana McDonald
14. Utah Starzz..LaNeishea Caufield
15. Miami Sol..Tamara Moore
16. Los Angeles Sparks ....Rosalind Ross

SECOND ROUND
17. Indiana Fever...Zuzi Klimesova
18. Detroit Shock ....Lenae Williams
19. Seattle Storm ....Lucienne Berthieu
20. Detroit Shock ....Ayana Walker
21. Detroit Shock ....Jill Chapman
22. Detroit Shock ....Kathy Wambe
23. Orlando Miracle...Davalyn Cunningham
24. Cleveland Rockers ....Brandi McCain
25. Phoenix Mercury ....Tootie Shaw

26. New York Liberty ....Linda Fröhlich
27. Utah Starzz..Andrea Gardner
28. Seattle Storm ....Felicia Ragland
29. Miami Sol..Lindsey Yamasaki
30. Los Angeles Sparks ....Gergana Slavtcheva*
31. Cleveland Rockers ....Angie Welle
32. Los Angeles Sparks ....Jackie Higgins

THIRD ROUND
33. Washington Mystics ....LaNisha Cartwell
34. Indiana Fever ....Kelly Komara
35. Seattle Storm ....Takeisha Lewis
36. Washington Mystics ....Teresa Geter
37. Portland Fire...Mandy Nightingale
38. Minnesota Lynx ....Lindsey Meder
39. Orlando Miracle..Saundra Jackson
40. Phoenix Mercury ....Kayte Christensen
41. Charlotte Sting ....Edniesha Curry
42. Houston Comets..Shondra Johnson
43. Utah Starzz..Edmarie Lumbsley
44. Sacramento Monarchs ....Alayne Ingram
45. Miami Sol..Jerica Watson
46. New York Liberty ....Tracy Gahan
47. Detroit Shock ....Ericka Haney
48. Los Angeles Sparks ....Rashana Barnes

FOURTH ROUND
49. Indiana Fever ....LaKeisha Taylor
50. Portland Fire...Melody Johnson
51. Sacramento Monarchs ....Jermisha Dosty
52. Indiana Fever ....Jillian Danker
53. Portland Fire...Monique Cardenas
54. Minnesota Lynx ....Shárron Francis
55. Orlando Miracle..Tomeka Brown
56. Phoenix Mercury ....Amba Kongolo
57. Charlotte Sting ....Jessie Stomski
58. Houston Comets..Cori Enghusen
59. Utah Starzz..Jaclyn Winfield
60. Sacramento Monarchs ....Elizabeth Pickney
61. Miami Sol..Jerkisha Dosty
62. New York Liberty ....Deedee Warley
63. Cleveland Rockers ....Marché Strickland
64. Los Angeles Sparks ....Tiffany Thompson

Note:
* — Portland traded Nikki Teasley and guard Sophia Witherspoon to Los Angeles for guards Gergana Slavtcheva and Ukari Figgs.
† — Shaunzinski Gortman was traded to Minnesota for forward Erin Buescher and center Maylana Martin.

2001 PLAYER ACQUISITION SUMMARIES
APRIL 20, 2001 - WNBA DRAFT

FIRST ROUND
1. Seattle Storm ....Lauren Jackson
2. Charlotte Sting ....Kelly Miller
3. Indiana Fever ....Tamika Catchings
4. Portland Fire...Jackie Stiles

5. Miami Sol ....Ruth Riley
6. Detroit Shock ....Deanna Nolan
7. Minnesota Lynx ....Svetlana Abrosimova
8. Utah Starzz..Marie Ferdinand
9. Washington Mystics ....Coco Miller
10. Orlando Miracle...Katie Douglas
11. Cleveland Rockers ....Penny Taylor
12. Portland Fire..LaQuanda Barksdale
13. Phoenix Mercury ....Kristen Veal
14. Indiana Fever ....Kelly Schumacher
15. Houston Comets..Amanda Lassiter
16. Los Angeles Sparks ....Camille Cooper

SECOND ROUND
17. Seattle Storm ....Semeka Randall
18. Charlotte Sting ....Tammy Sutton-Brown
19. Indiana Fever ....Niele Ivey
20. Portland Fire...Jenny Mowe
21. Miami Sol..Georgia Schweitzer*
22. Detroit Shock ....Jae Kingi
23. Minnesota Lynx ....Erin Buescher
24. Utah Starzz..Michaela Pavlickova
25. Washington Mystics ....Tamara Stocks
26. Orlando Miracle..Brooke Wyckoff
27. Cleveland Rockers ....Jaynetta Saunders
28. Minnesota Lynx ....Janell Burse
29. Phoenix Mercury ....Ilona Korstine
30. Sacramento Monarchs ....Jackie Moore
31. Houston Comets..Tynesha Lewis
32. Los Angeles Sparks ....Nicole Levandusky

THIRD ROUND
33. Houston Comets..ShaRae Mansfield
34. Charlotte Sting ....Jennifer Phillips
35. Indiana Fever ....Marlena Williams
36. Portland Fire...Rasheeda Clark
37. Miami Sol..Levys Torres
38. Detroit Shock ....Svetlana Volnaya
39. Minnesota Lynx ....Tombi Bell
40. Utah Starzz..Shea Ralph
41. Washington Mystics ....Jamie Lewis
42. Orlando Miracle..Jaclyn Johnson
43. Cleveland Rockers ....Angelina Wolvert
44. Washington Mystics ....Elena Karpova
45. Phoenix Mercury ....Tere Williams
46. Sacramento Monarchs ....Maren Walseth
47. Houston Comets..Shala Crawford
48. Los Angeles Sparks ....Kelley Siemon

FOURTH ROUND
49. Seattle Storm ....Juana Brown
50. Charlotte Sting ....Reshea Bristol
51. Indiana Fever ....April Brown
52. Portland Fire...Natasha Pointer
53. Phoenix Mercury ....Carolyn Moos
54. Detroit Shock ....Kelly Santos
55. Minnesota Lynx ....Megan Taylor

56. Utah Starzz..Cara Consuegra
57. New York Libery...Taru Tuukkanen
58. Orlando Miracle...Anne Thorius
59. Cleveland Rockers ....Erin Batth
60. New York Libery...Tara Mitchem
61. Phoenix Mercury ....Megan Franza
62. Sacramento Monarchs ....Katie Smrcka-Duffy
63. Houston Comets...Kristen Clement
64. Los Angeles Sparks ....Beth Record

Note:
* — Traded to Minnesota for Marla Brumfield.

2000 PLAYER ACQUISITION SUMMARIES
DECEMBER 15, 1999 - EXPANSION DRAFT

FIRST ROUND
1. Indiana Fever ....Gordana Grubin ....(Los Angeles)
2. Seattle Storm ....Edna Campbell ....(Phoenix)
3. Miami Sol...Kate Starbird ....(Sacramento)*
4. Portland Fire......................................Alisa Burras ....(Cleveland)

SECOND ROUND
5. Portland Fire......................................Sophia Witherspoon ....(New York)†
6. Miami Sol...Stephanie McCarty ....(Charlotte)‡
7. Seattle Storm ....Sonja Henning..................................(Houston)
8. Indiana Fever ....Sandy Brondello ....(Detroit)‡

THIRD ROUND
9. Indiana Fever ....Nyree Roberts ....(Washington)∞
10. Seattle Storm ....Angela Aycock...................................(Minnesota)
11. Miami Sol..Debbie Black....................................(Utah)
12. Portland Fire.....................................Tari Phillips ....(Orlando)

FOURTH ROUND
13. Portland Fire ....Coquese Washington ....(New York)†
14. Miami Sol..Sharon Manning ....(Charlotte)
15. Seattle Storm ....Nina Bjedov ....(Los Angeles)
16. Indiana Fever ....Kara Wolters ....(Houston)

FIFTH ROUND
17. Indiana Fever ....Rita Williams ....(Washington)
18. Seattle Storm ....Toni Foster ....(Phoenix)
19. Miami Sol..Lesley Brown ....(Detroit)
20. Portland Fire.....................................Molly Goodenbour ....(Sacramento)

SIXTH ROUND
21. Portland Fire.....................................Jamila Wideman ....(Cleveland)
22. Miami Sol..Yolanda Moore ....(Orlando)
23. Seattle Storm ....Charmin Smith..................................(Minnesota)
24. Indiana Fever ....Chantel Tremitiere ....(Utah)

Notes:
* — Kate Starbird was traded with Miami's first-round draft pick (eighth overall) in the 2000 WNBA Draft to the Utah Starzz in exchange for center Elena Baranova and Utah's second round pick (19th overall) in the 2000 WNBA Draft.

† — In exchange for selecting Sophia Witherspoon and Coquese Washington, Portland acquired Michele VanGorp from New York.

‡ — Stephanie McCarty was traded by Miami to Indiana for Sandy Brondello and Indiana's first-round pick (10th overall) in the 2000 WNBA Draft.

∞ — In exchange for selecting Nyree Roberts, Indiana acquired Monica Maxwell and a fourth-round pick in the 2000 WNBA Draft from Washington.

APRIL 25, 2000 - WNBA DRAFT

FIRST ROUND
1. Cleveland Rockers ....Ann Wauters
2. Washington Mystics ....Tausha Mills
3. Detriot Shock (from Utah) ....Edwina Brown
4. Orlando Miracle..Cintia Dos Santos
5. Minnesota Lynx (from Phoenix) ....Grace Daley
6. Minnesota Lynx ....Betty Lennox
7. Portland Fire..Lynn Pride
8. Detroit Shock (from Utah/Miami) ....Tamicha Jackson
9. Seattle Storm ....Kamila Vodichkova
10. Minnesota Lynx (from Miami/Indiana) ....Maylana Martin
11. Charlotte Sting ....Summer Erb
12. Utah Starzz (from Detroit)......................................Naomi Mulitauaopele
13. New York Liberty ....Olga Firsova
14. Sacramento Monarchs ....Katy Steding
15. Los Angeles Sparks...Nicole Kubik
16. Houston Comets..Elen Chakirova

SECOND ROUND
17. Cleveland Rockers ....Helen Darling
18. Washington Mystics ....Tonya Washington
19. Miami Sol (from Utah) ....Jameka Jones
20. Orlando Miracle..Jannon Roland
21. Phoenix Mercury ....Adrain Williams
22. Minnesota Lynx ....Marla Brumfield
23. Portland Fire..Stacey Thomas
24. Minnesota Lynx (from Miami)................................Keitha Dickerson
25. Seattle Storm ....Charisse Sampson
26. Indiana Fever ....Jurgita Streimikyte
27. Charlotte Sting ....Tiffany Travis
28. Detroit Shock ....Madinah Slaise
29. New York Liberty ....Desiree Francis
30. Sacramento Monarchs ....Stacy Clinesmith
31. Los Angeles Sparks...Paige Sauer
32. Houston Comets..Andrea Garner

THIRD ROUND
33. Cleveland Rockers ....Monique Morehouse
34. Charlotte Sting (from Washington) ....Jill Morton
35. Utah Starzz...Stacy Frese
36. Orlando Miracle..Shawnetta Stewart
37. Phoenix Mercury ....Tauja Catchings
38. Minnesota Lynx ....Phylesha Whaley
39. Portland Fire..Maxann Reese
40. Miami Sol...Milena Flores
41. Seattle Storm ....Kirra Jordan
42. Indiana Fever ....Usha Gilmore

43.	Charlotte Sting	Peppi Browne
44.	Detroit Shock	Chavonne Hammond
45.	New York Liberty	Jessica Bibby
46.	Sacramento Monarchs	Rhonda Banchero
47.	Los Angeles Sparks	Marte Alexander
48.	Houston Comets	Latavia Coleman*

FOURTH ROUND

49.	Cleveland Rockers	Sophie Von Saldern
50.	Indiana Fever (from Washington)	Latina Davis*
51.	Utah Starzz	Kristi Rasmussen
52.	Orlando Miracle	Romana Hamzova
53.	Phoenix Mercury	Shantia Owens †
54.	Minnesota Lynx	Jana Lichnerova
55.	Portland Fire	Rhonda LaCher Smith
56.	Minnesota Lynx (from Miami)	Shanele Stires
57.	Seattle Storm	Katrina Hibbert
58.	Indiana Fever	Renee Robinson*
59.	Charlotte Sting	Shaka Massey
60.	Detroit Shock	Cal Bouchard
61.	New York Liberty	Natalie Porter
62.	Sacramento Monarchs	Jessica Zinobile
63.	Los Angeles Sparks	Nicky McCrimmon
64.	Houston Comets	Abbie Willenborg

Notes:

* — Houston traded Latavia Coleman to Indiana in exchange for Latina Davis and Renee Robinson.

† — Phoenix traded Shantia Owens to Miami in exchange for a fourth-round pick in the 2001 WNBA Draft.

1999 PLAYER ACQUISITION SUMMARIES
SEPTEMBER 15, 1998 - PLAYER ALLOCATIONS

| Minnesota Lynx | Kristin Folkl |
| Orlando Miracle | Nykesha Sales |

APRIL 6, 1999 - EXPANSION DRAFT

Minnesota	Orlando
1. Brandy Reed (Phoenix)	2. Andrea Congreaves (Charlotte)
3. Kim Williams (Utah)	4. Kisha Ford (New York)
5. Octavia Blue (Los Angeles)	6. Yolanda Moore (Houston)
7. Adia Barnes (Sacramento)	8. Adrienne Johnson (Cleveland)

MAY 3, 1999 - PLAYER ALLOCATIONS

| Minnesota Lynx | Katie Smith |
| Orlando Miracle | Shannon Johnson |

MAY 4, 1999 - WNBA DRAFT

FIRST ROUND

1.	Washington Mystics	Chamique Holdsclaw
2.	Sacramento Monarchs	Yolanda Griffith
3.	Utah Starzz	Natalie Williams
4.	Los Angeles Sparks	DeLisha Milton
5.	Detroit Shock	Jennifer Azzi
6.	New York Liberty	Crystal Robinson

7. Minnesota Lynx ....Tonya Edwards
8. Orlando Miracle...Tari Phillips
9. Charlotte Sting ....Dawn Staley
10. Phoenix Mercury ....Edna Campbell
11. Cleveland Rockers ....Chasity Melvin
12. Houston Comets...Natalia Zasulskaya

SECOND ROUND
13. Washington Mystics ....Shalonda Enis
14. Sacramento Monarchs ....Kedra Holland-Corn
15. Utah Starzz...Debbie Black
16. Los Angeles Sparks ....Clarisse Machanguana
17. Detroit Shock ....Val Whiting
18. New York Liberty ....Michele VanGorp
19. Minnesota Lynx ....Trisha Fallon
20. Orlando Miracle...Sheri Sam
21. Charlotte Sting ....Stephanie McCarty
22. Phoenix Mercury ....Clarissa Davis-Wrightsil
23. Cleveland Rockers ....Mery Andrade
24. Houston Comets...Sonja Henning

THIRD ROUND
25. Washington Mystics ....Andrea Nagy
26. Sacramento Monarchs ....Kate Starbird
27. Utah Starzz...Adrienne Goodson
28. Los Angeles Sparks ....Ukari Figgs
29. Detroit Shock ....Dominique Canty
30. New York Liberty ....Tamika Whitmore
31. Minnesota Lynx ....Andrea Lloyd-Curry
32. Orlando Miracle...Taj McWilliams
33. Charlotte Sting ....Charlotte Smith
34. Phoenix Mercury ....Lisa Harrison
35. Cleveland Rockers ....Tracy Henderson
36. Houston Comets...Kara Wolters

FOURTH ROUND
37. Washington Mystics ....Jennifer Whittle
38. Sacramento Monarchs ....Amy Herrig
39. Utah Starzz...Dalma Ivanyi
40. Los Angeles Sparks ....La'Keshia Frett
41. Detroit Shock ....Astou Ndiaye
42. New York Liberty ....Carolyn Jones-Young
43. Minnesota Lynx ....Sonja Tate
44. Orlando Miracle...Carla McGhee
45. Charlotte Sting ....Angie Braziel
46. Phoenix Mercury ....Amanda Wilson
47. Cleveland Rockers ....Kellie Jolly Harper
48. Houston Comets...Jennifer Rizzotti
49. Minnesota Lynx ....Angie Potthoff
50. Orlando Miracle...Elaine Powel

1998 PLAYER ACQUISITION SUMMARIES
JANUARY 27, 1998 - PLAYER ALLOCATIONS

Detroit Shock — Cindy Brown, Razija Mujanivic
Washington Mystics — Nikki McCray, Alessandra Santos de Oliveira

Detroit
1. Rhonda Blades (New York)
3. Tajama Abraham (Sacramento)
5. Tara Williams (Phoenix)
7. Lynette Woodard (Cleveland)

Washington
2. Heidi Burge (Los Angeles)
4. Penny Moore (Charlotte)
6. Deborah Carter (Utah)
8. Tammy Jackson (Houston)

APRIL 29, 1998 - WNBA DRAFT

FIRST ROUND
1. Utah Starzz...Margo Dydek
2. Sacramento Monarchs ....Ticha Penicheiro
3. Washington Mystics ....Murriel Page
4. Detroit Shock ....Korie Hlede
5. Los Angeles Sparks ....Allison Feaster
6. Cleveland Rockers ....Cindy Blodgett
7. Charlotte Sting ....Tracy Reid
8. Phoenix Mercury ....Maria Stepanova
9. New York Liberty ....Alicia Thompson
10. Houston Comets...................................Polina Tzekova

SECOND ROUND
11. Utah Starzz...Olympia Scott
12. Sacramento Monarchs ....Tangela Smith
13. Washington Mystics ....Rita Williams
14. Detroit Shock ....Rachael Sporn
15. Los Angeles Sparks ....Octavia Blue
16. Cleveland Rockers ....Suzie McConnell Serio
17. Charlotte Sting ....Christy Smith
18. Phoenix Mercury ....Andrea Kuklova
19. New York Liberty ....Nadine Domond
20. Houston Comets...................................Nyree Roberts

THIRD ROUND
21. Utah Starzz...LaTonya Johnson
22. Sacramento Monarchs ....Quacy Barnes
23. Washington Mystics ....Angela Hamblin
24. Detroit Shock ....Gergana Branzova
25. Los Angeles Sparks ....Rehema Stephens
26. Cleveland Rockers ....Tanja Kostic
27. Charlotte Sting ....Pollyanna Johns
28. Phoenix Mercury ....Brandy Reed
29. New York Liberty ....Albena Branzova
30. Houston Comets...................................Amaya Valdemoro

FOURTH ROUND
31. Utah Starzz...Tricia Bader
32. Sacramento Monarchs ....Adia Barnes
33. Washington Mystics ....Angela Jackson
34. Detroit Shock ....Sandy Brondello
35. Los Angeles Sparks ....Erica Kienast
36. Cleveland Rockers ....Tammye Jenkins
37. Charlotte Sting ....Sonia Chase
38. Phoenix Mercury ....Karen Wilkins
39. New York Liberty ....Vanessa Nygaard
40. Houston Comets...................................Monica Lamb

REVIEW Player Acquisitions

1997 PLAYER ACQUISITION SUMMARIES
JANUARY 22, 1997 - INITIAL PLAYER ALLOCATIONS

EASTERN CONFERENCE

Charlotte Sting	Vicky Bullett, Andrea Stinson
Cleveland Rockers	Janice Braxton, Michelle Edwards
Houston Comets	Cynthia Cooper, Sheryl Swoopes
New York Liberty	Rebecca Lobo, Teresa Weatherspoon

WESTERN CONFERENCE

Los Angeles Sparks	Lisa Leslie, Penny Toler
Phoenix Mercury	Jennifer Gillom, Michelle Timms
Sacramento Monarchs	Ruthie Bolton-Holifield, Bridgette Gordon
Utah Starzz	Elena Baranova, Lady Harmon

FEBRUARY 27, 1997 - WNBA ELITE DRAFT

FIRST ROUND
1. Utah Starzz...Dena Head
2. Cleveland Rockers ....Isabelle Fijalkowski
3. Charlotte Sting ....Rhonda Mapp
4. New York Liberty ....Kym Hampton
5. Houston Comets...Wanda Guyton
6. Sacramento Monarchs ....Judy Mosley-McAfee
7. Phoenix Mercury ....Bridget Pettis
8. Los Angeles Sparks ....Daedra Charles

SECOND ROUND
9. Utah Starzz...Wendy Palmer
10. Cleveland Rockers ....Lynette Woodard
11. Charlotte Sting ....Michi Atkins
12. New York Liberty ....Vickie Johnson
13. Houston Comets...Janeth Arcain
14. Sacramento Monarchs ....Mikiko Hagiwara
15. Phoenix Mercury ....Nancy Lieberman-Cline
16. Los Angeles Sparks ....Haixia Zheng

APRIL 28, 1997 - WNBA DRAFT

FIRST ROUND
1. Houston Comets...Tina Thompson
2. Sacramento Monarchs ....Pamela McGee
3. Los Angeles Sparks ....Jamila Wideman
4. Cleveland Rockers ....Eva Nemcova
5. Utah Starzz...Tammi Reiss
6. New York Liberty ....Sue Wicks
7. Charlotte Sting ....Tora Suber
8. Phoenix Mercury ....Toni Foster

SECOND ROUND
9. Phoenix Mercury ....Tia Jackson
10. Charlotte Sting ....Sharon Manning
11. New York Liberty ....Sophia Witherspoon
12. Utah Starzz...Jessie Hicks
13. Cleveland Rockers ....Merlakia Jones
14. Los Angeles Sparks ....Tamecka Dixon
15. Sacramento Monarchs ....Denique Graves
16. Houston Comets...Tammy Jackson

THIRD ROUND
17. Houston Comets ....Racquel Spurlock
18. Sacramento Monarchs ....Chantel Tremitiere
19. Los Angeles Sparks ....Katrina Colleton
20. Cleveland Rockers ....Tina Nicholson
21. Utah Starzz...Raegan Scott
22. New York Liberty ....Trena Trice
23. Charlotte Sting ....Debra Williams
24. Phoenix Mercury ....Umeki Webb

FOURTH ROUND
25. Phoenix Mercury ....Monique Ambers
26. Charlotte Sting ....Andrea Congreaves
27. New York Liberty ....Kisha Ford
28. Utah Starzz...Kim Williams
29. Cleveland Rockers ....Anita Maxwell
30. Los Angeles Sparks ....Travesa Gant
31. Sacramento Monarchs ....Tajama Abraham
32. Houston Comets ....Catarina Pollini

MAY 22, 1997 - FINAL ROSTER ALLOCATIONS

EASTERN CONFERENCE
Charlotte Sting ....Katasha Artis, Milica Vukadinovic
Cleveland Rockers ....Jenny Boucek, Donna Harrington
Houston Comets..Pietra Gay, Patty Jo Hedges-Ward,
Nekeshia Henderson
New York Liberty ....Rhonda Blades, Jasmina Perazic-Gipe

WESTERN CONFERENCE
Los Angeles Sparks ....Linda Burgess, Mwadi Mabika
Phoenix Mercury ....Marlies Askamp, Tara Williams
Sacramento Monarchs ....Eliza Sokolowska, Corissa Yasen
Utah Starzz..Deborah Carter, Megan Compain

2003 WNBA Player of the Year presented by Chevy

2003 Voting Results

406	Lauren Jackson, Seattle Storm
242	Tamika Catchings, Indiana Fever
218	Lisa Leslie, Los Angeles Sparks
173	Katie Smith, Minnesota Lynx
160	Swin Cash, Detroit Shock
83	Sheryl Swoopes, Houston Comets
71	Chamique Holdsclaw, Washington Mystics
28	Tina Thompson, Houston Comets
10	Yolanda Griffith, Sacramento Monarchs
6	Cheryl Ford, Detroit Shock
3	Ticha Penicheiro, Sacramento Monarchs
1	Vickie Johnson, New York Liberty
1	Dawn Staley, Charlotte Sting
1	Shannon Johnson, Connecticut Sun
1	Tamecka Dixon, Los Angeles Sparks

Past Winners

1997	Cynthia Cooper, Houston Comets
1998	Cynthia Cooper, Houston Comets
1999	Yolanda Griffith, Sacramento Monarchs
2000	Sheryl Swoopes, Houston Comets
2001	Lisa Leslie, Los Angeles Sparks
2002	Sheryl Swoopes, Houston Comets

WNBA Coach of the Year

2003 Voting Results

45	Bill Laimbeer, Detroit Shock
4	Suzie McConnell-Serio, Minnesota Lynx
2	Van Chancellor, Houston Comets
2	John Whisenant, Sacramento Monarchs
1	Michael Cooper, Los Angeles Sparks

Past Winners

1997	Van Chancellor, Houston Comets
1998	Van Chancellor, Houston Comets
1999	Van Chancellor, Houston Comets
2000	Michael Cooper, Los Angeles Sparks
2001	Dan Hughes, Cleveland Rockers
2002	Marianne Stanley, Washington Mystics

WNBA Rookie of the Year

2003 Voting Results

49	Cheryl Ford, Detroit Shock
2	LaToya Thomas, Cleveland Rockers
2	Gwen Jackson, San Antonio Silver Stars
1	Kara Lawson, Sacramento Monarchs

Past Winners

1998	Tracy Reid, Charlotte Sting
1999	Chamique Holdsclaw, Wash. Mystics
2000	Betty Lennox, Minnesota Lynx
2001	Jackie Stiles, Portland Fire
2002	Tamika Catchings, Indiana Fever

WNBA Defensive Player of the Year

2003 Voting Results

35	Sheryl Swoopes, Houston Comets
4	Tamika Catchings, Indiana Fever
3	Lisa Leslie, Los Angeles Sparks
2	Margo Dydek, San Antonio Silver Stars
2	Katie Smith, Minnesota Lynx
2	Yolanda Griffith, Sacramento Monarchs
1	Chamique Holdsclaw, Washington Mystics
1	Lauren Jackson, Seattle Storm
1	Allison Feaster, Charlotte Sting
1	Deanna Nolan, Detroit Shock
1	Teresa Edwards, Minnesota Lynx
1	DeMya Walker, Sacramento Monarchs

Past Winners

1997	Teresa Weatherspoon, NY Liberty
1998	Teresa Weatherspoon, NY Liberty
1999	Yolanda Griffith, Sacramento Monarchs
2000	Sheryl Swoopes, Houston Comets
2001	Debbie Black, Miami Sol
2002	Sheryl Swoopes, Houston Comets

REVIEW Award Winners

WNBA Newcomer of the Year

1998   Suzie McConnell Serio, Cleveland Rockers
1999   Yolanda Griffith, Sacramento Monarchs

WNBA Most Improved Player

2003 Voting Results

22	Michelle Snow, Houston Comets	2000	Tari Phillips, New York Liberty
12	Deanna Nolan, Detroit Shock	2001	Janeth Arcain, Houston Comets
10	Anna DeForge, Phoenix Mercury	2002	Coco Miller, Washington Mystics
5	Nikki Teasley, Los Angeles Sparks		
1	Becky Hammon, New York Liberty		
1	Ruth Riley, Detroit Shock		
1	Swin Cash, Detroit Shock		
1	Tamecka Dixon, Los Angeles Sparks		

Kim Perrot Sportsmanship Award presented by Secret

2003   Edna Campbell, Sacramento Monarchs
2002   Jennifer Gillom, Phoenix Mercury
2001   Sue Wicks, New York Liberty
2000   Suzie McConnell Serio, Cleveland Rockers
1999   Dawn Staley, Charlotte Sting
1998   Suzie McConnell Serio, Cleveland Rockers
1997   Haixia Zheng, Los Angeles Sparks

American Express Small Business Service WNBA Entrepreneurial Award Winners

1999 - Dawn Staley, Charlotte Sting
        Michele Petrillo, Ridgefield, N.J.
2000 - Monica Lamb, Houston Comets
        Amy Cameron, Orlando, Fla.

WNBA Finals Most Valuable Player

1997 - Cynthia Cooper, Houston Comets
1998 - Cynthia Cooper, Houston Comets
1999 - Cynthia Cooper, Houston Comets
2000 - Cynthia Cooper, Houston Comets
2001 - Lisa Leslie, Los Angeles Sparks
2002 - Lisa Leslie, Los Angeles Sparks
2003 - Ruth Riley, Detroit Shock

WNBA All-Star Game Most Valuable Player

1999 - Lisa Leslie, Los Angeles Sparks
2000 - Tina Thompson, Houston Comets
2001 - Lisa Leslie, Los Angeles Sparks
2002 - Lisa Leslie, Los Angeles Sparks
2003 - Nikki Teasley, Los Angeles Sparks

ALL-WNBA TEAMS PRESENTED BY BUD LIGHT

1997

	FIRST		SECOND
Center	Lisa Leslie, Los Angeles Sparks	Center	Jennifer Gillom, Phoenix Mercury
Forward	Tina Thompson, Houston Comets	Forward	Wendy Palmer, Utah Starzz
Forward	Eva Nemcova, Cleveland Rockers	Forward	Rebecca Lobo, New York Liberty
Guard	Cynthia Cooper, Houston Comets	Guard	Teresa Weatherspoon, New York Liberty
Guard	Ruthie Bolton, Sacramento Monarchs	Guard	Andrea Stinson, Charlotte Sting

1998

	FIRST		SECOND
Center	Jennifer Gillom, Phoenix Mercury	Center	Lisa Leslie, Los Angeles Sparks
Forward	Tina Thompson, Houston Comets	Forward	Cindy Brown, Detroit Shock
Forward	Sheryl Swoopes, Houston Comets	Forward	Eva Nemcova, Cleveland Rockers
Guard	Cynthia Cooper, Houston Comets	Guard	Andrea Stinson, Charlotte Sting
Guard	Suzie McConnell Serio, Cle. Rockers	Guard	Teresa Weatherspoon, New York Liberty

1999

	FIRST		SECOND
Center	Yolanda Griffith, Sacramento Monarchs	Center	Lisa Leslie, Los Angeles Sparks
Forward	Natalie Williams, Utah Starzz	Forward	Chamique Holdsclaw, Wash. Mystics
Forward	Sheryl Swoopes, Houston Comets	Forward	Tina Thompson, Houston Comets
Guard	Ticha Penicheiro, Sacramento Monarchs	Guard	Teresa Weatherspoon, New York Liberty
Guard	Cynthia Cooper, Houston Comets	Guard	Shannon Johnson, Orlando Miracle

2000

	FIRST		SECOND
Center	Lisa Leslie, Los Angeles Sparks	Center	Yolanda Griffith, Sacramento Monarchs
Forward	Sheryl Swoopes, Houston Comets	Forward	Tina Thompson, Houston Comets
Forward	Natalie Williams, Utah Starzz	Forward	Katie Smith, Minnesota Lynx
Guard	Cynthia Cooper, Houston Comets	Guard	Teresa Weatherspoon, New York Liberty
Guard	Ticha Penicheiro, Sacramento Monarchs	Guard	Betty Lennox, Minnesota Lynx
			Shannon Johnson, Orlando Miracle

2001

	FIRST		SECOND
Center	Lisa Leslie, Los Angeles Sparks	Center	Yolanda Griffith, Sacramento Monarchs
Forward	Katie Smith, Minnesota Lynx	Forward	Tina Thompson, Houston Comets
Forward	Natalie Williams, Utah Starzz	Forward	Chamique Holdsclaw, Wash. Mystics
Guard	Janeth Arcain, Houston Comets	Guard	Ticha Penicheiro, Sacramento Monarchs
Guard	Merlakia Jones, Cleveland Rockers	Guard	Tamecka Dixon, Los Angeles Sparks

2002

	FIRST		SECOND
Center	Lisa Leslie, Los Angeles Sparks	Center	Tari Phillips, New York Liberty
Forward	Sheryl Swoopes, Houston Comets	Forward	Chamique Holdscaw, Wash.Mystics
Forward	Tamika Catchings, Indiana Fever	Forward	Tina Thompson, Houston Comets
Guard	Sue Bird, Seattle Storm	Guard	Shannon Johnson, Orlando Miracle
Guard	Mwadi Mabika, Los Angeles Sparks	Guard	Katie Smith, Minnesota Lynx

2003

	FIRST		SECOND
Center	Lisa Leslie, Los Angeles Sparks	Center	Cheryl Ford, Detroit Shock
Forward	Lauren Jackson, Seattle Storm	Forward	Sheryl Swoopes, Houston Comets
Forward	Tamika Catchings, Indiana Fever	Forward	Swin Cash, Detroit Shock
Guard	Katie Smith, Minnesota Lynx	Guard	Nikki Teasley, Los Angeles Sparks
Guard	Sue Bird, Seattle Storm	Guard	Deanna Nolan, Detroit Shock

REVIEW Award Winners

CHARLOTTE STING

Season	Coach	Finish	Regular Season W	L	Playoffs W	L
1997	Marynell Meadors	T3rd/East	15	13	0	1
1998	Marynell Meadors	T2nd/East	18	12	0	2
1999	Marynell Meadors (5-7)					
	Dan Hughes (10-10)	T2nd/East	15	17	2	2
2000	T.R. Dunn	8th/East	8	24	—	—
2001	Anne Donovan	4th/East	18	14	4	4
2002	Anne Donovan	T1st/East	18	14	0	2
2003	Trudi Lacey	T2nd/East	18	16	0	2
		Totals	110	110	6	13

CLEVELAND ROCKERS

Season	Coach	Finish	Regular Season W	L	Playoffs W	L
1997	Linda Hill-MacDonald	T3rd/East	15	13	—	—
1998	Linda Hill-MacDonald	1st/East	20	10	1	2
1999	Linda Hill-MacDonald	6th/East	7	25	—	—
2000	Dan Hughes	2nd/East	17	15	3	3
2001	Dan Hughes	1st/East	22	10	1	2
2002	Dan Hughes	7th/East	10	22	—	—
2003	Dan Hughes	4th/East	17	17	1	2
		Totals	108	112	6	9

CONNECTICUT SUN (formerly Orlando Miracle—1999-02)

Season	Coach	Finish	Regular Season W	L	Playoffs W	L
1999	Carolyn Peck	T2nd/East	15	17	—	—
2000	Carolyn Peck	3rd/East	16	16	1	2
2001	Carolyn Peck	5th/East	13	19	—	—
2002	Dee Brown	T4th/East	16	16	—	—
2003	Mike Thibault	T2nd/East	18	16	2	2
		Totals	78	84	3	4

DETROIT SHOCK

Season	Coach	Finish	Regular Season W	L	Playoffs W	L
1998	Nancy Lieberman	4th/East	17	13	—	—
1999	Nancy Lieberman	T2nd/East	15	17	0	1
2000	Nancy Lieberman	T4th/East	14	18	—	—
2001	Greg Williams	T6th/East	10	22	—	—
2002	Greg Williams (0-10)					
	Bill Laimbeer (9-13)	8th/East	9	23	—	—
2003	Bill Laimbeer	1st/East	25	9	6	2
		Totals	90	102	6	3

HOUSTON COMETS

Season	Coach	Finish	Regular Season W	L	Playoffs W	L
1997	Van Chancellor	1st/East	18	10	2	0
1998	Van Chancellor	1st/West	27	3	4	1
1999	Van Chancellor	1st/West	26	6	4	2
2000	Van Chancellor	2nd/West	27	5	6	0
2001	Van Chancellor	T3rd/West	19	13	0	2
2002	Van Chancellor	2nd/West	24	8	1	2
2003	Van Chancellor	2nd/West	20	14	1	2
		Totals	161	59	18	9

INDIANA FEVER

Season	Coach	Finish	Regular Season W	L	Playoffs W	L
2000	Anne Donovan	7th/East	9	23	—	—
2001	Nell Fortner	T6th/West	10	22	—	—
2002	Nell Fortner	T4th/East	16	16	1	2
2003	Nell Fortner	T5th/East	16	18	-	-
		Totals	51	79	1	2

LOS ANGELES SPARKS

Season	Coach	Finish	Regular Season W	L	Playoffs W	L
1997	Linda Sharp (4-7)					
	Julie Rousseau (10-7)	2nd/West	14	14	—	—
1998	Julie Rousseau (7-13)					
	Orlando Woolridge (5-5)	3rd/West	12	18	—	—
1999	Orlando Woolridge	2nd/West	20	12	2	2
2000	Michael Cooper	1st/West	28	4	2	2
2001	Michael Cooper	1st/West	28	4	6	1
2002	Michael Cooper	1st/West	25	7	6	0
2003	Michael Cooper	1st/West	24	10	5	4
	Totals		151	69	21	9

MIAMI SOL

Season	Coach	Finish	Regular Season W	L	Playoffs W	L
2000	Ron Rothstein	6th/East	13	19	—	—
2001	Ron Rothstein	3rd/East	20	12	1	2
2002	Ron Rothstein	6th/East	15	17	—	—
	Totals		48	48	1	2

MINNESOTA LYNX

Season	Coach	Finish	Regular Season W	L	Playoffs W	L
1999	Brian Agler	T4th/West	15	17	—	—
2000	Brian Agler	6th/West	15	17	—	—
2001	Brian Agler	6th/West	12	20	—	—
2002	Brian Agler (6-13)					
	Heidi VanDerveer (4-9)	8th/West	10	22	—	—
2003	Suzie McConnell Serio	T4th/West	18	16	1	2
	Totals		70	92	1	2

NEW YORK LIBERTY

Season	Coach	Finish	Regular Season W	L	Playoffs W	L
1997	Nancy Darsch	2nd/East	17	11	1	1
1998	Nancy Darsch	T2nd/East	18	12	—	—
1999	Richie Adubato	1st/East	18	14	3	3
2000	Richie Adubato	1st/East	20	12	4	3
2001	Richie Adubato	2nd/East	21	11	3	3
2002	Richie Adubato	T1st/East	18	14	4	4
2003	Richie Adubato	T5th/East	16	18	-	-
	Totals		128	92	15	14

PHOENIX MERCURY

Season	Coach	Finish	Regular Season W	L	Playoffs W	L
1997	Cheryl Miller	1st/West	16	12	0	1
1998	Cheryl Miller	2nd/West	19	11	3	3
1999	Cheryl Miller	T4th/West	15	17	—	—
2000	Cheryl Miller	4th/West	20	12	0	2
2001	Cynthia Cooper	5th/West	13	19	—	—
2002	Cynthia Cooper (6-4)					
	Linda Sharp (5-17)	7th/West	11	21	—	—
2003	John Shumate	7th/West	8	26	-	-
	Totals		102	118	3	6

PORTLAND FIRE

Season	Coach	Finish	Regular Season W	L	Playoffs W	L
2000	Linda Hargrove	7th/West	10	22	—	—
2001	Linda Hargrove	7th/West	11	21	—	—
2002	Linda Hargrove	5th/West	16	16	—	—
	Totals		37	59	—	—

SACRAMENTO MONARCHS

Season	Coach	Finish	Regular Season W	L	Playoffs W	L
1997	Mary Murphy (5-10)					
	Heidi VanDerveer (5-8)	3rd/West	10	18	—	—
1998	Heidi VanDerveer	T4th/West	8	22	—	—
1999	Sonny Allen	3rd/West	19	13	0	1
2000	Sonny Allen	3rd/West	21	11	0	2
2001	Sonny Allen (6-6)					
	Maura McHugh (14-6)	2nd/West	20	12	3	2
2002	Maura McHugh	6th/West	14	18	—	—
2003	Maura McHugh (7-11)					
	John Whisenant (12-4)	3rd/West	19	15	3	3
		Totals	111	109	6	8

SAN ANTONIO SILVER STARS (formerly Utah Starzz—1997-02)

Season	Coach	Finish	Regular Season W	L	Playoffs W	L
1997	Denise Taylor	4th/West	7	21	—	—
1998	Denise Taylor (6-13)					
	Frank Layden (2-9)	T4th/West	8	22	—	—
1999	Frank Layden (2-2)					
	Fred Williams (13-15)	T4th/West	15	17	—	—
2000	Fred Williams	5th/West	18	14	—	—
2001	Fred Williams (5-8)					
	Candi Harvey (14-5)	T3rd/West	19	13	0	2
2002	Candi Harvey	3rd/West	20	12	2	3
2003	Candi Harvey (6-16)					
	Shell Dailey (6-6)	6th/West	12	22	-	-
		Totals	99	121	2	5

SEATTLE STORM

Season	Coach	Finish	Regular Season W	L	Playoffs W	L
2000	Lin Dunn	8th/West	6	26	—	—
2001	Lin Dunn	8th/West	10	22	—	—
2002	Lin Dunn	4th/West	17	15	0	2
2003	Anne Donovan	T4th/West	18	16	-	-
		Totals	51	79	0	2

WASHINGTON MYSTICS

Season	Coach	Finish	Regular Season W	L	Playoffs W	L
1998	Jim Lewis (2-16)					
	Cathy Parson (1-11)	5th/East	3	27	—	—
1999	Nancy Darsch	5th/East	12	20	—	—
2000	Nancy Darsch (9-11)					
	Darrell Walker (5-7)	T4th/East	14	18	0	2
2001	Tom Maher	T6th/East	10	22	—	—
2002	Marianne Stanley	3rd/East	17	15	3	2
2003	Marianne Stanley	7th/East	9	25	-	-
		Totals	65	127	3	4

TEAM WINNING, LOSING STREAKS

Team	G	Winning Streak Dates	G	Losing Streak Dates
Charlotte	7	Jul. 31-Aug. 14, 2001	7	Jun. 12-24, 2001
Cleveland	8	Jul. 17-Aug. 2, 1997	8	Aug. 2-19, 1999
Connecticut *	6	Jun. 28-Jul. 9, 2000*	7	Jul. 21-Aug. 4, 2000
	4	Jul. 19-26, 2003	3	Jun. 26-Jul. 1, 2003
				Jul. 8-17, 2003
				Aug. 5-12, 2003
Detroit	8	Jun.5-27,2003	13	May 30-Jun. 28, 2002
Houston	15	Jun. 27-Jul. 30, 1998	3	Aug. 21-25, 2003
Indiana	4	Jul. 31-Aug. 7, 2002	10	Jun. 18-Jul. 8, 2000
Los Angeles	18	Jun. 26-Aug.11, 2001	5	Jun. 21-Jul. 2, 1998
Miami	7	Jul. 7-22, 2001	5	Jun. 22-Jul. 1, 2001
				May 28-Jun. 9, 2002
Minnesota	5	Jun. 5-17, 2000	8	Jul. 5-21, 2000
New York	7	Jun. 21-Jul. 5, 1997	4	Aug. 17-23, 1997
				Jun. 10-24, 2001 Jul. 8-16, 1998
				Jul. 19-26, 2001
Phoenix	5	Jul. 14-27, 2001	7	Jul. 29-Aug. 10, 2001
				Jul. 2-25, 2003
Portland	7	Jun. 26-Jul. 10, 2002	10	Jul. 27-Aug. 14, 2001
Sacramento	6	Jul. 21-Aug. 1, 2002	9	Jul. 16-Aug. 4, 1997
San Antonio	+8	Jul. 24-Aug. 7, 2001	+6	Aug. 6-17, 1997
				Jun. 19-30, 1998
				Jul. 30-Aug. 10, 1998
				Jul. 10-21, 1999
	3	Jul. 27-Aug. 1, 2003	6	Jul. 10-25, 2003
Seattle	5	Jul. 25-Aug. 1, 2002	8	Jun. 15-Jul. 3, 2000
Washington	6	Aug. 2-14, 1999	11	Jul. 13-Aug. 7, 1998
		Jun. 4-18, 2002		Jun. 13-Jul. 9, 2003

*Club located in Orlando. +Club located in Utah.

OVERALL

	W	L	PCT
Houston Comets	161	59	.732
Los Angeles Sparks	151	69	.686
New York Liberty	128	92	.582
Sacramento Monarchs	111	109	.505
Charlotte Sting	110	110	.500
Miami Sol	48	48	.500
Cleveland Rockers	108	112	.491
Orlando Miracle	60	68	.469
Connecticut Sun	18	16	.529
Detroit Shock	90	102	.469
Phoenix Mercury	102	118	.464
Utah Starzz	87	99	.468
Minnesota Lynx	70	92	.432
Indiana Fever	51	79	.392
Seattle Storm	51	79	.392
Portland Fire	37	59	.385
San Antonio Silver Stars	12	22	.353
Washington Mystics	65	127	.339
Totals	1460	1460	.500

HOME

	W	L	PCT
Houston Comets	91	19	.827
Los Angeles Sparks	83	27	.755
New York Liberty	80	30	.727
Phoenix Mercury	72	38	.655
Sacramento Monarchs	70	40	.636
Charlotte Sting	69	41	.627
Orlando Miracle	39	25	.609
Cleveland Rockers	66	44	.600
Connecticut Sun	10	7	.588
Miami Sol	28	20	.583
Detroit Shock	52	44	.542
San Antonio Silver Stars	9	8	.529
Indiana Fever	33	32	.508
Minnesota Lynx	40	41	.494
Seattle Storm	32	33	.492
Portland Fire	21	27	.438
Washington Mystics	36	60	.375
Utah Starzz	54	39	.581
Totals	885	575	.606

ROAD

	W	L	PCT
Houston Comets	70	40	.636
Los Angeles Sparks	68	42	.618
Connecticut Sun	8	9	.470
New York Liberty	48	62	.436
Miami Sol	20	28	.417
Detroit Shock	38	58	.396
Cleveland Rockers	42	68	.382
Charlotte Sting	41	69	.373
Sacramento Monarchs	41	69	.373
Minnesota Lynx	30	51	.370
Utah Starzz	33	60	.355
Portland Fire	16	32	.333
Orlando Miracle	21	43	.328
Washington Mystics	29	67	.302
Seattle Storm	19	46	.292
Indiana Fever	18	47	.277
Phoenix Mercury	30	80	.273
San Antonio Silver Stars	3	14	.214
Totals	575	885	.394

BY VICTORIES

COACH	W-L	PCT
Van Chancellor	161 - 59	.732
Michael Cooper	105 - 25	.808
Richie Adubato	93 - 69	.574
Dan Hughes	76 - 74	.507
Cheryl Miller	70 - 52	.574
Anne Donovan	63 - 67	.485
Nancy Darsch	56 - 54	.509
Brian Agler	48 - 67	.417
Ron Rothstein	48 - 48	.500
Sonny Allen	46 - 30	.605
Nancy Lieberman-Cline	46 - 48	.489
Carolyn Peck	44 - 52	.458
Nell Fortner	42 - 56	.429
Linda Hill-MacDonald	42 - 48	.467
Candi Harvey	40 - 33	.548

BY GAMES

COACH	G
Van Chancellor	220
Richie Adubato	162
Dan Hughes	150
Michael Cooper	130
Anne Donovan	130
Cheryl Miller	122
Brian Agler	115
Nancy Darsch	110
Nell Fortner	98
Lin Dunn	96
Linda Hargrove	96
Carolyn Peck	96
Ron Rothstein	96
Nancy Lieberman-Cline	94
Linda Hill-MacDonald	90

BY WINNING PERCENTAGE
(MIN: 75 GAMES)

COACH	PCT	W-L
Michael Cooper	.808	105 - 25
Van Chancellor	.732	161 - 59
Sonny Allen	.605	46 - 30
Richie Adubato	.574	93 - 69
Cheryl Miller	.574	70 - 52
Nancy Darsch	.509	56 - 54
Dan Hughes	.507	76 - 74
Ron Rothstein	.500	48 - 48
Nancy Lieberman-Cline	.489	46 - 48
Anne Donovan	.485	63 - 67
Linda Hill-MacDonald	.467	42 - 48
Carolyn Peck	.458	44 - 52
Nell Fortner	.429	42 - 56
Brian Agler	.417	48 - 67
Linda Hargrove	.385	37 - 59

RECORDS Regular Season

WNBA ALL-TIME LEADERS

GAMES

Janeth Arcain	220
Andrea Stinson	220
Teresa Weatherspoon	220
Merlakia Jones	218
Lady Grooms	217
Bridget Pettis	217
Jennifer Gillom	216
Vickie Johnson	214
Rushia Brown	210
Sophia Witherspoon	207

MINUTES

Andrea Stinson	7,177
Tina Thompson	7,048
Teresa Weatherspoon	6,842
Vickie Johnson	6,808
Lisa Leslie	6,643
Janeth Arcain	6,559
Janeth Arcain	6,559
Vicky Bullett	5,950
Jennifer Gillom	5,886
Merlakia Jones	5,837
Mwadi Mabika	5,833

FIELD GOALS MADE

Lisa Leslie	1,316
Andrea Stinson	1,223
Tina Thompson	1,138
Sheryl Swoopes	1,065
Jennifer Gillom	1,049
Vickie Johnson	994
Chamique Holdsclaw	974
Tangela Smith	913
Katie Smith	890
Merlakia Jones	883

FIELD GOAL ATTEMPTS

Lisa Leslie	2,859
Tina Thompson	2,715
Andrea Stinson	2,691
Jennifer Gillom	2,464
Sheryl Swoopes	2,374
Vickie Johnson	2,290
Chamique Holdsclaw	2,238
Mwadi Mabika	2,152
Katie Smith	2,149
Tangela Smith	2,099

FIELD GOAL PERCENTAGE
(MINIMUM: 400 FG)

	FG	FGA	PCT
Yolanda Griffith	839	1,610	.521
Latasha Byears	701	1,363	.514
Natalie Williams	830	1,709	.486
Taj McWilliams-Franklin	657	1,363	.482
Murriel Page	611	1,268	.482
Brandy Reed	465	966	.481
Rhonda Mapp	540	1,127	.479
DeLisha Milton	680	1,424	.478
Rushia Brown	470	989	.475
Lisa Harrison	452	968	.467

FREE THROWS MADE

Lisa Leslie	889
Cynthia Cooper	758
Katie Smith	722
Yolanda Griffith	665
Jennifer Gillom	643
Natalie Williams	626
Tina Thompson	612
Shannon Johnson	585
Margo Dydek	584
Nikki McCray	544

FREE THROW ATTEMPTS

Lisa Leslie	1,236
Yolanda Griffith	932
Cynthia Cooper	870
Jennifer Gillom	847
Katie Smith	840
Natalie Williams	832
Shannon Johnson	793
Tina Thompson	744
Margo Dydek	737
Wendy Palmer	734

FREE THROW PERCENTAGE
(MINIMUM: 200 FT)

	FT	FTA	PCT
Eva Nemcova	227	253	.897
Cynthia Cooper	758	870	.871
Janeth Arcain	497	575	.864
Katie Smith	722	840	.860
Dawn Staley	339	396	.856
Sandy Brondello	316	370	.854
Ukari Figgs	204	239	.854
Crystal Robinson	211	248	.851
Jennifer Azzi	348	412	.845
Sheryl Swoopes	537	645	.833

THREE-POINT FIELD GOALS

Katie Smith	365
Crystal Robinson	311
Tina Thompson	291
Ruthie Bolton	282
Mwadi Mabika	281
Sophia Witherspoon	260
Allison Feaster	251
Kedra Holland-Corn	248
Cynthia Cooper	239
Nykesha Sales	207

THREE-POINT FIELD GOAL

ATTEMPTS

Katie Smith	996
Ruthie Bolton	905
Mwadi Mabika	854
Tina Thompson	818
Crystal Robinson	793
Sophia Witherspoon	741
Kedra Holland-Corn	720
Allison Feaster	714
Cynthia Cooper	634
Nykesha Sales	594

THREE-POINT PERCENTAGE
(MINIMUM: 100 FG3)

	3FG	3GA	PCT
Jennifer Azzi	158	345	.458
Nikki Teasley	110	265	.415
Sandy Brondello	114	278	.410
Eva Nemcova	131	326	.402
Crystal Robinson	311	793	.392
Edna Campbell	140	357	.392
Tamika Catchings	150	384	.391
Becky Hammon	172	453	.380
Cynthia Cooper	239	634	.377
Sue Bird	106	282	.376

OFFENSIVE REBOUNDS

Yolanda Griffith	609
Natalie Williams	566
Lisa Leslie	529
Tina Thompson	457
Latasha Byears	448
Murriel Page	419
Taj McWilliams-Franklin	384
Wendy Palmer	377
Adrienne Goodson	371
Tari Phillips	369

DEFENSIVE REBOUNDS

Lisa Leslie	1,427
Margo Dydek	1,125
Tina Thompson	985
Chamique Holdsclaw	939
Wendy Palmer	890
Natalie Williams	845
Vicky Bullett	831
Yolanda Griffith	804
Andrea Stinson	748
Mwadi Mabika	725

TOTAL REBOUNDS

Lisa Leslie	1,956
Tina Thompson	1,442
Yolanda Griffith	1,413
Natalie Williams	1,411
Margo Dydek	1,362
Chamique Holdsclaw	1,268
Wendy Palmer	1,267

Vicky Bullett	1,191
Murriel Page	1,113
Tari Phillips	1,073

ASSISTS

Teresa Weatherspoon	1,306
Ticha Penicheiro	1,279
Dawn Staley	884
Andrea Stinson	748
Shannon Johnson	737
Jennifer Azzi	638
Cynthia Cooper	602
Tamecka Dixon	580
Vickie Johnson	571
Debbie Black	565

STEALS

Teresa Weatherspoon	453
Sheryl Swoopes	407
Ticha Penicheiro	369
Vicky Bullett	353
Andrea Stinson	312
Debbie Black	296
Janeth Arcain	292
Yolanda Griffith	292
Nykesha Sales	292
Rita Williams	278

PERSONAL FOULS

Lisa Leslie	838
Margo Dydek	672
Jennifer Gillom	629
Natalie Williams	620
Mwadi Mabika	607
Latasha Byears	605
Tina Thompson	594
Tangela Smith	592
Wendy Palmer	590
Murriel Page	571

DISQUALIFICATIONS

Lisa Leslie	28
Latasha Byears	18
Natalie Williams	15
Isabelle Fijalkowski	10
Tari Phillips	10
Margo Dydek	9
DeLisha Milton	9
Murriel Page	9
Tangela Smith	9
Sue Wicks	8

BLOCKED SHOTS

Margo Dydek	607
Lisa Leslie	466
Vicky Bullett	288
Tangela Smith	281
Elena Baranova	216
Lauren Jackson	209

Yolanda Griffith 204
Tina Thompson 174
Taj McWilliams-Franklin 166
Sue Wicks 155

POINTS

Lisa Leslie 3,617
Tina Thompson 3,179
Andrea Stinson 3,126
Jennifer Gillom 2,896
Katie Smith 2,867
Sheryl Swoopes 2,821
Cynthia Cooper 2,601
Vickie Johnson 2,572
Chamique Holdsclaw 2,523
Nikki McCray 2,421

SCORING AVERAGE
(MINIMUM: 100 GAMES)

	G	FG	FT	PTS	AVG
Cynthia Cooper	124	802	758	2,601	21.0
Chamique Holdsclaw	...139	974	532	2,523	18.2
Katie Smith	159	890	722	2,867	18.0
Lisa Leslie	205	1,316	889	3,617	17.6
Sheryl Swoopes	164	1,065	537	2,821	17.2
Yolanda Griffith	144	839	665	2,343	16.3
Tina Thompson	206	1,138	612	3,179	15.4
Natalie Williams	153	830	626	2,294	15.0
Adrienne Goodson	154	849	451	2,191	14.2
Andrea Stinson	220	1,223	486	3,126	14.2

ALL-TIME TOP 50 SCORERS

PLAYER	YRS	G	MIN	FG	FGA	PCT	FT	FTA	PCT	REB	AST	STL	PF	BLK	PTS	AVG
Lisa Leslie	7	205	6643	1316	2859	.460	889	1236	.719	1956	462	259	838	466	3617	17.6
Tina Thompson	7	206	7048	1138	2715	.419	612	744	.823	1442	299	202	594	174	3179	15.4
Andrea Stinson	7	220	7177	1223	2691	.454	486	662	.734	996	748	312	445	110	3126	14.2
Jennifer Gillom	7	216	5886	1049	2464	.426	643	847	.759	968	255	221	629	104	2896	13.4
Katie Smith	5	159	5721	890	2149	.414	722	840	.860	533	383	143	470	35	2867	18.0
Sheryl Swoopes	6	164	5494	1065	2374	.449	537	645	.833	862	543	407	269	146	2821	17.2
Cynthia Cooper	5	124	4363	802	1749	.459	758	870	.871	403	602	193	264	35	2601	21.0
Vickie Johnson	7	214	6808	994	2290	.434	410	502	.817	814	571	207	434	32	2572	12.0
Chamique Holdsclaw	5	139	4749	974	2238	.435	532	687	.774	1268	354	182	314	80	2523	18.2
Nikki McCray	6	191	5678	854	2043	.418	544	705	.772	431	419	213	454	13	2421	12.7
Mwadi Mabika	7	206	5833	840	2152	.390	436	543	.803	951	537	262	607	86	2397	11.6
Yolanda Griffith	5	144	4674	839	1610	.521	665	932	.714	1413	211	292	510	204	2343	16.3
Wendy Palmer	7	205	5401	852	2004	.425	504	734	.687	1267	239	163	590	48	2314	11.3
Janeth Arcain	7	220	6559	869	1977	.440	497	575	.864	826	416	292	428	22	2310	10.5
Tamecka Dixon	7	201	5795	865	2028	.427	466	582	.801	611	580	220	480	44	2303	11.5
Natalie Williams	5	153	5119	830	1709	.486	626	832	.752	1411	215	195	620	87	2294	15.0
Nykesha Sales	5	162	5221	838	2003	.418	396	504	.786	711	370	292	502	46	2279	14.1
Margo Dydek	6	190	5119	815	1778	.458	584	737	.792	1362	356	114	672	607	2232	11.7
Sophia Witherspoon	7	207	4862	735	1934	.380	489	610	.802	449	313	210	345	31	2219	10.7
Adrienne Goodson	5	154	4921	849	1937	.438	451	611	.738	820	352	164	395	27	2191	14.2
Merlakia Jones	7	218	5837	883	2078	.425	348	462	.753	875	339	220	469	24	2173	10.0
Tangela Smith	6	189	5225	913	2099	.435	312	416	.750	980	224	177	592	281	2172	11.5
Shannon Johnson	5	155	5275	658	1600	.411	585	793	.738	645	737	241	383	35	2049	13.2
Sheri Sam	5	161	5118	790	1942	.407	308	450	.684	712	402	238	399	34	2041	12.7
Ruthie Bolton	7	184	4624	710	1934	.367	321	430	.747	627	322	231	392	7	2023	11.0
Vicky Bullett	6	186	5950	813	1799	.452	322	415	.776	1191	297	353	507	288	2018	10.8
Tari Phillips	5	160	4404	755	1633	.462	356	569	.626	1073	168	240	505	88	1869	11.7
DeLisha Milton	5	159	4808	680	1424	.478	386	498	.775	970	295	239	568	151	1804	11.3
Sandy Brondello	5	155	4583	665	1606	.414	316	370	.854	300	349	148	298	16	1760	11.4
Chasity Melvin	5	157	4483	645	1385	.466	441	628	.702	862	258	129	499	96	1741	11.1
Crystal Robinson	5	156	4749	603	1381	.437	211	248	.851	411	324	187	433	54	1728	11.1
Taj McWilliams-Franklin	5	143	4565	657	1363	.482	371	513	.723	1016	236	230	399	166	1725	12.1
Latasha Byears	7	185	4007	701	1363	.514	245	388	.631	1030	173	209	605	51	1654	8.9
Lauren Jackson	3	90	2992	589	1394	.423	323	416	.776	690	147	122	298	209	1622	18.0

Kedra Holland-Corn	5	162	4438	554	1356	.409	265	369	.718	360	327	239	325	28	1621	10.0
Allison Feaster	6	165	3979	497	1290	.385	295	357	.826	529	248	160	348	40	1540	9.3
Dawn Staley	5	162	5463	500	1282	.390	339	396	.856	334	884	224	348	9	1495	9.2
Murriel Page	6	192	5506	611	1268	.482	257	406	.633	1113	259	128	571	150	1490	7.8
Elena Baranova	5	142	3990	529	1285	.412	232	280	.829	863	304	153	334	216	1428	10.1
Tamika Whitmore	5	156	3814	543	1211	.448	305	446	.684	561	105	112	452	98	1394	8.9
Bridget Pettis	7	217	3835	451	1321	.341	339	417	.813	447	306	175	337	32	1394	6.4
Rhonda Mapp	6	163	3462	540	1127	.479	275	358	.768	788	237	112	483	69	1369	8.4
Marie Ferdinand	3	98	3045	458	1045	.438	377	507	.744	320	260	149	243	17	1325	13.5
Eva Nemcova	5	111	3397	474	1072	.442	227	253	.897	386	215	120	218	64	1306	11.8
Jennifer Azzi	5	141	4889	391	878	.445	348	412	.845	360	638	112	435	42	1288	9.1
Tamik Catchings	2	66	2377	405	951	.426	305	367	.831	548	232	166	227	78	1265	19.2
Betty Lennox	4	108	2504	462	1205	.383	179	229	.782	410	193	107	320	22	1261	11.7
Teresa Weatherspoon	7	220	6842	432	1045	.413	310	471	.658	750	1306	453	564	22	1247	5.7
Rushia Brown	7	210	3857	470	989	.475	297	388	.765	707	192	219	507	81	1239	5.9
Korie Hlede	5	133	3048	430	1039	.414	243	302	.805	375	273	120	313	11	1186	8.9

INDIVIDUAL RECORDS

SEASONS

Most Seasons

7 — 17 tied

GAMES

Most games, career

220 — Janeth Arcain, Houston, 1997-2003
Andrea Stinson, Charlotte, 1997-2003
Teresa Weatherspoon, New York, 1997-2003

218 — Merlakia Jones, Cleveland, 1997-2003

217 — Lady Grooms, Utah, 1997; Sacramento, 1998-2003
Bridget Pettis, Phoenix, 1997-2001; Indiana, 2002-03

Most consecutive games, career

220 — Janeth Arcain, Houston, June 21, 1997-August 25, 2003 (current)
Andrea Stinson, Charlotte, June 22, 1997-August 25, 2003 (current)
Teresa Weatherspoon, New York, June 21, 1997-August 24, 2003 (current)

203 — Bridget Pettis, Phoenix-Indiana, June 22, 1997-July 10, 2003

192 — Murriel Page, Washington, June 11, 1998-August 25, 2003 (current)

Most games, season

34 — By many

MINUTES

Most seasons leading league, minutes

2 — Katie Smith, Minnesota, 2000-01
Tamika Catchings, Indiana, 2002-03

1 — Chantel Tremitiere, Sacramento, 1997
Ticha Penicheiro, Sacramento, 1998
Shannon Johnson, Orlando, 1999

Most minutes, career

7,177 — Andrea Stinson, Charlotte, 1997-2003

7,048 — Tina Thompson, Houston, 1997-2003

6,842 — Teresa Weatherspoon, New York, 1997-2003

Highest average, minutes per game, career (Minimum 100 games)

36.0 — Katie Smith, Minnesota, 1999-2003 (5,721/159)

35.2 — Cynthia Cooper, Houston, 1997-00, 2003 (4,363/124)

34.7 — Jennifer Azzi, Detroit, 1999; Utah, 2000-03 (4,889/141)

Most minutes, season

1,234 — Katie Smith, Minnesota, 2001

1,210 — Tamika Catchings, Indiana, 2003

1,205 — Jennifer Azzi, Utah, 2001

Highest average, minutes per game, season

38.6 — Katie Smith, Minnesota, 2001 (1,234/32)

37.7 — Jennifer Azzi, Utah, 2001 (1,205/32)

37.5 — Chantel Tremitiere, Sacramento, 1997 (1,051/28)

Most minutes, game

55 — Vicky Bullett, Washington at Seattle, July 3, 2001 (4 ot)
Lauren Jackson, Seattle vs. Washington, July 3, 2001 (4 ot)

54 — Chamique Holdsclaw, Washington at Seattle, July 3, 2001 (4 ot)
Audrey Sauret, Washington at Seattle, July 3, 2001 (4 ot)

53 — Chasity Melvin, Cleveland at Orlando, June 8, 2002 (3 ot)

COMPLETE GAMES

Most complete games, season

13 — Jennifer Azzi, Utah, 2001

10 — Tamika Catchings, Indiana, 2002

9 — DeLisha Milton, Los Angeles, 2003

SCORING

Most seasons leading league
3 — Cynthia Cooper, Houston, 1997-99
1 — Sheryl Swoopes, Houston, 2000
Katie Smith, Minnesota, 2001
Chamique Holdsclaw, Washington, 2002
Lauren Jackson, Seattle, 2003

Most points, lifetime
3,617 — Lisa Leslie, Los Angeles, 1997-2003
3,179 — Tina Thompson, Houston, 1997-2003
3,126 — Andrea Stinson, Charlotte, 1997-2003

Highest average, points per game, career
(Minimum 100 games)
21.0 — Cynthia Cooper, Houston, 1997-2000, 2003 (2,601/124)
18.2 — Chamique Holdsclaw, Washington, 1999-2003 (2,523/139)
18.0 — Katie Smith, Minnesota, 1997-2003 (2,867/159)

Most points, season
739 — Katie Smith, Minnesota, 2001
698 — Lauren Jackson, Seattle, 2003
686 — Cynthia Cooper, Houston, 1999

Highest average, points per game, season
23.1 — Katie Smith, Minnesota, 2001 (739/32)
22.7 — Cynthia Cooper, Houston, 1998 (680/30)
22.2 — Cynthia Cooper, Houston, 1997 (621/28)

Most points, game
46 — Katie Smith, Minnesota at Los Angeles, July 8, 2001 (ot)
44 — Cynthia Cooper, Houston at Sacramento, July 25, 1997
42 — Cynthia Cooper, Houston vs. Utah, August 16, 1999

Most games, 40 or more points, career
2 — Cynthia Cooper, Houston 1997-2000, 2003
Katie Smith, Minnesota, 1999-2003

Most games, 30 or more points, career
16 — Cynthia Cooper, Houston, 1997-2000, 2003
10 — Katie Smith, Minnesota, 1999-2003
9 — Lisa Leslie, Los Angeles, 1997-2003

Most consecutive games, 30 or more points
3 — Cynthia Cooper, Houston, July 18-25, 1997

2 — Cynthia Cooper, Houston, August 5-7, 1997
Sheryl Swoopes, Houston, August 8-10, 2002

Most games, 20 or more points, career
77 — Lisa Leslie, Los Angeles, 1997-2003
72 — Cynthia Cooper, Houston, 1997-2000, 2003
67 — Katie Smith, Minnesota, 1999-2003

Most consecutive games, 20 or more points
11 — Cynthia Cooper, Houston, August 17, 1998-June 30, 1999
8 — Sheryl Swoopes, Houston, May 29-June 12, 2000
Brandy Reed, Phoenix, July 13-28, 2000
7 — Ruthie Bolton-Holifield, Sacramento, June 23-July 10, 1997
Lauren Jackson, Seattle, July 17-31, 2003

Most consecutive games, 10 or more points
92 — Cynthia Cooper, Houston, June 21, 1997-June 1, 2000
54 — Lisa Leslie, Los Angeles, June 17, 2000-August 8, 2001
53 — Lauren Jackson, Seattle, June 26, 2002-August 25, 2003 (current)

Most points, one half
31 — Cynthia Cooper, Houston at Sacramento, July 25, 1997
29 — Katie Smith, Minnesota vs. Los Angeles, June 3, 2000

Most points, overtime period
11 — Shannon Johnson, Orlando vs. Cleveland, June 8, 2002
10 — Chamique Holdsclaw, Washington at Sacramento, June 25, 2002

FIELD GOAL PERCENTAGE

Most seasons leading league
2 — Murriel Page, Washington, 1999-00
1 — Haixia Zheng, Los Angeles, 1997
Isabelle Fijalkowski, Cleveland, 1998
Latasha Byears, Los Angeles, 2001
Alisa Burras, Portland, 2002
Tamika Williams, Minnesota, 2003

Highest field goal percentage, career
(Minimum 400 field goals)
.521 — Yolanda Griffith, Sacramento, 1999-2003 (839/1,610)
.514 — Latasha Byears, Sacramento, 1997-2000; Los Angeles, 2001-03 (701/1,363)
.486 — Natalie Williams, Utah, 1999-2002; Indiana, 2003 (830/1,709)

Highest field goal percentage, season (qualifiers)
.668 — Tamika Williams, Minnesota, 2003
(129/193)
.629 — Alisa Burras, Portland, 2002
(117/186)
.618 — Haixia Zheng, Los Angeles, 1997
(110/178)
Highest field goal percentage, game
(Minimum 10 field goals made)
.917 — Sheryl Swoopes, Houston at
Portland, August 4, 2000 (11/12)
.909 — Haixia Zheng, Los Angeles vs.
Sacramento, August 22, 1997
(10/11)
Kamila Vodichkova, Seattle vs.
Detroit, June 28, 2000 (10/11)
Tracy Reid, Charlotte vs. Utah, August
5, 2000 (10/11)
Vicky Bullett, Washington vs.
Detroit, July 18, 2002 (10/11)
LaToya Thomas, Cleveland vs.
Indiana, June 29, 2003 (10/11)
.857 — Tari Phillips, New York vs.
Charlotte, June 12, 2001 (12/14)
Adrienne Goodson, Utah at Portland,
August 6, 2002 (12/14)
Most field goals, none missed, game
8 — Becky Hammon, New York at
Phoenix, June 21, 2001
Crystal Robinson, New York at
Cleveland, August 17, 2003
7 — Taj McWilliams, Orlando at
Washington, July 21, 2000
Kara Wolters, Indiana at Portland,
July 28, 2000
Pollyan Johns Kimbrough, Miami
vs. Phoenix, July 3, 2002
6 — By many
Most field goal attempts, none made, game
12 — Tina Thompson, Houston at
Phoenix, July 19, 1999
11 — Kamila Vodichkova, Seattle vs.
Portland, August 9, 2002
Slobodanka Tuvic, Phoenix at
Seattle, July 25, 2003
Elena Baranova, New York vs.
Detroit, August 1, 2003
10 — By Many

FIELD GOALS

Most seasons leading league
3 — Sheryl Swoopes, Houston,
1999-2000, 2002
1 — Cynthia Cooper, Houston, 1997
Jennifer Gillom, Phoenix, 1998
Lisa Leslie, Los Angeles, 2001
Lauren Jackson, Seattle, 2003
Most field goals, career

1,316 — Lisa Leslie, Los Angeles,
1997-2003
1,223 — Andrea Stinson, Charlotte,
1997-2003
1,138 — Tina Thompson, Houston,
1997-2003
Most field goals, season
254 — Lauren Jackson, Seattle, 2003
245 — Sheryl Swoopes, Houston, 2000
232 — Chamique Holdsclaw,
Washington, 2000
Most consecutive field goals made
14 — Tammy Sutton-Brown, Charlotte,
June 1-8, 2002
13 — Tina Thompson, Houston,
June 23-25, 2002
Tamika Whitmore, New York, June
30-July 8, 2002
12 — DeLisha Milton, Los Angeles,
August 20-21, 1999
Kelly Schumacher, Indiana,
July 16-23, 2003
Most field goals, game
17 — Lauren Jackson, Seattle vs.
Los Angeles, August 6, 2003
15 — Cynthia Cooper, Houston at
Charlotte, August 11, 1997
14 — by many
Most field goals, one half
11 — Linda Burgess, Sacramento vs.
Utah, August 15, 1998
Lauren Jackson, Seattle vs.
Los Angeles, August 6, 2003
10 — By many

FIELD GOAL ATTEMPTS

Most seasons leading league
2 — Sheryl Swoopes, Houston, 1999, 2002
1 — Wendy Palmer, Utah, 1997
Jennifer Gillom, Phoenix, 1998
Chamique Holdsclaw, Washington,
2000
Tina Thompson, Houston, 2001
Lauren Jackson, Seattle, 2003
Most field goal attempts, career
2,859 — Lisa Leslie, Los Angeles, 1997-
2003
2,715 — Tina Thompson, Houston, 1997-
2003
2,691 — Andrea Stinson, Charlotte, 1997-
2003
Most field goal attempts, season
528 — Tina Thompson, Houston, 2001
526 — Lauren Jackson, Seattle, 2003
519 — Katie Smith, Minnesota, 2001
Most field goal attempts, game
31 — Wendy Palmer, Utah vs. Los

Angeles,   August 16, 1997
29 — Sheryl Swoopes, Houston at
   Los Angeles, August 20, 1999
   Lauren Jackson, Seattle vs.
   Washington, July 3, 2001 (4 ot)
28 — Cynthia Cooper, Houston at Utah,
   June 30, 1998 (2 ot)
   Sandy Brondello, Detroit at Utah,
   July 6, 1999 (2 ot)
   Mwadi Mabika, Los Angeles vs.
   Phoenix, July 15, 2003 (2 ot)
Most field goal attempts, one half
20 — Wendy Palmer, Utah vs. Los
   Angeles, August 16, 1997
19 — Sheryl Swoopes, Houston at Los
   Angeles, August 20, 1999
   Chamique Holdsclaw, Washington vs.
   Los Angeles, June 26, 2000

THREE-POINT FIELD-GOAL PER-CENTAGE

Most seasons leading league
2 — Eva Nemcova, Cleveland, 1997-98
   Jennifer Azzi, Detroit, 1999; Utah, 2001
1 — Korie Hlede, Utah, 2000
   Kelly Miller, Charlotte, 2002
   Becky Hammon, New York, 2003
Highest three-point field goal percentage, career
(Minimum 100 three-point field goals)
.458 — Jennifer Azzi, Detroit, 1999;
   Utah, 2000-03 (158/345)
.415 — Nikki Teasley, Los Angeles,
   2002-03 (110/265)
.410 — Sandy Brondello, Detroit, 1998-99;
   Miami, 2001-02; Seattle, 2003
(114/278)
Highest three-point field goal percentage, season
(qualifiers)
.517 — Jennifer Azzi, Detroit, 1999
   (30/58)
.514 — Jennifer Azzi, Utah, 2001 (38/74)
.487 — Sandy Brondello, Detroit, 1999
   (37/76)
Most three-point field goals, none missed, game
6 — Tamika Catchings, Indiana at
   Orlando, July 3, 2002 (ot)
5 — Andrea Lloyd-Curry, Minnesota at
   Sacramento, June 22, 1999
   Crystal Robinson, New York vs.
   Phoenix, July 1, 1999
   Tina Thompson, Houston at
   Phoenix, August 7, 2000
   Becky Hammon, New York at
   Phoenix, June 21, 2001
   Sheri Sam, Miami at Charlotte,
   July 9, 2002
   Nikki Teasley, Los Angeles at

Houston, June 24, 2003
   Shalonda Enis, Charlotte at
   Detroit, July 3, 2003
   Kara Lawson, Sacramento vs.
   Charlotte, August 3, 2003
4 — By many
Most three-point field goal attempts, none made,
game
8 — Tina Thompson, Houston at Utah,
   June 30, 1998 (2 ot)
   Crystal Robinson, New York vs.
   Detroit, June 21, 2000
   Crystal Robinson, New York vs.
   Cleveland, August 4, 2001
7 — Ruthie Bolton-Holifield,
   Sacramento vs. Los Angeles, July
   27, 1997
   Sophia Witherspoon, New York at
   Utah, August 19, 1997
   Cynthia Cooper, Houston vs.
   Sacramento, August 24, 1997
   Kim Perrot, Houston at Charlotte,
   June 15, 1998
   Michele Timms, Phoenix at
   Houston, August 6, 1998
   Cynthia Cooper, Houston vs.
   Cleveland, July 1, 1999
   Becky Hammon, New York vs.
Cleveland, July 29, 2000
   Lauren Jackson, Seattle vs.
   Houston, August 8, 2001
   Rita Williams, Indiana at Orlando,
   July 3, 2002 (ot)
   Katie Smith, Minnesota vs. Miami,
   July 19, 2002

THREE-POINT FIELD GOALS

Most seasons leading league
3 — Katie Smith, Minnesota, 2000-01,
   2003
2 — Cynthia Cooper, Houston, 1997-98
1 — Crystal Robinson, New York, 1999
   Allison Feaster, Charlotte, 2002
Most three-point field goals, career
365 — Katie Smith, Minnesota, 1999-
   2003
311 — Crystal Robinson, New York,
   1999-2003
291 — Tina Thompson, Houston, 1997-
   2003
Most three-point field goals, season
88 — Katie Smith, Minnesota, 2000
85 — Katie Smith, Minnesota, 2001
79 — Allison Feaster, Charlotte, 2002
Most three-point field goals, game
7 — Elena Baranova, Utah at New York,
   July 22, 1997
   Cynthia Cooper, Houston at

Sacramento, July 25, 1997
Crystal Robinson, New York at
Los Angeles, July 24, 1999 (ot)
Nykesha Sales, Orlando at
Sacramento, July 27, 2000
Sophia Witherspoon, Portland at
Miami, June 29, 2001 (ot)
Katie Smith, Minnesota at Seattle,
June 14, 2003
Deanna Nolan, Detroit vs. New York,
August 10, 2003 (ot)
6 — By many
Most consecutive three-point field goals made
8 — Crystal Robinson, June 28, 1999-
July 1,1999
Lisa Leslie, Los Angeles,
June 5-16, 2001
7 — Many tied
Most consecutive games, three-point field goals
made
32 — Katie Smith, Minnesota, July 31,
2002-August 2, 2003
25 — Katie Smith, Minnesota, June 22,
2000-June 9, 2001
23 — Tamika Catchings, Indiana, July 3,
2002-June 12, 2003
Most three-point field goals made, one half
5 — By many. Most recent:
Katie Douglas, Connecticut vs.
Indiana, June 26, 2003

THREE-POINT FIELD GOAL ATTEMPTS

Most seasons leading league
2 — Katie Smith, Minnesota, 2000-01
1 — Ruthie Bolton-Holifield,
Sacramento, 1997
Cynthia Cooper, Houston, 1998
Tonya Edwards, Minnesota, 1999
Tamika Catchings, Indiana, 2002
Allison Feaster, Charlotte, 2003
Most three-point field goal attempts, career
996 — Katie Smith, Minnesota, 1999-2003
905 — Ruthie Bolton, Sacramento, 1997-2003
854 — Mwadi Mabika, Los Angeles, 1997-2003
Most three-point field goal attempts, season
240 — Katie Smith, Minnesota, 2001
232 — Katie Smith, Minnesota, 2000
205 — Allison Feaster, Charlotte, 2003
Most three-point field goal attempts, game
15 — Ruthie Bolton-Holifield,
Sacramento at Cleveland, July 10, 1997
14 — Ruthie Bolton-Holifield,
Sacramento vs. Utah, July 2, 1997 (ot)
Crystal Robinson, New York at Los
Angeles, July 24, 1999 (ot)
13 — Cynthia Cooper, Houston vs.
Cleveland, July 29, 1997

Cynthia Cooper, Houston at Utah,
August 4, 1998
Katie Smith, Minnesota vs. Los
Angeles, June 3, 2000
Most three-point field goal attempts, one half
10 — Cynthia Cooper, Houston vs.
Cleveland, July 29, 1997
9 — by many

FREE THROW PERCENTAGE

Most seasons leading league
1 — Bridget Pettis, Phoenix, 1997
Sandy Brondello, Detroit, 1998
Eva Nemcova, Cleveland, 1999
Jennifer Azzi, Utah, 2000
Elena Baranova, Miami, 2001
Sue Bird, Seattle, 2002
Becky Hammon, New York, 2003
Highest free-throw percentage, career
(Minimum 200 free throws)
.897 — Eva Nemcova, Cleveland,
1997-2002 (227/253)
.871 — Cynthia Cooper, Houston,
1997-2000, 2003 (758/870)
.864 — Janeth Arcain, Houston, 1997-
2003 (497/575)
Highest free-throw percentage, season (qualifiers)
.984 — Eva Nemcova, Cleveland, 1999 (62/63)
.951 — Becky Hammon, New York, 2003 (39/41)
.937 — Stephanie White, Indiana, 2003 (45/48)
Most free throws made, none missed, game
14 — Lisa Leslie, Los Angeles vs.
Minnesota, July 15, 2000
13 — Yolanda Griffith, Sacramento at
Charlotte, June 24, 2001 (ot)
Sheryl Swoopes, Houston at
Los Angeles, August 8, 2002
Tina Thompson, Houston at
Minnesota, June 17, 2003
Chamique Holdsclaw, Washington vs.
Indiana, July 24, 2003
12 — By Many
Most free throw attempts, none made, game
6 — Wendy Palmer, Utah at Los
Angeles, June 28, 1999
Tangela Smith, Sacramento vs.
Utah, August 14, 1999
Swin Cash, Detroit at San Antonio,
June 7, 2003
5 — Tammy Jackson, Houston at Miami,
July 20, 2001
Audrey Sauret, Washington vs.
Portland, August 3, 2001
Pollyan Johns Kimbrough, Miami vs.
Phoenix, July 3, 2002
4 — By many

FREE THROWS MADE

Most seasons leading league
- 3 — Cynthia Cooper, Houston, 1997-99
- 1 — Natalie Williams, Utah, 2000
  Katie Smith, Minnesota, 2001
  Swin Cash, Detroit, 2002
  Marie Ferdinand, San Antonio, 2003

Most free throws made, career
- 889 — Lisa Leslie, Los Angeles, 1997-2003
- 758 — Cynthia Cooper, Houston, 1997-2000, 2003
- 722 — Katie Smith, Minnesota, 1999-2003

Most free throws made, season
- 246 — Katie Smith, Minnesota, 2001
- 210 — Cynthia Cooper, Houston, 1998
- 204 — Cynthia Cooper, Houston, 1999

Most consecutive free throws made
- 66 — Eva Nemcova, Cleveland, June 14, 1999-June 5, 2000
- 47 — Cynthia Cooper, Houston, August 16, 1999-June 1, 2000
- 46 — Lisa Leslie, Los Angeles, July 9-25, 2000

Most free throws made, game
- 22 — Cynthia Cooper, Houston vs. Sacramento, July 3, 1998
- 18 — Katie Smith, Minnesota at Los Angeles,   July 8, 2001 (ot)
- 17 — Cynthia Cooper, Houston vs. Utah, August 16, 1999

Most free throws made, one half
- 13 — Ruthie Bolton-Holifield, Sacramento at Washington, July 2, 1999
  Yolanda Griffith, Sacramento at Charlotte, June 24, 2001
- 12 — By many

FREE THROW ATTEMPTS

Most seasons leading league
- 2 — Cynthia Cooper, Houston, 1997-98
- 1 — Yolanda Griffith, Sacramento, 1999
  Natalie Williams, Utah, 2000
  Katie Smith, Minnesota, 2001
  Swin Cash, Detroit, 2002
  Marie Ferdinand, San Antonio, 2003

Most free throw attempts, career
- 1,236 — Lisa Leslie, Los Angeles, 1997-2003
- 932 — Yolanda Griffith, Sacramento, 1999-2003
- 870 — Cynthia Cooper, Houston, 1997-2000, 2003

Most free throw attempts, season
- 275 — Katie Smith, Minnesota, 2001
- 246 — Cynthia Cooper, Houston, 1998
- 235 — Yolanda Griffith, Sacramento, 1999

Most free throw attempts, game
- 24 — Cynthia Cooper, Houston vs. Sacramento, July 3, 1998
- 21 — Swin Cash, Detroit vs. Miami,

June 28, 2002 (ot)
- 19 — Yolanda Griffith, Sacramento vs. Phoenix, June 12, 1999
  Katie Smith, Minnesota at Los Angeles, July 8, 2001 (ot)
  Lisa Leslie, Los Angeles vs. Utah, August 4, 2002
  Plenette Pierson, Phoenix vs. Los Angeles, August 8, 2003

Most free throw attempts, one half
- 16 — Lisa Leslie, Los Angeles at New York, June 25, 2000
  Kayte Christensen, Phoenix vs. San Antonio, August 22, 2003
- 14 — Cynthia Cooper, Houston vs. Sacramento, July 3, 1998
  Ruthie Bolton-Holifield, Sacramento at Washington, July 2, 1999
  Katie Smith, Minnesota at Miami, June 10, 2000
  Natalie Williams, Utah vs. Los Angeles, August 9, 2000
  Lisa Leslie, Los Angeles vs. Utah, August 4, 2002

REBOUNDS

Most seasons leading league
- 2 — Lisa Leslie, Los Angeles, 1997-98
  Yolanda Griffith, Sacramento, 1999, 2001
  Chamique Holdsclaw, Washington, 2002-03
- 1 — Natalie Williams, Utah, 2000

Most rebounds, career
- 1,956 — Lisa Leslie, Los Angeles, 1997-2003
- 1,442 — Tina Thompson, Houston, 1997-2003
- 1,413 — Yolanda Griffith, Sacramento, 1999-2003

Highest average, rebounds per game, career (Minimum 100 games)
- 9.8 — Yolanda Griffith, Sacramento, 1999-2003 (1,413/144)
- 9.5 — Lisa Leslie, Los Angeles, 1997-2003 (1,956/205)
- 9.2 — Natalie Williams, Utah, 1999-2002; Indiana, 2003 (1,411/153)

Most rebounds, season
- 357 — Yolanda Griffith, Sacramento, 2001
- 336 — Natalie Williams, Utah, 2000
- 334 — Cheryl Ford, Detroit, 2003

Highest average, rebounds per game, season (qualifiers)
- 11.60 — Chamique Holdsclaw, Washington, 2002 (232/20)
- 11.59 — Natalie Williams, Utah, 2000 (336/29)
- 11.3 — Yolanda Griffith, Sacramento, 1999 (329/29)

Most rebounds, game
- 24 — Chamique Holdsclaw, Washington

at Charlotte, May 23, 2003
21 — Lisa Leslie, Los Angeles vs. New
    York, June 19, 1998
    Cindy Brown, Detroit at Utah,
    August 10, 1998
    Chamique Holdsclaw, Washington at
    Sacramento, June 25, 2002 (2 ot)
    Lisa Leslie, Los Angeles vs.
    Orlando, July 22, 2002
    Cheryl Ford, Detroit at
    Connecticut, June 22, 2003 (ot)
20 — Yolanda Griffith, Sacramento at
    Washington, June 5, 2001
    Natalie Williams, Utah at
    Sacramento, June 22, 2002
    Lauren Jackson, Seattle vs.
    Charlotte, July 31, 2003
Most games, 10+ rebounds, career
99 — Lisa Leslie, Los Angeles, 1997-2003
73 — Yolanda Griffith, Sacramento, 1999-2003
65 — Natalie Williams, Utah, 1999-2002;
    Indiana, 2003
Most consecutive games, 10+ rebounds
7 — Lisa Leslie, Los Angeles, August 22,
    1997—June 21, 1998
    Natalie Williams, Utah, July 15-
    August 2, 2000
    Lauren Jackson, Seattle, July 25-
    August 12, 2003
    Lisa Leslie, Los Angeles, August 13,
    2002-June 7, 2003
6 — Cindy Brown, Detroit, July 31-
    August 11, 1998
5 — By many
Most rebounds, one half
14 — Lisa Leslie, Los Angeles vs. New
    York, June 19, 1998
    Latasha Byears, Los Angeles vs.
    Houston, August 11, 2001
13 — By Many

OFFENSIVE REBOUNDS

Most seasons leading league
3 — Yolanda Griffith, Sacramento, 1999-01
2 — Latasha Byears, Sacramento, 1997-98
    Natalie Williams, Utah, 2002; Indiana,
    2003
Most offensive rebounds, career
609 — Yolanda Griffith, Sacramento, 1999-2003
566 — Natalie Williams, Utah, 1999-2002;
    Indiana, 2003
529 — Lisa Leslie, Los Angeles, 1997-2003
Highest average, offensive rebounds per game,
career (Minimum 100 games)
4.2 — Yolanda Griffith, Sacramento,
    1999-2003 (609/144)
3.7 — Natalie Williams, Utah, 1999-2002;

Indiana, 2003 (566/153)
2.7 — Taj McWilliams-Franklin, Orlando,
    1999-2003 (384/143)
Most offensive rebounds, season
162 — Yolanda Griffith, Sacramento, 2001
148 — Yolanda Griffith, Sacramento, 2000
141 — Yolanda Griffith, Sacramento, 1999
Most offensive rebounds, game
11 — Yolanda Griffith, Sacramento vs. Los
    Angeles, June 26, 1999
    Yolanda Griffith, Sacramento vs.
    Houston, August 6, 2000
10 — Marlies Askamp, Miami vs. Seattle,
    July 10, 2000
    Marlies Askamp, Miami vs. Orlando,
    August 9, 2000 (2 ot)
    Yolanda Griffith, Sacramento at
    Washington, June 5, 2001
    Taj McWilliams-Franklin, Orlando vs.
    Houston, July 18, 2001
    Latasha Byears, Los Angeles vs.
    Sacramento, July 25, 2001
    Natalie Williams, Utah at
    Sacramento, June 22, 2002
    Tamika Williams, Minnesota at
    Phoenix, June 23, 2002
    Gwen Jackson, San Antonio vs.
    Charlotte, June 14, 2003
9 — By many
Most offensive rebounds, one half
8 — Tausha Mills, Washington at
    Sacramento, July 8, 2000
    Tamika Williams, Minnesota at
    Phoenix, June 23, 2002
7 — By many

DEFENSIVE REBOUNDS

Most seasons leading league
3 — Lisa Leslie, Los Angeles, 1997, 2000, 2002
1 — Cindy Brown, Detroit, 1998
    Yolanda Griffith, Sacramento, 1999
    Margo Dydek, Utah, 2001
    Cheryl Ford, Detroit, 2003
Most defensive rebounds, career
1,427 — Lisa Leslie, Los Angeles, 1997-2003
1,128 — Margo Dydek, Utah, 1998-2002;
    San Antonio, 2003
985 — Tina Thompson, Houston, 1997-2003
Highest average, defensive rebounds per game,
career (Minimum 100 games)
7.0 — Lisa Leslie, Los Angeles, 1997-
    2003 (1,427/205)
6.8 — Chamique Holdsclaw, Washington,
    1999-2003 (939/139)
5.9 — Margo Dydek, Utah, 1998-2002;
    San Antonio, 2003 (1,128/190)

Most defensive rebounds, season
244 — Lisa Leslie, Los Angeles, 2002
235 — Cheryl Ford, Detroit, 2003
231 — Cindy Brown, Detroit, 1998
      Lisa Leslie, Los Angeles, 2000
Most defensive rebounds, game
18 — Cindy Brown, Detroit at Utah,
      August 10, 1998
17 — Chamique Holdsclaw, Washington
      at Charlotte, May 23, 2003
      Cheryl Ford, Detroit at
      Connecticut, une 22, 2003 (ot)
16 — Lisa Leslie, Los Angeles vs. New
      York, June 19, 1998
      Lisa Leslie, Los Angeles vs.
      Orlando, July 22, 2002
Most defensive rebounds, one half
11 — Tari Phillips, New York at Houston,
      July 26, 2003
10 — By many

ASSISTS

Most seasons leading league
6 — Ticha Penicheiro, Sacramento,
    1998-2003
1 — Teresa Weatherspoon, New York, 1997
Most assists, career
1,306 — Teresa Weatherspoon, New York,
        1997-2003
1,279 — Ticha Penicheiro, Sacramento,
        1998-2003
884 — Dawn Staley, Charlotte, 1999-2003
Highest average, assists per game, career
(Minimum 100 games)
7.4 — Ticha Penicheiro, Sacramento,
     1998-2003 (1,279/173)
5.9 — Teresa Weatherspoon, New York,
     1997-2003 (1,306/220)
5.5 — Dawn Staley, Charlotte, 1999-2003
     (884/162)
Most assists, season
236 — Ticha Penicheiro, Sacramento, 2000
229 — Ticha Penicheiro, Sacramento, 2003
226 — Ticha Penicheiro, Sacramento, 1999
Highest average, assists per game, season
(qualifiers)
8.0 — Ticha Penicheiro, Sacramento,
     2002 (192/24)
7.9 — Ticha Penicheiro, Sacramento,
     2000 (236/30)
7.5 — Ticha Penicheiro, Sacramento,
     2001 (172/23)
Most assists, game
16 — Ticha Penicheiro, Sacramento at
      Cleveland, July 29, 1998
      Ticha Penicheiro, Sacramento vs. Los
      Angeles, August 3, 2002

15 — Ticha Penicheiro, Sacramento at
      Cleveland, July 15, 2003
14 — By many
Most games, 10+ assists, career
47 — Ticha Penicheiro, Sacramento, 1998-
      2003
18 — Teresa Weatherspoon, New York,
      1997-2003
12 — Sue Bird, Seattle, 2002-03
Most assists, one half
11 — Ticha Penicheiro, Sacramento at
      Cleveland, July 29, 1998
      Ticha Penicheiro, Sacramento at Utah,
      June 26, 2000
      Ticha Penicheiro, Sacramento vs.
      Los Angeles, August 3, 2002
10 — Ticha Penicheiro, Sacramento at
      Charlotte, July 27, 1998
      Michele Timms, Phoenix at
      Sacramento, June 12, 1999
      Dawn Staley, Charlotte vs.
      Washington, July 26, 2000

PERSONAL FOULS

Most seasons leading league
3 — Lisa Leslie, Los Angeles, 1999-01
1 — Isabelle Fijalkowski, Cleveland, 1997
    Margo Dydek, Utah, 1998
    Olympia Scott-Richardson, Indiana,
    2002
    Natalie Williams, Indiana, 2003
Most personal fouls, career
838 — Lisa Leslie, Los Angeles, 1997-2003
672 — Margo Dydek, Utah, 1998-2002;
      San Antonio, 2003
629 — Jennifer Gillom, Phoenix, 1997-2002;
      Los Angeles, 2003
Most personal fouls, season
138 — Natalie Williams, Indiana, 2003
136 — Lisa Leslie, Los Angeles, 1999
134 — Lisa Leslie, Los Angeles, 2000
Most personal fouls, game
6 — by many
Most personal fouls, one half
6 — by many

DISQUALIFICATIONS

Most seasons leading league
2 — Latasha Byears, Sacramento, 1998;
    Los Angeles, 2001
    Lisa Leslie, Los Angeles, 2000, 2002
1 — Isabelle Fijalkowski, Cleveland, 1997
    Tonya Edwards, Minnesota, 1999
    Natalie Williams, Utah, 2001
    Kayte Christensen, Phoenix, 2003
    Kamila Vodichkova, Seattle, 2003
Most disqualifications, career

28 — Lisa Leslie, Los Angeles, 1997-2003
18 — Latasha Byears, Sacramento, 1997-00;
    Los Angeles, 2001-03
15 — Natalie Williams, Utah, 1999-2002;
    Indiana, 2003

Highest percentage, games disqualified, career
(Minimum 100 games)
13.7 — Lisa Leslie, Los Angeles, 1997-2003
    (28/205)
9.8 — Natalie Williams, Utah, 1999-2002;
    Indiana, 2003 (15/153)
9.7 — Latasha Byears, Sacramento, 1997-00;
    Los Angeles, 2001-03 (18/185)

Lowest percentage, games disqualified, career
(Minimum 100 games)
0.00 — by many

Most consecutive games without disqualification,
career
220 — Andrea Stinson, Charlotte, June 22,
    1997-August 25, 2003 (current)
217 — Lady Grooms, Utah-Sacramento, June
    21, 1997-August 25, 2003 (current)
184 — Tina Thompson, Houston, August 12,
    1997-August 25, 2003 (current)

Most disqualifications, season
7 — Isabelle Fijalkowski, Cleveland, 1997
    Lisa Leslie, Los Angeles, 2000
    Lisa Leslie, Los Angeles, 2002
6 — Tonya Edwards, Minnesota, 1999
5 — Pam McGee, Sacramento, 1997
    Sue Wicks, New York, 1999
    Tari Phillips, Portland-New York, 2000

Fewest minutes, disqualified, game
5 — Sharon Manning, Miami at Detroit,
    July 26, 2000
7 — Rushia Brown, Cleveland vs. Utah, July
    24, 1999
8 — Asjha Jones, Washington at Portland,
    June 28, 2002
    LaTonya Johnson, Utah vs. Los
    Angeles, August 9, 2002

STEALS

Most seasons leading league
2 — Teresa Weatherspoon, New York,
    1997-98
1 — Yolanda Griffith, Sacramento, 1999
    Sheryl Swoopes, Houston, 2000
    Debbie Black, Miami, 2001
    Tamika Catchings, Indiana, 2002
    Sheryl Swoopes, Houston, 2003

Most steals, career
453 — Teresa Weatherspoon, New York,
    1997-2003
407 — Sheryl Swoopes, Houston, 1997-2000,
    2002-03
369 — Ticha Penicheiro, Sacramento, 1998-
    2003

Highest average, steals per game, career
(Minimum 100 games)
2.48 — Sheryl Swoopes, Houston, 1997-2000,
    2002-03 (407/164)
2.13 — Ticha Penicheiro, Sacramento, 1998-
    2003 (369/173)
2.06 — Teresa Weatherspoon, New York,
    1997-2003 (453/220)

Most steals, season
100 — Teresa Weatherspoon, New York, 1998
94 — Tamika Catchings, Indiana, 2002
88 — Sheryl Swoopes, Houston, 2002

Highest average, steals per game, season
(qualifiers)
3.33 — Teresa Weatherspoon, New York, 1998
    (100/30)
3.04 — Teresa Weatherspoon, New York, 1997
    (85/28)
2.94 — Tamika Catchings, Indiana, 2002
    (94/32)

Most steals, game
10 — Ticha Penicheiro, Sacramento vs. San
    Antonio, July 10, 2003
9 — Michelle Griffiths, Phoenix at Utah,
    July 27, 1998
    Tamika Catchings, Indiana vs.
    Minnesota, July 26, 2002
8 — By Many

Most steals, one half
7 — Cynthia Cooper, Houston at Charlotte,
    August 11, 1997
    Michelle Brogan, Phoenix at Utah, July
    27, 1998
6 — By many

BLOCKED SHOTS

Most seasons leading league
6 — Margo Dydek, Utah, 1998-2002;
    San Antonio, 2003
1 — Elena Baranova, Utah, 1997

Most blocked shots, career
607 — Margo Dydek, Utah, 1998-2002;
    San Antonio, 2003
466 — Lisa Leslie, Los Angeles, 1997-2003
288 — Vicky Bullett, Charlotte, 1997-99;
    Washington, 2000-02

Highest average, blocked shots per game, career
(Minimum: 100 games)
3.19 — Margo Dydek, Utah, 1998-2002; San
    Antonio, 2003 (607/190)
2.27 — Lisa Leslie, Los Angeles, 1997-2003
    (466/205)
1.55 — Vicky Bullett, Charlotte, 1997-99;
    Washington, 2000-02 (288/186)

Most blocked shots, season
114 — Margo Dydek, Utah, 1998
113 — Margo Dydek, Utah, 2001
107 — Margo Dydek, Utah, 2002

Highest average, blocked shots per game, season
(qualifiers)

3.80 — Margo Dydek, Utah, 1998 (114/30)

3.57 — Margo Dydek, Utah, 2002 (107/30)

3.53 — Margo Dydek, Utah, 2001 (113/32)

Most blocked shots, game

10 — Margo Dydek, Utah vs. Orlando,
June 7, 2001

9 — Margo Dydek, Utah vs. Cleveland,
August 6, 1998

8 — Margo Dydek, Utah at Detroit,
July 17, 1998
Margo Dydek, Utah vs. Sacramento,
August 12, 1998
Margo Dydek, Utah vs. Sacramento,
July 14, 2001
Lauren Jackson, Seattle vs. Utah,
August 11, 2002
Michelle Snow, Houston at San
Antonio, June 20, 2003

Most blocked shots, one half

6 — Margo Dydek, Utah at Detroit, July 17,
1998
Margo Dydek, Utah vs. Cleveland,
August 6, 1998
Margo Dydek, Utah vs. Minnesota,
June 1, 2000
Margo Dydek, Utah vs. Orlando, June
13, 2000
Margo Dydek, Utah vs. Charlotte, June
15, 2000
Margo Dydek, Utah vs. Orlando, June
7, 2001
Margo Dydek, Utah vs. Minnesota,
June 23, 2001
Lauren Jackson, Seattle vs. Utah,
August 11, 2002
Margo Dydek, San Antonio vs.
Houston, August 1, 2003

5 — by many

TURNOVERS

Most turnovers, career

679 — Lisa Leslie, Los Angeles, 1997-2003

577 — Teresa Weatherspoon, New York,
1997-2003

547 — Margo Dydek, Utah, 1998-2002; San
Antonio, 2003

Most turnovers, season

135 — Ticha Penicheiro, Sacramento, 1999

125 — Nikki McCray, Washington, 1998

122 — Chantel Tremitiere, Sacramento, 1997

Most turnovers, game

11 — Michelle Edwards, Cleveland vs.
Sacramento, August 2, 1997
Chamique Holdsclaw, Washington vs.
Utah, July 8, 1999

Betty Lennox, Minnesota at Houston,
August 9, 2000

10 — Nikki McCray, Washington vs. New
York, July 5, 1998 (ot)

9 — By Many

TEAM OFFENSE

SCORING

Highest average, points per game, season

77.3 — Houston, 2000 (2,475/32)

76.6 — Los Angeles, 2002 (2,452/32)

76.5 — Los Angeles, 1999 (2,449/32)

Lowest average, points per game, season

56.9 — Seattle, 2000 (1,822/32)

57.2 — Miami, 2000 (1,831/32)

60.0 — Seattle, 2001 (1,921/32)

Most points, game

111 — Detroit vs. Indiana, June 18, 2000

110 — Houston at Washington,
August 17, 1998

108 — Sacramento vs. Detroit, July 1, 2000

Fewest points, game

34 — Washington at Cleveland,
May 31, 2001

35 — Miami vs. Cleveland, June 24, 2001

36 — Seattle vs. Cleveland, June 14, 2001
Washington vs. Miami, August 8, 2001

Most points, both teams, game

204 — Sacramento (108) vs. Detroit (96),
July 1, 2000

202 — Orlando (103) vs. Cleveland (99),
June 8, 2002 (3 ot)

198 — Utah (104) vs. Detroit (94),
July 6, 1999 (2 ot)

Fewest points, both teams, game

78 — Washington (36) vs. Miami (42),
August 8, 2001

86 — Seattle (38) at Charlotte (48), July 7, 2001

89 — Miami (35) vs. Cleveland (54),
June 24, 2001
Miami (41) vs. Charlotte (48),
August 14, 2001

Largest margin of victory, game

45 — Houston (110) at Washington (65),
August 17, 1998

43 — New York (88) vs. Washington (45),
August 13, 1998

41 — Seattle (89) vs. Phoenix (48),
July 19, 2002

BY HALF

Most points, first half

56 — Detroit vs. San Antonio, July 1, 2003

55 — Los Angeles vs. Utah, August 4, 2002
Los Angeles at Connecticut,
May 24, 2003
Cleveland vs. Washington,

July 26, 2003
54 — Los Angeles vs. Sacramento,
August 22, 1997
Houston vs. Indiana, July 6, 2001
Fewest points, first half
8 — Detroit at Houston, July 6, 2002
11 — Minnesota vs. Houston,
June 30, 2001
12 — Miami vs. Cleveland, June 24, 2001
Charlotte at Cleveland, July 21, 2001
Most points, both teams, first half
106 — Cleveland (53) at Detroit (53),
June 15, 1998
103 — Detroit (56) vs. San Antonio (47),
July 1, 2003
99 — Utah (50) vs. Los Angeles (49),
June 23, 1997
Fewest points, both teams, first half
26 — Detroit (8) at Houston (18),
July 6, 2002
31 — Miami (15) vs. Charlotte (16),
August 14, 2001
33 — Washington (16) vs. Los Angeles (17),
August 14, 1999
Miami (12) vs. Cleveland (21),
June 24, 2001
Minnesota (11) vs. Houston (22),
June 30, 2001
Largest lead at halftime
31 — Houston vs. Miami, June 15, 2000
(led 44-13; won 77-53)
Sacramento at Minnesota,
July 3, 2001 (led 46-15; won 91-52)
28 — Cleveland vs. Phoenix, July 31, 1997
(led 43-15; won 79-67)
Phoenix vs. Washington,
August 4, 1998 (led 48-20; won 88-59)
Cleveland vs. Charlotte,
July 10, 1999 (led 47-19; won 82-56)
Houston vs. Indiana, July 6, 2001
(led 54-26; won 79-64)
26 — By many
Largest deficit at halftime overcome to win game
18 — Utah at Phoenix, August 20, 1999
(trailed 38-20; won 70-62)
17 — Los Angeles at San Antonio, June 26,
2003 (trailed 41-24; won 67-58)
15 — Detroit at Cleveland, June 27, 1998
(trailed 36-51; won 84-73)
New York vs. Indiana, June 30, 2000
(trailed 25-40; won 72-70)
New York at Connecticut, August 12,
2003 (trailed 36-21; won 74-73)
Most points, second half
66 — Detroit vs. Indiana, June 18, 2000
63 — Washington vs. Utah, July 19, 1998
60 — Houston at Washington,

August 17, 1998
Utah vs. Sacramento, June 26, 2000
Fewest points, second half
9 — Seattle vs. Cleveland, June 14, 2001
14 — Seattle at Phoenix, August 15, 2003
15 — Washington at Seattle, July 3, 2001
Most points, both teams, second half
115 — Washington (63) vs. Utah (52),
July 19, 1998
111 — Utah (60) vs. Sacramento (51),
June 26, 2000
108 — Sacramento (56) vs. Detroit (52),
July 1, 2000
Fewest points, both teams, second half
35 — Washington (16) vs. Miami (19),
August 8, 2001
37 — Utah (17) vs. Houston (20),
June 30, 1998
Miami (18) vs. Cleveland (19),
July 7, 2000
Washington (15) at Seattle (22),
July 3, 2001
Miami (18) at Cleveland (19),
July 25, 2001
39 — Charlotte (18) at Washington (21),
July 29, 2001
Charlotte (18) vs. New York (21),
August 24, 2003

OVERTIME

Most points, overtime period
19 — Los Angeles vs. Minnesota,
July 8, 2001
18 — Indiana vs. Phoenix, July 1, 2001
Detroit at Connecticut,
June 22, 2003
17 — New York at Orlando, July 29, 1999
Orlando vs. Cleveland, June 8, 2002
Fewest points, overtime period
0 — Miami at Cleveland, July 25, 2001
1 — Detroit at Utah, July 6, 1999
2 — By many
Most points, both teams, overtime period
33 — Los Angeles (19) vs. Minnesota (14),
July 8, 2001
30 — Orlando (17) vs. Cleveland (13),
June 8, 2002
28 — Indiana (18) vs. Phoenix (10),
July 1, 2001
Fewest points, both teams, overtime period
4 — Seattle (2) vs. Washington (2),
July 3, 2001
Miami (0) at Cleveland (4),
July 25, 2001
7 — Indiana (2) vs. Seattle (5),
June 4, 2001
8 — Many times

Largest margin of victory, overtime period
11 — Miami (74) at Charlotte (63),
  June 3, 2000
10 — Utah (104) vs. Detroit (94),
  July 6, 1999
  Seattle (69) vs. Los Angeles (59),
  June 13, 2000
  Seattle (78) vs. Minnesota (68),
  June 4, 2002
9 — By many

FIELD GOAL PERCENTAGE
Highest field-goal percentage, season
.470 — Houston, 2000 (891/1,894)
.468 — Cleveland, 1998 (804/1,719)
.459 — Washington, 2000 (832/1,813)
Lowest field-goal percentage, season
.365 — Miami, 2000 (647/1,774)
.371 — Minnesota, 2001 (671/1,810)
.373 — Phoenix, 1997 (660/1,768)
Highest field-goal percentage, game
.636 — Phoenix vs. Seattle,
  August 3, 2000 (28/44)
.632 — Cleveland at Washington,
  July 21, 1999 (36/57)
.625 — Charlotte at Washington,
  August 19, 1998 (40/64)
Lowest field-goal percentage, game
.182 — Miami vs. Cleveland,
  June 24, 2001 (10/55)
.196 — Washington vs. Miami,
  August 8, 2001 (10/51)
.200 — Minnesota vs. Houston,
  July 23, 2001 (11/55)
Highest field-goal percentage, both teams, game
.576 — Cleveland (.611) vs. Detroit (.547),
  June 16, 2000 (68/118)
.563 — Cleveland (.593) at Los Angeles
  (.538), July 23, 1997 (67/119)
.556 — Sacramento (.586) vs. Utah (.530),
  August 14, 1999 (69/124)
Lowest field-goal percentage, both teams, game
.245 — Washington (.196) vs. Miami (.294),
  August 8, 2001 (25/102)
.252 — Minnesota (.200) vs. Houston (.300),
  July 23, 2001 (29/115)
.268 — New York (.250) at Washington
  (.288), August 11, 1999 (ot) (33/123)

FIELD GOALS
Most field goals per game, season
28.6 — Los Angeles, 2001 (916/32)
28.4 — Los Angeles, 1997 (794/28)
27.8 — Houston, 2000 (891/32)
  Los Angeles, 2002 (891/32)
Fewest field goals per game, season
20.2 — Miami, 2000 (647/32)
20.8 — Seattle, 2000 (667/32)

21.0 — Minnesota, 2001 (671/32)
Most field goals, game
41 — Houston at Washington,
  August 17, 1998
40 — Charlotte at Washington,
  August 19, 1998
  Utah vs. Detroit, July 6, 1999 (2 ot)
39 — New York at Phoenix, June 21, 2001
  Los Angeles at Detroit, June 26, 2001 (ot)
Fewest field goals, game
10 — Miami vs. Seattle, July 10, 2000
  Miami vs. Cleveland, June 24, 2001
  Washington vs. Miami, August 8, 2001
11 — Minnesota vs. Houston, July 23, 2001
12 — Portland at New York, July 5, 2000
Most field goals, both teams, game
70 — Utah (40) vs. Detroit (30),
  July 6, 1999 (2 ot)
69 — Cleveland (38) at Detroit (31),
  June 15, 1998
  Utah (35) at Sacramento (34),
  August 14, 1999
  Sacramento (36) vs. Detroit (33),
  July 1, 2000
68 — Utah (35) vs. Charlotte (33),
  June 25, 1998
  Detroit (35) at Cleveland (33),
  June 16, 2000
  Orlando (35) vs. Cleveland (33),
  June 8, 2002 (3 ot)
Fewest field goals, both teams, game
23 — Miami (10) vs. Seattle (13),
  July 10, 2000
25 — Washington (10) vs. Miami (15),
  August 8, 2001
29 — Minnesota (11) vs. Houston (18),
  July 23, 2001
Most field goals, one half
23 — Houston at Washington,
  August 17, 1998
  New York at Phoenix, June 21, 2001
  Portland at Utah, June 25, 2002
22 — By many

FIELD GOAL ATTEMPTS
Most field-goal attempts per game, season
64.4 — Washington, 2003 (2,191/34)
63.9 — Los Angeles, 1999 (2,044/32)
63.8 — Los Angeles, 1998 (1,914/30)
Fewest field-goal attempts per game, season
54.4 — Seattle, 2000 (1,740/32)
  New York, 2002 (1,740/32)
55.31 — Cleveland, 2001 (1,770/32)
55.32 — Charlotte, 2003 (1,881/34)
Most field-goal attempts, game
94 — Detroit vs. Washington,
  July 10, 1999 (2 ot)
93 — Phoenix at Los Angeles,

July 15, 2003 (2 ot)
    91 — Seattle vs. Washington,
        July 3, 2001 (4 ot)
Regulation Game:
    84 — Sacramento at Los Angeles,
        August 22, 1997
        Connecticut vs. Los Angeles,
        May 24, 2003
Fewest field-goal attempts, game
    36 — Portland vs. Miami, August 1, 2000
        Minnesota at Miami, May 28, 2002
    39 — Washington at Cleveland,
        June 3, 2000
        New York vs. Miami, June 2, 2002
    40 — Minnesota vs. Portland, July 10, 2002
Most field-goal attempts, both teams, game
    169 — Utah (87) vs. Detroit (82),
        July 6, 1999 (2 ot)
        Phoenix (93) at Los Angeles (76),
        July 15, 2003 (2 ot)
    165 — Seattle (91) vs. Washington (74),
        July 3, 2001 (4 ot)
    162 — Washington (84) at Sacramento (78),
        June 25, 2002 (2 ot)
Regulation Game:
    156 — Connecticut (84) vs. Los Angeles
        (72), May 24, 2003
Fewest field-goal attempts, both teams, game
    84 — Miami (41) vs. Seattle (43),
        July 10, 2000
    89 — New York (39) at Miami (50),
        June 2, 2002
    90 — Portland (36) vs. Miami (54),
        August 1, 2000
        Seattle (42) at Charlotte (48),
        July 7, 2001
Most field-goal attempts, one half
    49 — Sacramento at Los Angeles,
        August 22, 1997
    48 — Washington vs. Utah, July 19, 1998

THREE-POINT FIELD-GOAL PERCENTAGE

Highest three-point field-goal percentage, season
    .400 — Charlotte, 2002 (211/527)
    .387 — Detroit, 2003 (125/323)
    .385 — Sacramento, 2001 (163/423)
Lowest three-point field-goal percentage, season
    .260 — Sacramento, 1998 (72/277)
    .264 — Washington, 1998 (114/432)
    .269 — Los Angeles, 1997 (65/242)
Most three-point field goals, none missed, game
    9 — New York at Phoenix, June 21, 2001
    3 — Cleveland vs. Sacramento,
        August 2, 1997
    2 — Utah vs. Charlotte, June 8, 2002
Most three-point field goal attempts, none made,

game
    17 — New York at Phoenix, July 7, 1997
    16 — Washington at New York,
        August 13, 1998
        Washington vs. Miami, August 8, 2001
    13 — Charlotte vs. Cleveland, June 5, 2000
        New York vs. Cleveland, August 4, 2001

THREE-POINT FIELD GOALS

Most three-point field goals per game, season
    6.6 — Charlotte, 2002 (211/32)
    6.4 — Minnesota, 2000 (204/32)
    6.3 — Minnesota, 1999 (200/32)
Fewest three-point field goals per game, season
    2.3 — Cleveland, 1997 (65/28)
        Los Angeles, 1997 (65/28)
    2.38 — Detroit, 2000 (76/32)
    2.40 — Sacramento, 1998 (72/30)
Most three-point field goals, game
    14 — Minnesota at Utah, June 26, 1999
        Sacramento at Minnesota,
        July 3, 2001
    13 — Orlando at Sacramento,
        July 27, 2000
        Seattle vs. Los Angeles, July 11, 2002
        Charlotte at Detroit, July 3, 2003
        Indiana at Washington,
        July 29, 2003 (ot)
    12 — By many
Fewest three-point field goals, game
    0 — By many
Most three-point field goals, both teams, game
    22 — Connecticut (12) vs. Indiana (10),
        June 26, 2003 (2 ot)
    21 — Minnesota (11) vs. Sacramento (10),
        June 29, 1999
    20 — Orlando (13) at Sacramento (7),
        July 27, 2000
Fewest three-point field goals, both teams, game
    0 — Washington vs. Miami,
        August 8, 2001
    1 — Cleveland (0) vs. New York (1),
        July 14, 1997
        Sacramento (0) vs. Phoenix (1),
        July 21, 1997
        Utah (0) at Phoenix (1),
        May 30, 2001
        Miami (0) vs. Detroit (1),
        June 12, 2001 (ot)
        Miami (0) vs. Cleveland (1),
        June 24, 2001
        Utah (0) vs. Seattle (1), June 25, 2001
        Cleveland (0) at Indiana (1),
        August 23, 2003
    2 — By many
Most three-point field goals, one half
    9 — Houston at New York, July 8, 1998

Washington vs. Utah, July 19, 1998
Seattle vs. Los Angeles, July 11, 2002
8 — By many

THREE-POINT FIELD GOAL ATTEMPTS

Most three-point field goal attempts per game, season
  18.8 — Minnesota, 1999 (603/32)
  17.8 — Minnesota, 2000 (571/32)
  17.7 — Indiana, 2003 (600/34)
Fewest three-point field goal attempts per game, season
  6.3 — Cleveland, 1997 (177/28)
  7.6 — Utah, 2001 (244/32)
  7.7 — Utah, 2002 (247/32)
Most three-point field goal attempts, game
  30 — Houston at Utah, June 30, 1998 (2 ot)
       Orlando at Sacramento, July 27, 2000
       Portland vs. Los Angeles, July 28, 2001
       Indiana at Washington, July 29, 2003 (ot)
  29 — Phoenix at Orlando, June 21, 1999
       Washington vs. Los Angeles, July 14, 2001
       Minnesota vs. Los Angeles, May 28, 2003
  28 — By many
Fewest three-point field goal attempts, game
  1 — Los Angeles at New York, August 5, 1997
      New York vs. Detroit, July 6, 1998
      Sacramento at Washington, July 26, 1998
      Utah at Detroit, August 7, 2001
  2 — By many
Most three-point field goal attempts, both teams, game
  50 — Connecticut (27) vs. Indiana (23), June 26, 2003 (2 ot)
  49 — Houston (30) at Utah (19), June 30, 1998 (2 ot)
  48 — Orlando (30) at Sacramento (18), July 27, 2000
Fewest three-point field goal attempts, both teams, game
  8 — Miami (2) vs. Detroit (6), June 12, 2001 (ot)
  9 — Cleveland (3) vs. New York (6), July 14, 1997
  10 — Los Angeles (5) vs. New York (5), August 20, 1997
       Utah (2) at Sacramento (8), July 12, 2001
Most three-point field goal attempts, one half
  23 — Washington vs. Utah, July 19, 1998
  20 — Houston vs. Cleveland, July 29, 1997
       Minnesota at Cleveland, July 12, 1999

FREE THROW PERCENTAGE

Highest free-throw percentage, season
  .822 — Houston, 2000 (521/634)
  .818 — Houston, 1999 (509/622)
  .802 — Houston, 1998 (518/646)
Lowest free-throw percentage, season
  .645 — Washington, 1998 (400/620)
  .661 — Washington, 2001 (333/504)
  .663 — Minnesota, 2002 (383/578)
Most free throws made, no misses, game
  27 — Portland vs. Los Angeles, July 28, 2001
       Los Angeles vs. Phoenix, July 24, 2003
  21 — Washington at New York, August 8, 2002
  20 — Los Angeles at Minnesota, May 28, 2003
       Minnesota vs. Phoenix, August 4, 2003
Lowest free-throw percentage, game
  .000 — Washington at Detroit, August 25, 2003 (0/1)
  .167 — Phoenix vs. Houston, August 14, 2001 (1/6)
  .200 — Minnesota at Portland, July 14, 2000 (1/5)
Highest free-throw percentage, both teams, game
  1.000 — Cleveland (1.000) vs. Orlando (1.000), June 22, 1999 (15/15)
          Cleveland (1.000) vs. Washington (1.000), May 31, 2001 (11/11)
  .958 — Washington (1.000) vs. Charlotte (.875), July 12, 1999 (23/24)
          Washington (1.000) vs. Charlotte (.933), June 30, 2002 (23/24)
          Orlando (1.000) at Houston (.941), August 3, 2002 (23/24)
  .947 — Houston (1.000) vs. Phoenix (.875), July 31, 1999 (18/19)
Lowest free-throw percentage, both teams, game
  .423 — Utah (.389) vs. Los Angeles (.500), August 13, 2001 (ot) (11/26)
  .435 — Minnesota (.200) at Portland (.500), July 14, 2000 (10/23)
  .448 — Washington (.313) vs. Portland (.615), August 3, 2001 (13/29)

FREE THROWS MADE

Most free throws made per game, season
  20.1 — Utah, 2002 (643/32)
  19.0 — Utah, 2000 (609/32)
  18.4 — Detroit, 2003 (624/34)
Fewest free throws made per game, season
  10.4 — Washington, 2001 (333/32)
  10.5 — New York, 2001 (336/32)
  10.6 — Minnesota, 1999 (339/32)

Most free throws made, game
42 — Utah vs. Los Angeles, June 23, 1997
40 — Los Angeles vs. Washington,
August 3, 1998
Detroit vs. Indiana, June 18, 2000
Detroit vs. San Antonio, July 1, 2003
38 — Miami vs. Seattle, July 10, 2000
Fewest free throws made, game
0 — Washington vs. Charlotte,
July 7, 2003
Washington at Detroit,
August 25, 2003
1 — Minnesota at Portland, July 14, 2000
Miami at Seattle, July 30, 2000
Phoenix vs. Houston,
August 14, 2001
Indiana at Houston, July 8, 2003
Sacramento at Seattle,
August 25, 2003
2 — By many
Most free throws made, both teams, game
61 — Los Angeles (33) vs. Houston (28),
June 20, 2000
Sacramento (34) vs. Detroit (27),
July 1, 2000
Detroit (40) vs. San Antonio (21),
July 1, 2003
60 — Utah (42) vs. Los Angeles (18),
June 23, 1997
Minnesota (37) at Los Angeles (23),
July 8, 2001 (ot)
59 — Detroit (40) vs. Indiana (19),
June 18, 2000
Fewest free throws made, both teams, game
7 — Indiana (1) at Houston (6),
July 8, 2003
8 — Washington (0) vs. Charlotte (8),
July 7, 2003
9 — New York (3) vs. Cleveland (6),
August 8, 2000
Most free throws made, one half
30 — Los Angeles vs. Washington,
August 3, 1998
28 — Utah vs. Los Angeles, June 23, 1997

FREE THROW ATTEMPTS
Most free throw attempts per game, season
26.5 — Sacramento, 1999 (847/32)
26.4 — Utah, 2002 (844/32)
25.9 — Detroit, 2003 (882/34)
Fewest free throw attempts per game, season
14.66 — Miami, 2001 (469/32)
14.69 — Minnesota, 1999 (470/32)
14.9 — Washington, 2003 (507/34)
Most free throw attempts, game
56 — Utah vs. Los Angeles, June 23, 1997

55 — Miami vs. Seattle, July 10, 2000
54 — Detroit vs. Indiana, June 18, 2000
Fewest free throw attempts, game
0 — Washington vs. Charlotte,
July 7, 2003
1 — Miami at Seattle, July 30, 2000
Washington at Detroit,
August 25, 2003
2 — Sacramento at Phoenix,
July 20, 1998
Phoenix at Washington, July 9, 2002
Washington vs. Connecticut,
June 24, 2003
Indiana at Houston, July 8, 2003
Most free throw attempts, both teams, game
88 — Detroit (54) vs. Indiana (34),
June 18, 2000
87 — Phoenix (47) vs. San Antonio (40),
August 22, 2003
80 — Utah (56) vs. Los Angeles (24),
June 23, 1997
Fewest free throw attempts, both teams, game
9 — Washington (0) vs. Charlotte (9),
July 7, 2003
10 — New York (4) vs. Cleveland (6),
August 8, 2000
11 — Cleveland (4) vs. Washington (7),
May 31, 2001
Indiana (2) at Houston (9),
July 8, 2003
Most free throw attempts, one half
39 — Los Angeles vs. Washington,
August 3, 1998
Miami vs. Seattle, July 10, 2000
38 — Sacramento at Detroit, July 4, 1999

REBOUNDS
Most rebounds per game, season
36.2 — Detroit, 2003 (1,230/34)
35.9 — Detroit, 1998 (1,077/30)
35.7 — Los Angeles, 2002 (1,143/32)
Fewest rebounds per game, season
24.8 — Seattle, 2000 (793/32)
27.16 — Miami, 2002 (869/32)
27.19 — Minnesota, 2000 (870/32)
New York, 2002 (870/32)
Most rebounds, game
54 — Utah vs. Detroit, July 6, 1999 (2 ot)
51 — Houston at Utah, June 30, 1998 (2 ot)
Houston vs. Orlando, August 3, 2001
Washington at Sacramento,
June 25, 2002 (2 ot)
50 — Los Angeles vs. Houston,
July 16, 1997
Los Angeles at Sacramento,
July 27, 1997
Washington at Seattle,
July 3, 2001 (4 ot)

Fewest rebounds, game
    13 — Miami at Orlando, August 11, 2001
    14 — New York at Charlotte, July 30, 1999
         Detroit vs. Utah, August 7, 2001
    15 — Seattle at Sacramento, August 9, 2000

Most rebounds, both teams, game
    95 — Washington (50) at Seattle (45),
         July 3, 2001 (4 ot)
    94 — Houston (51) at Utah (43),
         June 30, 1998 (2 ot)
    93 — Detroit (48) at Connecticut (45),
         June 22, 2003 (ot)

Regulation Game:
    89 — Sacramento (48) at Washington (41),
         June 5, 2001
         Connecticut (46) vs. Los Angeles
         (43), May 24, 2003

Fewest rebounds, both teams, game
    40 — New York (14) at Charlotte (26),
         July 30, 1999
    41 — Miami (13) at Orlando (28),
         August 11, 2001
         Houston (19) vs. Indiana (22),
         July 8, 2003
    42 — Miami (20) at Phoenix (22),
         July 4, 2001
         Detroit (18) at Cleveland (24),
         August 8, 2001
         Phoenix (19) vs. Sacramento (23),
         July 27, 2002
         Washington (20) vs. Indiana (22),
         July 24, 2003

Most rebounds, one half
    33 — Los Angeles vs. Houston,
         July 16, 1997
    31 — Connecticut vs. Los Angeles,
         May 24, 2003

OFFENSIVE REBOUNDS

Most offensive rebounds per game, season
    12.9 — Sacramento, 1999 (412/32)
    12.2 — Sacramento, 1997 (341/28)
    12.1 — Sacramento, 2000 (388/32)

Fewest offensive rebounds per game, season
    7.6 — Cleveland, 1998 (227/30)
    7.8 — Houston, 2003 (266/34)
    8.0 — New York, 2001 (255/32)

Most offensive rebounds, game
    23 — Cleveland vs. Los Angeles,
         August 7, 1997 (2 ot)
    22 — Phoenix at Cleveland, July 31, 1997
         Houston vs. Orlando, August 3, 2001
         Minnesota vs. Utah, May 25, 2002 (ot)
         Detroit vs. Charlotte, July 3, 2003
    21 — By many

Fewest offensive rebounds, game
    1 — Cleveland vs. Utah, July 25, 1998
      New York at Charlotte, July 30, 1999

Houston at New York, August 8, 1999
Washington at Cleveland, June 3, 2000
Indiana at Portland, July 28, 2000
Portland vs. Miami, August 1, 2000
Houston at Phoenix, August 7, 2000
Indiana at Detroit, June 23, 2001
New York at Detroit, July 18, 2001
Miami at Orlando, August 11, 2001
New York vs. Seattle, July 2, 2002
New York vs. Sacramento,
      June 17, 2003
    2 — By many

Most offensive rebounds, both teams, game
    37 — Sacramento (19) at Washington (18),
         June 5, 2001
    35 — Sacramento (19) at Utah (16),
         June 21, 1997
         Phoenix (19) at New York (16),
         August 2, 1997
         Orlando (19) at Miami (16),
         August 9, 2000 (2 ot)
    33 — Many times

Fewest offensive rebounds, both teams, game
    5 — New York (2) at Minnesota (3),
        July 6, 2001
    7 — Houston (2) vs. Indiana (5),
        July 8, 2003
    8 — New York (1) at Charlotte (7),
        July 30, 1999
        Seattle (2) at Houston (6),
        July 25, 2000

Most offensive rebounds, one half
    16 — Phoenix at Cleveland, July 31, 1997
         Seattle at Utah, June 15, 2002
    14 — By many

DEFENSIVE REBOUNDS

Most defensive rebounds per game, season
    25.4 — Los Angeles, 2002 (814/32)
    25.0 — Detroit, 2003 (851/34)
    24.5 — Los Angeles, 2000 (783/32)

Fewest defensive rebounds per game, season
    16.8 — Seattle, 2000 (537/32)
    17.9 — Miami, 2002 (573/32)
    18.3 — Seattle, 2001 (585/32)

Most defensive rebounds, game
    40 — Utah vs. Detroit, July 6, 1999 (2 ot)
    39 — San Antonio vs. Connecticut,
         June 1, 2003
    38 — Los Angeles at Sacramento,
         July 27, 1997

Fewest defensive rebounds, game
    8 — Washington at New York,
        August 13, 1998
        Miami vs. Minnesota, May 28, 2002
    10 — Seattle at Sacramento,
         August 9, 2000

Charlotte at Orlando, June 9, 2001
Sacramento at Miami, July 7, 2001
Detroit vs. Utah, August 7, 2001
Phoenix at Minnesota,
August 4, 2003
11 — By many
Most defensive rebounds, both teams, game
67 — Los Angeles (35) vs. Phoenix (32),
July 15, 2003 (2 ot)
66 — Washington (35) at Los Angeles (31),
June 27, 2002
San Antonio (39) vs. Connecticut
(27), June 1, 2003
Detroit (36) at Connecticut (30),
June 22, 2003 (ot)
65 — Houston (33) at Utah (32),
June 30, 1998 (2 ot)
Utah (40) vs. Detroit (25),
July 6, 1999 (2 ot)
Fewest defensive rebounds, both teams, game
23 — Seattle (11) at Cleveland (12),
July 5, 2002
25 — New York (11) at Indiana (14),
July 19, 2002
Cleveland (11) at Charlotte (14),
June 25, 2003
27 — Many times
Most defensive rebounds, one half
22 — Los Angeles vs. New York,
July 20, 2000
Los Angeles vs. Portland,
July 24, 2002
San Antonio vs. Connecticut,
June 1, 2003
21 — Many times

ASSISTS

Most assists per game, season
19.2 — Cleveland, 1998 (575/30)
18.6 — Los Angeles, 2001 (596/32)
18.3 — Los Angeles, 2000 (586/32)
Fewest assists per game, season
12.2 — Seattle, 2000 (390/32)
12.6 — San Antonio, 2003 (428/34)
12.9 — Seattle, 2001 (412/32)
Most assists, game
32 — New York at Phoenix, June 21, 2001
31 — Charlotte at Washington,
August 19, 1998
Cleveland vs. Detroit, June 16, 2000
30 — Charlotte vs. Orlando, July 17, 2002
Fewest assists, game
3 — Cleveland at Detroit, July 28, 2001
Minnesota at Seattle, August 8, 2003
4 — Houston at Phoenix, June 24, 1998
5 — By many
Most assists, both teams, game
57 — Cleveland (31) vs. Detroit (26),
June 16, 2000

53 — Cleveland (28) vs. Washington (25),
August 15, 1998
51 — Washington (28) at Charlotte (23),
July 26, 2000
Fewest assists, both teams, game
11 — Seattle (5) at Miami (6), July 10, 2000
12 — Portland (5) at Houston (7),
June 24, 2001
14 — Charlotte (6) at Detroit (8),
July 6, 2001
Cleveland (3) at Detroit (11),
July 28, 2001
Most assists, one half
18 — Los Angeles vs. Utah, July 7, 2002
17 — By many

PERSONAL FOULS

Most personal fouls per game, season
23.8 — Portland, 2000 (761/32)
23.13 — Utah, 1999 (740/32)
23.07 — Washington, 1998 (692/30)
Fewest personal fouls per game, season
14.4 — Houston, 2003 (490/34)
14.6 — Houston, 2002 (467/32)
15.9 — Houston, 2001 (509/32)
Most personal fouls, game
39 — Indiana at Detroit, June 18, 2000
36 — Los Angeles at Utah, June 23, 1997
Washington at Los Angeles,
August 3, 1998
San Antonio at Phoenix,
August 22, 2003
35 — By many
Fewest personal fouls, game
6 — Seattle vs. Miami, July 30, 2000
7 — Houston vs. Minnesota, June 15, 2002
Houston vs. Seattle, May 22, 2003
Detroit vs. Washington,
August 25, 2003
8 — By many
Most personal fouls, both teams, game
70 — Indiana (39) at Detroit (31),
June 18, 2000
66 — Orlando (34) vs. Cleveland (32),
June 8, 2002 (3 ot)
64 — Phoenix (35) at Sacramento (29),
June 12, 1999
Minnesota (34) at Utah (30),
July 28, 2001 (ot)
San Antonio (36) at Phoenix (28),
August 22, 2003
Fewest personal fouls, both teams, game
20 — Orlando (8) vs. Washington (12),
August 15, 1999
21 — Washington (10) vs. Cleveland (11),
August 9, 2000
Phoenix (9) at Los Angeles (12),
July 5, 2001
Houston (8) at Orlando (13),

177

July 18, 2001
Los Angeles (10) vs. Indiana (11),
August 6, 2001
Washington (9) vs. Detroit (12),
July 18, 2002
22 — Houston (7) vs. Minnesota (15),
June 15, 2002
Charlotte (10) at Washington (12),
July 7, 2003

Most personal fouls, one half
25 — Indiana at Detroit, June 18, 2000
Portland at Miami, July 19, 2000
24 — Detroit vs. Sacramento, July 4, 1999
Miami vs. Minnesota, June 10, 2000

DISQUALIFICATIONS

Most disqualifications per game, season
0.56 — Los Angeles, 2002 (18/32)
0.50 — Sacramento, 1997 (14/28)
0.44 — Detroit, 1999 (14/32)

Fewest disqualifications per game, season
0.00 — Charlotte, 1997 (0/28)
0.03 — Cleveland, 2001 (1/32)
Houston, 2002 (1/32)
Phoenix, 2002 (1/32)
Portland, 2002 (1/32)
Detroit, 2002 (1/32)

Most disqualifications, game
3 — Washington at Los Angeles,
August 3, 1998
Phoenix at Sacramento,
June 12, 1999
Charlotte vs. Miami, June 3, 2000 (ot)
Los Angeles at Seattle, June 13, 2000 (ot)
Portland at Minnesota, July 23, 2000
2 — By many

Most disqualifications, both teams, game
5 — Phoenix (3) at Sacramento (2),
June 12, 1999
4 — Detroit (2) vs. Washington (2),
July 10, 1999 (2 ot)
Los Angeles (3) at Seattle (1),
June 13, 2000 (ot)
Orlando (2) vs. Cleveland (2),
June 8, 2002 (3 ot)
3 — By many

STEALS

Most steals per game, season
12.3 — Phoenix, 1997 (343/28)
11.11 — Houston, 1997 (311/28)
11.07 — Houston, 1998 (332/30)

Fewest steals per game, season
5.5 — San Antonio, 2003 (187/34)
6.26 — Washington, 2003 (213/34)
6.28 — Detroit, 2002 (201/32)

Most steals, game
21 — Houston vs. Washington,

June 29, 1998
20 — Los Angeles at Cleveland,
July 3, 1997
Phoenix vs. Utah, August 17, 1997 (ot)
Detroit vs. Indiana, June 18, 2000
Indiana vs. Detroit, July 6, 2003
19 — Sacramento at Orlando,
July 17, 1999
Washington vs. Cleveland,
August 9, 2000
Houston vs. Minnesota, August 9, 2000

Fewest steals, game
0 — Minnesota at Charlotte, July 21, 1999
Indiana at New York, June 2, 2001
Charlotte at Miami, August 14, 2001
San Antonio vs. Connecticut,
June 1, 2003
1 — By many

Most steals, both teams, game
34 — Los Angeles (20) at Cleveland (14),
July 3, 1997
32 — New York (18) at Phoenix (14),
July 7, 1997
31 — Phoenix (20) vs. Utah (11),
August 17, 1997 (ot)
Houston (16) vs. Cleveland (15),
August 1, 1998 (ot)
Sacramento (16) at Indiana (15),
June 21, 2000
Houston (19) vs. Minnesota (12),
August 9, 2000

Fewest steals, both teams, game
2 — Minnesota (0) at Charlotte (2),
July 21, 1999
Indiana (0) at New York (2),
June 2, 2001
4 — Charlotte (0) at Miami (4),
August 14, 2001
5 — Los Angeles (2) at Utah (3),
August 16, 1997
Seattle (2) at Charlotte (3),
July 7, 2001
San Antonio (1) at Washington (4),
June 10, 2003
San Antonio (1) vs. Washington (4),
July 19, 2003

Most steals, one half
14 — New York at Phoenix, July 7, 1997
13 — Phoenix vs. Los Angeles,
August 24, 1997
Orlando vs. Los Angeles, June 1, 2001
Phoenix at Minnesota, June 27, 2003
Phoenix vs. San Antonio,
August 22, 2003

BLOCKED SHOTS

Most blocked shots per game, season

5.7 — Utah, 1998 (170/30)
5.6 — Utah, 2002 (178/32)
5.0 — Los Angeles, 2002 (161/32)
Fewest blocked shots per game, season
2.0 — Minnesota, 2000 (63/32)
2.1 — Sacramento, 1997 (60/28)
2.4 — Houston, 1997 (67/28)
Most blocked shots, game
13 — Los Angeles at Phoenix, July 11, 2001
12 — Utah vs. Sacramento, July 14, 2001
       Seattle vs. Utah, August 11, 2002
11 — By many
Fewest blocked shots, game
0 — By many: Last:
       Cleveland vs. Charlotte,
       August 25, 2003
Most blocked shots, both teams, game
21 — Los Angeles (13) at Phoenix (8),
       July 11, 2001
18 — Utah (11) vs. Sacramento (7),
       August 12, 1998
       Indiana (10) at Utah (8),
       July 29, 2000
       Utah (10) vs. Portland (8),
       June 2, 2001
       Sacramento (9) vs. Portland (9),
       June 16, 2001 (ot)
       Seattle (12) vs. Utah (6),
       August 11, 2002
       Houston (10) at San Antonio (8),
       June 20, 2003
17 — Many times
Fewest blocked shots, both teams, game
0 — Houston vs. Cleveland,
       August 21, 1997
       Minnesota vs. Cleveland,
       May 31, 2000
       Miami vs. Portland,
       June 29, 2001 (ot)
       Portland vs. Houston, June 23, 2002
       Portland vs. Houston, July 19, 2002
       Houston vs. Connecticut,
       May 30, 2003
1 — By many
Most blocked shots, one half
10 — Los Angeles at Phoenix, July 11, 2001
9 — Detroit at Charlotte, July 10, 2003
       Los Angeles at Phoenix, June 21, 2003

TURNOVERS

Most turnovers per game, season
20.8 — Washington, 1998 (625/30)
20.1 — Sacramento, 1997 (562/28)
19.1 — New York, 1997 (536/28)
Fewest turnovers per game, season
12.75 — Charlotte, 2002 (408/32)
12.76 — Connecticut, 2003 (434/34)

13.2 — Houston, 2003 (450/34)
Most turnovers, game
33 — Utah at New York, July 17, 1997
       Utah at Phoenix, August 17, 1997 (ot)
       Washington at Houston, June 29, 1998
30 — New York vs. Phoenix,
       August 11, 1998 (ot)
       Cleveland at New York, June 10, 1999
       Utah at Los Angeles, June 28, 1999
Fewest turnovers, game
4 — Orlando vs. Washington,
       August 15, 1999
5 — Houston vs. Washington,
       June 27, 2001
       Miami vs. Indiana, June 30, 2002
       Indiana vs. Utah, July 10, 2002
       Connecticut at San Antonio,
       June 1, 2003
       Seattle at Charlotte, June 30, 2003
6 — By many
Most turnovers, both teams, game
56 — Houston (28) vs. New York (28),
       June 26, 1997 (ot)
53 — New York (30) vs. Phoenix (23),
       August 11, 1998 (ot)
51 — Washington (33) at Houston (18),
       June 29, 1998
Fewest turnovers, both teams, game
12 — Houston (5) vs. Washington (7),
       June 27, 2001
14 — Houston (6) at Los Angeles (8),
       August 11, 2001
15 — Seattle (7) vs. Minnesota (8),
       June 14, 2003
       Seattle (6) vs. Houston (9),
       August 23, 2003
Most turnovers, one half
20 — Cleveland at New York, June 10, 1999

TEAM DEFENSE

POINTS

Fewest points allowed per game, season
55.9 — Cleveland, 2001 (1,788/32)
59.1 — Houston, 2002 (1,892/32)
59.3 — Miami, 2001 (1,898/32)
Most points allowed per game, season
80.5 — Washington, 1998 (2,415/30)
77.1 — Utah, 1999 (2,467/32)
76.5 — Utah, 1998 (2,294/30)

FIELD GOAL PERCENTAGE

Lowest opponents' field-goal percentage, season
.375 — Houston, 2002 (705/1,880)
.381 — Cleveland, 2001 (664/1,745)
.390 — Los Angeles, 2002 (796/2,040)
Highest opponents' field-goal percentage, season
.468 — Washington, 1998 (876/1,870)

.462 — Detroit, 2001 (848/1,837)
.460 — Detroit, 2000 (905/1,967)

TURNOVERS

Most opponents' turnovers per game, season
21.4 — Phoenix, 1997 (599/28)
20.4 — New York, 1997 (570/28)
19.4 — Phoenix, 1998 (581/30)
Fewest opponents' turnovers per game, season
12.2 — Utah, 2001 (390/32)
12.5 — San Antonio, 2003 (424/34)
12.7 — Houston, 2003 (430/34)

TEAM MISCELLANEOUS

GAME WON AND LOST

Highest winning percentage, season
.900 — Houston, 1998 (27-3)
.875 — Los Angeles, 2000 (28-4)
Los Angeles, 2001 (28-4)
.844 — Houston, 2000 (27-5)
Lowest winning percentage, season
.100 — Washington, 1998 (3-27)
.188 — Seattle, 2000 (6-26)
.219 — Cleveland, 1999 (7-25)
Most consecutive games won
18 — Los Angeles, June 26-August 11, 2001
15 — Houston, June 27-July 30, 1998
12 — Los Angeles, June 17-July 9, 2000
Los Angeles, July 14-August 8, 2000
Los Angeles, August 9, 2002-
June 14, 2003
Most consecutive games won, one season
18 — Los Angeles, June 26-August 11, 2001
15 — Houston, June 27-July 30, 1998
12 — Los Angeles, June 17-July 9, 2000
Los Angeles, July 14-August 8, 2000
Most consecutive games won, start of season
9 — Los Angeles, May 28-June 19, 2001
Los Angeles, May 24-June 14, 2003
7 — New York, June 21-July 5, 1997
Houston, June 10-25, 1999
5 — Houston, June 13-21, 1998
Most consecutive games won, end of season
7 — Charlotte, July 31-August 14, 2001
5 — Houston, August 1-9, 2000
Los Angeles, August 14-25, 2003
4 — By many
Most consecutive game lost
14 — Portland, July 27, 2001-June 3, 2002
13 — Detroit, May 30-June 28, 2002
11 — Washington, July 13-August 7, 1998
Washington, June 13-July 9, 2003
Most consecutive game lost, one season
13 — Detroit, May 30-June 28, 2002
11 — Washington, July 13-August 7, 1998
Washington, June 13-July 9, 2003
10 — Indiana, June 18-July 8, 2000

Portland, July 27-August 14, 2001
Most consecutive game lost, start of season
13 — Detroit, May 30-June 28, 2002
7 — Cleveland, June 10-25, 1999
5 — Charlotte, June 1-10, 2000
Indiana, May 31-June 9, 2001
Miami, May 28-June 9, 2002
Most consecutive game lost, end of season
10 — Portland, July 27-August 14, 2001
6 — Cleveland, August 3-13, 2002
5 — Washington, August 12-19, 1998
Charlotte, August 9-20, 1999
Highest winning percentage, home games, season
1.000 — Los Angeles, 2001 (16-0)
.938 — Houston, 1999 (15-1)
Los Angeles, 2000 (15-1)
.933 — Houston, 1998 (14-1)
Lowest winning percentage, home games, season
.176 — Washington, 2003 (3-14)
.200 — Washington, 1998 (3-12)
.250 — Seattle, 2000 (4-12)
Cleveland, 2002 (4-12)
Most consecutive home games won
28 — Los Angeles, July 14, 2000-
June 27, 2002
16 — Cleveland, July 22, 2000-
July 25, 2001
13 — Houston, July 1, 1999-May 29, 2000
Charlotte, July 14, 2001-July 1, 2002
Houston, May 29-August 6, 2002
Indiana, July 22, 2002-July 10, 2003
Most consecutive home games won, start of season
16 — Los Angeles, June 5-August 11, 2001
(entire season)
12 — Cleveland, May 31-July 25, 2001
10 — Houston, June 13-July 30, 1998
Most consecutive home games won, end of season
16 — Los Angeles, June 5-August 11, 2001
(entire season)
12 — Houston, July 1-August 18, 1999
10 — New York, June 28-August 8, 2000
Most consecutive home games lost
10 — Cleveland, June 30-May 27, 2003
9 — Charlotte, August 20, 1999-
July 1, 2000
8 — Washington, August 12, 1998-
July 2, 1999
Indiana, June 10-July 8, 2000
Most consecutive home games lost, start of season
8 — Charlotte, June 3-July 1, 2000
5 — Washington, June 10-July 2, 1999
Portland, May 31-June 20, 2000
Detroit, June 2-28, 2002
4 — Cleveland, June 12-25, 1999
Charlotte, June 2-24, 2001
Most consecutive home games lost, end of season
9 — Cleveland, June 30-August 13, 2002

6 — Washington, July 20-August 9, 2002
5 — Portland, July 28-August 14, 2001
Highest winning percentage, road games, season
.867 — Houston, 1998 (13-2)
.813 — Houston, 2000 (13-3)
        Los Angeles, 2000 (13-3)
        Los Angeles, 2002 (13-3)
.765 — Los Angeles, 2003 (13-4)
Lowest winning percentage, road games, season
.000 — Washington, 1998 (0-15)
.063 — Phoenix, 2002 (1-15)
.118 — Phoenix, 2003 (2-15)
Most consecutive road games won
12 — Los Angeles, June 17-August 8, 2000
11 — Los Angeles, July 20, 2002-
        June 14, 2003
9 — Houston, June 30-August 7, 1998
Most consecutive road games won, start of season
6 — Los Angeles, May 24-June 14, 2003
5 — New York, June 21-July 5, 1997
        Houston, June 10-30, 1999
        Los Angeles, May 28-June 16, 2001
4 — By many
Most consecutive road games won, end of season
6 — Cleveland, August 1-17, 1998
5 — Los Angeles, July 20-August 13, 2002
4 — Charlotte, August 3-14, 2001
Most consecutive road games lost
21 — Phoenix, July 29, 2001-August 6, 2002
17 — Detroit, July 24, 2001-July 18, 2002
16 — Washington, June 11, 1998-
        June 12, 1999
Most consecutive road games lost, start of season
15 — Washington, June 11-August 15, 1998
        Phoenix, May 29-August 6, 2002
12 — Detroit, May 30-July 18, 2002
10 — Sacramento, June 6-July 7, 2002
Most consecutive road games lost, end of season
15 — Washington, June 11-August 15, 1998
9 — Seattle, July 6-August 9, 2000
8 — Orlando, July 12-August 9, 2000
        Seattle, July 7-August 11, 2001

OVERTIME GAMES

Most overtime games, season
7 — Miami, 2001
5 — New York, 1999
        Detroit, 2001
        Portland, 2001
4 — By many
Most consecutive overtime games, season
3 — New York, July 24-29, 1999
2 — By many
Most overtime games won, season
4 — Portland, 2001
        Detroit, 2003
3 — New York, 1997

Cleveland, 2000
Detroit, 2001
Miami, 2001
Utah, 2001
Orlando, 2002
Most overtime games won, no losses, season
4 — Detroit, 2003
3 — New York, 1997
        Utah, 2001
        Orlando, 2002
2 — By many
Most consecutive overtime games won
6 — New York, June 26, 1997-
        July 18, 1999
        Utah-San Antonio, June 27, 2001-
        August 20, 2003 (current)
4 — Portland, June 4-29, 2001
        Washington, July 10, 1999-
        June 25, 2002
        Miami, July 27, 2001-July 7, 2002
        Detroit, June 17-August 23, 2003
        (current)
Most overtime games lost, season
4 — Portland, 2000
        Miami, 2001
        Cleveland, 2002
3 — New York, 1999
        Orlando, 2000
        Charlotte, 2001
2 — By many
Most overtime games lost, no wins, season
4 — Portland, 2000
        Cleveland, 2002
3 — Orlando, 2000
        Charlotte, 2001
2 — By many
Most consecutive overtime games lost
5 — Orlando, June 7, 2000-July 27, 2001
        New York, August 11, 1999-
        August 24, 2003 (current)
4 — Portland, May 31-August 6, 2000
        Sacramento, July 2, 1997-
        June 16, 2001
        Cleveland, June 1-July 28, 2002
3 — By many
Most overtime periods, game
4 — Washington (72) at Seattle (69),
        July 3, 2001
3 — Orlando (103) vs. Cleveland (99),
        June 8, 2002
2 — By many

181

*Denotes number of overtime periods

POINTS

	FG	FT	PTS
Katie Smith, Minnesota at Los Angeles, July 8, 2001	*11	23	46
Cynthia Cooper, Houston at Sacramento, July 25, 1997	14	9	44
Cynthia Cooper, Houston vs. Utah, August 16, 1999	11	17	42
Katie Smith, Minnesota at Detroit, June 17, 2001	13	19	40
Cynthia Cooper, Houston at Charlotte, August 11, 1997	15	4	39
Jennifer Gillom, Phoenix at Cleveland, August 10, 1998	**13	9	36
Cynthia Cooper, Houston vs. Los Angeles, June 22, 1999	11	13	36
Katie Smith, Minnesota at Phoenix, August 1, 2001	11	16	36
Shannon Johnson, Orlando vs. Cleveland, June 8, 2002	***11	11	35
Cynthia Cooper, Houston at Los Angeles, August 1, 1997	9	11	34
Cynthia Cooper, Houston vs. Phoenix, August 7, 1997	10	10	34
Ruthie Bolton-Holifield, Sacramento vs. Utah, August 8, 1997	11	7	34
Ruthie Bolton-Holifield, Sacramento vs. Cleveland, August 12, 1997	12	4	34
Cynthia Cooper, Houston vs. Sacramento, July 3, 1998	6	22	34
Cynthia Cooper, Houston at Detroit, August 7, 1998	13	4	34
Ruthie Bolton-Holifield, Sacramento at Washington, July 2, 1999	9	13	34
Katie Smith, Minnesota vs. Cleveland, May 31, 2000	9	10	34
Katie Smith, Minnesota vs. Connecticut, July 10, 2003	12	5	34
Chamique Holdsclaw, Washington vs. Indiana, July 24, 2003	10	13	34
Lauren Jackson, Seattle vs. Los Angeles, August 6, 2003	17	0	34

FIELD GOALS

	FG	FGA
Lauren Jackson, Seattle vs. Los Angeles, August 6, 2003	17	23
Cynthia Cooper, Houston at Charlotte, August 11, 1997	15	19
Cynthia Cooper, Houston at Sacramento, July 25, 1997	14	21
Wendy Palmer, Utah vs. Chicago, July 8, 1998	14	20
Latasha Byears, Sacramento at Phoenix, July 20, 1998	14	20
Linda Burgess, Sacramento vs. Utah, August 15, 1998	14	20
Tangela Smith, Sacramento vs. Utah, August 14, 1999	14	23
Wendy Palmer, Detroit at Seattle, June 28, 2000	14	21
Lisa Leslie, Los Angeles vs. Seattle, August 1, 2002	14	17
Margo Dydek, Utah vs. Houston, June 30, 1998	**13	25
Cynthia Cooper, Houston at Detroit, August 7, 1998	13	21
Jennifer Gillom, Phoenix at Cleveland, August 10, 1998	**13	27
Sandy Brondello, Detroit at Utah, July 6, 1999	**13	28
Sheryl Swoopes, Houston at Utah, July 16, 1999	*13	21
Brandy Reed, Phoenix at Houston, June 3, 2000	13	18
Tari Phillips, New York vs. Indiana, June 30, 2000	13	19
Sheryl Swoopes, Houston vs. Charlotte, July 7, 2000	13	22
Yolanda Griffith, Sacramento vs. Utah, July 15, 2000	13	19
Tina Thompson, Houston at Detroit, June 2, 2001	13	18
Katie Smith, Minnesota at Detroit, June 17, 2001	13	19
Tamika Catchings, Indiana vs. Orlando, August 7, 2002	13	20

FREE THROWS

	FT	FTA
Cynthia Cooper, Houston vs. Sacramento, July 3, 1998	22	24
Katie Smith, Minnesota at Los Angeles, July 8, 2001	*18	19
Cynthia Cooper, Houston vs. Utah, August 16, 1999	17	18
Katie Smith, Minnesota at Utah, July 28, 2001	*16	18
Swin Cash, Detroit vs. Miami, June 28, 2002	*15	21

Lisa Leslie, Los Angeles vs. Utah, August 4, 2002	15	19
Katie Smith, Minnesota at Miami, June 10, 2000	14	16
Lisa Leslie, Los Angeles vs. Minnesota, July 15, 2000	14	14
Tina Thompson, Houston vs. Minnesota, August 9, 2000	14	16
Tamika Catchings, Indiana vs. New York, June 8, 2002	14	16
Sheryl Swoopes, Houston at Los Angeles, June 30, 2002	14	15
Lauren Jackson, Seattle vs. San Antonio, August 12, 2003	14	16

REBOUNDS

	REB
Chamique Holdsclaw, Washington at Charlotte, May 23, 2003	24
Lisa Leslie, Los Angeles vs. New York, June 19, 1998	21
Cindy Brown, Detroit at Utah, August 10, 1998	21
Chamique Holdsclaw, Washington at Sacramento, June 25, 2002	**21
Lisa Leslie, Los Angeles vs. Orlando, July 22, 2002	21
Cheryl Ford, Detroit at Connecticut, June 22, 2003	*21
Yolanda Griffith, Sacramento at Washington, June 5, 2001	20
Natalie Williams, Utah at Sacramento, June 22, 2002	20
Lauren Jackson, Seattle vs. Charlotte, July 31, 2003	20
Yolanda Griffith, Sacramento vs. Cleveland, June 17, 1999	19
Yolanda Griffith, Sacramento at Utah, June 19, 1999	19
Yolanda Griffith, Sacramento vs. New York, July 22, 1999	19
Natalie Williams, Utah vs. Cleveland, July 26, 2000	19
Yolanda Griffith, Sacramento vs. Houston, August 6, 2000	19

ASSISTS

	AST
Ticha Penicheiro, Sacramento at Cleveland, July 29, 1998	16
Ticha Penicheiro, Sacramento vs. Los Angeles, August 3, 2002	16
Ticha Penicheiro, Sacramento at Cleveland, July 15, 2003	15
Penny Toler, Los Angeles vs. Utah, August 14, 1998	14
Ticha Penicheiro, Sacramento vs. Minnesota, June 22, 1999	14
Ticha Penicheiro, Sacramento vs. Detroit, July 1, 2000	14
Ticha Penicheiro, Sacramento vs. Minnesota, August 7, 2001	14
Jennifer Rizzotti, Cleveland vs. New York, June 21, 2002	14
Ticha Penicheiro, Sacramento vs. Phoenix, May 30, 2003	14
Teresa Weatherspoon, New York at Los Angeles, July 21, 1998	13
Ticha Penicheiro, Sacramento vs. Washington, August 7, 1998	13
Ticha Penicheiro, Sacramento at Minnesota, June 29, 1999	13
Ticha Penicheiro, Sacramento at Houston, August 2, 1999	13
Teresa Weatherspoon, New York at Houston, May 29, 2000	13
Ticha Penicheiro, Sacramento at Utah, June 26, 2000	13
Dawn Staley, Charlotte vs. Washington, July 26, 2000	13
Ticha Penicheiro, Sacramento vs. Orlando, July 27, 2000	13
Ticha Penicheiro, Sacramento vs. Indiana, July 30, 2002	13
Nikki Teasley, Los Angeles at New York, June 14, 2003	13

STEALS

Ticha Penicheiro, Sacramento vs. San Antonio, July 10, 2003	10
Michelle Griffiths, Phoenix at Utah, July 27, 1998	9
Tamika Catchings, Indiana vs. Minnesota, July 26, 2002	9
Janice Lawrence Braxton, Cleveland vs. Los Angeles, July 3, 1997	8
Michele Timms, Phoenix at Utah, July 3, 1997	8
Teresa Weatherspoon, New York vs. Charlotte, July 10, 1997	8
Cynthia Cooper, Houston at Charlotte, August 11, 1997	8
Michele Timms, Phoenix vs. Utah, August 17, 1997	*8
Yolanda Griffith, Sacramento vs. Washington, July 29, 1999	8
Chamique Holdsclaw, Washington vs. Indiana, July 20, 2000	8
Rita Williams, Indiana at Miami, August 10, 2001	*8

BLOCKED SHOTS

	BLK
Margo Dydek, Utah vs. Orlando, June 7, 2001	10
Margo Dydek, Utah vs. Cleveland, August 6, 1998	9
Margo Dydek, Utah at Detroit, July 17, 1998	8
Margo Dydek, Utah vs. Sacramento, August 12, 1998	8
Margo Dydek, Utah vs. Sacramento, July 14, 2001	8
Lauren Jackson, Seattle vs. Utah, August 11, 2002	8
Michelle Snow, Houston at San Antonio, June 20, 2003	8
Margo Dydek, Utah at Phoenix, August 8, 1998	7
Margo Dydek, Utah vs. Phoenix, August 13, 1999	7
Margo Dydek, Utah vs. Minnesota, June 1, 2000	7
Margo Dydek, Utah vs. Orlando, June 13, 2000	7
Margo Dydek, Utah vs. Charlotte, June 15, 2000	7
Lisa Leslie, Los Angeles at Utah, August 13, 2001	*7
Margo Dydek, Utah at Sacramento, July 12, 2001	7
Lisa Leslie, Los Angeles vs. New York, May 25, 2002	7
Margo Dydek, Utah vs. Detroit, July 8, 2002	7
Margo Dydek, Utah at Detroit, July 23, 2002	7
Margo Dydek, San Antonio at Minnesota, July 16, 2003	7
Margo Dydek, San Antonio vs. Houston, August 1, 2003	7

ALL-TIME POST-SEASON STANDINGS

OVERALL

TEAM	W-L	PCT
Los Angeles Sparks	21 - 9	.700
Detroit Shock	6 - 3	.667
Houston Comets	18 - 9	.667
New York Liberty	15 - 14	.517
Connecticut Sun	2 - 2	.500
Sacramento Monarchs	6 - 8	.429
Washington Mystics	3 - 4	.429
Cleveland Rockers	6 - 9	.400
Indiana Fever	1 - 2	.333
Miami Sol	1 - 2	.333
Minnesota Lynx	1 - 2	.333
Orlando Miracle	1 - 2	.333
Phoenix Mercury	3 - 6	.333
Charlotte Sting	6 - 13	.316
Utah Starzz	2 - 5	.286
Seattle Storm	0 - 2	.000
Totals	92 - 92	.500

HOME

TEAM	W-L	PCT
Indiana Fever	1 - 0	1.000
Minnesota Lynx	1 - 0	1.000
Orlando Miracle	1 - 0	1.000
Los Angeles Sparks	14 - 2	.875
Houston Comets	13 - 4	.765
Detroit Shock	4 - 2	.667
Washington Mystics	2 - 1	.667
Cleveland Rockers	5 - 3	.625
New York Liberty	10 - 6	.625
Sacramento Monarchs	3 - 2	.600
Connecticut Sun	1 - 1	.500
Phoenix Mercury	2 - 2	.500
Utah Starzz	1 - 2	.333
Charlotte Sting	2 - 5	.286
Miami Sol	0 - 1	.000
Seattle Storm	0 - 1	.000
Totals	60 - 32	.652

ROAD

TEAM	W-L	PCT
Detroit Shock	2 - 1	.667
Connecticut Sun	1 - 1	.500
Houston Comets	5 - 5	.500
Los Angeles Sparks	7 - 7	.500
Miami Sol	1 - 1	.500
New York Liberty	5 - 8	.385
Charlotte Sting	4 - 8	.333
Sacramento Monarchs	3 - 6	.333
Utah Starzz	1 - 3	.250
Washington Mystics	1 - 3	.250
Phoenix Mercury	1 - 4	.200
Cleveland Rockers	1 - 6	.143
Indiana Fever	0 - 2	.000
Minnesota Lynx	0 - 2	.000
Orlando Miracle	0 - 2	.000
Seattle Storm	0 - 1	.000
Totals	32 - 60	.348

SERIES

TEAM	W-L	PCT
Los Angeles Sparks	10 - 3	.769
Detroit Shock	3 - 1	.750
Houston Comets	9 - 3	.750
New York Liberty	7 - 5	.583
Connecticut Sun	1 - 1	.500
Charlotte Sting	3 - 6	.333
Orlando Miracle	0 - 1	.333
Sacramento Monarchs	2 - 4	.333
Utah Starzz	1 - 2	.333
Washington Mystics	1 - 2	.333
Phoenix Mercury	1 - 3	.250
Cleveland Rockers	1 - 4	.200
Indiana Fever	0 - 1	.000
Miami Sol	0 - 1	.000
Minnesota Lynx	0 - 1	.000
Seattle Storm	0 - 1	.000
Totals	39 - 39	.500

WNBA ALL-TIME PLAYOFF LEADERS

GAMES

Lisa Leslie	30
Mwadi Mabika	30
DeLisha Milton	30
Tamecka Dixon	29
Vickie Johnson	29
Teresa Weatherspoon	29
Sue Wicks	29
Five tied	27

MINUTES

Lisa Leslie	1,103
Mwadi Mabika	1,050
DeLisha Milton	1,031
Tina Thompson	1,003
Teresa Weatherspoon	970
Vickie Johnson	952
Tamecka Dixon	885
Sheryl Swoopes	875
Crystal Robinson	837
Janeth Arcain	816

FIELD GOALS MADE

Lisa Leslie	235
Mwadi Mabika	147
DeLisha Milton	147
Sheryl Swoopes	142
Cynthia Cooper	136
Vickie Johnson	132
Tamecka Dixon	129
Tina Thompson	120
Tari Phillips	119
Tamika Whitmore	115

185

RECORDS Playoffs

FIELD GOAL ATTEMPTS

Lisa Leslie 458
Mwadi Mabika 360
Sheryl Swoopes 343
Cynthia Cooper 327
DeLisha Milton 307
VVickie Johnson 304
Tina Thompson 299
Tamecka Dixon 287
Andrea Stinson 250
Tari Phillips 248

FIELD GOAL PERCENTAGE
(MINIMUM: 30 FG)

	FG	FGA	PCT
Natalie Williams	33	63	.524
Latasha Byears	37	71	.521
Lisa Leslie	235	458	.513
Yolanda Griffith	80	157	.510
Tammy Sutton-Brown	34	67	.507
Taj McWilliams-Franklin	42	85	.494
Tamika Whitmore	115	233	.494
Rushia Brown	36	73	.493
Rhonda Mapp	36	74	.486
Tari Phillips	119	248	.480

FREE THROWS MADE

Cynthia Cooper 138
Lisa Leslie 127
Sheryl Swoopes 98
Yolanda Griffith 78
DeLisha Milton 68
Tina Thompson 67
Tari Phillips 59
Tamika Whitmore 55
Tamecka Dixon 53
Vickie Johnson 49

FREE THROW ATTEMPTS

Lisa Leslie 171
Cynthia Cooper 163
Sheryl Swoopes 113
Yolanda Griffith 97
Tari Phillips 92
DeLisha Milton 89
Tamika Whitmore 85
Tina Thompson 83
Chasity Melvin 63
Vickie Johnson 61

FREE THROW PERCENTAGE
(MINIMUM: 20 FT)

	FT	FTA	PCT
Crystal Robinson	24	25	.960
Ruthie Bolton	23	24	.958
Tamecka Dixon	53	58	.914
Becky Hammon	30	33	.909
Taj McWilliams-Franklin ...	23	26	.885
Charlotte Smith-Taylor ...	21	24	.875
Sheryl Swoopes	98	113	.867
Kedra Holland-Corn	24	28	.857
Cynthia Cooper	138	163	.847
Andrea Stinson	48	58	.828

THREE-POINT FIELD GOALS

Mwadi Mabika 50
Crystal Robinson 48
Tina Thompson 37
Cynthia Cooper 33
Kedra Holland-Corn 31
Vickie Johnson 30
Becky Hammon 26
Dawn Staley 26
Allison Feaster 22
DeLisha Milton 22

THREE-POINT FIELD GOAL
ATTEMPTS

Mwadi Mabika 148
Crystal Robinson 126
Cynthia Cooper 104
Tina Thompson 102
Vickie Johnson 82
Allison Feaster 76
Becky Hammon 75
Kedra Holland-Corn 69
Sheryl Swoopes 69
Nikki Teasley 67

THREE-POINT PERCENTAGE
(MINIMUM: 10 FG3)

	3FG	3GA	PCT
DeLisha Milton	22	42	.524
Kedra Holland-Corn	31	69	.449
Deanna Nolan	21	47	.447
Dawn Staley	26	60	.433
Tamecka Dixon	17	40	.425
Jennifer Gillom	10	24	.417
Lisa Leslie	13	34	.382
Crystal Robinson	48	126	.381
Vickie Johnson	30	82	.366
Ticha Penicheiro	12	33	.364

OFFENSIVE REBOUNDS

Lisa Leslie 76
Tina Thompson 59
DeLisha Milton 58
Tari Phillips 47
Yolanda Griffith 43
Sue Wicks 41
Mwadi Mabika 40
Sheryl Swoopes 36
Latasha Byears 35
Vickie Johnson 34

DEFENSIVE REBOUNDS

Lisa Leslie 212

Mwadi Mabika 136
Tina Thompson 133
DeLisha Milton 127
Sheryl Swoopes 114
Tari Phillips 102
Vickie Johnson 91
Yolanda Griffith 78
Andrea Stinson 78
Teresa Weatherspoon 78

TOTAL REBOUNDS
Lisa Leslie 288
Tina Thompson 192
DeLisha Milton 185
Mwadi Mabika 176
Sheryl Swoopes 150
Tari Phillips 149
Vickie Johnson 125
Yolanda Griffith 121
Andrea Stinson 109
Janeth Arcain 104
Sue Wicks 104

ASSISTS
Teresa Weatherspoon 185
Nikki Teasley 118
Vickie Johnson 98
Tamecka Dixon 96
Cynthia Cooper 94
Sheryl Swoopes 82
Mwadi Mabika 78
DeLisha Milton 75
Dawn Staley 75
Andrea Stinson 75

STEALS
Sheryl Swoopes 56
Mwadi Mabika 48
DeLisha Milton 47
Teresa Weatherspoon 44
Tamecka Dixon 41
Lisa Leslie 40
Andrea Stinson 37
Janeth Arcain 34
Vickie Johnson 32
Crystal Robinson 31

PERSONAL FOULS
DeLisha Milton 110
Lisa Leslie 109
Mwadi Mabika 105
Tina Thompson 93
Teresa Weatherspoon 83
Sue Wicks 78

Tamecka Dixon 72
Tari Phillips 69
Tamika Whitmore 69
Crystal Robinson 64

DISQUALIFICATIONS
DeLisha Milton 3
Mwadi Mabika 2
Tari Phillips 2
Natalie Williams 2
14 tied 1

BLOCKED SHOTS
Lisa Leslie 87
DeLisha Milton 40
Vicky Bullett 26
Tina Thompson 26
Sue Wicks 26
Margo Dydek 24
Ruth Riley 24
Tamika Whitmore 19
Tari Phillips 16
Tammy Sutton-Brown 15
Sheryl Swoopes 15

POINTS
Lisa Leslie 610
Cynthia Cooper 443
Sheryl Swoopes 403
Mwadi Mabika 387
DeLisha Milton 384
Tina Thompson 344
Vickie Johnson 343
Tamecka Dixon 328
Tari Phillips 297
Tamika Whitmore 287

SCORING AVERAGE
(MINIMUM: 10 GAMES)

	G	FG	FT	PTS	AVG
Cynthia Cooper ..	19	136	138	443	23.3
Lisa Leslie	30	235	127	610	20.3
Yolanda Griffith ..	13	80	78	238	18.3
Sheryl Swoopes ..	25	142	98	403	16.1
Andrea Stinson ...	19	108	48	282	14.8
Tari Phillips	21	119	59	297	14.1
Mwadi Mabika ...	30	147	43	387	12.9
DeLisha Milton ...	30	147	68	384	12.8
Tina Thompson ...	27	120	67	344	12.7
Tangela Smith	14	67	28	167	11.9

TOP 25 CAREER PLAYOFF SCORERS

NAME	YRS	G	MIN	FG	FGA	PCT	FT	FTA	PCT	REB	AST	STL	PF	BLK	PTS	AVG
Lisa Leslie	5	30	1103	235	458	.513	127	171	.743	288	74	40	109	87	610	20.3
Cynthia Cooper..........	4	19	723	136	327	.416	138	163	.847	66	94	30	38	13	443	23.3
Sheryl Swoopes..........	6	25	875	142	343	.414	98	113	.867	150	82	56	46	15	403	16.1
Mwadi Mabika...........	5	30	1050	147	360	.408	43	58	.741	176	78	48	105	14	387	12.9
DeLisha Milton	5	30	1031	147	307	.479	68	89	.764	185	75	47	110	40	384	12.8

NAME	YRS	G	MIN	FG	FGA	PCT	FT	FTA	PCT	REB	AST	STL	PF	BLK	PTS	AVG
Tina Thompson 7		27	1003	120	299	.401	67	83	.807	192	39	28	93	26	344	12.7
Vickie Johnson 5		29	952	132	304	.434	49	61	.803	125	98	32	56	5	343	11.8
Tamecka Dixon 5		29	885	129	287	.449	53	58	.914	85	96	41	72	4	328	11.3
Tari Phillips 3		21	673	119	248	.480	59	92	.641	149	28	30	69	16	297	14.1
Tamika Whitmore........4		27	733	115	233	.494	55	85	.647	95	23	14	69	19	287	10.6
Andrea Stinson............6		19	665	108	250	.432	48	58	.828	109	75	37	47	3	282	14.8
Crystal Robinson 4		27	837	98	222	.441	24	25	.960	85	40	31	64	7	268	9.9
Yolanda Griffith..........3		13	459	80	157	.510	78	97	.804	121	16	16	38	13	238	18.3
Janeth Arcain...............7		27	816	91	221	.412	39	48	.812	104	35	34	51	3	230	8.5
Dawn Staley................4		16	594	57	155	.368	37	50	.740	33	75	19	34	2	177	11.1
Becky Hammon 4		27	487	58	132	.439	30	33	.909	31	38	15	28	0	172	6.4
Teresa Weatherspoon ..5		29	970	63	164	.384	32	43	.744	100	185	44	83	0	169	5.8
Tangela Smith..............4		14	437	67	171	.392	28	41	.683	80	20	15	42	10	167	11.9
Kedra Holland-Corn....4		16	396	50	122	.410	24	28	.857	43	29	23	22	2	155	9.7
Merlakia Jones 4		15	412	62	147	.422	19	23	.826	78	21	8	28	1	151	10.1
Jennifer Gillom............4		15	331	50	131	.382	27	36	.750	59	5	12	35	13	137	9.1
Swin Cash 1		8	289	43	104	.413	42	52	.808	51	35	4	21	5	130	16.3
Allison Feaster.............5		20	452	48	145	.331	11	12	.917	65	26	16	38	5	129	6.5
Chasity Melvin 3		12	368	40	85	.471	47	63	.746	65	22	9	35	9	127	10.6
Ruth Riley 2		11	368	49	125	.392	29	45	.644	65	23	6	38	24	127	11.5

INDIVIDUAL RECORDS

MINUTES

Most minutes, game

50 — Adrienne Goodson, Utah at Houston, August 18, 2002 (2 ot)

48 — Margo Dydek, Utah at Houston, August 18, 2002 (2 ot)
Marie Ferdinand, Utah at Houston, August 18, 2002 (2 ot)
Tina Thompson, Houston vs. Utah, August 18, 2002 (2 ot)

47 — Janeth Arcain, Houston vs. Utah, August 18, 2002 (2 ot)
Sheryl Swoopes, Houston vs. Utah, August 18, 2002 (2 ot)

SCORING

Most points, game

35 — Lisa Leslie, Los Angeles vs. Sacramento, August 27, 2001

31 — Cynthia Cooper, Houston vs. Charlotte, August 28, 1997
Sheryl Swoopes, Houston vs. New York, August 26, 2000 (ot)

30 — Yolanda Griffith, Sacramento vs. Utah, August 19, 2001

Most consecutive games, 20 or more points

7 — Cynthia Cooper, Houston, August 28, 1997-September 1, 1998

5 — Lisa Leslie, Los Angeles, August 27, 2001-August 17, 2002

4 — Cynthia Cooper, Houston, August 17-26, 2000

Lisa Leslie, Los Angeles, August 28-September 5, 2003

Most consecutive games, 10 or more points

30 — Lisa Leslie, Los Angeles, August 24, 1999-September 16, 2003 (current)

19 — Cynthia Cooper, Houston, August 28, 1997-August 26, 2000

12 — Tamecka Dixon, Los Angeles, August 20, 2000-August 24, 2002

Most points, one half

22 — Lisa Leslie, Los Angeles vs. Sacramento, August 27, 2001

20 — Cynthia Cooper, Houston at New York, September 2, 1999
Sheryl Swoopes, Houston vs. Utah, August 20, 2002

Most points, overtime period

7 — Sheryl Swoopes, Houston vs. New York, August 26, 2000

6 — Tina Thompson, Houston vs. Utah, August 18, 2002

FIELD GOALS

Highest field-goal percentage, game
(Minimum: 8 field goals made)

.846 — Tari Phillips, New York vs. Washington, August 24, 2002 (11/13)

.833 — Tamika Whitmore, New York vs. Indiana, August 18, 2002 (10/12)

.769 — Tari Phillips, New York at Washington, August 22, 2002 (10/13)
Deanna Nolan, Detroit vs. Cleveland, September 2, 2003 (10/13)

RECORDS Playoffs

Most field goals, none missed, game
  7 — Taj McWilliams, Orlando vs.
    Cleveland, August 11, 2000
  6 — Tammy Sutton-Brown, Charlotte at
    Cleveland, August 20, 2001
  5 — Yolanda Moore, Houston at Charlotte,
    August 22, 1998
Most field goals, game
  15 — Lisa Leslie, Los Angeles vs.
    Sacramento, August 27, 2001
  12 — Lisa Leslie, Los Angeles vs. Phoenix,
    August 13, 2000
  11 — By many
Most field goals, one half
  9 — Lisa Leslie, Los Angeles vs.
    Sacramento, August 27, 2001
  7 — By many
Most field goal attempts, game
  24 — Cynthia Cooper, Houston at Phoenix,
    August 27, 1998
    Merlakia Jones, Cleveland at Orlando,
    August 11, 2000
  23 — Cynthia Cooper, Houston at
    Los Angeles, August 20, 2000
    Cynthia Cooper, Houston at
    New York, August 24, 2000
  22 — Lisa Leslie, Los Angeles vs.
    Sacramento, August 27, 2001
    Sheryl Swoopes, Houston vs. Utah,
    August 18, 2002 (2 ot)
    Sheryl Swoopes, Houston vs. Utah,
    August 20, 2002
Most field goal attempts, none made, game
  8 — Ticha Penicheiro, Sacramento at
    Los Angeles, August 27, 2001
    Allison Feaster, Charlotte vs.
    Washington, August 17, 2002
  7 — Coquese Washington, Houston vs.
    Los Angeles, August 18, 2001
    Ticha Penicheiro, Sacramento vs.
    Utah, August 19, 2001
    Edna Campbell, Sacramento at
    Los Angeles, August 26, 2001
  6 — By many
Most field goal attempts, one half
  14 — Cynthia Cooper, Houston at Phoenix,
    August 27, 1998
    Adrienne Johnson, Orlando at
    Cleveland, August 13, 2000
    Lisa Leslie, Los Angeles vs.
    Sacramento, August 27, 2001
  13 — By many

THREE POINT FIELD GOALS
Most three-point field goals, none missed, game
  5 — Vickie Johnson, New York vs.
    Washington, August 24, 2002
  4 — Kedra Holland-Corn, Detroit at
    Connecticut, September 5, 2003

  3 — Michele Timms, Phoenix vs.
    Cleveland, August 22, 1998
    Edna Campbell, Sacramento vs.
    Los Angeles, August 24, 2001
    Tamecka Dixon, Los Angeles vs.
    Sacramento, August 27, 2001
Most three-point field goals, game
  7 — Mwadi Mabika, Los Angeles at
    Houston, August 17, 2000
  6 — Deanna Nolan, Detroit vs. Cleveland,
    September 2, 2003
  5 — Ticha Penicheiro, Sacramento at
    Los Angeles, August 26, 2001
    Vickie Johnson, New York vs.
    Washington, August 24, 2002
Most three-point field goals, one half
  4 — Bridget Pettis, Phoenix vs.
    Los Angeles, August 11, 2000
    Mwadi Mabika, Los Angeles at
    Houston, August 17, 2000
    Dawn Staley, Charlotte at New York,
    August 26, 2001
    Stacey Dales-Schuman, Washington
    at Charlotte, August 17, 2002
    Vickie Johnson, New York vs.
    Washington, August 24, 2002
    Deanna Nolan, Detroit vs. Cleveland,
    September 2, 2003
    Deanna Nolan, Detroit vs.
    Connecticut, September 7, 2003
  3 — By many
Most three-point field goal attempts, game
  11 — Mwadi Mabika, Los Angeles at
    Houston, August 17, 2000
  10 — Crystal Robinson, New York at
    Washington, August 22, 2002
    Nikki Teasley, Los Angeles vs. Detroit,
    September 12, 2003
  9 — By Many
Most three-point field goal attempts, none made,
game
  9 — Nikki Teasley, Los Angeles vs.
    Minnesota, August 30, 2003
  6 — Charlotte Smith, Charlotte at
    Washington, August 15, 2002
  5 — by many
Most three-point field goal attempts, one half
  7 — Bridget Pettis, Phoenix vs.
    Los Angeles, August 11, 2000
    Kedra Holland-Corn, Sacramento vs.
    Los Angeles, August 24, 2001
    Stacey Dales-Schuman, Washington
    at Charlotte, August 17, 2002
    Deanna Nolan, Detroit vs. Cleveland,
    August 31, 2003
  6 — By many

FREE THROWS
Most free throws made, none missed, game
  10 — Cynthia Cooper, Houston at
    New York, September 2, 1999

Nykesha Sales, Connecticut vs.
Detroit, September 5, 2003
Yolanda Griffith, Sacramento at
Los Angeles, September 7, 2003
8 — Cynthia Cooper, Houston at Charlotte,
August 22, 1998
Andrea Stinson, Charlotte at
New York, August 29, 1999
Sheryl Swoopes, Houston vs.
Sacramento, August 14, 2000
Lisa Leslie, Los Angeles vs. Houston,
August 20, 2000
Cynthia Cooper, Houston vs.
New York, August 26, 2000 (ot)
Vickie Johnson, New York vs. Miami,
August 21, 2001
7 — Tari Phillips, New York vs.
Washington, August 25, 2002
Andrea Stinson, Charlotte vs.
Connecticut, August 30, 2003

Most free throws made, game
18 — Yolanda Griffith, Sacramento vs. Utah,
August 19, 2001
13 — Cynthia Cooper, Houston vs.
New York, September 5, 1999
11 — Cynthia Cooper, Houston vs.
New York, August 30, 1997
Cynthia Cooper, Houston vs. Phoenix,
August 29, 1998 (ot)
Marie Ferdinand, Utah at Sacramento,
August 19, 2001
Chasity Melvin, Cleveland at Detroit,
September 2, 2003

Most free throws made, one half
10 — Yolanda Griffith, Sacramento vs. Utah,
August 19, 2001
9 — Sheryl Swoopes, Houston vs. Phoenix,
September 1, 1998
Chasity Melvin, Cleveland vs. Detroit,
August 29, 2003
Tamika Williams, Minnesota at
Los Angeles, August 30, 2003

Most free throw attempts, game
24 — Yolanda Griffith, Sacramento vs. Utah,
August 19, 2001
15 — Cynthia Cooper, Houston vs.
New York, August 30, 1997
Cynthia Cooper, Houston vs.
New York, September 5, 1999
14 — Cynthia Cooper, Houston vs. Phoenix,
August 29, 1998 (ot)
Marie Ferdinand, Utah at Sacramento,
August 19, 2001
Natalie Williams, Utah at Houston,
August 18, 2002 (2 ot)
Chasity Melvin, Cleveland at Detroit,
September 2, 2003

Most free throw attempts, one half
13 — Yolanda Griffith, Sacramento vs. Utah,
August 19, 2001

Tamika Williams, Minnesota at Los
Angeles, August 30, 2003
12 — Cynthia Cooper, Houston vs.
New York, August 30, 1997
Natalie Williams, Utah at Houston,
August 18, 2002
Chasity Melvin, Cleveland vs. Detroit,
August 29, 2003

REBOUNDS

Most rebounds, game
18 — Lisa Leslie, Los Angeles vs. Houston,
August 20, 2001
17 — Yolanda Griffith, Sacramento at
Houston, September 2, 2003
16 — Lisa Leslie, Los Angeles vs.
Sacramento, August 27, 2001

Most rebounds, one half
14 — Lisa Leslie, Los Angeles vs.
Sacramento, August 27, 2001
12 — Lisa Leslie, Los Angeles vs. Houston,
August 20, 2001
Cheryl Ford, Detroit vs. Cleveland,
September 2, 2003

Most offensive rebounds, game
8 — Swin Cash, Detroit vs. Connecticut,
September 7, 2003
7 — Yolanda Griffith, Sacramento vs. Utah,
August 19, 2001
Lisa Leslie, Los Angeles vs.
Sacramento, August 27, 2001
Tina Thompson, Houston vs. Utah,
August 18, 2002 (2 ot)
Cheryl Ford, Detroit vs. Los Angeles,
September 12, 2003
6 — By many

Most offensive rebounds, one half
5 — Janeth Arcain, Houston vs. Charlotte,
August 28, 1997
Natalie Williams, Utah vs.
Sacramento, August 17, 2001
Yolanda Griffith, Sacramento vs. Utah,
August 19, 2001
Lisa Leslie, Los Angeles vs.
Sacramento, August 27, 2001
Tamika Catchings, Indiana at
New York, August 18, 2002
Michelle Snow, Houston vs.
Sacramento, September 2, 2003
Swin Cash, Detroit vs. Connecticut,
September 7, 2003
4 — By many

Most defensive rebounds, game
14 — Tina Thompson, Houston vs.
Charlotte, August 24, 1998
13 — Margo Dydek, Utah vs. Houston,
August 16, 2002
Cheryl Ford, Detroit vs. Cleveland,
September 2, 2003
12 — Kym Hampton, New York at Phoenix,
August 28, 1997

Andrea Stinson, Charlotte at Detroit,
August 24, 1999
Lisa Leslie, Los Angeles vs. Houston,
August 20, 2001
Chamique Holdsclaw, Washington vs.
Charlotte, August 15, 2002
Most defensive rebounds, one half
10 — Cheryl Ford, Detroit vs. Cleveland,
September 2, 2003
9 — Lisa Leslie, Los Angeles vs. Houston,
August 20, 2001
Lisa Leslie, Los Angeles vs.
Sacramento, August 27, 2001
Chamique Holdsclaw, Washington at
Charlotte, August 17, 2002

ASSISTS

Most assists, game
12 — Cynthia Cooper, Houston vs.
Los Angeles, August 30, 1999
Jennifer Azzi, Utah at Los Angeles,
August 24, 2002
Teresa Weatherspoon, New York vs.
Washington, August 24, 2002
11 — Teresa Weatherspoon, New York vs.
Charlotte, August 30, 1999
Nikki McCray, Washington vs.
New York, August 12, 2000
Nikki Teasley, Los Angeles at
New York, August 29, 2002
Nikki Teasley, Los Angeles vs.
New York, August 31, 2002
Nikki Teasley, Los Angeles vs. Detroit,
September 12, 2003
10 — By many
Most assists, one half
9 — Teresa Weatherspoon, New York vs.
Washington, August 24, 2002
7 — By many

PERSONAL FOULS

Most personal fouls, game
6 — By many
Most personal fouls, one half
6 — Maria Stepanova, Phoenix at
Cleveland, August 25, 1998
5 — By many
Most minutes played, no personal fouls, game
40 — Cynthia Cooper, Houston vs.
Los Angeles, August 30, 1999
Dawn Staley, Charlotte vs.
Washington, August 17, 2002
39 — Cynthia Cooper, Houston at Phoenix,
August 27, 1998
Annie Burgess, Washington vs.
New York, August 22, 2002
37 — Sheryl Swoopes, Houston vs.
New York, September 5, 1999
Ukari Figgs, Los Angeles vs. Houston,
August 20, 2001

Vickie Johnson, New York vs.
Charlotte, August 26, 2001

DISQUALIFICATIONS

Fewest minutes played, disqualified player, game
9 — Maria Stepanova, Phoenix at
Cleveland, August 25, 1998
14 — Tamecka Dixon, Los Angeles vs.
New York, August 31, 2002
19 — Nadine Malcolm, Indiana vs.
New York, August 16, 2002

STEALS

Most steals, game
6 — Mwadi Mabika, Los Angeles vs.
Sacramento, August 24, 1999
Vickie Johnson, New York
at Charlotte, August 24, 2001
Sheryl Swoopes, Houston vs. Utah,
August 18, 2002 (2 ot)
Tamecka Dixon, Los Angeles vs.
Minnesota, August 30, 2003
5 — By many
Most steals, one half
4 — Suzie McConnell Serio, Cleveland vs.
Phoenix, August 25, 1998
DeLisha Milton, Los Angeles vs.
Sacramento, August 24, 1999
Sheryl Swoopes, Houston vs.
Los Angeles, August 17, 2000
Penny Taylor, Cleveland vs. Charlotte,
August 18, 2001
Tamecka Dixon, Los Angeles
at Houston, August 18, 2001
Lisa Leslie, Los Angeles vs. Seattle,
August 17, 2002
Sheryl Swoopes, Houston vs. Utah,
August 18, 2002 (2 ot)
Tamika Williams, Minnesota vs.
Los Angeles, August 28, 2003
Tamecka Dixon, Los Angeles vs.
Minnesota, August 30, 2003
Sheri Sam, Minnesota at Los Angeles,
September 1, 2003

BLOCKED SHOTS

Most blocked shots, game
7 — Lisa Leslie, Los Angeles vs.
Sacramento, August 27, 2001
Lisa Leslie, Los Angeles vs. Charlotte,
September 1, 2001
Lisa Leslie, Los Angeles at Utah,
August 22, 2002
6 — Lisa Leslie, Los Angeles vs.
Sacramento, August 26, 2001
5 — By Many
Most blocked shots, one half
4 — Vicky Bullett, Washington vs.
New York, August 12, 2000
Lisa Leslie, Los Angeles vs.
Sacramento, August 26, 2001
Lisa Leslie, Los Angeles vs.

Sacramento, August 27, 2001
Lisa Leslie, Los Angeles vs. Charlotte, September 1, 2001
Lisa Leslie, Los Angeles at Utah, August 22, 2002
Lisa Leslie, Los Angeles at Sacramento, September 5, 2003
Lisa Leslie, Los Angeles vs. Sacramento, September 7, 2003
3 — By many

TURNOVERS

Most turnovers, game
    8 — Olympia Scott-Richardson, Indiana at New York, August 20, 2002
       Swin Cash, Detroit at Cleveland, August 29, 2003
    7 — Teresa Weatherspoon, New York at Phoenix, August 28, 1997
       Nikki McCray, Washington vs. New York, August 12, 2000
       Tina Thompson, Houston vs. Los Angeles, August 18, 2001
       Dawn Staley, Charlotte at New York, August 26, 2001
       Nikki Teasley, Los Angeles at New York, August 29, 2002
       Mwadi Mabika, Los Angeles at Minnesota, August 28, 2003
    6 — By many
Most turnovers, one half
    6 — Mwadi Mabika, Los Angeles at Minnesota, August 28, 2003
    5 — By Many

TEAM RECORDS

WON-LOST

Highest won-lost percentage, one postseason
    1.000 — Houston, 1997 (2-0)
       Houston, 2000 (6-0)
       Los Angeles, 2002 (6-0)
    .857 — Los Angeles, 2001 (6-1)
    .800 — Houston, 1998 (4-1)
Most games, one postseason
    9 — Los Angeles, 2003
    8 — Charlotte, 2001
       New York, 2002
       Detroit, 2003
    7 — New York, 2000
       Los Angeles, 2001
Most home games, one postseason
    5 — New York, 2002
       Detroit, 2003
       Los Angeles, 2003
    4 — Houston, 1999
       New York, 2000

       Los Angeles, 2001
       New York, 2001
    3 — By many
Most road games, one postseason
    5 — Charlotte, 2001
    4 — Phoenix, 1998
       Los Angeles, 2003
       Sacramento, 2003
    3 — By many
Most wins, one postseason
    6 — Houston, 2000
       Los Angeles, 2001
       Los Angeles, 2002
       Detroit, 2003
    5 — Los Angeles, 2003
    4 — By many
Most wins at home, one postseason
    5 — Los Angeles, 2003
    4 — New York, 2002
       Detroit, 2003
    3 — By many
Most wins on road, one postseason
    3 — Houston, 2000
       Charlotte, 2001
       Los Angeles, 2001
       Los Angeles, 2002
    2 — New York, 2001
       Sacramento, 2001
       Detroit, 2003
    1 — By many
Most games lost, one postseason
    4 — Charlotte, 2001
       New York, 2002
       Los Angeles, 2003
    3 — Phoenix, 1998
       New York, 1999
       Cleveland, 2000
       New York, 2000
       New York, 2001
       Utah, 2002
       Sacramento, 2003
    2 — By many
Most games lost at home, one postseason
    3 — New York, 2001
    2 — Charlotte, 2001
    1 — By many
Most games lost on road, one postseason
    4 — Los Angeles, 2003
    3 — Phoenix, 1998
       Cleveland, 2000
       New York, 2002
       Sacramento, 2003
    2 — By many
Most consecutive games won
    9 — Los Angeles, 2001-02
    7 — Houston, 1999-00

4 — Houston, 1997-98

Most consecutive games won, one postseason
6 — Houston, 2000
Los Angeles, 2002
3 — By many

Most consecutive games won at home
10 — Los Angeles, 2001-03 (current)
7 — Houston, 1997-99
4 — By many

Most consecutive games won at home,
one postseason
5 — Los Angeles, 2003
4 — New York, 2002
Detroit, 2003
3 — By many

Most consecutive games won on road
6 — Los Angeles, 2001-02
4 — Houston, 1999-00
3 — Charlotte, 2001

Most consecutive games won on road,
one postseason
3 — Houston, 2000
Charlotte, 2001
Los Angeles, 2001
Los Angeles, 2002
2 — New York, 2001
Sacramento, 2001
Detroit, 2003
1 — By many

Most consecutive games lost
6 — Charlotte, 2001-03 (current)
4 — Phoenix, 1998, 2000 (current)
3 — By many

Most consecutive games lost, one postseason
2 — By many

Most consecutive games lost at home
4 — Charlotte, 2001-03 (current)
2 — New York, 2000-01
New York, 2001
Cleveland, 2001, 2003 (current)
Detroit, 1999, 2003 (current)
1 — By many

Most consecutive games lost at home,
one postseason
2 — Charlotte, 2001
New York, 2001
1 — By many

Most consecutive games lost on road
5 — Cleveland, 1998, 2000-01
4 — Los Angeles, 2003 (current)
3 — By many

Most consecutive games lost on road,
one postseason
4 — Los Angeles, 2003
3 — Cleveland, 2000
New York, 2002

2 — By many

SCORING

Most points, game
103 — Los Angeles vs. Utah,
August 24, 2002
101 — Los Angeles vs. Phoenix,
August 13, 2000
96 — New York vs. Washington,
August 24, 2002

Fewest points, game
41 — Phoenix vs. New York,
August 28, 1997
43 — Orlando at Cleveland,
August 15, 2000
New York at Cleveland,
August 17, 2000
44 — New York vs. Charlotte,
August 27, 2001

Most points, both teams, game
180 — Los Angeles (103) vs. Utah (77),
August 24, 2002
177 — Los Angeles (101) vs. Phoenix (76),
August 13, 2000
175 — New York (96) vs. Washington (79),
August 24, 2002

Fewest points, both teams, game
92 — New York (44) vs. Charlotte (48),
August 27, 2001
96 — Cleveland (45) at New York (51),
August 20, 2000
99 — New York (43) at Cleveland (56),
August 17, 2000
Cleveland (46) at Charlotte (53),
August 16, 2001

Largest margin of victory, game
31 — Los Angeles (93) vs. Sacramento (62),
August 27, 2001
29 — Cleveland (72) vs. Orlando (43),
August 15, 2000
28 — Houston (83) vs. Los Angeles (55),
August 29, 1999
Los Angeles (82) vs. Charlotte (54),
September 1, 2001

BY HALF

Most points, first half
50 — New York vs. Washington,
August 24, 2002
49 — Los Angeles at Minnesota,
August 28, 2003
48 — Detroit vs. Connecticut,
September 7, 2003

Fewest points, first half
15 — Orlando at Cleveland,
August 13, 2000
17 — Cleveland at New York,
August 20, 2000

18 — Phoenix vs. New York,
August 28, 1997

Most points, both teams, first half
90 — Detroit (46) at Cleveland (44),
August 29, 2003
89 — New York (50) vs. Washington (39),
August 24, 2002
85 — Detroit (48) vs. Connecticut (37),
September 7, 2003

Fewest points, both teams, first half
41 — Phoenix (18) vs. New York (23),
August 28, 1997
42 — New York (21) vs. Charlotte (21),
August 27, 2001
48 — Charlotte (22) at Detroit (26),
August 24, 1999
Miami (20) at New York (28),
August 19, 2001

Largest lead at halftime
22 — Cleveland vs. Charlotte, August 18,
2001 (led 43-21; won 69-51)
21 — Cleveland vs. Orlando, August 13,
2000 (led 36-15; won 63-54)
Los Angeles vs. Detroit, September
12, 2003 (led 42-21; won 75-63)
20 — Los Angeles vs. Sacramento,
September 7, 2003
(led 46-26; won 79-54)

Largest deficit at halftime overcome to win game
17 — Minnesota vs. Los Angeles, August
28, 2003 (trailed 32-49; won 74-72)
14 — New York at Houston, September 4,
1999 (trailed 23-37; won 68-67)
11 — Los Angeles vs. Sacramento, August
24, 1999 (trailed 21-32; won 71-58)

Most points, second half
59 — Los Angeles vs. Phoenix,
August 13, 2000
Los Angeles vs. Utah, August 24, 2002
51 — Los Angeles vs. Sacramento,
August 27, 2001
50 — Los Angeles vs. Sacramento,
August 24, 1999

Fewest points, second half
15 — New York vs. Cleveland,
August 20, 2000
17 — Miami vs. New York,
August 17, 2001
18 — Cleveland at Charlotte,
August 16, 2001

Most points, both teams, second half
107 — Los Angeles (59) vs. Utah (48),
August 24, 2002
99 — Los Angeles (59) vs. Phoenix (40),
August 13, 2000
93 — Houston (48) vs. Phoenix (45),
September 1, 1998

Fewest points, both teams, second half
43 — Phoenix (21) vs. Houston (22),
August 27, 1998
New York (15) vs. Cleveland (28),
August 20, 2000
46 — Cleveland (18) at Charlotte (28),
August 16, 2001
47 — Miami (17) vs. New York (30),
August 17, 2001

OVERTIME PERIOD

Most points, overtime period
15 — Houston vs. New York,
August 26, 2000
10 — Houston vs. Utah,
August 18, 2002

Fewest points, overtime period
3 — Phoenix at Houston, August 29, 1998
4 — Utah at Houston, August 18, 2002
8 — Houston vs. Phoenix, August 29, 1998
Houston vs. Utah, August 18, 2002
Utah at Houston, August 18, 2002

Most points, both teams, overtime period
24 — Houston (15) vs. New York (9),
August 26, 2000

Fewest points, both teams, overtime period
11 — Phoenix (3) at Houston (8),
August 29, 1998

PLAYERS SCORING

Most players, 20 or more points, game
2 — By many. Last:
Los Angeles at Sacramento,
September 5, 2003

Most players, 20 or more points, both teams,
game
3 — Phoenix (2) at Houston (1),
September 1, 1998
Houston (2) vs. Los Angeles (1),
August 30, 1999
New York (2) at Washington (1),
August 12, 2000
Houston (2) vs. Sacramento (1),
August 14, 2000
Houston (2) vs. Los Angeles (1),
August 17, 2000
Houston (2) vs. New York (1),
August 26, 2000 (ot)
New York (2) vs. Indiana (1),
August 18, 2002
Utah (2) at Houston (1),
August 18, 2002 (2 ot)
New York (2) at Washington (1),
August 22, 2002

Most players, 10 or more points, game
5 — By many. Last:
Los Angeles vs. Minnesota,
September 1, 2003

Fewest players, 10 or more points, game
  0 — Phoenix vs. New York,
    August 28, 1997
Most players, 10 or more points, both teams, game
  10 — Sacramento (5) vs. Los Angeles (5),
    August 24, 2001
  9 — Houston (5) at Charlotte (4),
    August 22, 1998
    Phoenix (5) vs. Los Angeles (4),
    August 11, 2000
    Los Angeles (5) vs. Phoenix (4),
    August 13, 2000
    Washington (5) at New York (4),
    August 24, 2002
  8 — Many times
Fewest players, 10 or more points, both teams, game
  2 — Houston (1) at Phoenix (1),
    August 27, 1998
  3 — Phoenix (0) vs. New York (3),
    August 28, 1997

FIELD GOAL PERCENTAGE

Highest field-goal percentage, game
  .660 — New York vs. Washington,
    August 24, 2002 (35/53)
  .593 — New York vs. Indiana,
    August 18, 2002 (32/54)
  .586 — New York vs. Cleveland,
    August 21, 2000 (34/58)
Lowest field-goal percentage, game
  .224 — Phoenix vs. New York,
    August 28, 1997 (15/67)
  .268 — Sacramento vs. Utah,
    August 19, 2001 (15/56)
  .276 — Orlando at Cleveland,
    August 15, 2000 (16/58)
Highest field-goal percentage, both teams, game
  .549 — New York (.660) vs. Washington
    (.450), August 24, 2002 (62/113)
  .500 — New York (.536) at Washington
    (.468), August 22, 2002 (59/118)
  .496 — Los Angeles (.514) vs. Utah (.477),
    August 24, 2002 (69/139)
Lowest field-goal percentage, both teams, game
  .299 — Houston (.288) vs. New York (.309),
    September 5, 1999 (32/107)
  .325 — Phoenix (.224) vs. New York (.460),
    August 28, 1997 (38/117)
  .333 — Detroit (.286) vs. Cleveland (.383),
    August 31, 2003 (41/123)

FIELD GOALS

Most field-goals, game
  38 — Los Angeles vs. Utah,
    August 24, 2002

  37 — Los Angeles vs. Sacramento,
    August 27, 2001
  35 — New York vs. Washington,
    August 24, 2002
Fewest field-goals, game
  14 — Charlotte at New York,
    August 27, 2001
  15 — Phoenix vs. New York,
    August 28, 1997
    Houston vs. New York,
    September 4, 1999
    Houston vs. New York,
    September 5, 1999
    Sacramento vs. Utah,
    August 19, 2001
  16 — Orlando at Cleveland, August 15, 2000
    New York at Cleveland,
    August 17, 2000
Most field-goals, both teams, game
  69 — Los Angeles (38) vs. Utah (31),
    August 24, 2002
  62 — New York (35) vs. Washington (27),
    August 24, 2002
  61 — Houston (31) at Charlotte (30),
    August 22, 1998
    Los Angeles (34) at Phoenix (27),
    August 11, 2000
Fewest field-goals, both teams, game
  32 — Houston (15) vs. New York (17),
    September 5, 1999
  33 — Charlotte (14) at New York (19),
    August 27, 2001
  37 — Houston (15) vs. New York (22),
    September 4, 1999
    New York (16) at Cleveland (21),
    August 17, 2000
    Cleveland (17) at Charlotte (20),
    August 16, 2001
    Sacramento (15) vs. Utah (22),
    August 19, 2001
Most field goals, one half
  21 — Los Angeles vs. Sacramento,
    August 24, 1999
    New York vs. Indiana,
    August 20, 2002
    Los Angeles at Minnesota,
    August 28, 2003
  20 — Los Angeles vs. Sacramento,
    August 27, 2001
    New York vs. Washington,
    August 24, 2002
    Los Angeles vs. Utah, August 24, 2002
    Los Angeles vs. Sacramento,
    September 7, 2003

FIELD GOAL ATTEMPTS

Most field-goal attempts, game
  79 — Houston vs. Utah, August 18, 2002 (2 ot)

195

74 — Los Angeles vs. Sacramento,
August 24, 1999
Los Angeles at Houston,
August 29, 1999
Los Angeles vs. Utah, August 24, 2002
Detroit vs. Cleveland,
September 2, 2003
73 — Cleveland vs. Phoenix,
August 24, 1998
Fewest field-goal attempts, game
45 — Charlotte at New York, August 27, 2001
46 — Miami at New York, August 19, 2001
Utah at Sacramento, August 19, 2001
47 — Washington at New York,
August 14, 2000
Charlotte at Cleveland, August 18, 2001
Most field-goal attempts, both teams, game
147 — Houston (79) vs. Utah (68),
August 18, 2002 (2 ot)
140 — Los Angeles (74) vs. Sacramento (66),
August 24, 1999
139 — Los Angeles (74) vs. Utah (65),
August 24, 2002
Detroit (70) at Los Angeles (69),
September 12, 2003
Fewest field-goal attempts, both teams, game
94 — Charlotte (45) at New York (49),
August 27, 2001
99 — Charlotte (48) vs. New York (51),
August 24, 2001
101 — Charlotte (49) vs. Cleveland (52),
August 16, 2001
Most field goal attempts, one half
42 — Detroit vs. Cleveland,
September 2, 2003
41 — Cleveland vs. Phoenix,
August 24, 1998
Los Angeles vs. Detroit,
September 12, 2003

THREE-POINT FIELD GOALS

Most three-point field goals, game
11 — Los Angeles vs. Utah,
August 24, 2002
Washington at New York,
August 24, 2002
10 — Sacramento at Los Angeles,
August 26, 2001
9 — By many
Fewest three-point field goals, game
0 — New York vs. Houston,
August 24, 2000
Utah vs. Sacramento,
August 17, 2001
1 — By many
Most three-point field goals, both teams, game
18 — Washington (11) at New York (7),

August 24, 2002
16 — Sacramento (10) at Los Angeles (6),
August 26, 2001
15 — Sacramento (9) vs. Los Angeles (6),
August 24, 2001
Los Angeles (11) vs. Utah (4),
August 24, 2002
Fewest three-point field goals, both teams, game
2 — New York (1) at Phoenix (1),
August 28, 1997
3 — New York (1) vs. Cleveland (2),
August 20, 2000
4 — Charlotte (1) at Detroit (3),
August 24, 1999
Cleveland (2) vs. New York (2),
August 17, 2000
Sacramento (2) vs. Utah (2),
August 19, 2001
Most three-point field goals, one half
8 — Los Angeles vs. Utah,
August 24, 2002
7 — Charlotte at New York,
August 26, 2001
Charlotte at Washington,
August 15, 2002
New York vs. Los Angeles,
August 29, 2002

THREE-POINT FIELD-GOAL ATTEMPTS

Most three-point field goal attempts, game
29 — Charlotte at Washington,
August 15, 2002
25 — Los Angeles vs. Houston,
August 20, 2000
24 — Houston at Charlotte,
August 22, 1998
Fewest three-point field goal attempts, game
4 — New York at Phoenix,
August 28, 1997
6 — Utah at Sacramento,
August 19, 2001
Utah at Houston, August 18, 2002 (2 ot)
Connecticut at Charlotte,
August 30, 2003
7 — Cleveland vs. Phoenix,
August 25, 1998
Washington vs. Charlotte,
August 15, 2002
Los Angeles vs. Minnesota,
September 1, 2003
Most three-point field goal attempts, both teams, game
46 — Los Angeles (23) vs. Sacramento (23),
August 26, 2001
39 — Los Angeles (23) vs. Utah (16),

August 24, 2002
38 — Los Angeles (25) vs. Houston (13),
August 20, 2000
Fewest three-point field goal attempts, both
teams, game
14 — Utah (6) at Sacramento (8),
August 19, 2001
15 — New York (4) at Phoenix (11),
August 28, 1997
17 — Cleveland (8) vs. Phoenix (9),
August 24, 1998
Most three-point field goal attempts, one half
16 — Houston at Charlotte,
August 22, 1998
Charlotte at Washington,
August 15, 2002
15 — Washington at Charlotte,
August 17, 2002

FREE-THROW PERCENTAGE

Highest free-throw percentage, game
1.000 — Phoenix vs. Cleveland,
August 22, 1998 (16/16)
New York vs. Charlotte,
August 30, 1999 (8/8)
Cleveland at New York,
August 20, 2000 (7/7)
Los Angeles vs. Houston,
August 20, 2000 (15/15)
Los Angeles at Seattle,
August 15, 2002 (6/6)
Los Angeles at Minnesota,
August 28, 2003 (11/11)
.955 — Houston vs. Los Angeles,
August 17, 2000 (21/22)
.950 — Detroit at Los Angeles,
September 12, 2003 (19/20)
Lowest free-throw percentage, game
.333 — New York vs. Charlotte,
August 27, 2001 (2/6)
.400 — New York at Houston,
August 30, 1997 (4/10)
.417 — New York vs. Charlotte,
August 29, 1999 (5/12)
Highest free-throw percentage, both teams, game
.970 — Phoenix (1.000) vs. Cleveland (.941),
August 22, 1998 (32/33)
.931 — Houston (.955) vs. Los Angeles
(.857), August 17, 2000 (27/29)
.917 — Detroit (.950) at Los Angeles (.875),
September 12, 2003 (33/36)
Lowest free-throw percentage, both teams, game
.478 — Miami (.467) vs. New York (.500),
August 17, 2001 (11/23)
.567 — Cleveland (.444) vs. Orlando (.750),
August 15, 2000 (17/30)

.588 — Miami (.500) at New York (.714),
August 19, 2001 (20/34)

FREE THROWS MADE

Most free throws made, game
39 — Sacramento vs. Utah, August 19, 2001
32 — Houston vs. New York,
September 4, 1999
27 — Houston vs. New York,
September 5, 1999
Fewest free throws made, game
2 — New York vs. Charlotte,
August 27, 2001
3 — Charlotte at Los Angeles,
September 1, 2001
4 — By many
Most free throws made, both teams, game
59 — Sacramento (39) vs. Utah (20),
August 19, 2001
48 — Houston (32) vs. New York (16),
September 4, 1999
46 — Los Angeles (23) vs. Minnesota (23),
August 30, 2003
Fewest free throws made, both teams, game
11 — New York (4) at Miami (7),
August 17, 2001
12 — Charlotte (4) at New York (8),
August 30, 1999
New York (6) vs. Indiana (6),
August 20, 2002
13 — Houston (6) at Phoenix (7),
August 27, 1998
Orlando (6) vs. Cleveland (7),
August 11, 2000
Most free throws made, one half
24 — Sacramento vs. Utah, August 19, 2001
23 — Los Angeles vs. Phoenix,
August 13, 2000

FREE THROW ATTEMPTS

Most free throw attempts, game
47 — Sacramento vs. Utah,
August 19, 2001
42 — Houston vs. New York,
September 4, 1999
33 — Los Angeles vs. Phoenix,
August 13, 2000
Utah at Houston, August 18, 2002 (2 ot)
Los Angeles at Utah, August 22, 2002
Fewest free throw attempts, game
4 — Charlotte at Los Angeles,
September 1, 2001
5 — Detroit vs. Los Angeles,
September 14, 2003
6 — New York vs. Charlotte,
August 27, 2001
Los Angeles at Seattle,
August 15, 2002

Sacramento at Houston,
August 31, 2003

Most free throw attempts, both teams, game
73 — Sacramento (47) vs. Utah (26),
August 19, 2001
64 — Houston (42) vs. New York (22),
September 4, 1999
58 — Los Angeles (33) vs. Phoenix (25),
August 13, 2000
Minnesota (30) at Los Angeles (28),
August 30, 2003

Fewest free throw attempts, both teams, game
15 — Charlotte (7) at New York (8),
August 30, 1999
17 — Charlotte (8) at New York (9),
August 26, 2001
19 — Houston (8) at Phoenix (11),
August 27, 1998
Cleveland (7) at New York (12),
August 20, 2000
New York (9) vs. Indiana (10),
August 20, 2002

Most free throw attempts, one half
29 — Sacramento vs. Utah,
August 19, 2001
28 — Los Angeles vs. Phoenix,
August 13, 2000

TOTAL REBOUNDS

Highest rebound percentage, game
.673 — Cleveland vs. Charlotte,
August 18, 2001 (35/52)
.656 — Houston vs. Charlotte,
August 28, 1997 (42/64)
.648 — Charlotte at Cleveland,
August 20, 2001 (35/54)

Most rebounds, game
44 — Los Angeles vs. Sacramento,
August 27, 2001
Houston vs. Utah, August 18, 2002 (2 ot)
43 — Houston vs. Los Angeles,
August 29, 1999
42 — Houston vs. Charlotte,
August 28, 1997

Fewest rebounds, game
17 — Charlotte at Cleveland,
August 18, 2001
19 — Washington at New York,
August 14, 2000
Cleveland vs. Charlotte,
August 20, 2001
Washington at New York,
August 24, 2002
20 — Charlotte vs. Houston,
August 22, 1998
Charlotte at New York,
August 30, 1999

Most rebounds, both teams, game

81 — Houston (44) vs. Utah (37),
August 18, 2002 (2 ot)
80 — Detroit (41) at Los Angeles (39),
September 12, 2003
78 — Houston (43) vs. Los Angeles (35),
August 29, 1999

Fewest rebounds, both teams, game
47 — New York (21) at Charlotte (26),
August 24, 2001
48 — Houston (24) vs. Phoenix (24),
September 1, 1998
49 — Washington (19) at New York (30),
August 24, 2002
Los Angeles (22) vs. Sacramento (27),
September 8, 2003

Most rebounds, one half
26 — Cleveland vs. Orlando,
August 13, 2000
25 — Cleveland vs. Orlando,
August 15, 2000
Los Angeles vs. Sacramento,
August 27, 2001
Detroit vs. Cleveland,
September 2, 2003

OFFENSIVE REBOUNDS

Highest offensive rebound percentage, game
.630 — Charlotte at Cleveland,
August 20, 2001 (17/27)
.538 — Detroit vs. Charlotte,
September 7, 2003 (21/39)
.522 — New York vs. Charlotte,
August 30, 1999 (12/23)

Most offensive rebounds, game
21 — Cleveland vs. Phoenix,
August 24, 1998
Detroit vs. Connecticut,
September 7, 2003
18 — Houston vs. Utah, August 18, 2002 (2 ot)
17 — Cleveland at New York,
August 21, 2000
Charlotte at Cleveland, August 20, 2001

Fewest offensive rebounds, game
3 — Houston vs. Phoenix,
September 1, 1998
Los Angeles at Seattle, August 15, 2002
4 — By many

Most offensive rebounds, both teams, game
30 — Houston (18) vs. Utah (12),
August 18, 2002 (2 ot)
29 — Detroit (21) vs. Connecticut (8),
September 7, 2003
28 — Cleveland (21) vs. Phoenix (7),
August 24, 1998
Los Angeles (16) at Houston (12),
August 29, 1999
New York (14) vs. Miami (14),
August 21, 2001

RECORDS Playoffs

198

Fewest offensive rebounds, both teams, game
8 — Los Angeles (3) at Seattle (5),
August 15, 2002
10 — Houston (3) vs. Phoenix (7),
September 1, 1998
Connecticut (4) vs. Detroit (6),
September 5, 2003
11 — New York (4) at Cleveland (7),
August 17, 2000
New York (5) vs. Washington (6),
August 24, 2002
Sacramento (4) vs. Houston (7),
August 29, 2003
Most offensive rebounds, one half
16 — Cleveland vs. Phoenix,
August 24, 1998
13 — Cleveland at New York,
August 21, 2000

DEFENSIVE REBOUNDS

Highest defensive rebound percentage, game
.879 — Detroit at Connecticut,
September 5, 2003 (29/33)
.875 — Detroit vs. Cleveland,
September 2, 2003 (28/42)
.871 — Cleveland vs. New York,
August 17, 2000 (27/31)
Most defensive rebounds, game
34 — New York at Phoenix,
August 28, 1997
33 — Los Angeles vs. Sacramento,
August 27, 2001
31 — Houston vs. Charlotte,
August 24, 1998
Houston vs. Los Angeles,
August 29, 1999
Los Angeles vs. Houston,
August 20, 2001
Utah vs. Houston, August 16, 2002
Fewest defensive rebounds, game
10 — Cleveland vs. Charlotte,
August 20, 2001
11 — Charlotte at New York,
August 30, 1999
12 — Miami vs. New York, August 17, 2001
Most defensive rebounds, both teams, game
55 — Los Angeles (31) vs. Houston (24),
August 20, 2001
54 — Cleveland (28) at Detroit (26),
August 31, 2003
Detroit (29) at Connecticut (25),
September 5, 2003
Los Angeles (29) vs. Detroit (25),
September 12, 2003
52 — Many times
Fewest defensive rebounds, both teams, game
28 — Cleveland (10) vs. Charlotte (18),
August 20, 2001

30 — Washington (15) vs. New York (15),
August 22, 2002
31 — Charlotte (11) at New York (20),
August 30, 1999
Indiana (13) at New York (18),
August 18, 2002
Most defensive rebounds, one half
20 — Los Angeles vs. Sacramento,
September 7, 2003
19 — New York at Phoenix,
August 28, 1997
Los Angeles vs. Houston,
August 20, 2001

ASSISTS

Most assists, game
31 — Los Angeles vs. Utah,
August 24, 2002
26 — Los Angeles vs. Sacramento,
September 7, 2003
25 — New York vs. Cleveland,
August 21, 2000
Los Angeles vs. Sacramento,
August 27, 2001
Los Angeles vs. Minnesota,
September 1, 2003
Fewest assists, game
6 — Houston vs. New York,
August 30, 1997
Houston vs. New York,
September 5, 1999
8 — Houston at Los Angeles,
August 20, 2001
Cleveland at Detroit,
September 2, 2003
9 — Phoenix vs. New York,
August 28, 1997
Orlando at Cleveland, August 15, 2000
Sacramento vs. Utah, August 19, 2001
New York vs. Charlotte,
August 27, 2001
Most assists, both teams, game
51 — Los Angeles (31) vs. Utah (20),
August 24, 2002
44 — Los Angeles (25) vs. Minnesota (19),
September 1, 2003
43 — Charlotte (23) vs. New York (20),
August 27, 1999
Fewest assists, both teams, game
16 — Houston (6) vs. New York (10),
September 5, 1999
19 — Houston (6) vs. New York (13),
August 30, 1997
New York (9) vs. Charlotte (10),
August 27, 2001
20 — Sacramento (10) vs. Houston (10),
August 29, 2003

Most assists, one half
  17 — Los Angeles vs. Sacramento,
       August 27, 2001
       Los Angeles vs. Sacramento,
       September 7, 2003
  16 — Los Angeles vs. Sacramento,
       August 24, 1999
       New York vs. Washington,
       August 24, 2002
       Los Angeles vs. Utah, August 24, 2002
       Los Angeles vs. Minnesota,
       September 1, 2003

PERSONAL FOULS

Most personal fouls, game
  31 — Utah at Sacramento, August 19, 2001
  28 — New York at Houston,
       September 5, 1999
  26 — New York at Houston,
       September 4, 1999
       Phoenix at Los Angeles,
       August 13, 2000
       Minnesota at Los Angeles,
       August 30, 2003
Fewest personal fouls, game
  7 — Houston vs. Los Angeles,
       August 17, 2000
  9 — New York vs. Charlotte,
       August 26, 2001
  10 — Houston at Sacramento,
       August 12, 2000
Most personal fouls, both teams, game
  51 — Utah (31) at Sacramento (20),
       August 19, 2001
  50 — Minnesota (26) at Los Angeles (24),
       August 30, 2003
  49 — Phoenix (26) at Los Angeles (23),
       August 13, 2000
Fewest personal fouls, both teams, game
  22 — New York (9) vs. Charlotte (13),
       August 26, 2001
  25 — Houston (10) at Sacramento (15),
       August 12, 2000
  26 — New York (12) vs. Charlotte (14),
       August 30, 1999
       Los Angeles (12) at Detroit (14),
       September 14, 2003
Most personal fouls, one half
  19 — Utah at Sacramento,
       August 19, 2001
  17 — Phoenix at Los Angeles,
       August 13, 2000

DISQUALIFICATIONS

Most disqualifications, game
  2 — Los Angeles at Houston,
       August 29, 1999
       New York at Houston,
       August 26, 2000 (ot)

  1 — By many
Most disqualifications, both teams, game
  2 — Los Angeles (2) at Houston (0),
       August 29, 1999
       New York (2) at Houston (0),
       August 26, 2000 (ot)
       New York (1) vs. Miami (1),
       August 21, 2001
  1 — By many

STEALS

Most steals, game
  15 — Los Angeles vs. Sacramento,
       August 24, 1999
       Houston vs. Los Angeles,
       August 17, 2000
       Los Angeles vs. Minnesota,
       August 30, 2003
  14 — New York vs. Cleveland,
       August 20, 2000
       Utah at Houston, August 18, 2002 (2 ot)
       Los Angeles vs. Sacramento,
       September 7, 2003
  13 — By many
Fewest steals, game
  1 — Indiana at New York,
       August 18, 2002
  2 — Utah at Houston, August 20, 2002
       Washington at New York,
       August 25, 2002
       New York vs. Los Angeles,
       August 29, 2002
       Sacramento at Houston,
       August 31, 2003
  3 — By many
Most steals, both teams, game
  28 — Los Angeles (15) vs. Sacramento (13),
       August 24, 1999
  25 — Utah (14) at Houston (11),
       August 18, 2002 (2 ot)
  23 — New York (14) vs. Cleveland (9),
       August 20, 2000
Fewest steals, both teams, game
  5 — Indiana (1) at New York (4),
       August 18, 2002
  6 — Phoenix (3) vs. Los Angeles (3),
       August 11, 2000
  7 — Los Angeles (3) vs. Sacramento (4),
       August 27, 2001
Most steals, one half
  12 — Los Angeles vs. Sacramento,
       August 24, 1999
  10 — Houston vs. Los Angeles,
       August 17, 2000
       New York vs. Cleveland,
       August 20, 2000
       Minnesota vs. Los Angeles,
       August 28, 2003

BLOCKED SHOTS

Most blocked shots, game
  13 — Los Angeles vs. Sacramento,

August 27, 2001
11 — Los Angeles vs. Sacramento,
August 24, 1999
10 — Los Angeles vs. Charlotte,
September 1, 2001
Los Angeles at Utah,
August 22, 2002

Fewest blocked shots, game
0 — Cleveland vs. Orlando,
August 13, 2000
New York at Miami, August 17, 2001
New York vs. Indiana,
August 20, 2002
Minnesota vs. Los Angeles,
August 28, 2003
Houston vs. Sacramento,
September 2, 2003
1 — By many

Most blocked shots, both teams, game
19 — Los Angeles (10) at Utah (9),
August 22, 2002
17 — Los Angeles (13) vs. Sacramento (4),
August 27, 2001
16 — Los Angeles (10) vs. Charlotte (6),
September 1, 2001

Fewest blocked shots, both teams, game
2 — Phoenix (1) vs. Cleveland (1),
August 22, 1998
Sacramento (1) vs. Houston (1),
August 12, 2000
Indiana (1) vs. New York (1),
August 16, 2002
Charlotte (1) vs. Washington (1),
August 17, 2002
New York (0) vs. Indiana (2),
August 20, 2002
Minnesota (0) vs. Los Angeles (2),
August 28, 2003
3 — Many times

Most blocked shots, one half
8 — Los Angeles vs. Sacramento,
August 27, 2001
6 — Los Angeles vs. Sacramento,
August 24, 1999
New York at Houston,
September 4, 1999
Los Angeles at Sacramento,
August 24, 2001
Utah vs. Los Angeles,
August 22, 2002
Los Angeles vs. Detroit,
September 12, 2003

TURNOVERS

Most turnovers, game
25 — Los Angeles at Houston,
August 17, 2000
24 — Minnesota at Los Angeles,
August 30, 2003
21 — Sacramento at Los Angeles,

August 24, 1999
Indiana at New York,
August 20, 2002
Utah vs. Los Angeles,
August 22, 2002

Fewest turnovers, game
5 — New York at Charlotte,
August 27, 1999
6 — Los Angeles at Houston,
August 29, 1999
Orlando at Cleveland,
August 13, 2000
Sacramento at Los Angeles,
August 27, 2001
New York vs. Indiana,
August 18, 2002
Houston vs. Utah, August 20, 2002
7 — Washington vs. New York,
August 22, 2002
Washington at New York,
August 24, 2002

Most turnovers, both teams, game
39 — Minnesota (24) at Los Angeles (15),
August 30, 2003
37 — Los Angeles (19) at Seattle (18),
August 15, 2002
36 — Sacramento (21) at Los Angeles (15),
August 24, 1999
Charlotte (20) vs. New York (16),
August 24, 2001

Fewest turnovers, both teams, game
14 — New York (5) at Charlotte (9),
August 27, 1999
16 — Los Angeles (6) at Houston (10),
August 29, 1999
Orlando (6) at Cleveland (10),
August 13, 2000
Sacramento (6) at Los Angeles (10),
August 27, 2001
Connecticut (8) vs. Charlotte (8),
August 28, 2003
17 — New York (6) vs. Indiana (11),
August 18, 2002
Houston (6) vs. Utah (11),
August 20, 2002
Washington (7) at New York (10),
August 24, 2002

Most turnovers, one half
16 — Los Angeles at Houston,
August 17, 2000
15 — Minnesota at Los Angeles,
August 30, 2003

PLAYOFFS SINGLE GAME BESTS

POINTS

	FG	FT	PTS
Lisa Leslie, Los Angeles vs. Sacramento, August 27, 2001	15	5	35
Cynthia Cooper, Houston vs. Charlotte, August 28, 1997	9	9	31
Sheryl Swoopes, Houston vs. New York, August 26, 2000	11	6	31*
Yolanda Griffith, Sacramento vs. Utah, August 19, 2001	6	18	30
Cynthia Cooper, Houston at Phoenix, August 27, 1998	11	5	29
Cynthia Cooper, Houston at New York, September 2, 1999	8	10	29
Lisa Leslie, Los Angeles vs. Phoenix, August 13, 2000	12	5	29
Cynthia Cooper, Houston at Los Angeles, August 20, 2000	10	7	29
Tamika Catchings, Indiana vs. New York, August 16, 2002	11	3	29
Mwadi Mabika, Los Angeles at Detroit, September 16, 2003	11	5	29
Yolanda Griffith, Sacramento at Utah, August 17, 2001	10	8	28
Lisa Leslie, Los Angeles vs. Houston, August 20, 2001	8	10	28
Sheryl Swoopes, Houston vs. Utah, August 18, 2002	11	6	28**
Sheryl Swoopes, Houston vs. Utah, August 20, 2002	9	8	28
Cynthia Cooper, Houston at Charlotte, August 22, 1998	8	8	27
Jennifer Gillom, Phoenix at Cleveland, August 24, 1998	10	4	27
Bridget Pettis, Phoenix at Cleveland, August 25, 1998	9	8	27
Cynthia Cooper, Houston vs. Phoenix, August 29, 1998	7	11	27*
Andrea Stinson, Charlotte at New York, August 29, 1999	9	8	27
Sheryl Swoopes, Houston vs. Sacramento, August 14, 2000	9	8	27
Sheryl Swoopes, Houston at Sacramento, August 29, 2003	9	8	27
Yolanda Griffith, Sacramento at Houston, September 2, 2003	11	5	27
Ruth Riley, Detroit vs. Los Angeles, September 16, 2003	11	5	27

FIELD GOALS

	FG	FGA
Lisa Leslie, Los Angeles vs. Sacramento, August 27, 2001	15	22
Lisa Leslie, Los Angeles vs. Phoenix, August 13, 2000	12	17
Cynthia Cooper, Houston at Phoenix, August 27, 1998	11	24
Sheryl Swoopes, Houston vs. New York, August 26, 2000	11	18*
Lisa Leslie, Los Angeles at Seattle, August 15, 2002	11	17
Tamika Catchings, Indiana vs. New York, August 16, 2002	11	19
Sheryl Swoopes, Houston vs. Utah, August 18, 2002	11	22**
Natalie Williams, Utah at Houston, August 20, 2002	11	16
Tari Phillips, New York vs. Washington, August 24, 2002	11	13
Yolanda Griffith, Sacramento at Houston, September 2, 2003	11	15
Mwadi Mabika, Los Angeles at Detroit, September 16, 2003	11	20
Ruth Riley, Detroit vs. Los Angeles, September 16, 2003	11	19
Jennifer Gillom, Phoenix at Cleveland, August 24, 1998	10	19
Michelle Griffiths, Phoenix at Houston, September 1, 1998	10	16
Andrea Stinson, Charlotte at New York, August 30, 1999	10	19
Sheryl Swoopes, Houston vs. Los Angeles, August 30, 1999	10	19
Cynthia Cooper, Houston at Los Angeles, August 20, 2000	10	23
Tari Phillips, New York vs. Houston, August 24, 2000	10	19
Yolanda Griffith, Sacramento at Utah, August 17, 2001	10	17
Lisa Leslie, Los Angeles vs. Seattle, August 17, 2002	10	16
Tamika Whitmore, New York vs. Indiana, August 18, 2002	10	12
Tari Phillips, New York at Washington, August 22, 2002	10	13
Lisa Leslie, Los Angeles vs. Utah, August 24, 2002	10	17
Deanna Nolan, Detroit vs. Cleveland, September 2, 2003	10	13
Mwadi Mabika, Los Angeles vs. Sacramento, September 7, 2003	10	18
Lisa Leslie, Los Angeles vs. Sacramento, September 8, 2003	10	16

* Denotes overtime. ** Denotes double overtime.

202

RECORDS Playoffs

	FT	FTA
Lisa Leslie, Los Angeles vs. Detroit, September 12, 2003 10		18

FREE THROWS

	FT	FTA
Yolanda Griffith, Sacramento vs. Utah, August 19, 2001 18		24
Cynthia Cooper, Houston vs. New York, September 5, 1999 13		15
Cynthia Cooper, Houston vs. New York, August 30, 1997 11		15
Cynthia Cooper, Houston vs. Phoenix, August 29, 1998 11		14*
Marie Ferdinand, Utah at Sacramento, August 19, 2001 11		14
Chasity Melvin, Cleveland at Detroit, September 2, 2003 11		14
Cynthia Cooper, Houston at New York, September 2, 1999 10		10
Cynthia Cooper, Houston vs. New York, September 4, 1999 10		12
Lisa Leslie, Los Angeles vs. Houston, August 20, 2001 10		12
Swin Cash, Detroit at Cleveland, August 29, 2003 10		13
Nykesha Sales, Connecticut vs. Detroit, September 5, 2003 10		10
Yolanda Griffith, Sacramento at Los Angeles, September 7, 2003 10		10
Cynthia Cooper, Houston vs. Charlotte, August 28, 1997 9		12
Cynthia Cooper, Houston vs. Charlotte, August 24, 1998 9		10
Sheryl Swoopes, Houston vs. Phoenix, September 1, 1998 9		10
Kedra Holland-Corn, Sacramento vs. Utah, August 19, 2001 9		10
Lisa Lesle, Los Angeles vs. Charlotte, September 1, 2001 9		10
Natalie Williams, Utah at Houston, August 18, 2002 9		14**
Chasity Melvin, Cleveland vs. Detroit, August 29, 2003 9		12
LaToya Thomas, Cleveland vs. Detroit, August 29, 2003 9		11
Tamika Williams, Minnesota at Los Angeles, August 30, 2003 9		13
Yolanda Griffith, Sacramento vs. Los Angeles, September 5, 2003 9		10

REBOUNDS

	REB
Lisa Leslie, Los Angeles vs. Houston, August 20, 2001 18
Yolanda Griffith, Sacramento at Houston, September 2, 2003 17
Lisa Leslie, Los Angeles vs. Sacramento, August 27, 2001 16
Tari Phillips, New York vs. Houston, August 24, 2000 15
Tari Phillips, New York vs. Miami, August 19, 2001 15
Cheryl Ford, Detroit vs. Cleveland, September 2, 2003 15
Michelle Snow, Houston vs. Sacramento, September 2, 2003 15
Lisa Leslie, Los Angeles at Detroit, September 14, 2003 15
Kym Hampton, New York at Phoenix, August 28, 1997 14
Tina Thompson, Houston vs. Charlotte, August 24, 1998 14
Andrea Stinson, Charlotte at Detroit, August 24, 1999 14
Yolanda Griffith, Sacramento vs. Houston, August 12, 2000 14
Tina Thompson, Houston vs. Sacramento, August 14, 2000 14
Lisa Leslie, Los Angeles vs. Houston, August 20, 2000 14
Yolanda Griffith, Sacramento vs. Utah, August 19, 2001 14
Olympia Scott-Richardson, Indiana vs. New York, August 16, 2002 14
Tina Thompson, Houston vs. Utah, August 18, 2002 ....14**
Tamika Catchings, Indiana at New York, August 18, 2002 14
Cheryl Ford, Detroit vs. Connecticut, September 7, 2003 14

ASSISTS

	AST
Cynthia Cooper, Houston vs. Los Angeles, August 30, 1999 12
Jennifer Azzi, Utah at Los Angeles, August 24, 2002 12
Teresa Weatherspoon, New York vs. Washington, August 24, 2002 12
Teresa Weatherspoon, New York vs. Charlotte, August 30, 1999 11
Nikki McCray, Washington vs. New York, August 12, 2000 11
Nikki Teasley, Los Angeles at New York, August 29, 2002 11

* Denotes overtime. ** Denotes double overtime.

Nikki Teasley, Los Angeles vs. New York, August 31, 2002 11
Nikki Teasley, Los Angeles vs. Detroit, September 12, 2003 11
Teresa Weatherspoon, New York vs. Houston, September 2, 1999 10
Ticha Penicheiro, Sacramento at Houston, August 14, 2000 10
Teresa Weatherspoon, New York vs. Washington, August 14, 2000 10
Vickie Johnson, New York vs. Cleveland, August 21, 2000 10
Helen Darling, Cleveland vs. Charlotte, August 20, 2001 10
Ukari Figgs, Los Angeles vs. Sacramento, August 27, 2001 10
Jennifer Azzi, Utah at Houston, August 20, 2002 10
Nikki Teasley, Los Angeles vs. Sacramento, September 7, 2003 10
Nikki Teasley, Los Angeles vs. Sacramento, September 8, 2003 10

STEALS

STL

Mwadi Mabika, Los Angeles vs. Sacramento, August 24, 1999 6
Vickie Johnson, New York at Charlotte, August 24, 2001 6
Sheryl Swoopes, Houston vs. Utah, August 18, 2002 ....6**
Tamecka Dixon, Los Angeles vs. Minnesota, August 30, 2003 6
Andrea Stinson, Charlotte at Detroit, August 24, 1999 5
Sheryl Swoopes, Houston vs. Los Angeles, August 30, 1999 5
Sheryl Swoopes, Houston vs. Los Angeles, August 17, 2000 5
Helen Darling, Cleveland at Charlotte, August 16, 2001 5
Penny Taylor, Cleveland vs. Charlotte, August 18, 2001 5
Chamique Holdsclaw, Washington vs. Charlotte, August 15, 2002 5
Marie Ferdinand, Utah at Houston, August 18, 2002 ....5**
Adrienne Goodson, Utah at Houston, August 18, 2002 ....5**
Tamika Williams, Minnesota vs. Los Angeles, August 28, 2003 5
Sheri Sam, Minnesota at Los Angeles, September 1, 2003 5

BLOCKED SHOTS

BLK

Lisa Leslie, Los Angeles vs. Sacramento, August 27, 2001 7
Lisa Leslie, Los Angeles vs. Charlotte, September 1, 2001 7
Lisa Leslie, Los Angeles at Utah, August 22, 2002 7
Lisa Leslie, Los Angeles vs. Sacramento, August 26, 2001 6
DeLisha Milton, Los Angeles vs. Sacramento, August 24, 1999 5
Vicky Bullett, Washington vs. New York, August 12, 2000 5
Margo Dydek, Utah at Houston, August 18, 2002 ....5**
Lisa Leslie, Los Angeles vs. Minnesota, September 1, 2003 5
Lisa Leslie, Los Angeles vs. Sacramento, September 7, 2003 5
Vicky Bullett, Charlotte at Houston, August 28, 1997 4
Vicky Bullett, Charlotte at Detroit, August 24, 1999 4
Cintia Dos Santos, Orlando at Cleveland, August 13, 2000 4
Jennifer Gillom, Phoenix at Los Angeles, August 13, 2000 4
Margo Dydek, Utah vs. Sacramento, August 17, 2001 4
Lisa Leslie, Los Angeles at Sacramento, August 24, 2001 4
Tammy Sutton-Brown, Charlotte at Los Angeles, September 1, 2001 4
Margo Dydek, Utah vs. Houston, August 16, 2002 4
Tiffani Johnson, Houston vs. Utah, August 18, 2002 ....4**
Margo Dydek, Utah vs. Los Angeles, August 22, 2002 4
Lisa Leslie, Los Angeles at Sacramento, September 5, 2003 4
Ruth Riley, Detroit vs. Los Angeles, September 14, 2003 4

* Denotes overtime. ** Denotes double overtime.

FINALS RECORDS

RESULTS

Year	Dates	Winner (coach)	Loser (coach)	Games
1997	August 30	Houston (Van Chancellor)	New York (Nancy Darsch)	1-0
1998	Aug. 27-Sep. 1	Houston (Van Chancellor)	Phoenix (Cheryl Miller)	2-1
1999	Sep. 2-5	Houston (Van Chancellor)	New York (Richie Adubato)	2-1
2000	Aug. 24-26	Houston (Van Chancellor)	New York (Richie Adubato)	2-0
2001	Aug. 30-Sep. 1	Los Angeles (Michael Cooper)	Charlotte (Anne Donovan)	2-0
2002	Aug. 29-31	Los Angeles (Michael Cooper)	New York (Richie Adubato)	2-0
2003	Sept. 12-16	Detroit (Bill Laimbeer)	Los Angeles (Michael Cooper)	2-1

SERIES

TEAM	W-L	PCT
Houston Comets	4 - 0	1.000
Detroit Shock	1 - 0	1.000
Los Angeles Sparks	2 - 1	.667
Charlotte Sting	0 - 1	.000
Phoenix Mercury	0 - 1	.000
New York Liberty	0 - 4	.000
Total	7 - 7	.500

HOME

TEAM	W-L	PCT
Los Angeles Sparks	3 - 0	1.000
Detroit Shock	2 - 0	1.000
Phoenix Mercury	1 - 0	1.000
Houston Comets	5 - 1	.833
Charlotte Sting	0 - 1	.000
New York Liberty	0 - 3	.000
Total	11 - 5	.688

OVERALL

TEAM	W-L	PCT
Houston Comets	7 - 2	.778
Los Angeles Sparks	5 - 2	.714
Detroit Shock	2 - 1	.667
Phoenix Mercury	1 - 2	.333
New York Liberty	1 - 7	.125
Charlotte Sting	0 - 2	.000
Total	16 - 16	.500

ROAD

TEAM	W-L	PCT
Houston Comets	2 - 1	.667
Los Angeles Sparks	2 - 2	.500
New York Liberty	1 - 4	.200
Charlotte Sting	0 - 1	.000
Detroit Shock	0 - 1	.000
Phoenix Mercury	0 - 2	.000
Total	5 - 11	.313

ALL-TIME FINALS LEADERS

GAMES
Janeth Arcain 9
Cynthia Cooper 9
Sheryl Swoopes 9
Tina Thompson 9
Tammy Jackson 8
Vickie Johnson 8
Teresa Weatherspoon 8
Sue Wicks 8
Sophia Witherspoon 8
Six tied 7

FIELD GOALS MADE
Cynthia Cooper 63
Lisa Leslie 49
DeLisha Milton 41
Sheryl Swoopes 39
Tina Thompson 39
Vickie Johnson 33
Mwadi Mabika 28
Tamecka Dixon 26
Tari Phillips 24
Crystal Robinson 23

MINUTES
Cynthia Cooper 354
Tina Thompson 339
Sheryl Swoopes 312
Teresa Weatherspoon 276
Lisa Leslie 275
Vickie Johnson 263
DeLisha Milton 257
Mwadi Mabika 253
Janeth Arcain 250
Crystal Robinson 217

FIELD GOAL ATTEMPTS
Cynthia Cooper 157
Lisa Leslie 109
Sheryl Swoopes 105
Tina Thompson 96
Mwadi Mabika 84
DeLisha Milton 84
Vickie Johnson 82
Crystal Robinson 63
Tari Phillips 60
Tamecka Dixon 56

205

RECORDS Finals

FIELD GOAL PERCENTAGE
(MINIMUM: 15 FG)

	FG	FGA	PCT
DeLisha Milton	41	84	.488
Tamecka Dixon	26	56	.464
Lisa Leslie	49	109	.450
Deanna Nolan	15	35	429
Ruth Riley	18	43	.419
Tina Thompson	39	96	.406
Vickie Johnson	33	82	.402
Cynthia Cooper	63	157	.401
Tari Phillips	24	60	.400
Teresa Weatherspoon	18	45	.400

FREE THROWS MADE

Cynthia Cooper	77
Sheryl Swoopes	36
Lisa Leslie	34
DeLisha Milton	25
Tina Thompson	25
Mwadi Mabika	23
Tari Phillips	20
Tamika Whitmore	20
Tamecka Dixon	13
Jennifer Gillom	12

FREE THROW ATTEMPTS

Cynthia Cooper	92
Lisa Leslie	45
Sheryl Swoopes	41
DeLisha Milton	31
Tina Thompson	31
Tamika Whitmore	31
Mwadi Mabika	26
Tari Phillips	25
Jennifer Gillom	15
Vickie Johnson	15

FREE THROW PERCENTAGE
(MINIMUM: 10 FT)

	FT	FTA	PCT
Tamecka Dixon	13	13	1.000
Becky Hammon	10	10	1.000
Deanna Nolan	10	10	1.000
Crystal Robinson	10	10	1.000
Mwadi Mabika	23	26	.885
Sheryl Swoopes	36	41	.878
Cynthia Cooper	77	92	.837
DeLisha Milton	25	31	.806
Tina Thompson	25	31	.806
Jennifer Gillom	12	15	.800
Tari Phillips	20	25	.800

THREE-POINT FIELD GOALS

Tina Thompson	14
Crystal Robinson	13
Cynthia Cooper	11
Mwadi Mabika	9
DeLisha Milton	8
Becky Hammon	7
Kedra Holland-Corn	7
Sheryl Swoopes	7
Four tied	6

THREE-POINT FIELD GOAL ATTEMPTS

Crystal Robinson	41
Cynthia Cooper	39
Tina Thompson	37
Mwadi Mabika	30
Nikki Teasley	27
Sheryl Swoopes	22
Vickie Johnson	20
Becky Hammon	19
Kim Perrot	18
Deanna Nolan	16

THREE-POINT PERCENTAGE
(MINIMUM: 5 FG3)

	3FG	3GA	PCT
Kedra Holland-Corn	7	12	.583
DeLisha Milton	8	14	.571
Tina Thompson	14	37	.378
Deanna Nolan	6	16	.375
Becky Hammon	7	19	.368
Kim Perrot	6	18	.333
Teresa Weatherspoon	5	15	.333
Sophia Witherspoon	5	15	.333
Sheryl Swoopes	7	22	.318
Crystal Robinson	13	41 .	317

OFFENSIVE REBOUNDS

Tina Thompson	20
Lisa Leslie	18
Sue Wicks	18
Tammy Jackson	16
Vickie Johnson	16
DeLisha Milton	15
Latasha Byears	13
Sheryl Swoopes	13
Cheryl Ford	11
Kym Hampton	11
Tari Phillips	11

DEFENSIVE REBOUNDS

Lisa Leslie	57
Tina Thompson	42
Sheryl Swoopes	41
Mwadi Mabika	34
DeLisha Milton	31
Tammy Jackson	28
Janeth Arcain	24
Kym Hampton	24
Sue Wicks	24
Teresa Weatherspoon	24

TOTAL REBOUNDS

Lisa Leslie	75
Tina Thompson	62
Sheryl Swoopes	54

DeLisha Milton 46
Tammy Jackson 44
Mwadi Mabika 42
Sue Wicks 42
Vickie Johnson 37
Kym Hampton 35
Tari Phillips 34

ASSISTS

Nikki Teasley 46
Teresa Weatherspoon 43
Cynthia Cooper 42
Sheryl Swoopes 24
Lisa Leslie 20
Mwadi Mabika 19
Tamecka Dixon 17
Vickie Johnson 17
DeLisha Milton 17
Swin Cash 16

STEALS

Cynthia Cooper 18
Sheryl Swoopes 15
DeLisha Milton 13
Teresa Weatherspoon 13
Tina Thompson 10
Janeth Arcain 9
Tammy Jackson 9
Lisa Leslie 9
Mwadi Mabika 8
Crystal Robinson 8

PERSONAL FOULS

Teresa Weatherspoon 30
Tina Thompson 29
DeLisha Milton 28
Lisa Leslie 26
Vickie Johnson 24
Tamecka Dixon 23
Sue Wicks 23
Tamika Whitmore 22
Crystal Robinson 21
Janeth Arcain 20

DISQUALIFICATIONS

Tamecka Dixon 1

INDIVIDUAL RECORDS

MINUTES

Most minutes, game
   44 — Cynthia Cooper, Houston vs. Phoenix,
        August 29, 1998 (ot)
        Cynthia Cooper, Houston vs.
        New York, August 26, 2000 (ot)
Regulation game:
   40 — By Many. Most recent:
        Swin Cash, Detroit vs. Los Angeles,
        September 16, 2003
        Mwadi Mabika, Los Angeles at
        Detroit, September 16, 2003

Lisa Leslie 1
Tari Phillips 1
Crystal Robinson 1
Michele Timms 1
Teresa Weatherspoon 1

BLOCKED SHOTS

Lisa Leslie 20
DeLisha Milton 12
Ruth Riley 10
Tammy Jackson 9
Tina Thompson 7
Jennifer Gillom 6
Tari Phillips 6
Sheryl Swoopes 6
Four tied 5

POINTS

Cynthia Cooper 214
Lisa Leslie 134
Sheryl Swoopes 121
Tina Thompson 117
DeLisha Milton 115
Mwadi Mabika 88
Vickie Johnson 82
Crystal Robinson 69
Tamecka Dixon 68
Tari Phillips 68

SCORING AVERAGE
(MINIMUM: 5 G)

	G	FG	FT	PTS	AVG
Cynthia Cooper 9		63	77	214	23.8
Lisa Leslie 7		49	34	134	19.1
DeLisha Milton 7		41	25	115	16.4
Sheryl Swoopes 9		39	36	121	13.4
Tina Thompson 9		39	25	117	13.0
Mwadi Mabika 7		28	23	88	12.6
Tamecka Dixon 6		26	13	68	11.3
Vickie Johnson 8		33	10	82	10.3
Crystal Robinson 7		23	10	69	9.9
Nikki Teasley 5		12	8	38	7.6

DeLisha Milton, Los Angeles at
Detroit, September 16, 2003

SCORING

Most points, game
   31 — Sheryl Swoopes, Houston vs.
        New York, August 26, 2000 (ot)
   29 — Cynthia Cooper, Houston at Phoenix,
        August 27, 1998
        Cynthia Cooper, Houston at
        New York, September 2, 1999
        Mwadi Mabika, Los Angeles at
        Detroit, September 16, 2003
   27 — Cynthia Cooper, Houston vs. Phoenix,
        August 29, 1998 (ot)

Ruth Riley, Detroit vs. Los Angeles,
September 16, 2003
Most consecutive games, 20 or more points
   5 — Cynthia Cooper, Houston,
      August 30, 1997-September 2, 1999
   3 — Cynthia Cooper, Houston,
      September 5, 1999-August 26, 2000
   2 — Tari Phillips, New York,
      August 24-26, 2000
      Lisa Leslie, Los Angeles,
      August 30-September 1, 2001
Most consecutive games, 10 or more points
   9 — Cynthia Cooper, Houston,
      August 30, 1997-August 26, 2000
   7 — Sheryl Swoopes, Houston,
      August 29, 1998-August 26, 2000
      Tina Thompson, Houston, August 29,
      1998-August 26, 2000
      Lisa Leslie, Los Angeles, August 30,
      2001-September 16, 2003
   4 — Tari Phillips, New York, August 24,
      2000-August 31, 2002
Most points, one half
  20 — Cynthia Cooper, Houston at
      New York, September 2, 1999
  18 — Crystal Robinson, New York
      at Houston, September 4, 1999
Most points, overtime period
   7 — Sheryl Swoopes, Houston vs. New
      York, August 26, 2000
   4 — By many

FIELD GOALS

Highest field-goal percentage, game
(Minimum: 8 field goals made)
 .625 — Michelle Griffiths, Phoenix at
      Houston, September 1, 1998 (10/16)
 .611 — Sheryl Swoopes, Houston vs.
      New York, August 26, 2000 (ot) (11/18)
 .579 — Ruth Riley, Detroit vs. Los Angeles,
      September 16, 2003 (11/19)
Most field goals, none missed, game
   3 — Tiffani Johnson, Houston vs.
      New York, August 26, 2000 (ot)
      Latasha Byears, Los Angeles vs.
      Charlotte, September 1, 2001
      Summer Erb, Charlotte at Los Angeles,
      September 1, 2001
      Tamecka Dixon, Los Angeles vs.
      New York, August 31, 2002
   2 — Monica Lamb, Houston vs.
      Phoenix, September 1, 1998
Most field goals, game
  11 — Cynthia Cooper, Houston at Phoenix,
      August 27, 1998
      Sheryl Swoopes, Houston vs.
      New York, August 26, 2000 (ot)

Mwadi Mabika, Los Angeles at
Detroit, September 16, 2003
Ruth Riley, Detroit vs. Los Angeles,
September 16, 2003
  10 — Michelle Griffiths, Phoenix at
      Houston, September 1, 1998
      Tari Phillips, New York vs. Houston,
      August 24, 2000
      Lisa Leslie, Los Angeles vs. Detroit,
      September 12, 2003
Most field goals, one half
   7 — Tari Phillips, New York vs. Houston,
      August 24, 2000
      Tari Phillips, New York at Houston,
      August 26, 2000
      Lisa Leslie, Los Angeles vs. Detroit,
      September 12, 2003
      Mwadi Mabika, Los Angeles at
      Detroit, September 16, 2003
   6 — By many
Most field goal attempts, game
  24 — Cynthia Cooper, Houston at Phoenix,
      August 27, 1998
  23 — Cynthia Cooper, Houston at New
      York, August 24, 2000
  21 — Cynthia Cooper, Houston vs. New
      York, August 26, 2000 (ot)
Most field goal attempts, none made, game
   6 — Crystal Robinson, New York at Los
      Angeles, August 31, 2002
   4 — Tamika Whitmore, New York at
      Houston, September 4, 1999
      Sonja Henning, Houston vs.
      New York, September 5, 1999
      Tamika Whitmore, New York at
      Houston, September 5, 1999
      Tammy-Sutton Brown, Charlotte vs.
      Los Angeles, August 30, 2001
      Teresa Weatherspoon, New York vs.
      Los Angeles, August 29, 2002
Most field goal attempts, one half
  14 — Cynthia Cooper, Houston at Phoenix,
      August 27, 1998
  13 — Cynthia Cooper, Houston vs.
      New York, August 26, 2000
      Tari Phillips, New York at Houston,
      August 26, 2000

THREE POINT FIELD GOALS

Most three-point field goals, none missed, game
   2 — Kristi Harrower, Phoenix at Houston,
      August 29, 1998 (ot)
   1 — By many
Most three-point field goals, game
   4 — Tina Thompson, Houston vs. Phoenix,
      September 1, 1998
      Crystal Robinson, New York at
      Houston, September 4, 1999

Becky Hammon, New York vs.
Los Angeles, August 29, 2002
Kedra Holland-Corn, Detroit vs.
Los Angeles, September 14, 2003
3 — By many

Most three-point field goals, one half
3 — Crystal Robinson, New York at
Houston, September 4, 1999
Crystal Robinson, New York vs.
Los Angeles, August 29, 2002
Becky Hammon, New York vs.
Los Angeles, August 29, 2002
Nikki Teasley, Los Angeles at Detroit,
September 14, 2003
2 — By many

Most three-point field goal attempts, game
10 — Nikki Teasley, Los Angeles vs. Detroit,
September 12, 2003
9 — Kim Perrot, Houston vs. New York,
August 30, 1997
Crystal Robinson, New York
at Houston, September 4, 1999
8 — Michele Timms, Phoenix at Houston,
August 29, 1998 (ot)

Most three-point field goal attempts, none made,
game
5 — Tina Thompson, Houston vs.
New York, September 5, 1999
4 — By many

Most three-point field goal attempts, one half
6 — Crystal Robinson, New York at
Houston, September 4, 1999
5 — By Many

FREE THROWS

Most free throws made, none missed, game
10 — Cynthia Cooper, Houston at
New York, September 2, 1999
8 — Cynthia Cooper, Houston vs.
New York, August 26, 2000 (ot)
6 — By Many

Most free throws made, game
13 — Cynthia Cooper, Houston vs.
New York, September 5, 1999
11 — Cynthia Cooper, Houston vs.
New York, August 30, 1997
Cynthia Cooper, Houston vs. Phoenix,
August 29, 1998 (ot)
10 — Cynthia Cooper, Houston at
New York, September 2, 1999
Cynthia Cooper, Houston vs.
New York, September 4, 1999

Most free throws made, one half
9 — Sheryl Swoopes, Houston vs. Phoenix,
September 1, 1998
8 — Cynthia Cooper, Houston vs.
New York, August 30, 1997

Cynthia Cooper, Houston at
New York, September 2, 1999
Cynthia Cooper, Houston vs.
New York, September 5, 1999
Cynthia Cooper, Houston vs.
New York, August 26, 2000

Most free throw attempts, game
15 — Cynthia Cooper, Houston vs.
New York, August 30, 1997
Cynthia Cooper, Houston vs.
New York, September 5, 1999
14 — Cynthia Cooper, Houston vs. Phoenix,
August 29, 1998 (ot)
12 — Cynthia Cooper, Houston vs.
New York, September 4, 1999

Most free throw attempts, one half
12 — Cynthia Cooper, Houston vs.
New York, August 30, 1997
10 — Sheryl Swoopes, Houston vs. Phoenix,
September 1, 1998
Cynthia Cooper, Houston vs.
New York, September 5, 1999

REBOUNDS

Most rebounds, game
15 — Tari Phillips, New York vs. Houston,
August 24, 2000
Lisa Leslie, Los Angeles at Detroit,
September 14, 2003
13 — Kym Hampton, New York at Houston,
August 30, 1997
Sheryl Swoopes, Houston vs. Phoenix,
August 29, 1998 (ot)
Lisa Leslie, Los Angeles vs. Charlotte,
September 1, 2001
12 — By Many

Most rebounds, one half
10 — Tari Phillips, New York vs. Houston,
August 24, 2000
9 — Kym Hampton, New York at Houston,
August 30, 1997
Tammy Jackson, Houston vs.
New York, September 5, 1999
Lisa Leslie, Los Angeles vs. Charlotte,
September 1, 2001
Lisa Leslie, Los Angeles at Detroit,
September 14, 2003
Swin Cash, Detroit vs. Los Angeles,
September 16, 2003

Most offensive rebounds, game
7 — Cheryl Ford, Detroit at Los Angeles,
September 12, 2003
5 — By Many

Most offensive rebounds, one half
4 — Tammy Jackson, Houston vs.
New York, September 5, 1999
Lisa Leslie, Los Angeles vs. Charlotte,
September 1, 2001

Charlotte Smith, Charlotte at
Los Angeles, September 1, 2001
Cheryl Ford, Detroit at Los Angeles,
September 12, 2003
3 — By many

Most defensive rebounds, game
11 — Sheryl Swoopes, Houston vs. Phoenix,
August 29, 1998 (ot)
Tari Phillips, New York vs. Houston,
August 24, 2000
Lisa Leslie, Los Angeles at Detroit,
September 14, 2003
10 — Kym Hampton, New York at Houston,
August 30, 1997
Lisa Leslie, Los Angeles vs. Detroit,
September 12, 2003

Most defensive rebounds, one half
7 — Kym Hampton, New York at Houston,
August 30, 1997
Tari Phillips, New York vs. Houston,
August 24, 2000
Swin Cash, Detroit vs. Los Angeles,
September 16, 2003
6 — Tina Thompson, Houston vs. Phoenix,
August 29, 1998
Lisa Leslie, Los Angeles vs.
Detroit, September 12, 2003
Lisa Leslie, Los Angeles at Detroit,
September 14, 2003

ASSISTS

Most assists, game
11 — Nikki Teasley, Los Angeles at
New York, August 29, 2002
Nikki Teasley, Los Angeles vs.
New York, August 31, 2002
Nikki Teasley, Los Angeles vs.
Detroit, September 12, 2003
10 — Teresa Weatherspoon, New York vs.
Houston, September 2, 1999
9 — Swin Cash, Detroit vs. Los Angeles,
September 16, 2003

Most assists, one half
7 — Nikki Teasley, Los Angeles at
New York, August 29, 2002
6 — Teresa Weatherspoon, New York vs.
Houston, September 2, 1999
Nikki Teasley, Los Angeles vs.
New York, August 31, 2002
Nikki Teasley, Los Angeles vs. Detroit,
September 12, 2003
Swin Cash, Detroit vs. Los Angeles,
September 16, 2003

PERSONAL FOULS

Most personal fouls, game
6 — Michele Timms, Phoenix at Houston,
August 29, 1998 (ot)

Crystal Robinson, New York vs.
Houston, September 2, 1999
Tari Phillips, New York at Houston,
August 26, 2000 (ot)
Teresa Weatherspoon, New York at
Houston, August 26, 2000 (ot)
Tamecka Dixon, Los Angeles vs.
New York, August 31, 2002
Lisa Leslie, Los Angeles at Detroit,
September 16, 2003
5 — by many

Most personal fouls, one half
5 — Teresa Weatherspoon, New York
at Houston, September 5, 1999
Dawn Staley, Charlotte vs.
Los Angeles, August 30, 2001
4 — By many

Most minutes played, no personal fouls, game
39 — Cynthia Cooper, Houston at Phoenix,
August 27, 1998
37 — Sheryl Swoopes, Houston vs. New
York, September 5, 1999
34 — Kim Perrot, Houston vs. Phoenix,
September 1, 1998

DISQUALIFICATIONS

Fewest minutes played, disqualified player, game
14 — Tamecka Dixon, Los Angeles vs.
New York, August 31, 2002
34 — Crystal Robinson, New York vs.
Houston, September 2, 1999
37 — Tari Phillips, New York at Houston,
August 26, 2000 (ot)

STEALS

Most steals, game
4 — Teresa Weatherspoon, New York at
Houston, August 30, 1997
Cynthia Cooper, Houston at
New York, September 2, 1999
Sue Wicks, New York vs. Houston,
September 2, 1999
Sheryl Swoopes, Houston vs.
New York, September 4, 1999
3 — By many

Most steals, one half
3 — Kim Perrot, Houston vs. New York,
August 30, 1997
Tammy Jackson, Houston vs.
New York, September 5, 1999
Cynthia Cooper, Houston vs.
New York, September 5, 1999
Allison Feaster, Charlotte at
Los Angeles, September 1, 2001
DeLisha Milton, Los Angeles
at Detroit, September 14, 2003

BLOCKED SHOTS
Most blocked shots, game
7 — Lisa Leslie, Los Angeles vs. Charlotte,
September 1, 2001
4 — Tammy Sutton-Brown, Charlotte at
Los Angeles, September 1, 2001
Ruth Riley, Detroit vs. Los Angeles,
September 14, 2003
3 — By many
Most blocked shots, one half
4 — Lisa Leslie, Los Angeles vs. Charlotte,
September 1, 2001
3 — Kym Hampton, New York at Houston,
September 4, 1999
Lisa Leslie, Los Angeles vs. Charlotte,
September 1, 2001
Lisa Leslie, Los Angeles vs. Detroit,
September 12, 2003
2 — By many

TURNOVERS
Most turnovers, game
7 — Nikki Teasley, Los Angeles at
New York, August 29, 2002
6 — Sheryl Swoopes, Houston vs. Phoenix,
August 29, 1998 (ot)
Cynthia Cooper, Houston vs. Phoenix,
September 1, 1998
Cynthia Cooper, Houston vs.
New York, September 5, 1999
Tari Phillips, New York vs. Houston,
August 24, 2000
Dawn Staley, Charlotte vs.
Los Angeles, August 30, 2001
5 — By many
Most turnovers, one half
5 — Sheryl Swoopes, Houston vs. Phoenix,
August 29, 1998
4 — By many

TEAM RECORDS

WON-LOST
Most consecutive games won
5 — Los Angeles, 2001-03
3 — Houston, 1998-99
Houston, 1999-00 (current)
Most consecutive games won at home
3 — Houston, 1997-98
Los Angeles, 2001-03 (current)
2 — Houston, 1999-00 (current)
Detroit, 2003 (current)
Most consecutive games won on road
2 — Houston, 1999-00 (current)
Los Angeles, 2001-02
1 — New York, 1999
Most consecutive games lost
5 — New York, 1999-00, 2002 (current)

2 — Phoenix, 1998 (current)
New York, 1997, 1999
Charlotte, 2001 (current)
Los Angeles, 2003 (current)
Most consecutive games lost at home
3 — New York, 1999-00, 2002 (current)
1 — Houston, 1999
Charlotte, 2001 (current)
Most consecutive games lost on road
3 — New York, 1999-00, 2002 (current)
2 — Phoenix, 1998 (current)
Los Angeles, 2003 (current)

SCORING
Most points, game
83 — Detroit vs. Los Angeles,
September 16, 2003
82 — Los Angeles vs. Charlotte,
September 1, 2001
Fewest points, game
47 — New York at Houston,
September 5, 1999
51 — New York at Houston,
August 30, 1997
Houston at Phoenix, August 27, 1998
Most points, both teams, game
161 — Detroit (83) vs. Los Angeles (78),
September 16, 2003
152 — Houston (79) vs. New York (73),
August 26, 2000 (ot)
Fewest points, both teams, game
105 — Houston (51) at Phoenix (54),
August 27, 1998
106 — New York (47) at Houston (59),
September 5, 1999
Largest margin of victory, game
28 — Los Angeles (82) vs. Charlotte (54),
September 1, 2001
14 — Houston (65) vs. New York (51),
August 30, 1997

BY HALF
Most points, first half
42 — Los Angeles vs. Detroit,
September 12, 2003
Detroit vs. Los Angeles,
September 16, 2003
39 — Charlotte vs. Los Angeles,
August 30, 2001
Fewest points, first half
20 — New York vs. Houston,
September 2, 1999
21 — Detroit at Los Angeles,
September 12, 2003
Most points, both teams, first half
79 — Detroit (42) vs. Los Angeles (37),
September 16, 2003
74 — Charlotte (39) vs. Los Angeles (35),
August 30, 2001

Fewest points, both teams, first half
49 — New York (20) vs. Houston (29),
September 2, 1999
51 — New York (22) vs. Houston (29),
August 24, 2000
Largest lead at halftime
21 — Los Angeles vs. Detroit, September
12, 2003 (led 42-21; won 75-63)
16 — Detroit vs. Los Angeles, September
14, 2003 (led 38-22; won 62-61)
Largest deficit at halftime overcome to win game
14 — New York at Houston, September 4,
1999 (trailed 23-37; won 68-67)
5 — Houston vs. Phoenix, August 29,
1998 (trailed 32-37; won 74-69 in ot)
Most points, second half
48 — Houston vs. Phoenix, September 1, 1998
45 — Phoenix at Houston, September 1, 1998
New York at Houston,
September 4, 1999
Fewest points, second half
21 — Phoenix vs. Houston, August 27, 1998
22 — Houston at Phoenix, August 27, 1998
New York at Houston,
September 5, 1999
Most points, both teams, second half
93 — Houston (48) vs. Phoenix (45),
September 1, 1998
84 — Houston (44) at New York (40),
September 2, 1999
Fewest points, both teams, second half
43 — Phoenix (21) vs. Houston (22),
August 27, 1998
48 — New York (22) at Houston (26),
September 5, 1999

OVERTIME PERIOD

Most points, overtime period
15 — Houston vs. New York,
August 26, 2000
9 — New York at Houston,
August 26, 2000
Fewest points, overtime period
3 — Phoenix at Houston, August 29, 1998
8 — Houston vs. Phoenix, August 29, 1998
Most points, both teams, overtime period
24 — Houston (15) vs. New York (9),
August 26, 2000
Fewest points, both teams, overtime period
11 — Phoenix (3) at Houston (8),
August 29, 1998

PLAYERS SCORING

Most players, 20 or more points, game
2 — Phoenix at Houston, September 1, 1998
Houston vs. New York, August 26, 2000 (ot)
1 — by many

Most players, 20 or more points, both teams,
game
3 — Phoenix (2) at Houston (1),
September 1, 1998
Houston (2) vs. New York (1),
August 26, 2000 (ot)
2 — Houston (1) vs. Phoenix (1),
August 29, 1998 (ot)
New York (1) vs. Houston (1),
August 24, 2000
Detroit (1) vs. Los Angeles (1),
September 16, 2003
Most players, 10 or more points, game
5 — Houston vs. New York,
September 4, 1999
Charlotte vs. Los Angeles,
August 30, 2001
4 — By Many
Most players, 10 or more points, both teams,
game
8 — Houston (5) vs. New York (3),
September 4, 1999
Charlotte (5) vs. Los Angeles (3),
August 30, 2001
Detroit (4) vs. Los Angeles (4),
September 16, 2003
7 — Houston (4) vs. Phoenix (3),
September 1, 1998
New York (4) at Houston (3),
August 26, 2000 (ot)
Los Angeles (4) vs. New York (3),
August 31, 2002

FIELD GOAL PERCENTAGE

Highest field-goal percentage, game
.519 — Houston vs. Phoenix,
September 1, 1998 (28/54)
.509 — Los Angeles at Charlotte,
August 30, 2001 (29/57)
Lowest field-goal percentage, game
.286 — Detroit at Los Angeles,
September 12, 2003 (20/70)
.288 — Houston vs. New York,
September 5, 1999 (15/52)
Highest field-goal percentage, both teams, game
.496 — Houston (.519) vs. Phoenix (.475),
September 1, 1998 (57/115)
.478 — Los Angeles (.509) at Charlotte (.448),
August 30, 2001 (55/115)
Lowest field-goal percentage, both teams, game
.299 — Houston (.288) vs. New York (.309),
September 5, 1999 (32/107)
.336 — Houston (.323) at Phoenix (.349),
August 27, 1998 (43/128)

FIELD GOALS

Most field-goals, game
29 — Phoenix at Houston, September 1, 1998

Los Angeles at Charlotte,
August 30, 2001
28 — Houston vs. Phoenix,
August 29, 1998 (ot)
Houston vs. Phoenix, September 1, 1998
Houston vs. New York,
August 26, 2000 (ot)
Los Angeles at Detroit,
September 16, 2003
Detroit vs. Los Angeles,
September 16, 2003
Fewest field-goals, game
15 — Houston vs. New York,
September 4, 1999
Houston vs. New York,
September 5, 1999
17 — New York at Houston,
September 5, 1999
Most field-goals, both teams, game
57 — Phoenix (29) at Houston (28),
September 1, 1998
56 — Detroit (28) vs. Los Angeles (28),
September 16, 2003
Fewest field-goals, both teams, game
32 — Houston (15) vs. New York (17),
September 5, 1999
37 — Houston (15) vs. New York (22),
September 4, 1999
Most field goals, one half
19 — Phoenix at Houston,
September 1, 1998
17 — New York vs. Houston,
September 2, 1999
Los Angeles vs. Detroit,
September 12, 2003
Detroit vs. Los Angeles,
September 14, 2003

FIELD GOAL ATTEMPTS

Most field-goal attempts, game
71 — Los Angeles at Detroit,
September 16, 2003
70 — Detroit at Los Angeles,
September 12, 2003
Fewest field-goal attempts, game
50 — Houston at New York,
September 2, 1999
Houston vs. New York,
September 4, 1999
Los Angeles vs. New York,
August 31, 2002
52 — Houston vs. New York,
September 5, 1999
Most field-goal attempts, both teams, game
139 — Detroit (70) at Los Angeles (69),
September 12, 2003
133 — Los Angeles (71) at Detroit (62),
September 16, 2003

Fewest field-goal attempts, both teams, game
106 — Houston (50) vs. New York (56),
September 4, 1999
107 — Houston (52) vs. New York (55),
September 5, 1999
Most field-goal attempts, one half
41 — Los Angeles vs. Detroit,
September 12, 2003
38 — Los Angeles at Detroit,
September 16, 2003

THREE-POINT FIELD GOALS

Most three-point field goals, game
9 — New York vs. Los Angeles,
August 29, 2002
8 — New York at Houston,
September 4, 1999
Fewest three-point field goals, game
0 — New York vs. Houston,
August 24, 2000
1 — New York at Houston,
August 30, 1997
Charlotte at Los Angeles,
September 1, 2001
Most three-point field goals, both teams, game
14 — New York (9) vs. Los Angeles (5),
August 29, 2002
13 — New York (8) at Houston (5),
September 4, 1999
Fewest three-point field goals, both teams, game
5 — New York (1) at Houston (4),
August 30, 1997
New York (0) vs. Houston (5),
August 24, 2000
6 — Phoenix (3) vs. Houston (3),
August 27, 1998
Charlotte (1) at Los Angeles (5),
September 1, 2001
Most three-point field goals, one half
7 — New York vs. Los Angeles,
August 29, 2002
6 — Phoenix at Houston, August 29, 1998
New York at Houston, September 4, 1999

THREE-POINT FIELD-GOAL ATTEMPTS

Most three-point field goal attempts, game
23 — Los Angeles vs. Detroit,
September 12, 2003
19 — New York vs. Los Angeles,
August 29, 2002
Fewest three-point field goal attempts, game
8 — New York at Houston,
August 30, 1997
New York vs. Houston,
August 24, 2000
9 — Los Angeles at Charlotte,
August 30, 2001

Most three-point field goal attempts, both teams, game
- 36 — Los Angeles (23) vs. Detroit (13), September 12, 2003
- 33 New York (18) vs. Houston (15), September 2, 1999
  New York (19) vs. Los Angeles (14), August 29, 2002

Fewest three-point field goal attempts, both teams, game
- 22 — New York (8) at Houston (14), August 30, 1997
- 23 — New York (8) vs. Houston (15), August 24, 2000
  Los Angeles (9) at Charlotte (14), August 30, 2001

Most three-point, field goal attempts, one half
- 14 — Los Angeles vs. Detroit, September 12, 2003
- 11 — Los Angeles at New York, August 29, 2002
  Los Angeles at Detroit, September 14, 2003

FREE-THROW PERCENTAGE

Highest free-throw percentage, game
- .950 — Detroit at Los Angeles, September 12, 2003 (19/20)
- .947 — Houston vs. New York, August 26, 2000 (ot) (18/19)

Lowest free-throw percentage, game
- .400 — New York at Houston, August 30, 1997 (4/10)
- .467 — New York vs. Houston, September 2, 1999 (7/15)

Highest free-throw percentage, both teams, game
- .917 — Detroit (.950) at Los Angeles (.875), September 12, 2003 (33/36)
- .900 — Houston (.947) vs. New York (.857), August 26, 2000 (ot) (36/40)

Lowest free-throw percentage, both teams, game
- .600 — New York (.400) at Houston (.680), August 30, 1997 (21/35)
- .682 — New York (.467) vs. Houston (.793), September 2, 1999 (30/44)

FREE THROWS MADE

Most free throws made, game
- 32 — Houston vs. New York, September 4, 1999
- 27 — Houston vs. New York, September 5, 1999

Fewest free throws made, game
- 3 — Charlotte at Los Angeles, September 1, 2001
- 4 — New York at Houston, August 30, 1997
  Detroit vs. Los Angeles, September 14, 2003

Most free throws made, both teams, game
- 48 — Houston (32) vs. New York (16), September 4, 1999
- 40 — Detroit (23) vs. Los Angeles (17), September 16, 2003

Fewest free throws made, both teams, game
- 13 — Houston (6) at Phoenix (7), August 27, 1998
- 17 — Detroit (4) vs. Los Angeles (13), September 14, 2003

Most free throws made, one half
- 17 — Houston at New York, September 2, 1999
- 16 — Houston vs. New York, September 4, 1999 (both halves)

FREE THROW ATTEMPTS

Most free throw attempts, game
- 42 — Houston vs. New York, September 4, 1999
- 32 — Houston vs. New York, September 5, 1999

Fewest free throw attempts, game
- 4 — Charlotte at Los Angeles, September 1, 2001
- 5 — Detroit vs. Los Angeles, September 14, 2003

Most free throw attempts, both teams, game
- 64 — Houston (42) vs. New York (22), September 4, 1999
- 50 — New York (28) at Los Angeles (22), August 31, 2002

Fewest free throw attempts, both teams, game
- 19 — Houston (8) at Phoenix (11), August 27, 1998
- 21 — Detroit (5) vs. Los Angeles (16), September 14, 2003

Most free throw attempts, one half
- 21 — Houston at New York, September 2, 1999
  Houston vs. New York, September 4, 1999 (both halves)
- 19 — Houston vs. New York, September 5, 1999

TOTAL REBOUNDS

Highest rebound percentage, game
- .597 — Los Angeles at New York, August 29, 2002 (37/62)
- .579 — Houston vs. New York, August 26, 2000 (ot) (33/57)

Most rebounds, game
- 41 — Phoenix vs. Houston, August 27, 1998
  Detroit at Los Angeles, September 12, 2003
- 39 — Los Angeles vs. Detroit, September 12, 2003

Fewest rebounds, game
    24 — Houston vs. Phoenix,
        September 1, 1998
        Phoenix at Houston,
        September 1, 1998
        New York at Houston,
        August 26, 2000 (ot)
        Charlotte vs. Los Angeles,
        August 30, 2001
    25 — New York vs. Los Angeles,
        August 29, 2002
Most rebounds, both teams, game
    80 — Detroit (41) at Los Angeles (39),
        September 12, 2003
    73 — Phoenix (41) vs. Houston (32),
        August 27, 1998
Fewest rebounds, both teams, game
    48 — Houston (24) vs. Phoenix (24),
        September 1, 1998
    50 — Charlotte (24) vs. Los Angeles (26),
        August 30, 2001
Most rebounds, one half
    24 — Detroit at Los Angeles,
        September 12, 2003
    22 — Los Angeles vs. Detroit,
        September 12, 2003

OFFENSIVE REBOUNDS

Highest offensive rebound percentage, game
    .464 — Houston vs. New York, August 26,
        2000 (ot) (13/28)
    .412 — Houston vs. New York,
        September 5, 1999 (14/34)
Most offensive rebounds, game
    16 — Detroit at Los Angeles,
        September 12, 2003
    14 — Houston vs. New York,
        September 5, 1999
Fewest offensive rebounds, game
    3 — Houston vs. Phoenix,
        September 1, 1998
    5 — New York vs. Los Angeles,
        August 29, 2002
        Detroit vs. Los Angeles,
        September 14, 2003
Most offensive rebounds, both teams, game
    26 — Detroit (16) at Los Angeles (10),
        September 12, 2003
    23 — Phoenix (13) vs. Houston (10),
        August 27, 1998
        Houston (12) at New York (11),
        August 24, 2000
        Los Angeles (12) at Detroit (11),
        September 16, 2003
Fewest offensive rebounds, both teams, game
    10 — Houston (3) vs. Phoenix (7),
        September 1, 1998

    13 — Detroit (5) vs. Los Angeles (8),
        September 14, 2003
Most offensive rebounds, one half
    10 — Houston vs. New York,
        September 5, 1999
        Detroit at Los Angeles,
        September 12, 2003
        Los Angeles at Detroit,
        September 16, 2003
    9 — New York at Houston,
        August 30, 1997
        Los Angeles at New York,
        August 29, 2002
        New York at Los Angeles,
        August 31, 2002

DEFENSIVE REBOUNDS

Highest defensive rebound percentage, game
    .850 — Phoenix at Houston,
        September 1, 1998 (17/20)
    .833 — Los Angeles at Detroit,
        September 14, 2003 (25/30)
Most defensive rebounds, game
    29 — Los Angeles vs. Detroit,
        September 12, 2003
    28 — Phoenix vs. Houston,
        August 27, 1998
Fewest defensive rebounds, game
    15 — New York at Houston,
        August 26, 2000 (ot)
    17 — Phoenix at Houston,
        September 1, 1998
        Charlotte vs. Los Angeles,
        August 30, 2001
Most defensive rebounds, both teams, game
    54 — Los Angeles (29) vs. Detroit (25),
        September 12, 2003
    51 — Houston (26) vs. Phoenix (25),
        August 29, 1998 (ot)
Fewest defensive rebounds, both teams, game
    35 — New York (15) at Houston (20),
        August 26, 2000 (ot)
    36 — Charlotte (17) vs. Los Angeles (19),
        August 30, 2001
Most defensive rebounds, one half
    17 — Detroit vs. Los Angeles,
        September 14, 2003
    16 — Los Angeles vs. New York,
        August 31, 2002
        Los Angeles vs. Detroit,
        September 12, 2003

ASSISTS

Most assists, game
    24 — Los Angeles vs. Charlotte,
        September 1, 2001
    22 — Los Angeles vs. Detroit,
        September 12, 2003

Fewest assists, game
6 — Houston vs. New York,
August 30, 1997
Houston vs. New York,
September 5, 1999
10 — Houston vs. New York,
September 4, 1999
New York at Houston,
September 5, 1999
New York vs. Houston,
August 24, 2000
New York at Los Angeles,
August 31, 2002
Most assists, both teams, game
38 — Los Angeles (24) vs. Charlotte (14),
September 1, 2001
Detroit (21) vs. Los Angeles (17),
September 16, 2003
36 — Houston (18) vs. Phoenix (18),
September 1, 1998
Los Angeles (22) vs. Detroit (14),
September 12, 2003
Fewest assists, both teams, game
16 — Houston (6) vs. New York (10),
September 5, 1999
19 — Houston (6) vs. New York (13),
August 30, 1997
Most assists, one half
15 — Los Angeles vs. Charlotte,
September 1, 2001
14 — Detroit vs. Los Angeles,
September 14, 2003

PERSONAL FOULS
Most personal fouls, game
28 — New York at Houston,
September 5, 1999
26 — New York at Houston,
September 4, 1999
Fewest personal fouls, game
12 — Houston vs. Phoenix, September 1, 1998
Detroit at Los Angeles,
September 12, 2003
Los Angeles at Detroit,
September 14, 2003
13 — Houston at New York,
September 2, 1999
Most personal fouls, both teams, game
45 — Los Angeles (25) vs. New York (20),
August 31, 2002
44 — New York (26) at Houston (18),
September 4, 1999
Fewest personal fouls, both teams, game
26 — Los Angeles (12) at Detroit (14),
September 14, 2003
29 — Houston (12) vs. Phoenix (17),
September 1, 1998

Most personal fouls, one half
16 — New York at Houston,
September 5, 1999
14 — New York at Houston,
August 30, 1997
New York at Houston,
September 4, 1999

DISQUALIFICATIONS
Most disqualifications, game
2 — New York at Houston,
August 26, 2000 (ot)
1 — Phoenix at Houston, August 29, 1998
New York vs. Houston,
September 2, 1999
Los Angeles vs. New York,
August 31, 2002
Los Angeles at Detroit,
September 16, 2003
Most disqualifications, both teams, game
2 — New York (2) at Houston (0),
August 26, 2000 (ot)
1 — Phoenix (1) at Houston (0),
August 29, 1998 (ot)
New York (1) vs. Houston (0),
September 2, 1999
Los Angeles (1) vs. New York (0),
August 31, 2002
Los Angeles (1) at Detroit (0),
September 16, 2003

STEALS
Most steals, game
12 — Houston vs. New York,
September 4, 1999
11 — Houston vs. New York,
September 5, 1999
Fewest steals, game
2 — New York vs. Los Angeles,
August 29, 2002
3 — New York at Houston,
September 5, 1999
Most steals, both teams, game
18 — Houston (10) at New York (8),
September 2, 1999
17 — Houston (10) at Phoenix (7),
August 27, 1998
Houston (10) vs. Phoenix (7),
August 29, 1998 (ot)
Fewest steals, both teams, game
10 — Los Angeles (5) vs. Charlotte (5),
September 1, 2001
11 — Phoenix (5) at Houston (6),
September 1, 1998
New York (2) vs. Los Angeles (9),
August 29, 2002
Most steals, one half
7 — Houston vs. New York,
September 4, 1999

6 — By Many

BLOCKED SHOTS

Most blocked shots, game
10 — Los Angeles vs. Charlotte,
September 1, 2001
8 — New York at Houston, September 4, 1999
Fewest blocked shots, game
1 — Houston at New York,
September 2, 1999
New York at Houston,
September 5, 1999
New York at Los Angeles,
August 31, 2002
2 — New York at Houston, August 30, 1997
New York vs. Houston,
September 2, 1999
New York vs. Houston,
August 24, 2000
Most blocked shots, both teams, game
16 — Los Angeles (10) vs. Charlotte (6),
September 1, 2001
13 — Detroit (7) at Los Angeles (6),
September 12, 2003
Fewest blocked shots, both teams, game
3 — Houston (1) at New York (2),
September 2, 1999
5 — New York (2) at Houston (3),
August 30, 1997
New York (2) vs. Houston (3),
August 24, 2000
New York (1) at Los Angeles (4),
August 31, 2002
Most blocked shots, one half
6 — New York at Houston,
September 4, 1999
Los Angeles vs. Detroit,
September 12, 2003

5 — Los Angeles vs. Charlotte,
September 1, 2001 (both halves)

TURNOVERS

Most turnovers, game
18 — New York at Houston,
September 4, 1999
16 — New York vs. Houston,
September 2, 1999
New York at Houston,
September 5, 1999
New York at Houston,
August 26, 2000 (ot)
Houston vs. New York,
August 26, 2000 (ot)
Los Angeles vs. New York,
August 31, 2002
Fewest turnovers, game
8 — Los Angeles vs. Charlotte,
September 1, 2001
9 — New York at Los Angeles,
August 31, 2002
Los Angeles at Detroit,
September 16, 2003
Most turnovers, both teams, game
32 — Houston (16) vs. New York (16),
August 26, 2000 (ot)
29 — Phoenix (15) at Houston (14),
August 29, 1998 (ot)
New York (16) vs. Houston (13),
September 2, 1999
New York (18) at Houston (11),
September 4, 1999
Fewest turnovers, both teams, game
20 — Los Angeles (9) at Detroit (11),
September 16, 2003
22 — Los Angeles (8) vs. Charlotte (14),
September 1, 2001

FINALS SINGLE GAME BESTS

POINTS

	FG	FT	PTS
Sheryl Swoopes, Houston vs. New York, August 26, 2000	11	6	31*
Cynthia Cooper, Houston at Phoenix, August 27, 1998	11	5	29
Cynthia Cooper, Houston at New York, September 2, 1999	8	10	29
Mwadi Mabika, Los Angeles at Detroit, September 16, 2003	11	5	29
Cynthia Cooper, Houston vs. Phoenix, August 29, 1998	7	11	27*
Ruth Riley, Detroit vs. Los Angeles, September 16, 2003	11	5	27
Cynthia Cooper, Houston vs. New York, August 30, 1997	7	11	25
Cynthia Cooper, Houston vs. New York, August 26, 2000	8	8	25*
Michelle Griffiths, Phoenix at Houston, September 1, 1998	10	3	24
Cynthia Cooper, Houston vs. New York, September 5, 1999	5	13	24
Tari Phillips, New York vs. Houston, August 24, 2000	10	4	24
Lisa Leslie, Los Angeles at Charlotte, August 30, 2001	9	6	24
Lisa Leslie, Los Angeles vs. Charlotte, September 1, 2001	7	9	24
Cynthia Cooper, Houston vs. Phoenix, September 1, 1998	9	5	23
Lisa Leslie, Los Angeles vs. Detroit, September 12, 2003	10	3	23
Michele Timms, Phoenix at Houston, August 29, 1998	7	5	21*
Crystal Robinson, New York at Houston, September 4, 1999	6	5	21

RECORDS Finals

FIELD GOALS

	FG	FGA
Cynthia Cooper, Houston at Phoenix, August 27, 1998	11	24
Sheryl Swoopes, Houston vs. New York, August 26, 2000	11	18*
Mwadi Mabika, Los Angeles at Detroit, September 16, 2003	11	20
Ruth Riley, Detroit vs. Los Angeles, September 16, 2003	11	19
Michelle Griffiths, Phoenix at Houston, September 1, 1998	10	16
Tari Phillips, New York vs. Houston, August 24, 2000	10	19
Lisa Leslie, Los Angeles vs. Detroit, September 12, 2003	10	18
Cynthia Cooper, Houston vs. Phoenix, September 1, 1998	9	20
Lisa Leslie, Los Angeles at Charlotte, August 30, 2001	9	16
Cynthia Cooper, Houston at New York, September 2, 1999	8	16
Cynthia Cooper, Houston vs. New York, August 26, 2000	8	21*
Andrea Stinson, Charlotte vs. Los Angeles, August 30, 2001	8	17

FREE THROWS

	FT	FTA
Cynthia Cooper, Houston vs. New York, September 5, 1999	13	15
Cynthia Cooper, Houston vs. New York, August 30, 1997	11	15
Cynthia Cooper, Houston vs. Phoenix, August 29, 1998	11	14*
Cynthia Cooper, Houston at New York, September 2, 1999	10	10
Cynthia Cooper, Houston vs. New York, September 4, 1999	10	12
Sheryl Swoopes, Houston vs. Phoenix, September 1, 1998	9	10
Lisa Leslie, Los Angeles vs. Charlotte, September 1, 2001	9	10
Cynthia Cooper, Houston vs. New York, August 26, 2000	8	8*
Sheryl Swoopes, Houston vs. New York, September 4, 1999	7	8
Tamika Whitmore, New York at Los Angeles, August 31, 2002	7	9

REBOUNDS

	REB
Tari Phillips, New York vs. Houston, August 24, 2000	15
Lisa Leslie, Los Angeles at Detroit, September 14, 2003	15
Kym Hampton, New York at Houston, August 30, 1997	13
Sheryl Swoopes, Houston vs. Phoenix, August 29, 1998	13*
Lisa Leslie, Los Angeles vs. Charlotte, September 1, 2001	13
Michelle Griffiths, Phoenix vs. Houston, August 27, 1998	12
Tina Thompson, Houston vs. Phoenix, August 29, 1998	12*
Cheryl Ford, Detroit at Los Angeles, September 12, 2003	12
Lisa Leslie, Los Angeles vs. Detroit, September 12, 2003	12
Swin Cash, Detroit vs. Los Angeles, September 16, 2003	12
Tammy Jackson, Houston vs. New York, August 30, 1997	11
Sheryl Swoopes, Houston at Phoenix, August 27, 1998	11
Sue Wicks, New York vs. Houston, September 2, 1999	11
Tammy Jackson, Houston vs. New York, September 5, 1999	11
Latasha Byears, Los Angeles at New York, August 29, 2002	11
Latasha Byears, Los Angeles vs. New York, August 31, 2002	11
Chery Ford, Detroit vs. Los Angeles, September 16, 2003	11
Lisa Leslie, Los Angeles at Detroit, September 16, 2003	11

ASSISTS

	AST
Nikki Teasley, Los Angeles at New York, August 29, 2002	11
Nikki Teasley, Los Angeles vs. New York, August 31, 2002	11
Nikki Teasley, Los Angeles vs. Detroit, September 12, 2003	11
Teresa Weatherspoon, New York vs. Houston, September 2, 1999	10
Swin Cash, Detroit vs. Los Angeles, September 16, 2003	9
Teresa Weatherspoon, New York at Houston, August 26, 2000	8*
Michele Timms, Phoenix at Houston, September 1, 1998	7

Cynthia Cooper, Houston vs. New York, August 26, 2000 ....7*
Tamecka Dixon, Los Angeles vs. Charlotte, September 1, 2001 7
Nikki Teasley, Los Angeles at Detroit, September 16, 2003 7
Kim Perrot, Houston at Phoenix, August 27, 1998 6
Sheryl Swoopes, Houston at Phoenix, August 27, 1998 6
Cynthia Cooper, Houston vs. Phoenix, August 29, 1998 ....6*
Cynthia Cooper, Houston vs. Phoenix, September 1, 1998 6
Sheryl Swoopes, Houston vs. Phoenix, September 1, 1998...6
Cynthia Cooper, Houston at New York, September 2, 1999 6
Cynthia Cooper, Houston vs. New York, September 4, 1999 6
Lisa Leslie, Los Angeles vs. Charlotte, September 1, 2001 6
Nikki Teasley, Los Angeles at Detroit, September 14, 2003 6

STEALS

STL

Teresa Weatherspoon, New York at Houston, August 30, 1997 4
Cynthia Cooper, Houston at New York, September 2, 1999 4
Sue Wicks, New York vs. Houston, September 2, 1999 4
Sheryl Swoopes, Houston vs. New York, September 4, 1999 4
Kim Perrot, Houston vs. New York, August 30, 1997 3
Cynthia Cooper, Houston vs. Phoenix, August 29, 1998 ....3*
Tammy Jackson, Houston vs. New York, September 4, 1999 3
Cynthia Cooper, Houston vs. New York, September 5, 1999 3
Tammy Jackson, Houston vs. New York, September 5, 1999 3
Cynthia Cooper, Houston vs. New York, August 26, 2000 ....3*
Tari Phillips, New York at Houston, August 26, 2000 ....3*
Allison Feaster, Charlotte vs. Los Angeles, August 30, 2001 3
Allison Feaster, Charlotte at Los Angeles, September 1, 2001 3
Latasha Byears, Los Angeles at New York, August 29, 2002 3
Kedra Holland-Corn, Detroit at Los Angeles, September 12, 2003 3
Lisa Leslie, Los Angeles at Detroit, September 14, 2003 3
DeLisha Milton, Los Angeles at Detroit, September 14, 2003 3
Deanna Nolan, Detroit vs. Los Angeles, September 14, 2003 3

BLOCKED SHOTS

BLK

Lisa Leslie, Los Angeles vs. Charlotte, September 1, 2001 7
Tammy Sutton-Brown, Charlotte at Los Angeles, September 1, 2001 4
Ruth Riley, Detroit vs. Los Angeles, September 14, 2003 4
Jennifer Gillom, Phoenix at Houston, August 29, 1998 ....3*
Kym Hampton, New York at Houston, September 4, 1999 3
Tammy Jackson, Houston vs. New York, September 5, 1999 3
Allison Feaster, Charlotte vs. Los Angeles, August 30, 2001 3
DeLisha Milton, Los Angeles at New York, August 29, 2002 3
Lisa Leslie, Los Angeles at New York, August 29, 2002 3
Cheryl Ford, Detroit at Los Angeles, September 12, 2003 3
Lisa Leslie, Los Angeles vs. Detroit, September 12, 2003 3
Ruth Riley, Detroit at Los Angeles, September 12, 2003 3
Ruth Riley, Detroit vs. Los Angeles, September 16, 2003 3

*Overtime

RECORDS Finals

ALL-STAR GAME RECORDS
RESULTS

Year	Result	Winning coach	Losing coach	MVP
1999	West 79, East 61 at New York	Van Chancellor	Linda Hill-McDonald	Lisa Leslie, Los Angeles
2000	West 73, East 61 at Phoenix.	Van Chancellor	Richie Adubato	Tina Thompson, Houston
2001	West 80, East 72 at Orlando	Van Chancellor	Richie Adubato	Lisa Leslie, Los Angeles
2002	West 81, East 76 at Washington	Michael Cooper	Anne Donovan	Lisa Leslie, Los Angeles
2003	West 84, East 75 at New York.	Michael Cooper	Richie Adubato	Nikki Teasley, Los Angeles

ALL-TIME ALL-STAR GAME LEADERS

GAMES
Lisa Leslie 5
Nykesha Sales 5
Teresa Weatherspoon 5
Yolanda Griffith 4
Shannon Johnson 4
Ticha Penicheiro 4
Tari Phillips 4
Katie Smith 4
Sheryl Swoopes 4
Tina Thompson 4

MINUTES
Lisa Leslie 105
Teresa Weatherspoon 89
Tari Phillips 88
Ticha Penicheiro 87
Sheryl Swoopes 84
Tina Thompson 84
Taj McWilliams-Franklin 81
Yolanda Griffith 80
Shannon Johnson 75
Nykesha Sales 65

FIELD GOALS MADE
Lisa Leslie 34
Yolanda Griffith 21
Tina Thompson 18
Tari Phillips 16
Nykesha Sales 15
Lauren Jackson 13
Sheryl Swoopes 12
Tamika Catchings 10
Taj McWilliams-Franklin 10
Chamique Holdsclaw 9
Merlakia Jones 9

FIELD GOAL ATTEMPTS
Lisa Leslie 63
Tina Thompson 50
Tari Phillips 43
Nykesha Sales 38
Yolanda Griffith 34
Sheryl Swoopes 30
Nikki McCray 29
Tamika Catchings 27

Lauren Jackson 27
Chamique Holdsclaw 25
Andrea Stinson 25

FIELD GOAL PERCENTAGE (MINIMUM: 8 FG)

	FG	FGA	PCT
Yolanda Griffith	21	34	.618
Lisa Leslie	34	63	.540
Natalie Williams	8	15	.533
Taj McWilliams-Franklin	10	20	.500
Lauren Jackson	13	27	.481
Merlakia Jones	9	20	.450
Sheryl Swoopes	12	30	.400
Nykesha Sales	15	38	.395
Tari Phillips	16	43	.372
Tamika Catchings	10	27	.370

FREE THROWS MADE
Lisa Leslie 14
Yolanda Griffith 9
Natalie Williams 9
Taj McWilliams-Franklin 7
Tina Thompson 7
Sheryl Swoopes 5
Seven tied 4

FREE THROW ATTEMPTS
Lisa Leslie 20
Yolanda Griffith 13
Tari Phillips 12
Natalie Williams 12
Taj McWilliams-Franklin 10
Sheryl Swoopes 8
Tina Thompson 8
Nykesha Sales 7
Merlakia Jones 6
Ticha Penicheiro 6

FREE THROW PERCENTAGE (MINIMUM: 4 FT)

	FT	FTA	PCT
Jackie Stiles	4	4	1.000
Nikki Teasley	4	4	1.000
Tina Thompson	7	8	.875
Sue Bird	4	5	.800

Lauren Jackson 4	5	.800
Natalie Williams 9	12	.750
Taj McWilliams-Franklin ..7	10	.700
Lisa Leslie 14	20	.700
Yolanda Griffith 9	13	.692
Merlakia Jones 4	6	.667

THREE-POINT FIELD GOALS THREE-POINT FIELD GOAL ATTEMPTS

Tamika Catchings 6
Lauren Jackson 5
Shannon Johnson 4
Deanna Nolan 3
Nykesha Sales 3
Vickie Johnson 2
Lisa Leslie 2
Mwadi Mabika 2
Nikki Teasley 2
Tina Thompson 2

THREE-POINT FIELD GOAL ATTEMPTS

Shannon Johnson 16
Nykesha Sales 14
Tamika Catchings 11
Sue Bird 9
Lauren Jackson 9
Tina Thompson 9
Vickie Johnson 8
Nikki McCray 8
Andrea Stinson 8
Three tied 7

THREE-POINT PERCENTAGE (MINIMUM: 2 FG3)

	3FG	3GA	PCT
Lauren Jackson 5		9	.556
Tamika Catchings 6		11	.545
Deanna Nolan 3		7	.429
Nikki Teasley 2		5	.400
Lisa Leslie 2		6	.333
Mwadi Mabika 2		6	.333
Shannon Johnson 4		16	.250
Vickie Johnson 2		8	.250
Tina Thompson 2		9	.222
Nykesha Sales 3		14	.214

OFFENSIVE REBOUNDS

Tari Phillips 19
Natalie Williams 15
Lisa Leslie 14
Yolanda Griffith 12
Taj McWilliams-Franklin 11
Tina Thompson 10
Sheryl Swoopes 7
Sue Bird 5
Tamika Catchings 5
Lauren Jackson 5

DEFENSIVE REBOUNDS

Lisa Leslie 23
Yolanda Griffith 17
Sheryl Swoopes 17
Tari Phillips 16
Tina Thompson 16
Natalie Williams 14
Chamique Holdsclaw 9
Taj McWilliams-Franklin 9
Teresa Weatherspoon 9
Three tied 8

TOTAL REBOUNDS

Lisa Leslie 37
Tari Phillips 35
Yolanda Griffith 29
Natalie Williams 29
Tina Thompson 26
Sheryl Swoopes 24
Taj McWilliams-Franklin 20
Tamika Catchings 13
Lauren Jackson 13
Merlakia Jones 11
Teresa Weatherspoon 11

ASSISTS

Dawn Staley 15
Ticha Penicheiro 14
Teresa Weatherspoon 13
Sheryl Swoopes 10
Sue Bird 9
Shannon Johnson 9
Katie Smith 6
Nikki Teasley 6
Tamecka Dixon 5
Andrea Stinson 5

STEALS

Teresa Weatherspoon 9
Tina Thompson 8
Ruthie Bolton 7
Shannon Johnson 7
Nikki McCray 6
Taj McWilliams-Franklin 6
Sheryl Swoopes 6
Six tied 5

PERSONAL FOULS

Tari Phillips 15
Shannon Johnson 10
Lisa Leslie 10
Tina Thompson 8
Tamika Catchings 7
Yolanda Griffith 7
Lauren Jackson 7
Taj McWilliams-Franklin 7
Nykesha Sales 6
Teresa Weatherspoon 6

DISQUALIFICATIONS

Tari Phillips 1

BLOCKED SHOTS

Lisa Leslie	9
Yolanda Griffith	5
Tari Phillips	5
Elena Baranova	4
Tamika Catchings	4
Lauren Jackson	4
Tammy Sutton-Brown	3
Vicky Bullett	2
Shannon Johnson	2
Taj McWilliams-Franklin	2
Tina Thompson	2

POINTS

Lisa Leslie	84
Yolanda Griffith	51
Tina Thompson	45
Nykesha Sales	37
Tari Phillips	36

INDIVIDUAL RECORDS

Most minutes, game
    31 — Taj McWilliams, 1999
    30 — Tamika Catchings, 2003
    28 — Lisa Leslie, 2002
         Tina Thompson, 2002
Most points, game
    20 — Lisa Leslie, 2001
         Tina Thompson, 2002
    18 — Lisa Leslie, 2002
    17 — Yolanda Griffith, 2001
         Tamika Catchings, 2003
         Lisa Leslie, 2003
Most field goals, game
    8 — Lisa Leslie, 2000
        Lisa Leslie, 2001
    7 — Yolanda Griffith, 2001
        Tina Thompson, 2002
        Lisa Leslie, 2003
    6 — By many
Most field goal attempts, game
    16 — Tina Thompson, 2002
    15 — Lisa Leslie, 2000
         Tamika Catchings, 2003
    14 — Tari Phillips, 2000
         Tina Thompson, 2000
         Lisa Leslie, 2001
Highest field goal percentage, game
(Minimum: 4 FG)
    .875 — Yolanda Griffith, 2001 (7/8)
    .750 — Yolanda Griffith, 2003 (6/8)
    .700 — Lisa Leslie, 2003 (7/10)
Most free throws, game
    8 — Natalie Williams, 1999
    6 — Lisa Leslie, 2002
    5 — Tina Thompson, 2002
Most free throw attempts, game
    10 — Natalie Williams, 1999
         Lisa Leslie, 2002
    6 — Yolanda Griffith, 2000
        Merlakia Jones, 2001

Lauren Jackson	35
Tamika Catchings	29
Sheryl Swoopes	29
Taj McWilliams-Franklin	28
Natalie Williams	25

SCORING AVERAGE
(MINIMUM: 3 G)

	G	FG	FT	PTS	AVG
Lisa Leslie	5	34	14	84	16.8
Yolanda Griffith	4	21	9	51	12.8
Lauren Jackson	3	13	4	35	11.7
Tina Thompson	4	18	7	45	11.3
Taj McWilliams-Franklin	3	10	7	28	9.3
Tari Phillips	4	16	4	36	9.0
Natalie Williams	3	8	9	25	8.3
Nykesha Sales	5	15	4	37	7.4
Merlakia Jones	3	9	4	22	7.3
Sheryl Swoopes	4	12	5	29	7.3

        Tari Phillips, 2001
        Tina Thompson, 2002
Most free throw made, no misses, game
    4 — Jackie Stiles, 2001
        Nikki Teasley, 2003
    3 — Nykesha Sales, 2002
    2 — By many
Most three-point field goals, game
    4 — Tamika Catchings, 2003
    3 — Deanna Nolan, 2003
    2 — By many
Most three-point field goal attempts, game
    7 — Deanna Nolan, 2003
    6 — Nikki McCray, 2000
        Shannon Johnson, 2002
        Tamika Catchings, 2003
    5 — By many
Most rebounds, game
    14 — Lisa Leslie, 2002
    11 — Tina Thompson, 2000
         Natalie Williams, 2003
    10 — Yolanda Griffith, 2000
         Natalie Williams, 2000
         Tari Phillips, 2002
Most offensive rebounds, game
    8 — Tari Phillips, 2000
    7 — Taj McWilliams, 2000
Natalie Williams, 2003
    6 — Tina Thompson, 2000
Most defensive rebounds, game
    11 — Lisa Leslie, 2002
    7 — Sheryl Swoopes, 1999
Elena Baranova, 2001
    6 — Natalie Williams, 2000
        Lisa Leslie, 2001
        Tamika Catchings, 2002
        Nikki Teasley, 2003
Most assists, game
    7 — Sue Bird, 2002
        Dawn Staley, 2003
    6 — Nikki Teasley, 2003
    5 — Ticha Penicheiro, 2001

Dawn Staley, 2002
Most personal fouls, game
6 — Tari Phillips, 2002
5 — Vicky Bullett, 1999
Tina Thompson, 2001
4 — By many
Most steals, game
6 — Ruthie Bolton-Holifield, 2001
5 — Nikki Teasley, 2003
4 — Dawn Staley, 2001
Most blocked shots, game
4 — Elena Baranova, 2001
Tamika Catchings, 2002
Lisa Leslie, 2002
3 — Tari Phillips, 2000
Lisa Leslie, 2001
Tammy Sutton-Brown, 2002
Lauren Jackson, 2003
Most turnovers, game
7 — Ticha Penicheiro, 2000
Tari Phillips, 2001
6 — Yolanda Griffith, 2003
5 — Ticha Penicheiro, 2001
Tari Phillips, 2002

TEAM RECORDS

SCORING

Most points, game
84 — West, 2003
81 — West, 2002
Fewest points, game
61 — East, 1999, 2000
72 — East, 2001
Most points, both teams, game
159 — West (84) vs. East (75), 2003
Fewest points, both teams, game
134 — East (61) vs. West (73), 2000
Most points, first half
46 — East, 2003
43 — West, 1999
Fewest points, first half
29 — East, 1999
30 — East, 2001
Most points, both teams, first half
84 — East (46) vs. West (38), 2003
Fewest points, both teams, first half
70 — East (30) vs. West (40), 2001
Most points, second half
46 — West, 2003
42 — East, 2001
Fewest points, second half
28 — East, 2000
29 — East, 2003
Most points, both teams, second half
82 — East (42) vs. West (40), 2001
Fewest points, both teams, second half
61 — East (28) vs. West (33), 2000
Most points, overtime period
None
Fewest points, overtime period
None
Most points, both teams, overtime period
None

FIELD GOALS

Most field goals, game
31 — West, 1999, 2001, 2002, 2003
Fewest field goals, game
25 — East, 2000
26 — East, 1999
Most field goals, both teams, game
61 — West (31) vs. East (30), 2003
Fewest field goals, both teams, game
54 — East (25) vs. West (29), 2000

FIELD GOAL ATTEMPTS

Most field goal attempts, game
85 — East, 2000
84 — East, 2003
Fewest field goal attempts, game
65 — West, 2003
69 — East, 2001
Most field goal attempts, both teams, game
165 — East (84) vs. West (81), 2002
Fewest field goal attempts, both teams, game
144 — West (70) vs. East (74), 1999
East (69) vs. West (75), 2001

FIELD GOAL PERCENTAGE

Highest field goal percentage, game
.477 — West, 2003 (31/65)
.443 — West, 1999 (31/70)
Lowest field goal percentage, game
.294 — East, 2000 (25/85)
.333 — East, 2002 (28/84)
Highest field goal percentage, both teams, game
.412 — West (.477) vs. East (.361),
2003 (61/148)
Lowest field goal percentage, both teams, game
.333 — East (.294) vs. West (.377),
2000 (54/162)

THREE-POINT FIELD GOALS

Most three-point field goals, game
9 — East, 2003
7 — East, 2002
Fewest three-point field goals, game
2 — West, 1999
East, 2000
Most three-point field goals, both teams, game
14 — East (9) vs. West (5), 2003
Fewest three-point field goals, both teams, game
6 — West (2) vs. East (4), 1999
East (2) vs. West (4), 2000

THREE-POINT FIELD GOALS ATTEMPTS

Most three-point field goal attempts, game
27 — East, 2002
26 — East, 2003
Fewest three-point field goal attempts, game
14 — West, 1999
15 — West, 2000, 2003
Most three-point field goal attempts, both teams, game
49 — East (27) vs. West (22), 2002
Fewest three-point field goal attempts, both teams, game
32 — West (14) vs. East (18), 1999

FREE THROWS

Most free throws, game
    17 — West, 2003
    15 — West, 1999, 2002
Fewest free throws, game
    5 — East, 1999
    6 — East, 2003
Most free throws, both teams, game
    28 — West (15) vs. East (13), 2002
Fewest free throws, both teams, game
    20 — East (5) vs. West (15), 1999
        East (9) vs. West (11), 2000

FREE THROW ATTEMPTS

Most free throw attempts, game
    24 — East, 2001
    23 — West, 2003
Fewest free throw attempts, game
    9 — East, 1999
    10 — East, 2003
Most free throw attempts, both teams, game
    41 — East (24) vs. West (17), 2001
Fewest free throw attempts, both teams, game
    28 — East (9) vs. West (19), 1999

REBOUNDS

Most rebounds, game
    60 — West, 2000
    50 — West, 2002
Fewest rebounds, game
    36 — East, 1999, 2001
        West, 2001
Most rebounds, both teams, game
    100 — West (60) vs. East (40), 2000
Fewest rebounds, both teams, game
    72 — East (36) vs. West (36), 2001

OFFENSIVE REBOUNDS

Most offensive rebounds, game
    25 — West, 2000
    22 — East, 2000
Fewest offensive rebounds, game
    8 — West, 2003
    9 — East, 1999, 2001
Most offensive rebounds, both teams, game
    47 — West (25) vs. East (22), 2000
Fewest offensive rebounds, both teams, game
    19 — East (9) vs. West (10), 2001

DEFENSIVE REBOUNDS

Most defensive rebounds, game
    37 — West, 1999
    35 — West, 2000
Fewest defensive rebounds, game
    18 — East, 2000
    26 — West, 2001
        East, 2003
Most defensive rebounds, both teams, game
    64 — West (37) vs. East (27), 1999
Fewest defensive rebounds, both teams, game
    53 — East (18) vs. West (35), 2000
        West (26) vs. East (27), 2001

ASSISTS

Most assists, game
    19 — West, 1999

18 — West, 2002
Fewest assists, game
    11 — East, 2000
    14 — East, 2001
        West, 2001
Most assists, both teams, game
    35 — West (19) vs. East (16), 1999
Fewest assists, both teams, game
    27 — East (11) vs. West (16), 2000

PERSONAL FOULS

Most personal fouls, game
    21 — West, 2001
    20 — East, 2002
Fewest personal fouls, game
    8 — West, 2000
    10 — West, 1999
Most personal fouls, both teams, game
    36 — West (21) vs. East (15), 2001
Fewest personal fouls, both teams, game
    24 — West (8) vs. East (16), 2000

STEALS

Most steals, game
    18 — West, 2001
    14 — East, 2000
West, 2003
Fewest steals, game
    9 — West, 2002
    10 — West, 2000
Most steals, both teams, game
    30 — West (18) vs. East (12), 2001
Fewest steals, both teams, game
    20 — West (9) vs. East (11), 2002

BLOCKED SHOTS

Most blocked shots, game
    8 — East, 2002
    7 — West, 2002
Fewest blocked shots, game
    3 — West, 1999, 2000
    4 — East, 1999, 2003
Most blocked shots, both teams, game
    15 — East (8) vs. West (7), 2002
Fewest blocked shots, both teams, game
    7 — West (3) vs. East (4), 1999

DISQUALIFICATIONS

Most disqualifications, game
    1 — East, 2002
Most disqualifications, both teams, game
    1 — East (1) vs. West (0), 2002

TURNOVERS

Fewest turnovers, game
    14 — East, 2002
    15 — East, 1999, 2000
Most turnovers, game
    23 — West, 2000
    21 — East, 2001
Fewest turnovers, both teams, game
    31 — East (14) vs. West (17), 2002
Most turnovers, both teams, game
    40 — East (21) vs. West (19), 2001
        East (20) vs. West (20), 2003

CHARLOTTE STING

TEAM OFFENSE

SCORING

Highest average, points per game, season
71.4 — 1998 (2143/30)
70.0 — 2002 (2241/32)
Lowest average, points per game, season
64.2 — 2001 (2055/32)
65.2 — 2003 (2217/34)
Most points, game
105 — at Washington, August 19, 1998
94 — vs. Los Angeles, June 1, 2002 (ot)
Fewest points, game
41 — at Cleveland, July 21, 2001
42 — at Washington, July 29, 2001
Largest margin of victory, game
36 — at Washington, August 19, 1998
(105—69)
30 — vs. Washington, July 17, 1998 (86-56)
vs. Indiana, August 20, 2003 (80-50)
Largest margin of defeat, game
33 — vs. Phoenix, June 22, 2000 (57-90)
32 — at Cleveland, August 17, 1997 (49-81)

BY HALF

Most points, first half
51 — at Washington, August 19, 1998
47 — vs. Phoenix, July 1, 2002
Fewest points, first half
12 — at Cleveland, July 21, 2001
15 — at Phoenix, August 15, 1999
Largest lead at halftime
20 — at Minnesota, August 3, 2001
(led 33-13; won 72-64)
at Miami, July 5, 2002 (led 41-21; won 72-68)
19 — at Washington, August 19, 1998
(led 51-32; won 105-69)
Largest deficit at halftime overcome to win game
13 — vs. Detroit, August 3, 1998
(trailed 27-40; won 71-68)
10 — vs. Connecticut, August 9, 2003
(trailed 30-40; won 69-68)
Most points, second half
55 — vs. New York, July 9, 1997
54 — at Washington, August 19, 1998
Fewest points, second half
18 — vs. Utah, July 22, 1998
at Washington, July 29, 2001
vs. New York, August 24, 2003
19 — at Cleveland, June 25, 1999
at Washington, June 30, 2002

OVERTIME

Most points, overtime period
14 — vs. Los Angeles, June 1, 2002
13 — at Cleveland, July 24, 2002
Fewest points, overtime period
4 — vs. Miami, June 3, 2000
5 — vs. Cleveland, July 20, 2003
Largest margin of victory, overtime period
7 — vs. Los Angeles, June 1, 2002 (94-87)
at Cleveland, July 24, 2002 (73-66)
6 — at New York, July 26, 1999 (75-69)

FIELD GOAL PERCENTAGE

Highest field—goal percentage, season
.439 — 1999 (793/1805)
.435 — 1997 (719/1651)
Lowest field—goal percentage, season
.418 — 2003 (787/1881)
.419 — 2001 (746/1780)
Highest field—goal percentage, game
.625 — at Washington, August 19, 1998 (40/64)
.603 — vs. Orlando, July 17, 2002 (35/58)
Lowest field—goal percentage, game
.246 — at Detroit, June 29, 1998 (16/65)
.254 — at Washington, July 29, 2001 (15/59)

FIELD GOALS

Most field goals per game, season
26.6 — 1998 (798/30)
25.7 — 1997 (719/28)
Fewest field goals per game, season
23.2 — 2003 (787/34)
23.3 — 2001 (746/32)
Most field goals, game
40 — at Washington, August 19, 1998
35 — vs. Orlando, July 17, 2002
Fewest field goals, game
15 — at Washington, July 29, 2001
16 — at Cleveland, July 17, 1997
at Detroit, June 29, 1998
at Cleveland, July 21, 2001
vs. Miami, July 9, 2002
at Orlando, July 12, 2002

FIELD GOAL ATTEMPTS

Most field—goal attempts per game, season
61.8 — 1998 (1855/30)
59.5 — 2000 (1903/32)
Fewest field—goal attempts per game, season
55.3 — 2003 (1881/34)
55.6 — 2001 (1780/32)
Most field—goal attempts, game
73 — at Cleveland, July 19, 1998

72 — at Utah, June 15, 2000

Fewest field—goal attempts, game
41 — vs. Miami, July 31, 2001
44 — vs. Minnesota, June 20, 2003

THREE-POINT FIELD-GOAL PERCENTAGE

Highest three-point field-goal percentage, season
.400 — 2002 (211/527)
.362 — 2003 (187/517)
Lowest three-point field-goal percentage, season
.279 — 1998 (105/377)
.293 — 1999 (108/369)

THREE-POINT FIELD GOALS

Most three-point field goals per game, season
6.6 — 2002 (211/32)
5.5 — 2003 (187/34)
Fewest three-point field goals per game, season
3.4 — 1999 (108/32)
3.5 — 1998 (105/30)
Most three-point field goals, game
13 — at Detroit, July 3, 2003
12 — vs. Los Angeles, June 1, 2002 (ot)
Fewest three-point field goals, game
0 — at Los Angeles, June 24, 1998
vs. Utah, July 22, 1998
vs. Cleveland, June 5, 2000
1 — many times

THREE-POINT FIELD GOAL ATTEMPTS

Most three-point field goal attempts per game, season
16.5 — 2002 (527/32)
15.2 — 2003 (517/34)
Fewest three-point field goal attempts per game, season
11.46— 1997 (321/28)
11.53— 1999 (369/32)
Most three-point field goal attempts, game
24 — vs. Cleveland, July 6, 2002
23 — vs. New York, August 4, 2002
Fewest three-point field goal attempts, game
3 — at Sacramento, June 26, 1997
4 — at Los Angeles, June 24, 1998

FREE THROW PERCENTAGE

Highest free-throw percentage, season
.777 — 2001 (410/528)
.773 — 2003 (456/590)
Lowest free-throw percentage, season
.692 — 1997 (337/487)
.708 — 1998 (442/624)
Highest free-throw percentage, game
1.000 — vs. Sacramento, August 4, 1999 (11/11)
at New York, June 12, 2001 (6/6)
.955 — vs. Sacramento, June 27, 1998 (21/22)
Lowest free-throw percentage, game
.412 — vs. Cleveland, August 14, 1998 (7/17)
.444 — at Cleveland, August 8, 1998 (4/9)

FREE THROWS MADE

Most free throws made per game, season
15.3 — 2002 (490/32)
14.7 — 1998 (442/30)
Fewest free throws made per game, season
12.0 — 1997 (337/28)
12.8 — 1999 (410/32)
2001 (410/32)
Most free throws made, game
33 — at Orlando, July 12, 2002
27 — vs. Washington, July 26, 2000
vs. Connecticut, June 28, 2003
Fewest free throws made, game
4 — at Phoenix, August 22, 1997
at Cleveland, August 8, 1998
vs. Orlando, June 10, 2000
at Cleveland, July 10, 2000
at Seattle, June 18, 2001
at Orlando, August 1, 2002
5 — vs. Houston, June 28, 2000
at Phoenix, June 12, 2003

FREE THROW ATTEMPTS

Most free throw attempts per game, season
20.8 — 1998 (624/30)
20.7 — 2002 (663/32)
Fewest free throw attempts per game, season
16.5 — 2001 (528/32)
16.7 — 1999 (535/32)
Most free throw attempts, game
44 — at Orlando, July 12, 2002
35 — vs. Washington, July 26, 2000
Fewest free throw attempts, game
5 — at Seattle, June 18, 2001
6 — at Cleveland, July 10, 2000
at New York, June 12, 2001
at Orlando, August 1, 2002
at Phoenix, June 12, 2003

REBOUNDS

Most rebounds per game, season
32.7 — 1998 (981/30)
32.6 — 1997 (914/28)
Fewest rebounds per game, season
28.6 — 2003 (971/34)
29.2 — 2000 (935/32)
Most rebounds, game
47 — vs. Cleveland, July 12, 1997
45 — vs. Phoenix, August 9, 1997
Fewest rebounds, game
16 — at Cleveland, August 25, 2003
17 — vs. Utah, August 5, 2000

OFFENSIVE REBOUNDS

Most offensive rebounds per game, season
10.13— 1998 (304/30)
10.06— 2003 (342/34)
Fewest offensive rebounds per game, season
8.4 — 1999 (268/32)

9.4 — 2002 (302/32)

Most offensive rebounds, game
    19 — vs. Cleveland, August 14, 1998
    18 — at New York, June 22, 2003

Fewest offensive rebounds, game
    2 — vs. Sacramento, August 4, 1999
    3 — at Los Angeles, August 3, 1997
       at Washington, July 12, 1999
       at Houston, July 7, 2000
       vs. Utah, August 5, 2000

DEFENSIVE REBOUNDS

Most defensive rebounds per game, season
    22.7 — 1997 (635/28)
    22.6 — 1998 (677/30)

Fewest defensive rebounds per game, season
    18.5 — 2003 (629/34)
    19.7 — 2000 (630/32)

Most defensive rebounds, game
    35 — vs. Detroit, June 16, 2001 (2 ot)
    34 — at New York, July 26, 1999 (ot)

Regulation Game:
    33 — vs. Cleveland, July 12, 1997
       at New York, July 12, 1998

Fewest defensive rebounds, game
    10 — at Orlando, June 9, 2001
    11 — vs. Cleveland, July 8, 2000
       vs. Cleveland, July 25, 2002
       at Cleveland, August 25, 2003

ASSISTS

Most assists per game, season
    17.8 — 1999 (568/32)
    17.3 — 1997 (485/28)

Fewest assists per game, season
    14.6 — 2001 (467/32)
    14.7 — 2003 (499/34)

Most assists, game
    31 — at Washington, August 19, 1998
    30 — vs. Orlando, July 17, 2002

Fewest assists, game
    5 — at Washington, July 29, 2001
    6 — at Detroit, July 6, 2001
       at Miami, July 18, 2001
at Seattle, July 31, 2003

PERSONAL FOULS

Most personal fouls per game, season
    22.3 — 2000 (713/32)
    20.5 — 2003 (697/34)

Fewest personal fouls per game, season
    16.6 — 1997 (465/28)
    16.9 — 1998 (507/30)

Most personal fouls, game
    32 — vs. Miami, June 3, 2000 (ot)
    30 — at Cleveland, July 10, 2000

Fewest personal fouls, game
    9 — vs. Sacramento, June 27, 1998
    10 — at Washington, July 7, 2003

DISQUALIFICATIONS

Most disqualifications per game, season
    0.28 — 2002 (9/32)
    0.25 — 2000 (8/32)

Fewest disqualifications per game, season
    0.00 — 1997 (0/28)
    0.09 — 2003 (3/34)

Most disqualifications, game
    3 — vs. Miami, June 3, 2000 (ot)
    2 — vs. Houston, June 15, 1998
       at Utah, June 8, 2002
       at Indiana, July 22, 2002

STEALS

Most steals per game, season
    9.1 — 1998 (273/30)
    8.2 — 2003 (279/34)

Fewest steals per game, season
    6.8 — 2001 (217/32)
    6.9 — 2000 (222/32)

Most steals, game
    17 — vs. Washington, June 11, 1998
    16 — vs. Seattle, June 9, 2000
vs. Detroit, July 10, 2003

Fewest steals, game
    0 — at Miami, August 14, 2001
    1 — vs. Orlando, July 20, 2001
       at Cleveland, July 21, 2001

BLOCKED SHOTS

Most blocked shots per game, season
    4.1 — 1997 (116/28)
    3.6 — 2001 (114/32)

Most blocked shots per game, season
    2.8 — 2000 (90/32)
    3.0 — 1999 (97/32)

Most blocked shots, game
    9 — vs. Detroit, June 16, 2001 (2 ot)
    8 — vs. Orlando, July 17, 2002
       at Washington, July 17, 2003

Fewest blocked shots, game
    0 — Many times. Most recent:
       at Los Angeles, August 2, 2003

TURNOVERS

Most turnovers per game, season
    17.7 — 1997 (496/28)
    15.5 — 2000 (496/32)

Fewest turnovers per game, season
    12.8 — 2002 (408/32)
    14.6 — 2003 (497/34)

Most turnovers, game
    28 — at New York, July 26, 1997
    24 — at New York, July 10, 1997
       vs. Phoenix, July 30, 1997
       at Cleveland, July 21, 2001

FEWEST TURNOVERS, GAME

6 — vs. Cleveland, June 30, 2001
    at New York, August 11, 2002
8 — vs. Sacramento, August 1, 1997
    at New York, July 12, 1998
    at Houston, June 11, 2002
    vs. Miami, June 22, 2002
    at Connecticut, July 26, 2003

TEAM DEFENSE

POINTS

Fewest points allowed per game, season
62.8 — 2001 (2009/32)
64.6 — 2003 (2195/34)
Most points allowed per game, season
75.9 — 2000 (2429/32)
68.4 — 1998 (2051/30)
Fewest points allowed, game
38 — vs. Seattle, July 7, 2001
41 — at Miami, August 14, 2001
Fewest points allowed, first half
13 — at Minnesota, August 3, 2001
15 — at Miami, August 14, 2001
Fewest points allowed, second half
19 — at Phoenix, June 12, 2003
       vs. Indiana, August 20, 2003
21 — Many times
Fewest points allowed, overtime period
5 — at New York, July 26, 1999
6 — at Portland, June 20, 2000
       vs. Indiana, July 24, 2000
       at Cleveland, July 24, 2002

FIELD GOAL PERCENTAGE

Lowest opponents' field—goal percentage, season
.397 — 2001 (732/1846)
.402 — 1997 (686/1707)
Highest opponents' field—goal percentage, season
.455 — 2000 (879/1930)
.431 — 2002 (778/1807)
Lowest opponents' field goal percentage, game
.254 — vs. Houston, August 4, 2001 (15/59)
.270 — vs. Cleveland, July 12, 1997 (17/63)

TURNOVERS

Most opponents' turnovers per game, season
16.7 — 1998 (501/30)
16.6 — 1997 (464/28)
Fewest opponents' turnovers per game, season
13.25— 2002 (424/32)
13.31— 2000 (426/32)
Most opponents' turnovers, game
25 — vs. Sacramento, June 27, 1998
       vs. Utah, July 22, 1998
23 — vs. Cleveland, June 29, 1997
       vs. Washington, June 11, 1998

TEAM MISCELLANEOUS

GAME WON AND LOST

Highest winning percentage, season
.600 — 1998 (18-12)
.563 — 2001 (18-14)
       2002 (18-14)
Lowest winning percentage, season
.250 — 2000 (8-24)
.469 — 1999 (15-17)
Most consecutive games won
9 — July 31, 2001-June 3, 2002
6 — July 25-August 2, 1999
       June 27-July 7, 2001
Most consecutive games won, one season
7 — July 31-August 14, 2001
6 — July 25-August 2, 1999
       June 27-July 7, 2001
Most consecutive games lost
10 — August 9, 199-June 10, 2000
7 — June 12-24, 2001
Most consecutive games lost, one season
7 — June 12-24, 2001
5 — Many times
Highest winning percentage, home games, season
.857 — 1997 (12-2)
.765 — 2003 (13-4)
Lowest winning percentage, home games, season
.313 — 2000 (5-11)
.500 — 1999 (8-8)
Most consecutive home games won
13 — July 14, 2001-July 1, 2002
6 — June 29-July 21, 1997
May 29—June 28, 2003
Most consecutive home games lost
9 — August 20, 1999-July 1, 2000
5 — August 8, 2000-June 24, 2001
Highest winning percentage, road games, season
.600 — 1998 (9—6)
.438 — 1999 (7—9)
       2001 (7—9)
       2002 (7—9)
Lowest winning percentage, road games, season
.188 — 2000 (3—13)
.214 — 1997 (3—11)
Most consecutive road games won
4 — June 13—25, 1998
       July 16—31, 1999
       August 3—14, 2001
       August 6, 2002—May 31, 2003
3 — July 8—12, 1998
Most consecutive road games lost
7 — July 22, 2000-June 7, 2001
6 — June 22-July 17, 1997
       August 6, 1999-June 1, 2000

OVERTIME GAMES

Most overtime games, season
3 — 2000, 2001
2 — 2002, 2003

Most consecutive overtime games, season
2 — June 22-24, 2001
Most overtime games won, season
2 — 2000, 2002
1 — 1999, 2003
Most overtime games won, no losses, season
2 — 2002
1 — 1999
Most consecutive overtime games won
2 — June 20—July 24, 2000
   June 1-July 24, 2002
Most overtime games lost, season
3 — 2001
1 — 2000, 2003
Most overtime games lost, no wins, season
3 — 2001
Most consecutive overtime games lost
3 — June 16-24, 2001
Most overtime periods, game
2 — vs. Detroit, June 16, 2001

INDIVIDUAL RECORDS

SEASONS

Most Seasons
7 — Andrea Stinson
5 — Charlotte Smith-Taylor
Dawn Staley
4 — Shalonda Enis
   Rhonda Mapp

GAMES

Most game, career
220 — Andrea Stinson
162 — Dawn Staley
151 — Charlotte Smith-Taylor
Most consecutive games, career
220 — Andrea Stinson, June 22, 1997
   August 25, 2003 (current)
162 — Dawn Staley, June 10, 1999—August
   25, 2003 (current)
98 — Allison Feaster, June 2, 2001—August
   25, 2003 (current)
Most games, season
34 — By many

MINUTES

Most minutes, career
7,177 — Andrea Stinson
5,463 — Dawn Staley
3,416 — Charlotte Smith—Taylor

Highest average, minutes per game, career
(Minimum 90 games)
33.7 — Dawn Staley (5463/162)
32.6 — Andrea Stinson (7177/220)
31.4 — Vicky Bullett (2830/90)

Most minutes, season
1,152 — Dawn Staley, 2001
1,123 — Andrea Stinson, 2000
1,099 — Dawn Staley, 2000
Highest average, minutes per game, season
36.1 — Andrea Stinson, 1997 (1011/28)
36.0 — Dawn Staley, 2001 (1152/32)
35.1 — Andrea Stinson, 2000 (1123/32)
Most minutes, game
45 — Allison Feaster, vs. Los Angeles, June 1,
   2002 (ot)
44 — Dawn Staley, vs. Sacramento, June 24,
   2001 (ot)
43 — Dawn Staley, at Portland, June 20,
   2000 (ot)

SCORING

Most points, lifetime
3,126 — Andrea Stinson
1,495 — Dawn Staley
1,181 — Rhonda Mapp
Highest average, points per game, career
(Minimum 90 games)
14.2 — Andrea Stinson (3126/220)
12.5 — Vicky Bullett (1127/90)
11.9 — Allison Feaster (1166/98)
Most points, season
565 — Andrea Stinson, 2000
450 — Andrea Stinson, 1998
Andrea Stinson, 2001
439 — Andrea Stinson, 1997
Highest average, points per game, season
17.7 — Andrea Stinson, 2000 (565/32)
15.7 — Andrea Stinson, 1997 (439/28)
15.0 — Andrea Stinson, 1998 (450/30)
Most points, game
33 — Andrea Stinson, vs. Washington, July
   26, 2000
29 — Andrea Stinson, vs. New York, July 9, 1997
   Shalonda Enis, at Detroit, July 3, 2003
27 — Andrea Stinson, vs. Detroit, July 28, 1999
   Andrea Stinson, vs. Washington, June
   19, 2002
Most games, 30 or more points, career
1 — Andrea Stinson
Most games, 20 or more points, career
37 — Andrea Stinson
9 — Allison Feaster
8 — Vicky Bullett
Most consecutive games, 20 or more points
2 — Many times
Most consecutive games, 10 or more points
20 — Andrea Stinson, August 16, 1999-July 8, 2000
19 — Andrea Stinson, July 12, 2000-June 14, 2001
14 — Andrea Stinson, July 10-August 4, 1999

FIELD GOAL PERCENTAGE

Highest field goal percentage, career
(Minimum 350 field goals)
.486 — Rhonda Mapp (459/944)

.457 — Vicky Bullett (449/983)
.454 — Andrea Stinson (1223/2691)
Highest field goal percentage, season (qualifiers)
  .531 — Tammy Sutton—Brown, 2002 (129/243)
  .500 — Rhonda Mapp, 1999 (118/236)
  .492 — Rhonda Mapp, 1997 (120/244)
Highest field goal percentage, game
(Minimum 8 field goals made)
  .909 — Tracy Reid, vs. Utah, August 5, 2000 (10/11)
  .889 — Andrea Stinson, vs. Houston, June 3, 2002 (8/9)
  .833 — Rhonda Mapp, vs. Cleveland, July 30, 1998
    (10/12)
Most field goals, none missed, game
    5 — Tammy Sutton—Brown, at Seattle, June
      6, 2002
      Tammy Sutton—Brown, vs. Indiana,
      June 13, 2002
    4 — Sharon Manning, at Detroit, July 25, 1999
      Summer Erb, vs. Indiana, June 13, 2002
      Erin Buescher, vs. Detroit, July 27, 2002
Most field goal attempts, none made, game
    8 — Kelly Miller, vs. Detroit, July 10, 2003
    7 — Tora Suber, vs. Houston, July 25, 1998
      Tammy Sutton—Brown, at Washington,
      July 29, 2001
      Charlotte Smith, at Miami, July 5, 2002
      Shalonda Enis, vs. New York, August 7,
      2003

FIELD GOALS
Most field goals, career
1,223 — Andrea Stinson
  500 — Dawn Staley
  459 — Rhonda Mapp
Most field goals, season
  214 — Andrea Stinson, 2000
  179 — Andrea Stinson, 2001
  177 — Andrea Stinson, 1997
Most field goals, game
    12 — Andrea Stinson, vs. Washington, June
      19, 2002
    11 — Andrea Stinson, vs. New York, July 9, 1997
      Andrea Stinson, vs. Houston, August 16, 1997
      Vicky Bullett, at Los Angeles, June 24, 1998
      Andrea Stinson, vs. Phoenix, June 24, 1999
      Andrea Stinson, vs. Washington, July 26, 2000

FIELD GOAL ATTEMPTS

Most field goal attempts, career
2,691 — Andrea Stinson
1,282 — Dawn Staley
1,006 — Allison Feaster
Most field goal attempts, season
  463 — Andrea Stinson, 2000
  414 — Andrea Stinson, 1998
  396 — Andrea Stinson, 1997
Most field goal attempts, game
    23 — Andrea Stinson, vs. Los Angeles,
      August 12, 1998

Andrea Stinson, vs. Cleveland, August 14, 1998
    22 — Vicky Bullett, at Los Angeles, June 24,
      1998
      Andrea Stinson, at Los Angeles, July 7,
      1998
THREE-POINT FIELD-GOAL PERCENTAGE
Highest three-point field goal percentage, career
(Minimum 90 three-point field goals)
  .367 — Allison Feaster (206/562)
  .358 — Dawn Staley (156/436)
  .344 — Andrea Stinson (194/564)
Highest three-point field goal percentage, season
(qualifiers)
  .471 — Kelly Miller, 2002 (24/51)
  .446 — Andrea Stinson, 2001 (29/65)
  .423 — Kelly Miller, 2003 (22/52)
Most three-point field goals, none missed, game
    5 — Shalonda Enis, at Detroit, July 3, 2003
    4 — Kelly Miller, vs. Los Angeles, June 1,
      2002 (ot)
      Dawn Staley, vs. New York, August 4,
      2002
Most three-point field goal attempts, none made, game
    6 — Allison Feaster, vs. New York, August
      4, 2002
    5 — Tora Suber, vs. Houston, July 25, 1998
      Stephanie McCarty, vs. Washington,
      June 30, 1999
      Charlotte Smith, at Detroit, July 29, 2000
      Allison Feaster, at Cleveland, July 21, 2001
      Andrea Stinson, at Houston, June 11, 2002
      Allison Feaster, at Connecticut, August 22,
      2003

THREE—POINT FIELD GOALS

Most three—point field goals, career
  206 — Allison Feaster
  194 — Andrea Stinson
  156 — Dawn Staley
Most three—point field goals, season
  79 — Allison Feaster, 2002
  72 — Allison Feaster, 2003
  55 — Allison Feaster, 2001
Most three-point field goals, game
    6 — Allison Feaster, vs. Cleveland, July 6,
      2002
    5 — By many
Most consecutive games, three-point field goals made
  16 — Allison Feaster, June 30—August 3, 2002
  15 — Allison Feaster, May 31—July 7, 2003
  13 — Allison Feaster, July 17—August 20, 2003

THREE-POINT FIELD GOAL ATTEMPTS

Most three-point field goal attempts, career
  564 — Andrea Stinson
  562 — Allison Feaster
  436 — Dawn Staley

Most three—point field goal attempts, season
205 — Allison Feaster, 2003
189 — Allison Feaster, 2002
168 — Allison Feaster, 2001
Most three—point field goal attempts, game
11 — Tora Suber, vs. Cleveland, August 14, 1998
Allison Feaster, vs. San Antonio, June 4, 2003
10 — By many

FREE THROW PERCENTAGE

Highest free—throw percentage, career
(Minimum 175 free throws)
.858 — Allison Feaster (194/226)
.856 — Dawn Staley (339/396)
.791 — Vicky Bullett (208/263)
Highest free—throw percentage, season (qualifiers)
.934 — Dawn Staley, 1999 (85/91)
.921 — Allison Feaster, 2001 (58/63)
.895 — Dawn Staley, 2001 (51/57)
Most free throws made, none missed, game
10 — Tammy Sutton—Brown, at Orlando, July 12, 2002
8 — By many
Most free throw attempts, none made, game
3 — Tracy Reid, vs. Houston, July 25, 1998
Tracy Reid, vs. Minnesota, July 21, 1999
Tracy Reid, vs. Houston, June 28, 2000
Rhonda Mapp, vs. New York, July 28, 2000
2 — by many

FREE THROWS MADE

Most free throws made, career
486 — Andrea Stinson
339 — Dawn Staley
266 — Tammy Sutton—Brown
Most free throws made, season
124 — Tammy Sutton—Brown, 2002
111 — Tracy Reid, 1998
99 — Andrea Stinson, 2000
Most free throws made, game
11 — Tracy Reid, at Phoenix, June 21, 1998
Andrea Stinson, vs. Washington, July 26, 2000
10 — Tracy Reid, at Washington, July 21, 1998
Andrea Stinson, at New York, July 12, 2000
Dawn Staley, vs. Los Angeles, June 1, 2002 (ot)
Tammy Sutton—Brown, at Orlando, July 12, 2002

FREE THROW ATTEMPTS

Most free throw attempts, career
662 — Andrea Stinson
396 — Dawn Staley
377 — Tammy Sutton—Brown
Most free throw attempts, season
181 — Tracy Reid, 1998
174 — Tammy Sutton—Brown, 2002
134 — Andrea Stinson, 2000

Most free throw attempts, game
16 — Tracy Reid, at Phoenix, June 21, 1998
14 — Tracy Reid, at Washington, July 21, 1998
Andrea Stinson, at New York, July 12, 2000
13 — Tracy Reid, at Los Angeles, June 24, 1998
Tracy Reid, vs. Los Angeles, August 12, 1998
Andrea Stinson, vs. Sacramento, June 24, 2001 (ot)

REBOUNDS

Most rebounds, career
996 — Andrea Stinson
641 — Rhonda Mapp
591 — Vicky Bullett
Highest average, rebounds per game, career
(Minimum 90 games)
6.6 — Vicky Bullett (591/90)
5.9 — Rhonda Mapp (641/109)
5.5 — Tammy Sutton—Brown (521/95)
Most rebounds, season
219 — Vicky Bullett, 1999
205 — Rhonda Mapp, 2000
201 — Tammy Sutton-Brown, 2003
Highest average, rebounds per game, season (qualifiers)
6.84— Vicky Bullett, 1999 (219/32)
6.83— Rhonda Mapp, 2000 (205/30)
6.5 — Vicky Bullett, 1998 (194/30)
Most rebounds, game
18 — Rhonda Mapp, at New York, July 26, 1999 (ot)
16 — Andrea Congreaves, vs. Phoenix, July 30, 1997
15 — By many
Most games, 10+ rebounds, career
16 — Vicky Bullett
13 — Rhonda Mapp
9 — Andrea Stinson
Most consecutive games, 10+ rebounds
3 — Vicky Bullett, July 30-August 3, 1998
2 — By many

OFFENSIVE REBOUNDS

Most offensive rebounds, career
248 — Andrea Stinson
200 — Tammy Sutton-Brown
196 — Rhonda Mapp

Highest average, offensive rebounds per game, career (Minimum 90 games)
2.11— Tammy Sutton-Brown (200/95)
2.09— Vicky Bullett (188/90)
1.8 — Rhonda Mapp (196/109)
Most offensive rebounds, season
76 — Tammy Sutton-Brown, 2002
73 — Tammy Sutton-Brown, 2003
66 — Vicky Bullett, 1997

Most offensive rebounds, game
  9 — Sharon Manning, at Los Angeles, June 24, 1998
  8 — Vicky Bullett, vs. Detroit, August 3, 1998
  7 — Andrea Congreaves, vs. Phoenix, July 30, 1997
     Sharon Manning, vs. Houston, July 25, 1998
     Andrea Stinson, vs. Sacramento, June 24, 2001 (ot)
     Shalonda Enis, at Washington, July 17, 2003

DEFENSIVE REBOUNDS

Most defensive rebounds, career
  748 — Andrea Stinson
  445 — Rhonda Mapp
  403 — Vicky Bullett
Highest average, defensive rebounds per game, career (Minimum 90 games)
  4.5 — Vicky Bullett (403/90)
  4.1 — Rhonda Mapp (445/109)
  3.4 — Andrea Stinson (748/220)
Most defensive rebounds, season
  159 — Vicky Bullett, 1999
  145 — Rhonda Mapp, 1999
Rhonda Mapp, 2000
  140 — Andrea Stinson, 2002
Most defensive rebounds, game
  15 — Rhonda Mapp, at New York, July 26, 1999 (ot)
  13 — Rhonda Mapp, at Detroit, June 12, 2000
  11 — Tracy Reid, at Sacramento, July 10, 1998
     Andrea Stinson, at Cleveland, July 24, 2002 (ot)

ASSISTS

Most assists, career
  884 — Dawn Staley
  748 — Andrea Stinson
  234 — Charlotte Taylor-Smith
Highest average, assists per game, career (Minimum 90 games)
  5.5 — Dawn Staley (884/162)
  3.4 — Andrea Stinson (748/220)
  2.0 — Rhonda Mapp (217/109)
Most assists, season
  190 — Dawn Staley, 2000
  179 — Dawn Staley, 2001
  177 — Dawn Staley, 1999
Highest average, assists per game, season (qualifiers)
  5.9 — Dawn Staley, 2000 (190/32)
  5.6 — Dawn Staley, 2001 (179/32)
  5.5 — Dawn Staley, 1999 (177/32)
Most assists, game
  13 — Dawn Staley, vs. Washington, July 26, 2000

  11 — Dawn Staley, vs. Detroit, June 27, 2001
  10 — By many
Most games, 10+ assists, career
  9 — Dawn Staley
  1 — Andrea Stinson

PERSONAL FOULS

Most personal fouls, career
  445 — Andrea Stinson
  415 — Charlotte Smith-Taylor
  378 — Rhonda Mapp
Most personal fouls, season
  132 — Tammy Sutton-Brown, 2003
  125 — Tammy Sutton-Brown, 2002
  113 — Charlotte Smith, 2002
Most personal fouls, game
  6 — By many

DISQUALIFICATIONS

Most disqualifications, career
  7 — Charlotte Smith-Taylor
  6 — Tammy Sutton-Brown
  3 — Vicky Bullett
     Rhonda Mapp
Highest percentage, games disqualified, career (Minimum: 90 games)
  6.3 — Tammy Sutton-Brown (6/95)
  4.6 — Charlotte Smith (7/151)
  3.3 — Vicky Bullett (3/90)
Lowest percentage, games disqualified, career (Minimum: 90 games)
  0.0 — Andrea Stinson (0/220)
     Kelly Miller (0/92)
     Sharon Manning (0/90)
Most consecutive games without disqualification, career
  220 — Andrea Stinson, June 22, 1997-August 25, 2003 (current)
  128 — Dawn Staley, June 5, 2000-August 25, 2003 (current)
  94 — Allison Feaster, June 12, 2001-August 25, 2003 (current)
Most disqualifications, season
  3 — Rhonda Mapp, 2000
     Charlotte Smith, 2002
     Tammy Sutton-Brown, 2002
  2 — By many
Fewest minutes, disqualified, game
  11 — Summer Erb, vs. Orlando, July 17, 2002
  12 — Rushia Brown, at Seattle, July 31, 2003
  18 — Rhonda Mapp, vs. New York, July 28, 2000
     Charlotte Smith, vs. Los Angeles, June 2, 2001

STEALS

Most steals, career
  312 — Andrea Stinson
  224 — Dawn Staley

182 — Vicky Bullett

Highest average, steals per game, career
(Minimum 90 games)

2.02 — Vicky Bullett (182/90)
1.42 — Andrea Stinson (312/220)
1.38 — Dawn Staley (224/162)

Most steals, season

66 — Vicky Bullett, 1998
62 — Vicky Bullett, 1999
55 — Andrea Stinson, 2000

Highest average, steals per game, season
(qualifiers)

2.20 — Vicky Bullett, 1998 (66/30)
1.94 — Vicky Bullett, 1999 (62/32)
1.93 — Vicky Bullett, 1997 (54/28)

Most steals, game

6 — Vicky Bullett, vs. Orlando,
    August 7, 1999
    Andrea Stinson, vs. Seattle,
    June 9, 2000
    Dawn Staley, vs. Washington,
    July 26, 2001
    Andrea Stinson, at Washington,
    July 7, 2003
5 — By many

BLOCKED SHOTS

Most blocked shots, career

146 — Vicky Bullett
125 — Tammy Sutton-Brown
110 — Andrea Stinson

Highest average, blocked shots per game, career
(Minimum: 90 games)

1.62 — Vicky Bullett (146/90)

1.32 — Tammy Sutton-Brown (125/95)
0.52 — Rhonda Mapp (57/109)

Most blocked shots, season

55 — Vicky Bullett, 1997
50 — Tammy Sutton-Brown, 2003
46 — Vicky Bullett, 1998

Highest average, blocked shots per game, season
(qualifiers)

1.96 — Vicky Bullett, 1997 (55/28)
1.53 — Vicky Bullett, 1998 (46/30)
1.47 — Tammy Sutton-Brown, 2003 (50/34)

Most blocked shots, game

5 — Andrea Stinson, at Utah, August 4, 1997
    Vicky Bullett, vs. New York,
    June 12, 1999
    Tammy Sutton—Brown, at Cleveland,
    July 24, 2002 (ot)
4 — by many

TURNOVERS

Most turnovers, career

526 — Andrea Stinson
439 — Dawn Staley
226 — Rhonda Mapp

Most turnovers, season

100 — Dawn Staley, 2001
99 — Andrea Stinson, 1997
91 — Dawn Staley, 2000

Most turnovers, game

8 — Nicole Levesque, at New York,
    July 26, 1997
    Andrea Stinson, vs. Houston,
    August 11, 1997
7 — by many

CLEVELAND ROCKERS

REGULAR SEASON TEAM RECORDS

TEAM OFFENSE

SCORING

Highest average, points per game, season
73.2 — 1998 (2197/30)
70.2 — 1997 (1965/28)
Lowest average, points per game, season
62.6 — 2001 (2004/32)
62.9 — 1999 (2014/32)
Most points, game
99 — at Orlando, June 8, 2002 (3 ot)
96 — at Detroit, June 15, 1998
Fewest points, game
43 — at Charlotte, July 12, 1997
44 — at Charlotte, June 29, 1997
at New York, August 8, 2000
Largest margin of victory, game
35 — vs. Washington, May 31, 2001 (69-34)
32 — vs. Charlotte, August 17, 1997 (81-49)
Largest margin of defeat, game
35 — vs. New York, July 8, 1999 (49-84)
at Washington, August 8, 1999 (45-80)
29 — at Charlotte, July 12, 1997 (43-72)

BY HALF

Most points, first half
55 — vs. Washington, July 26, 2003
53 — at Detroit, June 15, 1998
vs. Sacramento, June 19, 2000
Fewest points, first half
18 — at New York, July 22, 2002
19 — at New York, June 10, 1999
at New York, August 8, 2000
Largest lead at halftime
28 — vs. Phoenix, July 31, 1997
(led 43-15; won 79-67)
vs. Charlotte, July 10, 1999
(led 47-19; won 82-56)
26 — vs. Charlotte, August 17, 1997
(led 47-21; won 81-49)
Largest deficit at halftime overcome to win game
8 — vs. New York, August 23, 1997
(trailed 32-40; won 72-71)
7 — at Detroit, July 31, 2000
(trailed 28-35; won 76-65)
vs. Portland, June 26, 2001
(trailed 27-34; won 61-57)
Most points, second half
54 — at Utah, August 6, 1998
52 — at Charlotte, August 14, 1998
at Charlotte, July 25, 2002
Fewest points, second half
19 — at Miami, July 7, 2000
vs. Miami, July 25, 2001

vs. Indiana, August 13, 2002
21 — Many times

OVERTIME

Most points, overtime period
13 — at Orlando, June 8, 2002 (3rd OT)
10 — vs. Los Angeles, August 7, 1997
(2nd OT)
vs. Orlando, June 7, 2000
Fewest points, overtime period
3 — at New York, August 24, 1997
4 — vs. Minnesota, June 24, 2000
vs. Miami, July 25, 2001
vs. Houston, June 1, 2002
Largest margin of victory, overtime game
4 — vs. Orlando, June 7, 2000 (83-79)
vs. Miami, July 25, 2001 (52-48)
3 — at Houston, August 1, 1998 (74-71)

FIELD GOAL PERCENTAGE

Highest field-goal percentage, season
.468 — 1998 (804/1719)
.444 — 1997 (725/1633)
Lowest field-goal percentage, season
.413 — 2003 (815/1975)
.414 — 1999 (766/1852)
Highest field-goal percentage, game
.632 — at Washington, July 21, 1999 (36/57)
.611 — vs. Detroit, June 16, 2000 (33/54)
Lowest field-goal percentage, game
.241 — vs. New York, July 8, 1999 (14/58)
.261 — vs. Los Angeles, July 20, 2002 (18/69)

FIELD GOALS

Most field goals per game, season
26.8 — 1998 (804/30)
25.9 — 1997 (725/28)
Fewest field goals per game, season
23.75 — 2002 (760/32)
23.84 — 2001 (763/32)
Most field goals, game
38 — at Detroit, June 15, 1998
36 — vs. Utah, July 19, 1997
at Washington, July 21, 1999
Fewest field goals, game
14 — vs. New York, July 8, 1999
at Washington, August 8, 1999
16 — at Charlotte, June 29, 1997

FIELD GOAL ATTEMPTS

Most field-goal attempts per game, season
58.3 — 1997 (1633/28)
58.1 — 2003 (1975/34)
Fewest field-goal attempts per game, season
55.3 — 2001 (1770/32)
56.9 — 2002 (1820/32)

Most field-goal attempts, game
    86 — vs. Los Angeles, August 7, 1997 (2 ot)
    79 — vs. Orlando, June 7, 2000 (ot)
Regulation game:
    76 — at Sacramento, June 2, 2001
Fewest field-goal attempts, game
    42 — at Minnesota, August 16, 1999
    44 — at Phoenix, August 14, 1997
        vs. Phoenix, July 13, 2001

THREE-POINT FIELD-GOAL PERCENTAGE

Highest three-point field-goal percentage, season
    .380 — 1998 (106/279)
    .367 — 1997 (65/177)
Lowest three-point field-goal percentage, season
    .285 — 1999 (88/309)
    .316 — 2001 (106/335)

THREE-POINT FIELD GOALS

Most three-point field goals per game, season
    4.4 — 2000 (141/32)
    4.0 — 2003 (135/34)
Fewest three-point field goals per game, season
    2.3 — 1997 (65/28)
    2.8 — 1999 (88/32)
Most three-point field goals, game
    11 — vs. Orlando, July 12, 2000 (ot)
    10 — at Indiana, July 11, 2001
        at Los Angeles, July 7, 2003
Fewest three-point field goals, game
    0 — vs. Los Angeles, July 3, 1997
        at Charlotte, July 12, 1997
        vs. New York, July 14, 1997
        at Sacramento, June 17, 1999
        vs. Utah, June 30, 2002
        at Indiana, August 23, 2003

THREE-POINT FIELD GOAL ATTEMPTS

Most three-point field goal attempts per game, season
    12.7 — 2000 (407/32)
    12.5 — 2003 (425/34)
Fewest three-point field goal attempts per game, season
    6.3 — 1997 (177/28)
    9.3 — 1998 (279/30)
Most three-point field goal attempts, game
    27 — vs. Orlando, June 7, 2000 (ot)
    24 — at Portland, June 28, 2000
Fewest three-point field goal attempts, game
    3 — vs. New York, July 14, 1997
       vs. Sacramento, August 2, 1997
       at Phoenix, August 14, 1997
       vs. Portland, July 2, 2002
    4 — at Los Angeles, July 7, 1997
       at Los Angeles, July 23, 1997
       vs. Phoenix, August 1, 2003

FREE THROW PERCENTAGE

Highest free-throw percentage, season
    .778 — 2002 (430/553)
    .765 — 1998 (483/631)
Lowest free-throw percentage, season
    .7223 — 1997 (450/623)
    .7216 — 2003 (464/643)
Highest free-throw percentage, game
    1.000 — vs. Orlando, June 22, 1999 (5/5)
        at New York, August 8, 2000 (6/6)
        vs. Washington, May 31, 2001 (4/4)
        at Washington, June 17, 2001 (5/5)
        vs. New York, August 17, 2003 (11/11)
    .941 — at Utah, August 6, 1998 (16/17)
Lowest free-throw percentage, game
    .357 — at Miami, June 24, 2001 (5/14)
    .455 — at Charlotte, June 25, 2003 (5/11)

FREE THROWS MADE

Most free throws made per game, season
    16.10 — 1998 (483/30)
    16.07 — 1997 (450/28)
Fewest free throws made per game, season
    11.6 — 2001 (372/32)
    12.3 — 1999 (394/32)
Most free throws made, game
    33 — vs. Utah, June 22, 1998
    30 — at Charlotte, July 25, 2002
Fewest free throws made, game
    2 — at Houston, July 1, 1999
    3 — at Washington, August 9, 2000

FREE THROW ATTEMPTS

Most free throw attempts per game, season
    22.3 — 1997 (623/28)
    21.0 — 1998 (631/30)
Fewest free throw attempts per game, season
    15.8 — 2001 (505/32)
    17.0 — 1999 (545/32)
Most free throw attempts, game
    40 — at Indiana, June 12, 2000
    39 — vs. Utah, June 22, 1998
Fewest free throw attempts, game
    4 — at Houston, July 1, 1999
       at Washington, August 9, 2000
       vs. Washington, May 31, 2001
    5 — vs. Orlando, June 22, 1999
       at Washington, June 17, 2001

REBOUNDS

Most rebounds per game, season
    31.8 — 1997 (891/28)
    31.4 — 2003 (1069/34)
Fewest rebounds per game, season
    29.19 — 2000 (934/32)
    29.20 — 1998 (876/30)
Most rebounds, game
    49 — vs. Los Angeles, August 7, 1997 (2 ot)

45 — vs. Sacramento, August 2, 1997
      vs. Phoenix, August 10, 1998 (2 ot)
Fewest rebounds, game
17 — vs. Houston, August 5, 1997
19 — at Charlotte, July 7, 1999
      at Minnesota, May 31, 2000
      vs. Utah, June 30, 2002

OFFENSIVE REBOUNDS

Most offensive rebounds per game, season
10.34 — 2000 (331/32)
10.26 — 2003 (349/34)
Fewest offensive rebounds per game, season
7.6 — 1998 (227/30)
9.0 — 1999 (289/32)
Most offensive rebounds, game
23 — vs. Los Angeles, August 7, 1997 (2 ot)
19 — vs. New York, July 3, 2000 (ot)
Regulation game:
17 — at Sacramento, August 4, 1998
Fewest offensive rebounds, game
1 — vs. Utah, July 25, 1998
3 — at Washington, August 12, 2001

DEFENSIVE REBOUNDS

Most defensive rebounds per game, season
22.3 — 1997 (624/28)
21.6 — 1998 (649/30)
Fewest defensive rebounds per game, season
18.8 — 2000 (603/32)
20.7 — 2001 (662/32)
Most defensive rebounds, game
34 — vs. Charlotte, August 17, 1997
32 — vs. Sacramento, August 2, 1997
Fewest defensive rebounds, game
11 — at New York, August 24, 1997 (ot)
at Charlotte, June 25, 2003
12 — Many times

ASSISTS

Most assists per game, season
19.2 — 1998 (575/30)
16.8 — 2000 (539/32)
Fewest assists per game, season
15.0 — 2002 (480/32)
15.2 — 2003 (517/34)
Most assists, game
31 — vs. Detroit, June 16, 2000
29 — at Washington, July 21, 1999
Fewest assists, game
3 — at Detroit, July 28, 2001
5 — at Detroit, July 18, 1998

PERSONAL FOULS

Most personal fouls per game, season
20.2 — 2000 (647/32)
20.0 — 1998 (600/30)
Fewest personal fouls per game, season
16.6 — 2001 (532/32)
17.7 — 2002 (567/32)

Most personal fouls, game
32 — at Orlando, June 8, 2002 (3 ot)
31 — at Portland, June 28, 2000
Fewest personal fouls, game
9 — vs. Miami, June 25, 2002
10 — vs. Charlotte, August 8, 1998
      vs. Orlando, July 30, 2001
      vs. Detroit, August 8, 2001
      at Minnesota, July 17, 2002

DISQUALIFICATIONS

Most disqualifications per game, season
0.29 — 1997 (8/24)
0.25 — 2002 (8/32)
Fewest disqualifications per game, season
0.03 — 2001 (1/32)
0.09 — 1999 (3/32)
Most disqualifications, game
2 — at Phoenix, August 14, 1997
      vs. Detroit, July 23, 1999
      at Phoenix, July 24, 2000
      vs. Houston, June 1, 2002 (ot)
      at Orlando, June 8, 2002 (3 ot)
1 — many times

STEALS

Most steals per game, season
9.1 — 1997 (256/28)
9.0 — 1998 (270/30)
Fewest steals per game, season
6.7 — 2003 (226/34)
6.9 — 2002 (221/32)
Most steals, game
17 — vs. Orlando, June 7, 2000 (ot)
16 — at Sacramento, August 4, 1998
Fewest steals, game
1 — vs. Los Angeles, May 27, 2003
2 — at Charlotte, June 30, 2001
      at Miami, June 11, 2002
      at New York, June 28, 2002
      at Sacramento, July 11, 2002
      vs. Washington, June 20, 2003

BLOCKED SHOTS

Most blocked shots per game, season
3.6 — 1999 (116/32)
3.3 — 1998 (99/30)
Fewest blocked shots per game, season
2.5 — 2003 (86/34)
2.6 — 2001 (83/32)
      2002 (83/32)
Most blocked shots, game
9 — vs. Detroit, July 23, 1999
      vs. Detroit, July 28, 2000
8 — at Sacramento, July 14, 1998
      vs. Orlando, August 14, 1999
      vs. New York, August 21, 1999
Fewest blocked shots, game
0 — Many times

TURNOVERS

Most turnovers per game, season
18.8 — 1997 (526/28)
17.6 — 1998 (528/30)
Fewest turnovers per game, season
13.7 — 2003 (466/34)
13.9 — 2001 (444/32)
Most turnovers, game
30 — at New York, June 10, 1999
28 — vs. Los Angeles, July 3, 1997
Fewest turnovers, game
6 — vs. Washington, July 26, 2003
vs. Detroit, July 29, 2003
7 — at Utah, August 6, 1998
at Utah, July 6, 2001

TEAM DEFENSE

POINTS

Fewest points allowed per game, season
55.9 — 2001 (1788/32)
65.0 — 2003 (2210/34)
Most points allowed per game, season
70.3 — 1998 (2110/30)
69.3 — 1999 (2217/32)
Fewest points allowed, game
34 — vs. Washington, May 31, 2001
35 — at Miami, June 24, 2001
Fewest points allowed, first half
12 — at Miami, June 24, 2001
vs. Charlotte, July 21, 2001
14 — at Washington, June 6, 2003
Fewest points allowed, second half
9 — at Seattle, June 14, 2001
18 — at Miami, July 7, 2000
vs. Washington, May 31, 2001
vs. Miami, July 25, 2001
vs. Orlando, July 30, 2001
Fewest points allowed, overtime period
0 — vs. Miami, July 25, 2001
3 — at Houston, August 1, 1998

FIELD GOAL PERCENTAGE

Lowest opponents' field-goal percentage, season
.381 — 2001 (664/1745)
.413 — 1997 (709/1715)
Highest opponents' field-goal percentage, season
.440 — 2000 (774/1761)
.435 — 2002 (797/1834)
Lowest opponents' field goal percentage, game
.182 — at Miami, June 24, 2001 (10/55)
.245 — vs. Washington, May 31, 2001 (13/53)

TURNOVERS

Most opponents' turnovers per game, season
18.2 — 1998 (546/30)
17.6 — 1997 (494/28)
Fewest opponents' turnovers per game, season
13.4 — 2002 (428/32)

13.7 — 2003 (467/34)
Most opponents' turnovers, game
27 — vs. Washington, July 8, 1998
at Washington, August 12, 1998
vs. Washington, June 3, 2000
vs. Orlando, June 7, 2000 (ot)

TEAM MISCELLANEOUS

GAME WON AND LOST

Highest winning percentage, season
.688 — 2001 (22-10)
.667 — 1998 (20-10)
Lowest winning percentage, season
.219 — 1999 (7-25)
.313 — 2002 (10-22)
Most consecutive games won
8 — July 17-August 2, 1997
7 — June 14-27, 2001
July 8-25, 2001
Most consecutive games won, one season
8 — July 17-August 2, 1997
7 — June 14-27, 2001
July 8-25, 2001
Most consecutive games lost
8 — August 2-19, 1999
7 — June 10-25, 1999
August 3, 2002-May 27, 2003
Most consecutive games lost, one season
8 — August 2-19, 1999
7 — June 10-25, 1999
Highest winning percentage, home games, season
.875 — 2001 (14-2)
.813 — 2000 (13-3)
Lowest winning percentage, home games, season
.250 — 2002 (4-12)
.313 — 1999 (5-11)
Most consecutive home games won
16 — July 22, 2000-July 25, 2001
7 — July 8-August 8, 1998
Most consecutive home games lost
10 — June 3, 2002-May 27, 2003 (current)
6 — July 16-August 14, 1999
Highest winning percentage, road games, season
.600 — 1998 (9-6)
.500 — 1997 (7-7)
2001 (8-8)
Lowest winning percentage, road games, season
.125 — 1999 (2-14)
.250 — 2000 (4-12)
Most consecutive road games won
6 — August 1-17, 1998
5 — July 23-August 11, 1997
Most consecutive road games lost
8 — June 10-July 17, 1999
7 — August 2, 1999-May 31, 2000

OVERTIME GAMES

Most overtime games, season
4 — 2000, 2002
2 — 1997, 1998
Most consecutive overtime games, season
1 — Many times
Most overtime games won, season
3 — 2000
1 — 1998, 2001, 2003
Most overtime games won, no losses, season
1 — 2001, 2003
Most consecutive overtime games won
3 — July 3, 2000-July 25, 2001
Most overtime games lost, season
4 — 2002
2 — 1997
Most overtime games lost, no wins, season
4 — 2002
2 — 1997
Most consecutive overtime games lost
4 — June 1-July 28, 2002
2 — August 7-24, 1997
Most overtime periods, game
3 — at Orlando, June 8, 2002
2 — vs. Los Angeles, August 7, 1997
vs. Phoenix, August 10, 1998

INDIVIDUAL RECORDS

SEASONS

Most Seasons
7 — Merlakia Jones
6 — Rushia Brown
5 — Chasity Melvin
Eva Nemcova

GAMES

Most game, career
218 — Merlakia Jones
176 — Rushia Brown
157 — Chasity Melvin
Most consecutive games, career
139 — Merlakia Jones, June 21, 1997-
July 8, 2001
128 — Mery Andrade, June 10, 1999-
August 13, 2002
81 — Chasity Melvin, June 10, 1999-
July 8, 2001
Most games, season
34 — By many

MINUTES

Most minutes, career
5,837 — Merlakia Jones
4,483 — Chasity Melvin
3,397 — Eva Nemcova
Highest average, minutes per game, career
(Minimum 90 games)
30.6 — Eva Nemcova (3397/111)
28.6 — Chasity Melvin (4483/157)

26.8 — Merlakia Jones (5837/218)
Most minutes, season
1,094 — Merlakia Jones, 2002
1,061 — Chasity Melvin, 2003
1,055 — Chasity Melvin, 2002
Highest average, minutes per game, season
34.2 — Merlakia Jones, 2002 (1094/32)
33.7 — Eva Nemcova, 1997 (944/28)
33.3 — Merlakia Jones, 2001 (998/30)
Most minutes, game
53 — Chasity Melvin, at Orlando,
June 8, 2002 (3 ot)
50 — Merlakia Jones, at Orlando,
June 8, 2002 (3 ot)
47 — Eva Nemcova, vs. Los Angeles,
August 7, 1997 (2 ot)

SCORING

Most points, lifetime
2,173 — Merlakia Jones
1,741 — Chasity Melvin
1,306 — Eva Nemcova
Highest average, points per game, career
(Minimum 90 games)
11.8 — Eva Nemcova (1306/111)
11.1 — Chasity Melvin (1741/157)
10.6 — Penny Taylor (1019/96)
Most points, season
444 — Chasity Melvin, 2003
404 — Merlakia Jones, 2001
399 — Chasity Melvin, 2002
Highest average, points per game, season
13.71 — Eva Nemcova, 1997 (384/28)
13.68 — Isabelle Fijalkowski, 1998 (383/28)
13.5 — Merlakia Jones, 2001 (404/30)
Most points, game
33 — Penny Taylor, vs. Phoenix,
August 1, 2003
30 — Chasity Melvin, vs. New York,
June 21, 2002
Deanna Jackson, at Minnesota,
July 5, 2003
28 — Chasity Melvin, vs. Detroit,
June 16, 2000
Most games, 30 or more points, career
1 — Deanna Jackson
Chasity Melvin
Penny Taylor
Most games, 20 or more points, career
12 — Merlakia Jones
10 — Penny Taylor
8 — Chasity Melvin
Eva Nemcova
Most consecutive games, 20 or more points
2 — Penny Taylor, June 27-28, 2002
Merlakia Jones, July 24-25, 2002
Penny Taylor, August 14, 2001-
June 1, 2002
Most consecutive games, 10 or more points
13 — Chasity Melvin, July 17-
August 17, 2003

11 — Penny Taylor, June 27-July 20, 2002
10 — Mery Andrade, June 28-July 22, 2000
     LaToya Thomas, August 1-25, 2003
     (current)

FIELD GOAL PERCENTAGE

Highest field goal percentage, career
(Minimum 350 field goals)
.478 — Rushia Brown (417/873)
.466 — Chasity Melvin (645/1385)
.442 — Eva Nemcova (474/1072)
Highest field goal percentage, season (qualifiers)
.569 — Ann Wauters, 2001 (87/153)
.553 — Ann Wauters, 2002 (120/217)
.547 — Isabelle Fijalkowski, 1998 (146/267)
Highest field goal percentage, game
(Minimum 8 field goals made)
.909 — LaToya Thomas, vs. Indiana,
     June 29, 2003 (10/11)
.900 — Janice Braxton, at Detroit, June 15,
     1998 (9/10)
.889 — Isabelle Fijalkowski, vs. Utah,
     June 26, 1997 (8/9)
     Chasity Melvin, at Washington,
     July 21, 1999 (8/9)
     Rushia Brown, vs. Washington,
     August 6, 2000 (8/9)
Most field goals, none missed, game
  6 — Janice Braxton, vs. Phoenix,
     July 31, 1997
Ann Wauters, vs. Detroit, July 28, 2000
  5 — Adrienne Johnson, vs. Utah,
     July 19, 1997
     Eva Nemcova, at New York,
     June 23, 1998
     Chasity Melvin, at Orlando,
     June 27, 2001
     Pollyan Johns Kimbrough,
     vs. New York, May 31, 2003
Most field goal attempts, none made, game
  7 — Vicki Hall, at Charlotte, June 5, 2000
     Mery Andrade, vs. Orlando,
     July 30, 2001
     Betty Lennox, at San Antonio,
     July 27, 2003
  6 — By many

FIELD GOALS

Most field goals, career
883 — Merlakia Jones
645 — Chasity Melvin
474 — Eva Nemcova
Most field goals, season
165 — Merlakia Jones, 2001
159 — Chasity Melvin, 2003
157 — Merlakia Jones, 2002
Most field goals, game
  12 — Chasity Melvin, vs. New York,
     June 21, 2002

11 — Merlakia Jones, vs. Utah, July 24, 1999
     Merlakia Jones, at Indiana,
     June 15, 2002
     Deanna Jackson, at Minnesota,
     July 5, 2003
     Penny Taylor, vs. Phoenix,
     August 1, 2003

FIELD GOAL ATTEMPTS

Most field goal attempts, career
2,078 — Merlakia Jones
1,385 — Chasity Melvin
1,072 — Eva Nemcova
Most field goal attempts, season
393 — Merlakia Jones, 2002
377 — Merlakia Jones, 2001
340 — Penny Taylor, 2003
Most field goal attempts, game
  23 — Penny Taylor, at Orlando,
     June 8, 2002 (3 ot)
  22 — Eva Nemcova, vs. Orlando,
     June 7, 2000 (ot)
  21 — Merlakia Jones, vs. Portland,
     June 26, 2001

THREE-POINT FIELD-GOAL PERCENTAGE

Highest three-point field goal percentage, career
(Minimum 90 three-point field goals)
.402 — Eva Nemcova (131/326)
.332 — Penny Taylor (94/283)
Highest three-point field goal percentage, season
(qualifiers)
.452 — Eva Nemcova, 1998 (28/62)
.435 — Eva Nemcova, 1997 (37/85)
.414 — Deanna Jackson, 2003 (29/70)
Most three-point field goals, none missed, game
  4 — Suzie McConnell Serio, vs. Detroit,
     June 14, 1999
     Mery Andrade, vs. Orlando,
     July 12, 2000 (ot)
     Deanna Jackson, at Detroit,
     July 22, 2003
  3 — By many
Most three-point field goal attempts, none made,
game
  6 — Vicki Hall, at Sacramento,
     June 2, 2001
     Penny Taylor, vs. Los Angeles,
     July 20, 2002
  5 — By many

THREE-POINT FIELD GOALS

Most three-point field goals, career
131 — Eva Nemcova
94 — Penny Taylor
87 — Suzie McConnell Serio
Most three-point field goals, season

38 — Suzie McConnell Serio, 2000
Jennifer Rizzotti, 2002
Penny Taylor, 2002
37 — Eva Nemcova, 1997
34 — Eva Nemcova, 1999
Penny Taylor, 2003
Most three-point field goals, game
5 — Suzie McConnell Serio, vs.
Washington, August 15, 1998
Eva Nemcova, vs. Orlando,
June 7, 2000 (ot)
Betty Lennox, at Los Angeles,
July 7, 2003
4 — By many
Most consecutive games, three-point field goals made
18 — Eva Nemcova, July 17, 1997-
June 11, 1998
16 — Suzie McConnell Serio, July 8-
August 9, 2000
14 — Eva Nemcova, August 12, 1999-
June 19, 2000

THREE-POINT FIELD GOAL ATTEMPTS

Most three-point field goal attempts, career
326 — Eva Nemcova
283 — Penny Taylor
228 — Suzie McConnell Serio
Most three-point field goal attempts, season
111 — Penny Taylor, 2002
103 — Betty Lennox, 2003
99 — Jennifer Rizzotti, 2002
Penny Taylor, 2003
Most three-point field goal attempts, game
12 — Eva Nemcova, vs. Orlando,
June 7, 2000 (ot)
8 — Suzie McConnell Serio, vs.
New York, July 8, 1999
Michelle Edwards, vs. Orlando,
August 14, 1999
Betty Lennox, at New York,
June 10, 2003
Betty Lennox, at Los Angeles,
July 7, 2003
7 — By many

FREE THROW PERCENTAGE

Highest free-throw percentage, career
(Minimum 175 free throws)
.897 — Eva Nemcova (227/253)
.827 — Penny Taylor (201/243)
.805 — Ann Wauters (177/220)
Highest free-throw percentage, season (qualifiers)
.984 — Eva Nemcova, 1999 (62/63)
.893 — Eva Nemcova, 1998 (67/75)
.855 — Eva Nemcova, 1997 (71/83)

Most free throws made, none missed, game
10 — Merlakia Jones, vs. Phoenix,
July 13, 2001
9 — Eva Nemcova, vs. Sacramento,
August 2, 1997
LaToya Thomas, vs. Connecticut,
August 19, 2003
8 — By many
Most free throw attempts, none made, game
3 — Pollyan Johns Kimbrough, vs. Miami,
June 16, 2001
2 — By many

FREE THROWS MADE

Most free throws made, career
441 — Chasity Melvin
348 — Merlakia Jones
278 — Rushia Brown
Most free throws made, season
123 — Chasity Melvin, 2003
106 — Janice Braxton, 1997
100 — Chasity Melvin, 2000
Most free throws made, game
13 — Janice Braxton, at Phoenix,
July 28, 1997
11 — Janice Braxton, vs. Utah,
June 22, 1998
Penny Taylor, vs. Charlotte,
August 25, 2003
10 — Merlakia Jones, vs. Phoenix,
July 13, 2001

FREE THROW ATTEMPTS

Most free throw attempts, career
628 — Chasity Melvin
462 — Merlakia Jones
365 — Rushia Brown
Most free throw attempts, season
176 — Chasity Melvin, 2003
138 — Janice Braxton, 1997
137 — Chasity Melvin, 2000
Most free throw attempts, game
15 — Janice Braxton, at Phoenix,
July 28, 1997
13 — Janice Braxton, vs. Utah,
June 22, 1998
Penny Taylor, vs. Charlotte,
August 25, 2003
12 — By many

REBOUNDS

Most rebounds, career
875 — Merlakia Jones
862 — Chasity Melvin
624 — Rushia Brown
Highest average, rebounds per game, career
(Minimum 90 games)
5.5 — Chasity Melvin (862/157)

4.4 — Penny Taylor (418/96)
4.0 — Merlakia Jones (875/218)
Most rebounds, season
215 — Chasity Melvin, 2003
194 — Chasity Melvin, 2002
192 — Isabelle Fijalkowski, 1998
Highest average, rebounds per game, season
(qualifiers)
7.6 — Janice Braxton, 1997 (189/25)
6.9 — Isabelle Fijalkowski, 1998 (192/28)
6.3 — Chasity Melvin, 2003 (215/34)
Most rebounds, game
15 — Janice Braxton, vs. Charlotte,
August 17, 1997
14 — Janice Braxton, vs. Utah,
June 26, 1997
13 — Janice Braxton, vs. Detroit,
June 27, 1998
LaToya Thomas, at Connecticut,
June 18, 2003
Most games, 10+ rebounds, career
17 — Chasity Melvin
7 — Janice Braxton
5 — Isabelle Fijalkowski
Merlakia Jones
Most consecutive games, 10+ rebounds
3 — Chasity Melvin, June 14-17, 2001
2 — Janice Braxton, June 26-28, 1997
Chasity Melvin, July 12-17, 2002

OFFENSIVE REBOUNDS

Most offensive rebounds, career
354 — Chasity Melvin
252 — Merlakia Jones
245 — Rushia Brown
Highest average, offensive rebounds per game,
career (Minimum 90 games)
2.3 — Chasity Melvin (354/157)
1.39 — Rushia Brown (245/176)
1.36 — Penny Toler (131/96)
Most offensive rebounds, season
84 — Chasity Melvin, 2002
82 — Chasity Melvin, 2003
69 — Chasity Melvin, 2000
Most offensive rebounds, game
7 — Chasity Melvin, vs. Sacramento,
July 16, 1999
Chasity Melvin, at Charlotte,
July 25, 2002
LaToya Thomas, at Connecticut,
June 18, 2003
6 — By many

DEFENSIVE REBOUNDS

Most defensive rebounds, career
623 — Merlakia Jones
508 — Chasity Melvin
379 — Rushia Brown

Highest average, defensive rebounds per game,
career (Minimum 90 games)
3.2 — Chasity Melvin (508/157)
3.0 — Penny Taylor (287/96)
2.9 — Merlakia Jones (623/218)
Most defensive rebounds, season
151 — Janice Braxton, 1997
143 — Merlakia Jones, 2002
133 — Isabelle Fijalkowski, 1998
Chasity Melvin, 2003
Most defensive rebounds, game
12 — Janice Braxton, vs. Charlotte,
August 17, 1997
11 — Janice Braxton, vs. Utah,
June 26, 1997
10 — By many

ASSISTS

Most assists, career
373 — Suzie McConnell Serio
339 — Merlakia Jones
302 — Helen Darling
Highest average, assists per game, career
(Minimum 90 games)
3.1 — Helen Darling (302/98)
2.3 — Mery Andrade (291/128)
2.2 — Jennifer Rizzotti (201/91)
Most assists, season
178 — Suzie McConnell Serio, 1998
128 — Helen Darling, 2003
119 — Suzie McConnell Serio, 2000
Highest average, assists per game, season
(qualifiers)
6.4 — Suzie McConnell Serio, 1998 (178/28)
4.5 — Michelle Edwards, 1997 (89/20)
3.8 — Helen Darling, 2003 (128/34)
Most assists, game
14 — Jennifer Rizzotti, vs. New York,
June 21, 2002
12 — Suzie McConnell Serio, vs. Phoenix,
July 2, 1998
11 — Suzie McConnell Serio, at Detroit,
June 15, 1998
Most games, 10+ assists, career
4 — Suzie McConnell Serio
1 — Jennifer Rizzotti

PERSONAL FOULS

Most personal fouls, career
499 — Chasity Melvin
469 — Merlakia Jones
419 — Rushia Brown
Most personal fouls, season
129 — Isabelle Fijalkowski, 1997
115 — Isabelle Fijalkowski, 1998
113 — Chasity Melvin, 2000
Most personal fouls, game

6 — by many

DISQUALIFICATIONS

Most disqualifications, career
10 — Isabelle Fijalkowski
7 — Chasity Melvin
3 — By many

Highest percentage, games disqualified, career
(Minimum 90 games)
4.5 — Chasity Melvin (7/157)
3.3 — Jennifer Rizzotti (3/91)
2.3 — Mery Andrade (3/128)

Lowest percentage, games disqualified, career
(Minimum 90 games)
0.00 — Eva Nemcova (0/111)
Penny Taylor (0/96)
1.4 — Merlakia Jones (3/218)
1.7 — Rushia Brown (3/176)

Most consecutive games without disqualification, career
111 — Eva Nemcova, June 21, 1997-
July 21, 2001
105 — Merlakia Jones, July 26, 2000-
August 25, 2003 (current)
96 — Penny Taylor, May 31, 2001-
August 25, 2003 (current)

Most disqualifications, season
7 — Isabelle Fijalkowski, 1997
4 — Chasity Melvin, 2000
3 — Isabelle Fijalkowski, 1998
Jennifer Rizzotti, 2002

Fewest minutes, disqualified, game
7 — Rushia Brown, vs. Utah, July 24, 1999
16 — Chasity Melvin, vs. Detroit,
July 23, 1999
18 — Isabelle Fijalkowski, at Charlotte,
July 12, 1997
Rushia Brown, vs. Utah, June 22, 1998

STEALS

Most steals, career
220 — Merlakia Jones
190 — Rushia Brown
139 — Mery Andrade

Highest average, steals per game, career
(Minimum 90 games)
1.15 — Penny Taylor (110/96)
1.12 — Helen Darling (110/98)
1.09 — Mery Andrade (139/128)

Most steals, season
51 — Janice Braxton, 1998
Mery Andrade, 2001
49 — Suzie McConnell Serio, 1998
46 — Lynette Woodard, 1997

Highest average, steals per game, season
(qualifiers)
1.75 — Suzie McConnell Serio, 1998 (49/28)
1.70 — Michelle Edwards, 1997 (34/20)
Janice Braxton, 1998 (51/30)

1.64 — Lynette Woodard, 1997 (46/28)

Most steals, game
8 — Janice Braxton, vs. Los Angeles,
July 3, 1997
7 — Rushia Brown, vs. Orlando,
June 7, 2000 (ot)
6 — Janice Braxton, at Los Angeles,
July 23, 1997
Merlakia Jones, vs. New York,
August 21, 1999

BLOCKED SHOTS

Most blocked shots, career
96 — Chasity Melvin
71 — Rushia Brown
64 — Eva Nemcova

Highest average, blocked shots per game, career
(Minimum: 90 games)
0.61 — Chasity Melvin (96/157)
0.58 — Eva Nemcova (64/111)
0.40 — Rushia Brown (71/176)

Most blocked shots, season
28 — Janice Braxton, 1997
27 — Isabelle Fijalkowski, 1998
24 — Ann Wauters, 2000

Highest average, blocked shots per game, season
(qualifiers)
1.12 — Janice Braxton, 1997 (28/25)
0.96 — Isabelle Fijalkowski, 1998 (27/28)
0.75 — Ann Wauters, 2000 (24/32)
Ann Wauters, 2002 (21/28)

Most blocked shots, game
4 — Janice Braxton, vs. Utah, July 19, 1997
Tracy Henderson, at Washington,
August 8, 1999
Chasity Melvin, vs. Phoenix,
June 25, 2000
Ann Wauters, vs. Detroit,
July 28, 2000
3 — by many

TURNOVERS

Most turnovers, career
376 — Merlakia Jones
290 — Chasity Melvin
256 — Eva Nemcova

Most turnovers, season
104 — Suzie McConnell Serio, 1998
81 — Isabelle Fijalkowski, 1998
Eva Nemcova, 1999
78 — Eva Nemcova, 1997

Most turnovers, game
11 — Michelle Edwards, vs. Sacramento,
August 2, 1997
8 — Isabelle Fijalkowski, at Sacramento,
August 12, 1997
Suzie McConnell Serio, at Houston,
August 1, 1998 (ot)
7 — By many

CONNECTICUT SUN

REGULAR SEASON TEAM RECORDS

TEAM OFFENSE

SCORING

Highest average, points per game, season
70.4 — 2002 (2254/32)
70.1 — 2003 (2384/34)
Lowest average, points per game, season
66.9 — 2001 (2140/32)
68.9 — 1999 (2206/32)
Most points, game
103 — vs. Cleveland, June 8, 2002 (3 ot)
93 — vs. Detroit, August 18, 1999
Fewest points, game
41 — vs. Cleveland, June 27, 2001
45 — vs. Washington, August 1, 2003
Largest margin of victory, game
29 — vs. Detroit, August 6, 2000 (92-63)
27 — vs. Washington, August 15, 1999 (81-54)

Largest margin of defeat, game
28 — at Cleveland, June 14, 2003 (56-84)
27 — at Charlotte, July 17, 2002 (62-89)

BY HALF

Most points, first half
49 — at Houston, May 30, 2003
46 — vs. Detroit, August 18, 1999
Fewest points, first half
17 — vs. Minnesota, June 8, 2000
18 — vs. Seattle, July 17, 2003

LARGEST LEAD AT HALFTIME

18 — vs. Detroit, August 6, 2000 (led 43-25; won 92-63)
17 — vs. Detroit, August 18, 1999 (led 46-29; won 93-81)
vs. Washington, July 24, 2001 (led 40-23; won 71-63)

LARGEST DEFICIT AT HALFTIME OVERCOME TO WIN GAME

12 — vs. New York, July 6, 2003 (trailed 20-32; won 62-58)
11 — vs. Los Angeles, June 15, 1999 (trailed 39-50; won 88-86)

MOST POINTS, SECOND HALF

54 — at Indiana, June 3, 2000
vs. New York, June 23, 2002
49 — vs. Los Angeles, June 15, 1999
vs. Detroit, August 6, 2000
at San Antonio, June 1, 2003

Fewest points, second half
16 — at Detroit, July 8, 2003
18 — at Cleveland, July 30, 2001

OVERTIME

Most points, overtime period
17 — vs. Cleveland, June 8, 2002
16 — vs. Indiana, July 3, 2002
Fewest points, overtime period
4 — vs. Miami, July 10, 2001
6 — at Cleveland, June 7, 2000
at Miami, July 27, 2001
vs. Cleveland, June 8, 2002
Largest margin of victory, overtime period
8 — vs. Indiana, July 3, 2002 (79-71)
6 — at Cleveland, July 28, 2002 (76-70)

FIELD GOAL PERCENTAGE

Highest field—goal percentage, season
.436 — 2000 (833/1911)
.424 — 1999 (793/1869)
Lowest field—goal percentage, season
.401 — 2001 (768/1914)
.411 — 2003 (864/2102)
Highest field—goal percentage, game
.600 — at Indiana, June 18, 2001 (30/50)
.577 — at Cleveland, June 7, 2000 (ot) (30/52)
Lowest field—goal percentage, game
.238 — vs. Washington, August 1, 2003 (15/63)
.263 — vs. Cleveland, June 27, 2001 (15/57)

FIELD GOALS

Most field goals per game, season
26.0 — 2000 (833/32)
25.4 — 2003 (864/34)
Fewest field goals per game, season
24.0 — 2001 (768/32)
24.8 — 1999 (793/32)
Most field goals, game
37 — vs. Detroit, July 19, 2000
at Detroit, June 5, 2001
35 — vs. Detroit, August 6, 2000
vs. Cleveland, June 8, 2002 (3 ot)
Fewest field goals, game
15 — vs. Cleveland, June 27, 2001
vs. Washington, August 1, 2003
17 — at Cleveland, June 14, 2003

FIELD GOAL ATTEMPTS

Most field—goal attempts per game, season
61.8 — 2003 (2102/34)
59.8 — 2001 (1914/32)
2002 (1914/32)

Fewest field—goal attempts per game, season
    58.4 — 1999 (1869/32)
    59.7 — 2000 (1911/32)
Most field—goal attempts, game
    84 — vs. Los Angeles, May 24, 2003
    82 — at Utah, June 7, 2001
        vs. Detroit, June 22, 2003 (ot)
Fewest field—goal attempts, game
    43 — at Portland, July 30, 2000
    44 — at Charlotte, August 9, 2003

THREE-POINT FIELD-GOAL PERCENTAGE

Highest three-point field-goal percentage, season
    .342 — 2000 (145/424)
    .336 — 1999 (155/461)
Lowest three-point field-goal percentage, season
    .315 — 2002 (145/461)
    .322 — 2003 (177/549)

THREE-POINT FIELD GOALS

Most three-point field goals per game, season
    5.4 — 2001 (174/32)
    5.2 — 2003 (177/34)
Fewest three-point field goals per game, season
    4.5 — 2000 (145/32)
          2002 (145/32)
Most three-point field goals, game
    13 — at Sacramento, July 27, 2000
    12 — vs. Indiana, June 26, 2003 (2 ot)
Fewest three-point field goals, game
    0 — vs. Houston, June 26, 2000
    1 — Many times

THREE-POINT FIELD GOAL ATTEMPTS

Most three-point field goal attempts per game, season
    16.6 — 2001 (532/32)
    16.2 — 2003 (549/34)
Fewest three-point field goal attempts per game, season
    13.3 — 2000 (424/32)
    14.4 — 1999 (461/32)
            2002 (461/32)
Most three-point field goal attempts, game
    30 — at Sacramento, July 27, 2000
    28 — at Utah, June 12, 1999
Fewest three-point field goal attempts, game
    6 — at Seattle, June 27, 2002
    7 — Many times

FREE THROW PERCENTAGE

Highest free-throw percentage, season
    .763 — 2002 (493/646)
    .741 — 2003 (479/646)

Lowest free-throw percentage, season
    .692 — 1999 (465/672)
    .727 — 2000 (397/546)
Highest free-throw percentage, game
    1.000 — at Cleveland, June 22, 1999 (10/10)
            at Houston, August 3, 2002 (7/7)
    .955 — at Miami, June 30, 2000 (21/22)
Lowest free-throw percentage, game
    .455 — at Charlotte, July 17, 2002 (10/22)
    .462 — vs. Portland, August 1, 2001 (6/13)

FREE THROWS MADE

Most free throws made per game, season
    15.4 — 2002 (493/32)
    14.5 — 1999 (465/32)
Fewest free throws made per game, season
    12.4 — 2000 (397/32)
    13.4 — 2001 (430/32)
Most free throws made, game
    35 — vs. Detroit, August 18, 1999
    28 — vs. Cleveland, June 8, 2002
          vs. New York, June 23, 2002
Fewest free throws made, game
    2 — at Cleveland, July 30, 2001
    3 — at Sacramento, July 27, 2000

FREE THROW ATTEMPTS

Most free throw attempts per game, season
    21.0 — 1999 (672/32)
    20.2 — 2002 (646/32)
Fewest free throw attempts per game, season
    17.1 — 2000 (546/32)
    18.3 — 2001 (587/32)
Most free throw attempts, game
    47 — vs. Detroit, August 18, 1999
    42 — at Detroit, June 17, 1999
Fewest free throw attempts, game
    4 — at Cleveland, July 30, 2001
    5 — at Sacramento, July 27, 2000

REBOUNDS

Most rebounds per game, season
    32.2 — 2003 (1095/34)
    30.3 — 2001 (970/32)
Fewest rebounds per game, season
    28.6 — 2002 (915/32)
    28.9 — 2000 (925/32)
Most rebounds, game
    46 — vs. Los Angeles, May 24, 2003
    45 — vs. Detroit, June 22, 2003 (ot)
Fewest rebounds, game
    16 — vs. Charlotte, July 16, 1999
    18 — vs. Seattle, July 8, 2000
          vs. Utah, July 19, 2002

OFFENSIVE REBOUNDS

Most offensive rebounds per game, season
11.1 — 2001 (356/32)
10.3 — 1999 (329/32)
Fewest offensive rebounds per game, season
9.8 — 2003 (333/34)
10.0 — 2000 (319/32)
Most offensive rebounds, game
21 — at Charlotte, July 12, 2001
19 — at Miami, August 9, 2000 (2 ot)
Fewest offensive rebounds, game
3 — at Seattle, June 12, 2001
at Indiana, June 18, 2000
at Los Angeles, July 22, 2002
at Indiana, August 25, 2003
4 — at Detroit, June 17, 1999
vs. Detroit, July 19, 2000

DEFENSIVE REBOUNDS

Most defensive rebounds per game, season
22.4 — 2003 (762/34)
19.9 — 1999 (637/32)
Fewest defensive rebounds per game, season
18.6 — 2002 (595/32)
18.9 — 2000 (606/32)
Most defensive rebounds, game
32 — vs. Los Angeles, May 24, 2003
31 — vs. New York, July 6, 2003
Fewest defensive rebounds, game
11 — vs. Charlotte, July 16, 1999
12 — vs. Seattle, July 8, 2000

ASSISTS

Most assists per game, season
15.3 — 2003 (520/34)
14.8 — 2000 (473/32)
Fewest assists per game, season
13.9 — 2002 (446/32)
14.1 — 2001 (452/32)
Most assists, game
26 — at Minnesota, August 20, 1999 (ot)
22 — vs. Los Angeles, June 15, 1999
vs. Sacramento, July 17, 1999
at Charlotte, June 10, 2000
at Phoenix, June 16, 2001
Fewest assists, game
5 — at Detroit, June 17, 1999
6 — vs. Cleveland, June 27, 2001

PERSONAL FOULS

Most personal fouls per game, season
20.9 — 2002 (669/32)
20.3 — 1999 (648/32)
Fewest personal fouls per game, season
18.2 — 2000 (583/32)

19.5 — 2003 (663/34)
Most personal fouls, game
34 — at Utah, June 7, 2001
vs. Cleveland, June 8, 2002 (3 ot)
31 — at Detroit, June 17, 1999
Fewest personal fouls, game
8 — vs. Washington, August 15, 1999
11 — vs. Charlotte, August 1, 2002

DISQUALIFICATIONS

Most disqualifications per game, season
0.31 — 1999 (10/32)
0.19 — 2002 (6/32)
Fewest disqualifications per game, season
0.09 — 2001 (3/32)
0.15 — 2003 (5/34)
Most disqualifications, game
2 — at Detroit, June 17, 1999
at Phoenix, July 23, 1999
at Detroit, August 21, 1999
at Phoenix, August 1, 2000
vs. Cleveland, June 8, 2002 (3 ot)
vs. Indiana, June 26, 2003 (2 ot)

STEALS

Most steals per game, season
10.0 — 2001 (320/32)
9.3 — 1999 (297/32)
Fewest steals per game, season
7.9 — 2003 (270/34)
8.0 — 2000 (255/32)
Most steals, game
17 — vs. Los Angeles, June 1, 2001
16 — vs. Miami, July 10, 2001 (ot)
Fewest steals, game
2 — at Portland, July 30, 2000
3 — Many times

BLOCKED SHOTS

Most blocked shots per game, season
4.1 — 2000 (130/32)
3.9 — 2001 (125/32)
Fewest blocked shots per game, season
2.9 — 1999 (93/32)
3.3 — 2003 (111/34)
Most blocked shots, game
10 — vs. Charlotte, June 24, 2000
vs. Detroit, July 19, 200
at Indiana, August 25, 2003
9 — vs. Sacramento, July 4, 2003
Fewest blocked shots, game
0 — Many times. Most recent:
vs. New York, August 12, 2003

TURNOVERS

Most turnovers per game, season
16.6 — 2001 (532/32)
16.3 — 1999 (521/32)
Fewest turnovers per game, season
12.8 — 2003 (434/34)
14.3 — 2002 (456/32)
Most turnovers, game
27 — at Cleveland, June 7, 2000 (ot)
24 — vs. Sacramento, July 17, 1999
      at Minnesota, June 15, 2000
Fewest turnovers, game
4 — vs. Washington, August 15, 1999
5 — at San Antonio, June 1, 2003

TEAM DEFENSE

POINTS

Fewest points allowed per game, season
68.9 — 2001 (2205/32)
69.3 — 1999 (2216/32)
Most points allowed per game, season
70.9 — 2003 (2409/34)
70.5 — 2002 (2255/32)
Fewest points allowed, game
48 — vs. Washington, August 1, 2003
49 — vs. Minnesota, July 21, 2001
Fewest points allowed, first half
21 — vs. Seattle, July 8, 2000
      vs. Washington, August 1, 2003
      vs. New York, August 12, 2003
23 — Many times
Fewest points allowed, second half
20 — vs. Houston, June 7, 2003
22 — vs. Washington, June 23, 2001
      vs. Minnesota, July 21, 2001
Fewest points allowed, overtime period
5 — at Cleveland, July 28, 2002
6 — at Minnesota, August 20, 1999
      vs. Miami, July 10, 2001
      vs. Cleveland, June 8, 2002

FIELD GOAL PERCENTAGE

Lowest opponents' field-goal percentage, season
.411 — 2003 (864/2104)
.429 — 1999 (812/1892)
Highest opponents' field-goal percentage, season
.440 — 2001 (806/1831)
.433 — 2000 (851/1964)
Lowest opponents' field goal percentage, game
.254 — vs. Minnesota, July 21, 2001 (16/63)
.281 — at Washington, July 19, 1999 (16/57)

TURNOVERS

Most opponents' turnovers per game, season
17.1 — 2001 (546/32)

16.9 — 2002 (541/32)
Fewest opponents' turnovers per game, season
14.0 — 2003 (476/34)
15.6 — 2000 (500/32)
Most opponents' turnovers, game
26 — vs. Detroit, May 30, 2002
25 — vs. Miami, July 10, 2001 (ot)
      vs. Washington, July 24, 2001
      vs. Washington, July 8, 2002

TEAM MISCELLANEOUS

GAME WON AND LOST

Highest winning percentage, season
.529 — 2003 (18—16)
.500 — 2000 (16—16)
      2002 (16—16)
Lowest winning percentage, season
.406 — 2001 (13—19)
.469 — 1999 (15—17)
Most consecutive games won
6 — June 28-July 9, 2000
5 — August 12-20, 1999
Most consecutive games won, one season
6 — June 28-July 9, 2000
5 — August 12-20, 1999
Most consecutive game lost
7 — July 21-August 4, 2000
5 — June 7-16, 2001
Most consecutive game lost, one season
7 — July 21-August 4, 2000
5 — June 7-16, 2001
Highest winning percentage, home games, season
.688 — 2000 (11-5)
.625 — 2001 (10-6)
      2002 (10-6)
Lowest winning percentage, home games, season
.500 — 1999 (8-8)
.588 — 2003 (10-7)
Most consecutive home games won
6 — July 18-August 7, 2001
5 — August 12, 1999-June 5, 2000
Most consecutive home games lost
4 — July 12-29, 1999
2 — Many times
Highest winning percentage, road games, season
.471 — 2003 (8-9)
.438 — 1999 (7-9)
Lowest winning percentage, road games, season
.188 — 2001 (3-13)
.313 — 2000 (5-11)
Most consecutive road games won
4 — June 22-July 19, 1999
      June 4-21, 2002

2 — Many times

Most consecutive road games lost
8 — July 12-August 9, 2000
July 13, 2001-June 1, 2002
7 — June 26-July 22, 2002

OVERTIME GAMES

Most overtime games, season
3 — 2000, 2002
2 — 1999, 2001, 2003

Most consecutive overtime games, season
1 — Many times

Most overtime games won, season
3 — 2002
1 — 1999

Most overtime games won, no losses, season
3 — 2002

Most consecutive overtime games won
3 — June 8—July 28, 2002

Most overtime games lost, season
3 — 2000
2 — 2001, 2003

Most overtime games lost, no wins, season
3 — 2000
2 — 2001, 2003

Most consecutive overtime games lost
5 — June 7, 2000-July 27, 2001
2 — June 22-26, 2003 (current)

Most overtime periods, game
3 — vs. Cleveland, June 8, 2002
2 — at Miami, August 9, 2000
vs. Indiana, June 26, 2003

INDIVIDUAL RECORDS

SEASONS

Most Seasons
5 — Shannon Johnson
Taj McWilliams-Franklin
Nykesha Sales
4 — By many

GAMES

Most games, career
162 — Nykesha Sales
155 — Shannon Johnson
143 — Taj McWilliams-Franklin

Most consecutive games, career
162 — Nykesha Sales, June 10, 1999-August
25, 2003 (current)
109 — Taj McWilliams-Franklin, June 10,
1999-June 29, 2002
98 — Brooke Wyckoff, June 1, 2001-August
25, 2003 (current)

Most games, season
34 — By many

MINUTES

Most minutes, career
5,275 — Shannon Johnson
5,221 — Nykesha Sales
4,565 — Taj McWilliams-Franklin

Highest average, minutes per game, career
(Minimum 60 games)
34.0 — Shannon Johnson (5275/155)
32.2 — Nykesha Sales (5221/162)
31.9 — Taj McWilliams-Franklin (4565/143)

Most minutes, season
1,147 — Shannon Johnson, 1999
1,126 — Shannon Johnson, 2000
1,110 — Shannon Johnson, 2002

Highest average, minutes per game, season
35.84— Shannon Johnson, 1999 (1147/32)
35.81— Shannon Johnson, 2002 (1110/31)
35.2 — Shannon Johnson, 2000 (1126/32)

Most minutes, game
51 — Shannon Johnson, vs. Cleveland,
June 8, 2002 (3 ot)
50 — Adrienne Johnson, at Miami,
August 9, 2000 (2 ot)
49 — Shannon Johnson, at Miami,
August 9, 2000 (2 ot)

SCORING

Most points, lifetime
2,279 — Nykesha Sales
2,049 — Shannon Johnson
1,725 — Taj McWilliams-Franklin

Highest average, points per game, career
(Minimum 60 games)
14.1 — Nykesha Sales (2279/162)
13.2 — Shannon Johnson (2049/155)
12.1 — Taj McWilliams-Franklin (1725/143)

Most points, season
548 — Nykesha Sales, 2003
499 — Shannon Johnson, 2002
447 — Shannon Johnson, 1999

Highest average, points per game, season
16.12— Nykesha Sales, 2003 (548/34)
16.10— Shannon Johnson, 2002 (499/31)
14.0 — Shannon Johnson, 1999 (447/32)

Most points, game
35 — Shannon Johnson, vs. Cleveland,
June 8, 2002 (3 ot)
31 — Shannon Johnson, at Sacramento,
July 24, 1999
Shannon Johnson, at Houston,
May 30, 2003
Nykesha Sales, vs. New York,
August 12, 2003

29 — Nykesha Sales, vs. Los Angles, June
15, 1999
Nykesha Sales, vs. New York,
June 23, 2002
Nykesha Sales, at Charlotte,
August 9, 2003
Most games, 30 or more points, career
3 — Shannon Johnson
1 — Nykesha Sales
Most games, 20 or more points, career
38 — Nykesha Sales
27 — Shannon Johnson
13 — Taj McWilliams-Franklin
Most consecutive games, 20 or more points
3 — Shannon Johnson, July 19-22, 2002
Nykesha Sales, May 30-June 5, 2003
Shannon Johnson, June 5-13, 2003
Nykesha Sales, August 9-16, 2003
2 — By many
Most consecutive games, 10 or more points
15 — Taj McWilliams-Franklin,
August 1, 2000-June 25, 2001
Nykesha Sales, August 7, 2002-June 24, 2003
14 — Shannon Johnson,
July 12-August 8, 2002
12 — Adrienne Johnson,
July 14-August 9, 2000
Nykesha Sales, July 25, 2000-
June 9, 2001

FIELD GOAL PERCENTAGE

Highest field goal percentage, career
(Minimum 225 field goals)
.482 — Taj McWilliams-Franklin (657/1363)
.424 — Katie Douglas (263/620)
.418 — Nykesha Sales (838/2003)
Highest field goal percentage, season (qualifiers)
.524 — Taj McWilliams—Franklin, 2000
(173/330)
.480 — Taj McWilliams—Franklin, 1999
(153/319)
.474 — Taj McWilliams—Franklin, 2001
(157/331)
Highest field goal percentage, game
(Minimum 8 field goals made)
.889 — Elaine Powell, vs. Washington,
June 23, 2001 (8/9)
.818 — Taj McWilliams-Franklin, vs.
Cleveland, June 22, 2000 (9/11)
Taj McWilliams-Franklin, vs.
Charlotte, June 9, 2001 (9/11)
.800 — Katie Douglas, vs. Phoenix, July 6,
2002 (8/10)

Most field goals, none missed, game
7 — Taj McWilliams-Franklin, at
Washington, July 21, 2000
4 — By many
Most field goal attempts, none made, game
9 — Elaine Powell, at New York,
June 30, 2001
8 — Nykesha Sales, at Los Angeles,
July 27, 1999
Adrienne Johnson, at Portland,
June 26, 2002
Adrienne Johnson, at Detroit,
July 8, 2003
6 — By many

FIELD GOALS

Most field goals, career
838 — Nykesha Sales
658 — Shannon Johnson
657 — Taj McWilliams-Franklin
Most field goals, season
194 — Nykesha Sales, 2003
175 — Adrienne Johnson, 2000
173 — Taj McWilliams-Franklin, 2000
Most field goals, game
12 — Shannon Johnson, at Sacramento,
July 24, 1999
11 — Taj McWilliams-Franklin, at Miami,
August 9, 2000 (2 ot)
Shannon Johnson, vs. Cleveland,
June 8, 2002 (3 ot)
Nykesha Sales, vs. New York,
August 12, 2003
Katie Douglas, at Washington,
August 23, 2003
10 — By many

FIELD GOAL ATTEMPTS

Most field goal attempts, career
2,003 — Nykesha Sales
1,600 — Shannon Johnson
1,363 — Taj McWilliams-Franklin
Most field goal attempts, season
468 — Nykesha Sales, 2003
397 — Nykesha Sales, 1999
393 — Adrienne Johnson, 2000
Most field goal attempts, game
23 — Taj McWilliams-Franklin, at Miami,
August 9, 2000 (2 ot)
22 — Shannon Johnson, at Sacramento,
July 21, 2002
21 — Nykesha Sales, vs. Charlotte,
June 24, 2000
Nykesha Sales, at Sacramento, July 27, 2000

THREE-POINT FIELD-GOAL PERCENTAGE

Highest three-point field goal percentage, career (Minimum 60 three-point field goals)
.363 — Katie Douglas (94/259)
.348 — Nykesha Sales (207/594)
.331 — Adrienne Johnson (88/266)

Highest three-point field goal percentage, season (qualifiers)
.444 — Taj McWilliams-Franklin, 1999 (20/45)
.395 — Nykesha Sales, 2000 (47/119)
.386 — Nykesha Sales, 2003 (44/114)

Most three-point field goals, none missed, game
4 — Andrea Congreaves, at Minnesota, August 20, 1999 (ot)
Elaine Powell, vs. Washington, June 23, 2001
3 — Sheri Sam, vs. Phoenix, June 21, 1999
Adrienne Johnson, at Indiana, June 3, 2000
Nykesha Sales, at Utah, June 13, 2000
Adrienne Johnson, at Phoenix, July 19, 2003

Most three-point field goal attempts, none made, game
6 — Katie Douglas, at Houston, August 3, 2002
5 — By many

THREE-POINT FIELD GOALS

Most three-point field goals, career
207 — Nykesha Sales
148 — Shannon Johnson
94 — Katie Douglas

Most three-point field goals, season
52 — Adrienne Johnson, 2000
47 — Nykesha Sales, 2000
Katie Douglas, 2003
44 — Nykesha Sales, 2003

Most three-point field goals, game
7 — Nykesha Sales, at Sacramento, July 27, 2000
6 — Katie Douglas, vs. Indiana, June 26, 2003 (2 ot)
Nykesha Sales, at New York, July 1, 2003
5 — By many

Most consecutive games, three-point field goals made
18 — Adrienne Johnson, June 30-August 9, 2000
15 — Nykesha Sales, July 17-August 25, 2003 (current)
14 — Shannon Johnson, July 21-June 1, 2002
Katie Douglas, July 2—August 9, 2003

THREE-POINT FIELD GOAL ATTEMPTS

Most three-point field goal attempts, career
594 — Nykesha Sales
454 — Shannon Johnson
266 — Adrienne Johnson

Most three-point field goal attempts, season
148 — Adrienne Johnson, 2000
137 — Nykesha Sales, 2001
125 — Sheri Sam, 1999

Most three-point field goal attempts, game
11 — Nykesha Sales, at Sacramento, July 27, 2000
10 — Sheri Sam, at Cleveland, June 22, 1999
Adrienne Johnson, at Sacramento, July 27, 2000
Shannon Johnson, at Indiana, July 13, 2001
9 — By many

FREE THROW PERCENTAGE

Highest free-throw percentage, career (Minimum 125 free throws)
.786 — Nykesha Sales (396/504)
.775 — Katie Douglas (141/182)
.738 — Shannon Johnson (585/793)

Highest free-throw percentage, season (qualifiers)
.866 — Katie Douglas, 2002 (58/67)
.830 — Andrea Congreaves, 1999 (44/53)
.806 — Nykesha Sales, 2003 (116/144)

Most free throws made, none missed, game
10 — Shannon Johnson, at Miami, June 30, 2000
9 — Taj McWilliams-Franklin, vs. Detroit, July 8, 2001
Nykesha Sales, at New York, August 16, 2003
8 — Nykesha Sales, vs. Los Angeles, June 1, 2001
Nykesha Sales, at Cleveland, July 28, 2002 (ot)
Taj McWilliams-Franklin, vs. Indiana, June 26, 2003 (2 ot)

Most free throw attempts, none made, game
4 — Sheri Sam, vs. Utah, July 10, 1999
3 — Tari Phillips, vs. Utah, July 10, 1999
Clarisse Machanguana, at Charlotte, July 17, 2002
Rebecca Lobo, at Los Angeles, July 20, 2003
2 — By many

FREE THROWS MADE

Most free throws made, career
- 585 — Shannon Johnson
- 396 — Nykesha Sales
- 371 — Taj McWilliams-Franklin

Most free throws made, season
- 164 — Shannon Johnson, 2002
- 125 — Shannon Johnson, 2003
- 116 — Nykesha Sales, 2003

Most free throws made, game
- 13 — Nykesha Sales, at Charlotte, August 9, 2003
- 12 — Shannon Johnson, vs. New York, June 23, 2002
- 11 — Shannon Johnson, vs. Cleveland, June 8, 2002 (3 ot)
  Shannon Johnson, at Houston, May 30, 2003
  Shannon Johnson, vs. Minnesota, July 23, 2003

FREE THROW ATTEMPTS

Most free throw attempts, career
- 793 — Shannon Johnson
- 513 — Taj McWilliams-Franklin
- 504 — Nykesha Sales

Most free throw attempts, season
- 214 — Shannon Johnson, 2002
- 171 — Shannon Johnson, 2003
- 153 — Shannon Johnson, 1999

Most free throw attempts, game
- 16 — Nykesha Sales, at Charlotte, August 9, 2003
- 15 — Shannon Johnson, vs. New York, June 23, 2002
  Shannon Johnson, at Houston, May 30, 2003
- 14 — Shannon Johnson, at New York, June 18, 2002
  Taj McWilliams-Franklin, vs. Detroit, June 22, 2003 (ot)
  Shannon Johnson, vs. Minnesota, July 23, 2003

REBOUNDS

Most rebounds, career
- 1,016 — Taj McWilliams-Franklin
- 711 — Nykesha Sales
- 645 — Shannon Johnson

Highest average, rebounds per game, career (Minimum 60 games)
- 7.1 — Taj McWilliams-Franklin (1016/143)
- 4.4 — Nykesha Sales (711/162)
- 4.2 — Shannon Johnson (645/155)

Most rebounds, season
- 244 — Taj McWilliams-Franklin, 2000
- 243 — Taj McWilliams-Franklin, 2001
- 239 — Taj McWilliams-Franklin, 1999

Highest average, rebounds per game, season (qualifiers)
- 7.63— Taj McWilliamsFranklin, 2000 (244/32)
- 7.59— Taj McWilliamsFranklin, 2001 (243/32)
- 7.5 — Taj McWilliamsFranklin, 1999 (239/32)

Most rebounds, game
- 15 — Taj McWilliams-Franklin, vs. Cleveland, August 12, 1999
- 14 — Taj McWilliams-Franklin, at New York, August 4, 2000
- 13 — By many

Most games, 10+ rebounds, career
- 27 — Taj McWilliams-Franklin
- 5 — Nykesha Sales
- 3 — Shannon Johnson

Most consecutive games, 10+ rebounds
- 2 — Taj McWilliams-Franklin, June 17-19, 1999
  Taj McWilliams-Franklin, June 14-16, 2001
  Taj McWilliams-Franklin, July 17-19, 2003

OFFENSIVE REBOUNDS

Most offensive rebounds, career
- 384 — Taj McWilliams-Franklin
- 207 — Nykesha Sales
- 200 — Shannon Johnson

Highest average, offensive rebounds per game, career (Minimum 60 games)
- 2.7 — Taj McWilliams-Franklin (384/143)
- 1.29— Shannon Johnson (200/155)
- 1.28— Nykesha Sales (207/162)

Most offensive rebounds, season
- 114 — Taj McWilliams-Franklin, 2001
- 90 — Taj McWilliams-Franklin, 2000
- 81 — Taj McWilliams-Franklin, 1999

Most offensive rebounds, game
- 10 — Taj McWilliams-Franklin, vs. Houston, July 18, 2001
- 8 — Taj McWilliams-Franklin, at Phoenix, June 16, 2001
  Nykesha Sales, at Charlotte, July 12, 2001
  Taj McWilliams-Franklin, vs. Washington, July 24, 2001
  Taj McWilliams-Franklin, at Detroit, July 29, 2001
- 7 — Andrea Congreaves, vs. Los Angeles, June 15, 1999

DEFENSIVE REBOUNDS

Most defensive rebounds, career
- 632 — Taj McWilliams-Franklin

504 — Nykesha Sales
445 — Shannon Johnson
Highest average, defensive rebounds per game,
career (Minimum 60 games)
4.4 — Taj McWilliams-Franklin (632/143)
3.1 — Nykesha Sales (504/162)
2.9 — Shannon Johnson (445/155)
Most defensive rebounds, season
158 — Taj McWilliams-Franklin, 1999
154 — Taj McWilliams-Franklin, 2000
149 — Taj McWilliams-Franklin, 2003
Most defensive rebounds, game
11 — Taj McWilliams-Franklin, at Detroit,
June 17, 1999
10 — Taj McWilliams—Franklin, vs.
Washington, June 19, 1999
Taj McWilliams-Franklin, vs.
Sacramento, June 5, 2000
Taj McWilliams-Franklin, vs. Detroit,
July 19, 2000
Taj McWilliams-Franklin, at Detroit,
June 5, 2001
Nykesha Sales, vs. Minnesota,
July 21, 2001
Nykesha Sales, vs. Washington,
June 13, 2003

ASSISTS

Most assists, career
737 — Shannon Johnson
370 — Nykesha Sales
236 — Taj McWilliams-Franklin
Highest average, assists per game, career
(Minimum 60 games)
4.8 — Shannon Johnson (737/155)
2.4 — Elaine Powell (202/85)
2.3 — Nykesha Sales (370/162)
Most assists, season
196 — Shannon Johnson, 2003
169 — Shannon Johnson, 2000
163 — Shannon Johnson, 2002
Highest average, assists per game,
season (qualifiers)
5.8 — Shannon Johnson, 2003 (196/34)
5.28— Shannon Johnson, 2000 (169/32)
5.26— Shannon Johnson, 2002 (163/31)
Most assists, game
12 — Shannon Johnson, at Utah,
June 13, 2000
Shannon Johnson, vs. Utah, July 19, 2002
11 — Shannon Johnson, at Minnesota,
July 10, 2003
10 — By many
Most games, 10+ assists, career

8 — Shannon Johnson

PERSONAL FOULS

Most personal fouls, career
502 — Nykesha Sales
399 — Taj McWilliams-Franklin
383 — Shannon Johnson
Most personal fouls, season
112 — Sheri Sam, 1999
Cintia dos Santos, 2000
109 — Nykesha Sales, 2001
Brooke Wyckoff, 2003
107 — Nykesha Sales, 2003
Most personal fouls, game
6 — By many

DISQUALIFICATIONS

Most disqualifications, career
7 — Nykesha Sales
6 — Taj McWilliams-Franklin
4 — Sheri Sam
Brooke Wyckoff
Highest percentage, games disqualified, career
(Minimum 60 games)
4.4 — Cintia dos Santos (3/68)
4.3 — Nykesha Sales (7/162)
4.2 — Taj McWilliams-Franklin (6/143)
Lowest percentage, games disqualified, career
(Minimum 60 games)
0.0 — Elaine Powell (0/85)
Carla McGhee (0/81)
Tiffany McCain (0/73)
0.6 — Shannon Johnson (1/155)
Most consecutive games without
disqualification, career
94 — Shannon Johnson, June 10, 1999-
June 8, 2002
85 — Elaine Powell, July 16, 1999-
July 6, 2002
81 — Carla McGhee, June 12, 1999-
August 13, 2002
Most disqualifications, season
4 — Sheri Sam, 1999
3 — Taj McWilliams-Franklin, 1999
Cintia dos Santos, 2000
Nykesha Sales, 2003
2 — Nykesha Sales, 1999
Brooke Wyckoff, 2001
Fewest minutes, disqualified, game
13 — Cintia dos Santos, vs. Utah,
July 19, 2002
19 — Brooke Wyckoff, at Washington,
July 1, 2001
20 — Brooke Wyckoff, at Washington,
June 1, 2002

STEALS

Most steals, career
  292 — Nykesha Sales
  241 — Shannon Johnson
  230 — Taj McWilliams-Franklin
Highest average, steals per game, career
(Minimum 60 games)
  1.80 — Nykesha Sales (292/162)
  1.61 — Taj McWilliams-Franklin (230/143)
  1.55 — Shannon Johnson (241/155)
Most steals, season
  70 — Nykesha Sales, 2001
  69 — Nykesha Sales, 1999
  60 — Nykesha Sales, 2002
Highest average, steals per game, season
(qualifiers)
  2.19 — Nykesha Sales, 2001 (70/32)
  2.16 — Nykesha Sales, 1999 (69/32)
  1.88 — Nykesha Sales, 2002 (60/32)
Most steals, game
  6 — Nykesha Sales, vs. Washington,
      June 19, 1999
      Shannon Johnson, at New York,
      August 1, 1999
      Nykesha Sales, vs. Detroit,
      August 18, 1999
  5 — By many

BLOCKED SHOTS

Most blocked shots, career
  166 — Taj McWilliams-Franklin
  81 — Cintia dos Santos
  58 — Jessie Hicks
Highest average, blocked shots per game, career
(Minimum: 60 games)
  1.19 — Cintia dos Santos (81/68)
  1.16 — Taj McWilliams-Franklin (166/143)
  0.53 — Brooke Wyckoff (52/98)
Most blocked shots, season
  63 — Cintia dos Santos, 2000
  50 — Taj McWilliams-Franklin, 2001
  38 — Taj McWilliams-Franklin, 1999
Highest average, blocked shots per game,
season (qualifiers)
  1.97 — Cintia dos Santos, 2000 (63/320
  1.56 — Taj McWilliams-Franklin, 2001 (50/32)
  1.19 — Taj McWilliams-Franklin, 1999 (38/32)
Most blocked shots, game
  5 — Cintia dos Santos, vs. Indiana,
      June 17, 2000
      Cintia dos Santos, vs. Detroit,
      July 19, 2000
      Taj McWilliams-Franklin, vs. Detroit,
      July 8, 2001
      Taj McWilliams-Franklin, vs.
      Sacramento, July 4, 2003
      Taj McWilliams-Franklin, vs. Indiana,
      August 3, 2003
  4 — By many

TURNOVERS

Most turnovers, career
  482 — Shannon Johnson
  352 — Nykesha Sales
  319 — Taj McWilliams-Franklin
Most turnovers, season
  121 — Shannon Johnson, 1999
  107 — Shannon Johnson, 2003
  102 — Shannon Johnson, 2000
Most turnovers, game
  8 — Shannon Johnson, at Cleveland,
      August 14, 1999
      Shannon Johnson, at Miami,
      August 9, 2000 (2 ot)
      Elaine Powell, at Miami, June 4, 2002
      Shannon Johnson, vs. New York,
      August 13, 2002
  7 — Many times

DETROIT SHOCK

REGULAR SEASON TEAM RECORDS

TEAM OFFENSE

SCORING

Highest average, points per game, season
75.1 — 2003 (2553/34)
72.8 — 2000 (2331/32)
Lowest average, points per game, season
65.7 — 2001 (2103/32)
66.1 — 2002 (2114/32)
Most points, game
111 — vs. Indiana, June 18, 2000
103 — vs. Connecticut, June 5, 2003
Fewest points, game
40 — at Houston, July 6, 2002
46 — at Houston, July 27, 1999
Largest margin of victory, game
37 — vs. Indiana, June 18, 2000 (111-74)
at Washington, June 14, 2003 (93—56)
30 — vs. Miami, July 14, 2000 (80-50)
Largest margin of defeat, game
39 — at Houston, July 27, 1999 (46-85)
31 — at Indiana, July 6, 2003 (54-85)

BY HALF

Most points, first half
56 — vs. San Antonio, July 1, 2003
53 — vs. Cleveland, June 15, 1998
Fewest points, first half
8 — at Houston, July 6, 2002
16 — at Minnesota, June 12, 1999
at Miami, July 14, 2001
Largest lead at halftime
19 — at Los Angeles, August 16, 1998 (42-23)
vs. Cleveland, July 17, 1999 (42-23)
at Connecticut, August 5, 2003 (47-28)
17 — vs. Miami, July 20, 2002 (36-19)
Largest deficit at halftime overcome to win game
15 — at Cleveland, June 27, 1998
(trailed 36-51; won 84-73)
12 — at Minnesota, August 23, 2003
(trailed 23-35; won 86-77 in OT)
Most points, second half
66 — vs. Indiana, June 18, 2000
58 — at Seattle, August 17, 2003
Fewest points, second half
19 — vs. Indiana, August 9, 2002
20 — at Washington, June 19, 2000

OVERTIME

Most points, overtime period
18 — at Connecticut, June 22, 2003

15 — at Minnesota, August 23, 2003
Fewest points, overtime period
1 — at Utah, July 6, 1999 (2nd OT)
2 — at Seattle, July 24, 2001
Largest margin of victory, overtime period
9 — vs. Los Angeles, June 17, 2003 (87-78)
at Connecticut, June 22, 2003 (82-73)
at Minnesota, August 23, 2003 (86-77)

FIELD GOAL PERCENTAGE

Highest field-goal percentage, season
.450 — 2003 (902/2004)
.438 — 2000 (868/1981)
Lowest field-goal percentage, season
.399 — 2002 (766/1919)
.401 — 1999 (791/1972)
Highest field-goal percentage, game
.619 — at Phoenix, July 26, 2001 (26/42)
.593 — vs. Indiana, June 18, 2000 (35/59)
Lowest field-goal percentage, game
.259 — at Houston, July 6, 2002 (15/58)
.262 — at Houston, July 27, 1999 (17/65)

FIELD GOALS

Most field goals per game, season
27.1 — 2000 (868/32)
26.5 — 2003 (902/34)
Fewest field goals per game, season
23.9 — 2002 (766/32)
24.2 — 2001 (774/32)
Most field goals, game
36 — at Charlotte, June 25, 2000
35 — at Cleveland, June 16, 2000
vs. Indiana, June 18, 2000
Fewest field goals, game
15 — at Houston, July 6, 2002
16 — vs. Orlando, June 21, 2002

FIELD GOAL ATTEMPTS

Most field—goal attempts per game, season
62.5 — 1998 (1875/30)
61.9 — 2000 (1980/32)
Fewest field—goal attempts per game, season
58.9 — 2003 (2004/34)
59.8 — 2001 (1914/32)
Most field—goal attempts, game
94 — vs. Washington, July 10, 1999 (2 ot)
84 — at Portland, July 22, 2001 (ot)
Regulation game:
78 — vs. Phoenix, June 29, 2001
Fewest field-goal attempts, game
42 — at Phoenix, July 26, 2001

45 — at Sacramento, August 11, 1998

THREE-POINT FIELD-GOAL PERCENTAGE

Highest three-point field-goal percentage, season
.387 — 2003 (125/323)
.360 — 1999 (121/336)
Lowest three-point field-goal percentage, season
.278 — 2000 (76/273)
.302 — 2002 (110/364)

THREE-POINT FIELD GOALS

Most three-point field goals per game, season
4.5 — 2001 (143/32)
3.8 — 1999 (121/32)
Fewest three-point field goals per game, season
2.4 — 2000 (76/32)
3.2 — 1998 (97/30)
Most three-point field goals, game
10 — at Indiana, June 1, 2002
vs. New York, August 10, 2003 (ot)
9 — at Orlando, August 18, 1999
vs. Orlando, June 5, 2001
vs. Los Angeles, June 26, 2001 (ot)
vs. New York, June 9, 2002
Fewest three-point field goals, game
0 — Many times

THREE-POINT FIELD GOAL ATTEMPTS

Most three-point field goal attempts per game, season
12.7 — 2001 (405/32)
11.4 — 2002 (364/32)
Fewest three-point field goal attempts per game, season
8.5 — 2000 (273/32)
9.5 — 2003 (323/34)
Most three-point field goal attempts, game
27 — vs. Orlando, June 5, 2001
26 — at Indiana, June 1, 2002
Fewest three-point field goal attempts, game
3 — at Phoenix, July 15, 1998
vs. Sacramento, June 3, 2000
at Seattle, June 28, 2000
vs. New York, August 9, 2000
vs. New York, July 10, 2002
4 — By many

FREE THROW PERCENTAGE

Highest free-throw percentage, season
.760 — 2001 (412/542)
.742 — 2000 (519/699)
Lowest free-throw percentage, season
.7016— 1999 (536/764)
.7022— 1998 (448/638)
Highest free-throw percentage, game
1.000 — vs. Houston, August 7, 1998 (4/4)
at Charlotte, June 27, 2001 (8/8)

.952 — at Orlando, August 18, 1999 (20/21)
Lowest free-throw percentage, game
.385 — at Washington, June 21, 1998 (5/13)
.400 — vs. Orlando, July 9, 2000 (4/10)

FREE THROWS MADE

Most free throws made per game, season
18.4 — 2003 (624/34)
16.8 — 1999 (536/32)
Fewest free throws made per game, season
12.9 — 2001 (412/32)
14.8 — 2002 (472/32)
Most free throws made, game
40 — vs. Indiana, June 18, 2000
vs. San Antonio, July 1, 2003
30 — vs. Miami, June 28, 2002 (ot)
vs. Connecticut, June 5, 2003
Fewest free throws made, game
3 — at Phoenix, July 6, 2000
4 — vs. Houston, August 7, 1998
vs. Orlando, July 9, 2000
at Indiana, June 1, 2002

FREE THROW ATTEMPTS

Most free throw attempts per game, season
25.9 — 2003 (882/34)
23.9 — 1999 (764/32)
Fewest free throw attempts per game, season
16.9 — 2001 (542/32)
20.3 — 2002 (651/32)
Most free throw attempts, game
54 — vs. Indiana, June 18, 2000
51 — vs. San Antonio, July 1, 2003
Fewest free throw attempts, game
4 — vs. Houston, August 7, 1998
5 — at Phoenix, July 6, 2000

REBOUNDS

Most rebounds per game, season
36.2 — 2003 (1230/34)
35.9 — 1998 (1077/30)
Fewest rebounds per game, season
29.5 — 2001 (945/32)
30.8 — 2000 (985/32)
Most rebounds, game
48 — at Connecticut, June 22, 2003 (ot)
47 — at Utah, August 10, 1998
Fewest rebounds, game
14 — vs. Utah, August 7, 2001
18 — at Cleveland, August 8, 2001

OFFENSIVE REBOUNDS

Most offensive rebounds per game, season
11.5 — 1998 (345/30)
11.3 — 2002 (360/32)
Fewest offensive rebounds per game, season
10.0 — 1999 (321/32)
10.1 — 2001 (324/32)

Most offensive rebounds, game
  22 — vs. Charlotte, July 3, 2003
  21 — vs. New York, June 9, 2002
Fewest offensive rebounds, game
  4 — vs. Utah, August 7, 2001
     at Cleveland, August 8, 2001
     at New York, June 27, 2003
  5 — By many

DEFENSIVE REBOUNDS

Most defensive rebounds per game, season
  25.1 — 2003 (851/34)
  24.4 — 1998 (732/30)
Fewest defensive rebounds per game, season
  19.4 — 2001 (621/32)
  20.1 — 2000 (644/32)
Most defensive rebounds, game
  36 — at Connecticut, June 22, 2003 (ot)
  35 — at Washington, June 14, 2003
Fewest defensive rebounds, game
  10 — vs. Utah, August 7, 2001
  13 — at Cleveland, July 28, 2000
     vs. Charlotte, July 3, 2003
     at Charlotte, July 24, 2003

ASSISTS

Most assists per game, season
  16.0 — 2003 (545/34)
  15.7 — 2000 (503/32)
Fewest assists per game, season
  14.4 — 1998 (432/30)
  14.5 — 1999 (464/32)
Most assists, game
  26 — at Cleveland, June 16, 2000
  25 — at Washington, June 14, 2003
Fewest assists, game
  6 — vs. Orlando, June 21, 2002
  7 — vs. Houston, June 24, 1999
     vs. Minnesota, August 4, 1999
     vs. New York, August 13, 1999
     at Houston, July 6, 2002

PERSONAL FOULS

Most personal fouls per game, season
  22.8 — 1999 (728/32)
  21.9 — 2000 (701/32)
Fewest personal fouls per game, season
  17.8 — 2003 (605/34)
  18.8 — 2001 (602/32)
Most personal fouls, game
  34 — at Orlando, August 18, 1999
  32 — vs. Sacramento, July 4, 1999
Fewest personal fouls, game
  7 — vs. Washington, August 25, 2003
  11 — vs. Seattle, July 28, 2002
     at Orlando, August 11, 2002

DISQUALIFICATIONS

Most disqualifications per game, season
  0.44 — 1999 (14/32)
  0.13 — 2000 (4/32)
Fewest disqualifications per game, season
  0.03 — 2002 (1/32)
  0.09 — 2003 (3/34)
Most disqualifications, game
  2 — at Utah, July 6, 1999 (2 ot)
     vs. Washington, July 10, 1999 (2 ot)
     at Phoenix, August 11, 1999

STEALS

Most steals per game, season
  8.1 — 2000 (260/32)
  7.7 — 2003 (263/34)
Fewest steals per game, season
  6.3 — 2002 (201/32)
  6.6 — 1998 (197/30)
Most steals, game
  20 — vs. Indiana, June 18, 2000
  18 — vs. Washington, June 24, 2000
Fewest steals, game
  1 — vs. Charlotte, June 26, 2002
  2 — vs. Sacramento, June 23, 1998
     at Orlando, August 18, 1999
     vs. Cleveland, July 28, 2001
     vs. Utah, July 23, 2002
     at Cleveland, July 29, 2003

BLOCKED SHOTS

Most blocked shots per game, season
  4.7 — 2003 (158/34)
  4.1 — 2002 (132/32)
Fewest blocked shots per game, season
  2.6 — 2001 (82/32)
  2.7 — 1998 (81/30)
Most blocked shots, game
  11 — at Charlotte, July 10, 2003
  10 — at Indiana, July 16, 2003
     vs. Indiana, August 2, 2003
Fewest blocked shots, game
  0 — Many times

TURNOVERS

Most turnovers per game, season
  17.9 — 2003 (608/34)
  16.9 — 2002 (541/32)
Fewest turnovers per game, season
  15.1 — 1999 (483/32)
  15.6 — 2001 (498/32)
Most turnovers, game
  27 — at Minnesota, July 1, 2002 (ot)
  26 — at Utah, July 7, 2000
     at Phoenix, July 26, 2001
     at Orlando, May 30, 2002
     at Miami, August 13, 2002
     at Indiana, July 6, 2003

Fewest turnovers, game
>8 — vs. Washington, July 10, 1999 (2 ot)
vs. Utah, August 7, 2001
>9 — at Cleveland, June 14, 1999
>>vs. Indiana, June 18, 2000
>>vs. Phoenix, June 29, 2001
>>vs. Utah, July 23, 2002

TEAM DEFENSE

POINTS

Fewest points allowed per game, season
>69.3 — 1998 (2078/30)
>70.4 — 2003 (2395/34)
Most points allowed per game, season
>75.8 — 2000 (2426/32)
>72.0 — 1999 (2303/32)
Fewest points allowed, game
>41 — at Sacramento, August 11, 1998
>48 — vs. Miami, July 20, 2002
Fewest points allowed, first half
>16 — at Sacramento, August 11, 1998
>18 — at Houston, July 6, 2002
Fewest points allowed, second half
>16 — vs. Connecticut, July 8, 2003
>20 — at New York, August 1, 2003
Fewest points allowed, overtime period
>2 — vs. Los Angeles, June 17, 2003
>4 — vs. Washington, July 10, 1999

FIELD GOAL PERCENTAGE

Lowest opponents' field-goal percentage, season
>.399 — 2003 (911/2286)
>.411 — 1998 (768/1869)
Highest opponents' field-goal percentage, season
>.462 — 2001 (848/1837)
>.460 — 2000 (905/1967)
Lowest opponents' field-goal percentage, game
>.246 — vs. Charlotte, June 29, 1998 (16/65)
>.257 — at San Antonio, June 7, 2003 (18/70)

TURNOVERS

Most opponents' turnovers per game, season
>17.0 — 2000 (543/32)
>16.6 — 1999 (532/32)
Fewest opponents' turnovers per game, season
>13.8 — 2002 (443/32)
>14.6 — 2003 (497/34)
Most opponents' turnovers, game
>28 — vs. Washington, July 10, 1999 (2 ot)
>>vs. Indiana, June 18, 2000
>25 — vs. Indiana, June 24, 2003

TEAM MISCELLANEOUS

GAME WON AND LOST

Highest winning percentage, season
>.735 — 2003 (25-9)
>.567 — 1998 (17-13)

Lowest winning percentage, season
>.281 — 2002 (9-23)
>.313 — 2001 (10-22)
Most consecutive games won
>8 — June 5-27, 2003
>6 — June 21-July 1, 1998
Most consecutive games won, one season
>8 — June 5-27, 2003
>6 — June 21-July 1, 1998
Most consecutive game lost
>13 — May 30-June 28, 2002
>5 — July 25-August 2, 1999
>>June 17-27, 2001
Most consecutive game lost, one season
>13 — May 30-June 28, 2002
>5 — July 25-August 2, 1999
>>June 17-27, 2001
Highest winning percentage, home games, season
>.765 — 2003 (13-4)
>.733 — 1998 (11-4)
Lowest winning percentage, home games, season
>.375 — 2001 (6-10)
>.438 — 1999, 2002 (7-9)
Most consecutive home games won
>6 — July 17-August 5, 1998
>5 — July 8-August 2, 2003
Most consecutive home games lost
>5 — June 2-28, 2002
>4 — July 6-28, 2001
Highest winning percentage, road games, season
>.706 — 2003 (12-5)
>.500 — 1999 (8-8)
Lowest winning percentage, road games, season
>.125 — 2002 (2-14)
>.250 — 2001 (4-12)
Most consecutive road games won
>4 — June 7-27, 2003
>3 — July 12-23, 1999
>>June 21-28, 2000
>>July 29-August 5, 2003
Most consecutive road games lost
>17 — July 24, 2001-July 18, 2002
>4 — July 19-August 6, 2000
>>June 22—July 8, 2001

OVERTIME GAMES

Most overtime games, season
>5 — 2001
>4 — 2003
Most consecutive overtime games, season
>2 — July 6-10, 1999
>>July 22-24, 2001
Most overtime games won, season
>4 — 2003
>3 — 2001
Most overtime games won, no losses, season
>4 — 2003

Most consecutive overtime games won
    4 — June 17-August 23, 2003 (current)
    2 — June 12-16, 2001
Most overtime games lost, season
    2 — 1999, 2001, 2002
    1 — 2000
Most overtime games lost, no wins, season
    2 — 1999, 2002
    1 — 2000
Most consecutive overtime games lost
    3 — July 6, 1999-July 21, 2000
        July 24, 2001-July 1, 2002 (current)
Most overtime periods, game
    2 — at Utah, July 6, 1999
        vs. Washington, July 10, 1999
        at Charlotte, June 16, 2001

INDIVIDUAL RECORDS

SEASONS

Most Seasons
    5 — Astou Ndiaye-Diatta
    4 — Dominique Canty
        Barbara Farris
        Wendy Palmer

GAMES

Most games, career
    138 — Astou Ndiaye-Diatta
    114 — Dominique Canty
    111 — Barbara Farris
Most consecutive games, career
    108 — Astou Ndiaye-Diatta, July 28, 1999
         August 13, 2002
     77 — Edwina Brown, June 3, 2000-
         June 28, 2002
     75 — Barbara Farris, July 28, 2001-
         August 25, 2003 (current)
Most games, season
    34 — Barbara Farris, 2003
        Kedra Holland—Corn, 2003
        Ruth Riley, 2003
        Ayana Walker, 2003

MINUTES

Most minutes, career
    3,065 — Astou Ndiaye-Diatta
    2,680 — Dominique Canty
    2,324 — Wendy Palmer
Highest average, minutes per game, career
(Minimum 75 games)
    28.7 — Wendy Palmer (2324/81)
    25.3 — Deanna Nolan (2303/91)
    23.5 — Dominique Canty (2680/114)
Most minutes, season
    1,097 — Swin Cash, 2003
    1,079 — Swin Cash, 2002
    1,002 — Sandy Brondello, 1999

Highest average, minutes per game, season
    33.8 — Korie Hlede, 1998 (912/27)
    33.7 — Swin Cash, 2002 (1079/32)
    33.2 — Swin Cash, 2003 (1097/33)
Most minutes, game
    46 — Sandy Brondello, at Utah,
        July 6, 1999 (2 ot)
    43 — Wendy Palmer, vs. Houston,
        July 21, 2000 (ot)
        Swin Cash, at Minnesota,
        July 1, 2002 (ot)
    42 — Claudia Maria das Neves,
        at Charlotte, June 16, 2001 (2 ot)
        Ruth Riley, at Connecticut,
        June 22, 2003 (ot)

SCORING

Most points, lifetime
    1,181 — Astou Ndiaye-Diatta
    1,022 — Swin Cash
    998 — Wendy Palmer
Highest average, points per game, career
(Minimum 75 games)
    12.3 — Wendy Palmer (998/81)
    9.5 — Deanna Nolan (865/91)
    8.8 — Elena Tornikidou (657/75)
Most points, season
    548 — Swin Cash, 2003
    474 — Swin Cash, 2002
    441 — Wendy Palmer, 2000
Highest average, points per game, season
    16.6 — Swin Cash, 2003 (548/33)
    14.8 — Swin Cash, 2002 (474/32)
    14.2 — Sandy Brondello, 1998 (426/30)
Most points, game
    33 — Sandy Brondello, at Utah,
        July 6, 1999 (2 ot)
    32 — Wendy Palmer, at Seattle,
        June 28, 2000
    27 — Wendy Palmer, at New York,
        August 15, 1999
        Jennifer Azzi, vs. Orlando,
        August 21, 1999
        Astou Ndiaye-Diatta, vs. Utah,
        August 7, 2001
        Deanna Nolan, at Indiana,
        July 16, 2003
Most games, 30 or more points, career
    1 — Sandy Brondello
        Wendy Palmer
Most games, 20 or more points, career
    14 — Swin Cash
    11 — Sandy Brondello
    9 — Wendy Palmer
Most consecutive games, 20 or more points
    2 — Many times

Most consecutive games, 10 or more points
24 — Sandy Brondello, July 31, 1998-
July 16, 1999
20 — Swin Cash, July 8-August 23, 2003
(current)
14 — Swin Cash, July 8-August 9,2002

FIELD GOAL PERCENTAGE

Highest field goal percentage, career
(Minimum 300 field goals)
.462 — Astou Ndiaye-Diatta (520/1125)
.440 — Wendy Palmer (370/841)
.433 — Swin Cash (339/783)
Highest field goal percentage, season (qualifiers)
.520 — Razija Mujanovic, 1998 (106/204)
.514 — Jennifer Azzi, 1999 (93/181)
.506 — Elena Tornikidou, 2000 (122/241)
Highest field goal percentage, game
(Minimum 8 field goals made)
.846 — Elena Tornikidou, at Charlotte,
June 25, 2000 (11/13)
.818 — Lynette Woodard, vs. New York,
August 19, 1998 (9/11)
Wendy Palmer, vs. Indiana,
June 18, 2000 (9/11)
Astou Ndiaye-Diatta, at Washington,
August 4, 2000 (9/11)
Most field goals, none missed, game
5 — Jennifer Azzi, at Minnesota,
June 12, 1999
Cheryl Ford, vs. Connecticut,
July 8, 2003
Elaine Powell, at Connecticut, August 5, 2003
4 — Val Whiting—Raymond,
at New York, August 15, 1999
Dominique Canty, at Sacramento,
July 1, 2000
Carla Boyd, at Phoenix,
July 26, 2001
3 — By many
Most field goal attempts, none made, game
10 — Dominique Canty, at Houston,
July 27, 1999
9 — Dominique Canty, at Charlotte,
August 20, 1999
Astou Ndiaye—Diatta, vs. Miami,
July 14, 2000
8 — by many

FIELD GOALS

Most field goals, career
520 — Astou Ndiaye-Diatta
370 — Wendy Palmer
339 — Swin Cash
Most field goals, season
195 — Swin Cash, 2003
167 — Wendy Palmer, 2000
158 — Astou Ndiaye-Diatta, 2000

Most field goals, game
14 — Wendy Palmer, at Seattle,
June 28, 2000
13 — Sandy Brondello, at Utah,
July 6, 1999 (2 ot)
11 — Elena Tornikidou, at Charlotte,
June 25, 2000
Astou Ndiaye-Diatta, vs. Houston,
June 2, 2001
Astou Ndiaye-Diatta, at Seattle,
July 24, 2001 (ot)
Astou Ndiaye-Diatta, vs. Utah,
August 7, 2001
Swin Cash, at Cleveland, July 29, 2003

FIELD GOAL ATTEMPTS

Most field goal attempts, career
1,125 — Astou Ndiaye-Diatta
841 — Wendy Palmer
783 — Swin Cash
Most field goal attempts, season
430 — Swin Cash, 2003
374 — Wendy Palmer, 2000
367 — Sandy Brondello, 1998
Most field goal attempts, game
28 — Sandy Brondello, at Utah,
July 6, 1999 (2 ot)
23 — Astou Ndiaye-Diatta, vs. Utah,
August 7, 2001
22 — Dominique Canty, vs. Washington,
July 10, 1999 (2 ot)

THREE-POINT FIELD-GOAL PERCENTAGE

Highest three-point field goal percentage, career
(Minimum 75 three—point field goals)
.369 — Deanna Nolan (111/301)
Highest three-point field goal percentage,
season (qualifiers)
.517 — Jennifer Azzi, 1999 (30/58)
.487 — Sandy Brondello, 1999 (37/76)
.449 — Elena Tornikidou, 2001 (22/49)
Most three-point field goals, none missed, game
4 — Jennifer Azzi, vs. Orlando,
August 21, 1999
3 — Many times
Most three-point field goal attempts, none made,
game
6 — Tamicha Jackson, vs. Charlotte,
June 12, 2000
Kedra Holland-Corn,
at Sacramento, August 15, 2003
5 — Korie Hlede, vs. Houston,
August 7, 1998
Claudia Maria das Neves,
at Minnesota, June 12, 1999
Claudia Maria das Neves,

at Washington, August 4, 2000
Swin Cash, at Cleveland, June 6, 2002
4 — Many times

THREE-POINT FIELD GOALS

Most three-point field goals, career
111 — Deanna Nolan
61 — Claudia Neves
53 — Sandy Brondello
Most three-point field goals, season
50 — Kedra Holland-Corn, 2003
48 — Deanna Nolan, 2003
42 — Deanna Nolan, 2002
Most three-point field goals, game
7 — Deanna Nolan, vs. New York,
August 10, 2003 (ot)
6 — Sandy Brondello, at Utah,
July 6, 1999 (2 ot)
5 — Claudia Maria das Neves,
at Orlando, July 19, 2000
Jae Kingi, vs. Phoenix, June 29, 2001
Deanna Nolan, at Indiana, June 1, 2002
Kedra Holland—Corn,
at Washington, August 6, 2003
Most consecutive games, three-point field goals made
10 — Deanna Nolan, May 31-
June 28, 2003
7 — Korie Hlede, June 15-27, 1998
Jae Kingi, July 21-August 1, 2001
Deanna Nolan, May 30-June 11, 2002

THREE-POINT FIELD GOAL ATTEMPTS

Most three-point field goal attempts, career
301 — Deanna Nolan
204 — Claudia Neves
157 — Wendy Palmer
Most three-point field goal attempts, season
124 — Kedra Holland-Corn, 2003
114 — Deanna Nolan, 2002
Deanna Nolan, 2003
92 — Claudia Maria das Neves, 2000
Most three-point field goal attempts, game
10 — Anna DeForge, vs. Cleveland,
July 31, 2000
Deanna Nolan, at Indiana,
June 1, 2002
Deanna Nolan, vs. New York,
August 10, 2003 (ot)
9 — By many

FREE THROW PERCENTAGE

Highest free—throw percentage, career
(Minimum 150 free throws)
.886 — Sandy Brondello (179/202)
.882 — Elena Tornikidou (150/170)
.723 — Swin Cash (319/441)
Highest free-throw percentage, season (qualifiers)

.923 — Sandy Brondello, 1998 (96/104)
.914 — Elena Tornikidou, 2000 (85/93)
.887 — Elena Tornikidou, 2001 (63/71)
Most free throws made, none missed, game
11 — Wendy Palmer, at New York,
August 15, 1999
10 — Wendy Palmer, at Orlando,
August 18, 1999
Wendy Palmer, vs. Charlotte, July 29, 2000
9 — By many
Most free throw attempts, none made, game
6 — Swin Cash, at San Antonio,
June 7, 2003
4 — Lenae Williams, vs. Indiana,
August 9, 2002
3 — Cindy Brown, at New York,
July 6, 1998
Rhonda Blades, vs. Washington,
July 22, 1998
Dominique Canty, at Sacramento,
August 6, 1999
Rachael Sporn, at New York,
July 2, 2001

FREE THROWS MADE

Most free throws made, career
319 — Swin Cash
296 — Dominique Canty
212 — Wendy Palmer
Most free throws made, season
173 — Swin Cash, 2002
146 — Swin Cash, 2003
97 — Ruth Riley, 2003
Most free throws made, game
15 — Swin Cash, vs. Miami, June 28, 2002 (ot)
13 — Swin Cash, at Utah, July 8, 2002
11 — Wendy Palmer, at New York,
August 15, 1999
Swin Cash, vs. Orlando, June 21, 2002

FREE THROW ATTEMPTS

Most free throw attempts, career
441 — Swin Cash
417 — Dominique Canty
302 — Wendy Palmer
Most free throw attempts, season
227 — Swin Cash, 2002
214 — Swin Cash, 2003
136 — Dominique Canty, 1999
Most free throw attempts, game
21 — Swin Cash, vs. Miami, June 28, 2002 (ot)
15 — Swin Cash, at Utah, July 8, 2002
Swin Cash, at Cleveland, August 3, 2002
14 — Dominique Canty, at Cleveland,
June 16, 2000

REBOUNDS

Most rebounds, career
- 633 — Astou Ndiaye-Diatta
- 574 — Wendy Palmer
- 415 — Swin Cash

Highest average, rebounds per game, career (Minimum 75 games)
- 7.1 — Wendy Palmer (574/81)
- 4.6 — Astou Ndiaye-Diatta (633/138)
- 2.9 — Edwina Brown (271/92)

Most rebounds, season
- 334 — Cheryl Ford, 2003
- 301 — Cindy Brown, 1998
- 222 — Swin Cash, 2002

Highest average, rebounds per game, season (qualifiers)
- 10.4 — Cheryl Ford, 2003 (334/32)
- 10.0 — Cindy Brown, 1998 (301/30)
- 7.0 — Wendy Palmer, 2001 (154/22)

Most rebounds, game
- 21 — Cindy Brown, at Utah, August 10, 1998
  Cheryl Ford, at Connecticut, June 22, 2003 (ot)
- 16 — Cindy Brown, vs. Charlotte, June 29, 1998
  Val Whiting—Raymond, at Minnesota, June 12, 1999
- 15 — By many

Most games, 10+ rebounds, career
- 21 — Cindy Brown
- 20 — Cheryl Ford
- 17 — Wendy Palmer

Most consecutive games, 10+ rebounds
- 6 — Cindy Brown, July 31—August 11, 1998
- 5 — Wendy Palmer, August 9—18, 1999
  Cheryl Ford, July 10—22, 2003

OFFENSIVE REBOUNDS

Most offensive rebounds, career
- 199 — Astou Ndiaye-Diatta
- 159 — Wendy Palmer
- 142 — Swin Cash

Highest average, offensive rebounds per game, career (Minimum 75 games)
- 2.0 — Wendy Palmer (159/81)
- 1.4 — Astou Ndiaye-Diatta (199/138)
- 1.2 — Dominique Canty (135/114)

Most offensive rebounds, season
- 99 — Cheryl Ford, 2003
- 77 — Swin Cash, 2002
- 70 — Cindy Brown, 1998

Most offensive rebounds, game
- 7 — Rachael Sporn, vs. Washington, July 10, 1999 (2 ot)
  Wendy Palmer, vs. Los Angeles, August 2, 2000
  Cheryl Ford, vs. San Antonio, July 1, 2003

- 6 — Many times

DEFENSIVE REBOUNDS

Most defensive rebounds, career
- 434 — Astou Ndiaye-Diatta
- 415 — Wendy Palmer
- 309 — Cindy Brown

Highest average, defensive rebounds per game, career (Minimum 75 games)
- 5.1 — Wendy Palmer (415/81)
- 3.1 — Astou Ndiaye-Diatta (434/138)
- 2.2 — Deanna Nolan (202/91)

Most defensive rebounds, season
- 235 — Cheryl Ford, 2003
- 231 — Cindy Brown, 1998
- 152 — Wendy Palmer, 2000

Most defensive rebounds, game
- 18 — Cindy Brown, at Utah, August 10, 1998
- 17 — Cheryl Ford, at Connecticut, June 22, 2003 (ot)
- 14 — Cheryl Ford, vs. Los Angeles, June 17, 2003 (ot)

ASSISTS

Most assists, career
- 273 — Dominique Canty
- 217 — Edwina Brown
- 205 — Swin Cash

Highest average, assists per game, career (Minimum 75 games)
- 2.39 — Dominique Canty (273/114)
- 2.36 — Edwina Brown (217/92)
- 1.9 — Elena Tornikidou (146/75)

Most assists, season
- 129 — Elaine Powell, 2003
- 119 — Swin Cash, 2003
- 106 — Jennifer Azzi, 1999

Highest average, assists per game, season (qualifiers)
- 3.9 — Elaine Powell, 2003 (129/33)
- 3.8 — Jennifer Azzi, 1999 (106/28)
- 3.6 — Swin Cash, 2003 (119/33)

Most assists, game
- 9 — Carla Boyd, vs. Sacramento, July 31, 1998
- 8 — By many

Most games, 10+ assists, career
None

PERSONAL FOULS

Most personal fouls, career
- 288 — Astou Ndiaye-Diatta
- 264 — Wendy Palmer
- 249 — Dominque Canty

Most personal fouls, season
- 128 — Ruth Riley, 2003
- 112 — Wendy Palmer, 2000
- 109 — Cheryl Ford, 2003

Most personal fouls, game
    6 — Many times

DISQUALIFICATIONS

Most disqualifications, career
    4 — Sandy Brondello
        Wendy Palmer
    3 — Jennifer Azzi
        Carla Boyd
    2 — Olympia Scott-Richardson
        Ruth Riley
Highest percentage, games disqualified, career
(Minimum 75 games)
    4.9 — Wendy Palmer (4/81)
    3.6 — Carla Boyd (3/83)
    1.1 — Deanna Nolan (1/91)
Lowest percentage, games disqualified, career
(Minimum 75 games)
    0.0 — Claudia Neves (0/82)
        Elena Tornikidou (0/75)
    0.7 — Astou Ndiaye—Diatta (1/138)
Most consecutive games without disqualification,
career
    109 — Dominique Canty, July 4, 1999
          August 13, 2002
    84 — Barbara Farris, July 6, 2001-
         August 25, 2003 (current)
    82 — Claudia Neves, June 12, 1999-
         August 14, 2001
Most disqualifications, season
    4 — Sandy Brondello, 1999
    3 — Jennifer Azzi, 1999
    2 — By many
Fewest minutes, disqualified, game
    15 — Olympia Scott—Richardson,
        at Los Angeles, July 2, 2000
    17 — Wendy Palmer, vs. Cleveland,
        July 31, 1999
        Barbara Farris, at New York,
        July 2, 2001
    18 — Olympia Scott—Richardson,
        vs. Washington, June 24, 2000

STEALS

Most steals, career
    127 — Dominique Canty
    85 — Deanna Nolan
    82 — Edwina Brown
Highest average, steals per game, career
(Minimum 75 games)
    1.11 — Dominique Canty (127/114)
    0.93 — Deanna Nolan (85/91)
    0.89 — Edwina Brown (82/92)
Most steals, season
    51 — Cindy Brown, 1998

    49 — Dominique Canty, 2000
    45 — Elaine Powell, 2003
Highest average, steals per game, season
(qualifiers)
    1.75 — Dominique Canty, 2000 (49/28)
    1.70 — Cindy Brown, 1998 (51/30)
    1.36 — Elaine Powell, 2003 (45/33)
Most steals, game
    6 — Claudia Maria das Neves, vs.
Washington, June 24, 2000
    5 — by many

BLOCKED SHOTS

Most blocked shots, career
    81 — Astou Ndiaye-Diatta
    58 — Ruth Riley
    54 — Swin Cash
Highest average, blocked shots per game, career
(Minimum: 75 games)
    0.59 — Astou Ndiaye—Diatta (81/138)
    0.37 — Elena Tornikidou (28/75)
    0.35 — Deanna Nolan (32/91)
Most blocked shots, season
    58 — Ruth Riley, 2003
    34 — Ayana Walker, 2002
    31 — Val Whiting—Raymond, 1999
        Swin Cash, 2002
        Cheryl Ford, 2003
Highest average, blocked shots per game,
season (qualifiers)
    1.71 — Ruth Riley, 2003 (58/43)
    1.06 — Ayana Walker, 2002 (34/32)
    1.00 — Val Whiting—Raymond, 1999 (31/31)
Most blocked shots, game
    5 — Ayana Walker, vs. Connecticut,
        July 8, 2003
    4 — Many times

TURNOVERS

Most turnovers, career
    236 — Astou Ndiaye-Diatta
    208 — Swin Cash
    207 — Dominique Canty
Most turnovers, season
    108 — Swin Cash, 2003
    100 — Swin Cash, 2002
    88 — Korie Hlede, 1998
Most turnovers, game
    8 — Swin Cash, vs. Indiana, June 24, 2003
Cheryl Ford, at Indiana, July 6, 2003
    7 — Korie Hlede, at Charlotte, June 18, 1998
        Elena Tornikidou, vs. Sacramento,
        June 3, 2000
        Swin Cash, at Houston, July 6, 2002
        Cheryl Ford, at Charlotte, July 10, 2003

HOUSTON COMETS

TEAM OFFENSE

SCORING

Highest average, points per game, season
  77.3 — 2000 (2475/32)
  76.2 — 1998 (2285/30)
Lowest average, points per game, season
  64.0 — 2001 (2047/32)
  64.8 — 2002 (2072/32)
Most points, game
  110 — at Washington, August 17, 1998
  107 — vs. Utah, June 12, 2000
Fewest points, game
  38 — at Phoenix, August 14, 2001
  48 — at Phoenix, July 19, 1999
Largest margin of victory, game
  45 — at Washington, August 17, 1998
       (110-65)
  40 — vs. Portland, June 30, 2000 (79-39)
Largest margin of defeat, game
  25 — at Los Angeles, July 16, 1997 (52-77)
  18 — vs. Phoenix, June 3, 2000 (62-80)
       at Phoenix, August 14, 2001 (38-56)

BY HALF

Most points, first half
  54 — vs. Indiana, July 6, 2001
  53 — vs. Sacramento, July 12, 1997
       vs. Utah, June 17, 1999
Fewest points, first half
  16 — at Miami, June 18, 2002
  17 — at Miami, July 20, 2001
       at Phoenix, August 14, 2001
Largest lead at halftime
  31 — vs. Miami, June 15, 2000 (44-13)
  28 — vs. Indiana, July 6, 2001 (54-26)
Largest deficit at halftime overcome to win game
  14 — vs. Seattle, July 9, 2002
       (trailed 27-41; won 67-59)
  13 — at Detroit, August 7, 1998
       (trailed 20-33; won 61-57)
Most points, second half
  60 — at Washington, August 17, 1998
  55 — vs. Utah, June 12, 2000
Fewest points, second half
  20 — at Utah, June 30, 1998
       at Phoenix, July 19, 1999
       at Connecticut, June 7, 2003
  21 — at Sacramento, June 28, 2001
       at Phoenix, August 14, 2001

OVERTIME

Most points, overtime period
  14 — at Utah, July 16, 1999
  12 — at Utah, June 30, 1998 (2nd ot)
       at Portland, May 31, 2000 (2nd ot)
Fewest points, overtime period
  3 — vs. Cleveland, August 1, 1998
      at Minnesota, June 1, 2003
  4 — vs. New York, June 26, 1997
Largest margin of victory, overtime period
  5 — vs. Los Angeles, June 30, 1997 (71-66)
  4 — at Utah, July 16, 1999 (88-84)
      at Portland, May 31, 2000 (93-89) (2 ot)
      at Cleveland, June 1, 2002 (69-65)

FIELD GOAL PERCENTAGE

Highest field-goal percentage, season
  .470 — 2000 (891/1894)
  .440 — 1999 (841/1912)
Lowest field-goal percentage, season
  .392 — 2001 (747/1908)
  .422 — 1997 (700/1660)
Highest field-goal percentage, game
  .609 — at Phoenix, August 7, 2000 (28/46)
  .593 — at Washington, June 7, 2000 (32/54)
Lowest field-goal percentage, game
  .236 — at Phoenix, August 14, 2001 (13/55)
  .254 — at Charlotte, August 4, 2001 (15/59)

FIELD GOALS

Most field goals per game, season
  27.8 — 2000 (891/32)
  26.5 — 1998 (795/30)
Fewest field goals per game, season
  23.3 — 2001 (747/32)
  23.6 — 2002 (755/32)
Most field goals, game
  41 — at Washington, August 17, 1998
  36 — vs. Washington, July 13, 1998
       vs. Portland, July 30, 2002
Fewest field goals, game
  13 — at Phoenix, August 14, 2001
  15 — at Charlotte, August 4, 2001

FIELD GOAL ATTEMPTS

Most field-goal attempts per game, season
  60.8 — 1998 (1824/30)
  59.8 — 1999 (1912/32)
Fewest field-goal attempts per game, season
  55.6 — 2002 (1778/32)
  56.4 — 2003 (1916/34)

Most field-goal attempts, game
82 — at Portland, May 31, 2000 (2 ot)
79 — vs. Washington, June 12, 1999
Fewest field-goal attempts, game
45 — at Minnesota, July 25, 1999
46 — at Phoenix, July 9, 1999
at Phoenix, August 7, 2000

THREE-POINT FIELD-GOAL PERCENTAGE

Highest three-point field-goal percentage, season
.350 — 2000 (172/491)
.348 — 1997 (169/485)
Lowest three-point field-goal percentage, season
.317 — 2001 (138/435)
.322 — 1999 (176/547)

THREE-POINT FIELD GOALS

Most three-point field goals per game, season
6.0 — 1997 (169/28)
5.9 — 1998 (177/30)
Fewest three-point field goals per game, season
3.38 — 2003 (115/34)
3.41 — 2002 (109/32)
Most three-point field goals, game
12 — at Phoenix, July 22, 1997
at Sacramento, July 25, 1997
11 — at Cleveland, July 6, 1998
at Charlotte, July 25, 1998
vs. Los Angeles, August 12, 1999
Fewest three-point field goals, game
0 — at Phoenix, July 21, 1998
vs. Los Angeles, July 29, 2000
at Los Angeles, August 8, 2002
1 — Many times

THREE-POINT FIELD GOAL ATTEMPTS

Most three-point field goal attempts per game, season
17.4 — 1998 (523/30)
17.3 — 1997 (485/28)
Fewest three-point field goal attempts per game, season
10.1 — 2003 (344/34)
10.4 — 2002 (332/32)
Most three-point field goal attempts, game
30 — at Utah, June 30, 1998 (2 ot)
28 — at Sacramento, July 8, 1999
Fewest three-point field goal attempts, game
4 — vs. Phoenix, June 3, 2003
5 — at Charlotte, June 3, 2002
at Seattle, July 15, 2003

FREE THROW PERCENTAGE

Highest free-throw percentage, season
.822 — 2000 (521/634)
.818 — 1999 (509/622)

Lowest free-throw percentage, season
.745 — 1997 (441/592)
.770 — 2001 (415/539)
Highest free-throw percentage, game
1.000 — vs. Phoenix, July 31, 1999 (11/11)
at Minnesota, July 9, 2000 (15/15)
at Portland, August 4, 2000 (11/11)
at Phoenix, June 10, 2001 (12/12)
.955 — at Phoenix, July 22, 1997 (21/22)
Lowest free-throw percentage, game
.455 — at Washington, June 13, 2002 (5/11)
.500 — vs. Charlotte, August 6, 1999 (5/10)
at Miami, July 20, 2001 (10/20)

FREE THROWS MADE

Most free throws made per game, season
17.3 — 1998 (518/30)
16.3 — 2000 (521/32)
Fewest free throws made per game, season
13.0 — 2001 (415/32)
13.9 — 2003 (473/34)
Most free throws made, game
33 — vs. Sacramento, July 3, 1998
31 — vs. Utah, June 12, 2000
Fewest free throws made, game
5 — vs. Washington, July 13, 1998
vs. Charlotte, August 6, 1999
at Washington, June 13, 2002
at Charlotte, June 6, 2003
6 — Many times

FREE THROW ATTEMPTS

Most free throw attempts per game, season
21.5 — 1998 (646/30)
21.1 — 1997 (592/28)
Fewest free throw attempts per game, season
16.8 — 2001 (539/32)
17.7 — 2003 (600/34)
Most free throw attempts, game
39 — vs. Utah, June 12, 2000
37 — at Los Angeles, June 20, 2000
Fewest free throw attempts, game
7 — vs. Washington, July 13, 1998
8 — at Phoenix, July 11, 2002
at Charlotte, June 6, 2003

REBOUNDS

Most rebounds per game, season
33.1 — 2001 (1058/32)
31.3 — 2002 (1001/32)
Fewest rebounds per game, season
30.3 — 2003 (1030/34)
30.7 — 1997 (859/28)
Most rebounds, game
51 — at Utah, June 30, 1998 (2 ot)
vs. Orlando, August 3, 2001
47 — at Sacramento, July 10, 2001 (ot)
at Minnesota, July 23, 2001

Fewest rebounds, game
19 — vs. Indiana, July 8, 2003
21 — at Utah, August 2, 1997
at Charlotte, August 16, 1997
at New York, August 8, 1999
at New York, July 28, 2002

OFFENSIVE REBOUNDS

Most offensive rebounds per game, season
11.3 — 1997 (316/28)
10.9 — 2001 (348/32)
Fewest offensive rebounds per game, season
7.8 — 2003 (266/34)
8.5 — 2000 (273/32)
Most offensive rebounds, game
22 — vs. Orlando, August 3, 2001
19 — at Minnesota, July 23, 2001
Fewest offensive rebounds, game
1 — at New York, August 8, 1999
at Phoenix, August 7, 2000
2 — vs. Indiana, July 8, 2003

DEFENSIVE REBOUNDS

Most defensive rebounds per game, season
22.6 — 2000 (724/32)
22.5 — 2003 (764/34)
Fewest defensive rebounds per game, season
19.4 — 1997 (543/28)
21.0 — 1998 (630/30)
Most defensive rebounds, game
33 — at Utah, June 30, 1998 (2 ot)
32 — at Sacramento, July 10, 2001 (2 ot)
Regulation game:
31 — vs. Detroit, July 27, 1999
Fewest defensive rebounds, game
11 — at Charlotte, August 16, 1997
13 — vs. Los Angeles, August 9, 1997

ASSISTS

Most assists per game, season
15.6 — 1999 (499/32)
15.4 — 2000 (494/32)
Fewest assists per game, season
13.3 — 2001 (426/32)
13.7 — 2003 (465/34)
Most assists, game
26 — at Washington, August 17, 1998
24 — vs. Charlotte, August 6, 1999
Fewest assists, game
4 — at Phoenix, June 24, 1998
5 — at New York, August 15, 1998
vs. Seattle, August 19, 2003

PERSONAL FOULS

Most personal fouls per game, season
19.1 — 1997 (535/28)
18.3 — 1999 (586/32)
Fewest personal fouls per game, season
14.4 — 2003 (490/34)

14.6 — 2002 (467/32)
Most personal fouls, game
32 — at Los Angeles, June 20, 2000
27 — Many times
Fewest personal fouls, game
7 — vs. Minnesota, June 15, 2002
vs. Seattle, May 22, 2003
8 — vs. Sacramento, July 12, 2000
at Orlando, July 18, 2001
vs. San Antonio, June 28, 2003

DISQUALIFICATIONS

Most disqualifications per game, season
0.13 — 1999 (4/32)
0.10 — 1998 (3/30)
Fewest disqualifications per game, season
0.03 — 2002 (1/32)
0.04 — 1997 (1/28)
Most disqualifications, game
1 — Many times

STEALS

Most steals per game, season
11.11 — 1997 (311/28)
11.07 — 1998 (332/30)
Fewest steals per game, season
6.8 — 2003 (231/34)
7.8 — 2001 (251/32)
Most steals, game
21 — vs. Washington, June 29, 1998
19 — vs. Minnesota, August 9, 2000
Fewest steals, game
1 — vs. Orlando, August 3, 2002
2 — vs. Orlando, August 3, 2001

BLOCKED SHOTS

Most blocked shots per game, season
4.3 — 1999 (139/32)
3.9 — 2002 (126/32)
Fewest blocked shots per game, season
2.4 — 1997 (67/28)
2.7 — 1998 (81/30)
Most blocked shots, game
11 — at Utah, July 3, 2002
10 — at Utah, June 5, 2001
at San Antonio, June 20, 2003
Fewest blocked shots, game
0 — Many times. Last:
at Seattle, July 15, 2003

TURNOVERS

Most turnovers per game, season
17.6 — 1997 (492/28)
14.5 — 1998 (435/30)
Fewest turnovers per game, season
13.2 — 2003 (450/34)
13.6 — 2001 (436/32)
Most turnovers, game
28 — vs. New York, June 26, 1997 (ot)

26 — vs. New York, June 13, 1998
Fewest turnovers, game
    5 — vs. Washington, June 27, 2001
    6 — at Los Angeles, August 11, 2001
        vs. Minnesota, July 1, 2003

TEAM DEFENSE
POINTS

Fewest points allowed per game, season
    59.1 — 2002 (1892/32)
    62.3 — 2001 (1994/32)
Most points allowed per game, season
    65.5 — 1997 (1833/28)
    64.7 — 1999 (2070/32)
Fewest points allowed, game
    39 — vs. Portland, June 30, 2000
    40 — vs. Detroit, July 6, 2002
Fewest points allowed, first half
    8 — vs. Detroit, July 6, 2002
    11 — at Minnesota, June 30, 2001
Fewest points allowed, second half
    17 — at Utah, June 30, 1998
        vs. Portland, June 30, 2000
    18 — vs. Seattle, July 9, 2002
        vs. Sacramento, August 5, 2003
Fewest points allowed, overtime period
    4 — vs. Los Angeles, June 30, 1997
        at Cleveland, June 1, 2002
    6 — many times

FIELD GOAL PERCENTAGE

Lowest opponents' field-goal percentage, season
    .375 — 2002 (705/1880)
    .390 — 1999 (763/1954)
Highest opponents' field-goal percentage, season
    .417 — 1997 (679/1630)
    .406 — 2003 (2030/824)
Lowest opponents' field goal percentage, game
    .200 — at Minnesota, July 23, 2001 (11/55)
    .217 — at Indiana, June 5, 2002 (13/60)

TURNOVERS

Most opponents' turnovers per game, season
    19.2 — 1997 (537/28)
    18.7 — 1998 (560/30)
Fewest opponents' turnovers per game, season
    12.7 — 2003 (430/34)
    13.5 — 2001 (433/32)
Most opponents' turnovers, game
    33 — vs. Washington, June 29, 1998
    28 — vs. New York, June 26, 1997 (ot)

TEAM MISCELLANEOUS
GAME WON AND LOST

Highest winning percentage, season
    .900 — 1998 (27-3)
    .844 — 2000 (27-5)

Lowest winning percentage, season
    .588 — 2003 (20-14)
    .594 — 2001 (19-13)
Most consecutive games won
    15 — June 27-July 30, 1998
    10 — June 23-July 12, 2000
        June 15-July 9, 2002
Most consecutive games won, one season
    15 — June 27-July 30, 1998
    10 — June 23-July 12, 2000
        June 15-July 9, 2002
Most consecutive game lost
    3 — August 21-25, 2003 (current)
    2 — Many times
Most consecutive game lost, one season
    3 — August 21-25, 2003
    2 — Many times
Highest winning percentage, home games, season
    .938 — 1999 (15-1)
    .933 — 1998 (14-1)
Lowest winning percentage, home games, season
    .643 — 1997 (9-5)
    .688 — 2001 (11-5)
Most consecutive home games won
    13 — July 1, 1999-May 29, 2000
May 29-August 6, 2002
    11 — June 6-July 25, 2000
Most consecutive home games lost
    3 — July 8-28, 2001
    2 — August 21-24, 1997
Highest winning percentage, road games, season
    .867 — 1998 (13-2)
    .813 — 2000 (13-3)
Lowest winning percentage, road games, season
    .353 — 2003 (6-11)
    .500 — 2001 (8-8)
Most consecutive road games won
    9 — June 30-August 7, 1998
    7 — August 4, 2000-June 10, 2001
Most consecutive road games lost
    4 — August 4-14, 2001
        June 1-14, 2003
        August 18-25, 2003 (current)
    3 — July 2-16, 1997

OVERTIME GAMES

Most overtime games, season
    2 — 1997, 1998, 2000
Most consecutive overtime games, season
    1 — Many times
Most overtime games won, season
    2 — 2000
Most overtime games won, no losses, season
    2 — 2000
Most consecutive overtime games won
    3 — July 16, 1999-July 21, 2000
    2 — June 30, 1997-June 30, 1998

RECORDS Houston Comets

Most overtime games lost, season
   1 — 1997, 1998, 2001, 2003
Most overtime games lost, no wins, season
   1 — 2001, 2003
Most consecutive overtime games lost
   1 — Many times
Most overtime periods, game
   2 — at Utah, June 30, 1998
       at Portland, May 31, 2000
       at Sacramento, July 10, 2001

INDIVIDUAL RECORDS

SEASONS

Most Seasons
   7 — Janeth Arcain
       Tina Thompson
   6 — Tammy Jackson
       Sheryl Swoopes
   5 — Cynthia Cooper

GAMES

Most games, career
   220 — Janeth Arcain
   206 — Tina Thompson
   164 — Sheryl Swoopes
Most consecutive games, career
   220 — Janeth Arcain, June 21, 1997-
         August 25, 2003 (current)
   88 — Cynthia Cooper, June 21, 1997
         August 18, 1999
   87 — Tina Thompson, August 10, 1998
         July 18, 2001
Most games, season
   34 — Janeth Arcain, 2003
       Ukari Figgs, 2003
       Michelle Snow, 2003

MINUTES

Most minutes, career
   7,048 — Tina Thompson
   6,559 — Janeth Arcain
   5,494 — Sheryl Swoopes
Highest average, minutes per game, career
(Minimum 90 games)
   35.2 — Cynthia Cooper (4363/124)
   34.2 — Tina Thompson (7048/206)
   33.5 — Sheryl Swoopes (5494/164)
Most minutes, season
   1,154 — Janeth Arcain, 2001
Sheryl Swoopes, 2002
   1,136 — Janeth Arcain, 2003
   1,116 — Janeth Arcain, 2002
Highest average, minutes per game, season
   36.7 — Tina Thompson, 2001 (1102/30)
   36.3 — Tina Thompson, 2002 (1052/29)
   36.1 — Janeth Arcain, 2001 (1154/32)
         Sheryl Swoopes, 2002 (1154/32)

Most minutes, game
   50 — Tina Thompson, at Utah,
         June 30, 1998 (2 ot)
   48 — Cynthia Cooper, at Portland,
         May 31, 2000 (2 ot)
         Sheryl Swoopes, at Portland,
         May 31, 2000 (2 ot)

SCORING

Most points, lifetime
   3,179 — Tina Thompson
   2,821 — Sheryl Swoopes
   2,601 — Cynthia Cooper
Highest average, points per game, career
(Minimum 90 games)
   21.0 — Cynthia Cooper (2601/124)
   17.2 — Sheryl Swoopes (2821/164)
   15.4 — Tina Thompson (3179/206)
Most points, season
   686 — Cynthia Cooper, 1999
   680 — Cynthia Cooper, 1998
   643 — Sheryl Swoopes, 2000
Highest average, points per game, season
   22.7 — Cynthia Cooper, 1998 (680/30)
   22.2 — Cynthia Cooper, 1997 (621/28)
   22.1 — Cynthia Cooper, 1999 (686/31)
Most points, game
   44 — Cynthia Cooper, at Sacramento,
         July 25, 1997
   42 — Cynthia Cooper, vs. Utah,
         August 16, 1999
   39 — Cynthia Cooper, at Charlotte,
         August 11, 1997
Most games, 30 or more points, career
   16 — Cynthia Cooper
   5 — Sheryl Swoopes
   2 — Tina Thompson
Most games, 20 or more points, career
   72 — Cynthia Cooper
   61 — Sheryl Swoopes
   42 — Tina Thompson
Most consecutive games, 20 or more points
   11 — Cynthia Cooper, August 17, 1998
         June 30, 1999
   8 — Sheryl Swoopes, May 29-
         June 12, 2000
   6 — By many
Most consecutive games, 10 or more points
   92 — Cynthia Cooper, June 21, 1997-
         June 1, 2000
   44 — Tina Thompson, July 6, 2000-
         August 13, 2001
   39 — Tina Thompson, June 21, 2002
         August 7, 2003

FIELD GOAL PERCENTAGE

Highest field goal percentage, career
(Minimum 350 field goals)
   .459 — Cynthia Cooper (802/1749)

.449 — Sheryl Swoopes (1065/2374)
.440 — Janeth Arcain (869/1977)
Highest field goal percentage, season (qualifiers)
.506 — Sheryl Swoopes, 2000 (245/484)
.498 — Michelle Snow, 2003 (126/253)
.470 — Cynthia Cooper, 1997 (191/406)
Highest field goal percentage, game
(Minimum 8 field goals made)
.917 — Sheryl Swoopes, at Portland,
August 4, 2000 (11/12)
.800 — Michelle Snow, at Detroit,
August 8, 2003 (8/10)
.789 — Cynthia Cooper, at Charlotte,
August 11, 1997 (15/19)
Most field goals, none missed, game
4 — By many. Most recent:
Ukari Figgs, at Phoenix,
June 14, 2003
Most field goal attempts, none made, game
12 — Tina Thompson, at Phoenix,
July 19, 1999
10 — Sheryl Swoopes, at Los Angeles,
June 21, 1998
8 — Tina Thompson, at Los Angeles,
July 18, 1999

FIELD GOALS

Most field goals, career
1,138 — Tina Thompson
1,065 — Sheryl Swoopes
869 — Janeth Arcain
Most field goals, season
245 — Sheryl Swoopes, 2000
226 — Sheryl Swoopes, 1999
221 — Sheryl Swoopes, 2002
Most field goals, game
15 — Cynthia Cooper, at Charlotte,
August 11, 1997
14 — Cynthia Cooper, at Sacramento,
July 25, 1997
13 — Cynthia Cooper, at Detroit,
August 7, 1998
Sheryl Swoopes, at Utah,
July 16, 1999 (ot)
Sheryl Swoopes, vs. Charlotte,
July 7, 2000
Tina Thompson, at Detroit,
June 2, 2001

FIELD GOAL ATTEMPTS

Most field goal attempts, career
2,715 — Tina Thompson
2,374 — Sheryl Swoopes
1,977 — Janeth Arcain
Most field goal attempts, season
528 — Tina Thompson, 2001
509 — Janeth Arcain, 2001
Sheryl Swoopes, 2002

489 — Sheryl Swoopes, 1999
Most field goal attempts, game
29 — Sheryl Swoopes, at Los Angeles,
August 20, 1999
28 — Cynthia Cooper, at Utah,
June 30, 1998 (2 ot)
27 — Sheryl Swoopes, at Portland,
May 31, 2000 (2 ot)
Tina Thompson, vs. Portland,
July 2, 2001

THREE-POINT FIELD-GOAL PERCENTAGE

Highest three-point field goal percentage, career
(Minimum 90 three-point field goals)
.377 — Cynthia Cooper (239/634)
.356 — Tina Thompson (291/818)
.332 — Sheryl Swoopes (154/464)
Highest three-point field goal percentage,
season (qualifiers)
.417 — Tina Thompson, 2000 (55/132)
.414 — Cynthia Cooper, 1997 (67/162)
.400 — Cynthia Cooper, 1998 (64/160)
Most three-point field goals, none missed, game
5 — Tina Thompson, at Phoenix,
August 7, 2000
4 — Sheryl Swoopes, vs. Phoenix,
June 21, 2002
3 — By many
Most three-point field goal attempts,
none made, game
8 — Tina Thompson, at Utah,
June 30, 1998 (2 ot)
7 — Cynthia Cooper, vs. Sacramento,
August 24, 1997
Kim Perrot, at Charlotte,
June 15, 1998
Cynthia Cooper, vs. Cleveland,
July 1, 1999
THREE-POINT FIELD GOALS
Most three-point field goals, career
291 — Tina Thompson
239 — Cynthia Cooper
154 — Sheryl Swoopes
Most three-point field goals, season
67 — Cynthia Cooper, 1997
64 — Cynthia Cooper, 1998
58 — Cynthia Cooper, 1999
Most three-point field goals, game
7 — Cynthia Cooper, at Sacramento,
July 25, 1997
6 — by many
Most consecutive games, three-point field goals
made
21 — Cynthia Cooper, July 25, 1998-
June 30, 1999
15 — Cynthia Cooper, July 2-August 7, 1997

Tina Thompson, June 6-August 1, 2003
11 — Tina Thompson, June 6-
June 28, 2000
Cynthia Cooper, June 28-July 25, 2000

THREE-POINT FIELD GOAL ATTEMPTS

Most three-point field goal attempts, career
818 — Tina Thompson
634 — Cynthia Cooper
464 — Sheryl Swoopes
Most three-point field goal attempts, season
173 — Cynthia Cooper, 1999
162 — Cynthia Cooper, 1997
160 — Cynthia Cooper, 1998
Most three-point field goal attempts, game
13 — Cynthia Cooper, vs. Cleveland,
July 29, 1997
Cynthia Cooper, at Utah, August 4, 1998
11 — Cynthia Cooper, at Portland,
May 31, 2000 (2 ot)
10 — by many

FREE THROW PERCENTAGE

Highest free-throw percentage, career
(Minimum 175 free throws)
.871 — Cynthia Cooper (758/870)
.864 — Janeth Arcain (497/575)
.833 — Sheryl Swoopes (537/645)
Highest free-throw percentage, season (qualifiers)
.900 — Janeth Arcain, 2001 (135/150)
.894 — Janeth Arcain, 1997 (76/85)
.891 — Cynthia Cooper, 1999 (204/229)
Most free throws made, none missed, game
13 — Sheryl Swoopes, at Los Angeles,
August 8, 2002
Tina Thompson, at Minnesota, June 17, 2003
12 — Cynthia Cooper, at Los Angeles,
July 17, 1998
Cynthia Cooper, at Minnesota,
June 19, 1999
Sheryl Swoopes, at Sacramento, July 19, 2003
11 — Cynthia Cooper, at Charlotte,
July 23, 1999
Most free throw attempts, none made, game
5 — Tammy Jackson, at Miami,
July 20, 2001
4 — Kim Perrot, vs. Phoenix,
August 7, 1997
Sheryl Swoopes, at Washington,
June 13, 2002
3 — Tina Thompson, at Los Angeles,
July 17, 1998

FREE THROWS MADE

Most free throws made, career
758 — Cynthia Cooper
612 — Tina Thompson

537 — Sheryl Swoopes
Most free throws made, season
210 — Cynthia Cooper, 1998
204 — Cynthia Cooper, 1999
172 — Cynthia Cooper, 1997
Most free throws made, game
22 — Cynthia Cooper, vs. Sacramento,
July 3, 1998
17 — Cynthia Cooper, vs. Utah,
August 16, 1999
14 — Tina Thompson, vs. Minnesota,
August 9, 2000
Sheryl Swoopes, at Los Angeles,
June 30, 2002

FREE THROW ATTEMPTS

Most free throw attempts, career
870 — Cynthia Cooper
744 — Tina Thompson
645 — Sheryl Swoopes
Most free throw attempts, season
246 — Cynthia Cooper, 1998
229 — Cynthia Cooper, 1999
199 — Cynthia Cooper, 1997
Most free throw attempts, game
24 — Cynthia Cooper, vs. Sacramento,
July 3, 1998
18 — Cynthia Cooper, vs. Utah,
August 16, 1999
16 — Cynthia Cooper, at Utah,
June 30, 1998 (2 ot)
Tina Thompson, vs. Minnesota,
August 9, 2000

REBOUNDS

Most rebounds, career
1,442 — Tina Thompson
862 — Sheryl Swoopes
826 — Janeth Arcain
Highest average, rebounds per game, career
(Minimum 90 games)
7.0 — Tina Thompson (1442/206)
5.3 — Sheryl Swoopes (862/164)
4.5 — Tiffani Johnson (521/117)
Most rebounds, season
263 — Michelle Snow, 2003
245 — Tina Thompson, 2000
233 — Tina Thompson, 2001
Highest average, rebounds per game, season
(qualifiers)
7.8 — Tina Thompson, 2001 (233/30)
7.74 — Michelle Snow, 2003 (263/34)
7.66 — Tina Thompson, 2000 (245/32)
Most rebounds, game
16 — Michelle Snow, at Phoenix,
May 24, 2003
15 — Sheryl Swoopes, vs. Detroit,
July 27, 1999

Tiffani Johnson, at Detroit,
July 21, 2000 (ot)
14 — Tina Thompson, at Utah,
June 30, 1998 (2 ot)
Tiffani Johnson, at Los Angeles,
June 30, 2002

Most games, 10+ rebounds, career
42 — Tina Thompson
11 — Michelle Snow
Sheryl Swoopes
7 — Tiffani Johnson

Most consecutive games, 10+ rebounds
4 — Tina Thompson, June 2-10, 2001
Michelle Snow, July 29-
August 5, 2003
3 — Tina Thompson, August 4-7, 2000
Michelle Snow, May 22-30, 2003

OFFENSIVE REBOUNDS

Most offensive rebounds, career
457 — Tina Thompson
267 — Janeth Arcain
195 — Tiffani Johnson
Sheryl Swoopes

Highest average, offensive rebounds per game,
career (Minimum 90 games)
2.2 — Tina Thompson (457/206)
1.7 — Tiffani Johnson (195/117)
1.2 — Janeth Arcain (267/220)

Most offensive rebounds, season
84 — Tina Thompson, 2001
76 — Wanda Guyton, 1997
Michelle Snow, 2003
73 — Tiffani Johnson, 2002

Most offensive rebounds, game
9 — Tiffani Johnson, at Detroit,
July 21, 2000 (ot)
8 — Tina Thompson, vs. Orlando,
August 3, 2001
7 — Wanda Guyton, at Utah,
June 28, 1997
Wanda Guyton, vs. Cleveland,
August 21, 1997
Monica Lamb, vs. Sacramento,
August 2, 1998
Tiffani Johnson, vs. Seattle,
July 9, 2002

DEFENSIVE REBOUNDS

Most defensive rebounds, career
985 — Tina Thompson
667 — Sheryl Swoopes
559 — Janeth Arcain

Highest average, defensive rebounds per game,
career (Minimum 90 games)
4.8 — Tina Thompson (985/206)
4.1 — Sheryl Swoopes (667/164)
2.8 — Tiffani Johnson (326/117)

Most defensive rebounds, season
187 — Michelle Snow, 2003
177 — Tina Thompson, 2000
155 — Sheryl Swoopes, 2000

Most defensive rebounds, game
12 — Tina Thompson, at Detroit,
July 21, 2000 (ot)
11 — Sheryl Swoopes, vs. Detroit,
July 27, 1999
Michelle Snow, at Phoenix,
May 24, 2003
10 — By many

ASSISTS

Most assists, career
602 — Cynthia Cooper
543 — Sheryl Swoopes
416 — Janeth Arcain

Highest average, assists per game, career
(Minimum 90 games)
4.9 — Cynthia Cooper (602/124)
3.3 — Sheryl Swoopes (543/164)
1.9 — Janeth Arcain (416/220)

Most assists, season
162 — Cynthia Cooper, 1999
156 — Cynthia Cooper, 2000
142 — Kim Perrot, 1998

Highest average, assists per game, season
(qualifiers)
5.2 — Cynthia Cooper, 1999 (162/31)
5.0 — Cynthia Cooper, 2000 (156/31)
4.7 — Kim Perrot, 1998 (142/30)

Most assists, game
10 — Cynthia Cooper, vs. Utah,
July 30, 1998
Sheryl Swoopes, vs. Detroit,
July 27, 1999
Cynthia Cooper, at Sacramento,
August 21, 1999
Cynthia Cooper, at Charlotte,
June 28, 2000
Sheryl Swoopes, vs. Seattle,
July 23, 2002
Sheryl Swoopes, vs. Phoenix,
June 3, 2003
9 — By many

Most games, 10+ assists, career
3 — Cynthia Cooper
Sheryl Swoopes

PERSONAL FOULS

Most personal fouls, career
594 — Tina Thompson
428 — Janeth Arcain
312 — Tammy Jackson

Most personal fouls, season
120 — Michelle Snow, 2003
118 — Polina Tzekova, 1999

107 — Tina Thompson, 1997
Most personal fouls, game
  6 — By many

DISQUALIFICATIONS

Most disqualifications, career
  4 — Polina Tzekova
  3 — Monica Lamb
  2 — Janeth Arcain
     Michelle Snow
     Coquese Washington
Highest percentage, games disqualified, career
(Minimum 90 games)
  0.91 — Janeth Arcain (2/220)
  0.85 — Tiffani Johnson (1/117)
  0.5 — Tina Thompson (1/206)
Lowest percentage, games disqualified, career
(Minimum 90 games)
  0.00 — Sheryl Swoopes (0/164)
     Tammy Jackson (0/141)
     Cynthia Cooper (0/124)
     Kelley Gibson (0/100)
Most consecutive games without disqualification,
career
  184 — Tina Thompson, August 12, 1997
     August 25, 2003 (current)
  164 — Sheryl Swoopes, August 7, 1997
     August 25, 2003 (current)
  141 — Tammy Jackson, June 21, 1997
     August 13, 2002
Most disqualifications, season
  4 — Polina Tzekova, 1999
  3 — Monica Lamb, 1998
  2 — Michelle Snow, 2003
Fewest minutes, disqualified, game
  15 — Monica Lamb, at Utah,
     June 30, 1998 (2 ot)
  17 — Monica Lamb, at Sacramento,
     June 20, 1998
  20 — Monica Lamb, vs. New York,
     June 13, 1998

STEALS

Most steals, career
  407 — Sheryl Swoopes
  292 — Janeth Arcain
  202 — Tina Thompson
Highest average, steals per game, career
(Minimum 90 games)
  2.48 — Sheryl Swoopes (407/164)
  1.56 — Cynthia Cooper (193/124)
  1.33 — Janeth Arcain (292/220)
Most steals, season
  88 — Sheryl Swoopes, 2002
  87 — Sheryl Swoopes, 2000
  84 — Kim Perrot, 1998
Highest average, steals per game, season
(qualifiers)
  2.81 — Sheryl Swoopes, 2000 (87/31)
  2.80 — Kim Perrot, 1998 (84/30)

2.75 — Sheryl Swoopes, 2002 (88/32)
Most steals, game
  8 — Cynthia Cooper, at Charlotte,
     August 11, 1997
  7 — Kim Perrot, vs. Utah, July 14, 1997
     Kim Perrot, vs. New York,
     June 13, 1998
     Kim Perrot, vs. Washington,
     June 29, 1998
     Sheryl Swoopes, vs. Portland,
     June 30, 2000

BLOCKED SHOTS

Most blocked shots, career
  174 — Tina Thompson
  146 — Sheryl Swoopes
  88 — Michelle Snow
Highest average, blocked shots per game, career
(Minimum: 90 games)
  0.89 — Sheryl Swoopes (146/164)
  0.84 — Tina Thompson (174/206)
  0.53 — Tiffani Johnson (62/117)
Most blocked shots, season
  62 — Michelle Snow, 2003
  46 — Sheryl Swoopes, 1999
  33 — Sheryl Swoopes, 2000
Highest average, blocked shots per game, season
(qualifiers)
  1.82 — Michelle Snow, 2003 (62/34)
  1.44 — Sheryl Swoopes, 1999 (46/32)
  1.06 — Sheryl Swoopes, 2000 (33/31)
Most blocked shots, game
  8 — Michelle Snow, at San Antonio,
     June 20, 2003
  5 — Michelle Snow, vs. San Antonio,
     August 2, 2003
  4 — By many

TURNOVERS

Most turnovers, career
  513 — Tina Thompson
  421 — Cynthia Cooper
  401 — Janeth Arcain
Most turnovers, season
  109 — Cynthia Cooper, 1997
  104 — Cynthia Cooper, 1999
  99 — Cynthia Cooper, 2000
Most turnovers, game
  8 — Cynthia Cooper, at Cleveland,
     June 21, 1997
     Cynthia Cooper, at Charlotte,
     July 25, 1998
     Cynthia Cooper, vs. Sacramento,
     August 2, 1999
     Tina Thompson, at Phoenix,
     June 10, 2001
     Janeth Arcain, at Orlando,
     July 18, 2001
     Sheryl Swoopes, vs. Minnesota,
     June 15, 2002
  7 — by many

INDIANA FEVER

TEAM OFFENSE

SCORING

Highest average, points per game, season
69.2 — 2000 (2213/32)
Lowest average, points per game, season
65.5 — 2002 (2097/32)
Most points, game
94 — at Connecticut, June 26, 2003 (2 ot)
92 — at Washington, July 29, 2003 (ot)
Regulation game:
87 — vs. Cleveland, August 4, 2000
Fewest points, game
45 — vs. Houston, June 5, 2002
50 — vs. Washington, July 6, 2002
at Charlotte, August 20, 2003
Largest margin of victory, game
34 — vs. San Antonio, July 23, 2003 (81-47)
31 — vs. Detroit, July 6, 2003 (85-54)
Largest margin of defeat, game
37 — at Detroit, June 18, 2000 (74-111)
30 — at Charlotte, August 20, 2003 (50-80)

BY HALF

Most points, first half
48 — at Orlando, June 17, 2000
at Washington, July 20, 2000
vs. Connecticut, June 20, 2003
46 — vs. Charlotte, July 22, 2000
vs. New York, June 7, 2003
Fewest points, first half
18 — at Seattle, June 10, 2003
19 — at Cleveland, July 15, 2000
at New York, June 25, 2002
Largest lead at halftime
25 — vs. New York, June 7, 2003
(led 46-21; won 86-66)
18 — vs. Detroit, July 6, 2003
(led 42-24; won 85-54)
Largest deficit at halftime overcome to win game
13 — at Miami, June 1, 2000
(trailed 20-33; won 57-54)
10 — at Cleveland, August 13, 2002
(trailed 27-37; won 60-56)
Most points, second half
59 — at Portland, June 20, 2002
50 — vs. Cleveland, August 4, 2000
Fewest points, second half
19 — at Charlotte, August 20, 2003
21 — vs. Washington, July 6, 2002

at Detroit, August 9, 2002

OVERTIME

Most points, overtime period
18 — vs. Phoenix, July 1, 2001
14 — at Connecticut, June 26, 2003
Fewest points, overtime period
2 — vs. Seattle, June 4, 2001
5 — at Miami, August 10, 2001
Largest margin of victory, overtime game
8 — vs. Phoenix, July 1, 2001 (86-78)
4 — at Washington, June 26, 2003 (94-90)

FIELD GOAL PERCENTAGE

Highest field-goal percentage, season
.433 — 2000 (796/1838)
Lowest field-goal percentage, season
.401 — 2002 (731/1825)
Highest field-goal percentage, game
.549 — at Sacramento, June 14, 2003 (28/51)
.544 — at Portland, July 28, 2000 (31/57)
vs. Cleveland, August 4, 2000 (31/57)
Lowest field-goal percentage, game
.217 — vs. Houston, June 5, 2002 (13/60)
.266 — at Detroit, August 9, 2002 (17/64)

FIELD GOALS

Most field goals per game, season
24.9 — 2000 (796/32)
Fewest field goals per game, season
22.8 — 2002 (731/32)
Most field goals, game
33 — vs. Detroit, July 6, 2003
at Washington, July 29, 2003 (ot)
32 — vs. Detroit, August 12, 2001
vs. New York, June 7, 2003
at Connecticut, June 26, 2003 (2 ot)
Fewest field goals, game
13 — vs. Houston, June 5, 2002
16 — at Charlotte, August 20, 2003

FIELD GOAL ATTEMPTS

Most field-goal attempts per game, season
59.2 — 2003 (2011/34)
Fewest field-goal attempts per game, season
56.9 — 2001 (1822/32)
Most field-goal attempts, game
73 — vs. Utah, July 10, 2002
70 — at Washington, July 29, 2003 (ot)
Fewest field-goal attempts, game
44 — at Detroit, June 2, 2002
vs. New York, June 8, 2002

at Portland, June 20, 2002
45 — at Phoenix, July 31, 2002

THREE-POINT FIELD-GOAL PERCENTAGE

Highest three-point field-goal percentage, season
.370 — 2000 (193/521)
Lowest three-point field-goal percentage, season
.331 — 2002 (180/543)

THREE-POINT FIELD GOALS

Most three-point field goals per game, season
6.2 — 2003 (210/34)
Fewest three-point field goals per game, season
4.9 — 2001 (157/32)
Most three-point field goals, game
13 — at Washington, July 29, 2003 (ot)
11 — at Seattle, June 10, 2003
vs. Detroit, July 6, 2003
at New York, July 20, 2003
Fewest three-point field goals, game
1 — at Charlotte, August 20, 2003
vs. Cleveland, August 23, 2003
2 — By many

THREE-POINT FIELD GOAL ATTEMPTS

Most three-point field goal attempts per game, season
17.7 — 2003 (600/34)
Fewest three-point field goal attempts per game, season
13.9 — 2001 (446/32)
Most three-point field goal attempts, game
30 — at Washington, July 29, 2003 (ot)
28 — at New York, July 20, 2003
Fewest three-point field goal attempts, game
6 — at Miami, June 1, 2000
7 — at Phoenix, July 31, 2002

FREE THROW PERCENTAGE

Highest free-throw percentage, season
.799 — 2001 (472/591)
Lowest free-throw percentage, season
.752 — 2000 (428/569)
Highest free-throw percentage, game
1.000 — Many times. Last:
at Connecticut, August 3, 2003 (11/11)
Lowest free-throw percentage, game
.462 — at Minnesota, August 6, 2000 (6/13)
.500 — at Houston, July 8, 2003 (1/2)

FREE THROWS MADE

Most free throws made per game, season
14.8 — 2001 (472/32)
Fewest free throws made per game, season
13.2 — 2003 (449/34)
Most free throws made, game
34 — vs. Phoenix, July 1, 2001 (ot)

31 — at Portland, June 20, 2002
Fewest free throws made, game
1 — at Houston, July 8, 2003
2 — at New York, July 20, 2003

FREE THROW ATTEMPTS

Most free throw attempts per game, season
18.5 — 2001 (591/32)
Fewest free throw attempts per game, season
16.6 — 2003 (563/34)
Most free throw attempts, game
39 — vs. Phoenix, July 1, 2001 (ot)
38 — vs. Miami, June 5, 2000
vs. New York, June 8, 2002
Fewest free throw attempts, game
2 — at Houston, July 8, 2003
3 — at New York, July 20, 2003

REBOUNDS

Most rebounds per game, season
29.6 — 2002 (948/32)
Fewest rebounds per game, season
29.1 — 2003 (988/34)
Most rebounds, game
43 — vs. Orlando, June 3, 2000
vs. San Antonio, July 23, 2003
40 — vs. Detroit, June 1, 2002
at Connecticut, June 26, 2003 (2 ot)
Fewest rebounds, game
17 — vs. Minnesota, July 26, 2002
18 — at Cleveland, July 15, 2000

OFFENSIVE REBOUNDS

Most offensive rebounds per game, season
9.8 — 2002 (315/32)
Fewest offensive rebounds per game, season
8.9 — 2000 (285/32)
Most offensive rebounds, game
17 — vs. Sacramento, June 28, 2002
vs. Utah, July 10, 2002
at Charlotte, May 29, 2003
at Detroit, June 24, 2003
16 — vs. Orlando, June 3, 2000
vs. Charlotte, August 3, 2002
Fewest offensive rebounds, game
1 — at Portland, July 28, 2000
at Detroit, June 23, 2001
4 — at New York, June 30, 2000
vs. Minnesota, July 26, 2002
vs. Orlando, August 7, 2002
at Los Angeles, June 12, 2003

DEFENSIVE REBOUNDS

Most defensive rebounds per game, season
20.3 — 2001 (649/32)
Fewest defensive rebounds per game, season
19.2 — 2003 (654/34)
Most defensive rebounds, game
34 — vs. San Antonio, July 23, 2003

31 — at Connecticut, June 26, 2003 (2 ot)
Fewest defensive rebounds, game
  11 — vs. Washington, August 12, 2003
  12 — at Cleveland, July 15, 2000
      at Charlotte, June 13, 2002
      at Seattle, June 10, 2003

ASSISTS

Most assists per game, season
  15.9 — 2003 (539/34)
Fewest assists per game, season
  14.0 — 2002 (447/32)
Most assists, game
  26 — at Washington, July 29, 2003 (ot)
  25 — vs. Washington, August 12, 2003
Fewest assists, game
  5 — at Miami, June 5, 2001
      at Detroit, August 2, 2003
  6 — at Miami, August 10, 2001 (ot)
      at Charlotte, August 20, 2003

PERSONAL FOULS

Most personal fouls per game, season
  20.1 — 2000 (642/32)
Fewest personal fouls per game, season
  17.5 — 2002 (559/32)
Most personal fouls, game
  39 — at Detroit, June 18, 2000
  33 — vs. Cleveland, June 12, 2000
Fewest personal fouls, game
  9 — vs. Detroit, June 1, 2002
  10 — vs. Cleveland, August 4, 2000
      vs. Washington, July 20, 2001

DISQUALIFICATIONS

Most disqualifications per game, season
  0.28 — 2000 (9/32)
Fewest disqualifications per game, season
  0.15 — 2003 (5/34)
Most disqualifications, game
  2 — at Detroit, June 9, 2000
      at Detroit, June 18, 2000
      vs. Connecticut, August 25, 2003
  1 — Many times

STEALS

Most steals per game, season
  8.8 — 2003 (299/34)
Fewest steals per game, season
  7.6 — 2001 (242/32)
Most steals, game
  20 — vs. Detroit, July 6, 2003
  16 — vs. Minnesota, July 26, 2002
      vs. New York, June 7, 2003
Fewest steals, game
  0 — at New York, June 2, 2001
  2 — vs. Orlando, June 3, 2000
at Miami, June 30, 2002
at Sacramento, June 14, 2003

BLOCKED SHOTS

Most blocked shots per game, season
  3.9 — 2000 (126/32)
Fewest blocked shots per game, season
  3.1 — 2002 (100/32)
Most blocked shots, game
  10 — at Utah, July 29, 2000
  8 — at Portland, July 28, 2000
Fewest blocked shots, game
  0 — Many times. Most recent:
      vs. Washington, August 12, 2003

TURNOVERS

Most turnovers per game, season
  16.2 — 2000 (518/32)
Fewest turnovers per game, season
  13.7 — 2002 (438/32)
Most turnovers, game
  28 — at Detroit, June 18, 2000
  26 — vs. Cleveland, June 12, 2000
Fewest turnovers, game
  5 — vs. Utah, July 10, 2002
  7 — vs. Sacramento, June 28, 2002

TEAM DEFENSE

POINTS

Fewest points allowed per game, season
  66.5 — 2002 (2129/32)
Most points allowed per game, season
  71.6 — 2000 (2290/32)
Fewest points allowed, game
  45 — vs. Seattle, July 14, 2000
      vs. Washington, July 6, 2002
  46 — vs. Cleveland, August 23, 2003
Fewest points allowed, first half
  19 — vs. Seattle, July 14, 2000
  20 — at Phoenix, July 31, 2002
      vs. Charlotte, August 3, 2002
Fewest points allowed, second half
  19 — at Detroit, August 9, 2002
at Cleveland, August 13, 2002
  20 — vs. Charlotte, August 9, 2000
      vs. Washington, July 6, 2002
      vs. San Antonio, July 23, 2003
Fewest points allowed, overtime period
  5 — vs. Seattle, June 4, 2001
  7 — at Connecticut, June 26, 2003

FIELD GOAL PERCENTAGE

Lowest opponents' field-goal percentage, season
  .439 — 2003 (837/1908)
Highest opponents' field-goal percentage, season
  .449 — 2001 (853/1899)
Lowest opponents' field goal percentage, game
  .242 — vs. San Antonio, July 23, 2003 (16/66)
  .303 — at Miami, June 1, 2000 (20/66)

TURNOVERS

Most opponents' turnovers per game, season
  15.1 — 2003 (512/34)
Fewest opponents' turnovers per game, season
  14.6 — 2001 (466/32)
Most opponents' turnovers, game
  26 — vs. Detroit, July 6, 2003
  24 — vs. Minnesota, July 26, 2002

TEAM MISCELLANEOUS

GAME WON AND LOST

Highest winning percentage, season
  .500 — 2002 (16-16)
Lowest winning percentage, season
  .281 — 2000 (9-23)
Most consecutive games won
  4 — July 31-August 7, 2002
  3 — June 14-20, 2003
Most consecutive games won, one season
  4 — July 31-August 7, 2002
  3 — June 14-20, 2003
Most consecutive game lost
  10 — June 18-July 8, 2000
  6 — August 2-12, 2003
Most consecutive game lost, one season
  10 — June 18-July 8, 2000
  6 — August 2-12, 2003
Highest winning percentage, home games, season
  .647 — 2003 (11-6)
Lowest winning percentage, home games, season
  .313 — 2000 (5-11)
Most consecutive home games won
  13 — July 22, 2002-July 10, 2003
  3 — August 1, 2001-June 1, 2002
      June 28-July 8, 2002
Most consecutive home games lost
  8 — June 10-July 8, 2000
  4 — July 10-19, 2002
      July 26-August 12, 2003
Highest winning percentage, road games, season
  .375 — 2002 (6-10)
Lowest winning percentage, road games, season
  .188 — 2001 (3-13)
Most consecutive road games won
  2 — June 12-23, 2001
      July 31-August 6, 2002
      July 24-29, 2003
Most consecutive road games lost
  6 — July 29, 2000-June 9, 2001
      June 21-July 30, 2002
  5 — July 6-24, 2001
      August 3-14, 2001

OVERTIME GAMES

Most overtime games, season
  3 — 2001
  2 — 2003

Most consecutive overtime games, season
  1 — Many times
Most overtime games won, season
  2 — 2003
  1 — 2001
Most overtime games won, no losses, season
  2 — 2003
Most consecutive overtime games won
  2 — June 26-July 29, 2003 (current)
Most overtime games lost, season
  2 — 2001
  1 — 2000, 2002
Most overtime games lost, no wins, season
  1 — 2000, 2002
Most consecutive overtime games lost
  2 — July 24, 2000-June 4, 2001
      August 10, 2001-July 3, 2002
Most overtime periods, game
  2 — at Connecticut, June 26, 2003

INDIVIDUAL RECORDS

SEASONS

Most Seasons
  3 — Niele Ivey
      Monica Maxwell
      Kelly Schumacher
      Alicia Thompson
      Stephanie White
      Rita Williams
  2 — By many

GAMES

Most games, career
  93 — Kelly Schumacher
  90 — Niele Ivey
Stephanie White
  84 — Rita Williams
Most consecutive games, career
  66 — Tamika Catchings, June 1, 2002-
       August 25, 2003 (current)
       Nikki McCray, June 1, 2002-
       August 25, 2003 (current)
  65 — Rita Williams, June 1, 2000-
       June 1, 2002
  63 — Olympia Scott-Richardson,
       May 31, 2001-August 11, 2002
Most games, season
  34 — Tamika Catchings, 2003
       Nikki McCray, 2003
       Kelly Schumacher, 2003
       Natalie Williams, 2003

MINUTES

Most minutes, career
  2,540 — Rita Willias
  2,377 — Tamika Catchings
  1,798 — Niele Ivey

Highest average, minutes per game, career
(Minimum 50 games)
36.0 — Tamika Catchings (2377/66)
30.2 — Rita Williams (2540/84)
27.8 — Olmpia Scott-Richardson (1750/63)
Most minutes, season
1,210 — Tamika Catchings, 2003
1,167 — Tamika Catchings, 2002
1,058 — Nikki McCray, 2002
Highest average, minutes per game, season
36.5 — Tamika Catchings, 2002 (1167/32)
35.6 — Tamika Catchings, 2003 (1210/34)
33.1 — Nikki McCray, 2002 (1058/32)
Most minutes, game
45 — Rita Williams, vs. Phoenix,
July 1, 2001 (ot)
Tamika Catchings, at Connecticut,
June 26, 2003 (2 ot)
Tamika Catchings, at Washington,
July 29, 2003 (ot)
42 — Rita Williams, at Miami,
August 10, 2001 (ot)

SCORING

Most points, lifetime
1,265 — Tamika Catchings
852 — Rita Williams
593 — Alicia Thompson
Stephanie White
Highest average, points per game, career
(Minimum 50 games)
19.2 — Tamika Catchings (1265/66)
10.1 — Rita Williams (852/84)
9.1 — Olympia Scott-Richardson (572/63)
Most points, season
671 — Tamika Catchings, 2003
594 — Tamika Catchings, 2002
457 — Natalie Williams, 2003
Highest average, points per game, season
19.7 — Tamika Catchings, 2003 (1671/34)
18.6 — Tamika Catchings, 2002 (594/32)
13.4 — Natalie Williams, 2003 (457/34)
Most points, game
32 — Tamika Catchings, vs. New York,
June 8, 2002
Tamika Catchings, vs. Orlando,
August 7, 2002
Tamika Catchings, at New York,
August 22, 2003
31 — Olympia Scott-Richardson, vs. Utah,
July 10, 2002
Tamika Catchings, vs. New York,
July 10, 2003
30 — Nikki McCray, at Portland, June 20, 2002
Tamika Catchings, at Washington,
July 29, 2003 (ot)
Most games, 30 or more points, career

5 — Tamika Catchings
1 — Nikki McCray
Olympia Scott-Richardson
Most games, 20 or more points, career
36 — Tamika Catchings
5 — Rita Williams
4 — Nikki McCray
Natalie Williams
Most consecutive games, 20 or more points
4 — Tamika Catchings, August 6-11, 2002
Tamika Catchings, July 24-
August 2, 2003
Tamika Catchings, August 7-12, 2003
3 — Tamika Catchings, July 8-16, 2003
Most consecutive games, 10 or more points
25 — Tamika Catchings, June 24-
August 25, 2003 (current)
15 — Tamika Catchings, June 7-
July 10, 2002
12 — Tamika Catchings, July 17-
August 11, 2002

FIELD GOAL PERCENTAGE

Highest field goal percentage, career
(Minimum 200 field goals)
.472 — Olympia Scott-Richardson (212/449)
.457 — Alicia Thompson (246/538)
.426 — Tamika Catchings (405/951)
Highest field goal percentage, season (qualifiers)
.561 — Kara Wolters, 2000 (148/264)
.514 — Alicia Thompson, 2000 (131/255)
.487 — Olympia Scott-Richardson,
2002 (113/232)
Highest field goal percentage, game
(Minimum 8 field goals made)
.846 — Nikki McCray, at Portland,
June 20, 2002 (11/13)
Natalie Williams, vs. Phoenix,
July 2, 2003 (11/13)
.800 — Nadine Malcolm, vs. Minnesota,
June 16, 2001 (8/10)
.750 — Jurgita Streimikyte, at Charlotte,
July 24, 2001 (9/12)
Natalie Williams, at Sacramento,
June 14, 2003 (9/12)
Most field goals, none missed, game
7 — Kara Wolters, at Portland,
July 28, 2000
5 — Kelly Schumacher, at Seattle,
June 21, 2002
4 — Jackie Moore, at Charlotte,
June 13, 2002
Kelly Schumacher, vs. Charlotte,
August 3, 2002
Kelly Schumacher, at New York,
July 20, 2003

Most field goal attempts, none made, game
7 — Nadine Malcolm, vs. Washington,
August 1, 2001
Alicia Thompson, vs. Houston, June 5, 2002
6 — Stephanie McCarty, at Orlando,
June 17, 2000
Monica Maxwell, vs. Washington,
July 6, 2002

FIELD GOALS

Most field goals, career
405 — Tamika Catchings
266 — Rita Williams
246 — Alicia Thompson
Most field goals, season
221 — Tamika Catchings, 2003
184 — Tamika Catchings, 2002
176 — Natalie Williams, 2003
Most field goals, game
13 — Tamika Catchings, vs. Orlando,
August 7, 2002
11 — Nikki McCray, at Portland,
June 20, 2002
Olympia Scott-Richardson, vs. Utah,
July 10, 2002
Natalie Williams, vs. Phoenix,
July 2, 2003
Tamika Catchings, vs. New York,
July 10, 2003
Tamika Catchings, at New York,
August 22, 2003
10 — By many

FIELD GOAL ATTEMPTS

Most field goal attempts, career
951 — Tamika Catchings
702 — Rita Williams
538 — Alicia Thompson
Most field goal attempts, season
512 — Tamika Catchings, 2003
439 — Tamika Catchings, 2002
363 — Natalie Williams, 2003
Most field goal attempts, game
22 — Tamika Catchings, at Detroit,
August 9, 2002
21 — Tamika Catchings, at Connecticut,
June 26, 2003 (2 ot)
Tamika Catchings, at Washington,
July 29, 2003 (ot)
20 — By many

THREE-POINT FIELD-GOAL PERCENTAGE

Highest three-point field goal percentage, career
(Minimum 50 three-point field goals)
.391 — Tamika Catchings (150/384)
.377 — Niele Ivey (77/204)
.374 — Stephanie McCarty (79/211)

Highest three-point field goal percentage, season
(qualifiers)
.411 — Nadine Malcolm, 2001 (23/56)
.404 — Stephanie McCarty, 2001 (23/57)
.397 — Monica Maxwell, 2000 (62/156)
Most three-point field goals, none missed, game
6 — Tamika Catchings, at Orlando,
July 3, 2002 (ot)
4 — Nadine Malcolm, at New York,
July 9, 2001
Alicia Thompson, vs. Miami,
July 28, 2001
Niele Ivey, vs. Washington,
May 31, 2003
3 — By many
Most three-point field goal attempts, none made, game
7 — Rita Williams, at Orlando, July 3, 2002 (ot)
6 — Tamika Catchings, vs. Houston,
June 5, 2002
5 — Rita Williams, vs. Los Angeles,
June 28, 2000
Gordana Grubin, at Charlotte,
July 24, 2000 (ot)
Niele Ivey, at Los Angeles,
August 6, 2001
Stephanie White, at Houston,
July 8, 2003

THREE-POINT FIELD GOALS

Most three-point field goals, career
150 — Tamika Catchings
107 — Rita Williams
79 — Stephanie White
Most three-point field goals, season
76 — Tamika Catchings, 2002
74 — Tamika Catchings, 2003
62 — Monica Maxwell, 2000
Most three-point field goals, game
6 — Tamika Catchings, at Orlando,
July 3, 2002 (ot)
5 — By many
Most consecutive games, three-point field goals made
23 — Tamika Catchings, July 3, 2002-
June 12, 2003
22 — Monica Maxwell, June 12-
August 1, 2000
12 — Tamika Catchings, June 24-
July 24, 2003

THREE-POINT FIELD GOAL ATTEMPTS

Most three-point field goal attempts, career
384 — Tamika Catchings
307 — Rita Williams
211 — Stephanie White

Most three-point field goal attempts, season
  193 — Tamika Catchings, 2002
  191 — Tamika Catchings, 2003
  156 — Monica Maxwell, 2000
Most three-point field goal attempts, game
  12 — Tamika Catchings, at Washington,
      August 6, 2002
  11 — Tamika Catchings, vs. Washington,
      July 6, 2002
      Tamika Catchings, at Washington,
      July 29, 2003 (ot)
  10 — By many

FREE THROW PERCENTAGE

Highest free-throw percentage, career
(Minimum 100 free throws)
  .836 — Stephanie White (158/189)
  .831 — Tamika Catchings (305/367)
  .819 — Nikki McCray (104/127)
Highest free-throw percentage, season (qualifiers)
  .938 — Stephanie White, 2003 (45/48)
  .871 — Nadine Malcolm, 2001 (54/62)
  .862 — Monica Maxwell, 2000 (50/58)
Most free throws made, none missed, game
  12 — Tamika Catchings, at Detroit,
      June 2, 2002
  9 — Stephanie McCarty, vs. Phoenix,
      July 1, 2001 (ot)
  8 — By many
Most free throw attempts, none made, game
  4 — Ales Santos de Oliveira, at Detroit,
      June 18, 2000
  2 — By many

FREE THROWS MADE

Most free throws made, career
  305 — Tamika Catchings
  213 — Rita Williams
  158 — Stephanie White
Most free throws made, season
  155 — Tamika Catchings, 2003
  150 — Tamika Catchings, 2002
  109 — Rita Williams, 2001
Most free throws made, game
  14 — Tamika Catchings, vs. New York,
      June 8, 2002
  13 — Rita Williams, vs. Phoenix,
      July 1, 2001 (ot)
  12 — Tamika Catchings, at Detroit,
      June 2, 2002
      Tamika Catchings, at Portland,
      June 20, 2002
      Tamika Catchings, vs. Charlotte,
      June 17, 2003

FREE THROW ATTEMPTS

Most free throw attempts, career
  367 — Tamika Catchings
  272 — Rita Willams

  193 — Olympia Scott-Richardson
Most free throw attempts, season
  184 — Tamika Catchings, 2002
  183 — Tamika Catchings, 2003
  148 — Natalie Williams, 2003
Most free throw attempts, game
  16 — Tamika Catchings, vs. New York,
      June 8, 2002
  14 — Olympia Scott-Richardson, vs.
      Minnesota, June 16, 2001
      Rita Williams, vs. Phoenix,
      July 1, 2001 (ot)
      Tamika Catchings, at Portland,
      June 20, 2002
      Tamika Catchings, vs. Connecticut,
      August 25, 2003
  13 — Tamika Catchings, at Phoenix,
      July 31, 2002
      Tamika Catchings, vs. Charlotte,
      June 17, 2003

REBOUNDS

Most rebounds, career
  548 — Tamika Catchings
  372 — Olympia Scott-Richardson
  262 — Alicia Thompson
Highest average, rebounds per game, career
(Minimum 50 games)
  8.3 — Tamika Catchings (548/66)
  5.9 — Olympia Scott-Richardson (372/63)
  3.9 — Jurgita Streimkyte (210/54)
Most rebounds, season
  276 — Tamika Catchings, 2002
  272 — Tamika Catchings, 2003
  255 — Natalie Williams, 2003
Highest average, rebounds per game, season
(qualifiers)
  8.6 — Tamika Catchings, 2002 (276/32)
  8.0 — Tamika Catchings, 2003 (272/34)
  7.5 — Natalie Williams, 2003 (255/34)
Most rebounds, game
  17 — Olympia Scott-Richardson, vs.
      Houston, June 5, 2002
      Natalie Williams, vs. Charlotte,
      August 16, 2003
  16 — Tamika Catchings, at Connecticut,
      June 26, 2003 (2 ot)
  15 — Alicia Thompson, vs. Orlando,
      June 3, 2000
      Tamika Catchings, vs. Charlotte,
      August 3, 2002
      Tamika Catchings, vs. Washington,
      August 12, 2003
Most games, 10+ rebounds, career
  22 — Tamika Catchings
  9 — Natalie Williams
  8 — Olympia Scott-Richardson

Most consecutive games, 10+ rebounds
    4 — Tamika Catchings, August 3-9, 2002
    3 — Natalie Williams, June 20-24, 2003
    2 — By many

OFFENSIVE REBOUNDS

Most offensive rebounds, career
    174 — Tamika Catchings
    132 — Olympia Scott-Richardson
    109 — Natalie Williams
Highest average, offensive rebounds per game,
career (Minimum 50 games)
    2.6 — Tamika Catchings (174/66)
    2.1 — Olympia Scott-Richardson (132/63)
    1.3 — Jurgita Streimikyte (70/54)
Most offensive rebounds, season
    109 — Natalie Williams, 2003
    92 — Tamika Catchings, 2002
    82 — Tamika Catchings, 2003
Most offensive rebounds, game
    9 — Olympia Scott-Richardson, vs.
        Houston, June 5, 2002
        Tamika Catchings, vs. Washington,
        August 12, 2003
    8 — Olympia Scott-Richardson, vs. Utah,
        July 10, 2002
        Natalie Williams, vs. Charlotte,
        August 16, 2003
    7 — By many

DEFENSIVE REBOUNDS

Most defensive rebounds, career
    374 — Tamika Catchings
    240 — Olympia Scott-Richardson
    181 — Alicia Thompson
Highest average, defensive rebounds per game,
career (Minimum 50 games)
    5.7 — Tamika Catchings (374/66)
    3.8 — Olympia Scott-Richardson (240/63)
    2.6 — Jurgita Streimikyte (140/54)
Most defensive rebounds, season
    190 — Tamika Catchings, 2003
    184 — Tamika Catchings, 2002
    146 — Natalie Williams, 2003
Most defensive rebounds, game
    11 — Tamika Catchings, vs. Orlando,
        August 7, 2002
        Tamika Catchings, at Connecticut,
        June 26, 2003 (2 ot)
        Tamika Catchings, vs. Houston,
        August 7, 2003
    10 — Tamika Catchings, vs. Detroit,
        June 1, 2002
        Olympia Scott-Richardson, vs. Miami,
        July 12, 2002
    9 — By many

ASSISTS

Most assists, career
    258 — Rita Williams

    232 — Tamika Catchings
    180 — Niele Ivey
Highest average, assists per game, career
(Minimum 40 games)
    3.5 — Tamika Catchings (232/66)
    3.1 — Rita Williams (258/84)
    2.0 — Niele Ivey (180/90)
Most assists, season
    118 — Tamika Catchings, 2002
    114 — Rita Williams, 2001
Tamika Catchings, 2003
    101 — Rita Williams, 2000
Highest average, assists per game, season
(qualifiers)
    3.7 — Tamika Catchings, 2002 (118/32)
    3.6 — Rita Williams, 2001 (114/32)
    3.4 — Tamika Catchings, 2003 (114/34)
Most assists, game
    11 — Coquese Washington, vs. Orlando,
        August 7, 2002
    10 — Rita Williams, vs. Detroit,
        August 12, 2001
        Coquese Washington, at Washington,
        July 24, 2003
        Tamika Catchings, at Cleveland,
        August 10, 2003
    9 — Rita Williams, vs. Phoenix,
        July 1, 2001 (ot)
Most games, 10+ assists, career
    2 — Coquese Washington
    1 — Tamika Catchings
        Rita Williams

PERSONAL FOULS

Most personal fouls, career
    235 — Olympia Scott-Richardson
    227 — Tamika Catchings
    174 — Rita Williams
Most personal fouls, season
    138 — Natalie Williams, 2003
    127 — Olympia Scott-Richardson, 2002
    122 — Tamika Catchings, 2003
Most personal fouls, game
    6 — By many

DISQUALIFICATIONS

Most disqualifications, career
    4 — Alicia Thompson
Tamika Catchings
    3 — Nikki McCray
        Olympia Scott-Richardson
        Jurgita Streimikyte
Highest percentage, games disqualified, career
(Minimum 50 games)
    6.1 — Tamika Catchings (4/66)
    5.63 — Alicia Thompson (4/71)
    5.56 — Jurgita Streimikyte (3/54)
Lowest percentage, games disqualified, career

(Minimum 50 games)
  0.0 — Kelly Schumacher (0/93)
       Niele Ivey (0/90)
       Stephanie White (0/90)
       Monica Maxwell (0/65)
       Gordana Grubin (0/56)
Most consecutive games without disqualification,
career
  93 — Kelly Schumacher, May 31, 2001
       August 25, 2003 (current)
  90 — Stephanie White, June 1, 2000-
       August 22, 2003 (current)
       Niele Ivey, May 31, 2001-
       August 25, 2003 (current)
  76 — Rita Williams, June 21, 2000-
       July 19, 2002
Most disqualifications, season
  4 — Alicia Thompson, 2000
  2 — By many
Fewest minutes, disqualified, game
  11 — Alicia Thompson, at Houston,
       June 24, 2000
  22 — Rita Williams, at Detroit,
       June 18, 2000
Danielle McCulley, at Detroit, June 18, 2000
  23 — Kara Wolters, at Detroit, June 9, 2000
       Jurgita Streimikyte, at Minnesota,
       June 12, 2001

STEALS

Most steals, career
  169 — Rita Williams
  166 — Tamika Catchings
  91 — Stephanie White
Highest average, steals per game, career
(Minimum 50 games)
  2.52 — Tamika Catchings (166/66)
  2.01 — Rita Williams (169/84)
  1.01 — Stephanie White (91/90)
Most steals, season
  94 — Tamika Catchings, 2002
  76 — Rita Williams, 2000
  72 — Rita Williams, 2001
       Tamika Catchings, 2003
Highest average, steals per game, season
(qualifiers)
  2.94 — Tamika Catchings, 2002 (94/32)
  2.38 — Rita Williams, 2000 (76/32)
  2.25 — Rita Williams, 2001 (72/32)
Most steals, game
  9 — Tamika Catchings, vs. Minnesota,
       July 26, 2002
  8 — Rita Williams, at Miami,
       August 10, 2001 (ot)
  7 — Rita Williams, at New York,

June 30, 2000
Tamika Catchings, vs. Houston,
June 5, 2002
Tamika Catchings, at Cleveland,
August 10, 2003

BLOCKED SHOTS

Most blocked shots, career
  78 — Tamika Catchings
  76 — Kelly Schumacher
  49 — Kara Wolters
Highest average, blocked shots per game, career
(Minimum: 50 games)
  1.18 — Tamika Catchings (78/66)
  0.82 — Kelly Schumacher (76/93)
  0.78 — Jurgita Streimikyte (42/54)
Most blocked shots, season
  49 — Kara Wolters, 2000
  43 — Tamika Catchings, 2002
  35 — Tamika Catchings, 2003
Highest average, blocked shots per game, season
(qualifiers)
  1.58 — Kara Wolters, 2000 (49/31)
  1.34 — Tamika Catchings, 2002 (43/32)
  1.04 — Kelly Schumacher, 2001 (29/28)
Most blocked shots, game
  5 — Kara Wolters, vs. Portland,
       July 3, 2000
       Kara Wolters, vs. Cleveland,
       August 4, 2000
       Natalie Williams, vs. Charlotte,
       June 17, 2003
  4 — By many

TURNOVERS

Most turnovers, career
  198 — Rita Williams
  184 — Tamika Catchings
  141 — Olympia Scott-Richardson
Most turnovers, season
  102 — Tamika Catchings, 2003
  100 — Rita Williams, 2001
  82 — Tamika Catchings, 2002
       Nikki McCray, 2002
Most turnovers, game
  8 — Rita Williams, vs. Sacramento,
       June 21, 2000
       Rita Williams, at Cleveland,
       July 27, 2001
       Tamika Catchings, at Portland,
       June 20, 2002
       Natalie Williams, at Detroit,
       June 24, 2003
  7 — By many

LOS ANGELES SPARKS

REGULAR SEASON TEAM RECORDS

TEAM OFFENSE

SCORING

Highest average, points per game, season
76.6 — 2002 (2452/32)
76.5 — 1999 (2449/32)
Lowest average, points per game, season
71.6 — 1998 (2148/30)
73.5 — 2003 (2499/34)
Most points, game
102 — vs. Utah, June 28, 1999
vs. Utah, July 7, 2002
100 — vs. Sacramento, June 10, 1999
vs. Minnesota, July 8, 2001 (ot)
Fewest points, game
52 — at San Antonio, August 9, 2003
53 — at Washington, August 14, 1999
Largest margin of victory, game
32 — vs. Utah, June 28, 1999 (102-70)
27 — vs. Utah, July 7, 2002 (102-75)
Largest margin of defeat, game
36 — at Seattle, August 6, 2003 (56-92)
25 — vs. Detroit, August 9, 1999 (59-84)

BY HALF

Most points, first half
55 — vs. Utah, August 4, 2002
at Connecticut, May 24, 2003
54 — vs. Sacramento, August 22, 1997
Fewest points, first half
16 — at San Antonio, August 9, 2003
17 — at Washington, August 14, 1999
Largest lead at halftime
26 — vs. Minnesota, August 21, 2003 (50-24)
25 — vs. Phoenix, July 21, 1999 (50-25)
Largest deficit at halftime overcome to win game
17 — at San Antonio, June 26, 2003
(trailed 24-41; won 67-58)
13 — at Minnesota, July 1, 1999
(trailed 28-41; won 81-77 in 2 OT)
Most points, second half
53 — vs. Detroit, August 16, 1998
at Sacramento, July 19, 2001
at Sacramento, August 3, 2002
at Washington, July 9, 2003
52 — vs. Sacramento, June 10, 1999
Fewest points, second half
19 — vs. Houston, August 1, 1997
21 — at Sacramento, June 30, 1998

OVERTIME

Most points, overtime period
19 — vs. Minnesota, July 8, 2001
15 — at Detroit, June 26, 2001
at Sacramento, June 15, 2002
Fewest points, overtime period
2 — at Detroit, June 17, 2003
4 — at Houston, June 30, 1997
at Phoenix, August 24, 1997
at Seattle, June 13, 2000
at Utah, August 13, 2001
Largest margin of victory, overtime period
9 — at Detroit, June 26, 2001 (98-89)
8 — at Seattle, August 8, 2000 (60-52)

FIELD GOAL PERCENTAGE

Highest field-goal percentage, season
.451 — 2001 (916/2031)
.446 — 1997 (794/1782)
Lowest field-goal percentage, season
.416 — 1998 (797/1914)
.418 — 2003 (894/2140)
Highest field-goal percentage, game
.607 — vs. New York, July 20, 2000 (34/56)
.583 — vs. Sacramento,
August 22, 1997 (35/60)
Lowest field-goal percentage, game
.257 — vs. Houston, August 8, 2002 (19/74)
.279 — vs. Detroit, August 9, 1999 (19/68)

FIELD GOALS

Most field goals per game, season
28.6 — 2001 (916/32)
28.4 — 1997 (794/28)
Fewest field goals per game, season
26.3 — 2003 (894/34)
26.6 — 1998 (797/30)
Most field goals, game
39 — at Detroit, June 26, 2001 (ot)
38 — vs. Utah, July 7, 2002
Fewest field goals, game
16 — at Seattle, July 11, 2002
at San Antonio, August 9, 2003
17 — at Houston, August 12, 1999

FIELD GOAL ATTEMPTS

Most field-goal attempts per game, season
63.9 — 1999 (2044/32)
63.8 — 1998 (1914/30)
Fewest field-goal attempts per game, season
61.1 — 2000 (1956/32)

62.6 — 2002 (2002/32)

Most field-goal attempts, game
  82 — vs. Minnesota, July 8, 2001 (ot)
  78 — at Detroit, July 25, 1998

Fewest field-goal attempts, game
  45 — at Sacramento, June 30, 1998
  48 — at Miami, June 23, 2000

THREE-POINT FIELD-GOAL PERCENTAGE

Highest three-point field-goal percentage, season
  .377 — 2002 (194/515)
  .367 — 2001 (160/436)

Lowest three-point field-goal percentage, season
  .269 — 1997 (65/242)
  .330 — 2003 (174/528)

THREE-POINT FIELD GOALS

Most three-point field goals per game, season
  6.1 — 2002 (194/32)
  5.1 — 2003 (174/34)

Fewest three-point field goals per game, season
  2.3 — 1997 (65/28)
  3.7 — 1998 (111/30)

Most three-point field goals, game
  11 — at Sacramento, August 3, 2002
  10 — at Houston, August 19, 1998
       vs. Sacramento, June 10, 1999
       vs. Detroit, June 11, 2002
       vs. Utah, July 7, 2002

Fewest three-point field goals, game
  0 — vs. Utah, July 11, 1997
      vs. Houston, August 1, 1997
      at New York, August 5, 1997
      vs. Sacramento, August 22, 1997
      vs. Phoenix, July 11, 1999
      vs. Phoenix, July 15, 2003 (2 ot)

THREE-POINT FIELD GOAL ATTEMPTS

Most three-point field goal attempts per game, season
  16.1 — 2002 (515/32)
  15.5 — 2003 (528/34)

Fewest three-point field goal attempts per game, season
  8.6 — 1997 (242/28)
  11.2 — 1998 (335/30)

Most three-point field goal attempts, game
  25 — at New York, June 18, 1999
       at Utah, August 13, 2001 (ot)
       vs. Orlando, July 22, 2002
       vs. Miami, July 30, 2002
  23 — Many times

Fewest three-point field goal attempts, game
  1 — at New York, August 5, 1997
  2 — vs. Sacramento, August 22, 1997

FREE THROW PERCENTAGE

Highest free-throw percentage, season
  .792 — 2003 (537/678)
  .786 — 2000 (545/693)

Lowest free-throw percentage, season
  .676 — 1997 (419/620)
  .727 — 1998 (443/609)

Highest free-throw percentage, game
  1.000 — at Houston, August 19, 1998 (5/5)
          vs. Minnesota, July 15, 2000 (16/16)
          at Minnesota, August 11, 2002 (8/8)
          at Minnesota, May 28, 2003 (20/20)
          vs. Phoenix, July 24, 2003 (27/27)
          vs. Charlotte, August 2, 2003 (17/17)
  .955 — vs. Sacramento, June 27, 1997 (21/22)

Lowest free-throw percentage, game
  .375 — at Houston, June 21, 2001 (3/8)
  .400 — vs. Cleveland, July 5, 1999 (4/10)

FREE THROWS MADE

Most free throws made per game, season
  17.0 — 2000 (545/32)
  15.8 — 1999 (506/32)

Fewest free throws made per game, season
  14.0 — 2001 (449/32)
  14.8 — 1998 (443/30)

Most free throws made, game
  40 — vs. Washington, August 3, 1998
  33 — vs. Houston, June 20, 2000

Fewest free throws made, game
  3 — at Houston, June 21, 2001
      vs. Seattle, August 1, 2002
  4 — vs. Cleveland, July 5, 1999
      at Utah, August 13, 2001 (ot)

FREE THROW ATTEMPTS

Most free throw attempts per game, season
  22.1 — 1997 (620/28)
  21.7 — 2000 (693/32)

Fewest free throw attempts per game, season
  18.6 — 2001 (594/32)
  19.9 — 2003 (678/34)

Most free throw attempts, game
  51 — vs. Washington, August 3, 1998
  42 — vs. Houston, June 20, 2000
       vs. Utah, August 4, 2002

Fewest free throw attempts, game
  5 — at Houston, August 19, 1998
  7 — vs. Seattle, August 1, 2002

REBOUNDS

Most rebounds per game, season
  35.7 — 2002 (1143/32)
  34.8 — 1997 (973/28)

Fewest rebounds per game, season
  33.3 — 1999 (1067/32)
  33.8 — 2003 (1149/34)

Most rebounds, game
50 — vs. Houston, July 16, 1997
at Sacramento, July 27, 1997
48 — vs. Seattle, August 4, 2001
Fewest rebounds, game
17 — at Utah, August 21, 1999
19 — at Detroit, August 2, 2000

OFFENSIVE REBOUNDS

Most offensive rebounds per game, season
11.2 — 1998 (337/30)
10.9 — 2001 (350/32)
Fewest offensive rebounds per game, season
9.6 — 2000 (308/32)
9.9 — 2003 (336/34)
Most offensive rebounds, game
19 — vs. Houston, July 16, 1997
18 — at Houston, June 27, 1998
vs. Portland, June 6, 2000
Fewest offensive rebounds, game
4 — vs. Phoenix, July 23, 1998
at Utah, August 5, 1999
vs. Washington, July 6, 2000
at Cleveland, July 20, 2002
5 — Many times

DEFENSIVE REBOUNDS

Most defensive rebounds per game, season
25.4 — 2002 (814/32)
24.5 — 2000 (783/32)
Fewest defensive rebounds per game, season
22.7 — 1999 (725/32)
22.8 — 1998 (683/30)
Most defensive rebounds, game
38 — at Sacramento, July 27, 1997
37 — vs. Portland, July 24, 2002
Fewest defensive rebounds, game
12 — at Utah, August 21, 1999
13 — at Sacramento, July 15, 1997
at Detroit, August 2, 2000

ASSISTS

Most assists per game, season
18.6 — 2001 (596/32)
18.3 — 2000 (586/32)
Fewest assists per game, season
15.7 — 1998 (472/30)
17.3 — 2003 (587/34)
Most assists, game
29 — vs. Indiana, August 6, 2001
28 — vs. New York, July 20, 2000
Fewest assists, game
6 — at New York, August 5, 1997
at San Antonio, August 9, 2003
7 — at Detroit, July 25, 1998
at Seattle, August 6, 2003

PERSONAL FOULS

Most personal fouls per game, season
22.5 — 1998 (675/30)

22.0 — 2000 (705/32)
Fewest personal fouls per game, season
19.3 — 2001 (616/32)
20.1 — 2003 (682/34)
Most personal fouls, game
36 — at Utah, June 23, 1997
35 — at Portland, June 17, 2000
Fewest personal fouls, game
10 — vs. Indiana, August 6, 2001
12 — vs. Charlotte, June 25, 1997
vs. Phoenix, July 5, 2001
at Houston, June 24, 2003

DISQUALIFICATIONS

Most disqualifications per game, season
0.56 — 2002 (18/32)
0.41 — 2000 (13/32)
Fewest disqualifications per game, season
0.19 — 1999 (6/32)
0.21 — 1997 (6/28)
Most disqualifications, game
3 — at Seattle, June 13, 2000 (ot)
2 — Many times

STEALS

Most steals per game, season
9.3 — 1997 (259/28)
8.8 — 2001 (281/32)
Fewest steals per game, season
7.1 — 2003 (242/34)
7.4 — 1999 (237/32)
Most steals, game
20 — at Cleveland, July 3, 1997
17 — at Portland, August 14, 2001
Fewest steals, game
1 — vs. New York, June 19, 1998
2 — many times

BLOCKED SHOTS

Most blocked shots per game, season
5.0 — 2002 (161/32)
4.9 — 1998 (148/30)
Fewest blocked shots per game, season
3.9 — 1999 (124/32)
4.3 — 2001 (138/32)
Most blocked shots, game
13 — at Phoenix, July 11, 2001
11 — vs. Washington, July 31, 1999
Fewest blocked shots, game
0 — vs. Houston, July 18, 1999
vs. New York, July 24, 1999 (ot)
vs. Portland, June 17, 2001
1 — Many times

TURNOVERS

Most turnovers per game, season
18.9 — 1997 (528/28)
17.0 — 1998 (511/30)
Fewest turnovers per game, season
13.7 — 2001 (438/32)

13.8 — 2003 (470/34)
Most turnovers, game
    27 — vs. Portland, July 24, 2002
    26 — vs. Sacramento, June 5, 2003
Fewest turnovers, game
    7 — vs. Charlotte, June 19, 2001
        vs. San Antonio, August 23, 2003
    8 — Many times

TEAM DEFENSE

POINTS

Fewest points allowed per game, season
    67.7 — 2001 (2166/32)
    67.8 — 2000 (2169/32)
Most points allowed per game, season
    72.4 — 1999 (2318/32)
    72.3 — 1998 (2169/30)
Fewest points allowed, game
    48 — at Phoenix, June 21, 2003
    50 — at New York, August 5, 1997
        vs. Cleveland, June 5, 2001
        vs. Phoenix, July 5, 2001
        at Washington, July 14, 2001
        at Cleveland, July 20, 2002
Fewest points allowed, first half
    16 — at Washington, August 14, 1999
    18 — vs. Houston, July 16, 1997
Fewest points allowed, second half
    17 — at San Antonio, June 26, 2003
    19 — at Minnesota, August 6, 1999
        at Phoenix, June 21, 2003
Fewest points allowed, overtime period
    2 — at Seattle, August 8, 2000
    4 — at Phoenix, July 25, 1997

FIELD GOAL PERCENTAGE

Lowest opponents' field-goal percentage, season
    .390 — 2002 (796/2040)
    .392 — 2001 (779/1985)
Highest opponents' field-goal percentage, season
    .411 — 1998 (780/1898)
    .410 — 1999 (818/1993)
Lowest opponents' field goal percentage, game
    .261 — at Cleveland, July 20, 2002 (18/69)
    .270 — at Miami, June 23, 2000 (17/63)

TURNOVERS

Most opponents' turnovers per game, season
    18.0 — 1997 (505/28)
    16.0 — 1998 (481/30)
Fewest opponents' turnovers per game, season
    13.8 — 2003 (468/34)
    14.2 — 2001 (453/32)
        2002 (453/32)
Most opponents' turnovers, game
    30 — vs. Utah, June 28, 1999
    28 — at Cleveland, July 3, 1997

TEAM MISCELLANEOUS

GAME WON AND LOST

Highest winning percentage, season
    .875 — 2000 (28-4)
        2001 (28-4)
    .781 — 2002 (25-7)
Lowest winning percentage, season
    .400 — 1998 (12-18)
    .500 — 1997 (14-14)
Most consecutive games won
    18 — June 26-August 11, 2001
    12 — June 17-July 9, 2000
        July 14-August 8, 2000
        August 9, 2002-June 14, 2003
Most consecutive games won, one season
    18 — June 26-August 11, 2001
    12 — June 17-July 9, 2000
        July 14-August 8, 2000
Most consecutive game lost
    5 — June 21-July 2, 1998
    4 — August 9-14, 1999
        July 30-August 6, 2003
Most consecutive game lost, one season
    5 — June 21-July 2, 1998
    4 — August 9-14, 1999
        July 30-August 6, 2003
Highest winning percentage, home games, season
    1.000 — 2001 (16-0)
    .938 — 2000 (15-1)
Lowest winning percentage, home games, season
    .533 — 1998 (8-7)
    .571 — 1997 (8-6)
Most consecutive home games won
    28 — July 14, 2000-June 27, 2002
    12 — August 16, 1999-July 9, 2000
Most consecutive home games lost
    3 — June 21-July 2, 1998
    2 — Many times
Highest winning percentage, road games, season
    .813 — 2000 (13-3)
        2002 (13-3)
    .765 — 2003 (13-4)
Lowest winning percentage, road games, season
    .267 — 1998 (4-11)
    .429 — 1997 (6-8)
Most consecutive road games won
    12 — June 17-August 8, 2000
    11 — July 20, 2002-June 14, 2003
Most consecutive road games lost
    7 — June 14-July 27, 1998
    4 — July 5-21, 1997
        August 10-21, 1999

OVERTIME GAMES

Most overtime games, season
    4 — 1997

3 — 2001, 2002, 2003
Most consecutive overtime games, season
   1 — many times
Most overtime games won, season
   2 — 1997, 1999, 2001, 2002, 2003
Most overtime games won, no losses, season
   2 — 1999
   1 — 1998
Most consecutive overtime games won
   3 — July 15, 1998-July 24, 1999
      August 8, 2000-July 8, 2001
      June 15, 2002-May 30, 2003
   2 — July 25-August 7, 1997
Most overtime games lost, season
   2 — 1997
   1 — 2000, 2001, 2002, 2003
Most overtime games lost, no wins, season
   None
Most consecutive overtime games lost
   2 — August 13, 2001-June 1, 2002
Most overtime periods, game
   2 — at Cleveland, August 7, 1997
      at Minnesota, July 1, 1999
      vs. Phoenix, July 15, 2003

INDIVIDUAL RECORDS

SEASONS

Most Seasons
   7 — Tamecka Dixon
      Lisa Leslie
      Mwadi Mabika
   5 — DeLisha Milton-Jones
   4 — Nicky McCrimmon

GAMES

Most game, career
   206 — Mwadi Mabika
   205 — Lisa Leslie
   201 — Tamecka Dixon
Most consecutive games, career
   154 — DeLisha Milton-Jones,
      June 10, 1999-August 2, 2003
   98 — Lisa Leslie, July 27, 1998-
      July 21, 2001
   81 — Penny Toler, June 21, 1997-
      August 5, 1999
Most games, season
   34 — Nikki Teasley, 2003
   33 — Jennifer Gillom, 2003
      Nicky McCrimmon, 2003

MINUTES

Most minutes, career
   6,643 — Lisa Leslie
   5,833 — Mwadi Mabika
   5,795 — Tamecka Dixon

Highest average, minutes per game, career
(Minimum 90 games)
   32.4 — Lisa Leslie (6643/205)
   30.2 — DeLisha Milton-Jones (4808/159)
   28.8 — Tamecka Dixon (5795/201)
Most minutes, season
   1,189 — Nikki Teasley, 2003
   1,086 — DeLisha Milton-Jones, 2003
   1,060 — Lisa Leslie, 2002
Highest average, minutes per game, season
   35.03 — DeLisha Milton-Jones,
      2003 (1086/31)
   34.97 — Nikki Teasley, 2003 (1189/34)
   34.7 — Tamecka Dixon, 2003 (1042/30)
Most minutes, game
   50 — Nikki Teasley, vs. Phoenix,
      July 15, 2003 (2 ot)
   45 — DeLisha Milton-Jones, at Seattle,
      May 30, 2003 (ot)
      Lisa Leslie, at Seattle,
      May 30, 2003 (ot)
      Mwadi Mabika, vs. Phoenix,
      July 15, 2003 (2 ot)
      Tamecka Dixon, vs. Phoenix,
      July 15, 2003 (2 ot)

SCORING

Most points, lifetime
   3,617 — Lisa Leslie
   2,397 — Mwadi Mabika
   2,303 — Tamecka Dixon
Highest average, points per game, career
(Minimum 90 games)
   17.6 — Lisa Leslie (3617/205)
   11.6 — Mwadi Mabika (2397/206)
   11.5 — Tamecka Dixon (2303/201)
Most points, season
   606 — Lisa Leslie, 2001
   570 — Lisa Leslie, 2000
   549 — Lisa Leslie, 1998
Highest average, points per game, season
   19.6 — Lisa Leslie, 1998 (549/28)
   19.5 — Lisa Leslie, 2001 (606/31)
   18.4 — Lisa Leslie, 2003 (424/23)
Most points, game
   32 — Lisa Leslie, vs. Minnesota,
      July 8, 2001 (ot)
      Mwadi Mabika, at Portland,
      July 12, 2002 (ot)
   31 — Lisa Leslie, at Portland, July 28, 2001
      Lisa Leslie, vs. San Antonio,
      August 23, 2003
   30 — By many
Most games, 30 or more points, career
   9 — Lisa Leslie
   1 — Mwadi Mabika

Most games, 20 or more points, career
   77 — Lisa Leslie
   28 — Mwadi Mabika
   19 — Tamecka Dixon
Most consecutive games, 20 or more points
   6 — Lisa Leslie, July 28-August 8, 2001
   4 — Lisa Leslie, July 15-23, 2000
Mwadi Mabika, July 15-22, 2003
   3 — By many
Most consecutive games, 10 or more points
   54 — Lisa Leslie, June 17, 2000-
      August 8, 2001
   40 — Lisa Leslie, August 16, 1997-
      June 24, 1999
   18 — Lisa Leslie, August 4, 2002-
      June 24, 2003

FIELD GOAL PERCENTAGE

Highest field goal percentage, career
(Minimum 350 field goals)
   .478 — DeLisha Milton-Jones (680/1424)
   .460 — Lisa Leslie (1316/2859)
   .427 — Tamecka Dixon (865/2028)
Highest field goal percentage, season (qualifiers)
   .618 — Haixia Zheng, 1997 (110/178)
   .602 — Latasha Byears, 2001 (133/221)
   .530 — DeLisha Milton, 1999 (125/236)
Highest field goal percentage, game
(Minimum 8 field goals made)
   .909 — Haixia Zheng, vs. Sacramento,
      August 22, 1997 (10/11)
   .900 — Lisa Leslie, vs. Seattle,
      August 4, 2001 (9/10)
   .889 — Tamecka Dixon, at Sacramento,
      July 27, 1997 (8/9)
      DeLisha Milton, vs. Houston,
      August 20, 1999 (8/9)
      Latasha Byears, at Orlando,
      June 1, 2001 (8/9)
Most field goals, none missed, game
   6 — Latasha Byears, at Phoenix,
      June 28, 2002
   5 — Linda Burgess, at Charlotte,
      July 5, 1997
      Ukari Figgs, vs. New York,
      July 20, 2000
      Vedra Grgin Fonseca, at Cleveland,
      June 22, 2001
      Rhonda Mapp, vs. Indiana,
      August 6, 2001
   4 — By many
Most field goal attempts, none made, game
   7 — Jamila Wideman, vs. Phoenix,
      July 13, 1997
      Mwadi Mabika, at Charlotte,
      August 12, 1998
      Tamecka Dixon, vs. Cleveland,
      June 5, 2001

Nikki Teasley, at San Antonio, August 9, 2003
   6 — By many

FIELD GOALS

Most field goals, career
   1,316 — Lisa Leslie
   865 — Tamecka Dixon
   840 — Mwadi Mabika
Most field goals, season
   221 — Lisa Leslie, 2001
   202 — Lisa Leslie, 1998
   197 — Lisa Leslie, 2000
Most field goals, game
   14 — Lisa Leslie, vs. Seattle,
      August 1, 2002
   12 — Lisa Leslie, at Cleveland,
      June 12, 1999
      Lisa Leslie, at New York,
      June 14, 2003
      Lisa Leslie, vs. San Antonio,
      August 23, 2003
   11 — Many times

FIELD GOAL ATTEMPTS

Most field goal attempts, career
   2,859 — Lisa Leslie
   2,152 — Mwadi Mabika
   2,028 — Tamecka Dixon
Most field goal attempts, season
   467 — Lisa Leslie, 2001
   444 — Mwadi Mabika, 2002
   430 — Lisa Leslie, 2000
Most field goal attempts, game
   28 — Mwadi Mabika, vs. Phoenix,
      July 15, 2003 (2 ot)
   24 — Lisa Leslie, vs. San Antonio,
      August 23, 2003
   23 — By many

THREE-POINT FIELD-GOAL PERCENTAGE

Highest three-point field goal percentage, career
(Minimum 90 three-point field goals)
   .415 — Nikki Teasley (110/265)
   .394 — Ukari Figgs (97/246)
   .334 — Lisa Leslie (96/287)
Highest three-point field goal percentage, season
(qualifiers)
   .462 — Ukari Figgs, 2001 (54/117)
   .430 — Gordana Grubin, 1999 (40/93)
   .424 — Nikki Teasley, 2003 (70/165)
Most three-point field goals, none missed, game
   5 — Nikki Teasley, at Houston,
      June 24, 2003
   4 — Nina Bjedov, at Utah, August 5, 1999
      Lisa Leslie, at Seattle, June 16, 2001
   3 — By many

Most three-point field goal attempts, none made, game
6 — Lisa Leslie, at Utah, August 13, 2001 (ot)
5 — Mwadi Mabika, vs. Phoenix,
July 11, 1999
Allison Feaster, at Minnesota,
July 31, 2000
Nikki Teasley, vs. Sacramento,
June 28, 2003
4 — By many

THREE-POINT FIELD GOALS

Most three-point field goals, career
281 — Mwadi Mabika
110 — Nikki Teasley
107 — Tamecka Dixon
Most three-point field goals, season
70 — Nikki Teasley, 2003
64 — Mwadi Mabika, 2002
61 — Mwadi Mabika, 2000
Most three-point field goals, game
5 — Mwadi Mabika, at Sacramento,
August 10, 1999
Sophia Witherspoon, vs. Orlando,
July 22, 2002
Nikki Teasley, at Sacramento,
August 3, 2002
Nikki Teasley, at Seattle,
May 30, 2003 (ot)
Nikki Teasley, at Houston,
June 24, 2003
Nikki Teasley, at Sacramento,
July 31, 2003
4 — by many
Most consecutive games, three-point field goals made
16 — Mwadi Mabika, June 11-
July 14, 2000
Mwadi Mabika, June 8-July 20, 2002
15 — Mwadi Mabika, July 20, 2000-
June 5, 2001
Ukari Figgs, July 8-August 13, 2001
14 — Mwadi Mabika, June 30-
July 31, 1998

THREE-POINT FIELD GOAL ATTEMPTS

Most three-point field goal attempts, career
854 — Mwadi Mabika
336 — Tamecka Dixon
287 — Lisa Leslie
Most three-point field goal attempts, season
175 — Mwadi Mabika, 2002
165 — Nikki Teasley, 2003
159 — Mwadi Mabika, 2000
Most three-point field goal attempts, game
11 — Mwadi Mabika, at Minnesota,
July 1, 1999 (2 ot)

Sophia Witherspoon, vs. Orlando,
July 22, 2002
Mwadi Mabika, vs. Miami,
July 30, 2002
Mwadi Mabika, vs. Houston,
August 8, 2002
10 — Mwadi Mabika, vs. Minnesota,
July 30, 2001
Mwadi Mabika, at Sacramento,
August 3, 2002
Nikki Teasley, at Sacramento,
July 31, 2003

FREE THROW PERCENTAGE

Highest free-throw percentage, career
(Minimum 175 FT)
.803 — Mwadi Mabika (436/543)
.801 — Tamecka Dixon (466/582)
.775 — DeLisha Milton-Jones (386/498)
Highest free-throw percentage, season (qualifiers)
.883 — Tamecka Dixon, 2003 (83/94)
.875 — Nikki Teasley, 2003 (98/112)
.867 — Penny Toler, 1999 (39/45)
Most free throws made, none missed, game
14 — Lisa Leslie, vs. Minnesota,
July 15, 2000
11 — Mwadi Mabika, at Portland,
June 17, 2000
10 — Mwadi Mabika, at Portland,
July 12, 2002 (ot)
Mwadi Mabika, vs. Houston,
July 18, 2003
DeLisha Milton-Jones,
vs. Phoenix, July 24, 2003
Nikki Teasley, at Phoenix,
August 8, 2003
Most free throw attempts, none made, game
4 — Sophia Witherspoon, at Miami,
May 30, 2002
3 — Vedra Grgin Fonseca, at New York,
June 24, 2001
2 — By many
FREE THROWS MADE
Most free throws made, career
889 — Lisa Leslie
466 — Tamecka Dixon
436 — Mwadi Mabika
Most free throws made, season
169 — Lisa Leslie, 2000
142 — Lisa Leslie, 2001
136 — Lisa Leslie, 1998
Most free throws made, game
15 — Lisa Leslie, vs. Utah, August 4, 2002
14 — Lisa Leslie, vs. Minnesota,
July 15, 2000
12 — Lisa Leslie, at New York,
June 25, 2000

FREE THROW ATTEMPTS

Most free throw attempts, career
1,236 — Lisa Leslie
582 — Tamecka Dixon
543 — Mwadi Mabika

Most free throw attempts, season
205 — Lisa Leslie, 2000
193 — Lisa Leslie, 2001
189 — Lisa Leslie, 1997

Most free throw attempts, game
19 — Lisa Leslie, vs. Utah, August 4, 2002
16 — Lisa Leslie, at New York,
June 25, 2000
15 — Lisa Leslie, at Houston,
June 30, 1997 (ot)
Lisa Leslie, at Cleveland, July 3, 1997
Lisa Leslie, at Sacramento,
June 30, 1998

REBOUNDS

Most rebounds, career
1,956 — Lisa Leslie
970 — DeLisha Milton-Jones
951 — Mwadi Mabika

Highest average, rebounds per game, career
(Minimum 90 games)
9.5 — Lisa Leslie (1956/205)
6.1 — DeLisha Milton-Jones (970/159)
4.6 — Mwadi Mabika (951/206)

Most rebounds, season
322 — Lisa Leslie, 2002
306 — Lisa Leslie, 2000
298 — Lisa Leslie, 2001

Highest average, rebounds per game, season
(qualifiers)
10.4 — Lisa Leslie, 2002 (322/31)
10.2 — Lisa Leslie, 1998 (285/28)
10.0 — Lisa Leslie, 2003 (231/23)

Most rebounds, game
21 — Lisa Leslie, vs. New York, June 19, 1998
Lisa Leslie, vs. Orlando,
July 22, 2002
18 — Lisa Leslie, at Cleveland,
June 12, 1999
Lisa Leslie, vs. Portland, June 3, 2002
17 — Latasha Byears, vs. Houston,
August 11, 2001
Lisa Leslie, at Houston, May 27, 2002

Most games, 10+ rebounds, career
99 — Lisa Leslie
18 — DeLisha Milton-Jones
9 — Mwadi Mabika

Most consecutive games, 10+ rebounds
7 — Lisa Leslie, August 22, 1997-
June 21, 1998
Lisa Leslie, August 13, 2002-
June 7, 2003

4 — Lisa Leslie, August 9-16, 1998
Lisa Leslie, August 13, 2001-
May 27, 2002
Lisa Leslie, August 16-25, 2003 (current)
3 — By many

OFFENSIVE REBOUNDS

Most offensive rebounds, career
529 — Lisa Leslie
310 — DeLisha Milton-Jones
226 — Mwadi Mabika

Highest average, offensive rebounds per game,
career (Minimum 90 games)
2.6 — Lisa Leslie (529/205)
2.0 — DeLisha Milton-Jones (310/159)
1.1 — Mwadi Mabika (226/206)

Most offensive rebounds, season
88 — Lisa Leslie, 2001
80 — Latasha Byears, 2001
78 — Lisa Leslie, 2002

Most offensive rebounds, game
10 — Latasha Byears, vs. Sacramento,
July 25, 2001
8 — Lisa Leslie, at New York,
June 24, 2001
7 — By many

DEFENSIVE REBOUNDS

Most defensive rebounds, career
1,427 — Lisa Leslie
725 — Mwadi Mabika
660 — DeLisha Milton-Jones

Highest average, defensive rebounds per game,
career (Minimum 90 games)
7.0 — Lisa Leslie (1427/205)
4.2 — DeLisha Milton-Jones (660/159)
3.5 — Mwadi Mabika (725/206)

Most defensive rebounds, season
244 — Lisa Leslie, 2002
231 — Lisa Leslie, 2000
210 — Lisa Leslie, 2001

Most defensive rebounds, game
16 — Lisa Leslie, vs. New York, June 19, 1998
Lisa Leslie, vs. Orlando, July 22, 2002
15 — Lisa Leslie, vs. Portland, June 3, 2002
14 — Lisa Leslie, at Minnesota, June 9, 2001

ASSISTS

Most assists, career
580 — Tamecka Dixon
537 — Mwadi Mabika
462 — Lisa Leslie

Highest average, assists per game, career
(Minimum 90 games)
2.9 — Tamecka Dixon (580/201)
2.6 — Mwadi Mabika (537/206)
2.3 — Lisa Leslie (462/205)

Most assists, season
  214 — Nikki Teasley, 2003
  143 — Penny Toler, 1997
Penny Toler, 1998
  140 — Nikki Teasley, 2002
Highest average, assists per game, season
(qualifiers)
  6.3 — Nikki Teasley, 2003 (214/34)
  5.1 — Penny Toler, 1997 (143/28)
  4.8 — Penny Toler, 1998 (143/30)
Most assists, game
  14 — Penny Toler, vs. Utah,
       August 14, 1998
  13 — Nikki Teasley, at New York,
       June 14, 2003
  11 — Nikki Teasley, vs. Indiana,
       June 12, 2003
       Nikki Teasley, vs. Cleveland,
       July 7, 2003
       Nikki Teasley, at Minnesota,
       August 14, 2003
Most games, 10+ assists, career
  5 — Nikki Teasley
  2 — Penny Toler

PERSONAL FOULS

Most personal fouls, career
  838 — Lisa Leslie
  607 — Mwadi Mabika
  568 — DeLisha Milton-Jones
Most personal fouls, season
  136 — Lisa Leslie, 1999
  134 — Lisa Leslie, 2000
  132 — Lisa Leslie, 2001
Most personal fouls, game
  6 — by many

DISQUALIFICATIONS

Most disqualifications, career
  28 — Lisa Leslie
  9 — DeLisha Milton-Jones
  8 — Latasha Byears
Highest percentage, games disqualified, career
(Minimum 90 games)
  13.7 — Lisa Leslie (28/205)
  5.7 — DeLisha Milton-Jones (9/159)
  3.4 — Mwadi Mabika (7/206)
Lowest percentage, games disqualified, career
(Minimum 90 games)
  0.00 — Nicky McCrimmon (0/125)
  3.0 — Tamecka Dixon (6/201)
Most consecutive games without disqualification,
career
  125 — Nicky McCrimmon, May 31, 2000
        August 25, 2003 (current)
  86 — Ukari Figgs, June 10, 1999-
       August 14, 2001
  82 — Tamecka Dixon, July 21, 1998-
       June 24, 2001

Most disqualifications, season
  7 — Lisa Leslie, 2000
      Lisa Leslie, 2002
  4 — Lisa Leslie, 1999
      Latasha Byears, 2001
      Latasha Byears, 2002
  3 — Many times
Fewest minutes, disqualified, game
  14 — Latasha Byears, vs. Phoenix,
       June 25, 2002
       Lynn Pride, at Phoenix,
       August 8, 2003
  15 — DeLisha Milton, at Miami,
       June 23, 2000
  16 — Latasha Byears, at Houston,
       May 27, 2002

STEALS

Most steals, career
  262 — Mwadi Mabika
  259 — Lisa Leslie
  239 — DeLisha Milton-Jones
Highest average, steals per game, career
(Minimum 90 games)
  1.50 — DeLisha Milton-Jones (239/159)
  1.27 — Mwadi Mabika (262/206)
  1.26 — Lisa Leslie (259/205)
Most steals, season
  58 — Mwadi Mabika, 2000
  50 — DeLisha Milton, 2002
  49 — Tamecka Dixon, 1997
       DeLisha Milton, 2001
       DeLisha Milton-Jones, 2003
Highest average, steals per game, season
(qualifiers)
  1.815 — Tamecka Dixon, 1997 (49/27)
  1.813 — Mwadi Mabika, 2000 (58/32)
  1.58 — DeLisha Milton-Jones, 2003 (49/31)
Most steals, game
  6 — Lisa Leslie, vs. Cleveland,
      July 12, 1998
      Lisa Leslie, at Utah, August 1, 1998
      Penny Toler, vs. Washington,
      August 3, 1998
      Mwadi Mabika, at Detroit, July 2, 1999
      Lisa Leslie, vs. Utah, July 30, 1999
      Latasha Byears, at Portland,
      July 28, 2001

BLOCKED SHOTS

Most blocked shots, career
  466 — Lisa Leslie
  151 — DeLisha Milton-Jones
  86 — Mwadi Mabika
Highest average, blocked shots per game, career
(Minimum: 90 games)
  2.27 — Lisa Leslie (466/205)
  0.95 — DeLisha Milton-Jones (151/159)

RECORDS Los Angeles Sparks

0.42 — Mwadi Mabika (86/206)

Most blocked shots, season
    90 — Lisa Leslie, 2002
    74 — Lisa Leslie, 2000
    71 — Lisa Leslie, 2001

Highest average, blocked shots per game, season (qualifiers)
    2.90 — Lisa Leslie, 2002 (90/31)
    2.74 — Lisa Leslie, 2003 (63/23)
    2.31 — Lisa Leslie, 2000 (74/32)

Most blocked shots, game
    7 — Lisa Leslie, at Utah, August 13, 2001 (ot)
Lisa Leslie, vs. New York, May 25, 2002
    6 — By many

TURNOVERS

Most turnovers, career
    679 — Lisa Leslie

    436 — Tamecka Dixon
    369 — DeLisha Milton-Jones

Most turnovers, season
    109 — Lisa Leslie, 1997
    108 — Lisa Leslie, 2002
Nikki Teasley, 2003
    107 — Penny Toler, 1997

Most turnovers, game
    9 — Nikki Teasley, vs. Phoenix, July 15, 2003 (2 ot)
    8 — Lisa Leslie, at Detroit, June 26, 2001 (ot)
    Mwadi Mabika, vs. Sacramento, June 5, 2003
    7 — By many

MINNESOTA LYNX

REGULAR SEASON TEAM RECORDS

TEAM OFFENSE

SCORING

Highest average, points per game, season
70.0 — 2003 (2380/34)
68.5 — 2000 (2193/32)
Lowest average, points per game, season
62.6 — 2002 (2003/32)
63.6 — 1999 (2035/32)
Most points, game
95 — at Los Angeles, July 8, 2001 (ot)
88 — vs. Detroit, June 5, 2000
Fewest points, game
45 — at Phoenix, July 29, 2002
46 — at Phoenix, July 29, 1999
vs. Houston, July 23, 2001
Largest margin of victory, game
27 — vs. San Antonio, July 25, 2003 (81-54)
24 — vs. Utah, June 14, 1999 (78-54)
vs. Miami, July 28, 2000 (68-44)
vs. Phoenix, August 2, 2002 (75-51)
Largest margin of defeat, game
39 — vs. Sacramento, July 3, 2001 (52-91)
33 — at Phoenix, July 29, 1999 (46-79)

BY HALF

Most points, first half
48 — vs. Utah, June 14, 1999
at Seattle, June 14, 2003
46 — vs. Los Angeles, May 28, 2003
Fewest points, first half
11 — vs. Houston, June 30, 2001
13 — vs. Charlotte, August 3, 2001
Largest lead at halftime
24 — at Orlando, June 8, 2000
(led 41-17; won 71-57)
23 — vs. Utah, June 14, 1999
(led 48-25; won 78-54)
Largest deficit at halftime overcome to win game
9 — at Sacramento, June 1, 2002
(trailed 26-35; won 63-61)
8 — vs. Houston, June 1, 2003
(trailed 27-35; won 68-64 in OT)
Most points, second half
52 — at Los Angeles, July 8, 2001
51 — vs. Charlotte, August 3, 2001
Fewest points, second half
19 — vs. Los Angeles, August 6, 1999
at Washington, August 21, 1999
20 — Many times

OVERTIME

Most points, overtime period
14 — at Los Angeles, July 8, 2001
10 — vs. Detroit, July 1, 2002
Fewest points, overtime period
2 — at Utah, July 28, 2001
at Seattle, June 4, 2002
6 — Many times
Largest margin of victory, overtime period
5 — vs. Detroit, July 1, 2002 (85-80)
4 — vs. Houston, June 1, 2003 (68-64)

FIELD GOAL PERCENTAGE

Highest field-goal percentage, season
.442 — 2003 (875/1978)
.421 — 2000 (770/1831)
Lowest field-goal percentage, season
.371 — 2001 (671/1810)
.389 — 1999 (748/1925)
Highest field-goal percentage, game
.556 — at Miami, May 28, 2002 (20/36)
.548 — vs. Seattle, July 20, 2003 (23/42)
Lowest field-goal percentage, game
.200 — vs. Houston, July 23, 2001 (11/55)
.254 — at Orlando, July 21, 2001 (16/63)

FIELD GOALS

Most field goals per game, season
25.7 — 2003 (875/34)
24.1 — 2000 (770/32)
Fewest field goals per game, season
21.0 — 2001 (671/32)
22.7 — 2002 (727/32)
Most field goals, game
32 — vs. Orlando, August 20, 1999 (ot)
vs. Indiana, August 6, 2000
vs. Connecticut, July 10, 2003
vs. San Antonio, July 25, 2003
31 — vs. Utah, June 22, 2000
vs. Phoenix, August 2, 2002
Fewest field goals, game
11 — vs. Houston, July 23, 2001
14 — vs. New York, July 6, 2001

FIELD GOAL ATTEMPTS

Most field-goal attempts per game, season
60.2 — 1999 (1925/32)
58.2 — 2003 (1978/34)
Fewest field-goal attempts per game, season
55.5 — 2002 (1775/32)
56.6 — 2001 (1810/32)
Most field-goal attempts, game
77 — vs. Detroit, August 23, 2003 (ot)
76 — vs. Utah, May 25, 2002 (ot)
72 — at San Antonio, May 30, 2003

Fewest field-goal attempts, game
    36 — at Miami, May 28, 2002
    40 — vs. Portland, July 10, 2002

THREE-POINT FIELD-GOAL PERCENTAGE
Highest three-point field-goal percentage, season
    .357 — 2000 (204/571)
    .344 — 2003 (180/524)
Lowest three-point field-goal percentage, season
    .319 — 2001 (176/552)
    .332 — 1999 (200/603)

THREE-POINT FIELD GOALS
Most three-point field goals per game, season
    6.4 — 2000 (204/32)
    6.3 — 1999 (200/32)
Fewest three-point field goals per game, season
    5.2 — 2002 (166/32)
    5.3 — 2003 (180/34)
Most three-point field goals, game
    14 — at Utah, June 26, 1999
    12 — at Los Angeles, July 8, 2001 (ot)
Fewest three-point field goals, game
    1 — vs. Indiana, June 12, 2001
        vs. Sacramento, July 3, 2001
        at Orlando, July 21, 2001
        vs. Houston, July 23, 2001
        at Seattle, August 8, 2003
    2 — Many times

THREE-POINT FIELD GOAL ATTEMPTS
Most three-point field goal attempts per game, season
    18.8 — 1999 (603/32)
    17.8 — 2000 (571/32)
Fewest three-point field goal attempts per game, season
    15.4 — 2003 (524/34)
    15.6 — 2002 (500/32)
Most three-point field goal attempts, game
    29 — vs. Los Angeles, May 28, 2003
    28 — at Utah, June 26, 1999
        vs. Orlando, August 20, 1999 (ot)
        at Connecticut, July 23, 2003
Fewest three-point field goal attempts, game
    8 — vs. Detroit, June 12, 1999
        vs. Seattle, July 18, 2001
        vs. Portland, July 10, 2002
    9 — vs. Seattle, July 5, 2000
        at Seattle, August 8, 2003
        at Phoenix, August 20, 2003

FREE THROW PERCENTAGE
Highest free-throw percentage, season
    .769 — 2001 (559/727)
    .758 — 2000 (449/592)
Lowest free-throw percentage, season
    .663 — 2002 (383/578)
    .721 — 2003 (450/624)

Highest free-throw percentage, game
    1.000 — vs. Los Angeles, August 6, 1999 (6/6)
        at Houston, August 9, 2000 (11/11)
        vs. Phoenix, August 4, 2003 (20/20)
    .957 — vs. Orlando, June 15, 2000 (22/23)
Lowest free-throw percentage, game
    .200 — at Portland, July 14, 2000 (1/5)
    .286 — at Los Angeles, August 18, 1999 (2/7)

FREE THROWS MADE
Most free throws made per game, season
    17.5 — 2001 (559/32)
    14.0 — 2000 (449/32)
Fewest free throws made per game, season
    10.6 — 1999 (339/32)
    12.0 — 2002 (383/32)
Most free throws made, game
    37 — at Los Angeles, July 8, 2001 (ot)
    30 — at Sacramento, August 9, 2003
Fewest free throws made, game
    1 — at Portland, July 14, 2000
    2 — at Phoenix, July 29, 1999
        at Los Angeles, August 18, 1999

FREE THROW ATTEMPTS
Most free throw attempts per game, season
    22.7 — 2001 (727/32)
    18.5 — 2000 (592/32)
Fewest free throw attempts per game, season
    14.7 — 1999 (470/32)
    18.1 — 2002 (578/32)
Most free throw attempts, game
    45 — at Sacramento, August 9, 2003
    43 — at Los Angeles, July 8, 2001 (ot)
Fewest free throw attempts, game
    4 — at Phoenix, July 29, 1999
    5 — vs. Houston, July 25, 1999
        at Portland, July 14, 2000

REBOUNDS
Most rebounds per game, season
    31.8 — 2003 (1079/34)
    31.3 — 2001 (1001/32)
Fewest rebounds per game, season
    27.2 — 2000 (870/32)
    28.3 — 1999 (906/32)
Most rebounds, game
    47 — vs. Sacramento, August 5, 2001 (ot)
    41 — vs. Los Angeles, July 1, 1999 (2 ot)
        at Utah, July 28, 2001 (ot)
        vs. Utah, May 25, 2002 (ot)
        at Connecticut, July 23, 2003
Fewest rebounds, game
    19 — vs. Cleveland, August 16, 1999
    20 — vs. Los Angeles, August 6, 1999

OFFENSIVE REBOUNDS
Most offensive rebounds per game, season
    10.6 — 2003 (361/34)
    9.7 — 2002 (309/32)

Fewest offensive rebounds per game, season
8.1 — 2000 (258/32)
9.3 — 1999 (298/32)
Most offensive rebounds, game
22 — vs. Utah, May 25, 2002 (ot)
19 — at Utah, June 23, 2001
at Connecticut, July 23, 2003
Fewest offensive rebounds, game
2 — vs. Los Angeles, August 6, 1999
3 — at Portland, July 14, 2000
vs. New York, July 6, 2001

DEFENSIVE REBOUNDS

Most defensive rebounds per game, season
21.7 — 2001 (693/32)
21.1 — 2003 (718/34)
Fewest defensive rebounds per game, season
19.0 — 1999 (608/32)
19.1 — 2000 (612/32)
Most defensive rebounds, game
33 — vs. Sacramento, August 5, 2001 (ot)
31 — at Utah, July 28, 2001 (ot)
Regulation game:
30 — at Seattle, August 10, 2001
Fewest defensive rebounds, game
11 — vs. Charlotte, August 3, 2001
12 — vs. New York, June 6, 2003

ASSISTS

Most assists per game, season
17.1 — 2003 (580/34)
16.4 — 1999 (525/32)
Fewest assists per game, season
13.7 — 2001 (437/32)
14.6 — 2002 (466/32)
Most assists, game
25 — vs. Indiana, August 6, 2000
23 — Many times
Fewest assists, game
3 — at Seattle, August 8, 2003
6 — vs. Orlando, June 15, 2000

PERSONAL FOULS

Most personal fouls per game, season
21.7 — 2001 (695/32)
21.6 — 2000 (690/32)
Fewest personal fouls per game, season
18.7 — 2003 (634/34)
19.3 — 2002 (617/32)
Most personal fouls, game
34 — at Utah, July 28, 2001 (ot)
33 — at Utah, July 5, 2002
Fewest personal fouls, game
9 — vs. Los Angeles, August 11, 2002
11 — at Seattle, June 14, 2003

DISQUALIFICATIONS

Most disqualifications per game, season
0.34 — 1999 (11/32)
2000 (11/32)

Fewest disqualifications per game, season
0.18 — 2003 (6/34)
0.22 — 2002 (7/32)
Most disqualifications, game
2 — at Charlotte, July 21, 1999
at Seattle, July 21, 2000
at Utah, July 28, 2001 (ot)
at San Antonio, August 16, 2003
1 — many times

STEALS

Most steals per game, season
7.4 — 2000 (237/32)
7.1 — 2003 (242/34)
Fewest steals per game, season
6.4 — 1999 (204/32)
6.6 — 2001 (210/32)
Most steals, game
15 — vs. Cleveland, August 16, 1999
14 — vs. Orlando, June 15, 2000
at Houston, June 15, 2002
vs. Sacramento, July 8, 2003
Fewest steals, game
0 — at Charlotte, July 21, 1999
2 — at Houston, July 1, 2003
at Indiana, July 26, 2003

BLOCKED SHOTS

Most blocked shots per game, season
4.0 — 2001 (127/32)
3.2 — 2002 (102/32)
Fewest blocked shots per game, season
2.0 — 2000 (63/32)
2.4 — 1999 (78/32)
Most blocked shots, game
9 — vs. Phoenix, August 2, 2002
8 — at Los Angeles, July 8, 2001 (ot)
at Washington, June 29, 2003
at Indiana, July 26, 2003
Fewest blocked shots, game
0 — Many times. Most recent:
at Los Angeles, August 21, 2003

TURNOVERS

Most turnovers per game, season
16.5 — 2002 (529/32)
16.4 — 2003 (558/34)
Fewest turnovers per game, season
13.6 — 1999 (437/32)
15.5 — 2000 (497/32)
Most turnovers, game
27 — vs. Phoenix, June 27, 2003
26 — at Houston, August 9, 2000
Fewest turnovers, game
6 — at Charlotte, July 21, 1999
7 — vs. Charlotte, July 31, 1999

TEAM DEFENSE
POINTS

Fewest points allowed per game, season
    65.8 — 2002 (2104/32)
    66.0 — 1999 (2111/32)
Most points allowed per game, season
    69.7 — 2003 (2370/34)
    68.4 — 2000 (2188/32)
Fewest points allowed, game
    44 — vs. Miami, July 28, 2000
    45 — at Washington, August 21, 1999
Fewest points allowed, first half
    16 — vs. Detroit, June 12, 1999
    17 — at Orlando, June 8, 2000
       at Miami, June 10, 2000
       at New York, August 6, 2002
Fewest points allowed, second half
    16 — vs. Portland, June 13, 2002
    21 — vs. Cleveland, August 16, 1999
       at Cleveland, June 24, 2000
       at Washington, June 25, 2001
       vs. Portland, July 10, 2001
Fewest points allowed, overtime period
    3 — vs. Houston, June 1, 2003
    4 — at Cleveland, June 24, 2000

FIELD GOAL PERCENTAGE

Lowest opponents' field-goal percentage, season
    .390 — 2001 (752/1927)
    .413 — 2002 (747/1807)
Highest opponents' field-goal percentage, season
    .429 — 2000 (755/1758)
    .425 — 1999 (749/1763)
Lowest opponents' field goal percentage, game
    .262 — at Washington,
       June 25, 2001 (16/61)
    .274 — vs. Phoenix, July 3, 1999 (17/62)

TURNOVERS

Most opponents' turnovers per game, season
    17.1 — 2000 (547/32)
    15.4 — 1999 (492/32)
Fewest opponents' turnovers per game, season
    13.9 — 2003 (471/34)
    14.5 — 2002 (465/32)
Most opponents' turnovers, game
    28 — vs. Portland, July 2, 2000
       vs. Utah, May 25, 2002 (ot)
    27 — vs. Detroit, July 1, 2002 (ot)

TEAM MISCELLANEOUS
GAME WON AND LOST

Highest winning percentage, season
    .529 — 2003 (18-16)
    .469 — 1999 (15-17)
       2000 (15-17)

Lowest winning percentage, season
    .313 — 2002 (10-22)
    .375 — 2001 (12-20)
Most consecutive games won
    5 — June 5-17, 2000
    3 — Many times
Most consecutive games won, one season
    5 — June 5-17, 2000
    3 — Many times
Most consecutive game lost
    8 — July 5-21, 2000
    7 — July 3-19, 2002
Most consecutive game lost, one season
    8 — July 5-21, 2000
    7 — July 3-19, 2002
Highest winning percentage, home games, season
    .647 — 2003 (11-6)
    .500 — 1999 (8-8)
       2000 (8-8)
Lowest winning percentage, home games, season
    .375 — 2001 (6-10)
    .438 — 2002 (7-9)
Most consecutive home games won
    7 — July 8-August 4, 2003
    3 — July 3-19, 1999
       July 24-August 4, 2002
Most consecutive home games lost
    4 — July 3-19, 2002
    3 — Many times
Highest winning percentage, road games, season
    .438 — 1999 (7-9)
       2000 (7-9)
Lowest winning percentage, road games, season
    .188 — 2002 (3-13)
    .375 — 2001 (6-10)
Most consecutive road games won
    3 — June 8-17, 2000
August 9-20, 2003
    2 — Many times
Most consecutive road games lost
    12 — June 4-July 31, 2002
    6 — July 29-August 18, 1999
       July 1-30, 2001

OVERTIME GAMES

Most overtime games, season
    3 — 2001, 2002
    2 — 1999, 2003Most consecutive
Overtime games, season
    1 — Many times
Most overtime games won, season
    1 — 2000, 2001, 2002, 2003
Most overtime games won, no losses, season
    1 — 2000
Most consecutive overtime games won
    2 — July 1, 2002-June 1, 2003

Most overtime games lost, season
   2 — 1999, 2001, 2002
Most overtime games lost, no wins, season
   2 — 1999
Most consecutive overtime games lost
   2 — July 1-August 20, 1999
      July 8-28, 2001
      May 25-June 4, 2002
Most overtime periods, game
   2 — vs. Los Angeles, July 1, 1999

INDIVIDUAL RECORDS

SEASONS
Most Seasons
   5 — Katie Smith
   3 — By many

GAMES
Most games, career
   159 — Katie Smith
   83 — Svetlana Abrosimova
   80 — Janell Burse
Most consecutive games, career
   94 — Katie Smith, June 19, 1999-
      August 13, 2001
   65 — Katie Smith, May 28, 2002-
      August 23, 2003 (current)
   64 — Kristin Folkl, June 12, 1999-
      August 9, 2000
Most games, season
   34 — Teresa Edwards, 2003
      Sheri Sam, 2003
      Katie Smith, 2003
      Tamika Williams, 2003

MINUTES
Most minutes, career
   5,721 — Katie Smith
   2,443 — Svetlana Abrosimova
   2,144 — Tamika Williams
Highest average, minutes per game, career
(Minimum 60 games)
   36.0 — Katie Smith (5721/159)
   33.0 — Tamika Williams (2144/65)
   29.4 — Svetlana Abrosimova (2443/83)
Most minutes, season
   1,234 — Katie Smith, 2001
   1,193 — Katie Smith, 2000
   1,185 — Katie Smith, 2003
Highest average, minutes per game, season
   38.6 — Katie Smith, 2001 (1234/32)
   37.3 — Katie Smith, 2000 (1193/32)
   36.7 — Katie Smith, 2002 (1138/31)
Most minutes, game
   49 — Sonja Tate, vs. Los Angeles,
      July 1, 1999 (2 ot)
   45 — Katie Smith, at Los Angeles,
      July 8, 2001 (ot)

      Katie Smith, vs. Sacramento,
      August 5, 2001 (ot)
Regulation game:
   .40 — By many

SCORING
Most points, lifetime
   2,867 — Katie Smith
   975 — Svetlana Abrosimova
   693 — Betty Lennox
Highest average, points per game, career
(Minimum 60 games)
   18.0 — Katie Smith (2867/159)
   11.7 — Svetlana Abrosimova (975/83)
   9.5 — Tamika Williams (617/65)
Most points, season
   739 — Katie Smith, 2001
   646 — Katie Smith, 2000
   620 — Katie Smith, 2003
Highest average, points per game, season
   23.1 — Katie Smith, 2001 (739/32)
   20.2 — Katie Smith, 2000 (646/32)
   18.2 — Katie Smith, 2003 (620/34)
Most points, game
   46 — Katie Smith, at Los Angeles,
      July 8, 2001 (ot)
   40 — Katie Smith, at Detroit,
      June 17, 2001
   36 — Katie Smith, at Phoenix,
      August 1, 2001
Most games, 30 or more points, career
   10 — Katie Smith
   1 — Betty Lennox
Most games, 20 or more points, career
   67 — Katie Smith
   13 — Svetlana Abrosimova
      Betty Lennox
   8 — Tonya Edwards
Brandy ReedMost consecutive games, 20 or
more points
   6 — Katie Smith, June 16-28, 2001
      Katie Smith, July 1-17, 2003
   5 — Katie Smith, August 8, 2000-
      June 9, 2001
      Katie Smith, July 6-14, 2001
Most consecutive games, 10 or more points
   35 — Katie Smith, July 7, 2000-
      July 18, 2001
   18 — Katie Smith, July 23, 2001-
      June 13, 2002
   17 — Katie Smith, August 20, 1999-
      July 2, 2000

FIELD GOAL PERCENTAGE
Highest field goal percentage, career
(Minimum 225 field goals)
   .611 — Tamika Williams (253/414)
   .414 — Katie Smith (890/2149)
   .401 — Betty Lennox (252/629)

Highest field goal percentage, season (qualifiers)
.668 — Tamika Williams, 2003 (129/193)
.561 — Tamika Williams, 2002 (124/221)
.459 — Brandy Reed, 1999 (168/366)
Highest field goal percentage, game
(Minimum 8 field goals made)
.900 — Katie Smith, vs. Phoenix, August 2,
2002 (9/10)
.889 — Svetlana Abrosimova, vs. Seattle,
July 18, 2001 (8/9)
.833 — Svetlana Abrosimova, vs.
Los Angeles, June 8, 2002 (10/12)
Most field goals, none missed, game
5 — Marla Brumfield, vs. Portland,
July 23, 2000
4 — Sonja Tate, at Utah, June 26, 1999
Tamika Williams, vs. Connecticut,
July 10, 2003
3 — By many
Most field goal attempts, none made, game
9 — Andrea Lloyd-Curry, vs. Houston,
June 19, 1999
Erin Buescher, at Utah, June 23, 2001
Lynn Pride, vs. Houston, July 23, 2001
7 — Grace Daley, at Los Angeles,
July 15, 2000
Val Whiting-Raymond, at Utah,
June 23, 2001
Tamara Moore, at Sacramento,
July 28, 2002
6 — By many

FIELD GOALS

Most field goals, career
890 — Katie Smith
345 — Svetlana Abrosimova
253 — Tamika Williams Most field goals, season
208 — Katie Smith, 2003
204 — Katie Smith, 2001
203 — Katie Smith, 2000 Most field goals, game
13 — Katie Smith, at Detroit, June 17, 2001
12 — Brandy Reed, vs. Washington,
July 23, 1999
Katie Smith, vs. Connecticut, July 10, 2003
11 — By many

FIELD GOAL ATTEMPTS

Most field goal attempts, career
2,149 — Katie Smith
894 — Svetlana Abrosimova
629 — Betty Lennox Most field goal
attempts, season
519 — Katie Smith, 2001
482 — Katie Smith, 2000
471 — Betty Lennox, 2000
Most field goal attempts, game
23 — Brandy Reed, vs. Charlotte,
July 31, 1999
Katie Smith, at Los Angeles,

July 8, 2001 (ot)
Svetlana Abrosimova, at Los Angeles,
July 30, 2001
22 — Tonya Edwards, vs. Houston,
July 25, 1999
Betty Lennox, vs. Los Angeles,
July 31, 2000
Betty Lennox, vs. Utah,
May 25, 2002 (ot)

THREE-POINT FIELD-GOAL PERCENTAGE

Highest three-point field goal percentage, career
(Minimum 60 three-point field goals)
.374 — Betty Lennox (80/214)
.366 — Katie Smith (365/996)
.344 — Tonya Edwards (66/192)
Highest three-point field goal percentage, season
(qualifiers)
.396 — Betty Lennox, 2000 (55/139)
.390 — Katie Smith, 2003 (78/200)
.385 — Betty Lennox, 2001 (20/52)
Most three-point field goals, none missed, game
5 — Andrea Lloyd-Curry, at Sacramento,
June 22, 1999
4 — Katie Smith, vs. Miami, July 28, 2000
3 — By many
Most three-point field goal attempts, none made,
game
7 — Katie Smith, vs. Miami, July 19, 2002
6 — Andrea Lloyd-Curry, vs. Washington,
July 23, 1999
Katie Smith, vs. Phoenix,
June 20, 2000
Katie Smith, at Phoenix,
July 29, 2002
Teresa Edwards, vs. Houston,
June 1, 2003 (ot)
5 — by many

THREE-POINT FIELD GOALS

Most three-point field goals, career
365 — Katie Smith
80 — Betty Lennox
66 — Tonya Edwards
Most three-point field goals, season
88 — Katie Smith, 2000
85 — Katie Smith, 2001
78 — Katie Smith, 2003
Most three-point field goals, game
7 — Katie Smith, at Seattle, June 14, 2003
6 — By many
Most consecutive games, three-point field goals made
32 — Katie Smith, July 31, 2002-
August 2, 2003
25 — Katie Smith, June 22, 2000-
June 9, 2001

22 — Katie Smith, August 1, 2001-
July 3, 2002

THREE-POINT FIELD GOAL ATTEMPTS

Most three-point field goal attempts, career
996 — Katie Smith
218 — Svetlana Abrosimova
214 — Betty Lennox
Most three-point field goal attempts, season
240 — Katie Smith, 2001
232 — Katie Smith, 2000
200 — Katie Smith, 2003
Most three-point field goal attempts, game
13 — Katie Smith, vs. Los Angeles,
June 3, 2000
12 — Tonya Edwards, vs. Charlotte,
July 31, 1999
Katie Smith, at Utah, June 23, 2001
Betty Lennox, vs. Utah,
May 25, 2002 (ot)
11 — Tonya Edwards, at Cleveland,
July 12, 1999
Katie Smith, vs. Portland,
July 10, 2001

FREE THROW PERCENTAGE

Highest free-throw percentage, career
(Minimum 125 free throws)
.860 — Katie Smith (722/840)
.639 — Svetlana Abrosimova (221/346)
Highest free-throw percentage, season (qualifiers)
.895 — Katie Smith, 2001 (246/275)
.881 — Katie Smith, 2003 (126/143)
.869 — Katie Smith, 2000 (152/175)
Most free throws made, none missed, game
12 — Katie Smith, vs. Orlando,
June 15, 2000
10 — Kristin Folkl, vs. Detroit,
June 5, 2000
Katie Smith, at Utah, June 23, 2001
Katie Smith, vs. Washington,
July 27, 2001
Katie Smith, vs. Cleveland,
July 5, 2003
Most free throw attempts, none made, game
4 — Maylana Martin, at Indiana,
June 16, 2001
Janell Burse, vs. Los Angeles,
June 8, 2002
Svetlana Abrosimova,
at Indiana, July 26, 2002
2 — by many

FREE THROWS MADE

Most free throws made, career
722 — Katie Smith
221 — Svetlana Abrosimova
109 — Betty Lennox

Most free throws made, season
246 — Katie Smith, 2001
152 — Katie Smith, 2000
126 — Katie Smith, 2002
Katie Smith, 2003
Most free throws made, game
18 — Katie Smith, at Los Angeles,
July 8, 2001 (ot)
16 — Katie Smith, at Utah,
July 28, 2001 (ot)
14 — Katie Smith, at Miami, June 10, 2000

FREE THROW ATTEMPTS

Most free throw attempts, career
840 — Katie Smith
346 — Svetlana Abrosimova
201 — Tamika Williams
Most free throw attempts, season
275 — Katie Smith, 2001
175 — Katie Smith, 2000
153 — Katie Smith, 2002
Most free throw attempts, game
19 — Katie Smith, at Los Angeles,
July 8, 2001 (ot)
18 — Katie Smith, at Utah,
July 28, 2001 (ot)
Svetlana Abrosimova, vs. Utah,
May 25, 2002 (ot)
16 — Katie Smith, at Miami, June 10, 2000
Katie Smith, vs. Portland, July 2, 2000
Svetlana Abrosimova, vs. Houston,
July 23, 2001

REBOUNDS

Most rebounds, career
533 — Katie Smith
461 — Svetlana Abrosimova
438 — Tamika Williams
Highest average, rebounds per game, career
(Minimum 60 games)
6.7 — Tamika Williams (438/65)
5.6 — Svetlana Abrosimova (461/83)
4.2 — Kristin Folkl (270/64)
Most rebounds, season
229 — Tamika Williams, 2002
209 — Tamika Williams, 2003
178 — Betty Lennox, 2000
Highest average, rebounds per game, season
(qualifiers)
7.4 — Tamika Williams, 2002 (229/31)
6.7 — Svetlana Abrosimova, 2001 (174/26)
6.1 — Tamika Williams, 2003 (209/34)
Most rebounds, game
15 — Svetlana Abrosimova,
vs. Sacramento, August 5, 2001 (ot)
13 — Brandy Reed, vs. Charlotte,
July 31, 1999
Svetlana Abrosimova, at Seattle,
August 10, 2001

Svetlana Abrosimova, vs. Portland,
    June 13, 2002
· 12 — By many
Most games, 10+ rebounds, career
    13 — Svetlana Abrosimova
    7 — Tamika Williams
    5 — Betty Lennox
Most consecutive games, 10+ rebounds
    3 — Svetlana Abrosimova,
        August 8-12, 2001
    2 — Svetlana Abrosimova,
        July 24-26, 2002
        Tamika Williams, July 10-16, 2003

OFFENSIVE REBOUNDS

Most offensive rebounds, career
    188 — Tamika Williams
    174 — Katie Smith
    132 — Svetlana Abrosimova
Highest average, offensive rebounds per game,
career (Minimum 60 games)
    2.9 — Tamika Williams (188/65)
    1.6 — Svetlana Abrosimova (132/83)
    1.2 — Kristin Folkl (79/64)
Most offensive rebounds, season
    96 — Tamika Williams, 2002
    92 — Tamika Williams, 2003
    55 — Brandy Reed, 1999
Most offensive rebounds, game
    10 — Tamika Williams, at Phoenix,
        June 23, 2002
    7 — Tamika Williams, at Houston,
        June 15, 2002
        Tamika Williams, at Seattle,
        August 8, 2003
    6 — By many

DEFENSIVE REBOUNDS

Most defensive rebounds, career
    359 — Katie Smith
    329 — Svetlana Abrosimova
    250 — Tamika Williams
Highest average, defensive rebounds per game,
career (Minimum 60 games)
    4.0 — Svetlana Abrosimova (329/83)
    3.9 — Tamika Williams (250/65)
    3.0 — Kristin Folkl (191/64)
Most defensive rebounds, season
    133 — Tamika Williams, 2002
    131 — Svetlana Abrosimova, 2001
    125 — Betty Lennox, 2000
Most defensive rebounds, game
    13 — Svetlana Abrosimova,
        vs. Sacramento, August 5, 2001 (ot)
    11 — Kristin Folkl, at Seattle, July 21, 2000
    10 — Betty Lennox, at Portland,
        July 14, 2000
        Svetlana Abrosimova, vs. Utah,
        July 24, 2002

ASSISTS

Most assists, career
    383 — Katie Smith
    195 — Svetlana Abrosimova
    148 — Teresa Edwards
Highest average, assists per game, career
(Minimum 60 games)
    2.4 — Katie Smith (383/159)
    2.35 — Svetlana Abrosimova (195/83)
    2.25 — Kate Paye (135/60)
Most assists, season
    148 — Teresa Edwards, 2003
    100 — Sonja Tate, 1999
    97 — Kate Paye, 2001
Highest average, assists per game, season
(qualifiers)
    4.4 — Teresa Edwards, 2003 (148/34)
    3.1 — Sonja Tate, 1999 (100/32)
    3.0 — Kate Paye, 2001 (97/32)
Most assists, game
    11 — Andrea Lloyd-Curry,
        at Charlotte, July 21, 1999
    9 — Svetlana Abrosimova,
        at San Antonio, May 30, 2003
    8 — By many
Most games, 10+ assists, career
    1 — Andrea Lloyd-Curry

PERSONAL FOULS

Most personal fouls, career
    470 — Katie Smith
    222 — Svetlana Abrosimova
    176 — Michele Van Gorp
Most personal fouls, season
    112 — Betty Lennox, 2000
Katie Smith, 2003
    107 — Keitha Dickerson, 2000
    106 — Katie Smith, 1999
Most personal fouls, game
    6 — by many

DISQUALIFICATIONS

Most disqualifications, career
    7 — Katie Smith
    6 — Tonya Edwards
    5 — Betty Lennox
        Katie Smith
Highest percentage, games disqualified, career
(Minimum 60 games)
    5.3 — Michele Van Gorp (4/75)
    4.9 — Maylana Martin (3/61)
    4.4 — Katie Smith (7/159)
Lowest percentage, games disqualified, career
(Minimum 60 games)
    0.0 — Tamika Williams (0/65)
        Kristi Harrower (0/62)
        Kate Paye (0/60)

Most consecutive games without disqualification, career
90 — Katie Smith, August 11, 1999-
July 19, 2002
69 — Janell Burse, May 31, 2001-
July 26, 2003
66 — Svetlana Abrosimova, July 30, 2001
August 23, 2003 (current)
Most disqualifications, season
6 — Tonya Edwards, 1999
4 — Keitha Dickerson, 2000
Betty Lennox, 2000
3 — Katie Smith, 1999
Fewest minutes, disqualified, game
16 — Janell Burse, at San Antonio,
August 16, 2003
17 — Maylana Martin, at Utah,
July 28, 2001 (ot)
19 — Lynn Pride, at Indiana, June 16, 2001

STEALS

Most steals, career
143 — Katie Smith
128 — Svetlana Abrosimova
78 — Tamika Williams
Highest average, steals per game, career
(Minimum 60 games)
1.54 — Svetlana Abrosimova (128/83)
1.20 — Tamika Williams (78/65)
0.90 — Katie Smith (143/159)
Most steals, season
53 — Betty Lennox, 2000
44 — Katie Smith, 2000
Tamika Williams, 2002
Svetlana Abrosimova, 2003
42 — Svetlana Abrosimova, 2001
Svetlana Abrosimova, 2002
Highest average, steals per game, season
(qualifiers)
1.66 — Betty Lennox, 2000 (53/32)
1.62 — Svetlana Abrosimova, 2001 (42/26)
1.56 — Svetlana Abrosimova, 2002 (42/27)
Most steals, game
6 — Sonja Tate, vs. Cleveland,
August 16, 1999
Lynn Pride, vs. Sacramento,
August 5, 2001 (ot)
Tamika Williams, at Houston,
June 15, 2002
Teresa Edwards, vs. Sacramento,
July 8, 2003
5 — Betty Lennox, at Cleveland,
June 24, 2000 (ot)
Svetlana Abrosimova, at Seattle,
June 4, 2002 (ot)
4 — By many

BLOCKED SHOTS

Most blocked shots, career
56 — Janell Burse

46 — Lynn Pride
37 — Michele Van Gorp
Highest average, blocked shots per game, career
(Minimum: 60 games)
0.70 — Janell Burse (56/80)
0.61 — Lynn Pride (46/76)
0.53 — Kristin Folkl (34/64)
Most blocked shots, season
29 — Erin Buescher, 2001
28 — Janell Burse, 2003
25 — Lynn Pride, 2002
Highest average, blocked shots per game, season
(qualifiers)
0.97 — Janell Burse, 2003 (28/29)
0.91 — Erin Buescher, 2001 (29/32)
0.81 — Lynn Pride, 2002 (25/31)
Most blocked shots, game
5 — Janell Burse, at Indiana,
July 26, 2003
4 — Kristin Folkl, vs. Detroit,
June 5, 2000
Kate Paye, at Los Angeles,
July 15, 2000
Janell Burse, vs. Sacramento,
August 5, 2001 (ot)
Janell Burse, at Sacramento,
August 7, 2001
Lynn Pride, vs. Utah,
August 12, 2001
Janell Burse, vs. Seattle,
August 2, 2003
3 — By many

TURNOVERS

Most turnovers, career
355 — Katie Smith
267 — Svetlana Abrosimova
142 — Betty LennoxMost turnovers, season
97 — Betty Lennox, 2000
92 — Svetlana Abrosimova, 2002
Teresa Edwards, 2003
90 — Svetlana Abrosimova, 2003
Most turnovers, game
11 — Betty Lennox, at Houston,
August 9, 2000
9 — Keitha Dickerson, at Seattle,
July 21, 2000
Svetlana Abrosimova, at Portland,
August 8, 2001
Betty Lennox, vs. Utah,
May 25, 2002 (ot)
8 — Tamara Moore, vs. Portland,
July 10, 2002
Svetlana Abrosimova, vs. Portland,
July 10, 2002
Tamara Moore, at Houston,
August 13, 2002

RECORDS Minnesota Lynx

298

NEW YORK LIBERTY

REGULAR SEASON TEAM RECORDS

TEAM OFFENSE

SCORING

Highest average, points per game, season
68.6 — 1998 (2058/30)
68.3 — 1997 (1911/28)
Lowest average, points per game, season
65.3 — 2002 (2089/32)
66.0 — 2003 (2243/34)
Most points, game
95 — at Phoenix, June 21, 2001
92 — at Los Angeles, July 21, 1998
Fewest points, game
41 — at Miami, August 6, 2000
43 — vs. Cleveland, August 4, 2001
Largest margin of victory, game
43 — vs. Washington, August 13, 1998 (88-45)
35 — at Cleveland, July 8, 1999 (84-49)
Largest margin of defeat, game
25 — vs. Houston, July 8, 1998 (54-79)
24 — at Cleveland, May 31, 2003 (50-74)

BY HALF

Most points, first half
52 — at Phoenix, June 21, 2001
50 — vs. Charlotte, August 2, 1998
Fewest points, first half
15 — at Houston, July 3, 1999
16 — vs. Portland, June 30, 2002
at Cleveland, May 31, 2003
Largest lead at halftime
26 — at Phoenix, June 21, 2001 (52-26)
25 — vs. Charlotte, August 2, 1998 (50-25)
Largest deficit at halftime overcome to win game
15 — vs. Indiana, June 30, 2000
(trailed 25-40; won 72-70)
at Connecticut, August 12, 2003
(trailed 21-36; won 74-73)
14 — at Washington, August 21, 2003
(trailed 19-33; won 65-60)
Most points, second half
53 — at Connecticut, August 12, 2003
52 — at Portland, May 29, 2002
Fewest points, second half
20 — vs. Detroit, August 1, 2003
21 — at Miami, August 6, 2000
at Charlotte, August 24, 2003

OVERTIME

Most points, overtime period
17 — at Orlando, July 29, 1999

13 — vs. Utah, July 18, 1999
Fewest points, overtime period
4 — at Washington, August 11, 1999
5 — vs. Charlotte, July 26, 1999
Largest margin of victory, overtime period
8 — at Orlando, July 29, 1999 (73-65)
7 — vs. Cleveland, August 24, 1997 (79-72)

FIELD GOAL PERCENTAGE

Highest field-goal percentage, season
.456 — 2001 (833/1828)
.444 — 2002 (772/1740)
Lowest field-goal percentage, season
.412 — 1997 (707/1715)
.418 — 1999 (800/1914)
Highest field-goal percentage, game
.621 — vs. Connecticut, July 1, 2003 (36/58)
.600 — vs. Orlando, August 10, 2001 (30/50)
Lowest field-goal percentage, game
.219 — at Houston, July 3, 1999 (14/64)
.250 — at Washington,
August 11, 1999 (16/64) (ot)

FIELD GOALS

Most field goals per game, season
26.0 — 2001 (833/32)
25.3 — 1998 (758/30)
Fewest field goals per game, season
24.1 — 2002 (772/32)
24.3 — 2003 (825/34)
Most field goals, game
39 — at Phoenix, June 21, 2001
36 — vs. Connecticut, July 1, 2003
Fewest field goals, game
14 — at Houston, July 3, 1999
16 — at Washington, August 11, 1999 (ot)
at Phoenix, May 31, 2000
at Miami, July 23, 2002
at Cleveland, May 31, 2003

FIELD GOAL ATTEMPTS

Most field-goal attempts per game, season
61.3 — 1997 (1715/28)
59.8 — 1999 (1914/32)
Fewest field-goal attempts per game, season
54.4 — 2002 (1740/32)
56.6 — 2003 (1923/34)
Most field-goal attempts, game
79 — at Utah, August 19, 1997
78 — at Washington, July 5, 1998 (ot)
Fewest field-goal attempts, game
39 — vs. Miami, June 2, 2002

43 — at Charlotte, July 23, 1997

THREE-POINT FIELD-GOAL PERCENTAGE

Highest three-point field-goal percentage, season
.380 — 2001 (160/421)
.370 — 1999 (175/473)
Lowest three-point field-goal percentage, season
.274 — 1997 (93/339)
.327 — 1998 (92/281)

THREE-POINT FIELD GOALS

Most three-point field goals per game, season
5.5 — 1999 (175/32)
5.3 — 2003 (181/34)
Fewest three-point field goals per game, season
3.1 — 1998 (92/30)
3.3 — 1997 (93/28)
Most three-point field goals, game
10 — vs. Los Angeles, June 18, 1999
     vs. Sacramento, June 17, 2003
9 — Many times
Fewest three-point field goals, game
0 — at Phoenix, July 7, 1997
     at Washington, July 5, 1998 (ot)
     at Detroit, July 18, 2001
     vs. Cleveland, August 4, 2001
1 — many times

THREE-POINT FIELD GOAL ATTEMPTS

Most three-point field goal attempts per game, season
14.8 — 1999 (473/32)
14.7 — 2003 (500/34)
Fewest three-point field goal attempts per game, season
9.4 — 1998 (281/30)
12.1 — 1997 (339/28)
Most three-point field goal attempts, game
24 — at Houston, July 3, 1999
23 — at Connecticut, August 12, 2003
Fewest three-point field goal attempts, game
1 — vs. Detroit, July 6, 1998
2 — at Phoenix, July 18, 1998

FREE THROW PERCENTAGE

Highest free-throw percentage, season
.767 — 2003 (412/537)
.757 — 2000 (429/567)
Lowest free-throw percentage, season
.666 — 1997 (404/607)
.672 — 2001 (336/500)
Highest free-throw percentage, game
1.000 — vs. Minnesota, July 11, 1999 (9/9)
         vs. Sacramento, June 17, 2003 (8/8)
         at Seattle, July 23, 2003 (7/7)
         at Phoenix, July 29, 2003 (16/16)

vs. Detroit, August 1, 2003 (3/3)
Lowest free-throw percentage, game
.364 — at Charlotte, August 24, 2003 (4/11) (ot)
.375 — at Utah, July 26, 2001 (3/8)

FREE THROWS MADE

Most free throws made per game, season
15.0 — 1998 (450/30)
14.4 — 1997 (404/28)
Fewest free throws made per game, season
10.5 — 2001 (336/32)
12.1 — 2003 (412/34)
Most free throws made, game
30 — vs. Cleveland, June 10, 2003
28 — vs. Utah, June 3, 2000
Fewest free throws made, game
3 — at Phoenix, August 6, 1999
     vs. Cleveland, August 8, 2000
     at Cleveland, July 19, 2001
     at Utah, July 26, 2001
     at Houston, July 26, 2003
     vs. Detroit, August 1, 2003
4 — Many times

FREE THROW ATTEMPTS

Most free throw attempts per game, season
21.7 — 1997 (607/28)
21.0 — 1998 (629/30)
Fewest free throw attempts per game, season
15.6 — 2001 (500/32)
15.8 — 2003 (537/34)
Most free throw attempts, game
41 — vs. Cleveland, June 10, 2003
35 — vs. Utah, June 3, 2000
Fewest free throw attempts, game
3 — vs. Detroit, August 1, 2003
4 — at Phoenix, August 6, 1999
     vs. Cleveland, August 8, 2000
     at Houston, July 26, 2003

REBOUNDS

Most rebounds per game, season
32.9 — 1997 (920/28)
31.5 — 1998 (944/30)
Fewest rebounds per game, season
27.2 — 2002 (870/32)
28.2 — 2003 (957/34)
Most rebounds, game
43 — vs. Washington, August 13, 1998
41 — at Washington, July 5, 1998 (ot)
     vs. Houston, August 15, 1998
Fewest rebounds, game
14 — at Charlotte, July 30, 1999
17 — at Charlotte, July 23, 1997

OFFENSIVE REBOUNDS

Most offensive rebounds per game, season
11.4 — 1997 (320/28)
10.7 — 1998 (320/30)

Fewest offensive rebounds per game, season
7.969 — 2001 (255/32)
7.971 — 2003 (271/34)
Most offensive rebounds, game
20 — vs. Charlotte, July 26, 1997
19 — at Cleveland, August 21, 1999
vs. Sacramento, June 9, 2000
Fewest offensive rebounds, game
1 — at Charlotte, July 30, 1999
at Detroit, July 18, 2001
vs. Seattle, July 2, 2002
vs. Sacramento, June 17, 2003
2 — Many times

DEFENSIVE REBOUNDS

Most defensive rebounds per game, season
21.4 — 1997 (600/28)
20.8 — 1998 (624/30)
Fewest defensive rebounds per game, season
19.1 — 2002 (610/32)
19.5 — 1999 (625/32)
Most defensive rebounds, game
33 — vs. Charlotte, July 12, 2000
31 — vs. Cleveland, July 15, 1997
vs. Seattle, July 11, 2001
Fewest defensive rebounds, game
11 — at Detroit, August 9, 2000
at Indiana, July 19, 2002
12 — at Houston, June 13, 1998
vs. Cleveland, August 17, 1998
vs. Houston, August 18, 2003

ASSISTS

Most assists per game, season
17.29 — 1997 (484/28)
17.28 — 2001 (553/32)
Fewest assists per game, season
14.9 — 2000 (477/32)
15.5 — 2003 (527/34)
Most assists, game
32 — at Phoenix, June 21, 2001
29 — vs. Connecticut, July 1, 2003
Fewest assists, game
6 — at Houston, July 3, 1999
vs. Sacramento, June 9, 2000
7 — at Washington, August 11, 1999 (ot)
at Miami, June 17, 2001

PERSONAL FOULS

Most personal fouls per game, season
21.9 — 1999 (700/32)
21.0 — 1998 (630/30)
Fewest personal fouls per game, season
17.3 — 2003 (587/34)
19.3 — 2000 (617/32)
Most personal fouls, game
32 — at Los Angeles, July 24, 1999 (ot)
30 — at Washington, June 4, 2000

Fewest personal fouls, game
8 — at Washington, August 21, 2003
10 — vs. Washington, June 13, 2000
vs. Indiana, July 20, 2003

DISQUALIFICATIONS

Most disqualifications per game, season
0.28 — 1999 (9/32)
0.22 — 2000 (7/32)
Fewest disqualifications per game, season
0.10 — 1998 (3/30)
0.14 — 1997 (4/28)
Most disqualifications, game
2 — at Detroit, August 19, 1998
vs. Washington, June 14, 1999
at Orlando, July 29, 1999 (ot)
1 — Many times

STEALS

Most steals per game, season
10.3 — 1997 (289/28)
9.7 — 1998 (291/30)
Fewest steals per game, season
7.69 — 2000 (246/32)
7.71 — 2003 (262/34)
Most steals, game
18 — at Phoenix, July 7, 1997
17 — vs. Phoenix, August 11, 1998 (ot)
vs. Los Angeles, June 24, 2001
Fewest steals, game
2 — vs. Indiana, June 2, 2001
at Cleveland, July 19, 2001
3 — Many times

BLOCKED SHOTS

Most blocked shots per game, season
4.1 — 1997 (116/28)
3.8 — 2003 (128/34)
Fewest blocked shots per game, season
2.6 — 2001 (82/32)
2.8 — 1998 (84/30)
Most blocked shots, game
8 — at Houston, July 4, 1997
vs. Sacramento, July 30, 1997 (ot)
vs. Phoenix, August 2, 1997
at Cleveland, August 21, 1999
at Indiana, June 7, 2003
7 — By many
Fewest blocked shots, game
0 — Many times

TURNOVERS

Most turnovers per game, season
19.1 — 1997 (536/28)
16.7 — 1998 (501/30)
Fewest turnovers per game, season
13.7 — 2001 (437/32)
13.8 — 2003 (470/34)

Most turnovers, game
30 — vs. Phoenix, August 11, 1998 (ot)
Regulation game:
26 — vs. Washington, August 13, 1998
at Phoenix, May 31, 2000
Fewest turnovers, game
6 — at Los Angeles, June 19, 1998
7 — vs. Washington, June 16, 2001

TEAM DEFENSE

POINTS

Fewest points allowed per game, season
63.0 — 2002 (2015/32)
63.6 — 2000 (2035/32)
Most points allowed per game, season
66.4 — 2003 (2256/34)
65.9 — 1997 (1844/28)
Fewest points allowed, game
44 — vs. Cleveland, August 8, 2000
45 — vs. Washington, August 13, 1998
vs. Portland, July 5, 2000
Fewest points allowed, first half
17 — at Sacramento, June 18, 1998
18 — at Miami, June 17, 2001
vs. Cleveland, July 22, 2002
Fewest points allowed, second half
18 — at Charlotte, August 24, 2003
21 — vs. Washington, August 13, 1998
vs. Portland, July 5, 2000
vs. Miami, June 2, 2002
Fewest points allowed, overtime period
3 — vs. Cleveland, August 24, 1997
4 — at Houston, June 26, 1997
vs. Sacramento, July 30, 1997

FIELD GOAL PERCENTAGE

Lowest opponents' field-goal percentage, season
.391 — 1997 (661/1690)
.399 — 2002 (691/1733)
Highest opponents' field-goal percentage, season
.423 — 2001 (744/1759)
.419 — 2003 (821/1959)
Lowest opponents' field goal percentage, game
.241 — at Cleveland, July 8, 1999 (14/58)
.245 — vs. Portland, July 5, 2000 (12/49)

TURNOVERS

Most opponents' turnovers per game, season
20.4 — 1997 (570/28)
17.9 — 1998 (538/30)
Fewest opponents' turnovers per game, season
14.1 — 2003 (480/34)
14.9 — 2002 (478/32)
Most opponents' turnovers, game
33 — vs. Utah, July 17, 1997
30 — vs. Cleveland, June 10, 1999

TEAM MISCELLANEOUS

GAME WON AND LOST

Highest winning percentage, season
.656 — 2001 (21-11)
.625 — 2000 (20-12)
Lowest winning percentage, season
.471 — 2003 (16-18)
.563 — 1999 (18-14)
2002 (18-14)
Most consecutive games won
7 — June 21-July 5, 1997
June 10-24, 2001
6 — Many times
Most consecutive games won, one season
7 — June 21-July 5, 1997
June 10-24, 2001
6 — Many times
Most consecutive game lost
5 — July 23-August 1, 2003
4 — August 17-23, 1997
July 8-16, 1998
July 19-26, 2001
Most consecutive game lost, one season
5 — July 23-August 1, 2003
4 — August 17-23, 1997
July 8-16, 1998
July 19-26, 2001
Highest winning percentage, home games,
season
.813 — 2001 (13-3)
.800 — 1998 (12-3)
Lowest winning percentage, home games, season
.625 — 2002 (10-6)
.647 — 2003 (11-6)
Most consecutive home games won
11 — June 28, 2000-June 2, 2001
8 — June 12-July 13, 2001
Most consecutive home games lost
3 — August 6-11, 2002
2 — Many times
Highest winning percentage, road games, season
.500 — 1997 (7-7)
2000 (8-8)
2001 (8-8)
2002 (8-8)
Lowest winning percentage, road games, season
.294 — 2003 (5-12)
.375 — 1999 (6-10)
Most consecutive road games won
5 — June 21-July 5, 1997
4 — July 18-August 1, 1998
June 10-21, 2001
Most consecutive road games lost
9 — June 7-August 7, 2003
8 — August 10, 1997-June 15, 1998

OVERTIME GAMES

Most overtime games, season
5 — 1999
3 — 1997

Most consecutive overtime games, season
3 — July 24-29, 1999

Most overtime games won, season
3 — 1997
2 — 1998
1999

Most overtime games won, no losses, season
3 — 1997
2 — 1998

Most consecutive overtime games won
6 — June 26, 1997-July 18, 1999

Most overtime games lost, season
3 — 1999
2 — 2003

Most overtime games lost, no wins, season
2 — 2003
1 — 2000, 2002

Most consecutive overtime games lost
5 — August 11, 1999-August 24, 2003
(current)
2 — July 24-26, 1999

Most overtime periods, game
2 — at Sacramento, June 13, 2002

INDIVIDUAL RECORDS

SEASONS

Most Seasons
7 — Vickie Johnson
Teresa Weatherspoon
6 — Sue Wicks
5 — Many tied

GAMES

Most games, career
220 — Teresa Weatherspoon
214 — Vickie Johnson
182 — Sue Wicks

Most consecutive games, career
220 — Teresa Weatherspoon, June 21, 1997
August 24, 2003 (current)
149 — Sue Wicks, June 21, 1997-
August 1, 2001
124 — Tamika Whitmore, July 17, 1999
June 22, 2003

Most games, season
34 — Teresa Weatherspoon, 2003
33 — By many

MINUTES

Most minutes, career
6,842 — Teresa Weatherspoon
6,808 — Vickie Johnson
4,749 — Crystal Robinson

Highest average, minutes per game, career
(Minimum 90 games)
31.81 — Vickie Johnson (6808/214)
31.79 — Tari Phillips (4069/128)
31.1 — Teresa Weatherspoon (6842/220)

Most minutes, season
1,086 — Teresa Weatherspoon, 1999
1,082 — Vickie Johnson, 1999
1,078 — Teresa Weatherspoon, 2000
Crystal Robinson, 2003

Highest average, minutes per game, season
33.9 — Teresa Weatherspoon,
1999 (1086/32)
33.8 — Vickie Johnson, 1999 (1082/32)
33.7 — Teresa Weatherspoon,
2000 (1078/32)

Most minutes, game
46 — Becky Hammon, at Sacramento,
June 13, 2002 (2 ot)
45 — Teresa Weatherspoon,
at Washington, July 5, 1998 (ot)
Crystal Robinson, at Sacramento,
June 13, 2002 (2 ot)

SCORING

Most points, lifetime
2,572 — Vickie Johnson
1,739 — Tari Phillips
1,728 — Crystal Robinson

Highest average, points per game, career
(Minimum 90 games)
13.6 — Tari Phillips (1739/128)
12.1 — Sophia Witherspoon (1091/90)
12.0 — Vickie Johnson (2572/214)

Most points, season
489 — Tari Phillips, 2001
451 — Tari Phillips, 2002
430 — Vickie Johnson, 2003

Highest average, points per game, season
15.3 — Tari Phillips, 2001 (489/32)
14.5 — Sophia Witherspoon, 1997 (407/28)
14.1 — Tari Phillips, 2002 (451/32)

Most points, game
33 — Becky Hammon, at Minnesota,
June 6, 2003
30 — Tari Phillips, vs. Indiana,
June 30, 2000
28 — Tamika Whitmore, vs. Phoenix,
July 8, 2002
Becky Hammon, vs. Cleveland,
June 10, 2003

Most games, 30 or more points, career
1 — Becky Hammon
Tari Phillips

Most games, 20 or more points, career
20 — Tari Phillips
19 — Vickie Johnson

14 — Sophia Witherspoon

Most consecutive games, 20 or more points
   3 — Sophia Witherspoon, July 26-
      August 2, 1997
      Vickie Johnson, July 1-5, 1999
      Tari Phillips, June 28-July 1, 2000
      Tari Phillips, July 6-9, 2001

Most consecutive games, 10 or more points
  23 — Tari Phillips, June 30-May 30, 2002
  19 — Vickie Johnson, July 6-
      August 18, 2003
  15 — Sophia Witherspoon, July 9-
      August 15, 1997

FIELD GOAL PERCENTAGE

Highest field goal percentage, career
(Minimum 350 field goals)
  .468 — Becky Hammon (373/797)
  .467 — Tari Phillips (703/1505)
  .448 — Tamika Whitmore (543/1211)
Highest field goal percentage, season (qualifiers)
  .507 — Tari Phillips, 2001 (208/410)
  .491 — Tari Phillips, 2002 (183/373)
  .484 — Rebecca Lobo, 1998 (136/281)
Highest field goal percentage, game
(Minimum 8 field goals made)
  1.000 — Becky Hammon, at Phoenix,
      June 21, 2001 (8/8)
      Crystal Robinson, at Cleveland,
      August 17, 2003 (8/8)
  .857 — Tari Phillips, vs. Charlotte,
      June 12, 2001 (12/14)
  .846 — Tamika Whitmore, vs. Phoenix,
      July 8, 2002 (11/13)
Most field goals, none missed, game
  8 — Becky Hammon, at Phoenix,
      June 21, 2001
      Crystal Robinson, at Cleveland,
      August 17, 2003
  6 — Tamika Whitmore, vs. Los Angeles,
      June 24, 2001
      Tamika Whitmore, vs. Seattle,
      July 2, 2002
      Tamika Whitmore, vs. Houston,
      August 18, 2003
Most field goal attempts, none made, game
  11 — Elena Baranova, vs. Detroit,
      August 1, 2003
  9 — Vickie Johnson, vs. Charlotte,
      July 12, 1998
  8 — Vickie Johnson, at Houston,
      May 29, 2000

FIELD GOALS

Most field goals, career
  994 — Vickie Johnson
  703 — Tari Phillips
  603 — Crystal Robinson

Most field goals, season
  208 — Tari Phillips, 2001
  183 — Tari Phillips, 2002
  170 — Tari Phillips, 2000
Most field goals, game
  13 — Tari Phillips, vs. Indiana,
      June 30, 2000
  12 — Sophia Witherspoon, at Los Angeles,
      August 20, 1997
      Vickie Johnson, vs. Cleveland,
      June 23, 1998
      Tari Phillips, vs. Charlotte,
      June 12, 2001
      Becky Hammon, at Minnesota,
      June 6, 2003
  11 — By many

FIELD GOAL ATTEMPTS

Most field goal attempts, career
  2,290 — Vickie Johnson
  1,505 — Tari Phillips
  1,381 — Crystal Robinson
Most field goal attempts, season
  410 — Tari Phillips, 2001
  394 — Vickie Johnson, 1999
  373 — Tari Phillips, 2002
Most field goal attempts, game
  21 — Tari Phillips, vs. Detroit,
      June 27, 2003
  20 — By many

THREE-POINT FIELD-GOAL PERCENTAGE

Highest three-point field goal percentage, career
(Minimum 90 three-point field goals)
  .392 — Crystal Robinson (311/793)
  .380 — Becky Hammon (172/453)
  .368 — Vickie Johnson (174/473)
Highest three-point field goal percentage, season
(qualifiers)
  .469 — Becky Hammon, 2003 (23/49)
  .437 — Crystal Robinson, 1999 (76/174)
  .421 — Vickie Johnson, 2002 (32/76)
Most three-point field goals, none missed, game
  5 — Crystal Robinson, vs. Phoenix,
      July 1, 1999
      Becky Hammon, at Phoenix,
      June 21, 2001
  3 — By many
Most three-point field goal attempts, none made,
game
  8 — Crystal Robinson, vs. Detroit,
      June 21, 2000
Crystal Robinson, vs. Cleveland, August 4, 2001
  7 — Sophia Witherspoon, at Utah,
      August 19, 1997
      Becky Hammon, vs. Cleveland,
      July 29, 2000

6 — By many

THREE-POINT FIELD GOALS

Most three-point field goals, career
311 — Crystal Robinson
174 — Vickie Johnson
172 — Becky Hammon
Most three-point field goals, season
76 — Crystal Robinson, 1999
70 — Crystal Robinson, 2001
67 — Crystal Robinson, 2002
Most three-point field goals, game
7 — Crystal Robinson, at Los Angeles,
July 24, 1999 (ot)
6 — Sophia Witherspoon,
at Detroit, August 19, 1998
Crystal Robinson, vs. Charlotte,
July 26, 1999 (ot)
Crystal Robinson, at Phoenix,
August 6, 1999
Crystal Robinson, vs. Indiana,
June 25, 2002
Becky Hammon, at Minnesota,
June 6, 2003
Most consecutive games, three-point field goals
made
18 — Crystal Robinson, June 18-
July 30, 1999
15 — Crystal Robinson, July 26-
August 4, 2003 (current)
13 — Sophia Witherspoon, July 9-
August 10, 1997

THREE-POINT FIELD GOAL ATTEMPTS

Most three-point field goal attempts, career
793 — Crystal Robinson
473 — Vickie Johnson
453 — Becky Hammon
Most three-point field goal attempts, season
181 — Crystal Robinson, 2002
174 — Crystal Robinson, 1999
168 — Crystal Robinson, 2001
Crystal Robinson, 2003
Most three-point field goal attempts, game
14 — Crystal Robinson, at Los Angeles,
July 24, 1999 (ot)
12 — Crystal Robinson, vs. Charlotte,
July 26, 1999 (ot)
11 — Crystal Robinson, vs. Portland,
June 30, 2002

FREE THROW PERCENTAGE

Highest free-throw percentage, career
(Minimum 175 free throws)
.851 — Crystal Robinson (211/248)
.825 — Becky Hammon (193/234)

.817 — Vickie Johnson (410/502)

Highest free-throw percentage, season (qualifiers)
.951 — Becky Hammon, 2003 (39/41)
.884 — Becky Hammon, 2000 (61/69)
.882 — Vickie Johnson, 2000 (67/76)
Most free throws made, none missed, game
8 — Teresa Weatherspoon, vs.
Sacramento, August 15, 1997
7 — Vickie Johnson, vs. Los Angeles,
June 18, 1999
Becky Hammon, at Indiana,
June 10, 2000
Becky Hammon, at Cleveland,
May 31, 2003
Becky Hammon, vs. Washington,
June 1, 2003
6 — by many
Most free throw attempts, none made, game
4 — Kym Hampton, vs. Charlotte,
July 26, 1997
3 — Sophia Witherspoon, vs. Los Angeles,
August 5, 1997
Kym Hampton, at Sacramento,
July 22, 1999
Vickie Johnson, at Los Angeles,
July 24, 1999 (ot)
Tari Phillips, vs. Miami, July 8, 2000

FREE THROWS MADE

Most free throws made, career
410 — Vickie Johnson
330 — Tari Phillips
310 — Teresa Weatherspoon
Most free throws made, season
110 — Tamika Whitmore, 2002
92 — Sophia Witherspoon, 1998
87 — Tari Phillips, 2003
Most free throws made, game
11 — Becky Hammon, vs. Utah,
June 3, 2000
10 — Sophia Witherspoon, at Phoenix,
July 18, 1998
Tamika Whitmore, vs. Washington,
August 17, 1999
9 — Crystal Robinson, at Washington,
August 11, 1999 (ot)
Tamika Whitmore, at Indiana,
July 19, 2002

FREE THROW ATTEMPTS

Most free throw attempts, career
515 — Tari Phillips
502 — Vickie Johnson
471 — Teresa Weatherspoon
Most free throw attempts, season
150 — Tamika Whitmore, 2002
134 — Tari Phillips, 2003

130 — Tari Phillips, 2000
Most free throw attempts, game
    12 — Kym Hampton, at Los Angeles,
        June 19, 1998
        Sophia Witherspoon, at Phoenix,
        July 18, 1998
        Crystal Robinson, at Washington,
        August 11, 1999 (ot)
        Becky Hammon, vs. Utah,
        June 3, 2000
        Tari Phillips, vs. Sacramento,
        June 9, 2000
        Tari Phillips, vs. Phoenix,
        June 25, 2003
    11 — By many

REBOUNDS

Most rebounds, career
    1,007 — Tari Phillips
    814 — Vickie Johnson
    788 — Sue Wicks
Highest average, rebounds per game, career
(Minimum 90 games)
    7.9 — Tari Phillips (1007/128)
    5.8 — Kym Hampton (523/90)
    4.3 — Sue Wicks (788/182)
Most rebounds, season
    280 — Tari Phillips, 2003
    257 — Tari Phillips, 2001
    247 — Tari Phillips, 2000
Highest average, rebounds per game, season
(qualifiers)
    8.5 — Tari Phillips, 2003 (280/33)
    8.03 — Tari Phillips, 2001 (257/32)
    7.96 — Tari Phillips, 2000 (247/31)
Most rebounds, game
    16 — Sue Wicks, at Washington,
        August 11, 1999 (ot)
        Tari Phillips, at Houston,
        July 26, 2003
    14 — Tari Phillips, vs. Indiana, July 9, 2001
        Tari Phillips, at Portland, July 24, 2001
    13 — By many
Most games, 10+ rebounds, career
    41 — Tari Phillips
    11 — Rebecca Lobo
    9 — Sue Wicks
Most consecutive games, 10+ rebounds
    4 — Tari Phillips, July 6-20, 2003
    3 — Tari Phillips, June 25-30, 2000
Tari Phillips, June 22-27, 2003
    2 — Many times

OFFENSIVE REBOUNDS

Most offensive rebounds, career
    343 — Tari Phillips
    268 — Vickie Johnson

    267 — Sue Wicks
Highest average, offensive rebounds per game,
career (Minimum 90 games)
    2.7 — Tari Phillips (343/128)
    1.8 — Kym Hampton (166/90)
    1.5 — Sue Wicks (267/182)
Most offensive rebounds, season
    99 — Tari Phillips, 2003
    89 — Tari Phillips, 2001
    86 — Tari Phillips, 2000
Most offensive rebounds, game
    9 — Tari Phillips, vs. Phoenix,
        June 25, 2003
    8 — Rebecca Lobo, vs. Charlotte,
        July 26, 1997
        Tari Phillips, at Portland,
        July 24, 2001
        Tari Phillips, at Charlotte,
        August 24, 2003 (ot)
    7 — Tari Phillips, at Charlotte,
        July 3, 2001
        Tari Phillips, vs. Washington,
        July 15, 2003

DEFENSIVE REBOUNDS

Most defensive rebounds, career
    664 — Tari Phillips
    596 — Teresa Weatherspoon
    546 — Vickie Johnson
Highest average, defensive rebounds per game,
career (Minimum 90 games)
    5.2 — Tari Phillips (664/128)
    4.0 — Kym Hampton (357/90)
    2.9 — Sue Wicks (521/182)
Most defensive rebounds, season
    181 — Tari Phillips, 2003
    168 — Tari Phillips, 2001
    161 — Tari Phillips, 2000
Most defensive rebounds, game
    12 — Sue Wicks, at Washington,
        August 11, 1999 (ot)
        Tari Phillips, vs. Orlando,
        June 30, 2001
        Tari Phillips, at Houston,
        July 26, 2003
    11 — Rebecca Lobo, vs. Charlotte,
        July 10, 1997
        Kym Hampton, at Charlotte,
        July 15, 1998
        Tamika Whitmore, vs. Washington,
        June 1, 2003
        Tari Phillips, vs. San Antonio,
        August 5, 2003

ASSISTS

Most assists, career
    1,307 — Teresa Weatherspoon
    571 — Vickie Johnson

324 — Crystal Robinson
Highest average, assists per game, career
(Minimum 90 games)
   5.9 — Teresa Weatherspoon (1306/220)
   2.7 — Vickie Johnson (571/214)
   2.1 — Crystal Robinson (324/156)
Most assists, season
   205 — Teresa Weatherspoon, 1999
          Teresa Weatherspoon, 2000
   203 — Teresa Weatherspoon, 2001
   191 — Teresa Weatherspoon, 1998
Highest average, assists per game, season
(qualifiers)
   6.41 — Teresa Weatherspoon, 1999 (205/32)
           Teresa Weatherspoon, 2000 (205/32)
   6.37 — Teresa Weatherspoon, 1998 (191/30)
   6.3 — Teresa Weatherspoon, 2001 (203/32)
Most assists, game
   13 — Teresa Weatherspoon,
      at Los Angeles, July 21, 1998
      Teresa Weatherspoon,
      at Houston, May 29, 2000
   12 — Teresa Weatherspoon,
      at Los Angeles, August 20, 1997
      Teresa Weatherspoon,
      at Los Angeles, July 24, 1999 (ot)
      Teresa Weatherspoon, vs. Indiana,
      June 30, 2000
      Teresa Weatherspoon,
      at Sacramento, June 13, 2002 (2 ot)
   11 — By many
Most games, 10+ assists, career
   18 — Teresa Weatherspoon

PERSONAL FOULS

Most personal fouls, career
   564 — Teresa Weatherspoon
   465 — Sue Wicks
   452 — Tamika Williams
Most personal fouls, season
   123 — Sue Wicks, 1999
   118 — Tari Phillips, 2003
   113 — Tari Phillips, 2002
Most personal fouls, game
   6 — by many

DISQUALIFICATIONS

Most disqualifications, career
   10 — Tari Phillips
   8 — Sue Wicks
   4 — Tamika Whitmore
      Teresa Weatherspoon
Highest percentage, games disqualified, career
(Minimum 90 games)
   7.8 — Tari Phillips (10/128)
   4.4 — Sue Wicks (8/182)
   3.3 — Kym Hampton (3/90)
Lowest percentage, games disqualified, career
(Minimum 90 games)

0.00 — Becky Hammon (0/137)
       Sophia Witherspoon (0/90)
   0.9 — Vickie Johnson (2/214)
   1.3 — Crystal Robinson (2/156)
Most consecutive games without disqualification,
career
   137 — Becky Hammon, June 10, 1999-
      June 27, 2003 (current)
   92 — Vickie Johnson, July 16, 1998-
      July 3, 2001
   90 — Sophia Witherspoon, June 21, 1997-
      August 21, 1999
Most disqualifications, season
   5 — Sue Wicks, 1999
      Tari Phillips, 2000
   3 — Tari Phillips, 2003
   2 — Sue Wicks, 2001
      Tari Phillips, 2002
      Teresa Weatherspoon, 2002
Fewest minutes, disqualified, game
   9 — Sue Wicks, vs. Sacramento,
      June 4, 2001
   11 — Lindsey Yamasaki, at Cleveland,
      May 31, 2003
   12 — Andrea Nagy, vs. Indiana,
      June 2, 2001

STEALS

Most steals, career
   453 — Teresa Weatherspoon
   221 — Tari Phillips
   207 — Vickie Johnson
Highest average, steals per game, career
(Minimum 90 games)
   2.06 — Teresa Weatherspoon (453/220)
   1.73 — Tari Phillips (221/128)
   1.36 — Sophia Witherspoon (122/90)
Most steals, season
   100 — Teresa Weatherspoon, 1998
   85 — Teresa Weatherspoon, 1997
   78 — Teresa Weatherspoon, 1999
Highest average, steals per game, season
(qualifiers)
   3.33 — Teresa Weatherspoon, 1998 (100/30)
   3.04 — Teresa Weatherspoon, 1997 (85/28)
   2.44 — Teresa Weatherspoon, 1999 (78/32)
Most steals, game
   8 — Teresa Weatherspoon, vs. Charlotte,
      July 10, 1997
   7 — Teresa Weatherspoon, at Sacramento,
      July 24, 1998
      Teresa Weatherspoon, vs. Phoenix,
      August 11, 1998 (ot)
   6 — By many

BLOCKED SHOTS

Most blocked shots, career
   155 — Sue Wicks
   98 — Tamika Whitmore

84 — Rebecca Lobo

Highest average, blocked shots per game, career
(Minimum: 90 games)
- 0.85 — Sue Wicks (155/182)
- 0.628 — Tamika Whitmore (98/156)
- 0.625 — Tari Phillips (80/128)

Most blocked shots, season
- 51 — Rebecca Lobo, 1997
- 43 — Sue Wicks, 1999
  - Tamika Whitmore, 2002
  - Elena Baranova, 2003
- 39 — Sue Wicks, 2000

Highest average, blocked shots per game, season
(qualifiers)
- 1.82 — Rebecca Lobo, 1997 (51/28)
- 1.34 — Sue Wicks, 1999 (43/32)
  - Tamika Whitmore, 2002 (43/32)
- 1.30 — Elena Baranova, 2003 (43/33)

Most blocked shots, game
- 5 — Rebecca Lobo, at Utah,
  August 19, 1997
  - Sue Wicks, vs. Sacramento,
  July 5, 1999
  - Tamika Whitmore, vs.
  Washington, August 8, 2002
- 4 — Kym Hampton, vs. Sacramento,
  July 30, 1997 (ot)
  - Rebecca Lobo, vs. Phoenix,
  August 2, 1997
  - Sue Wicks, vs. Orlando, August 1, 1999
  - Sue Wicks, vs. Indiana, July 9, 2001

TURNOVERS

Most turnovers, career
- 577 — Teresa Weatherspoon
- 369 — Vickie Johnson
- 354 — Tari Phillips

Most turnovers, season
- 96 — Teresa Weatherspoon, 1998
- 94 — Teresa Weatherspoon, 1997
- 93 — Tari Phillips, 2002

Most turnovers, game
- 8 — Teresa Weatherspoon, at Utah,
  July 5, 1997
  - Rebecca Lobo, at Sacramento,
  August 10, 1997
  - Teresa Weatherspoon, at Phoenix,
  August 12, 1997
- 7 — by many

PHOENIX MERCURY

TEAM OFFENSE

SCORING

Highest average, points per game, season
73.9 — 1998 (2217/30)
70.1 — 2000 (2243/32)
Lowest average, points per game, season
61.7 — 2003 (2097/34)
64.5 — 2001 (2064/32)
Most points, game
96 — vs. Utah, June 26, 1998
90 — at Charlotte, June 22, 2000
Fewest points, game
46 — at Houston, August 10, 2003
47 — at Minnesota, July 3, 1999
at Sacramento, July 29, 2001
Largest margin of victory, game
33 — vs. Utah, June 26, 1998 (96-63)
vs. Minnesota, July 29, 1999 (79-46)
vs. Seattle, June 7, 2000 (82-49)
at Charlotte, June 22, 2000 (90-57)
32 — vs. Utah, August 6, 1997 (78-46)
Largest margin of defeat, game
41 — at Seattle, July 19, 2002 (48-89)
29 — at Seattle, July 25, 2003 (53-82)

BY HALF

Most points, first half
52 — vs. Utah, June 26, 1998
50 — at Sacramento, June 12, 1999
Fewest points, first half
14 — at Sacramento, July 29, 2001
15 — at Cleveland, July 31, 1997
Largest lead at halftime
28 — vs. Washington, August 4, 1998 (48-20)
22 — at Miami, June 24, 2000 (39-17)
Largest deficit at halftime overcome to win game
14 — vs. Utah, August 17, 1997
(trailed 21-35; won 71-63 in OT)
12 — at Detroit, July 8, 1998
(trailed 32-44; won 78-76)
at Washington, June 22, 1999
(trailed 32-44; won 79-76)
Most points, second half
57 — vs. Sacramento, July 20, 1998
52 — at Cleveland, July 31, 1997
vs. Los Angeles, July 17, 1999
Fewest points, second half
18 — at San Antonio, June 5, 2003
19 — at Miami, August 3, 2001
vs. Charlotte, June 12, 2003
vs. Los Angeles, June 21, 2003

OVERTIME

Most points, overtime period
11 — vs. Utah, August 17, 1997
10 — at New York, August 11, 1998
at Indiana, July 1, 2001
Fewest points, overtime period
4 — vs. Los Angeles, July 25, 1997
5 — at Washington, August 3, 2003
Largest margin of victory, overtime period
8 — vs. Utah, August 17, 1997 (71-63)
5 — vs. Los Angeles,
August 24, 1997 (73-68)

FIELD GOAL PERCENTAGE

Highest field-goal percentage, season
.446 — 2000 (803/1800)
.424 — 1998 (787/1856)
Lowest field-goal percentage, season
.373 — 1997 (660/1768)
.382 — 2003 (801/2095)
Highest field-goal percentage, game
.636 — vs. Seattle, August 3, 2000 (28/44)
.569 — vs. Orlando, August 1, 2000 (29/51)
Lowest field-goal percentage, game
.255 — at Sacramento, July 29, 2001 (14/55)
.270 — at Seattle, July 25, 2003 (20/74)

FIELD GOALS

Most field goals per game, season
26.2 — 1998 (787/30)
25.1 — 2000 (803/32)
Fewest field goals per game, season
23.56 — 2003 (801/34)
23.57 — 1997 (660/28)
Most field goals, game
34 — vs. Utah, June 26, 1998
33 — at Houston, June 3, 2000
at Charlotte, June 22, 2000
at Los Angeles, July 15, 2003 (2 ot)
Fewest field goals, game
14 — at Sacramento, July 29, 2001
16 — at Charlotte, August 9, 1997

FIELD GOAL ATTEMPTS

Most field-goal attempts per game, season
63.1 — 1997 (1768/28)
61.9 — 1998 (1856/30)
Fewest field-goal attempts per game, season
56.3 — 2000 (1800/32)
59.0 — 2002 (1889/32)
Most field-goal attempts, game
93 — at Los Angeles, July 15, 2003 (2 ot)
81 — vs. Utah, August 17, 1997 (ot)
Regulation Game:
79 — at Orlando, June 21, 1999

Fewest field-goal attempts, game
    44 — at Sacramento, August 20, 1997
        vs. Minnesota, August 9, 1999
        vs. Seattle, August 3, 2000
    45 — at Miami, August 3, 2001
        vs. Los Angeles, August 8, 2003

THREE-POINT FIELD-GOAL PERCENTAGE

Highest three-point field-goal percentage, season
    .332 — 2003 (116/349)
    .323 — 2001 (101/313)
Lowest three-point field-goal percentage, season
    .294 — 1999 (134/456)
    .305 — 2002 (100/328)

THREE-POINT FIELD GOALS

Most three-point field goals per game, season
    4.8 — 1997 (134/28)
    4.3 — 1998 (130/30)
Fewest three-point field goals per game, season
    3.1 — 2002 (100/32)
    3.2 — 2001 (101/32)
Most three-point field goals, game
    10 — at Orlando, June 21, 1999
    9 — at Cleveland, July 2, 1998
        at Washington, June 22, 1999
Fewest three-point field goals, game
    0 — Many times. Most recent:
        at Houston, August 10, 2003

THREE-POINT FIELD GOAL ATTEMPTS

Most three-point field goal attempts per game, season
    15.6 — 1997 (436/28)
    14.3 — 1999 (456/32)
Fewest three-point field goal attempts per game, season
    9.8 — 2001 (313/32)
    10.3 — 2002 (328/32)
Most three-point field goal attempts, game
    29 — at Orlando, June 21, 1999
    23 — at Los Angeles, July 21, 1999
        at New York, June 28, 2000
Fewest three-point field goal attempts, game
    3 — at Seattle, July 28, 2000
    4 — vs. Minnesota, June 23, 2002
        at Detroit, June 28, 2003

FREE THROW PERCENTAGE

Highest free-throw percentage, season
    .776 — 2000 (513/661)
    .763 — 1997 (484/634)
Lowest free-throw percentage, season
    .682 — 2003 (379/556)
    .724 — 1998 (513/709)
Highest free-throw percentage, game
  1.000 — at Washington, July 9, 2002 (2/2)

        at Sacramento, August 23, 2003 (5/5)
    .952 — at Minnesota, June 2, 2001 (20/21)
Lowest free-throw percentage, game
    .167 — vs. Houston, August 14, 2001 (1/6)
    .480 — vs. Los Angeles, July 7, 1999 (12/25)

FREE THROWS MADE

Most free throws made per game, season
    17.3 — 1997 (484/28)
    17.1 — 1998 (513/30)
Fewest free throws made per game, season
    11.2 — 2003 (379/34)
    12.7 — 2002 (405/32)
Most free throws made, game
    35 — vs. Sacramento, August 4, 1997
    34 — vs. Los Angeles, July 17, 1999
Fewest free throws made, game
    1 — vs. Houston, August 14, 2001
    2 — at Washington, July 9, 2002

FREE THROW ATTEMPTS

Most free throw attempts per game, season
    23.6 — 1998 (709/30)
    22.6 — 1997 (634/28)
Fewest free throw attempts per game, season
    16.4 — 2003 (556/34)
    16.8 — 2002 (538/32)
Most free throw attempts, game
    47 — vs. San Antonio, August 22, 2003
    45 — vs. Sacramento, August 4, 1997
Fewest free throw attempts, game
    2 — at Washington, July 9, 2002
    4 — vs. Sacramento, August 17, 1999

REBOUNDS

Most rebounds per game, season
    32.9 — 1997 (921/28)
    31.4 — 1998 (941/30)
Fewest rebounds per game, season
    27.9 — 2000 (894/32)
    28.7 — 2002 (918/32)
Most rebounds, game
    48 — at Portland, June 4, 2001 (ot)
    47 — vs. New York, July 7, 1997
        at Los Angeles, July 15, 2003 (2 ot)
Fewest rebounds, game
    18 — at Minnesota, June 27, 2003
    19 — at Utah, June 6, 2000
        at Portland, June 13, 2000
        vs. Sacramento, July 27, 2002

OFFENSIVE REBOUNDS

Most offensive rebounds per game, season
    11.5 — 1997 (322/28)
    10.9 — 1998 (327/30)
Fewest offensive rebounds per game, season
    8.6 — 2000 (275/32)
    9.1 — 2002 (292/32)
Most offensive rebounds, game
    22 — at Cleveland, July 31, 1997

21 — at New York, June 29, 1997
Fewest offensive rebounds, game
    4 — Many times. Most recent:
        vs. Cleveland, August 7, 2002

DEFENSIVE REBOUNDS

Most defensive rebounds per game, season
    21.4 — 1997 (599/28)
    20.6 — 1999 (659/32)
Fewest defensive rebounds per game, season
    18.9 — 2003 (643/34)
    19.3 — 2000 (619/32)
Most defensive rebounds, game
    33 — vs. Charlotte, June 22, 1997
        vs. New York, July 7, 1997
    32 — at Portland, June 4, 2001 (ot)
        at Los Angeles, July 15, 2003 (2 ot)
Fewest defensive rebounds, game
    10 — at Minnesota, August 4, 2003
    11 — at Utah, June 6, 2000
        vs. Detroit, July 26, 2001
        at Minnesota, June 27, 2003
        vs. Connecticut, July 19, 2003

ASSISTS

Most assists per game, season
    18.1 — 1998 (543/30)
    16.1 — 2001 (514/32)
Fewest assists per game, season
    13.3 — 2002 (427/32)
    13.6 — 2003 (461/34)
Most assists, game
    27 — vs. Utah, June 26, 1998
    25 — at Utah, July 3, 1997
        vs. Minnesota, July 29, 1999
Fewest assists, game
    5 — at Seattle, July 25, 2003
    7 — vs. Los Angeles, August 13, 2002

PERSONAL FOULS

Most personal fouls per game, season
    20.38 — 1999 (652/32)
    20.36 — 1997 (570/28)
Fewest personal fouls per game, season
    19.47 — 2002 (623/32)
    19.53 — 2003 (664/34)
Most personal fouls, game
    35 — at Sacramento, June 12, 1999
    32 — at Indiana, July 1, 2001 (ot)
Fewest personal fouls, game
    9 — vs. Sacramento, July 20, 1998
        at Minnesota, June 20, 2000
        at Los Angeles, July 5, 2001
    10 — vs. Minnesota, July 29, 1999

DISQUALIFICATIONS

Most disqualifications per game, season
    0.25 — 1999 (8/32)
    0.24 — 2003 (8/34)
Fewest disqualifications per game, season

0.03 — 2002 (1/32)
0.10 — 1998 (3/30)
Most disqualifications, game
    3 — at Sacramento, June 12, 1999
    2 — at Seattle, July 25, 2003

STEALS

Most steals per game, season
    12.3 — 1997 (343/28)
    9.6 — 1998 (288/30)
Fewest steals per game, season
    7.2 — 1999 (229/32)
    8.3 — 2002 (267/32)
Most steals, game
    20 — vs. Utah, August 17, 1997 (ot)
    18 — at Cleveland, July 31, 1997
        at Minnesota, June 27, 2003
Fewest steals, game
    2 — vs. Minnesota, August 9, 1999
    3 — at Houston, July 28, 1998
        at Sacramento, June 12, 1999
        at Orlando, June 21, 1999
        at Indiana, July 8, 2000
        vs. New York, June 21, 2001

BLOCKED SHOTS

Most blocked shots per game, season
    4.3 — 2001 (138/32)
    3.8 — 1999 (121/32)
Fewest blocked shots per game, season
    2.84 — 2000 (91/32)
    2.86 — 1997 (80/28)
Most blocked shots, game
    9 — at Sacramento, June 12, 1999
        at Indiana, July 1, 2001 (ot)
    8 — vs. Los Angeles, July 11, 2001
        vs. Portland, July 19, 2001
        at Utah, August 10, 2001
        vs. Detroit, June 13, 2002
Fewest blocked shots, game
    0 — Many times. Most recent:
        at Seattle, June 7, 2003

TURNOVERS

Most turnovers per game, season
    17.0 — 1997 (475/28)
    16.2 — 2001 (519/32)
Fewest turnovers per game, season
    13.4 — 2000 (429/32)
    14.1 — 2003 (479/34)
Most turnovers, game
    24 — at Cleveland, July 31, 1997
        at Houston, August 6, 1998
        at Miami, August 3, 2001
    23 — many times
Fewest turnovers, game
    6 — vs. Los Angeles, August 5, 2000
    7 — at Los Angeles, July 21, 1999

TEAM DEFENSE

POINTS

Fewest points allowed per game, season
65.2 — 1997 (1826/28)
65.7 — 2000 (2102/32)
Most points allowed per game, season
71.6 — 2002 (2291/32)
68.2 — 1999 (2182/32)
Fewest points allowed, game
38 — vs. Houston, August 14, 2001
44 — at Miami, June 24, 2000
Fewest points allowed, first half
15 — vs. Charlotte, August 15, 1999
16 — vs. Minnesota, July 29, 1999
Fewest points allowed, second half
14 — vs. Seattle, August 15, 2003
17 — vs. Seattle, June 7, 2000
Fewest points allowed, overtime period
3 — vs. Utah, August 17, 1997
4 — vs. Los Angeles, August 24, 1997
   at Washington, August 3, 2003

FIELD GOAL PERCENTAGE

Lowest opponents' field-goal percentage, season
.413 — 1997 (670/1622)
.415 — 2001 (785/1892)
Highest opponents' field-goal percentage, season
.455 — 2002 (850/1870)
.447 — 2003 (834/1867)
Lowest opponents' field goal percentage, game
.226 — at Miami, June 24, 2000 (14/62)
.236 — vs. Houston, August 14, 2001 (13/55)

TURNOVERS

Most opponents' turnovers per game, season
21.4 — 1997 (599/28)
19.4 — 1998 (581/30)
Fewest opponents' turnovers per game, season
15.0 — 1999 (479/32)
15.3 — 2002 (491/32)
Most opponents' turnovers, game
33 — vs. Utah, August 17, 1997 (ot)
30 — at New York, August 11, 1998 (ot)
Regulation game:
27 — at Utah, July 3, 1997
   vs. Washington, June 15, 1998
   at Minnesota, June 27, 2003

TEAM MISCELLANEOUS

GAME WON AND LOST

Highest winning percentage, season
.633 — 1998 (19-11)
.625 — 2000 (20-12)
Lowest winning percentage, season
.235 — 2003 (8-26)
.344 — 2002 (11-21)
Most consecutive games won
6 — August 20, 1997—June 15, 1998
5 — July 14-27, 2001
Most consecutive games won, one season
5 — July 14-27, 2001

4 — Many times
Most consecutive game lost
7 — July 29-August 10, 2001
   July 2-25, 2003
6 — Many times
Most consecutive game lost, one season
7 — July 29-August 10, 2001
   July 2-25, 2003
6 — Many times
Highest winning percentage, home games, season
.800 — 1998 (12-3)
.786 — 1997 (11-3)
Lowest winning percentage, home games, season
.353 — 2003 (6-11)
.625 — 2001 (10-6)
   2002 (10-6)
Most consecutive home games won
11 — July 17-August 17, 1999
9 — August 4, 1997-June 15, 1998
Most consecutive home games lost
4 — June 17-July 19, 2003
3 — July 22-28, 1997
   August 5, 2000-May 30, 2001
   August 13, 2002-May 24, 2003
Highest winning percentage, road games, season
.563 — 2000 (9-7)
.467 — 1998 (7-8)
Lowest winning percentage, road games, season
.063 — 2002 (1-15)
.118 — 2003 (2-15)
Most consecutive road games won
4 — June 13-24, 2000
3 — August 20, 1997—June 28, 1998
Most consecutive road games lost
21 — July 29, 2001-August 6, 2002
6 — Many times

OVERTIME GAMES

Most overtime games, season
3 — 1997, 2003
2 — 1998, 2001
Most consecutive overtime games, season
2 — August 10-11, 1998
Most overtime games won, season
2 — 1997
1 — 1998, 2000, 2003
Most overtime games won, no losses, season
1 — 2000
Most consecutive overtime games won
3 — August 17, 1997-August 10, 1998
Most overtime games lost, season
2 — 2001, 2003
1 — 1997, 1998
Most overtime games lost, no wins, season
2 — 2001
Most consecutive overtime games lost
3 — June 4, 2001-July 15, 2003

Most overtime periods, game
2 — at Cleveland, August 10, 1998
at Los Angeles, July 15, 2003
at Washington, August 3, 2003

INDIVIDUAL RECORDS

SEASONS

Most Seasons
6 — Jennifer Gillom
5 — Lisa Harrison
Bridget Pettis
Michele Timms
4 — By many

GAMES

Most game, career
183 — Jennifer Gillom
160 — Lisa Harrison
154 — Bridget Pettis
Most consecutive games, career
154 — Bridget Pettis, June 22, 1997-
August 14, 2001
105 — Jennifer Gillom, June 22, 1997-
July 2, 2000
104 — Lisa Harrison, June 24, 2000-
July 15, 2003
Most games, season
34 — Edwina Brown, 2003
Anna DeForge, 2003
Tamicha Jackson, 2003
Adrian Williams, 2003

MINUTES

Most minutes, career
5,489 — Jennifer Gillom
4,230 — Lisa Harrison
3,312 — Bridget Pettis
Highest average, minutes per game, career
(Minimum 90 games)
30.0 — Jennifer Gillom (5489/183)
28.3 — Michele Timms (3288/116)
26.4 — Lisa Harrison (4230/160)
Most minutes, season
1,095 — Jennifer Gillom, 1999
1,090 — Brandy Reed, 2000
1,065 — Anna DeForge, 2003
Highest average, minutes per game, season
35.8 — Michele Timms, 1997 (966/27)
34.2 — Jennifer Gillom, 1999 (1095/32)
34.1 — Brandy Reed, 2000 (1090/32)
Most minutes, game
46 — Adrian Williams, at Los Angeles,
July 15, 2003 (2 ot)
45 — Umeki Webb, at Cleveland,
August 10, 1998 (2 ot)
44 — Jennifer Gillom, at Cleveland,
August 10, 1998 (2 ot)
Jennifer Gillom, vs. Portland,
June 14, 2000 (ot)

SCORING

Most points, lifetime
2,793 — Jennifer Gillom
1,232 — Bridget Pettis
1,084 — Lisa Harrison
Highest average, points per game, career
(Minimum 90 games)
15.3 — Jennifer Gillom (2793/183)
8.0 — Bridget Pettis (1232/154)
7.5 — Michele Timms (866/116)
Most points, season
624 — Jennifer Gillom, 1998
608 — Brandy Reed, 2000
485 — Jennifer Gillom, 1999
Highest average, points per game, season
20.8 — Jennifer Gillom, 1998 (624/30)
19.0 — Brandy Reed, 2000 (608/32)
15.7 — Jennifer Gillom, 1997 (440/28)
Most points, game
36 — Jennifer Gillom, at Cleveland,
August 10, 1998 (2 ot)
32 — Brandy Reed, at Houston,
June 3, 2000
Brandy Reed, at Charlotte,
June 22, 2000
31 — Jennifer Gillom, at Utah,
July 27, 1998
Brandy Reed, vs. Utah, July 19, 2000
Brandy Reed, vs. Cleveland, July 24, 2000
Most games, 30 or more points, career
4 — Brandy Reed
2 — Jennifer Gillom
Most games, 20 or more points, career
48 — Jennifer Gillom
19 — Brandy Reed
10 — Bridget Pettis
Most consecutive games, 20 or more points
8 — Brandy Reed, July 13-28, 2000
6 — Jennifer Gillom, July 21-
August 4, 1998
5 — Jennifer Gillom, July 2-13, 1998
Jennifer Gillom, August 10-17, 1998
Most consecutive games, 10 or more points
27 — Jennifer Gillom, June 29, 1998-
June 21, 1999
22 — Jennifer Gillom, July 25, 1997-
June 26, 1998
17 — Brandy Reed, July 6-August 9, 2000

FIELD GOAL PERCENTAGE

Highest field goal percentage, career
(Minimum 350 field goals)
.467 — Lisa Harrison (452/968)
.426 — Jennifer Gillom (1009/2367)
.343 — Bridget Pettis (398/1162)
Highest field goal percentage, season (qualifiers)
.5071 — Maria Stepanova, 2001 (143/282)
.5066 — Brandy Reed, 2000 (231/456)
.505 — Michelle Brogan, 1998 (93/184)
Highest field goal percentage, game
(Minimum 8 field goals made)
.900 — Maria Stepanova, vs. Detroit,

July 26, 2001 (9/10)
.833 — Lisa Harrison, vs. Charlotte,
August 15, 1999 (10/12)
Jennifer Gillom, vs. Orlando,
August 1, 2000 (10/12)
.800 — Jennifer Gillom, at Houston,
August 7, 1997 (8/10)
Most field goals, none missed, game
6 — Lisa Harrison, at Seattle,
May 31, 2001
4 — Maria Stepanova, vs. Utah,
July 27, 1999
Lisa Harrison, at Minnesota,
July 14, 2001
Slobodanka Tuvic, vs. Seattle,
June 14, 2002
Kaye Christensen,
at Washington, July 9, 2002
Izia Castro Marques, at Indiana,
July 2, 2003
3 — By many
Most field goal attempts, none made, game
11 — Slobodanka Tuvic, at Seattle,
July 25, 2003
10 — Umeki Webb, vs. Utah,
August 6, 1997
9 — Tonya Edwards, vs. Houston,
August 7, 2000
Gordana Grubin, vs. Seattle,
June 14, 2002

FIELD GOALS

Most field goals, career
1,009 — Jennifer Gillom
452 — Lisa Harrison
398 — Bridget Pettis
Most field goals, season
231 — Brandy Reed, 2000
228 — Jennifer Gillom, 1998
166 — Jennifer Gillom, 2002
Most field goals, game
13 — Jennifer Gillom, at Cleveland,
August 10, 1998 (2 ot)
Brandy Reed, at Houston,
June 3, 2000
12 — By many

FIELD GOAL ATTEMPTS

Most field goal attempts, career
2,367 — Jennifer Gillom
1,162 — Bridget Pettis
968 — Lisa Harrison
Most field goal attempts, season
492 — Jennifer Gillom, 1998
456 — Brandy Reed, 200
428 — Jennifer Gillom, 1999
Most field goal attempts, game
27 — Jennifer Gillom, vs. Los Angeles,
August 24, 1997 (ot)

Jennifer Gillom, at Cleveland,
August 10, 1998 (2 ot)
25 — Jennifer Gillom, at Utah,
July 27, 1998
24 — Jennifer Gillom, vs. Sacramento,
August 19, 1998
Anna DeForge, at Los Angeles,
July 15, 2003 (2 ot)

THREE-POINT FIELD-GOAL PERCENTAGE

Highest three-point field goal percentage, career
(Minimum 90 three-point field goals)
.328 — Jennifer Gillom (148/451)
.324 — Michele Timms (129/398)
.280 — Bridget Pettis (138/493)
Highest three-point field goal percentage, season
(qualifiers)
.412 — Anna DeForge, 2003 (61/148)
.387 — Jennifer Gillom, 2002 (36/93)
.378 — Jennifer Gillom, 1998 (31/82)
Most three-point field goals, none missed, game
4 — Jennifer Gillom, at Cleveland,
July 2, 1998
Anna DeForge, vs. Minnesota,
August 20, 2003
3 — Michele Timms, at Cleveland,
June 28, 1997
Anna DeForge, at New York,
June 25, 2003
2 — By many
Most three-point field goal attempts, none made,
game
7 — Michele Timms, at Houston,
August 6, 1998
6 — By many

THREE-POINT FIELD GOALS

Most three-point field goals, career
148 — Jennifer Gillom
138 — Bridget Pettis
129 — Michele Timms
Most three-point field goals, season
61 — Anna DeForge, 2003
49 — Michele Timms, 1997
41 — Bridget Pettis, 1997
Most three-point field goals, game
5 — Edna Campbell, vs. Cleveland,
June 19, 1999
Edna Campbell, vs. Utah,
July 27, 1999
Anna DeForge, vs. Detroit,
August 13, 2003
4 — By many
Most consecutive games, three-point field goals made
13 — Anna DeForge, July 2-August 8, 2003
11 — Michele Timms, August 6, 1997-
June 11, 1998
10 — Edna Campbell, July 19-
August 7, 1999

Anna DeForge, May 30-
June 27, 2003

THREE-POINT FIELD GOAL ATTEMPTS

Most three-point field goal attempts, career
493 — Bridget Pettis
451 — Jennifer Gillom
398 — Michele Timms

Most three-point field goal attempts, season
148 — Anna DeForge, 2003
142 — Michele Timms, 1997
134 — Bridget Pettis, 1997

Most three-point field goal attempts, game
11 — Bridget Pettis, at Utah, August 17, 1998
9 — Bridget Pettis, at Charlotte, July 30, 1997
Michele Timms, vs. Cleveland,
August 14, 1997
Bridget Pettis, vs. Detroit,
August 14, 1998
Anna DeForge, at Los Angeles,
July 15, 2003 (2 ot)

FREE THROW PERCENTAGE

Highest free-throw percentage, career
(Minimum 175 free throws)
.825 — Bridget Pettis (298/361)
.762 — Marlies Askamp (205/269)
.759 — Jennifer Gillom (627/826)

Highest free-throw percentage, season (qualifiers)
.901 — Brandy Reed, 2000 (128/142)
.898 — Bridget Pettis, 1997 (97/108)
.865 — Bridget Pettis, 1998 (77/89)

Most free throws made, none missed, game
12 — Kristi Harrower, vs. Los Angeles,
July 17, 1999
Jennifer Gillom, vs. Portland,
June 14, 2000 (ot)
10 — Bridget Pettis, vs. Sacramento,
August 4, 1997
Jennifer Gillom, vs. Sacramento,
June 18, 2002
9 — by many

Most free throw attempts, none made, game
4 — Michelle Brogan, vs. Cleveland,
July 10, 1998
Marlies Askamp, vs. New York,
July 18, 1998
Maria Stepanova, vs. Washington,
July 7, 2001
Tracy Reid, vs. Detroit,
June 13, 2002
3 — by many

FREE THROWS MADE

Most free throws made, career
627 — Jennifer Gillom
298 — Bridget Pettis
205 — Marlies Askamp

Most free throws made, season

141 — Jennifer Gillom, 1999
137 — Jennifer Gillom, 1998
128 — Brandy Reed, 2000

Most free throws made, game
12 — Kristi Harrower, vs. Los Angeles,
July 17, 1999
Jennifer Gillom, vs. Portland,
June 14, 2000 (ot)
Lisa Harrison, vs. Minnesota,
July 11, 2000
Plenette Pierson, vs. Los Angeles,
August 8, 2003
11 — By many

FREE THROW ATTEMPTS

Most free throw attempts, career
826 — Jennifer Gillom
361 — Bridget Pettis
269 — Marlies Askamp

Most free throw attempts, season
195 — Jennifer Gillom, 1998
177 — Jennifer Gillom, 1999
142 — Brandy Reed, 2000

Most free throw attempts, game
19 — Plenette Pierson, vs. Los Angeles,
August 8, 2003
16 — Kayte Christensen, vs. San Antonio,
August 22, 2003
15 — Jennifer Gillom, at Los Angeles,
July 23, 1998

REBOUNDS

Most rebounds, career
913 — Jennifer Gillom
634 — Lisa Harrison
618 — Adrian Williams

Highest average, rebounds per game, career
(Minimum 90 games)
5.2 — Adrian Williams (618/119)
5.0 — Jennifer Gillom (913/183)
4.6 — Maria Stepanova (451/99)

Most rebounds, season
252 — Adrian Williams, 2003
220 — Adrian Williams, 2002
219 — Jennifer Gillom, 1998

Highest average, rebounds per game, season
(qualifiers)
7.4 — Adrian Williams, 2003 (252/34)
7.3 — Jennifer Gillom, 1998 (219/30)
7.2 — Marlies Askamp, 1999 (215/30)

Most rebounds, game
16 — Adrian Williams, vs. San Antonio,
May 28, 2003
15 — Jennifer Gillom, vs. Sacramento,
June 14, 1999
Marlies Askamp, vs. Cleveland,
June 19, 1999
Adrian Williams, at Los Angeles,

July 15, 2003 (2 ot)
14 — Adrian Williams, vs. Los Angeles,
August 13, 2002
Adrian Williams, vs. Houston,
June 14, 2003

Most games, 10+ rebounds, career
14 — Adrian Williams
12 — Jennifer Gillom
11 — Marlies Askamp

Most consecutive games, 10+ rebounds
4 — Maria Stepanova, August 6-11, 1999
2 — By many

OFFENSIVE REBOUNDS

Most offensive rebounds, career
263 — Jennifer Gillom
209 — Lisa Harrison
194 — Marlies Askamp

Highest average, offensive rebounds per game,
career (Minimum 90 games)
1.6 — Maria Stepanova (160/99)
1.5 — Adrian Williams (177/119)
1.4 — Jennifer Gillom (263/183)

Most offensive rebounds, season
92 — Marlies Askamp, 1999
68 — Adrian Williams, 2003
66 — Marlies Askamp, 1997
Maria Stepanova, 2001

Most offensive rebounds, game
8 — Brandy Reed, at Charlotte,
June 22, 2000
7 — Marlies Askamp, at Minnesota,
July 3, 1999
Marlies Askamp, vs. Los Angeles,
July 17, 1999
Adrian Williams, vs. San Antonio, May 28, 2003
6 — by many

DEFENSIVE REBOUNDS

Most defensive rebounds, career
650 — Jennifer Gillom
441 — Adrian Williams
425 — Lisa Harrison

Highest average, defensive rebounds per game,
career (Minimum 90 games)
3.7 — Adrian Williams (441/119)
3.6 — Jennifer Gillom (650/183)
2.9 — Maria Stepanova (291/99)

Most defensive rebounds, season
184 — Adrian Williams, 2003
157 — Jennifer Gillom, 1998
156 — Adrian Williams, 2002

Most defensive rebounds, game
12 — Jennifer Gillom, vs. Sacramento,
June 14, 1999
Adrian Williams, vs. Houston, June 14, 2003
11 — Jennifer Gillom, at Houston,
July 28, 1998
Adrian Williams, vs. Los Angeles,

August 13, 2002
Adrian Williams, at Los Angeles,
July 15, 2003 (2 ot)
10 — By many

ASSISTS

Most assists, career
551 — Michele Timms
281 — Bridget Pettis
234 — Jennifer Gillom

Highest average, assists per game, career
(Minimum 90 games)
4.8 — Michele Timms (551/116)
1.8 — Bridget Pettis (281/154)
1.4 — Lisa Harrison (216/160)

Most assists, season
158 — Michele Timms, 1998
151 — Michele Timms, 1999
146 — Tamicha Jackson, 2003

Highest average, assists per game, season
(qualifiers)
5.3 — Michele Timms, 1998 (158/30)
5.1 — Michele Timms, 1997 (137/27)
5.0 — Michele Timms, 1999 (151/30)

Most assists, game
12 — Michelle Cleary, vs. Utah,
July 19, 2000
10 — Michele Timms, at Sacramento,
June 12, 1999
Michele Timms, vs. Sacramento,
August 17, 1999
Kristen Veal, vs. Houston,
June 10, 2001
9 — Many times

Most games, 10+ assists, career
2 — Michele Timms
1 — Michelle Cleary
Kristen Veal

PERSONAL FOULS

Most personal fouls, career
564 — Jennifer Gillom
322 — Michele Timms
305 — Lisa Harrison

Most personal fouls, season
110 — Maria Stepanova, 2001
105 — Umeki Webb, 1998
Jennifer Gillom, 1999
104 — Kayte Christensen, 2003

Most personal fouls, game
6 — by many

DISQUALIFICATIONS

Most disqualifications, career
5 — Kayte Christensen
Jennifer Gillom
Maria Stepanova
4 — Bridget Pettis
Umeki Webb
2 — By many

Highest percentage, games disqualified, career
(Minimum 90 games)
    5.1 — Maria Stepanova (5/99)
    2.7 — Jennifer Gillom (5/183)
    2.6 — Bridget Pettis (4/154)
Lowest percentage, games disqualified, career
(Minimum 90 games)
    0.00 — Michele Timms (0/116)
    0.6 — Lisa Harrison (1/160)
    0.8 — Adrian Williams (1/119)
Most consecutive games without disqualification,
career
    128 — Lisa Harrison, May 31, 2000-
        August 23, 2003 (current)
    116 — Michele Timms, June 22, 1997
        August 14, 2001
    105 — Adrian Williams, May 31, 2000-
        July 24, 2003
Most disqualifications, season
    4 — Kayte Christensen, 2003
    3 — Maria Stepanova, 2001
    2 — By many
Fewest minutes, disqualified, game
    9 — Bridget Pettis, at Indiana,
        July 1, 2001 (ot)
    13 — Plenette Pierson, vs. Sacramento,
        May 22, 2003
Kayte Christensen, at Los Angeles, July 24, 2003
    14 — Maria Stepanova, at Sacramento,
        June 12, 1999
        Maria Stepanova, at Miami,
        June 24, 2000

STEALS

Most steals, career
    205 — Jennifer Gillom
    188 — Michele Timms
    163 — Bridget Pettis
Highest average, steals per game, career
(Minimum 90 games)
    1.62 — Michele Timms (188/116)
    1.13 — Adrian Williams (134/119)
    1.12 — Jennifer Gillom (205/183)
Most steals, season
    71 — Michele Timms, 1997
    68 — Umeki Webb, 1997
    66 — Brandy Reed, 2000
Highest average, steals per game, season
(qualifiers)
    2.63 — Michele Timms, 1997 (71/27)
    2.43 — Umeki Webb, 1997 (68/28)
    2.06 — Brandy Reed, 2000 (66/32)
Most steals, game
    9 — Michelle Brogan, at Utah,
        July 27, 1998
    8 — Michele Timms, at Utah, July 3, 1997
        Michele Timms, vs. Utah,

August 17, 1997 (ot)
    7 — Brandy Reed, at Charlotte, June 22, 2000
        Brandy Reed, vs. Los Angeles,
        July 21, 2000

BLOCKED SHOTS

Most blocked shots, career
    146 — Maria Stepanova
    101 — Jennifer Gillom
    57 — Adrian Williams
Highest average, blocked shots per game, career
(Minimum: 90 games)
    1.47 — Maria Stepanova (146/99)
    0.55 — Jennifer Gillom (101/183)
    0.48 — Adrian Williams (57/119)
Most blocked shots, season
    64 — Maria Stepanova, 2001
    62 — Maria Stepanova, 1999
    29 — Jennifer Gillom, 2000
        Adrian Williams, 2002
Highest average, blocked shots per game, season
(qualifiers)
    2.00 — Maria Stepanova, 2001 (64/32)
    1.94 — Maria Stepanova, 1999 (62/32)
    0.97 — Jennifer Gillom, 2000 (29/30)
Most blocked shots, game
    6 — Maria Stepanova, at Detroit, June 26, 1999
    5 — Maria Stepanova, vs. Detroit,
        August 11, 1999
        Maria Stepanova, at Indiana,
        July 1, 2001 (ot)
        Maria Stepanova, at Sacramento,
        July 29, 2001
Adrian Williams, at Utah, July 13, 2002
    4 — By many

TURNOVERS

Most turnovers, career
    425 — Jennifer Gillom
    298 — Michele Timms
    251 — Bridget Pettis
Most turnovers, season
    90 — Brandy Reed, 2000
    89 — Jennifer Gillom, 1998
Michele Timms, 1999
    87 — Jennifer Gillom, 1999
Most turnovers, game
    8 — Bridget Pettis, at Cleveland,
        June 28, 1997
    7 — Jennifer Gillom, at Houston,
        August 6, 1998
        Michele Timms, at Sacramento,
        June 12, 1999
        Brandy Reed, at Cleveland,
        June 25, 2000
        Jennifer Gillom, vs. Utah,
        May 30, 2001
        Michele Timms, at Minnesota,
        July 14, 2001

SACRAMENTO MONARCHS

REGULAR SEASON TEAM RECORDS

TEAM OFFENSE

SCORING

Highest average, points per game, season
74.8 — 1999 (2392/32)
73.2 — 2000 (2343/32)
Lowest average, points per game, season
63.9 — 1998 (1916/30)
67.6 — 2003 (2299/34)
Most points, game
108 — vs. Detroit, July 1, 2000
107 — vs. Utah, June 24, 1999
Fewest points, game
41 — vs. Detroit, August 11, 1998
44 — vs. Houston, July 18, 1998
Largest margin of victory, game
39 — at Minnesota, July 3, 2001 (91-52)
38 — vs. Utah, June 24, 1999 (107-69)
Largest margin of defeat, game
31 — vs. Houston, July 18, 1998 (44-75)
28 — at Houston, July 12, 1997 (61-89)

BY HALF

Most points, first half
52 — vs. Detroit, July 1, 2000
48 — vs. Utah, June 24, 1999
vs. Utah, August 14, 1999
vs. Minnesota, June 28, 2000
Fewest points, first half
13 — vs. Houston, July 18, 1998
16 — vs. Detroit, August 11, 1998
Largest lead at halftime
31 — at Minnesota, July 3, 2001
(led 46-15; won 91-52)
24 — vs. Seattle, August 9, 2000
(led 47-23; won 79-46)
Largest deficit at halftime overcome to win game
11 — vs. Phoenix, June 12, 1999
(trailed 39-50; won 96-85)
at Portland, July 7, 2000
(trailed 25-36; won 63-60)
8 — vs. Utah, August 15, 1998
(trailed 30-38; won 82-55)
Most points, second half
59 — vs. Utah, June 24, 1999
58 — at Detroit, July 4, 1999
Fewest points, second half
18 — at Houston, August 5, 2003
21 — vs. Houston, July 12, 2002

OVERTIME

Most points, overtime period
13 — at Charlotte, June 24, 2001

12 — Many times
Fewest points, overtime period
2 — vs. Portland, June 16, 2001
4 — vs. Utah, July 2, 1997
at New York, July 30, 1997
Largest margin of victory, overtime period
4 — at Phoenix, August 16, 2003 (65-61)
3 — at Charlotte, June 24, 2001 (85-82)

FIELD GOAL PERCENTAGE

Highest field-goal percentage, season
.440 — 2000 (876/1993)
.424 — 2001 (837/1974)
Lowest field-goal percentage, season
.401 — 2002 (780/1945)
.406 — 1997 (704/1732)
Highest field-goal percentage, game
.600 — at San Antonio,
August 7, 2003 (36/60)
.586 — vs. Utah, August 14, 1999 (34/58)
Lowest field-goal percentage, game
.273 — vs. Houston, July 18, 1998 (18/66)
.281 — at Seattle, June 3, 2003 (18/64)

FIELD GOALS

Most field goals per game, season
27.4 — 2000 (876/32)
26.5 — 1999 (849/32)
Fewest field goals per game, season
24.4 — 2002 (780/32)
24.5 — 1998 (734/30)
Most field goals, game
36 — vs. Utah, June 24, 1999
vs. Detroit, July 1, 2000
at San Antonio, August 7, 2003
34 — vs. Utah, August 14, 1999
Fewest field goals, game
16 — at New York, June 26, 1998
at Charlotte, July 19, 2002
18 — Many times

FIELD GOAL ATTEMPTS

Most field-goal attempts per game, season
62.7 — 1999 (2006/32)
62.3 — 2000 (1993/32)
Fewest field-goal attempts per game, season
60.1 — 1998 (1802/30)
60.8 — 2002 (1945/32)
Most field-goal attempts, game
88 — at Los Angeles, July 15, 1998 (ot)
84 — at Los Angeles, August 22, 1997
Fewest field-goal attempts, game
43 — at New York, June 26, 1998

vs. Cleveland, June 2, 2001
at Seattle, June 30, 2001
45 — vs. Houston, July 18, 1997

THREE-POINT FIELD-GOAL PERCENTAGE

Highest three-point field-goal percentage, season
.385 — 2001 (163/423)
.317 — 2003 (150/473)
Lowest three-point field-goal percentage, season
.260 — 1998 (72/277)
.284 — 2002 (112/395)

THREE-POINT FIELD GOALS

Most three-point field goals per game, season
5.1 — 2001 (163/32)
4.4 — 2000 (142/32)
Fewest three-point field goals per game, season
2.4 — 1998 (72/30)
3.5 — 2002 (112/32)
Most three-point field goals, game
14 — at Minnesota, July 3, 2001
10 — at Minnesota, June 29, 1999
vs. Los Angeles, July 31, 2003
Fewest three-point field goals, game
0 — many times. Last:
at Phoenix, August 19, 1998

THREE-POINT FIELD GOAL ATTEMPTS

Most three-point field goal attempts per game, season
14.3 — 2000 (459/32)
13.9 — 2003 (473/34)
Fewest three-point field goal attempts per game, season
9.2 — 1998 (277/30)
12.3 — 1997 (345/28)
Most three-point field goal attempts, game
25 — at Los Angeles, July 25, 2001
24 — at Los Angeles, August 2, 2001
Fewest three-point field goal attempts, game
1 — at Washington, July 26, 1998
2 — at Charlotte, July 27, 1998

FREE THROW PERCENTAGE

Highest free-throw percentage, season
.757 — 2002 (494/653)
.739 — 2001 (457/618)
Lowest free-throw percentage, season
.6706 — 1999 (568/847)
.6714 — 1998 (376/560)
Highest free-throw percentage, game
1.000 — at Phoenix, July 20, 1998 (2/2)
at Los Angeles, July 25, 2001 (7/7)
at San Antonio, July 17, 2003 (15/15)
at San Antonio, August 7, 2003 (7/7)
.958 — vs. Utah, August 1, 2002 (23/24)

Lowest free-throw percentage, game
.250 — at Seattle, August 25, 2003 (1/4)
.286 — at Minnesota, May 24, 2003 (2/7)

FREE THROWS MADE

Most free throws made per game, season
17.8 — 1999 (568/32)
15.4 — 2002 (494/32)
Fewest free throws made per game, season
12.50 — 2003 (425/34)
12.53 — 1998 (376/30)
Most free throws made, game
34 — vs. Detroit, July 1, 2000
32 — at Washington, July 26, 1998
Fewest free throws made, game
1 — at Seattle, August 25, 2003
2 — at Phoenix, July 20, 1998
at Minnesota, May 24, 2003

FREE THROW ATTEMPTS

Most free throw attempts per game, season
26.5 — 1999 (847/32)
20.4 — 2002 (653/32)
Fewest free throw attempts per game, season
18.4 — 2003 (626/34)
18.7 — 1998 (560/30)
Most free throw attempts, game
48 — vs. Phoenix, June 12, 1999
46 — vs. Utah, June 24, 1999
vs. Detroit, July 1, 2000
Fewest free throw attempts, game
2 — at Phoenix, July 20, 1998
4 — at Seattle, August 25, 2003

REBOUNDS

Most rebounds per game, season
34.8 — 1999 (1112/32)
34.3 — 2001 (1097/32)
Fewest rebounds per game, season
29.7 — 2002 (949/32)
31.4 — 2003 (1067/34)
Most rebounds, game
48 — at Washington, June 5, 2001
vs. Portland, June 16, 2001 (ot)
46 — at Los Angeles, July 15, 1998 (ot)
vs. Utah, June 24, 1999
vs. Portland, July 25, 2002 (2 ot)
vs. Los Angeles, June 7, 2003
Fewest rebounds, game
19 — vs. Houston, July 18, 1997
20 — at Portland, June 6, 2002

OFFENSIVE REBOUNDS

Most offensive rebounds per game, season
12.9 — 1999 (412/32)
12.2 — 1997 (341/28)
Fewest offensive rebounds per game, season
9.4 — 2002 (301/32)
10.3 — 2003 (349/34)

Most offensive rebounds, game
  21 — vs. Los Angeles, June 30, 1998
  20 — at Los Angeles, July 15, 1998 (ot)
Fewest offensive rebounds, game
  3 — vs. Cleveland, June 2, 2001
  4 — at Portland, July 7, 2000
    at Orlando, July 6, 2001

DEFENSIVE REBOUNDS

Most defensive rebounds per game, season
  22.6 — 2001 (723/32)
  21.9 — 1999 (700/32)
Fewest defensive rebounds per game, season
  19.2 — 1997 (538/28)
  20.3 — 2002 (648/32)
Most defensive rebounds, game
  34 — vs. Los Angeles, June 7, 2003
  33 — vs. Phoenix, May 30, 2003
Fewest defensive rebounds, game
  10 — at Miami, July 7, 2001
  11 — at Cleveland, July 10, 1997

ASSISTS

Most assists per game, season
  17.7 — 2000 (567/32)
  17.4 — 2001 (558/32)
Fewest assists per game, season
  14.4 — 1997 (404/28)
  15.4 — 1998 (463/30)
Most assists, game
  27 — at Minnesota, May 24, 2003
  25 — at Los Angeles, July 25, 2001
Fewest assists, game
  6 — at Phoenix, August 19, 1998
  7 — vs. New York, June 18, 1998
    at New York, June 26, 1998

PERSONAL FOULS

Most personal fouls per game, season
  21.2 — 1997 (593/28)
  21.1 — 1998 (633/30)
Fewest personal fouls per game, season
  17.8 — 2000 (571/32)
  18.4 — 2001 (588/32)
Most personal fouls, game
  32 — at Phoenix, August 4, 1997
  31 — vs. Minnesota, August 9, 2003
Fewest personal fouls, game
  9 — vs. Detroit, July 21, 2001
    vs. Portland, July 27, 2001
  10 — vs. Orlando, July 27, 2000

DISQUALIFICATIONS

Most disqualifications per game, season
  0.50 — 1997 (14/28)
  0.25 — 2002 (8/32)
Fewest disqualifications per game, season
  0.13 — 1999 (4/32)
    2001 (4/32)

Most disqualifications, game
  2 — Many time. Most recent:
    vs. Minnesota, August 9, 2003

STEALS

Most steals per game, season
  10.4 — 2000 (332/32)
  10.3 — 1999 (329/32)
Fewest steals per game, season
  7.7 — 2002 (247/32)
  8.6 — 2001 (276/32)
Most steals, game
  19 — at Orlando, July 17, 1999
  18 — vs. Seattle, July 26, 2003
Fewest steals, game
  3 — vs. Phoenix, July 29, 2001
  4 — Many times

BLOCKED SHOTS

Most blocked shots per game, season
  4.94 — 2001 (158/32)
  4.91 — 2000 (157/32)
Fewest blocked shots per game, season
  2.1 — 1997 (60/28)
  3.4 — 2002 (109/32)
Most blocked shots, game
  11 — vs. Portland, July 27, 2001
    vs. Los Angeles, July 31, 2003
  10 — vs. Cleveland, June 2, 2001
Fewest blocked shots, game
  0 — Many times. Most recent:
    vs. Indiana, July 30, 2002

TURNOVERS

Most turnovers per game, season
  20.1 — 1997 (562/28)
  17.8 — 1998 (533/30)
Fewest turnovers per game, season
  13.6 — 2003 (461/34)
  14.3 — 2002 (456/32)
Most turnovers, game
  26 — vs. Cleveland, August 4, 1998
  25 — many times
Fewest turnovers, game
  6 — vs. Indiana, August 3, 2001
    vs. Cleveland, July 11, 2002
  7 — vs. Charlotte, June 17, 2000
    vs. Seattle, June 20, 2002
    vs. Indiana, June 14, 2003

TEAM DEFENSE

POINTS

Fewest points allowed per game, season
  65.2 — 2003 (2216/34)
  66.8 — 2001 (2139/32)
Most points allowed per game, season
  75.4 — 1997 (2112/28)
  71.7 — 2002 (2294/32)

Fewest points allowed, game
    46 — vs. Seattle, August 9, 2000
    47 — vs. Phoenix, July 29, 2001
Fewest points allowed, first half
    14 — vs. Phoenix, July 29, 2001
    15 — at Minnesota, July 3, 2001
Fewest points allowed, second half
    17 — vs. Utah, August 15, 1998
    20 — vs. Phoenix, August 23, 2003
Fewest points allowed, overtime period
    6 — vs. Houston, July 10, 2001
        vs. New York, June 13, 2002
        at Phoenix, August 16, 2003
    7 — vs. Houston, July 10, 2001

FIELD GOAL PERCENTAGE

Lowest opponents' field-goal percentage, season
    .401 — 2001 (804/2003)
    .410 — 2003 (816/1991)
Highest opponents' field-goal percentage, season
    .446 — 1997 (775/1738)
    .423 — 2000 (811/1918)
Lowest opponents' field goal percentage, game
    .255 — vs. Phoenix, July 29, 2001 (14/55)
    .269 — vs. Minnesota, August 7, 2001 (18/67)

TURNOVERS

Most opponents' turnovers per game, season
    18.1 — 1997 (508/28)
    17.8 — 1999 (569/32)
Fewest opponents' turnovers per game, season
    15.0 — 2001 (481/32)
    15.5 — 2002 (496/32)
Most opponents' turnovers, game
    27 — vs. Utah, July 2, 1997 (ot)
    26 — at Los Angeles, June 5, 2003

TEAM MISCELLANEOUS

GAME WON AND LOST

Highest winning percentage, season
    .656 — 2000 (21-11)
    .625 — 2001 (20-12)
Lowest winning percentage, season
    .267 — 1998 (8-22)
    .357 — 1997 (10-18)
Most consecutive games won
    6 — July 21-August 1, 2002
    5 — August 4-13, 1999
        July 26-August 4, 2000
        June 24-July 6, 2001
Most consecutive games won, one season
    6 — July 21-August 1, 2002
    5 — August 4-13, 1999
        July 26-August 4, 2000
        June 24-July 6, 2001
Most consecutive game lost
    9 — July 16-August 4, 1997

    8 — June 22-July 7, 2002
Most consecutive game lost, one season
    9 — July 16-August 4, 1997
    8 — June 22-July 7, 2002
Highest winning percentage, home games, season
    .813 — 2000 (13-3)
    .750 — 2001 (12-4)
Lowest winning percentage, home games, season
    .333 — 1998 (5-10)
    .500 — 1997 (7-7)
Most consecutive home games won
    7 — May 31-July 1, 2000
    6 — July 21-August 11, 2001
Most consecutive home games lost
    5 — July 10-August 4, 1998
    4 — July 18-27, 1997
Highest winning percentage, road games, season
    .500 — 1999 (8-8)
        2000 (8-8)
        2001 (8-8)
Lowest winning percentage, road games, season
    .200 — 1998 (3-12)
    .214 — 1997 (3-11)
Most consecutive road games won
    4 — July 26, 2000-June 4, 2001
        June 24-July 6, 2001
    3 — June 29-July 4, 1999
        July 27-August 10, 2002
Most consecutive road games lost
    10 — July 10-August 22, 1997
        June 6-July 7, 2002
    6 — July 29, 1998—June 10, 1999

OVERTIME GAMES

Most overtime games, season
    4 — 2001, 2002
    2 — 1997
Most consecutive overtime games, season
    2 — June 13-15, 2002
Most overtime games won, season
    2 — 2001, 2002
Most overtime games won, no losses, season
    1 — 2003
Most consecutive overtime games won
    2 — June 24-July 10, 2001
        July 25, 2002-August 16, 2003 (current)
Most overtime games lost, season
    2 — 1997, 2001, 2002
    1 — 1998
Most overtime games lost, no wins, season
    2 — 1997
    1 — 1998
Most consecutive overtime games lost
    4 — July 2, 1997-June 16, 2001
    2 — June 15-25, 2002

Most overtime periods, game
2 — vs. Houston, July 10, 2001
    vs. New York, June 13, 2002
    vs. Washington, June 25, 2002
    vs. Portland, July 25, 2002

INDIVIDUAL RECORDS

SEASONS

Most Seasons
7 — Ruthie Bolton-Holifield
6 — Lady Grooms
    Ticha Penicheiro
    Tangela Smith

GAMES

Most game, career
189 — Lady Grooms
Tangela Smith
184 — Ruthie Bolton
173 — Ticha Penicheiro
Most consecutive games, career
159 — Tangela Smith, June 17, 1999-
    August 25, 2003 (current)
128 — Kedra Holland-Corn, June 10, 1999
    August 13, 2002
122 — Latasha Byears, June 21, 1997
    August 9, 2000
Most games, season
34 — By many

MINUTES

Most minutes, career
5,822 — Ticha Penicheiro
5,225 — Tangela Smith
4,674 — Yolanda Griffith
Highest average, minutes per game, career
(Minimum 90 games)
33.7 — Ticha Penicheiro (5822/173)
32.5 — Yolanda Griffith (4674/144)
29.3 — Kedra Holland-Corn (3744/128)
Most minutes, season
1,120 — Ticha Penicheiro, 1999
1,089 — Ticha Penicheiro, 2003
1,080 — Ticha Penicheiro, 1998
Highest average, minutes per game, season
(qualifiers)
37.5 — Chantel Tremitiere, 1997 (1051/28)
36.0 — Ticha Penicheiro, 1998 (1080/30)
35.5 — Ticha Penicheiro, 2002 (853/24)
Most minutes, game
50 — La'Keshia Frett, vs. New York,
    June 13, 2002 (2 ot)
49 — Andrea Nagy, vs. Washington,
    June 25, 2002 (2 ot)
48 — Ticha Penicheiro, vs. New York,
    June 13, 2002 (2 ot)

SCORING

Most points, lifetime
2,343 — Yolanda Griffith
2,172 — Tangela Smith
2,023 — Ruthie Bolton
Highest average, points per game, career
(Minimum 90 games)
16.3 — Yolanda Griffith (2343/144)
11.5 — Tangela Smith (2172/189)
11.0 — Ruthie Bolton (2023/184)
Most points, season
545 — Yolanda Griffith, 1999
523 — Yolanda Griffith, 2000
518 — Yolanda Griffith, 2001
Highest average, points per game, season
19.4 — Ruthie Bolton-Holifield, 1997 (447/23)
18.8 — Yolanda Griffith, 1999 (545/29)
16.3 — Yolanda Griffith, 2000 (523/32)
Most points, game
34 — Ruthie Bolton-Holifield, vs. Utah,
    August 8, 1997
    Ruthie Bolton-Holifield, vs. Cleveland,
    August 12, 1997
    Ruthie Bolton-Holifield, at Washington,
    July 2, 1999
33 — Linda Burgess, vs. Utah,
    August 15, 1998
31 — Yolanda Griffith, vs. Phoenix,
    June 12, 1999
Most games, 30 or more points, career
4 — Yolanda Griffith
3 — Ruthie Bolton
1 — Linda Burgess
Most games, 20 or more points, career
45 — Yolanda Griffith
27 — Ruthie Bolton
18 — Tangela Smith
Most consecutive games, 20 or more points
7 — Ruthie Bolton-Holifield, June 23-
    July 10, 1997
4 — Yolanda Griffith, July 16-22, 1999
3 — By many
Most consecutive games, 10 or more points
25 — Ruthie Bolton-Holifield,
    June 21, 1997—June 16, 1998
20 — Tangela Smith, June 18-
    August 1, 2002
19 — Latasha Byears, June 30-
    August 11, 1998

FIELD GOAL PERCENTAGE

Highest field goal percentage, career
(Minimum 350 field goals)
.521 — Yolanda Griffith (839/1610)
.485 — Latasha Byears (482/994)
.435 — Tangela Smith (913/2099)

Highest field goal percentage, season (qualifiers)
.541 — Yolanda Griffith, 1999 (200/370)
.537 — Latasha Byears, 1999 (130/242)
.535 — Yolanda Griffith, 2000 (193/361)
Highest field goal percentage, game
(Minimum 8 field goals made)
.889 — Yolanda Griffith, at Seattle,
August 14, 2001 (8/9)
.833 — Tangela Smith, at Washington,
June 23, 2000 (10/12)
.818 — Latasha Byears, at Los Angeles,
June 10, 1999 (9/11)
Most field goals, none missed, game
5 — Latasha Byears, vs. Phoenix,
August 7, 1999
4 — Latasha Byears, vs. Cleveland,
August 12, 1997
Lady Hardmon, at Phoenix,
July 20, 1998
DeMya Walker, vs. Charlotte,
August 3, 2003
Most field goal attempts, none made, game
9 — Ticha Penicheiro, at New York,
June 17, 2003
8 — Chantel Tremitiere, vs. Cleveland,
August 12, 1997
Ruthie Bolton-Holifield, at Utah,
June 19, 1999
7 — Ticha Penicheiro, vs. Detroit,
August 11, 1998
Kedra Holland-Corn, at Houston,
August 10, 2002
Ticha Penicheiro, vs. Minnesota,
August 9, 2003

FIELD GOALS

Most field goals, career
913 — Tangela Smith
839 — Yolanda Griffith
710 — Ruthie Bolton
Most field goals, season
200 — Yolanda Griffith, 1999
193 — Yolanda Griffith, 2000
192 — Yolanda Griffith, 2001
Most field goals, game
14 — Latasha Byears, at Phoenix,
July 20, 1998
Linda Burgess, vs. Utah,
August 15, 1998
Tangela Smith, vs. Utah,
August 14, 1999
13 — Yolanda Griffith, vs. Utah,
July 15, 2000
12 — Ruthie Bolton-Holifield, vs.
Cleveland, August 12, 1997
Yolanda Griffith, vs. Houston,
July 10, 2001 (2 ot)

FIELD GOAL ATTEMPTS

Most field goal attempts, career
2,099 — Tangela Smith
1,934 — Ruthie Bolton
1,610 — Yolanda Griffith
Most field goal attempts, season
435 — Tangela Smith, 2002
427 — Tangela Smith, 2003
408 — Ruthie Bolton-Holifield, 1997
Most field goal attempts, game
24 — Ruthie Bolton-Holifield,
at Cleveland, July 10, 1997
Ruthie Bolton-Holifield, vs. Orlando,
July 27, 2000
23 — By many

THREE-POINT FIELD-GOAL PERCENTAGE

Highest three-point field goal percentage, career
(Minimum 90 three-point field goals)
.332 — Kedra Holland-Corn (198/596)
.312 — Ruthie Bolton (282/905)
Highest three-point field goal percentage, season
(qualifiers)
.457 — Edna Campbell, 2001 (43/94)
.414 — Edna Campbell, 2003 (46/111)
.400 — Kara Lawson, 2003 (54/135)
Most three-point field goals, none missed, game
5 — Kara Lawson, vs. Charlotte,
August 3, 2003
4 — Kedra Holland-Corn, at Phoenix,
July 13, 2000
3 — By many
Most three-point field goal attempts, none made,
game
7 — Ruthie Bolton-Holifield,
vs. Los Angeles, July 27, 1997
6 — By many

THREE-POINT FIELD GOALS

Most three-point field goals, career
282 — Ruthie Bolton
198 — Kedra Holland-Corn
89 — Edna Campbell
Most three-point field goals, season
66 — Ruthie Bolton-Holifield, 1997
60 — Ruthie Bolton-Holifield, 1999
59 — Kedra Holland-Corn, 2001
Most three-point field goals, game
6 — By many. Most recent:
Kara Lawson, vs. Los Angeles,
July 31, 2003
Most consecutive games, three-point field goals
made
20 — Ruthie Bolton-Holifield,
June 21-August 2, 2000
18 — Kedra Holland-Corn, June 10-
July 19, 1999

14 — Kedra Holland-Corn,
    August 11, 2001-June 25, 2002

THREE-POINT FIELD GOAL ATTEMPTS

Most three-point field goal attempts, career
    905 — Ruthie Bolton
    596 — Kedra Holland-Corn
    265 — Ticha Penicheiro
Most three-point field goal attempts, season
    192 — Ruthie Bolton-Holifield, 1997
    187 — Ruthie Bolton-Holifield, 1999
    167 — Kedra Holland-Corn, 1999
Most three-point field goal attempts, game
    15 — Ruthie Bolton-Holifield,
        at Cleveland, July 10, 1997
    14 — Ruthie Bolton-Holifield, vs. Utah,
        July 2, 1997 (ot)
    12 — Ruthie Bolton-Holifield, vs.
        New York, June 23, 1997
        Ruthie Bolton-Holifield, vs. Orlando,
        July 27, 2000

FREE THROW PERCENTAGE

Highest free-throw percentage, career
(Minimum 175 free throws)
    .750 — Tangela Smith (312/416)
    .748 — Lady Grooms (288/385)
    .747 — Ruthie Bolton (321/430)
Highest free-throw percentage, season (qualifiers)
    .855 — Lady Grooms, 2002 (71/83)
    .851 — Tangela Smith, 2002 (86/101)
    .803 — Yolanda Griffith, 2002 (102/127)
Most free throws made, none missed, game
    13 — Yolanda Griffith, at Charlotte,
        June 24, 2001 (ot)
    10 — Tangela Smith, vs. Orlando,
        July 21, 2002
    9 — Ticha Penicheiro, at Minnesota,
        June 11, 2002
Most free throw attempts, none made, game
    6 — Tangela Smith, vs. Utah,
        August 14, 1999
    4 — Ticha Penicheiro, vs. New York,
        June 18, 1998
        Pauline Jordan, at Detroit,
        July 31, 1998
    3 — Chantelle Anderson, vs. Los Angeles,
        June 7, 2003

FREE THROWS MADE

Most free throws made, career
    665 — Yolanda Griffith
    387 — Ticha Penicheiro
    321 — Ruthie Bolton
Most free throws made, season
    147 — Yolanda Griffith, 2003
    145 — Yolanda Griffith, 1999

137 — Yolanda Griffith, 2000
Most free throws made, game
    13 — Ruthie Bolton-Holifield,
        at Washington, July 2, 1999
        Yolanda Griffith, vs. Los Angeles,
        August 10, 1999
        Yolanda Griffith, at Charlotte,
        June 24, 2001 (ot)
        Yolanda Griffith, at Phoenix,
        May 22, 2003
    12 — By many

FREE THROW ATTEMPTS

Most free throw attempts, career
    932 — Yolanda Griffith
    590 — Ticha Penicheiro
    430 — Ruthie Bolton
Most free throw attempts, season
    235 — Yolanda Griffith, 1999
    194 — Yolanda Griffith, 2000
    190 — Yolanda Griffith, 2003
Most free throw attempts, game
    19 — Yolanda Griffith, vs. Phoenix,
        June 12, 1999
    17 — Yolanda Griffith, vs. Minnesota,
        August 7, 2001
    16 — Yolanda Griffith, vs. Los Angeles,
        August 10, 1999

REBOUNDS

Most rebounds, career
    1,413 — Yolanda Griffith
    980 — Tangela Smith
    692 — Ticha Penicheiro
Highest average, rebounds per game, career
(Minimum 90 games)
    9.8 — Yolanda Griffith (1413/144)
    5.6 — Latasha Byears (685/122)
    5.2 — Tangela Smith (980/189)
Most rebounds, season
    357 — Yolanda Griffith, 2001
    331 — Yolanda Griffith, 2000
    329 — Yolanda Griffith, 1999
Highest average, rebounds per game, season
(qualifiers)
    11.3 — Yolanda Griffith, 1999 (329/29)
    11.2 — Yolanda Griffith, 2001 (357/32)
    10.3 — Yolanda Griffith, 2000 (331/32)
Most rebounds, game
    20 — Yolanda Griffith, at Washington,
        June 5, 2001
    19 — Yolanda Griffith, vs. Cleveland,
        June 17, 1999
        Yolanda Griffith, at Utah,
        June 19, 1999
        Yolanda Griffith, vs. New York,
        July 22, 1999
        Yolanda Griffith, vs. Houston,
        August 6, 2000

Most games, 10+ rebounds, career
   73 — Yolanda Griffith
   17 — Latasha Byears
   12 — Tangela Smith
Most consecutive games, 10+ rebounds
   5 — Yolanda Griffith, June 24-July 4, 1999
       Yolanda Griffith, June 12-21, 2001
   4 — Yolanda Griffith, July 8-16, 1999
       Yolanda Griffith, July 13-22, 2000
   3 — By many

OFFENSIVE REBOUNDS

Most offensive rebounds, career
   609 — Yolanda Griffith
   317 — Tangela Smith
   291 — Latasha Byears
Highest average, offensive rebounds per game,
career (Minimum 90 games)
   4.2 — Yolanda Griffith (609/144)
   2.4 — Latasha Byears (291/122)
   1.7 — Tangela Smith (317/189)
Most offensive rebounds, season
   162 — Yolanda Griffith, 2001
   148 — Yolanda Griffith, 2000
   141 — Yolanda Griffith, 1999
Most offensive rebounds, game
   11 — Yolanda Griffith, vs. Los Angeles,
        June 26, 1999
        Yolanda Griffith, vs. Houston,
        August 6, 2000
   10 — Yolanda Griffith, at Washington,
        June 5, 2001
   9 — By many

DEFENSIVE REBOUNDS

Most defensive rebounds, career
   804 — Yolanda Griffith
   663 — Tangela Smith
   596 — Ticha Penicheiro
Highest average, defensive rebounds per game,
career (Minimum 90 games)
   5.6 — Yolanda Griffith (804/144)
   3.51 — Tangela Smith (663/189)
   3.45 — Ticha Penicheiro (596/173)
Most defensive rebounds, season
   195 — Yolanda Griffith, 2001
   188 — Yolanda Griffith, 1999
   183 — Yolanda Griffith, 2000
Most defensive rebounds, game
   13 — Yolanda Griffith, vs. Portland,
        June 16, 2001 (ot)
   12 — Ticha Penicheiro, vs. Utah,
        August 15, 1998
        Ticha Penicheiro, at Los Angeles,
        June 10, 1999
        Yolanda Griffith, at Phoenix,
        June 14, 1999

Yolanda Griffith, vs. Cleveland, June 17, 1999

ASSISTS

Most assists, career
   1,279 — Ticha Penicheiro
   322 — Ruthie Bolton
   264 — Kedra Holland-Corn
Highest average, assists per game, career
(Minimum 90 games)
   7.4 — Ticha Penicheiro (1279/173)
   2.1 — Kedra Holland-Corn (264/128)
   1.8 — Ruthie Bolton-Holifield (322/184)
Most assists, season
   236 — Ticha Penicheiro, 2000
   229 — Ticha Penicheiro, 2003
   226 — Ticha Penicheiro, 1999
Highest average, assists per game, season
(qualifiers)
   8.0 — Ticha Penicheiro, 2002 (192/24)
   7.9 — Ticha Penicheiro, 2000 (236/30)
   7.5 — Ticha Penicheiro, 2001 (172/23)
Most assists, game
   16 — Ticha Penicheiro, at Cleveland,
        July 29, 1998
        Ticha Penicheiro,
        vs. Los Angeles, August 3, 2002
   15 — Ticha Penicheiro, at Cleveland,
        July 15, 2003
   14 — Ticha Penicheiro, vs. Minnesota,
        June 22, 1999
        Ticha Penicheiro, vs. Detroit,
        July 1, 2000
        Ticha Penicheiro, vs. Minnesota,
        August 7, 2001
        Ticha Penicheiro, vs. Phoenix,
        May 30, 2003
Most games, 10+ assists, career
   47 — Ticha Penicheiro
   2 — Chantel Tremitiere
   1 — Andrea Nagy

PERSONAL FOULS

Most personal fouls, career
   592 — Tangela Smith
   510 — Yolanda Griffith
   431 — Ticha Penicheiro
Most personal fouls, season
   126 — Tangela Smith, 2002
   125 — Yolanda Griffith, 2003
   121 — Latasha Byears, 1998
Most personal fouls, game
   6 — by many

DISQUALIFICATIONS

Most disqualifications, career
   10 — Latasha Byears
   9 — Tangela Smith
   5 — Yolanda Griffith
       Pam McGee
       Ticha Penicheiro

Highest percentage, games disqualified, career
(Minimum 90 games)
  8.2 — Latasha Byears (10/122)
  4.8 — Tangela Smith (9/189)
  3.5 — Yolanda Griffith (5/144)
Lowest percentage, games disqualified, career
(Minimum 90 games)
  0.0 — Lady Grooms (0/189)
  1.6 — Ruthie Bolton (3/184)
  2.9 — Ticha Penicheiro (5/173)
Most consecutive games without disqualification,
career
  189 — Lady Grooms, June 11, 1998-
        August 25, 2003 (current)
  163 — Ruthie Bolton, August 22, 1997
        August 25, 2003 (current)
   71 — Tangela Smith, June 11, 1998-
        June 25, 2000
Most disqualifications, season
    5 — Pam McGee, 1997
    4 — Latasha Byears, 1997
        Latasha Byears, 1998
        Tangela Smith, 2002
    3 — By many
Fewest minutes, disqualified, game
   13 — Yolanda Griffith, vs. Los Angeles,
        June 7, 2003
   14 — Chantelle Anderson, vs. Los Angeles,
        June 7, 2003
   16 — Pauline Jordan, at Charlotte,
        July 27, 1998

STEALS

Most steals, career
  369 — Ticha Penicheiro
  292 — Yolanda Griffith
  231 — Ruthie Bolton
Highest average, steals per game, career
(Minimum 90 games)
  2.13 — Ticha Penicheiro (369/173)
  2.03 — Yolanda Griffith (292/144)
  1.59 — Kedra Holland-Corn (203/128)
Most steals, season
   83 — Yolanda Griffith, 2000
   73 — Yolanda Griffith, 1999
   70 — Ticha Penicheiro, 2000
Highest average, steals per game, season
(qualifiers)
  2.67 — Ticha Penicheiro, 2002 (64/24)
  2.59 — Yolanda Griffith, 2000 (83/32)
  2.52 — Yolanda Griffith, 1999 (73/29)
Most steals, game
   10 — Ticha Penicheiro, vs. San Antonio,

July 10, 2003
    8 — Yolanda Griffith, vs. Washington,
        July 29, 1999
    7 — Yolanda Griffith, at Detroit, June 3, 2000
        Ticha Penicheiro, at Houston,
        June 6, 2000
        Ticha Penicheiro, vs. Phoenix,
        August 6, 2002

BLOCKED SHOTS

Most blocked shots, career
  281 — Tangela Smith
  204 — Yolanda Griffith
   32 — Latasha Byears
Highest average, blocked shots per game, career
(Minimum: 90 games)
  1.49 — Tangela Smith (281/189)
  1.42 — Yolanda Griffith (204/144)
  0.26 — Latasha Byears (32/122)
Most blocked shots, season
   64 — Tangela Smith, 2000
   61 — Yolanda Griffith, 2000
   55 — Tangela Smith, 2001
Highest average, blocked shots per game, season
(qualifiers)
  2.00 — Tangela Smith, 2000 (64/32)
  1.91 — Yolanda Griffith, 2000 (61/32)
  1.86 — Yolanda Griffith, 1999 (54/29)
Most blocked shots, game
    6 — Yolanda Griffith, vs. New York,
        July 22, 1999
        Yolanda Griffith, vs. Orlando,
        July 24, 1999
        Yolanda Griffith, vs. Minnesota,
        July 20, 2000
        Tangela Smith, vs. Seattle,
        August 9, 2000
    5 — By many

TURNOVERS

Most turnovers, career
  536 — Ticha Penicheiro
  343 — Yolanda Griffith
  325 — Tangela Smith
Most turnovers, season
  135 — Ticha Penicheiro, 1999
  122 — Chantel Tremitiere, 1997
  116 — Ticha Penicheiro, 1998
Most turnovers, game
    8 — By many. Most recent:
        Ticha Penicheiro, vs. Houston,
        August 21, 1999

SAN ANTONIO SILVER STARS

REGULAR SEASON TEAM RECORDS AS UTAH STARZZ

TEAM OFFENSE

SCORING

Highest average, points per game, season
75.6 — 2002 (2418/32)
75.4 — 2000 (2413/32)
Lowest average, points per game, season
64.6 — 1997 (1809/28)
65.2 — 2003 (2215/34)
Most points, game
104 — vs. Detroit, July 6, 1999 (2 ot)
102 — vs. Los Angeles, June 23, 1997
Fewest points, game
46 — at Phoenix, August 6, 1997
47 — vs. Seattle, June 25, 2001
at Indiana, July 23, 2003
Largest margin of victory, game
31 — vs. Minnesota, July 5, 2002 (87-56)
28 — vs. Charlotte, June 15, 2000 (96-68)
Largest margin of defeat, game
40 — at Seattle, June 22, 2003 (53-93)
38 — at Sacramento, June 24, 1999
(69-107)

BY HALF

Most points, first half
51 — vs. Detroit, July 8, 2002
50 — vs. Los Angeles, June 23, 1997
Fewest points, first half
17 — vs. Seattle, June 25, 2001
18 — vs. Cleveland, August 11, 1997
at Seattle, June 18, 2000
at Sacramento, June 24, 2003
Largest lead at halftime
22 — at Washington, July 19, 1998
(led 47-25; won 99-88)
19 — vs. Detroit, July 8, 2002
(led 51-32; won 94-76)
Largest deficit at halftime overcome to win game
18 — at Phoenix, August 20, 1999
(trailed 20-38; won 70-62)
14 — at Portland, July 8, 2001
(trailed 30-44; won 65-63)
Most points, second half
60 — vs. Sacramento, June 26, 2000
54 — vs. Charlotte, June 15, 2000
at Detroit, July 23, 2002
Fewest points, second half
17 — vs. Houston, June 30, 1998
at Sacramento, August 15, 1998
vs. Los Angeles, June 26, 2003
18 — at Phoenix, August 6, 1997

OVERTIME

Most points, overtime period
14 — vs. Miami, July 31, 2002
vs. Seattle, August 20, 2003
13 — vs. Detroit, July 6, 1999 (1st OT)
Fewest points, overtime period
3 — at Phoenix, August 17, 1997
6 — vs. Los Angeles, August 13, 2001
Largest margin of victory, overtime period
10 — vs. Detroit, July 6, 1999(104-94) (2 ot)
8 — vs. Minnesota, July 28, 2001 (68-60)
vs. Seattle, August 20, 2003 (78-70)

FIELD GOAL PERCENTAGE

Highest field-goal percentage, season
.453 — 2000 (858/1896)
.441 — 2002 (843/1911)
Lowest field-goal percentage, season
.374 — 1997 (666/1781)
.383 — 2003 (792/2068)
Highest field-goal percentage, game
.614 — vs. Phoenix, July 14, 2000 (35/57)
.604 — at Indiana, July 10, 2002 (29-48)
Lowest field-goal percentage, game
.242 — at Indiana, July 23, 2003 (16/66)
.250 — vs. New York, July 5, 1997 (17/68)

FIELD GOALS

Most field goals per game, season
26.8 — 2000 (858/32)
26.4 — 1999 (845/32)
Fewest field goals per game, season
23.3 — 2003 (792/34)
23.8 — 1997 (666/28)
Most field goals, game
40 — vs. Detroit, July 6, 1999 (2 ot)
35 — vs. Charlotte, June 25, 1998
at Sacramento, August 14, 1999
vs. Charlotte, June 15, 2000
vs. Phoenix, July 14, 2000
Fewest field goals, game
15 — vs. New York, August 3, 1999
16 — at Charlotte, June 4, 2003
at Indiana, July 23, 2003

FIELD GOAL ATTEMPTS

Most field-goal attempts per game, season
63.6 — 1997 (1781/28)
61.2 — 1998 (1837/30)
Fewest field-goal attempts per game, season
57.8 — 2001 (1849/32)
59.3 — 2000 (1896/32)
Most field-goal attempts, game
87 — vs. Detroit, July 6, 1999 (2 ot)

79 — vs. Houston, June 30, 1998 (2 ot)
Regulation game:
78 — vs. Washington, July 19, 2003
Fewest field-goal attempts, game
43 — vs. New York, July 26, 2001
45 — vs. Seattle, May 24, 2003

THREE-POINT FIELD-GOAL PERCENTAGE

Highest three-point field-goal percentage, season
.360 — 2002 (89/247)
.336 — 2000 (88/262)
Lowest three-point field-goal percentage, season
.295 — 2003 (93/315)
.296 — 1999 (107/362)

THREE-POINT FIELD GOALS

Most three-point field goals per game, season
3.79 — 1997 (106/28)
3.77 — 1998 (113/30)
Fewest three-point field goals per game, season
2.4 — 2001 (78/32)
2.7 — 2003 (93/34)
Most three-point field goals, game
10 — vs. Washington, June 13, 1998
9 — at Minnesota, August 2, 2000
Fewest three-point field goals, game
0 — Many times. Most recent:
at Phoenix, August 22, 2003

THREE-POINT FIELD GOAL ATTEMPTS

Most three-point field goal attempts per game, season
12.5 — 1997 (349/28)
11.5 — 1998 (346/30)
Fewest three-point field goal attempts per game, season
7.6 — 2001 (244/32)
7.7 — 2002 (247/32)
Most three-point field goal attempts, game
25 — vs. Charlotte, August 21, 1997
20 — at Sacramento, July 10, 2003
Fewest three-point field goal attempts, game
1 — at Detroit, August 7, 2001
2 — at Phoenix, May 30, 2001
at Miami, June 27, 2001 (ot)
at Sacramento, July 12, 2001
vs. Charlotte, June 8, 2002

FREE THROW PERCENTAGE

Highest free-throw percentage, season
.771 — 2000 (609/790)
.768 — 1999 (570/742)
Lowest free-throw percentage, season
.701 — 1998 (426/608)
.703 — 1997 (371/528)
Highest free-throw percentage, game
1.000 — vs. Sacramento, July 7, 1997 (11/11)
at Houston, July 11, 1998 (11/11)
.950 — at Detroit, July 21, 1999 (19/20)

Lowest free-throw percentage, game
.364 — vs. Charlotte, August 9, 1999 (4/11)
.389 — vs. Los Angeles,
August 13, 2001 (7/18) (ot)

FREE THROWS MADE

Most free throws made per game, season
20.1 — 2002 (643/32)
19.0 — 2000 (609/32)
Fewest free throws made per game, season
13.3 — 1997 (371/28)
14.2 — 1998 (426/30)
Most free throws made, game
42 — vs. Los Angeles, June 23, 1997
33 — vs. Orlando, June 7, 2001
Fewest free throws made, game
3 — at Houston, June 28, 2003
4 — vs. Charlotte, August 9, 1999

FREE THROW ATTEMPTS

Most free throw attempts per game, season
26.4 — 2002 (844/32)
24.7 — 2000 (790/32)
Fewest free throw attempts per game, season
18.9 — 1997 (528/28)
20.3 — 1998 (608/30)
Most free throw attempts, game
56 — vs. Los Angeles, June 23, 1997
40 — vs. Portland, August 7, 2000
vs. Orlando, June 7, 2001
at Phoenix, August 22, 2003
Fewest free throw attempts, game
4 — at Houston, June 28, 2003
7 — vs. Houston, June 30, 1998 (2 ot)

REBOUNDS

Most rebounds per game, season
34.0 — 1997 (951/28)
33.8 — 2000 (1080/32)
Fewest rebounds per game, season
33.2 — 1999 (1061/32)
33.4 — 1998 (1001/30)
Most rebounds, game
54 — vs. Detroit, July 6, 1999 (2 ot)
47 — at Sacramento, July 2, 1997 (ot)
vs. Charlotte, June 15, 2000
Fewest rebounds, game
19 — at Phoenix, August 6, 1997
22 — at Cleveland, July 19, 1997
at New York, June 21, 1998
at Seattle, June 22, 2003

OFFENSIVE REBOUNDS

Most offensive rebounds per game, season
12.1 — 1997 (339/28)
10.9 — 2000 (348/32)
Fewest offensive rebounds per game, season
9.2 — 2001 (295/32)
10.1 — 1998 (302/30)
Most offensive rebounds, game
20 — vs. New York, July 5, 1997

vs. Phoenix, June 6, 2000
vs. Portland, May 30, 2002
19 — at Houston, July 14, 1997
vs. Washington, July 19, 2003
Fewest offensive rebounds, game
2 — at Phoenix, August 6, 1997
3 — at New York, June 21, 1998
at Phoenix, August 8, 1998
at Sacramento, June 24, 2003

DEFENSIVE REBOUNDS

Most defensive rebounds per game, season
24.2 — 2001 (775/32)
23.4 — 2003 (795/34)
Fewest defensive rebounds per game, season
21.9 — 1997 (612/28)
22.4 — 1999 (717/32)
Most defensive rebounds, game
40 — vs. Detroit, July 6, 1999 (2 ot)
39 — vs. Connecticut, June 1, 2003
Fewest defensive rebounds, game
11 — at Cleveland, July 19, 1997
12 — vs. Sacramento, July 7, 1997
vs. Sacramento, August 7, 2003

ASSISTS

Most assists per game, season
17.3 — 1999 (552/32)
16.4 — 2001 (524/32)
Fewest assists per game, season
12.6 — 2003 (428/34)
14.9 — 2002 (478/32)
Most assists, game
28 — vs. Detroit, July 6, 1999 (2 ot)
26 — at Seattle, July 1, 2000
Fewest assists, game
6 — at Miami, July 21, 2000
7 — at New York, August 8, 2001
vs. Phoenix, June 5, 2003

PERSONAL FOULS

Most personal fouls per game, season
23.1 — 1999 (740/32)
21.8 — 2000 (698/32)
Fewest personal fouls per game, season
19.4 — 2001 (622/32)
20.3 — 1997 (567/28)
Most personal fouls, game
36 — at Phoenix, August 22, 2003
35 — at Detroit, July 1, 2003
Fewest personal fouls, game
11 — vs. Miami, July 2, 2001
12 — vs. Sacramento, July 6, 1998
at Charlotte, July 22, 1998
at Charlotte, August 5, 2000

DISQUALIFICATIONS

Most disqualifications per game, season
0.30 — 1998 (9/30)
0.24 — 2003 (8/34)

Fewest disqualifications per game, season
0.14 — 1997 (4/28)
0.16 — 1999 (5/32)
Most disqualifications, game
2 — vs. Detroit, August 10, 1998
vs. Portland, July 12, 2000
at Seattle, August 12, 2003
1 — many times

STEALS

Most steals per game, season
9.0 — 1997 (252/28)
7.5 — 1999 (240/32)
Fewest steals per game, season
5.5 — 2003 (187/34)
6.3 — 2001 (202/32)
Most steals, game
17 — at Los Angeles, July 11, 1997
14 — vs. New York, July 5, 1997
vs. Detroit, July 13, 1998
vs. Detroit, July 7, 2000
vs. Phoenix, June 5, 2003
Fewest steals, game
0 — vs. Connecticut, June 1, 2003
1 — at Indiana, July 10, 2002
vs. Detroit, June 7, 2003
at Washington, June 10, 2003
vs. Washington, July 19, 2003

BLOCKED SHOTS

Most blocked shots per game, season
5.7 — 1998 (170/30)
5.6 — 2002 (178/32)
Fewest blocked shots per game, season
4.4 — 1997 (123/28)
4.9 — 2001 (156/32)
Most blocked shots, game
12 — vs. Sacramento, July 14, 2001
11 — vs. Sacramento, August 12, 1998
vs. Sacramento, June 19, 1999
vs. Sacramento, July 31, 1999
vs. Portland, June 25, 2002
10 — Many times
Fewest blocked shots, game
0 — vs. Houston, June 23, 2000
at Charlotte, August 5, 2000
at New York, August 8, 2001
1 — Many times

TURNOVERS

Most turnovers per game, season
18.6 — 1997 (520/28)
18.1 — 1998 (543/30)
Fewest turnovers per game, season
15.1 — 2003 (513/34)
15.4 — 2001 (493/32)
Most turnovers, game
33 — at New York, July 17, 1997
at Phoenix, August 17, 1997 (ot)
30 — at Los Angeles, June 28, 1999

Fewest turnovers, game
8 — vs. Los Angeles, June 23, 1997
vs. Los Angeles, August 9, 2000
9 — Many times

POINTS

Fewest points allowed per game, season
68.5 — 2001 (2192/32)
71.4 — 2003 (2427/34)
Most points allowed per game, season
77.1 — 1999 (2467/32)
76.5 — 1998 (2294/30)
Fewest points allowed, game
51 — vs. Phoenix, July 12, 1997
at Phoenix, May 28, 2003
52 — vs. Charlotte, June 14, 2003
vs. Los Angeles, August 9, 2003
Fewest points allowed, first half
16 — vs. Los Angeles, August 9, 2003
18 — vs. Phoenix, July 12, 1997
Fewest points allowed, second half
18 — at Charlotte, July 22, 1998
vs. Phoenix, June 5, 2003
19 — at Portland, July 8, 2001
Fewest points allowed, overtime period
1 — vs. Detroit, July 6, 1999 (2nd ot)
2 — at Miami, June 27, 2001
vs. Minnesota, July 28, 2001

FIELD GOAL PERCENTAGE

Lowest opponents' field-goal percentage, season
.398 — 2003 (867/2176)
.399 — 2001 (789/1976)
Highest opponents' field-goal percentage, season
.4379 — 2000 (860/1964)
.4377 — 1999 (860/1965)
Lowest opponents' field goal percentage, game
.259 — vs. Minnesota, July 28, 2001 (15/58) (ot)
.284 — vs. Seattle, June 15, 2002 (19/67)

TURNOVERS

Most opponents' turnovers per game, season
16.4 — 1997 (458/28)
14.9 — 1999 (477/32)
Fewest opponents' turnovers per game, season
12.2 — 2001 (390/32)
12.5 — 2003 (424/34)
Most opponents' turnovers, game
26 — vs. Detroit, July 7, 2000
24 — Many times

TEAM MISCELLANEOUS

GAME WON AND LOST

Highest winning percentage, season
.625 — 2002 (20-12)
.594 — 2001 (19-13)

Lowest winning percentage, season
.250 — 1997 (7-21)
.267 — 1998 (8-22)
Most consecutive games won
8 — July 24-August 7, 2001
4 — Many times
Most consecutive games won, one season
8 — July 24-August 7, 2001
4 — Many times
Most consecutive game lost
6 — August 6-17, 1997
June 19-30, 1998
July 30-August 10, 1998
July 10-21, 1999
July 10-25, 2003
Most consecutive game lost, one season
6 — August 6-17, 1997
June 19-30, 1998
July 30-August 10, 1998
July 10-21, 1999
July 10-25, 2003
Highest winning percentage, home games, season
.750 — 2000 (12-4)
2002 (12-4)
.688 — 1999 (11-5)
Lowest winning percentage, home games, season
.333 — 1998 (5-10)
.357 — 1997 (5-9)
Most consecutive home games won
7 — August 5, 1999-June 6, 2000
July 14, 2001-May 30, 2002
6 — July 12-August 9, 2000
July 5-31, 2002
Most consecutive home games lost
4 — June 28-July 7, 1997
August 1-10, 1998
Highest winning percentage, road games, season
.625 — 2001 (10-6)
.500 — 2002 (8-8)
Lowest winning percentage, road games, season
.143 — 1997 (2-12)
.176 — 2003 (3-14)
Most consecutive road games won
5 — July 24-August 7, 2001
3 — May 30-June 27, 2001
Most consecutive road games lost
10 — July 30, 1997-June 26, 1998
9 — July 25, 1998-June 28, 1999

OVERTIME GAMES

Most overtime games, season
3 — 1999, 2001
2 — 1997, 2002
Most consecutive overtime games, season
2 — July 16-18, 1999
Most overtime games won, season
3 — 2001
2 — 2002

RECORDS San Antonio Silver Stars

Most overtime games won, no losses, season
  3 — 2001
  2 — 2002
Most consecutive overtime games won
  6 — June 27, 2001-August 20, 2003
     (current)
Most overtime games lost, season
  2 — 1999
  1 — 1997, 1998
Most overtime games lost, no wins, season
  1 — 1998
Most consecutive overtime games lost
  2 — August 17, 1997-June 30, 1998
     July 16-18, 1999
Most overtime periods, game
  2 — vs. Houston, June 30, 1998
     vs. Detroit, July 6, 1999

INDIVIDUAL RECORDS

SEASONS
Most Seasons
  6 — Margo Dydek
LaTonya Johnson
  5 — Adrienne Goodson
  4 — Jennifer Azzi
     Natalie Williams

GAMES
Most game, career
  190 — Margo Dydek
  173 — LaTonya Johnson
  154 — Adrienne Goodson
Most consecutive games, career
  139 — Margo Dydek, June 11, 1998-
     June 30, 2002
  113 — Jennifer Azzi, July 7, 2000-
     August 23, 2003 (current)
  98 — Marie Ferdinand, May 30, 2001
     August 23, 2003 (current)
Most games, season
  34 — Jennifer Azzi, 2003
     Margo Dydek, 2003
     Marie Ferdinand, 2003

MINUTES
Most minutes, career
  5,119 — Margo Dydek
  4,921 — Adrienne Goodson
  4,065 — Natalie Williams
Highest average, minutes per game, career
(Minimum: 90 games)
  35.8 — Jennifer Azzi (4051/113)
  34.2 — Natalie Williams (4065/119)
  32.0 — Adrienne Goodson (4921/154)
Most minutes, season
  1,205 — Jennifer Azzi, 2001
  1,151 — Jennifer Azzi, 2002

1,136 — Jennifer Azzi, 2003
Highest average, minutes per game, season
  37.7 — Jennifer Azzi, 2001 (1205/32)
  37.3 — Jennifer Azzi, 2000 (559/15)
  36.0 — Jennifer Azzi, 2002 (1151/32)
Most minutes, game
  46 — Adrienne Goodson, vs. Detroit,
     July 6, 1999 (2 ot)
  45 — Debbie Black, vs. Houston,
     July 16, 1999 (ot)
     Natalie Williams, at New York,
     July 18, 1999 (ot)
     Jennifer Azzi, vs. Los Angeles,
     August 13, 2001 (ot)

SCORING
Most points, lifetime
  2,232 — Margo Dydek
  2,191 — Adrienne Goodson
  1,837 — Natalie Williams
Highest average, points per game, career
(Minimum 90 games)
  15.4 — Natalie Williams (1837/119)
  14.2 — Adrienne Goodson (2191/154)
  13.5 — Marie Ferdinand (1325/98)
Most points, season
  543 — Natalie Williams, 2000
  504 — Natalie Williams, 1999
  503 — Adrienne Goodson, 2002
Highest average, points per game, season
  18.7 — Natalie Williams, 2000 (543/29)
  18.0 — Natalie Williams, 1999 (504/28)
  17.2 — Adrienne Goodson, 2000 (498/29)
Most points, game
  31 — Wendy Palmer, vs. Sacramento,
     August 12, 1998
     Natalie Williams, vs. Detroit,
     July 6, 1999 (2 ot)
  30 — Wendy Palmer, vs. Charlotte,
     July 8, 1998
     Natalie Williams, vs. Washington,
     June 17, 2000
     Adrienne Goodson, vs. Portland,
     June 25, 2002
  29 — Natalie Williams, at Sacramento,
     July 15, 2000
     Adrienne Goodson, vs. Indiana,
     July 29, 2000
Most games, 30 or more points, career
  2 — Wendy Palmer
     Natalie Williams
  1 — Adrienne Goodson
Most games, 20 or more points, career
  30 — Natalie Williams
  27 — Adrienne Goodson
  18 — Margo Dydek
Most consecutive games, 20 or more points
  3 — Elena Baranova, July 19-26, 1997

Wendy Palmer, August 10-14, 1998
Natalie Williams, July 23-29, 2000
Natalie Williams, August 5-9, 2000
2 — By many
Most consecutive games, 10 or more points
36 — Adrienne Goodson, June 28, 1999
June 17, 2000
23 — Natalie Williams, June 12-
August 11, 1999
Adrienne Goodson, July 24, 2001
June 25, 2002
19 — Marie Ferdinand, June 9-July 24, 2002

FIELD GOAL PERCENTAGE

Highest field goal percentage, career
(Minimum 350 field goals)
.486 — Natalie Williams (654/1346)
.458 — Margo Dydek (815/1778)
.438 — Adrienne Goodson (849/1937)
Highest field goal percentage, season (qualifiers)
.519 — Natalie Williams, 1999 (180/347)
.498 — Margo Dydek, 1999 (141/283)
.493 — Marie Ferdinand, 2001 (143/290)
Highest field goal percentage, game
(Minimum 8 field goals made)
.900 — Korie Hlede, at Minnesota,
August 11, 1999 (9/10)
.889 — Natalie Williams, vs. Phoenix,
July 14, 2000 (8/9)
.857 — Adrienne Goodson, at Portland,
August 6, 2002 (12/14)
Most field goals, none missed, game
6 — Margo Dydek, at New York,
June 21, 1998
5 — Wendy Palmer, at Houston,
July 30, 1998
4 — Amy Herrig, at Minnesota,
June 22, 2000
Most field goal attempts, none made, game
10 — Adrienne Goodson, vs. Orlando,
June 7, 2001
8 — Tammi Reiss, vs. New York,
July 5, 1997
Natalie Williams, vs. Seattle,
June 15, 2002
Marie Ferdinand, vs. Connecticut,
June 1, 2003
7 — Tai Dillard, at Phoenix,
August 22, 2003

FIELD GOALS

Most field goals, career
849 — Adrienne Goodson
815 — Margo Dydek
654 — Natalie Williams
Most field goals, season
199 — Adrienne Goodson, 2000
189 — Adrienne Goodson, 2002

182 — Adrienne Goodson, 1999
Most field goals, game
14 — Wendy Palmer, vs. Charlotte,
July 8, 1998
13 — Margo Dydek, vs. Houston,
June 30, 1998 (2 ot)
12 — Adrienne Goodson, at Portland,
August 6, 2002
Margo Dydek, at Los Angeles,
August 23, 2003

FIELD GOAL ATTEMPTS

Most field goal attempts, career
1,937 — Adrienne Goodson
1,778 — Margo Dydek
1,346 — Natalie Williams
Most field goal attempts, season
427 — Adrienne Goodson, 1999
420 — Wendy Palmer, 1997
419 — Adrienne Goodson, 2002
Most field goal attempts, game
31 — Wendy Palmer, vs. Los Angeles,
August 16, 1997
25 — Margo Dydek, vs. Houston,
June 30, 1998 (2 ot)
22 — Natalie Williams, vs. Detroit,
July 6, 1999 (2 ot)

THREE-POINT FIELD-GOAL PERCENTAGE

Highest three-point field goal percentage, career
(Minimum 90 three-point field goals)
.446 — Jennifer Azzi (128/287)
Highest three-point field goal percentage, season
(qualifiers)
.514 — Jennifer Azzi, 2001 (38/74)
.446 — Jennifer Azzi, 2002 (41/92)
.431 — Korie Hlede, 2000 (25/58)
Most three-point field goals, none missed, game
3 — By many. Most recent:
Jennifer Azzi, at Washington,
July 20, 2002
Most three-point field goal attempts, none made,
game
6 — Marie Ferdinand, vs. Houston,
July 3, 2002
4 — By many

THREE-POINT FIELD GOALS

Most three-point field goals, career
128 — Jennifer Azzi
75 — Elena Baranova
71 — LaTonya Johnson
Most three-point field goals, season
41 — Jennifer Azzi, 2002
40 — Elena Baranova, 1997
39 — Jennifer Azzi, 2003

Most three-point field goals, game
7 — Elena Baranova, at New York,
July 22, 1997
6 — LaQuanda Quick, at Sacramento,
July 10, 2003
5 — Elena Baranova, at Cleveland,
July 19, 1997
Jennifer Azzi, at Los Angeles,
July 3, 2001
Most consecutive games, three-point field goals
made
10 — Elena Baranova, August 2-
August 21, 1997
7 — Jennifer Azzi, July 21-August 3, 2001
Jennifer Azzi, July 1-23, 2003
6 — Jennifer Azzi, June 29-July 10, 2001
Jennifer Azzi, July 5-17, 2002

THREE-POINT FIELD GOAL ATTEMPTS

Most three-point field goal attempts, career
287 — Jennifer Azzi
252 — LaTonya Johnson
202 — Elena Baranova
Most three-point field goal attempts, season
106 — Elena Baranova, 1997
101 — Tammi Reiss, 1997
97 — Jennifer Azzi, 2003
Most three-point field goal attempts, game
10 — Jennifer Azzi, at Los Angeles,
July 3, 2001
LaQuanda Quick, at Sacramento, July 10, 2003
9 — Elena Baranova, at Cleveland,
July 19, 1997
Elena Baranova, at New York,
July 22, 1997
Elena Baranova, at Sacramento,
August 8, 1997
8 — Elena Baranova, vs. Cleveland,
July 26, 1997
Elena Baranova, at Phoenix,
August 6, 1997

FREE THROW PERCENTAGE

Highest free-throw percentage, career
(Minimum: 175 free throws)
.851 — Jennifer Azzi (262/308)
.792 — Margo Dydek (584/737)
.762 — Natalie Williams (521/684)
Highest free-throw percentage, season (qualifiers)
.930 — Jennifer Azzi, 2000 (40/43)
.917 — Jennifer Azzi, 2001 (88/96)
.857 — Margo Dydek, 1999 (114/133)
Most free throws made, none missed, game
11 — Jennifer Azzi, at Seattle,
August 12, 2003
10 — Margo Dydek, vs. Houston,

July 16, 1999 (ot)
Margo Dydek, at Seattle,
June 18, 2000
Margo Dydek, at Minnesota,
May 25, 2002 (ot)
Marie Ferdinand, vs. Miami,
July 31, 2002 (ot)
9 — Margo Dydek, vs. Minnesota,
June 26, 1999
Marie Ferdinand, vs. Portland,
May 30, 2002
Most free throw attempts, none made, game
6 — Wendy Palmer, at Los Angeles,
June 28, 1999
4 — Dena Head, vs. Phoenix, July 3, 1997
Lady Hardmon, at Phoenix,
August 17, 1997 (ot)
Semeka Randall, vs. Charlotte,
June 14, 2003
3 — By many

FREE THROWS MADE

Most free throws made, career
584 — Margo Dydek
521 — Natalie Williams
451 — Adrienne Goodson
Most free throws made, season
182 — Natalie Williams, 2000
176 — Marie Ferdinand, 2003
144 — Natalie Williams, 1999
Most free throws made, game
13 — Kim Williams, vs. Los Angeles,
June 23, 1997
12 — By many

FREE THROW ATTEMPTS

Most free throw attempts, career
737 — Margo Dydek
684 — Natalie Williams
611 — Adrienne Goodson
Most free throw attempts, season
228 — Natalie Williams, 2000
223 — Marie Ferdinand, 2003
191 — Natalie Williams, 1999
Most free throw attempts, game
18 — Wendy Palmer, vs. Los Angeles,
June 23, 1997
16 — Natalie Williams, vs. Los Angeles,
August 9, 2000
15 — Kim Williams, vs. Los Angeles,
June 23, 1997

REBOUNDS

Most rebounds, career
1,362 — Margo Dydek
1,156 — Natalie Williams
820 — Adrienne Goodson
Highest average, rebounds per game, career

(Minimum 90 games)
    9.7 — Natalie Williams (1156/119)
    7.2 — Margo Dydek (1362/190)
    5.3 — Adrienne Goodson (820/154)
Most rebounds, season
    336 — Natalie Williams, 2000
    308 — Natalie Williams, 2001
    262 — Margo Dydek, 2002
Highest average, rebounds per game, season
(qualifiers)
    11.6 — Natalie Williams, 2000 (336/29)
    9.9 — Natalie Williams, 2001 (308/31)
    9.3 — Elena Baranova, 1998 (186/20)
Most rebounds, game
    20 — Natalie Williams, at Sacramento,
        June 22, 2002
    19 — Natalie Williams, vs. Cleveland,
        July 26, 2000
    18 — Natalie Williams, vs. Charlotte,
        June 15, 2000
Most games, 10+ rebounds, career
    56 — Natalie Williams
    45 — Margo Dydek
    17 — Elena Baranova
        Wendy Palmer
Most consecutive games with 10+ rebounds
    7 — Natalie Williams, July 15-
        August 2, 2000
    5 — Elena Baranova, August 24, 1997-
        June 19, 1998
        Natalie Williams, June 29-July 8, 2001
    4 — By many

OFFENSIVE REBOUNDS
Most offensive rebounds, career
    457 — Natalie Williams
    371 — Adrienne Goodson
    234 — Margo Dydek
Highest average, offensive rebounds per game,
career (Minimum 90 games)
    3.8 — Natalie Williams (457/119)
    2.4 — Adrienne Goodson (371/154)
    1.2 — Margo Dydek (234/190)
Most offensive rebounds, season
    132 — Natalie Williams, 2000
    111 — Natalie Williams, 2001
    109 — Natalie Williams, 1999
Most offensive rebounds, game
    10 — Natalie Williams, at Sacramento,
        June 22, 2002
Gwen Jackson, vs. Charlotte, June 14, 2003
    9 — Natalie Williams, vs. Charlotte,
        June 15, 2000
        Natalie Williams, vs. Portland,
        July 12, 2000
    8 — Natalie Williams, vs. Indiana,
        July 29, 2000
        Adrienne Goodson, vs. Portland,
        May 30, 2002

DEFENSIVE REBOUNDS
Most defensive rebounds, career
    1,128 — Margo Dydek
    699 — Natalie Williams
    449 — Adrienne Goodson
Highest average, defensive rebounds per game,
career (Minimum 90 games)
    5.94 — Margo Dydek (1128/190)
    5.87 — Natalie Williams (699/119)
    2.9 — Adrienne Goodson (449/154)
Most defensive rebounds, season
    214 — Margo Dydek, 2001
    210 — Margo Dydek, 2002
    206 — Margo Dydek, 2003
Most defensive rebounds, game
    15 — Margo Dydek, vs. Phoenix,
        July 26, 2002
    14 — Natalie Williams, vs. Cleveland,
        July 26, 2000
    13 — By many

ASSISTS
Most assists, career
    532 — Jennifer Azzi
    356 — Margo Dydek
    352 — Adrienne Goodson
Highest average, assists per game, career
(Minimum 90 games)
    4.7 — Jennifer Azzi (532/113)
    2.7 — Marie Ferdinand (260/98)
    2.3 — Adrienne Goodson (352/154)
Most assists, season
    171 — Jennifer Azzi, 2001
    161 — Debbie Black, 1999
    158 — Jennifer Azzi, 2002
Highest average, assists per game, season
(qualifiers)
    5.3 — Jennifer Azzi, 2001 (171/32)
    5.0 — Debbie Black, 1999 (161/32)
    4.9 — Jennifer Azzi, 2002 (158/32)
Most assists, game
    11 — Debbie Black, at Cleveland,
        July 24, 1999
    10 — Debbie Black, vs. Detroit,
        July 6, 1999 (2 ot)
        Jennifer Azzi, at Sacramento,
        July 12, 2001
        Jennifer Azzi, vs. Indiana,
        August 4, 2001
    9 — By many
Most games, 10+ assists, career
    2 — Jennifer Azzi
        Debbie Black

PERSONAL FOULS
Most personal fouls, career
    672 — Margo Dydek

482 — Natalie Williams
395 — Adrienne Goodson
Most personal fouls, season
128 — Natalie Williams, 2001
126 — Margo Dydek, 1998
124 — Natalie Williams, 2000
Most personal fouls, game
6 — by many
DISQUALIFICATIONS
Most disqualifications, career
13 — Natalie Williams
9 — Margo Dydek
3 — Jennifer Azzi
Kim Williams
Highest percentage, games disqualified, career
(Minimum: 90 games)
10.9 — Natalie Williams (13/119)
4.7 — Margo Dydek (9/190)
2.7 — Jennifer Azzi (3/113)
Lowest percentage, games disqualified, career
(Minimum: 90 games)
1.0 — Marie Ferdinand (1/98)
1.2 — LaTonya Johnson (2/173)
1.3 — Adrienne Goodson (2/154)
Most consecutive games without disqualification,
career
150 — Adrienne Goodson, June 12, 1999
August 12, 2003
104 — LaTonya Johnson, July 2, 1999-
August 6, 2002
87 — Marie Ferdinand, July 2, 2001-
August 23, 2003 (current)
Most disqualifications, season
4 — Natalie Williams, 2001
Natalie Williams, 2002
3 — Margo Dydek, 1998
Natalie Williams, 2000
2 — By many
Fewest minutes, disqualified, game
8 — LaTonya Johnson, vs. Los Angeles,
August 9, 2002
10 — Jessie Hicks, at Los Angeles, July 11, 1997
11 — Tausha Mills, at Indiana, July 23, 2003

STEALS

Most steals, career
164 — Adrienne Goodson
152 — Natalie Williams
149 — Marie Ferdinand
Highest average, steals per game, career
(Minimun 90 games)
1.52 — Marie Ferdinand (149/98)
1.28 — Natalie Williams (152/119)
1.06 — Adrienne Goodson (164/154)
Most steals, season
77 — Debbie Black, 1999
58 — Marie Ferdinand, 2003
51 — Marie Ferdinand, 2002

Highest average, steals per game, season
(qualifiers)
2.41 — Debbie Black, 1999 (77/32)
1.71 — Marie Ferdinand, 2003 (58/34)
1.68 — Wendy Palmer, 1997 (47/28)
Most steals, game
7 — Wendy Palmer, vs. New York,
July 5, 1997
Debbie Black, at Washington,
July 8, 1999
6 — Karen Booker, at Cleveland,
June 26, 1997
Elena Baranova, at Los Angeles,
July 11, 1997
Debbie Black, at Phoenix, July 27, 1999

BLOCKED SHOTS

Most blocked shots, career
607 — Margo Dydek
116 — Elena Baranova
66 — Natalie Williams
Highest average, blocked shots per game, career
(Minimum: 90 games)
3.19 — Margo Dydek (607/190)
0.55 — Natalie Williams (66/119)
0.34 — Jennifer Azzi (38/113)
Most blocked shots, season
114 — Margo Dydek, 1998
113 — Margo Dydek, 2001
107 — Margo Dydek, 2002
Highest average, blocked shots per game, season
(qualifiers)
3.80 — Margo Dydek, 1998 (114/30)
3.57 — Margo Dydek, 2002 (107/30)
3.53 — Margo Dydek, 2001 (113/32)
Most blocked shots, game
10 — Margo Dydek, vs. Orlando, June 7, 2001
9 — Margo Dydek, vs. Cleveland,
August 6, 1998
8 — Margo Dydek, at Detroit, July 17, 1998
Margo Dydek, vs. Sacramento,
August 12, 1998
Margo Dydek, vs. Sacramento,
July 14, 2001

TURNOVERS

Most turnovers, career
547 — Margo Dydek
441 — Adrienne Goodson
289 — Natalie Williams
Most turnovers, season
108 — Margo Dydek, 1998
102 — Adrienne Goodson, 2002
98 — Adrienne Goodson, 1999
Most turnovers, game
9 — Adrienne Goodson, vs. Los Angeles,
June 26, 2003
8 — By many

SEATTLE STORM

TEAM OFFENSE

SCORING

Highest average, points per game, season
70.2 — 2003 (2388/34)
Lowest average, points per game, season
56.9 — 2000 (1822/32)
Most points, game
93 — vs. San Antonio, June 22, 2003
92 — vs. Los Angeles, August 6, 2003
Fewest points, game
36 — vs. Cleveland, June 14, 2001
38 — at Charlotte, July 7, 2001
Largest margin of victory, game
41 — vs. Phoenix, July 19, 2002 (89-48)
40 — vs. San Antonio, June 22, 2003 (93-53)
Largest margin of defeat, game
33 — at Phoenix, June 7, 2000 (49-82)
at Sacramento, August 9, 2000 (46-79)
30 — vs. Houston, June 1, 2000 (47-77)
at Houston, July 6, 2000 (50-80)

BY HALF

Most points, first half
48 — at Phoenix, June 14, 2002
46 — vs. Phoenix, May 31, 2001
vs. Phoenix, July 19, 2002
Fewest points, first half
17 — at Miami, July 10, 2000
at Charlotte, July 7, 2001
19 — at Houston, July 6, 2000
at Indiana, July 14, 2000
at Sacramento, August 13, 2002
Largest lead at halftime
24 — vs. Phoenix, July 19, 2002
(led 46-22; won 89-48)
22 — vs. Los Angeles, July 11, 2002
(led 45-23; won 79-60)
Largest deficit at halftime overcome to win game
8 — vs. Portland, August 6, 2000
(trailed 24-32; won 66-58 in OT)
vs. Charlotte, June 6, 2002
(trailed 21-29; won 65-59)
5 — at Phoenix, June 22, 2001
(trailed 28-33; won 58-55)
at Cleveland, July 5, 2002
(trailed 29-34; won 73-65)
vs. Washington, July 3, 2003
(trailed 32-37; won 76-72)
Most points, second half
56 — vs. Los Angeles, August 6, 2003
51 — vs. San Antonio, June 22, 2003

Fewest points, second half
9 — vs. Cleveland, June 14, 2001
14 — at Phoenix, August 15, 2003

OVERTIME

Most points, overtime period
14 — vs. Los Angeles, June 13, 2000
vs. Portland, August 6, 2000
12 — vs. Minnesota, June 4, 2002
Fewest points, overtime period
2 — vs. Los Angeles, August 8, 2000
vs. Washington, July 3, 2001
Largest margin of victory, overtime period
10 — vs. Los Angeles, June 13, 2000 (69-59)
vs. Minnesota, June 4, 2002 (78-68)
8 — vs. Portland, August 6, 2000 (66-58)

FIELD GOAL PERCENTAGE

Highest field-goal percentage, season
.435 — 2003 (890/2045)
Lowest field-goal percentage, season
.378 — 2001 (689/1821)
Highest field-goal percentage, game
.569 — at Phoenix, June 14, 2002 (33/58)
.552 — vs. Los Angeles, August 6, 2003
(37/67)
Lowest field-goal percentage, game
.241 — vs. Phoenix, July 27, 2001 (13/54)
.276 — at Phoenix, June 7, 2000 (16/58)

FIELD GOALS

Most field goals per game, season
26.3 — 2003 (890/34)
Fewest field goals per game, season
20.8 — 2000 (667/32)
Most field goals, game
37 — vs. Los Angeles, August 6, 2003
34 — vs. Detroit, June 28, 2000
Fewest field goals, game
13 — at Miami, July 10, 2000
vs. Phoenix, July 27, 2001
14 — vs. Cleveland, June 14, 2001
at Portland, June 19, 2001
at Charlotte, July 7, 2001

FIELD GOAL ATTEMPTS

Most field-goal attempts per game, season
60.9 — 2002 (1948/32)
Fewest field-goal attempts per game, season
54.4 — 2000 (1741/32)
Most field-goal attempts, game
91 — vs. Washington, July 3, 2001 (ot)
78 — vs. Sacramento, August 14, 2001

Fewest field-goal attempts, game
    42 — at Charlotte, July 7, 2001
    43 — at Cleveland, June 10, 2000
        at Miami, July 10, 2000
        vs. Minnesota, July 21, 2000

THREE-POINT FIELD-GOAL PERCENTAGE

Highest three-point field-goal percentage, season
  .360 — 2002 (182/506)
Lowest three-point field-goal percentage, season
  .299 — 2000 (109/364)

THREE-POINT FIELD GOALS

Most three-point field goals per game, season
  5.7 — 2002 (182/32)
Fewest three-point field goals per game, season
  3.4 — 2000 (109/32)
Most three-point field goals, game
    13 — vs. Los Angeles, July 11, 2002
    10 — at Detroit, July 12, 2000
Fewest three-point field goals, game
    0 — at Indiana, July 14, 2000
    1 — Many times

THREE-POINT FIELD GOAL ATTEMPTS

Most three-point field goal attempts per game, season
  15.8 — 2002 (506/32)
Fewest three-point field goal attempts per game, season
  11.4 — 2000 (364/32)
Most three-point field goal attempts, game
    27 — vs. Houston, July 20, 2002
    25 — vs. Los Angeles, July 11, 2002
Fewest three-point field goal attempts, game
    6 — at Indiana, July 14, 2000
        at Portland, July 4, 2001
    7 — vs. Houston, June 1, 2000
        at Charlotte, June 9, 2000
        at Cleveland, June 10, 2000
        vs. Los Angeles, June 13, 2000 (ot)

FREE THROW PERCENTAGE

Highest free-throw percentage, season
  .780 — 2003 (442/567)
Lowest free-throw percentage, season
  .676 — 2000 (379/561)
Highest free-throw percentage, game
  1.000 — vs. Cleveland, July 12, 2002 (8/8)
        at Houston, July 23, 2002 (6/6)
  .933 — vs. Houston, August 8, 2001 (14/15)
        at Sacramento, August 13, 2002 (14/15)
Lowest free-throw percentage, game
  .400 — at Houston, August 19, 2003 (4/10)
  .412 — vs. Minnesota, July 21, 2000 (14/34)

FREE THROWS MADE

Most free throws made per game, season
  13.1 — 2002 (418/32)
Fewest free throws made per game, season
  11.8 — 2000 (379/32)
Most free throws made, game
    26 — at Utah, June 25, 2001
        vs. Phoenix, July 27, 2001
    25 — vs. San Antonio, August 12, 2003
Fewest free throws made, game
    4 — at Phoenix, June 26, 2002
        at Houston, July 9, 2002
        at Houston, August 19, 2003
    5 — vs. Utah, July 1, 2000
        at Houston, July 6, 2000
        at Houston, May 22, 2003

FREE THROW ATTEMPTS

Most free throw attempts per game, season
  18.9 — 2001 (606/32)
Fewest free throw attempts per game, season
  16.7 — 2003 (567/34)
Most free throw attempts, game
    34 — vs. Minnesota, July 21, 2000
        vs. Phoenix, May 31, 2001
    33 — at Utah, June 25, 2001
Fewest free throw attempts, game
    6 — at Phoenix, June 26, 2002
        at Houston, July 9, 2002
        at Houston, July 23, 2002
    7 — vs. Los Angeles, July 11, 2002
        at Cleveland, June 27, 2003
        vs. Houston, July 15, 2003

REBOUNDS

Most rebounds per game, season
  31.6 — 2003 (1074/34)
Fewest rebounds per game, season
  24.8 — 2000 (793/32)
Most rebounds, game
    49 — vs. Phoenix, July 19, 2002
    48 — vs. Portland, August 9, 2002
Fewest rebounds, game
    15 — at Sacramento, August 9, 2000
    16 — vs. Sacramento, June 30, 2001

OFFENSIVE REBOUNDS

Most offensive rebounds per game, season
  11.3 — 2002 (362/32)
Fewest offensive rebounds per game, season
  8.0 — 2000 (256/32)
Most offensive rebounds, game
    20 — vs. Phoenix, July 19, 2002
    19 — at Utah, June 15, 2002
Fewest offensive rebounds, game
    2 — at Houston, July 25, 2000
        at Los Angeles, July 27, 2000
    3 — at Miami, July 10, 2000

DEFENSIVE REBOUNDS

Most defensive rebounds per game, season
    21.5 — 2003 (732/34)
Fewest defensive rebounds per game, season
    16.8 — 2000 (537/32)
Most defensive rebounds, game
    35 — vs. Phoenix, July 25, 2003
    34 — vs. Portland, August 9, 2002
Fewest defensive rebounds, game
    10 — at Sacramento, August 9, 2000
    11 — vs. Utah, July 1, 2000
        at Cleveland, July 5, 2002
        at Charlotte, June 30, 2003

ASSISTS

Most assists per game, season
    16.1 — 2003 (548/34)
Fewest assists per game, season
    12.2 — 2000 (390/32)
Most assists, game
    24 — vs. Sacramento, June 23, 2002
    22 — vs. Phoenix, May 31, 2001
        vs. Phoenix, July 19, 2002
        vs. Indiana, June 10, 2003
        vs. Washington, July 3, 2003
Fewest assists, game
    5 — at Miami, July 10, 2000
        vs. Phoenix, July 27, 2001
    6 — at Portland, June 19, 2001

PERSONAL FOULS

Most personal fouls per game, season
    20.3 — 2000 (648/32)
Fewest personal fouls per game, season
    18.9 — 2001 (605/32)
Most personal fouls, game
    35 — at Miami, July 10, 2000
    30 — at Portland, June 23, 2000
        at San Antonio, May 24, 2003
Fewest personal fouls, game
    6 — vs. Miami, July 30, 2000
    9 — at Phoenix, June 22, 2001
        vs. Sacramento, August 25, 2003

DISQUALIFICATIONS

Most disqualifications per game, season
    0.24 — 2003 (8/34)
Fewest disqualifications per game, season
    0.13 — 2000 (4/32)
Most disqualifications, game
    2 — at Utah, June 9, 2001
at Sacramento, June 21, 2003
    1 — Many times

STEALS

Most steals per game, season
    8.8 — 2002 (282/32)
Fewest steals per game, season
    6.8 — 2003 (232/34)

Most steals, game
    16 — at Utah, June 25, 2001
    15 — vs. Minnesota, July 21, 2000
        at Sacramento, August 9, 2000
        vs. Houston, July 20, 2002
Fewest steals, game
    2 — at Charlotte, July 7, 2001
    3 — at Sacramento, June 20, 2002
        vs. Indiana, June 10, 2003
        vs. Minnesota, June 14, 2003
        vs. Houston, August 23, 2003

BLOCKED SHOTS

Most blocked shots per game, season
    4.7 — 2002 (151/32)
Fewest blocked shots per game, season
    2.9 — 2000 (93/32)
Most blocked shots, game
    12 — vs. Utah, August 11, 2002
    10 — vs. Minnesota, August 8, 2003
Fewest blocked shots, game
    0 — vs. Utah, July 1, 2000
        at Indiana, July 14, 2000
        vs. Charlotte, June 6, 2002
        at New York, July 2, 2002
        vs. Houston, July 20, 2002
    1 — By many

TURNOVERS

Most turnovers per game, season
    16.4 — 2000 (525/32)
Fewest turnovers per game, season
    13.5 — 2001 (431/32)
Most turnovers, game
    24 — vs. Los Angeles, June 13, 2000 (ot)
    23 — at Sacramento, August 9, 2000
        at Sacramento, August 13, 2002
Fewest turnovers, game
    5 — at Charlotte, June 30, 2003
    6 — vs. Charlotte, June 6, 2002
        vs. Houston, August 23, 2003

TEAM DEFENSE

POINTS

Fewest points allowed per game, season
    64.0 — 2001 (2048/32)
Most points allowed per game, season
    67.8 — 2000 (2171/32)
Fewest points allowed, game
    47 — at Utah, June 25, 2001
        at Portland, June 2, 2002
    48 — at Charlotte, July 7, 2001
        vs. Phoenix, July 19, 2002
Fewest points allowed, first half
    17 — at Utah, June 25, 2001
    18 — vs. Utah, June 18, 2000
        at Miami, July 10, 2000

vs. Indiana, June 10, 2003
at Connecticut, July 17, 2003
Fewest points allowed, second half
15 — vs. Washington, July 3, 2001
20 — vs. Portland, August 6, 2000
Fewest points allowed, overtime period
2 — at Indiana, June 4, 2001
vs. Detroit, July 24, 2001
vs. Washington, July 3, 2001
vs. Minnesota, June 4, 2002

FIELD GOAL PERCENTAGE

Lowest opponents' field-goal percentage, season
.414 — 2003 (844/2039)
Highest opponents' field-goal percentage, season
.452 — 2000 (778/1721)
Lowest opponents' field goal percentage, game
.244 — at Miami, July 10, 2000 (10/41)
.270 — vs. Phoenix, July 25, 2003 (20/74)

TURNOVERS

Most opponents' turnovers per game, season
16.6 — 2002 (531/32)
Fewest opponents' turnovers per game, season
13.5 — 2003 (459/34)
Most opponents' turnovers, game
26 — vs. Utah, June 18, 2000
24 — at Utah, June 25, 2001

TEAM MISCELLANEOUS

GAME WON AND LOST

Highest winning percentage, season
.531 — 2002 (17-15)
Lowest winning percentage, season
.188 — 2000 (6-26)
Most consecutive games won
5 — July 25-August 1, 2002
3 — June 2-6, 2002
June 3-10, 2003
Most consecutive games won, one season
5 — July 25-August 1, 2002
3 — June 2-6, 2002
June 3-10, 2003
Most consecutive game lost
8 — June 15-July 3, 2000
7 — July 7-21, 2001
Most consecutive game lost, one season
8 — June 15-July 3, 2000
7 — July 7-21, 2001
Highest winning percentage, home games, season
.765 — 2003 (13-4)
Lowest winning percentage, home games, season
.250 — 2000 (4-12)
Most consecutive home games won
8 — June 22-August 8, 2003
4 — June 21-July 11, 2002

Most consecutive home games lost
7 — June 15-July 19, 2000
4 — June 30-July 20, 2001
Highest winning percentage, road games, season
.438 — 2002 (7-9)
Lowest winning percentage, road games, season
.125 — 2000 (2-14)
Most consecutive road games won
4 — July 25-August 1, 2002
2 — Many times
Most consecutive road games lost
10 — July 6, 2000-June 3, 2001
8 — July 7-August 11, 2001

OVERTIME GAMES

Most overtime games, season
3 — 2000, 2001
Most consecutive overtime games, season
2 — August 6-8, 2000
Most overtime games won, season
2 — 2000, 2001
Most overtime games won, no losses, season
None
Most consecutive overtime games won
2 — June 13-August 6, 2000
July 24, 2001-June 4, 2002
Most overtime games lost, season
2 — 2003
Most overtime games lost, no wins, season
2 — 2003
Most consecutive overtime games lost
3 — July 7-August 20, 2003 (current)
Most overtime periods, game
4 — vs. Washington, July 3, 2001

INDIVIDUAL RECORDS

SEASONS

Most Seasons
4 — Simone Edwards
Kamila Vodichkova
3 — Sonja Henning
Lauren Jackson
Jamie Redd

GAMES

Most games, career
127 — Simone Edwards
112 — Kamila Vodichkova
90 — Lauren Jackson
Most consecutive games, career
116 — Simone Edwards, July 3, 2000-
August 25, 2003 (current)
72 — Sonja Henning, May 31, 2000-
June 15, 2002
66 — Sue Bird, May 30, 2002-
August 25, 2003 (current)
Most games, season
34 — Sue Bird, 2003

Sandy Brondello, 2003
Simone Edwards, 2003
33 — Lauren Jackson, 2003

MINUTES

Most minutes, career
2,992 — Lauren Jackson
2,726 — Simone Edwards
2,420 — Kamila Vodichkova
Highest average, minutes per game, career
(Minimum 50 games)
34.2 — Sue Bird (2257/66)
33.2 — Lauren Jackson (2992/90)
29.0 — Sonja Henning (2089/72)
Most minutes, season
1,136 — Sue Bird, 2003
1,121 — Sue Bird, 2002
1,109 — Lauren Jackson, 2003
Highest average, minutes per game, season
35.0 — Sue Bird, 2002 (1121/32)
34.5 — Lauren Jackson, 2001 (1001/29)
33.6 — Lauren Jackson, 2003 (1109/33)
Most minutes, game
55 — Lauren Jackson, vs. Washington,
July 3, 2001 (4 ot)
43 — Semeka Randall, vs. Washington,
July 3, 2001 (4 ot)
Sonja Henning, vs. Minnesota,
June 4, 2002 (ot)
Sue Bird, vs. Minnesota,
June 4, 2002 (ot)
Regulation Game:
40 — Sonja Henning, vs. Miami,
July 30, 2002
Sue Bird, at Sacramento, July 26, 2003

SCORING

Most points, lifetime
1,622 — Lauren Jackson
929 — Kamila Vodichkova
881 — Sue Bird
Highest average, points per game, career
(Minimum 50 games)
18.0 — Lauren Jackson (1,622/90)
13.3 — Sue Bird (881/66)
8.3 — Kamila Vodichkova (929/112)
Most points, season
698 — Lauren Jackson, 2003
482 — Lauren Jackson, 2002
461 — Sue Bird, 2002
Highest average, points per game, season
21.2 — Lauren Jackson, 2003 (698/33)
17.2 — Lauren Jackson, 2002 (482/28)
15.2 — Lauren Jackson, 2001 (442/29)
Most points, game
34 — Lauren Jackson, vs. Los Angeles,
August 6, 2003
33 — Sue Bird, vs. Portland, August 9, 2002

32 — Lauren Jackson, vs. San Antonio,
August 12, 2003
Most games, 30 or more points, career
3 — Lauren Jackson
1 — Sue Bird
Most games, 20 or more points, career
33 — Lauren Jackson
10 — Sue Bird
3 — Edna Campbell
Jamie Redd
Kamila Vodichkova
Most consecutive games, 20 or more points
7 — Lauren Jackson, July 17-31, 2003
3 — Lauren Jackson, July 11-19, 2002
Lauren Jackson, June 3-10, 2003
Most consecutive games, 10 or more points
53 — Lauren Jackson, June 26, 2002-
August 25, 2003 (current)
15 — Lauren Jackson, May 31-July 4, 2001
10 — Lauren Jackson, July 24, 2001-
June 14, 2002

FIELD GOAL PERCENTAGE

Highest field goal percentage, career
(Minimum 200 field goals)
.480 — Simone Edwards (319/664)
.445 — Kamila Vodichkova (334/751)
.423 — Lauren Jackson (589/1394)
Highest field goal percentage, season (qualifiers)
.483 — Lauren Jackson, 2003 (254/526)
.479 — Simone Edwards, 2001 (91/190)
.474 — Kamila Vodichkova, 2003 (101/213)
Highest field goal percentage, game
(Minimum 8 field goals made)
.909 — Kamila Vodichkova, vs. Detroit,
June 28, 2000 (10/11)
.800 — Simone Edwards, at Orlando,
July 25, 2002 (8/10)
.769 — Robin Threatt, vs. Utah,
July 1, 2000 (10/13)
Most field goals, none missed, game
4 — Felicia Ragland, vs. Sacramento,
June 23, 2002
3 — By many
Most field goal attempts, none made, game
11 — Kamila Vodichkova, vs. Portland,
August 9, 2002
9 — Stacey Lovelace, at Sacramento,
August 9, 2000
8 — Lauren Jackson, at New York,
July 11, 2001

FIELD GOALS

Most field goals, career
589 — Lauren Jackson
334 — Kamila Vodichkova
319 — Simone Edwards

Most field goals, season
- 254 — Lauren Jackson, 2003
- 186 — Lauren Jackson, 2002
- 155 — Sue Bird, 2003

Most field goals, game
- 17 — Lauren Jackson, vs. Los Angeles,
  August 6, 2003
- 11 — Lauren Jackson, at Orlando,
  July 25, 2002
  Lauren Jackson, vs. Utah,
  August 11, 2002
  Lauren Jackson, vs. Washington,
  July 3, 2003
  Sue Bird, at Los Angeles, July 5, 2003
- 10 — By many

FIELD GOAL ATTEMPTS

Most field goal attempts, career
- 1,394 — Lauren Jackson
- 751 — Kamila Vodichkova
- 743 — Sue Bird

Most field goal attempts, season
- 526 — Lauren Jackson, 2003
- 462 — Lauren Jackson, 2002
- 406 — Lauren Jackson, 2001

Most field goal attempts, game
- 29 — Lauren Jackson, vs. Washington,
  July 3, 2001 (4 ot)
- 23 — Lauren Jackson, vs. Utah,
  August 11, 2002
  Lauren Jackson, vs. Los Angeles,
  August 6, 2003
- 21 — By many

THREE-POINT FIELD-GOAL PERCENTAGE

Highest three-point field goal percentage, career
(Minimum 50 three-point field goals)
- .376 — Sue Bird (106/282)
- .325 — Lauren Jackson (121/372)

Highest three-point field goal percentage, season
(qualifiers)
- .438 — Sandy Brondello, 2003 (21/48)
- .401 — Sue Bird, 2002 (57/142)
- .400 — Felicia Ragland, 2002 (22/55)

Most three-point field goals, none missed, game
- 4 — Amanda Lassiter, vs. New York,
  July 23, 2003
- 3 — By many

Most three-point field goal attempts, none made,
game
- 7 — Lauren Jackson, vs. Houston,
  August 8, 2001
- 6 — Edna Campbell, vs. Portland,
  June 3, 2000
  Sue Bird, at Portland, June 2, 2002
  Lauren Jackson, vs. Minnesota,
  July 31, 2002

THREE-POINT FIELD GOALS

Most three-point field goals, career
- 121 — Lauren Jackson
- 106 — Sue Bird
- 49 — Jamie Redd

Most three-point field goals, season
- 57 — Sue Bird, 2002
- 49 — Sue Bird, 2003
- 42 — Lauren Jackson, 2002

Most three-point field goals, game
- 6 — Sonja Henning, at Los Angeles,
  July 27, 2000
- 5 — Lauren Jackson, at Houston,
  July 30, 2001
  Felicia Ragland, vs. Los Angeles,
  July 11, 2002
  Sue Bird, at Los Angeles,
  July 5, 2003
- 4 — By many

Most consecutive games, three-point field goals
made
- 13 — Lauren Jackson, June 27-
  July 28, 2002
- 11 — Sue Bird, June 11-July 5, 2002
- 9 — Sue Bird, June 7-28, 2003

THREE-POINT FIELD GOAL ATTEMPTS

Most three-point field goal attempts, career
- 372 — Lauren Jackson
- 282 — Sue Bird
- 147 — Jamie Redd

Most three-point field goal attempts, season
- 142 — Sue Bird, 2002
- 140 — Sue Bird, 2003
- 129 — Lauren Jackson, 2001

Most three-point field goal attempts, game
- 10 — Sonja Henning, at Los Angeles,
  July 27, 2000
  Sue Bird, vs. Los Angeles,
  May 30, 2003 (ot)
- 9 — Sue Bird, vs. Houston, July 20, 2002
  Lauren Jackson, vs. Sacramento,
  June 3, 2003
- 8 — By many

FREE THROW PERCENTAGE

Highest free-throw percentage, career
(Minimum 100 free throws)
- .901 — Sue Bird (163/181)
- .807 — Kamila Vodichkova (234/290)
- .766 — Lauren Jackson (323/416)

Highest free-throw percentage, season (qualifiers)
- .911 — Sue Bird, 2002 (102/112)
- .884 — Sue Bird, 2003 (61/69)
- .864 — Kamila Vodichkova, 2001 (38/44)

Most free throws made, none missed, game
- 11 — Lauren Jackson, vs. Phoenix,
  July 27, 2001

8 — Kamila Vodichkova, vs. Los Angeles,
June 16, 2001
Lauren Jackson, at Utah,
June 25, 2001
Lauren Jackson, vs. Los Angeles,
May 30, 2003 (ot)
Simone Edwards, vs. San Antonio,
June 22, 2003
7 — Simone Edwards, vs. Houston,
August 8, 2001
Kamila Vodichkova, vs. Sacramento,
June 23, 2002

Most free throw attempts, none made, game
4 — Quacy Barnes, vs. Sacramento,
June 15, 2000
Charmin Smith, vs. Minnesota,
July 21, 2000
Semeka Randall, vs. Phoenix,
July 19, 2002
3 — Sonja Henning, vs. Portland,
June 3, 2000
Simone Edwards, vs. Phoenix,
May 31, 2001

FREE THROWS MADE

Most free throws made, career
323 — Lauren Jackson
234 — Kamila Vodichkova
194 — Simone Edwards

Most free throws made, season
151 — Lauren Jackson, 2003
104 — Lauren Jackson, 2001
102 — Sue Bird, 2002

Most free throws made, game
14 — Lauren Jackson, vs. San Antonio,
August 12, 2003
11 — Lauren Jackson, vs. Phoenix,
July 27, 2001
Sue Bird, vs. Minnesota,
June 4, 2002 (ot)
Lauren Jackson, at Minnesota,
July 20, 2003
Lauren Jackson, vs. Charlotte,
July 31, 2003

FREE THROW ATTEMPTS

Most free throw attempts, career
416 — Lauren Jackson
292 — Simone Edwards
290 — Kamila Vodichkova

Most free throw attempts, season
183 — Lauren Jackson, 2003
143 — Lauren Jackson, 2001
112 — Sue Bird, 2002

Most free throw attempts, game
16 — Lauren Jackson, vs. San Antonio,
August 12, 2003
15 — Lauren Jackson, vs. Charlotte,
July 31, 2003

13 — Semeka Randall, vs. Orlando,
June 12, 2001

REBOUNDS

Most rebounds, career
690 — Lauren Jackson
538 — Simone Edwards
487 — Kamila Vodichkova

Highest average, rebounds per game, career
(Minimum 50 games)
7.7 — Lauren Jackson (690/90)
4.3 — Kamila Vodichkova (487/112)
4.2 — Simone Edwards (538/127)

Most rebounds, season
307 — Lauren Jackson, 2003
193 — Lauren Jackson, 2001
190 — Lauren Jackson, 2002

Highest average, rebounds per game, season
(qualifiers)
9.3 — Lauren Jackson, 2003 (307/33)
6.8 — Lauren Jackson, 2002 (190/28)
6.7 — Lauren Jackson, 2001 (193/29)

Most rebounds, game
20 — Lauren Jackson, vs. Charlotte,
July 31, 2003
18 — Lauren Jackson, vs. San Antonio,
August 12, 2003
15 — Lauren Jackson, at Houston,
August 19, 2003

Most games, 10+ rebounds, career
23 — Lauren Jackson
5 — Kamila Vodichkova
2 — Simone Edwards

Most consecutive games, 10+ rebounds
7 — Lauren Jackson, July 25-
August 12, 2003
3 — Lauren Jackson, June 15-20, 2002
Lauren Jackson, August 17-20, 2003

OFFENSIVE REBOUNDS

Most offensive rebounds, career
205 — Simone Edwards
Lauren Jackson
169 — Kamila Vodichkova
71 — Adia Barnes

Highest average, offensive rebounds per game,
career (Minimum 50 games)
2.3 — Lauren Jackson (205/90)
1.6 — Simone Edwards (205/127)
1.5 — Kamila Vodichkova (169/112)

Most offensive rebounds, season
82 — Lauren Jackson, 2003
67 — Simone Edwards, 2001
66 — Lauren Jackson, 2002

Most offensive rebounds, game
8 — Semeka Randall, at Cleveland,
July 5, 2002
7 — Felicia Ragland, vs. New York,
May 30, 2002

Lauren Jackson, at Utah,
June 15, 2002
Kamila Vodichkova, at Minnesota,
August 2, 2003
Lauren Jackson, vs. San Antonio,
August 12, 2003

DEFENSIVE REBOUNDS

Most defensive rebounds, career
485 — Lauren Jackson
333 — Simone Edwards
318 — Kamila Vodichkova
Highest average, defensive rebounds per game,
career (Minimum 50 games)
5.4 — Lauren Jackson (485/90)
2.8 — Kamila Vodichkova (318/112)
2.6 — Simone Edwards (333/127)
Most defensive rebounds, season
225 — Lauren Jackson, 2003
136 — Lauren Jackson, 2001
124 — Lauren Jackson, 2002
Most defensive rebounds, game
15 — Lauren Jackson, vs. Charlotte,
July 31, 2003
13 — Lauren Jackson, at Houston,
August 19, 2003
12 — Lauren Jackson, vs. Los Angeles,
August 6, 2003

ASSISTS

Most assists, career
412 — Sue Bird
187 — Sonja Henning
147 — Lauren Jackson
Highest average, assists per game, career
(Minimum 50 games)
6.2 — Sue Bird (412/66)
2.6 — Sonja Henning (187/72)
1.7 — Amanda Lassiter (97/56)
Most assists, season
221 — Sue Bird, 2003
191 — Sue Bird, 2002
93 — Sonja Henning, 2001
Highest average, assists per game, season
(qualifiers)
6.5 — Sue Bird, 2003 (221/34)
6.0 — Sue Bird, 2002 (191/32)
2.9 — Sonja Henning, 2001 (93/32)
Most assists, game
12 — Sue Bird, at Cleveland, July 5, 2002
Sue Bird, at Los Angeles, June 19, 2003
Sue Bird, at Cleveland, June 27, 2003
11 — Sue Bird, at Miami, July 7, 2002
Sue Bird, at Orlando, July 25, 2002
Sue Bird, at Indiana, June 28, 2003
Most games, 10+ assists, career
12 — Sue Bird

PERSONAL FOULS

Most personal fouls, career
316 — Kamila Vodichkova
298 — Lauren Jackson
232 — Simone Edwards
Most personal fouls, season
106 — Lauren Jackson, 2003
103 — Quacy Barnes, 2000
101 — Jamie Redd, 2001
Kamila Vodichkova, 2003
Most personal fouls, game
6 — By many

DISQUALIFICATIONS

Most disqualifications, career
5 — Lauren Jackson
Kamila Vodichkova
3 — Sonja Henning
Amanda Lassiter
2 — Quacy Barnes
Adia Barnes
Highest percentage, games disqualified, career
(Minimum 50 games)
5.6 — Lauren Jackson (5/90)
5.4 — Amanda Lassiter (3/56)
4.5 — Kamila Vodichkova (5/112)
Lowest percentage, games disqualified, career
(Minimum 50 games)
0.00 — By many
Most consecutive games without disqualification,
career
127 — Simone Edwards, May 31, 2000
August 25, 2003 (current)
68 — Jamie Redd, May 31, 2000-
July 2, 2002
66 — Sue Bird, May 30, 2002-
August 25, 2003 (current)
Most disqualifications, season
4 — Kamila Vodichkova, 2003
3 — Lauren Jackson, 2001
2 — Quacy Barnes, 2000
Sonja Henning, 2001
Amanda Lassiter, 2003
Fewest minutes, disqualified, game
15 — Sonja Henning, at Portland,
June 23, 2000
20 — Kate Paye, at Sacramento,
June 20, 2002
21 — Amanda Lassiter, vs. Detroit,
August 17, 2003

STEALS

Most steals, career
122 — Sonja Henning
Lauren Jackson
103 — Sue Bird
85 — Kamila Vodichkova

Highest average, steals per game, career
(Minimum 50 games)
    1.69 — Sonja Henning (122/72)
    1.56 — Sue Bird (103/66)
    1.36 — Lauren Jackson (122/90)
Most steals, season
    61 — Sonja Henning, 2000
    55 — Sue Bird, 2002
    54 — Lauren Jackson, 2001
Highest average, steals per game, season
(qualifiers)
    1.91 — Sonja Henning, 2000 (61/32)
    1.86 — Lauren Jackson, 2001 (54/29)
    1.72 — Sue Bird, 2002 (55/32)
Most steals, game
    6 — Sonja Henning, vs. Portland,
        July 20, 2001
        Adia Barnes, vs. Houston,
        July 20, 2002
    5 — By many

BLOCKED SHOTS

Most blocked shots, career
    209 — Lauren Jackson
    58 — Kamila Vodichkova
    51 — Simone Edwards
Highest average, blocked shots per game, career
(Minimum: 50 games)
    2.32 — Lauren Jackson (209/90)
    0.80 — Amanda Lassiter (45/56)
    0.76 — Quacy Barnes (39/51)

Most blocked shots, season
    81 — Lauren Jackson, 2002
    64 — Lauren Jackson, 2001
Lauren Jackson, 2003
    33 — Quacy Barnes, 2000
Highest average, blocked shots per game, season
(qualifiers)
    2.89 — Lauren Jackson, 2002 (81/28)
    2.21 — Lauren Jackson, 2001 (64/29)
    1.94 — Lauren Jackson, 2003 (64/33)
Most blocked shots, game
    8 — Lauren Jackson, vs. Utah,
        August 11, 2002
    5 — By many

TURNOVERS

Most turnovers, career
    219 — Sue Bird
    199 — Kamila Vodichkova
    169 — Lauren Jackson
Most turnovers, season
    110 — Sue Bird, 2003
    109 — Sue Bird, 2002
    73 — Semeka Randall, 2001
Most turnovers, game
    8 — Sue Bird, at Phoenix, June 26, 2002
        Sue Bird, vs. Sacramento, June 3, 2003
        Sue Bird, at Phoenix, August 15, 2003
    7 — Sonja Henning, at Orlando, July 8, 2000
        Sue Bird, vs. Houston, July 20, 2002
        Sue Bird, at Sacramento, July 26, 2003
    6 — By many

WASHINGTON MYSTICS

REGULAR SEASON TEAM RECORDS

TEAM OFFENSE

SCORING

Highest average, points per game, season
68.5 — 2003 (2330/34)
68.0 — 2000 (2176/32)
Lowest average, points per game, season
60.3 — 2001 (1928/32)
65.1 — 1998 (1954/30)
Most points, game
97 — at Utah, June 4, 2002
96 — vs. Detroit, August 4, 2000
Fewest points, game
34 — at Cleveland, May 31, 2001
36 — vs. Miami, August 8, 2001
Largest margin of victory, game
35 — vs. Cleveland, August 8, 1999 (80-45)
26 — vs. Orlando, May 31, 2000 (92-66)
Largest margin of defeat, game
45 — vs. Houston, August 17, 1998 (65-110)
43 — at New York, August 13, 1998 (45-88)

BY HALF

Most points, first half
50 — at Utah, June 13, 1998
vs. Orlando, June 1, 2002
vs. Indiana, June 7, 2002
49 — at Utah, June 4, 2002
Fewest points, first half
14 — vs. Cleveland, June 6, 2003
16 — vs. Los Angeles, August 14, 1999
at Cleveland, May 31, 2001
Largest lead at halftime
19 — vs. Detroit, August 4, 2000
(led 45-26; won 96-72)
17 — vs. Detroit, July 11, 1998
(led 41-24; won 78-53)
vs. Indiana, June 7, 2002
(led 50-33; won 89-68)
Largest deficit at halftime overcome to win game
12 — vs. Charlotte, June 30, 2002
(trailed 24-36; won 56-55)
11 — at Indiana, August 12, 2003
(trailed 29-40; won 84-80)
Most points, second half
63 — vs. Utah, July 19, 1998
55 — at Indiana, August 12, 2003
Fewest points, second half
15 — at Seattle, July 3, 2001
16 — vs. Miami, August 8, 2001

OVERTIME

Most points, overtime period
13 — at Sacramento, June 25, 2002

12 — at Seattle, July 3, 2001
Fewest points, overtime period
2 — at Seattle, July 3, 2001
4 — Many times
Largest margin of victory, overtime period
5 — at Detroit, July 10, 1999 (83-78)
3 — vs. New York, August 11, 1999 (59-56)
at Seattle, July 3, 2001 (72-69)

FIELD GOAL PERCENTAGE

Highest field-goal percentage, season
.459 — 2000 (832/1813)
.423 — 1999 (759/1794)
Lowest field-goal percentage, season
.386 — 2001 (739/1915)
.395 — 1998 (720/1821)
Highest field-goal percentage, game
.603 — vs. Indiana, June 7, 2002 (35/58)
.567 — vs. Orlando, May 31, 2000 (38/67)
Lowest field-goal percentage, game
.196 — vs. Miami, August 8, 2001 (10/51)
.245 — at Cleveland, May 31, 2001 (13/53)

FIELD GOALS

Most field goals per game, season
26.4 — 2003 (896/34)
26.0 — 2000 (832/32)
Fewest field goals per game, season
23.1 — 2001 (739/32)
23.7 — 1999 (759/32)
Most field goals, game
38 — vs. Orlando, May 31, 2000
35 — vs. Indiana, June 7, 2002
vs. Detroit, August 6, 2003
Fewest field goals, game
10 — vs. Miami, August 8, 2001
13 — at Cleveland, May 31, 2001

FIELD GOAL ATTEMPTS

Most field-goal attempts per game, season
64.4 — 2003 (2191/34)
60.7 — 1998 (1821/30)
Fewest field-goal attempts per game, season
56.1 — 1999 (1794/32)
56.7 — 2000 (1813/32)
Most field-goal attempts, game
84 — at Sacramento, June 25, 2002 (2 ot)
79 — at Detroit, August 25, 2003
Fewest field-goal attempts, game
39 — at Cleveland, June 3, 2000
42 — at New York, August 17, 1999

THREE-POINT FIELD-GOAL PERCENTAGE

Highest three-point field-goal percentage, season
.370 — 2002 (164/443)
.325 — 2000 (109/335)
Lowest three-point field-goal percentage, season
.264 — 1998 (114/432)
.280 — 2001 (117/418)

THREE-POINT FIELD GOALS

Most three-point field goals per game, season
5.1 — 2002 (164/32)
4.6 — 2003 (157/34)
Fewest three-point field goals per game, season
3.1 — 1999 (100/32)
3.4 — 2000 (109/32)
Most three-point field goals, game
10 — vs. Utah, July 19, 1998
at Utah, June 4, 2002
9 — Many times
Fewest three-point field goals, game
0 — at New York, August 13, 1998
at Charlotte, July 1, 2000
vs. Miami, August 8, 2001
1 — Many time

THREE-POINT FIELD GOAL ATTEMPTS

Most three-point field goal attempts per game, season
14.9 — 2003 (505/34)
14.4 — 1998 (432/30)
Fewest three-point field goal attempts per game, season
10.5 — 2000 (335/32)
10.8 — 1999 (345/32)
Most three-point field goal attempts, game
29 — vs. Los Angeles, July 14, 2001
27 — vs. Utah, July 19, 1998
Fewest three-point field goal attempts, game
5 — at Houston, July 13, 1998
vs. Phoenix, June 22, 1999
at Charlotte, June 30, 1999
6 — By many

FREE THROW PERCENTAGE

Highest free-throw percentage, season
.7515 — 2003 (381/507)
.7511 — 2002 (359/478)
Lowest free-throw percentage, season
.645 — 1998 (400/620)
.661 — 2001 (333/504)
Highest free-throw percentage, game
1.000 — Many times. Most recent:
vs. Detroit, August 6, 2003 (14/14)
Lowest free-throw percentage, game
.000 — at Detroit, August 25, 2003 (0/1)

.313 — vs. Portland, August 3, 2001 (5/16)

FREE THROWS MADE

Most free throws made per game, season
15.1 — 1999 (482/32)
13.3 — 1998 (400/30)
Fewest free throws made per game, season
10.4 — 2001 (333/32)
11.2 — 2003 (381/34)
Most free throws made, game
30 — at New York, June 14, 1999
vs. Detroit, August 4, 2000
29 — vs. Orlando, June 1, 2002
at Utah, June 4, 2002
Fewest free throws made, game
0 — vs. Charlotte, July 7, 2003
at Detroit, August 25, 2003
2 — at Houston, June 27, 2001
vs. Connecticut, June 24, 2003

FREE THROW ATTEMPTS

Most free throw attempts per game, season
21.2 — 1999 (679/32)
20.7 — 1998 (620/30)
Fewest free throw attempts per game, season
14.91 — 2003 (507/34)
14.94 — 2002 (478/32)
Most free throw attempts, game
37 — at New York, June 14, 1999
vs. Cleveland, July 21, 1999
vs. Orlando, June 1, 2002
36 — at Utah, June 4, 2002
Fewest free throw attempts, game
0 — vs. Charlotte, July 7, 2003
1 — at Detroit, August 25, 2003

REBOUNDS

Most rebounds per game, season
33.0 — 2001 (1055/32)
32.4 — 2002 (1038/32)
Fewest rebounds per game, season
29.6 — 2000 (946/32)
30.8 — 1998 (924/30)
Most rebounds, game
51 — at Sacramento, June 25, 2002 (2 ot)
50 — at Seattle, July 3, 2001 (4 ot)
Regulation game:
48 — vs. Detroit, July 11, 1998
Fewest rebounds, game
17 — at Cleveland, June 3, 2000
at Detroit, June 14, 2001
19 — at New York, August 13, 1998

OFFENSIVE REBOUNDS

Most offensive rebounds per game, season
11.2 — 2003 (382/34)
11.1 — 2001 (356/32)
Fewest offensive rebounds per game, season
9.4 — 2000 (300/32)
9.8 — 1999 (312/32)

Most offensive rebounds, game
    20 — at Orlando, June 19, 1999
        at Minnesota, July 27, 2001
        vs. Orlando, July 30, 2002
    19 — vs. Detroit, August 4, 2000
        at Sacramento, June 25, 2002 (2 ot)
        at Sacramento, July 2, 2003
Fewest offensive rebounds, game
    1 — at Cleveland, June 3, 2000
    3 — at Orlando, August 15, 1999

DEFENSIVE REBOUNDS

Most defensive rebounds per game, season
    22.1 — 2002 (708/32)
    21.9 — 1999 (701/32)
Fewest defensive rebounds per game, season
    20.0 — 1998 (599/30)
    20.2 — 2000 (646/32)
Most defensive rebounds, game
    37 — at Detroit, July 10, 1999 (2 ot)
    36 — at Seattle, July 3, 2001 (4 ot)
Regulation Game:
    35 — at Los Angeles, June 27, 2002
Fewest defensive rebounds, game
    8 — at New York, August 13, 1998
    12 — at New York, July 3, 1998
        vs. Charlotte, August 19, 1998
        at Utah, July 26, 1999

ASSISTS

Most assists per game, season
    16.7 — 2003 (568/34)
    16.3 — 2000 (521/32)
Fewest assists per game, season
    13.2 — 1998 (397/30)
    13.3 — 2001 (424/32)
Most assists, game
    29 — vs. Detroit, August 6, 2003
    28 — vs. Orlando, May 31, 2000
        at Charlotte, July 26, 2000
Fewest assists, game
    5 — vs. Orlando, July 19, 1999
        at Charlotte, July 26, 2001
        at Miami, August 5, 2001
        vs. Miami, August 8, 2001
    7 — at New York, August 13, 1998

PERSONAL FOULS

Most personal fouls per game, season
    23.1 — 1998 (692/30)
    20.2 — 1999 (646/32)
Fewest personal fouls per game, season
    16.8 — 2001 (537/32)
    18.2 — 2002 (583/32)
Most personal fouls, game
    36 — at Los Angeles, August 3, 1998
    33 — at Detroit, July 10, 1999 (2 ot)

Fewest personal fouls, game
    9 — vs. Detroit, July 18, 2002
    10 — vs. Cleveland, August 9, 2000
        vs. Phoenix, July 9, 2002

DISQUALIFICATIONS

Most disqualifications per game, season
    0.30 — 1998 (9/30)
    0.22 — 1999 (7/32)
Fewest disqualifications per game, season
    0.09 — 2000 (3/32)
        2001 (3/32)
        2002 (3/32)
Most disqualifications, game
    3 — at Los Angeles, August 3, 1998
    2 — at Phoenix, June 15, 1998
        vs. Utah, July 19, 1998
        at Detroit, July 10, 1999 (2 ot)

STEALS

Most steals per game, season
    8.9 — 1998 (266/30)
    8.0 — 2001 (257/32)
Fewest steals per game, season
    6.26 — 2003 (213/34)
    6.34 — 1999 (203/32)
Most steals, game
    19 — vs. Cleveland, August 9, 2000
    18 — at New York, August 13, 1998
Fewest steals, game
    1 — at Miami, July 13, 2000
    2 — Many times

BLOCKED SHOTS

Most blocked shots per game, season
    4.0 — 2001 (127/32)
    3.9 — 2000 (126/32)
Fewest blocked shots per game, season
    2.7 — 1999 (87/32)
    2.9 — 2003 (99/34)
Most blocked shots, game
    9 — vs. Sacramento, June 5, 2001
        at Indiana, May 31, 2003
    8 — at Houston, August 1, 2000
        vs. Indiana, August 6, 2002
        at Indiana, August 12, 2003
        vs. New York, August 21, 2003
Fewest blocked shots, game
    0 — Many times. Most recent:
        vs. Connecticut, August 23, 2003

TURNOVERS

Most turnovers per game, season
    20.8 — 1998 (625/30)
    17.9 — 1999 (574/32)
Fewest turnovers per game, season
    13.6 — 2003 (462/34)
    14.2 — 2002 (455/32)

Most turnovers, game
  33 — at Houston, June 29, 1998
  28 — vs. New York, July 5, 1998 (ot)
       at Detroit, July 10, 1999 (2 ot)
Fewest turnovers, game
  7 — at Houston, June 27, 2001
      vs. San Antonio, June 10, 2003
  8 — at Cleveland, June 20, 2003
      vs. Charlotte, July 17, 2003
      vs. Connecticut, August 23, 2003

TEAM DEFENSE

POINTS

Fewest points allowed per game, season
  64.8 — 2001 (2075/32)
  66.1 — 2002 (2116/32)
Most points allowed per game, season
  80.5 — 1998 (2415/30)
  73.5 — 2003 (2498/34)
Fewest points allowed, game
  42 — vs. Charlotte, July 29, 2001
       vs. Miami, August 8, 2001
  45 — vs. Cleveland, August 8, 1999
       vs. Cleveland, June 23, 2002
       at Connecticut, August 1, 2003
Fewest points allowed, first half
  17 — vs. New York, July 5, 1998
       vs. New York, August 11, 1999
       vs. Los Angeles, August 14, 1999
  19 — at Charlotte, July 17, 1999
       vs. Charlotte, July 7, 2003
       vs. New York, August 21, 2003
Fewest points allowed, second half
  18 — vs. Charlotte, July 29, 2001
  19 — vs. Minnesota, August 21, 1999
       vs. Miami, August 8, 2001
       vs. Charlotte, June 30, 2002
Fewest points allowed, overtime period
  2 — at Seattle, July 3, 2001
  4 — Many times

FIELD GOAL PERCENTAGE

Lowest opponents' field-goal percentage, season
  .407 — 2001 (791/1945)
  .413 — 2002 (786/1903)
Highest opponents' field-goal percentage, season
  .468 — 1998 (876/1870)
  .451 — 2000 (845/1875)
Lowest opponents' field goal percentage, game
  .238 — at Connecticut, August 1, 2003 (15/63)
  .250 — vs. New York, August 11, 1999
         (ot) (16/64)

TURNOVERS

Most opponents' turnovers per game, season
  17.0 — 1998 (511/30)
  14.3 — 2000 (456/32)

Fewest opponents' turnovers per game, season
  13.6 — 1999 (436/32)
  13.8 — 2003 (468/34)
Most opponents' turnovers, game
  26 — at New York, August 13, 1998
  24 — vs. Indiana, July 22, 2001

TEAM MISCELLANEOUS

GAME WON AND LOST

Highest winning percentage, season
  .531 — 2002 (17-15)
  .438 — 2000 (14-18)
Lowest winning percentage, season
  .100 — 1998 (3-27)
  .265 — 2003 (9-25)
Most consecutive games won
  6 — August 2-14, 1999
      June 4-18, 2002
  3 — June 29-July 3, 2001
      June 21-25, 2002
      July 15-19, 2003
Most consecutive games won, one season
  6 — August 2-14, 1999
      June 4-18, 2002
  3 — June 29-July 3, 2001
      June 21-25, 2002
      July 15-19, 2003
Most consecutive game lost
  11 — July 13-August 7, 1998
       June 13-July 9, 2003
  8 — June 21-July 8, 1998
      June 10-27, 2001
Most consecutive game lost, one season
  11 — July 13-August 7, 1998
       June 13-July 9, 2003
  8 — June 21-July 8, 1998
      June 10-27, 2001
Highest winning percentage, home games, season
  .563 — 2002 (9-7)
  .500 — 2001 (8-8)
Lowest winning percentage, home games, season
  .176 — 2003 (3-14)
  .200 — 1998 (3-12)
Most consecutive home games won
  9 — August 12, 2001-July 9, 2002
  4 — August 5-14, 1999
      August 4, 2000-June 5, 2001
Most consecutive home games lost
  8 — August 12, 1998-July 2, 1999
  7 — July 20, 2002-June 6, 2003
Highest winning percentage, road games, season
  .500 — 2002 (8-8)
  .438 — 2000 (7-9)
Lowest winning percentage, road games, season
  .000 — 1998 (0-15)
  .125 — 2001 (2-14)

RECORDS Washington Mystics

Most consecutive road games won
3 — June 24-July 3, 2000
August 1-14, 2003
2 — Many times
Most consecutive road games lost
16 — June 11, 1998-June 12, 1999
7 — August 6, 2000-June 27, 2001
May 31-July 5, 2003

OVERTIME GAMES

Most overtime games, season
2 — 1999, 2003
1 — 1998, 2001, 2002
Most consecutive overtime games, season
1 — Many times
Most overtime games won, season
2 — 1999
1 — 2001, 2002
Most overtime games won, no losses, season
2 — 1999
1 — 2001, 2002
Most consecutive overtime games won
4 — July 10, 1999-June 25, 2002
Most overtime games lost, season
2 — 2003
1 — 1998
Most overtime games lost, no wins, season
2 — 2003
1 — 1998
Most consecutive overtime games lost
2 — July 29-August 3, 2003 (current)
Most overtime periods, game
4 — at Seattle, July 3, 2001
2 — at Detroit, July 10, 1999
at Sacramento, June 25, 2002
vs. Phoenix, August 3, 2003

INDIVIDUAL RECORDS

SEASONS

Most Seasons
6 — Murriel Page
5 — Chamique Holdsclaw
4 — LaTonya Massaline
Nikki McCray

GAMES

Most games, career
192 — Murriel Page
139 — Chamique Holdsclaw
125 — Nikki McCray
Most consecutive games, career
192 — Murriel Page, June 11, 1998-
August 25, 2003 (current)
111 — Nikki McCray, July 19, 1998-
August 14, 2001
96 — Vicky Bullett, May 31, 2000-
August 13, 2002

Most games, season
34 — Annie Burgess, 2003
Stacey Dales-Schuman, 2003
Ashja Jones, 2003
Murriel Page, 2003

MINUTES

Most minutes, career
5,506 — Murriel Page
4,749 — Chamique Holdsclaw
3,886 — Nikki McCray
Highest average, minutes per game, career
(Minimum 75 games)
34.2 — Chamique Holdsclaw (4749/139)
32.5 — Vicky Bullett (3120/96)
31.1 — Nikki McCray (3886/125)
Most minutes, season
1,131 — Chamique Holdsclaw, 2000
1,094 — Vicky Bullett, 2000
1,076 — Coco Miller, 2003
Highest average, minutes per game, season
35.3 — Chamique Holdsclaw,
2000 (1131/32)
35.1 — Chamique Holdsclaw,
2003 (948/27)
34.23 — Chamique Holdsclaw,
1999 (1061/31)
Most minutes, game
55 — Vicky Bullett, at Seattle,
July 3, 2001 (4 ot)
54 — Audrey Sauret, at Seattle,
July 3, 2001 (4 ot)
Chamique Holdsclaw, at Seattle,
July 3, 2001 (4 ot)
49 — Nikki McCray, at Seattle,
July 3, 2001 (4 ot)

SCORING

Most points, lifetime
2,523 — Chamique Holdsclaw
1,921 — Nikki McCray
1,490 — Murriel Page
Highest average, points per game, career
(Minimum 75 games)
18.2 — Chamique Holdsclaw (2523/139)
15.4 — Nikki McCray (1921/125)
9.3 — Vicky Bullett (891/96)
Most points, season
561 — Nikki McCray, 1999
Chamique Holdsclaw, 2000
554 — Chamique Holdsclaw, 2003
525 — Chamique Holdsclaw, 1999
Highest average, points per game, season
20.5 — Chamique Holdsclaw,
2003 (554/27)
19.9 — Chamique Holdsclaw,
2002 (397/20)
17.7 — Nikki McCray, 1998 (512/29)

Most points, game
- 34 — Chamique Holdsclaw, vs. Indiana,
  July 24, 2003
- 32 — Chamique Holdsclaw, vs. Seattle,
  July 27, 2002
- 31 — Chamique Holdsclaw, vs. New York,
  June 10, 2001

Most games, 30 or more points, career
- 4 — Chamique Holdsclaw

Most games, 20 or more points, career
- 56 — Chamique Holdsclaw
- 35 — Nikki McCray
- 7 — Vicky Bullett

Most consecutive games, 20 or more points
- 6 — Chamique Holdsclaw,
  July 9-24, 2003
- 5 — Nikki McCray, August 5-14, 1999
- 4 — Chamique Holdsclaw,
  August 14-23, 2003

Most consecutive games, 10 or more points
- 19 — Chamique Holdsclaw,
  August 1, 2001-June 27, 2002
- 18 — Chamique Holdsclaw,
  May 23-July 29, 2003
- 17 — Nikki McCray,
  July 23, 1999-June 4, 2000

FIELD GOAL PERCENTAGE

Highest field goal percentage, career
(Minimum 300 field goals)
- .482 — Murriel Page (611/1268)
- .446 — Vicky Bullett (364/816)
- .435 — Chamique Holdsclaw (974/2238)

Highest field goal percentage, season (qualifiers)
- .590 — Murriel Page, 2000 (131/222)
- .574 — Murriel Page, 1999 (105/183)
- .486 — Vicky Bullett, 2000 (143/294)

Highest field goal percentage, game
(Minimum 8 field goals made)
- .909 — Vicky Bullett, vs. Detroit,
  July 18, 2002 (10/11)
- .800 — Nikki McCray, at Cleveland,
  June 3, 2000 (8/10)
  Murriel Page, vs. New York,
  July 24, 2000 (8/10)
- .727 — Heidi Burge, at Phoenix,
  August 4, 1998 (8/11)
  Nikki McCray, vs. Cleveland,
  August 8, 1999 (8/11)
  Murriel Page, vs. Detroit,
  August 4, 2000 (8/11)

Most field goals, none missed, game
- 5 — Murriel Page, vs. Utah,
  June 19, 1998
  Murriel Page, at Miami,
  July 13, 2000
  Stacey Dales-Schuman, at Indiana,
  August 12, 2003

- 4 — Andrea Nagy, at Cleveland,
  June 26, 1999
  Murriel Page, vs. Orlando,
  August 5, 1999

Most field goal attempts, none made, game
- 8 — Shalonda Enis, vs. Orlando,
  July 19, 1999
- 7 — Nikki McCray, vs. Miami,
  August 8, 2001
- 6 — By many

FIELD GOALS

Most field goals, career
- 974 — Chamique Holdsclaw
- 670 — Nikki McCray
- 611 — Murriel Page

Most field goals, season
- 232 — Chamique Holdsclaw, 2000
- 204 — Chamique Holdsclaw, 2003
- 202 — Chamique Holdsclaw, 1999

Most field goals, game
- 12 — Chamique Holdsclaw, vs. Orlando,
  May 31, 2000
  Chamique Holdsclaw, vs. Indiana,
  July 20, 2000
  Chamique Holdsclaw, vs. New York,
  June 10, 2001
  Chamique Holdsclaw, vs. Indiana,
  June 7, 2002
- 11 — Many times

FIELD GOAL ATTEMPTS

Most field goal attempts, career
- 2,238 — Chamique Holdsclaw
- 1,587 — Nikki McCray
- 1,268 — Murriel Page

Most field goal attempts, season
- 499 — Chamique Holdsclaw, 2000
- 480 — Chamique Holdsclaw, 2003
- 467 — Chamique Holdsclaw, 2001

Most field goal attempts, game
- 27 — Chamique Holdsclaw,
  vs. Los Angeles, June 26, 2000
  Chamique Holdsclaw,
  at Sacramento, June 25, 2002 (2 ot)
- 26 — Chamique Holdsclaw,
  at Charlotte, May 23, 2003
- 25 — Chamique Holdsclaw,
  vs. Sacramento, June 5, 2001
  Chamique Holdsclaw,
  vs. Seattle, July 27, 2002

THREE-POINT FIELD-GOAL PERCENTAGE

Highest three-point field goal percentage, career
(Minimum 75 three-point field goals)
- .377 — Helen Luz (86/228)
- .372 — Stacey Dales-Schuman (100/269)

.299 — Nikki McCray (141/472)
Highest three-point field goal percentage, season (qualifiers)
  .396 — Helen Luz, 2002 (42/106)
  .394 — Stacey Dales-Schuman,
      2002 (43/109)
  .390 — Helen Luz, 2001 (32/82)
Most three-point field goals, none missed, game
  3 — Nikki McCray, at Utah,
      June 13, 1998
      Helen Luz, at Seattle, July 3, 2001 (4 ot)
      Helen Luz, at Utah, June 4, 2002
      Coco Miller, at Orlando, July 8, 2002
      Stacey Dales-Schuman,
      at Indiana, August 12, 2003
      Coco Miller,
      vs. Connecticut, August 23, 2003
  2 — By many
Most three-point field goal attempts, none made, game
  6 — Penny Moore, vs. Sacramento,
      July 26, 1998
      Stacey Dales-Schuman, at New York,
      June 1, 2003
  5 — By many

THREE-POINT FIELD GOALS

Most three-point field goals, career
  141 — Nikki McCray
  100 — Stacey Dales-Schuman
  86 — Helen Luz
Most three-point field goals, season
  57 — Stacey Dales-Schuman, 2003
  50 — Nikki McCray, 2000
  46 — Nikki McCray, 1999
Most three-point field goals, game
  6 — Nikki McCray, vs. Orlando,
      May 31, 2000
      Nikki McCray, at Cleveland, June 3, 2000
  5 — Keri Chaconas, vs. Cleveland,
      July 1, 1998
      Stacey Dales-Schuman, vs. Charlotte,
      July 17, 2003
  4 — By many
Most consecutive games, three-point field goals made
  13 — Nikki McCray, August 5, 1999-
      June 8, 2000
  10 — Keri Chaconas, July 1-22, 1998
  8 — Helen Luz, June 4-21, 2002
      Stacey Dales-Schuman, June 13-
      July 3, 2003
      Stacey Dales-Schuman,
      July 7-26, 2003

THREE-POINT FIELD GOAL ATTEMPTS

Most three-point field goal attempts, career
  472 — Nikki McCray

269 — Stacey Dales-Schuman
228 — Helen Luz
Most three-point field goal attempts, season
  160 — Stacey Dales-Schuman, 2003
  153 — Nikki McCray, 1999
  151 — Nikki McCray, 2000
Most three-point field goal attempts, game
  10 — Keri Chaconas, vs. Cleveland,
      July 1, 1998
      Nikki McCray, vs. Orlando,
      May 31, 2000
      Nikki McCray, at Minnesota,
      July 27, 2001
  9 — By many

FREE THROW PERCENTAGE

Highest free-throw percentage, career
(Minimum 150 free throws)
  .774 — Chamique Holdsclaw (532/687)
  .761 — Nikki McCray (440/578)
  .633 — Murriel Page (257/406)
Highest free-throw percentage, season (qualifiers)
  .903 — Chamique Holdsclaw,
      2003 (140/155)
  .830 — Chamique Holdsclaw,
      2002 (88/106)
  .821 — Coco Miller, 2002 (46/56)
Most free throws made, none missed, game
  13 — Chamique Holdsclaw, vs. Indiana,
      July 24, 2003
  10 — Chamique Holdsclaw, vs. Seattle,
      July 27, 2002
      Chamique Holdsclaw, at New York,
      August 8, 2002
  9 — Chamique Holdsclaw, at Cleveland,
      June 20, 2003
Most free throw attempts, none made, game
  5 — Audrey Sauret, vs. Portland,
      August 3, 2001
  4 — Aiysha Smith, vs. Phoenix,
      August 3, 2003 (2 ot)
  3 — Murriel Page, at New York,
      August 17, 1999

FREE THROWS MADE

Most free throws made, career
  532 — Chamique Holdsclaw
  440 — Nikki McCray
  257 — Murriel Page
Most free throws made, season
  140 — Chamique Holdsclaw, 2003
  129 — Nikki McCray, 1999
  116 — Chamique Holdsclaw, 1999
Most free throws made, game
  13 — Chamique Holdsclaw, at New York,
      July 15, 2003
      Chamique Holdsclaw, vs. Indiana,
      July 24, 2003

12 — Nikki McCray, vs. Minnesota,
July 29, 2000
11 — Stacey Dales-Schuman, vs. Orlando,
June 1, 2002

FREE THROW ATTEMPTS

Most free throw attempts, career
687 — Chamique Holdsclaw
578 — Nikki McCray
406 — Murriel Page
Most free throw attempts, season
160 — Nikki McCray, 1999
155 — Chamique Holdsclaw, 2003
150 — Chamique Holdsclaw, 1999
Most free throw attempts, game
17 — Chamique Holdsclaw, at New York,
July 15, 2003
16 — Nikki McCray, vs. Minnesota,
July 29, 2000
Nikki McCray, vs. Seattle,
June 3, 2001
14 — Alessandra Santos de Oliveira,
at Utah, June 13, 1998
Chamique Holdsclaw, vs. New York,
June 10, 2001

REBOUNDS

Most rebounds, career
1,268 — Chamique Holdsclaw
1,113 — Murriel Page
600 — Vicky Bullett
Highest average, rebounds per game, career
(Minimum 75 games)
9.1 — Chamique Holdsclaw (1268/139)
6.3 — Vicky Bullett (600/96)
5.8 — Murriel Page (1113/192)
Most rebounds, season
294 — Chamique Holdsclaw, 2003
256 — Chamique Holdsclaw, 2001
246 — Chamique Holdsclaw, 1999
Highest average, rebounds per game, season
(qualifiers)
11.6 — Chamique Holdsclaw,
2002 (232/20)
10.9 — Chamique Holdsclaw,
2003 (294/27)
8.8 — Chamique Holdsclaw,
2001 (256/29)
Most rebounds, game
24 — Chamique Holdsclaw, at Charlotte,
May 23, 2003
21 — Chamique Holdsclaw,
at Sacramento, June 25, 2002 (2 ot)
18 — Alessandra Santos de Oliveira,
at Utah, June 13, 1998
Most games, 10+ rebounds, career
56 — Chamique Holdsclaw
18 — Murriel Page
10 — Vicky Bullett
Most consecutive games, 10+ rebounds
5 — Chamique Holdsclaw,
June 9-19, 2002
Chamique Holdsclaw,
July 27-August 9, 2003
3 — Many times

OFFENSIVE REBOUNDS

Most offensive rebounds, career
419 — Murriel Page
329 — Chamique Holdsclaw
172 — Vicky Bullett
Highest average, offensive rebounds per game,
career (Minimum 75 games)
2.4 — Chamique Holdsclaw (329/139)
2.2 — Murriel Page (419/192)
1.8 — Vicky Bullett (172/96)
Most offensive rebounds, season
81 — Murriel Page, 1998
79 — Murriel Page, 2000
74 — Chamique Holdsclaw, 1999
Murriel Page, 2001
Most offensive rebounds, game
9 — Tausha Mills, at Sacramento,
July 8, 2000
8 — Alessandra Santos de Oliveira,
at Houston, July 13, 1998
Chamique Holdsclaw,
vs. Cleveland, August 12, 2001
7 — many times

DEFENSIVE REBOUNDS

Most defensive rebounds, career
939 — Chamique Holdsclaw
694 — Murriel Page
428 — Vicky Bullett
Highest average, defensive rebounds per game,
career (Minimum 75 games)
6.8 — Chamique Holdsclaw (939/139)
4.5 — Vicky Bullett (428/96)
3.6 — Murriel Page (694/192)
Most defensive rebounds, season
222 — Chamique Holdsclaw, 2003
184 — Chamique Holdsclaw, 2001
183 — Chamique Holdsclaw, 2000
Most defensive rebounds, game
17 — Chamique Holdsclaw, at Charlotte,
May 23, 2003
14 — Chamique Holdsclaw,
at Sacramento, June 25, 2002 (2 ot)
Chamique Holdsclaw,
at Los Angeles, July 22, 2003
13 — Chamique Holdsclaw, at Detroit,
July 10, 1999 (2 ot)
Chamique Holdsclaw,
at Los Angeles, June 27, 2002
Chamique Holdsclaw, at Cleveland,
August 11, 2002

ASSISTS

Most assists, career
354 — Chamique Holdsclaw
300 — Nikki McCray
293 — Annie Burgess
Highest average, assists per game, career
(Minimum 75 games)
3.2 — Annie Burgess (293/91)
2.5 — Chamique Holdsclaw (354/139)
2.4 — Nikki McCray (300/125)
Most assists, season
146 — Andrea Nagy, 1999
118 — Andrea Nagy, 2000
114 — Stacey Dales-Schuman, 2003
Highest average, assists per game, season
(qualifiers)
5.1 — Andrea Nagy, 2000 (118/23)

4.6 — Andrea Nagy, 1999 (146/32)
3.6 — Annie Burgess, 2002 (93/26)
Most assists, game
　12 — Andrea Nagy, vs. Charlotte,
　　　　June 10, 1999
　11 — Andrea Nagy, at Cleveland,
　　　　August 7, 1999
　　　　Keisha Anderson, at Charlotte,
　　　　July 26, 2000
　　　　Annie Burgess, at Connecticut,
　　　　June 13, 2003
　10 — Andrea Nagy, vs. Orlando,
　　　　May 31, 2000
　　　　Andrea Nagy, vs. Sacramento,
　　　　June 23, 2000
Most games, 10+ assists, career
　4 — Andrea Nagy
　1 — Keisha Anderson
　　　 Annie Burgess

PERSONAL FOULS

Most personal fouls, career
　571 — Murriel Page
　314 — Chamique Holdsclaw
　　　　 Nikki McCray
　258 — Vicky Bullett
Most personal fouls, season
　111 — Andrea Nagy, 1999
　109 — Ashja Jones, 2003
　103 — Murriel Page, 1999
　　　　 Murriel Page, 2000
Most personal fouls, game
　6 — many times

DISQUALIFICATIONS

Most disqualifications, career
　9 — Murriel Page
　4 — Nikki McCray
　3 — Stacey Dales-Schuman
　　　 Ashja Jones
Highest percentage, games disqualified, career
(Minimum 75 games)
　4.8 — Murriel Page (9/192)
　3.2 — Nikki McCray (4/125)
　1.2 — Coco Miller (1/85)
Lowest percentage, games disqualified, career
(Minimum 75 games)
　0.00 — By many
Most consecutive games without disqualification,
career
　139 — Chamique Holdsclaw,
　　　　　June 10, 1999-August 25, 2003 (current)
　96 — Vicky Bullett, May 31, 2000-
　　　　August 13, 2002
　87 — LaTonya Massaline, May 31, 2000
　　　　July 5, 2003 (current)
Most disqualifications, season
　4 — Murriel Page, 1999
　2 — By many
Fewest minutes, disqualified, game
　8 — Asjha Jones, at Portland,
　　　 June 28, 2002
　9 — Heidi Burge, at Phoenix,
　　　 June 15, 1998
　10 — Asjha Jones, at Utah, June 4, 2002

STEALS

Most steals, career
　182 — Chamique Holdsclaw

171 — Vicky Bullett
148 — Nikki McCray
Highest average, steals per game, career
(Minimum 75 games)
　1.78 — Vicky Bullett (171/96)
　1.31 — Chamique Holdsclaw (182/139)
　1.18 — Nikki McCray (148/125)
Most steals, season
　64 — Vicky Bullett, 2000
　63 — Rita Williams, 1998
　54 — Vicky Bullett, 2002
Highest average, steals per game, season
(qualifiers)
　2.10 — Rita Williams, 1998 (63/30)
　2.00 — Vicky Bullett, 2000 (64/32)
　1.69 — Vicky Bullett, 2002 (54/32)
Most steals, game
　8 — Chamique Holdsclaw, vs. Indiana,
　　　 July 20, 2000
　7 — Rita Williams, vs. Sacramento,
　　　 July 26, 1998
　5 — By many

BLOCKED SHOTS

Most blocked shots, career
　150 — Murriel Page
　142 — Vicky Bullett
　80 — Chamique Holdsclaw
Highest average, blocked shots per game, career
(Minimum: 75 games)
　1.48 — Vicky Bullett (142/96)
　0.78 — Murriel Page (150/192)
　0.58 — Chamique Holdsclaw (80/139)
Most blocked shots, season
　58 — Vicky Bullett, 2001
　47 — Vicky Bullett, 2000
　37 — Vicky Bullett, 2002
Highest average, blocked shots per game, season
(qualifiers)
　1.81 — Vicky Bullett, 2001 (58/32)
　1.47 — Vicky Bullett, 2000 (47/32)
　1.16 — Vicky Bullett, 2002 (37/32)
Most blocked shots, game
　5 — La'Shawn Brown, vs. Sacramento,
　　　 July 26, 1998
　　　 Vicky Bullett, at Charlotte, July 1,
　　　 2000
　　　 Vicky Bullett, vs. Minnesota,
　　　 July 29, 2000
　　　 Vicky Bullett, at Orlando, July 24, 2001
　4 — By many

TURNOVERS

Most turnovers, career
　412 — Chamique Holdsclaw
　394 — Nikki McCray
　315 — Murriel Page
Most turnovers, season
　125 — Nikki McCray, 1998
　108 — Chamique Holdsclaw, 1999
　107 — Nikki McCray, 1999
Most turnovers, game
　11 — Chamique Holdsclaw, vs. Utah,
　　　　July 8, 1999
　10 — Nikki McCray, vs. New York,
　　　　July 5, 1998 (ot)
　9 — Nikki McCray, at Utah, June 13, 1998

OFFICIAL WNBA RULES

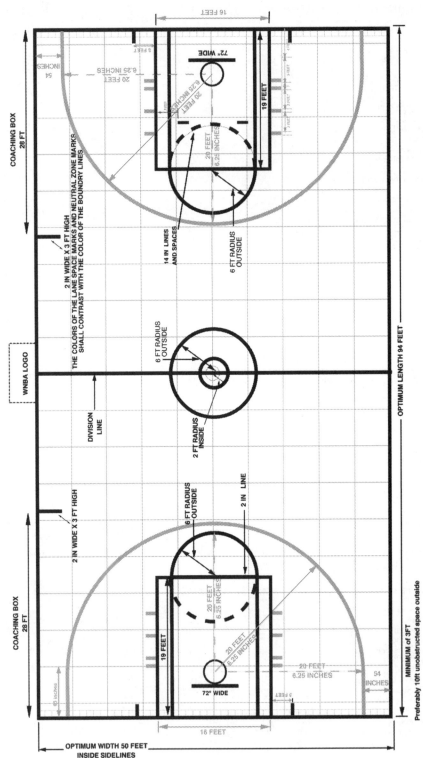

OFFICIAL WNBA COURT DIAGRAM

COACHING BOX 28 FT

COACHING BOX 28 FT

WNBA LOGO

2 IN WIDE X 3 FT HIGH

THE COLORS OF THE LANE SPACE MARKS AND NEUTRAL ZONE MARKS SHALL CONTRAST WITH THE COLOR OF THE BOUNDRY LINES

14 IN LINES AND SPACES

6 FT RADIUS OUTSIDE

6 FT RADIUS OUTSIDE

DIVISION LINE

2 FT RADIUS INSIDE

6 FT RADIUS OUTSIDE

2 IN LINE

72" WIDE

19 FEET

16 FEET

20 FEET 6.25 INCHES

28 FEET 6.25 INCHES

54 INCHES

3 FEET

OPTIMUM LENGTH 94 FEET

MINIMUM of 3FT
Preferably 10ft unobstructed space outside

OPTIMUM WIDTH 50 FEET
INSIDE SIDELINES

358

OFFICIAL RULES
RULE NO. 1—COURT DIMENSIONS—EQUIPMENT

SECTION I—COURT AND DIMENSIONS

a. The playing court shall be measured and marked as shown in the court diagram. (See page 10)

b. A free throw lane, shall be marked at each end of the court with dimensions and markings as shown on the court diagram. All boundary lines are part of the lane; lane space marks and neutral zone marks are not. The color of the lane space marks and neutral zones shall contrast with the color of the boundary lines. The areas identified by the lane space markings are 2" by 8" inches and the neutral zone marks are 12" by 8".

c. A free throw line shall be drawn (2" wide) across each of the circles indicated in the court diagram. It shall be parallel to the end line and shall be 15' from the plane of the face of the backboard.

d. The three-point field goal area has parallel lines 54" from the sidelines, extending 63" from the baseline and an arc of 20'61/4' from the middle of the basket which intersects the parallel lines.

e. Four hash marks shall be drawn (2" wide) perpendicular to the sideline on each side of the court and 28' from the baseline. These hash marks shall extend 3' onto the court.

f. Two hash marks shall be drawn (2" wide) perpendicular to the sideline, in front of the scorer's table, and 4' on each side of the midcourt line. This will designate the Substitution Box area.

g. Four hash marks shall be drawn (2" wide) perpendicular to the baseline on each side of the free throw lane line. These hash marks shall be 3' from the free throw lane line and extend 6" onto the court.

SECTION II—EQUIPMENT

a. The backboard shall be a rectangle measuring 6' horizontally and 311/42' vertically. The front surface shall be flat and transparent.

b. Atransparent backboard shall be marked with a 2" white rectangle centered behind the ring. This rectangle shall have outside dimensions of 24" horizontally and 18" vertically.

c. Home management is required to have a spare board with supporting unit on hand for emergencies, and a steel tape or extension ruler and a level for use if necessary.

d. Each basket shall consist of a pressure-release WNBA approved metal safety ring 18" in inside diameter with a white cord net 15" to 18" in length. The cord of the net shall not be less than 30 thread nor more than 120 thread and shall be constructed to check the ball momentarily as it passes through the basket.

e. Each basket ring shall be securely attached to the backboard with its upper edge 10' above and parallel to the floor and equidistant from the vertical edges of the board. The nearest point of the inside edge of the ring shall be 6" from the plane of the face of the board. The ring shall be painted orange.

f. (1) The ball shall be an officially approved WNBA ball with a weight not less than 18 ounces nor more than 20 ounces. The circumference of the ball shall be within a maximum of 29 inches and a minimum of 28.5 inches.

(2) Six balls must be made available to each team for pre-game warmup.

g. At least one electric light is to be placed behind the backboard, obvious to officials and synchronized to light up when the horn sounds at the expiration of time for each period. The electric light is to be "red."

RULE NO. 2—OFFICIALS AND THEIR DUTIES

SECTION I—THE GAME OFFICIALS

a. The game officials shall be a crew chief and two referees. They will be assisted by an official scorer and two trained timers. One timer will operate the game clock and the other will operate the 30-second clock. All officials shall be approved by the Operations Department.

b. The officials shall wear the uniform prescribed by the WNBA.

SECTION II—DUTIES OF THE OFFICIALS

a. The officials shall, prior to the start of the game, inspect and approve all equipment, including court, baskets, balls, backboards, timers and scorer's equipment.

b. The officials shall not permit players to play with any type of hand, arm, face, nose, ear, head or neck jewelry.

c. The officials shall not permit any player to wear equipment which, in his/her judgment, is dangerous to other players. Any equipment which is of hard substance (casts, splints, guards and braces) must be padded or foam covered and have no exposed sharp or cutting edge. All the face masks and eye or nose protectors must conform to the contour of the face and have no sharp or protruding edges. Approval is on a game-to-game basis.

d. All equipment used must be appropriate for basketball. Equipment that is unnatural and designed to increase a player's height or reach, or to gain an advantage, shall not be used.

e. The officials must check the game ball to see that it is properly inflated. The recommended ball pressure should be between 7 1/2 and 8 1/2 pounds.

f. The crew chief shall be the official in charge.

g. If a coach desires to discuss a rule or interpretation of a rule prior to the start of a game or between periods, it will be mandatory for the officials to ask the other coach to be present during the discussion. The same procedure shall be followed if the officials wish to discuss a game situation with either coach.

h. The designated official shall toss the ball at the start of the game. The crew chief shall decide whether or not a goal shall count if the officials disagree, and he/she shall decide matters upon which scorers and timers disagree.

i. All officials will report on the floor eighteen (18) minutes prior to game time, or await the arrival of the first team on the floor.

j. Officials must meet with team captains prior to the start of the game.

k. Officials must report any atypical or unique incident to the Operations Department. Flagrant, punching, fighting fouls or a team's failure to have eight players to begin the game must also be reported.

SECTION III—ELASTIC POWER

The officials shall have the power to make decisions on any point not specifically covered in the rules. The Operations Department will be advised of all such decisions at the earliest possible moment.

SECTION IV—DIFFERENT DECISIONS BY OFFICIALS

a. The crew chief shall have the authority to set aside or question decisions regarding a rule interpretation made by either of the other officials.

b. If the officials give conflicting signals as to who caused the ball to go outof- bounds, a jump ball shall be called between the two players involved. However, if an official offers assistance, the calling official may change the call.

c. In the event that a violation and foul occur at the same time, the foul will take precedence.

d. Double Foul (See Rule 12-B—Section VI-f).

SECTION V—TIME AND PLACE FOR DECISIONS

a. The officials have the power to render decisions for infractions of rules committed inside or outside the boundary lines. This includes periods when the game may be stopped for any reason.

b. When a personal foul or violation occurs, an official will blow his/her whistle to terminate play. The whistle is the signal for the timer to stop the game clock. If a personal foul has occurred, the official: (1) will indicate the number of the offender to the official scorer (2) the nature of the personal foul (3) the number of free throws, if any, to be attempted or point to the spot of the throw-in.

If a violation has occurred, the official will indicate: (1) the nature of the violation by giving the correct signal; (2) the number of the offender, if applicable; and (3) the direction in which the ball will be advanced.

c. When a team is entitled to a throw-in, an official shall clearly signal
(1) the act which caused the ball to become dead
(2) the spot of the throw-in
(3) the team entitled to the throw-in, unless it follows a successful or awarded field goal.

d. When a whistle is erroneously sounded, whether the ball is in a possession or non-possession status, it is an inadvertent whistle and shall be interpreted as a suspension-of-play.

e. An official may suspend play for any unusual circumstance.

a. The officials have the power to render decisions for infractions of rules committed inside or outside the boundary lines. This includes periods when the game may be stopped for any reason.

b. When a personal foul or violation occurs, an official will blow his/her whistle to terminate play. The whistle is the signal for the timer to stop the game clock. If a personal foul has occurred, the official: (1) will indicate the number of the offender to the official scorer (2) the nature of the personal foul (3) the number of free throws, if any, to be attempted or point to the spot of the throw-in. If a violation has occurred, the official will indicate: (1) the nature of the violation by giving the correct signal; (2) the number of the offender, if applicable; and (3) the direction in which the ball will be advanced.

    c. When a team is entitled to a throw-in, an official shall clearly signal

        (1) the act which caused the ball to become dead

        (2) the spot of the throw-in

        (3) the team entitled to the throw-in, unless it follows a successful or awarded field goal.

    d. When a whistle is erroneously sounded, whether the ball is in a possession or non-possession status, it is an inadvertent whistle and shall be interpreted as a suspension-of-play.

    e. An official may suspend play for any unusual circumstance.

SECTION VI—CORRECTING ERRORS

A. FREE THROWS

    Officials may correct an error if a rule is inadvertently set aside and results in the following:

        (1) A team not shooting a merited free throw that will remain in play.

    EXCEPTION: If the offensive team scores or shoots earned free throws as a result of a personal foul prior to possession by the defensive team the error shall be ignored if more than 30 seconds have expired.

        (2) A team not shooting a merited free throw that will not remain in play. The error shall be corrected, all play shall stand and play will resume from the point of interruption with the clocks remaining the same.

        (3) A team shooting an unmerited free throw.

        (4) Permitting the wrong player to attempt a free throw.

    a. Officials shall be notified of a possible error at the first dead ball.

    b. Errors which occur in the first half must be discovered and the scorer's table notified prior to the officials leaving the floor at the end of the half. The errors must be rectified prior to the start of the second half.

    c. Errors which occur in the second half or overtime(s) must be discovered and rectified prior to the end of the period.

    d. The ball is not in play on corrected free throw attempt(s). Play is resumed at the same spot and under the same conditions as would have prevailed had the error not been discovered.

    e. All play that occurs is to be nullified if the error is discovered within a 30-second time period. The game clock shall be reset to the time that the error occurred.

    EXCEPTION (1): Acts of unsportsmanlike conduct, flagrant fouls and points scored there from, shall not be nullified.

    EXCEPTION (2): If the error to be corrected is for a free throw attempt, where there is to be no line-up of players on the free throw lane line (technical foul, flagrant foul, punching foul, clear-path foul and away from the play foul in last one minute), the error shall be corrected, all play shall stand and play shall resume from the point of interruption with the clocks remaining the same.

B. LINEUP POSITIONS

    In any jump ball situation, if the jumpers are lined up incorrectly and the error is discovered:

        (1) After more than 30 seconds has elapsed, the teams will continue to shoot for that basket.

        (2) If 30 seconds or less has elapsed, all play shall be nullified.

    EXCEPTION: Acts of unsportsmanlike conduct, flagrant fouls and points scored therefrom, shall not be nullified.

    a. The game clock shall be reset to the time of the original jump ball.

    b. The 30-second clock shall be reset to 30.

C. RECORD KEEPING

    A record keeping error by the official scorer which involves the score, number of personal fouls and/or timeouts may be corrected by the officials at any time prior to the end of the second half. Any such error which occurs in overtime must be corrected prior to the end of that period.

SECTION VII—DUTIES OF SCORERS

    a. The scorers shall record the field goals made, the free throws made and missed and shall keep a running summary of the points scored. They shall record the personal and technical fouls called on each player and shall notify the officials immediately when a sixth personal foul is called on any player. They shall record the timeouts charged to each team, shall notify a team and its coach through an official whenever that team is granted a team charged timeout and shall notify the nearest official when the team is granted a charged timeout in excess of the legal number. In case there is a question about an error in the scoring, the scorer shall check with the crew chief at once to find the discrepancy. If the error cannot be found, the official shall accept the record of the official scorer, unless he/she has knowledge that forces him/her to decide otherwise.

b. The scorers shall keep a record of the names, numbers and positions of the players who are to start the game and of all substitutes who enter the game. When there is an infraction of the rules pertaining to submission of the lineup, substitutions or numbers of players, they shall notify the nearest official immediately if the ball is dead, or as soon as it becomes dead if it is in play when the infraction is discovered. The scorer shall mark the time at which players are disqualified by reason of receiving six personal fouls, so that it may be easy to ascertain the order in which the players are eligible to go back into the game in accordance with Rule 3—Section I.

c. The scorers shall use a horn or other device unlike that used by the officials or timers to signal the officials. This may be used when the ball is dead or in certain specified situations when the ball is in control of a given team.

d. When a player is disqualified from the game, or whenever a penalty free throw is being awarded, a buzzer, siren or some other clearly audible sound must be used by the scorer or timer to notify the game officials. It is the duty of the scorekeeper to be certain the officials have acknowledged the sixth personal foul buzzer and the penalty shot buzzer.

e. The scorer shall not signal the officials while the ball is in play, except to notify them of the necessity to correct an error.

f. Should the scorer sound the horn while the ball is in play, it shall be ignored by the players on the court. The officials must use their judgment in stopping play to consult with the scorer's table.

g. Scorers shall record on the scoreboard the number of team fouls up to a total of eight, which will indicate that the team is in a penalty situation.

SECTION VIII—DUTIES OF TIMERS

a. The timers shall note when each half is to start and shall notify the crew chief and both coaches five minutes before this time, or cause them to be notified at least five minutes before the half is to start. They shall signal the scorers two minutes before starting time. They shall record playing time and time of stoppages as provided in the rules. The official timer and the 30-second clock operator shall be provided with digital stop watches to be used with the timing of timeouts and in case the official game clock, 30-second clocks/game clocks located above the backboards fail to work properly.

b. At the beginning of the first half, second half and any overtime period or whenever play is resumed by a jump ball, the game clock shall be started when the ball is legally tapped by either of the jumpers. No time will be removed from the game clock and/or 30-second clock if there is an illegal tap.

c. If the game clock has been stopped for a violation, successful field goal or free throw attempt and the ball is put in play by a throw-in, the game clock and the 30-second clock shall be started when the ball is legally touched by any player on the court. The starting of the game clock and the 30-second clock will be under the control of the official timer.

d. During an unsuccessful free throw attempt, the game clock will be started by the official timer when the ball is legally touched. The 30-second clock will be reset when player possession of the ball is obtained.

e. The game clock shall be stopped at the expiration of time for each half and when an official signals timeout. For a charged timeout, the timer shall start a digital stop watch and shall signal the official when it is time to resume play.

f. The game clock and the scoreboard will combine to cause a horn or buzzer to sound, automatically, when playing time for the period has expired. If the horn or buzzer fails to sound, or is not heard, the official timer shall use any other means to notify the officials immediately.

g. In a dead ball situation, if the clock shows :00.0, the half or game is considered to have ended although the buzzer may not have sounded.

EXCEPTION: See Rule 13—Section II–a(6).

h. Record only the actual playing time in the last minute of the first half.

i. Record only the actual playing time in the last minute of the second half and the last minute of any overtime period(s).

j. Timers are responsible for contents in Comments On The Rules—Section L.

RULE NO. 3—PLAYERS, SUBSTITUTES AND COACHES

SECTION I—TEAM

a. Each team shall consist of five players. No team may be reduced to less than five players. If a player in the game receives her sixth personal foul and all substitutes have already been disqualified, said player shall remain in the game and shall be charged with a personal and team foul. A technical foul also shall be assessed against her team. All subsequent personal fouls, including offensive fouls, shall be treated similarly. All players who have six or more personal fouls and remain in the game shall be treated similarly.

b. In the event that there are only five eligible players remaining and one of these players is injured and must leave the game or is ejected, she must be replaced by the last player who was disqualified by reason of receiving six personal fouls. Each subsequent requirement to replace an injured or ejected player will be treated in this inverse order. Any such re-entry into a game by a disqualified player shall be penalized by a technical foul.

c. In the event that a player becomes ill and must leave the court while the ball is in play, the official will stop play immediately when her team gains new possession. The player will be replaced and no technical foul will be assessed. The opposing team is also permitted to substitute one player.

SECTION II—STARTING LINE-UPS

At least ten minutes before the game is scheduled to begin, the scorer shall be supplied with the name and number of each player who may participate in the game. Starting line-ups will be indicated. Failure to comply with this provision shall be reported to the Operations Department.

SECTION III—THE CAPTAIN

a. A team may have a captain and a co-captain numbering a maximum of two. The designated captain may be anyone on the squad who is in uniform, except a player-coach.

b. The designated captain is the only player who may talk to an official during a regular or 20-second timeout charged to her team. She may discuss a rule interpretation, but not a judgment decision.

c. If the designated captain continues to sit on the bench, she remains the captain for the entire game.

d. In the event that the captain is absent from the court and bench, her coach shall immediately designate a new captain.

SECTION IV—THE COACH AND OTHERS

a. A coach's position may be on or off the bench from the 28' hash mark to the baseline. They are permitted between the 28' hash mark and the midcourt line to relay information to players but must return to the bench side of the 28' hash mark immediately or be called for a non-unsportsmanlike technical foul. A coach is not permitted to cross the midcourt line and violators will be assessed an unsportsmanlike technical foul immediately. All assistants and trainers must remain in the vicinity of the bench. Coaches and trainers are not permitted to go to the scorer's table, for any reason, except during a dead ball.

b. A player-coach will have no special privileges. She is to conduct herself in the same manner as any other player.

c. Any club personnel not seated on the bench must conduct themselves in a manner that would reflect favorably on the dignity of the game or that of the officials. Violations by any of the personnel indicated shall require a written report to the Operations Department for subsequent action.

d. The bench shall be occupied only by a league-approved head coach, a maximum of two assistant coaches, players and trainer. During an altercation the head coach and assistant coaches are permitted on the court as "peacemakers."

e. If a player, coach or assistant coach is suspended from a game or games, he/she shall not at any time before, during or after such game or games appear in any part of the arena or stands where his/her team is playing. A player, coach or assistant coach who is ejected may only remain in the dressing room of his/her team during the remainder of the game, or leave the building. A violation of this rule shall result in a fine.

SECTION V—SUBSTITUTES

a. A substitute shall report to the scorer and position herself in the 8' Substitution Box located in front of the scorer's table. She shall inform the scorer whom she is to replace. The scorer shall sound the horn as soon as the ball is dead to indicate a substitution. The horn does not have to be sounded if the substitution occurs between periods or during timeouts. No substitute may enter the game after a successful field goal by either team, unless the ball is dead due to a personal foul, technical foul, timeout or violation. She may enter the game after the first of multiple free throws, whether made or missed.

b. The substitute shall remain in the Substitution Box until she is beckoned onto the court by an official. If the ball is about to become live, the beckoning signal shall be withheld. Any player who enters the court prior to being beckoned by an official shall be assessed a non-unsportsmanlike technical foul.

c. A substitute must be ready to enter the game when beckoned. No delays for removal of warm-up clothing will be permitted.

d. The substitute shall not replace a free throw shooter or a player involved in a jump ball unless dictated to do so by an injury whereby she is selected by the opposing coach. At no time may she be allowed to attempt a free throw awarded as a result of a technical foul.

e. A substitute shall be considered as being in the game when she is beckoned onto the court or recognized as being in the game by an official. Once a player is in the game, she cannot be removed until the ball is legally touched by a player on the court unless: (1) a personal foul or technical is called, (2) there is a change of possession, (3) administration of infection control.

EXCEPTION: Rule 3—Section V—f and Comments on the Rules—N.

f. Any substitute may be removed after a successful free throw attempt which is to remain in play, if the offensive team requests and is granted a timeout.

g. A substitute may be recalled from the scorer's table prior to being beckoned onto the court by an official.

h. A player may be replaced and allowed to re-enter the game as a substitute during the same dead ball.

i. A player must be in the Substitution Box at the time a violation occurs if the throw-in is to be administered in the backcourt. If a substitute fails to meet the requirement, she may not enter the game until the next legal opportunity.

EXCEPTION: In the last minute of each half or overtime, a reasonable amount of time will be allowed for a substitution.

j. Notification of all above infractions and ensuing procedures shall be in accordance with Rule 2—Section VII.

k. No substitutes are allowed to enter the game during an official's suspension-of-play for (1) a delay-of-game warning, (2) retrieving an errant ball (3) an inadvertent whistle or (4) any other unusual circumstance.

EXCEPTION: Suspension of play for a player bleeding. See Comments on the Rules—N.

SECTION VI—UNIFORMS (PLAYERS JERSEYS)

a. Each player shall be numbered on the front and back of her jersey with a number of solid color contrasting with the color of the shirt.

b. Each number must be not less than 3/4" in width and not less than 4" in height on both the front and back. Each player shall have her surname affixed to the back of her game jersey in letters at least 2" in height. If a team has more than one player with the same surname, each such player's first initial must appear before the surname on the back of the game jersey.

c. The home team shall wear light color jerseys and the visitors dark jerseys. For neutral court games and doubleheaders, the second team named in the official schedule shall be regarded as the home team and shall wear the light colored jerseys.

RULE NO. 4—DEFINITIONS

SECTION I—BASKET/BACKBOARD

a. A team's basket consists of the basket ring and net through which its players try to shoot the ball. The visiting team has the choice of baskets for the first half. The basket selected by the visiting team when it first enters onto the court shall be its basket for the first half.

b. The teams change baskets for the second half. All overtime periods are considered extensions of the second half.

c. Five sides of the backboard (front, two sides, bottom and top) are considered in play when contacted by the basketball. The back of the backboard and the area directly behind it are out of bounds.

SECTION II—BLOCKING

Blocking is illegal personal contact which impedes the progress of an opponent.

SECTION III—DRIBBLE

A dribble is movement of the ball, caused by a player in control, who throws or taps the ball to the floor.

a. The dribble ends when the dribbler:
    (1) Touches the ball simultaneously with both hands
    (2) Permits the ball to come to rest while she is in control of it
    (3) Tries for a field goal
    (4) Throws a pass
    (5) Touches the ball more than once while dribbling, before it
        touches the floor
    (6) Loses control
    (7) Allows the ball to become dead

SECTION IV—FOULS

a. A common personal foul is illegal physical contact which occurs with an opponent after the ball has become live, or before the horn sounds to end the period. If time expires before the personal foul occurs, the personal foul should be disregarded, unless it was unsportsmanlike.

EXCEPTION: If the foul is committed on or by a player in the act of shooting, and the shooter released the ball prior to the expiration of time on the game clock, then the foul should be administered in the same manner as with any similar play during the course of the game. See: Rule 13—Section II–a(6)

b. A technical foul is the penalty for unsportsmanlike conduct or violations by team members on the floor or seated on the bench. It may be assessed for illegal contact which occurs with an opponent before the ball becomes live.

c. A double foul is a situation in which two opponents commit personal or technical fouls against each other at approximately the same time.

d. An offensive foul is illegal contact, committed by an offensive player, after the ball is live.

e. A loose ball foul is illegal contact, after the ball is live, when team control does not exist.

f. An elbow foul is making contact with the elbow in an unsportsmanlike manner, whether the ball is dead or alive.

g. A flagrant foul is unnecessary and/or excessive contact committed by a player against an opponent, whether the ball is dead or alive.

h. A punching foul is a punch by a player which makes contact with an opponent, whether the ball is dead or alive.

i. An away-from-the-play foul is illegal contact by the defense in the last minute of the game, and/or overtime, which occurs (1) deliberately away from the immediate area of the ball, and/or (2) prior to the ball being released on a throw-in.

SECTION V—FREE THROW

A free throw is the privilege given a player to score one point by an unhindered attempt for the goal from a position directly behind the free throw line. This attempt must be made within 10 seconds.

SECTION VI—FRONTCOURT/BACKCOURT

a. A team's frontcourt consists of that part of the court between its endline and the nearer edge of the midcourt line, including the basket and inbounds part of the backboard.

b. A team's backcourt consists of the entire midcourt line and the rest of the court to include the opponent's basket and inbounds part of the backboard.

c. A ball being held by a player: (1) is in the frontcourt if neither the ball nor the player is touching the backcourt, (2) is in the backcourt if either the ball or the player is touching the backcourt.

365

d. A ball being dribbled is (1) in the frontcourt when the ball and both feet of the player are in the frontcourt, (2) in the backcourt if the ball or either foot of the player is in the backcourt.

e. The ball is considered in the frontcourt once it has broken the plane of the midcourt line and is not in player control.

f. The team on the offense must bring the ball across the midcourt line within 10 seconds.

EXCEPTION: (1) kicked ball, (2) punched ball, (3) personal or technical foul on the defensive team, (4) delay of game warning on the defensive team or (5) infection control.

g. Frontcourt/backcourt status is not attained until a player with the ball has established a positive position in either half during (1) a jump ball, (2) a steal by a defensive player or (3) any time the ball is loose.

h. The defensive team has no "frontcourt/backcourt."

SECTION VII—HELD BALL

A held ball occurs when two opponents have one or both hands firmly on the ball. A held ball should not be called until both players have hands so firmly on the ball that neither can gain sole possession without undue roughness. If a player is lying or sitting on the floor, while in possession, she should have an opportunity to throw the ball, but a held ball should be called if there is danger of injury.

SECTION VIII—PIVOT

a. A pivot takes place when a player, who is holding the ball, steps once or more than once in any direction with the same foot, with the other foot (pivot foot) in contact with the floor.

b. If the player wishes to dribble after a pivot, the ball must be out of her hand before the pivot foot is raised off the floor.

c. If the player raises her pivot off the floor, she must pass or attempt a field goal. If she fails to follow these guidelines, she has committed a traveling violation.

SECTION IX—TRAVELING

Traveling is progressing in any direction while in possession of the ball, which is in excess of prescribed limits as noted in Rule 4—Section VIII and Rule 10—Section XIV.

SECTION X—SCREEN

A screen is the legal action of a player who, without causing undue contact, delays or prevents an opponent from reaching a desired position.

SECTION XI—FIELD GOAL ATTEMPT

A field goal attempt is a player's attempt to shoot the ball into her basket for a field goal. The act of shooting starts when, in the official's judgment, the player has started her shooting motion and continues until the shooting motion ceases and she returns to a normal floor position. It is not essential that the ball leave the shooter's hand. Her arm(s) might be held so that she cannot actually make an attempt.

The term is also used to include the flight of the ball until it becomes dead or is touched by a player. A tap during a jump ball or rebound is not considered a field goal attempt. However, any time a live ball is in flight from the playing court, the goal, if made, shall count, even if time expires or the official's whistle sounds. The field goal will not be scored if time on the game clock expires before the ball leaves the player's hand.

EXCEPTION: —Rule 5—Section III(2).

SECTION XII—THROW-IN

A throw-in is a method of putting the ball in play from out-of-bounds in accordance with Rule 8—Section III. The throw-in begins when the ball is at the disposal of the team or player entitled to it, and ends when the ball is released by the thrower-in.

SECTION XIII—LAST MINUTE

When the game clock shows 1:00, the half or overtime is considered to be in the one-minute period.

SECTION XIV—DISCONCERTION OF FREE THROW SHOOTER

Disconcertion of the free throw shooter is any of the following:

a. During multiple free throw attempts which are not going to remain in play, an opponent may not, while located on the lane lines, be allowed to raise her arms above her head.

b. During any free throw attempt, an opponent in the game who is in the visual field of the free throw shooter, may not (1) wave her arms, (2) make a sudden dash upcourt, (3) talk to the free throw shooter, or (4) talk loudly in a disruptive manner.

SECTION XV—SUSPENSION OF PLAY

An official can suspend play for retrieving an errant ball, re-setting the timing devices, wiping the floor, delay-of-game warning, inadvertent whistle, or any other unusual circumstance. During a suspension of play, neither team is allowed to substitute and the defensive team may not be granted a timeout. Play shall be resumed from the point of interruption.

EXCEPTION: See Comments on Rules-N.

SECTION XVI—POINT OF INTERRUPTION

Where the ball is located when the whistle sounds.

SECTION XVII—TEAM CONTROL

A team is in control when a player is holding, dribbling or passing the ball. Team control ends when the defensive team deflects the ball or there is a field goal attempt.

SECTION XVIII—TEAM POSSESSION

A team is in possession when a player is holding, dribbling or passing the ball. Team possession ends when the defensive team gains possession or there is a field goal attempt.

RULE NO. 5—SCORING AND TIMING

SECTION I—SCORING

a. A legal field goal or free throw attempt shall be scored when a live ball from the playing area enters the basket from above and remains in or passes through the net.

b. A successful field goal attempt from the area on or inside the three-point field goal line shall count two points.

c. A successful field goal attempt from the area outside the three-point field goal line shall count three points.

(1) The shooter must have at least one foot on the floor outside the three-point field goal line prior to the attempt.

(2) The shooter may not be touching the floor on or inside the threepoint field goal line.

(3) The shooter may contact the three-point field goal line, or land in the two-point field goal area, after the ball is released.

d. A field goal accidentally scored in an opponent's basket shall be added to the opponent's score, credited to the opposing player nearest the shooter and mentioned in a footnote. This is not considered a field goal attempt.

e. It is a violation for a player to attempt a field goal at an opponent's basket. A field goal intentionally scored in the wrong basket shall be disallowed. The ball shall be awarded to the opposing team out-of-bounds at the free throw line extended.

f. A successful free throw attempt shall count one point.

g. An unsuccessful free throw attempt which is tapped into the basket shall count two points and shall be credited to the player who tapped the ball in.

h. If there is a discrepancy in the score and it cannot be resolved, the running score shall be official.

SECTION II—TIMING

a. Regulation play in the WNBA will be two twenty-minute halves.

b. All overtime periods of play will be five minutes.

c. Fifteen minutes will be permitted between halves of all games.

d. 120 seconds will be permitted for regular timeouts and between the second half and or any overtime period.

e. A team is permitted a total of 30 seconds to replace a disqualified player.

f. The half or overtime is considered to be in the one-minute period when the game clock shows 1:00 or less time remaining.

g. The public address operator is required to announce that there is one minute remaining in each half and any overtime period.

h. The game clock shall be equipped to show tenths-of-a-second during the last minute of each half and any overtime period.

SECTION III—END OF PERIOD

a. Each period ends when time expires.

EXCEPTIONS:

(1) If a live ball is in flight, the period ends when the goal is made, missed or touched by an offensive player.

(2) If the official's whistle sounds prior to the horn or :00.0 on the clock, the period is not over and time must be added to the clock.

(3) If the ball is in the air when the horn sounds ending a period, and it subsequently is touched by: (a) a defensive player, the goal, if successful, shall count; or (b) an offensive player, the period has ended.

(4) If a timeout request is made at approximately the instant time expires for a period, the period ends and the timeout shall not be granted.

(5) If there is a foul called on or by a player in the act of shooting, the period will end after the foul is penalized.

b. If the ball is dead and the game clock shows :00.0, the period has ended even though the horn may not have sounded.

EXCEPTION: See Rule 13—Section II–a(6).

SECTION IV—TIE SCORE—OVERTIME

If the score is tied at the end of the second half, play shall resume in 120 seconds without change of baskets for any of the overtime periods required. (See Rule 5—Section II–d for the amount of time between overtime periods.)

SECTION V—STOPPAGE OF TIMING DEVICES

a. The timing devices shall be stopped whenever the official's whistle sounds indicating one of the following:

(1) A personal or technical foul.

(2) A jump ball.

(3) A floor violation.

(4) An unusual delay.

(5) A suspension-of-play.

(6) A regular or 20-second timeout.

b. The timing devices shall be stopped during the last minute of each half and/or overtime(s) following a successful field goal attempt.

c. Officials may not use official time to permit a player to change or repair equipment.

SECTION VI—20-SECOND TIMEOUT

A player's request for a 20-second timeout shall be granted only when the ball is dead or in control by a player on the team making the request. A request at any other time shall be ignored.

A team is in control when one of its players has possession of the ball on the floor, in the air or following a successful field goal by the opposing team. A request at any other time is to be ignored. Timeouts are considered regular unless the player calls "20-second timeout."

EXCEPTION: The head coach may request a 20-second timeout if there is a suspension of play to administer Comments on the Rules—N—Guidelines for Infection Control.

a. Each team is entitled to one (1) 20-second timeout in the first half and two (2) 20-second timeouts in the second half. Timeouts unused in the first half may not be utilized in the second half.

b. For the overtime period, each team is entitled to one additional 20-second timeout plus one unused 20-second timeout carried over from the second half for a maximum of two 20-second timeouts per team.

c. During a 20-second timeout, both teams may have unlimited substitutions.

d. The official shall instruct the timer to record the 20 seconds and to inform him/her when the time has expired. A regular timeout will be charged if play is unable to resume at the expiration of that 20-second timeout limit.

EXCEPTIONS: No regular time-out remaining or an injured player is on the court.

e. This rule may be used for any reason, including a request for a rule interpretation. If the correction is sustained, no timeout shall be charged.

f. Players should say "20-second timeout" when requesting 20-second timeout.

g. If a 20-second timeout is awarded to the offensive team during the last minute of the second half and/or any overtime period and (1) the ball is out-ofbounds in the backcourt (except for a suspension of play after a team had advanced the ball), or (2) after securing the ball from a rebound in the backcourt and prior to any advance of the ball (3) after the offensive team secures the ball from a change of possession in the backcourt and prior to any advance of the ball, the timeout shall be granted. Upon resumption of play, the team granted the timeout shall have the option of putting the ball into play at the 28' hash mark in the frontcourt, with the ball having to be passed into the frontcourt, or at the designated spot out-of-bounds.

However, once the ball is (1) thrown in from out-of-bounds, or (2) dribbled or passed after receiving it from a rebound or a change of possession, the timeout shall be granted, and, upon resumption of play, the ball shall be in-bounded on the sideline where play was interrupted. In the last minute of second half play and/or any overtime period, the official shall ask the head coach the type of time-out desired—(regular or 20-second)—prior to notifying the scorer's table. This applies only to a requested timeout.

The time on the game clock and the 30-second clock shall remain as when the timeout was called. In order for the option to be available under the conditions in Section VI(g), the offensive team must call two successive timeouts.

h. If a 20-second timeout has been granted and a mandatory timeout is due, the mandatory time-out will be taken on the next dead ball following the resumption of play.

i. A 20-second timeout shall not be granted to the defensive team during an official's suspension-of-play for (1) delay-of-game warning, (2) retrieving an errant ball, (3) an inadvertent whistle or (4) any other unusual circumstance.

EXCEPTION: Suspension of play for a player bleeding. See Comments on the Rules—N.

SECTION VII—REGULAR TIMEOUTS–120 SECONDS

A player's request for a timeout shall be granted only when the ball is dead or in control by a player on the team making the request. A request at any other time shall be ignored.

A team is in control when one of its players has possession of the ball on the floor, in the air or following a successful field goal by the opposing team. A request at any other time is to be ignored. Timeouts are considered regular unless the player calls, "20-second timeout."

EXCEPTION: The head coach may request a regular timeout if there is a suspension of play to administer Comments on the Rules—N—Guidelines for Infection Control.

a. There must be four (4) timeouts per half. If neither team has taken a regular timeout prior to the 16-, 12-, 8- and 4-minute marks in each half, it shall be mandatory for the Official Scorer to take a regular timeout at the next dead ball.

b. Each team is entitled to one (1) regular timeout per half during regulation play. Unused timeouts will not carryover from the first half to the second half. Each team will also be granted one (1) 20-second timeout in the first half (no carryover) and two (2) 20-second timeouts in the second half.

c. In overtime periods, each team shall be allowed one (1) regular timeout plus one 20-second timeout. Unused regular timeouts from the 2nd half will not be carried over into overtime. However, unused 20-second timeouts can be carried over, with a maximum of two 20-second timeouts per team permitted in any overtime period. There is no restriction as to when a team must call its timeouts during any overtime period.

No regular timeout shall be granted to the defensive team during an official's suspension-of-play for (1) a delay-of-game warning, (2) retrieving an errant ball, (3) an inadvertent whistle, or (4) any other unusual circumstance.

EXCEPTION: Suspension-of-play for player bleeding. See Comments on the Rules—N.

d. If a regular timeout is awarded to the offensive team during the last minute of the second half and/or any overtime period and (1) the ball is out-of-bounds in the backcourt (except for a suspension of play after the team had advanced the ball), or (2) after securing the ball from a rebound in the backcourt and prior to any advance of the ball, or (3) after securing the ball from a change of possession in the backcourt and prior to any advance of the ball, the timeout shall be granted. Upon resumption of play, the team granted the timeout shall have the option of putting the ball into play at the 28' hash mark in the frontcourt, with the ball having to be passed into the frontcourt, or at the designated spot out-of-bounds.

However, once the ball is (1) thrown in from out-of-bounds, or (2) dribbled or passed after receiving it from a rebound or a change of possession, the timeout shall be granted, and, upon resumption of play, the ball shall be in-bounded on the sideline where play was interrupted. In the last minute of the second half and/or any overtime period, the official shall ask the head coach the type of timeout desired—(regular or 20-second)—prior to notifying the scorer's table. This applies only to a requested timeout. The time on the game clock and the 30-second clock shall remain as when the timeout was called. In order for the option to be available under the conditions in Section VII(d), the offensive team must call two successive timeouts.

e. No timeout shall be charged if it is called to question a rule interpretation and the correction is sustained.

f. Requests for a timeout in excess of the authorized number shall be granted and a technical foul shall be assessed. Following the timeout, the ball will be awarded to the opposing team and play shall resume with a throw-in nearest the spot where play was interrupted. If a player is injured and cannot be removed from the playing court during stoppage of play, no excessive timeout will be charged and play will resume when playing conditions are safe.

g. During a regular timeout, both teams may have unlimited substitutions.

SECTION VIII—TIMEOUT REQUESTS

a. If an official, upon receiving a timeout request (regular or 20-second) by the defensive team, inadvertently signals for a timeout while the play is in progress, play shall be suspended and the team in possession shall put the ball in play immediately at the sideline nearest where the ball was when the signal was given. The team in possession shall have only the time remaining of the original ten seconds in which to move the ball into the frontcourt. The 30-second clock shall remain the same.

b. If an official, upon receiving a timeout request (regular or 20-second) from the defensive team, inadvertently signals for a timeout during: (1) a successful field goal or free throw attempt, the point(s) shall be scored; (2) an unsuccessful field goal attempt, play shall be resumed with a jump ball at the center circle between any two opponents; (3) an unsuccessful free throw attempt, the official shall rule disconcerting and award a substitute free throw.

c. If an official inadvertently blows his/her whistle during (1) a successful field goal or free throw attempt, the points shall be scored, or (2) an unsuccessful field goal or free throw attempt, play shall be resumed with a jump ball at the center circle between any two opponents.

d. When a team is granted a regular or 20-second time-out, play shall not resume until the full 120 seconds or 20 seconds, as the case may be, have elapsed. The throw-in shall be nearest the spot where play was suspended. The throw-in shall be on the sideline, if the ball was in play when the request was granted.

e. A player shall not be granted a timeout (regular or 20-second) if both of her feet are in the air and any part of her body has broken the vertical plane of the boundary line (including the midcourt line).

f. If a player calls a timeout to stop play (or after a stoppage of play) due to an injury to herself or one of her teammates, a 20-second timeout will be charged to the team. If the team has exhausted its allotment of 20-second timeouts, a regular timeout will be charged. No more than one timeout (20-second or regular) will be charged during an injury timeout situation. Officials will not suspend play after an injury unless bleeding occurs. See Comments on the Rules—N—Guidelines for Infection Control.

SECTION IX—TIME-IN

a. After time has been out, the game clock shall be started when the ball is legally touched by any player within the playing area of the court. The timer is authorized to start the game clock if officials neglect to signal.

b. On a free throw that is unsuccessful and the ball continues in play, the game clock shall be started when the missed free throw is legally touched by any player.

c. If play is resumed by a throw-in from out-of-bounds, the game clock shall be started when the ball is legally touched by any player within the playing area of the court.

d. If play is resumed with a jump ball, the game clock shall be started when the ball is legally tapped.

RULE NO. 6—PUTTING BALL IN PLAY—LIVE/DEAD BALL

SECTION I—START OF GAMES/PERIODS AND OTHERS

a. The game, second half and overtime(s) shall be started with a jump ball in the center circle.

b. After a score, the thrower-in may run along the endline or pass it to a teammate who is also out-of-bounds at the endline.

c. After any dead ball, play shall be resumed by a jump ball, a throw-in or by placing the ball at the disposal of a free-thrower.

d. On the following infractions, the ball shall be awarded to the opposing team out-of-bounds on the nearest sideline at the free throw line extended:

(1) Three-seconds
(2) Ball entering basket from below
(3) Illegal assist in scoring
(4) Offensive screen set out-of-bounds
(5) Free throw violation by the offensive team
(6) Flagrant foul-penalty (1) or (2)
(7) Jump ball violation at free throw circle
(8) Ball passing directly behind backboard
(9) Offensive basket interference
(10) Ball hitting horizontal basket support
(11) Loose ball fouls which occur inside the free throw line extended

e. On the following infractions, the ball shall be awarded to the opposing team on the baseline at the nearest spot outside the three-second area extended:

(1) Ball out-of-bounds on baseline
(2) Ball hitting vertical basket support
(3) Defensive goaltending (all privileges remain)
(4) During a throw-in violation on the baseline
(5) Suspension of play which is prior to a baseline throw-in (all privileges remain)

f. On the following infractions, the ball shall be awarded to the opposing team on the sidelines out-of-bounds at the nearest spot but no nearer to the baseline than the free throw line extended:

(1) Traveling
(2) Double dribble
(3) Swinging of elbows
(4) 30-second violation
(5) Suspension of play when player control exists and the ball is in play
(6) Non-shooting fouls on the defense
(7) Offensive fouls
(8) Double fouls where the offensive team retains possession
(9) Striking with fist or intentionally kicking the ball on any situation except a throw-in

g. Following a regular or 20-second timeout that was called while the ball was alive, the ball shall be awarded out-of-bounds on the sidelines at the nearest spot. For all other timeouts, play shall resume where it was interrupted.

EXCEPTION: Rule 5—Section VII—d.

h. On a violation which requires putting the ball in play in the backcourt, the official will give the ball to the offensive player as soon as she is in a position out-of-bounds and ready to accept the ball.

EXCEPTION: In the last minute of each half or overtime, a reasonable amount of time shall be allowed for a substitution.

i. On any play where the ball goes out of bounds on the sideline, the ball shall be awarded to the opposing team at that spot.

j. In a throw-on situation if the ball is intentionally kicked or struck with the fist, the ball will be returned to the original spot with all privileges remaining, if any.

SECTION II—LIVE BALL

a. The ball becomes live when:
 (1) It is tossed by an official on any jump ball.
 (2) It is at the disposal of the offensive player for a throw-in.
 (3) It is placed at the disposal of a free throw shooter.

SECTION III—BALL IS ALIVE

a. The ball becomes alive when:
 (1) It is legally tapped by one of the participants of a jump ball
 (2) It is released by the thrower-in
 (3) It is released by the free throw shooter on a free throw which will remain in play

SECTION IV—DEAD BALL

a. The ball becomes dead and/or remains dead when the following occurs:
 (1) Official blows his/her whistle
 (2) Free throw which will not remain in play (free throw which will be followed by another free throw, technical, flagrant, etc.)
 (3) Following a successful field goal or free throw that will remain in play, until player possession out-of-bounds. Contact which is not considered unsportsmanlike will be ignored
 (4) Time expiring at the end of any period
EXCEPTION: If a live ball is in flight, the ball becomes dead when the goal is made, missed or touched by an offensive player.

SECTION V—JUMP BALLS IN CENTER CIRCLE

a. The ball shall be put into play in the center circle by a jump ball between any two opponents:
 (1) At the start of the game
 (2) At the start of the second half
 (3) At the start of each overtime period
 (4) A double free throw violation
 (5) Double foul during a loose ball situation
 (6) The ball becomes dead when neither team is in control and no field goal or infraction is involved
 (7) The ball comes to rest on the basket flange or becomes lodged between the basket ring and the backboard
 (8) A double foul which occurs as a result of a difference in opinion between officials
 (9) A suspension of play which occurs during a loose ball
 (10) A fighting foul occurs during a loose ball situation
 (11) If it is not possible to identify the two players involved.
b. In all cases above, the jump ball shall be between any two opponents in the game at that time. If injury, ejection or disqualification makes it necessary for any player to be replaced, her substitute may not participate in the jump ball.

SECTION VI—OTHER JUMP BALLS

a. The ball shall be put into play by a jump ball at the circle which is closest to the spot where:
 (1) A held ball occurs
 (2) A ball out-of-bounds caused by both teams
 (3) An official is in doubt as to who last touched the ball
b. The jump ball shall be between the two involved players unless injury or ejection precludes one of the jumpers from participation. If the injured or ejected player must leave the game, the coach of the opposing team shall select from his/her opponent's bench a player who will replace the injured or ejected player. The injured player will not be permitted to re-enter the game.
EXCEPTION: Excessive bleeding. See Comments on the Rules—N.

SECTION VII—RESTRICTIONS GOVERNING JUMP BALLS

a. Each jumper must have at least one foot on or inside that half of the jumping circle which is farthest from her own basket. Each jumper must have both feet within the restraining circle.

b. The ball must be tapped by one or both of the players participating in the jump ball after it reaches its highest point. If the ball falls to the floor without being tapped by at least one of the jumpers, the official off the ball shall whistle the ball dead and signal another toss.

c. Neither jumper may tap the tossed ball before it reaches its highest point.

d. Neither jumper may leave her half of the jumping circle until the ball has been tapped.

e. Neither jumper may catch the tossed or tapped ball until it touches one of the eight non-jumpers, the floor, the basket or the backboard.

f. Neither jumper is permitted to tap the ball more than twice on any jump ball.

g. The eight non-jumpers will remain outside the restraining circle until the ball has been tapped. Teammates may not occupy adjacent positions around the restraining circle if an opponent desires one of the positions. No player may position herself immediately behind an opponent on the restraining circle.

Penalty for c., d., e., f., g.: Ball awarded out-of-bounds to the opponent.

h. Player position on the restraining circle is determined by the direction of a player's basket. The player whose basket is nearest shall have first choice of position, with position being alternated thereafter.

RULE NO. 7—30-SECOND CLOCK

SECTION I—DEFINITION

For the purpose of clarification, the 30-second device shall be referred to as "the 30-second clock."

SECTION II—STARTING AND STOPPING OF 30-SECOND CLOCK

a. The 30-second clock will start when a team gains new possession of a ball which is in play.

b. On a throw-in, the 30-second clock shall start when the ball is legally touched on the court by a player.

c. A team must attempt a field goal within 30 seconds after gaining possession of the ball. To constitute a legal field goal attempt, the following conditions must be complied with:

(1) The ball must leave the player's hand prior to the expiration of 30 seconds.

(2) After leaving the player's hand(s), the ball must make contact with the basket ring. If it fails to do so within 30 seconds, a 30-second violation has occurred.

d. A team is considered in possession of the ball when holding, passing or dribbling. The team is considered in possession of the ball even though the ball has been batted away but the opponent has not gained possession. No 3-second violation can occur under these conditions.

e. Team possession ends when:

(1) There is a legal field goal attempt

(2) The opponent gains possession

f. If a ball is touched by a defensive player who does not gain possession of the ball, the 30-second clock shall continue to run.

g. If a defensive player causes the ball to go out-of-bounds or causes the ball to enter the basket ring from below, the 30-second clock is stopped and the offensive team shall be awarded the ball.

The offensive team shall have only the unexpired time remaining on the 30-second clock in which to attempt a field goal. If the 30-second clock reads 0, a 30-second violation has occurred, even though the horn may not have sounded.

h. If during any period there are 30 seconds OR LESS left to play in the period, the 30-second clock shall not function following a new possession.

i. If an official inadvertently blows his/her whistle and the 30-second clock buzzer sounds while the ball is in the air, play shall be suspended and play resumed by a jump ball between any two opponents at the center circle, if the shot hits the rim and is unsuccessful. If the shot does not hit the rim a 30-second violation has occurred. If the shot is successful, the goal shall count and the whistle is ignored. The ball shall be inbounded as after any successful field goal. It should be noted that even though the official blows his/her whistle, all provisions of the above rule apply.

j. If there is a question whether or not an attempt to score has been made within the 30 seconds allowed, the final decision shall be made by the officials.

k. Whenever the 30-second clock reads 0 and the ball is dead for any reason other than a kicking violation, struck with the fist violation, personal foul or a technical foul by the defensive team, a 30-second violation has occurred.

SECTION III—PUTTING BALL IN PLAY AFTER VIOLATION

If a team fails to attempt a field goal within the time allotted, a 30-second violation shall be called. The ball is awarded to the defensive team on the sideline nearest the spot where play was suspended, but no nearer to the baseline than the free throw line extended.

SECTION IV—RESETTING 30-SECOND CLOCK

a. The 30-second clock shall be reset when a special situation occurs which warrants such action.

b. The 30-second clock is never reset on technical fouls and/or delay-ofgame warnings called on the offensive team.

c. The 30-second clock shall be reset to 30 seconds anytime the following occurs:

(1) Change of possession

(2) Personal foul that results in the ball being inbounded in the backcourt

(3) Jump balls which are not the result of a held ball caused by the defense

(4) Violation that results in the ball being inbounded in the backcourt

(5) Ball from the playing court contacting the basket ring of the team which is in possession

(6) All flagrant and punching fouls

d. The 30-second clock shall remain the same as when play was interrupted or reset to 20 seconds, whichever is greater, anytime the following occurs:

(1) Personal foul by the defense that results in the ball being inbounded in the frontcourt

(2) Technical foul and/or delay-of-game warnings on the defensive team

(3) Kicked or punched ball by the defensive team that results in the ball being inbounded in the offensive team's frontcourt

(4) Infection control

(5) Jump balls retained by the offensive team as the result of any violation by the defensive team during a jump ball which results in a frontcourt throw-in

e. The 30-second clock shall remain the same as when play was stopped, or reset to 5 seconds, whichever is greater, on jump balls retained by the offensive team as a result of a held ball caused by the defense.

RULE NO. 8—OUT-OF-BOUNDS AND THROW-IN

SECTION I—PLAYER

The player is out-of-bounds when she touches the floor or any object on or outside a boundary. For location of a player in the air, her position is that from which she last touched the floor.

SECTION II—BALL

a. The ball is out-of-bounds when it touches a player who is out-of-bounds or any other person, the floor, or any object on, above or outside of a boundary or the supports or back of the backboard.

b. Any ball that rebounds or passes directly behind the backboard, in either direction, from any point is considered out-of-bounds.

c. The ball is caused to go out-of-bounds by the last player to touch it before it goes out, provided it is out-of-bounds because of touching something other than a player. If the ball is out-of-bounds because of touching a player who is on or outside a boundary, such player caused it to go out.

d. If the ball goes out-of-bounds and was last touched simultaneously by two opponents, both of whom are inbounds or out-of-bounds, or if the official is in doubt as to who last touched the ball, or if the officials disagree, play shall be resumed by a jump ball between the two involved players in the nearest restraining circle.

e. After the ball is out-of-bounds, the team shall designate a player to make the throw-in. She shall make the throw-in at the spot out-of-bounds nearest where the ball crossed the boundary. The designated thrower-in or her substitute shall not be changed except following a regular or 20-second timeout.

f. If the ball is interfered with by an opponent seated on the bench or standing on the sideline (Rule 12A—Section II—a[7]), it shall be awarded to the offended team nearest the spot of the violation.

SECTION III—THE THROW-IN

a. The throw-in starts when the ball is at the disposal of a player entitled to the throw-in. She shall release the ball inbounds within 5 seconds from the time the throw-in starts. Until the passed ball has crossed the plane of the boundary, no player shall have any part of her person over the boundary line and teammates shall not occupy positions parallel or adjacent to the baseline if an opponent desires one of those positions. The defensive player shall have the right to be between her opponent and the basket.

b. On a throw-in which goes out of bounds and is not touched inbounds, the ball is returned to the original throw-in spot.

c. After a score, field goal or free throw, the latter coming as the result of a personal foul, any player of the team not credited with the score shall put the ball into play from any point out-of-bounds at the endline of the court where the point(s) were scored. She may pass the ball to a teammate behind the endline; however, the five-second throw-in rule applies.

d. After a free throw violation by the shooter or her teammate, the throw-in is made from out-of-bounds at either end of the free throw line extended.

e. Any ball out-of-bounds in a team's frontcourt or at the midcourt line cannot be passed into the backcourt. On all backcourt and midcourt violations, the ball shall be awarded to the opposing team at the midcourt line, and must be passed into the frontcourt.

f. A throw-in which touches the floor, or any object on or outside the boundary line, or touches anything above the playing surface is a violation. The ball must be thrown directly inbounds.

EXCEPTION: Rule 8—Section III—c.

PENALTY: Violation of this rule is loss of possession, and the ball must be inbounded at the previous spot of the throw-in.

RULE NO. 9—FREE THROW

SECTION I—POSITIONS AND VIOLATIONS

a. When a free throw is awarded, an official shall put the ball in play by placing it at the disposal of the free throw shooter. The shooter shall be above the free throw line and within the upper half of the free throw circle. She shall attempt the free throw within 10 seconds in such a way that the ball enters the basket or touches the ring.

PENALTY: If the free throw attempt is remaining in play, the opposing team shall inbound on either sideline at the free throw line extended. If an opponent also commits a violation (double violation) during this free throw, a jump ball shall be administered at midcourt between any two opponents in the game. If the opponent's violation is disconcertion, then a substitute free throw shall be awarded.

If the free throw attempt is not remaining in play then play will continue from that point. If an opponent also commits a violation (double violation), then play will also continue from that point. If the opponent's violation is disconcertion, then a substitute free throw shall be awarded.

b. The free throw shooter may not step over the plane of the free throw line until the ball touches the basket ring, backboard or the free throw ends.

PENALTY: This is a violation by the shooter on all free throw attempts and no point can be scored.

If the free throw attempt is remaining in play, the opposing team shall inbound on either sideline at the free throw line extended. If an opponent also commits a violation (double violation) during this free throw, a jump ball shall be administered at midcourt between any two opponents in the game.

If the free throw attempt is not remaining in play, then play will continue from that point. If an opponent also commits a violation (double violation), then play will also continue from that point.

c. The free throw shooter shall not purposely fake a free throw attempt.

PENALTY: This is a violation by the shooter on all free throw attempts and a double violation should not be called if an opponent violates any free throw rules.

If the free throw attempt is to remain in play, the opposing team shall inbound on either sideline at the free throw line extended.

If the free throw attempt is not remaining in play, then play will continue from that point.

d. During a free throw attempt for a personal foul, each of the spaces nearest the end-line must be occupied by an opponent of the free throw shooter. Teammates of the free throw shooter must occupy the next adjacent spaces on each side. Only one of the third spaces may be occupied by an opponent of the free throw shooter. It is not mandatory that either of the third spaces be occupied by an opponent but may not be occupied by a teammate. If there is a discrepancy, teammates of the free throw shooter will occupy the spaces first.

Players occupying lane spaces may not be touching the lane line or floor inside the line when the ball is released by the shooter. They may not vacate their lane space more than 3' from the lane line before the ball is released.

Players not occupying lane spaces must remain behind the free throw line and at least 3' from the three-point arc.

PENALTY: If the free throw attempt is to remain in play and a teammate of the shooter violates, no point can be scored and the opposing team will inbound on either sideline at the free throw line extended. If an opponent violates, the shooter shall receive a substitute free throw if her attempt is unsuccessful but shall be ignored if the attempt is successful. If a teammate and opponent both violate, a jump ball shall be administered at midcourt between any two opponents in the game.

If the free throw attempt is not remaining in play, no violation can occur regardless of which player or players violate since no advantage is gained unless there is a disconcertion violation by an opponent to which a substitute free throw will be awarded.

e. If the ball is to become dead after the last free throw attempt, players shall not occupy positions along the free throw lanes. All players must remain behind the three point line above the free throw line extended until the ball is released.

PENALTY: No violations can occur regardless of which player or players violate since no advantage is gained unless there is a disconcertion violation by an opponent to which a substitute free throw will be awarded.

f. During all free throw attempts, no opponent in the game shall disconcert the shooter once the ball is placed at her disposal. The following are acts of disconcertion:

(1) Raising her arms when positioned on the lane line on a free throw which will not remain in play.

(2) Waiving her arms or making a sudden movement when in the visual field of the shooter during any free throw attempt.

(3) Talking to the free throw shooter or talking in a loud disruptive manner during any free throw attempt.

PENALTY: No penalty is assessed if the free throw is successful. A substitute free throw will be administered if the attempt is unsuccessful.

g. A player shall not touch the ball or the basket ring when the ball is using the basket ring as its lower base nor touch the ball while it is in the imaginary cylinder above the ring after touching the basket ring or backboard.

PENALTY: If the free throw attempt is to remain in play and a teammate of the shooter violates, no point can be scored and the opposing team will inbound on either sideline at the free throw line extended. If an opponent violates, the shooter shall be scored and play will continue as after any successful free throw with the official administering the throw-in.

If the free throw attempt is not remaining in play, no point can be scored if the violation is by a teammate and the shooter will attempt her next free throw. One point shall be scored if the violation is by an opponent and the shooter will attempt her next free throw.

h. No player shall touch the ball before it touches the basket ring or backboard.

PENALTY: If the free throw attempt is to remain in play and a teammate of the shooter violates, no point can be scored and the opposing team will inbound on either sideline at the free throw line extended. If an opponent violates, one point shall be scored and an additional free throw shall be awarded the same shooter.

If the free throw attempt is not remaining in play, no point can be scored if the violation is by a teammate and the shooter will attempt her next free throw. One point shall be scored if the violation is by an opponent and the shooter will attempt her next free throw.

i. During all free throw attempts, if an official suspends play before the free throw attempt is released, no violations can occur.

SECTION II—SHOOTING OF FREE THROW

a. The free throw(s) awarded because of a personal foul shall be attempted by the offended player.
EXCEPTIONS:

(1) If the offended player is injured or ejected from the game and cannot attempt the awarded

freethrow(s), the opposing coach shall select, from the opponents bench, the replacement player. That player will attempt the free throw(s) and the injured player will not be permitted to re-enter the game. The substitute must remain in the game until the ball is legally touched by a player on the court.

(2) If the offended player is injured and unable to attempt the awarded free throw(s) due to any unsportsmanlike act, her coach may designate any eligible member of the squad to attempt the free throw(s). The injured player will be permitted to re-enter the game.

(3) If the offended player is disqualified and unable to attempt the awarded free throw(s), her coach shall designate an eligible substitute from the bench. That substitute will attempt the free throw(s) and cannot be removed until the ball is legally touched by a player on the court.

EXCEPTION: Rule 3—Section V—e.

(4) Away from play foul—Rule 12B—Section X-a(1).

b. A free throw attempt, personal or technical, shall be illegal if an official does not handle the ball and is in the free throw lane area during the actual attempt.

c. If multiple free throws are awarded, all those which remain must be attempted, if the first and/or second attempt is nullified by an offensive player's violation.

SECTION III—TIME LIMIT

Each free throw attempt shall be made within 10 seconds after the ball has been placed at the disposal of the free-thrower.

SECTION IV—NEXT PLAY

After a successful free throw which is not followed by another free throw, the ball shall be put into play by a throw-in, as after any successful field goal.

EXCEPTION: After a free throw for a foul which occurs during a dead ball which immediately precedes any period, the ball shall be put into play by a jump ball in the period which follows. (See Rule 6—Section I—c). This includes flagrant and punching fouls.

RULE NO. 10—VIOLATIONS AND PENALTIES

SECTION I—OUT-OF-BOUNDS

a. A player shall not cause the ball to go out-of-bounds.

PENALTY: Loss of ball. The ball is awarded to opponents at the boundary line nearest the spot of the violation.

EXCEPTION: On a throw-in which goes out of bounds and is not touched by a player in the game, the ball is returned to the original throw-in spot.

SECTION II—DRIBBLE

a. A player shall not run with the ball without dribbling it.

b. A player in control of a dribble who steps on or outside a boundary line, even though not touching the ball while on or outside that boundary line, shall not be allowed to return inbounds and continue her dribble. She may not even be the first player to touch the ball after she has re-established a position inbounds.

c. A player may not dribble a second time after she has voluntarily ended her first dribble.

d. A player may dribble a second time if she lost control of the ball because of:
(1) A field goal attempt at her basket, provided the ball touches the backboard, basket ring, or another player
(2) An opponent touching the ball
(3) A pass or fumble which has then touched another player

PENALTY: Loss of ball. Ball is awarded to opponent on the sideline nearest the spot of the violation but no nearer to the baseline than the free throw line extended.

SECTION III—THROWER-IN

a. A thrower-in shall not (1) carry the ball onto the court; (2) fail to release the ball within 5 seconds; (3) touch it on the court before it has touched another player; (4) leave the designated throw-in spot; (5) throw the ball so that it enters the basket before touching anyone on the court; (6) step over the boundary line while inbounding the ball; (7) cause the ball to go out-of-bounds without being touched inbounds; (8) leave the playing surface to gain an advantage on a throwin; (9) hand the ball to a player on the court.

EXCEPTION: After a field goal or free throw as a result of a personal foul, the thrower-in may run the end line or pass to a teammate behind the end line.

b. Once an official recognizes the designated player to throw the ball in, there shall be no change of the thrower-in unless the offensive team makes a substitution or uses a regular or 20-second timeout, or there is a suspension of play.

PENALTY: Loss of ball. The ball is awarded to the opponent at the original spot of the throw-in.

SECTION IV—STRIKE THE BALL

a. A player shall not kick the ball or strike it with the fist.

b. Kicking the ball or striking it with any part of the leg is a violation when it is an intentional act. The ball accidentally striking the foot, the leg or fist is not a violation.

c. A player may not use any part of her leg to intentionally move or secure the ball.

PENALTY: (1) If the violation is by the offense, the ball is awarded to the opponent nearest the spot of the violation but no nearer the baseline than the free throw line extended.

(2) If the violation is by the defense, the offensive team retains possession of the ball at the side line nearest the spot of the violation but no nearer the baseline than the free throw line extended. The 30-second clock is reset to 30 seconds and if the violation occurred in the backcourt, a new 10-second count is awarded.

(3) If the violation occurs during a throw-in, the opposing team retains possession at the spot of the original throw-in with all privileges remaining.

SECTION V—JUMP BALL

a. A player shall not violate the jump ball rule (Rule 6—Section V).

b. During a jump ball, a personal foul committed prior to either team obtaining possession shall be ruled a "loose ball" foul. If the violation or foul occurs prior to the ball being legally tapped, neither the game clock or 30-second clock shall be started.

PENALTY: (1) In (a) above, the ball is awarded to the opponent on the sideline nearest the spot of the violation.

(2) In (a) above, if there is a violation by each team, or if the official makes a bad toss, the toss shall be repeated with the same jumpers.

(3) In (b) above, free throws may or may not be awarded, consistent with whether the penalty is in effect (Rule 12B—Section VIII).

SECTION VI—THREE-SECOND RULE

a. A player shall not remain for more than three seconds in that part of her free throw lane between the endline and extended 4' (imaginary) off the court and the farther edge of the free throw line while the ball is in control of her team.

b. Allowance may be made for a player who, having been in this area for less than three seconds, is in the act of shooting at the end of the third second. Under these conditions, the 3-second count is discontinued while her continuous motion is toward the basket. If that continuous motion ceases, the previous 3-second count is continued. This is also true if it is imminent the offensive player will exit this area.

c. The 3-second count shall not begin until the ball is in control in the offensive team's frontcourt. No violation can occur if the ball is batted away by an opponent.

PENALTY: Loss of ball. The ball is awarded to the opponent at the sideline at the free throw line extended.

SECTION VII—TEN-SECOND RULE

A team shall not be in continuous possession of a ball which is in its backcourt for more than 10 consecutive seconds.

EXCEPTION (1): A new 10 seconds is awarded if the defense: (1) kicks or strikes the ball with the fist, (2) is assessed a personal or technical foul, or (3) is issued a delay of game warning.

EXCEPTION (2): A new 10 seconds is awarded if play is suspended to administer Comments on the Rules—N—Infection Control and all jump balls.

PENALTY: Loss of ball. The ball is awarded to the opponent at the midcourt line, with the ball having to be passed into the frontcourt.

SECTION VIII—BALL IN BACKCOURT

a. A player shall not be the first to touch a ball which she or a teammate caused to go from frontcourt to backcourt while her team was in control of the ball.

b. During a jump ball, a try for a goal, or a situation in which a player taps the ball away from a congested area, as during rebounding, in an attempt to get the ball out where player control may be secured, the ball is not in control of either team. Hence, the restriction on first touching does not apply.

c. Following a jump ball, a player who secures a positive position and control of the ball in her frontcourt cannot pass the ball to a teammate or dribble the ball into the backcourt.

PENALTY: Loss of ball. The ball is awarded to the opponent at the midcourt line, and the ball must be passed into the frontcourt. If the violation occurs on a throw-in, the game clock shall not start.

SECTION IX—SWINGING OF ELBOWS

A player shall not be allowed excessive and/or a vigorous swinging motion of the elbows. When a defensive player is nearby and the offensive player has the ball, it is considered a violation.

PENALTY: Loss of ball. The ball is awarded to the opponent on the sideline nearest the spot of the violation, but no nearer the baseline than the free throw line extended. If the violation occurs on a throw-in, the game clock shall not be started.

SECTION X—ENTERING BASKET FROM BELOW

A player shall not cause the ball to enter the basket from below.

PENALTY: Loss of ball. The ball is awarded to the opponent at the sideline at the free throw line extended.

SECTION XI—ILLEGAL ASSIST IN SCORING

a. A player may not assist herself to score by using the basket ring or backboard to lift, hold or raise herself.

b. A player may not assist a teammate to gain height while attempting to score.

PENALTY: Loss of ball. The ball is awarded to the opponent at the free throw line extended.

SECTION XII—TRAVELING

a. A player who receives the ball while standing still may pivot, using either foot as the pivot foot.

b. A player who receives the ball while she is progressing or upon completion of a dribble, may use a two-count rhythm in coming to a stop, passing or shooting the ball.

The first count occurs:

(1) As she receives the ball, if either foot is touching the floor at the time she receives it.

(2) As the foot touches the floor, or as both feet touch the floor simultaneously after she receives the ball, if both feet are off the floor when she receives it.

The second occurs:

(1) After the count of one when either foot touches the floor, or both feet touch the floor simultaneously.

c. A player who comes to a stop on the count of one may pivot, using either foot as the pivot foot.

d. A player who comes to a stop on the count of two, with one foot in advance of the other, may pivot using only the rear foot as the pivot foot.

e. A player who comes to a stop on the count of two, with neither foot in advance of the other, may use either foot as the pivot foot.

f. In starting a dribble after (1) receiving the ball while standing still, or (2) coming to a legal stop, the ball must be out of the player's hand before the pivot foot is raised off the floor.

g. If a player, with the ball in her possession, raises her pivot foot off the floor, she must pass or shoot before her pivot foot returns to the floor. If she drops the ball while in the air, she may not be the first to touch the ball.

h. A player who falls to the floor while holding the ball, or while coming to a stop, may not gain an advantage by sliding.

i. A player who attempts a field goal may not be the first to touch the ball if it fails to touch the backboard, basket ring or another player.

j. A player may not be the first to touch her own pass.

PENALTY: Loss of ball. The ball is awarded to the opponent at the sideline, nearest spot of the violation but no nearer the baseline than the free throw line extended.

SECTION XIII—OFFENSIVE SCREEN SET OUT-OF-BOUNDS

An offensive player shall not leave the playing area of the floor on the endline in the frontcourt for the purpose of setting a screen.

PENALTY: Loss of ball. The ball is awarded to the opponent at the sideline at the free throw line extended.

RULE NO. 11—BASKETBALL INTERFERENCE—GOALTENDING

SECTION I—A PLAYER SHALL NOT:

a. Touch the ball or the basket ring when the ball is using the basket ring as its lower base.

EXCEPTION: If a player near her own basket has her hand(s) legally in contact with the ball, it is not a violation if her contact with the ball continues after the ball enters the cylinder, or if, in such action, she touches the basket.

b. Touch the ball when it is above the basket ring and within the imaginary cylinder.

c. During a field goal attempt, touch a ball after it has touched any part of the backboard above ring level, whether the ball is considered on its upward or downward flight.

d. During a field goal attempt, touch a ball after it has touched the backboard below the ring level and while the ball is on its upward flight.

e. Trap the ball against the face of the backboard after it has been released. (To be a trapped ball, three elements must exist simultaneously. The hand, the ball and the backboard must all occur at the same time. A batted ball against the backboard is not a trapped ball.)

f. Touch any live ball from within the playing area that is on its downward flight with an opportunity to score. This is considered to be a "field goal attempt" or trying for a goal.

g. Touch the ball at any time with a hand which is through the basket ring.

h. Vibrate the rim, net or backboard so as to cause the ball to make an unnatural bounce.

i. Touch the ball while in the net preventing it from clearing the basket.

PENALTY: If the violation is at the opponent's basket, the offended team is awarded two points, if the attempt is from the two point zone and three points if it is from the three point zone. The crediting of the score and subsequent procedure is the same as if the awarded score has resulted from the ball having gone through the basket, except that the official shall hand the ball to a player of the team entitled to the throw-in. If the violation is at a team's own basket, no points can be scored and the ball is awarded to the offended team at either sideline at the free throw line extended. If there is a violation by both teams, play shall be resumed by a jump ball between any two opponents at the center circle.

RULE NO. 12—FOULS AND PENALTIES

A. TECHNICAL FOUL

SECTION I—EXCESSIVE TIMEOUTS

a. Requests for a timeout in excess of the authorized number shall be granted and a technical foul shall be assessed. Following the timeout and free throw attempt, the ball will be awarded to the team which shot the free throw and play shall resume with a throw-in nearest the spot where play was interrupted.

b. If the excessive timeout is granted prior to free throw attempt(s), there will be no lineup for the remaining free throws and play shall resume with a throw-in at the point of interruption by the team which shot the technical foul.

c. If the excessive timeout is granted prior to a jump ball, the ball shall be awarded to the team shooting the technical foul at the point of interruption.

SECTION II—DELAY-OF-GAME

a. A delay-of-game shall be called for:

(1) Preventing the ball from being promptly put into play.

(2) Interfering with the ball after a successful field goal or free throw.

(3) Failing to immediately pass the ball to the nearest official when a personal foul or violation is assessed.

(4) Touching the ball before the throw-in has been released.

(5) A defender crossing the boundary line prior to the ball being released on a throw-in.

(6) A team preventing play from commencing at any time.

(7) Any player, coach or trainer interfering with a ball which has crossed the boundary line (Rule 8—Section II—f).

PENALTY: The first offense is a warning. A technical foul shall be assessed with each successive offense and charged to the team. An announcement will be made by the public address announcer. The 30-second clock shall remain the same or reset to 20, whichever is greater, if the violation is assessed against the defensive team. The offensive team shall be awarded a new 10 seconds to advance the ball if it is in the backcourt. If repeated acts become a travesty, the head coach shall be notified that he/she is being held responsible.

SECTION III—SUBSTITUTIONS

a. A substitute shall report to the official scorer while standing in the "substitution box."

b. A substitute shall not enter onto the court until she is beckoned by an official.

c. A substitute shall not be allowed to re-enter the game after being disqualified.

EXCEPTION: Rule 3—Section I—b.

d. It is the responsibility of each team to have the proper number of players on the court at all times. Failure to do so will result in a technical foul being assessed and charged to the team.

EXCEPTION: If the violation occurs on (1) a free throw attempt which is to be followed by another free throw attempt, or (2) a free throw attempt that is not going to remain in play.

SECTION IV—BASKET RING, BACKBOARD OR SUPPORT

a. An offensive player who deliberately hangs on her basket ring, net, backboard or support during the game shall be assessed a non-unsportsmanlike technical foul.

b. A defensive player who deliberately gains or maintains height or hangs on her opponent's basket ring, net, backboard or support, shall be assessed a nonunsportsmanlike technical foul. If she touches the ball during a field goal attempt, points shall be awarded consistent with the type of shot.

EXCEPTION: An offensive or defensive player may hang on the basket ring, backboard or support to prevent an injury to herself or another player, with no technical foul assessed.

c. Should a defensive player deliberately hang on the basket ring, backboard or support to successfully touch a ball which is in possession of an opponent, an unsportsmanlike technical foul shall be assessed.

d. See Rule 10—Section XI—with regard to an offensive player assisting herself to score.

SECTION V—CONDUCT

a. An official may assess a technical foul, without prior warning, at any time. A technical foul(s) may be assessed to any player on the court or anyone seated on the bench for conduct which, in the opinion of an official, is detrimental to the game. A technical foul cannot be assessed for physical contact when the ball is alive

EXCEPTION: Fighting fouls and/or taunting with physical contact.

b. A maximum of two technicals for unsportsmanlike acts may be assessed to any player, coach or trainer. Any of these offenders may be ejected for committing only one unsportsmanlike act, and they must be ejected for committing two unsportsmanlike acts.

c. A technical foul called for (1) delay of game, (2) coaches box violations, (3) having a team total of less or more than five players when the ball is alive, or (4) a player hanging on her basket ring or backboard, is not considered an act of unsportsmanlike conduct.

d. A technical foul shall be assessed for unsportsmanlike tactics such as:

(1) Disrespectfully addressing an official

(2) Physically contacting an official

(3) Overt actions indicating resentment to a call

(4) Use of profanity

(5) A coach entering onto the court without permission of an official

(6) A deliberately-thrown elbow or any attempted physical act with no contact involved

(7) Taunting

e. Cursing or blaspheming an official shall not be considered the only cause for imposing technical fouls. Running tirades, continuous criticism or griping may be sufficient cause to assess a technical. Excessive misconduct shall result in ejection from the game.

f. Assessment of a technical foul shall be avoided whenever and wherever possible; but, when necessary they are to be assessed without delay or procrastination. Once a player has been ejected or the game is over, technicals cannot be assessed regardless of the provocation. Any additional unsportsmanlike conduct shall be reported immediately to the Operations Department.

g. If a technical foul is assessed to a team following a personal foul on the same team, the free throw attempt for the technical foul shall be administered first.

h. The ball shall be awarded to the team which had possession at the time the technical foul was assessed, whether the free throw attempt is successful or not. Play shall be resumed by a throw-in nearest the spot where play was interrupted.

EXCEPTION: Rule 12A—Section I.

i. Anyone guilty of illegal contact which occurs during a dead ball may be assessed (1) a technical foul, if the contact is deemed to be unsportsmanlike in nature, or (2) a flagrant foul, if unnecessary and/or excessive contact occurs.

j. Free throws awarded for a technical foul must be attempted by a player in the game when the technical foul is assessed.

(1) If a substitute has been beckoned into the game or has been recognized by the officials as being in the game prior to a technical foul being assessed, she is eligible to attempt the free throw(s).

(2) If the technical foul is assessed before the opening tap, any player listed in the scorebook as a starter is eligible to attempt the free throw(s).

(3) If a technical foul is assessed before the starting lineup is indicated, any player on the squad may attempt the free throw(s).

k. A technical foul, unsportsmanlike act or flagrant foul must be called for a participant to be ejected. A player, coach or trainer may be ejected for:

(1) An elbow foul which makes contact shoulder level or below

(2) Any unsportsmanlike conduct where a technical foul is assessed

(3) A flagrant foul where unnecessary and/or excessive contact occurs

EXCEPTION: Rule 12A—Section V—1(5)

l. A player, coach or trainer must be ejected for:

(1) A punching foul

(2) A fighting foul

(3) An elbow foul which makes contact above shoulder level

(4) An attempted punch which does not make contact

(5) Deliberately entering the stands other than as a continuance of play

m. Eye guarding (placing a hand in front of the opponent's eyes when guarding from the rear) a player who does not have possession of the ball is illegal and an unsportsmanlike technical shall be assessed.

n. A free throw attempt is awarded when one technical foul is assessed.

o. No free throw attempts are awarded when a double technical foul is assessed. Technical fouls assessed to members of opposing teams during the same deadball and prior to the administering of any free throw attempt for the first technical foul shall be interpreted as a double technical foul.

p. The deliberate act of throwing the ball or any object at an official by a player, coach or trainer is a technical foul and violators are subject to ejection from the game.

q. Elbow fouls, which make contact above shoulder level, and punching fouls, although recorded as both personal and team fouls, are unsportsmanlike acts. The player will be ejected immediately.

SECTION VI—FIGHTING FOULS

a. Technical fouls shall be assessed to players, coaches or trainers for fighting. No free throws will be attempted. The participants will be ejected immediately.

b. This rule applies whether play is in progress or the ball is dead.

c. If a fighting foul occurs with a team in possession of the ball, that team will retain possession on the sideline nearest the spot where play was interrupted but no nearer to the baseline than the free throw line extended.

d. If a fighting foul occurs with neither team in possession, play will be resumed with a jump ball between any two opponents who were in the game at the center circle.

e. A fine and/or suspension may be imposed upon such person(s) by the President at her sole discretion. Any fine imposed by the League Office upon a player who is involved in an altercation will be accompanied by a fine to that player's team.

SECTION VII—FINES

a. Recipients of technical fouls for unsportsmanlike conduct will be assessed a $150 fine for the first offense and an additional $150 for the second offense in any one given game, for a minimum total of $300. If a player is ejected on (1) the first technical foul for unsportsmanlike conduct, (2) a punching foul, (3) a fighting foul, (4) an elbow foul, or (5) a flagrant foul, she shall be fined a minimum of $300. Whether or not said player(s) is ejected, a fine and/or suspension may be imposed upon such person(s) by the President at her sole discretion.

b. During an altercation, all players not participating in the game must remain in the immediate vicinity of their bench. Violators will be suspended, without pay, for a minimum of one game and fined a minimum of $500. Any such suspension will commence prior to the start of the player's next game.

c. A team must have a minimum of eight players dressed and ready to play in every game.

d. If four or more players leave the bench, the players will serve their suspensions alphabetically according to the letters of their last names.

e. If six bench players are suspended (assuming no participants are included), three of them will be suspended for the first game following the altercation. The remaining three will be suspended for the second game following the altercation.

f. A player, coach, or assistant coach, upon being notified by an official that he/she has been ejected from the game, must leave the playing area IMMEDIATELY and remain in the dressing room of his/her team during such suspension until completion of the game or leave the building. Violation of this rule shall result in an automatic fine of $250, an additional fine not to exceed $5,000, suspension, and possible forfeiture of the game. The use of messengers and/or telephones to transmit information from an ejected coach to the bench violates the spirit of this rule, and may result in appropriate penalties.

g. At halftime and the end of each game, the coach and his/her players are to leave the court and go directly to their dressing room without pause or delay. There is to be absolutely no talking to game officials.

h. Each player, when introduced prior to the start of the game, must be uniformly dressed.

i. Any player who is assessed a flagrant foul—penalty (2)—shall be ejected and will be fined a minimum of $300.

B. PERSONAL FOUL

SECTION I—TYPES

a. A player shall not hold, push, charge into, impede the progress of an opponent by extending a hand, forearm, leg or knee or by bending the body into a position that is not normal. Contact that results in re-routing of an opponent is a foul which must be called immediately.

b. Offensive and defensive players have equal rights to any position they have legally obtained.

c. Contact initiated by a defensive player guarding a player with the ball is not legal. This contact includes, but is not limited to, forearms, hands or body check.

EXCEPTIONS:

(1) A defender may apply contact with a forearm to an offensive player with the ball who has her back to the basket below the free throw line extended outside the Lower Defensive Box.

(2) A defender may apply contact with forearm and/or one hand with a bent elbow to an offensive player in the post-up position with the ball in the Lower Defensive Box.

(3) A defender may apply contact with a forearm to an offensive player with the ball at any time in the Lower Defensive Box. The forearm in the above exceptions is solely for the purpose of maintaining a defensive position.

(4) A defender may position her leg between the legs of an offensive player in a post-up position in the lower Lower Defensive Box for the purpose of maintaining defensive position. If her foot leaves the floor in an attempt to dislodge her opponent, it is a foul immediately.

(5) Incidental contact with the hand against an offensive player shall be ignored if it does not

affect a player's speed, quickness, balance and/or rhythm.

d. Any player whose actions against an opponent cause illegal contact with yet another opponent has committed the personal foul.

e. A personal foul committed by the offensive team during a throw-in shall be an offensive foul, regardless of whether the ball has been released.

f. Contact which occurs on the shooting hand of the offensive player, while that hand is in contact with the ball, is legal.

g. One free throw attempt and possession of the ball on the sideline nearest the spot where play was interrupted if an offensive player, or a teammate is fouled while having a clear-path-to-the-basket. The ball and an offensive player must be positioned between the tip-of-circle extended in the backcourt and the basket in the frontcourt, with no defender between the ball and the basket when the personal foul occurs. There must be team control and the new play must originate in the backcourt, including throw-ins, and the offended team must be deprived an opportunity to score an uncontested basket.

EXCEPTION: Flagrant, elbow and punching fouls.

PENALTY: The offender is charged with a personal foul. The offended team is charged with a team foul if the illegal contact was caused by the defender. There is no team foul if there are personal fouls on one member of each team or the personal foul is on an offensive player. The offended team is awarded

(1) The ball out-of-bounds on the sideline at the spot nearest the foul but no nearer to the base line than the free throw line extended, if an offensive foul is assessed.

(2) The ball out-of-bounds on the sideline nearest to where the play was interrupted but no nearer to the baseline than the free throw line extended if the personal foul is on the defender and if the penalty situation is not in effect.

(3) One free throw attempt if the personal foul is on the defender and there is a successful field goal or free throw on the play.

(4) Two/three free throw attempts if the personal foul is on the defender and the offensive player is in the act of shooting an unsuccessful field goal.

(5) One free throw attempt plus a penalty free throw attempt if the personal foul is on the defender and the offensive player is not in the act of attempting a field goal if the penalty situation is in effect.

(6) Two free throw attempts shall be awarded if a personal foul is for illegal contact with an elbow. The elbow foul may be assessed whether the ball is dead or alive. Free throw attempts are awarded whether the ball is dead, alive, loose, or away-from-the-play in the last minute of regulation or overtime(s).

Contact must occur for an elbow foul to be assessed. It is an unsportsmanlike act whether or not there is contact. (See Rule 12A—Section V—d[6] for non-contact.)

If the deliberate elbow contact is above shoulder level, the player will be ejected. If the elbow contact is shoulder level or below, the player may be ejected at the discretion of the official.

In all of the situations, the official has the discretion of assessing a flagrant foul-penalty (1) or (2).

(7) Two free throw attempts shall be awarded if a personal foul is committed by a defender prior to the ball being released on a throw-in.

EXCEPTION: Rule 12B—Section X

(8) One (1) free throw attempt and possession of the ball on the sideline nearest the spot where play was interrupted if an offensive player, or teammate, is fouled while having a clear-path-to-thebasket. The ball and the offensive player must be positioned between the tip-of-circle extended in the backcourt and the basket in the frontcourt, with no defender between the ball and the basket when the personal foul occurs. There must be team control (including throw-ins), and the new play must originate in the backcourt, and the offended team must be deprived of an opportunity to score an uncontested basket.

(9) Two free throw attempts are awarded if a personal foul is committed against an offensive player without the ball when her team has at least a one-woman advantage on a fast break and the defensive player takes a foul to stop play.

SECTION II—BY DRIBBLER

a. A dribbler shall not (1) charge into an opponent who has established a legal guarding position,

384

or (2) attempt to dribble between two opponents, or (3) attempt to dribble between an opponent and a boundary, where sufficient space is not available for illegal contact to be avoided.

b. If a defender is able to establish a legal position in the straight line path of the dribbler, the dribbler must avoid contact by changing direction or ending her dribble.

c. The dribbler must be in control of her body at all times. If illegal contact occurs, the responsibility is on the dribbler.

PENALTY: The offender is assessed an offensive foul. There is no team foul. The ball is awarded to the offended team on the sideline nearest the spot where play was interrupted, but no nearer to the baseline than the free throw line extended.

EXCEPTION: Rule 3—Section I—a.

d. If a dribbler has sufficient space to have her head and shoulders in advance of her defender, the responsibility for illegal contact is on the defender.

e. If a dribbler has established a straight line path, a defender may not crowd her out of that path.

PENALTY: The defender shall be assessed a personal foul and a team foul. If the penalty is not in effect, the offended team is awarded the ball on the sideline nearest the spot where play was interrupted, but no nearer to the baseline than the free throw line extended. If the penalty is in effect, one free throw attempt plus a penalty free throw attempt is awarded.

f. A field goal attempt cannot be scored if a dribble follows the contact for a personal foul.

SECTION III—BY SCREENING

A player who sets a screen shall not (1) assume a position nearer than a normal step from an opponent, if that opponent is stationary and unaware of the screener's position, or (2) make illegal contact with an opponent when she assumes a position at the side or front of an opponent, or (3) assume a position so near to a moving opponent that illegal contact cannot be avoided by the opponent without changing direction or stopping, or (4) move laterally or toward an opponent being screened, after having assumed a legal position. The screener may move in the same direction and path of the opponent being screened.

In (3) above, the speed of the opponent being screened will determine what the screener's stationary position may be. This position will vary and may be one to two normal steps or strides from her opponent.

SECTION IV—FLAGRANT FOUL

a. If contact committed against a player, with or without the ball, is interpreted to be unnecessary, a flagrant foul—penalty 1 will be assessed. A personal foul is charged to the offender and a team foul is charged to the team.

PENALTY: (1) Two free throws shall be attempted and the ball awarded to the offended team on either side of the court at the free throw line extended. (2) If the offended player is injured and unable to attempt her free throws, the opposing coach will select any player from the bench to attempt the free throws. (3) This substitute may not be replaced until the ball is legally touched by a player on the court. (EXCEPTION: RULE 3—Section V—e.) (4) The injured player may not return to the game. (5) A player will be ejected if she commits two flagrant fouls in the same game.

b. If contact committed against a player, with or without the ball, is interpreted to be unnecessary and excessive, a flagrant foul—penalty 2 will be assessed. A personal foul is charged to the offender and a team foul is charged to the team.

PENALTY: (1) Two free throws shall be attempted and the ball awarded to the offended team on either side of the court at the free throw line extended. (2) If the offended player is injured and unable to attempt her free throws, her coach will select a substitute and any player from the team is eligible to attempt the free throws. (3) This substitute may not be replaced until the ball is legally touched by a player on the court. (EXCEPTION: RULE 3—Section V—e.. (4) The injured player may return to the game at any time after the free throws are attempted. (5) This is an unsportsmanlike act and the offender is ejected.

c. A flagrant foul may be assessed whether the ball is dead or alive.

SECTION V—FREE THROW PENALTY SITUATIONS

a. Each team is limited to seven team fouls per regulation half without additional penalties.

Common fouls charged as team fouls, in excess of seven, will be penalized by one free throw attempt plus a penalty free throw attempt.

(1) The first seven common fouls committed by a team in any regulation half shall result in the ball being awarded to the opponent on the sideline nearest where play was interrupted but no nearer the baseline than the free throw line extended.

(2) The first three common fouls committed by a team in any overtime period, shall result in the ball being awarded to the opponent on the sideline nearest where play was interrupted but no nearer the baseline than the free throw line extended.

(3) In the final minute of each half, if a team has not reached eight team fouls or its quota of three team fouls during the first four minutes of any overtime period, it shall be permitted to incur one more team foul without penalty.

(4) During any overtime period, common fouls charged as team fouls in excess of three will be penalized by one free throw plus a penalty free throw attempt.

(5) Personal fouls which are flagrant, punching, elbowing or awayfrom- the-play or clear-path-to-the-basket will carry their own separate penalties and are included in the team foul total.

(6) Personal fouls committed against an offensive player in the act of attempting a two-point field goal will result in two free throw attempts being awarded. If the offensive player is attempting a three-point field goal, three free throw attempts will be awarded.

(7) Personal fouls committed during a successful field goal attempt, which result in one free throw attempt being awarded, will not result in an additional free throw attempt if the penalty situation exists.

b. A maximum of three points may be scored by the same team on a successful two-point field goal attempt.

c. A maximum of four points may be scored by the same team on a successful three-point field goal attempt.

SECTION VI—DOUBLE FOULS

a. No free throw attempts will be awarded on double fouls, whether they are personal or technical.

b. Double personal fouls shall add to a player's total, but not to the team total.

c. If a double foul occurs, the team in possession of the ball at the time of the call shall retain possession. Play is resumed on the sideline nearest the point where play was interrupted, but no nearer to the baseline than the free throw line extended. The 30-second clock is reset to 30 seconds if the ball is to be inbounded in the team's backcourt or stay the same or reset to 20, whichever is greater, if the ball is to be inbounded in the frontcourt.

d. If a double foul occurs with neither team in possession, or when the ball is in the air on an unsuccessful field goal or free throw attempt, play will be resumed with a jump ball at the center circle between any two opponents in the game at that time. If injury, ejection or disqualification makes it necessary for any player to be replaced, no substitute may participate in the jump ball. The jumper shall be selected from one of the remaining players in the game.

e. If a double foul occurs on a successful field goal or free throw attempt, the team that has been scored upon will inbound the ball at the baseline as after any other score.

f. If a double foul occurs as a result of a difference in opinion by the officials, no points can be scored and play shall resume with a jump ball at the center circle between any two opponents in the game at that time. No substitute may participate in the jump ball.

SECTION VII—OFFENSIVE FOULS

A personal foul assessed against an offensive player which is neither an elbow, punching or flagrant foul shall be penalized in the following manner:

(1) No points can be scored by the offensive team

(2) The offending player is charged with a personal foul

(3) The offending team is not charged with a team foul No free throws are awarded.

EXCEPTION: Rule 3—Section I—a.

SECTION VIII—LOOSE BALL FOULS

a. A personal foul, which is neither a punching, flagrant or an elbow foul, committed while there is no team control shall be administered in the following manner:

(1) Offending team is charged with a team foul

(2) Offending player is charged with a personal foul

(3) Offended team will be awarded possession at the sideline, nearest the spot of the foul, but no nearer to the baseline than the free throw line extended, if no penalty exists

(4) Offended player is awarded one free throw attempt plus a penalty free throw attempt if the offending team is in a penalty situation

b. If a "loose ball" foul called against the defensive team is then followed by a successful field goal, one free throw attempt will be awarded to the offended player, allowing for the three-point or four-point play. This interpretation applies:

(1) Regardless of which offensive player is fouled

(2) Whether or not the penalty situation exists. The ball can never be awarded to the scoring team out-of-bounds following a personal foul which occurs on the same play

c. If a "loose ball" foul called against the defensive team is followed by a successful free throw, one free throw will be awarded to the offended player whether or not the penalty is in effect.

d. If a "loose ball" foul called against the offensive team is then followed by a successful field goal attempt by the same offensive player, no points may be scored.

SECTION IX—PUNCHING FOULS

a. Illegal contact called on a player for punching is a personal foul and a team foul. One free throw attempt shall be awarded, regardless of the number of previous fouls in the period. The ball shall be awarded to the offended team out of- bounds on either side of the court at the free throw line-extended, whether the free throw is successful or unsuccessful.

b. Any player who throws a punch, whether it connects or not, has committed an unsportsmanlike act. She will be ejected immediately and suspended for a minimum of one game.

c. This rule applies whether play is in progress or the ball is dead.

d. In the case where one punching foul is followed by another, all aspects of the rule are applied in both cases, and the team last offended is awarded possession on the sideline at the free throw line extended in the frontcourt.

SECTION X—AWAY-FROM-THE-PLAY FOUL

a. During the last minute of the second half or overtime period(s) with the offensive team in possession of the ball, all personal fouls which are assessed against the defensive team prior to the ball being released on a throw-in and/or away-from-the-play, shall be administered as follows:

(1) A personal foul and team foul shall be assessed and one free throw attempt shall be awarded. The free throw may be attempted by any player in the game at the time the personal foul was committed.

(2) If the foul occurs when the ball is inbounds, the offended team shall be awarded the ball at the nearest point where play was interrupted but no nearer to the baseline than the free throw line extended.

(3) If the foul occurs prior to the release on a throw-in, the offended team shall be awarded the ball at the original throw-in spot, with all privileges, if any, remaining.
EXCEPTION: Rule 12-B—Section X—b & c.

b. In the event that the personal foul committed is an elbow foul, the play shall be administered as follows:

(1) A personal foul and team foul shall be assessed and the free throw shooter shall be awarded two free throw attempts. The free throw(s) may be attempted by any player in the game at the time the personal foul was committed.

(2) In the event that the offended player is unable to participate in the game, the free throw shooter may be selected by her coach from any eligible player on the team. Any substitute must remain in the game until the ball is legally touched by a player on the court.
EXCEPTION: RULE 3—Section V—e.

(3) The offended team shall be awarded the ball at the nearest point where play was interrupted with all privileges if any remaining.

c. In the event that the personal foul committed is a flagrant foul, the play shall be administered as follows:

(1) A personal foul and team foul shall be assessed and the free throw shooter shall be awarded two free throw attempts. The free throws may be attempted by any player in the game at the

time the flagrant foul was committed.

(2) If a flagrant foul—penalty (1) is assessed and the offended player is unable to participate in the game, the substitute will be selected by her coach. The two free throws may be attempted by any of the four remaining players in the game. The ball will be awarded to the offended team at the free throw line extended in the frontcourt. The injured player may return to the game.

(3) If a flagrant foul—penalty (2) is assessed and the offended player is unable to participate in the game, the substitute will be selected by her coach. The two free throws may be attempted by the substitute or any of the four remaining players in the game. The ball will be awarded to the offended team at the free throw line extended in the frontcourt. The injured player may return to the game.

RULE NO. 13—INSTANT REPLAY

SECTION I—INSTANT REPLAY REVIEW TRIGGERS

a. Instant replay would be triggered automatically in the following situations:

(1) A field goal made with no time remaining on the clock (0:00) at the end of the second half or any overtime period that, if scored, would affect or potentially could affect, the outcome of the game.

(2) A field goal made with no time remaining on the clock (0:00) at the end of the first half.

(3) A foul called with no time remaining on the clock (0:00) at the end of the second half or any overtime period, provided that it could affect the outcome of the game.

(4) A foul called with no time remaining on the clock (0:00) at the end of the first half.

SECTION II—REVIEWABLE MATTERS

a. If an instant replay review is triggered as described in Section I-a (1) and (2) above, the officials would review the tape to determine only the following issues:

(1) Whether time on the game clock expired before the ball left the shooter's hand.

(2) If the shot was timely, whether the successful field goal was scored correctly as a two-point or three-point field goal.

(3) If the shot was timely, whether the shooter committed a boundary line violation. For purposes of this review, the officials would look only at the position of the shooter's feet at the moment they last touched the floor immediately prior to (or, if applicable, during) the release of the shot.

(4) Whether the 30-second clock expired before the ball left the shooter's hand.

(5) Whether a 10-second backcourt violation occurred before the ball left the shooter's hand.

(6) Whether a called foul that is not committed on or by a player in the act of shooting occurred prior to the expiration on the game clock. For a called foul that is committed on or by a player in the act of shooting, where the shooter releases the ball prior to expiration of time on the game clock, the foul should be administered regardless of whether it occurred prior to or after the expiration of time.

b. If an instant replay review is triggered as described in Section I-a (3) and (4) above, the officials would review the tape to determine only the following issue:

(1) Whether the called foul occurred prior to the expiration of time on the game clock.

NOTE: The officials would be permitted to utilize instant replay to determine whether (and how much) time should be put on the game clock but only when it is determined through replay that (i) the shooter committed a boundary line violation, (ii) a 30-second violation occurred, (iii) a 10-second backcourt violation occurred, or (iv) a called foul occurred prior to the expiration of time on the game clock.

SECTION III—REPLAY REVIEW PROCESS

a. All replay reviews would be conducted by the officials as a crew after gathering as much information as possible. In cases of conflict, the crew chief would make the final decision.

b. The call made by the game officials during play would be reversed only when the replay provides the officials with "clear and conclusive" visual evidence to do so.

I. GUIDES FOR ADMINISTRATION AND APPLICATION OF THE RULES

Each official should have a definite and clear conception of his/her overall responsibilities. It is essential for them to know, understand and implement the rules as intended. If all officials possess the same conception there will be a guaranteed uniformity in the administration of all contests.

The restrictions placed upon the player by the rules are intended to create a balance of play, equal opportunity for the defense and the offense, provide reasonable safety and protection for all players and emphasize cleverness and skill without unduly limiting freedom of action of players or teams.

The purpose of penalties is to compensate a player who has been placed at a disadvantage through an illegal act of an opponent and to restrain players from committing acts which, if ignored, might lead to roughness even though they do not affect the immediate play. To implement this philosophy, there are times during a game where "degrees of certainty" are necessary to determine a foul during physical contact. This practice may be necessary throughout the game with a higher degree implemented during impact times when the intensity has risen, especially nearing the end of a game.

II. BASIC PRINCIPLES

A. CONTACT SITUATIONS

1. Incidental Contact

a. The mere fact that contact occurs does not necessarily constitute a foul. Contact which is incidental to an effort by a player to play an opponent, reach a loose ball, or perform normal defensive or offensive movements, should not be considered illegal. If, however, a player attempts to play an opponent from a position where she has no reasonable chance to perform without making contact with her opponent, the responsibility is on the player in this position.

b. The hand is considered "part of the ball" when it is in contact with the ball. Therefore, contact on that hand by a defender while it is in contact with the ball is not illegal.

2. Guarding an Opponent

a. In all guarding situations, a player is entitled to any spot on the court she desires, provided she legally gets to that spot first and without contact with an opponent.

b. If a defensive or offensive player has established position on the floor and her opponent initiates contact that results in dislodging, a foul should be called IMMEDIATELY.

c. During all throw-ins, the defensive player(s) must be allowed to take a position between her opponent and the basket.

d. A player may continue to move after gaining a guarding position in the path of an opponent provided she is not moving directly or obliquely toward her opponent when contact occurs. A player is never permitted to move into the path of an opponent after the opponent has jumped into the air.

e. A player who extends a hand, forearm, shoulder, hip or leg into the path of an opponent and thereby causes contact is not considered to have a legal position in the path of an opponent.

f. A player is entitled to a vertical position even to the extent of holding her arms above her shoulders, as in post play or when double-teaming in pressing tactics.

g. Any player who conforms to the above is absolved from responsibility for any contact by an opponent which may dislodge or tend to dislodge such player from the position which she has attained and is maintaining legally. If contact occurs, the official must decide whether the contact is incidental or a foul has been committed.

3. Screening

When a player screens in front of or at the side of a stationary opponent, she may be as close as she desires providing she does not make illegal contact. Because her opponent can see the screener, the screened player is expected to detour around the screen.

If she screens behind a stationary opponent, the opponent must be able to take a normal step backward without contact. Because the opponent is not expected to see a screener behind her, the player screened is given latitude of movement. The defender must be given an opportunity to change direction and avoid contact with the screener.

To screen a moving opponent, the player must stop soon enough to permit her opponent to stop or change direction. The distance between the player screening and her opponent will depend upon the speed at which the players are moving.

If two opponents are moving in the same direction and path, the player who is behind is responsible for contact. The player in front may stop or slow her pace, but she may not move backward or sideways into her opponent. The player in front may or may not have the ball. This situation assumes the two players have been moving in identically the same direction and path before contact.

4. The Dribble

If the dribbler's path is blocked, she is expected to pass or shoot; that is, she should not try to dribble by an opponent unless there is a reasonable chance of getting by without contact.

B. FOULS: FLAGRANT—UNSPORTSMANLIKE

To be unsportsmanlike is to act in a manner unbecoming to the image of professional basketball. It consists of acts of deceit, disrespect of officials and profanity. The penalty for such action is a technical foul. Repeated acts shall result in expulsion from the game and potentially a fine.

A flagrant foul—penalty (1) is unnecessary contact committed by a player against an opponent.

A flagrant foul—penalty (2) is unnecessary and excessive contact committed by a player against an opponent. It is an unsportsmanlike act and the offender is ejected immediately.

The offender will be subject to a fine and/or suspension by the President. See Rule 12B—Section IV—b(1-5) for interpretation and penalties.

C. BLOCK-CHARGE

A defensive player is permitted to establish a legal guarding position in the path of a dribbler regardless of her speed and distance.

A defensive player is not permitted to move into the path of an offensive player once she has started her shooting motion.

A defensive player must allow a moving player the distance to stop or change direction when the offensive player receives a pass outside the lower defensive box. The lower defensive box is the area between the 3 ft. posted up marks, the bottom tip of the circle and the endline.

A defensive player must allow an alighted player the distance to land and then stop or change direction when the offensive player is outside the lower defensive box.

A defensive player is permitted to establish a legal guarding position in the path of an offensive player who receives a pass inside the lower defensive box regardless of her speed and distance.

A defensive player must allow an alighted player who received a pass the space to land when the offensive player is inside the lower defensive box.

A player must allow a moving opponent without the ball the distance to stop and change direction. The speed of the offensive player will determine the amount of distance a defensive player must allow.

If a defensive player acquires a position directly under the basket/backboard on anything but a "baseline drive," she shall be responsible if contact occurs. An offensive foul should never be called under these conditions. The offensive player remains a shooter until she has regained a normal playing position on the floor. Many times this type of play is allowed to continue if the goal is successful.

The opposite is also true. If an offensive player causes contact with a defensive player who has established a legal position prior to the offensive player having picked up the ball in an effort to either pass or shoot, and it is anything but negligible and/or incidental, an offensive foul shall be called, and no points may be scored. A defensive player may turn slightly to protect herself, but is never allowed to bend over and submarine an opponent.

On a "drive to the basket," if the defensive player has established a legal position in front of the basket/backboard, the offensive player shall be responsible for any illegal contact which occurs prior to her having regained her balance on the floor. An offensive foul shall be called and no points are to be awarded if the field goal is successful.

The mere fact that contact occurs on these type of plays, or any other similar play, does not necessarily mean that a personal foul has been committed. The officials must decide whether the contact is negligible and/or incidental, judging each situation separately.

In judging this play, the officials must be aware that if EITHER player has been placed at a disadvantage by the contact which has occurred, then a personal foul MUST be called on the player responsible for that contact.

D. GAME CANCELLATION

For the purpose of game cancellation, the officials' jurisdiction begins with the opening tipoff.

Prior to this, it shall be the decision of the home team's management whether or not playing conditions are such to warrant postponement.

However, once the game begins, if because of extremely hazardous playing conditions the question arises whether or not the game should be canceled, the crew chief shall see that EVERY effort is made to continue the game before making the decision to terminate it.

E. PHYSICAL CONTACT—SUSPENSION

Any player or coach guilty of intentional physical contact with an official shall automatically be suspended without pay for one game. A fine and/or longer period of suspension will result if circumstances so dictate.

F. PROTEST

Protests are not permitted during the course of a game. In order to file a protest, a team must adhere to the following procedure:

(a) In order to protest against or appeal from the result of a game, notice thereof must be given to the President within forty-eight (48) hours after the conclusion of such game, by fax or e-mail, stating the grounds for protest. No protest may be filed in connection with any game played during the regular season after midnight of the day of the last game of the regular season schedule. A protest in connection with a playoff game must be filed not later than midnight of the day of the game protested. A game may be protested only by a Governor, Alternate Governor, the general manager or the head coach. The right of protest shall inure not only to the immediately allegedly aggrieved contestants, but to any other team who can show an interest in the grounds of protest and the results that might be attained if the protest were allowed. Each fax or e-mail of protest shall be immediately confirmed by letter, and no protest shall be valid unless the letter of confirmation is accompanied by a check in the sum of $5000 payable to the WNBA. If the team filing the protest prevails, the $5000 is to be refunded. If the team does not prevail, the $5000 is to be forfeited and retained by the WNBA.

(b) Upon receipt of a protest, the President shall at once notify the opposing team in the game protested and require both of said teams within five (5) days to file with her such evidence as she may desire bearing upon the issue. The President shall decide the question raised within five (5) days after receipt of such evidence.

G. SHATTERING BACKBOARDS

Any player whose contact with the basket ring or backboard causes the backboard to shatter will be penalized in the following manner:

(1) Pre-game and/or Half-time warm-ups—No penalty to be assessed by officials.

(2) During the game—Non-unsportsmanlike conduct technical foul. Under NO circumstances will that player be ejected from the game.

The President will review all actions and plays involved in the shattering of a backboard.

H. PLAYER/TEAM CONDUCT AND DRESS

(1) Each player when introduced, prior to the game, must be uniformly dressed.

(2) Players, coaches and trainers are to stand and line up in a dignified posture along the sidelines or on the foul line during the playing of the National Anthem.

(3) Coaches and assistant coaches must wear business attire or other apparel as may be designated by the WNBA.

(4) While playing, players must keep their uniform shirts untucked (worn outside of shorts), and no T-shirts are allowed.

(5) The only article bearing a commercial logo which can be worn by players is their shoes, subject to WNBA rules.

I. OFFENSIVE 3-SECONDS

The offensive player cannot be allowed in the 3-second lane for more than the allotted time. This causes the defensive player to "hand-check" because she cannot control the offensive player for that extended period of time.

If the offensive player is in the 3-second lane for less than three seconds and receives the ball, she must make a move toward the hoop for the official to discontinue his/her three second count. If she attempts to back the defensive player down to secure a better position in relation to the basket, offensive three seconds or an offensive foul must be called. If she passes off and immediately makes a move out of the lane, there should be no whistle.

J. PLAYER CONDUCT—SPECTATORS

Any coach, player or trainer who deliberately enters the spectator stands during the game will be automatically ejected and the incident reported via e-mail to the President. Entering the stands to keep a ball in play by a player or the momentum which carries the player into the stands is not considered deliberate. The first row of seats is considered the beginning of the stands.

K. PUNCHING, FIGHTING AND ELBOW FOULS

Violent acts of any nature on the court will not be tolerated. Players involved in altercations will be ejected, fined and/or suspended.

Officials have been instructed to eject a player who throws a punch, whether or not it connects, or an elbow which makes contact above shoulder level. If elbow contact is shoulder level or below, it shall be left to the discretion of the official as to whether the player is ejected. Even if a punch or an elbow goes undetected by the officials during the game, but is detected during a review of a videotape, that player will be penalized.

There is absolutely no justification for fighting in a WNBA game. The fact that a player believes she was provoked by another player is not an acceptable excuse. If a player takes it upon herself to retaliate, she can expect to be subject to appropriate penalties.

L. EXPIRATION OF TIME

NO LESS THAN :00.3 must expire on the game clock when a ball is thrown inbounds and then hit instantly out-of-bounds. If less than :00.3 expires in such a situation, the timer will be instructed to deduct AT LEAST :00.3 from the game clock. If, in the judgment of the official, the play took longer than :00.3, he/she will instruct the timer to deduct more time. If less than :00.3 remain on the game clock when this situation occurs, the period is over.

NO LESS THAN :00.3 must expire on the game clock when a player secures possession of an inbounds pass and then attempts a field goal. If less than :00.3 expires in such a situation, the timer will be instructed to deduct AT LEAST :00.3 from the game clock. If less than :00.3 remain on the game clock when this situation occurs, the period is over, and the field goal attempt will be disallowed immediately whether successful or unsuccessful.

This guideline shall apply to any field goal attempted by a player after she receives an inbounds pass, OTHER THAN what will be called, for this purpose, a "tip-in" or "alley oop."

A "tip-in" is defined as any action in which the ball is deflected, not controlled, by a player and then enters the basket ring. This type of action shall be deemed legal if :00.1 or more remains in a period.

A "high lob" is defined as a pass which is received by an offensive player while in mid-air, and is followed instantaneously by a field goal attempt. If the reception of the pass and the subsequent "slam dunk" is immediately adjacent to the basket ring, this type of action shall be deemed legal if :00.1 or more remains in a period. However, if the "high lob" attempt is a distance from the basket ring whereby the ball must be controlled in mid-air, either one-handed or two-handed, a minimum of :00.3 is necessary for a field goal to score if successful.

NO LESS than :00.3 must expire on the game clock when a player secures possession of an unsuccessful free throw attempt and immediately requests a timeout.

If LESS than :00.3 expires in such a circumstance, the time on the game clock shall be reduced by at least :00.3. Therefore, if :00.3 OR LESS remain on the game clock when the above situation exists, and a player requests a timeout upon securing possession of the ball, the period is over.

During ANY regular or 20-second timeout taken during the FINAL minute of ANY period, the crew chief must meet with his/her fellow officials to discuss possible timing scenarios, fouls being taken if either team is under the penalty limit, number of timeouts, assistance by all officials on 3-point field goal attempts, rotation or away-from-the play foul.

Regardless of when the horn or red light operates to signify the end of period, the officials will ultimately make the final decision whether to allow or disallow a successful field goal. THE CREW CHIEF MUST TAKE CHARGE OF THE SITUATION.

M. VERBAL FAN INTERFERENCE

Any spectator who verbally abuses players and/or coaches in a manner which, in the opinion of the game officials, interferes with the ability of a coach to communicate with his/her players during the game and/or huddles, will, at the direction of the crew chief, be given one warning by a building security officer. If the same spectator continues to behave in a like manner, the crew chief shall direct a building security officer to eject the spectator from the arena.

N. GUIDELINES FOR INFECTION CONTROL

If a player suffers a laceration or a wound where bleeding occurs, the officials shall suspend the game at the earliest appropriate time and allow a maximum of 30 seconds for treatment. After that time, the head coach shall be informed that she/he has the option to substitute for the player, call a regular timeout or a 20-second timeout. If a substitute replaces the player, the opposing team shall be allowed to substitute one player. The bleeding player may return to the game when she has received appropriate treatment by medical staff personnel.

If the player returns to the game, the officials shall make certain that any lesion, wound or dermatitis is covered with a dressing that will prevent contamination to and/or from other sources. A wrist or sweat band is not considered a suitable bandage.

If the bleeding player is awarded a free throw attempt(s) as a result of a personal foul, or is involved in a jump ball, the bleeding player will be given 30 seconds for treatment. If the treatment is not completed, play will resume and will then be suspended at the first appropriate time.

Mandatory timeouts shall not be granted at any time play is suspended.

If treatment is not completed within the allotted time, the head coach may call another timeout (regular or 20 second) or substitute for the bleeding player. Substitutes are permitted consistent with existing rules on substitution.

If a team has no timeouts remaining when play is suspended, the officials will allow 30 seconds for appropriate treatment. If the treatment is not completed in accordance with paragraph one above, the bleeding player must be removed immediately. ONLY the bleeding player on that team may be removed from the game under these circumstances. If so, the opponent may also substitute one player.

The offensive team will receive a full ten seconds to advance the ball into the frontcourt. The 30 second clock will remain as is or reset to 10, whichever is greater.

O. DEAD BALL, LIVE BALL, BALL IS ALIVE

After the ball has been dead, it is put into play by a jump ball, throw-in or a free throw attempt. The game clock does not start until the ball is legally touched on the court by a player. However, any floor violation or personal foul which may occur will be penalized.

The ball is live when it is placed at the disposal of the thrower-in, free throw shooter or is tossed by the official on a jump ball. Illegal contact, which occurs prior to the ball becoming live, will be ignored if it is not unsportsmanlike.

The ball is alive when it is legally tapped by one of the participants of a jump ball, released by a thrower-in or released on a free throw attempt that will remain in play.

P. TAUNTING

If a player blatantly taunts an opponent, a technical foul shall be assessed. The opponent WILL NOT, automatically, be assessed a technical foul. Her behavior will be the determining factor.

Simultaneous taunting is a verbal altercation. Verbal altercations and unsportsmanlike conduct will be administered as a double technical foul and no free throws will be attempted.

Technical fouls assessed opponents during the same dead ball and prior to the administering of any free throw attempt for the first technical foul, shall be interpreted as a double technical foul.

A PLAYER(S) GUILTY OF TAUNTING MUST BE SINGLED OUT AND PENALIZED.

If a previous unsportsmanlike act has been committed and if this situation is BLATANT, a technical foul must be assessed and the guilty player(s) must be ejected.

VETERAN PLAYERS

ABROSIMOVA, SVETLANA   F   LYNX

PERSONAL: Born July 9, 1980, in St. Petersburg, Russia ... 6-2/169. (1.88 m/77 kg). **Full name:** Svetlana Olegovna Abrosimova.
HIGH SCHOOL: Petrogradskoi N86 (St. Petersburg, Russia).
COLLEGE: Connecticut.
TRANSACTIONS/CAREER NOTES: Selected by Minnesota in first round (seventh overall) of WNBA Draft, April 20, 2001.

COLLEGIATE RECORD

NOTES: Member of NCAA Division I championship team (2000). ... Kodak All-America first team (1999, 2000).

Season Team	G	Min.	FGM	FGA	Pct.	FTM	FTA	Pct.	Reb.	Ast.	Pts.	RPG	AVERAGES APG	PPG
97-98—Connecticut	37	972	191	372	.513	122	184	.663	235	114	538	6.4	3.1	14.5
98-99—Connecticut	34	888	204	425	.480	118	186	.634	226	127	564	6.6	3.7	16.6
99-00—Connecticut	37	1051	181	369	.491	91	122	.746	229	154	496	6.2	4.2	13.4
00-01—Connecticut	19	466	100	186	.538	41	58	.707	124	78	267	6.5	4.1	14.1
Totals	127	3377	676	1352	.500	372	550	.676	814	473	1865	6.4	3.7	14.7

Three-point field goals: 1997-98, 34-for-80 (.425). 1998-99, 38-for-101 (.376). 1999-00, 43-for-108 (.398). 2000-01, 26-for-58 (.448). Totals, 141-for-347 (.406)

OLYMPICS

Season Team	G	Min.	FGM	FGA	Pct.	FTM	FTA	Pct.	Reb.	Ast.	Pts.	RPG	AVERAGES APG	PPG
2000—Russia	7	151	23	43	.535	8	15	.533	23	13	58	3.3	1.9	8.3
Totals	7	151	23	43	.535	8	15	.533	23	13	58	3.3	1.9	8.3

Three-point field goals: 2000-01, 4-for-10 (.400).

WNBA REGULAR-SEASON RECORD

Season Team	G	Min.	FGM	FGA	Pct.	FTM	FTA	Pct.	REBOUNDS Off.	Def.	Tot.	Ast.	St.	Blk.	TO	Pts.	AVERAGES RPG	APG	PPG
2001—Minnesota	26	846	114	293	.389	96	132	.727	43	131	174	53	42	9	85	343	6.7	2.0	13.2
2002—Minnesota	27	805	119	316	.377	56	116	.483	45	101	146	60	42	10	92	314	5.4	2.2	11.6
2003—Minnesota	30	792	112	285	.393	69	98	.704	44	97	141	82	44	11	90	318	4.7	2.7	10.6
Totals	83	2443	345	894	.386	221	346	.639	132	329	461	195	128	30	267	975	5.6	2.3	11.7

Three-point field goals: 2001, 19-for-76 (.250). 2002, 20-for-60 (.333). 2003, 25-for-82 (.305). Totals, 64-for-218 (.294).
Personal fouls/disqualifications: 2001, 70/2. 2002, 73/0. 2003, 79/0. Totals, 222/2.

WNBA PLAYOFF RECORD

Season Team	G	Min.	FGM	FGA	Pct.	FTM	FTA	Pct.	REBOUNDS Off.	Def.	Tot.	Ast.	St.	Blk.	TO	Pts.	AVERAGES RPG	APG	PPG
2003—Minnesota	3	69	6	22	.273	8	8	1.000	1	4	5	4	4	1	8	23	1.7	1.3	7.7
Totals	3	69	6	22	.273	8	8	1.000	1	4	5	4	4	1	8	23	1.7	1.3	7.7

Three-point field goals: 2003, 3-for-7 (.429). Totals, 3-for-7 (.429)
Personal fouls/disqualifications: 2003, 8/0. Totals, 8/0.

ADAMS, JORDAN   C   LYNX

PERSONAL: Born May 24, 1981, in Spokane, Wash. ... 6-3. (1.91 m/ kg).
HIGH SCHOOL: Moapa Valley (Overton, Nev.).
COLLEGE: New Mexico.
TRANSACTIONS/CAREER NOTES: Selected by Minnesota in second round (18th overall) of WNBA Draft, April 25, 2003.

COLLEGIATE RECORD

NOTES: First Team All-Mountain West Conference (2003). ... Named Second Team All-Mountain West Conference (2002, 2001). ... Mountain West Conference Newcomer of the Year (2000). ... UNM's all-time shot blocker for both the men's and women's basketball.

Season Team	G	Min.	FGM	FGA	Pct.	FTM	FTA	Pct.	Reb.	Ast.	Pts.	RPG	AVERAGES APG	PPG
99-00—New Mexico	29	554	131	271	.483	59	97	.608	...	17	321	4.8	0.6	11.1
00-01—New Mexico	35	895	182	371	.491	129	163	.791	...	44	509	5.5	1.3	14.5
01-02—New Mexico	30	846	162	381	.425	92	120	.767	...	66	433	6.0	2.2	14.4
02-03—New Mexico	33	975	209	426	.491	95	135	.704	...	84	528	6.6	2.5	16.0
Totals	127	3270	684	1449	.472	375	515	.728	0	211	1791	0.0	1.7	14.1

Three-point field goals: 1999-00, 7-for-24 (.292). 2000-01, 16-for-49 (.327). 2001-02, 17-for-50 (.340). 2002-03, 15-for-49 (.306). Totals, 55-for-172 (.320)

WNBA REGULAR-SEASON RECORD

Season Team	G	Min.	FGM	FGA	Pct.	FTM	FTA	Pct.	REBOUNDS Off.	Def.	Tot.	Ast.	St.	Blk.	TO	Pts.	AVERAGES RPG	APG	PPG
2003—Minnesota.....	10	96	13	33	.394	2	2	1.000	10	13	23	4	2	3	10	33	2.3	0.4	3.3
Totals.................	10	96	13	33	.394	2	2	1.000	10	13	23	4	2	3	10	33	2.3	0.4	3.3

Three-point field goals: 2003, 5-for-12 (.417). Totals, 5-for-12 (.417)
Personal fouls/disqualifications: 2003, 10/0. Totals, 10/0.

AMACHREE, MACTABENE   F

PERSONAL: Born January 30, 1978, in Nigeria. ... 6-2/172. (1.88 m/78 kg).
TRANSACTIONS/CAREER NOTES: Signed by the WNBA and added by Phoenix, May 1, 2000. ... Waived by Phoenix, June 19, 2000. ... Added by New York, July 9, 2001. ... Signed by Seattle, July 14, 2003.
MISCELLANEOUS: Member of the Nigerian National Team.

WNBA REGULAR-SEASON RECORD

Season Team	G	Min.	FGM	FGA	Pct.	FTM	FTA	Pct.	REBOUNDS Off.	Def.	Tot.	Ast.	St.	Blk.	TO	Pts.	AVERAGES RPG	APG	PPG
2001—New York......	2	3	0	0	...	1	2	.500	1	0	1	0	0	1	1	1	0.5	0.0	0.5
2003—Seattle	7	47	3	10	.300	2	4	.500	4	10	14	0	5	2	9	8	2.0	0.0	1.1
Totals.................	9	50	3	10	.300	3	6	.500	5	10	15	0	5	3	10	9	1.7	0.0	1.0

ANDERSON, CHANTELLE   C   MONARCHS

PERSONAL: Born January 22, 1981, in Loma Linda, Calif. ... 6-6/192. (1.98 m/87 kg). ... **Full name:** Chantelle Denise Anderson.
HIGH SCHOOL: Hudson Bay (Vancouver, Wash.).
COLLEGE: Vanderbilt.
TRANSACTIONS/CAREER NOTES: Selected by Sacramento in first round (second overall) of WNBA Draft, April 25, 2003.

COLLEGIATE RECORD

NOTES: Associated Press All-America Second Team (2003). ... Named a Top 20 finalist for the 2003 Naismith Award. ... All-SEC First Team (2003, 2002, 2001). ... All-SEC Second Team (2000). ... Vanderbilt's all-time leading scorer (2,604). ... Led NCAA in field-goal percentage (.723) in 2000-01. ... Led SEC in field-goal percentage (.647) in 2001-02. ... NCAA Midwest Regional MVP (2002). ... SEC Tournament MVP (2001).

Season Team	G	Min.	FGM	FGA	Pct.	FTM	FTA	Pct.	Reb.	Ast.	Pts.	AVERAGES RPG	APG	PPG
99-00—Vanderbilt	34	935	216	367	.589	104	150	.693	...	25	536	5.6	0.7	15.8
00-01—Vanderbilt	34	1034	292	404	.723	135	185	.730	...	37	722	6.3	1.1	21.2
01-02—Vanderbilt	37	1106	295	456	.647	170	220	.773	...	54	765	6.8	1.5	20.7
02-03—Vanderbilt	32	901	217	341	.636	147	196	.750	...	57	581	5.2	1.8	18.2
Totals	137	3976	1020	1568	.651	556	751	.740	...	173	2604	—	1.3	19.0

Three-point field goals: 1999-2000, 0-for-1. 2000-01, 4-for-7 (.571). 2001-02, 5-for-13 (.385). Totals, 9-for-21 (.429)

WNBA REGULAR-SEASON RECORD

Season Team	G	Min.	FGM	FGA	Pct.	FTM	FTA	Pct.	REBOUNDS Off.	Def.	Tot.	Ast.	St.	Blk.	TO	Pts.	AVERAGES RPG	APG	PPG
2003—Sacramento	26	171	19	44	.432	4	12	.333	7	17	24	5	5	5	17	42	0.9	0.2	1.6
Totals.................	26	171	19	44	.432	4	12	.333	7	17	24	5	5	5	17	42	0.9	0.2	1.6

WNBA PLAYOFF RECORD

Season Team	G	Min.	FGM	FGA	Pct.	FTM	FTA	Pct.	REBOUNDS Off.	Def.	Tot.	Ast.	St.	Blk.	TO	Pts.	AVERAGES RPG	APG	PPG
2003—Sacramento	5	29	3	5	.600	1	2	.500	0	3	3	0	0	2	4	7	0.6	0.0	1.4
Totals.................	5	29	3	5	.600	1	2	.500	0	3	3	0	0	2	4	7	0.6	0.0	1.4

ANDRADE, MERY   F   STING

PERSONAL: Born December 31, 1975, in Cape Verde, Portugal ... 6-0/169. (1.83 m/77 kg). ... **Full name:** Mery Elizabeth Fernandes Andrade.
HIGH SCHOOL: Lisbon, Portugal.
COLLEGE: Old Dominion.
TRANSACTIONS/CAREER NOTES: Selected by Cleveland in second round (23rd overall) of WNBA Draft, May 4, 1999. ... Selected by Charlotte in Dispersal Draft, January 6, 2004.

COLLEGIATE RECORD

Season Team	G	Min.	FGM	FGA	Pct.	FTM	FTA	Pct.	Reb.	Ast.	Pts.	AVERAGES RPG	APG	PPG
95-96—Old Dominion 32		120	232	.517	85	120	.708	153	87	352	4.8	2.7	11.0
96-97—Old Dominion 36		142	317	.448	94	128	.734	226	129	407	6.3	3.6	11.3
97-98—Old Dominion 32		152	314	.484	147	202	.728	217	113	455	6.8	3.5	14.2
98-99—Old Dominion 32		131	291	.450	127	162	.784	218	118	408	6.8	3.7	12.8
Totals 132		545	1154	.472	453	612	.740	814	447	1622	6.2	3.4	12.3

Three-point field goals: 1995-96, 27-for-60 (.450). 1996-97, 29-for-86 (.337). 1997-98, 4-for-22 (.182). 1998-99, 19-for-72 (.264).

Totals, 79-for-240 (.329)

A

WNBA REGULAR-SEASON RECORD

Season Team	G	Min.	FGM	FGA	Pct.	FTM	FTA	Pct.	REBOUNDS Off.	Def.	Tot.	Ast.	St.	Blk.	TO	Pts.	AVERAGES RPG	APG	PPG
1999—Cleveland 32	364	23	59	.390	18	26	.692	15	35	50	49	18	4	40	71	1.6	1.5	2.2
2000—Cleveland 32	797	89	195	.456	60	80	.750	32	63	95	75	41	10	65	265	3.0	2.3	8.3
2001—Cleveland 2	893	58	171	.339	30	45	.667	21	66	87	100	51	10	61	152	2.7	3.1	4.8
Totals......................96	2054	170	425	.400	108	151	.715	68	164	232	224	110	24	166	488	2.4	2.3	5.1

Three-point field goals: 1999, 7-for-24 (.292). 2000, 27-for-75 (.360). 2001, 6-for-30 (.200). Totals, 40-for-129 (.310)
Personal fouls/disqualifications: 1999, 73/0. 2000, 91/1. 2001, 77/0. Totals, 241/1.

WNBA PLAYOFF RECORD

Season Team	G	Min.	FGM	FGA	Pct.	FTM	FTA	Pct.	REBOUNDS Off.	Def.	Tot.	Ast.	St.	Blk.	TO	Pts.	AVERAGES RPG	APG	PPG
2000—Cleveland	6	166	8	33	.242	5	9	.556	5	12	17	14	6	3	11	21	2.8	3.5	3.5
2001—Cleveland......	3	72	6	17	.353	0	0	—	5	4	9	1	2	2	7	13	3.0	0.3	4.3
Totals.................	9	238	14	50	.280	5	9	.556	10	16	26	15	8	5	18	34	2.9	1.7	3.8

Three-point field goals: 2000, 0-for-9. 2001, 1-for-2 (.500). Totals, 1-for-11 (.091)
Personal fouls/disqualifications: 2000, 17/0. 2001, 9/0. Totals, 26/0.

ARCAIN, JANETH   G   COMETS

PERSONAL: Born April 11, 1969, in Sao Paulo, Brazil ... 5-11/147 (1.80 m/67 kg).
HIGH SCHOOL: Minas Gerais (Sto Andres, Brazil).
TRANSACTIONS/CAREER NOTES: Selected by Houston in second round (12th overall) of the WNBA Elite Draft, February 27, 1997.
MISCELLANEOUS: Member of WNBA Championship Team (1997, 1998, 1999, 2000).

OLYMPICS

NOTES: Member of silver medal-winning Brazilian Olympic Team (1996). ... Member of bronze medal-winning Brazilian Olympic Team (2000).

Season Team	G	Min.	FGM	FGA	Pct.	FTM	FTA	Pct.	Reb.	Ast.	Pts.	AVERAGES RPG	APG	PPG
1992—Brazil	5	...	33	63	.524	19	24	.792	39	13	85	7.8	2.6	17.0
1996—Brazil	8	...	56	122	.459	29	37	.784	52	35	142	6.5	4.4	17.8
2000—Brazil	8	274	60	118	.508	43	53	.811	46	21	164	5.8	2.6	20.5
Totals	21	274	149	303	.492	91	114	.798	137	69	391	6.5	3.3	18.6

Three-point field goals: 1996-97, 1-for-7 (.143). 2000-01, 1-for-5 (.200). Totals, 2-for-12 (.167)

WNBA REGULAR-SEASON RECORD

NOTES: WNBA Most Improved Player (2001). ... All-WNBA first team (2001).

Season Team	G	Min.	FGM	FGA	Pct.	FTM	FTA	Pct.	REBOUNDS Off.	Def.	Tot.	Ast.	St.	Blk.	TO	Pts.	AVERAGES RPG	APG	PPG
1997—Houston	28	784	110	250	.440	76	85	.894	41	69	110	45	43	4	67	305	3.9	1.6	10.9
1998—Houston	30	657	83	195	.426	34	45	.756	43	65	108	26	25	3	38	205	3.6	0.9	6.8
1999—Houston	32	735	71	164	.433	34	41	.829	32	59	91	38	30	2	39	187	2.8	1.2	5.8
2000—Houston	32	977	109	233	.468	41	49	.837	36	83	119	60	42	3	53	268	3.7	1.9	8.4
2001—Houston	32	1154	217	509	.426	135	150	.900	49	87	136	94	60	3	83	591	4.3	2.9	18.5
2002—Houston	32	1116	128	302	.424	98	111	.883	42	84	126	86	51	6	71	364	3.9	2.7	11.4
2003—Houston	34	1136	151	324	.466	79	94	.840	24	112	136	67	41	1	50	390	4.0	2.0	11.5
Totals.................	220	6559	869	1977	.440	497	575	.864	267	559	826	416	292	22	401	2310	3.8	1.9	10.5

Three-point field goals: 1997, 9-for-33 (.273). 1998, 5-for-33 (.152). 1999, 11-for-44 (.250). 2000, 9-for-45 (.200). 2001, 22-for-66 (.333). 2002, 10-for-37 (.270). 2003, 9-for-37 (.243). Totals, 75-for-295 (.254)
Personal fouls/disqualifications: 1997, 56/0. 1998, 48/0. 1999, 60/0. 2000, 66/1. 2001, 82/1. 2002, 49/0. 2003, 64/0. Totals, 428/2.

WNBA PLAYOFF RECORD

Season Team	G	Min.	FGM	FGA	Pct.	FTM	FTA	Pct.	REBOUNDS Off.	Def.	Tot.	Ast.	St.	Blk.	TO	Pts.	AVERAGES RPG	APG	PPG
1997—Houston	2	70	9	27	.333	2	2	1.000	7	8	15	1	1	0	1	21	7.5	0.5	10.5
1998—Houston	5	92	8	18	.444	0	0	...	1	7	8	4	2	1	3	16	1.6	0.8	3.2
1999—Houston	6	156	13	29	.448	10	16	.625	4	14	18	6	6	1	2	38	3.0	1.0	6.3
2000—Houston	6	201	21	47	.447	6	7	.857	6	21	27	12	10	0	16	50	4.5	2.0	8.3
2001—Houston	2	71	13	34	.382	2	2	1.000	2	9	11	5	2	0	5	29	5.5	2.5	14.5
2002—Houston	3	119	15	35	.429	7	8	.875	2	9	11	4	5	1	5	39	3.7	1.3	13.0
2003—Houston	3	107	12	31	.387	12	13	.923	6	8	14	3	8	0	7	37	4.7	1.0	12.3
Totals.................	27	816	91	221	.412	39	48	.813	28	76	104	35	34	3	39	230	3.9	1.3	8.5

Three-point field goals: 1997, 1-for-3 (.333). 1998, 0-for-2. 1999, 2-for-9 (.222). 2000, 2-for-7 (.286). 2001, 1-for-8 (.125). 2002, 2-for-7 (.286). 2003, 1-for-5 (.200). Totals, 9-for-41 (.220)
Personal fouls/disqualifications: 1997, 4/0. 1998, 5/0. 1999, 7/0. 2000, 14/0. 2001, 5/0. 2002, 11/0. 2003, 5/0. Totals, 51/0.

WNBA ALL-STAR GAME RECORD

Season Team	Min.	FGM	FGA	Pct.	FTM	FTA	Pct.	REBOUNDS Off.	Def.	Tot.	Ast.	PF	Dq.	St.	Blk.	TO	Pts.
2001—Houston	20	2	7	.286	2	2	1.000	1	0	1	0	0	0	0	0	...	7
Totals.................	20	2	7	.286	2	2	1.000	1	0	1	0	0	0	0	0	2	7

Three-point field goals: 2001, 1-for-2 (.500). Totals, 1-for-2 (.500)

AZIZ, LEIGH   F   FEVER

PERSONAL: Born February 28, 1979 ... 6-3/177 (1.91 m/80 kg).
HIGH SCHOOL: Auburn HS (Auburn, NY)
COLLEGE: Syracuse.
TRANSACTIONS/CAREER NOTES: Signed with Indiana as a free agent, May 1, 2003.

A

COLLEGIATE RECORD

Season Team	G	Min.	FGM	FGA	Pct.	FTM	FTA	Pct.	Off.	Def.	Tot.	Ast.	St.	Blk.	TO	Pts.	RPG	APG	PPG
									REBOUNDS								AVERAGES		
97-98—Syracuse	16	95	6	20	.300	11	19	.579	10	10	20	0	4	9	1	23	1.3	0.0	1.4
98-99—Syracuse	27	512	60	135	.444	31	56	.554	43	75	118	13	19	51	10	151	4.4	0.5	5.6
99-00—Syracuse	27	802	101	214	.472	36	62	.581	81	121	202	26	11	84	13	238	7.5	1.0	8.8
00-01—Syracuse	24	502	67	137	.500	25	45	.556	73	88	161	22	15	59	22	159	6.7	0.9	6.6
Totals	94	1911	234	506	.462	103	182	.566	207	294	501	61	49	203	46	571	5.3	0.6	6.1

WNBA REGULAR-SEASON RECORD

Season Team	G	Min.	FGM	FGA	Pct.	FTM	FTA	Pct.	Off.	Def.	Tot.	Ast.	St.	Blk.	TO	Pts.	RPG	APG	PPG
									REBOUNDS								AVERAGES		
2003—Indiana	7	44	4	14	.286	2	4	.500	2	7	9	1	0	4	3	10	1.3	0.1	1.4
Totals	7	44	4	14	.286	2	4	.500	2	7	9	1	0	4	3	10	1.3	0.1	1.4

AZZI, JENNIFER   G   SILVER STARS

PERSONAL: Born August 31, 1968, in Oak Ridge, Tenn. ... 5-8/144 (1.73 m/65 kg). ... **Full name:** Jennifer Lynn Azzi.
HIGH SCHOOL: Oak Ridge (Oak Ridge, Tenn.).
COLLEGE: Stanford.
TRANSACTIONS/CAREER NOTES: Selected by Detroit in first round (fifth overall) of WNBA Draft, May 4, 1999. ... Traded by Detroit with the 12th pick in the 2000 WNBA Draft to Utah for the third and eighth picks in the draft (April 24, 2000).

NOTES: Kodak All-America first team (1989, 1990). ... Member of NCAA Division I championship team (1990). ... Naismith Player of the Year (1990). ... Wade Trophy recipient (1990).

COLLEGIATE RECORD

Season Team	G	Min.	FGM	FGA	Pct.	FTM	FTA	Pct.	Reb.	Ast.	Pts.	RPG	APG	PPG
												AVERAGES		
86-87—Stanford	27	...	91	201	.453	65	95	.684	100	165	247	3.7	6.1	9.1
87-88—Stanford	32	...	139	321	.433	57	72	.792	126	191	405	3.9	6.0	12.7
88-89—Stanford	31	...	180	331	.544	100	127	.787	129	203	513	4.2	6.5	16.5
89-90—Stanford	32	...	159	320	.497	83	104	.798	121	192	469	3.8	6.0	14.7
Totals	122	...	569	1173	.485	305	398	.766	476	751	1634	3.9	6.2	13.4

Three-point field goals: 1988-89, 53-for-107 (.495). 1989-90, 68-for-154 (.442). Totals, 121-for-261 (.464).

ABL REGULAR-SEASON RECORD

Season Team	G	Min.	FGM	FGA	Pct.	FTM	FTA	Pct.	Reb.	Ast.	Pts.	RPG	APG	PPG
												AVERAGES		
96-97—San Jose	11	...	57	100	.570	52	61	.852	38	52	183	3.5	4.7	16.6
97-98—San Jose	44	...	205	463	.443	196	230	.852	135	219	651	3.1	5.0	14.8
98-99—San Jose	15	...	67	140	.479	75	86	.872	54	72	217	3.6	4.8	14.5
Totals	70	...	329	703	.468	323	377	.857	227	343	1051	3.2	4.9	15.0

Three-point field goals: 1996-97, 17-for-41 (.415). 1997-98, 45-for-126 (.357). 1998-99, 8-for-24 (.333). Totals, 70-for-191 (.366).

OLYMPICS

Season Team	G	Min.	FGM	FGA	Pct.	FTM	FTA	Pct.	Reb.	Ast.	Pts.	RPG	APG	PPG
												AVERAGES		
1996—United States	8	...	17	30	.567	9	11	.818	10	15	47	1.3	1.9	5.9
Totals	8	...	17	30	.567	9	11	.818	10	15	47	1.3	1.9	5.9

Three-point field goals: 1996-97, 4-for-6 (.667).

WNBA REGULAR-SEASON RECORD

NOTES: Led WNBA in three-point field goal percentage (.514) in 2001.

Season Team	G	Min.	FGM	FGA	Pct.	FTM	FTA	Pct.	Off.	Def.	Tot.	Ast.	St.	Blk.	TO	Pts.	RPG	APG	PPG
									REBOUNDS								AVERAGES		
1999—Detroit	28	838	93	181	.514	86	104	.827	5	56	61	106	24	4	56	302	2.2	3.8	10.8
2000—Utah	15	559	47	104	.452	40	43	.930	5	36	41	92	12	5	28	144	2.7	6.1	9.6
2001—Utah	32	1205	75	184	.408	88	96	.917	10	88	98	171	22	10	69	276	3.1	5.3	8.6
2002—Utah	32	1151	91	198	.460	83	104	.798	15	54	69	158	27	14	67	306	2.2	4.9	9.6
2003—San Antonio	34	1136	85	211	.403	51	65	.785	10	81	91	111	27	9	61	260	2.7	3.3	7.6
Totals	141	4889	391	878	.445	348	412	.845	45	315	360	638	112	42	281	1288	2.6	4.5	9.1

Three-point field goals: 1999, 30-for-58 (.517). 2000, 10-for-24 (.417). 2001, 38-for-74 (.514). 2002, 41-for-92 (.446). 2003, 39-for-97 (.402). Totals, 158-for-345 (.458)
Personal fouls/disqualifications: 1999, 103/3. 2000, 89/1. 2001, 89/1. 2002, 102/0. 2003, 98/2. Totals, 435/6.

WNBA PLAYOFF RECORD

Season Team	G	Min.	FGM	FGA	Pct.	FTM	FTA	Pct.	Off.	Def.	Tot.	Ast.	St.	Blk.	TO	Pts.	RPG	APG	PPG
									REBOUNDS								AVERAGES		
1999—Detroit	1	40	2	13	.154	0	0	...	0	5	5	3	0	1	2	5	5.0	3.0	5.0
2001—Utah	2	75	3	12	.250	1	1	1.000	0	3	3	10	1	1	5	9	1.5	5.0	4.5
2002—Utah	5	186	13	33	.394	7	8	.875	2	11	13	34	4	5	8	40	2.6	6.8	8.0
Totals	8	301	18	58	.310	8	9	.889	2	19	21	47	5	7	15	54	2.6	5.9	6.8

Three-point field goals: 1999, 1-for-6 (.167). 2001, 2-for-7 (.286). 2002, 7-for-19 (.368). Totals, 10-for-32 (.313).
Personal fouls/disqualifications: 1999, 3/0. 2001, 7/0. 2002, 20/0. Totals, 30/0.

BADER BINFORD, TRICIA   G

PERSONAL: Born February 26, 1973, in Boise, Idaho ... 5-4/125 (1.63 m/57 kg). ... **Full name:** Tricia Lynne Bader Binford.
COLLEGE: Boise State.
TRANSACTIONS/CAREER NOTES: Selected by Utah in the fourth round (31st overall) in the 1998 WNBA Draft, April 29, 1998. ... Waived by Utah, July 6, 1999. ... Added to Cleveland, July 23, 1999.

COLLEGIATE RECORD

Season Team	G	Min.	FGM	FGA	Pct.	FTM	FTA	Pct.	Reb.	Ast.	Pts.	RPG	APG	PPG
91-92—Boise State	29	...	62	162	.383	56	97	.577	75	66	106	2.6	2.3	3.7
92-93—Boise State	27	...	100	265	.377	90	124	.726	89	127	305	3.3	4.7	11.3
93-94—Boise State	29	...	113	295	.383	76	105	.724	106	139	306	3.7	4.8	10.6
94-95—Boise State	3	...	16	47	.340	11	19	.579	8	10	48	2.7	3.3	16.0
95-96—Boise State	27	...	120	312	.385	44	63	.698	72	106	316	2.7	3.9	11.7
Totals	115	...	411	1081	.380	277	408	.679	350	448	1081	3.0	3.9	9.4

Three-point field goals: 1991-92, 16-for-57 (.281). 1992-93, 15-for-60 (.250). 1993-94, 4-for-30 (.133). 1994-95, 5-for-13 (.385). 1995-96, 32-for-109 (.294). Totals, 72-for-269 (.268)

WNBA REGULAR-SEASON RECORD

Season Team	G	Min.	FGM	FGA	Pct.	FTM	FTA	Pct.	Off.	Def.	Tot.	Ast.	St.	Blk.	TO	Pts.	RPG	APG	PPG
1998—Utah	22	206	16	53	.302	4	8	.500	0	10	10	20	13	0	26	46	0.5	0.9	2.1
1999—Utah-Cleveland	16	106	2	16	.125	2	2	1.000	3	10	13	12	6	1	7	7	0.8	0.8	0.4
2000—Cleveland	25	201	17	48	.354	5	6	.833	2	9	11	21	17	1	18	47	0.4	0.8	1.9
2001—Cleveland	19	114	8	20	.400	0	0	...	2	10	12	11	5	0	8	21	0.6	0.6	1.1
2002—Cleveland	18	132	4	26	.154	5	6	.833	1	6	7	15	6	1	7	14	0.4	0.8	0.8
Totals	100	759	47	163	.288	16	22	.727	8	45	53	79	47	3	66	135	0.5	0.8	1.4

Three-point field goals: 1998, 10-for-27 (.370). 1999, 1-for-10 (.100). 2000, 8-for-24 (.333). 2001, 5-for-13 (.385). 2002, 1-for-14 (.071). Totals, 25-for-88 (.284)
Personal fouls/disqualifications: 1998, 34/1. 1999, 20/0. 2000, 16/0. 2001, 7/0. 2002, 3/0. Totals, 80/1.

WNBA PLAYOFF RECORD

Season Team	G	Min.	FGM	FGA	Pct.	FTM	FTA	Pct.	Off.	Def.	Tot.	Ast.	St.	Blk.	TO	Pts.	RPG	APG	PPG
2000—Cleveland	5	36	3	9	.333	0	1	.000	0	1	1	2	0	1	8	0.2	0.2	1.6
2001—Cleveland	1	4	0	2	.000	0	0	...	1	0	1	0	0	0	0	0	1.0	0.0	0.0
Totals	6	40	3	11	.273	0	1	1.000	1	1	2	1	2	0	1	8	0.3	0.2	1.3

Three-point field goals: 2000, 2-for-3 (.667). 2001, 0-for-2. Totals, 2-for-5 (.400)
Personal fouls/disqualifications: 2000, 1/0. 2001, 0/0. Totals, 1/0.

BARANOVA, ELENA   F   LIBERTY

PERSONAL: Born January 28, 1972, in Bishkek, Kyrgyzstan ... 6-5/182. (1.96 m/83 kg).
TRANSACTIONS/CAREER NOTES: Signed by WNBA and assigned to Utah, January 22, 1997. ... Traded by Utah with Utah's second-round pick in 2000 WNBA Draft to Miami Sol for G Kate Starbird and Miami's first-round pick in 2000 WNBA Draft, December 15, 1999. ... Selected by New York in dispersal draft, April 24, 2003.

OLYMPICS

Season Team	G	Min.	FGM	FGA	Pct.	FTM	FTA	Pct.	Reb.	Ast.	Pts.	RPG	APG	PPG
1996—Russia	8	...	62	177	.350	37	44	.841	105	10	162	13.1	1.3	20.3
Totals	8	...	62	177	.350	37	44	.841	105	10	162	13.1	1.3	20.3

Three-point field goals: 1996-97, 1-for-11 (.091).

WNBA REGULAR-SEASON RECORD

NOTES: Bud Light Free Throw Shooting Champion (2001).

Season Team	G	Min.	FGM	FGA	Pct.	FTM	FTA	Pct.	Off.	Def.	Tot.	Ast.	St.	Blk.	TO	Pts.	RPG	APG	PPG
1997—Utah	28	913	129	331	.390	43	62	.694	56	151	207	62	43	63	82	341	7.4	2.2	12.2
1998—Utah	20	671	92	219	.420	59	71	.831	61	125	186	70	21	30	55	258	9.3	3.5	12.9
1999—Utah	29	572	60	148	.405	33	41	.805	25	73	98	45	20	23	44	173	3.4	1.6	6.0
2001—Miami	32	984	141	330	.427	66	71	.930	40	151	191	63	33	57	62	378	6.0	2.0	11.8
2003—New York	33	850	107	257	.416	31	35	.886	45	136	181	64	36	43	62	278	5.5	1.9	8.4
Totals	142	3990	529	1285	.412	232	280	.829	227	636	863	304	153	216	305	1428	6.1	2.1	10.1

Three-point field goals: 1997, 40-for-106 (.377). 1998, 15-for-48 (.313). 1999, 20-for-48 (.417). 2001, 30-for-80 (.375). 2003, 33-for-91. Totals, 138-for-373 (.373).
Personal fouls/disqualifications: 1997, 82/0. 1998, 44/1. 1999, 58/0. 2001, 81/2. 2003, 69/0. Totals, 334/3.

WNBA PLAYOFF RECORD

Season Team	G	Min.	FGM	FGA	Pct.	FTM	FTA	Pct.	Off.	Def.	Tot.	Ast.	St.	Blk.	TO	Pts.	RPG	APG	PPG
2001—Miami	3	105	15	33	.455	8	11	.727	7	11	18	7	2	2	9	44	6.0	2.3	14.7
Totals	3	105	15	33	.455	8	11	.727	7	11	18	7	2	2	9	44	6.0	2.3	14.7

Three-point field goals: 2001, 6-for-11 (.545). Totals, 6-for-11 (.545)
Personal fouls/disqualifications: 2001, 9/0. Totals, 9/0.

WNBA ALL-STAR GAME RECORD

Season Team	Min.	FGM	FGA	Pct.	FTM	FTA	Pct.	Off.	Def.	Tot.	Ast.	PF	Dq.	St.	Blk.	TO	Pts.
2001 —Miami	25	4	8	.500	1	2	.500	0	7	7	2	2	0	1	4	...	10
Totals	25	4	8	.500	1	2	.500	0	7	7	2	2	0	1	4	2	10

Three-point field goals: 2001, 1-for-2 (.500). Totals, 1-for-2 (.500)

BARNES, ADIA   F   STORM

PERSONAL: Born February 3, 1977, in San Diego, Calif. ... 5-11/165. (1.80 m/75 kg). ... **Full name:** Adia Oshun Barnes.
COLLEGE: Arizona.
TRANSACTIONS/CAREER NOTES: Selected by Sacramento in fourth round (32nd overall) of WNBA Draft, April 29, 1998. ... Selected by Minnesota with the seventh pick in WNBA Expansion Draft, April 6, 1999. ... Traded by Minnesota with G Tonya Edwards and G/F Trisha Fallon to Phoenix for F/C Marlies Askamp, G Angela Aycock and G Kristi Harrower, October 27, 1999. ... Waived by Phoenix, May 28, 2000. ...

Added by Cleveland, July 6, 2000. ... Waived by Cleveland, June 16, 2001. ... Allotted as free agent to Seattle April 25, 2002.

COLLEGIATE RECORD

Season Team	G	Min.	FGM	FGA	Pct.	FTM	FTA	Pct.	Reb.	Ast.	Pts.	AVERAGES RPG	APG	PPG
94-95—Arizona	30	...	191	411	.465	81	131	.618	233	18	464	7.8	0.6	15.5
95-96—Arizona	30	...	209	396	.528	104	154	.675	221	38	522	7.4	1.3	17.4
96-97—Arizona	31	...	232	452	.513	133	182	.731	255	51	598	8.2	1.6	19.3
97-98—Arizona	30	...	249	472	.528	154	204	.755	212	40	653	7.1	1.3	21.8
Totals	**121**	...	**881**	**1731**	**.509**	**472**	**671**	**.703**	**921**	**147**	**2237**	**7.6**	**1.2**	**18.5**

Three-point field goals: 1994-95, 1-for-3 (.333). 1995-96, 0-for-3. 1996-97, 1-for-5 (.200). 1997-98, 1-for-4 (.250). Totals, 3-for-15 (.200)

WNBA REGULAR-SEASON RECORD

Season Team	G	Min.	FGM	FGA	Pct.	FTM	FTA	Pct.	REBOUNDS Off.	Def.	Tot.	Ast.	St.	Blk.	TO	Pts.	AVERAGES RPG	APG	PPG
1998—Sacramento	29	619	88	223	.395	29	39	.744	35	49	84	22	14	10	53	219	2.9	0.8	7.6
1999—Minnesota	19	91	7	23	.304	6	12	.500	8	12	20	6	5	0	8	21	1.1	0.3	1.1
2000—Phoenix-Cleveland	5	18	3	5	.600	2	4	.500	2	0	2	4	0	0	2	8	0.4	0.8	1.6
2001—Cleveland	3	3	1	1	1.000	0	0	...	0	1	1	0	0	0	0	2	0.3	0.0	0.7
2002—Seattle	26	493	37	111	.333	15	29	.517	45	57	102	28	32	9	25	90	3.9	1.1	3.5
2003—Seattle	16	396	32	84	.381	12	21	.571	26	39	65	23	11	7	18	88	4.1	1.4	5.5
Totals	**98**	**1620**	**168**	**447**	**.376**	**64**	**105**	**.610**	**116**	**158**	**274**	**83**	**62**	**26**	**106**	**428**	**2.8**	**0.8**	**4.4**

Three-point field goals: 1998, 14-for-47 (.298). 1999, 1-for-3 (.333). 2000, 0-for-1. 2002, 1-for-4 (.250). 2003, 12-for-31 (.387). Totals, 28-for-86 (.326).
Personal fouls/disqualifications: 1998, 70/1. 1999, 16/0. 2000, 2/0. 2002, 64/1. 2003, 36/1. Totals, 188/3.

WNBA PLAYOFF RECORD

Season Team	G	Min.	FGM	FGA	Pct.	FTM	FTA	Pct.	REBOUNDS Off.	Def.	Tot.	Ast.	St.	Blk.	TO	Pts.	AVERAGES RPG	APG	PPG
2000—Cleveland	4	6	1	2	.500	0	0	...	0	1	1	2	0	0	1	2	0.3	0.5	0.5
2002—Seattle	2	50	4	9	.444	0	0	...	3	5	8	3	3	0	7	10	4.0	1.5	5.0
Totals	**6**	**56**	**5**	**11**	**.455**	**0**	**0**	...	**3**	**6**	**9**	**5**	**3**	**0**	**8**	**12**	**1.5**	**0.8**	**2.0**

Three-point field goals: 2000, 0-for-1. 2002, 2-for-4 (.500). Totals, 2-for-5 (.400)
Personal fouls/disqualifications: 2000, 0/0. 2002, 4/0. Totals, 4/0.

BERTHIEU, LUCIENNE F   COMETS

PERSONAL: Born March 31, 1978, in Duala, Cameroon, Africa ... 6-0/188 (1.83 m/85 kg). ... **Full name:** Lucienne Claudine Berthieu.
HIGH SCHOOL: Rennes Club (France).
COLLEGE: Old Dominion.
TRANSACTIONS/CAREER NOTES: Selected by Seattle in second round (19th overall) of WNBA Draft, April 19, 2002. ... Waived by Seattle, May 28, 2002. ... Added by Cleveland, May 30, 2002. ... Selected by Houston in Dispersal Draft, January 6, 2004.
MISCELLANEOUS: Member of the French National Team. ... Previously attended Rennes University in France.

COLLEGIATE RECORD

Season Team	G	Min.	FGM	FGA	Pct.	FTM	FTA	Pct.	Reb.	Ast.	Pts.	AVERAGES RPG	APG	PPG
98-99—Old Dominion	31	...	180	293	.614	81	151	.536	246	...	441	7.9	0.0	14.2
99-00—Old Dominion	26	...	167	275	.607	130	206	.631	231	...	464	8.9	0.0	17.8
00-01—Old Dominion						Did not play—injured								
01-02—Old Dominion	34	799	178	302	.589	121	208	.582	257	42	477	7.6	1.2	14.0
Totals	**91**	**799**	**525**	**870**	**.603**	**332**	**565**	**.588**	**734**	**42**	**1382**	**8.1**	**0.5**	**15.2**

WNBA REGULAR-SEASON RECORD

Season Team	G	Min.	FGM	FGA	Pct.	FTM	FTA	Pct.	REBOUNDS Off.	Def.	Tot.	Ast.	St.	Blk.	TO	Pts.	AVERAGES RPG	APG	PPG
2002—Cleveland	5	16	3	7	.429	2	4	.500	3	1	4	0	0	0	0	8	0.8	0.0	1.6
2003—Cleveland	22	201	27	52	.519	30	46	.652	20	22	42	6	10	4	22	84	1.9	0.3	3.8
Totals	**27**	**217**	**30**	**59**	**.508**	**32**	**50**	**.640**	**23**	**23**	**46**	**6**	**10**	**4**	**22**	**92**	**1.7**	**0.2**	**3.4**

Three-point field goals: 2002, 0-for-1. 2003, 0-for-1. Totals, 0-for-2.
Personal fouls/disqualifications: 2002, 5/0. 2003, 38/0. Totals, 43/0.

WNBA PLAYOFF RECORD

Season Team	G	Min.	FGM	FGA	Pct.	FTM	FTA	Pct.	REBOUNDS Off.	Def.	Tot.	Ast.	St.	Blk.	TO	Pts.	AVERAGES RPG	APG	PPG
2003—Cleveland	3	13	2	9	.222	0	0	...	2	2	4	1	1	1	2	4	1.3	0.3	1.3
Totals	**3**	**13**	**2**	**9**	**.222**	**0**	**0**	...	**2**	**2**	**4**	**1**	**1**	**1**	**2**	**4**	**1.3**	**0.3**	**1.3**

BEVILAQUA, TULLY G   STORM

PERSONAL: Born July 19, 1972, in Australia ... 5-6/145. (1.68 m/66 kg).
TRANSACTIONS/CAREER NOTES: Signed by the WNBA and assigned to Cleveland, May 30, 1998. ... Waived by Cleveland, July 16, 1998. ... Signed by the WNBA and assigned to Portland, May 1, 2000. ... Signed by the Seattle Storm as a free agent on April 29, 2003.

WNBA REGULAR-SEASON RECORD

Season Team	G	Min.	FGM	FGA	Pct.	FTM	FTA	Pct.	REBOUNDS Off.	Def.	Tot.	Ast.	St.	Blk.	TO	Pts.	AVERAGES RPG	APG	PPG
2000—Portland	32	796	40	112	.357	56	72	.778	19	76	95	89	41	6	66	153	3.0	2.8	4.8
2001—Portland	31	788	39	119	.328	52	71	.732	27	61	88	103	59	6	52	153	2.8	3.3	4.9
2002—Portland	27	421	25	61	.410	19	29	.655	7	26	33	44	22	3	27	84	1.2	1.6	3.1
2003—Seattle	31	252	17	51	.333	16	21	.762	9	17	26	32	14	1	20	58	0.8	1.0	1.9
Totals	**121**	**2257**	**121**	**343**	**.353**	**143**	**193**	**.741**	**62**	**180**	**242**	**268**	**136**	**16**	**165**	**448**	**2.0**	**2.2**	**3.7**

Three-point field goals: 2000, 17-for-60 (.283). 2001, 23-for-73 (.315). 2002, 15-for-36 (.417). 2003, 8-for-21 (.381). Totals, 63-for-190 (.332)
Personal fouls/disqualifications: 2000, 93/1. 2001, 102/0. 2002, 49/0. 2003, 30/0. Totals, 274/1.

BIRD, SUE   G   STORM

PERSONAL: Born October 16, 1980, in Syosset, N.Y. ... 5-9/155 (1.75 m/70 kg). ... **Full name:** Suzanne Brigit Bird.
HIGH SCHOOL: Christ the King (Middle Village, N.Y.).
COLLEGE: Connecticut.
TRANSACTIONS/CAREER NOTES: Selected by Seattle in first round (first overall) of WNBA Draft, April 19, 2002.

COLLEGIATE RECORD

NOTES: Member of NCAA Division I Championship Team (2002, 2000). ... Naismith Award winner (2002). ... Wade Trophy recipient (2002). ... USBWA and AP National Player of the Year (2002). ... Kodak All-America first team (2002).

Season Team	G	Min.	FGM	FGA	Pct.	FTM	FTA	Pct.	Reb.	Ast.	Pts.	RPG	APG	PPG
98-99—Connecticut	8	160	16	41	.390	3	4	.750	16	25	41	2.0	3.1	5.1
99-00—Connecticut	37	1052	140	279	.502	53	59	.898	94	160	405	2.5	4.3	10.9
00-01—Connecticut	34	941	137	309	.443	35	45	.778	89	169	369	2.6	5.0	10.9
01-02—Connecticut	39	1168	198	392	.505	98	104	.942	131	231	563	3.4	5.9	14.4
Totals	118	3321	491	1021	.481	189	212	.892	330	585	1378	2.8	5.0	11.7

Three-point field goals: 1998-99, 6-for-19 (.316). 1999-00, 72-for-145 (.497). 2000-01, 60-for-139 (.432). 2001-02, 69-for-148 (.466). Totals, 207-for-451 (.459)

WNBA REGULAR-SEASON RECORD

NOTES: All-WNBA first team (2002, 2003). ... Led WNBA in free throw percentage (.911) in 2002.

Season Team	G	Min.	FGM	FGA	Pct.	FTM	FTA	Pct.	Off.	Def.	Tot.	Ast.	St.	Blk.	TO	Pts.	RPG	APG	PPG
2002—Seattle	32	1121	151	375	.403	102	112	.911	17	66	83	191	55	3	109	461	2.6	6.0	14.4
2003—Seattle	34	1136	155	368	.421	61	69	.884	22	91	113	221	48	1	110	420	3.3	6.5	12.4
Totals	66	2257	306	743	.412	163	181	.901	39	157	196	412	103	4	219	881	3.0	6.2	13.3

Three-point field goals: 2002, 57-for-142 (.401). 2003, 49-for-140 (.350). Totals, 106-for-282 (.376)
Personal fouls/disqualifications: 2002, 48/0. 2003, 47/0. Totals, 95/0.

WNBA PLAYOFF RECORD

Season Team	G	Min.	FGM	FGA	Pct.	FTM	FTA	Pct.	Off.	Def.	Tot.	Ast.	St.	Blk.	TO	Pts.	RPG	APG	PPG
2002—Seattle	2	73	9	22	.409	7	7	1.000	0	0	0	12	5	0	5	28	0.0	6.0	14.0
Totals	2	73	9	22	.409	7	7	1.000	0	0	0	12	5	0	5	28	0.0	6.0	14.0

Three-point field goals: 2002, 3-for-11 (.273). Totals, 3-for-11 (.273)
Personal fouls/disqualifications: 2002, 6/0. Totals, 6/0.

WNBA ALL-STAR GAME RECORD

Season Team	Min.	FGM	FGA	Pct.	FTM	FTA	Pct.	Off.	Def.	Tot.	Ast.	PF	Dq.	St.	Blk.	TO	Pts.
2002 —Seattle	21	1	8	.125	0	0	...	4	1	5	7	0	0	1	0	...	2
2003 —Seattle	21	3	8	.375	4	5	.800	1	3	4	2	1	0	0	0	...	11
Totals	42	4	16	.250	4	5	.800	5	4	9	9	1	0	1	0	3	13

Three-point field goals: 2002, 0-for-5. 2003, 1-for-4 (.250). Totals, 1-for-9 (.111)

BLACK, DEBBIE   G   SUN

PERSONAL: Born July 29, 1966, in New Ulm, Minn. ... 5-3/124 (1.60 m/56 kg). ... **Full name:** Deborah Anne Black.
HIGH SCHOOL: Archbishop Wood (Warminster, Pa.).
COLLEGE: St. Joseph's (Pa.).
TRANSACTIONS/CAREER NOTES: Selected by Utah in second round (15th overall) of WNBA Draft, May 4, 1999. ... Selected by Miami in third round (11th overall) of the WNBA Expansion Draft, December 15, 1999. ... Selected by Connecticut in dispersal draft, April 24, 2003.

COLLEGIATE RECORD

Season Team	G	Min.	FGM	FGA	Pct.	FTM	FTA	Pct.	Reb.	Ast.	Pts.	RPG	APG	PPG
84-85—St. Joseph's (Pa.)	30	...	66	169	.391	35	56	.625	63	83	167	2.1	2.8	5.6
85-86—St. Joseph's (Pa.)	29	...	89	192	.464	27	42	.643	89	231	205	3.1	8.0	7.1
86-87—St. Joseph's (Pa.)	32	...	91	183	.497	51	67	.761	122	194	235	3.8	6.1	7.3
87-88—St. Joseph's (Pa.)	32	...	139	256	.543	28	35	.800	176	210	311	5.5	6.6	9.7
Totals	123	...	385	800	.481	141	200	.705	450	718	918	3.7	5.8	7.5

Three-point field goals: 1986-87, 2-for-14 (.143). 1987-88, 5-for-16 (.313). Totals, 7-for-30 (.233)

ABL REGULAR-SEASON RECORD

Season Team	G	Min.	FGM	FGA	Pct.	FTM	FTA	Pct.	Reb.	Ast.	Pts.	RPG	APG	PPG
96-97—Colorado	40	...	107	275	.389	65	87	.747	240	275	306	6.0	6.9	7.7
97-98—Colorado	44	...	108	260	.415	62	75	.827	191	268	296	4.3	6.1	6.7
98-99—Colorado	13	...	41	85	.482	7	13	.538	60	65	92	4.6	5.0	7.1
Totals	97	...	256	620	.413	134	175	.766	491	608	694	5.1	6.3	7.2

Three-point field goals: 1996-97, 27-for-85 (.318). 1997-98, 18-for-62 (.290). 1998-99, 3-for-12 (.250). Totals, 48-for-159 (.302)

WNBA REGULAR-SEASON RECORD

NOTES: WNBA Defensive Player of the Year (2001). ... Led WNBA in steals (2.56 spg) in 2001.

Season Team	G	Min.	FGM	FGA	Pct.	FTM	FTA	Pct.	Off.	Def.	Tot.	Ast.	St.	Blk.	TO	Pts.	RPG	APG	PPG
1999—Utah	32	1014	62	163	.380	31	50	.620	31	80	111	161	77	6	67	163	3.5	5.0	5.1
2000—Miami	32	820	57	150	.380	29	42	.690	23	69	92	98	58	1	50	152	2.9	3.1	4.8

Season Team	G	Min.	FGM	FGA	Pct.	FTM	FTA	Pct.	Off.	Def.	Tot.	Ast.	St.	Blk.	TO	Pts.	RPG	APG	PPG
2001—Miami	32	946	70	187	.374	37	48	.771	43	83	126	123	82	2	51	180	3.9	3.8	5.6
2002—Miami	32	899	64	160	.400	25	33	.758	41	82	123	137	59	5	32	153	3.8	4.3	4.8
2003—Connecticut ...	34	373	24	68	.353	6	9	.667	16	35	51	46	20	2	18	55	1.5	1.4	1.6
Totals................	162	4052	277	728	.380	128	182	.703	154	349	503	565	296	16	218	703	3.1	3.5	4.3

Three-point field goals: 1999, 8-for-40 (.200). 2000, 9-for-42 (.214). 2001, 3-for-20 (.150). 2002, 0-for-3. 2003, 1-for-3 (.333). Totals, 21-for-108 (.194)

Personal fouls/disqualifications: 1999, 116/0. 2000, 86/0. 2001, 69/0. 2002, 75/1. 2003, 33/0. Totals, 379/1.

WNBA PLAYOFF RECORD

Season Team	G	Min.	FGM	FGA	Pct.	FTM	FTA	Pct.	REBOUNDS Off.	Def.	Tot.	Ast.	St.	Blk.	TO	Pts.	AVERAGES RPG	APG	PPG
2001—Miami	3	95	7	18	.389	0	0	...	7	9	16	11	5	1	4	14	5.3	3.7	4.7
2003—Connecticut ...	4	29	4	10	.400	0	0	...	1	1	2	2	2	0	0	8	0.5	0.5	2.0
Totals................	7	124	11	28	.393	0	0	...	8	10	18	13	7	1	4	22	2.6	1.9	3.1

Three-point field goals: 2001, 0-for-3. Totals, 0-for-3.
Personal fouls/disqualifications: 2001, 7/0. Totals, 9/0.

BOLTON, RUTHIE   G   MONARCHS

B

PERSONAL: Born May 25, 1967, in Lucedale, Miss. ... 5-9/150 (1.75 m/68 kg). ... **Full name:** Alice Ruth Bolton.
COLLEGE: Auburn.
TRANSACTIONS/CAREER NOTES: Assigned to Sacramento, January 22, 1997.

COLLEGIATE RECORD

Season Team	G	Min.	FGM	FGA	Pct.	FTM	FTA	Pct.	Reb.	Ast.	Pts.	AVERAGES RPG	APG	PPG
85-86—Auburn	30	...	137	257	.533	22	35	.629	143	41	296	4.8	1.4	9.9
86-87—Auburn	33	...	125	240	.521	25	34	.735	96	77	275	2.9	2.3	8.3
87-88—Auburn	35	...	145	265	.547	40	54	.741	108	213	335	3.1	6.1	9.6
88-89—Auburn	34	...	123	276	.446	21	34	.618	143	195	270	4.2	5.7	7.9
Totals	132	...	530	1038	.511	108	157	.688	490	526	1176	3.7	4.0	8.9

Three-point field goals: 1987-88, 5-for-8 (.625). 1988-89, 3-for-8 (.375). Totals, 8-for-16 (.500)

OLYMPICS

NOTES: Member of gold medal-winning Olympic Team (1996, 2000). ... USA Basketball's Female Athlete of the Year (1991).

Season Team	G	Min.	FGM	FGA	Pct.	FTM	FTA	Pct.	Reb.	Ast.	Pts.	AVERAGES RPG	APG	PPG
1996—United States...............	8	...	21	47	.447	15	21	.714	34	16	102	4.3	2.0	12.8
2000—United States...............	8	118	15	46	.326	3	6	.500	16	14	40	2.0	1.8	5.0
Totals	16	118	36	93	.387	18	27	.667	50	30	142	3.1	1.9	8.9

Three-point field goals: 1996-97, 15-for-34 (.441). 2000-01, 7-for-27 (.259). Totals, 22-for-61 (.361)

WNBA REGULAR-SEASON RECORD

NOTES: Named to First-Team All WNBA (1997).

Season Team	G	Min.	FGM	FGA	Pct.	FTM	FTA	Pct.	REBOUNDS Off.	Def.	Tot.	Ast.	St.	Blk.	TO	Pts.	AVERAGES RPG	APG	PPG
1997—Sacramento....	23	813	164	408	.402	53	69	.768	31	103	134	59	54	1	58	447	5.8	2.6	19.4
1998—Sacramento....	5	133	17	58	.293	17	28	.607	5	6	11	6	6	0	7	55	2.2	1.2	11.0
1999—Sacramento....	31	970	143	393	.364	75	94	.798	46	86	132	73	31	0	44	421	4.3	2.4	13.6
2000—Sacramento....	29	868	133	368	.361	64	84	.762	42	64	106	57	34	1	45	380	3.7	2.0	13.1
2001—Sacramento....	31	582	73	216	.338	36	52	.692	34	59	93	55	28	1	39	222	3.0	1.8	7.2
2002—Sacramento....	32	737	125	316	.396	56	77	.727	31	63	94	37	45	2	35	349	2.9	1.2	10.9
2003—Sacramento....	33	521	55	175	.314	20	26	.769	15	42	57	35	33	2	21	149	1.7	1.1	4.5
Totals................	184	4624	710	1934	.367	321	430	.747	204	423	627	322	231	7	249	2023	3.4	1.8	11.0

Three-point field goals: 1997, 66-for-192 (.344). 1998, 4-for-26 (.154). 1999, 60-for-187 (.321). 2000, 50-for-160 (.313). 2001, 40-for-110 (.364). 2002, 43-for-132 (.326). 2003, 19-for-98 (.194). Totals, 282-for-905 (.312)

Personal fouls/disqualifications: 1997, 71/3. 1998, 12/0. 1999, 68/0. 2000, 60/0. 2001, 55/0. 2002, 74/0. 2003, 52/0. Totals, 392/3.

WNBA PLAYOFF RECORD

Season Team	G	Min.	FGM	FGA	Pct.	FTM	FTA	Pct.	REBOUNDS Off.	Def.	Tot.	Ast.	St.	Blk.	TO	Pts.	AVERAGES RPG	APG	PPG
1999—Sacramento....	1	32	6	15	.400	2	2	1.000	1	0	1	4	1	0	2	15	1.0	4.0	15.0
2000—Sacramento....	2	70	13	34	.382	9	9	1.000	4	5	9	7	4	0	5	39	4.5	3.5	19.5
2001—Sacramento....	5	121	17	44	.386	12	13	.923	10	12	22	9	4	0	10	55	4.4	1.8	11.0
2003—Sacramento....	6	91	6	28	.214	0	0	...	2	8	10	6	2	0	5	15	1.7	1.0	2.5
Totals................	14	314	42	121	.347	23	24	.958	17	25	42	26	11	0	22	124	3.0	1.9	8.9

Three-point field goals: 1999, 1-for-6 (.167). 2000, 4-for-14 (.286). 2001, 9-for-23 (.391). 2003, 3-for-12 (.250). Totals, 17-for-55 (.309)
Personal fouls/disqualifications: 1999, 1/0. 2000, 6/0. 2001, 11/0. 2003, 10/0. Totals, 28/0.

WNBA ALL-STAR GAME RECORD

Season Team	Min.	FGM	FGA	Pct.	FTM	FTA	Pct.	REBOUNDS Off.	Def.	Tot.	Ast.	PF	Dq.	St.	Blk.	TO	Pts.
1999 —Sacramento.....	20	1	7	.143	0	0	...	1	2	3	1	0	0	1	0	...	2
2001 —Sacramento.....	20	3	8	.375	0	0	...	0	4	4	3	2	0	6	0	...	6
Totals................	40	4	15	.267	0	0	...	1	6	7	4	2	0	7	0	1	8

Three-point field goals: 1999, 0-for-4. 2001, 0-for-3. Totals, 0-for-7.

BRONDELLO, SANDY   G   STORM

PERSONAL: Born August 20, 1968, in Mackay QLD., Australia ... 5-7/136 (1.70 m/62 kg). ... **Full name:** Sandra Anne Brondello.
HIGH SCHOOL: Mirani State (Mirani, QLD., Australia).
TRANSACTIONS/CAREER NOTES: Selected by Detroit in fourth round (34th overall) of WNBA Draft, April 29, 1998. ... Selected by Indiana in second round (eighth overall) of WNBA Expansion Draft, December 15, 1999. ... Traded by Indiana with first round pick in 2000 WNBA Draft to Miami for F Stephanie

McCarty, December 15, 1999. ... Became an unrestricted free agent when the Miami Sol ceased operation during the 2003-03 offseason. ... Signed as a free agent by Seattle on April 29, 2003.

OLYMPICS

NOTES: Member of bronze medal-winning Australian Olympic Team (1996). ... Member of silver medal-winning Australian Olympic Team (2000).

AVERAGES

Season Team	G	Min.	FGM	FGA	Pct.	FTM	FTA	Pct.	Reb.	Ast.	Pts.	RPG	APG	PPG
1996—Australia	8	...	22	66	.333	22	25	.880	15	13	69	1.9	1.6	8.6
2000—Australia	8	168	38	74	.514	13	16	.813	10	7	90	1.3	0.9	11.3
Totals	16	168	60	140	.429	35	41	.854	25	20	159	1.6	1.3	9.9

Three-point field goals: 1996-97, 1-for-2 (.500). 2000-01, 1-for-1. Totals, 2-for-3 (.667)

WNBA REGULAR-SEASON RECORD

HONORS: Led WNBA in free throw percentage in 1998 (.923).

Season Team	G	Min.	FGM	FGA	Pct.	FTM	FTA	Pct.	REBOUNDS Off.	Def.	Tot.	Ast.	St.	Blk.	TO	Pts.	AVERAGES RPG	APG	PPG
1998—Detroit	30	993	157	367	.428	96	104	.923	18	69	87	98	38	1	64	426	2.9	3.3	14.2
1999—Detroit	32	1002	152	347	.438	83	98	.847	29	37	66	73	25	5	75	424	2.1	2.3	13.3
2000—Miami								Did not play											
2001—Miami	29	850	142	344	.413	57	70	.814	10	40	50	63	28	4	36	367	1.7	2.2	12.7
2002—Miami	30	763	97	266	.365	55	67	.821	7	34	41	46	26	4	40	263	1.4	1.5	8.8
2003—Seattle	34	975	117	282	.415	25	31	.806	19	37	56	69	31	2	37	280	1.6	2.0	8.2
Totals	155	4583	665	1606	.414	316	370	.854	83	217	300	349	148	16	252	1760	1.9	2.3	11.4

Three-point field goals: 1998, 16-for-44 (.364). 1999, 37-for-76 (.487). 2001, 26-for-66 (.394). 2002, 14-for-44 (.318). 2003, 21-for-48 (.438). Totals, 114-for-278 (.410)
Personal fouls/disqualifications: 1998, 58/0. 1999, 81/4. 2001, 61/0. 2002, 40/0. 2003, 58/0. Totals, 298/4.

WNBA PLAYOFF RECORD

Season Team	G	Min.	FGM	FGA	Pct.	FTM	FTA	Pct.	REBOUNDS Off.	Def.	Tot.	Ast.	St.	Blk.	TO	Pts.	AVERAGES RPG	APG	PPG
1999—Detroit	1	29	4	12	.333	0	0	...	2	1	3	0	2	1	1	9	3.0	0.0	9.0
2001—Miami	3	107	13	36	.361	5	6	.833	1	9	10	7	2	0	3	34	3.3	2.3	11.3
Totals	4	136	17	48	.354	5	6	.833	3	10	13	7	4	1	4	43	3.3	1.8	10.8

Three-point field goals: 1999, 1-for-4 (.250). 2001, 3-for-10 (.300). Totals, 4-for-14 (.286)
Personal fouls/disqualifications: 1999, 2/0. 2001, 5/0. Totals, 7/0.

WNBA ALL-STAR GAME RECORD

Season Team	Min.	FGM	FGA	Pct.	FTM	FTA	Pct.	REBOUNDS Off.	Def.	Tot.	Ast.	PF	Dq.	St.	Blk.	TO	Pts.
1999—Detroit	11	4	8	.500	0	0	...	2	1	3	1	0	0	0	0	...	8
Totals	11	4	8	.500	0	0	...	2	1	3	1	0	0	0	0	...	8

Three-point field goals: 1999, 0-for-1. Totals, 0-for-1.

BROWN, CORETTA   G   FEVER

PERSONAL: Born October 21, 1980, in Statesboro, Ga. ... 5-9/150. (1.75 m/68 kg). ... **Full name:** Coretta Renay Brown.
HIGH SCHOOL: Southeast Bulloch (Brooklet, Ga.).
COLLEGE: North Carolina.
TRANSACTIONS/CAREER NOTES: Selected by San Antonio in first round (11th overall) of WNBA Draft, April 25, 2003. ... Traded by San Antonio to Indiana, along with Natalie Williams, to Indiana in exchange for Sylvia Crawley and Gwen Jackson, May 1, 2003.

COLLEGIATE RECORD

NOTES: Associated Press All-America Honorable Mention (2003). ... All-ACC First Team (2003, 2002). ... Holds UNC Record for career three-point percentage (.380). ... Set ACC record with 99 three-pointers made as a junior.

Season Team	G	Min.	FGM	FGA	Pct.	FTM	FTA	Pct.	Reb.	Ast.	Pts.	AVERAGES RPG	APG	PPG
99-00—North Carolina	33	543	48	160	.300	26	41	.634	...	59	135	1.7	1.8	4.1
00-01—North Carolina	29	1121	156	408	.382	99	145	.683	...	193	462	4.8	6.7	15.9
01-02—North Carolina	35	1203	216	469	.461	67	93	.720	...	118	598	5.0	3.4	17.1
02-03—North Carolina	34	1152	157	396	.396	90	108	.833	...	147	492	3.6	4.3	14.5
Totals	131	4019	577	1433	.403	282	387	.729	0	517	1687	0.0	3.9	12.9

Three-point field goals: 1999-00, 13-for-49 (.265). 2000-01, 51-for-138 (.370). 2001-02, 99-for-251 (.394). 2002-03, 88-for-223 (.395). Totals, 251-for-661 (.380)

WNBA REGULAR-SEASON RECORD

Season Team	G	Min.	FGM	FGA	Pct.	FTM	FTA	Pct.	REBOUNDS Off.	Def.	Tot.	Ast.	St.	Blk.	TO	Pts.	AVERAGES RPG	APG	PPG
2003—Indiana	30	522	61	164	.372	28	33	.848	11	30	41	31	21	4	36	186	1.4	1.0	6.2
Totals	30	522	61	164	.372	28	33	.848	11	30	41	31	21	4	36	186	1.4	1.0	6.2

Three-point field goals: 2003, 36-for-100 (.360). Totals, 36-for-100 (.360).
Personal fouls/disqualifications: 2003, 30/0. Totals, 30/0.

BROWN, EDWINA   G/F   MERCURY

PERSONAL: Born July 1, 1978, in Dallas, Texas ... 5-9/163 (1.75 m/74 kg). ... **Full name:** Edwina Lynn Brown.
HIGH SCHOOL: Lockhart (Lockhart, Texas).
COLLEGE: Texas.
TRANSACTIONS/CAREER NOTES: Selected by Detroit in first round (third overall) of WNBA Draft, April 25, 2000. ... Traded to Phoenix along with Lenae Williams in exchange for Petra Ujhelyi and Telisha

Quarles, the Mercury's second and third round draft picks in the 2003 WNBA Draft on April 29, 2003.

COLLEGIATE RECORD

NOTES: Kodak All-America first team (2000). ... Wade Trophy winner (2000).

Season Team	G	Min.	FGM	FGA	Pct.	FTM	FTA	Pct.	Reb.	Ast.	Pts.	AVERAGES RPG	APG	PPG
96-97—Texas	30	...	76	177	.429	29	48	.604	115	52	181	3.8	1.7	6.0
97-98—Texas	24	...	142	284	.500	68	97	.701	167	103	352	7.0	4.3	14.7
98-99—Texas	28	...	172	349	.493	104	138	.754	211	159	450	7.5	5.7	16.1
99-00—Texas	34	...	274	589	.465	172	225	.764	284	203	722	8.4	6.0	21.2
Totals	116	...	664	1399	.475	373	508	.734	777	517	1705	6.7	4.5	14.7

Three-point field goals: 1996-97, 0-for-1. 1997-98, 0-for-4. 1998-99, 2-for-9 (.222). 1999-2000, 2-for-5 (.400). Totals, 4-for-19 (.211)

WNBA REGULAR-SEASON RECORD

Season Team	G	Min.	FGM	FGA	Pct.	FTM	FTA	Pct.	REBOUNDS Off.	Def.	Tot.	Ast.	St.	Blk.	TO	Pts.	AVERAGES RPG	APG	PPG
2000—Detroit	32	619	60	168	.357	67	80	.838	36	52	88	72	24	5	68	188	2.8	2.3	5.9
2001—Detroit	32	800	85	232	.366	47	60	.783	31	70	101	87	33	7	68	237	3.2	2.7	7.4
2002—Detroit	28	549	43	131	.328	23	32	.719	29	53	82	58	25	7	60	115	2.9	2.1	4.1
2003—Phoenix	34	524	41	152	.270	36	44	.818	29	42	71	62	30	7	47	118	2.1	1.8	3.5
Totals	126	2492	229	683	.335	173	216	.801	125	217	342	279	112	26	243	658	2.7	2.2	5.2

Three-point field goals: 2000, 1-for-4 (.250). 2001, 20-for-53 (.377). 2002, 6-for-12 (.500). 2003, 0-for-3. Totals, 27-for-72 (.375)
Personal fouls/disqualifications: 2000, 77/0. 2001, 83/1. 2002, 73/0. 2003, 44/0. Totals, 277/1.

BROWN, KIESHA   G   MYSTICS

PERSONAL: Born January 13, 1979 ... 5-10/142 (1.78 m/64 kg).
COLLEGE: Georgia.
TRANSACTIONS/CAREER NOTES: Signed by the WNBA and added by Los Angeles, April 30, 2001. ... Waived by Los Angeles, May 24, 2001. ... Added by Washington, April 25, 2002.

COLLEGIATE RECORD

Season Team	G	Min.	FGM	FGA	Pct.	FTM	FTA	Pct.	Reb.	Ast.	Pts.	AVERAGES RPG	APG	PPG
96-97—Georgia	8	...	19	41	.463	13	19	.684	20	36	52	2.5	4.5	6.5
97-98—Georgia							Did not play—injured							
98-99—Georgia	34	...	65	147	.442	58	81	.716	102	109	196	3.0	3.2	5.8
99-00—Georgia	36	...	36	100	.360	15	24	.625	68	55	87	1.9	1.5	2.4
00-01—Georgia	33	...	53	159	.333	53	71	.746	102	60	160	3.1	2.8	4.8
Totals	111	...	173	447	.387	139	195	.713	292	293	495	2.6	2.6	4.5

Three-point field goals: 1996-97, 1-for-9 (.111). 1998-99, 8-for-34 (.235). 1999-2000, 0-for-4. 2000-1, 1-for-12 (.083). Totals, 10-for-59 (.169)

WNBA REGULAR-SEASON RECORD

Season Team	G	Min.	FGM	FGA	Pct.	FTM	FTA	Pct.	REBOUNDS Off.	Def.	Tot.	Ast.	St.	Blk.	TO	Pts.	AVERAGES RPG	APG	PPG
2002—Washington	18	108	12	35	.343	3	3	1.000	4	8	12	6	5	0	5	28	0.7	0.3	1.6
2003—Washington	27	269	24	72	.333	2	3	.667	6	26	32	28	13	1	22	60	1.2	1.0	2.2
Totals	45	377	36	107	.336	5	6	.833	10	34	44	34	18	1	27	88	1.0	0.8	2.0

Three-point field goals: 2002, 1-for-11 (.091). 2003, 10-for-33 (.303). Totals, 11-for-44 (.250)
Personal fouls/disqualifications: 2002, 10/0. 2003, 23/0. Totals, 33/0.

WNBA PLAYOFF RECORD

Season Team	G	Min.	FGM	FGA	Pct.	FTM	FTA	Pct.	REBOUNDS Off.	Def.	Tot.	Ast.	St.	Blk.	TO	Pts.	AVERAGES RPG	APG	PPG
2002—Washington	2	15	3	6	.500	0	0	...	0	1	1	1	2	0	0	6	0.5	0.5	3.0
Totals	2	15	3	6	.500	0	0	...	0	1	1	1	2	0	0	6	0.5	0.5	3.0

Three-point field goals: 2002, 0-for-2. Totals, 0-for-2 (.000)
Personal fouls/disqualifications: 2002, 3/0. Totals, 3/0.

BROWN, RUSHIA   F   STING

PERSONAL: Born May 5, 1972, in New York, N.Y. ... 6-2/175. (1.88 m/79 kg). ... **Full name:** Yerushia Brown.
HIGH SCHOOL: Summerville (Summerville, S.C.).
COLLEGE: Furman.
TRANSACTIONS/CAREER NOTES: Selected as developmental player and assigned to Cleveland, May 27, 1997. ... Earned an active roster position, June 17, 1997. ... Traded by the Cleveland to Charlotte for Pollyanna Johns Kimbrough, May 19, 2003.

COLLEGIATE RECORD

Season Team	G	Min.	FGM	FGA	Pct.	FTM	FTA	Pct.	Reb.	Ast.	Pts.	AVERAGES RPG	APG	PPG
89-90—Furman	29	...	191	336	.568	75	132	.568	236	22	457	8.1	0.8	15.8
90-91—Furman	4	...	28	51	.549	17	27	.630	28	3	73	7.0	0.8	18.3
91-92—Furman	26	...	216	371	.582	114	181	.630	243	29	546	9.3	1.1	21.0
92-93—Furman	28	...	231	384	.602	65	119	.546	269	41	527	9.6	1.5	18.8
93-94—Furman	27	...	242	394	.614	82	135	.607	247	30	566	9.1	1.1	21.0
Totals	114	...	908	1536	.591	353	594	.594	1023	125	2169	9.0	1.1	19.0

Three-point field goals: 1991-92, 0-for-1. 1992-93, 0-for-3. 1993-94, 0-for-2. Totals, 0-for-6.

WNBA REGULAR-SEASON RECORD

Season Team	G	Min.	FGM	FGA	Pct.	FTM	FTA	Pct.	REBOUNDS Off.	Def.	Tot.	Ast.	St.	Blk.	TO	Pts.	AVERAGES RPG	APG	PPG
1997—Cleveland	28	511	64	123	.520	47	64	.734	48	65	113	20	34	14	27	175	4.0	0.7	6.3
1998—Cleveland	30	522	64	139	.460	66	85	.776	34	59	93	28	34	16	49	194	3.1	0.9	6.5
1999—Cleveland	30	434	53	124	.427	25	37	.676	31	56	87	20	19	10	34	131	2.9	0.7	4.4
2000—Cleveland	30	679	93	187	.497	66	78	.846	54	70	124	44	38	13	59	253	4.1	1.5	8.4
2001—Cleveland	30	760	101	195	.518	46	63	.730	49	83	132	37	44	10	37	249	4.4	1.2	8.3
2002—Cleveland	28	468	42	105	.400	28	38	.737	29	46	75	27	21	8	39	112	2.7	1.0	4.0
2003—Charlotte	34	483	53	116	.457	19	23	.826	34	49	83	16	29	10	35	125	2.4	0.5	3.7
Totals	210	3857	470	989	.475	297	388	.765	279	428	707	192	219	81	280	1239	3.4	0.9	5.9

Three-point field goals: 1998, 0-for-1. 1999, 0-for-1. 2000, 1-for-2 (.500). 2001, 1-for-1. 2002, 0-for-1. 2003, 0-for-2. Totals, 2-for-8 (.250)
Personal fouls/disqualifications: 1998, 79/1. 1999, 60/1. 2000, 81/0. 2001, 73/1. 2002, 54/0. 2003, 88/1. Totals, 507/4.

WNBA PLAYOFF RECORD

Season Team	G	Min.	FGM	FGA	Pct.	FTM	FTA	Pct.	REBOUNDS Off.	Def.	Tot.	Ast.	St.	Blk.	TO	Pts.	AVERAGES RPG	APG	PPG
1998—Cleveland	3	21	2	6	.333	1	2	.500	3	0	3	0	5	0	5	5	1.0	0.0	1.7
2000—Cleveland	6	167	21	45	.467	21	24	.875	19	15	34	10	17	2	17	63	5.7	1.7	10.5
2001—Cleveland	3	62	10	15	.667	5	6	.833	2	6	8	5	4	2	3	25	2.7	1.7	8.3
2003—Charlotte	2	46	3	7	.429	1	2	.500	3	5	8	4	2	0	4	7	4.0	2.0	3.5
Totals	14	296	36	73	.493	28	34	.824	27	26	53	19	28	4	29	100	3.8	1.4	7.1

Three-point field goals: 2000, 0-for-1. Totals, 0-for-1.
Personal fouls/disqualifications: 2000, 17/0. Totals, 32/0.

BRUMFIELD, MARLA   G   STING

PERSONAL: Born June 6, 1978, in Aurora, Ill. ... 5-8/133. (1.73 m/60 kg). ... **Full name:** Marla Tanishe Brumfield.
HIGH SCHOOL: Alief Elsik (Texas).
COLLEGE: Rice.
TRANSACTIONS/CAREER NOTES: Selected by Minnesota in second round (22nd overall) of WNBA Draft, April 25, 2000. ... Traded to Miami for G Georgia Schweitzer, April 20, 2001. ... Traded to Portland with Katrina Colleton in exchange for Vanessa Nygaard, May 22, 2002. ... Signed by Charlotte as a free agent, April 30, 2003.

COLLEGIATE RECORD

Season Team	G	Min.	FGM	FGA	Pct.	FTM	FTA	Pct.	Reb.	Ast.	Pts.	AVERAGES RPG	APG	PPG
96-97—Rice	27	...	129	307	.420	81	118	.686	159	75	350	5.9	2.8	13.0
97-98—Rice	30	...	146	378	.386	91	144	.632	141	86	407	4.7	2.9	13.6
98-99—Rice	32	...	180	436	.413	127	176	.722	187	101	464	5.8	3.2	14.5
99-00—Rice	32	...	185	424	.436	97	143	.678	136	143	482	4.3	4.5	15.1
Totals	121	...	640	1545	.414	396	581	.682	623	405	1703	5.1	3.3	14.1

Three-point field goals: 1996-97, 11-for-36 (.306). 1997-98, 24-for-76 (.316). 1998-99, 17-for-64 (.266). 1999-000, 15-for-52 (.288). Totals, 67-for-228 (.294)

WNBA REGULAR-SEASON RECORD

Season Team	G	Min.	FGM	FGA	Pct.	FTM	FTA	Pct.	REBOUNDS Off.	Def.	Tot.	Ast.	St.	Blk.	TO	Pts.	AVERAGES RPG	APG	PPG
2000—Minnesota	32	613	47	101	.465	29	42	.690	22	38	60	42	22	2	40	124	1.9	1.3	3.9
2001—Miami	27	247	17	60	.283	5	5	1.000	8	17	25	32	20	0	24	44	0.9	1.2	1.6
2003—Charlotte	25	123	6	16	.375	6	6	1.000	1	9	10	14	1	1	6	18	0.4	0.6	0.7
Totals	84	983	70	177	.395	40	53	.755	31	64	95	88	43	3	70	186	1.1	1.0	2.2

Three-point field goals: 2000, 1-for-9 (.111). 2001, 5-for-15 (.333). Totals, 6-for-24 (.250)
Personal fouls/disqualifications: 2000, 70/1. 2001, 27/0. Totals, 97/1.

WNBA PLAYOFF RECORD

Season Team	G	Min.	FGM	FGA	Pct.	FTM	FTA	Pct.	REBOUNDS Off.	Def.	Tot.	Ast.	St.	Blk.	TO	Pts.	AVERAGES RPG	APG	PPG
2001—Miami	2	4	1	2	.500	0	0	...	0	0	0	0	1	0	0	2	0.0	0.0	1.0
Totals	2	4	1	2	.500	0	0	...	0	0	0	0	1	0	0	2	0.0	0.0	1.0

Three-point field goals: 2001, 0-for-1. Totals, 0-for-1.
Personal fouls/disqualifications: 2001, 0/0.

BUESCHER, ERIN   G   STING

PERSONAL: Born June 5, 1979, in San Francisco, Calif. ... 6-2/181. (1.88 m/82 kg). ... **Full name:** Erin Rebecca Buescher.
HIGH SCHOOL: Rincon Valley Christian (Santa Rosa, Calif.).
COLLEGE: Master's College.
TRANSACTIONS/CAREER NOTES: Selected by Minnesota in second round (23rd overall) of WNBA Draft, April 20, 2001. ... Traded by Minnesota with F Maylana Martin to Charlotte for G Shaunzinski Gortman, April 19, 2002.

COLLEGIATE RECORD

NOTES: NAIA All-America first team (2001).

Season Team	G	Min.	FGM	FGA	Pct.	FTM	FTA	Pct.	Reb.	Ast.	Pts.	AVERAGES RPG	APG	PPG
97-98—Cal.-Santa Barbara	31	...	210	406	.517	89	131	.679	269	93	530	8.7	3.0	17.1

Season Team	G	Min.	FGM	FGA	Pct.	FTM	FTA	Pct.	Off.	Def.	Tot.	Ast.					RPG	APG	PPG
98-99—Cal.-Santa Barbara	30	...	207	395	.524	140	195	.718			274	102			597		9.1	3.4	19.9
99-00—Cal.-Santa Barbara	33	...	216	436	.495	119	183	.650			321	95			570		9.7	2.9	17.3
00-01—Master's College	25	700	158	323	.489	116	147	.789			233	77			439		9.3	3.1	17.6
Totals	119	700	791	1560	.507	464	656	.707			1097	367			2136		9.2	3.1	17.9

Three-point field goals: 1997-98, 21-for-54 (.389). 1998-99, 43-for-91 (.473). 1999-000, 19-for-71 (.268). 2000-01, 7-for-32 (.219). Totals, 90-for-248 (.363).

WNBA REGULAR-SEASON RECORD

Season Team	G	Min.	FGM	FGA	Pct.	FTM	FTA	Pct.	REBOUNDS Off.	Def.	Tot.	Ast.	St.	Blk.	TO	Pts.	AVERAGES RPG	APG	PPG
2001—Minnesota	32	725	64	184	.348	47	76	.618	42	76	118	62	27	29	65	183	3.7	1.9	5.7
2002—Charlotte	29	392	33	82	.402	25	36	.694	32	59	91	18	13	15	27	95	3.1	0.6	3.3
2003—Charlotte	14	44	3	8	.375	3	4	.750	2	2	4	3	0	0	2	9	0.3	0.2	0.6
Totals	75	1161	100	274	.365	75	116	.647	76	137	213	83	40	44	94	287	2.8	1.1	3.8

Three-point field goals: 2001, 8-for-29 (.276). 2002, 4-for-11 (.364). Totals, 12-for-40 (.300). Personal fouls/disqualifications: 2001, 101/2. 2002, 61/1. Totals, 168/3.

WNBA PLAYOFF RECORD

Season Team	G	Min.	FGM	FGA	Pct.	FTM	FTA	Pct.	REBOUNDS Off.	Def.	Tot.	Ast.	St.	Blk.	TO	Pts.	AVERAGES RPG	APG	PPG
2002—Charlotte	2	31	7	8	.875	2	4	.500	2	5	7	1	0	1	3	17	3.5	0.5	8.5
Totals	2	31	7	8	.875	2	4	.500	2	5	7	1	0	1	3	17	3.5	0.5	8.5

Three-point field goals: 2002, 1-for-1. Totals, 1-for-1 (1.000). Personal fouls/disqualifications: 2002, 6/0. Totals, 6/0.

BURGESS, ANNIE   G   MYSTICS

PERSONAL: Born November 3, 1969, in Port Moresby, Papua, New Guinea ... 5-7/141 (1.70 m/64 kg). ... **Full name:** Annie Lilian Burgess.
TRANSACTIONS/CAREER NOTES: Signed by WNBA and assigned to Minnesota, May 12, 1999. ... Traded by Minnesota to Washington for the 28th pick in the 2001 WNBA Draft, April 17, 2001.

WNBA REGULAR-SEASON RECORD

Season Team	G	Min.	FGM	FGA	Pct.	FTM	FTA	Pct.	REBOUNDS Off.	Def.	Tot.	Ast.	St.	Blk.	TO	Pts.	AVERAGES RPG	APG	PPG
1999—Minnesota	25	333	23	66	.348	2	8	.250	14	24	38	36	8	0	20	59	1.5	1.4	2.4
2000—Minnesota								Did not play											
2001—Washington ...	31	731	47	141	.333	16	27	.593	27	49	76	88	26	2	60	124	2.5	2.8	4.0
2002—Washington ...	26	632	39	101	.386	35	45	.778	16	46	62	93	34	4	41	125	2.4	3.6	4.8
2003—Washington ...	34	841	50	134	.373	15	25	.600	24	55	79	112	27	1	52	131	2.3	3.3	3.9
Totals	116	2537	159	442	.360	68	105	.648	81	174	255	329	95	7	173	439	2.2	2.8	3.8

Three-point field goals: 1999, 11-for-24 (.458). 2001, 14-for-47 (.298). 2002, 12-for-33 (.364). 2003, 16-for-58 (.276). Totals, 53-for-162 (.327).
Personal fouls/disqualifications: 1999, 19/0. 2001, 45/0. 2002, 39/0. 2003, 47/1. Totals, 150/1.

WNBA PLAYOFF RECORD

Season Team	G	Min.	FGM	FGA	Pct.	FTM	FTA	Pct.	REBOUNDS Off.	Def.	Tot.	Ast.	St.	Blk.	TO	Pts.	AVERAGES RPG	APG	PPG
2002—Washington ...	5	160	11	29	.379	6	9	.667	7	8	15	27	2	0	10	30	3.0	5.4	6.0
Totals	5	160	11	29	.379	6	9	.667	7	8	15	27	2	0	10	30	3.0	5.4	6.0

Three-point field goals: 2002, 2-for-8 (.250). Totals, 2-for-8 (.250).
Personal fouls/disqualifications: 2002, 4/0. Totals, 4/0.

OLYMPICS

NOTES: Member of silver medal-winning Australian Olympic Team (2000).

Season Team	G	Min.	FGM	FGA	Pct.	FTM	FTA	Pct.	Reb.	Ast.	Pts.	AVERAGES RPG	APG	PPG
2000—Australia......................	8	107	9	25	.360	2	4	.500	15	13	22	1.9	1.6	2.8
Totals	8	107	9	25	.360	2	4	.500	15	13	22	1.9	1.6	2.8

Three-point field goals: 2000, 2-for-4 (.500).

BURRAS, ALISA   F   STORM

PERSONAL: Born June 23, 1975, in Chicago, Ill. ... 6-3/218. (1.91 m/99 kg). ... **Full name:** Alisa Marzatte Burras.
HIGH SCHOOL: John Marshall (Chicago, Ill.).
COLLEGE: Louisiana Tech.
TRANSACTIONS/CAREER NOTES: Signed by the WNBA and assigned to Cleveland, May 11, 1999. ... Selected by Portland in first round (4th overall) of 2000 WNBA Expansion Draft, December 15, 1999. ... Selected in the first round (ninth overall) of the 2003 WNBA Dispersal Draft by the Seattle Storm.

COLLEGIATE RECORD

NOTES: Associated Press All-America second team (1998). ... Kodak All-America Honorable Mention (1998). ... Kodak Junior College All-America (1996).

Season Team	G	Min.	FGM	FGA	Pct.	FTM	FTA	Pct.	Reb.	Ast.	Pts.	AVERAGES RPG	APG	PPG
96-97—Louisiana Tech	35	...	272	452	.602	93	162	.574	333	17	637	9.5	0.5	18.2

B

97-98—Louisiana Tech	35	...	205	339	.605	87	150	.580	283	25	497	8.1	0.7	14.2
Totals	70	...	477	791	.603	180	312	.577	616	42	1134	8.8	0.6	16.2

ABL REGULAR-SEASON RECORD

Season Team	G	Min.	FGM	FGA	Pct.	FTM	FTA	Pct.	Reb.	Ast.	Pts.	AVERAGES		
												RPG	APG	PPG
98-99—Colorado	13	...	36	74	.486	16	23	.696	52	2	88	4.0	0.2	6.8
Totals	13	...	36	74	.486	16	23	.696	52	2	88	4.0	0.2	6.8

Three-point field goals: 1998-99, 0-for-1.

WNBA REGULAR-SEASON RECORD

Season Team	G	Min.	FGM	FGA	Pct.	FTM	FTA	Pct.	REBOUNDS			Ast.	St.	Blk.	TO	Pts.	AVERAGES		
									Off.	Def.	Tot.						RPG	APG	PPG
1999—Cleveland	31	563	103	191	.539	26	47	.553	40	84	124	17	17	10	38	232	4.0	0.5	7.5
2000—Portland	21	314	64	109	.587	31	41	.756	20	54	74	6	3	7	36	159	3.5	0.3	7.6
2001—Portland	26	272	44	83	.530	18	31	.581	22	37	59	10	5	3	30	106	2.3	0.4	4.1
2002—Portland	32	633	117	186	.629	44	52	.846	52	95	147	7	10	7	49	278	4.6	0.2	8.7
2003—Seattle	27	270	35	75	.467	19	27	.704	27	34	61	5	5	5	25	89	2.3	0.2	3.3
Totals	137	2052	363	644	.564	138	198	.697	161	304	465	45	40	32	178	864	3.4	0.3	6.3

C

BURSE, JANELL   C   STORM

PERSONAL: Born May 19, 1979, in New Orleans, La. ... 6-5/199. (1.96 m/90 kg). ... **FULL NAME:** Janell Latrice Burse.
HIGH SCHOOL: Redeemer-Seton (New Orleans).
COLLEGE: Tulane.
TRANSACTIONS/CAREER NOTES: Selected by Minnesota in second round (28th overall) of WNBA Draft, April 20, 2001.

COLLEGIATE RECORD

Season Team	G	Min.	FGM	FGA	Pct.	FTM	FTA	Pct.	Reb.	Ast.	Pts.	AVERAGES		
												RPG	APG	PPG
97-98—Tulane	22	186	37	78	.474	19	41	.463	66	5	93	3.0	0.2	4.2
98-99—Tulane	30	455	133	237	.561	58	104	.558	148	10	324	4.9	0.3	10.8
99-00—Tulane	32	913	233	392	.594	139	228	.610	315	26	605	9.8	0.8	18.9
00-01—Tulane	32	905	233	391	.596	136	252	.540	342	30	603	10.7	0.9	18.8
Totals	116	2459	636	1098	.579	352	625	.563	871	71	1625	7.5	0.6	14.0

Three-point field goals: 2000-01, 1-for-1 (1.000).

WNBA REGULAR-SEASON RECORD

Season Team	G	Min.	FGM	FGA	Pct.	FTM	FTA	Pct.	REBOUNDS			Ast.	St.	Blk.	TO	Pts.	AVERAGES		
									Off.	Def.	Tot.						RPG	APG	PPG
2001—Minnesota	20	169	16	48	.333	15	20	.750	23	19	42	5	2	15	20	47	2.1	0.3	2.4
2002—Minnesota	31	344	31	83	.373	21	36	.583	29	31	60	7	7	13	18	83	1.9	0.2	2.7
2003—Minnesota	29	438	76	155	.490	54	70	.771	40	68	108	19	13	28	42	206	3.7	0.7	7.1
Totals	80	951	123	286	.430	90	126	.714	92	118	210	31	22	56	80	336	2.6	0.4	4.2

Three-point field goals: 2001, 0-for-1. 2002, 0-for-1. 2003, 0-for-2. Totals, 0-for-4.
Personal fouls/disqualifications: 2001, 20/0. 2002, 60/0. 2003, 81/2. Totals, 161/2.

WNBA PLAYOFF RECORD

Season Team	G	Min.	FGM	FGA	Pct.	FTM	FTA	Pct.	REBOUNDS			Ast.	St.	Blk.	TO	Pts.	AVERAGES		
									Off.	Def.	Tot.						RPG	APG	PPG
2003—Minnesota	3	42	6	18	.333	4	6	.667	2	7	9	2	4	2	3	16	3.0	0.7	5.3
Totals	3	42	6	18	.333	4	6	.667	2	7	9	2	4	2	3	16	3.0	0.7	5.3

CAMPBELL, EDNA   G   MONARCHS

PERSONAL: Born November 26, 1968, in Philadelphia, Pa. ... 5-8/152 (1.73 m/69 kg). ... **Full name:** Edna L. Campbell.
HIGH SCHOOL: Allderdice (Pittsburgh, Pa.).
COLLEGE: Texas.
TRANSACTIONS/CAREER NOTES: Selected by Phoenix in first round (10th overall) of WNBA Draft, May 4, 1999. ... Seleted by Seattle in first round (2nd overall) of WNBA 2000 Expansion Draft, December 15, 1999. ... Traded to Sacramento with a first-round pick in the 2002 WNBA Draft for F Katy Steding and a second-round pick in the 2002 WNBA Draft, April 24, 2001.

COLLEGIATE RECORD

Season Team	G	Min.	FGM	FGA	Pct.	FTM	FTA	Pct.	Reb.	Ast.	Pts.	AVERAGES		
												RPG	APG	PPG
86-87—Maryland	29	...	201	399	.504	64	87	.736	90	86	466	3.1	3.0	16.1
87-88—Maryland	32	...	123	261	.471	41	56	.732	153	94	287	4.8	2.9	9.0
89-90—Texas	29	...	180	318	.566	72	95	.758	107	57	432	3.7	2.0	14.9
90-91—Texas	26	...	181	324	.559	69	86	.802	99	69	434	3.8	2.7	16.7
Totals	116	...	685	1302	.526	246	324	.759	449	306	1619	3.9	2.6	14.0

Three-point field goals: 1990-91, 3-for-7 (.429).

ABL REGULAR-SEASON RECORD

												AVERAGES		
Season Team	G	Min.	FGM	FGA	Pct.	FTM	FTA	Pct.	Reb.	Ast.	Pts.	RPG	APG	PPG
96-97—Colorado....................	40	...	227	506	.449	62	78	.795	189	109	566	4.7	2.7	14.2
97-98—Colorado....................	44	...	233	545	.428	80	94	.851	126	109	613	2.9	2.5	13.9
98-99—Colorado....................	13	...	75	189	.397	38	41	.927	40	37	225	3.1	2.8	17.3
Totals	97	...	535	1240	.431	180	213	.845	355	255	1404	3.7	2.6	14.5

Three-point field goals: 1996-97, 50-for-124 (.403). 1997-98, 67-for-167 (.401). 1998-99, 37-for-85 (.435). Totals, 154-for-376 (.410)

WNBA REGULAR-SEASON RECORD

NOTES: Kim Perrot Sportsmanship Award (2003).

								REBOUNDS							AVERAGES		
Season Team	G	Min.	FGM	FGA	Pct.	FTM	FTA	Pct.	Off.	Def.	Tot.	Ast.	St.	Blk.	TO	Pts.	RPG APG PPG
1999—Phoenix.........	28	750	95	261	.364	40	56	.714	11	42	53	37	25	10	48	268	1.9 1.3 9.6
2000—Seattle...........	16	510	84	215	.391	41	58	.707	8	26	34	37	19	4	40	222	2.1 2.3 13.9
2001—Sacramento....	32	854	92	244	.377	33	43	.767	11	74	85	74	19	9	64	260	2.7 2.3 8.1
2002—Sacramento....	1	12	2	5	.400	0	0	...	0	1	1	0	1	0	0	4	1.0 0.0 4.0
2003—Sacramento....	34	724	98	244	.402	25	33	.758	17	53	70	43	21	5	43	267	2.1 1.3 7.9
Totals.................	111	2850	371	969	.383	139	190	.732	47	196	243	191	85	28	195	1021	2.2 1.7 9.2

Three-point field goals: 1999, 38-for-101 (.376). 2000, 13-for-49 (.265). 2001, 43-for-94 (.457). 2002, 0-for-2. 2003, 46-for-111 (.414). Totals, 140-for-357 (.392)

Personal fouls/disqualifications: 1999, 53/0. 2000, 35/0. 2001, 45/0. 2002, 0/0. 2003, 42/0. Totals, 175/0.

WNBA PLAYOFF RECORD

								REBOUNDS							AVERAGES		
Season Team	G	Min.	FGM	FGA	Pct.	FTM	FTA	Pct.	Off.	Def.	Tot.	Ast.	St.	Blk.	TO	Pts.	RPG APG PPG
2001—Sacramento....	5	115	11	31	.355	2	3	.667	4	7	11	11	5	1	5	28	2.2 2.2 5.6
2003—Sacramento....	6	148	17	36	.472	2	2	1.000	1	3	4	11	1	0	8	40	0.7 1.8 6.7
Totals.................	11	263	28	67	.418	4	5	.800	5	10	15	22	6	1	13	68	1.4 2.0 6.2

Three-point field goals: 2001, 4-for-9 (.444). 2003, 4-for-16 (.250). Totals, 8-for-25 (.320).
Personal fouls/disqualifications: 2001, 9/0. 2003, 11/0. Totals, 20/0.

CANTY, DOMINIQUE G/F   COMETS

PERSONAL: Born March 2, 1977, in Chicago, Ill. ... 5-9/162. (1.75 m/73 kg). ... **Full name:** Dominique Danyell Canty.
HIGH SCHOOL: Whitney Young (Chicago, Ill.).
COLLEGE: Alabama.
TRANSACTIONS/CAREER NOTES: Selected by Detroit in third round (29th overall) of WNBA Draft, May 4, 1999. ... Traded by Detroit to Houston for the draft rights to Allison Curtin, April 28, 2003.

COLLEGIATE RECORD

NOTES: Associated Press All-America first team (1999) and second team (1998).

												AVERAGES		
Season Team	G	Min.	FGM	FGA	Pct.	FTM	FTA	Pct.	Reb.	Ast.	Pts.	RPG	APG	PPG
95-96—Alabama	31	...	176	332	.530	100	151	.662	210	75	452	6.8	2.4	14.6
96-97—Alabama	31	...	177	345	.513	144	218	.661	226	90	498	7.3	2.9	16.1
97-98—Alabama	34	...	262	506	.518	203	270	.752	241	164	732	7.1	4.8	21.5
98-99—Alabama	31	...	213	445	.479	181	236	.767	232	130	612	7.5	4.2	19.7
Totals	127	...	828	1628	.509	628	875	.718	909	459	2294	7.2	3.6	18.1

Three-point field goals: 1995-96, 0-for-7. 1996-97, 0-for-5. 1997-98, 5-for-24 (.208). 1998-99, 5-for-16 (.313). Totals, 10-for-52 (.192)

WNBA REGULAR-SEASON RECORD

								REBOUNDS							AVERAGES		
Season Team	G	Min.	FGM	FGA	Pct.	FTM	FTA	Pct.	Off.	Def.	Tot.	Ast.	St.	Blk.	TO	Pts.	RPG APG PPG
1999—Detroit	26	646	76	229	.332	94	136	.691	35	45	80	38	26	1	45	249	3.1 1.5 9.6
2000—Detroit	28	784	83	203	.409	91	131	.695	31	39	70	82	49	5	51	257	2.5 2.9 9.2
2001—Detroit	32	625	70	193	.363	56	74	.757	45	38	83	70	31	1	55	197	2.6 2.2 6.2
2002—Detroit	28	625	52	154	.338	55	76	.724	24	45	69	83	21	4	56	160	2.5 3.0 5.7
2003—Houston	32	648	55	145	.379	62	93	.667	36	64	100	56	22	1	49	172	3.1 1.8 5.4
Totals.................	146	3328	336	924	.364	358	510	.702	171	231	402	329	149	12	256	1035	2.8 2.3 7.1

Three-point field goals: 1999, 3-for-17 (.176). 2000, 0-for-5. 2001, 1-for-5 (.200). 2002, 1-for-5 (.200). 2003, 0-for-1. Totals, 5-for-33 (.152)

Personal fouls/disqualifications: 1999, 57/1. 2000, 64/0. 2001, 69/0. 2002, 59/0. 2003, 62/0. Totals, 311/1.

WNBA PLAYOFF RECORD

								REBOUNDS							AVERAGES		
Season Team	G	Min.	FGM	FGA	Pct.	FTM	FTA	Pct.	Off.	Def.	Tot.	Ast.	St.	Blk.	TO	Pts.	RPG APG PPG
1999—Detroit	1	21	2	6	.333	2	2	1.000	1	2	3	1	1	0	2	6	3.0 1.0 6.0
2003—Houston	3	48	3	9	.333	5	8	.625	7	4	11	5	1	0	3	11	3.7 1.7 3.7
Totals.................	4	69	5	15	.333	7	10	.700	8	6	14	6	2	0	5	17	3.5 1.5 4.3

CASH, SWIN   F   SHOCK

PERSONAL: Born September 22, 1979, in McKeesport, Pa. ... 6-2/162 (1.88 m/73 kg). ... **Full name:** Swintayla Marie Cash.
HIGH SCHOOL: McKeesport (Pa.).
COLLEGE: Connecticut.
TRANSACTIONS/CAREER NOTES: Selected by Detroit in first round (second overall) of WNBA Draft, April 19, 2002.
MISCELLANEOUS: Member of WNBA Championship Team (2003).

C

COLLEGIATE RECORD

NOTES: Member of NCAA Division I Championship Team (2002, 2000). ... Kodak All-America first team (2002).

Season Team	G	Min.	FGM	FGA	Pct.	FTM	FTA	Pct.	Reb.	Ast.	Pts.	RPG	APG	PPG
98-99—Connecticut	22	332	75	127	.591	59	92	.641	115	14	209	5.2	0.6	9.5
99-00—Connecticut	37	768	141	265	.532	85	132	.644	196	24	367	5.3	0.6	9.9
00-01—Connecticut	35	832	162	292	.555	103	174	.592	263	51	427	7.5	1.5	12.2
01-02—Connecticut	39	1085	220	401	.549	140	200	.700	336	86	580	8.6	2.2	14.9
Totals	133	3017	598	1085	.551	387	598	.647	910	175	1583	6.8	1.3	11.9

Three-point field goals: 2001-02, 0-for-1.

WNBA REGULAR-SEASON RECORD

NOTES: All-WNBA second team (2003).

Season Team	G	Min.	FGM	FGA	Pct.	FTM	FTA	Pct.	Off.	Def.	Tot.	Ast.	St.	Blk.	TO	Pts.	RPG	APG	PPG
2002—Detroit	32	1079	144	353	.408	173	227	.762	77	145	222	86	37	31	100	474	6.9	2.7	14.8
2003—Detroit	33	1097	195	430	.453	146	214	.682	65	128	193	119	43	23	108	548	5.8	3.6	16.6
Totals	65	2176	339	783	.433	319	441	.723	142	273	415	205	80	54	208	1022	6.4	3.2	15.7

Three-point field goals: 2002, 13-for-63 (.206). 2003, 12-for-40 (.300). Totals, 25-for-103 (.243).
Personal fouls/disqualifications: 2002, 85/0. 2003, 76/0. Totals, 161/0.

WNBA PLAYOFF RECORD

Season Team	G	Min.	FGM	FGA	Pct.	FTM	FTA	Pct.	Off.	Def.	Tot.	Ast.	St.	Blk.	TO	Pts.	RPG	APG	PPG
2003—Detroit	8	289	43	104	.413	42	52	.808	24	27	51	35	4	5	28	130	6.4	4.4	16.3
Totals	8	289	43	104	.413	42	52	.808	24	27	51	35	4	5	28	130	6.4	4.4	16.3

Three-point field goals: 2003, 2-for-10 (.200). Totals, 2-for-10 (.200).
Personal fouls/disqualifications: 2003, 21/0. Totals, 21/0.

WNBA ALL-STAR GAME RECORD

Season Team	Min.	FGM	FGA	Pct.	FTM	FTA	Pct.	Off.	Def.	Tot.	Ast.	PF	Dq.	St.	Blk.	TO	Pts.
2003—Detroit	19	3	13	.231	0	0	...	1	1	2	1	1	0	2	0	...	6
Totals	19	3	13	.231	0	0	...	1	1	2	1	1	0	2	0	1	6

Three-point field goals: 2003, 0-for-4. Totals, 0-for-4.

CASTRO MARQUES, IZIANE   G   MERCURY

PERSONAL: Born March 13, 1982, in Sao Luis, Brazil ... 6-0/140. (1.83 m/64 kg).
TRANSACTIONS/CAREER NOTES: Signed by the WNBA and added by Miami, April 25, 2002. ... Became an unrestricted free agent when the Miami Sol ceased operation during the 2002-03 offseason. ... Signed by the Phoenix Mercury as a free agent, April 15, 2003.
MISCELLANEOUS: Member of Brazilian National Team.

WNBA REGULAR-SEASON RECORD

Season Team	G	Min.	FGM	FGA	Pct.	FTM	FTA	Pct.	Off.	Def.	Tot.	Ast.	St.	Blk.	TO	Pts.	RPG	APG	PPG
2002—Miami	19	182	24	72	.333	17	25	.680	7	10	17	7	7	0	18	66	0.9	0.4	3.5
2003—Phoenix	16	178	25	71	.352	11	18	.611	6	6	12	9	6	1	10	69	0.8	0.6	4.3
Totals	35	360	49	143	.343	28	43	.651	13	16	29	16	13	1	28	135	0.8	0.5	3.9

Three-point field goals: 2002, 1-for-17 (.059). 2003, 8-for-27 (.296). Totals, 9-for-44 (.205).
Personal fouls/disqualifications: 2002, 22/0. 2003, 11/0. Totals, 33/0.

CATCHINGS, TAMIKA   F   FEVER

PERSONAL: Born July 21, 1979, in Stratford, N.J. ... 6-0/166 (1.83 m/75 kg). ... **Full name:** Tamika Devonne Catchings.
HIGH SCHOOL: Duncanville (Duncanville, Texas).
COLLEGE: Tennessee.
TRANSACTIONS/CAREER NOTES: Selected by Indiana in first round (third overall) of WNBA Draft, April 20, 2001.

COLLEGIATE RECORD

NOTES: Member of NCAA Division I championship team (1998). ... Naismith Award winner (2000). ... Kodak All-America first team (1998, 1999, 2000, 2001).

												AVERAGES		
Season Team	G	Min.	FGM	FGA	Pct.	FTM	FTA	Pct.	Reb.	Ast.	Pts.	RPG	APG	PPG
97-98—Tennessee	39	1123	253	471	.537	165	217	.760	313	92	711	8.0	2.4	18.2
98-99—Tennessee	34	991	205	400	.513	134	173	.775	249	95	563	7.3	2.8	16.6
99-00—Tennessee	37	1143	209	440	.475	122	159	.767	292	101	580	7.9	2.7	15.7
00-01—Tennessee	17	465	93	195	.477	50	62	.806	150	50	259	8.8	2.9	15.2
Totals	127	3722	760	1506	.505	471	611	.771	1004	338	2113	7.9	2.7	16.6

Three-point field goals: 1997-98, 40-for-110 (.364). 1998-99, 19-for-68 (.279). 1999-000, 40-for-121 (.331). 2000-01, 23-for-67 (.343). Totals, 122-for-366 (.333).

WNBA REGULAR-SEASON RECORD

NOTES: WNBA Rookie of the Year (2002). ... All-WNBA first team (2002, 2003). ... Led WNBA in steals (2.94 spg) in 2002.

									REBOUNDS								AVERAGES		
Season Team	G	Min.	FGM	FGA	Pct.	FTM	FTA	Pct.	Off.	Def.	Tot.	Ast.	St.	Blk.	TO	Pts.	RPG	APG	PPG
2001—Indiana..........						Did not play—injured.													
2002—Indiana..........	32	1167	184	439	.419	150	184	.815	92	184	276	118	94	43	82	594	8.6	3.7	18.6
2003—Indiana..........	34	1210	221	512	.432	155	183	.847	82	190	272	114	72	35	102	671	8.0	3.4	19.7
Totals..................	66	2377	405	951	.426	305	367	.831	174	374	548	232	166	78	184	1265	8.3	3.5	19.2

Three-point field goals: 2002, 76-for-193 (.394). 2003, 74-for-191 (.387). Totals, 150-for-384 (.391).
Personal fouls/disqualifications: 2002, 105/2. 2003, 122/2. Totals, 227/4.

WNBA PLAYOFF RECORD

									REBOUNDS								AVERAGES		
Season Team	G	Min.	FGM	FGA	Pct.	FTM	FTA	Pct.	Off.	Def.	Tot.	Ast.	St.	Blk.	TO	Pts.	RPG	APG	PPG
2002—Indiana..........	3	103	22	45	.489	9	11	.818	12	20	32	7	4	1	11	61	10.7	2.3	20.3
Totals..................	3	103	22	45	.489	9	11	.818	12	20	32	7	4	1	11	61	10.7	2.3	20.3

Three-point field goals: 2002, 8-for-21 (.381). Totals, 8-for-21 (.381).
Personal fouls/disqualifications: 2002, 7/0. Totals, 7/0.

WNBA ALL-STAR GAME RECORD

								REBOUNDS								
Season Team	Min.	FGM	FGA	Pct.	FTM	FTA	Pct.	Off.	Def.	Tot.	Ast.	PF	Dq.	St.	Blk.	TO	Pts.
2002 —Indiana...........	21	4	12	.333	2	2	1.000	3	6	9	1	3	0	1	4	...	12
2003 —Indiana...........	30	6	15	.400	1	2	.500	2	2	4	2	4	0	2	0	...	17
Totals.................	51	10	27	.370	3	4	.750	5	8	13	3	7	0	3	4	6	29

Three-point field goals: 2002, 2-for-5 (.400). 2003, 4-for-6 (.667). Totals, 6-for-11 (.545).

CHRISTENSEN, KAYTE   F   MERCURY

PERSONAL: Born November 16, 1980, in Lakeview, Ore. ... 6-3/185. (1.91 m/84 kg). ... **Full name:** Kayte Lauren Christensen.
HIGH SCHOOL: Modoc (Calif.).
COLLEGE: California-Santa Barbara.
TRANSACTIONS/CAREER NOTES: Selected by Phoenix in third round (40th overall) of WNBA Draft, April 19, 2002.

COLLEGIATE RECORD

												AVERAGES		
Season Team	G	Min.	FGM	FGA	Pct.	FTM	FTA	Pct.	Reb.	Ast.	Pts.	RPG	APG	PPG
98-99—Cal.-Santa Barbara..........	30	508	87	158	.551	64	103	.621	167	12	239	5.6	0.4	8.0
99-00—Cal.-Santa Barbara	18	367	78	138	.565	32	63	.508	113	7	188	6.3	0.4	10.4
00-01—Cal.-Santa Barbara	31	786	163	297	.549	100	150	.667	236	27	426	7.6	0.9	13.7
01-02—Cal.-Santa Barbara	32	834	184	339	.543	97	148	.655	291	27	465	9.1	0.8	14.5
Totals	111	2495	512	932	.549	293	464	.631	807	73	1318	7.3	0.7	11.9

Three-point field goals: 1998-99, 1-for-1. 1999-000, 0-for-2. 2000-01, 0-for-4. 2001-02, 0-for-2. Totals, 1-for-9 (.111)

WNBA REGULAR-SEASON RECORD

									REBOUNDS								AVERAGES		
Season Team	G	Min.	FGM	FGA	Pct.	FTM	FTA	Pct.	Off.	Def.	Tot.	Ast.	St.	Blk.	TO	Pts.	RPG	APG	PPG
2002—Phoenix........	30	413	48	95	.505	24	35	.686	39	41	80	15	24	13	32	120	2.7	0.5	4.0
2003—Phoenix........	30	659	78	161	.484	50	83	.602	61	65	126	16	25	16	39	206	4.2	0.5	6.9
Totals.................	60	1072	126	256	.492	74	118	.627	100	106	206	31	49	29	71	326	3.4	0.5	5.4

Three-point field goals: 2002, 0-for-1. Totals, 0-for-1.
Personal fouls/disqualifications: 2002, 73/1. Totals, 177/5.

COLEMAN, COURTNEY   C   SUN

PERSONAL: Born April 13, 1981, in Cincinnati. ... 6-1/170. (1.85 m/77 kg). ... **Full name:** Courtney Michelle Coleman.
HIGH SCHOOL: Hughes (Cincinnati).
COLLEGE: Ohio State.
TRANSACTIONS/CAREER NOTES: Selected by Connecticut in second round (13th overall) of WNBA Draft, April 25, 2003.

NOTES: Second Team All-Big Ten (2003, 2002, 2001). ... Chosen to participate in the 2003 WBCA All-Star Challenge.

Season Team	G	Min.	FGM	FGA	Pct.	FTM	FTA	Pct.	Reb.	Ast.	Pts.	AVERAGES RPG	APG	PPG
99-00—Ohio State	28	428	50	100	.500	45	75	.600	...	3	145	3.3	0.1	5.2
00-01—Ohio State	33	981	182	314	.580	123	209	.589	...	16	487	7.5	0.5	14.8
01-02—Ohio State	28	896	180	296	.608	98	183	.536	...	27	458	7.8	1.0	16.4
02-03—Ohio State	32	1020	184	278	.662	82	137	.599	...	49	450	6.7	1.5	14.1
Totals	121	3325	596	988	.603	348	604	.576	0	95	1540	0.0	0.8	12.7

Three-point field goals: 2002-03, 0-for-1.

WNBA REGULAR-SEASON RECORD

Season Team	G	Min.	FGM	FGA	Pct.	FTM	FTA	Pct.	REBOUNDS Off.	Def.	Tot.	Ast.	St.	Blk.	TO	Pts.	AVERAGES RPG	APG	PPG
2003—Connecticut	20	141	11	20	.550	14	30	.467	8	14	22	1	8	2	13	36	1.1	0.1	1.8
Totals	20	141	11	20	.550	14	30	.467	8	14	22	1	8	2	13	36	1.1	0.1	1.8

COOPER, CAMILLE   C

PERSONAL: Born February 5, 1979, in Georgetown, Ky. ... 6-4/176 (1.93 m/80 kg). ... **Full name:** Camille Kaye Cooper.
HIGH SCHOOL: Scott County (Georgetown, Ky.).
COLLEGE: Purdue.
TRANSACTIONS/CAREER NOTES: Selected by Los Angeles in first round (16th overall) of WNBA Draft, April 20, 2001. ... Traded by Los Angeles to New York for a second-round pick in the 2002 WNBA Draft, June 5, 2001. ... Waived by New York May 21, 2003.

COLLEGIATE RECORD

NOTES: Member of NCAA Division I championship team (1999).

Season Team	G	Min.	FGM	FGA	Pct.	FTM	FTA	Pct.	Reb.	Ast.	Pts.	AVERAGES RPG	APG	PPG
97-98—Purdue	33	552	87	146	.596	45	111	.405	108	4	219	3.3	0.1	6.6
98-99—Purdue	35	792	149	232	.642	43	86	.500	171	5	341	4.9	0.1	9.7
99-00—Purdue	31	885	196	337	.582	82	134	.612	233	5	474	7.5	0.2	15.3
00-01—Purdue	38	1053	225	366	.615	91	155	.587	248	22	541	6.5	0.6	14.2
Totals	137	3282	657	1081	.608	261	486	.537	760	36	1575	5.5	0.3	11.5

WNBA REGULAR-SEASON RECORD

Season Team	G	Min.	FGM	FGA	Pct.	FTM	FTA	Pct.	REBOUNDS Off.	Def.	Tot.	Ast.	St.	Blk.	TO	Pts.	AVERAGES RPG	APG	PPG
2001—New York	4	51	8	12	.667	10	13	.769	7	4	11	1	0	2	3	26	2.8	0.3	6.5
2002—New York	23	119	11	28	.393	5	8	.625	5	11	16	3	4	5	10	27	0.7	0.1	1.2
Totals	27	170	19	40	.475	15	21	.714	12	15	27	4	4	7	13	53	1.0	0.1	2.0

WNBA PLAYOFF RECORD

Season Team	G	Min.	FGM	FGA	Pct.	FTM	FTA	Pct.	REBOUNDS Off.	Def.	Tot.	Ast.	St.	Blk.	TO	Pts.	AVERAGES RPG	APG	PPG
2001—New York	3	8	0	2	.000	0	0	...	0	1	1	0	0	0	0	0	0.3	0.0	0.0
2002—New York	3	15	1	2	.500	1	2	.500	1	1	2	0	2	0	2	3	0.7	0.0	1.0
Totals	6	23	1	4	.250	1	2	.500	1	2	3	0	2	0	2	3	0.5	0.0	0.5

CRAWLEY, SYLVIA   C   SILVER STARS

PERSONAL: Born September 27, 1972, in Wintersville, Ohio ... 6-5/187. (1.96 m/85 kg). ... **Full name:** Sylvia Yvonne Crawley.
HIGH SCHOOL: Steubenville (Steubenville, Ohio).
COLLEGE: North Carolina.
TRANSACTIONS/CAREER NOTES: Signed by the WNBA and assigned to Portland, May 2, 2000. ... Selected by the Indiana Fever in the 2003 WNBA Dispersal Draft on April 23, 2003. ... Traded along with Gwen Jackson in exchange for Natalie Williams and Coretta Brown to the San Antonio Silver Stars on May 1, 2003.

COLLEGIATE RECORD

NOTES: Member of NCAA National Championship team (1994).

Season Team	G	Min.	FGM	FGA	Pct.	FTM	FTA	Pct.	Reb.	Ast.	Pts.	AVERAGES RPG	APG	PPG
90-91—North Carolina	28	...	48	104	.462	15	46	.326	100	8	111	3.6	0.3	4.0
91-92—North Carolina	31	...	110	240	.458	34	63	.540	137	7	254	4.4	0.2	8.2
92-93—North Carolina	30	...	137	255	.537	42	63	.667	163	15	316	5.4	0.5	10.5
93-94—North Carolina	35	...	195	354	.551	87	139	.626	182	32	477	5.2	0.9	13.6
Totals	124	...	490	953	.514	178	311	.572	582	62	1158	4.7	0.5	9.3

Three-point field goals: 1990-91, 0-for-1.

ABL REGULAR-SEASON RECORD

NOTES: Played for Portland Power and Colorado Xplosion of ABL. ... Won first ABL Slam Dunk Contest at 1998 All-Star Weekend.

Season Team	G	Min.	FGM	FGA	Pct.	FTM	FTA	Pct.	Reb.	Ast.	Pts.	AVERAGES RPG	APG	PPG
96-97—Colorado	40	...	184	385	.478	105	139	.755	223	47	473	5.6	1.2	11.8
97-98—Portland	43	...	68	153	.444	39	57	.684	87	26	175	2.0	0.6	4.1
98-99—Portland	12	...	12	36	.333	4	5	.800	24	2	28	2.0	0.2	2.3
Totals	95	...	264	574	.460	148	201	.736	334	75	676	3.5	0.8	7.1

WNBA REGULAR-SEASON RECORD

Season Team	G	Min.	FGM	FGA	Pct.	FTM	FTA	Pct.	Off.	Def.	Tot.	Ast.	St.	Blk.	TO	Pts.	RPG	APG	PPG
									REBOUNDS								AVERAGES		
2000—Portland	31	930	143	298	.480	71	102	.696	64	121	185	34	29	24	88	357	6.0	1.1	11.5
2001—Portland	32	921	120	267	.449	59	77	.766	63	140	203	54	19	26	61	299	6.3	1.7	9.3
2002—Portland	32	819	114	284	.401	44	63	.698	46	88	134	47	18	37	62	279	4.2	1.5	8.7
2003—San Antonio ...	33	564	50	130	.385	15	22	.682	39	66	105	19	18	19	40	115	3.2	0.6	3.5
Totals.................	128	3234	427	979	.436	189	264	.716	212	415	627	154	84	106	251	1050	4.9	1.2	8.2

Three-point field goals: 2000, 0-for-2. 2001, 0-for-1. 2002, 7-for-17 (.412). Totals, 7-for-20 (.350).
Personal fouls/disqualifications: 2000, 96/2. 2001, 85/3. 2002, 90/0. Totals, 347/6.

CROSS, JAE   G   SHOCK

PERSONAL: Born January 20, 1976, in Wellington, New Zealand ... 5-9/148 (1.75 m/67 kg).
HIGH SCHOOL: Maroochydore (Queensland, Australia).
COLLEGE: Canberra (Canberra, Australia).
TRANSACTIONS/CAREER NOTES: Selected by Detroit in second round (22nd overall) of WNBA Draft, April 20, 2001.

AUSTRALIAN LEAGUE RECORD

Season Team	G	Min.	FGM	FGA	Pct.	FTM	FTA	Pct.	Reb.	Ast.	Pts.	RPG	APG	PPG
													AVERAGES	
00-01—Adelaide AUS	19	...	102	216	.472	52	70	.743	116	59	284	6.1	3.1	14.9
Totals	19	...	102	216	.472	52	70	.743	116	59	284	6.1	3.1	14.9

Three-point field goals: 2000-01, 28-for-66 (.424).

WNBA REGULAR-SEASON RECORD

Season Team	G	Min.	FGM	FGA	Pct.	FTM	FTA	Pct.	Off.	Def.	Tot.	Ast.	St.	Blk.	TO	Pts.	RPG	APG	PPG
									REBOUNDS								AVERAGES		
2001—Detroit	29	625	55	142	.387	26	36	.722	20	43	63	74	31	8	53	169	2.2	2.6	5.8
Totals	29	625	55	142	.387	26	36	.722	20	43	63	74	31	8	53	169	2.2	2.6	5.8

Three-point field goals: 2001, 33-for-88 (.375). Totals, 33-for-88 (.375).
Personal fouls/disqualifications: 2001, 42/0. Totals, 42/0.

CURRY, EDNIESHA   G   MERCURY

PERSONAL: Born July 9, 1979, in Panorama City, Calif. ... 5-6 (1.68 m/ kg).
HIGH SCHOOL: Palmdale (Palmdale, Calif.).
COLLEGE: Oregon.
TRANSACTIONS/CAREER NOTES: Selected by Charlotte in third round (41st overall) of WNBA Draft, April 19, 2002. ... Waived by Charlotte. Waived by Phoenix, May 21, 2003. ... Signed by Phoenix, July 2, 2003.

COLLEGIATE RECORD

Season Team	G	Min.	FGM	FGA	Pct.	FTM	FTA	Pct.	Reb.	Ast.	Pts.	RPG	APG	PPG
													AVERAGES	
97-98—CS Northridge	28	964	167	439	.380	78	117	.667	131	118	477	4.7	4.2	17.0
98-99—CS Northridge	29	876	186	444	.419	95	118	.805	108	92	533	3.7	3.2	18.4
99-00—CS Northridge	16	507	89	241	.369	29	45	.644	56	67	244	3.5	4.2	15.3
01-02—Oregon	29	864	112	280	.400	56	79	.709	95	104	313	3.3	3.6	10.8
Totals	102	3211	554	1404	.395	258	359	.719	390	381	1567	3.8	3.7	15.4

Three-point field goals: 1997-98, 65-for-199 (.327). 1998-99, 66-for-170 (.388). 1999-000, 37-for-123 (.301). 2001-02, 33-for-117 (.282). Totals, 201-for-609 (.330).

WNBA REGULAR-SEASON RECORD

Season Team	G	Min.	FGM	FGA	Pct.	FTM	FTA	Pct.	Off.	Def.	Tot.	Ast.	St.	Blk.	TO	Pts.	RPG	APG	PPG
									REBOUNDS								AVERAGES		
2003—Phoenix.........	20	205	13	35	.371	2	3	.667	1	10	11	24	9	0	15	33	0.6	1.2	1.7
Totals.................	20	205	13	35	.371	2	3	.667	1	10	11	24	9	0	15	33	0.6	1.2	1.7

Three-point field goals: 2003, 5-for-22 (.227). Totals, 5-for-22 (.227).
Personal fouls/disqualifications: 2003, 25/0. Totals, 25/0.

CURTIN, ALLISON   G   SHOCK

PERSONAL: Born March 31, 1980, in Taylorville, Ill. ... 5-11/151 (1.80 m/68 kg). ... **Full name:** Allison Dianne Curtin.
HIGH SCHOOL: Taylorville (Ill.).
COLLEGE: Illinois, then Tulsa.
TRANSACTIONS/CAREER NOTES: Selected by Houston in first round (12th overall) of WNBA Draft, April 25, 2003. ... Traded by Houston to Detroit Shock, April 28, 2003.

NOTES: Associated Press All-America Honorable Mention (2003). ... Named to the 2003 Western Athletics Conference first team and the all-WAC Newcomer squad. ... All Big-Ten First Team (coaches: 2001, 2000; media: 2001). ... All Big-Ten Second Team (media: 2000). ... All Big-Ten Freshman Team (1999). ... Illinois' all-time steals leader (252). ... Finished career at Illinois fifth in career scoring (1,529 points) and fourth in three-pointers attempted.

Season Team	G	Min.	FGM	FGA	Pct.	FTM	FTA	Pct.	Reb.	Ast.	Pts.	RPG	APG	PPG
98-99—Illinois	31	806	126	282	.447	121	146	.829	124	75	400	4.0	2.4	12.9
99-00—Illinois	34	1135	213	453	.470	133	162	.821	194	95	599	5.7	2.8	17.6
00-01—Illinois	33	1122	200	432	.463	84	109	.771	187	141	530	5.7	4.3	16.1
02-03—Tulsa	30	1053	231	516	.448	174	207	.841	227	138	692	7.6	4.6	23.1
Totals	128	4116	770	1683	.458	512	624	.821	732	449	2221	5.7	3.5	17.4

Three-point field goals: 1998-99, 28-for-72 (.389). 1999-000, 40-for-97 (.412). 2000-01, 46-for-114 (.404). 2002-03, 54-for-146 (.370). Totals, 168-for-429 (.392)

DALES-SCHUMAN, STACEY G   MYSTICS

PERSONAL: Born September 6, 1979, in Collingwood, Ontario, Canada ... 6-0/155 (1.83 m/70 kg). ... **FULL NAME:** Stacey Anne Dales-Schuman.
HIGH SCHOOL: Thousand Islands Secondary School (Canada).
COLLEGE: Oklahoma.
TRANSACTIONS/CAREER NOTES: Selected by Washington in first round (third overall) of WNBA Draft, April 19, 2002.
MISCELLANEOUS: Member of Canadian National Team.

COLLEGIATE RECORD

NOTES: Kodak All-American first team (2002, 2001).

Season Team	G	Min.	FGM	FGA	Pct.	FTM	FTA	Pct.	Reb.	Ast.	Pts.	RPG	APG	PPG
98-99—Oklahoma	29	929	129	331	.390	64	97	.660	201	150	346	6.9	5.2	11.9
99-00—Oklahoma	33	1058	153	371	.412	71	115	.617	168	190	420	5.1	5.8	12.7
00-01—Oklahoma	34	1087	209	439	.476	97	147	.660	172	248	543	5.1	7.3	16.0
01-02—Oklahoma	36	1123	228	479	.476	114	145	.786	180	176	611	5.0	4.9	17.0
Totals	132	4197	719	1620	.444	346	504	.687	721	764	1920	5.5	5.8	14.5

Three-point field goals: 1998-99, 24-for-77 (.312). 1999-000, 43-for-122 (.352). 2000-01, 28-for-86 (.326). 2001-02, 41-for-106 (.387). Totals, 136-for-391 (.348).

OLYMPICS

Season Team	G	Min.	FGM	FGA	Pct.	FTM	FTA	Pct.	Reb.	Ast.	Pts.	RPG	APG	PPG
2000—Canada	6	184	31	73	.425	6	10	.600	23	10	71	3.8	1.7	11.8
Totals	6	184	31	73	.425	6	10	.600	23	10	71	3.8	1.7	11.8

Three-point field goals: 2000, 3-for-13 (.231).

WNBA REGULAR-SEASON RECORD

Season Team	G	Min.	FGM	FGA	Pct.	FTM	FTA	Pct.	Off.	Def.	Tot.	Ast.	St.	Blk.	TO	Pts.	RPG	APG	PPG
2002—Washington	31	805	93	230	.404	74	100	.740	26	55	81	84	16	4	68	303	2.6	2.7	9.8
2003—Washington	34	998	122	298	.409	39	55	.709	44	57	101	114	29	12	72	340	3.0	3.4	10.0
Totals	65	1803	215	528	.407	113	155	.729	70	112	182	198	45	16	140	643	2.8	3.0	9.9

Three-point field goals: 2002, 43-for-109 (.394). 2003, 57-for-160 (.356). Totals, 100-for-269 (.372).
Personal fouls/disqualifications: 2002, 79/1. 2003, 97/2. Totals, 176/3.

WNBA PLAYOFF RECORD

Season Team	G	Min.	FGM	FGA	Pct.	FTM	FTA	Pct.	Off.	Def.	Tot.	Ast.	St.	Blk.	TO	Pts.	RPG	APG	PPG
2002—Washington	5	98	13	30	.433	4	4	1.000	5	3	8	16	2	0	5	38	1.6	3.2	7.6
Totals	5	98	13	30	.433	4	4	1.000	5	3	8	16	2	0	5	38	1.6	3.2	7.6

Three-point field goals: 2002, 8-for-18 (.444). Totals, 8-for-18 (.444).
Personal fouls/disqualifications: 2002, 8/0. Totals, 8/0.

WNBA ALL-STAR GAME RECORD

Season Team	Min.	FGM	FGA	Pct.	FTM	FTA	Pct.	Off.	Def.	Tot.	Ast.	PF	Dq.	St.	Blk.	TO	Pts.
2002 —Washington	11	1	5	.200	0	0	...	1	2	3	0	0	0	0	0	...	3
Totals	11	1	5	.200	0	0	...	1	2	3	0	0	0	0	0	0	3

Three-point field goals: 2002, 1-for-3 (.333). Totals, 1-for-3 (.333).

DALEY, GRACE   G

PERSONAL: Born June 26, 1978, in Miami, Fla. ... 5-6/147 (1.68 m/67 kg). ... **Full name:** Grace Elizabeth Daley.
HIGH SCHOOL: Lake Weir (Ocala, Fla.).
COLLEGE: Tulane.
TRANSACTIONS/CAREER NOTES: Selected by Minnesota in first round (fifth overall) of WNBA Draft, April 25, 2000. ... Traded by Minnesota to New York for the 12th pick in 2001 WNBA Draft, September 18, 2000. ... Waived by Phoenix, June 9, 2002. ... Signed by Phoenix, May 5, 2003.

COLLEGIATE RECORD

NOTES: All-Conference USA first team (1998, 1999, 2000). ... Associated Press All-America third team (2000). ... Conference USA Defensive Player of Year (1998). ... Conference USA Player of Year (2000). ... Conference USA record for career steals (289), free throws made (578) attempted (744). ... Kodak/District V All-America (1998, 1999, 2000). ... Led Conference USA scoring in 2000 (21.6 ppg). ... Women's Basketball News Service All-American third team (2000).

Season Team	G	Min.	FGM	FGA	Pct.	FTM	FTA	Pct.	Reb.	Ast.	Pts.	AVERAGES RPG	APG	PPG
96-97—Tulane	32	...	143	289	.495	108	142	.761	127	51	422	4.0	1.6	13.2
97-98—Tulane	28	...	193	376	.513	121	162	.747	122	74	563	4.4	2.6	20.1
98-99—Tulane	30	...	184	359	.513	164	201	.816	156	96	572	5.2	3.2	19.1
99-00—Tulane	32	...	227	465	.488	185	239	.774	189	124	692	5.9	3.9	21.6
Totals	122	...	747	1489	.502	578	744	.777	594	345	2249	4.9	2.8	18.4

Three-point field goals: 1996-97, 38-for-85 (.447). 1997-98, 56-for-152 (.368). 1998-99, 40-for-123 (.325). 1999-000, 53-for-165 (.321). Totals, 187-for-525 (.356).

WNBA REGULAR-SEASON RECORD

Season Team	G	Min.	FGM	FGA	Pct.	FTM	FTA	Pct.	REBOUNDS Off.	Def.	Tot.	Ast.	St.	Blk.	TO	Pts.	AVERAGES RPG	APG	PPG
2000—Minnesota	30	577	57	147	.388	42	65	.646	32	40	72	57	12	0	50	173	2.4	1.9	5.8
2001—New York	15	66	10	21	.476	5	9	.556	3	5	8	10	8	1	7	25	0.5	0.7	1.7
2002—Houston	23	185	16	37	.432	29	47	.617	13	10	23	16	3	1	17	63	1.0	0.7	2.7
2003—Phoenix	3	28	1	5	.200	0	0		1	1	2	3	0	1	3	2	0.7	1.0	0.7
Totals	71	856	84	210	.400	76	121	.628	49	56	105	86	23	3	77	263	1.5	1.2	3.7

Three-point field goals: 2000, 17-for-56 (.304). 2001, 0-for-5. 2002, 2-for-8 (.250). 2003, 0-for-2. Totals, 19-for-71 (.268). Personal fouls/disqualifications: 2000, 49/0. 2001, 12/0. 2002, 15/0. 2003, 2/0. Totals, 78/0.

WNBA PLAYOFF RECORD

Season Team	G	Min.	FGM	FGA	Pct.	FTM	FTA	Pct.	REBOUNDS Off.	Def.	Tot.	Ast.	St.	Blk.	TO	Pts.	AVERAGES RPG	APG	PPG
2001—New York	1	1	0	0	...	0	0	...	0	0	0	0	0	0	1	0	0.0	0.0	0.0
2002—Houston	1	7	0	2	.000	2	2	1.000	2	0	2	0	0	0	1	2	2.0	0.0	2.0
Totals	2	8	0	2	.000	2	2	1.000	2	0	2	0	0	0	2	2	1.0	0.0	1.0

DARLING, HELEN G LYNX

D

PERSONAL: Born August 29, 1978, in Columbus, Ohio ... 5-6/164 (1.68 m/74 kg). ... **Full name:** Helen Marie Darling.

HIGH SCHOOL: Brookhaven (Columbus, Ohio).

COLLEGE: Penn State.

TRANSACTIONS/CAREER NOTES: Selected by Cleveland in second round (17th overall) of WNBA Draft, April 25, 2000. ... Selected by Minnesota in dispersal draft, January 6, 2004.

COLLEGIATE RECORD

NOTES: Kodak All-America first team (2000). ... Naismith Award for small player of year (2000). ... Led NCAA in assists (7.8 apg) in 2000.

Season Team	G	Min.	FGM	FGA	Pct.	FTM	FTA	Pct.	Reb.	Ast.	Pts.	AVERAGES RPG	APG	PPG
96-97—Penn State	27	...	60	199	.302	90	127	.709	118	119	210	4.4	4.4	7.8
97-98—Penn State	34	...	114	288	.396	111	171	.649	178	172	343	5.2	5.1	10.1
98-99—Penn State	30	...	113	289	.391	146	191	.764	175	226	373	5.8	7.5	12.4
99-00—Penn State	35	...	111	280	.396	131	169	.775	201	274	368	5.7	7.8	10.5
Totals	26	...	398	1056	.377	478	658	.726	672	791	1294	5.3	6.3	10.3

Three-point field goals: 1996-97, 0-for-4. 1997-98, 4-for-15 (.267). 1998-99, 1-for-7 (.143). 1999-000, 15-for-52 (.288). Totals, 20-for-78 (.256).

WNBA REGULAR-SEASON RECORD

Season Team	G	Min.	FGM	FGA	Pct.	FTM	FTA	Pct.	REBOUNDS Off.	Def.	Tot.	Ast.	St.	Blk.	TO	Pts.	AVERAGES RPG	APG	PPG
2000—Cleveland	32	556	47	150	.313	48	65	.738	24	39	63	65	37	5	67	155	2.0	2.0	4.8
2001—Cleveland	2	778	59	166	.355	55	72	.764	18	58	76	109	34	4	70	196	2.4	3.4	6.1
2003—Cleveland	34	832	44	143	.308	23	71	.732	25	62	87	128	39	6	74	141	2.6	3.8	4.1
Totals	98	2166	150	459	.327	133	178	.747	67	159	226	302	110	15	211	492	2.3	3.1	5.0

Three-point field goals: 2000, 13-for-38 (.342). 2001, 23-for-70 (.329). Totals, 36-for-108 (.333). Personal fouls/disqualifications: 2000, 52/0. 2001, 59/0. Totals, 111/0.

WNBA PLAYOFF RECORD

Season Team	G	Min.	FGM	FGA	Pct.	FTM	FTA	Pct.	REBOUNDS Off.	Def.	Tot.	Ast.	St.	Blk.	TO	Pts.	AVERAGES RPG	APG	PPG
2000—Cleveland	6	106	9	28	.321	10	14	.714	7	13	20	13	7	0	6	33	3.3	2.2	5.5
2001—Cleveland	3	80	5	27	.185	5	6	.833	5	6	11	19	7	1	5	18	3.7	6.3	6.0
Totals	9	186	14	55	.255	15	20	.750	12	19	31	32	14	1	11	51	3.4	3.6	5.7

Three-point field goals: 2000, 5-for-13 (.385). 2001, 3-for-9 (.333). Totals, 8-for-22 (.364). Personal fouls/disqualifications: 2000, 5/0. 2001, 9/0. Totals, 14/0.

DeFORGE, ANNA   G   MERCURY

PERSONAL: Born April 14, 1976, in Iron Mountain, Mich. ... 5-10/160 (1.78 m/73 kg). ... **Full name:** Anna Louise DeForge.
HIGH SCHOOL: Niagara (Niagara, Wis.).
COLLEGE: Nebraska.
TRANSACTIONS/CAREER NOTES: Signed by the WNBA and assigned to Detroit, May 3, 2000. ... Traded to Houston for G Jennifer Rizzotti, April 23, 2001. ... Waived by Houston, May 14, 2001. ... Assigned to Charlotte as a free agent, April 25, 2002. ... Waived by Charlotte, May 20, 2002. ... Signed by Phoenix as a free agent, May 9, 2003.

COLLEGIATE RECORD

Season Team	G	Min.	FGM	FGA	Pct.	FTM	FTA	Pct.	Reb.	Ast.	Pts.	RPG	APG	PPG
94-95—Nebraska	27	...	128	311	.412	37	55	.673	185	86	339	6.9	3.2	12.6
95-96—Nebraska	29	...	159	370	.430	73	89	.820	197	100	420	6.8	3.4	14.5
96-97—Nebraska	28	...	185	402	.460	83	114	.728	162	86	489	5.8	3.1	17.5
97-98—Nebraska	33	...	222	543	.409	117	151	.775	260	120	611	7.9	3.6	18.5
Totals	117	...	694	1626	.427	310	409	.758	804	392	1859	6.9	3.4	15.9

Three-point field goals: 1994-95, 46-for-138 (.333). 1995-96, 29-for-94 (.309). 1996-97, 30-for-78 (.385). 1997-98, 50-for-154 (.325). Totals, 155-for-464 (.334).

WNBA REGULAR-SEASON RECORD

Season Team	G	Min.	FGM	FGA	Pct.	FTM	FTA	Pct.	Off.	Def.	Tot.	Ast.	St.	Blk.	TO	Pts.	RPG	APG	PPG
2000—Detroit	27	433	51	126	.405	25	32	.781	9	38	47	47	27	4	33	145	1.7	1.7	5.4
2003—Phoenix	34	1,065	147	357	.412	50	69	.725	32	73	105	72	51	12	53	405	3.9	2.7	1.5
Totals	61	1498	198	483	.410	75	101	.743	41	111	152	119	78	16	86	550	2.5	2.0	9.1

Three-point field goals: 2000, 18-for-56 (.321). Totals, 18-for-56 (.321).
Personal fouls/disqualifications: 2000, 34/0. Totals, 34/0.

D

DILLARD, TAI   G   SILVER STARS

PERSONAL: Born May 6, 1981 ... 5-9/146 (1.75 m/66 kg).
COLLEGE: Texas.
TRANSACTIONS/CAREER NOTES: Signed by San Antonio as a free agent on May 1, 2003.

COLLEGIATE RECORD

Season Team	G	Min.	FGM	FGA	Pct.	FTM	FTA	Pct.	Off.	Def.	Tot.	Ast.	St.	Blk.	TO	Pts.	RPG	APG	PPG
99-00—Texas	32	357	43	111	.387	18	24	.750	16	30	46	31	20	29	0	104	1.4	0.9	3.3
00-01—Texas	25	724	112	288	.389	34	56	.607	38	76	114	80	33	52	6	259	4.6	3.2	10.4
01-02—Texas	28	322	44	113	.389	5	8	.625	14	31	45	19	20	14	3	95	1.6	0.6	3.4
02-03—Texas	35	969	121	326	.371	22	30	.733	48	116	164	83	50	47	6	266	4.7	2.3	7.6
Totals	120	2372	320	838	.382	79	118	.669	116	253	369	213	123	142	15	724	3.1	1.7	6.0

Three-point field goals: 1999-2000, 0-for-2. 2000-01, 1-for-10 (.100). 2001-02, 2-for-5 (.400). 2002-03, 2-for-11 (.181). Totals, 5-for-28 (.179).

WNBA REGULAR-SEASON RECORD

Season Team	G	Min.	FGM	FGA	Pct.	FTM	FTA	Pct.	Off.	Def.	Tot.	Ast.	St.	Blk.	TO	Pts.	RPG	APG	PPG
2003—San Antonio	24	168	16	65	.246	5	6	.833	1	14	15	15	7	4	14	41	0.6	0.6	1.7
Totals	24	168	16	65	.246	5	6	.833	1	14	15	15	7	4	14	41	0.6	0.6	1.7

Three-point field goals: 2003, 4-for-23 (.174). Totals, 4-for-23 (.174).
Personal fouls/disqualifications: 2003, 22/0. Totals, 22/0.

DIXON, TAMECKA   G   SPARKS

PERSONAL: Born December 14, 1975, in Linden, N.J. ... 5-9/148 (1.75 m/67 kg). ... **Full name:** Tamecka Michele Dixon.
HIGH SCHOOL: Linden (Linden, N.J.).
COLLEGE: Kansas.
TRANSACTIONS/CAREER NOTES: Selected by Los Angeles in second round (14th overall) of WNBA Draft, April 28, 1997.
MISCELLANEOUS: Member of WNBA Championship Team (2001, 2002).

NOTES: Kodak All-America first team (1997).

COLLEGIATE RECORD

Season Team	G	Min.	FGM	FGA	Pct.	FTM	FTA	Pct.	Reb.	Ast.	Pts.	RPG	APG	PPG
93-94—Kansas	27	...	71	169	.420	39	75	.520	113	42	184	4.2	1.6	6.8
94-95—Kansas	30	...	131	276	.475	71	111	.640	120	80	338	4.0	2.7	11.3
95-96—Kansas	32	...	207	441	.469	123	159	.774	135	103	543	4.2	3.2	17.0
96-97—Kansas	30	...	226	502	.450	152	205	.741	167	112	624	5.6	3.7	20.8
Totals	119	...	635	1388	.457	385	550	.700	535	337	1689	4.5	2.8	14.2

Three-point field goals: 1993-94, 3-for-16 (.188). 1994-95, 5-for-14 (.357). 1995-96, 6-for-30 (.200). 1996-97, 20-for-58 (.345). Totals, 34-for-118 (.288).

WNBA REGULAR-SEASON RECORD

Season Team	G	Min.	FGM	FGA	Pct.	FTM	FTA	Pct.	REBOUNDS Off.	Def.	Tot.	Ast.	St.	Blk.	TO	Pts.	AVERAGES RPG	APG	PPG
1997—Los Angeles....	27	715	115	252	.456	68	88	.773	22	59	81	55	49	5	58	320	3.0	2.0	11.9
1998—Los Angeles....	22	710	124	283	.438	88	113	.779	13	43	56	54	24	8	57	357	2.5	2.5	16.2
1999—Los Angeles....	32	563	77	199	.387	48	65	.738	17	49	66	53	17	4	39	217	2.1	1.7	6.8
2000—Los Angeles....	31	882	132	291	.454	62	77	.805	34	71	105	96	40	10	60	338	3.4	3.1	10.9
2001—Los Angeles....	29	925	133	319	.417	68	86	.791	19	66	85	114	27	2	71	340	2.9	3.9	11.7
2002—Los Angeles....	30	958	125	320	.391	49	59	.831	18	74	92	119	28	5	82	319	3.1	4.0	10.6
2003—Los Angeles....	30	1042	159	364	.437	83	94	.883	41	85	126	89	35	10	69	412	4.2	3.0	13.7
Totals.................	201	5795	865	2028	.427	466	582	.801	164	447	611	580	220	44	436	2303	3.0	2.9	11.5

Three-point field goals: 1997, 22-for-52 (.423). 1998, 21-for-59 (.356). 1999, 15-for-48 (.313). 2000, 12-for-34 (.353). 2001, 6-for-34 (.176). 2002, 20-for-57 (.351). 2003, 11-for-52 (.212). Totals, 107-for-336 (.318).
Personal fouls/disqualifications: 1997, 76/0. 1998, 67/2. 1999, 42/0. 2000, 86/0. 2001, 52/2. 2002, 74/2. 2003, 83/0. Totals, 480/6.

WNBA PLAYOFF RECORD

Season Team	G	Min.	FGM	FGA	Pct.	FTM	FTA	Pct.	REBOUNDS Off.	Def.	Tot.	Ast.	St.	Blk.	TO	Pts.	AVERAGES RPG	APG	PPG
1999—Los Angeles....	4	42	7	20	.350	1	1	1.000	4	4	8	5	3	0	5	15	2.0	1.3	3.8
2000—Los Angeles....	4	127	17	46	.370	8	9	.889	4	7	11	16	3	0	8	47	2.8	4.0	11.8
2001—Los Angeles....	7	253	40	83	.482	9	11	.818	5	12	17	29	9	2	20	95	2.4	4.1	13.6
2002—Los Angeles....	5	147	25	44	.568	9	10	.900	2	18	20	17	12	0	13	61	4.0	3.4	12.2
2003—Los Angeles....	9	316	40	94	.426	26	27	.963	8	21	29	29	14	2	11	110	3.2	3.2	12.2
Totals.................	29	885	129	287	.449	53	58	.914	23	62	85	96	41	4	57	328	2.9	3.3	11.3

Three-point field goals: 1999, 0-for-1. 2000, 5-for-10 (.500). 2001, 6-for-13 (.462). 2002, 2-for-4 (.500). 2003, 4-for-12 (.333). Totals, 17-for-40 (.425).
Personal fouls/disqualifications: 1999, 4/0. 2000, 12/0. 2001, 14/0. 2002, 15/1. 2003, 27/0. Totals, 72/1.

WNBA ALL-STAR GAME RECORD

Season Team	Min.	FGM	FGA	Pct.	FTM	FTA	Pct.	REBOUNDS Off.	Def.	Tot.	Ast.	PF	Dq.	St.	Blk.	TO	Pts.
2001 —Los Angeles.....	20	4	7	.571	0	0	...	0	2	2	4	0	0	0	0	...	8
2002 —Los Angeles.....	13	2	6	.333	0	0	...	0	1	1	0	0	0	0	0	...	5
2003 —Los Angeles.....	14	0	2	.000	0	0	...	1	2	3	1	0	0	0	0	...	
Totals.................	47	6	15	.400	0	0	...	1	5	6	5	0	0	0	0	5	13

Three-point field goals: 2001, 0-for-1. 2002, 1-for-3 (.333). Totals, 1-for-4 (.250).

DONAPHIN, BETHANY   F/C   LIBERTY   D

PERSONAL: Born August 27, 1980 ... 6-2/195 (1.88 m/88 kg).
HIGH SCHOOL: Horace Mann HS (New York, NY)
COLLEGE: Stanford.
TRANSACTIONS/CAREER NOTES: Signed by New York as a free agent, August 6, 2003. ...Waived by New York, May 21, 2003.

COLLEGIATE RECORD

Notes: Pac-10 All-Academic honorable mention (2001, 2000).

Season Team	G	Min.	FGM	FGA	Pct.	FTM	FTA	Pct.	REBOUNDS Off.	Def.	Tot.	Ast.	St.	Blk.	TO	Pts.	AVERAGES RPG	APG	PPG
98-99—Stanford	27	592	76	142	.560	49	81	.605	72	99	171	14	18	40	26	201	6.3	0.5	7.2
99-00—Stanford	30	649	111	212	.524	67	112	.598	64	97	161	17	15	60	31	289	5.4	0.6	9.6
00-01—Stanford	29	531	89	177	.503	36	65	.554	37	54	91	15	14	48	26	214	3.1	0.5	7.4
01-02—Stanford	32	712	137	232	.591	32	85	.376	59	112	171	23	18	20	53	306	5.3	0.7	8.7
Totals	118	2484	413	763	.545	184	343	.533	232	362	594	69	65	168	136	1010	5.0	0.6	8.6

WNBA REGULAR-SEASON RECORD

Season Team	G	Min.	FGM	FGA	Pct.	FTM	FTA	Pct.	REBOUNDS Off.	Def.	Tot.	Ast.	St.	Blk.	TO	Pts.	AVERAGES RPG	APG	PPG
2003—New York......	1	2	0	0	...	0	0	...	0	0	0	0	0	0	0	0	0.0	0.0	0.0
Totals.................	1	2	0	0	...	0	0	...	0	0	0	0	0	0	0	0	0.0	0.0	0.0

DOUGLAS, KATIE   G/F   SUN

PERSONAL: Born May 7, 1979, in Indianapolis ... 6-0/165 (1.83 m/75 kg). ... Full name: Kathryn Elizabeth Douglas.
HIGH SCHOOL: Perry Meridian (Indianapolis).
COLLEGE: Purdue.
TRANSACTIONS/CAREER NOTES: Selected by Orlando in first round (10th overall) of WNBA Draft, April 20, 2001.

COLLEGIATE RECORD

NOTES: Member of NCAA Division I championship team (1999). ... Kodak All-America first team (2000,2001).

Season Team	G	Min.	FGM	FGA	Pct.	FTM	FTA	Pct.	Reb.	Ast.	Pts.	AVERAGES RPG	APG	PPG
97-98—Purdue	33	865	96	214	.449	92	122	.754	141	123	285	4.3	3.7	8.6
98-99—Purdue	35	1178	175	376	.465	121	148	.818	217	124	493	6.2	3.5	14.1
99-00—Purdue	30	1124	196	461	.425	188	227	.828	196	142	613	6.5	4.7	20.4
00-01—Purdue	37	1187	188	421	.447	149	192	.776	173	137	574	4.7	3.7	15.5
Totals	135	4354	655	1472	.445	550	689	.798	727	526	1965	5.4	3.9	14.6

Three-point field goals: 1997-98, 1-for-4 (.250). 1998-99, 22-for-63 (.349). 1999-000, 33-for-102 (.324). 2000-01, 49-for-137 (.358). Totals, 105-for-306 (.343).

WNBA REGULAR-SEASON RECORD

Season Team	G	Min.	FGM	FGA	Pct.	FTM	FTA	Pct.	REBOUNDS Off.	Def.	Tot.	Ast.	St.	Blk.	TO	Pts.	AVERAGES RPG	APG	PPG
2001—Orlando	22	439	51	141	.362	34	47	.723	16	35	51	39	37	7	44	154	2.3	1.8	7.0
2002—Orlando	32	830	92	205	.449	58	67	.866	41	94	135	53	49	13	42	271	4.2	1.7	8.5
2003—Connecticut ...	28	843	120	274	.438	49	68	.721	33	73	106	56	31	11	28	336	3.8	2.0	12.0
Totals.................	82	2112	263	620	.424	141	182	.775	90	202	292	148	117	31	114	761	3.6	1.8	9.3

Three-point field goals: 2001, 18-for-57 (.316). 2002, 29-for-79 (.367). 2003, 47-for-123 (.382). Totals, 94-for-259 (.363).
Personal fouls/disqualifications: 2001, 34/0. 2002, 66/1. 2003, 38/0. Totals, 138/1.

WNBA PLAYOFF RECORD

Season Team	G	Min.	FGM	FGA	Pct.	FTM	FTA	Pct.	REBOUNDS Off.	Def.	Tot.	Ast.	St.	Blk.	TO	Pts.	AVERAGES RPG	APG	PPG
2003—Connecticut....	4	126	10	30	.333	6	7	.857	2	8	10	12	3	1	1	29	2.5	3.0	7.3
Totals.................	4	126	10	30	.333	6	7	.857	2	8	10	12	3	1	1	29	2.5	3.0	7.3

Three-point field goals: 2003, 3-for-12 (.250). Totals, 3-for-12 (.250).
Personal fouls/disqualifications: 2003, 9/0. Totals, 9/0.

DYDEK, MARGO   C   SILVER STARS

PERSONAL: Born April 28, 1974, in Warsaw, Poland ... 7-2/223 (2.18 m/101 kg). ... **Full name:** Malgorzata Dydek.
TRANSACTIONS/CAREER NOTES: Selected by Utah in first round (first overall) of WNBA Draft, April 29, 1998.

WNBA REGULAR-SEASON RECORD

NOTES: Led WNBA in blocked shots in 1998 (3.8 bpg), 1999 (2.41 bpg), 2000 (3.00 bpg), 2001 (3.53 bpg), 2002 (3.57 bpg) and 2003 (2.94 bpg).

Season Team	G	Min.	FGM	FGA	Pct.	FTM	FTA	Pct.	REBOUNDS Off.	Def.	Tot.	Ast.	St.	Blk.	TO	Pts.	AVERAGES RPG	APG	PPG
1998—Utah..............	30	839	146	303	.482	93	127	.732	41	186	227	53	14	114	108	386	7.6	1.8	12.9
1999—Utah..............	32	733	141	283	.498	114	133	.857	38	166	204	59	13	77	91	403	6.4	1.8	12.6
2000—Utah..............	32	775	105	236	.445	82	103	.796	29	146	175	51	18	96	82	294	5.5	1.6	9.2
2001—Utah..............	32	970	128	291	.440	87	109	.798	29	214	243	64	25	113	90	349	7.6	2.0	10.9
2002—Utah..............	30	876	139	319	.436	114	135	.844	52	210	262	71	25	107	96	394	8.7	2.4	13.1
2003—San Antonio ..	34	926	156	346	.451	94	130	.723	45	206	251	58	19	100	80	406	7.4	1.7	11.9
Totals.................	190	5119	815	1778	.458	584	737	.792	234	1128	1362	356	114	607	547	2232	7.2	1.9	11.7

Three-point field goals: 1998, 1-for-7 (.143). 1999, 7-for-20 (.350). 2000, 2-for-14 (.143). 2001, 6-for-15 (.400). 2002, 2-for-8 (.250). 2003, 0-for-1. Totals, 18-for-65 (.277).
Personal fouls/disqualifications: 1998, 126/3. 1999, 112/1. 2000, 114/1. 2001, 108/1. 2002, 99/2. 2003, 113/1. Totals, 672/9.

WNBA PLAYOFF RECORD

Season Team	G	Min.	FGM	FGA	Pct.	FTM	FTA	Pct.	REBOUNDS Off.	Def.	Tot.	Ast.	St.	Blk.	TO	Pts.	AVERAGES RPG	APG	PPG
2001—Utah..............	2	69	9	21	.429	10	13	.769	1	13	14	3	1	7	4	28	7.0	1.5	14.0
2002—Utah..............	5	171	22	55	.400	13	15	.867	3	41	44	12	1	17	16	60	8.8	2.4	12.0
Totals.................	7	240	31	76	.408	23	28	.821	4	54	58	15	2	24	20	88	8.3	2.1	12.6

Three-point field goals: 2002, 3-for-5 (.600). Totals, 3-for-5 (.600)
Personal fouls/disqualifications: 2002, 17/0. Totals, 27/1.

WNBA ALL-STAR GAME RECORD

Season Team	Min.	FGM	FGA	Pct.	FTM	FTA	Pct.	REBOUNDS Off.	Def.	Tot.	Ast.	PF	Dq.	St.	Blk.	TO	Pts.
2003 —San Antonio	7	1	3	.333	0	0	...	1	1	2	0	0	0	1	0	...	2
Totals.................	7	1	3	.333	0	0	...	1	1	2	0	0	0	1	0	1	2

OLYMPICS

Season Team	G	Min.	FGM	FGA	Pct.	FTM	FTA	Pct.	Reb.	Ast.	Pts.	AVERAGES RPG	APG	PPG
2000—Poland	7	245	49	110	.445	44	56	.786	85	10	143	12.1	1.4	20.4
Totals	7	245	49	110	.445	44	56	.786	85	10	143	12.1	1.4	20.4

Three-point field goals: 2000-01, 1-for-6 (.167).

EDWARDS, SIMONE   C   STORM

PERSONAL: Born November 17, 1973, in Kingston, Jamaica ... 6-4/164 (1.93 m/74 kg). ... **Full name:** Simone Ann Marie Edwards.
HIGH SCHOOL: Kingston Technical (Kingston, Jamaica).
COLLEGE: Iowa.
TRANSACTIONS/CAREER NOTES: Selected as developmental player and assigned to New York, May 27, 1997. ... Waived by New York, May 18, 1998. ... Signed by WNBA and assigned to Seattle Storm, May 2, 2000.

COLLEGIATE RECORD

Season Team	G	Min.	FGM	FGA	Pct.	FTM	FTA	Pct.	Reb.	Ast.	Pts.	AVERAGES RPG	APG	PPG
93-94—Iowa	27	...	47	103	.456	8	22	.364	102	1	102	3.8	0.0	3.8
95-96—Iowa	6	...	15	27	.556	7	14	.500	31	1	37	5.2	0.2	6.2
96-97—Iowa	26	...	83	149	.557	18	46	.391	112	23	184	4.3	0.9	7.1
Totals	59	...	145	279	.520	33	82	.402	245	25	323	4.2	0.4	5.5

E

WNBA REGULAR-SEASON RECORD

								REBOUNDS								AVERAGES		
Season Team	G	Min.	FGM	FGA	Pct.	FTM	FTA	Pct.	Off.	Def.	Tot.	Ast.	St.	Blk.	TO	Pts.	RPG	APG	PPG
2000—Seattle..........	29	645	83	182	.456	50	80	.625	38	69	107	22	16	10	45	216	3.7	0.8	7.4
2001—Seattle..........	32	810	91	190	.479	55	83	.663	67	90	157	26	24	20	37	237	4.9	0.8	7.4
2002—Seattle..........	32	694	84	158	.532	54	73	.740	46	95	141	19	21	12	44	223	4.4	0.6	7.0
2003—Seattle..........	34	577	61	134	.455	35	56	.625	54	79	133	16	10	9	31	157	3.9	0.5	4.6
Totals.................	127	2726	319	664	.480	194	292	.664	205	333	538	83	71	51	157	833	4.2	0.7	6.6

Three-point field goals: 2002, 1-for-1. Totals, 1-for-1 (1.000).
Personal fouls/disqualifications: 2002, 66/0. Totals, 232/0.

WNBA PLAYOFF RECORD

								REBOUNDS								AVERAGES		
Season Team	G	Min.	FGM	FGA	Pct.	FTM	FTA	Pct.	Off.	Def.	Tot.	Ast.	St.	Blk.	TO	Pts.	RPG	APG	PPG
2002—Seattle..........	2	31	1	8	.125	2	4	.500	2	1	3	0	0	0	2	4	1.5	0.0	2.0
Totals.................	2	31	1	8	.125	2	4	.500	2	1	3	0	0	0	2	4	1.5	0.0	2.0

EDWARDS, TERESA   G   LYNX

PERSONAL: Born July 19, 1964, in Cairo, Ga. ... 5-11/155 (1.80 m/70 kg).
HIGH SCHOOL: Cairo (Cairo, Ga.).
COLLEGE: Georgia.
TRANSACTIONS/CAREER NOTES: Selected by Minnesota in second round (14th overall) of WNBA Draft, April 25, 2003.
MISCELLANEOUS: Named USA Basketball Female Athlete of the Year in 1996, 1990 and 1987.

COLLEGIATE RECORD

											AVERAGES		
Season Team	G	Min.	FGM	FGA	Pct.	FTM	FTA	Pct.	Reb.	Ast.	Pts.	RPG	APG	PPG
82-83—Georgia......................	33	...	189	412	.459	52	82	.634	73	100	430	2.2	3.0	13.0
83-84—Georgia......................	33	...	207	395	.524	51	65	.785	81	189	465	2.5	5.7	14.1
84-85—Georgia......................	30	...	203	385	.527	58	79	.734	84	188	464	2.8	6.3	15.5
85-86—Georgia......................	32	...	274	491	.558	82	104	.788	146	176	630	4.6	5.5	19.7
Totals	128	...	873	1683	.519	243	330	.736	384	653	1989	3.0	5.1	15.5

OLYMPICS

NOTES: Member of gold-medal-winning U.S. Olympic Team (1984, 1988, 1996, 2000). ... Member of bronze-medal-winning U.S. Olympic Team (1992). ... The first and only American basketball player, male or female, to compete in five Olympics. ... Co-captain of the 1996 and 1992 Olympic gold medal team.

											AVERAGES		
Season Team	G	Min.	FGM	FGA	Pct.	FTM	FTA	Pct.	Reb.	Ast.	Pts.	RPG	APG	PPG
1984—United States...............	6	...	6	22	.273	3	9	.333	12	8	15	2.0	1.3	2.5
1988—United States...............	5	...	33	57	.579	17	21	.810	9	17	83	1.8	3.4	16.6
1992—United States...............	5	...	26	70	.371	6	10	.600	2	27	63	0.4	5.4	12.6
1996—United States...............	8	...	24	40	.600	6	13	.462	30	64	55	3.8	8.0	6.9
2000—United States...............	8	...	19	31	.613	8	10	.800	15	27	49	1.9	3.4	6.1
Totals	32	...	108	220	.491	40	63	.635	68	143	265	2.1	4.5	8.3

Three-point field goals: 1988-89, 0-for-3. 1992-93, 5-for-24 (.208). 1996-97, 1-for-4 (.250). 2000-01, 3-for-6 (.500). Totals, 9-for-37 (.243).

ABL REGULAR-SEASON RECORD

NOTES: Named 1998 All-ABL first team, finished season ranked as the ABL leader in assists (6.7 apg), second in steals (2.7 spg), third in scoring (20.4 ppg), fourth in free-throw percentage (.858) and 13th in rebounding (6.4 rpg). ... On April 17, 1997, named Player/Head Coach of the ABL Atlanta Glory. ... Named 1997 All-ABL first team and runner-up to 1996 Olympic team-mate Nikki McCray in league MVP voting. ... Selected as 1998 and 1997 ABL All-Star as Eastern Conference starting guard. ... Scored an ABL All-Star Game record-tying 20 points in 1998, adding two rebounds, three assists and one steal in 27 minutes.

											AVERAGES		
Season Team	G	Min.	FGM	FGA	Pct.	FTM	FTA	Pct.	Reb.	Ast.	Pts.	RPG	APG	PPG
96-97—Atlanta	40	1518	291	688	.423	161	189	.852	...	252	842	6.7	6.3	21.1
97-98—Atlanta	44	1667	297	708	.419	217	253	.858	...	293	899	6.5	6.7	20.4
98-99—Philadelphia...............	14	508	103	207	.498	69	84	.821	...	79	294	4.8	5.6	21.0
Totals	98	3693	691	1603	.431	447	526	.850	0	624	2035	0.0	6.4	20.8

Three-point field goals: 1996-97, 99-for-264 (.375). 1997-98, 88-for-308 (.286). 1998-99, 19-for-55 (.345). Totals, 206-for-627 (.329).

WNBA REGULAR-SEASON RECORD

								REBOUNDS								AVERAGES		
Season Team	G	Min.	FGM	FGA	Pct.	FTM	FTA	Pct.	Off.	Def.	Tot.	Ast.	St.	Blk.	TO	Pts.	RPG	APG	PPG
2003—Minnesota	34	854	63	168	.375	31	40	.775	24	81	105	148	41	11	92	181	3.1	4.4	5.3
Totals.................	34	854	63	168	.375	31	40	.775	24	81	105	148	41	11	92	181	3.1	4.4	5.3

Three-point field goals: 2003, 24-for-80 (.300). Totals, 24-for-80 (.300).
Personal fouls/disqualifications: 2003, 60/0.

WNBA PLAYOFF RECORD

								REBOUNDS								AVERAGES		
Season Team	G	Min.	FGM	FGA	Pct.	FTM	FTA	Pct.	Off.	Def.	Tot.	Ast.	St.	Blk.	TO	Pts.	RPG	APG	PPG
2003—Minnesota	3	83	6	19	.316	4	4	1.000	1	9	10	19	5	1	8	20	3.3	6.3	6.7
Totals.................	3	83	6	19	.316	4	4	1.000	1	9	10	19	5	1	8	20	3.3	6.3	6.7

Three-point field goals: 2003, 4-for-12 (.333). Totals, 4-for-12 (.333).
Personal fouls/disqualifications: 2003, 6/0. Totals, 6/0.

E

EDWARDS, TONYA   G   MERCURY

PERSONAL: Born March 13, 1968, in Flint, Mich. ... 5-10/160 (1.78 m/73 kg). ... **Full name:** Tonya LaRay Edwards.
COLLEGE: Tennessee.
TRANSACTIONS/CAREER NOTES: Selected by Minnesota in first round (seventh overall) of WNBA Draft, May 4, 1999. ... Traded to Phoenix with F Adia Barnes and G Trisha Fallon for C Marlies Askamp, G Angela Aycock and G Kristi Harrower, October 27, 1999. ... Traded by Phoenix to Charlotte for a second-round pick in the 2002 WNBA Draft, June 22, 2001. ... Waived by Charlotte, May 2003. ... Signed by Phoenix as a free agent, May 10, 2004.

COLLEGIATE RECORD

NOTES: Member of NCAA Championship team (1987, 1989).

Season Team	G	Min.	FGM	FGA	Pct.	FTM	FTA	Pct.	Reb.	Ast.	Pts.	RPG	APG	PPG
86-87—Tennessee	34	...	107	248	.431	89	113	.788	91	7	303	2.7	0.2	8.9
87-88—Tennessee	34	...	151	331	.456	115	155	.742	166	111	438	4.9	3.3	12.9
88-89—Tennessee	20	...	66	146	.452	59	74	.797	59	69	194	3.0	3.5	9.7
89-90—Tennessee	33	...	112	263	.426	108	142	.761	104	111	374	3.2	3.4	11.3
Totals	121	...	436	988	.441	371	484	.767	420	298	1309	3.5	2.5	10.8

Three-point field goals: 1987-88, 7-for-14 (.500). 1988-89, 1-for-9 (.111). 1989-90, 14-for-38 (.368). Totals, 22-for-61 (.361).

ABL REGULAR-SEASON RECORD

NOTES: Member of ABL Championship Columbus Quest (1997, 1998).

Season Team	G	Min.	FGM	FGA	Pct.	FTM	FTA	Pct.	Reb.	Ast.	Pts.	RPG	APG	PPG
96-97—Columbus	40	...	203	507	.400	145	191	.759	128	108	624	3.2	2.7	15.6
97-98—Columbus	38	...	183	509	.360	109	130	.838	130	80	541	3.4	2.1	14.2
98-99—Columbus	14	...	75	210	.357	57	73	.781	41	25	227	2.9	1.8	16.2
Totals	92	...	461	1226	.376	311	394	.789	299	213	1392	3.3	2.3	15.1

Three-point field goals: 1996-97, 73-for-202 (.361). 1997-98, 66-for-197 (.335). 1998-99, 20-for-75 (.267). Totals, 159-for-474 (.335).

WNBA REGULAR-SEASON RECORD

Season Team	G	Min.	FGM	FGA	Pct.	FTM	FTA	Pct.	REBOUNDS Off.	Def.	Tot.	Ast.	St.	Blk.	TO	Pts.	RPG	APG	PPG
1999—Minnesota	32	1031	165	462	.357	79	98	.806	15	97	112	84	27	13	68	475	3.5	2.6	14.8
2000—Phoenix	32	926	112	298	.376	79	101	.782	19	57	76	58	36	9	63	338	2.4	1.8	10.6
2001—Charlotte	32	580	60	171	.351	64	84	.762	16	46	62	48	19	7	62	194	1.9	1.5	6.1
2002—Charlotte	29	303	36	99	.364	33	46	.717	11	30	41	24	16	2	17	112	1.4	0.8	3.9
Totals	125	2840	373	1030	.362	255	329	.775	61	230	291	214	98	31	210	1119	2.3	1.7	9.0

Three-point field goals: 1999, 66-for-192 (.344). 2000, 35-for-114 (.307). 2001, 10-for-36 (.278). 2002, 7-for-25 (.280). Totals, 118-for-367 (.322).
Personal fouls/disqualifications: 1999, 104/6. 2000, 80/0. 2001, 79/1. 2002, 28/0. Totals, 291/7.

WNBA PLAYOFF RECORD

Season Team	G	Min.	FGM	FGA	Pct.	FTM	FTA	Pct.	REBOUNDS Off.	Def.	Tot.	Ast.	St.	Blk.	TO	Pts.	RPG	APG	PPG
2000—Phoenix	2	61	5	20	.250	4	6	.667	1	5	6	5	4	0	2	17	3.0	2.5	8.5
2001—Charlotte	8	119	9	21	.429	2	2	1.000	6	10	16	12	5	0	11	22	2.0	1.5	2.8
2002—Charlotte	2	19	1	5	.200	0	2	.000	0	1	1	1	0	0	1	3	0.5	0.5	1.5
Totals	12	199	15	46	.326	6	10	.600	7	16	23	18	9	0	14	42	1.9	1.5	3.5

Three-point field goals: 2000, 3-for-13 (.231). 2001, 2-for-4 (.500). 2002, 1-for-3 (.333). Totals, 6-for-20 (.300).
Personal fouls/disqualifications: 2000, 8/1. 2001, 8/0. 2002, 2/0. Totals, 18/1.

WNBA ALL-STAR GAME RECORD

Season	Team	Min.	FGM	FGA	Pct.	FTM	FTA	Pct.	REBOUNDS Off.	Def.	Tot.	Ast.	PF	Dq.	St.	Blk.	TO	Pts.
1999	—Minnesota	15	3	8	.375	0	0	...	0	1	1	1	1	0	0	0	...	7
	Totals	15	3	8	.375	0	0	...	0	1	1	1	1	0	0	0	2	7

Three-point field goals: 1999, 1-for-4 (.250). Totals, 1-for-4 (.250).

ENIS, SHALONDA   F   STING

PERSONAL: Born December 3, 1974, in Shezman, Texas ... 6-1/185 (1.85 m/84 kg). ... **Full name:** Shalonda Mochea Enis.
HIGH SCHOOL: Celeste (Celeste, Texas).
COLLEGE: Alabama.
TRANSACTIONS/CAREER NOTES: Selected by Washington in second round (13th overall) of WNBA Draft, May 4, 1999. ... Traded by Washington with 34th overall pick in 2000 WNBA Draft to Charlotte for F Vicky Bullett (January 19, 2000).

COLLEGIATE RECORD

NOTES: Kodak All-America first team (1996).

Season Team	G	Min.	FGM	FGA	Pct.	FTM	FTA	Pct.	Reb.	Ast.	Pts.	RPG	APG	PPG
95-96—Alabama	32	...	296	629	.471	145	212	.684	305	60	766	9.5	1.9	23.9
96-97—Alabama	32	...	202	455	.444	106	152	.697	284	79	543	8.9	2.5	17.0
Totals	64	...	498	1084	.459	251	364	.690	589	139	1309	9.2	2.2	20.5

Three-point field goals: 1995-96, 29-for-89 (.326). 1996-97, 33-for-93 (.355). Totals, 62-for-182 (.341).

ABL REGULAR-SEASON RECORD

Season Team	G	Min.	FGM	FGA	Pct.	FTM	FTA	Pct.	Reb.	Ast.	Pts.	RPG	APG	PPG
97-98—Seattle	42	...	244	524	.466	214	270	.793	321	72	754	7.6	1.7	18.0
98-99—Seattle	15	...	78	156	.500	43	53	.811	120	19	205	8.0	1.3	13.7
Totals	57	...	322	680	.474	257	323	.796	441	91	959	7.7	1.6	16.8

Three-point field goals: 1997-98, 52-for-129 (.403). 1998-99, 6-for-18 (.333). Totals, 58-for-147 (.395).

WNBA REGULAR-SEASON RECORD

Season Team	G	Min.	FGM	FGA	Pct.	FTM	FTA	Pct.	Off.	Def.	Tot.	Ast.	St.	Blk.	TO	Pts.	RPG	APG	PPG
1999—Washington	29	844	83	228	.364	39	57	.684	53	104	157	47	23	4	60	216	5.4	1.6	7.4
2000—Charlotte	12	323	41	104	.394	46	60	.767	21	24	45	10	10	1	16	139	3.8	0.8	11.6
2001—Charlotte	32	623	66	158	.418	45	63	.714	48	65	113	14	10	5	36	191	3.5	0.4	6.0
2002—Charlotte	4	59	5	18	.278	9	9	1.000	6	3	9	3	1	2	1	19	2.3	0.8	4.8
2003—Charlotte	29	613	82	188	.436	62	77	.805	62	63	125	16	29	2	41	252	4.3	0.6	8.7
Totals	106	2462	277	696	.398	201	266	.756	190	259	449	90	73	14	154	817	4.2	0.8	7.7

Three-point field goals: 1999, 11-for-40 (.275). 2000, 11-for-32 (.344). 2001, 14-for-31 (.452). 2002, 0-for-3. 2003, 26-for-62 (.419). Totals, 62-for-168 (.369).
Personal fouls/disqualifications: 1999, 82/0. 2000, 30/0. 2001, 60/0. 2002, 4/0. 2003, 63/0. Totals, 239/0.

WNBA PLAYOFF RECORD

Season Team	G	Min.	FGM	FGA	Pct.	FTM	FTA	Pct.	Off.	Def.	Tot.	Ast.	St.	Blk.	TO	Pts.	RPG	APG	PPG
2001—Charlotte	8	101	11	22	.500	9	12	.750	6	9	15	4	2	1	7	34	1.9	0.5	4.3
2002—Charlotte	1	3	0	3	.000	0	0	...	2	0	2	0	0	0	0	0	2.0	0.0	0.0
2003—Charlotte	2	58	4	10	.400	6	6	1.000	5	7	12	1	2	2	6	15	6.0	0.5	7.5
Totals	11	162	15	35	.429	15	18	.833	13	16	29	5	4	3	13	49	2.6	0.5	4.5

Three-point field goals: 2001, 3-for-4 (.750). 2002, 0-for-1. 2003, 1-for-3 (.333). Totals, 4-for-8 (.500).
Personal fouls/disqualifications: 2001, 16/0. 2002, 0/0. 2003, 9/1. Totals, 25/1.

ERB, SUMMER   C   STING

PERSONAL: Born July 25, 1977, in Cleveland, Ohio ... 6-6/240 (1.98 m/109 kg). ... **Full name:** Summer Elizabeth Erb.
HIGH SCHOOL: Lakewood (Lakewood, Ohio).
COLLEGE: North Carolina State.
TRANSACTIONS/CAREER NOTES: Selected by Charlotte in first round (11th overall) of WNBA Draft, April 25, 2000.

COLLEGIATE RECORD

NOTES: ACC Player of Year (1999). ... All-ACC first team (1999, 2000). ... Kodak/District 3 All-America (1999, 2000). ... Led ACC scoring (21.5 ppg) rebounding (9.9 rpg) in 1999. ... Women's Basketball Journal All-America third team (1999).

Season Team	G	Min.	FGM	FGA	Pct.	FTM	FTA	Pct.	Reb.	Ast.	Pts.	RPG	APG	PPG
95-96—Purdue	28	...	37	80	.463	22	34	.647	55	5	96	2.0	0.2	3.4
97-98—N.C. State	32	...	105	206	.510	31	42	.738	137	24	244	4.3	0.8	7.6
98-99—N.C. State	29	...	254	425	.598	115	163	.706	288	24	624	9.9	0.8	21.5
99-00—N.C. State	22	...	135	247	.547	80	105	.762	186	28	353	8.5	1.3	16.0
Totals	111	...	531	958	.554	248	344	.721	666	81	1317	6.0	0.7	11.9

Three-point field goals: 1995-96, 0-for-3. 1997-98, 3-for-7 (.429). 1998-99, 1-for-3 (.333). 1999-000, 3-for-4 (.750). Totals, 7-for-17 (.412).

WNBA REGULAR-SEASON RECORD

Season Team	G	Min.	FGM	FGA	Pct.	FTM	FTA	Pct.	Off.	Def.	Tot.	Ast.	St.	Blk.	TO	Pts.	RPG	APG	PPG
2000—Charlotte	29	275	32	73	.438	28	43	.651	26	37	63	10	8	6	17	92	2.2	0.3	3.2
2001—Charlotte	18	148	18	42	.429	18	21	.857	8	27	35	4	1	5	10	54	1.9	0.2	3.0
2002—Charlotte	31	342	35	62	.565	18	25	.720	20	51	71	10	13	11	35	88	2.3	0.3	2.8
Totals	78	765	85	177	.480	64	89	.719	54	115	169	24	22	22	62	234	2.2	0.3	3.0

Three-point field goals: 2000, 0-for-1. Totals, 0-for-1.
Personal fouls/disqualifications: 2000, 68/0. Totals, 161/2.

WNBA PLAYOFF RECORD

Season Team	G	Min.	FGM	FGA	Pct.	FTM	FTA	Pct.	Off.	Def.	Tot.	Ast.	St.	Blk.	TO	Pts.	RPG	APG	PPG
2001—Charlotte	4	15	4	5	.800	0	0	...	2	2	4	0	0	0	3	8	1.0	0.0	2.0
2002—Charlotte	2	17	3	5	.600	1	1	1.000	0	1	1	0	0	1	0	7	0.5	0.0	3.5
Totals	6	32	7	10	.700	1	1	1.000	2	3	5	0	0	1	3	15	0.8	0.0	2.5

FARRIS, BARBARA   F   SHOCK

PERSONAL: Born September 10, 1976, in Harvey, La. ... 6-3/195 (1.91 m/88 kg). ... **Full name:** Barbara Farris.
HIGH SCHOOL: St. Martin's (Harvey, La.).
COLLEGE: Tulane.
TRANSACTIONS/CAREER NOTES: Signed by the WNBA and assigned to Detroit, May 2, 2000.
MISCELLANEOUS: Member of WNBA Championship Team (2003).

COLLEGIATE RECORD

NOTES: Finished second in NCAA in field goal percentage during her senior at Tulane. ... First Team All-Conference USA (1996-97). ... Kodak District IV All-America (1996-97). ... Named to Conference USA All-Tournament Team (1996-97). ... Ranks in the top five in six different statistical categories. ... Second Team All-Conference USA Selection (1997-98).

F

Season Team	G	Min.	FGM	FGA	Pct.	FTM	FTA	Pct.	Reb.	Ast.	Pts.	RPG	APG	PPG
												AVERAGES		
94-95—Tulane	28	...	161	269	.599	116	198	.586	224	13	438	8.0	0.5	15.6
95-96—Tulane	31	...	178	284	.627	109	194	.562	248	22	465	8.0	0.7	15.0
96-97—Tulane	32	...	170	273	.623	97	161	.602	246	40	437	7.7	1.3	13.7
97-98—Tulane	27	...	151	210	.719	86	131	.656	221	30	389	8.2	1.1	14.4
Totals	118	...	660	1036	.637	408	684	.596	939	105	1729	8.0	0.9	14.7

Three-point field goals: 1994-95, 0-for-1. 1997-98, 1-for-1. Totals, 1-for-2 (.500)

ABL REGULAR-SEASON RECORD

Season Team	G	Min.	FGM	FGA	Pct.	FTM	FTA	Pct.	Reb.	Ast.	Pts.	RPG	APG	PPG
												AVERAGES		
98-99—New England	13	...	25	74	.338	45	65	.692	7	95	...	0.5	7.3	0.0
Totals	13	...	25	74	.338	45	65	.692	7	95	0	0.5	7.3	0.0

WNBA REGULAR-SEASON RECORD

Season Team	G	Min.	FGM	FGA	Pct.	FTM	FTA	Pct.	Off.	Def.	Tot.	Ast.	St.	Blk.	TO	Pts.	RPG	APG	PPG
									REBOUNDS								**AVERAGES**		
2000—Detroit	14	130	15	30	.500	15	27	.556	16	16	32	2	6	1	14	45	2.3	0.1	3.2
2001—Detroit	31	559	46	98	.469	37	58	.638	41	68	109	16	7	5	30	129	3.5	0.5	4.2
2002—Detroit	32	564	49	117	.419	45	61	.738	29	65	94	16	12	9	38	143	2.9	0.5	4.5
2003—Detroit	34	522	43	99	.434	41	63	.651	29	53	82	23	10	4	41	127	2.4	0.7	3.7
Totals	111	1775	153	344	.445	138	209	.660	115	202	317	57	35	19	123	444	2.9	0.5	4.0

Three-point field goals: 2000, 0-for-1. 2002, 0-for-1. Totals, 0-for-2.
Personal fouls/disqualifications: 2000, 30/0. 2002, 62/0. Totals, 222/1.

WNBA PLAYOFF RECORD

Season Team	G	Min.	FGM	FGA	Pct.	FTM	FTA	Pct.	Off.	Def.	Tot.	Ast.	St.	Blk.	TO	Pts.	RPG	APG	PPG
									REBOUNDS								**AVERAGES**		
2003—Detroit	8	133	10	25	.400	11	17	.647	8	12	20	4	1	0	10	31	2.5	0.5	3.9
Totals	8	133	10	25	.400	11	17	.647	8	12	20	4	1	0	10	31	2.5	0.5	3.9

Three-point field goals: 2003, 0-for-1. Totals, 0-for-1.
Personal fouls/disqualifications: 2003, 14/0. Totals, 14/0.

FEASTER, ALLISON   G/F   STING

PERSONAL: Born February 11, 1976, in Chester, S.C. ... 5-11/168 (1.80 m/76 kg). ... **Full name:** Allison Sharlene Feaster.

HIGH SCHOOL: Chester (Chester, S.D.).

COLLEGE: Harvard.

TRANSACTIONS/CAREER NOTES: Selected by Los Angeles in first round (fifth overall) of WNBA Draft, April 29, 1998. ... Traded by Los Angeles to Charlotte with C/F Clarisse Machanguana for C Rhonda Mapp and G E.C. Hill, October 10, 2000.

COLLEGIATE RECORD

NOTES: Kodak All-America first team (1998). ... Led NCAA in scoring with 28.5 ppg (1997-98).

Season Team	G	Min.	FGM	FGA	Pct.	FTM	FTA	Pct.	Reb.	Ast.	Pts.	RPG	APG	PPG
												AVERAGES		
94-95—Harvard	26	...	160	302	.530	113	145	.779	290	49	445	11.2	1.9	17.0
95-96—Harvard	27	...	175	369	.474	110	146	.753	275	61	490	10.2	2.3	18.1
96-97—Harvard	27	...	227	471	.482	87	114	.763	289	60	582	10.7	2.2	21.6
97-98—Harvard	28	...	272	524	.519	195	245	.796	303	73	797	10.8	2.6	28.5
Totals	108	...	834	1666	.501	505	650	.777	1157	243	2312	10.7	2.3	21.4

Three-point field goals: 1994-95, 10-for-32 (.313). 1995-96, 30-for-84 (.357). 1996-97, 45-for-139 (.324). 1997-98, 58-for-143 (.406). Totals, 143-for-398 (.359).

WNBA REGULAR-SEASON RECORD

Season Team	G	Min.	FGM	FGA	Pct.	FTM	FTA	Pct.	Off.	Def.	Tot.	Ast.	St.	Blk.	TO	Pts.	RPG	APG	PPG
									REBOUNDS								**AVERAGES**		
1998—Los Angeles	3	41	3	14	.214	2	2	1.000	1	1	2	3	2	0	4	10	0.7	1.0	3.3
1999—Los Angeles	32	410	51	103	.495	39	57	.684	28	30	58	32	15	7	28	162	1.8	1.0	5.1
2000—Los Angeles	32	469	60	167	.359	60	72	.833	36	49	85	33	23	2	35	202	2.7	1.0	6.3
2001—Charlotte	32	1007	126	336	.375	58	63	.921	55	98	153	46	29	10	59	365	4.8	1.4	11.4
2002—Charlotte	32	956	115	292	.394	70	85	.824	37	81	118	61	39	12	40	379	3.7	1.9	11.8
2003—Charlotte	34	1096	142	378	.376	66	78	.846	37	76	113	73	52	9	72	422	3.3	2.1	12.4
Totals	165	3979	497	1290	.385	295	357	.826	194	335	529	248	160	40	238	1540	3.2	1.5	9.3

Three-point field goals: 1998, 2-for-10 (.200). 1999, 21-for-57 (.368). 2000, 22-for-85 (.259). 2001, 55-for-168 (.327). 2002, 79-for-189 (.418). 2003, 72-for-205 (.351). Totals, 251-for-714 (.352).
Personal fouls/disqualifications: 1998, 10/0. 1999, 51/0. 2000, 47/0. 2001, 86/1. 2002, 79/0. 2003, 75/0. Totals, 348/1.

WNBA PLAYOFF RECORD

Season Team	G	Min.	FGM	FGA	Pct.	FTM	FTA	Pct.	Off.	Def.	Tot.	Ast.	St.	Blk.	TO	Pts.	RPG	APG	PPG
									REBOUNDS								**AVERAGES**		
1999—Los Angeles	4	32	4	15	.267	5	5	1.000	1	1	2	1	1	0	1	14	0.5	0.3	3.5
2000—Los Angeles	4	44	5	16	.313	2	2	1.000	3	6	9	3	2	1	5	15	2.3	0.8	3.8
2001—Charlotte	8	248	26	74	.351	1	1	1.000	8	26	34	14	9	4	9	64	4.3	1.8	8.0
2002—Charlotte	2	65	6	20	.300	0	0	...	3	12	15	7	2	0	4	15	7.5	3.5	7.5
2003—Charlotte	2	63	7	20	.350	3	4	.750	2	3	5	1	2	0	0	21	2.5	0.5	10.5
Totals	20	452	48	145	.331	11	12	.917	17	48	65	26	16	5	19	129	3.3	1.3	6.5

Three-point field goals: 1999, 1-for-5 (.200). 2000, 3-for-13 (.231). 2001, 11-for-35 (.314). 2002, 3-for-13 (.231). 2003, 4-for-10 (.400). Totals, 22-for-76 (.289).
Personal fouls/disqualifications: 1999, 3/0. 2000, 11/0. 2001, 18/0. 2002, 1/0. 2003, 5/0. Totals, 38/0.

FERDINAND, MARIE   G   SILVER STARS

PERSONAL: Born October 13, 1978, in Miami, Fla. ... 5-9/153 (1.75 m/69 kg). ... **Full name:** Marie Ferdinand.
HIGH SCHOOL: Edison (Miami).
COLLEGE: Louisiana State.
TRANSACTIONS/CAREER NOTES: Selected by Utah in first round (eighth overall) of WNBA Draft, April 20, 2001.

COLLEGIATE RECORD

NOTES: Kodak All-America first team (2001).

Season Team	G	Min.	FGM	FGA	Pct.	FTM	FTA	Pct.	Reb.	Ast.	Pts.	RPG	APG	PPG
												AVERAGES		
97-98—Louisiana State	27	243	26	69	.377	14	24	.583	61	17	66	2.3	0.6	2.4
98-99—Louisiana State	30	883	149	322	.463	69	104	.663	157	90	368	5.2	3.0	12.3
99-00—Louisiana State	32	1138	240	479	.501	76	114	.667	148	170	560	4.6	5.3	17.5
00-01—Louisiana State	31	1075	240	469	.512	173	234	.739	158	107	654	5.1	3.5	21.1
Totals	120	3339	655	1339	.489	332	476	.697	524	384	1648	4.4	3.2	13.7

Three-point field goals: 1998-99, 1-for-3 (.333). 1999-000, 4-for-13 (.308). 2000-01, 1-for-13 (.077). Totals, 6-for-29 (.207).

WNBA REGULAR-SEASON RECORD

Season Team	G	Min.	FGM	FGA	Pct.	FTM	FTA	Pct.	Off.	Def.	Tot.	Ast.	St.	Blk.	TO	Pts.	RPG	APG	PPG
									REBOUNDS								AVERAGES		
2001—Utah	32	864	143	290	.493	69	113	.611	23	63	86	79	40	4	63	366	2.7	2.5	11.4
2002—Utah	32	1065	176	371	.474	132	171	.772	19	88	107	91	51	7	89	489	3.3	2.8	15.3
2003—San Antonio	34	1116	139	384	.362	176	223	.789	28	99	127	90	58	6	85	470	3.7	2.6	13.8
Totals	98	3045	458	1045	.438	377	507	.744	70	250	320	260	149	17	237	1325	3.3	2.7	13.5

Three-point field goals: 2001, 11-for-42 (.262). 2002, 5-for-34 (.147). 2003, 16-for-52 (.308). Totals, 32-for-128 (.250).
Personal fouls/disqualifications: 2001, 70/1. 2002, 86/0. 2003, 87/0. Totals, 243/1.

WNBA PLAYOFF RECORD

Season Team	G	Min.	FGM	FGA	Pct.	FTM	FTA	Pct.	Off.	Def.	Tot.	Ast.	St.	Blk.	TO	Pts.	RPG	APG	PPG
									REBOUNDS								AVERAGES		
2001—Utah	2	69	7	16	.438	15	18	.833	2	6	8	7	3	0	2	29	4.0	3.5	14.5
2002—Utah	5	186	25	56	.446	23	34	.676	4	18	22	13	10	0	20	74	4.4	2.6	14.8
Totals	7	255	32	72	.444	38	52	.731	6	24	30	20	13	0	22	103	4.3	2.9	14.7

Three-point field goals: 2001, 0-for-2. 2002, 1-for-5 (.200). Totals, 1-for-7 (.143).
Personal fouls/disqualifications: 2001, 4/0. 2002, 16/0. Totals, 20/0.

WNBA ALL-STAR GAME RECORD

Season Team	Min.	FGM	FGA	Pct.	FTM	FTA	Pct.	Off.	Def.	Tot.	Ast.	PF	Dq.	St.	Blk.	TO	Pts.
								REBOUNDS									
2002 —Utah	9	1	3	.333	0	0	...	0	0	0	1	0	0	0	0	...	2
2003 —San Antonio	19	3	7	.429	0	0	...	0	0	0	1	4	0	2	0	...	6
Totals	28	4	10	.400	0	0	...	0	0	0	2	4	0	2	0	4	8

Three-point field goals: 2003, 0-for-1. Totals, 0-for-1.

FIGGS, UKARI   G   COMETS

PERSONAL: Born March 31, 1977, in Georgetown, Ky. ... 5-9/142 (1.75 m/64 kg). ... **Full name:** Ukari Okien Figgs.
HIGH SCHOOL: Scott County (Georgetown, Ky.).
COLLEGE: Purdue.
TRANSACTIONS/CAREER NOTES: Selected by Los Angeles in third round (28th overall) of WNBA Draft, May 4, 1999. ... Traded by Los Angeles with G Gergana Slavtcheva to Portland for G Nikki Teasley and G Sophia Witherspoon, April 19, 2002. ... Selected by Houston in dispersal draft, April 24, 2003.
MISCELLANEOUS: Member of WNBA Championship Team (2001).

COLLEGIATE RECORD

NOTES: Member of NCAA Division I championship team (1999).

Season Team	G	Min.	FGM	FGA	Pct.	FTM	FTA	Pct.	Reb.	Ast.	Pts.	RPG	APG	PPG
												AVERAGES		
95-96—Purdue	30	...	40	108	.370	20	25	.800	68	56	117	2.3	1.9	3.9
96-97—Purdue	27	...	86	254	.339	54	71	.761	95	85	258	3.5	3.1	9.6
97-98—Purdue	33	...	160	368	.435	134	156	.859	169	121	510	5.1	3.7	15.5
98-99—Purdue	35	...	175	441	.397	151	175	.863	158	147	570	4.5	4.2	16.3
Totals	125		461	1171	.394	359	427	.841	490	409	1455	3.9	3.3	11.6

Three-point field goals: 1995-96, 17-for-57 (.298). 1996-97, 32-for-93 (.344). 1997-98, 56-for-154 (.364). 1998-99, 69-for-202 (.342). Totals, 174-for-506 (.344).

WNBA REGULAR-SEASON RECORD

Season Team	G	Min.	FGM	FGA	Pct.	FTM	FTA	Pct.	Off.	Def.	Tot.	Ast.	St.	Blk.	TO	Pts.	RPG	APG	PPG
									REBOUNDS								AVERAGES		
1999—Los Angeles	22	330	30	82	.366	21	24	.875	8	27	35	33	15	0	31	95	1.6	1.5	4.3
2000—Los Angeles	32	803	66	153	.431	54	65	.831	14	41	55	127	21	3	43	215	1.7	4.0	6.7
2001—Los Angeles	32	930	76	179	.425	51	63	.810	14	86	100	126	43	4	55	257	3.1	3.9	8.0
2002—Portland	31	866	83	233	.356	59	65	.908	13	67	80	104	25	2	44	264	2.6	3.4	8.5
2003—Houston	34	952	52	124	.419	19	22	.864	11	70	81	82	26	1	59	149	2.4	2.4	4.4

F

Totals................ 151 3881 307 771 .398 204 239 .854 60 291 351 472 130 10 232 980 2.3 3.1 6.5
Three-point field goals: 1999, 14-for-47 (.298). 2000, 29-for-82 (.354). 2001, 54-for-117 (.462). 2002, 39-for-120 (.325). 2003, 26-for-69 (.377). Totals, 162-for-435 (.372).
Personal fouls/disqualifications: 1999, 27/0. 2000, 53/0. 2001, 42/0. 2002, 50/0. 2003, 33/0. Totals, 205/0.

WNBA PLAYOFF RECORD

Season Team	G	Min.	FGM	FGA	Pct.	FTM	FTA	Pct.	Off.	Def.	Tot.	Ast.	St.	Blk.	TO	Pts.	RPG	APG	PPG
1999—Los Angeles....	1	4	0	1	.000	0	0	...	1	0	1	0	0	0	0	0	1.0	0.0	0.0
2000—Los Angeles....	4	106	7	23	.304	6	6	1.000	6	10	16	19	2	0	11	24	4.0	4.8	6.0
2001—Los Angeles....	7	239	18	53	.340	12	16	.750	3	12	15	41	4	4	6	58	2.1	5.9	8.3
2003—Houston........	3	81	6	15	.400	0	0	...	1	5	6	7	1	0	3	17	2.0	2.3	5.7
Totals................	15	430	31	92	.337	18	22	.818	11	27	38	67	7	4	20	99	2.5	4.5	6.6

Three-point field goals: 1999, 0-for-1. 2000, 4-for-11 (.364). 2001, 10-for-36 (.278). 2003, 5-for-7 (.714). Totals, 19-for-55 (.345).
Personal fouls/disqualifications: 1999, 0/0. 2000, 10/0. 2001, 14/0. 2003, 4/0. Totals, 28/0.

FIJALKOWSKI, ISABELLE   C   SPARKS

PERSONAL: Born May 23, 1972 in Clermont Ferrand, France ... 6-5/200 (1.96 m/91 kg).
HIGH SCHOOL: La Charme (France)
COLLEGE: Universite de Blaise Pascal and Colorado
TRANSACTIONS/CAREER NOTES: Selected by Cleveland in the first round (second overall) in the WNBA Elite Draft, February 27, 1997. Selected by Los Angeles in dispersal draft, January 6, 2004. ... Selected by Los Angeles in Dispersal Draft, January 6, 2004.

COLLEGIATE RECORD

NOTES: Big Eight Newcomer of the Year (1995) ... All-Big Eight First Team (1995) ... All-Academic Team Big Ten (1995).

Season Team	G	Min.	FGM	FGA	Pct.	FTM	FTA	Pct.	Off.	Def.	Tot.	Ast.	St.	Blk.	TO	Pts.	RPG	APG	PPG
94-95—Colorado	32		219	368	.595	78	106	.736			207	38	37			516	6.5	1.2	16.1
Total	32		219	368	.595	78	106	.736			207	38	37			516	6.5	1.2	16.1

Three-point field goals: 0-for-0.

PROFESSIONAL

Notes: 1995-97, CJM Bourges. 1997-98, Pool Comense. Named 1998 European Player of the Year.

Season Team	G	FGM	FGA	Pct.	FTM	FTA	Pct.	Reb.	Ast.	St.	Pts.	RPG	APG	PPG
95-96......................	23	132	232	.570	80	92	.870	150	30	36	344	6.5	1.3	15.0
01-02......................	20	106	172	.616	36	49	.735	125	36	23	249	6.3	1.8	12.4
02-03......................	31	169	307	.550	98	119	.824	143	19	41	440	4.6	0.6	14.2
Totals	74	407	711	.572	214	260	.823	418	85	100	1033	5.6	1.1	14.0

Three-point field goals: 1995-96, 0-for-0. 1996-97, 1-for-1 (1.000). 1997-98, 4-for-9 (.444). Totals, 5-for-10 (.500).

WNBA REGULAR-SEASON RECORD

Season Team	G	Min.	FGM	FGA	Pct.	FTM	FTA	Pct.	Off.	Def.	Tot.	Ast.	St.	Blk.	TO	Pts.	RPG	APG	PPG
1997—Cleveland.......	28	803	125	246	.508	81	103	.786	62	94	156	68	17	18	73	332	5.6	2.4	11.9
1998—Cleveland......	28	806	146	267	.547	87	106	.821	59	133	192	58	17	27	81	383	6.9	2.1	13.7
Totals	56	1609	271	513	.528	168	209	.804	121	227	348	126	34	45	154	715	6.2	2.3	12.8º

F

FORD, CHERYL   C   SHOCK

PERSONAL: Born June 6, 1981, in Summerfield, La. ... 6-3/215 (1.91 m/98 kg).
HIGH SCHOOL: Summerfield (Summerfield, La.).
COLLEGE: Louisiana Tech.
TRANSACTIONS/CAREER NOTES: Selected by Detroit in first round (third overall) of WNBA Draft, April 25, 2003.
MISCELLANEOUS: 1998 U.S. Olympic 17-under team member. ... Member of WNBA Championship Team (2003).

COLLEGIATE RECORD

NOTES: Associated Press All-America Honorable Mention (2003). ... Western Athletic Conference Player of the Year (2003, 2002). ... All-WAC First Team (2003, 2002). ... Led the WAC in rebounding (8.7) as a junior.

Season Team	G	Min.	FGM	FGA	Pct.	FTM	FTA	Pct.	Reb.	Ast.	Pts.	RPG	APG	PPG
99-00—Louisiana Tech	34	418	83	143	.580	56	84	.667	...	4	222	5.2	0.1	6.5
00-01—Louisiana Tech	35	532	106	201	.527	75	125	.600	...	18	287	5.1	0.5	8.2
01-02—Louisiana Tech	30	602	128	275	.465	82	140	.586	...	13	338	8.7	0.4	11.3
02-03—Louisiana Tech	34	997	206	429	.480	121	192	.630	...	30	533	12.9	0.9	15.7
Totals	133	2549	523	1048	.499	334	541	.617	0	65	1380	0.0	0.5	10.4

WNBA REGULAR-SEASON RECORD

NOTES: WNBA Rookie of the Year (2003). ... All-WNBA second team (2003).

Season Team	G	Min.	FGM	FGA	Pct.	FTM	FTA	Pct.	Off.	Def.	Tot.	Ast.	St.	Blk.	TO	Pts.	RPG	APG	PPG
2003—Detroit	32	956	128	270	.474	88	129	.682	99	235	334	27	32	31	79	344	10.4	0.8	10.8
Totals................	32	956	128	270	.474	88	129	.682	99	235	334	27	32	31	79	344	10.4	0.8	10.8

WNBA PLAYOFF RECORD

Season Team	G	Min.	FGM	FGA	Pct.	FTM	FTA	Pct.	REBOUNDS Off.	Def.	Tot.	Ast.	St.	Blk.	TO	Pts.	AVERAGES RPG	APG	PPG
2003—Detroit	8	232	24	74	.324	19	23	.826	25	55	80	4	11	6	10	67	10.0	0.5	8.4
Totals.................	8	232	24	74	.324	19	23	.826	25	55	80	4	11	6	10	67	10.0	0.5	8.4

WNBA ALL-STAR GAME RECORD

Season Team	Min.	FGM	FGA	Pct.	FTM	FTA	Pct.	REBOUNDS Off.	Def.	Tot.	Ast.	PF	Dq.	St.	Blk.	TO	Pts.
2003—Detroit.............	9	0	2	.000	0	0	...	0	1	1	0	2	0	0	1	...	0
Totals.................	9	0	2	.000	0	0	...	0	1	1	0	2	0	0	1	2	0

FRETT, LA'KESHIA F STING

PERSONAL: Born June 12, 1975, in Carmel, Calif. ... 6-3/170 (1.91 m/77 kg). ... **Full name:** La'Keshia Frett.
HIGH SCHOOL: Phoebus (Hampton, Va.).
COLLEGE: Georgia.
TRANSACTIONS/CAREER NOTES: Seleted by Los Angeles in fourth round (40th overall) of WNBA Draft, May 4, 1999. ... Traded by Los Angeles to Sacramento for G/F Latasha Byears, October 11, 2000.

COLLEGIATE RECORD

NOTES: Associated Press All-America third team (1997).

Season Team	G	Min.	FGM	FGA	Pct.	FTM	FTA	Pct.	Reb.	Ast.	Pts.	AVERAGES RPG	APG	PPG
93-94—Georgia.....................	28	...	154	323	.477	85	111	.766	168	69	393	6.0	2.5	14.0
94-95—Georgia.....................	33	...	203	421	.482	116	155	.748	199	100	523	6.0	3.0	15.8
95-96—Georgia.....................	33	...	195	374	.521	90	107	.841	288	65	481	8.7	2.0	14.6
96-97—Georgia.....................	28	...	191	396	.482	70	90	.778	187	81	453	6.7	2.9	16.2
Totals.................................	122	...	743	1514	.491	361	463	.780	842	315	1850	6.9	2.6	15.2

Three-point field goals: 1994-95, 1-for-2 (.500). 1995-96, 1-for-1. 1996-97, 1-for-2 (.500). Totals, 3-for-5 (.600).

ABL REGULAR-SEASON RECORD

Season Team	G	Min.	FGM	FGA	Pct.	FTM	FTA	Pct.	Reb.	Ast.	Pts.	AVERAGES RPG	APG	PPG
97-98—Philadelphia...............	44	...	160	338	.473	104	120	.867	200	47	427	4.5	1.1	9.7
98-99—Philadelphia...............	14	...	40	106	.377	17	21	.810	48	15	97	3.4	1.1	6.9
Totals.................................	58	...	200	444	.450	121	141	.858	248	62	524	4.3	1.1	9.0

Three-point field goals: 1997-98, 3-for-5 (.600). 1998-99, 0-for-2. Totals, 3-for-7 (.429).

WNBA REGULAR-SEASON RECORD

Season Team	G	Min.	FGM	FGA	Pct.	FTM	FTA	Pct.	REBOUNDS Off.	Def.	Tot.	Ast.	St.	Blk.	TO	Pts.	AVERAGES RPG	APG	PPG
1999—Los Angeles	31	658	77	162	.475	34	43	.791	48	46	94	63	9	5	26	188	3.0	2.0	6.1
2000—Los Angeles	25	187	14	51	.275	12	16	.750	8	16	24	6	7	6	13	40	1.0	0.2	1.6
2001—Sacramento	30	403	49	126	.389	30	35	.857	23	32	55	18	10	6	32	128	1.8	0.6	4.3
2002—Sacramento	32	648	84	187	.449	14	17	.824	30	65	95	23	5	19	27	187	3.0	0.7	5.8
2003—Sacramento	24	150	17	47	.362	1	2	.500	9	14	23	12	2	3	10	36	1.0	0.5	1.5
Totals.................	142	2046	241	573	.421	91	113	.805	118	173	291	122	33	39	108	579	2.0	0.9	4.1

Three-point field goals: 2000, 0-for-1. 2002, 5-for-15 (.333). 2003, 1-for-2 (.500). Totals, 6-for-18 (.333).
Personal fouls/disqualifications: 2000, 10/0. 2002, 70/2. 2003, 16/0. Totals, 168/2.

WNBA PLAYOFF RECORD

Season Team	G	Min.	FGM	FGA	Pct.	FTM	FTA	Pct.	REBOUNDS Off.	Def.	Tot.	Ast.	St.	Blk.	TO	Pts.	AVERAGES RPG	APG	PPG
1999—Los Angeles	4	121	11	30	.367	6	7	.857	12	9	21	13	2	2	3	28	5.3	3.3	7.0
2000—Los Angeles	3	7	2	3	.667	3	4	.750	0	0	0	0	0	0	0	7	0.0	0.0	2.3
2001—Sacramento	5	18	1	8	.125	2	2	1.000	2	0	2	1	0	0	1	4	0.4	0.2	0.8
2003—Sacramento	1	9	1	2	.500	0	0	...	0	0	0	0	0	0	1	2	0.0	0.0	2.0
Totals.................	13	155	15	43	.349	11	13	.846	14	9	23	14	2	2	5	41	1.8	1.1	3.2

Three-point field goals: 2003, 0-for-1. Totals, 0-for-1 (.000).
Personal fouls/disqualifications: 2003, 1/0. Totals, 9/0.

FROHLICH, LINDA F MERCURY

PERSONAL: Born June 23, 1979, in Oldendorf, Germany ... 6-2/183 (1.88 m/83 kg).
HIGH SCHOOL: Vincent-Lubeck Gymnasium Stade (Germany).
COLLEGE: Nevada-Las Vegas.
TRANSACTIONS/CAREER NOTES: Selected by New York in second round (26th overall) of WNBA Draft, April 19, 2002. ... Signed by Phoenix as a restricted free agent March 5, 2004.

COLLEGIATE RECORD

Season Team	G	Min.	FGM	FGA	Pct.	FTM	FTA	Pct.	Reb.	Ast.	Pts.	AVERAGES RPG	APG	PPG
98-99—UNLV......................	28	1011	251	543	.462	125	163	.767	258	77	657	9.2	2.8	23.5
99-00—UNLV......................	28	1045	229	499	.459	109	138	.790	319	112	604	11.4	4.0	21.6
00-01—UNLV......................	26	919	195	409	.477	72	101	.713	346	85	500	13.3	3.3	19.2
01-02—UNLV......................	29	1004	211	461	.458	136	161	.845	301	84	594	10.4	2.9	20.5
Totals	111	3979	886	1912	.463	442	563	.785	1224	358	2355	11.0	3.2	21.2

F

Three-point field goals: 1998-99, 30-for-90 (.333). 1999-00, 37-for-101 (.366). 2000-01, 38-for-93 (.409). 2001-02, 36-for-109 (.330). Totals, 141-for-393 (.359).

WNBA REGULAR-SEASON RECORD

								REBOUNDS								AVERAGES		
Season Team	G	Min.	FGM	FGA	Pct.	FTM	FTA	Pct.	Off.	Def.	Tot.	Ast.	St.	Blk.	TO	Pts.	RPG	APG	PPG
2002—New York	16	67	1	10	.100	4	4	1.000	3	10	13	1	2	0	4	6	0.8	0.1	0.4
2003—New York	26	214	31	72	.431	14	22	.636	11	25	36	15	6	8	14	83	1.4	0.6	3.2
Totals	42	281	32	82	.390	18	26	.692	14	35	49	16	8	8	18	89	1.2	0.4	2.1

Three-point field goals: 2002, 0-for-4. 2003, 7-for-13 (.538). Totals, 7-for-17 (.412).
Personal fouls/disqualifications: 2002, 11/0. 2003, 26/0. Totals, 37/0.

WNBA PLAYOFF RECORD

								REBOUNDS								AVERAGES		
Season Team	G	Min.	FGM	FGA	Pct.	FTM	FTA	Pct.	Off.	Def.	Tot.	Ast.	St.	Blk.	TO	Pts.	RPG	APG	PPG
2002—New York	3	20	0	3	.000	1	2	.500	0	5	5	2	1	0	3	1	1.7	0.7	0.3
Totals	3	20	0	3	.000	1	2	.500	0	5	5	2	1	0	3	1	1.7	0.7	0.3

GIBSON, KELLEY   G/F   COMETS

PERSONAL: Born November 7, 1976, in Easton, Md. ... 5-9/137 (1.75 m/62 kg). ... **Full name:** Jawann Kelley Gibson.
HIGH SCHOOL: Easton (Md.).
COLLEGE: Maryland.
TRANSACTIONS/CAREER NOTES: Signed by the WNBA and assigned to Houston, May 2, 2000. ... Signed as a free agent with the Indiana Fever on May 2, 2003, and waived on May 6. Re-signed by Houston as a free agent, May 8, 2003.
MISCELLANEOUS: Member of WNBA Championship Team (2000).

COLLEGIATE RECORD

											AVERAGES		
Season Team	G	Min.	FGM	FGA	Pct.	FTM	FTA	Pct.	Reb.	Ast.	Pts.	RPG	APG	PPG
94-95—Maryland	3	...	9	36	.250	3	5	.600	10	2	24	3.3	0.7	8.0
95-96—Maryland	27	...	118	340	.347	74	97	.763	91	73	330	3.4	2.7	12.2
96-97—Maryland	19	...	66	167	.395	39	64	.609	79	35	178	4.2	1.8	9.4
97-98—Maryland	28	...	73	232	.315	73	57	1.281	123	119	189	4.4	4.3	6.8
Totals	77	...	266	775	.343	189	223	.848	303	229	721	3.9	3.0	9.4

Three-point field goals: 1994-95, 3-for-12 (.250). 1995-96, 20-for-84 (.238). 1996-97, 7-for-26 (.269). 1997-98, 6-for-33 (.182). Totals, 36-for-155 (.232).

WNBA REGULAR-SEASON RECORD

								REBOUNDS								AVERAGES		
Season Team	G	Min.	FGM	FGA	Pct.	FTM	FTA	Pct.	Off.	Def.	Tot.	Ast.	St.	Blk.	TO	Pts.	RPG	APG	PPG
2000—Houston	17	76	7	19	.368	7	8	.875	4	8	12	2	1	0	4	24	0.7	0.1	1.4
2001—Houston	28	288	13	57	.228	15	22	.682	6	23	29	13	8	6	15	44	1.0	0.5	1.6
2002—Houston	29	276	21	55	.382	4	6	.667	3	17	20	14	8	7	21	60	0.7	0.5	2.1
2003—Houston	26	209	14	42	.333	0	0	...	4	12	16	8	1	5	9	38	0.6	0.3	1.5
Totals	100	849	55	173	.318	26	36	.722	17	60	77	37	18	18	49	166	0.8	0.4	1.7

Three-point field goals: 2000, 3-for-7 (.429). 2001, 3-for-21 (.143). 2002, 14-for-36 (.389). 2003, 10-for-24 (.417). Totals, 30-for-88 (.341).
Personal fouls/disqualifications: 2000, 11/0. 2001, 20/0. 2002, 21/0. 2003, 14/0. Totals, 66/0.

WNBA PLAYOFF RECORD

								REBOUNDS								AVERAGES		
Season Team	G	Min.	FGM	FGA	Pct.	FTM	FTA	Pct.	Off.	Def.	Tot.	Ast.	St.	Blk.	TO	Pts.	RPG	APG	PPG
2000—Houston	1	3	0	1	.000	0	0	...	0	0	0	0	0	0	0	0	0.0	0.0	0.0
2001—Houston	2	23	3	7	.429	0	0	...	0	3	3	0	1	0	2	7	1.5	0.0	3.5
2002—Houston	2	22	4	8	.500	0	0	...	3	1	4	0	0	0	1	10	2.0	0.0	5.0
2003—Houston	2	18	2	5	.400	0	0	...	0	1	1	0	0	0	0	4	0.5	0.0	2.0
Totals	7	66	9	21	.429	0	0	...	3	5	8	0	1	0	3	21	1.1	0.0	3.0

Three-point field goals: 2001, 1-for-3 (.333). 2002, 2-for-3 (.667). 2003, 0-for-2. Totals, 3-for-8 (.375).
Personal fouls/disqualifications: 2001, 1/0. 2002, 3/0. 2003, 1/0. Totals, 5/0.

G

GILLOM, JENNIFER   F   SPARKS

PERSONAL: Born June 13, 1964, in Abbeville, Miss. ... 6-3/180 (1.91 m/82 kg). **Full name:** Jennifer Gillom.
COLLEGE: Mississippi.
TRANSACTIONS/CAREER NOTES: Assigned to Phoenix, January 22, 1997. ... Signed by Los Angeles, May 1, 2003.

COLLEGIATE RECORD

											AVERAGES		
Season Team	G	Min.	FGM	FGA	Pct.	FTM	FTA	Pct.	Reb.	Ast.	Pts.	RPG	APG	PPG
82-83—Mississippi	32	...	139	301	.462	37	67	.552	198	65	315	6.2	2.0	9.8
83-84—Mississippi	30	...	244	471	.518	58	100	.580	272	31	546	9.1	1.0	18.2
84-85—Mississippi	32	...	246	460	.535	91	135	.674	231	30	583	7.2	0.9	18.2
85-86—Mississippi	32	...	314	577	.544	113	181	.624	254	11	742	7.9	0.3	23.2
Totals	126	...	943	1809	.521	299	483	.619	955	137	2186	7.6	1.1	17.3

OLYMPICS

NOTES: USA Basketball's Female Athlete of the Year (1985). ... Member of gold medal-winning U.S. Olympic Team (1988).

Season Team	G	Min.	FGM	FGA	Pct.	FTM	FTA	Pct.	Reb.	Ast.	Pts.	AVERAGES RPG	APG	PPG
1988—United States	4	...	2	8	.250	7	10	.700	9	...	11	2.3	0.0	2.8
Totals	4	...	2	8	.250	7	10	.700	9	0	11	2.3	0.0	2.8

WNBA REGULAR-SEASON RECORD

NOTES: Kim Perrott Sportsmanship Award (2002).

									REBOUNDS								AVERAGES		
Season Team	**G**	**Min.**	**FGM**	**FGA**	**Pct.**	**FTM**	**FTA**	**Pct.**	**Off.**	**Def.**	**Tot.**	**Ast.**	**St.**	**Blk.**	**TO**	**Pts.**	**RPG**	**APG**	**PPG**
1997—Phoenix	28	874	163	376	.434	94	121	.777	45	106	151	21	37	15	58	440	5.4	0.8	15.7
1998—Phoenix	30	962	228	492	.463	137	195	.703	62	157	219	42	50	10	89	624	7.3	1.4	20.8
1999—Phoenix	32	1095	163	428	.381	141	177	.797	53	131	184	54	37	7	87	485	5.8	1.7	15.2
2000—Phoenix	30	826	139	316	.440	79	106	.745	31	85	116	45	21	29	59	376	3.9	1.5	12.5
2001—Phoenix	32	858	150	355	.423	71	96	.740	36	91	127	35	31	19	71	395	4.0	1.1	12.3
2002—Phoenix	31	874	166	400	.415	105	131	.802	36	80	116	37	29	21	61	473	3.7	1.2	15.3
2003—Los Angeles	33	397	40	97	.412	16	21	.762	18	37	55	21	16	3	9	103	1.7	0.6	3.1
Totals	216	5886	1049	2464	.426	643	847	.759	281	687	968	255	221	104	434	2896	4.5	1.2	13.4

Three-point field goals: 1997, 20-for-65 (.308). 1998, 31-for-82 (.378). 1999, 18-for-72 (.250). 2000, 19-for-69 (.275). 2001, 24-for-70 (.343). 2002, 36-for-93 (.387). 2003, 7-for-26 (.269). Totals, 155-for-477 (.325).

Personal fouls/disqualifications: 1997, 93/0. 1998, 94/1. 1999, 105/2. 2000, 91/1. 2001, 91/1. 2002, 90/0. 2003, 65/1. Totals, 629/6.

WNBA PLAYOFF RECORD

									REBOUNDS								AVERAGES		
Season Team	**G**	**Min.**	**FGM**	**FGA**	**Pct.**	**FTM**	**FTA**	**Pct.**	**Off.**	**Def.**	**Tot.**	**Ast.**	**St.**	**Blk.**	**TO**	**Pts.**	**RPG**	**APG**	**PPG**
1997—Phoenix	1	31	4	11	.364	0	0	...	2	5	7	1	2	0	2	9	7.0	1.0	9.0
1998—Phoenix	6	214	36	95	.379	22	26	.846	8	39	47	2	8	7	17	102	7.8	0.3	17.0
2000—Phoenix	2	64	10	20	.500	5	10	.500	1	3	4	2	1	5	4	26	2.0	1.0	13.0
2003—Los Angeles	6	22	0	5	.000	0	0	...	0	1	1	0	1	1	0	0	0.2	0.0	0.0
Totals	15	331	50	131	.382	27	36	.750	11	48	59	5	12	13	23	137	3.9	0.3	9.1

Three-point field goals: 1997, 1-for-3 (.333). 1998, 8-for-16 (.500). 2000, 1-for-5 (.200). Totals, 10-for-24 (.417).

Personal fouls/disqualifications: 1997, 2/0. 1998, 18/0. 2000, 10/0. Totals, 35/0.

WNBA ALL-STAR GAME RECORD

								REBOUNDS								
Season Team	**Min.**	**FGM**	**FGA**	**Pct.**	**FTM**	**FTA**	**Pct.**	**Off.**	**Def.**	**Tot.**	**Ast.**	**PF**	**Dq.**	**St.**	**Blk.**	**TO**	**Pts.**
1999 —Phoenix	18	2	6	.333	2	2	1.000	0	5	5	1	0	0	1	0	...	6
Totals	18	2	6	.333	2	2	1.000	0	5	5	1	0	0	1	0	0	6

Three-point field goals: 1999, 0-for-1. Totals, 0-for-1.

GOODSON, ADRIENNE G SILVER STARS

PERSONAL: Born October 19, 1966, in Jersey City, N.J. ... 6-0/160 (1.83 m/73 kg). **Full name:** Adrienne Maureen Goodson.

HIGH SCHOOL: Bayonne (Bayonne, N.J.).

COLLEGE: Old Dominion.

TRANSACTIONS/CAREER NOTES: Selected by Utah in third round (27th overall) of WNBA Draft, May 4, 1999.

COLLEGIATE RECORD

NOTES: Member of NCAA championship team (1985).

Season Team	G	Min.	FGM	FGA	Pct.	FTM	FTA	Pct.	Reb.	Ast.	Pts.	AVERAGES RPG	APG	PPG
84-85—Old Dominion	34	...	131	300	.437	61	90	.678	153	69	323	4.5	2.0	9.5
85-86—Old Dominion	26	...	156	327	.477	62	88	.705	226	22	374	8.7	0.8	14.4
86-87—Old Dominion	31	...	177	345	.513	77	116	.664	256	41	431	8.3	1.3	13.9
87-88—Old Dominion	26	...	188	344	.547	70	107	.654	228	103	446	8.8	4.0	17.2
Totals	117	...	652	1316	.495	270	401	.673	863	235	1574	7.4	2.0	13.5

ABL REGULAR-SEASON RECORD

Season Team	G	Min.	FGM	FGA	Pct.	FTM	FTA	Pct.	Reb.	Ast.	Pts.	AVERAGES RPG	APG	PPG
96-97—Philadelphia	40	...	250	515	.485	183	241	.759	291	100	690	7.3	2.5	17.3
97-98—Philadelphia	43	...	288	582	.495	180	243	.741	376	98	761	8.7	2.3	17.7
98-99—Chicago	12	...	75	166	.452	53	66	.803	86	20	207	7.2	1.7	17.3
Totals	95	...	613	1263	.485	416	550	.756	753	218	1658	7.9	2.3	17.5

Three-point field goals: 1996-97, 7-for-24 (.292). 1997-98, 5-for-32 (.156). 1998-99, 4-for-19 (.211). Totals, 16-for-75 (.213).

WNBA REGULAR-SEASON RECORD

									REBOUNDS								AVERAGES		
Season Team	**G**	**Min.**	**FGM**	**FGA**	**Pct.**	**FTM**	**FTA**	**Pct.**	**Off.**	**Def.**	**Tot.**	**Ast.**	**St.**	**Blk.**	**TO**	**Pts.**	**RPG**	**APG**	**PPG**
1999—Utah	32	1068	182	427	.426	99	129	.767	71	67	138	87	27	8	98	476	4.3	2.7	14.9
2000—Utah	29	929	199	415	.480	92	134	.687	69	95	164	69	41	7	81	498	5.7	2.4	17.2
2001—Utah	28	854	138	319	.433	62	89	.697	66	86	152	58	27	0	75	343	5.4	2.1	12.3
2002—Utah	32	1101	189	419	.451	117	157	.745	91	90	181	67	45	6	102	503	5.7	2.1	15.7
2003—San Antonio	33	969	141	357	.395	81	102	.794	74	111	185	71	24	6	85	371	5.6	2.2	11.2
Totals	154	4921	849	1937	.438	451	611	.738	371	449	820	352	164	27	441	2191	5.3	2.3	14.2

Three-point field goals: 1999, 13-for-53 (.245). 2000, 8-for-29 (.276). 2001, 5-for-31 (.161). 2002, 8-for-28 (.286). 2003, 8-for-36 (.222). Totals, 42-for-177 (.237).

Personal fouls/disqualifications: 1999, 76/0. 2000, 67/0. 2001, 64/0. 2002, 92/0. 2003, 96/2. Totals, 395/2.

WNBA PLAYOFF RECORD

Season Team	G	Min.	FGM	FGA	Pct.	FTM	FTA	Pct.	REBOUNDS Off.	Def.	Tot.	Ast.	St.	Blk.	TO	Pts.	AVERAGES RPG	APG	PPG
2001—Utah..............	2	71	13	29	.448	5	9	.556	6	10	16	3	3	2	4	31	8.0	1.5	15.5
2002—Utah..............	5	190	29	74	.392	12	17	.706	9	18	27	8	7	0	21	72	5.4	1.6	14.4
Totals................	7	261	42	103	.408	17	26	.654	15	28	43	11	10	2	25	103	6.1	1.6	14.7

Three-point field goals: 2001, 0-for-4. 2002, 2-for-7 (.286). Totals, 2-for-11 (.182).
Personal fouls/disqualifications: 2001, 7/0. 2002, 11/0. Totals, 18/0.

WNBA ALL-STAR GAME RECORD

Season Team	Min.	FGM	FGA	Pct.	FTM	FTA	Pct.	REBOUNDS Off.	Def.	Tot.	Ast.	PF	Dq.	St.	Blk.	TO	Pts.
2002 —Utah................	9	0	2	.000	0	0	...	0	1	1	0	0	0	0	0	...	0
Totals................	9	0	2	.000	0	0	...	0	1	1	0	0	0	0	0	0	0

Three-point field goals: 2002, 0-for-1. Totals, 0-for-1.

GORTMAN, SHAUNZINSKI   G   LYNX

PERSONAL: Born December 7, 1979, in Columbia, S.C. ... 6-1/158 (1.85 m/72 kg).
COLLEGE: South Carolina.
TRANSACTIONS/CAREER NOTES: Selected by Charlotte in first round (ninth overall) of WNBA Draft, April 19, 2002. ... Traded by Charlotte to Minnesota for F Maylana Martin and G Erin Buescher, April 19, 2002.

COLLEGIATE RECORD

Season Team	G	Min.	FGM	FGA	Pct.	FTM	FTA	Pct.	Reb.	Ast.	Pts.	AVERAGES RPG	APG	PPG
98-99—South Carolina..........	27	745	118	314	.376	53	90	.589	137	61	301	5.1	2.3	11.1
99-00—South Carolina..........	20	578	116	248	.468	51	85	.600	112	84	296	5.6	4.2	14.8
00-01—South Carolina..........	27	843	112	293	.382	40	57	.702	138	80	298	5.1	3.0	11.0
01-02—South Carolina..........	29	910	164	377	.435	59	90	.656	179	87	436	6.2	3.0	15.0
Totals	103	3076	510	1232	.414	203	322	.630	566	312	1331	5.5	3.0	12.9

Three-point field goals: 1998-99, 12-for-56 (.214). 1999-00, 13-for-34 (.382). 2000-01, 34-for-105 (.324). 2001-02, 49-for-132 (.371). Totals, 108-for-327 (.330).

WNBA REGULAR-SEASON RECORD

Season Team	G	Min.	FGM	FGA	Pct.	FTM	FTA	Pct.	REBOUNDS Off.	Def.	Tot.	Ast.	St.	Blk.	TO	Pts.	AVERAGES RPG	APG	PPG
2002—Minnesota.....	29	369	35	97	.361	7	9	.778	16	45	61	21	13	6	25	91	2.1	0.7	3.1
2003—Minnesota.....	25	200	21	49	.429	3	4	.750	9	23	32	14	11	1	20	50	1.3	0.6	2.0
Totals................	54	569	56	146	.384	10	13	.769	25	68	93	35	24	7	45	141	1.7	0.6	2.6

Three-point field goals: 2002, 14-for-43 (.326). 2003, 5-for-20 (.250). Totals, 19-for-63 (.302).
Personal fouls/disqualifications: 2002, 42/0. 2003, 25/0. Totals, 67/0.

GRIFFITH, YOLANDA   F   MONARCHS

PERSONAL: Born March 1, 1970, in Chicago. ... 6-3/176 (1.91 m/80 kg). ... **Full name:** Yolanda Evette Griffith.
HIGH SCHOOL: George Washington Carver (Chicago).
COLLEGE: Florida Atlantic.
TRANSACTIONS/CAREER NOTES: Selected by Sacramento in first round (second overall) of WNBA Draft, May 4, 1999.

COLLEGIATE RECORD

NOTES: Division II Kodak All American (1993).

Season Team	G	Min.	FGM	FGA	Pct.	FTM	FTA	Pct.	Reb.	Ast.	Pts.	AVERAGES RPG	APG	PPG
92-93—Florida Atlantic	22	...	262	415	.631	97	164	.591	352	45	621	16.0	2.0	28.2
Totals	22	...	262	415	.631	97	164	.591	352	45	621	16.0	2.0	28.2

Three-point field goals: 1992-93, 0-for-1.

ABL REGULAR-SEASON RECORD

NOTES: ABL Defensive player of year (1997-98).

Season Team	G	Min.	FGM	FGA	Pct.	FTM	FTA	Pct.	Reb.	Ast.	Pts.	AVERAGES RPG	APG	PPG
97-98—Chicago	44	...	310	573	.541	207	298	.695	493	65	827	11.2	1.5	18.8
98-99—Chicago	12	...	62	145	.428	82	113	.726	147	31	206	12.3	2.6	17.2
Totals	56	...	372	718	.518	289	411	.703	640	96	1033	11.4	1.7	18.4

Three-point field goals: 1997-98, 0-for-2. 1998-99, 0-for-1. Totals, 0-for-3.

WNBA REGULAR-SEASON RECORD

HONORS: All-WNBA second team (2000, 2001). ... WNBA Most Valuable Player (1999). ... All-WNBA first team (1999). ... WNBA Newcomer of Year (1999). ... WNBA Defensive Player of the Year (1999). ... Led WNBA with 11.2 rebounds per game (2001) and 11.3 rebounds per game (1999). ... Led WNBA with 2.52 steals per game (1999). ... Led WNBA with 18 double-doubles (2001) and 17 double-doubles (1999).

Season Team	G	Min.	FGM	FGA	Pct.	FTM	FTA	Pct.	REBOUNDS Off.	Def.	Tot.	Ast.	St.	Blk.	TO	Pts.	AVERAGES RPG	APG	PPG
1999—Sacramento	29	979	200	370	.541	145	235	.617	141	188	329	45	73	54	66	545	11.3	1.6	18.8
2000—Sacramento	32	1026	193	361	.535	137	194	.706	148	183	331	47	83	61	82	523	10.3	1.5	16.3
2001—Sacramento	32	1077	192	368	.522	134	186	.720	162	195	357	54	63	37	75	518	11.2	1.7	16.2
2002—Sacramento	17	577	93	179	.520	102	127	.803	66	82	148	19	16	13	45	288	8.7	1.1	16.9
2003—Sacramento	34	1015	161	332	.485	147	190	.774	92	156	248	46	57	39	75	469	7.3	1.4	13.8
Totals................	144	4674	839	1610	.521	665	932	.714	609	804	1413	211	292	204	343	2343	9.8	1.5	16.3

Three-point field goals: 1999, 0-for-1. 2003, 0-for-2. Totals, 0-for-3.
Personal fouls/disqualifications: 1999, 91/0. 2003, 125/3. Totals, 510/5.

G

WNBA PLAYOFF RECORD

Season Team	G	Min.	FGM	FGA	Pct.	FTM	FTA	Pct.	Off.	Def.	Tot.	Ast.	St.	Blk.	TO	Pts.	RPG	APG	PPG
2000—Sacramento....	2	78	12	23	.522	5	8	.625	6	18	24	2	1	1	4	29	12.0	1.0	14.5
2001—Sacramento....	5	181	32	67	.478	42	55	.764	18	26	44	7	8	6	11	106	8.8	1.4	21.2
2003—Sacramento....	6	200	36	67	.537	31	34	.912	19	34	53	7	7	6	12	103	8.8	1.2	17.2
Totals.................	13	459	80	157	.510	78	97	.804	43	78	121	16	16	13	27	238	9.3	1.2	18.3

WNBA ALL-STAR GAME RECORD

Season Team	Min.	FGM	FGA	Pct.	FTM	FTA	Pct.	Off.	Def.	Tot.	Ast.	PF	Dq.	St.	Blk.	TO	Pts.
1999—Sacramento	21	5	10	.500	0	0	...	2	3	5	1	2	0	1	1	...	10
2000—Sacramento	16	3	8	.375	4	6	.667	5	5	10	0	0	0	0	1	...	10
2001—Sacramento	18	7	8	.875	3	4	.750	3	4	7	0	2	0	2	1	...	17
2003—Sacramento	25	6	8	.750	2	3	.667	2	5	7	1	3	0	2	2	...	14
Totals.................	80	21	34	.618	9	13	.692	12	17	29	2	7	0	5	5	13	51

OLYMPICS

NOTES: Member of gold medal-winning U.S. Olympic Team (2000).

Season Team	G	Min.	FGM	FGA	Pct.	FTM	FTA	Pct.	Reb.	Ast.	Pts.	RPG	APG	PPG
2000—United States..............	8	168	37	54	.685	18	24	.750	70	3	92	8.8	0.4	11.5
Totals	8	168	37	54	.685	18	24	.750	70	3	92	8.8	0.4	11.5

GROOMS, LADY   G   MONARCHS

PERSONAL: Born September 12, 1970, in Raleigh, N.C. ... 5-10/160 (1.78 m/73 kg). **Full name:** LeJuana Anjanette Grooms.
HIGH SCHOOL: Brown (Atlanta).
COLLEGE: Georgia.
TRANSACTIONS/CAREER NOTES: Assigned to Utah, January 22, 1997. ... Traded by Utah to Sacramento for G Chantel Tremitiere, May 4, 1998).

COLLEGIATE RECORD

Season Team	G	Min.	FGM	FGA	Pct.	FTM	FTA	Pct.	Reb.	Ast.	Pts.	RPG	APG	PPG
88-89—Georgia......................	30	...	81	167	.485	52	82	.634	119	46	214	4.0	1.5	7.1
89-90—Georgia......................	29	...	155	331	.468	99	142	.697	165	112	409	5.7	3.9	14.1
90-91—Georgia......................	32	...	158	338	.467	97	150	.647	140	96	413	4.4	3.0	12.9
91-92—Georgia......................	30	...	135	313	.431	89	140	.636	114	179	361	3.8	6.0	12.0
Totals	121	...	529	1149	.460	337	514	.656	538	433	1397	4.4	3.6	11.5

Three-point field goals: 1989-90, 1-for-5 (.200). 1990-91, 0-for-2. 1991-92, 2-for-14 (.143). Totals, 3-for-21 (.143).

WNBA REGULAR-SEASON RECORD

Season Team	G	Min.	FGM	FGA	Pct.	FTM	FTA	Pct.	Off.	Def.	Tot.	Ast.	St.	Blk.	TO	Pts.	RPG	APG	PPG
1997—Utah..............	28	691	58	167	.347	36	55	.655	33	51	84	67	23	2	79	153	3.0	2.4	5.5
1998—Sacramento....	30	792	75	154	.487	63	94	.670	37	43	80	48	20	3	52	214	2.7	1.6	7.1
1999—Sacramento....	32	450	27	72	.375	44	63	.698	23	31	54	39	11	2	36	98	1.7	1.2	3.1
2000—Sacramento....	30	401	39	88	.443	46	61	.754	27	17	44	13	10	3	21	124	1.5	0.4	4.1
2001—Sacramento....	31	543	49	114	.430	43	58	.741	32	46	78	38	15	10	25	141	2.5	1.2	4.5
2002—Sacramento....	32	850	78	181	.431	71	83	.855	38	61	99	39	21	8	46	227	3.1	1.2	7.1
2003—Sacramento....	34	470	45	112	.402	21	26	.808	15	31	46	29	17	5	21	111	1.4	0.9	3.3
Totals.................	217	4197	371	888	.418	324	440	.736	205	280	485	273	117	33	280	1068	2.2	1.3	4.9

Three-point field goals: 1997, 1-for-10 (.100). 1998, 1-for-6 (.167). 1999, 0-for-2. 2000, 0-for-1. 2002, 0-for-1. 2003, 0-for-1. Totals, 2-for-21 (.095).
Personal fouls/disqualifications: 1997, 39/0. 1998, 35/0. 1999, 21/0. 2000, 27/0. 2002, 69/0. 2003, 27/0. Totals, 261/0.

WNBA PLAYOFF RECORD

Season Team	G	Min.	FGM	FGA	Pct.	FTM	FTA	Pct.	Off.	Def.	Tot.	Ast.	St.	Blk.	TO	Pts.	RPG	APG	PPG
1999—Sacramento....	1	25	3	7	.429	0	0	...	1	4	5	1	1	0	2	6	5.0	1.0	6.0
2000—Sacramento....	2	23	1	2	.500	1	1	1.000	0	2	2	0	0	0	1	3	1.0	0.0	1.5
2001—Sacramento....	5	31	2	7	.286	5	6	.833	1	3	4	1	0	0	3	9	0.8	0.2	1.8
2003—Sacramento....	6	65	7	12	.583	1	2	.500	2	3	5	3	1	0	1	15	0.8	0.5	2.5
Totals.................	14	144	13	28	.464	7	9	.778	6	10	16	5	2	0	7	33	1.1	0.4	2.4

G

GRUBIN, GORDANA   G   COMETS

PERSONAL: Born August 20, 1972, in Zrenjanin, Yugoslavia ... 5-11/165 (1.80 m/75 kg). **Full name:** Gordana Grubin.
TRANSACTIONS/CAREER NOTES: Drafted by Los Angeles, June 10, 1999. ... Selected by Indiana in first round (first overall) of 2000 WNBA Expansion Draft, December 15, 1999. ... Traded by Indiana to Phoenix for G Bridget Pettis and a first-round pick in the 2002 WNBA Draft, March 4, 2002. ... Signed by Houston as a free agent, March 1, 2004.

WNBA REGULAR-SEASON RECORD

									REBOUNDS								AVERAGES		
Season Team	G	Min.	FGM	FGA	Pct.	FTM	FTA	Pct.	Off.	Def.	Tot.	Ast.	St.	Blk.	TO	Pts.	RPG	APG	PPG
1999—Los Angeles....	32	708	96	238	.403	52	68	.765	18	54	72	90	24	2	53	284	2.3	2.8	8.9
2000—Indiana.........	29	720	90	239	.377	31	40	.775	20	56	76	63	31	0	60	239	2.6	2.2	8.2
2001—Indiana.........	27	481	62	167	.371	29	39	.744	18	31	49	33	7	0	34	170	1.8	1.2	6.3
2002—Phoenix.........	32	859	114	297	.384	60	79	.759	16	48	64	104	36	3	58	317	2.0	3.3	9.9
Totals.................	120	2768	362	941	.385	172	226	.761	72	189	261	290	98	5	205	1010	2.2	2.4	8.4

Three-point field goals: 1999, 40-for-93 (.430). 2000, 28-for-91 (.308). 2001, 17-for-58 (.293). 2002, 29-for-92 (.315). Totals, 114-for-334 (.341).

Personal fouls/disqualifications: 1999, 53/1. 2000, 47/0. 2001, 30/0. 2002, 59/0. Totals, 189/1.

WNBA PLAYOFF RECORD

									REBOUNDS								AVERAGES		
Season Team	G	Min.	FGM	FGA	Pct.	FTM	FTA	Pct.	Off.	Def.	Tot.	Ast.	St.	Blk.	TO	Pts.	RPG	APG	PPG
1999—Los Angeles....	4	119	13	37	.351	1	2	.500	3	9	12	23	5	0	8	31	3.0	5.8	7.8
Totals.................	4	119	13	37	.351	1	2	.500	3	9	12	23	5	0	8	31	3.0	5.8	7.8

Three-point field goals: 1999, 4-for-16 (.250). Totals, 4-for-16 (.250).

Personal fouls/disqualifications: 1999, 9/0. Totals, 9/0.

HAMMON, BECKY   G   LIBERTY

PERSONAL: Born March 11, 1977, in Rapid City, S.D. ... 5-6/136 (1.68 m/62 kg). ... **Full name:** Rebecca Lynn Hammon.

HIGH SCHOOL: Stevens (Rapids City, S.D.).

COLLEGE: Colorado State.

TRANSACTIONS/CAREER NOTES: Signed by WNBA and assigned to New York, May 12, 1999.

COLLEGIATE RECORD

NOTES: Kodak All-America first team (1999).

												AVERAGES		
Season Team	G	Min.	FGM	FGA	Pct.	FTM	FTA	Pct.	Reb.	Ast.	Pts.	RPG	APG	PPG
95-96—Colorado State	31	...	200	424	.472	106	131	.809	97	101	594	3.1	3.3	19.2
96-97—Colorado State	28	...	219	476	.460	97	125	.776	111	102	618	4.0	3.6	22.1
97-98—Colorado State	30	...	238	468	.509	148	167	.886	116	161	704	3.9	5.4	23.5
98-99—Colorado State	36	...	261	526	.496	188	218	.862	138	171	824	3.8	4.8	22.9
Totals	125	...	918	1894	.485	539	641	.841	462	535	2740	3.7	4.3	21.9

Three-point field goals: 1995-96, 88-for-206 (.427). 1996-97, 83-for-209 (.397). 1997-98, 80-for-199 (.402). 1998-99, 114-for-274 (.416). Totals, 365-for-888 (.411)

WNBA REGULAR-SEASON RECORD

NOTES: Led the WNBA in three point field goal percentage (.469) 2003. ... Led the WNBA in free throw percentage (.951) 2003.

									REBOUNDS								AVERAGES		
Season Team	G	Min.	FGM	FGA	Pct.	FTM	FTA	Pct.	Off.	Def.	Tot.	Ast.	St.	Blk.	TO	Pts.	RPG	APG	PPG
1999—New York......	30	202	27	64	.422	15	17	.882	2	17	19	17	6	0	24	80	0.6	0.6	2.7
2000—New York......	32	835	119	252	.472	61	69	.884	19	45	64	58	29	1	62	351	2.0	1.8	11.0
2001—New York......	32	619	90	197	.457	40	51	.784	10	42	52	51	27	1	48	262	1.6	1.6	8.2
2002—New York......	32	659	87	197	.442	38	56	.679	18	50	68	54	25	0	55	256	2.1	1.7	8.0
2003—New York......	11	257	50	87	.575	39	41	.951	1	20	21	18	10	1	27	162	1.9	1.6	14.7
Totals.................	137	2572	373	797	.468	193	234	.825	50	174	224	198	97	3	216	1111	1.6	1.4	8.1

Three-point field goals: 1999, 11-for-38 (.289). 2000, 52-for-141 (.369). 2001, 42-for-111 (.378). 2002, 44-for-114 (.386). 2003, 23-for-49 (.469). Totals, 172-for-453 (.380)

Personal fouls/disqualifications: 1999, 27/0. 2000, 55/0. 2001, 46/0. 2002, 49/0. 2003, 13/0. Totals, 190/0.

WNBA PLAYOFF RECORD

									REBOUNDS								AVERAGES		
Season Team	G	Min.	FGM	FGA	Pct.	FTM	FTA	Pct.	Off.	Def.	Tot.	Ast.	St.	Blk.	TO	Pts.	RPG	APG	PPG
1999—New York......	6	50	2	12	.167	6	6	1.000	0	1	1	5	0	0	6	12	0.2	0.8	2.0
2000—New York......	7	206	21	49	.429	17	19	.895	5	5	10	15	9	0	17	66	1.4	2.1	9.4
2001—New York......	6	48	6	17	.353	0	0	...	0	3	3	2	1	0	3	15	0.5	0.3	2.5
2002—New York......	8	183	29	54	.537	7	8	.875	2	15	17	16	5	0	11	79	2.1	2.0	9.9
Totals.................	27	487	58	132	.439	30	33	.909	7	24	31	38	15	0	37	172	1.1	1.4	6.4

Three-point field goals: 1999, 2-for-9 (.222). 2000, 7-for-23 (.304). 2001, 3-for-10 (.300). 2002, 14-for-33 (.424). Totals, 26-for-75 (.347)

Personal fouls/disqualifications: 1999, 3/0. 2000, 10/0. 2001, 3/0. 2002, 12/0. Totals, 28/0.

HARRISON, LISA   F   MERCURY

PERSONAL: Born January 2, 1971, in Louisville, Ky. ... 6-1/164 (1.85 m/74 kg). ... **Full name:** Lisa Darlene Harrison.

HIGH SCHOOL: Southern (Louisville, Ky.).

COLLEGE: Tennessee.

TRANSACTIONS/CAREER NOTES: Selected by Phoenix in third round (34th overall) of WNBA Draft, May 4, 1999.

H

COLLEGIATE RECORD

NOTES: Member of NCAA Divison I championship team (1991). ... Kodak All-America first team (1993).

Season Team	G	Min.	FGM	FGA	Pct.	FTM	FTA	Pct.	Reb.	Ast.	Pts.	AVERAGES RPG	APG	PPG
89-90—Tennessee	33	...	107	229	.467	41	65	.631	159	51	255	4.8	1.5	7.7
90-91—Tennessee	34	...	114	287	.397	31	61	.508	193	75	259	5.7	2.2	7.6
91-92—Tennessee	31	...	75	193	.389	24	33	.727	162	64	174	5.2	2.1	5.6
92-93—Tennessee	31	...	196	419	.468	54	87	.621	300	82	447	9.7	2.6	14.4
Totals	129	...	492	1128	.436	150	246	.610	814	272	1135	6.3	2.1	8.8

Three-point field goals: 1992-93, 1-for-2 (.500).

ABL REGULAR-SEASON RECORD

Season Team	G	Min.	FGM	FGA	Pct.	FTM	FTA	Pct.	Reb.	Ast.	Pts.	AVERAGES RPG	APG	PPG
96-97—Portland	40	...	168	382	.440	51	68	.750	176	79	393	4.4	2.0	9.8
97-98—Portland	44	...	142	331	.429	33	52	.635	146	68	323	3.3	1.5	7.3
98-99—Columbus	14	...	47	93	.505	23	27	.852	76	12	117	5.4	0.9	8.4
Totals	98	...	357	806	.443	107	147	.728	398	159	833	4.1	1.6	8.5

Three-point field goals: 1996-97, 6-for-21 (.286). 1997-98, 6-for-28 (.214). 1998-99, 0-for-1. Totals, 12-for-50 (.240)

WNBA REGULAR-SEASON RECORD

Season Team	G	Min.	FGM	FGA	Pct.	FTM	FTA	Pct.	REBOUNDS Off.	Def.	Tot.	Ast.	St.	Blk.	TO	Pts.	AVERAGES RPG	APG	PPG
1999—Phoenix........	32	828	81	170	.476	30	44	.682	47	83	130	52	23	5	35	193	4.1	1.6	6.0
2000—Phoenix........	31	750	81	154	.526	30	37	.811	38	83	121	36	30	4	22	200	3.9	1.2	6.5
2001—Phoenix........	32	915	96	223	.430	51	59	.864	39	100	139	52	39	1	49	246	4.3	1.6	7.7
2002—Phoenix........	32	899	120	242	.496	20	23	.870	43	83	126	40	31	3	45	262	3.9	1.3	8.2
2003—Phoenix........	33	838	74	179	.413	35	51	.686	42	76	118	36	29	6	34	183	3.6	1.1	5.5
Totals.................	160	4230	452	968	.467	166	214	.776	209	425	634	216	152	19	185	1084	4.0	1.4	6.8

Three-point field goals: 1999, 1-for-9 (.111). 2000, 8-for-12 (.667). 2001, 3-for-9 (.333). 2002, 2-for-6 (.333). 2003, 0-for-3. Totals, 14-for-39 (.359)

Personal fouls/disqualifications: 1999, 65/1. 2000, 62/0. 2001, 58/0. 2002, 62/0. 2003, 58/0. Totals, 305/1.

WNBA PLAYOFF RECORD

Season Team	G	Min.	FGM	FGA	Pct.	FTM	FTA	Pct.	REBOUNDS Off.	Def.	Tot.	Ast.	St.	Blk.	TO	Pts.	AVERAGES RPG	APG	PPG
2000—Phoenix........	2	68	12	17	.706	2	2	1.000	4	7	11	10	3	0	3	26	5.5	5.0	13.0
Totals.................	2	68	12	17	.706	2	2	1.000	4	7	11	10	3	0	3	26	5.5	5.0	13.0

Three-point field goals: 2000, 0-for-2. Totals, 0-for-2.
Personal fouls/disqualifications: 2000, 5/0. Totals, 5/0.

HARROWER, KRISTI   G   LYNX

PERSONAL: Born March 4, 1975, in Bendigo, Australia ... 5-4/139 (1.63 m/63 kg).
HIGH SCHOOL: Bendigo (Bendigo, Australia).
TRANSACTIONS/CAREER NOTES: Signed by WNBA and asigned to Phoenix, May 8, 1998. ... Traded by Phoenix to Minnesota with C Marlies Askamp and G Angela Aycock for F Adia Barnes, G Tonya Edwards and G/F Trisha Fallon, October 27, 1999.

WNBA REGULAR-SEASON RECORD

Season Team	G	Min.	FGM	FGA	Pct.	FTM	FTA	Pct.	REBOUNDS Off.	Def.	Tot.	Ast.	St.	Blk.	TO	Pts.	AVERAGES RPG	APG	PPG
1998—Phoenix........	30	355	19	52	.365	21	28	.750	2	19	21	52	15	3	31	70	0.7	1.7	2.3
1999—Phoenix........	32	666	36	99	.364	59	73	.808	9	54	63	96	25	4	45	143	2.0	3.0	4.5
2000—Phoenix........						Did not play due to injury..													
2001—Minnesota.....	4	72	7	15	.467	4	4	1.000	1	3	4	11	3	0	3	21	1.0	2.8	5.3
2002—Minnesota.....	27	481	37	95	.389	4	10	.400	9	37	46	54	12	0	28	96	1.7	2.0	3.6
2003—Minnesota.....	31	499	32	87	.368	8	13	.615	9	30	39	72	18	3	39	88	1.3	2.3	2.8
Totals.................	124	2073	131	348	.376	96	128	.750	30	143	173	285	73	10	146	418	1.4	2.3	3.4

Three-point field goals: 1998, 11-for-32 (.344). 1999, 12-for-43 (.279). 2001, 3-for-6 (.500). 2002, 18-for-54 (.333). 2003, 16-for-43 (.372). Totals, 60-for-178 (.337)
Personal fouls/disqualifications: 1998, 25/0. 1999, 45/0. 2001, 4/0. 2002, 24/0. 2003, 15/0. Totals, 113/0.

WNBA PLAYOFF RECORD

Season Team	G	Min.	FGM	FGA	Pct.	FTM	FTA	Pct.	REBOUNDS Off.	Def.	Tot.	Ast.	St.	Blk.	TO	Pts.	AVERAGES RPG	APG	PPG
1998—Phoenix........	6	78	12	20	.600	0	0	...	1	5	6	7	5	1	4	27	1.0	1.2	4.5
2003—Minnesota.....	3	65	4	11	.364	1	2	.500	1	6	7	5	1	0	3	11	2.3	1.7	3.7
Totals.................	9	143	16	31	.516	1	2	.500	2	11	13	12	6	1	7	38	1.4	1.3	4.2

Three-point field goals: 1998, 3-for-7 (.429). 2003, 2-for-7 (.286). Totals, 5-for-14 (.357)
Personal fouls/disqualifications: 1998, 4/0. 2003, 6/0. Totals, 10/0.

OLYMPICS

NOTES: Member of silver medal-winning Australian Olympic Team (2000).

Season Team	G	Min.	FGM	FGA	Pct.	FTM	FTA	Pct.	Reb.	Ast.	Pts.	AVERAGES RPG	APG	PPG
2000—Australia......................	8	195	17	47	.362	12	19	.632	23	30	50	2.9	3.8	6.3
Totals	8	195	17	47	.362	12	19	.632	23	30	50	2.9	3.8	6.3

Three-point field goals: 2000-01, 4-for-18 (.222).

H

HENDERSON, TRACY   C

PERSONAL: Born December 31, 1974, in Greenville, Miss. ... 6-3/200 (1.91 m/91 kg). ... **Full name:** Tracy Henderson.
HIGH SCHOOL: Patrick Henry (Minneapolis, Minn.).
COLLEGE: Georgia.
TRANSACTIONS/CAREER NOTES: Selected by Cleveland in third round (35th overall) of WNBA Draft, May 4, 1999.

COLLEGIATE RECORD

| | | | | | | | | | | | | AVERAGES | | |
Season Team	G	Min.	FGM	FGA	Pct.	FTM	FTA	Pct.	Reb.	Ast.	Pts.	RPG	APG	PPG
93-94—Georgia	28	...	148	289	.512	53	89	.596	174	7	349	6.2	0.3	12.5
94-95—Georgia	33	...	219	399	.549	72	125	.576	252	13	510	7.6	0.4	15.5
95-96—Georgia	33	...	208	359	.579	50	78	.641	211	22	466	6.4	0.7	14.1
96-97—Georgia	28	...	182	333	.547	75	108	.694	186	28	438	6.6	1.0	15.6
Totals	122	...	757	1380	.549	250	400	.625	823	70	1763	6.7	0.6	14.5

Three-point field goals: 1996-97, 0-for-1.

ABL REGULAR-SEASON RECORD

| | | | | | | | | | | | | AVERAGES | | |
Season Team	G	Min.	FGM	FGA	Pct.	FTM	FTA	Pct.	Reb.	Ast.	Pts.	RPG	APG	PPG
97-98—Atlanta	37	...	156	296	.527	55	82	.671	157	27	367	4.2	0.7	9.9
98-99—Nashville	14	...	63	136	.463	37	51	.725	74	14	164	5.3	1.0	11.7
Totals	51	...	219	432	.507	92	133	.692	231	41	531	4.5	0.8	10.4

Three-point field goals: 1998-99, 1-for-5 (.200).

WNBA REGULAR-SEASON RECORD

| | | | | | | | | REBOUNDS | | | | | | | | AVERAGES | | |
Season Team	G	Min.	FGM	FGA	Pct.	FTM	FTA	Pct.	Off.	Def.	Tot.	Ast.	St.	Blk.	TO	Pts.	RPG	APG	PPG
1999—Cleveland	27	308	27	87	.310	17	29	.586	28	51	79	9	9	20	25	71	2.9	0.3	2.6
2000—Cleveland								Did not play..											
2002—Cleveland	23	173	16	41	.390	3	3	1.000	12	22	34	3	3	7	18	35	1.5	0.1	1.5
2003—Cleveland	11	45	1	13	.077	0	0	...	6	8	14	3	1	1	4	2	1.3	0.3	0.2
Totals	61	526	44	141	.312	20	32	.625	46	81	127	15	13	28	47	108	2.1	0.2	1.8

WNBA PLAYOFF RECORD

| | | | | | | | | REBOUNDS | | | | | | | | AVERAGES | | |
Season Team	G	Min.	FGM	FGA	Pct.	FTM	FTA	Pct.	Off.	Def.	Tot.	Ast.	St.	Blk.	TO	Pts.	RPG	APG	PPG
2003—Cleveland	1	3	1	1	1.000	0	0	...	0	1	1	0	0	0	0	2	1.0	0.0	2.0
Totals	1	3	1	1	1.000	0	0	...	0	1	1	0	0	0	0	2	1.0	0.0	2.0

HENNING, SONJA   G

PERSONAL: Born October 4, 1969, in Jackson, Tenn. ... 5-7/143 (1.70 m/65 kg). ... **Full name:** Sonja Leneice Henning.
HIGH SCHOOL: William Horlick High (Racine, Wis.).
COLLEGE: Stanford.
TRANSACTIONS/CAREER NOTES: Selected by Houston in second round (24th overall) of WNBA Draft (May 4, 1999). ... Selected by Seattle in second round (8th overall) of 2000 WNBA Expansion Draft (December 15, 1999). ... Traded by Seattle to Houston for F Amanda Lassiter, June 17, 2002. ... Waived by Washington, May 26, 2003. ... Signed by Indiana June 2, 2003.

COLLEGIATE RECORD

NOTES: Member of NCAA Division I championship team (1990). ... Kodak All America first team (1991).

| | | | | | | | | | | | | AVERAGES | | |
Season Team	G	Min.	FGM	FGA	Pct.	FTM	FTA	Pct.	Reb.	Ast.	Pts.	RPG	APG	PPG
87-88—Stanford	32	...	123	278	.442	101	133	.759	138	128	347	4.3	4.0	10.8
88-89—Stanford	30	...	109	219	.498	70	96	.729	123	171	304	4.1	5.7	10.1
89-90—Stanford	33	...	101	224	.451	79	107	.738	291	221	291	8.8	6.7	8.8
90-91—Stanford	32	...	172	378	.455	113	179	.631	191	237	347	6.0	7.4	10.8
Totals	127	...	505	1099	.460	363	515	.705	743	757	1289	5.9	6.0	10.1

Three-point field goals: 1987-88, 0-for-1. 1988-89, 16-for-37 (.432). 1989-90, 10-for-39 (.256). 1990-91, 46-for-121 (.380). Totals, 72-for-198 (.364).

ABL REGULAR-SEASON RECORD

| | | | | | | | | | | | | AVERAGES | | |
Season Team	G	Min.	FGM	FGA	Pct.	FTM	FTA	Pct.	Reb.	Ast.	Pts.	RPG	APG	PPG
96-97—San Jose	40	...	107	270	.396	68	101	.673	210	126	299	5.3	3.2	7.5
97-98—San Jose	44	...	37	117	.316	20	40	.500	96	73	105	2.2	1.7	2.4
98-99—Portland	13	...	36	88	.409	14	26	.538	34	78	106	2.6	6.0	8.2
Totals	97	...	180	475	.379	102	167	.611	340	277	510	3.5	2.9	5.3

Three-point field goals: 1996-97, 17-for-62 (.274). 1997-98, 11-for-35 (.314). 1998-99, 20-for-47 (.426). Totals, 48-for-144 (.333).

H

WNBA REGULAR-SEASON RECORD

Season Team	G	Min.	FGM	FGA	Pct.	FTM	FTA	Pct.	REBOUNDS Off.	Def.	Tot.	Ast.	St.	Blk.	TO	Pts.	AVERAGES RPG	APG	PPG
1999—Houston	32	798	52	117	.444	11	18	.611	22	58	80	74	34	7	29	128	2.5	2.3	4.0
2000—Seattle	32	980	53	151	.351	37	61	.607	22	64	86	79	61	3	54	168	2.7	2.5	5.3
2001—Seattle	32	902	41	129	.318	18	35	.514	14	57	71	93	52	6	43	108	2.2	2.9	3.4
2002—Sea.-Hou.......	31	728	26	74	.351	7	15	.467	18	66	84	66	32	7	43	62	2.7	2.1	2.0
2003—Washington....	24	295	11	43	.256	2	8	.250	2	23	25	29	15	0	13	24	1.0	1.2	1.0
Totals.................	151	3703	183	514	.356	75	137	.547	78	268	346	341	194	23	182	490	2.3	2.3	3.2

Three-point field goals: 1999, 13-for-41 (.317). 2000, 25-for-66 (.379). 2001, 8-for-44 (.182). 2002, 3-for-16 (.188). 2003, 0-for-9. Totals, 49-for-176 (.278).
Personal fouls/disqualifications: 1999, 60/0. 2000, 73/1. 2001, 62/2. 2002, 57/0. 2003, 28/0. Totals, 280/3.

WNBA PLAYOFF RECORD

Season Team	G	Min.	FGM	FGA	Pct.	FTM	FTA	Pct.	REBOUNDS Off.	Def.	Tot.	Ast.	St.	Blk.	TO	Pts.	AVERAGES RPG	APG	PPG
1999—Houston	6	136	8	23	.348	2	6	.333	7	11	18	11	7	1	7	19	3.0	1.8	3.2
2002—Houston	3	48	0	9	.000	0	0	...	1	3	4	4	1	0	2	0	1.3	1.3	0.0
Totals.................	9	184	8	32	.250	2	6	.333	8	14	22	15	8	1	9	19	2.4	1.7	2.1

Three-point field goals: 1999, 1-for-9 (.111). 2002, 0-for-2. Totals, 1-for-11 (.091).
Personal fouls/disqualifications: 1999, 5/0. 2002, 2/0. Totals, 7/0.

HICKS, JESSIE   F/C   SILVER STARS

PERSONAL: Born December 2, 1971, in Richmond, Va. ... 6-4/188 (1.93 m/85 kg). ... **Full name:** Jessie Yvette Hicks.
HIGH SCHOOL: Thomas Jefferson (Richmond, Va.).
COLLEGE: Maryland.
TRANSACTIONS/CAREER NOTES: Selected by Utah in second round (12th overall) of WNBA Draft, April 28, 1997. ... Waived by Utah, April 30, 1999. ... Signed by WNBA and assigned to Orlando, May 2, 2000. ... Signed by Connecticut as a free agent February 6, 2003.

COLLEGIATE RECORD

NOTES: Honorable Mention Kodak All-America, 1992 and 1993. ... ACC All-Conference first team, 1991-92 and 1992-93. ... Selected to 1993 ACC All-Tournament team.

Season Team	G	Min.	FGM	FGA	Pct.	FTM	FTA	Pct.	Reb.	Ast.	Pts.	AVERAGES RPG	APG	PPG
89-90—Maryland	21	...	89	183	.486	33	59	.559	103	8	211	4.9	0.4	10.0
90-91—Maryland	30	...	177	296	.598	59	99	.596	147	27	413	4.9	0.9	13.8
91-92—Maryland	31	...	178	301	.591	92	149	.617	228	36	448	7.4	1.2	14.5
92-93—Maryland	30	...	205	324	.633	119	193	.617	225	25	529	7.5	0.8	17.6
Totals	112	...	649	1104	.588	303	500	.606	703	96	1601	6.3	0.9	14.3

WNBA REGULAR-SEASON RECORD

Season Team	G	Min.	FGM	FGA	Pct.	FTM	FTA	Pct.	REBOUNDS Off.	Def.	Tot.	Ast.	St.	Blk.	TO	Pts.	AVERAGES RPG	APG	PPG
1997—Utah..............	26	263	37	80	.463	9	16	.563	17	19	36	10	13	11	12	83	1.4	0.4	3.2
2000—Orlando	26	157	10	23	.435	18	29	.621	13	13	26	4	2	7	17	38	1.0	0.2	1.5
2001—Orlando	32	456	63	162	.389	43	66	.652	38	54	92	22	23	17	53	169	2.9	0.7	5.3
2002—Orlando	31	471	73	153	.477	44	63	.698	60	42	102	23	19	25	51	190	3.3	0.7	6.1
2003—Connecticut ...	27	253	37	80	.463	24	25	.960	23	25	48	6	11	9	26	98	1.8	0.2	3.6
Totals.................	142	1600	220	498	.442	138	199	.693	151	153	304	65	68	69	159	578	2.1	0.5	4.1

Three-point field goals: 1997, 0-for-1. Totals, 0-for-1.
Personal fouls/disqualifications: 1997, 57/1. Totals, 299/2.

WNBA PLAYOFF RECORD

Season Team	G	Min.	FGM	FGA	Pct.	FTM	FTA	Pct.	REBOUNDS Off.	Def.	Tot.	Ast.	St.	Blk.	TO	Pts.	AVERAGES RPG	APG	PPG
2003—Connecticut ..	4	27	5	8	.625	0	0	...	3	3	6	1	0	1	2	10	1.5	0.3	2.5
Totals.................	4	27	5	8	.625	0	0	...	3	3	6	1	0	1	2	10	1.5	0.3	2.5

HOLDSCLAW, CHAMIQUE   F   MYSTICS

PERSONAL: Born August 9, 1977, in Flushing, N.Y. ... 6-2/172 (1.88 m/78 kg). ... **Full name:** Chamique Shaunta Holdsclaw.
HIGH SCHOOL: Christ the King (Astoria, N.Y.).
COLLEGE: Tennessee.
TRANSACTIONS/CAREER NOTES: ... Selected by Washington in the first round (first overall) of WNBA Draft, May 4, 1999.

COLLEGIATE RECORD

NOTES: Member of NCAA Championship team (1996, 1997, 1998). ... Naismith Player of the Year (1998). ... Kodak All-America first team (1996, 1997, 1998, 1999).

Season Team	G	Min.	FGM	FGA	Pct.	FTM	FTA	Pct.	Reb.	Ast.	Pts.	AVERAGES RPG	APG	PPG
95-96—Tennessee	36	1057	237	507	.467	102	143	.713	326	75	583	9.1	2.1	16.2
96-97—Tennessee	39	1296	332	667	.498	122	183	.667	367	114	803	9.4	2.9	20.6
97-98—Tennessee	39	1168	370	678	.546	166	217	.765	328	117	915	8.4	3.0	23.5
98-99—Tennessee	34	1061	294	567	.519	133	188	.707	274	80	724	8.1	2.4	21.3
Totals	148	4582	1233	2419	.510	523	731	.715	1295	386	3025	8.8	2.6	20.4

Three-point field goals: 1995-96, 7-for-30 (.233). 1996-97, 17-for-50 (.340). 1997-98, 9-for-41 (.220). 1998-99, 3-for-21 (.143). Totals, 36-for-142 (.254).

H

431

WNBA REGULAR-SEASON RECORD

NOTES: WNBA Rookie of Year Award (1999). ... All-WNBA second team (1999, 2001, 2002). ... Led WNBA in scoring (19.9 ppg) and rebounding (11.6 rpg) in 2002. ... Led WNBA in rebounding (10.9 rpg) 2003. ... Bud Light Peak Performer, Rebounding (2002, 2003), Scoring (2002).

Season Team	G	Min.	FGM	FGA	Pct.	FTM	FTA	Pct.	Off.	Def.	Tot.	Ast.	St.	Blk.	TO	Pts.	RPG	APG	PPG
1999—Washington ...	31	1061	202	462	.437	116	150	.773	74	172	246	74	37	27	108	525	7.9	2.4	16.9
2000—Washington ...	32	1131	232	499	.465	87	128	.680	57	183	240	80	47	18	93	561	7.5	2.5	17.5
2001—Washington ...	29	975	187	467	.400	101	148	.682	72	184	256	66	44	14	94	486	8.8	2.3	16.8
2002—Washington ...	20	634	149	330	.452	88	106	.830	54	178	232	45	20	6	45	397	11.6	2.3	19.9
2003—Washington ...	27	948	204	480	.425	140	155	.903	72	222	294	89	34	15	72	554	10.9	3.3	20.5
Totals	139	4749	974	2238	.435	532	687	.774	329	939	1268	354	182	80	412	2523	9.1	2.5	18.2

Three-point field goals: 1999, 5-for-29 (.172). 2000, 10-for-39 (.256). 2001, 11-for-46 (.239). 2002, 11-for-28 (.393). 2003, 6-for-35 (.171). Totals, 43-for-177 (.243).

Personal fouls/disqualifications: 1999, 67/0. 2000, 74/0. 2001, 49/0. 2002, 50/0. 2003, 74/0. Totals, 314/0.

WNBA PLAYOFF RECORD

Season Team	G	Min.	FGM	FGA	Pct.	FTM	FTA	Pct.	Off.	Def.	Tot.	Ast.	St.	Blk.	TO	Pts.	RPG	APG	PPG
2000—Washington ...	2	75	13	29	.448	4	4	1.000	3	8	11	1	3	1	6	30	5.5	0.5	15.0
2002—Washington ...	5	173	35	78	.449	22	30	.733	10	33	43	16	10	3	10	94	8.6	3.2	18.8
Totals	7	248	48	107	.449	26	34	.765	13	41	54	17	13	4	16	124	7.7	2.4	17.7

Three-point field goals: 2000, 0-for-1. 2002, 2-for-11 (.182). Totals, 2-for-12 (.167).

Personal fouls/disqualifications: 2000, 2/0. 2002, 14/0. Totals, 16/0.

WNBA ALL-STAR GAME RECORD

Season Team	Min.	FGM	FGA	Pct.	FTM	FTA	Pct.	Off.	Def.	Tot.	Ast.	PF	Dq.	St.	Blk.	TO	Pts.
1999 —Washington.....	11	2	6	.333	1	1	1.000	0	5	5	0	0	0	0	0	...	5
2000 —Washington.....	25	4	11	.364	1	2	.500	1	3	4	1	0	0	0	0	...	9
2003 —Washington.....	15	3	8	.375	0	0	...	0	1	1	0	0	0	1	1	...	6
Totals	51	9	25	.360	2	3	.667	1	9	10	1	0	0	1	1	3	20

Three-point field goals: 2003, 0-for-1. Totals, 0-for-1.

HOLLAND-CORN, KEDRA   G   COMETS

PERSONAL: Born November 5, 1974, in Houston, Texas ... 5-7/136 (1.70 m/62 kg). ... **Full name:** Kedra Nicol Holland-Corn.

HIGH SCHOOL: Lutheran North (Houston, Texas).

COLLEGE: Georgia.

TRANSACTIONS/CAREER NOTES: Selected by Sacramento in second round (14th overall) of WNBA Draft, May 4, 1999. ... Traded by Sacramento with a second round pick in the 2004 WNBA Draft to Detroit for the draft rights to Kara Lawson, April 29, 2003. ... Traded along with a second round pick in the 2004 WNBA Draft by Detroit to Houston in exchange for first and third round picks in the 2004 WNBA Draft.

MISCELLANEOUS: Member of WNBA Championship Team (2003).

COLLEGIATE RECORD

NOTES: Associated Press All-America third team (1997).

Season Team	G	Min.	FGM	FGA	Pct.	FTM	FTA	Pct.	Reb.	Ast.	Pts.	RPG	APG	PPG
93-94—Georgia......................	28	...	90	223	.404	28	39	.718	69	34	246	2.5	1.2	8.8
94-95—Georgia......................	33	...	149	362	.412	40	58	.690	128	61	413	3.9	1.8	12.5
95-96—Georgia......................	33	...	137	300	.457	36	47	.766	109	87	373	3.3	2.6	11.3
96-97—Georgia......................	31	...	187	399	.469	83	108	.769	124	117	534	4.0	3.8	17.2
Totals	125	...	563	1284	.438	187	252	.742	430	299	1566	3.4	2.4	12.5

Three-point field goals: 1993-94, 38-for-108 (.352). 1994-95, 75-for-208 (.361). 1995-96, 63-for-155 (.406). 1996-97, 77-for-204 (.377). Totals, 253-for-675 (.375)

ABL REGULAR-SEASON RECORD

Season Team	G	Min.	FGM	FGA	Pct.	FTM	FTA	Pct.	Reb.	Ast.	Pts.	RPG	APG	PPG
97-98—San Jose	43	...	130	315	.413	70	93	.753	106	97	375	2.5	2.3	8.7
98-99—San Jose	15	...	69	149	.463	63	80	.788	62	33	220	4.1	2.2	14.7
Totals	58	...	199	464	.429	133	173	.769	168	130	595	2.9	2.2	10.3

Three-point field goals: 1997-98, 45-for-134 (.336). 1998-99, 19-for-52 (.365). Totals, 64-for-186 (.344).

WNBA REGULAR-SEASON RECORD

Season Team	G	Min.	FGM	FGA	Pct.	FTM	FTA	Pct.	Off.	Def.	Tot.	Ast.	St.	Blk.	TO	Pts.	RPG	APG	PPG
1999—Sacramento....	32	1034	123	321	.383	76	108	.704	24	44	68	51	63	10	72	379	2.1	1.6	11.8
2000—Sacramento....	32	934	111	253	.439	46	66	.697	28	42	70	81	43	5	74	312	2.2	2.5	9.8
2001—Sacramento....	32	874	111	251	.442	41	60	.683	33	42	75	69	56	5	66	322	2.3	2.2	10.1
2002—Sacramento....	32	902	102	299	.341	54	72	.750	28	62	90	63	41	5	81	296	2.8	2.0	9.3
2003—Detroit	34	694	107	232	.461	48	63	.762	12	45	57	63	36	3	59	312	1.7	1.9	9.2
Totals	162	4438	554	1356	.409	265	369	.718	125	235	360	327	239	28	352	1621	2.2	2.0	10.0

Three-point field goals: 1999, 57-for-167 (.341). 2000, 44-for-122 (.361). 2001, 59-for-150 (.393). 2002, 38-for-157 (.242). 2003, 50-for-124 (.403). Totals, 248-for-720 (.344).

Personal fouls/disqualifications: 1999, 100/2. 2000, 63/1. 2001, 62/0. 2002, 74/1. 2003, 26/0. Totals, 325/4.

WNBA PLAYOFF RECORD

								REBOUNDS								AVERAGES		
Season Team	G	Min.	FGM	FGA	Pct.	FTM	FTA	Pct.	Off.	Def.	Tot.	Ast.	St.	Blk.	TO	Pts.	RPG	APG	PPG
1999—Sacramento....	1	21	1	5	.200	0	0	...	2	3	5	1	2	0	4	2	5.0	1.0	2.0
2000—Sacramento....	2	60	7	16	.438	2	2	1.000	3	5	8	6	3	0	1	19	4.0	3.0	9.5
2001—Sacramento....	5	160	21	48	.438	14	16	.875	2	16	18	7	8	2	7	69	3.6	1.4	13.8
2003—Detroit	8	155	21	53	.396	8	10	.800	2	10	12	15	10	0	12	65	1.5	1.9	8.1
Totals.................	16	396	50	122	.410	24	28	.857	9	34	43	29	23	2	24	155	2.7	1.8	9.7

Three-point field goals: 1999, 0-for-1. 2000, 3-for-9 (.333). 2001, 13-for-27 (.481). 2003, 15-for-32 (.469). Totals, 31-for-69 (.449).
Personal fouls/disqualifications: 1999, 2/0. 2000, 3/0. 2001, 10/0. 2003, 7/0. Totals, 22/0.

HOPE, KYM   C   SILVER STARS

PERSONAL: Born November 23, 1977, in Hollywood, Fla. ... 6-2/165 (1.88 m/75 kg). ... **Full name:** Kymberly Nicole Hope.
HIGH SCHOOL: McArthur (Hollywood, Fla.).
COLLEGE: Miami (Fla.).
TRANSACTIONS/CAREER NOTES: Signed by the WNBA and assigned to Orlando, May 2, 2000. ... Waived by Orlando, May 15, 2000. ... Added by Utah, July 27, 2000. ... Waived by Utah, April 19, 2001. ... Signed by San Antonio as a free agent, April 16, 2004.

COLLEGIATE RECORD

											AVERAGES		
Season Team	G	Min.	FGM	FGA	Pct.	FTM	FTA	Pct.	Reb.	Ast.	Pts.	RPG	APG	PPG
95-96—Miami (Fla.)	26	...	28	68	.412	28	52	.538	95	11	84	3.7	0.4	3.2
96-97—Miami (Fla.)	9	...	143	265	.540	81	117	.692	234	33	367	8.1	1.1	12.7
97-98—Miami (Fla.)	29	...	191	358	.534	128	166	.771	306	53	511	10.6	1.8	17.6
98-99—Miami (Fla.)	29	...	184	348	.529	132	163	.810	253	52	500	8.7	1.8	17.2
Totals	13	...	546	1039	.526	369	498	.741	888	149	1462	7.9	1.3	12.9

Three-point field goals: 1996-97, 0-for-2. 1997-98, 1-for-1. 1998-99, 0-for-3. Totals, 1-for-6 (.167).

WNBA REGULAR-SEASON RECORD

								REBOUNDS								AVERAGES		
Season Team	G	Min.	FGM	FGA	Pct.	FTM	FTA	Pct.	Off.	Def.	Tot.	Ast.	St.	Blk.	TO	Pts.	RPG	APG	PPG
2000—Utah..............	3	4	0	1	.000	2	2	1.000	0	2	2	0	0	0	1	2	0.7	0.0	0.7
Total	3	4	0	1	.000	2	2	1.000	0	2	2	0	0	0	1	2	0.7	0.0	0.7

IVANYI, DALMA   G

PERSONAL: Born March 18, 1976, in Bekescsaba, Hungary ... 5-10/135 (1.78 m/61 kg). ... **Full name:** Dalma Erika Ivanyi.
HIGH SCHOOL: Janos Bolyai (Kecskemet, Hungary).
COLLEGE: Florida International.
TRANSACTIONS/CAREER NOTES: Selected by Utah in fourth round (39th overall) of WNBA Draft, May 4, 1999.

COLLEGIATE RECORD

											AVERAGES		
Season Team	G	Min.	FGM	FGA	Pct.	FTM	FTA	Pct.	Reb.	Ast.	Pts.	RPG	APG	PPG
95-96—Florida International...	28	...	148	359	.412	84	111	.757	158	186	398	5.6	6.6	14.2
96-97—Florida International...	17	...	72	180	.400	37	47	.787	77	151	198	4.5	8.9	11.6
97-98—Florida International...	31	...	170	360	.472	86	109	.789	159	294	453	5.1	9.5	14.6
98-99—Florida International...	29	...	146	333	.438	95	111	.856	108	261	427	3.7	9.0	14.7
Totals 105		...	536	1232	.435	302	378	.799	502	892	1476	4.8	8.5	14.1

Three-point field goals: 1995-96, 18-for-67 (.269). 1996-97, 17-for-46 (.370). 1997-98, 27-for-84 (.321). 1998-99, 40-for-92 (.435). Totals, 102-for-289 (.353).

WNBA REGULAR-SEASON RECORD

								REBOUNDS								AVERAGES		
Season Team	G	Min.	FGM	FGA	Pct.	FTM	FTA	Pct.	Off.	Def.	Tot.	Ast.	St.	Blk.	TO	Pts.	RPG	APG	PPG
1999—Utah..............	14	67	4	12	.333	3	4	.750	3	2	5	7	4	0	11	11	0.4	0.5	0.8
2000—Utah..............	27	489	30	96	.313	21	28	.750	12	42	54	63	25	3	50	93	2.0	2.3	3.4
2003—Phoenix........	4	34	3	8	.375	24	32	.750	2	2	4	2	0	1	2	6	1.0	0.5	2.4
Totals.................	45	590	37	116	.293	48	64	.750	17	46	63	72	29	4	63	110	1.4	1.6	2.4

Three-point field goals: 1999, 0-for-4. 2000, 12-for-43 (.279). Totals, 12-for-47 (.255).
Personal fouls/disqualifications: 1999, 18/0. 2000, 67/0. Totals, 85/0.

IVEY, NIELE   G   FEVER

PERSONAL: Born September 24, 1977, in St. Louis, Mo. ... 5-7/149 (1.70 m/68 kg). ... **Full name:** Niele Ivey.
HIGH SCHOOL: Cor Jesu (St. Louis).
COLLEGE: Notre Dame.
TRANSACTIONS/CAREER NOTES: Selected by Indiana in second round (19th overall) of WNBA Draft, April 20, 2001.

COLLEGIATE RECORD

Season Team	G	Min.	FGM	FGA	Pct.	FTM	FTA	Pct.	Reb.	Ast.	Pts.	RPG	APG	PPG
96-97—Notre Dame	5	...	6	16	.375	3	4	.750	12	15	15	2.4	3.0	3.0
97-98—Notre Dame	31	...	83	185	.449	63	80	.788	106	90	254	3.4	2.9	8.2
98-99—Notre Dame	28	...	121	241	.502	80	92	.870	106	181	369	3.8	6.5	13.2
99-00—Notre Dame	32	...	118	272	.434	61	81	.753	111	194	358	3.5	6.1	11.2
00-01—Notre Dame	36	...	149	322	.463	79	111	.712	147	247	434	4.1	6.9	12.1
Totals	132		477	1036	.460	286	368	.777	482	727	1430	3.7	5.5	10.8

Three-point field goals: 1996-97, 0-for-1. 1997-98, 25-for-67 (.373). 1998-99, 47-for-105 (.448). 1999-00, 61-for-167 (.365). 2000-01, 57-for-129 (.442). Totals, 190-for-469 (.405).

WNBA REGULAR-SEASON RECORD

Season Team	G	Min.	FGM	FGA	Pct.	FTM	FTA	Pct.	Off.	Def.	Tot.	Ast.	St.	Blk.	TO	Pts.	RPG	APG	PPG
2001—Indiana	32	708	38	102	.373	14	15	.933	16	39	55	70	33	5	35	115	1.7	2.2	3.6
2002—Indiana	31	439	25	71	.352	17	21	.810	6	22	28	39	16	3	22	86	0.9	1.3	2.8
2003—Indiana	27	651	45	116	.388	12	17	.706	5	27	32	71	29	7	28	135	1.2	2.6	5.0
Totals	90	1798	108	289	.374	43	53	.811	27	88	115	180	78	15	85	336	1.3	2.0	3.7

Three-point field goals: 2001, 25-for-70 (.357). 2002, 19-for-50 (.380). 2003, 33-for-84 (.393). Totals, 77-for-204 (.377).
Personal fouls/disqualifications: 2001, 51/0. 2002, 31/0. 2003, 40/0. Totals, 122/0.

WNBA PLAYOFF RECORD

Season Team	G	Min.	FGM	FGA	Pct.	FTM	FTA	Pct.	Off.	Def.	Tot.	Ast.	St.	Blk.	TO	Pts.	RPG	APG	PPG
2002—Indiana	3	9	0	1	.000	0	0	...	0	1	1	3	1	0	0	0	0.3	1.0	0.0
Totals	3	9	0	1	.000	0	0	...	0	1	1	3	1	0	0	0	0.3	1.0	0.0

Three-point field goals: 2002, 0-for-1. Totals, 0-for-1.
Personal fouls/disqualifications: 2002, 2/0. Totals, 2/0.

JACKSON, DEANNA   F   FEVER

PERSONAL: Born December 15, 1979, in Selma, Ala. ... 6-2/159 (1.88 m/72 kg). ... **Full name:** Deanna Renee Jackson.
HIGH SCHOOL: T.R. Miller (Ala.).
COLLEGE: Alabama-Birmingham.
TRANSACTIONS/CAREER NOTES: Selected by Cleveland in first round (eighth overall) of WNBA Draft, April 19, 2002. ... Selected by Indiana in dispersal draft, January 6, 2004.

COLLEGIATE RECORD

Season Team	G	Min.	FGM	FGA	Pct.	FTM	FTA	Pct.	Reb.	Ast.	Pts.	RPG	APG	PPG
98-99—Ala.-Birmingham	27	793	175	339	.516	84	118	.712	240	18	452	8.9	0.7	16.7
99-00—Ala.-Birmingham	33	1182	250	524	.477	97	151	.642	385	43	...	11.7	1.3	0.0
00-01—Ala.-Birmingham	31	1154	275	578	.476	180	242	.744	358	63	777	11.5	2.0	25.1
01-02—Ala.-Birmingham	11	374	105	197	.533	67	91	.736	135	52	288	12.3	4.7	26.2
Totals	102	3503	805	1638	.491	428	602	.711	1118	176	1517	11.0	1.7	14.9

Three-point field goals: 1998-99, 18-for-65 (.277). 1999-00, 30-for-88 (.341). 2000-01, 47-for-118 (.398). 2001-02, 11-for-43 (.256). Totals, 106-for-314 (.338).

WNBA REGULAR-SEASON RECORD

Season Team	G	Min.	FGM	FGA	Pct.	FTM	FTA	Pct.	Off.	Def.	Tot.	Ast.	St.	Blk.	TO	Pts.	RPG	APG	PPG
2002—Cleveland	18	143	19	46	.413	17	24	.708	10	17	27	6	2	1	9	55	1.5	0.3	3.1
2003—Cleveland	34	763	83	198	.419	50	70	.714	37	52	89	51	20	13	33	245	2.6	1.5	7.2
Totals	52	906	102	244	.418	67	94	.713	47	69	116	57	22	14	42	300	2.2	1.1	5.8

Three-point field goals: 2002, 0-for-3. 2003, 29-for-70 (.414). Totals, 29-for-73 (.397).
Personal fouls/disqualifications: 2002, 11/0. 2003, 92/1. Totals, 103/1.

WNBA PLAYOFF RECORD

Season Team	G	Min.	FGM	FGA	Pct.	FTM	FTA	Pct.	Off.	Def.	Tot.	Ast.	St.	Blk.	TO	Pts.	RPG	APG	PPG
2003—Cleveland	3	60	4	20	.200	4	6	.667	2	10	12	2	2	0	0	12	4.0	0.7	4.0
Totals	3	60	4	20	.200	4	6	.667	2	10	12	2	2	0	0	12	4.0	0.7	4.0

Three-point field goals: 2003, 0-for-2. Totals, 0-for-2.
Personal fouls/disqualifications: 2003, 7/0. Totals, 7/0.

JACKSON, GWEN   F   SILVER STARS

PERSONAL: Born October 23, 1980, in Eufaula, Ala. ... 6-2/184 (1.88 m/83 kg). ... **Full name:** Gwendolyn Michelle Jackson.
HIGH SCHOOL: Eufaula (Eufaula, Ala.).
COLLEGE: Tennessee.
TRANSACTIONS/CAREER NOTES: Selected by Indiana in first round (sixth overall) of WNBA Draft, April 25, 2003. ... Traded by Indiana along with Sylvia Crawley in exchange for Natalie Williams and Coretta Brown to San Antonio, May 1, 2003.

COLLEGIATE RECORD

NOTES: Associated Press All-America Honorable Mention (2003). ... All-SEC First Team (2003, 2001). ... NCAA Midwest Regional All-Tournament Team (2002). ... All-SEC Freshman Team (2000).

Season Team	G	Min.	FGM	FGA	Pct.	FTM	FTA	Pct.	Reb.	Ast.	Pts.	AVERAGES RPG	APG	PPG
99-00—Tennessee	37	601	71	155	.458	58	91	.637	...	20	204	4.5	0.5	5.5
00-01—Tennessee	34	833	144	296	.486	93	118	.788	...	27	397	6.3	0.8	11.7
01-02—Tennessee	28	634	105	223	.471	76	95	.800	...	27	295	6.2	1.0	10.5
02-03—Tennessee	38	944	234	409	.572	118	156	.756	...	34	612	6.2	0.9	16.1
Totals	137	3012	554	1083	.512	345	460	.750	0	108	1508	0.0	0.8	11.0

Three-point field goals: 1999-00, 4-for-13 (.308). 2000-01, 16-for-34 (.471). 2001-02, 9-for-28 (.321). 2002-03, 26-for-65 (.400). Totals, 55-for-140 (.393).

WNBA REGULAR-SEASON RECORD

Season Team	G	Min.	FGM	FGA	Pct.	FTM	FTA	Pct.	REBOUNDS Off.	Def.	Tot.	Ast.	St.	Blk.	TO	Pts.	AVERAGES RPG	APG	PPG
2003—San Antonio	33	975	114	286	.399	56	88	.636	86	119	205	20	15	17	46	289	6.2	0.6	8.8
Totals	33	975	114	286	.399	56	88	.636	86	119	205	20	15	17	46	289	6.2	0.6	8.8

Three-point field goals: 2003, 5-for-30 (.167). Totals, 5-for-30 (.167).
Personal fouls/disqualifications: 2003, 85/1. Totals, 85/1.

JACKSON, LAUREN F/C STORM

PERSONAL: Born May 11, 1981, in Albury, Australia ... 6-5/185 (1.96 m/84 kg). ... **Full name:** Lauren Jackson.
TRANSACTIONS/CAREER NOTES: Selected by Seattle in first round (first overall) of WNBA Draft, April 20, 2001.

OLYMPICS

NOTES: Member of silver medal-winning Australian Olympic Team (2000).

Season Team	G	Min.	FGM	FGA	Pct.	FTM	FTA	Pct.	Reb.	Ast.	Pts.	AVERAGES RPG	APG	PPG
2000—Australia	8	207	49	101	.485	25	33	.758	67	8	127	8.4	1.0	15.9
Totals	8	207	49	101	.485	25	33	.758	67	8	127	8.4	1.0	15.9

Three-point field goals: 2000-01, 4-for-14 (.286).

WNBA REGULAR-SEASON RECORD

NOTES: WNBA Most Valuable Player (2003). ... All-WNBA first team (2003). ... Led WNBA in scoring (21.2 ppg) in 2003. ... Bud Light Peak Performer, Scoring (2003).

Season Team	G	Min.	FGM	FGA	Pct.	FTM	FTA	Pct.	REBOUNDS Off.	Def.	Tot.	Ast.	St.	Blk.	TO	Pts.	AVERAGES RPG	APG	PPG
2001—Seattle	29	1001	149	406	.367	104	143	.727	57	136	193	44	54	64	53	442	6.7	1.5	15.2
2002—Seattle	28	882	186	462	.403	68	90	.756	66	124	190	41	30	81	47	482	6.8	1.5	17.2
2003—Seattle	33	1109	254	526	.483	151	183	.825	82	225	307	62	38	64	69	698	9.3	1.9	21.2
Totals	90	2992	589	1394	.423	323	416	.776	205	485	690	147	122	209	169	1622	7.7	1.6	18.0

Three-point field goals: 2001, 40-for-129 (.310). 2002, 42-for-120 (.350). 2003, 39-for-123 (.317). Totals, 121-for-372 (.325).
Personal fouls/disqualifications: 2001, 97/3. 2002, 95/1. 2003, 106/1. Totals, 298/5.

WNBA PLAYOFF RECORD

Season Team	G	Min.	FGM	FGA	Pct.	FTM	FTA	Pct.	REBOUNDS Off.	Def.	Tot.	Ast.	St.	Blk.	TO	Pts.	AVERAGES RPG	APG	PPG
2002—Seattle	2	68	9	26	.346	5	7	.714	5	5	10	3	3	6	4	23	5.0	1.5	11.5
Totals	2	68	9	26	.346	5	7	.714	5	5	10	3	3	6	4	23	5.0	1.5	11.5

Three-point field goals: 2002, 0-for-6. Totals, 0-for-6.
Personal fouls/disqualifications: 2002, 9/0. Totals, 9/0.

WNBA ALL-STAR GAME RECORD

Season Team	Min.	FGM	FGA	Pct.	FTM	FTA	Pct.	REBOUNDS Off.	Def.	Tot.	Ast.	PF	Dq.	St.	Blk.	TO	Pts.
2001—Seattle	19	4	9	.444	1	1	1.000	2	1	3	1	3	0	3	0	...	11
2002—Seattle	20	6	11	.545	1	1	1.000	2	4	6	0	4	0	1	1	...	15
2003—Seattle	19	3	7	.429	2	3	.667	1	3	4	0	0	0	0	3	...	9
Totals	58	13	27	.481	4	5	.800	5	8	13	1	7	0	4	4	1	35

Three-point field goals: 2001, 2-for-4 (.500). 2002, 2-for-3 (.667). 2003, 1-for-2 (.500). Totals, 5-for-9 (.556).

JACKSON, TAMICHA G MYSTICS

PERSONAL: Born April 22, 1978, in Dallas, Texas ... 5-6/118 (1.68 m/54 kg). ... **Full name:** Tamicha Renia Jackson.
HIGH SCHOOL: Lincoln (Texas).
COLLEGE: Louisiana Tech.
TRANSACTIONS/CAREER NOTES: Drafted by Detroit in the first round (8th overall) of the 2000 WNBA Draft. ... Traded to Portland from Detroit along with a fourth round pick in the 2002 WNBA Draft in exchange for a 2002 second round pick. ... Selected by Phoenix with the fourth pick in the 2003 WNBA Dispersal Draft. ... Traded to the Washington Mystics in a three-team deal that sent Asjha Jones from the Mystics to the Connecticut Sun and the Sun sent the 8th pick in the 2004 WNBA Draft to the Mercury.

NOTES: Kodak All-America first team (2000).

COLLEGIATE RECORD

Season Team	G	Min.	FGM	FGA	Pct.	FTM	FTA	Pct.	Reb.	Ast.	Pts.	AVERAGES RPG	APG	PPG
96-97—Louisiana Tech	35	...	172	472	.364	36	59	.610	92	132	428	2.6	3.8	12.2
97-98—Louisiana Tech	33	...	202	456	.443	20	33	.606	108	156	481	3.3	4.7	14.6
98-99—Louisiana Tech	33	...	157	382	.411	34	42	.810	62	72	384	1.9	2.2	11.6
99-0—Louisiana Tech	34	...	222	456	.487	39	53	.736	90	114	529	2.6	3.4	15.6
Totals	135	...	753	1766	.426	129	187	.690	352	474	1822	2.6	3.5	13.5

Three-point field goals: 1996-97, 48-for-145 (.331). 1997-98, 57-for-167 (.341). 1998-99, 36-for-134 (.269). 1999-00, 46-for-123 (.374). Totals, 187-for-569 (.329).

WNBA REGULAR-SEASON RECORD

									REBOUNDS								AVERAGES		
Season Team	G	Min.	FGM	FGA	Pct.	FTM	FTA	Pct.	Off.	Def.	Tot.	Ast.	St.	Blk.	TO	Pts.	RPG	APG	PPG
2000—Detroit	17	267	41	106	.387	26	35	.743	8	17	25	36	22	0	21	116	1.5	2.1	6.8
2001—Portland	32	497	55	169	.325	16	23	.696	10	34	44	50	28	0	45	132	1.4	1.6	4.1
2002—Portland	32	692	122	291	.419	46	66	.697	20	39	59	95	55	1	64	314	1.8	3.0	9.8
2003—Phoenix	34	958	124	361	.343	17	21	.810	24	58	82	146	52	4	76	300	2.4	4.3	8.8
Totals	115	2414	342	927	.369	105	145	.724	62	148	210	327	157	5	206	862	1.8	2.8	7.5

Three-point field goals: 2000, 8-for-32 (.250). 2001, 6-for-39 (.154). 2002, 24-for-76 (.316). 2003, 35-for-99 (.354). Totals, 73-for-246 (.297).

Personal fouls/disqualifications: 2000, 30/0. 2001, 35/0. 2002, 59/0. 2003, 62/0. Totals, 186/0.

JOHNS KIMBROUGH, POLLYANNA   F   COMETS

PERSONAL: Born November 6, 1975, in Nassau, Bahamas ... 6-3/165 (1.91 m/75 kg). ... **Full name:** Pollyanna Casanga Johns Kimbrough.

HIGH SCHOOL: Evanston Township (Evanston, Ill.).

COLLEGE: Michigan.

TRANSACTIONS/CAREER NOTES: Selected by Charlotte in third round (27th overall) of WNBA Draft, April 29, 1998. ... Waived by Charlotte, June 9, 1999. ... Assigned to Cleveland, May 2, 2000. ... Traded by Cleveland with first-round pick in 2002 draft to Phoenix for first-round pick in 2002 draft, March 4, 2002. ... Traded by Phoenix with first-round pick to Miami for F Tracy Reid and first-round pick in 2002 draft, March 4, 2002. ... Traded by Charlotte to Cleveland Rockers in exchange for Rashia Brown, May 19, 2003. ... Selected by Connecticut in dispersal draft, January 6, 2004.

COLLEGIATE RECORD

NOTES: Kodak All-America first team (1994, 1995).

												AVERAGES		
Season Team	G	Min.	FGM	FGA	Pct.	FTM	FTA	Pct.	Reb.	Ast.	Pts.	RPG	APG	PPG
94-95—Michigan	9	...	20	36	.556	5	16	.313	61	3	45	6.8	0.3	5.0
95-96—Michigan	24	...	132	283	.466	85	149	.570	238	30	349	9.9	1.3	14.5
96-97—Michigan	25	...	142	262	.542	77	135	.570	261	28	375	10.4	1.1	15.0
97-98—Michigan	28	...	176	283	.622	130	192	.677	267	21	482	9.5	0.8	17.2
Totals	86	...	470	864	.544	297	492	.604	827	82	1251	9.6	1.0	14.5

WNBA REGULAR-SEASON RECORD

									REBOUNDS								AVERAGES		
Season Team	G	Min.	FGM	FGA	Pct.	FTM	FTA	Pct.	Off.	Def.	Tot.	Ast.	St.	Blk.	TO	Pts.	RPG	APG	PPG
1998—Charlotte	24	180	22	45	.489	18	28	.643	14	23	37	6	3	2	9	62	1.5	0.3	2.6
2000—Cleveland	12	57	5	10	.500	7	12	.583	7	7	14	2	0	1	8	17	1.2	0.2	1.4
2001—Cleveland	18	119	12	27	.444	4	9	.444	12	19	31	4	0	2	10	28	1.7	0.2	1.6
2002—Miami	31	801	78	149	.523	61	97	.629	58	82	140	32	27	15	53	217	4.5	1.0	7.0
2003—Cleveland	30	416	35	63	.556	19	34	.559	31	51	82	19	12	10	19	89	2.7	0.6	3.0
Totals	115	1573	152	294	.517	109	180	.606	122	182	304	63	42	30	99	413	2.6	0.5	3.6

WNBA PLAYOFF RECORD

									REBOUNDS								AVERAGES		
Season Team	G	Min.	FGM	FGA	Pct.	FTM	FTA	Pct.	Off.	Def.	Tot.	Ast.	St.	Blk.	TO	Pts.	RPG	APG	PPG
2000—Cleveland	4	6	3	3	1.000	1	2	.500	1	1	2	1	0	0	0	7	0.5	0.3	1.8
2001—Cleveland	1	4	0	0	...	0	0	...	1	1	2	1	0	0	1	0	2.0	1.0	0.0
2003—Cleveland	3	20	1	1	1.000	0	0	...	0	4	4	3	1	2	0	2	1.3	1.0	0.7
Totals	8	30	4	4	1.000	1	2	.500	2	6	8	5	1	2	1	9	1.0	0.6	1.1

JOHNSON, ADRIENNE G   SUN

PERSONAL: Born February 5, 1974, in Louisville, Ky. ... 5-10/154 (1.78 m/70 kg). ... **Full name:** Adrienne Lynn Johnson.

HIGH SCHOOL: Butler (Louisville, Ky.).

COLLEGE: Ohio State.

TRANSACTIONS/CAREER NOTES: Signed as developmental player and assigned to Cleveland, May 27, 1997. ... Moved to active roster June 17, 1997. ... Selected by Orlando with eighth pick in WNBA Expansion Draft, April 16, 1999. ... Traded by Cleveland with the 15th overall pick in the 2002 WNBA Draft to Phoenix for the 8th pick, and subsequently traded by Phoenix with the 15th pick to Miami for F Tracy Reid and the 13th pick, March 4, 2002.

COLLEGIATE RECORD

												AVERAGES		
Season Team	G	Min.	FGM	FGA	Pct.	FTM	FTA	Pct.	Reb.	Ast.	Pts.	RPG	APG	PPG
92-93—Ohio State	30	...	58	147	.395	14	23	.609	49	25	132	1.6	0.8	4.4
93-94—Ohio State	28	...	118	293	.403	41	49	.837	91	50	300	3.3	1.8	10.7
94-95—Ohio State	20	...	59	153	.386	30	43	.698	40	26	155	2.0	1.3	7.8
95-96—Ohio State	34	...	190	408	.466	50	64	.781	131	106	443	3.9	3.1	13.0
Totals	112	...	425	1001	.425	135	179	.754	311	207	1030	2.8	1.8	9.2

Three-point field goals: 1992-93, 2-for-10 (.200). 1993-94, 23-for-72 (.319). 1994-95, 7-for-35 (.200). 1995-96, 13-for-49 (.265). Totals, 45-for-166 (.271).

WNBA REGULAR-SEASON RECORD

									REBOUNDS								AVERAGES		
Season Team	G	Min.	FGM	FGA	Pct.	FTM	FTA	Pct.	Off.	Def.	Tot.	Ast.	St.	Blk.	TO	Pts.	RPG	APG	PPG
1997—Cleveland	25	194	22	59	.373	7	9	.778	8	14	22	9	5	1	27	53	0.9	0.4	2.1
1998—Cleveland	29	330	53	116	.457	13	18	.722	17	31	48	15	7	4	24	133	1.7	0.5	4.6
1999—Orlando	29	224	25	62	.403	6	9	.667	12	16	28	14	5	2	14	57	1.0	0.5	2.0
2000—Orlando	32	1100	175	393	.445	34	38	.895	30	60	90	54	24	3	56	436	2.8	1.7	13.6

Season Team	G	Min.	FGM	FGA	Pct.	FTM	FTA	Pct.	Off.	Def.	Tot.	Ast.	St.	Blk.	TO	Pts.	RPG	APG	PPG
2001—Orlando							Did not play due to injury..												
2002—Orlando	32	602	68	181	.376	12	17	.706	14	32	46	22	15	2	26	166	1.4	0.7	5.2
2003—Connecticut ...	34	584	69	195	.354	18	24	.750	23	35	58	18	17	1	21	173	1.7	0.5	5.1
Totals..............	181	3034	412	1006	.410	90	115	.783	104	188	292	132	73	13	168	1018	1.6	0.7	5.6

Three-point field goals: 1997, 2-for-4 (.500). 1998, 14-for-33 (.424). 1999, 1-for-8 (.125). 2000, 52-for-148 (.351). 2002, 18-for-61 (.295). 2003, 17-for-49 (.347). Totals, 104-for-303 (.343).
Personal fouls/disqualifications: 1997, 12/0. 1998, 35/0. 1999, 21/0. 2000, 59/1. 2002, 40/0. 2003, 36/0. Totals, 203/1.

WNBA PLAYOFF RECORD

Season Team	G	Min.	FGM	FGA	Pct.	FTM	FTA	Pct.	REBOUNDS Off.	Def.	Tot.	Ast.	St.	Blk.	TO	Pts.	AVERAGES RPG	APG	PPG
1998—Cleveland......	2	12	0	3	.000	0	0	...	1	2	3	0	1	0	0	0	1.5	0.0	0.0
2000—Orlando	3	111	14	42	.333	3	4	.750	3	1	4	8	1	1	7	34	1.3	2.7	11.3
2003—Connecticut ...	3	43	6	9	.667	0	0	...	0	4	4	4	1	0	0	12	1.3	1.3	4.0
Totals..............	8	166	20	54	.370	3	4	.750	4	7	11	12	3	1	7	46	1.4	1.5	5.8

Three-point field goals: 1998, 0-for-2. 2000, 3-for-10 (.300). 2003, 0-for-1. Totals, 3-for-13 (.231).
Personal fouls/disqualifications: 1998, 0/0. 2000, 7/0. 2003, 2/0. Totals, 9/0.

JOHNSON, CHANDRA C

PERSONAL: Born March 19, 1981 ... 6-3/185 (1.91 m/84 kg).
HIGH SCHOOL: Eau Claire North High School
COLLEGE: Wis.-Green Bay.
TRANSACTIONS/CAREER NOTES: Signed as a free agent by Los Angeles, April 30, 2003.

COLLEGIATE RECORD

Notes: Named to Oneida Bingo & Casino Holiday All-Tournament team. ... Named to Horizon League All-Tournament team. ... Finished career as seventh all time in team history with 82 blocked shots.

Season Team	G	Min.	FGM	FGA	Pct.	FTM	FTA	Pct.	REBOUNDS Off.	Def.	Tot.	Ast.	St.	Blk.	TO	Pts.	AVERAGES RPG	APG	PPG
99-00 27		382	70	136	.515	59	88	.670	40	59	99	9	18	38	15	199	3.7	0.3	7.4
00-01 28		436	89	180	.494	39	51	.765	34	68	102	11	18	40	20	217	3.6	0.4	7.8
01-02 31		525	100	197	.508	42	75	.560	33	74	107	24	23	39	30	242	3.5	0.8	7.8
02-03 32		734	178	320	.556	83	123	.675	47	95	142	48	36	59	18	440	4.4	1.5	13.8
Totals 118		2077	437	833	.525	223	337	.662	154	296	450	92	95	176	83	1098	3.8	0.8	9.3

Three-point field goals: 2000-01, 0-for-1. 2002-03, 1-for-7 (.143). Totals, 1-for-8 (.125).

WNBA REGULAR-SEASON RECORD

Season Team	G	Min.	FGM	FGA	Pct.	FTM	FTA	Pct.	REBOUNDS Off.	Def.	Tot.	Ast.	St.	Blk.	TO	Pts.	AVERAGES RPG	APG	PPG
2003—Los Angeles...	8	45	1	5	.200	3	4	.750	2	4	6	3	0	1	4	6	0.8	0.4	0.8
Totals..............	8	45	1	5	.200	3	4	.750	2	4	6	3	0	1	4	6	0.8	0.4	0.8

Three-point field goals: 2003, 1-for-5 (.200). Totals, 1-for-5 (.200).
Personal fouls/disqualifications: 2003, 6/0. Totals, 6/0.

JOHNSON, LATONYA   F   SILVER STARS

PERSONAL: Born August 17, 1975, in Detroit, Mich. ... 6-1/149 (1.85 m/68 kg). ... **Full name:** LaTonya Marie Johnson.
COLLEGE: Memphis.
TRANSACTIONS/CAREER NOTES: Selected by Utah in third round (21st overall) of WNBA Draft, April 29, 1998.

COLLEGIATE RECORD

Season Team	G	Min.	FGM	FGA	Pct.	FTM	FTA	Pct.	Reb.	Ast.	Pts.	AVERAGES RPG	APG	PPG
94-95—Memphis..................	30	...	209	421	.496	64	91	.703	184	42	529	6.1	1.4	17.6
95-96—Memphis..................	29	...	229	456	.502	79	106	.745	189	29	601	6.5	1.0	20.7
96-97—Memphis..................	29	...	164	367	.447	71	102	.696	143	34	444	4.9	1.2	15.3
97-98—Memphis..................	30	...	231	481	.480	145	184	.788	170	60	658	5.7	2.0	21.9
Totals	118	...	833	1725	.483	359	483	.743	686	165	2232	5.8	1.4	18.9

Three-point field goals: 1994-95, 47-for-117 (.402). 1995-96, 64-for-152 (.421). 1996-97, 45-for-130 (.346). 1997-98, 51-for-126 (.405). Totals, 207-for-525 (.394)

WNBA REGULAR-SEASON RECORD

Season Team	G	Min.	FGM	FGA	Pct.	FTM	FTA	Pct.	REBOUNDS Off.	Def.	Tot.	Ast.	St.	Blk.	TO	Pts.	AVERAGES RPG	APG	PPG
1998—Utah..............	28	490	58	145	.400	21	34	.618	14	40	54	20	11	1	42	151	1.9	0.7	5.4
1999—Utah..............	31	718	66	181	.365	47	58	.810	14	40	54	50	21	8	40	203	1.7	1.6	6.5
2000—Utah..............	29	481	52	129	.403	28	43	.651	14	38	52	26	12	2	34	144	1.8	0.9	5.0
2001—Utah..............	26	228	17	65	.262	11	14	.786	4	15	19	7	2	1	13	50	0.7	0.3	1.9
2002—Utah..............	28	269	25	76	.329	15	20	.750	8	11	19	10	7	2	15	75	0.7	0.4	2.7
2003—San Antonio ...	31	279	18	71	.254	16	22	.727	7	18	25	9	3	1	14	58	0.8	0.3	1.9
Totals..............	173	2465	236	667	.354	138	191	.723	61	162	223	122	56	15	158	681	1.3	0.7	3.9

Three-point field goals: 1998, 14-for-49 (.286). 1999, 24-for-82 (.293). 2000, 12-for-36 (.333). 2001, 5-for-30 (.167). 2002, 10-for-32 (.313). 2003, 6-for-23 (.261). Totals, 71-for-252 (.282).
Personal fouls/disqualifications: 1998, 42/0. 1999, 65/1. 2000, 65/0. 2001, 26/0. 2002, 36/1. 2003, 31/0. Totals, 265/2.

WNBA PLAYOFF RECORD

Season Team	G	Min.	FGM	FGA	Pct.	FTM	FTA	Pct.	REBOUNDS Off.	Def.	Tot.	Ast.	St.	Blk.	TO	Pts.	AVERAGES RPG	APG	PPG
2001—Utah..............	2	15	1	4	.250	2	2	1.000	0	1	1	0	0	1	3	4	0.5	0.0	2.0
2002—Utah..............	5	40	7	14	.500	1	2	.500	2	2	4	2	0	0	1	17	0.8	0.4	3.4
Totals..............	7	55	8	18	.444	3	4	.750	2	3	5	2	0	1	4	21	0.7	0.3	3.0

Three-point field goals: 2001, 0-for-3. 2002, 2-for-9 (.222). Totals, 2-for-12 (.167).
Personal fouls/disqualifications: 2001, 4/0. 2002, 2/0. Totals, 6/0.

JOHNSON, SHANNON G   SILVER STARS

PERSONAL: Born August 18, 1974, in Hartsville, S.C. ... 5-7/144 (1.70 m/65 kg). ... **Full name:** Shannon Regina Johnson.
HIGH SCHOOL: Hartsville (Hartsville, S.C.).
COLLEGE: South Carolina.
TRANSACTIONS/CAREER NOTES: Signed by WNBA and allocated to Orlando, May 3, 1999. ... Traded by Connecticut with a second round (21st overall) and third round (34th overall) pick in the 2004 WNBA Draft to San Antonio for a first round (fourth overall), second round (16th overall) and a third round (29th overall) pick in the 2004 WNBA Draft, January 28, 2004.

COLLEGIATE RECORD

Season Team	G	Min.	FGM	FGA	Pct.	FTM	FTA	Pct.	Reb.	Ast.	Pts.	RPG	APG	PPG
92-93—South Carolina	27	...	89	212	.420	63	87	.724	98	83	259	3.6	3.1	9.6
93-94—South Carolina	27	...	231	506	.457	128	187	.684	160	133	634	5.9	4.9	23.5
94-95—South Carolina	27	...	214	497	.431	154	227	.678	172	138	...	6.4	5.1	0.0
95-96—South Carolina	28	...	238	544	.438	133	179	.743	167	113	691	6.0	4.0	24.7
Totals	109	...	772	1759	.439	478	680	.703	597	467	1584	5.5	4.3	14.5

Three-point field goals: 1992-93, 18-for-50 (.360). 1993-94, 44-for-111 (.396). 1994-95, 64-for-182 (.352). 1995-96, 82-for-202 (.406). Totals, 208-for-545 (.382).

ABL REGULAR-SEASON RECORD

NOTES: Named to ABL Eastern Conference All-Star Team (1998). ... Member of ABL championship teams (1997, 1998).

Season Team	G	Min.	FGM	FGA	Pct.	FTM	FTA	Pct.	Reb.	Ast.	Pts.	RPG	APG	PPG
96-97—Columbus	40	...	140	271	.517	60	74	.811	157	151	409	3.9	3.8	10.2
97-98—Columbus	44	...	153	357	.429	134	169	.793	210	215	484	4.8	4.9	11.0
98-99—Columbus	14	...	66	160	.413	56	72	.778	82	55	211	5.9	3.9	15.1
Totals	98	...	359	788	.456	250	315	.794	449	421	1104	4.6	4.3	11.3

Three-point field goals: 1996-97, 69-for-144 (.479). 1997-98, 44-for-127 (.346). 1998-99, 23-for-61 (.377). Totals, 136-for-332 (.410).

WNBA REGULAR-SEASON RECORD

HONORS: All-WNBA second team (1999, 2000, 2002). ... Led league with 35.8 minutes per game (1999).

Season Team	G	Min.	FGM	FGA	Pct.	FTM	FTA	Pct.	REBOUNDS Off.	Def.	Tot.	Ast.	St.	Blk.	TO	Pts.	AVERAGES RPG	APG	PPG
1999—Orlando	32	1147	151	338	.447	105	153	.686	44	106	150	141	54	12	121	447	4.7	4.4	14.0
2000—Orlando	32	1126	122	309	.395	107	144	.743	53	102	155	169	58	7	102	381	4.8	5.3	11.9
2001—Orlando	26	785	90	245	.367	84	111	.757	15	62	77	68	34	6	54	302	3.0	2.6	11.6
2002—Orlando	31	1110	157	389	.404	164	214	.766	49	80	129	163	51	7	98	499	4.2	5.3	16.1
2003—Connecticut	34	1107	138	319	.433	125	171	.731	39	95	134	196	44	3	107	420	3.9	5.8	12.4
Totals	155	5275	658	1600	.411	585	793	.738	200	445	645	737	241	35	482	2049	4.2	4.8	13.2

Three-point field goals: 1999, 40-for-110 (.364). 2000, 30-for-90 (.333). 2001, 38-for-104 (.365). 2002, 21-for-77 (.273). 2003, 19-for-73 (.260). Totals, 148-for-454 (.326).
Personal fouls/disqualifications: 1999, 79/0. 2000, 83/0. 2001, 66/0. 2002, 78/1. 2003, 77/0. Totals, 383/1.

WNBA PLAYOFF RECORD

Season Team	G	Min.	FGM	FGA	Pct.	FTM	FTA	Pct.	REBOUNDS Off.	Def.	Tot.	Ast.	St.	Blk.	TO	Pts.	AVERAGES RPG	APG	PPG
2000—Orlando	3	119	6	27	.222	4	8	.500	4	17	21	14	5	2	7	18	7.0	4.7	6.0
2003—Connecticut	4	131	13	29	.448	14	18	.778	3	9	12	19	7	1	11	45	3.0	4.8	11.3
Totals	7	250	19	56	.339	18	26	.692	7	26	33	33	12	3	18	63	4.7	4.7	9.0

Three-point field goals: 2000, 2-for-13 (.154). 2003, 5-for-10 (.500). Totals, 7-for-23 (.304).
Personal fouls/disqualifications: 2000, 9/0. 2003, 11/0. Totals, 20/0.

WNBA ALL-STAR GAME RECORD

Season Team	Min.	FGM	FGA	Pct.	FTM	FTA	Pct.	REBOUNDS Off.	Def.	Tot.	Ast.	PF	Dq.	St.	Blk.	TO	Pts.
1999—Orlando	23	3	6	.500	0	0	...	2	2	4	2	2	0	3	1	...	8
2000—Orlando	20	2	6	.333	2	2	1.000	0	3	3	2	4	0	3	1	...	6
2002—Orlando	20	2	7	.286	0	0	...	2	0	2	3	3	0	1	0	...	6
2003—Connecticut	12	0	5	.000	0	0	...	0	1	1	2	1	0	0	0	...	0
Totals	75	7	24	.292	2	2	1.000	4	6	10	9	10	0	7	2	4	20

Three-point field goals: 1999, 2-for-5 (.400). 2000, 0-for-4. 2002, 2-for-6 (.333). 2003, 0-for-1. Totals, 4-for-16 (.250).

JOHNSON, TIFFANI   C   COMETS

PERSONAL: Born December 27, 1975, in Charlotte, N.C. ... 6-4/240 (1.93 m/109 kg).
COLLEGE: Tennessee.
TRANSACTIONS/CAREER NOTES: Signed by the WNBA and assigned to Sacramento, May 8, 1998. ... Traded by Sacramento to Phoenix for C/F Pauline Jordan, July 6, 1998. ... Waived by Phoenix, July 8, 1998. ... Signed by WNBA and assigned to Houston, May 3, 2000.
MISCELLANEOUS: Member of WNBA Championship Team (2000).

COLLEGIATE RECORD

NOTES: Member of NCAA Divison I championship team (1996, 1997).

Season Team	G	Min.	FGM	FGA	Pct.	FTM	FTA	Pct.	Reb.	Ast.	Pts.	RPG	APG	PPG
94-95—Tennessee	37	...	126	246	.512	80	108	.741	241	19	334	6.5	0.5	9.0
95-96—Tennessee	35	...	110	226	.487	42	68	.618	219	25	263	6.3	0.7	7.5
96-97—Tennessee	38	...	143	269	.532	93	132	.705	282	23	379	7.4	0.6	10.0
Totals	110	...	379	741	.511	215	308	.698	742	67	976	6.7	0.6	8.9

Three-point field goals: 1994-95, 2-for-8 (.250). 1995-96, 1-for-5 (.200). 1996-97, 0-for-1. Totals, 3-for-14 (.214).

WNBA REGULAR-SEASON RECORD

Season Team	G	Min.	FGM	FGA	Pct.	FTM	FTA	Pct.	REBOUNDS Off.	Def.	Tot.	Ast.	St.	Blk.	TO	Pts.	AVERAGES RPG	APG	PPG
1998—Sacramento....	6	32	0	6	.000	2	4	.500	3	7	10	10	2	0	3	2	1.7	1.7	0.3
2000—Houston	31	687	48	100	.480	35	50	.700	59	88	147	10	10	16	17	131	4.7	0.3	4.2
2001—Houston	32	672	62	138	.449	24	28	.857	44	94	138	22	12	15	42	148	4.3	0.7	4.6
2002—Houston	32	815	77	178	.433	47	58	.810	73	100	173	39	17	24	38	201	5.4	1.2	6.3
2003—Houston	22	359	30	62	.484	17	23	.739	19	44	63	13	3	7	20	77	2.9	0.6	3.5
Totals.................	123	2565	217	484	.448	125	163	.767	198	333	531	94	44	62	120	559	4.3	0.8	4.5

Three-point field goals: 2002, 0-for-2. Totals, 0-for-2.
Personal fouls/disqualifications: 2002, 67/0. Totals, 253/1.

WNBA PLAYOFF RECORD

Season Team	G	Min.	FGM	FGA	Pct.	FTM	FTA	Pct.	REBOUNDS Off.	Def.	Tot.	Ast.	St.	Blk.	TO	Pts.	AVERAGES RPG	APG	PPG
2000—Houston	6	135	10	20	.500	2	2	1.000	12	17	29	1	3	2	7	22	4.8	0.2	3.7
2001—Houston	2	71	7	17	.412	4	7	.571	4	13	17	3	0	3	4	18	8.5	1.5	9.0
2002—Houston	3	51	4	9	.444	0	0	...	2	7	9	1	0	6	4	8	3.0	0.3	2.7
2003—Houston	3	31	0	6	.000	0	0	...	2	4	6	0	2	0	1	0	2.0	0.0	0.0
Totals.................	14	288	21	52	.404	6	9	.667	20	41	61	5	5	11	16	48	4.4	0.4	3.4

JOHNSON, VICKIE   G   LIBERTY

PERSONAL: Born April 15, 1972, in Shreveport, La. ... 5-9/150 (1.75 m/68 kg). ... **Full name:** Vickie Annette Johnson.
HIGH SCHOOL: Coushatta (Coushatta, La.).
COLLEGE: Louisiana Tech.
TRANSACTIONS/CAREER NOTES: Selected by New York in second round (12th overall) of WNBA Elite Draft, February 27, 1997.

NOTES: Kodak All-America first team (1995, 1996).

COLLEGIATE RECORD

Season Team	G	Min.	FGM	FGA	Pct.	FTM	FTA	Pct.	Reb.	Ast.	Pts.	AVERAGES RPG	APG	PPG
92-93—Louisiana Tech	31	...	165	372	.444	76	103	.738	194	70	417	6.3	2.3	13.5
93-94—Louisiana Tech	35	...	209	418	.500	87	118	.737	244	76	517	7.0	2.2	14.8
94-95—Louisiana Tech	33	...	224	421	.532	94	127	.740	227	91	542	6.9	2.8	16.4
95-96—Louisiana Tech	26	...	169	313	.540	77	97	.794	166	68	415	6.4	2.6	16.0
Totals	125	...	767	1524	.503	334	445	.751	831	305	1891	6.6	2.4	15.1

Three-point field goals: 1992-93, 11-for-35 (.314). 1993-94, 12-for-38 (.316). 1994-95, 0-for-4. 1995-96, 0-for-2. Totals, 23-for-79 (.291).

WNBA REGULAR-SEASON RECORD

Season Team	G	Min.	FGM	FGA	Pct.	FTM	FTA	Pct.	REBOUNDS Off.	Def.	Tot.	Ast.	St.	Blk.	TO	Pts.	AVERAGES RPG	APG	PPG
1997—New York	26	789	108	269	.401	27	35	.771	46	64	110	66	19	4	49	247	4.2	2.5	9.5
1998—New York	30	905	146	327	.446	63	82	.768	44	70	114	74	31	7	45	376	3.8	2.5	12.5
1999—New York	32	1082	165	394	.419	72	86	.837	43	99	142	106	44	1	66	427	4.4	3.3	13.3
2000—New York	31	1023	143	324	.441	67	76	.882	40	97	137	77	22	5	57	380	4.4	2.5	12.3
2001—New York	32	939	135	326	.414	53	70	.757	23	84	107	87	35	4	52	353	3.3	2.7	11.0
2002—New York	31	1028	139	305	.456	49	61	.803	42	67	109	86	27	4	45	359	3.5	2.8	11.6
2003—New York	32	1042	158	345	.458	79	92	.859	30	65	95	75	29	7	55	430	3.0	2.3	13.4
Totals.................	214	6808	994	2290	.434	410	502	.817	268	546	814	571	207	32	369	2572	3.8	2.7	12.0

Three-point field goals: 1997, 4-for-21 (.190). 1998, 21-for-56 (.375). 1999, 25-for-71 (.352). 2000, 27-for-71 (.380). 2001, 30-for-82 (.366). 2002, 32-for-76 (.421). 2003, 35-for-96 (.365). Totals, 174-for-473 (.368).
Personal fouls/disqualifications: 1997, 52/0. 1998, 70/1. 1999, 77/0. 2000, 48/0. 2001, 62/1. 2002, 60/0. 2003, 65/0. Totals, 434/2.

WNBA PLAYOFF RECORD

Season Team	G	Min.	FGM	FGA	Pct.	FTM	FTA	Pct.	REBOUNDS Off.	Def.	Tot.	Ast.	St.	Blk.	TO	Pts.	AVERAGES RPG	APG	PPG
1997—New York	2	68	11	26	.423	1	2	.500	5	7	12	4	2	1	2	23	6.0	2.0	11.5
1999—New York	6	185	24	57	.421	9	14	.643	4	17	21	18	2	2	15	61	3.5	3.0	10.2
2000—New York	7	237	27	71	.380	12	14	.857	10	25	35	24	8	0	13	72	5.0	3.4	10.3
2001—New York	6	218	34	75	.453	15	15	1.000	7	20	27	28	13	2	14	89	4.5	4.7	14.8
2002—New York	8	244	36	75	.480	12	16	.750	8	22	30	24	7	0	11	98	3.8	3.0	12.3
Totals.................	29	952	132	304	.434	49	61	.803	34	91	125	98	32	5	55	343	4.3	3.4	11.8

Three-point field goals: 1997, 0-for-1. 1999, 4-for-10 (.400). 2000, 6-for-22 (.273). 2001, 6-for-22 (.273). 2002, 14-for-27 (.519). Totals, 30-for-82 (.366).
Personal fouls/disqualifications: 1997, 6/0. 1999, 15/0. 2000, 14/0. 2001, 11/0. 2002, 10/0. Totals, 56/0.

WNBA ALL-STAR GAME RECORD

Season Team	Min.	FGM	FGA	Pct.	FTM	FTA	Pct.	REBOUNDS Off.	Def.	Tot.	Ast.	PF	Dq.	St.	Blk.	TO	Pts.
1999—New York	15	3	8	.375	0	0	...	0	2	2	3	0	0	0	0	...	6
2001—New York	19	2	8	.250	2	2	1.000	0	3	3	1	0	0	0	0	...	8
Totals.................	34	5	16	.313	2	2	1.000	0	5	5	4	0	0	0	0	5	14

Three-point field goals: 1999, 0-for-3. 2001, 2-for-5 (.400). Totals, 2-for-8 (.250).

JONES, ASJHA   F/C   SUN

PERSONAL: Born August 1, 1980, in Piscataway, N.J. ... 6-2/198 (1.88 m/90 kg). ... **Full name:** Asjha Takera Jones.
HIGH SCHOOL: Piscataway (N.J.).
COLLEGE: Connecticut.
TRANSACTIONS/CAREER NOTES: Selected by Washington in first round (fourth overall) of WNBA Draft, April 19, 2002. ... Traded to Connecticut in a three-team deal that sent Tamicha Jackson from Phoenix to Washington and Connecticut sent the eighth pick in the 2004 WNBA Draft to Phoenix, March 25, 2004.

COLLEGIATE RECORD

NOTES: Member of NCAA Division I Championship Team (2002, 2000).

Season Team	G	Min.	FGM	FGA	Pct.	FTM	FTA	Pct.	Reb.	Ast.	Pts.	RPG	APG	PPG
98-99—Connecticut	34	681	140	284	.493	52	73	.712	170	45	332	5.0	1.3	9.8
99-00—Connecticut	36	632	127	251	.506	60	95	.632	177	33	319	4.9	0.9	8.9
00-01—Connecticut	35	683	128	291	.440	44	73	.603	190	50	304	5.4	1.4	8.7
01-02—Connecticut	39	961	247	445	.555	45	75	.600	257	66	547	6.6	1.7	14.0
Totals	144	2957	642	1271	.505	201	316	.636	794	194	1502	5.5	1.3	10.4

Three-point field goals: 1999-00, 5-for-10 (.500). 2000-01, 4-for-16 (.250). 2001-02, 8-for-25 (.320). Totals, 17-for-51 (.333).

WNBA REGULAR-SEASON RECORD

Season Team	G	Min.	FGM	FGA	Pct.	FTM	FTA	Pct.	Off.	Def.	Tot.	Ast.	St.	Blk.	TO	Pts.	RPG	APG	PPG
2002—Washington	32	612	93	233	.399	20	33	.606	39	50	89	28	13	17	39	208	2.8	0.9	6.5
2003—Washington	34	748	121	279	.434	41	55	.745	62	73	135	52	16	25	63	290	4.0	1.5	8.5
Totals	66	1360	214	512	.418	61	88	.693	101	123	224	80	29	42	102	498	3.4	1.2	7.5

Three-point field goals: 2002, 2-for-10 (.200). 2003, 7-for-17 (.412). Totals, 9-for-27 (.333).
Personal fouls/disqualifications: 2002, 88/2. 2003, 109/1. Totals, 197/3.

WNBA PLAYOFF RECORD

Season Team	G	Min.	FGM	FGA	Pct.	FTM	FTA	Pct.	Off.	Def.	Tot.	Ast.	St.	Blk.	TO	Pts.	RPG	APG	PPG
2002—Washington	5	63	8	19	.421	1	2	.500	3	5	8	3	0	1	1	18	1.6	0.6	3.6
Totals	5	63	8	19	.421	1	2	.500	3	5	8	3	0	1	1	18	1.6	0.6	3.6

Three-point field goals: 2002, 1-for-2 (.500). Totals, 1-for-2 (.500).
Personal fouls/disqualifications: 2002, 13/0. Totals, 13/0.

JONES, MERLAKIA   G/F   SHOCK

PERSONAL: Born June 21, 1973, in Montgomery, Ala. ... 5-9/147 (1.75 m/67 kg). ... **Full name:** Merlakia Kenyatta Jones.
HIGH SCHOOL: George Washington Carver (Montgomery, Ala.).
COLLEGE: Florida.
TRANSACTIONS/CAREER NOTES: Selected by Cleveland in second round (13th overall) of WNBA Draft, April 28, 1997. ... Signed by Detroit as an unrestricted free agent, February 17, 2004.

COLLEGIATE RECORD

Season Team	G	Min.	FGM	FGA	Pct.	FTM	FTA	Pct.	Reb.	Ast.	Pts.	RPG	APG	PPG
91-92—Florida	28	...	178	329	.541	64	83	.771	139	25	420	5.0	0.9	15.0
92-93—Florida	29	...	196	415	.472	45	68	.662	202	42	438	7.0	1.4	15.1
93-94—Florida	29	...	224	436	.514	70	103	.680	282	49	520	9.7	1.7	17.9
94-95—Florida	33	...	257	590	.436	81	117	.692	207	54	623	6.3	1.6	18.9
Totals	119	...	855	1770	.483	260	371	.701	830	170	2001	7.0	1.4	16.8

Three-point field goals: 1992-93, 1-for-4 (.250). 1993-94, 2-for-8 (.250). 1994-95, 28-for-113 (.248). Totals, 31-for-125 (.248).

WNBA REGULAR-SEASON RECORD

NOTES: All-WNBA first team (2001).

Season Team	G	Min.	FGM	FGA	Pct.	FTM	FTA	Pct.	Off.	Def.	Tot.	Ast.	St.	Blk.	TO	Pts.	RPG	APG	PPG
1997—Cleveland	28	589	92	229	.402	40	56	.714	31	51	82	25	23	3	54	229	2.9	0.9	8.2
1998—Cleveland	30	683	109	235	.464	61	81	.753	28	67	95	39	32	3	52	286	3.2	1.3	9.5
1999—Cleveland	32	853	141	325	.434	60	78	.769	47	75	122	51	41	5	66	347	3.8	1.6	10.8
2000—Cleveland	32	948	153	323	.474	32	47	.681	52	87	139	63	29	2	60	352	4.3	2.0	11.0
2001—Cleveland	30	998	165	377	.438	65	82	.793	43	121	164	45	29	4	53	404	5.5	1.5	13.5
2002—Cleveland	32	1094	157	393	.399	62	79	.785	33	143	176	72	44	4	55	391	5.5	2.3	12.2
2003—Cleveland	34	672	66	196	.337	28	39	.718	18	79	97	44	22	3	36	164	2.9	1.3	4.8
Totals	218	5837	883	2078	.425	348	462	.753	252	623	875	339	220	24	376	2173	4.0	1.6	10.0

Three-point field goals: 1997, 5-for-12 (.417). 1998, 7-for-20 (.350). 1999, 5-for-18 (.278). 2000, 14-for-45 (.311). 2001, 9-for-34 (.265). 2002, 15-for-54 (.278). 2003, 4-for-13 (.308). Totals, 59-for-196 (.301).
Personal fouls/disqualifications: 1997, 55/0. 1998, 86/0. 1999, 81/1. 2000, 86/2. 2001, 59/0. 2002, 60/0. 2003, 59/0. Totals, 469/3.

WNBA PLAYOFF RECORD

Season Team	G	Min.	FGM	FGA	Pct.	FTM	FTA	Pct.	Off.	Def.	Tot.	Ast.	St.	Blk.	TO	Pts.	RPG	APG	PPG
1998—Cleveland	3	65	11	24	.458	4	4	1.000	5	7	12	1	0	0	3	27	4.0	0.3	9.0
2000—Cleveland	6	207	34	86	.395	9	12	.750	11	32	43	11	7	0	8	83	7.2	1.8	13.8
2001—Cleveland	3	103	15	32	.469	5	5	1.000	8	10	18	9	1	1	3	36	6.0	3.0	12.0
2003—Cleveland	3	37	2	5	.400	1	2	.500	3	2	5	0	0	0	2	5	1.7	0.0	1.7
Totals	15	412	62	147	.422	19	23	.826	27	51	78	21	8	1	16	151	5.2	1.4	10.1

Three-point field goals: 1998, 1-for-2 (.500). 2000, 6-for-20 (.300). 2001, 1-for-3 (.333). 2003, 0-for-1. Totals, 8-for-26 (.308).
Personal fouls/disqualifications: 1998, 7/0. 2000, 14/0. 2001, 5/0. 2003, 2/0. Totals, 28/0.

WNBA ALL-STAR GAME RECORD

Season Team	Min.	FGM	FGA	Pct.	FTM	FTA	Pct.	Off.	Def.	Tot.	Ast.	PF	Dq.	St.	Blk.	TO	Pts.
1999—Cleveland	13	2	4	.500	0	0	...	1	2	3	3	0	0	0	0	...	4
2000—Cleveland	14	3	8	.375	0	0	...	1	1	2	0	1	0	0	0	...	6
2001—Cleveland	18	4	8	.500	4	6	.667	1	5	6	1	3	0	1	0	...	12
Totals	45	9	20	.450	4	6	.667	3	8	11	4	4	0	1	0	2	22

Three-point field goals: 2001, 0-for-1. Totals, 0-for-1.

JUNG SUN-MIN　　　　C　　　STORM

PERSONAL: Born October 12, 1974, in Masan, Kyungnam ... 6-1/168. (1.85 m/76 kg).
HIGH SCHOOL: Masan Girl's (Masan City, Gyungsangnam Province, Republic of Korea).
TRANSACTIONS/CAREER NOTES: Selected by Seattle in first round (eighth overall) of WNBA Draft, April 25, 2003.
MISCELLANEOUS: Two time ABC (Asian Basketball Championship) Gold medalist. ... Led Korean basketball team into the semi-finals of 2000 Sydney Olympic Games. ... 5 years with Gwangju Sinsegye Coolcats of the Womens Korean Basketball League.

KOREAN LEAGUE RECORD

Season Team	G	Min.	FGM	FGA	Pct.	FTM	FTA	Pct.	Reb.	Ast.	Pts.	AVERAGES RPG	APG	PPG
00-01—Shinsegae	24	920	220	477	.461	138	160	.863	...	150	578	10.8	6.3	24.1
01-02—Shinsegae	28	1026	265	564	.470	173	196	.883	...	163	812	9.3	5.8	29.0
02-03—Shinsegae	15	544	138	310	.445	76	87	.874	...	56	358	8.3	3.7	23.9
98-99—Shinsegae	13	488	132	271	.487	71	78	.910	...	34	335	9.1	2.6	25.8
99-00—Shinsegae	7	276	72	156	.462	54	67	.806	...	26	201	13.1	3.7	28.7
00-01—Shinsegae	9	347	100	213	.469	56	62	.903	...	60	256	10.3	6.7	28.4
01-02—Shinsegae	23	815	180	401	.449	150	163	.920	...	102	518	9.3	4.4	22.5
02-03—Shinsegae	21	729	159	362	.439	135	152	.888	...	76	453	7.7	3.6	21.6
Totals	140	5145	1266	2754	.460	853	966	.883	...	667	3511	...	4.7	25.1

Three-point field goals: 1900-01, 0-for-2. 1901-02, 3-for-4 (.750). 1902-03, 2-for-4 (.500). 1998-99, 0-for-1. 1999-00, 1-for-5 (.200). 2000-01, 0-for-1. 2001-02, 0-for-5. 2002-03, 0-for-10.

OLYMPICS

Season Team	G	Min.	FGM	FGA	Pct.	FTM	FTA	Pct.	Reb.	Ast.	Pts.	AVERAGES RPG	APG	PPG
2000—Korea	8	250	46	94	.489	19	22	.864	39	19	111	4.9	2.4	13.9
Totals	8	250	46	94	.489	19	22	.864	39	19	111	4.9	2.4	13.9

Three-point field goals: 2000-01, 0-for-1.

WNBA REGULAR-SEASON RECORD

Season Team	G	Min.	FGM	FGA	Pct.	FTM	FTA	Pct.	REBOUNDS Off.	Def.	Tot.	Ast.	St.	Blk.	TO	Pts.	AVERAGES RPG	APG	PPG
2003—Seattle	17	118	13	32	.406	4	4	1.000	1	1	10	1	5	0	5	30	0.6	0.1	1.8
Totals	17	118	13	32	.406	4	4	1.000	1	1	10	1	5	0	5	30	0.6	0.1	1.8

Three-point field goals: 2003, 0-for-7. Total, 0-for-7.
Personal fouls/disqualifications: 2003, 13/0. Total, 13/0.

KLIMESOVA, ZUZI　　　F　　　FEVER

PERSONAL: Born January 21, 1979, in Prague, Czech Republic ... 6-2/181 (1.88 m/82 kg). ... **Full name:** Zuzana Klimesova.
HIGH SCHOOL: Pius XI (Wis.).
COLLEGE: Vanderbilt.
TRANSACTIONS/CAREER NOTES: Selected by Indiana in second round (17th overall) of WNBA Draft, April 19, 2002.

COLLEGIATE RECORD

Season Team	G	Min.	FGM	FGA	Pct.	FTM	FTA	Pct.	Reb.	Ast.	Pts.	AVERAGES RPG	APG	PPG
98-99—Vanderbilt	27	705	107	217	.493	55	88	.625	170	24	269	6.3	0.9	10.0
99-00—Vanderbilt	34	1142	211	379	.557	51	73	.699	250	80	475	7.4	2.4	14.0
00-01—Vanderbilt	34	1179	234	414	.565	80	111	.721	276	119	555	8.1	3.5	16.3
01-02—Vanderbilt	37	1223	227	399	.569	106	132	.803	268	112	568	7.2	3.0	15.4
Totals	132	4249	779	1409	.553	292	404	.723	964	335	1867	7.3	2.5	14.1

Three-point field goals: 1998-99, 0-for-2. 1999-00, 2-for-3 (.667). 2000-01, 7-for-21 (.333). 2001-02, 8-for-24 (.333). Totals, 17-for-50 (.340).

WNBA REGULAR-SEASON RECORD

Season Team	G	Min.	FGM	FGA	Pct.	FTM	FTA	Pct.	REBOUNDS Off.	Def.	Tot.	Ast.	St.	Blk.	TO	Pts.	AVERAGES RPG	APG	PPG
2002—Indiana	11	39	2	12	.167	1	1	1.000	1	4	5	2	1	1	2	5	0.5	0.2	0.5
2003—Indiana	1	3	0	1	.000	2	2	1.000	0	0	0	0	0	0	0	2	0.0	0.0	2.0
Totals	12	42	2	13	.154	3	3	1.000	1	4	5	2	1	1	2	7	0.4	0.2	0.6

LAMBERT, SHEILA　　　G

PERSONAL: Born July 21, 1980, in Seattle, Wash. ... 5-7/125 (1.70 m/57 kg). ... **Full name:** Sheila Monique Lambert.
HIGH SCHOOL: Chief Sealth (Seattle).
COLLEGE: Baylor.
TRANSACTIONS/CAREER NOTES: Selected by Charlotte in first round (seventh overall) of WNBA Draft, April 19, 2002. ... Waived by Charlotte, May 21, 2003. ... Signed by Detroit, May 23, 2003.
MISCELLANEOUS: Member of WNBA Championship Team (2003).

K
—
L

COLLEGIATE RECORD

NOTES: Kodak All-America first team (2002). ... Played first two seasons at Grayson County (Texas) Community College. ... NJCAA All-America first team (2000, 1999).

Season Team	G	Min.	FGM	FGA	Pct.	FTM	FTA	Pct.	Reb.	Ast.	Pts.	AVERAGES RPG	APG	PPG
00-01—Baylor	30	1062	242	599	.404	148	196	.755	168	182	622	5.6	6.1	20.7
01-02—Baylor	33	1109	253	516	.490	129	169	.763	145	216	653	4.4	6.5	19.8
Totals	63	2171	495	1115	.444	277	365	.759	313	398	1275	5.0	6.3	20.2

Three-point field goals: 2000-01, 30-for-118 (.254). 2001-02, 18-for-57 (.316). Totals, 48-for-175 (.274).

WNBA REGULAR-SEASON RECORD

Season Team	G	Min.	FGM	FGA	Pct.	FTM	FTA	Pct.	REBOUNDS Off.	Def.	Tot.	Ast.	St.	Blk.	TO	Pts.	AVERAGES RPG	APG	PPG
2002—Charlotte	3	16	1	3	.333	0	0	...	2	1	3	3	1	0	2	2	1.0	1.0	0.7
2003—Detroit	27	187	24	66	.364	32	41	.780	10	18	28	14	5	0	29	87	1.0	0.5	3.2
Totals	30	203	25	69	.362	32	41	.780	12	19	31	17	6	0	31	89	1.0	0.6	3.0

Three-point field goals: 2003, 7-for-16 (.438). Totals, 7-for-16 (.438).
Personal fouls/disqualifications: 2003, 15/0. Totals, 16/0.

WNBA PLAYOFF RECORD

Season Team	G	Min.	FGM	FGA	Pct.	FTM	FTA	Pct.	REBOUNDS Off.	Def.	Tot.	Ast.	St.	Blk.	TO	Pts.	AVERAGES RPG	APG	PPG
2003—Detroit	7	14	2	6	.333	0	0	...	0	2	2	1	0	0	4	5	0.3	0.1	0.7
Totals	7	14	2	6	.333	0	0	...	0	2	2	1	0	0	4	5	0.3	0.1	0.7

Three-point field goals: 2003, 1-for-3 (.333). Totals, 1-for-3 (.333).
Personal fouls/disqualifications: 2003, 3/0. Totals, 3/0.

LASSITER, AMANDA   F   LYNX

PERSONAL: Born June 9, 1979, in San Francisco, Calif. ... 6-0/148 (1.83 m/67 kg). ... Full name: Amanda D. Lassiter.
HIGH SCHOOL: George Washington (San Francisco).
COLLEGE: Missouri.
TRANSACTIONS/CAREER NOTES: Selected by Houston in first round (15th overall) of WNBA Draft, April 20, 2001. ... Traded by Houston to Seattle for F Sonja Henning, June 17, 2002. ... Acquired by Minnesota along with a first round pick in the 2004 WNBA Draft for Janelle Burse and Sheri Sam, April 15, 2004.

COLLEGIATE RECORD

NOTES: Member of NJCAA Division I championship team (1998). ... Kodak and NJCAA All-America first team (1999). ... NJCAA Tournament MVP (1998).

Season Team	G	Min.	FGM	FGA	Pct.	FTM	FTA	Pct.	Reb.	Ast.	Pts.	AVERAGES RPG	APG	PPG
97-98—Cent. Arizona Coll.	32	...	165	324	.509	35	51	.686	205	114	407	6.4	3.6	12.7
98-99—Cent. Arizona Coll.	30	...	195	390	.500	24	43	.558	207	111	486	6.9	3.7	16.2
99-00—Missouri	30	826	165	395	.418	53	69	.768	168	99	418	5.6	3.3	13.9
00-01—Missouri	32	935	238	567	.420	69	97	.711	197	75	610	6.2	2.3	19.1
Totals	62	1761	403	962	.419	122	166	.735	365	174	1028	5.9	2.8	16.6

Three-point field goals: 1997-98, 14-for-52 (.269). 1998-99, 24-for-60 (.400). 1999-00, 35-for-95 (.368). 2000-01, 65-for-187 (.348). Totals, 100-for-282 (.355).

WNBA REGULAR-SEASON RECORD

Season Team	G	Min.	FGM	FGA	Pct.	FTM	FTA	Pct.	REBOUNDS Off.	Def.	Tot.	Ast.	St.	Blk.	TO	Pts.	AVERAGES RPG	APG	PPG
2001—Houston	32	613	51	139	.367	10	15	.667	27	83	110	34	16	21	35	138	3.4	1.1	4.3
2002—Hou.-Sea.	30	600	47	140	.336	13	19	.684	24	45	69	57	29	21	51	127	2.3	1.9	4.2
2003—Seattle	32	733	60	156	.385	19	30	.633	33	79	112	42	27	26	42	163	3.5	1.3	5.1
Totals	94	1946	158	435	.363	42	64	.656	84	207	291	133	72	68	128	428	3.1	1.4	4.6

Three-point field goals: 2001, 26-for-67 (.388). 2002, 20-for-71 (.282). 2003, 24-for-73 (.329). Totals, 70-for-211 (.332).
Personal fouls/disqualifications: 2001, 66/0. 2002, 62/1. 2003, 92/2. Totals, 220/3.

WNBA PLAYOFF RECORD

Season Team	G	Min.	FGM	FGA	Pct.	FTM	FTA	Pct.	REBOUNDS Off.	Def.	Tot.	Ast.	St.	Blk.	TO	Pts.	AVERAGES RPG	APG	PPG
2001—Houston	2	54	7	16	.438	2	2	1.000	1	8	9	0	0	3	2	19	4.5	0.0	9.5
2002—Seattle	2	46	4	15	.267	0	0	...	0	7	7	4	3	1	5	10	3.5	2.0	5.0
Totals	4	100	11	31	.355	2	2	1.000	1	15	16	4	3	4	7	29	4.0	1.0	7.3

Three-point field goals: 2001, 3-for-9 (.333). 2002, 2-for-9 (.222). Totals, 5-for-18 (.278).
Personal fouls/disqualifications: 2001, 4/0. 2002, 4/0. Totals, 8/0.

LAWSON, KARA   G   MONARCHS

PERSONAL: Born February 14, 1981, in Alexandria, Va. ... 5-8 (1.73 m/ kg). ... Full name: Kara Marie Lawson.
HIGH SCHOOL: West Springfield (Alexandria, Va.).
COLLEGE: Tennessee.
TRANSACTIONS/CAREER NOTES: Selected by Detroit in first round (fifth overall) of WNBA Draft, April 25, 2003. ... Traded by Detroit to Sacramento for G Kedra Holland-Corn and a second round pick in the

2004 WNBA Draft, April 29, 2003.

MISCELLANEOUS: Captain of the gold-medal-winning U.S. World University Games Team (2001). ... Named the 1999 Naismith High School Player of the Year as a senior. ... Member of bronze-medal-winning U.S. Women's World Youth Games Team (1998).

COLLEGIATE RECORD

NOTES: Associated Press All-America Second Team (2003). ... All-SEC First Team (2003, 2002, 2001, 2000). ... Associated Press All-America Third Team (2002). ... USBWA All-America Team (2002). ... SEC All-Freshman Team (2000). ... Holds Tennessee career mark for three-pointers made (256). ... Led the SEC in three-point field-goal percentage as a freshamn (.436).

												AVERAGES		
Season Team	G	Min.	FGM	FGA	Pct.	FTM	FTA	Pct.	Reb.	Ast.	Pts.	RPG	APG	PPG
99-00—Tennessee	37	1036	168	367	.458	89	109	.817	...	102	504	4.1	2.8	13.6
00-01—Tennessee	34	899	132	305	.433	60	70	.857	...	113	386	3.5	3.3	11.4
01-02—Tennessee	34	1078	189	406	.466	96	115	.835	...	90	512	4.9	2.6	15.1
02-03—Tennessee	38	1185	186	397	.469	99	112	.884	...	151	548	4.9	4.0	14.4
Totals	143	4198	675	1475	.458	344	406	.847	...	456	1950	0.0	3.2	13.6

Three-point field goals: 1999-00, 78-for-181 (.431). 2000-01, 62-for-150 (.413). 2001-02, 38-for-115 (.330). 2002-03, 77-for-171 (.450). Totals, 255-for-617 (.413).

WNBA REGULAR-SEASON RECORD

									REBOUNDS								AVERAGES		
Season Team	G	Min.	FGM	FGA	Pct.	FTM	FTA	Pct.	Off.	Def.	Tot.	Ast.	St.	Blk.	TO	Pts.	RPG	APG	PPG
2003—Sacramento	34	769	89	227	.392	31	40	.775	30	77	107	56	15	5	42	263	3.1	1.6	7.7
Totals	34	769	89	227	.392	31	40	.775	30	77	107	56	15	5	42	263	3.1	1.6	7.7

Three-point field goals: 2003, 54-for-135 (.400). Totals, 54-for-135 (.400).

Personal fouls/disqualifications: 2003, 45/0. Totals, 45/0.

WNBA PLAYOFF RECORD

									REBOUNDS								AVERAGES		
Season Team	G	Min.	FGM	FGA	Pct.	FTM	FTA	Pct.	Off.	Def.	Tot.	Ast.	St.	Blk.	TO	Pts.	RPG	APG	PPG
2003—Sacramento	6	154	9	42	.214	7	8	.875	2	21	23	16	1	2	4	32	3.8	2.7	5.3
Totals	6	154	9	42	.214	7	8	.875	2	21	23	16	1	2	4	32	3.8	2.7	5.3

Three-point field goals: 2003, 7-for-23 (.304). Totals, 7-for-23 (.304).

Personal fouls/disqualifications: 2003, 8/0. Totals, 8/0.

LENNOX, BETTY G STORM

PERSONAL: Born December 4, 1976, in Oklahoma City, Okla. ... 5-8/135 (1.73 m/61 kg). ... Full name: Betty Bernice Lennox.

HIGH SCHOOL: Fort Osage (Independence, Mo.).

COLLEGE: Louisiana Tech.

TRANSACTIONS/CAREER NOTES: Selected by Minnesota in first round (sixth overall) of WNBA Draft, April 25, 2000. ... Traded by Minnesota with a first-round pick in the 2003 WNBA Draft to Miami for G Tamara Moore and a second-round pick, June 13, 2002. ... Selected by the Cleveland Rockers in first round (third pick overall) of the 2003 Dispersal Draft. ... Selected by the Seattle Storm in the first round (sixth overall) in the 2004 WNBA Dispersal Draft, January 6, 2004.

COLLEGIATE RECORD

NOTES: Associated Press All-America third team (2000). ... Member of NJCAA national championship team (1997). ... NCAA Midwest Regional All-Tournament team (2000). ... NCAA West Regional All-Tournament Team (1999). ... Sun Belt Conference Player of Year (2000). ... U.S. Basketball Writers Association All-America first team (2000). ... Women's Basketball News Service All-America first team (2000).

												AVERAGES		
Season Team	G	Min.	FGM	FGA	Pct.	FTM	FTA	Pct.	Reb.	Ast.	Pts.	RPG	APG	PPG
96-97—Trinity Valley CC	35	...	261	...	...	115	...	...	...	...	820	0.0	0.0	23.4
98-99—Louisiana Tech	33	...	137	335	.409	33	52	.635	136	59	333	4.1	1.8	10.1
99-00—Louisiana Tech	34	...	232	526	.441	61	78	.782	199	116	587	5.9	3.4	17.3
Totals	67	...	369	861	.429	94	130	.723	335	175	920	5.0	2.6	13.7

Three-point field goals: 1998-99, 26-for-88 (.295). 1999-00, 62-for-163 (.380). Totals, 88-for-251 (.351).

WNBA REGULAR-SEASON RECORD

HONORS: All-WNBA second team (2000). ... WNBA Rookie of the Year (2000).

									REBOUNDS								AVERAGES		
Season Team	G	Min.	FGM	FGA	Pct.	FTM	FTA	Pct.	Off.	Def.	Tot.	Ast.	St.	Blk.	TO	Pts.	RPG	APG	PPG
2000—Minnesota	32	984	201	471	.427	84	105	.800	53	125	178	82	53	9	97	541	5.6	2.6	16.9
2001—Minnesota	11	241	41	110	.373	19	20	.950	13	41	54	16	10	4	25	121	4.9	1.5	11.0
2002—Minn.-Miami	31	719	120	355	.338	50	68	.735	20	69	89	63	30	5	82	341	2.9	2.0	11.0
2003—Cleveland	34	560	100	269	.372	26	36	.722	19	70	89	32	14	4	58	258	2.6	0.9	7.6
Totals	108	2504	462	1205	.383	179	229	.782	105	305	410	193	107	22	262	1261	3.8	1.8	11.7

Three-point field goals: 2000, 55-for-139 (.396). 2001, 20-for-52 (.385). 2002, 51-for-154 (.331). 2003, 32-for-103 (.311). Totals, 158-for-448 (.353).

Personal fouls/disqualifications: 2000, 112/4. 2001, 29/0. 2002, 102/3. 2003, 77/0. Totals, 320/7.

WNBA PLAYOFF RECORD

									REBOUNDS								AVERAGES		
Season Team	G	Min.	FGM	FGA	Pct.	FTM	FTA	Pct.	Off.	Def.	Tot.	Ast.	St.	Blk.	TO	Pts.	RPG	APG	PPG
2003—Cleveland	3	45	9	19	.474	1	2	.500	1	6	7	3	3	0	4	21	2.3	1.0	7.0
Totals	3	45	9	19	.474	1	2	.500	1	6	7	3	3	0	4	21	2.3	1.0	7.0

Three-point field goals: 2003, 2-for-5 (.400). Totals, 2-for-5 (.400).

Personal fouls/disqualifications: 2003, 7/0. Totals, 7/0.

Season Team	Min.	FGM	FGA	Pct.	FTM	FTA	Pct.	REBOUNDS Off.	Def.	Tot.	Ast.	PF	Dq.	St.	Blk.	TO	Pts.
2000 —Minnesota.......	13	1	3	.333	0	0	...	2	3	5	1	1	0	0	0	...	3
Totals................	13	1	3	.333	0	0	...	2	3	5	1	1	0	0	0	4	3

Three-point field goals: 2000, 1-for-2 (.500). Totals, 1-for-2 (.500).

LESLIE, LISA　　　　C　　　　SPARKS

PERSONAL: Born July 7, 1972, in Gardena, Calif. ... 6-5/170 (1.96 m/77 kg). ... Full name: Lisa DeShaun Leslie.
HIGH SCHOOL: Morningside (Inglewood, Calif.).
COLLEGE: U.S.C..
TRANSACTIONS/CAREER NOTES: Signed by WNBA and assigned to Los Angeles, January 22, 1997.
MISCELLANEOUS: Member of WNBA Championship Team (2001, 2002). ... Recorded first dunk in WNBA history, July 22, 2002.

COLLEGIATE RECORD
NOTES: Naismith Award winner (1994). ... Kodak All-America (1994).

Season Team	G	Min.	FGM	FGA	Pct.	FTM	FTA	Pct.	Reb.	Ast.	Pts.	AVERAGES RPG	APG	PPG
90-91—Southern Cal.............	30	...	241	504	.478	98	145	.676	299	20	582	10.0	0.7	19.4
91-92—Southern Cal.............	31	...	262	476	.550	106	152	.697	261	46	632	8.4	1.5	20.4
92-93—Southern Cal.............	29	...	211	378	.558	119	162	.735	285	59	543	9.8	2.0	18.7
93-94—Southern Cal.............	30	...	259	464	.558	138	201	.687	369	83	657	12.3	2.8	21.9
Totals	120	...	973	1822	.534	461	660	.698	1214	208	2414	10.1	1.7	20.1

Three-point field goals: 1990-91, 2-for-8 (.250). 1991-92, 2-for-8 (.250). 1992-93, 2-for-8 (.250). 1993-94, 1-for-13 (.077). Totals, 7-for-37 (.189).

OLYMPICS
NOTES: Member of gold medal-winning U.S. Olmpic Team (1996, 2000). ... USA Basketball's Female Athlete of the Year (1993, 1998).

Season Team	G	Min.	FGM	FGA	Pct.	FTM	FTA	Pct.	Reb.	Ast.	Pts.	AVERAGES RPG	APG	PPG
1996—United States..............	8	...	64	97	.660	28	44	.636	58	19	156	7.3	2.4	19.5
2000—United States..............	8	210	48	98	.490	27	39	.692	63	11	126	7.9	1.4	15.8
Totals	16	210	112	195	.574	55	83	.663	121	30	282	7.6	1.9	17.6

Three-point field goals: 1996-97, 0-for-1. 2000-01, 3-for-7 (.429). Totals, 3-for-8 (.375).

WNBA REGULAR-SEASON RECORD
HONORS: WNBA Most Valuable Player (2001). ... All-WNBA first team (1997, 2000, 2001, 2002, 2003). ... All-WNBA second team (1998, 1999). ... Led WNBA in rebounds in 1997 (9.5 rpg) and 1998 (10.2 rpg). ... Led WNBA in double-doubles in 1998 (16).

Season Team	G	Min.	FGM	FGA	Pct.	FTM	FTA	Pct.	REBOUNDS Off.	Def.	Tot.	Ast.	St.	Blk.	TO	Pts.	AVERAGES RPG	APG	PPG
1997—Los Angeles....	28	902	160	371	.431	113	189	.598	63	203	266	74	39	59	109	445	9.5	2.6	15.9
1998—Los Angeles....	28	898	202	423	.478	136	177	.768	77	208	285	70	42	60	102	549	10.2	2.5	19.6
1999—Los Angeles....	32	930	182	389	.468	114	156	.731	72	176	248	56	36	49	94	500	7.8	1.8	15.6
2000—Los Angeles....	32	1028	197	430	.458	169	205	.824	75	231	306	60	31	74	103	570	9.6	1.9	17.8
2001—Los Angeles....	31	1033	221	467	.473	142	193	.736	88	210	298	73	34	71	98	606	9.6	2.4	19.5
2002—Los Angeles....	31	1060	189	406	.466	133	183	.727	78	244	322	83	46	90	108	523	10.4	2.7	16.9
2003—Los Angeles....	23	792	165	373	.442	82	133	.617	76	155	231	46	31	63	65	424	10.0	2.0	18.4
Totals..................	205	6643	1316	2859	.460	889	1236	.719	529	1427	1956	462	259	466	679	3617	9.5	2.3	17.6

Three-point field goals: 1997, 12-for-46 (.261). 1998, 9-for-23 (.391). 1999, 22-for-52 (.423). 2000, 7-for-32 (.219). 2001, 22-for-60 (.367). 2002, 12-for-37 (.324). 2003, 12-for-37 (.324). Totals, 96-for-287 (.334).
Personal fouls/disqualifications: 1997, 99/1. 1998, 121/3. 1999, 136/4. 2000, 134/7. 2001, 132/3. 2002, 123/7. 2003, 93/3. Totals, 838/28.

WNBA PLAYOFF RECORD
NOTES: WNBA Championship Most Valuable Player (2001, 2002).

Season Team	G	Min.	FGM	FGA	Pct.	FTM	FTA	Pct.	REBOUNDS Off.	Def.	Tot.	Ast.	St.	Blk.	TO	Pts.	AVERAGES RPG	APG	PPG
1999—Los Angeles....	4	145	29	60	.483	14	18	.778	6	28	34	11	4	6	14	76	8.5	2.8	19.0
2000—Los Angeles....	4	139	28	57	.491	19	23	.826	10	31	41	8	1	5	13	75	10.3	2.0	18.8
2001—Los Angeles....	7	260	58	118	.492	37	50	.740	28	58	86	21	12	31	26	156	12.3	3.0	22.3
2002—Los Angeles....	6	232	46	86	.535	19	26	.731	10	37	47	11	11	17	8	116	7.8	1.8	19.3
2003—Los Angeles....	9	327	74	137	.540	38	54	.704	22	58	80	23	12	28	24	187	8.9	2.6	20.8
Totals................	30	1103	235	458	.513	127	171	.743	76	212	288	74	40	87	85	610	9.6	2.5	20.3

Three-point field goals: 1999, 4-for-13 (.308). 2000, 0-for-3. 2001, 3-for-7 (.429). 2002, 5-for-8 (.625). 2003, 1-for-3 (.333). Totals, 13-for-34 (.382).
Personal fouls/disqualifications: 1999, 12/0. 2000, 14/0. 2001, 22/0. 2002, 22/0. 2003, 39/1. Totals, 109/1.

WNBA ALL-STAR GAME RECORD
NOTES: WNBA All-Star Most Valuable Player (1999, 2001). ... WNBA All-Star Most Valuable Player (2002).

Season Team	Min.	FGM	FGA	Pct.	FTM	FTA	Pct.	REBOUNDS Off.	Def.	Tot.	Ast.	PF	Dq.	St.	Blk.	TO	Pts.
1999 —Los Angeles.....	17	5	11	.455	3	4	.750	3	2	5	1	2	0	1	1	...	13
2000 —Los Angeles.....	21	8	15	.533	0	0	...	4	2	6	0	0	0	0	1	...	16
2001 —Los Angeles.....	23	8	14	.571	3	4	.750	3	6	9	1	4	0	1	3	...	20
2002 —Los Angeles.....	28	6	13	.462	6	10	.600	3	11	14	0	2	0	1	4	...	18
2003 —Los Angeles.....	16	7	10	.700	2	2	1.000	1	2	3	0	2	0	1	0	...	17
Totals.................	105	34	63	.540	14	20	.700	14	23	37	2	10	0	4	9	9	84

Three-point field goals: 1999, 0-for-1. 2001, 1-for-2 (.500). 2002, 0-for-1. 2003, 1-for-2 (.500). Totals, 2-for-6 (.333)

LEWIS, TYNESHA   G/F   STING

PERSONAL: Born May 8, 1979, in Macclesfield, N.C. ... 5-9/148 (1.75 m/67 kg). ... Full name: Tynesha Rashaun Lewis.
HIGH SCHOOL: Southwest Edgecomb (Pinetops, N.C.).
COLLEGE: North Carolina State.
TRANSACTIONS/CAREER NOTES: Selected by Houston in second round (31st overall) of WNBA Draft, April 20, 2001. ... Waived by Houston, May 21, 2003. ... Signed by Charlotte, June 2, 2003.

COLLEGIATE RECORD

Season Team	G	Min.	FGM	FGA	Pct.	FTM	FTA	Pct.	Reb.	Ast.	Pts.	AVERAGES RPG	APG	PPG
97-98—N.C. State	32	860	146	321	.455	60	91	.659	128	80	376	4.0	2.5	11.8
98-99—N.C. State	29	954	176	408	.431	84	118	.712	197	92	480	6.8	3.2	16.6
99-00—N.C. State	29	932	117	324	.361	42	70	.600	147	71	318	5.1	2.4	11.0
00-01—N.C. State	33	1105	164	422	.389	87	117	.744	180	102	447	5.5	3.1	13.5
Totals	123	3851	603	1475	.409	273	396	.689	652	345	1621	5.3	2.8	13.2

Three-point field goals: 1997-98, 24-for-75 (.320). 1998-99, 44-for-145 (.303). 1999-00, 42-for-133 (.316). 2000-01, 32-for-109 (.294). Totals, 142-for-462 (.307).

WNBA REGULAR-SEASON RECORD

Season Team	G	Min.	FGM	FGA	Pct.	FTM	FTA	Pct.	REBOUNDS Off.	Def.	Tot.	Ast.	St.	Blk.	TO	Pts.	AVERAGES RPG	APG	PPG
2001—Houston	29	419	39	92	.424	11	17	.647	21	41	62	15	11	4	26	97	2.1	0.5	3.3
2002—Houston	17	145	13	30	.433	5	8	.625	6	12	18	9	3	3	9	34	1.1	0.5	2.0
2003—Charlotte	23	234	26	62	.419	11	12	.917	11	22	33	20	10	6	16	70	1.4	0.9	3.0
Totals	69	798	78	184	.424	27	37	.730	38	75	113	44	24	13	51	201	1.6	0.6	2.9

Three-point field goals: 2001, 8-for-20 (.400). 2002, 3-for-8 (.375). 2003, 7-for-13 (.538). Totals, 18-for-41 (.439).
Personal fouls/disqualifications: 2001, 26/0. 2002, 18/0. 2003, 18/0. Totals, 62/0.

WNBA PLAYOFF RECORD

Season Team	G	Min.	FGM	FGA	Pct.	FTM	FTA	Pct.	REBOUNDS Off.	Def.	Tot.	Ast.	St.	Blk.	TO	Pts.	AVERAGES RPG	APG	PPG
2001—Houston	2	6	0	1	.000	0	0	...	0	0	0	2	0	0	0	0	0.0	1.0	0.0
2003—Charlotte	2	29	4	8	.500	5	6	.833	2	1	3	4	0	1	0	14	1.5	2.0	7.0
Totals	4	35	4	9	.444	5	6	.833	2	1	3	6	0	1	0	14	0.8	1.5	3.5

Three-point field goals: 2003, 1-for-1. Totals, 1-for-1 (1.000).
Personal fouls/disqualifications: 2003, 2/0. Totals, 3/0.

L

LOBO, REBECCA   F   SUN

PERSONAL: Born October 6, 1973, in Hartford, Conn. ... 6-4/185 (1.93 m/84 kg). ... Full name: Rebecca Rose Lobo.
HIGH SCHOOL: Southwick Tolland Regional (Southwick, Mass.).
COLLEGE: Connecticut.
TRANSACTIONS/CAREER NOTES: Signed by WNBA and assigned to New York, January 22, 1997. ... Traded by Houston to Connecticut for a second-round pick in 2003 WNBA Draft, February 13, 2002.

COLLEGIATE RECORD

NOTES: Member of NCAA Division I Championship Team (1995). ... NCAA Final Four Most Valuable Player (1995). ... Wade Trophy winner (1995). ... National Player of the Year (1995). ... Kodak All-America first team (1994, 1995). ... Associated Press All-America first team (1995). ... GTE/CoSIDA Women's Basketball National Academic All-American of the Year (1995).

Season Team	G	Min.	FGM	FGA	Pct.	FTM	FTA	Pct.	Reb.	Ast.	Pts.	AVERAGES RPG	APG	PPG
91-92—Connecticut	29	...	167	338	.494	82	117	.701	228	26	416	7.9	0.9	14.3
92-93—Connecticut	29	...	189	421	.449	77	119	.647	326	37	484	11.2	1.3	16.7
93-94—Connecticut	33	...	243	445	.546	138	187	.738	371	68	635	11.2	2.1	19.2
94-95—Connecticut	35	...	238	476	.500	104	154	.675	343	129	598	9.8	3.7	17.1
Totals	126	...	837	1680	.498	401	577	.695	1268	260	2133	10.1	2.1	16.9

Three-point field goals: 1991-92, 0-for-1. 1992-93, 29-for-85 (.341). 1993-94, 11-for-34 (.324). 1994-95, 18-for-51 (.353). Totals, 58-for-171 (.339).

OLYMPICS

NOTES: Member of gold medal-winning U.S. Olympic Team.

Season Team	G	Min.	FGM	FGA	Pct.	FTM	FTA	Pct.	Reb.	Ast.	Pts.	AVERAGES RPG	APG	PPG
1996—United States	8	...	10	16	.625	8	11	.727	16	5	31	2.0	0.6	3.9
1996—United States	8	...	10	16	.625	8	11	.727	16	5	31	2.0	0.6	3.9
Totals	16	...	20	32	.625	16	22	.727	32	10	62	2.0	0.6	3.9

Three-point field goals: 1996-97, 1-for-3 (.333). 1996-97, 1-for-3 (.333). Totals, 2-for-6 (.333).

WNBA REGULAR-SEASON RECORD

HONORS: All-WNBA second team (1997).

Season Team	G	Min.	FGM	FGA	Pct.	FTM	FTA	Pct.	REBOUNDS Off.	Def.	Tot.	Ast.	St.	Blk.	TO	Pts.	AVERAGES RPG	APG	PPG
1997—New York	28	939	133	354	.376	64	105	.610	62	141	203	53	26	51	88	348	7.3	1.9	12.4
1998—New York	30	875	136	281	.484	66	93	.710	70	137	207	44	17	33	67	350	6.9	1.5	11.7
1999—New York	1	1	0	0	...	0	0	...	1	0	1	0	0	0	1	0	1.0	0.0	0.0
2000—New York							Did not play due to injury..												
2001—New York	16	85	7	22	.318	2	4	.500	2	12	14	1	2	0	7	17	0.9	0.1	1.1
2002—Houston	21	132	15	32	.469	1	4	.250	9	14	23	12	1	5	11	34	1.1	0.6	1.6
2003—Connecticut	25	297	25	88	.284	2	9	.222	9	43	52	5	6	15	14	59	2.1	0.2	2.4
Totals	121	2329	316	777	.407	135	215	.628	153	347	500	115	52	104	188	808	4.1	1.0	6.7

Three-point field goals: 1997, 18-for-63 (.286). 1998, 12-for-39 (.308). 2001, 1-for-2 (.500). 2002, 3-for-7 (.429). 2003, 7-for-28 (.250). Totals, 41-for-139 (.295).
Personal fouls/disqualifications: 1997, 73/1. 1998, 98/1. 2001, 16/0. 2002, 10/0. 2003, 33/0. Totals, 230/2.

WNBA PLAYOFF RECORD

Season Team	G	Min.	FGM	FGA	Pct.	FTM	FTA	Pct.	REBOUNDS Off.	Def.	Tot.	Ast.	St.	Blk.	TO	Pts.	AVERAGES RPG	APG	PPG
1997—New York......	2	68	9	21	.429	7	12	.583	5	13	18	4	0	4	5	25	9.0	2.0	12.5
2003—Connecticut ...	2	38	4	10	.400	0	0	...	3	5	8	5	0	4	2	9	4.0	2.5	4.5
Totals.................	4	106	13	31	.419	7	12	.583	8	18	26	9	0	8	7	34	6.5	2.3	8.5

Three-point field goals: 1997, 0-for-3. 2003, 1-for-4 (.250). Totals, 1-for-7 (.143).
Personal fouls/disqualifications: 1997, 8/0. 2003, 4/0. Totals, 12/0.

LUZ, HELEN   G   MYSTICS

PERSONAL: Born November 23, 1972, in Aracatuba, Sao Paulo, Brazil ... 5-8/144 (1.73 m/65 kg). ... Full name: Helen Cristina Santos Luz.
TRANSACTIONS/CAREER NOTES: Signed by the WNBA and added by Washington, April 30, 2001.

OLYMPICS
NOTES: Member of bronze medal-winning Brazilian Olympic Team (2000).

Season Team	G	Min.	FGM	FGA	Pct.	FTM	FTA	Pct.	Reb.	Ast.	Pts.	AVERAGES RPG	APG	PPG
2000—Brazil	8	224	27	73	.370	3	5	.600	8	25	70	1.0	3.1	8.8
Totals	8	224	27	73	.370	3	5	.600	8	25	70	1.0	3.1	8.8

Three-point field goals: 2000-01, 13-for-41 (.317).

WNBA REGULAR-SEASON RECORD

Season Team	G	Min.	FGM	FGA	Pct.	FTM	FTA	Pct.	REBOUNDS Off.	Def.	Tot.	Ast.	St.	Blk.	TO	Pts.	AVERAGES RPG	APG	PPG
2001—Washington ...	32	489	55	136	.404	22	25	.880	10	27	37	55	28	5	43	164	1.2	1.7	5.1
2002—Washington ...	32	474	65	148	.439	15	19	.789	9	23	32	48	18	5	43	187	1.0	1.5	5.8
2003—Washington ...	20	165	19	53	.358	9	10	.900	2	8	10	21	6	2	11	59	0.5	1.1	3.0
Totals.................	84	1128	139	337	.412	46	54	.852	21	58	79	124	52	12	97	410	0.9	1.5	4.9

Three-point field goals: 2001, 32-for-82 (.390). 2002, 42-for-106 (.396). 2003, 12-for-40 (.300). Totals, 86-for-228 (.377).
Personal fouls/disqualifications: 2001, 47/0. 2002, 40/0. 2003, 16/0. Totals, 103/0.

WNBA PLAYOFF RECORD

Season Team	G	Min.	FGM	FGA	Pct.	FTM	FTA	Pct.	REBOUNDS Off.	Def.	Tot.	Ast.	St.	Blk.	TO	Pts.	AVERAGES RPG	APG	PPG
2002—Washington....	4	46	7	12	.583	0	0	...	0	3	3	8	2	0	3	18	0.8	2.0	4.5
Totals.................	4	46	7	12	.583	0	0	...	0	3	3	8	2	0	3	18	0.8	2.0	4.5

Three-point field goals: 2002, 4-for-8 (.500). Totals, 4-for-8 (.500).
Personal fouls/disqualifications: 2002, 2/0. Totals, 2/0.

M

MABIKA, MWADI   G   SPARKS

PERSONAL: Born July 27, 1976, in Kinshasa, Congo ... 5-11/165 (1.80 m/75 kg).
HIGH SCHOOL: Institute of Lemba (Kinshasa, Congo).
TRANSACTIONS/CAREER NOTES: Signed by WNBA and assigned to Los Angeles, May 22, 1997.
MISCELLANEOUS: Member of WNBA Championship Team (2001, 2002).

OLYMPICS

Season Team	G	Min.	FGM	FGA	Pct.	FTM	FTA	Pct.	Reb.	Ast.	Pts.	AVERAGES RPG	APG	PPG
1996—Zaire	7	...	51	146	.349	9	15	.600	22	13	121	3.1	1.9	17.3
Totals	7	...	51	146	.349	9	15	.600	22	13	121	3.1	1.9	17.3

Three-point field goals: 1996-97, 10-for-29 (.345).

WNBA REGULAR-SEASON RECORD
NOTES: All-WNBA first team (2002).

Season Team	G	Min.	FGM	FGA	Pct.	FTM	FTA	Pct.	REBOUNDS Off.	Def.	Tot.	Ast.	St.	Blk.	TO	Pts.	AVERAGES RPG	APG	PPG
1997—Los Angeles ...	21	325	53	136	.390	13	24	.542	22	32	54	22	23	6	27	126	2.6	1.0	6.0
1998—Los Angeles ...	29	710	87	257	.339	30	43	.698	29	98	127	44	30	9	37	237	4.4	1.5	8.2
1999—Los Angeles ...	32	938	125	336	.372	56	78	.718	42	111	153	112	44	15	58	347	4.8	3.5	10.8
2000—Los Angeles ...	32	940	130	335	.388	73	89	.820	45	134	179	98	58	18	51	394	5.6	3.1	12.3
2001—Los Angeles ...	28	828	99	256	.387	68	79	.861	22	108	130	87	39	11	44	313	4.6	3.1	11.2
2002—Los Angeles ...	32	1050	188	444	.423	99	118	.839	32	135	167	92	38	9	62	539	5.2	2.9	16.8
2003—Los Angeles ...	32	1042	158	388	.407	97	112	.866	34	107	141	82	30	18	74	441	4.4	2.6	13.8
Totals.................	206	5833	840	2152	.390	436	543	.803	226	725	951	537	262	86	353	2397	4.6	2.6	11.6

Three-point field goals: 1997, 7-for-38 (.184). 1998, 33-for-107 (.308). 1999, 41-for-146 (.281). 2000, 61-for-159 (.384). 2001, 47-for-123 (.382). 2002, 64-for-175 (.366). 2003, 28-for-106 (.264). Totals, 281-for-854 (.329).
Personal fouls/disqualifications: 1997, 48/0. 1998, 73/0. 1999, 100/1. 2000, 117/2. 2001, 74/0. 2002, 90/1. 2003, 105/3. Totals, 607/7.

WNBA PLAYOFF RECORD

Season Team	G	Min.	FGM	FGA	Pct.	FTM	FTA	Pct.	REBOUNDS Off.	Def.	Tot.	Ast.	St.	Blk.	TO	Pts.	AVERAGES RPG	APG	PPG
1999—Los Angeles....	4	127	17	45	.378	0	1	.000	7	11	18	11	13	1	10	37	4.5	2.8	9.3
2000—Los Angeles....	4	136	25	46	.543	3	4	.750	6	15	21	4	6	4	5	70	5.3	1.0	17.5
2001—Los Angeles....	7	231	21	66	.318	11	14	.786	6	40	46	17	7	6	10	63	6.6	2.4	9.0
2002—Los Angeles....	6	212	31	82	.378	18	26	.692	11	30	41	25	8	1	10	88	6.8	4.2	14.7
2003—Los Angeles....	9	344	53	121	.438	11	13	.846	10	40	50	21	14	2	20	129	5.6	2.3	14.3
Totals..................	30	1050	147	360	.408	43	58	.741	40	136	176	78	48	14	55	387	5.9	2.6	12.9

Three-point field goals: 1999, 3-for-17 (.176). 2000, 17-for-32 (.531). 2001, 10-for-40 (.250). 2002, 8-for-25 (.320). 2003, 12-for-34 (.353). Totals, 50-for-148 (.338).

Personal fouls/disqualifications: 1999, 22/2. 2000, 14/0. 2001, 21/0. 2002, 19/0. 2003, 29/0. Totals, 105/2.

WNBA ALL-STAR GAME RECORD

Season Team	Min.	FGM	FGA	Pct.	FTM	FTA	Pct.	REBOUNDS Off.	Def.	Tot.	Ast.	PF	Dq.	St.	Blk.	TO	Pts.
2000—Los Angeles.......	16	3	7	.429	2	2	1.000	0	1	1	2	1	0	1	0	...	10
2002—Los Angeles.......	16	1	5	.200	0	0	...	1	5	6	1	1	0	0	0	...	2
Totals..................	32	4	12	.333	2	2	1.000	1	6	7	3	2	0	1	0	2	12

Three-point field goals: 2000, 2-for-3 (.667). 2002, 0-for-3. Totals, 2-for-6 (.333).

MAIGA, HAMCHETOU F   MONARCHS

PERSONAL: Born April 25, 1978, in Bamako, Mali ... 6-1/167 (1.85 m/76 kg).
COLLEGE: Old Dominion.
TRANSACTIONS/CAREER NOTES: Selected by Sacramento in first round (12th overall) of WNBA Draft, April 19, 2002.
MISCELLANEOUS: Member of Mali National Team since 1994. ... Averaged 18 points, 10 rebounds, eight assists and three steals for Senegales champion Dakar Club in 1997-98. ... Named MVP of club play in Northwestern Africa and Senegal in 1998.

COLLEGIATE RECORD

Season Team	G	Min.	FGM	FGA	Pct.	FTM	FTA	Pct.	Reb.	Ast.	Pts.	AVERAGES RPG	APG	PPG
98-99—Old Dominion	32	...	81	158	.513	36	76	.474	130	...	199	4.1	0.0	6.2
99-00—Old Dominion	34	...	201	336	.598	75	128	.586	256	...	477	7.5	0.0	14.0
00-01—Old Dominion	30	...	168	293	.573	48	97	.495	223	...	410	7.4	0.0	13.7
01-02—Old Dominion	34	939	174	305	.570	48	97	.495	276	117	397	8.1	3.4	11.7
Totals	130	939	624	1092	.571	207	398	.520	885	117	1483	6.8	0.9	11.4

Three-point field goals: 1998-99, 1-for-6 (.167). 2001-02, 1-for-3 (.333). Totals, 2-for-9 (.222).

WNBA REGULAR-SEASON RECORD

Season Team	G	Min.	FGM	FGA	Pct.	FTM	FTA	Pct.	REBOUNDS Off.	Def.	Tot.	Ast.	St.	Blk.	TO	Pts.	AVERAGES RPG	APG	PPG
2002—Sacramento	23	197	13	53	.245	14	30	.467	18	19	37	9	15	3	23	40	1.6	0.4	1.7
2003—Sacramento	22	190	17	52	.327	8	20	.400	13	24	37	14	18	2	14	42	1.7	0.6	1.9
Totals..................	45	387	30	105	.286	22	50	.440	31	43	74	23	33	5	37	82	1.6	0.5	1.8

WNBA PLAYOFF RECORD

Season Team	G	Min.	FGM	FGA	Pct.	FTM	FTA	Pct.	REBOUNDS Off.	Def.	Tot.	Ast.	St.	Blk.	TO	Pts.	AVERAGES RPG	APG	PPG
2003—Sacramento	4	15	1	3	.333	0	0	...	1	2	3	2	0	0	5	2	0.8	0.5	0.5
Totals..................	4	15	1	3	.333	0	0	...	1	2	3	2	0	0	5	2	0.8	0.5	0.5

MALLORY, SONJA   C

PERSONAL: Born September 2, 1981, in Bronx, N.Y. ... 6-5/210 (1.96 m/95 kg).
HIGH SCHOOL: Brooklyn Technical (Brooklyn, N.Y.).
COLLEGE: Georgia Tech.
TRANSACTIONS/CAREER NOTES: Selected by New York in second round (24th overall) of WNBA Draft, April 25, 2003. ... Waived by New York, May 21, 2003. ... Signed by Phoenix, July 2, 2003.

COLLEGIATE RECORD

NOTES: All-ACC First Team (2003). ... ACC All-Defensive Team (2003). ... All-ACC Second Team (2002). ... Led the ACC with 1.58 bpg as a junior.

Season Team	G	Min.	FGM	FGA	Pct.	FTM	FTA	Pct.	Reb.	Ast.	Pts.	AVERAGES RPG	APG	PPG
99-00—Georgia Tech	28	228	32	80	.400	20	45	.444	...	3	84	2.4	0.1	3.0
00-01—Georgia Tech	26	584	105	204	.515	47	94	.500	...	10	257	6.6	0.4	9.9
01-02—Georgia Tech	29	853	166	345	.481	78	148	.527	...	15	410	8.0	0.5	14.1
02-03—Georgia Tech	31	984	196	427	.459	117	196	.597	...	20	503	9.0	0.6	16.2
Totals	114	2649	499	1056	.473	262	483	.542	0	48	1254	0.0	0.4	11.0

WNBA REGULAR-SEASON RECORD

Season Team	G	Min.	FGM	FGA	Pct.	FTM	FTA	Pct.	REBOUNDS Off.	Def.	Tot.	Ast.	St.	Blk.	TO	Pts.	AVERAGES RPG	APG	PPG
2003—Phoenix.........	6	44	4	9	.444	2	2	1.000	4	6	10	0	1	4	6	10	1.7	0.0	1.7
Totals..................	6	44	4	9	.444	2	2	1.000	4	6	10	0	1	4	6	10	1.7	0.0	1.7

MASSALINE, TONYA   G/F   STORM

PERSONAL: Born December 30, 1977, in Opp, Ala. ... 5-11/166 (1.80 m/75 kg). ... Full name: Latonya Felicia Washington.
HIGH SCHOOL: Paxton (Paxton, Fla.).
COLLEGE: Florida.
TRANSACTIONS/CAREER NOTES: Selected by Washington in second round (18th overall) of WNBA Draft, April 25, 2000. ... Waived by Washington, July 6, 2003. ... Signed by Seattle, July 28, 2003.

COLLEGIATE RECORD

NOTES: Did not play during the 1996-97 season.

Season Team	G	Min.	FGM	FGA	Pct.	FTM	FTA	Pct.	Reb.	Ast.	Pts.	RPG	APG	PPG
97-98—Florida	32	...	152	318	.478	44	71	.620	173	35	349	5.4	1.1	10.9
98-99—Florida	28	...	202	415	.487	40	58	.690	232	40	468	8.3	1.4	16.7
99-00—Florida	4	...	266	619	.430	51	72	.708	234	64	631	6.9	1.9	18.6
Totals	94	...	620	1352	.459	135	201	.672	639	139	1448	6.8	1.5	15.4

Three-point field goals: 1997-98, 1-for-3 (.333). 1998-99, 24-for-59 (.407). 1999-00, 48-for-141 (.340). Totals, 73-for-203 (.360).

WNBA REGULAR-SEASON RECORD

Season Team	G	Min.	FGM	FGA	Pct.	FTM	FTA	Pct.	REBOUNDS Off.	Def.	Tot.	Ast.	St.	Blk.	TO	Pts.	RPG	APG	PPG
2000—Washington	19	103	8	29	.276	4	6	.667	6	8	14	5	2	0	4	26	0.7	0.3	1.4
2003—Washington	24	222	20	63	.317	7	7	1.000	12	9	21	8	5	0	10	53	0.9	0.3	2.2
Totals	43	325	28	92	.304	11	13	.846	18	17	35	13	5	2	14	79	0.8	0.3	1.8

Three-point field goals: 2000, 6-for-14 (.429). Totals, 6-for-14 (.429); 2003, 6-for-20 (.300). Totals, 6-for-20 (.300).
Personal fouls/disqualifications: 2000, 4/0. Totals, 4/0; 2003, 12/0. Totals, 12/0.

WNBA PLAYOFF RECORD

Season Team	G	Min.	FGM	FGA	Pct.	FTM	FTA	Pct.	REBOUNDS Off.	Def.	Tot.	Ast.	St.	Blk.	TO	Pts.	RPG	APG	PPG
2000—Washington	1	4	0	0	...	0	0	...	0	0	0	0	0	0	1	0	0.0	0.0	0.0
Totals	1	4	0	0	...	0	0	...	0	0	0	0	0	0	1	0	0.0	0.0	0.0

MCCRAY, NIKKI   G   MERCURY

PERSONAL: Born December 17, 1971, in Collierville, Tenn. ... 5-11/158 (1.80 m/72 kg). ... Full name: Nikki Kesangane McCray.
COLLEGE: Tennessee.
TRANSACTIONS/CAREER NOTES: Signed by WNBA and assigned to Washington, January 27, 1998. ... Traded by Washington with a second-and third-round pick in the 2002 WNBA Draft to Indiana for F Angie Braziel and a first-and third-round pick, December 5, 2001. ... Signed by Phoenix as an unrestricted free agent, April 27, 2004

COLLEGIATE RECORD

Season Team	G	Min.	FGM	FGA	Pct.	FTM	FTA	Pct.	Reb.	Ast.	Pts.	RPG	APG	PPG
91-92—Tennessee	31	...	87	174	.500	39	53	.736	114	25	215	3.7	0.8	6.9
92-93—Tennessee	32	...	133	286	.465	83	115	.722	145	63	349	4.5	2.0	10.9
93-94—Tennessee	33	...	213	421	.506	111	158	.703	231	81	537	7.0	2.5	16.3
94-95—Tennessee	31	...	193	392	.492	83	122	.680	182	82	471	5.9	2.6	15.2
Totals	127	...	626	1273	.492	316	448	.705	672	251	1572	5.3	2.0	12.4

Three-point field goals: 1991-92, 2-for-10 (.200). 1994-95, 2-for-15 (.133). Totals, 4-for-25 (.160).

ABL REGULAR-SEASON RECORD

Notes: Member of ABL Championship Team (1997). ... ABL Most Valuable Player (1997).

Season Team	G	Min.	FGM	FGA	Pct.	FTM	FTA	Pct.	Reb.	Ast.	Pts.	RPG	APG	PPG
96-97—Columbus	40	...	300	664	.452	33	91	.363	164	210	781	4.1	5.3	19.5
Totals	40	...	300	664	.452	33	91	.363	164	210	781	4.1	5.3	19.5

OLYMPICS

NOTES: Member of gold medal-winning U.S. Olympic Team (1996, 2000).

Season Team	G	Min.	FGM	FGA	Pct.	FTM	FTA	Pct.	Reb.	Ast.	Pts.	RPG	APG	PPG
1996—United States	8	...	28	43	.651	18	26	.692	28	9	75	3.5	1.1	9.4
1996—United States	8	...	28	43	.651	18	26	.692	28	9	75	3.5	1.1	9.4
2000—United States	8	147	16	40	.400	8	10	.800	7	9	41	0.9	1.1	5.1
Totals	24	147	72	126	.571	44	62	.710	63	27	191	2.6	1.1	8.0

Three-point field goals: 1996-97, 1-for-3 (.333). 1996-97, 1-for-3 (.333). 2000-01, 1-for-2 (.500). Totals, 3-for-8 (.375).

WNBA REGULAR-SEASON RECORD

Season Team	G	Min.	FGM	FGA	Pct.	FTM	FTA	Pct.	REBOUNDS Off.	Def.	Tot.	Ast.	St.	Blk.	TO	Pts.	RPG	APG	PPG
1998—Washington	29	969	191	457	.418	107	143	.748	34	51	85	90	43	2	125	512	2.9	3.1	17.7
1999—Washington	32	1043	193	455	.424	129	160	.806	35	51	86	78	34	1	107	561	2.7	2.4	17.5
2000—Washington	32	1046	167	385	.434	113	147	.769	22	34	56	85	45	5	89	497	1.8	2.7	15.5

Season—Team	G	Min.	FGM	FGA	Pct.	FTM	FTA	Pct.	Off.	Def.	Tot.	Ast.	St.	Blk.	TO	Pts.	RPG	APG	PPG
2001—Washington ...	32	828	119	290	.410	91	128	.711	22	34	56	47	26	0	73	351	1.8	1.5	11.0
2002—Indiana.........	32	1058	132	318	.415	84	103	.816	29	68	97	70	28	3	82	369	3.0	2.2	11.5
2003—Indiana.........	34	734	52	138	.377	20	24	.833	18	33	51	49	37	2	44	131	1.5	1.4	3.9
Totals.................	191	5678	854	2043	.418	544	705	.772	160	271	431	419	213	13	520	2421	2.3	2.2	12.7

Three-point field goals: 1998, 23-for-73 (.315). 1999, 46-for-153 (.301). 2000, 50-for-151 (.331). 2001, 22-for-95 (.232). 2002, 21-for-66 (.318). 2003, 7-for-32 (.219). Totals, 169-for-570 (.296).
Personal fouls/disqualifications: 1998, 81/2. 1999, 86/1. 2000, 79/0. 2001, 68/1. 2002, 73/2. 2003, 67/1. Totals, 454/7.

WNBA PLAYOFF RECORD

Season—Team	G	Min.	FGM	FGA	Pct.	FTM	FTA	Pct.	REBOUNDS Off.	Def.	Tot.	Ast.	St.	Blk.	TO	Pts.	AVERAGES RPG	APG	PPG
2000—Washington ...	2	70	7	16	.438	0	0	...	2	4	6	13	1	0	10	15	3.0	6.5	7.5
2002—Indiana.........	3	99	10	27	.370	3	5	.600	1	3	4	11	1	0	5	24	1.3	3.7	8.0
Totals.................	5	169	17	43	.395	3	5	.600	3	7	10	24	2	0	15	39	2.0	4.8	7.8

Three-point field goals: 2000, 1-for-7 (.143). 2002, 1-for-6 (.167). Totals, 2-for-13 (.154).
Personal fouls/disqualifications: 2000, 6/0. 2002, 4/0. Totals, 10/0.

WNBA ALL-STAR GAME RECORD

Season—Team	Min.	FGM	FGA	Pct.	FTM	FTA	Pct.	REBOUNDS Off.	Def.	Tot.	Ast.	PF	Dq.	St.	Blk.	TO	Pts.
1999—Washington	16	2	11	.182	0	0	...	0	2	2	0	1	0	3	0	...	4
2000—Washington	19	1	11	.091	2	2	1.000	0	0	0	1	0	0	3	0	...	5
2001—Washington	22	2	7	.286	1	2	.500	0	0	0	2	1	0	0	0	...	5
Totals.................	57	5	29	.172	3	4	.750	0	2	2	3	2	0	6	0	4	14

Three-point field goals: 1999, 0-for-2. 2000, 1-for-6 (.167). Totals, 1-for-8 (.125).

MCCRIMMON, NICKY G

PERSONAL: Born March 22, 1972, in Harlem, N.Y. ... 5-8/125 (1.73 m/57 kg). ... **Full name:** Nicole Denise McCrimmon.
HIGH SCHOOL: Westside (New York, N.Y.).
COLLEGE: U.S.C..
TRANSACTIONS/CAREER NOTES: Selected by Los Angeles in fourth round (63rd overall) of WNBA Draft, April 25, 2000. ... Waived by Los Angeles, May8, 2004.
MISCELLANEOUS: Member of WNBA Championship Team (2001, 2002).

COLLEGIATE RECORD

NOTES: All-Pac-10 first team (1994). ... All-Western Junior College Athletic Conference (1991). ... Kodak Junior College All-America (1992). ... Western Junior College Athletic Conference Player of Year (1992).

Season—Team	G	Min.	FGM	FGA	Pct.	FTM	FTA	Pct.	Reb.	Ast.	Pts.	AVERAGES RPG	APG	PPG
92-93—Southern Cal.............	28	...	120	270	.444	53	77	.688	80	119	305	2.9	4.3	10.9
93-94—Southern Cal.............	26	...	119	238	.500	46	60	.767	60	162	285	2.3	6.2	11.0
Totals	54	...	239	508	.470	99	137	.723	140	281	590	2.6	5.2	10.9

Three-point field goals: 1992-93, 12-for-46 (.261). 1993-94, 1-for-7 (.143). Totals, 13-for-53 (.245).

ABL REGULAR-SEASON RECORD

NOTES: Assigned to expansion Long Beach Stringrays on April 25, 1997. ... Traded to Atlanta for Niesa Johnson on November 14, 1997.

Season—Team	G	Min.	FGM	FGA	Pct.	FTM	FTA	Pct.	Reb.	Ast.	Pts.	AVERAGES RPG	APG	PPG
97-98—Atlanta	32	...	69	149	.463	18	27	.667	54	76	161	1.7	2.4	5.0
97-98—Long Beach...............	10	...	6	21	.286	3	4	.750	15	17	15	1.5	1.7	1.5
Totals	42	...	75	170	.441	21	31	.677	69	93	176	1.6	2.2	4.2

Three-point field goals: 1997-98, 5-for-18 (.278). 1997-98, 0-for-2. Totals, 5-for-20 (.250)

WNBA REGULAR-SEASON RECORD

Season—Team	G	Min.	FGM	FGA	Pct.	FTM	FTA	Pct.	REBOUNDS Off.	Def.	Tot.	Ast.	St.	Blk.	TO	Pts.	AVERAGES RPG	APG	PPG
2000—Los Angeles....	32	488	39	77	.506	7	14	.500	9	23	32	65	29	8	48	101	1.0	2.0	3.2
2001—Los Angeles....	28	350	28	63	.444	3	7	.429	9	12	63	21	0	22	64	0.4	2.3	2.3
2002—Los Angeles....	32	356	20	49	.408	7	11	.636	9	14	23	53	22	3	24	51	0.7	1.7	1.6
2003—Los Angeles....	33	299	28	63	.444	7	8	.875	7	22	29	32	19	1	17	68	0.9	1.0	2.1
Totals.................	125	1493	115	252	.456	24	40	.600	28	68	96	213	91	12	111	284	0.8	1.7	2.3

Three-point field goals: 2000, 16-for-33 (.485). 2001, 5-for-12 (.417). 2002, 4-for-15 (.267). 2003, 5-for-12 (.417). Totals, 30-for-72 (.417).
Personal fouls/disqualifications: 2000, 41/0. 2001, 19/0. 2002, 22/0. 2003, 20/0. Totals, 102/0.

WNBA PLAYOFF RECORD

Season—Team	G	Min.	FGM	FGA	Pct.	FTM	FTA	Pct.	REBOUNDS Off.	Def.	Tot.	Ast.	St.	Blk.	TO	Pts.	AVERAGES RPG	APG	PPG
2000—Los Angeles....	4	49	3	12	.250	3	4	.750	3	4	7	10	1	0	5	10	1.8	2.5	2.5
2001—Los Angeles....	7	41	1	2	.500	2	4	.500	0	4	4	6	5	0	4	5	0.6	0.9	0.7
2002—Los Angeles....	5	22	3	7	.429	1	1	1.000	0	1	1	2	2	0	1	8	0.2	0.4	1.6
2003—Los Angeles....	7	54	4	18	.222	0	0	...	0	4	4	7	2	0	4	9	0.6	1.0	1.3
Totals.................	23	166	11	39	.282	6	9	.667	3	13	16	25	10	0	14	32	0.7	1.1	1.4

Three-point field goals: 2000, 1-for-4 (.250). 2001, 1-for-1. 2002, 1-for-2 (.500). 2003, 1-for-6 (.167). Totals, 4-for-13 (.308).
Personal fouls/disqualifications: 2000, 2/0. 2001, 5/0. 2002, 2/0. 2003, 5/0. Totals, 14/0.

MCCULLEY, DANIELLE   C

PERSONAL: Born January 18, 1975, in Gary, Ind. ... 6-3/180 (1.91 m/82 kg). ... Full name: Danielle McCulley.
HIGH SCHOOL: West Side (Gary, Ind.).
COLLEGE: Western Kentucky.
TRANSACTIONS/CAREER NOTES: Signed by WNBA and assigned to Indiana, May 2, 2000. ... Waived by Fever July 13, 2001. ... Allotted by the WNBA as a free agent to Seattle Storm on April 25, 2002. ... Waived by Seattle, May 3, 2004.

COLLEGIATE RECORD

NOTES: A two-time All-Sun Belt Team selection. ... Ranked second on Western Kentucky team as a senior in points (15.2 per game) rebounds (8.1 per game).

Season Team	G	Min.	FGM	FGA	Pct.	FTM	FTA	Pct.	Reb.	Ast.	Pts.	RPG	APG	PPG
93-94—Purdue	33	...	78	182	.429	39	53	.736	138	18	200	4.2	0.5	6.1
94-95—Purdue	32	...	112	274	.409	76	104	.731	203	38	307	6.3	1.2	9.6
96-97—Western Kentucky	31	...	147	335	.439	97	128	.758	270	89	397	8.7	2.9	12.8
97-98—Western Kentucky	35	...	197	486	.405	148	206	.718	283	84	533	8.1	2.4	15.2
Totals	131	...	534	1277	.418	360	491	.733	894	229	1437	6.8	1.7	11.0

Three-point field goals: 1993-94, 5-for-16 (.313). 1994-95, 7-for-22 (.318). 1996-97, 6-for-30 (.200). 1997-98, 19-for-46 (.413). Totals, 37-for-114 (.325).

ABL REGULAR-SEASON RECORD

NOTES: Selected as first overall draft pick in 1998 ABL Draft.

Season Team	G	Min.	FGM	FGA	Pct.	FTM	FTA	Pct.	Reb.	Ast.	Pts.	RPG	APG	PPG
98-99—Portland	13	...	11	43	.256	11	13	.846	20	6	34	1.5	0.5	2.6
Totals	13	...	11	43	.256	11	13	.846	20	6	34	1.5	0.5	2.6

Three-point field goals: 1998-99, 1-for-13 (.077).

WNBA REGULAR-SEASON RECORD

Season Team	G	Min.	FGM	FGA	Pct.	FTM	FTA	Pct.	Off.	Def.	Tot.	Ast.	St.	Blk.	TO	Pts.	RPG	APG	PPG
2000—Indiana	29	456	63	153	.412	46	63	.730	45	37	82	19	16	22	37	175	2.8	0.7	6.0
2001—Indiana	8	90	5	18	.278	17	18	.944	4	13	17	5	0	2	7	28	2.1	0.6	3.5
2002—Seattle	4	43	0	12	.000	2	2	1.000	3	4	7	1	1	0	2	2	1.8	0.3	0.5
2003—Seattle	7	26	1	6	.167	0	0	...	0	1	1	0	0	0	4	2	0.1	0.0	0.3
Totals	48	615	69	189	.365	65	83	.783	52	55	107	25	17	24	50	207	2.2	0.5	4.3

Three-point field goals: 2000, 3-for-17 (.176). 2001, 1-for-2 (.500). 2002, 0-for-3. 2003, 0-for-1. Totals, 4-for-23 (.174).
Personal fouls/disqualifications: 2000, 63/1. 2001, 12/0. 2002, 5/0. 2003, 3/0. Totals, 83/1.

MCKIVER, TEANA   C   STING

PERSONAL: Born October 5, 1980, in Wilmington, N.C. ... 6-3 (1.91 m/ kg). ... Full name: Clifeteana Rena McKiver.
HIGH SCHOOL: East Duplin (Beulaville, N.C.).
COLLEGE: East Carolina, then Tulane.
TRANSACTIONS/CAREER NOTES: Signed as a free agent, April 30, 2003.

COLLEGIATE RECORD

Season Team	G	Min.	FGM	FGA	Pct.	FTM	FTA	Pct.	Reb.	Ast.	Pts.	RPG	APG	PPG
98-99—East Carolina	19	299	72	132	.545	36	75	.480	...	6	180	5.5	0.3	9.5
00-01—Tulane	32	600	103	189	.545	52	99	.525	...	22	258	5.3	0.7	8.1
01-02—Tulane	35	916	235	377	.623	104	189	.550	...	25	574	7.4	0.7	16.4
02-03—Tulane	29	792	149	262	.569	72	121	.595	...	52	372	7.1	1.8	12.8
Totals	115	2607	559	960	.582	264	484	.545	0	105	1384	0.0	0.9	12.0

Three-point field goals: 2002-03, 2-for-2.

WNBA REGULAR-SEASON RECORD

Season Team	G	Min.	FGM	FGA	Pct.	FTM	FTA	Pct.	Off.	Def.	Tot.	Ast.	St.	Blk.	TO	Pts.	RPG	APG	PPG
2003—Charlotte	31	341	41	78	.526	23	31	.742	37	54	91	6	14	24	27	105	2.9	0.2	3.4
Totals	31	341	41	78	.526	23	31	.742	37	54	91	6	14	24	27	105	2.9	0.2	3.4

Three-point field goals: 2003, 0-for-1. Totals, 0-for-1.
Personal fouls/disqualifications: 2003, 58/0. Totals, 58/0.

WNBA PLAYOFF RECORD

Season Team	G	Min.	FGM	FGA	Pct.	FTM	FTA	Pct.	Off.	Def.	Tot.	Ast.	St.	Blk.	TO	Pts.	RPG	APG	PPG
2003—Charlotte	2	13	0	2	.000	0	0	...	2	0	2	0	0	1	0	0	1.0	0.0	0.0
Totals	2	13	0	2	.000	0	0	...	2	0	2	0	0	1	0	0	1.0	0.0	0.0

MCWILLIAMS-FRANKLIN, TAJ   F/C   SUN

PERSONAL: Born October 20, 1970, in El Paso, Texas ... 6-2/184 (1.88 m/83 kg). ... Full name: Taj Madona McWilliams-Franklin.
HIGH SCHOOL: T.W. Josey (Augusta, Ga.).
COLLEGE: St. Edward's.
TRANSACTIONS/CAREER NOTES: Selected by Orlando in third round (32nd overall) of WNBA Draft, May 4, 1999.

COLLEGIATE RECORD
NOTES: Kodak NAIA All-America (1993). ... NAIA National Player of Year (1993).

Season Team	G	Min.	FGM	FGA	Pct.	FTM	FTA	Pct.	Reb.	Ast.	Pts.	RPG	AVERAGES APG	PPG
90-91—St. Edward's	31	...	184	322	.571	47	93	.505	243	12	415	7.8	0.4	13.4
91-92—St. Edward's	32	...	278	485	.573	106	176	.602	342	33	662	10.7	1.0	20.7
92-93—St. Edward's	31	...	336	521	.645	85	146	.582	365	34	760	11.8	1.1	24.5
Totals	94	...	798	1328	.601	238	415	.573	950	79	1837	10.1	0.8	19.5

ABL REGULAR-SEASON RECORD
NOTES: All-ABL second team (1997).

Season Team	G	Min.	FGM	FGA	Pct.	FTM	FTA	Pct.	Reb.	Ast.	Pts.	RPG	AVERAGES APG	PPG
96-97—Richmond	40	...	203	376	.540	114	175	.651	340	42	521	8.5	1.1	13.0
97-98—Philadelphia	44	...	173	358	.483	122	171	.713	356	53	471	8.1	1.2	10.7
98-99—Philadelphia	14	...	75	142	.528	32	46	.696	112	13	184	8.0	0.9	13.1
Totals	98	...	451	876	.515	268	392	.684	808	108	1176	8.2	1.1	12.0

Three-point field goals: 1996-97, 1-for-8 (.125). 1997-98, 3-for-16 (.188). 1998-99, 2-for-3 (.667). Totals, 6-for-27 (.222).

WNBA REGULAR-SEASON RECORD

Season Team	G	Min.	FGM	FGA	Pct.	FTM	FTA	Pct.	REBOUNDS Off.	Def.	Tot.	Ast.	St.	Blk.	TO	Pts.	RPG	AVERAGES APG	PPG
1999—Orlando	32	1042	153	319	.480	94	141	.667	81	158	239	51	57	38	80	420	7.5	1.6	13.1
2000—Orlando	32	1098	173	330	.524	87	122	.713	90	154	244	54	59	31	83	438	7.6	1.7	13.7
2001—Orlando	32	1059	157	331	.474	87	117	.744	114	129	243	69	52	50	80	403	7.6	2.2	12.6
2002—Orlando	13	383	41	82	.500	27	31	.871	21	42	63	13	19	14	22	110	4.8	1.0	8.5
2003—Connecticut	34	983	133	301	.442	76	102	.745	78	149	227	49	43	33	54	354	6.7	1.4	10.4
Totals	143	4565	657	1363	.482	371	513	.723	384	632	1016	236	230	166	319	1725	7.1	1.7	12.1

Three-point field goals: 1999, 20-for-45 (.444). 2000, 5-for-17 (.294). 2001, 2-for-10 (.200). 2002, 1-for-3 (.333). 2003, 12-for-43 (.279). Totals, 40-for-118 (.339).
Personal fouls/disqualifications: 1999, 96/3. 2000, 86/0. 2001, 74/1. 2002, 40/1. 2003, 103/1. Totals, 399/6.

WNBA PLAYOFF RECORD

Season Team	G	Min.	FGM	FGA	Pct.	FTM	FTA	Pct.	REBOUNDS Off.	Def.	Tot.	Ast.	St.	Blk.	TO	Pts.	RPG	AVERAGES APG	PPG
2000—Orlando	3	107	18	38	.474	7	9	.778	6	17	23	5	2	3	5	43	7.7	1.7	14.3
2003—Connecticut	4	122	24	47	.511	16	17	.941	9	21	30	5	6	2	6	65	7.5	1.3	16.3
Totals	7	229	42	85	.494	23	26	.885	15	38	53	10	8	5	11	108	7.6	1.4	15.4

Three-point field goals: 2000, 0-for-2. 2003, 1-for-5 (.200). Totals, 1-for-7 (.143).
Personal fouls/disqualifications: 2000, 8/0. 2003, 10/0. Totals, 18/0.

WNBA ALL-STAR GAME RECORD

Season Team	Min.	FGM	FGA	Pct.	FTM	FTA	Pct.	REBOUNDS Off.	Def.	Tot.	Ast.	PF	Dq.	St.	Blk.	TO	Pts.
1999—Orlando	31	2	5	.400	3	4	.750	2	5	7	1	2	0	2	1	...	8
2000—Orlando	24	4	8	.500	2	2	1.000	2	7	9	0	2	0	2	0	...	10
2001—Orlando	26	4	7	.571	2	4	.500	2	2	4	1	3	0	2	1	...	10
Totals	81	10	20	.500	7	10	.700	11	9	20	2	7	0	6	2	3	28

Three-point field goals: 1999, 1-for-1. Totals, 1-for-1 (1.000).

MELVIN, CHASITY   F   MYSTICS

PERSONAL: Born May 3, 1976, in Roseboro, N.C. ... 6-3/185 (1.91 m/84 kg). ... Full name: Chasity Monique Melvin.
HIGH SCHOOL: Lakewood (Roseboro, N.C.).
COLLEGE: North Carolina State.
TRANSACTIONS/CAREER NOTES: Selected by Cleveland in first round (11th overall) of WNBA Draft, May 4, 1999. ... Selected by the Washington Mystics (2nd) in the 2004 Dispersal Draft, January 6, 2004.

COLLEGIATE RECORD
NOTES: Kodak All-America team (1996).

Season Team	G	Min.	FGM	FGA	Pct.	FTM	FTA	Pct.	Reb.	Ast.	Pts.	RPG	AVERAGES APG	PPG
94-95—N.C. State	31	...	208	345	.603	92	163	.564	217	35	508	7.0	1.1	16.4
95-96—N.C. State	30	...	205	365	.562	79	147	.537	230	37	489	7.7	1.2	16.3
96-97—N.C. State	31	...	195	334	.584	110	182	.604	268	44	500	8.6	1.4	16.1
97-98—N.C. State	32	...	230	397	.579	85	147	.578	305	83	545	9.5	2.6	17.0
Totals	124	...	838	1441	.582	366	639	.573	1020	199	2042	8.2	1.6	16.5

Three-point field goals: 1996-97, 0-for-7. 1997-98, 0-for-4. Totals, 0-for-11.

ABL REGULAR-SEASON RECORD

Season Team	G	Min.	FGM	FGA	Pct.	FTM	FTA	Pct.	Reb.	Ast.	Pts.	AVERAGES		
												RPG	APG	PPG
98-99—Philadelphia	14	...	65	117	.556	48	63	.762	78	8	178	5.6	0.6	12.7
Totals	14	...	65	117	.556	48	63	.762	78	8	178	5.6	0.6	12.7

Three-point field goals: 1998-99, 0-for-1.

WNBA REGULAR-SEASON RECORD

Season Team	G	Min.	FGM	FGA	Pct.	FTM	FTA	Pct.	REBOUNDS			Ast.	St.	Blk.	TO	Pts.	AVERAGES		
									Off.	Def.	Tot.						RPG	APG	PPG
1999—Cleveland	32	709	95	218	.436	68	98	.694	53	74	127	38	20	22	42	259	4.0	1.2	8.1
2000—Cleveland	32	904	136	289	.471	100	137	.730	69	103	172	61	29	18	62	373	5.4	1.9	11.7
2001—Cleveland	27	754	102	215	.474	60	86	.698	66	88	154	50	24	16	45	266	5.7	1.9	9.9
2002—Cleveland	32	1055	153	330	.464	90	131	.687	84	110	194	57	28	18	74	399	6.1	1.8	12.5
2003—Cleveland	34	1061	159	333	.477	123	176	.699	82	133	215	52	28	22	67	444	6.3	1.5	13.1
Totals	157	4483	645	1385	.466	441	628	.702	354	508	862	258	129	96	290	1741	5.5	1.6	11.1

Three-point field goals: 1999, 1-for-1. 2000, 1-for-7 (.143). 2001, 2-for-2. 2002, 3-for-6 (.500). 2003, 3-for-11 (.273). Totals, 10-for-27 (.370).
Personal fouls/disqualifications: 1999, 93/1. 2000, 113/4. 2001, 81/0. 2002, 104/2. 2003, 108/0. Totals, 499/7.

WNBA PLAYOFF RECORD

Season Team	G	Min.	FGM	FGA	Pct.	FTM	FTA	Pct.	REBOUNDS			Ast.	St.	Blk.	TO	Pts.	AVERAGES		
									Off.	Def.	Tot.						RPG	APG	PPG
2000—Cleveland	6	183	20	38	.526	13	18	.722	16	24	40	11	5	3	11	53	6.7	1.8	8.8
2001—Cleveland	3	81	8	16	.500	8	11	.727	6	6	12	6	2	2	6	24	4.0	2.0	8.0
2003—Cleveland	3	104	12	31	.387	26	34	.765	3	10	13	5	2	4	8	50	4.3	1.7	16.7
Totals	12	368	40	85	.471	47	63	.746	25	40	65	22	9	9	25	127	5.4	1.8	10.6

Three-point field goals: 2000, 0-for-1. 2003, 0-for-1. Totals, 0-for-2.
Personal fouls/disqualifications: 2000, 20/0. 2003, 10/0. Totals, 35/0.

MILLER, COCO   G   MYSTICS

PERSONAL: Born September 6, 1978, in Rochester, Minn. ... 5-9/140 (1.75 m/65 kg). ... Full name: Colleen Mary Miller.
HIGH SCHOOL: Mayo (Rochester, Minn.).
COLLEGE: Georgia.
TRANSACTIONS/CAREER NOTES: Selected by Washington in first round (ninth overall) of WNBA Draft, April 20, 2001.

COLLEGIATE RECORD

Season Team	G	Min.	FGM	FGA	Pct.	FTM	FTA	Pct.	Reb.	Ast.	Pts.	AVERAGES		
												RPG	APG	PPG
97-98—Georgia	27	854	179	415	.431	50	74	.676	123	104	432	4.6	3.9	16.0
98-99—Georgia	34	1046	263	536	.491	68	89	.764	132	77	626	3.9	2.3	18.4
99-00—Georgia	36	1080	215	487	.441	76	98	.776	114	114	555	3.2	3.2	15.4
00-01—Georgia	33	1017	207	452	.458	73	87	.839	134	101	518	4.1	3.1	15.7
Totals	130	3997	864	1890	.457	267	348	.767	503	396	2131	3.9	3.0	16.4

Three-point field goals: 1997-98, 24-for-61 (.393). 1998-99, 32-for-82 (.390). 1999-00, 49-for-122 (.402). 2000-01, 31-for-96 (.323). Totals, 136-for-361 (.377).

WNBA REGULAR-SEASON RECORD

NOTES: WNBA Most Improved Player (2002).

Season Team	G	Min.	FGM	FGA	Pct.	FTM	FTA	Pct.	REBOUNDS			Ast.	St.	Blk.	TO	Pts.	AVERAGES		
									Off.	Def.	Tot.						RPG	APG	PPG
2001—Washington	20	137	13	40	.325	6	11	.545	5	4	9	8	6	0	13	34	0.5	0.4	1.7
2002—Washington	32	904	114	263	.433	46	56	.821	44	72	116	82	33	2	59	298	3.6	2.6	9.3
2003—Washington	33	1076	172	382	.450	37	53	.698	55	72	127	86	39	7	53	413	3.8	2.6	12.5
Totals	85	2117	299	685	.436	89	120	.742	104	148	252	176	78	9	125	745	3.0	2.1	8.8

Three-point field goals: 2001, 2-for-6 (.333). 2002, 24-for-64 (.375). 2003, 32-for-89 (.360). Totals, 58-for-159 (.365).
Personal fouls/disqualifications: 2001, 10/0. 2002, 84/0. 2003, 95/1. Totals, 189/1.

WNBA PLAYOFF RECORD

Season Team	G	Min.	FGM	FGA	Pct.	FTM	FTA	Pct.	REBOUNDS			Ast.	St.	Blk.	TO	Pts.	AVERAGES		
									Off.	Def.	Tot.						RPG	APG	PPG
2002—Washington	5	163	21	50	.420	6	10	.600	7	8	15	12	2	0	7	54	3.0	2.4	10.8
Totals	5	163	21	50	.420	6	10	.600	7	8	15	12	2	0	7	54	3.0	2.4	10.8

Three-point field goals: 2002, 6-for-11 (.545). Totals, 6-for-11 (.545).
Personal fouls/disqualifications: 2002, 13/0. Totals, 13/0.

MILLER, KELLY   G   FEVER

PERSONAL: Born September 6, 1978, in Rochester, Minn. ... 5-9/144 (1.75 m/64 kg). ... Full name: Kelly Marie Miller.
HIGH SCHOOL: Mayo (Rochester, Minn.).
COLLEGE: Georgia.
TRANSACTIONS/CAREER NOTES: Selected by Charlotte in the first round (No. 2 overall) of the 2001 WNBA Draft on April 20, 2001. ... Traded by Charlotte along with a first round (9th overall) pick in the 2004 WNBA Draft to Indiana for a first round (3rd overall) pick and a second round (18th overall) pick in the 2004 WNBA Draft, February 5, 2004.

COLLEGIATE RECORD

NOTES: Kodak All-American first team (1999, 2001).

AVERAGES

Season Team	G	Min.	FGM	FGA	Pct.	FTM	FTA	Pct.	Reb.	Ast.	Pts.	RPG	APG	PPG
97-98—Georgia	28	999	166	414	.401	118	144	.819	159	164	489	5.7	5.9	17.5
98-99—Georgia	34	1119	219	477	.459	136	163	.834	205	150	628	6.0	4.4	18.5
99-00—Georgia	36	1169	203	456	.445	94	115	.817	168	162	544	4.7	4.5	15.1
00-01—Georgia	33	1079	193	378	.511	80	97	.825	179	163	516	5.4	4.9	15.6
Totals	131	4366	781	1725	.453	428	519	.825	711	639	2177	5.4	4.9	16.6

Three-point field goals: 1997-98, 39-for-110 (.355). 1998-99, 39-for-110 (.355). 1999-00, 44-for-122 (.361). 2000-01, 50-for-108 (.463). Totals, 172-for-450 (.382).

WNBA REGULAR-SEASON RECORD

Season Team	G	Min.	FGM	FGA	Pct.	FTM	FTA	Pct.	REBOUNDS Off.	Def.	Tot.	Ast.	St.	Blk.	TO	Pts.	AVERAGES RPG	APG	PPG
2001—Charlotte	26	225	22	57	.386	4	5	.800	11	17	28	14	9	0	9	55	1.1	0.5	2.1
2002—Charlotte	32	554	79	177	.446	29	38	.763	31	37	68	49	22	1	27	211	2.1	1.5	6.6
2003—Charlotte	34	523	68	167	.407	31	40	.775	20	33	53	47	18	2	35	189	1.6	1.4	5.6
Totals	92	1302	169	401	.421	64	83	.771	62	87	149	110	49	3	71	455	1.6	1.2	4.9

Three-point field goals: 2001, 7-for-19 (.368). 2002, 24-for-51 (.471). 2003, 22-for-52 (.423). Totals, 53-for-122 (.434).
Personal fouls/disqualifications: 2001, 14/0. 2002, 39/0. 2003, 44/0. Totals, 97/0.

WNBA PLAYOFF RECORD

Season Team	G	Min.	FGM	FGA	Pct.	FTM	FTA	Pct.	REBOUNDS Off.	Def.	Tot.	Ast.	St.	Blk.	TO	Pts.	AVERAGES RPG	APG	PPG
2001—Charlotte	2	8	0	2	.000	0	2	.000	0	0	0	0	0	0	0	0	0.0	0.0	0.0
2002—Charlotte	2	13	2	4	.500	0	0	...	0	2	2	0	0	0	1	5	1.0	0.0	2.5
2003—Charlotte	2	23	4	10	.400	0	0	...	0	1	1	2	0	0	1	8	0.5	1.0	4.0
Totals	6	44	6	16	.375	0	2	.000	0	3	3	2	0	0	2	13	0.5	0.3	2.2

Three-point field goals: 2002, 1-for-1. 2003, 0-for-2. Totals, 1-for-3 (.333).
Personal fouls/disqualifications: 2002, 3/0. 2003, 2/0. Totals, 5/0.

MILTON-JONES, DELISHA   F   SPARKS

PERSONAL: Born September 11, 1974, in Riceboro, Ga. ... 6-1/172 (1.85 m/78 kg). ... Full name: DeLisha Lachell Milton-Jones.
HIGH SCHOOL: Bradewell Institute (Hinesville, Ga.).
COLLEGE: Florida.
TRANSACTIONS/CAREER NOTES: Selected by Los Angeles in first round (fourth overall) of WNBA Draft, May 4, 1999.
MISCELLANEOUS: Member of WNBA Championship Team (2001, 2002).

COLLEGIATE RECORD

NOTES: Wade Trophy recipient (1997). ... Kodak All-America first team (1997).

Season Team	G	Min.	FGM	FGA	Pct.	FTM	FTA	Pct.	Reb.	Ast.	Pts.	AVERAGES RPG	APG	PPG
93-94—Florida	29	...	134	275	.487	71	116	.612	334	31	339	11.5	1.1	11.7
94-95—Florida	33	...	188	331	.568	68	110	.618	219	27	444	6.6	0.8	13.5
95-96—Florida	30	...	182	380	.479	99	142	.697	262	47	462	8.7	1.6	15.4
96-97—Florida	29	...	222	392	.566	119	158	.753	256	56	563	8.8	1.9	19.4
Totals	121	...	726	1378	.527	357	526	.679	1071	161	1808	8.9	1.3	14.9

Three-point field goals: 1994-95, 0-for-1. 1995-96, 0-for-7. Totals, 0-for-8.

ABL REGULAR-SEASON RECORD

Season Team	G	Min.	FGM	FGA	Pct.	FTM	FTA	Pct.	Reb.	Ast.	Pts.	AVERAGES RPG	APG	PPG
97-98—Portland	44	...	163	326	.500	48	70	.686	217	99	376	4.9	2.3	8.5
98-99—Portland	13	...	59	127	.465	36	46	.783	89	26	155	6.8	2.0	11.9
Totals	57	...	222	453	.490	84	116	.724	306	125	531	5.4	2.2	9.3

Three-point field goals: 1997-98, 2-for-12 (.167). 1998-99, 1-for-3 (.333). Totals, 3-for-15 (.200).

WNBA REGULAR-SEASON RECORD

Season Team	G	Min.	FGM	FGA	Pct.	FTM	FTA	Pct.	REBOUNDS Off.	Def.	Tot.	Ast.	St.	Blk.	TO	Pts.	AVERAGES RPG	APG	PPG
1999—Los Angeles	32	835	125	236	.530	68	86	.791	60	116	176	50	47	17	71	318	5.5	1.6	9.9
2000—Los Angeles	32	983	150	293	.512	76	102	.745	55	139	194	68	44	29	67	378	6.1	2.1	11.8
2001—Los Angeles	32	938	134	296	.453	50	63	.794	71	98	169	68	49	29	58	330	5.3	2.1	10.3
2002—Los Angeles	32	966	132	271	.487	77	104	.740	65	146	211	45	50	35	94	362	6.6	1.4	11.3
2003—Los Angeles	31	1086	139	328	.424	115	143	.804	59	161	220	64	49	41	79	416	7.1	2.1	13.4
Totals	159	4808	680	1424	.478	386	498	.775	310	660	970	295	239	151	369	1804	6.1	1.9	11.3

Three-point field goals: 1999, 0-for-1. 2000, 2-for-8 (.250). 2001, 12-for-35 (.343). 2002, 21-for-50 (.420). 2003, 23-for-61 (.377). Totals, 58-for-155 (.374).
Personal fouls/disqualifications: 1999, 112/0. 2000, 124/3. 2001, 101/0. 2002, 122/3. 2003, 109/3. Totals, 568/9.

WNBA PLAYOFF RECORD

Season Team	G	Min.	FGM	FGA	Pct.	FTM	FTA	Pct.	Off.	Def.	Tot.	Ast.	St.	Blk.	TO	Pts.	RPG	APG	PPG
1999—Los Angeles....	4	127	18	40	.450	3	7	.429	6	15	21	10	7	6	5	39	5.3	2.5	9.8
2000—Los Angeles....	4	136	20	37	.541	10	12	.833	11	11	22	12	6	2	10	50	5.5	3.0	12.5
2001—Los Angeles....	7	226	35	64	.547	13	19	.684	12	32	44	20	7	10	11	86	6.3	2.9	12.3
2002—Los Angeles....	6	204	27	60	.450	15	16	.938	9	32	41	8	10	9	11	78	6.8	1.3	13.0
2003—Los Angeles....	9	338	47	106	.443	27	35	.771	20	37	57	25	17	13	20	131	6.3	2.8	14.6
Totals.................	30	1031	147	307	.479	68	89	.764	58	127	185	75	47	40	57	384	6.2	2.5	12.8

Three-point field goals: 2001, 3-for-8 (.375). 2002, 9-for-16 (.563). 2003, 10-for-18 (.556). Totals, 22-for-42 (.524).
Personal fouls/disqualifications: 2001, 22/0. 2002, 22/0. 2003, 40/1. Totals, 110/3.

WNBA ALL-STAR GAME RECORD

Season Team	Min.	FGM	FGA	Pct.	FTM	FTA	Pct.	Off.	Def.	Tot.	Ast.	PF	Dq.	St.	Blk.	TO	Pts.
2000—Los Angeles	16	2	2	1.000	0	0	...	3	1	4	3	0	0	0	0	...	4
Totals.................	16	2	2	1.000	0	0	...	3	1	4	3	0	0	0	0	0	4

OLYMPICS

Season Team	G	Min.	FGM	FGA	Pct.	FTM	FTA	Pct.	Reb.	Ast.	Pts.	RPG	APG	PPG
2000—United States..............	8	91	16	31	.516	4	8	.500	19	0	36	2.4	0.0	4.5
Totals	8	91	16	31	.516	4	8	.500	19	0	36	2.4	0.0	4.5

MOORE, TAMARA　　　G/F　　　MERCURY

PERSONAL: Born April 11, 1980, in Minneapolis, Minn. ... 5-11/167 (1.80 m/76 kg). ... Full name: Tamara Tennell Moore.
HIGH SCHOOL: North Community.
COLLEGE: Wisconsin.
TRANSACTIONS/CAREER NOTES: Selected by Miami in first round (15th overall) of WNBA Draft, April 19, 2002. ... Traded by Miami with a second-round pick in 2003 WNBA Draft to Minnesota for G Betty Lennox and a first-round pick, June 13, 2002. ... Traded by Minnesota to Detroit for a third-round selection in the 2004 WNBA Draft, May 19, 2003.. ...Traded by Detroit to Phoenix in exchange for Stacey Thomas, July 31, 2003.

COLLEGIATE RECORD

Season Team	G	Min.	FGM	FGA	Pct.	FTM	FTA	Pct.	Reb.	Ast.	Pts.	RPG	APG	PPG
98-99—Wisconsin	32	928	121	273	.443	86	106	.811	158	107	347	4.9	3.3	10.8
99-00—Wisconsin	33	999	152	329	.462	117	152	.770	167	108	445	5.1	3.3	13.5
00-01—Wisconsin	28	869	122	271	.450	89	122	.730	129	151	354	4.6	5.4	12.6
01-02—Wisconsin	31	1052	186	378	.492	95	114	.833	159	188	516	5.1	6.1	16.6
Totals	124	3848	581	1251	.464	387	494	.783	613	554	1662	4.9	4.5	13.4

Three-point field goals: 1998-99, 19-for-56 (.339). 1999-00, 24-for-69 (.348). 2000-01, 21-for-63 (.333). 2001-02, 49-for-135 (.363). Totals, 113-for-323 (.350).

WNBA REGULAR-SEASON RECORD

Season Team	G	Min.	FGM	FGA	Pct.	FTM	FTA	Pct.	Off.	Def.	Tot.	Ast.	St.	Blk.	TO	Pts.	RPG	APG	PPG
2002—Miami-Minn.......	31	736	71	197	.360	54	63	.857	23	60	83	88	30	9	85	224	2.7	2.8	7.2
2003—Detroit	26	176	19	42	.452	16	19	.842	6	22	28	12	9	6	16	54	1.1	0.5	2.1
Totals.................	57	912	90	239	.377	70	82	.854	29	82	111	100	39	15	101	278	1.9	1.8	4.9

Three-point field goals: 2002, 28-for-77 (.364). 2003, 0-for-9. Totals, 28-for-86 (.326).
Personal fouls/disqualifications: 2002, 81/0. 2003, 14/0. Totals, 95/0.

MOWE, JENNY　　　C

PERSONAL: Born February 25, 1978, in Mission Viejo, Calif. ... 6-5/236 (1.96 m/107 kg). ... Full name: Jennifer Lee Mowe.
HIGH SCHOOL: Powers (Powers, Ore.).
COLLEGE: Oregon.
TRANSACTIONS/CAREER NOTES: Selected by Portland in second round (20th overall) of WNBA Draft, April 20, 2001. ... Signed by Los Angeles, August 7, 2003.

COLLEGIATE RECORD

Season Team	G	Min.	FGM	FGA	Pct.	FTM	FTA	Pct.	Reb.	Ast.	Pts.	RPG	APG	PPG
96-97—Oregon	29	419	81	152	.533	38	78	.487	114	11	200	3.9	0.4	6.9
97-98—Oregon	4	64	11	21	.524	11	19	.579	28	...	33	7.0	0.0	8.3
98-99—Oregon	31	570	95	159	.597	43	75	.573	149	18	233	4.8	0.6	7.5
99-00—Oregon	31	627	70	123	.569	37	53	.698	178	22	177	5.7	0.7	5.7
00-01—Oregon	29	635	100	168	.595	40	70	.571	163	26	240	5.6	0.9	8.3
Totals	124	2315	357	623	.573	169	295	.573	632	77	883	5.1	0.6	7.1

Season Team	G	Min.	FGM	FGA	Pct.	FTM	FTA	Pct.	REBOUNDS Off.	Def.	Tot.	Ast.	St.	Blk.	TO	Pts.	AVERAGES RPG	APG	PPG
2001—Portland	5	17	3	3	1.000	0	0	...	1	2	3	0	0	1	2	6	0.6	0.0	1.2
2002—Portland	5	16	0	1	.000	1	2	.500	1	0	1	0	0	0	1	1	0.2	0.0	0.2
2003—Los Angeles	1	21	0	2	.000	0	0	...	0	1	1	0	0	1	1	0	1.0	0.0	0.0
Totals	11	54	3	6	.500	1	2	.500	2	3	5	0	0	2	4	7	0.5	0.0	0.6

NDIAYE-DIATTA, ASTOU   C   FEVER

PERSONAL: Born November 5, 1973, in Kaolack, Senegal ... 6-3/182 (1.91 m/83 kg).
HIGH SCHOOL: Lycee T.S. Nouron Tall (Dakar, Senegal).
COLLEGE: Southern Nazarene.
TRANSACTIONS/CAREER NOTES: Selected by Detroit in fourth round (41st overall) of WNBA Draft, May 4, 1999. ... Signed with Indiana as a restricted free agent, March 11, 2004.
MISCELLANEOUS: Member of WNBA Championship Team (2003).

ABL REGULAR-SEASON RECORD

Season Team	G	Min.	FGM	FGA	Pct.	FTM	FTA	Pct.	Reb.	Ast.	Pts.	AVERAGES RPG	APG	PPG
97-98—Seattle	36	...	83	160	.519	29	46	.630	82	18	195	2.3	0.5	5.4
98-99—Seattle	15	...	28	60	.467	18	24	.750	39	10	74	2.6	0.7	4.9
Totals	51	...	111	220	.505	47	70	.671	121	28	269	2.4	0.5	5.3

Three-point field goals: 1997-98, 0-for-4. 1998-99, 0-for-1. Totals, 0-for-5.

WNBA REGULAR-SEASON RECORD

Season Team	G	Min.	FGM	FGA	Pct.	FTM	FTA	Pct.	REBOUNDS Off.	Def.	Tot.	Ast.	St.	Blk.	TO	Pts.	AVERAGES RPG	APG	PPG
1999—Detroit	31	438	70	160	.438	24	39	.615	25	74	99	17	11	18	32	164	3.2	0.5	5.3
2000—Detroit	32	868	158	333	.474	29	51	.569	65	122	187	40	23	22	64	346	5.8	1.3	10.8
2001—Detroit	32	913	156	341	.457	59	76	.776	60	111	171	49	22	28	73	376	5.3	1.5	11.8
2002—Detroit	32	776	126	270	.467	23	39	.590	44	118	162	39	17	12	58	275	5.1	1.2	8.6
2003—Detroit	11	70	10	21	.476	0	2	.000	5	9	14	1	3	1	9	20	1.3	0.1	1.8
Totals	138	3065	520	1125	.462	135	207	.652	199	434	633	146	76	81	236	1181	4.6	1.1	8.6

Three-point field goals: 1999, 0-for-1. 2000, 1-for-6 (.167). 2001, 5-for-15 (.333). 2002, 0-for-2. Totals, 6-for-24 (.250).
Personal fouls/disqualifications: 1999, 51/0. 2000, 87/0. 2001, 82/1. 2002, 65/0. Totals, 288/1.

WNBA PLAYOFF RECORD

Season Team	G	Min.	FGM	FGA	Pct.	FTM	FTA	Pct.	REBOUNDS Off.	Def.	Tot.	Ast.	St.	Blk.	TO	Pts.	AVERAGES RPG	APG	PPG
1999—Detroit	1	16	4	5	.800	0	0	...	3	3	6	0	1	0	3	8	6.0	0.0	8.0
2003—Detroit	2	6	0	0	...	1	2	.500	0	0	0	1	0	0	0	1	0.0	0.5	0.5
Totals	3	22	4	5	.800	1	2	.500	3	3	6	1	1	0	3	9	2.0	0.3	3.0

OLYMPICS

Season Team	G	Min.	FGM	FGA	Pct.	FTM	FTA	Pct.	Reb.	Ast.	Pts.	AVERAGES RPG	APG	PPG
2000—Senegal	6	196	31	64	.484	9	13	.692	44	7	71	7.3	1.2	11.8
Totals	6	196	31	64	.484	9	13	.692	44	7	71	7.3	1.2	11.8

NOLAN, DEANNA   G/F   SHOCK

N

PERSONAL: Born August 25, 1979, in Flint, Mich. ... 6-0/160 (1.83 m/73 kg). ... **Full name:** Deanna Nicole Nolan.
HIGH SCHOOL: Flint Northern (Flint, Mich.).
COLLEGE: Georgia.
TRANSACTIONS/CAREER NOTES: Selected by Detroit in the first round (sixth overall) of WNBA Draft, April 20, 2001.
MISCELLANEOUS: Member of WNBA Championship Team (2003).

COLLEGIATE RECORD

Season Team	G	Min.	FGM	FGA	Pct.	FTM	FTA	Pct.	Reb.	Ast.	Pts.	AVERAGES RPG	APG	PPG
98-99—Georgia	26	543	73	175	.417	36	57	.632	125	48	187	4.8	1.8	7.2
99-00—Georgia	36	1008	178	325	.548	70	89	.787	164	126	436	4.6	3.5	12.1
00-01—Georgia	24	614	126	278	.453	51	69	.739	94	78	321	3.9	3.3	13.4
Totals	86	2165	377	778	.485	157	215	.730	383	252	944	4.5	2.9	11.0

Three-point field goals: 1998-99, 5-for-32 (.156). 1999-00, 10-for-27 (.370). 2000-01, 18-for-55 (.327). Totals, 33-for-114 (.289).
NOTES: All-WNBA second team (2003).

WNBA REGULAR-SEASON RECORD

Season Team	G	Min.	FGM	FGA	Pct.	FTM	FTA	Pct.	REBOUNDS Off.	Def.	Tot.	Ast.	St.	Blk.	TO	Pts.	AVERAGES RPG	APG	PPG
2001—Detroit	27	545	64	194	.330	43	53	.811	16	37	53	30	17	6	35	192	2.0	1.1	7.1
2002—Detroit	32	804	103	248	.415	29	36	.806	17	70	87	62	27	12	61	277	2.7	1.9	8.7
2003—Detroit	32	954	136	312	.436	76	96	.792	12	95	107	83	41	14	69	396	3.3	2.6	12.4
Totals	91	2303	303	754	.402	148	185	.800	45	202	247	175	85	32	165	865	2.7	1.9	9.5

Three-point field goals: 2001, 21-for-73 (.288). 2002, 42-for-114 (.368). 2003, 48-for-114 (.421). Totals, 111-for-301 (.369).
Personal fouls/disqualifications: 2001, 43/0. 2002, 74/1. 2003, 65/0. Totals, 182/1.

WNBA PLAYOFF RECORD

Season Team	G	Min.	FGM	FGA	Pct.	FTM	FTA	Pct.	REBOUNDS Off.	Def.	Tot.	Ast.	St.	Blk.	TO	Pts.	AVERAGES RPG	APG	PPG
2003—Detroit	8	257	44	96	.458	15	16	.938	4	25	29	21	10	2	13	124	3.6	2.6	15.5
Totals................	8	257	44	96	.458	15	16	.938	4	25	29	21	10	2	13	124	3.6	2.6	15.5

Three-point field goals: 2003, 21-for-47 (.447). Totals, 21-for-47 (.447).
Personal fouls/disqualifications: 2003, 21/0. Totals, 21/0.

WNBA ALL-STAR GAME RECORD

Season Team	Min.	FGM	FGA	Pct.	FTM	FTA	Pct.	REBOUNDS Off.	Def.	Tot.	Ast.	PF	Dq.	St.	Blk.	TO	Pts.
2003—Detroit	22	5	10	.500	2	3	.667	2	4	6	1	1	0	1	0	...	15
Totals................	22	5	10	.500	2	3	.667	2	4	6	1	1	0	1	0	0	15

Three-point field goals: 2003, 3-for-7 (.429). Totals, 3-for-7 (.429).

NYGAARD, VANESSA   F   SILVER STARS

PERSONAL: Born March 13, 1975, in Scottsdale, Ariz. ... 6-1/175 (1.85 m/79 kg). ... Full name: Vanessa Ann Nygaard.
COLLEGE: Stanford.
TRANSACTIONS/CAREER NOTES: Selected by New York in fourth round (39th overall) of WNBA Draft, April 29, 1998. ... Waived by New York, May 24, 1999. ... Signed by Cleveland, May 26, 1999. ... Waived by Cleveland, June 23, 1999. ... Assigned to Portland, May 2, 2000. ... Traded by Portland to Miami for G Marla Brumfield and F Katrina Colleton, May 22, 2002. ... Signed by Charlotte as a free agent April 30, 2003. ... Waived by Charlotte, May 19, 2003. ... Signed by Los Angeles, July 26, 2003. ... Signed by San Antonio as an unrestricted free agent, March 4, 2004.

COLLEGIATE RECORD

Season Team	G	Min.	FGM	FGA	Pct.	FTM	FTA	Pct.	Reb.	Ast.	Pts.	AVERAGES RPG	APG	PPG
94-95—Stanford	29	...	36	103	.350	13	20	.650	65	18	94	2.2	0.6	3.2
95-96—Stanford	31	...	159	359	.443	46	78	.590	216	70	439	7.0	2.3	14.2
96-97—Stanford	31	...	128	296	.432	45	70	.643	214	68	359	6.9	2.2	11.6
97-98—Stanford	26	...	133	267	.498	53	70	.757	160	55	387	6.2	2.1	14.9
Totals	117	...	456	1025	.445	157	238	.660	655	211	1279	5.6	1.8	10.9

Three-point field goals: 1994-95, 9-for-37 (.243). 1995-96, 75-for-193 (.389). 1996-97, 58-for-158 (.367). 1997-98, 68-for-148 (.459). Totals, 210-for-536 (.392).

WNBA REGULAR-SEASON RECORD

Season Team	G	Min.	FGM	FGA	Pct.	FTM	FTA	Pct.	REBOUNDS Off.	Def.	Tot.	Ast.	St.	Blk.	TO	Pts.	AVERAGES RPG	APG	PPG
1999—N.Y.-Cleve.....	4	20	1	2	.500	0	0	...	1	2	3	1	2	0	2	3	0.8	0.3	0.8
2000—Portland	32	843	91	209	.435	41	54	.759	50	71	121	30	17	5	38	253	3.8	0.9	7.9
2001—Portland	31	259	28	72	.389	1	3	.333	13	22	35	10	6	2	14	76	1.1	0.3	2.5
2002—Miami	29	443	43	101	.426	10	13	.769	27	40	67	9	11	1	13	120	2.3	0.3	4.1
2003—Los Angeles ..	11	168	16	36	.444	3	4	.750	11	8	19	5	3	0	4	41	1.7	0.5	3.7
Totals.................	107	1733	179	420	.426	55	74	.743	102	143	245	55	39	8	71	493	2.3	0.5	4.6

Three-point field goals: 1999, 1-for-2 (.500). 2000, 30-for-90 (.333). 2001, 19-for-49 (.388). 2002, 24-for-64 (.375). 2003, 6-for-17 (.353). Totals, 80-for-222 (.360).
Personal fouls/disqualifications: 1999, 4/0. 2000, 98/2. 2001, 48/0. 2002, 49/0. 2003, 22/1. Totals, 221/3.

WNBA PLAYOFF RECORD

Season Team	G	Min.	FGM	FGA	Pct.	FTM	FTA	Pct.	REBOUNDS Off.	Def.	Tot.	Ast.	St.	Blk.	TO	Pts.	AVERAGES RPG	APG	PPG
2003—Los Angeles	5	24	3	5	.600	0	0	...	3	2	5	0	1	1	1	8	1.0	0.0	1.6
Totals.................	5	24	3	5	.600	0	0	...	3	2	5	0	1	1	1	8	1.0	0.0	1.6

Three-point field goals: 2003, 2-for-2. Totals, 2-for-2 (1.000).
Personal fouls/disqualifications: 2003, 1/0. Totals, 1/0.

P

PAGE, MURRIEL   F   MYSTICS

PERSONAL: Born September 18, 1975, in Laurel, Miss. ... 6-2/160 (1.88 m/73 kg). ... Full name: Murriel Page.
COLLEGE: Florida.
TRANSACTIONS/CAREER NOTES: Selected by Washington in first round (third overall) of WNBA Draft, April 29, 1998.

COLLEGIATE RECORD

NOTES: Kodak All America first team (1998).

Season Team	G	Min.	FGM	FGA	Pct.	FTM	FTA	Pct.	Reb.	Ast.	Pts.	AVERAGES RPG	APG	PPG
94-95—Florida	33	...	151	246	.614	47	90	.522	239	30	349	7.2	0.9	10.6
95-96—Florida	30	...	172	354	.486	88	140	.629	271	48	432	9.0	1.6	14.4
96-97—Florida	33	...	214	394	.543	94	157	.599	339	52	522	10.3	1.6	15.8
97-98—Florida	32	...	253	443	.571	105	156	.673	402	70	612	12.6	2.2	19.1
Totals	128	...	790	1437	.550	334	543	.615	1251	200	1915	9.8	1.6	15.0

Three-point field goals: 1997-98, 1-for-6 (.167).

WNBA REGULAR-SEASON RECORD

HONORS: Bud Light Shooting Champion (1999, 2000).

Season Team	G	Min.	FGM	FGA	Pct.	FTM	FTA	Pct.	Off.	Def.	Tot.	Ast.	St.	Blk.	TO	Pts.	RPG	APG	PPG
1998—Washington ...	30	955	104	217	.479	41	65	.631	81	127	208	40	19	13	57	249	6.9	1.3	8.3
1999—Washington ...	32	916	105	183	.574	71	104	.683	68	145	213	28	24	30	49	281	6.7	0.9	8.8
2000—Washington ...	32	1046	131	222	.590	52	92	.565	79	129	208	64	23	32	63	314	6.5	2.0	9.8
2001—Washington ...	32	989	100	231	.433	21	36	.583	74	103	177	55	30	36	60	225	5.5	1.7	7.0
2002—Washington ...	32	750	88	195	.451	30	53	.566	55	100	155	37	14	15	45	208	4.8	1.2	6.5
2003—Washington ...	34	850	83	220	.377	42	56	.750	62	90	152	35	18	24	41	213	4.5	1.0	6.3
Totals	192	5506	611	1268	.482	257	406	.633	419	694	1113	259	128	150	315	1490	5.8	1.3	7.8

Three-point field goals: 1998, 0-for-2. 2001, 4-for-17 (.235). 2002, 2-for-4 (.500). 2003, 5-for-12 (.417). Totals, 11-for-35 (.314).
Personal fouls/disqualifications: 1998, 97/1. 2001, 88/2. 2002, 79/0. 2003, 101/0. Totals, 571/9.

WNBA PLAYOFF RECORD

Season Team	G	Min.	FGM	FGA	Pct.	FTM	FTA	Pct.	Off.	Def.	Tot.	Ast.	St.	Blk.	TO	Pts.	RPG	APG	PPG
2000—Washington ...	2	69	4	9	.444	3	4	.750	2	4	6	1	2	0	4	11	3.0	0.5	5.5
2002—Washington ...	5	113	17	27	.630	14	15	.933	6	16	22	4	1	4	3	48	4.4	0.8	9.6
Totals	7	182	21	36	.583	17	19	.895	8	20	28	5	3	4	7	59	4.0	0.7	8.4

PALMER, WENDY   F   SUN

PERSONAL: Born August 12, 1974, in Timberlake, N.C. ... 6-2/165 (1.88 m/75 kg). ... Full name: Wendy LaWan Palmer.
COLLEGE: Virginia.
TRANSACTIONS/CAREER NOTES: Selected by Utah in second round (ninth overall) in WNBA Elite Draft, February 27, 1997. ... Traded by Utah with F Olympia Scott-Richardson to Detroit for G Korie Hlede and F Cindy Brown, July 29, 1999. ... Traded by Detroit with a second-round pick in 2003 WNBA Draft to Orlando for G Elaine Powell and a first-round pick, July 8, 2002.

COLLEGIATE RECORD

NOTES: Kodak All-America first team (1995, 1996).

Season Team	G	Min.	FGM	FGA	Pct.	FTM	FTA	Pct.	Reb.	Ast.	Pts.	RPG	APG	PPG
92-93—Virginia	31	...	156	254	.614	97	162	.599	213	21	409	6.9	0.7	13.2
93-94—Virginia	32	...	221	389	.568	97	162	.599	323	60	540	10.1	1.9	16.9
94-95—Virginia	31	...	227	401	.566	77	120	.642	327	63	546	10.5	2.0	17.6
95-96—Virginia	32	...	176	368	.478	101	170	.594	358	63	468	11.2	2.0	14.6
Totals	126	...	780	1412	.552	372	614	.606	1221	207	1963	9.7	1.6	15.6

Three-point field goals: 1993-94, 1-for-1. 1994-95, 15-for-37 (.405). 1995-96, 15-for-58 (.259). Totals, 31-for-96 (.323).

WNBA REGULAR-SEASON RECORD

HONORS: All WNBA second team (1997).

Season Team	G	Min.	FGM	FGA	Pct.	FTM	FTA	Pct.	Off.	Def.	Tot.	Ast.	St.	Blk.	TO	Pts.	RPG	APG	PPG
1997—Utah	28	936	157	420	.374	117	173	.676	76	149	225	48	47	6	71	443	8.0	1.7	15.8
1998—Utah	28	761	145	307	.472	81	124	.653	70	116	186	30	18	5	56	377	6.6	1.1	13.5
1999—Utah-Det.	31	741	104	241	.432	86	123	.699	50	138	188	42	9	12	58	307	6.1	1.4	9.9
2000—Detroit	32	914	167	373	.448	95	135	.704	67	152	219	39	20	10	65	441	6.8	1.2	13.8
2001—Detroit	22	651	91	215	.423	40	59	.678	38	116	154	23	23	4	48	233	7.0	1.0	10.6
2002—Det.-Orlando	32	965	130	301	.432	62	92	.674	47	142	189	41	35	8	57	364	5.9	1.3	11.4
2003—Connecticut	32	433	58	147	.395	23	28	.821	29	77	106	16	11	3	35	149	3.3	0.5	4.7
Totals	205	5401	852	2004	.425	504	734	.687	377	890	1267	239	163	48	390	2314	6.2	1.2	11.3

Three-point field goals: 1997, 12-for-48 (.250). 1998, 6-for-17 (.353). 1999, 13-for-46 (.283). 2000, 12-for-48 (.250). 2001, 11-for-33 (.333). 2002, 42-for-120 (.350). 2003, 10-for-46 (.217). Totals, 106-for-358 (.296).
Personal fouls/disqualifications: 1997, 86/0. 1998, 75/1. 1999, 101/3. 2000, 112/2. 2001, 64/0. 2002, 90/0. 2003, 62/0. Totals, 590/6.

WNBA PLAYOFF RECORD

Season Team	G	Min.	FGM	FGA	Pct.	FTM	FTA	Pct.	Off.	Def.	Tot.	Ast.	St.	Blk.	TO	Pts.	RPG	APG	PPG
1999—Detroit	1	37	4	11	.364	2	3	.667	4	5	9	2	1	1	1	10	9.0	2.0	10.0
2003—Connecticut ...	4	64	13	22	.591	2	3	.667	1	11	12	3	0	0	7	29	3.0	0.8	7.3
Totals	5	101	17	33	.515	4	6	.667	5	16	21	5	1	1	8	39	4.2	1.0	7.8

Three-point field goals: 1999, 0-for-2. 2003, 1-for-6 (.167). Totals, 1-for-6 (.167).
Personal fouls/disqualifications: 1999, 3/0. 2003, 9/0. Totals, 12/0.

WNBA ALL-STAR GAME RECORD

Season Team	Min.	FGM	FGA	Pct.	FTM	FTA	Pct.	Off.	Def.	Tot.	Ast.	PF	Dq.	St.	Blk.	TO	Pts.
2000—Detroit	14	1	6	.167	1	2	.500	0	2	2	0	1	0	0	0	...	3
Totals	14	1	6	.167	1	2	.500	0	2	2	0	1	0	0	0		3

Three-point field goals: 2000, 0-for-2. Totals, 0-for-2.

P

PAVLICKOVA, MICHAELA   F/C   MERCURY

PERSONAL: Born November 27, 1977, in Prague, Czech Republic ... 6-3/180 (1.91 m/82 kg). ... **Full name:** Michaela Vladimira Pavlickova.
HIGH SCHOOL: Gymnasium Nad Stolou (Prague); then Boulder (Boulder, Colo.).
COLLEGE: Denver.
TRANSACTIONS/CAREER NOTES: Selected by Utah in second round (24th overall) of WNBA Draft, April 20, 2001.

COLLEGIATE RECORD

Season Team	G	Min.	FGM	FGA	Pct.	FTM	FTA	Pct.	Reb.	Ast.	Pts.	RPG	APG	PPG
97-98—Denver	27	...	88	192	.458	28	43	.651	132	31	206	4.9	1.1	7.6
98-99—Denver	27	...	156	357	.437	49	63	.778	213	34	374	7.9	1.3	13.9
99-00—Denver	27	...	147	346	.425	50	71	.704	240	49	351	8.9	1.8	13.0
00-01—Denver	0	...	223	430	.519	67	83	.807	284	52	524	9.5	1.7	17.5
Totals	111	...	614	1325	.463	194	260	.746	869	166	1455	7.8	1.5	13.1

Three-point field goals: 1997-98, 2-for-6 (.333). 1998-99, 13-for-35 (.371). 1999-000, 7-for-25 (.280). 2000-01, 11-for-29 (.379). Totals, 33-for-95 (.347).

WNBA REGULAR-SEASON RECORD

Season Team	G	Min.	FGM	FGA	Pct.	FTM	FTA	Pct.	Off.	Def.	Tot.	Ast.	St.	Blk.	TO	Pts.	RPG	APG	PPG
2001—Utah	10	21	0	2	.000	1	2	.500	0	6	6	1	0	2	1	1	0.6	0.1	0.1
2003—Phoenix	8	2.8	3	7	.428	0	0	—	1	3	4	1	1	0	2	7	0.5	0.1	0.8
Totals	18	50	3	9	.333	1	2	.500	1	9	10	2	1	2	3	8	0.6	0.1	0.4

WNBA PLAYOFF RECORD

Season Team	G	Min.	FGM	FGA	Pct.	FTM	FTA	Pct.	Off.	Def.	Tot.	Ast.	St.	Blk.	TO	Pts.	RPG	APG	PPG
2001—Utah	1	2	0	0	...	0	0	...	0	0	0	0	0	0	0	0	0.0	0.0	0.0
Totals	1	2	0	0	...	0	0	...	0	0	0	0	0	0	0	0	0.0	0.0	0.0

PENICHEIRO, TICHA   G   MONARCHS

PERSONAL: Born September 18, 1974, in Figueira da Foz, Portugal ... 5-11/158 (1.80 m/72 kg). ... **Full name:** Ticha Nunes Penicheiro.
COLLEGE: Old Dominion.
TRANSACTIONS/CAREER NOTES: Selected by Sacramento in first round (second overall) of the WNBA Draft, April 29, 1998.

COLLEGIATE RECORD

NOTES: Wade Trophy recipient (1998). ... Kodak All-America first team (1997, 1998).

Season Team	G	Min.	FGM	FGA	Pct.	FTM	FTA	Pct.	Reb.	Ast.	Pts.	RPG	APG	PPG
94-95—Old Dominion	33	...	109	255	.427	48	87	.552	158	203	283	4.8	6.2	8.6
95-96—Old Dominion	32	...	107	218	.491	57	85	.671	226	226	284	7.1	7.1	8.9
96-97—Old Dominion	36	...	140	316	.443	87	134	.649	163	271	393	4.5	7.5	10.9
97-98—Old Dominion	32	...	117	287	.408	88	140	.629	163	239	344	5.1	7.5	10.8
Totals	133	...	473	1076	.440	280	446	.628	710	939	1304	5.3	7.1	9.8

Three-point field goals: 1994-95, 17-for-51 (.333). 1995-96, 13-for-45 (.289). 1996-97, 26-for-84 (.310). 1997-98, 22-for-67 (.328). Totals, 78-for-247 (.316).

WNBA REGULAR-SEASON RECORD

HONORS: All-WNBA first team (1999, 2000). ... All-WNBA second team (2001).
NOTES: Led WNBA in assists in 1998 (7.5 apg), 1999 (7.1 apg), 2000 (7.9 apg), 2001 (7.5 apg) and 2002 (8,0 apg) and 2003 (6.7 apg). ... Led WNBA in minutes in 1998 (36.0 mpg).

Season Team	G	Min.	FGM	FGA	Pct.	FTM	FTA	Pct.	Off.	Def.	Tot.	Ast.	St.	Blk.	TO	Pts.	RPG	APG	PPG
1998—Sacramento	30	1080	55	165	.333	70	109	.642	13	128	141	224	67	3	116	190	4.7	7.5	6.3
1999—Sacramento	32	1120	71	222	.320	87	131	.664	29	126	155	226	67	5	135	235	4.8	7.1	7.3
2000—Sacramento	30	936	68	185	.368	62	107	.579	12	77	89	236	70	6	71	208	3.0	7.9	6.9
2001—Sacramento	23	744	42	124	.339	49	64	.766	6	80	86	172	40	8	64	144	3.7	7.5	6.3
2002—Sacramento	24	853	60	159	.377	75	103	.728	7	95	102	192	64	1	69	203	4.3	8.0	8.5
2003—Sacramento	34	1089	62	205	.302	44	76	.579	29	90	119	229	61	1	81	183	3.5	6.7	5.4
Totals	173	5822	358	1060	.338	387	590	.656	96	596	692	1279	369	24	536	1163	4.0	7.4	6.7

Three-point field goals: 1998, 10-for-43 (.233). 1999, 6-for-38 (.158). 2000, 10-for-50 (.200). 2001, 11-for-42 (.262). 2002, 8-for-32 (.250). 2003, 15-for-60 (.250). Totals, 60-for-265 (.226).
Personal fouls/disqualifications: 1998, 90/1. 1999, 87/1. 2000, 71/1. 2001, 58/1. 2002, 49/0. 2003, 76/1. Totals, 431/5.

WNBA PLAYOFF RECORD

Season Team	G	Min.	FGM	FGA	Pct.	FTM	FTA	Pct.	Off.	Def.	Tot.	Ast.	St.	Blk.	TO	Pts.	RPG	APG	PPG
1999—Sacramento	1	20	1	5	.200	2	2	1.000	0	4	4	3	1	0	2	4	4.0	3.0	4.0
2000—Sacramento	2	77	4	16	.250	5	6	.833	2	5	7	14	4	0	6	16	3.5	7.0	8.0
2001—Sacramento	5	163	10	40	.250	4	4	1.000	3	16	19	33	3	4	9	31	3.8	6.6	6.2
2003—Sacramento	6	143	8	24	.333	7	8	.875	1	13	14	18	6	3	7	25	2.3	3.0	4.2
Totals	14	403	23	85	.271	18	20	.900	6	38	44	68	14	7	24	76	3.1	4.9	5.4

Three-point field goals: 2000, 3-for-6 (.500). 2001, 7-for-19 (.368). 2003, 2-for-8 (.250). Totals, 12-for-33 (.364).
Personal fouls/disqualifications: 2000, 10/1. 2001, 9/0. 2003, 12/0. Totals, 32/1.

P

WNBA ALL-STAR GAME RECORD

Season Team	Min.	FGM	FGA	Pct.	FTM	FTA	Pct.	REBOUNDS Off.	Def.	Tot.	Ast.	PF	Dq.	St.	Blk.	TO	Pts.
1999—Sacramento	19	0	3	.000	1	2	.500	0	0	0	3	2	0	0	0	...	1
2000—Sacramento	25	1	2	.500	1	2	.500	0	2	2	4	0	0	1	0	...	3
2001—Sacramento	21	0	2	.000	1	2	.500	0	3	3	5	1	0	2	0	...	1
2002—Sacramento	22	1	1	1.000	0	0	...	0	1	1	2	2	0	2	1	...	2
Totals.................	87	2	8	.250	3	6	.500	0	6	6	14	5	0	5	1	17	7

Three-point field goals: 1999, 0-for-1. 2000, 0-for-1. Totals, 0-for-2.

PENN, JOCELYN   F   MYSTICS

PERSONAL: Born September 10, 1979, in Tucker, Ga. ... 6-0 (1.83 m/ kg).
HIGH SCHOOL: Meadowcreek (Norcross, Ga.).
COLLEGE: South Carolina.
TRANSACTIONS/CAREER NOTES: Selected by Charlotte in first round (ninth overall) of WNBA Draft, April 25, 2003. ... Waived by Charlotte, May 21, 2003. ... Signed by Washington, June 9, 2003.

COLLEGIATE RECORD

NOTES: Associated Press All-America Second Team (2003). ... All-SEC First Team (coaches: 2003, 2002). ... Named to the 2003 USBWA All-American Team. ... SEC's all-time leader in steals (359).

Season Team	G	Min.	FGM	FGA	Pct.	FTM	FTA	Pct.	Reb.	Ast.	Pts.	AVERAGES RPG	APG	PPG
99-00—South Carolina	27	685	130	247	.526	91	132	.689	...	41	351	6.5	1.5	13.0
00-01—South Carolina	28	721	127	230	.552	93	138	.674	...	64	347	6.1	2.3	12.4
01-02—South Carolina	32	991	218	351	.621	89	140	.636	...	53	525	6.7	1.7	16.4
02-03—South Carolina	30	1088	282	449	.628	138	194	.711	...	58	716	8.1	1.9	23.9
Totals	117	3485	757	1277	.593	411	604	.680	0	216	1939	0.0	1.8	16.6

Three-point field goals: 2002-03, 14-for-37 (.378).

WNBA REGULAR-SEASON RECORD

Season Team	G	Min.	FGM	FGA	Pct.	FTM	FTA	Pct.	REBOUNDS Off.	Def.	Tot.	Ast.	St.	Blk.	TO	Pts.	AVERAGES RPG	APG	PPG
2003—Washington....	30	288	31	78	.397	22	33	.667	19	33	52	16	15	1	20	86	1.7	0.5	2.9
Totals.................	30	288	31	78	.397	22	33	.667	19	33	52	16	15	1	20	86	1.7	0.5	2.9

Three-point field goals: 2003, 2-for-13 (.154). Totals, 2-for-13 (.154).
Personal fouls/disqualifications: 2003, 28/0. Totals, 28/0.

PETTIS, BRIDGET   G   FEVER

PERSONAL: Born January 1, 1971, in East Chicago, Ind. ... 5-9/150 (1.75 m/68 kg).
COLLEGE: Florida.
TRANSACTIONS/CAREER NOTES: Selected by Phoenix in first round (seventh overall) in the WNBA Elite Draft, February 27, 1997. ... Traded by Phoenix with a first-round pick in the 2002 WNBA Draft to Indiana for G Gordana Grubin, March 4, 2002.

COLLEGIATE RECORD

Season Team	G	Min.	FGM	FGA	Pct.	FTM	FTA	Pct.	Reb.	Ast.	Pts.	AVERAGES RPG	APG	PPG
91-92—Florida	27	...	142	377	.377	57	77	.740	125	76	393	4.6	2.8	14.6
92-93—Florida	26	...	139	365	.381	79	103	.767	122	39	411	4.7	1.5	15.8
Totals	53	...	281	742	.379	136	180	.756	247	115	804	4.7	2.2	15.2

Three-point field goals: 1991-92, 52-for-163 (.319). 1992-93, 54-for-175 (.309). Totals, 106-for-338 (.314).

WNBA REGULAR-SEASON RECORD

NOTES: Led WNBA in free throw percentage in 1997 (.898).

Season Team	G	Min.	FGM	FGA	Pct.	FTM	FTA	Pct.	REBOUNDS Off.	Def.	Tot.	Ast.	St.	Blk.	TO	Pts.	AVERAGES RPG	APG	PPG
1997—Phoenix........	28	842	107	321	.333	97	108	.898	36	71	107	78	49	12	82	352	3.8	2.8	12.6
1998—Phoenix........	30	849	113	300	.377	77	89	.865	34	69	103	62	29	9	62	338	3.4	2.1	11.3
1999—Phoenix........	32	541	65	214	.304	29	47	.617	29	30	59	45	26	2	30	181	1.8	1.4	5.7
2000—Phoenix........	32	583	60	168	.357	49	61	.803	19	41	60	46	31	4	39	189	1.9	1.4	5.9
2001—Phoenix........	32	497	53	159	.333	46	56	.821	30	30	60	50	28	4	38	172	1.9	1.6	5.4
2002—Indiana........	32	375	38	107	.355	28	39	.718	17	22	39	17	8	0	24	113	1.2	0.5	3.5
2003—Indiana........	31	148	15	52	.288	13	17	.765	5	14	19	8	4	1	8	49	0.6	0.3	1.6
Totals.................	217	3835	451	1321	.341	339	417	.813	170	277	447	306	175	32	283	1394	2.1	1.4	6.4

Three-point field goals: 1997, 41-for-134 (.306). 1998, 35-for-123 (.285). 1999, 22-for-98 (.224). 2000, 20-for-75 (.267). 2001, 20-for-63 (.317). 2002, 9-for-43 (.209). 2003, 6-for-27 (.222). Totals, 153-for-563 (.272).
Personal fouls/disqualifications: 1997, 57/1. 1998, 75/0. 1999, 57/1. 2000, 62/1. 2001, 47/1. 2002, 22/0. 2003, 17/0. Totals, 337/4.

WNBA PLAYOFF RECORD

Season Team	G	Min.	FGM	FGA	Pct.	FTM	FTA	Pct.	REBOUNDS Off.	Def.	Tot.	Ast.	St.	Blk.	TO	Pts.	AVERAGES RPG	APG	PPG
1997—Phoenix........	1	27	2	15	.133	0	0	...	3	3	6	2	2	0	2	4	6.0	2.0	4.0
1998—Phoenix........	6	183	30	60	.500	15	19	.789	10	12	22	13	11	2	11	77	3.7	2.2	12.8

P

Season Team	G	Min.	FGM	FGA	Pct.	FTM	FTA	Pct.	Off.	Def.	Tot.	Ast.	St.	Blk.	TO	Pts.	RPG	APG	PPG
2000—Phoenix	2	41	7	18	.389	2	2	1.000	1	4	5	6	1	0	3	21	2.5	3.0	10.5
2002—Indiana	3	43	5	15	.333	5	7	.714	6	3	9	2	0	0	4	16	3.0	0.7	5.3
Totals	12	294	44	108	.407	22	28	.786	20	22	42	23	14	2	20	118	3.5	1.9	9.8

Three-point field goals: 1997, 0-for-5. 1998, 2-for-10 (.200). 2000, 5-for-11 (.455). 2002, 1-for-3 (.333). Totals, 8-for-29 (.276).
Personal fouls/disqualifications: 1997, 1/0. 1998, 11/0. 2000, 7/0. 2002, 0/0. Totals, 19/0.

PHILLIPS, TARI   C   LIBERTY

PERSONAL: Born March 6, 1969, in Orlando, Fla. ... 6-1/200 (1.85 m/91 kg). ... Full name: Tari L. Phillips.
HIGH SCHOOL: Edgewater (Orlando, Fla.).
COLLEGE: Central Florida.
TRANSACTIONS/CAREER NOTES: Selected by Orlando in first round (eighth overall) of WNBA Draft, May 4, 1999. ... Selected by Portland in third round (12th overall) of WNBA Expansion Draft, December 15, 1999. ... Traded by Portland to New York for G Carolyn Jones-Young, May 28, 2000.

COLLEGIATE RECORD

Season Team	G	Min.	FGM	FGA	Pct.	FTM	FTA	Pct.	Reb.	Ast.	Pts.	AVERAGES RPG	APG	PPG
86-87—Georgia	31	...	51	112	.455	24	37	.649	74	20	126	2.4	0.6	4.1
87-88—Georgia	31	...	112	244	.459	53	85	.624	132	35	278	4.3	1.1	9.0
88-89—Georgia	2	...	3	4	.750	...	...	...	1	...	6	0.5	0.0	3.0
90-91—Central Florida	21	...	213	412	.517	93	151	.616	261	24	532	12.4	1.1	25.3
Totals	85	...	379	772	.491	170	273	.623	468	79	942	5.5	0.9	11.1

Three-point field goals: 1987-88, 1-for-6 (.167). 1990-91, 13-for-35 (.371). Totals, 14-for-41 (.341).

ABL REGULAR-SEASON RECORD

NOTES: ABL All-Star Most Valuable Player (1997).

Season Team	G	Min.	FGM	FGA	Pct.	FTM	FTA	Pct.	Reb.	Ast.	Pts.	AVERAGES RPG	APG	PPG
96-97—Seattle	40	...	227	496	.458	99	186	.532	296	48	559	7.4	1.2	14.0
97-98—Colorado	44	...	247	492	.502	115	200	.575	360	37	610	8.2	0.8	13.9
98-99—Colorado	13	...	78	161	.484	26	45	.578	119	21	182	9.2	1.6	14.0
Totals	97	...	552	1149	.480	240	431	.557	775	106	1351	8.0	1.1	13.9

Three-point field goals: 1996-97, 6-for-27 (.222). 1997-98, 1-for-2 (.500). 1998-99, 0-for-3. Totals, 7-for-32 (.219).

WNBA REGULAR-SEASON RECORD

HONORS: WNBA Most Improved Player (2000). ... All-WNBA second team (2002).

Season Team	G	Min.	FGM	FGA	Pct.	FTM	FTA	Pct.	REBOUNDS Off.	Def.	Tot.	Ast.	St.	Blk.	TO	Pts.	AVERAGES RPG	APG	PPG
1999—Orlando	32	335	52	128	.406	26	54	.481	26	40	66	9	19	8	48	130	2.1	0.3	4.1
2000—Portland-N.Y.	31	978	170	364	.467	85	130	.654	86	161	247	28	59	21	85	427	8.0	0.9	13.8
2001—New York	32	1049	208	410	.507	73	125	.584	89	168	257	34	48	17	84	489	8.0	1.1	15.3
2002—New York	32	1009	183	373	.491	85	126	.675	69	154	223	41	58	14	93	451	7.0	1.3	14.1
2003—New York	33	1033	142	358	.397	87	134	.649	99	181	280	56	56	28	92	372	8.5	1.7	11.3
Totals	160	4404	755	1633	.462	356	569	.626	369	704	1073	168	240	88	402	1869	6.7	1.1	11.7

Three-point field goals: 1999, 0-for-3. 2000, 2-for-8 (.250). 2001, 0-for-4. 2002, 0-for-2. 2003, 1-for-5 (.200). Totals, 3-for-22 (.136).
Personal fouls/disqualifications: 1999, 54/0. 2000, 110/5. 2001, 110/0. 2002, 113/2. 2003, 118/3. Totals, 505/10.

WNBA PLAYOFF RECORD

Season Team	G	Min.	FGM	FGA	Pct.	FTM	FTA	Pct.	REBOUNDS Off.	Def.	Tot.	Ast.	St.	Blk.	TO	Pts.	AVERAGES RPG	APG	PPG
2000—New York	7	222	48	95	.505	18	23	.783	16	37	53	8	12	6	16	114	7.6	1.1	16.3
2001—New York	6	202	26	62	.419	16	34	.471	15	34	49	10	9	6	17	68	8.2	1.7	11.3
2002—New York	8	249	45	91	.495	25	35	.714	16	31	47	10	9	4	19	115	5.9	1.3	14.4
Totals	21	673	119	248	.480	59	92	.641	47	102	149	28	30	16	52	297	7.1	1.3	14.1

Three-point field goals: 2000, 0-for-1. 2001, 0-for-1. 2002, 0-for-3. Totals, 0-for-5.
Personal fouls/disqualifications: 2000, 26/1. 2001, 17/1. 2002, 26/0. Totals, 69/2.

WNBA ALL-STAR GAME RECORD

Season Team	Min.	FGM	FGA	Pct.	FTM	FTA	Pct.	REBOUNDS Off.	Def.	Tot.	Ast.	PF	Dq.	St.	Blk.	TO	Pts.
2000—New York	22	5	14	.357	0	3	.000	8	1	9	1	4	0	0	3	...	10
2001—New York	24	4	8	.500	1	6	.167	4	5	9	0	1	0	1	0	...	9
2002—New York	22	1	9	.111	2	2	1.000	5	5	10	0	6	1	0	0	...	4
2003—New York	20	6	12	.500	1	1	1.000	2	5	7	1	4	0	2	2	...	13
Totals	88	16	43	.372	4	12	.333	19	16	35	2	15	1	3	5	15	36

Three-point field goals: 2000, 0-for-2. Totals, 0-for-2.

P

PIERSON, PLENETTE   F/C   MERCURY

PERSONAL: Born August 31, 1981, in Houston. ... 6-2 (1.88 m/ kg). ... Full name: Plenette Michelle Pierson.
HIGH SCHOOL: Kingwood (Kingwood, Texas).
COLLEGE: Texas Tech.
TRANSACTIONS/CAREER NOTES: Selected by Phoenix in first round (fourth overall) of WNBA Draft, April 25, 2003.

COLLEGIATE RECORD

Season Team	G	Min.	FGM	FGA	Pct.	FTM	FTA	Pct.	Reb.	Ast.	Pts.	RPG	APG	PPG
99-00—Texas Tech	33	889	171	338	.506	107	188	.569	...	19	449	6.9	0.6	13.6
00-01—Texas Tech	32	877	170	343	.496	131	205	.639	...	36	471	7.4	1.1	14.7
01-02—Texas Tech	4	125	23	55	.418	12	18	.667	...	10	58	9.0	2.5	14.5
02-03—Texas Tech	35	1000	238	467	.510	148	233	.635	...	51	624	8.1	1.5	17.8
Totals	104	2891	602	1203	.500	398	644	.618	0	116	1602	0.0	1.1	15.4

Three-point field goals: 2000-01, 0-for-1. 2002-03, 0-for-1. Totals, 0-for-2.

WNBA REGULAR-SEASON RECORD

Season Team	G	Min.	FGM	FGA	Pct.	FTM	FTA	Pct.	Off.	Def.	Tot.	Ast.	St.	Blk.	TO	Pts.	RPG	APG	PPG
2003—Phoenix	33	602	67	177	.379	64	101	.634	37	43	80	22	19	13	42	198	2.4	0.7	6.0
Totals	33	602	67	177	.379	64	101	.634	37	43	80	22	19	13	42	198	2.4	0.7	6.0

Three-point field goals: 2003, 0-for-2. Totals, 0-for-2.
Personal fouls/disqualifications: 2003, 87/1. Totals, 87/1.

POWELL, ELAINE   G   SHOCK

PERSONAL: Born August 9, 1975, in Monroe, La. ... 5-9/147 (1.75 m/67 kg). ... Full name: Elaine Marie Powell.
HIGH SCHOOL: Carroll (Monroe, La.).
COLLEGE: Louisiana State.
TRANSACTIONS/CAREER NOTES: Selected by Orlando in fourth round (50th overall) of WNBA Draft, May 4, 1999. ... Traded by Orlando with a first-round pick in 2003 WNBA Draft to Detroit for F Wendy Palmer and a second-round pick, July 8, 2002.
MISCELLANEOUS: Member of WNBA Championship Team (2003).

COLLEGIATE RECORD

Season Team	G	Min.	FGM	FGA	Pct.	FTM	FTA	Pct.	Reb.	Ast.	Pts.	RPG	APG	PPG
95-96—Louisiana State	32	...	242	508	.476	125	167	.749	191	123	643	6.0	3.8	20.1
96-97—Louisiana State	29	...	203	413	.492	92	133	.692	130	118	520	4.5	4.1	17.9
Totals	61	...	445	921	.483	217	300	.723	321	241	1163	5.3	4.0	19.1

Three-point field goals: 1995-96, 34-for-92 (.370). 1996-97, 22-for-59 (.373). Totals, 56-for-151 (.371).

ABL REGULAR-SEASON RECORD

Season Team	G	Min.	FGM	FGA	Pct.	FTM	FTA	Pct.	Reb.	Ast.	Pts.	RPG	APG	PPG
97-98—Portland	44	...	183	439	.417	132	182	.725	166	164	539	3.8	3.7	12.3
98-99—Portland	13	...	50	117	.427	22	36	.611	51	50	133	3.9	3.8	10.2
Totals	57	...	233	556	.419	154	218	.706	217	214	672	3.8	3.8	11.8

Three-point field goals: 1997-98, 41-for-107 (.383). 1998-99, 11-for-34 (.324). Totals, 52-for-141 (.369).

WNBA REGULAR-SEASON RECORD

Season Team	G	Min.	FGM	FGA	Pct.	FTM	FTA	Pct.	Off.	Def.	Tot.	Ast.	St.	Blk.	TO	Pts.	RPG	APG	PPG
1999—Orlando	18	256	17	33	.515	12	22	.545	9	14	23	32	9	4	19	47	1.3	1.8	2.6
2000—Orlando	20	347	26	66	.394	17	22	.773	17	33	50	42	12	1	30	72	2.5	2.1	3.6
2001—Orlando	32	1055	119	296	.402	80	106	.755	32	66	98	98	49	7	79	357	3.1	3.1	11.2
2002—Orlando-Det.	30	705	89	220	.405	50	66	.758	33	62	95	90	43	12	71	236	3.2	3.0	7.9
2003—Detroit	33	938	105	233	.451	79	106	.745	43	63	106	129	45	9	79	296	3.2	3.9	9.0
Totals	133	3301	356	848	.420	238	322	.739	134	238	372	391	158	33	278	1008	2.8	2.9	7.6

Three-point field goals: 1999, 1-for-9 (.111). 2000, 3-for-9 (.333). 2001, 39-for-102 (.382). 2002, 8-for-33 (.242). 2003, 7-for-20 (.350). Totals, 58-for-173 (.335).
Personal fouls/disqualifications: 1999, 22/0. 2000, 21/0. 2001, 64/0. 2002, 50/0. 2003, 65/0. Totals, 222/0.

WNBA PLAYOFF RECORD

Season Team	G	Min.	FGM	FGA	Pct.	FTM	FTA	Pct.	Off.	Def.	Tot.	Ast.	St.	Blk.	TO	Pts.	RPG	APG	PPG
2003—Detroit	8	219	16	46	.348	7	11	.636	6	24	30	38	7	4	13	41	3.8	4.8	5.1
Totals	8	219	16	46	.348	7	11	.636	6	24	30	38	7	4	13	41	3.8	4.8	5.1

Three-point field goals: 2003, 2-for-10 (.200). Totals, 2-for-10 (.200).
Personal fouls/disqualifications: 2003, 17/0. Totals, 17/0.

PRIDE, LYNN   F   SPARKS

PERSONAL: Born October 16, 1978, in Vera Beach, Fla. ... 6-2/180 (1.88 m/82 kg).
HIGH SCHOOL: Sam Houston (Arlington, Texas).
COLLEGE: Kansas.
TRANSACTIONS/CAREER NOTES: Selected by Portland in first round (seventh overall) of WNBA Draft, April 25, 2000. ... Traded by Portland with C Michele VanGorp to Minnesota for F Kristen Folkl and the 12th pick in the 2001 WNBA Draft, February 20, 2001. ... Waived by Minnesota, July 6, 2003. ... Signed by Los Angeles, August 7, 2003.

P

COLLEGIATE RECORD

NOTES: All-Big 12 first team (1998, 1999, 2000). ... Among top five at KU in career points (1774, fifth), rebounding (863, third), steals (279, fourth), blocks (93, fourth) minutes (3,789, third). ... Women's Basketball Journal All-America third team (2000). ... Women's Basketball News Service All-America second team (2000), third team (1999).

Season Team	G	Min.	FGM	FGA	Pct.	FTM	FTA	Pct.	Reb.	Ast.	Pts.	RPG	APG	PPG
96-97—Kansas	27	...	82	177	.463	44	64	.688	173	39	211	6.4	1.4	7.8
97-98—Kansas	32	...	184	464	.397	88	126	.698	214	91	478	6.7	2.8	14.9
98-99—Kansas	33	...	220	493	.446	110	150	.733	239	84	563	7.2	2.5	17.1
99-00—Kansas	30	...	210	473	.444	92	117	.786	237	83	522	7.9	2.8	17.4
Totals	**122**	...	**696**	**1607**	**.433**	**334**	**457**	**.731**	**863**	**297**	**1774**	**7.1**	**2.4**	**14.5**

Three-point field goals: 1996-97, 3-for-7 (.429). 1997-98, 22-for-70 (.314). 1998-99, 13-for-46 (.283). 1999-00, 10-for-38 (.263). Totals, 48-for-161 (.298).

WNBA REGULAR-SEASON RECORD

Season Team	G	Min.	FGM	FGA	Pct.	FTM	FTA	Pct.	Off.	Def.	Tot.	Ast.	St.	Blk.	TO	Pts.	RPG	APG	PPG
2000—Portland	32	462	41	118	.347	29	42	.690	22	39	61	40	16	9	33	114	1.9	1.3	3.6
2001—Minnesota	32	713	68	174	.391	33	55	.600	47	99	146	28	28	20	46	170	4.6	0.9	5.3
2002—Minnesota	31	589	57	148	.385	8	17	.471	25	78	103	43	25	25	47	123	3.3	1.4	4.0
2003—Minnesota	17	94	7	19	.368	4	8	.500	11	12	23	1	3	1	11	18	1.4	0.1	1.1
Totals	**112**	**1858**	**173**	**459**	**.377**	**74**	**122**	**.607**	**105**	**228**	**333**	**112**	**72**	**55**	**137**	**425**	**3.0**	**1.0**	**3.8**

Three-point field goals: 2000, 3-for-9 (.333). 2001, 1-for-4 (.250). 2002, 1-for-10 (.100). Totals, 5-for-23 (.217).
Personal fouls/disqualifications: 2000, 59/1. 2001, 77/2. 2002, 73/1. Totals, 229/5.

WNBA PLAYOFF RECORD

Season Team	G	Min.	FGM	FGA	Pct.	FTM	FTA	Pct.	Off.	Def.	Tot.	Ast.	St.	Blk.	TO	Pts.	RPG	APG	PPG
2003—Los Angeles	6	36	2	6	.333	1	1	1.000	6	3	9	1	2	1	3	5	1.5	0.2	0.8
Totals	**6**	**36**	**2**	**6**	**.333**	**1**	**1**	**1.000**	**6**	**3**	**9**	**1**	**2**	**1**	**3**	**5**	**1.5**	**0.2**	**0.8**

QUICK, LAQUANDA   G/F   SILVER STARS

PERSONAL: Born October 3, 1979 ... 5-10/156 (1.78 m/71 kg). ... **Full name:** LaQuanda Shena Barksdale Quick.
HIGH SCHOOL: West Forsyth HS.
COLLEGE: North Carolina.
TRANSACTIONS/CAREER NOTES: Drafted by the Portland Fire in the first round (12th overall) of the 2001 WNBA Draft. ... Selected by San Antonio with the 12th overall pick in 2003 WNBA Dispersal Draft.

COLLEGIATE RECORD

Season Team	G	Min.	FGM	FGA	Pct.	FTM	FTA	Pct.	Reb.	Ast.	Pts.	RPG	APG	PPG
97-98—North Carolina	32	338	63	130	.485	20	27	.741	77	11	154	2.4	0.3	4.8
98-99—North Carolina	36	1036	213	435	.490	57	73	.781	281	30	500	7.8	0.8	13.9
99-00—North Carolina	33	1062	230	516	.446	105	135	.778	285	41	581	8.6	1.2	17.6
00-01—North Carolina	29	993	217	483	.449	85	118	.720	334	41	552	11.5	1.4	19.0
Totals	**130**	**3429**	**723**	**1564**	**.462**	**267**	**353**	**.756**	**977**	**123**	**1787**	**7.5**	**0.9**	**13.7**

Three-point field goals: 1997-98, 8-for-23 (.348). 1998-99, 17-for-54 (.315). 1999-000, 16-for-39 (.410). 2000-01, 33-for-92 (.359). Totals, 74-for-208 (.356).

WNBA REGULAR-SEASON RECORD

Season Team	G	Min.	FGM	FGA	Pct.	FTM	FTA	Pct.	Off.	Def.	Tot.	Ast.	St.	Blk.	TO	Pts.	RPG	APG	PPG
2001—Portland	5	35	1	10	.100	0	3	.000	1	5	6	4	2	0	1	2	1.2	0.8	0.4
2002—Portland	17	285	36	101	.356	23	26	.884	18	22	40	12	8	7	23	100	2.4	0.7	5.9
2003—San Antonio	26	168	21	79	.266	2	2	1.000	8	25	33	5	1	3	10	59	1.3	0.2	2.3
Totals	**48**	**488**	**58**	**190**	**.305**	**25**	**31**	**.806**	**27**	**52**	**79**	**21**	**11**	**10**	**34**	**161**	**1.6**	**0.4**	**3.4**

Three-point field goals: 2003, 15-for-52 (.288). Totals, 15-for-52 (.288).
Personal fouls/disqualifications: 2003, 21/0. Totals, 21/0.

RAGLAND, FELICIA   G   COMETS

PERSONAL: Born February 3, 1980, in Tulare, Calif. ... 5-9/135 (1.75 m/61 kg). ... Full name: Felicia Rae Ragland.
HIGH SCHOOL: Tulare Western (Calif.).
COLLEGE: Oregon State.
TRANSACTIONS/CAREER NOTES: Selected by Seattle in second round (28th overall) of WNBA Draft, April 19, 2002. ... Waived by Seattle, May 9, 2003. ... Signed by Phoenix as a free agent, May 25, 2003. ... Waived by Phoenix, August 2003. ... Signed by Houston as a free agent, March 3, 2004.

COLLEGIATE RECORD

Season Team	G	Min.	FGM	FGA	Pct.	FTM	FTA	Pct.	Reb.	Ast.	Pts.	RPG	APG	PPG
98-99—Oregon State	27	674	78	214	.364	31	47	.660	126	49	205	4.7	1.8	7.6
99-00—Oregon State	30	928	146	391	.373	68	91	.747	186	86	388	6.2	2.9	12.9
00-01—Oregon State	29	910	206	464	.444	97	129	.752	215	56	572	7.4	1.9	19.7

Q
R

Season Team	G	Min.	FGM	FGA	Pct.	FTM	FTA	Pct.	Reb.	Ast.	Pts.	RPG	APG	PPG
01-02—Oregon State	32	1037	229	581	.394	111	134	.828	212	73	638	6.6	2.3	19.9
Totals	118	3549	659	1650	.399	307	401	.766	739	264	1803	6.3	2.2	15.3

Three-point field goals: 1998-99, 18-for-57 (.316). 1999-00, 28-for-105 (.267). 2000-01, 63-for-136 (.463). 2001-02, 69-for-199 (.347). Totals, 178-for-497 (.358).

WNBA REGULAR-SEASON RECORD

Season Team	G	Min.	FGM	FGA	Pct.	FTM	FTA	Pct.	REBOUNDS Off.	Def.	Tot.	Ast.	St.	Blk.	TO	Pts.	AVERAGES RPG	APG	PPG
2002—Seattle	31	432	48	125	.384	23	28	.821	27	21	48	23	27	1	29	141	1.5	0.7	4.5
2003—Phoenix	3	39	1	12	.083	2	2	1.000	0	2	2	2	2	0	3	5	0.7	0.7	1.7
Totals	34	471	49	137	.358	25	30	.833	27	23	50	25	29	1	32	146	1.5	0.7	4.3

Three-point field goals: 2002, 22-for-55 (.400). 2003, 1-for-5 (.200). Totals, 23-for-60 (.383).
Personal fouls/disqualifications: 2002, 44/0. 2003, 4/0. Totals, 48/0.

WNBA PLAYOFF RECORD

Season Team	G	Min.	FGM	FGA	Pct.	FTM	FTA	Pct.	REBOUNDS Off.	Def.	Tot.	Ast.	St.	Blk.	TO	Pts.	AVERAGES RPG	APG	PPG
2002—Seattle	2	19	3	9	.333	0	0	...	2	4	6	1	0	0	2	7	3.0	0.5	3.5
Totals	2	19	3	9	.333	0	0	...	2	4	6	1	0	0	2	7	3.0	0.5	3.5

Three-point field goals: 2002, 1-for-3 (.333). Totals, 1-for-3 (.333).
Personal fouls/disqualifications: 2002, 0/0.

RANDALL, SEMEKA   G   SILVER STARS

PERSONAL: Born February 7, 1979, in Cleveland ... 5-8/170 (1.73 m/77 kg). ... Full name: Semeka Chantay Randall.
HIGH SCHOOL: Trinity (Cleveland).
COLLEGE: Tennessee.
TRANSACTIONS/CAREER NOTES: Selected by Seattle in second round (17th overall) of WNBA Draft, April 20, 2001. ... Traded by Seattle to Utah for G Kate Starbird, July 22, 2002.

COLLEGIATE RECORD

NOTES: Member of NCAA Division I championship team (1998). ... Kodak All-America first team (1999,2000).

Season Team	G	Min.	FGM	FGA	Pct.	FTM	FTA	Pct.	Reb.	Ast.	Pts.	AVERAGES RPG	APG	PPG
97-98—Tennessee	38	987	224	460	.487	155	213	.728	200	50	604	5.3	1.3	15.9
98-99—Tennessee	33	887	190	371	.512	82	139	.590	160	46	464	4.8	1.4	14.1
99-00—Tennessee	37	1072	187	447	.418	135	172	.785	196	69	518	5.3	1.9	14.0
00-01—Tennessee	32	775	130	312	.417	67	94	.713	160	71	329	5.0	2.2	10.3
Totals	140	3721	731	1590	.460	439	618	.710	716	236	1915	5.1	1.7	13.7

Three-point field goals: 1997-98, 1-for-11 (.091). 1998-99, 2-for-8 (.250). 1999-00, 9-for-35 (.257). 2000-01, 2-for-13 (.154). Totals, 14-for-67 (.209).

WNBA REGULAR-SEASON RECORD

Season Team	G	Min.	FGM	FGA	Pct.	FTM	FTA	Pct.	REBOUNDS Off.	Def.	Tot.	Ast.	St.	Blk.	TO	Pts.	AVERAGES RPG	APG	PPG
2001—Seattle	32	884	117	315	.371	66	100	.660	32	73	105	44	29	4	73	300	3.3	1.4	9.4
2002—Seattle-Utah	29	593	65	173	.376	58	80	.725	42	47	89	37	24	2	46	192	3.1	1.3	6.6
2003—San Antonio	33	339	32	90	.356	24	45	.533	25	28	53	23	11	0	44	88	1.6	0.7	2.7
Totals	94	1816	214	578	.370	148	225	.658	99	148	247	104	64	6	163	580	2.6	1.1	6.2

Three-point field goals: 2001, 0-for-4. 2002, 4-for-21 (.190). 2003, 0-for-1. Totals, 4-for-26 (.154).
Personal fouls/disqualifications: 2001, 45/0. 2002, 49/0. 2003, 41/0. Totals, 135/0.

WNBA PLAYOFF RECORD

Season Team	G	Min.	FGM	FGA	Pct.	FTM	FTA	Pct.	REBOUNDS Off.	Def.	Tot.	Ast.	St.	Blk.	TO	Pts.	AVERAGES RPG	APG	PPG
2002—Utah	5	62	8	22	.364	4	5	.800	3	9	12	5	1	0	3	20	2.4	1.0	4.0
Totals	5	62	8	22	.364	4	5	.800	3	9	12	5	1	0	3	20	2.4	1.0	4.0

RASMUSSEN, KRISTEN F   FEVER

PERSONAL: Born November 1, 1978, in East Lansing, Mich. ... 6-2/172 (1.88 m/78 kg).
HIGH SCHOOL: Okemos (Mich.).
COLLEGE: Michigan State.
TRANSACTIONS/CAREER NOTES: Selected by Utah in fourth round (51st overall) of WNBA Draft, April 25, 2000. ... Waived by Utah, June 8, 2000. ... Added by Miami, June 13, 2000.

COLLEGIATE RECORD

NOTES: All-Big Ten first team (2000). ... All-Big Ten second team (1999). ... Holds MSU career blocks record (194). ... Led Big Ten in blocks in 1999 (1.84 bpg). ... Led Big Ten in rebounding (9.8 rpg) double-doubles (16) in 2000.

Season Team	G	Min.	FGM	FGA	Pct.	FTM	FTA	Pct.	Reb.	Ast.	Pts.	AVERAGES RPG	APG	PPG
96-97—Michigan State	29	...	98	190	.516	46	67	.687	157	23	243	5.4	0.8	8.4
97-98—Michigan State	27	...	124	245	.506	74	91	.813	217	45	322	8.0	1.7	11.9
98-99—Michigan State	31	...	188	363	.518	87	109	.798	286	96	470	9.2	3.1	15.2
99-00—Michigan State	31	...	185	347	.533	81	101	.802	304	85	458	9.8	2.7	14.8
Totals	118	...	595	1145	.520	288	368	.783	964	249	1493	8.2	2.1	12.7

Three-point field goals: 1996-97, 1-for-1. 1997-98, 0-for-2. 1998-99, 7-for-21 (.333). 1999-00, 7-for-15 (.467). Totals, 15-for-39 (.385).

WNBA REGULAR-SEASON RECORD

Season Team	G	Min.	FGM	FGA	Pct.	FTM	FTA	Pct.	REBOUNDS Off.	Def.	Tot.	Ast.	St.	Blk.	TO	Pts.	AVERAGES RPG	APG	PPG
2000—Utah-Miami ..	26	463	35	100	.350	54	64	.844	45	53	98	28	25	14	30	126	3.8	1.1	4.8
2001—Miami	28	416	31	86	.360	12	16	.750	33	55	88	16	11	14	31	75	3.1	0.6	2.7
2002—Miami	31	674	64	116	.552	39	46	.848	41	76	117	41	18	16	37	170	3.8	1.3	5.5
2003—Indiana..........	33	814	94	200	.470	31	39	.795	44	71	115	64	24	15	48	226	3.5	1.9	6.8
Totals.................	118	2367	224	502	.446	136	165	.824	163	255	418	149	78	59	146	597	3.5	1.3	5.1

Three-point field goals: 2000, 2-for-7 (.286). 2001, 1-for-4 (.250). 2002, 3-for-7 (.429). 2003, 7-for-15 (.467). Totals, 13-for-33 (.394).
Personal fouls/disqualifications: 2000, 49/0. 2001, 48/0. 2002, 63/0. 2003, 65/0. Totals, 225/0.

WNBA PLAYOFF RECORD

Season Team	G	Min.	FGM	FGA	Pct.	FTM	FTA	Pct.	REBOUNDS Off.	Def.	Tot.	Ast.	St.	Blk.	TO	Pts.	AVERAGES RPG	APG	PPG
2001—Miami	3	23	0	5	.000	1	2	.500	3	3	6	0	1	0	6	1	2.0	0.0	0.3
Totals.................	3	23	0	5	.000	1	2	.500	3	3	6	0	1	0	6	1	2.0	0.0	0.3

R

REID, TRACY   F

PERSONAL: Born November 1, 1976, in Miami, Fla. ... 5-11/150 (1.80 m/68 kg). ... Full name: Tracy LaShawn Reid.
HIGH SCHOOL: Miami Central (Miami, Fla.).
COLLEGE: North Carolina.
TRANSACTIONS/CAREER NOTES: Selected by Charlotte in first round (7th overall) of WNBA Draft, April 28, 1999. ... Traded by Charlotte to Miami for C Shantia Owens, November 3, 2000. ... Traded by Miami with the 13th overall pick in the 2002 WNBA Draft to Phoenix for C Pollyanna Johns Kimbrough and the 15th pick, March 4, 2002. ... Waived by Phoenix, May 27, 2003.

COLLEGIATE RECORD

NOTES: Kodak All-America first team (1998).

Season Team	G	Min.	FGM	FGA	Pct.	FTM	FTA	Pct.	Reb.	Ast.	Pts.	AVERAGES RPG	APG	PPG
94-95—North Carolina..........	35	...	178	361	.493	91	151	.603	244	38	451	7.0	1.1	12.9
95-96—North Carolina..........	23	...	188	345	.545	61	98	.622	205	30	439	8.9	1.3	19.1
96-97—North Carolina..........	30	...	253	477	.530	115	189	.608	304	29	623	10.1	1.0	20.8
97-98—North Carolina..........	33	...	267	496	.538	152	250	.608	312	34	687	9.5	1.0	20.8
Totals	121	...	886	1679	.528	419	688	.609	1065	131	2200	8.8	1.1	18.2

Three-point field goals: 1994-95, 4-for-18 (.222). 1995-96, 2-for-6 (.333). 1996-97, 2-for-5 (.400). 1997-98, 1-for-3 (.333). Totals, 9-for-32 (.281).

WNBA REGULAR-SEASON RECORD

HONORS: WNBA Rookie of the Year (1998).

Season Team	G	Min.	FGM	FGA	Pct.	FTM	FTA	Pct.	REBOUNDS Off.	Def.	Tot.	Ast.	St.	Blk.	TO	Pts.	AVERAGES RPG	APG	PPG
1998—Charlotte	30	966	151	310	.487	111	181	.613	60	97	157	46	40	12	71	413	5.2	1.5	13.8
1999—Charlotte	10	154	21	49	.429	6	14	.429	7	16	23	9	1	2	17	48	2.3	0.9	4.8
2000—Charlotte	29	620	86	180	.478	39	72	.542	45	55	100	29	14	9	51	211	3.4	1.0	7.3
2001—Miami	21	278	32	63	.508	16	26	.615	10	27	37	13	15	5	25	80	1.8	0.6	3.8
2002—Phoenix.........	24	421	48	117	.410	17	28	.607	33	44	77	14	22	2	36	113	3.2	0.6	4.7
2003—Phoenix.........	2	12	1	3	.333	0	0	...	1	0	1	1	2	0	1	2	0.5	0.5	1.0
Totals.................	116	2451	339	722	.470	189	321	.589	156	239	395	112	94	30	201	867	3.4	1.0	7.5

Three-point field goals: 1998, 0-for-2. 1999, 0-for-1. 2000, 0-for-2. 2002, 0-for-1. Totals, 0-for-6.
Personal fouls/disqualifications: 1998, 59/1. 1999, 12/0. 2000, 47/1. 2002, 29/0. Totals, 179/2.

WNBA PLAYOFF RECORD

Season Team	G	Min.	FGM	FGA	Pct.	FTM	FTA	Pct.	REBOUNDS Off.	Def.	Tot.	Ast.	St.	Blk.	TO	Pts.	AVERAGES RPG	APG	PPG
1998—Charlotte	2	74	14	25	.560	4	11	.364	5	5	10	0	2	1	5	32	5.0	0.0	16.0
1999—Charlotte	3	7	1	2	.500	0	0	...	1	0	1	0	1	0	1	2	0.3	0.0	0.7
2001—Miami	3	21	2	5	.400	0	4	.000	1	4	5	1	1	0	2	4	1.7	0.3	1.3
Totals.................	8	102	17	32	.531	4	15	.267	7	9	16	1	4	1	8	38	2.0	0.1	4.8

RILEY, RUTH   C   SHOCK

PERSONAL: Born August 28, 1979, in Ranson, Kan. ... 6-5/195 (1.96 m/88 kg). ... Full name: Ruth Riley.
HIGH SCHOOL: North Miami (Macy, Ind.).
COLLEGE: Notre Dame.
TRANSACTIONS/CAREER NOTES: Selected by Miami in first round (fifth overall) of WNBA Draft, April 20, 2001. ... Slected first overall in Dispersal Draft, April 24, 2003.
MISCELLANEOUS: Member of WNBA Championship Team (2003).

COLLEGIATE RECORD

NOTES: Member of NCAA Division I championship team (2001). ... Naismith Award winner (2001). ... The Associated Press Player of the Year (2001) . ... Kodak All-America first team (2001). ... NCAA Final Four Most Outstanding Player (2001). ... Led NCAA in field goal percentage (.683) in 1998-99.

Season Team	G	Min.	FGM	FGA	Pct.	FTM	FTA	Pct.	Reb.	Ast.	Pts.	RPG	APG	PPG
97-98—Notre Dame	32	...	141	235	.600	86	115	.748	233	21	368	7.3	0.7	11.5
98-99—Notre Dame	31	...	198	290	.683	118	171	.690	260	40	514	8.4	1.3	16.6
99-00—Notre Dame	32	...	193	314	.615	132	164	.805	233	41	518	7.3	1.3	16.2
00-01—Notre Dame	36	...	245	390	.628	182	237	.768	281	70	672	7.8	1.9	18.7
Totals	131	...	777	1229	.632	518	687	.754	1007	172	2072	7.7	1.3	15.8

WNBA REGULAR-SEASON RECORD

Season Team	G	Min.	FGM	FGA	Pct.	FTM	FTA	Pct.	REBOUNDS Off.	Def.	Tot.	Ast.	St.	Blk.	TO	Pts.	AVERAGES RPG	APG	PPG
2001—Miami	32	799	77	162	.475	64	83	.771	51	79	130	26	25	46	63	218	4.1	0.8	6.8
2002—Miami	26	519	60	129	.465	28	46	.609	24	66	90	25	11	41	49	148	3.5	1.0	5.7
2003—Detroit	34	995	115	231	.498	97	127	.764	59	142	201	64	25	58	82	327	5.9	1.9	9.6
Totals	92	2313	252	522	.483	189	256	.738	134	287	421	115	61	145	194	693	4.6	1.3	7.5

WNBA PLAYOFF RECORD

NOTES: WNBA Finals Most Valuable Player (2003).

Season Team	G	Min.	FGM	FGA	Pct.	FTM	FTA	Pct.	REBOUNDS Off.	Def.	Tot.	Ast.	St.	Blk.	TO	Pts.	AVERAGES RPG	APG	PPG
2001—Miami	3	110	8	19	.421	8	19	.421	5	11	16	3	1	4	3	24	5.3	1.0	8.0
2003—Detroit	8	258	41	106	.387	21	26	.808	15	34	49	20	5	20	13	103	6.1	2.5	12.9
Totals	11	368	49	125	.392	29	45	.644	20	45	65	23	6	24	16	127	5.9	2.1	11.5

RIZZOTTI, JENNIFER   G   SHOCK

PERSONAL: Born May 15, 1974, in White Plains, N.Y. ... 5-6/146 (1.68 m/66 kg). ... **Full name:** Jennifer Marie Rizzotti.
HIGH SCHOOL: New Fairfield (New Fairfield, Conn.).
COLLEGE: Connecticut.
TRANSACTIONS/CAREER NOTES: Selected by Houston in fourth round (48th overall) of WNBA Draft, May 4, 1999. ... Traded to Detroit for G Anna DeForge, April 23, 2001. ... Traded by Detroit to Cleveland for a third-round pick in 2002 WNBA Draft, May 27, 2001. ... Selected by Detroit in the Dispersal Draft, January 6, 2004.
MISCELLANEOUS: Member of WNBA championship team (1999, 2000).

COLLEGIATE RECORD

NOTES: Wade Trophy recipient (1996). ... The Associated Press Player of the Year (1996). ... Kodak All-America first team (1995, 1996) . ... Member of NCAA Divison I championship team (1995) .

Season Team	G	Min.	FGM	FGA	Pct.	FTM	FTA	Pct.	Reb.	Ast.	Pts.	RPG	APG	PPG
92-93—Connecticut	29	...	116	288	.403	73	118	.619	125	104	358	4.3	3.6	12.3
93-94—Connecticut	33	...	110	239	.460	52	78	.667	111	150	326	3.4	4.5	9.9
94-95—Connecticut	35	...	156	308	.506	69	94	.734	97	161	438	2.8	4.6	12.5
95-96—Connecticut	38	...	148	355	.417	79	112	.705	126	222	418	3.3	5.8	11.0
Totals	135	...	530	1190	.445	273	402	.679	459	637	1540	3.4	4.7	11.4

Three-point field goals: 1992-93, 53-for-142 (.373). 1993-94, 54-for-126 (.429). 1994-95, 57-for-138 (.413). 1995-96, 43-for-158 (.272). Totals, 207-for-564 (.367).

ABL REGULAR-SEASON RECORD

NOTES: Member of ABL All-Star team (1997,1998).

Season Team	G	Min.	FGM	FGA	Pct.	FTM	FTA	Pct.	Reb.	Ast.	Pts.	RPG	APG	PPG
96-97—New England	40	...	101	250	.404	64	90	.711	130	231	314	3.3	5.8	7.9
97-98—New England	44	...	148	352	.420	127	166	.765	124	193	477	2.8	4.4	10.8
98-99—New England	13	...	43	113	.381	26	38	.684	55	56	128	4.2	4.3	9.8
Totals	97	...	292	715	.408	217	294	.738	309	480	919	3.2	4.9	9.5

Three-point field goals: 1996-97, 48-for-131 (.366). 1997-98, 54-for-172 (.314). 1998-99, 16-for-61 (.262). Totals, 118-for-364 (.324).

WNBA REGULAR-SEASON RECORD

Season Team	G	Min.	FGM	FGA	Pct.	FTM	FTA	Pct.	REBOUNDS Off.	Def.	Tot.	Ast.	St.	Blk.	TO	Pts.	AVERAGES RPG	APG	PPG
1999—Houston	25	242	14	40	.350	7	12	.583	2	25	27	19	18	1	16	42	1.1	0.8	1.7
2000—Houston	32	437	21	55	.382	6	9	.667	6	30	36	44	15	2	26	60	1.1	1.4	1.9
2001—Cleveland	32	476	42	110	.382	7	11	.636	2	28	30	51	25	2	41	119	0.9	1.6	3.7
2002—Cleveland	26	695	54	135	.400	32	40	.800	5	65	70	85	23	3	45	178	2.7	3.3	6.8
2003—Cleveland	33	525	20	72	.278	9	16	.563	4	38	42	65	14	0	35	59	1.3	2.0	1.8
Totals	148	2375	151	412	.367	61	88	.693	19	186	205	264	95	8	163	458	1.4	1.8	3.1

Three-point field goals: 1999, 7-for-26 (.269). 2000, 12-for-39 (.308). 2001, 28-for-73 (.384). 2002, 38-for-99 (.384). 2003, 10-for-51 (.196). Totals, 95-for-288 (.330).
Personal fouls/disqualifications: 1999, 21/0. 2000, 38/0. 2001, 30/0. 2002, 53/3. 2003, 22/0. Totals, 164/3.

WNBA PLAYOFF RECORD

Season Team	G	Min.	FGM	FGA	Pct.	FTM	FTA	Pct.	REBOUNDS Off.	Def.	Tot.	Ast.	St.	Blk.	TO	Pts.	AVERAGES RPG	APG	PPG
1999—Houston	2	5	0	1	.000	0	0	...	0	1	1	1	0	0	0	0	0.5	0.5	0.0
2000—Houston	1	3	0	1	.000	0	0	...	0	0	0	0	0	0	0	0	0.0	0.0	0.0
2001—Cleveland	3	45	2	6	.333	0	0	...	0	3	3	7	0	0		6	1.0	2.3	2.0
2003—Cleveland	3	36	4	6	.667	0	0	...	0	2	2	8	0	0	1	12	0.7	2.7	4.0
Totals	9	89	6	14	.429	0	0	...	0	6	6	16	0	0	1	18	0.7	1.8	2.0

Three-point field goals: 1999, 0-for-1. 2000, 0-for-1. 2001, 2-for-6 (.333). 2003, 4-for-6 (.667). Totals, 6-for-14 (.429).
Personal fouls/disqualifications: 1999, 0/0. 2000, 0/0. 2001, 2/0. 2003, 2/0. Totals, 4/0.

ROBINSON, CRYSTAL F LIBERTY

PERSONAL: Born January 22, 1974, in Atoka, Okla. ... 5-10/175 (1.78 m/79 kg).
HIGH SCHOOL: Atoka (Atoka, Okla.).
COLLEGE: Southeastern Oklahoma State.
TRANSACTIONS/CAREER NOTES: Selected by New York in first round (6th overall) of WNBA Draft, May 4, 1999.

COLLEGIATE RECORD

Season Team	G	Min.	FGM	FGA	Pct.	FTM	FTA	Pct.	Reb.	Ast.	Pts.	RPG	APG	PPG
92-93—SE Oklahoma St.	13	...	91	197	.462	54	75	.720	110	49	264	8.5	3.8	20.3
93-94—SE Oklahoma St.	28	...	307	609	.504	131	163	.804	289	120	830	10.3	4.3	29.6
94-95—SE Oklahoma St.	34	...	377	716	.527	162	185	.876	346	191	1032	10.2	5.6	30.4
95-96—SE Oklahoma St.	37	...	335	632	.530	123	153	.804	420	187	897	11.4	5.1	24.2
Totals	112	...	1110	2154	.515	470	576	.816	1165	547	3023	10.4	4.9	27.0

Three-point field goals: 1992-93, 28-for-72 (.389). 1993-94, 85-for-214 (.397). 1994-95, 116-for-260 (.446). 1995-96, 104-for-239 (.435). Totals, 333-for-785 (.424).

ABL REGULAR-SEASON RECORD

NOTES: Named ABL Rookie of the Year (1996-97).

Season Team	G	Min.	FGM	FGA	Pct.	FTM	FTA	Pct.	Reb.	Ast.	Pts.	RPG	APG	PPG
96-97—Colorado	40	...	236	486	.486	122	142	.859	263	108	684	6.6	2.7	17.1
97-98—Colorado	43	...	224	429	.522	92	114	.807	173	146	642	4.0	3.4	14.9
98-99—Colorado	9	...	22	68	.324	8	14	.571	27	29	63	3.0	3.2	7.0
Totals	92	...	482	983	.490	222	270	.822	463	283	1389	5.0	3.1	15.1

Three-point field goals: 1996-97, 90-for-208 (.433). 1997-98, 102-for-219 (.466). 1998-99, 11-for-32 (.344). Totals, 203-for-459 (.442).

WNBA REGULAR-SEASON RECORD

Season Team	G	Min.	FGM	FGA	Pct.	FTM	FTA	Pct.	REBOUNDS Off.	Def.	Tot.	Ast.	St.	Blk.	TO	Pts.	AVERAGES RPG	APG	PPG
1999—New York	32	901	125	285	.439	49	58	.845	38	51	89	49	44	11	46	375	2.8	1.5	11.7
2000—New York	27	722	86	201	.428	30	33	.909	26	42	68	48	23	10	33	238	2.5	1.8	8.8
2001—New York	32	980	123	267	.461	26	29	.897	23	69	92	83	32	8	28	342	2.9	2.6	10.7
2002—New York	32	1068	126	302	.417	59	72	.819	22	70	92	81	48	12	52	378	2.9	2.5	11.8
2003—New York	33	1078	143	326	.439	47	56	.839	13	57	70	63	40	13	43	395	2.1	1.9	12.0
Totals	156	4749	603	1381	.437	211	248	.851	122	289	411	324	187	54	202	1728	2.6	2.1	11.1

Three-point field goals: 1999, 76-for-174 (.437). 2000, 36-for-102 (.353). 2001, 70-for-168 (.417). 2002, 67-for-181 (.370). 2003, 62-for-168 (.369). Totals, 311-for-793 (.392).
Personal fouls/disqualifications: 1999, 78/1. 2000, 74/0. 2001, 86/1. 2002, 101/0. 2003, 94/0. Totals, 433/2.

WNBA PLAYOFF RECORD

Season Team	G	Min.	FGM	FGA	Pct.	FTM	FTA	Pct.	REBOUNDS Off.	Def.	Tot.	Ast.	St.	Blk.	TO	Pts.	AVERAGES RPG	APG	PPG
1999—New York	6	205	32	64	.500	7	7	1.000	7	11	18	13	6	2	10	86	3.0	2.2	14.3
2000—New York	7	150	16	39	.410	5	5	1.000	7	13	20	5	9	1	10	46	2.9	0.7	6.6
2001—New York	6	223	27	54	.500	3	4	.750	7	16	23	8	8	2	14	69	3.8	1.3	11.5
2002—New York	8	259	23	65	.354	9	9	1.000	8	16	24	14	8	2	5	67	3.0	1.8	8.4
Totals	27	837	98	222	.441	24	25	.960	29	56	85	40	31	7	39	268	3.1	1.5	9.9

Three-point field goals: 1999, 15-for-39 (.385). 2000, 9-for-19 (.474). 2001, 12-for-29 (.414). 2002, 12-for-39 (.308). Totals, 48-for-126 (.381).
Personal fouls/disqualifications: 1999, 20/1. 2000, 12/0. 2001, 15/0. 2002, 17/0. Totals, 64/1.

SALES, NYKESHA F SUN

PERSONAL: Born May 10, 1976, in Bloomfield, Conn. ... 6-0/184 (1.83 m/83 kg). ... **Full name:** Nykesha Simone Sales.
HIGH SCHOOL: Bloomfield (Bloomfield, Conn.).
COLLEGE: Connecticut.
TRANSACTIONS/CAREER NOTES: Signed by WNBA and assigned to Orlando, September 15, 1998.

COLLEGIATE RECORD

NOTES: Member of NCAA Division I championship team (1995). ... Kodak All-American first team (1997, 1998).

Season Team	G	Min.	FGM	FGA	Pct.	FTM	FTA	Pct.	Reb.	Ast.	Pts.	RPG	APG	PPG
94-95—Connecticut	35	...	159	294	.541	45	77	.584	162	73	398	4.6	2.1	11.4
95-96—Connecticut	38	...	237	459	.516	92	131	.702	168	101	596	4.4	2.7	15.7
96-97—Connecticut	34	...	215	420	.512	97	128	.758	192	111	556	5.6	3.3	16.4
97-98—Connecticut	30	...	241	426	.566	106	135	.785	166	86	628	5.5	2.9	20.9
Totals	137	...	852	1599	.533	340	471	.722	688	371	2178	5.0	2.7	15.9

Three-point field goals: 1994-95, 35-for-81 (.432). 1995-96, 30-for-89 (.337). 1996-97, 29-for-81 (.358). 1997-98, 40-for-105 (.381). Totals, 134-for-356 (.376)

WNBA REGULAR-SEASON RECORD

NOTES: Did not play during the 1998 WNBA season due to rehabilitation of Achilles tendon after rupture suffered on February 21, 1998.

Season Team	G	Min.	FGM	FGA	Pct.	FTM	FTA	Pct.	Off.	Def.	Tot.	Ast.	St.	Blk.	TO	Pts.	RPG	APG	PPG
1999—Orlando	32	1039	153	397	.385	95	118	.805	44	91	135	91	69	8	69	437	4.2	2.8	13.7
2000—Orlando	32	995	170	383	.444	43	62	.694	43	96	139	69	47	12	67	430	4.3	2.2	13.4
2001—Orlando	32	1039	166	379	.438	58	74	.784	57	115	172	58	70	6	72	433	5.4	1.8	13.5
2002—Orlando	32	1042	155	376	.412	84	106	.792	36	84	120	60	60	7	71	431	3.8	1.9	13.5
2003—Connecticut....	34	1106	194	468	.415	116	144	.806	27	118	145	92	46	13	73	548	4.3	2.7	16.1
Totals.................	162	5221	838	2003	.418	396	504	.786	207	504	711	370	292	46	352	2279	4.4	2.3	14.1

Three-point field goals: 1999, 36-for-109 (.330). 2000, 47-for-119 (.395). 2001, 43-for-137 (.314). 2002, 37-for-115 (.322). 2003, 44-for-114 (.386). Totals, 207-for-594 (.348).
Personal fouls/disqualifications: 1999, 97/2. 2000, 92/2. 2001, 109/0. 2002, 97/0. 2003, 107/3. Totals, 502/7.

WNBA PLAYOFF RECORD

Season Team	G	Min.	FGM	FGA	Pct.	FTM	FTA	Pct.	Off.	Def.	Tot.	Ast.	St.	Blk.	TO	Pts.	RPG	APG	PPG
2000—Orlando	3	106	15	31	.484	0	2	.000	1	8	9	4	3	0	9	33	3.0	1.3	11.0
2003—Connecticut ...	4	131	17	40	.425	13	18	.722	1	12	13	9	5	3	7	47	3.3	2.3	11.8
Totals.................	7	237	32	71	.451	13	20	.650	2	20	22	13	8	3	16	80	3.1	1.9	11.4

Three-point field goals: 2000, 3-for-10 (.300). 2003, 0-for-6. Totals, 3-for-16 (.188).
Personal fouls/disqualifications: 2000, 9/0. 2003, 12/0. Totals, 21/0.

WNBA ALL-STAR GAME RECORD

Season Team	Min.	FGM	FGA	Pct.	FTM	FTA	Pct.	Off.	Def.	Tot.	Ast.	PF	Dq.	St.	Blk.	TO	Pts.
1999—Orlando............	17	3	8	.375	0	2	.000	0	0	0	1	1	0	0	0	...	6
2000—Orlando............	13	2	5	.400	0	0	...	3	0	3	1	1	0	2	0	...	5
2001—Orlando............	10	4	8	.500	1	2	.500	0	1	1	0	1	0	0	0	...	10
2002—Orlando............	14	3	11	.273	3	3	1.000	1	0	1	0	2	0	2	0	...	9
2003—Connecticut......	11	3	6	.500	0	0	...	0	1	1	0	1	0	1	0	...	7
Totals.................	65	15	38	.395	4	7	.571	4	2	6	2	6	0	5	0	6	37

Three-point field goals: 1999, 0-for-3. 2000, 1-for-3 (.333). 2001, 1-for-3 (.333). 2002, 0-for-2. 2003, 1-for-3 (.333). Totals, 3-for-14 (.214).

SAM, SHERI   G/F   STORM

PERSONAL: Born May 5, 1974, in Duson, La. ... 6-0/160 (1.83 m/73 kg). ... **Full name:** Sheri Lynette Sam.
HIGH SCHOOL: Acadiana (Lafayette, La.).
COLLEGE: Vanderbilt.
TRANSACTIONS/CAREER NOTES: Selected by Orlando in second round (20th overall) of WNBA Draft, May 4, 1999. ... Waived by Orlando, May 28, 2000. ... Signed by Miami, June 1, 2000. ... Selected by Minnesota in the 2003 Dispersal Draft, April 24, 2003. ...Traded by Minnesota along with Janell Burse to the Storm in exchange for Amanda Lassiter and a first round pick (sixth overall) in the 2004 WNBA Draft on April 15, 2004.

COLLEGIATE RECORD

NOTES: Kodak All-America first team (1996).

Season Team	G	Min.	FGM	FGA	Pct.	FTM	FTA	Pct.	Reb.	Ast.	Pts.	RPG	APG	PPG
92-93—Vanderbilt	24	...	32	61	.525	13	27	.481	50	11	77	2.1	0.5	3.2
93-94—Vanderbilt	33	...	125	240	.521	51	75	.680	206	64	304	6.2	1.9	9.2
94-95—Vanderbilt	35	...	224	417	.537	88	118	.746	291	126	544	8.3	3.6	15.5
95-96—Vanderbilt	30	...	244	427	.571	111	147	.755	215	105	612	7.2	3.5	20.4
Totals	122	...	625	1145	.546	263	367	.717	762	306	1537	6.2	2.5	12.6

Three-point field goals: 1993-94, 3-for-6 (.500). 1994-95, 8-for-25 (.320). 1995-96, 13-for-41 (.317). Totals, 24-for-72 (.333).

ABL REGULAR-SEASON RECORD

NOTES: Member of ABL All-Star team (1997 and 1998).

Season Team	G	Min.	FGM	FGA	Pct.	FTM	FTA	Pct.	Reb.	Ast.	Pts.	RPG	APG	PPG
96-97—San Jose	39	...	210	487	.431	105	146	.719	210	117	561	5.4	3.0	14.4
97-98—San Jose	43	...	238	550	.433	98	154	.636	305	109	624	7.1	2.5	14.5
98-99—San Jose	15	...	87	181	.481	19	34	.559	88	36	203	5.9	2.4	13.5
Totals	97	...	535	1218	.439	222	334	.665	603	262	1388	6.2	2.7	14.3

Three-point field goals: 1996-97, 36-for-117 (.308). 1997-98, 50-for-127 (.394). 1998-99, 10-for-35 (.286). Totals, 96-for-279 (.344).

WNBA REGULAR-SEASON RECORD

Season Team	G	Min.	FGM	FGA	Pct.	FTM	FTA	Pct.	Off.	Def.	Tot.	Ast.	St.	Blk.	TO	Pts.	RPG	APG	PPG
1999—Orlando	32	1088	134	345	.388	55	80	.688	39	107	146	77	41	9	64	364	4.6	2.4	11.4
2000—Orlando-Mia..	31	904	147	380	.387	67	100	.670	38	94	132	66	35	5	74	396	4.3	2.1	12.8
2001—Miami	32	1100	180	417	.432	57	76	.750	41	96	137	88	55	8	87	444	4.3	2.8	13.9
2002—Miami	32	1073	191	440	.434	55	89	.618	58	97	155	83	69	6	71	463	4.8	2.6	14.5
2003—Minnesota	34	953	138	360	.383	74	105	.705	46	96	142	88	38	6	48	374	4.2	2.6	11.0
Totals.................	161	5118	790	1942	.407	308	450	.684	222	490	712	402	238	34	344	2041	4.4	2.5	12.7

Three-point field goals: 1999, 41-for-125 (.328). 2000, 35-for-120 (.292). 2001, 27-for-98 (.276). 2002, 26-for-76 (.342). 2003, 24-for-73 (.329). Totals, 153-for-492 (.311).
Personal fouls/disqualifications: 1999, 112/4. 2000, 67/0. 2001, 67/0. 2002, 83/0. 2003, 70/0. Totals, 399/4.

WNBA PLAYOFF RECORD

Season Team	G	Min.	FGM	FGA	Pct.	FTM	FTA	Pct.	Off.	Def.	Tot.	Ast.	St.	Blk.	TO	Pts.	RPG	APG	PPG
2001—Miami	3	109	10	31	.323	9	11	.818	4	6	10	4	5	0	8	31	3.3	1.3	10.3
2003—Minnesota	3	74	10	28	.357	6	8	.750	5	11	16	8	6	0	8	26	5.3	2.7	8.7
Totals.................	6	183	20	59	.339	15	19	.789	9	17	26	12	11	0	16	57	4.3	2.0	9.5

Three-point field goals: 2001, 2-for-9 (.222). 2003, 0-for-4. Totals, 2-for-13 (.154).
Personal fouls/disqualifications: 2001, 11/1. 2003, 6/0. Totals, 17/1.

Season Team	Min.	FGM	FGA	Pct.	FTM	FTA	Pct.	REBOUNDS Off.	Def.	Tot.	Ast.	PF	Dq.	St.	Blk.	TO	Pts.
2002—Miami.................	19	3	9	.333	0	0	...	2	3	5	2	1	0	1	0	...	7
Totals.................	19	3	9	.333	0	0	...	2	3	5	2	1	0	1	0	0	7

Three-point field goals: 2002, 1-for-4 (.250). Totals, 1-for-4 (.250).

SANFORD, NAKIA   F/C   MYSTICS

PERSONAL: Born May 10, 1976 in Lithaonia, Ga. ... 6-2/182 (1.88 m/83 kg).
HIGH SCHOOL: South Gwinnette (Atlanta).
COLLEGE: Kansas.
TRANSACTIONS: Signed with the Washington Mystics on April 30, 2003.

COLLEGIATE RECORD

Season Team	G	Min.	FGM	FGA	Pct.	FTM	FTA	Pct.	REBOUNDS Off.	Def.	Tot.	Ast.	St.	Blk.	TO	Pts.	AVERAGES RPG	APG	PPG
95-96—Kansas	32	807	86	174	.494	37	74	.400			211	16	39	71	26	209	6.5	0.5	6.5
96-97—Kansas	31	839	90	185	.486	45	93	.484			218	16	37	66	30	225	7.0	0.5	7.3
97-98—Kansas	32	806	76	176	.432	60	109	.550			194	28	20	69	18	212	6.0	0.8	6.6
98-99—Kanas	33	951	136	261	.521	51	96	.531			209	28	28	82	15	323	6.3	0.8	9.8
Totals	128	3403	388	796	.487	193	372	.519			832	88	124	288	89	969	6.5	0.6	7.6

Three-point field goals: 2003-04, 0-for-1. Totals, 0-for-1.

WNBA REGULAR-SEASON RECORD

Season Team	G	Min.	FGM	FGA	Pct.	FTM	FTA	Pct.	REBOUNDS Off.	Def.	Tot.	Ast.	St.	Blk.	TO	Pts.	AVERAGES RPG	APG	PPG
2003—Washington.....	17	134	20	40	.500	9	20	.450	10	16	26	1	3	2	14	49	1.5	0.1	2.9
Totals.......................	17	134	20	40	.500	9	20	.450	10	16	26	1	3	2	14	49	1.5	0.1	2.9

SCHUMACHER, KELLY   C   FEVER

PERSONAL: Born October 14, 1977, in Cincinnati, Ohio ... 6-4/189 (1.93 m/86 kg). ... **Full name:** Kelly Marie Schumacher.
HIGH SCHOOL: Pontiac (Guyon, Quebec, Canada).
COLLEGE: Connecticut.
TRANSACTIONS/CAREER NOTES: Selected by Indiana in first round (14th overall) of WNBA Draft, April 20, 2001.

COLLEGIATE RECORD

NOTES: Member of NCAA Division I championship team (2000).

Season Team	G	Min.	FGM	FGA	Pct.	FTM	FTA	Pct.	Reb.	Ast.	Pts.	AVERAGES RPG	APG	PPG
97-98—Connecticut	35	408	70	117	.598	37	70	.529	103	19	177	2.9	0.5	5.1
98-99—Connecticut	31	356	63	113	.558	46	70	.657	130	16	172	4.2	0.5	5.5
99-00—Connecticut	37	577	80	144	.556	26	38	.684	141	27	186	3.8	0.7	5.0
00-01—Connecticut	29	491	75	143	.524	30	39	.769	126	28	182	4.3	1.0	6.3
Totals	132	1832	288	517	.557	139	217	.641	500	90	717	3.8	0.7	5.4

Three-point field goals: 2000-01, 2-for-9 (.222).

WNBA REGULAR-SEASON RECORD

Season Team	G	Min.	FGM	FGA	Pct.	FTM	FTA	Pct.	REBOUNDS Off.	Def.	Tot.	Ast.	St.	Blk.	TO	Pts.	AVERAGES RPG	APG	PPG
2001—Indiana..........	28	380	46	93	.495	17	20	.850	23	47	70	10	5	29	21	112	2.5	0.4	4.0
2002—Indiana..........	31	352	45	89	.506	18	26	.692	18	41	59	13	7	23	21	108	1.9	0.4	3.5
2003—Indiana..........	34	480	81	169	.479	23	27	.852	40	59	99	20	7	24	32	189	2.9	0.6	5.6
Totals.................	93	1212	172	351	.490	58	73	.795	81	147	228	43	19	76	74	409	2.5	0.5	4.4

Three-point field goals: 2001, 3-for-5 (.600). 2002, 0-for-1. 2003, 4-for-9 (.444). Totals, 7-for-15 (.467).
Personal fouls/disqualifications: 2001, 41/0. 2002, 49/0. 2003, 63/0. Totals, 153/0.

WNBA PLAYOFF RECORD

Season Team	G	Min.	FGM	FGA	Pct.	FTM	FTA	Pct.	REBOUNDS Off.	Def.	Tot.	Ast.	St.	Blk.	TO	Pts.	AVERAGES RPG	APG	PPG
2002—Indiana..........	3	52	13	20	.650	4	8	.500	6	3	9	3	0	2	2	32	3.0	1.0	10.7
Totals.................	3	52	13	20	.650	4	8	.500	6	3	9	3	0	2	2	32	3.0	1.0	10.7

Three-point field goals: 2002, 2-for-2. Totals, 2-for-2 (1.000).
Personal fouls/disqualifications: 2002, 6/0. Totals, 6/0.

SCHWEITZER, GEORGIA   G/F   LYNX

PERSONAL: Born January 31, 1979, in Columbus, Ohio ... 5-11/161 (1.80 m/73 kg). ... **Full name:** Georgia Marie Schweitzer.
HIGH SCHOOL: Bishop Hartley (Columbus, Ohio).
COLLEGE: Duke.
TRANSACTIONS/CAREER NOTES: Selected by Miami in second round (21st overall) of WNBA Draft, April 20, 2001. ... Traded to Minnesota for G Marla Brumfield, April 20, 2001.

COLLEGIATE RECORD

NOTES: Kodak All-America first team (2001).

Season Team	G	Min.	FGM	FGA	Pct.	FTM	FTA	Pct.	Reb.	Ast.	Pts.	AVERAGES RPG	APG	PPG
97-98—Duke........................	32	816	85	205	.415	40	54	.741	89	73	247	2.8	2.3	7.7
98-99—Duke........................	36	958	132	270	.489	56	83	.675	147	103	360	4.1	2.9	10.0
99-00—Duke........................	34	1069	187	408	.458	98	127	.772	136	112	532	4.0	3.3	15.6

S

Season Team	G	Min.	FGM	FGA	Pct.	FTM	FTA	Pct.	Off.	Def.	Tot.	Ast.	St.	Blk.	TO	Pts.	RPG	APG	PPG
00-01—Duke	34	1100	175	365	.479	66	94	.702			161	140				481	4.7	4.1	14.1
Totals	136	3943	579	1248	.464	260	358	.726			533	428				1620	3.9	3.1	11.9

Three-point field goals: 1997-98, 37-for-104 (.356). 1998-99, 40-for-96 (.417). 1999-00, 60-for-149 (.403). 2000-01, 65-for-155 (.419). Totals, 202-for-504 (.401).

WNBA REGULAR-SEASON RECORD

Season Team	G	Min.	FGM	FGA	Pct.	FTM	FTA	Pct.	REBOUNDS Off.	Def.	Tot.	Ast.	St.	Blk.	TO	Pts.	AVERAGES RPG	APG	PPG
2001—Minnesota	24	423	33	103	.320	13	17	.765	15	35	50	34	11	6	17	87	2.1	1.4	3.6
2002—Minnesota	30	509	42	87	.483	26	30	.867	7	44	51	37	15	5	27	124	1.7	1.2	4.1
2003—Minnesota	16	118	6	17	.353	0	0	...	7	11	18	7	3	1	8	15	1.1	0.4	0.9
Totals	70	1050	81	207	.391	39	47	.830	29	90	119	78	29	12	52	226	1.7	1.1	3.2

Three-point field goals: 2001, 8-for-43 (.186). 2002, 14-for-33 (.424). 2003, 3-for-9 (.333). Totals, 25-for-85 (.294).
Personal fouls/disqualifications: 2001, 34/1. 2002, 47/1. 2003, 6/0. Totals, 87/2.

SCOTT-RICHARDSON, OLYMPIA   C   FEVER

PERSONAL: Born August 5, 1976, in Los Angelos, Calif. ... 6-2/175. (1.88 m/79 kg). ... **Full name:** Olympia Ranee Scott-Richardson.
HIGH SCHOOL: St. Bernard (Playa del Rey, Calif.).
COLLEGE: Stanford.
TRANSACTIONS/CAREER NOTES: Selected by Utah in second round (11th overall) of WNBA Draft, April 29, 1998 . ... Traded by Utah with F Wendy Palmer to the Detroit Shock for G Korie Hlede and F Cindy Brown, July 29, 1999. ... Traded by Detroit with a third-round pick the 2002 WNBA Draft to Indiana for a second-round pick in the 2002 WNBA Draft, May 27, 2001.

COLLEGIATE RECORD

Season Team	G	Min.	FGM	FGA	Pct.	FTM	FTA	Pct.	Reb.	Ast.	Pts.	AVERAGES RPG	APG	PPG
94-95—Stanford	23	...	55	118	.466	31	53	.585	106	18	141	4.6	0.8	6.1
95-96—Stanford	32	...	131	267	.491	67	105	.638	163	23	329	5.1	0.7	10.3
96-97—Stanford	36	...	226	411	.550	130	180	.722	281	37	582	7.8	1.0	16.2
97-98—Stanford	27	...	177	307	.577	118	172	.686	203	39	472	7.5	1.4	17.5
Totals	118	...	589	1103	.534	346	510	.678	753	117	1524	6.4	1.0	12.9

Three-point field goals: 1997-98, 0-for-1.

WNBA REGULAR-SEASON RECORD

Season Team	G	Min.	FGM	FGA	Pct.	FTM	FTA	Pct.	REBOUNDS Off.	Def.	Tot.	Ast.	St.	Blk.	TO	Pts.	AVERAGES RPG	APG	PPG
1998—Utah	29	466	58	135	.430	37	65	.569	37	48	85	22	24	10	49	154	2.9	0.8	5.3
1999—Utah-Detroit..	12	88	9	28	.321	7	12	.583	8	12	20	5	1	3	8	25	1.7	0.4	2.1
2000—Detroit	28	369	37	89	.416	26	40	.650	28	52	80	28	12	10	45	100	2.9	1.0	3.6
2001—Indiana	32	775	99	217	.456	82	111	.739	52	109	161	40	22	12	72	280	5.0	1.3	8.8
2002—Indiana	31	975	113	232	.487	66	82	.805	80	131	211	52	38	13	69	292	6.8	1.7	9.4
2003								Did not play.											
Totals	132	2673	316	701	.451	218	310	.703	205	352	557	147	97	48	243	851	4.2	1.1	6.4

Three-point field goals: 1998, 1-for-5 (.200). 2000, 0-for-2. 2001, 0-for-2. 2002, 0-for-4. Totals, 1-for-13 (.077).
Personal fouls/disqualifications: 1998, 78/2. 2000, 83/2. 2001, 108/1. 2002, 127/2. Totals, 417/7.

WNBA PLAYOFF RECORD

Season Team	G	Min.	FGM	FGA	Pct.	FTM	FTA	Pct.	REBOUNDS Off.	Def.	Tot.	Ast.	St.	Blk.	TO	Pts.	AVERAGES RPG	APG	PPG
2002—Indiana	3	99	8	16	.500	5	5	1.000	7	17	24	5	1	1	14	21	8.0	1.7	7.0
Totals	3	99	8	16	.500	5	5	1.000	7	17	24	5	1	1	14	21	8.0	1.7	7.0

Personal fouls/disqualifications: 2002, 11/0. Totals, 11/0.

SHARP, K.B.   G   LIBERTY

PERSONAL: Born April 18, 1981, in Columbus, Ohio. ... 5-9/149 (1.75 m/68 kg). ... **Full name:** Kristen Brooke Sharp.
HIGH SCHOOL: Bexley (Columbus, Ohio).
COLLEGE: Cincinnati.
TRANSACTIONS/CAREER NOTES: Selected by New York in second round (26th overall) of WNBA Draft, April 25, 2003.

COLLEGIATE RECORD
NOTES: All-Conference USA First Team (2003). ... All-Conference USA Third Team (2002). ... Broke her own UC single-season records for assists (205) and minutes (1,214) as a junior.

Season Team	G	Min.	FGM	FGA	Pct.	FTM	FTA	Pct.	Reb.	Ast.	Pts.	AVERAGES RPG	APG	PPG
99-00—Cincinnati	31	708	66	152	.434	20	31	.645	...	64	174	1.9	2.1	5.6
00-01—Cincinnati	32	1207	99	238	.416	46	72	.639	...	170	266	3.6	5.3	8.3
01-02—Cincinnati	32	1214	101	247	.409	70	87	.805	...	205	301	4.4	6.4	9.4
02-03—Cincinnati	31	1210	145	352	.412	105	128	.820	...	184	423	5.7	5.9	13.6
Totals	126	4339	411	989	.416	241	318	.758	0	623	1164	0.0	4.9	9.2

Three-point field goals: 1999-00, 22-for-73 (.301). 2000-01, 22-for-74 (.297). 2001-02, 29-for-93 (.312). 2002-03, 28-for-116 (.241). Totals, 101-for-356 (.284).

WNBA REGULAR-SEASON RECORD

Season Team	G	Min.	FGM	FGA	Pct.	FTM	FTA	Pct.	REBOUNDS Off.	Def.	Tot.	Ast.	St.	Blk.	TO	Pts.	AVERAGES RPG	APG	PPG
2003—New York	30	398	28	71	.394	31	39	.795	11	21	32	37	14	0	26	94	1.1	1.2	3.1
Totals	30	398	28	71	.394	31	39	.795	11	21	32	37	14	0	26	94	1.1	1.2	3.1

Three-point field goals: 2003, 7-for-24 (.292). Totals, 7-for-24 (.292).
Personal fouls/disqualifications: 2003, 15/0. Totals, 15/0.

S

SLAVTCHEVA, GERGANA G   MERCURY

PERSONAL: Born October 20, 1979, in Sofia, Bulgaria. ... 6-1/160 (1.85 m/73 kg). ... **Full name:** Gergana Danova Slavtcheva.
HIGH SCHOOL: Vania Voinova (Sofia, Bulgaria).
COLLEGE: Florida International.
TRANSACTIONS/CAREER NOTES: Selected by Los Angeles in second round (30th overall) of WNBA Draft, April 19, 2002. ... Signed by Phoenix, July 15, 2003.

COLLEGIATE RECORD

Season Team	G	Min.	FGM	FGA	Pct.	FTM	FTA	Pct.	Reb.	Ast.	Pts.	RPG	APG	PPG
98-99—Florida International...	28	444	57	131	.435	43	55	.782	76	36	171	2.7	1.3	6.1
99-00—Florida International...	29	994	170	405	.420	114	147	.776	231	126	511	8.0	4.3	17.6
00-01—Florida International...	30	1098	193	500	.386	149	182	.819	181	107	593	6.0	3.6	19.8
01-02—Florida International...	33	1115	179	439	.408	147	190	.774	252	107	548	7.6	3.2	16.6
Totals	120	3651	599	1475	.406	453	574	.789	740	376	1823	6.2	3.1	15.2

Three-point field goals: 1998-99, 14-for-35 (.400). 1999-00, 57-for-152 (.375). 2000-01, 58-for-178 (.326). 2001-02, 43-for-127 (.339). Totals, 172-for-492 (.350).

WNBA REGULAR-SEASON RECORD

Season Team	G	Min.	FGM	FGA	Pct.	FTM	FTA	Pct.	Off.	Def.	Tot.	Ast.	St.	Blk.	TO	Pts.	RPG	APG	PPG
2003—Phoenix.........	2	12	0	2	.000	0	0	...	0	0	0	1	0	0	1	0	0.0	0.5	0.0
Totals.................	2	12	0	2	.000	0	0	...	0	0	0	1	0	0	1	0	0.0	0.5	0.0

Three-point field goals: 2003, 0-for-2. Totals, 0-for-2.
Personal fouls/disqualifications: 2003, 2/0. Totals, 2/0.

SMITH, AIYSHA   F   MYSTICS

PERSONAL: Born July 18, 1980, in Detroit. ... 6-2/173 (1.88 m/78 kg). ... **Full name:** Aiysha Kenya Smith.
HIGH SCHOOL: Bishop Borgess (Detroit).
JUNIOR COLLEGE: Tyler (Texas) Junior College.
COLLEGE: St. John's, then Louisiana State.
TRANSACTIONS/CAREER NOTES: Selected by Washington in first round (sixth overall) of WNBA Draft, April 25, 2003.

COLLEGIATE RECORD

NOTES: All-SEC First Team (2002). ... All-SEC honorable mention (2003). ... Kodak All-America First Team (2001). ... NJCAA All-America (2001).

Season Team	G	Min.	FGM	FGA	Pct.	FTM	FTA	Pct.	Reb.	Ast.	Pts.	RPG	APG	PPG
99-00—St. John's.....................	29	828	106	280	.379	62	81	.765	...	49	276	7.1	1.7	9.5
00-01—Tyler JC	26	...	141	268	.526	65	88	.739	...	69	347	9.3	2.7	13.3
01-02—Louisiana State..........	30	986	189	370	.511	97	129	.752	...	34	476	7.7	1.1	15.9
02-03—Louisiana State..........	34	929	167	357	.468	101	131	.771	...	37	449	5.6	1.1	13.2
Totals	93	2743	462	1007	.459	260	341	.762	0	120	1201	0.0	1.3	12.9

Three-point field goals: 1999-00, 2-for-15 (.133). 2000-01, 0-for-7. 2001-02, 1-for-10 (.100). 2002-03, 14-for-54 (.259). Totals, 17-for-79 (.215).

WNBA REGULAR-SEASON RECORD

Season Team	G	Min.	FGM	FGA	Pct.	FTM	FTA	Pct.	Off.	Def.	Tot.	Ast.	St.	Blk.	TO	Pts.	RPG	APG	PPG
2003—Washington ...	31	422	41	120	.342	17	34	.500	21	44	65	10	11	9	26	104	2.1	0.3	3.4
Totals.................	31	422	41	120	.342	17	34	.500	21	44	65	10	11	9	26	104	2.1	0.3	3.4

Three-point field goals: 2003, 5-for-34 (.147). Totals, 5-for-34 (.147).
Personal fouls/disqualifications: 2003, 44/0. Totals, 44/0.

SMITH, CHARMIN   G

PERSONAL: Born May 2, 1975, in St. Louis, Mo. ... 5-10/145 (1.78 m/66 kg).
HIGH SCHOOL: Ladue (St. Louis, Mo.).
COLLEGE: Stanford.
TRANSACTIONS/CAREER NOTES: Signed as free agent by Minnesota, May 12, 1999. ... Selected by Seattle in sixth round (23rd overall) of WNBA Expansion Draft, December 15, 1999.

COLLEGIATE RECORD

Season Team	G	Min.	FGM	FGA	Pct.	FTM	FTA	Pct.	Reb.	Ast.	Pts.	RPG	APG	PPG
93-94—Stanford	24	...	10	23	.435	12	16	.750	26	4	36	1.1	0.2	1.5
94-95—Stanford	31	...	17	49	.347	14	21	.667	52	4	54	1.7	0.1	1.7
95-96—Stanford	32	...	31	106	.292	13	20	.650	111	8	89	3.5	0.3	2.8
96-97—Stanford	36	...	53	149	.356	36	52	.692	123	4	168	3.4	0.1	4.7
Totals	123	...	111	327	.339	75	109	.688	312	20	347	2.5	0.2	2.8

Three-point field goals: 1993-94, 4-for-11 (.364). 1994-95, 6-for-18 (.333). 1995-96, 14-for-54 (.259). 1996-97, 26-for-77 (.338). Totals, 50-for-160 (.313).

WNBA REGULAR-SEASON RECORD

Season Team	G	Min.	FGM	FGA	Pct.	FTM	FTA	Pct.	Off.	Def.	Tot.	Ast.	St.	Blk.	TO	Pts.	RPG	APG	PPG
1999—Minnesota	13	56	1	9	.111	8	10	.800	2	7	9	2	1	0	5	10	0.7	0.2	0.8
2000—Seattle	32	516	16	56	.286	10	18	.556	14	33	47	53	16	3	32	52	1.5	1.7	1.6

	G	Min.	FGM	FGA	Pct.	FTM	FTA	Pct.	Off.	Def.	Tot.	Ast.	St.	Blk.	TO	Pts.	RPG	APG	PPG
2001—Seattle	32	589	17	63	.270	13	21	.619	18	37	55	39	17	1	26	58	1.7	1.2	1.8
2003—Phoenix........	4	17	0	2	.000	0	0	...	1	3	4	1	0	0	0	0	1.0	0.3	0.0
Totals................	81	1178	34	80	.261	31	49	.633	35	80	115	95	34	4	63	120	1.4	1.2	1.5

Three-point field goals: 1999, 0-for-4. 2000, 10-for-32 (.313). 2001, 11-for-38 (.289). Totals, 21-for-74 (.284).
Personal fouls/disqualifications: 1999, 10/0. 2000, 52/0. 2001, 52/0. 2003, 2/0. Totals, 116/0.

SMITH, KATIE   F   LYNX

PERSONAL: Born June 4, 1974, in Lancaster, Ohio ... 5-11/181 (1.80 m/82 kg). ... **Full name:** Katherine May Smith.
HIGH SCHOOL: Logan (Logan, Ohio).
COLLEGE: Ohio State.
TRANSACTIONS/CAREER NOTES: Signed by WNBA and allocated to Minnesota Lynx, May 3, 1999.

COLLEGIATE RECORD

NOTES: Kodak All-America first team (1993, 1996).

Season Team	G	Min.	FGM	FGA	Pct.	FTM	FTA	Pct.	Reb.	Ast.	Pts.	RPG	APG	PPG
92-93—Ohio State.................	32	...	189	375	.504	164	203	.808	186	104	578	5.8	3.3	18.1
93-94—Ohio State.................	28	...	211	428	.493	149	182	.819	170	87	616	6.1	3.1	22.0
94-95—Ohio State.................	30	...	196	433	.453	190	225	.844	174	108	639	5.8	3.6	21.3
95-96—Ohio State.................	34	...	230	527	.436	205	235	.872	174	145	745	5.1	4.3	21.9
Totals	124	...	826	1763	.469	708	845	.838	704	444	2578	5.7	3.6	20.8

Three-point field goals: 1992-93, 36-for-80 (.450). 1993-94, 45-for-119 (.378). 1994-95, 57-for-155 (.368). 1995-96, 80-for-210 (.381). Totals, 218-for-564 (.387).

ABL REGULAR-SEASON RECORD

Season Team	G	Min.	FGM	FGA	Pct.	FTM	FTA	Pct.	Reb.	Ast.	Pts.	RPG	APG	PPG
96-97—Columbus	40	...	214	459	.466	112	136	.824	134	102	633	3.4	2.6	15.8
97-98—Columbus	44	...	243	523	.465	191	214	.893	149	108	764	3.4	2.5	17.4
98-99—Columbus	2	...	14	32	.438	3	3	1.000	6	8	36	3.0	4.0	18.0
Totals	86	...	471	1014	.464	306	353	.867	289	218	1433	3.4	2.5	16.7

Three-point field goals: 1996-97, 93-for-216 (.431). 1997-98, 87-for-217 (.401). 1998-99, 5-for-11 (.455). Totals, 185-for-444 (.417).

WNBA REGULAR-SEASON RECORD

NOTES: All-WNBA first team (2001, 2003). ... All-WNBA second team (2000, 2002). ... Led WNBA in scoring (23.1 ppg) in 2001.

									REBOUNDS								AVERAGES		
Season Team	G	Min.	FGM	FGA	Pct.	FTM	FTA	Pct.	Off.	Def.	Tot.	Ast.	St.	Blk.	TO	Pts.	RPG	APG	PPG
1999—Minnesota	30	971	113	292	.387	72	94	.766	42	46	88	60	19	10	55	350	2.9	2.0	11.7
2000—Minnesota	32	1193	203	482	.421	152	175	.869	28	65	93	90	44	7	76	646	2.9	2.8	20.2
2001—Minnesota	32	1234	204	519	.393	246	275	.895	40	82	122	70	23	5	87	739	3.8	2.2	23.1
2002—Minnesota	31	1138	162	401	.404	126	153	.824	24	68	92	79	32	7	70	512	3.0	2.5	16.5
2003—Minnesota	34	1185	208	455	.457	126	143	.881	40	98	138	84	25	6	67	620	4.1	2.5	18.2
Totals.................	159	5721	890	2149	.414	722	840	.860	174	359	533	383	143	35	355	2867	3.4	2.4	18.0

Three-point field goals: 1999, 52-for-136 (.382). 2000, 88-for-232 (.379). 2001, 85-for-240 (.354). 2002, 62-for-188 (.330). 2003, 78-for-200 (.390). Totals, 365-for-996 (.366).
Personal fouls/disqualifications: 1999, 106/3. 2000, 71/0. 2001, 94/0. 2002, 87/2. 2003, 112/2. Totals, 470/7.

WNBA PLAYOFF RECORD

									REBOUNDS								AVERAGES		
Season Team	G	Min.	FGM	FGA	Pct.	FTM	FTA	Pct.	Off.	Def.	Tot.	Ast.	St.	Blk.	TO	Pts.	RPG	APG	PPG
2003—Minnesota	3	120	18	42	.429	11	12	.917	3	10	13	9	1	0	8	52	4.3	3.0	17.3
Totals.................	3	120	18	42	.429	11	12	.917	3	10	13	9	1	0	8	52	4.3	3.0	17.3

Three-point field goals: 2003, 5-for-14 (.357). Totals, 5-for-14 (.357).
Personal fouls/disqualifications: 2003, 11/0. Totals, 11/0.

WNBA ALL-STAR GAME RECORD

								REBOUNDS								
Season Team	Min.	FGM	FGA	Pct.	FTM	FTA	Pct.	Off.	Def.	Tot.	Ast.	PF	Dq.	St.	Blk.	TO Pts.
2000 —Minnesota	18	0	2	.000	0	0	...	0	1	1	2	0	0	2	0	... 0
2001 —Minnesota	20	1	5	.200	0	0	...	0	2	2	0	1	0	1	1	... 2
2002 —Minnesota	11	2	4	.500	0	0	...	0	3	3	4	1	0	0	0	... 4
2003 —Minnesota	15	1	4	.250	0	0	...	0	0	0	0	1	0	0	0	... 2
Totals.................	64	4	15	.267	0	0	...	0	6	6	6	3	0	3	1	4 8

Three-point field goals: 2000, 0-for-2. 2001, 0-for-3. 2002, 0-for-2. Totals, 0-for-7.

OLYMPICS

NOTES: Member of gold medal-winning U.S. Olympic Team (2000).

												AVERAGES		
Season Team	G	Min.	FGM	FGA	Pct.	FTM	FTA	Pct.	Reb.	Ast.	Pts.	RPG	APG	PPG
2000—United States...............	8	155	20	39	.513	2	3	.667	5	9	54	0.6	1.1	6.8
Totals	8	155	20	39	.513	2	3	.667	5	9	54	0.6	1.1	6.8

Three-point field goals: 2000-01, 12-for-20 (.600).

SMITH, TANGELA   F/C   MONARCHS

PERSONAL: Born April 1, 1977, in Chicago, Ill. ... 6-4/160 (1.93 m/73 kg). ... **Full name:** Tangela Nicole Smith.
HIGH SCHOOL: Chicago Washington (Chicago).
COLLEGE: Iowa.
TRANSACTIONS/CAREER NOTES: Selected by Sacramento in the second round (12th overall) of the WNBA Draft, April 29, 1998.

COLLEGIATE RECORD

Season Team	G	Min.	FGM	FGA	Pct.	FTM	FTA	Pct.	Reb.	Ast.	Pts.	RPG	APG	PPG
94-95—Iowa	28	...	102	225	.453	47	73	.644	211	20	251	7.5	0.7	9.0
95-96—Iowa	31	...	172	365	.471	77	113	.681	218	25	422	7.0	0.8	13.6
96-97—Iowa	30	...	149	280	.532	50	73	.685	186	37	348	6.2	1.2	11.6
97-98—Iowa	29	...	240	429	.559	97	138	.703	244	39	577	8.4	1.3	19.9
Totals	118		663	1299	.510	271	397	.683	859	121	1598	7.3	1.0	13.5

Three-point field goals: 1994-95, 0-for-3. 1995-96, 1-for-9 (.111). 1996-97, 0-for-1. 1997-98, 0-for-2. Totals, 1-for-15 (.067).

WNBA REGULAR-SEASON RECORD

Season Team	G	Min.	FGM	FGA	Pct.	FTM	FTA	Pct.	REBOUNDS Off.	Def.	Tot.	Ast.	St.	Blk.	TO	Pts.	AVERAGES RPG	APG	PPG
1998—Sacramento	28	707	113	279	.405	40	54	.741	45	84	129	31	17	46	46	271	4.6	1.1	9.7
1999—Sacramento	31	632	104	235	.443	47	72	.653	46	73	119	17	26	38	38	256	3.8	0.5	8.3
2000—Sacramento	32	925	176	371	.474	36	46	.783	61	117	178	43	30	64	60	388	5.6	1.3	12.1
2001—Sacramento	32	912	148	352	.420	62	85	.729	48	131	179	41	34	55	66	358	5.6	1.3	11.2
2002—Sacramento	32	1063	184	435	.423	86	101	.851	56	132	188	40	27	46	59	469	5.9	1.3	14.7
2003—Sacramento	34	986	188	427	.440	41	58	.707	61	126	187	52	43	32	56	430	5.5	1.5	12.6
Totals	189	5225	913	2099	.435	312	416	.750	317	663	980	224	177	281	325	2172	5.2	1.2	11.5

Three-point field goals: 1998, 5-for-14 (.357). 1999, 1-for-2 (.500). 2001, 0-for-2. 2002, 15-for-42 (.357). 2003, 13-for-49 (.265). Totals, 34-for-109 (.312).

Personal fouls/disqualifications: 1998, 78/0. 1999, 72/0. 2001, 106/2. 2002, 126/4. 2003, 103/2. Totals, 592/9.

WNBA PLAYOFF RECORD

Season Team	G	Min.	FGM	FGA	Pct.	FTM	FTA	Pct.	REBOUNDS Off.	Def.	Tot.	Ast.	St.	Blk.	TO	Pts.	AVERAGES RPG	APG	PPG
1999—Sacramento	1	38	6	16	.375	2	6	.333	1	1	2	0	3	1	1	14	2.0	0.0	14.0
2000—Sacramento	2	59	9	22	.409	3	4	.750	0	8	8	1	2	1	2	21	4.0	0.5	10.5
2001—Sacramento	5	164	23	60	.383	9	11	.818	8	16	24	8	5	5	4	55	4.8	1.6	11.0
2003—Sacramento	6	176	29	73	.397	14	20	.700	9	37	46	11	5	3	11	77	7.7	1.8	12.8
Totals	14	437	67	171	.392	28	41	.683	18	62	80	20	15	10	18	167	5.7	1.4	11.9

Three-point field goals: 2003, 5-for-15 (.333). Totals, 5-for-15 (.333).
Personal fouls/disqualifications: 2003, 17/0. Totals, 42/0.

SMITH-TAYLOR, CHARLOTTE F   STING

PERSONAL: Born August 23, 1973, in Shelby, N.C. ... 6-0/148 (1.83 m/67 kg). ... **Full name:** Charlotte D. Smith-Taylor.
HIGH SCHOOL: Shelby (Shelby, N.C.).
COLLEGE: North Carolina.
TRANSACTIONS/CAREER NOTES: Selected by Charlotte in third round (33rd overall) of WNBA Draft, May 4, 1999.

COLLEGIATE RECORD

NOTES: Consensus first team All-America (1995). ... Most Valuable Player of the NCAA Final Four (1995). ... Member of the NCAA National championship team (1994). ... Holds record with 23 rebounds in championship game (1994).

Season Team	G	Min.	FGM	FGA	Pct.	FTM	FTA	Pct.	Reb.	Ast.	Pts.	RPG	APG	PPG
91-92—North Carolina	31	...	175	360	.486	99	155	.639	251	...	251	8.1	0.0	8.1
92-93—North Carolina	30	...	172	377	.456	96	157	.611	269	...	446	9.0	0.0	14.9
93-94—North Carolina	33	...	196	390	.503	112	159	.704	304	...	513	9.2	0.0	15.5
94-95—North Carolina	35	...	249	467	.533	174	267	.652	376	...	685	10.7	0.0	19.6
Totals	129	...	792	1594	.497	481	738	.652	1200	0	1895	9.3	0.0	14.7

Three-point field goals: 1991-92, 1-for-10 (.100). 1992-93, 6-for-21 (.286). 1993-94, 9-for-32 (.281). 1994-95, 13-for-46 (.283). Totals, 29-for-109 (.266).

ABL REGULAR-SEASON RECORD

Season Team	G	Min.	FGM	FGA	Pct.	FTM	FTA	Pct.	Reb.	Ast.	Pts.	RPG	APG	PPG
96-97—Colorado	40	...	208	497	.419	182	234	.778	259	106	626	6.5	2.7	15.7
97-98—San Jose	42	...	187	383	.488	135	183	.738	252	90	513	6.0	2.1	12.2
98-99—San Jose	13	...	33	78	.423	29	37	.784	47	21	99	3.6	1.6	7.6
Totals	95	...	428	958	.447	346	454	.762	558	217	1238	5.9	2.3	13.0

Three-point field goals: 1996-97, 28-for-102 (.275). 1997-98, 4-for-28 (.143). 1998-99, 4-for-16 (.250). Totals, 36-for-146 (.247).

WNBA REGULAR-SEASON RECORD

Season Team	G	Min.	FGM	FGA	Pct.	FTM	FTA	Pct.	REBOUNDS Off.	Def.	Tot.	Ast.	St.	Blk.	TO	Pts.	AVERAGES RPG	APG	PPG
1999—Charlotte	32	746	62	188	.330	41	58	.707	46	69	115	58	10	7	50	173	3.6	1.8	5.4
2000—Charlotte	30	659	56	159	.352	20	25	.800	29	77	106	55	15	17	48	156	3.5	1.8	5.2
2001—Charlotte	30	678	57	146	.390	47	64	.734	36	65	101	50	16	13	41	171	3.4	1.7	5.7
2002—Charlotte	32	890	91	222	.410	40	54	.741	39	82	121	53	21	17	60	256	3.8	1.7	8.0
2003—Charlotte	27	443	31	98	.316	24	36	.667	23	37	60	18	10	2	24	95	2.2	0.7	3.5
Totals	151	3416	297	813	.365	172	237	.726	173	330	503	234	72	56	223	851	3.3	1.5	5.6

Three-point field goals: 1999, 8-for-56 (.143). 2000, 24-for-76 (.316). 2001, 10-for-32 (.313). 2002, 34-for-91 (.374). 2003, 9-for-32 (.281). Totals, 85-for-287 (.296).
Personal fouls/disqualifications: 1999, 87/1. 2000, 88/2. 2001, 73/1. 2002, 113/3. 2003, 54/0. Totals, 415/7.

WNBA PLAYOFF RECORD

Season Team	G	Min.	FGM	FGA	Pct.	FTM	FTA	Pct.	REBOUNDS Off.	Def.	Tot.	Ast.	St.	Blk.	TO	Pts.	AVERAGES RPG	APG	PPG
1999—Charlotte	4	106	13	31	.419	9	11	.818	8	10	18	3	4	0	7	36	4.5	0.8	9.0
2001—Charlotte	8	224	16	54	.296	10	11	.909	13	19	32	14	6	8	7	47	4.0	1.8	5.9

S

Season Team	G	Min.	FGM	FGA	Pct.	FTM	FTA	Pct.	Off.	Def.	Tot.	Ast.	St.	Blk.	TO	Pts.	RPG	APG	PPG
2002—Charlotte	2	53	5	17	.294	2	2	1.000	0	7	7	0	1	2	2	12	3.5	0.0	6.0
2003—Charlotte	2	7	1	1	1.000	0	0	...	1	0	1	1	0	0	0	2	0.5	0.5	1.0
Totals	16	390	35	103	.340	21	24	.875	22	36	58	18	11	10	16	97	3.6	1.1	6.1

Three-point field goals: 1999, 1-for-6 (.167). 2001, 5-for-20 (.250). 2002, 0-for-7. Totals, 6-for-33 (.182).
Personal fouls/disqualifications: 1999, 11/0. 2001, 24/0. 2002, 7/0. Totals, 42/0.

SNOW, MICHELLE   C   COMETS

PERSONAL: Born March 20, 1980, in Pensacola, Fla. ... 6-5/158 (1.96 m/72 kg). ... **Full name:** Donette JeMichelle Snow.
HIGH SCHOOL: Pensacola (Fla.).
COLLEGE: Tennessee.
TRANSACTIONS/CAREER NOTES: Selected by Houston in first round (10th overall) of WNBA Draft, April 19, 2002.

COLLEGIATE RECORD

NOTES: Recorded her third dunk in 2002.

Season Team	G	Min.	FGM	FGA	Pct.	FTM	FTA	Pct.	Reb.	Ast.	Pts.	RPG	APG	PPG
98-99—Tennessee	34	740	117	195	.600	56	108	.519	218	12	290	6.4	0.4	8.5
99-00—Tennessee	37	919	181	326	.555	73	116	.629	232	16	290	6.3	0.4	7.8
00-01—Tennessee	33	771	143	250	.572	79	130	.608	224	26	365	6.8	0.8	11.1
01-02—Tennessee	33	823	144	286	.503	119	158	.753	214	17	407	6.5	0.5	12.3
Totals	137	3253	585	1057	.553	327	512	.639	888	71	1352	6.5	0.5	9.9

Three-point field goals: 1999-00, 0-for-1.

WNBA REGULAR-SEASON RECORD

NOTES: WNBA Most Improved Player (2003).

Season Team	G	Min.	FGM	FGA	Pct.	FTM	FTA	Pct.	Off.	Def.	Tot.	Ast.	St.	Blk.	TO	Pts.	RPG	APG	PPG
2002—Houston	32	480	45	96	.469	34	57	.596	31	88	119	13	12	26	22	125	3.7	0.4	3.9
2003—Houston	34	1025	126	253	.498	62	85	.729	76	187	263	42	35	62	68	314	7.7	1.2	9.2
Totals	66	1505	171	349	.490	96	142	.676	107	275	382	55	47	88	90	439	5.8	0.8	6.7

Three-point field goals: 2002, 1-for-2 (.500). 2003, 0-for-1. Totals, 1-for-3 (.333).
Personal fouls/disqualifications: 2002, 59/0. 2003, 120/2. Totals, 179/2.

WNBA PLAYOFF RECORD

Season Team	G	Min.	FGM	FGA	Pct.	FTM	FTA	Pct.	Off.	Def.	Tot.	Ast.	St.	Blk.	TO	Pts.	RPG	APG	PPG
2002—Houston	3	79	6	18	.333	7	8	.875	6	15	21	4	0	2	5	19	7.0	1.3	6.3
2003—Houston	3	89	10	25	.400	5	8	.625	12	17	29	5	4	4	5	25	9.7	1.7	8.3
Totals	6	168	16	43	.372	12	16	.750	18	32	50	9	4	6	10	44	8.3	1.5	7.3

Three-point field goals: 2002, 0-for-1. Totals, 0-for-1.
Personal fouls/disqualifications: 2002, 9/0. Totals, 19/0.

STALEY, DAWN   G   STING

PERSONAL: Born May 4, 1970, in Philadelphia, Pa. ... 5-6/134 (1.68 m/61 kg). ... **Full name:** Dawn Michelle Staley.
HIGH SCHOOL: Dobbins Tech (Philadelphia, Pa.).
COLLEGE: Virginia.
TRANSACTIONS/CAREER NOTES: Selected by Charlotte in first round (ninth overall) of WNBA Draft, May 4, 1999.

COLLEGIATE RECORD

NOTES: Kodak All-America first team (1990, 1991, 1992).

Season Team	G	Min.	FGM	FGA	Pct.	FTM	FTA	Pct.	Reb.	Ast.	Pts.	RPG	APG	PPG
88-89—Virginia	31	...	197	431	.457	147	177	.831	158	144	574	5.1	4.6	18.5
89-90—Virginia	32	...	203	449	.452	132	169	.781	214	141	574	6.7	4.4	17.9
90-91—Virginia	34	...	176	391	.450	108	131	.824	209	235	495	6.1	6.9	14.6
91-92—Virginia	34	...	177	366	.484	118	146	.808	191	209	492	5.6	6.1	14.5
Totals	131	...	753	1637	.460	505	623	.811	772	729	2135	5.9	5.6	16.3

Three-point field goals: 1988-89, 33-for-93 (.355). 1989-90, 36-for-104 (.346). 1990-91, 35-for-108 (.324). 1991-92, 20-for-66 (.303). Totals, 124-for-371 (.334).

OLYMPICS

NOTES: USA Basketball Female Player of the Year (1994). ... Member of gold medal-winning U.S. Olympic Team (1996, 2000).

Season Team	G	Min.	FGM	FGA	Pct.	FTM	FTA	Pct.	Reb.	Ast.	Pts.	RPG	APG	PPG
1996—United States	8	...	6	18	.333	19	23	.826	5	28	33	0.6	3.5	4.1
2000—United States	8	140	9	19	.474	12	12	1.000	10	29	32	1.3	3.6	4.0
Totals	16	140	15	37	.405	31	35	.886	15	57	65	0.9	3.6	4.1

Three-point field goals: 1996-97, 2-for-5 (.400). 2000-01, 2-for-4 (.500). Totals, 4-for-9 (.444).

WNBA REGULAR-SEASON RECORD

HONORS: Winner of WNBA Sportsmanship Award (1999). ... Winner of WNBA Entrepreneurial Award (1999).

Season Team	G	Min.	FGM	FGA	Pct.	FTM	FTA	Pct.	Off.	Def.	Tot.	Ast.	St.	Blk.	TO	Pts.	RPG	APG	PPG
1999—Charlotte	32	1065	125	301	.415	89	95	.934	12	60	72	177	38	3	90	368	2.3	5.5	11.5
2000—Charlotte	32	1099	94	253	.372	65	74	.878	21	56	77	190	37	1	91	282	2.4	5.9	8.8
2001—Charlotte	32	1152	107	281	.381	51	57	.895	11	60	71	179	52	1	100	298	2.2	5.6	8.7
2002—Charlotte	32	1061	84	231	.364	77	101	.762	8	48	56	164	48	0	80	278	1.8	5.1	8.7
2003—Charlotte	34	1086	90	216	.417	61	73	.836	14	44	58	174	49	4	78	269	1.7	5.1	7.9
Totals	162	5463	500	1282	.390	339	396	.856	66	268	334	884	224	9	439	1495	2.1	5.5	9.2

Three-point field goals: 1999, 33-for-104 (.317). 2000, 29-for-88 (.330). 2001, 33-for-89 (.371). 2002, 33-for-83 (.398). 2003, 28-for-72 (.389). Totals, 156-for-436 (.358)

Personal fouls/disqualifications: 1999, 71/0. 2000, 80/1. 2001, 54/0. 2002, 67/0. 2003, 76/0. Totals, 348/1.

WNBA PLAYOFF RECORD

								REBOUNDS								AVERAGES		
Season Team	G	Min.	FGM	FGA	Pct.	FTM	FTA	Pct.	Off.	Def.	Tot.	Ast.	St.	Blk.	TO	Pts.	RPG	APG PPG
1999—Charlotte......	4	157	13	40	.325	15	18	.833	2	3	5	23	3	0	11	48	1.3	5.8 12.0
2001—Charlotte......	8	301	32	77	.416	17	21	.810	3	15	18	35	9	2	34	94	2.3	4.4 11.8
2002—Charlotte......	2	78	6	21	.286	3	6	.500	2	3	5	10	3	0	4	17	2.5	5.0 8.5
2003—Charlotte......	2	58	6	17	.353	2	5	.400	1	4	5	7	4	0	4	18	2.5	3.5 9.0
Totals..................	16	594	57	155	.368	37	50	.740	8	25	33	75	19	2	53	177	2.1	4.7 11.1

Three-point field goals: 1999, 7-for-16 (.438). 2001, 13-for-26 (.500). 2002, 2-for-10 (.200). 2003, 4-for-8 (.500). Totals, 26-for-60 (.433)

Personal fouls/disqualifications: 1999, 7/0. 2001, 19/0. 2002, 2/0. 2003, 6/0. Totals, 34/0.

WNBA ALL-STAR GAME RECORD

								REBOUNDS							
Season Team	Min.	FGM	FGA	Pct.	FTM	FTA	Pct.	Off.	Def.	Tot.	Ast.	PF	Dq.	St.	Blk. TO Pts.
2001—Charlotte	15	2	3	.667	0	0	...	0	0	0	3	2	0	4	0 ... 4
2002—Charlotte	18	2	5	.400	0	0	...	1	3	4	5	0	0	1	0 ... 4
2003—Charlotte	24	1	6	.167	2	2	1.000	0	4	4	7	1	0	0	0 ... 5
Totals..................	57	5	14	.357	2	2	1.000	1	7	8	15	3	0	5	0 5 13

Three-point field goals: 2003, 1-for-4 (.250). Totals, 1-for-4 (.250).

S

STINSON, ANDREA   G   STING

PERSONAL: Born November 25, 1967, in Mooresville, N.C. ... 5-10/158 (1.78 m/72 kg). ... **Full name:** Andrea Maria Stinson.

HIGH SCHOOL: North Mecklenburg (Charlotte, N.C.).

COLLEGE: North Carolina State.

TRANSACTIONS/CAREER NOTES: Signed by WNBA and assigned to Charlotte, January 22, 1997.

COLLEGIATE RECORD

NOTES: Kodak All-America first team (1990, 1991).

											AVERAGES		
Season Team	G	Min.	FGM	FGA	Pct.	FTM	FTA	Pct.	Reb.	Ast.	Pts.	RPG	APG PPG
88-89—N.C. State	31	...	320	605	.529	80	121	.661	141	113	733	4.5	3.6 23.6
89-90—N.C. State	30	...	283	514	.551	76	110	.691	197	149	651	6.6	5.0 21.7
90-91—N.C. State	33	...	314	577	.544	91	151	.603	208	140	752	6.3	4.2 22.8
Totals	94	...	917	1696	.541	247	382	.647	546	402	2136	5.8	4.3 22.7

Three-point field goals: 1988-89, 13-for-50 (.260). 1989-90, 9-for-23 (.391). 1990-91, 33-for-91 (.363). Totals, 55-for-164 (.335).

WNBA REGULAR-SEASON RECORD

HONORS: All-WNBA second team (1997, 1998).

									REBOUNDS								AVERAGES		
Season Team	G	Min.	FGM	FGA	Pct.	FTM	FTA	Pct.	Off.	Def.	Tot.	Ast.	St.	Blk.	TO	Pts.	RPG	APG PPG
1997—Charlotte......	28	1011	177	396	.447	60	89	.674	48	107	155	124	43	21	99	439	5.5	4.4 15.7
1998—Charlotte......	30	1046	173	414	.418	75	100	.750	29	109	138	134	54	15	77	450	4.6	4.5 15.0
1999—Charlotte......	32	1041	174	378	.460	65	88	.739	32	81	113	93	32	18	67	434	3.5	2.9 13.6
2000—Charlotte......	32	1123	204	463	.462	99	134	.739	35	101	136	121	55	23	86	565	4.3	3.8 17.7
2001—Charlotte......	32	1006	179	370	.484	63	79	.797	39	98	137	88	43	19	70	450	4.3	2.8 14.1
2002—Charlotte......	32	950	159	349	.456	64	93	.688	37	140	177	91	37	9	52	411	5.5	2.8 12.8
2003—Charlotte......	34	1000	147	321	.458	60	79	.759	28	112	140	97	48	5	75	377	4.1	2.9 11.1
Totals..................	220	7177	1223	2691	.454	486	662	.734	248	748	996	748	312	110	526	3126	4.5	3.4 14.2

Three-point field goals: 1997, 25-for-77 (.325). 1998, 29-for-103 (.282). 1999, 21-for-68 (.309). 2000, 38-for-106 (.358). 2001, 29-for-65 (.446). 2002, 29-for-70 (.414). 2003, 23-for-75 (.307). Totals, 194-for-564 (.344).

Personal fouls/disqualifications: 1997, 55/0. 1998, 72/0. 1999, 56/0. 2000, 77/0. 2001, 59/0. 2002, 56/0. 2003, 70/0. Totals, 445/0.

WNBA PLAYOFF RECORD

									REBOUNDS								AVERAGES		
Season Team	G	Min.	FGM	FGA	Pct.	FTM	FTA	Pct.	Off.	Def.	Tot.	Ast.	St.	Blk.	TO	Pts.	RPG	APG PPG
1997—Charlotte......	1	34	3	11	.273	2	2	1.000	0	0	0	3	0	0	3	8	0.0	3.0 8.0
1998—Charlotte......	2	71	12	27	.444	3	5	.600	2	8	10	13	4	0	6	29	5.0	6.5 14.5
1999—Charlotte......	4	153	32	64	.500	15	19	.789	6	24	30	17	11	1	5	83	7.5	4.3 20.8
2001—Charlotte......	8	278	37	95	.389	17	21	.810	12	37	49	26	13	2	18	96	6.1	3.3 12.0
2002—Charlotte......	2	65	12	25	.480	2	2	1.000	7	4	11	9	7	0	4	30	5.5	4.5 15.0
2003—Charlotte......	2	64	12	28	.429	9	9	1.000	4	5	9	7	2	0	4	36	4.5	3.5 18.0
Totals................	19	665	108	250	.432	48	58	.828	31	78	109	75	37	3	40	282	5.7	3.9 14.8

Three-point field goals: 1997, 0-for-2. 1998, 2-for-7 (.286). 1999, 4-for-14 (.286). 2001, 5-for-13 (.385). 2002, 4-for-7 (.571). 2003, 3-for-7 (.429). Totals, 18-for-50 (.360).

Personal fouls/disqualifications: 1997, 4/0. 1998, 9/0. 1999, 8/0. 2001, 18/0. 2002, 4/0. 2003, 4/0. Totals, 47/0.

WNBA ALL-STAR GAME RECORD

								REBOUNDS							
Season Team	Min.	FGM	FGA	Pct.	FTM	FTA	Pct.	Off.	Def.	Tot.	Ast.	PF	Dq.	St.	Blk. TO Pts.
2000—Charlotte	13	1	6	.167	1	1	1.000	1	1	2	2	0	0	1	0 ... 3
2001—Charlotte	17	2	9	.222	0	0	...	2	3	5	1	2	0	0	0 ... 4
2002—Charlotte	20	3	10	.300	2	2	1.000	0	1	1	2	3	0	1	0 ... 9
Totals.................	50	6	25	.240	3	3	1.000	3	5	8	5	5	0	2	0 5 16

Three-point field goals: 2000, 0-for-1. 2001, 0-for-3. 2002, 1-for-4 (.250). Totals, 1-for-8 (.125).

STOCKS, TAMARA   F/C   SPARKS

PERSONAL: Born January 29, 1979, in Akron, Ohio ... 6-2/165 (1.88 m/75 kg). ... **Full name:** Tamara Celeste Stocks.
HIGH SCHOOL: Pickerington (Pickerington, Ohio).
COLLEGE: Florida.
TRANSACTIONS/CAREER NOTES: Selected by Washington in second round (25th overall) of WNBA Draft, April 20, 2001. ... Signed by Los Angeles as a free agent, May 22, 2004.

COLLEGIATE RECORD

Season Team	G	Min.	FGM	FGA	Pct.	FTM	FTA	Pct.	Reb.	Ast.	Pts.	RPG	APG	PPG
97-98—Florida	32	764	130	242	.537	79	107	.738	149	25	339	4.7	0.8	10.6
98-99—Florida	33	775	140	264	.530	88	138	.638	197	26	368	6.0	0.8	11.2
99-00—Florida	34	767	120	261	.460	78	107	.729	165	21	318	4.9	0.6	9.4
00-01—Florida	30	714	113	259	.436	98	127	.772	153	34	324	5.1	1.1	10.8
Totals	129	3020	503	1026	.490	343	479	.716	664	106	1349	5.1	0.8	10.5

WNBA REGULAR-SEASON RECORD

Season Team	G	Min.	FGM	FGA	Pct.	FTM	FTA	Pct.	Off.	Def.	Tot.	Ast.	St.	Blk.	TO	Pts.	RPG	APG	PPG
2001—Washington	3	11	1	3	.333	1	2	.500	0	2	2	0	0	0	0	3	0.7	0.0	1.0
Totals	3	11	1	3	.333	1	2	.500	0	2	2	0	0	0	0	3	0.7	0.0	1.0

S

SUBER, TORA   G   COMETS

PERSONAL: Born November 23, 1974, in Coatesville, Pa. ... 5-7/137 (1.70 m/62 kg). ... **Full name:** Tora Annette Suber.
HIGH SCHOOL: Dowingtown (Dowingtown, Pa.).
COLLEGE: Virginia.
TRANSACTIONS/CAREER NOTES: Selected by Charlotte in first round (seventh overall) of WNBA Draft, April 28, 1997. ... Waived by Charlotte, May 28, 1999. ... Signed as free agent by Orlando, June 1, 1999. ... Waived by Orlando, May 11, 2000 ... Signed by Orlando, April 30, 2001 ... Waived by Orlando, May 15, 2001 ... Assigned to Houston, April 25, 2002 ... Waived by Houston, May 8, 2002 ... Signed by Houston as a free agent.

COLLEGIATE RECORD

Season Team	G	Min.	FGM	FGA	Pct.	FTM	FTA	Pct.	Reb.	Ast.	Pts.	RPG	APG	PPG
93-94—Virginia	32	...	144	319	.451	60	83	.723	92	126	405	2.9	3.9	12.7
94-95—Virginia	32	...	115	330	.348	61	93	.656	118	143	334	3.7	4.5	10.4
95-96—Virginia	33	...	193	423	.456	135	178	.758	112	124	582	3.4	3.8	17.6
96-97—Virginia	30	...	149	349	.427	89	118	.754	96	111	446	3.2	3.7	14.9
Totals	127	...	601	1421	.423	345	472	.731	418	504	1767	3.3	4.0	13.9

Three-point field goals: 1993-94, 57-for-154 (.370). 1994-95, 43-for-165 (.261). 1995-96, 61-for-170 (.359). 1996-97, 59-for-177 (.333). Totals, 220-for-666 (.330).

WNBA REGULAR-SEASON RECORD

Season Team	G	Min.	FGM	FGA	Pct.	FTM	FTA	Pct.	Off.	Def.	Tot.	Ast.	St.	Blk.	TO	Pts.	RPG	APG	PPG
1997—Charlotte	28	475	40	108	.370	28	41	.683	5	37	42	56	13	3	51	131	1.5	2.0	4.7
1998—Charlotte	30	682	58	185	.314	29	46	.630	12	41	53	86	30	1	44	181	1.8	2.9	6.0
1999—Char.-Orl	25	114	7	24	.292	5	10	.500	4	9	13	9	5	0	10	20	0.5	0.4	0.8
Totals	83	1271	105	317	.331	62	97	.639	21	87	108	151	48	4	105	332	1.3	1.8	4.0

Three-point field goals: 1997, 23-for-58 (.397). 1998, 36-for-116 (.310). 1999, 1-for-9 (.111). Totals, 60-for-183 (.328).
Personal fouls/disqualifications: 1997, 32/0. 1998, 55/1. 1999, 14/0. Totals, 101/1.

WNBA PLAYOFF RECORD

Season Team	G	Min.	FGM	FGA	Pct.	FTM	FTA	Pct.	Off.	Def.	Tot.	Ast.	St.	Blk.	TO	Pts.	RPG	APG	PPG
1997—Charlotte	1	7	0	1	.000	0	0	...	0	0	0	1	0	0	1	0	0.0	1.0	0.0
1998—Charlotte	2	74	9	23	.391	2	3	.667	1	1	2	10	5	0	7	23	1.0	5.0	11.5
Totals	3	81	9	24	.375	2	3	.667	1	1	2	11	5	0	8	23	0.7	3.7	7.7

Three-point field goals: 1997, 0-for-0. 1998, 3-for-12 (.250). Totals, 3-for-12 (.250).
Personal fouls/disqualifications: 1997, 2/0. 1998, 5/0. Totals, 7/0.

SUTTON-BROWN, TAMMY   C   STING

PERSONAL: Born January 27, 1978, in Markham, Ontario, Canada ... 6-4/203 (1.93 m/92 kg). ... **Full name:** Tamara Kim Sutton-Brown.
HIGH SCHOOL: Markham District (Markham, Ontario, Canada).
COLLEGE: Rutgers.
TRANSACTIONS/CAREER NOTES: Selected by Charlotte in second round (18th overall) of WNBA Draft, April 20, 2001.

COLLEGIATE RECORD

Season Team	G	Min.	FGM	FGA	Pct.	FTM	FTA	Pct.	Reb.	Ast.	Pts.	AVERAGES RPG	APG	PPG
97-98—Rutgers	32	570	93	172	.541	40	89	.449	158	15	226	4.9	0.5	7.1
98-99—Rutgers	35	745	132	196	.673	91	141	.645	205	16	355	5.9	0.5	10.1
99-00—Rutgers	32	762	109	211	.517	75	118	.636	164	11	293	5.1	0.3	9.2
00-01—Rutgers	31	736	137	237	.578	98	146	.671	158	10	372	5.1	0.3	12.0
Totals	130	2813	471	816	.577	304	494	.615	685	52	1246	5.3	0.4	9.6

Three-point field goals: 2000-01, 0-for-1.

OLYMPICS

Season Team	G	Min.	FGM	FGA	Pct.	FTM	FTA	Pct.	Reb.	Ast.	Pts.	AVERAGES RPG	APG	PPG
2000—Canada	6	159	20	42	.476	22	30	.733	44	1	62	7.3	0.2	10.3
Totals	6	159	20	42	.476	22	30	.733	44	1	62	7.3	0.2	10.3

WNBA REGULAR-SEASON RECORD

Season Team	G	Min.	FGM	FGA	Pct.	FTM	FTA	Pct.	REBOUNDS Off.	Def.	Tot.	Ast.	St.	Blk.	TO	Pts.	AVERAGES RPG	APG	PPG
2001—Charlotte	29	602	72	147	.490	52	72	.722	51	78	129	11	21	39	40	196	4.4	0.4	6.8
2002—Charlotte	32	885	129	243	.531	124	174	.713	76	115	191	15	29	36	49	382	6.0	0.5	11.9
2003—Charlotte	34	864	98	233	.421	90	131	.687	73	128	201	15	19	50	59	286	5.9	0.4	8.4
Totals	95	2351	299	623	.480	266	377	.706	200	321	521	41	69	125	148	864	5.5	0.4	9.1

WNBA PLAYOFF RECORD

Season Team	G	Min.	FGM	FGA	Pct.	FTM	FTA	Pct.	REBOUNDS Off.	Def.	Tot.	Ast.	St.	Blk.	TO	Pts.	AVERAGES RPG	APG	PPG
2001—Charlotte	8	167	25	46	.543	10	14	.714	10	16	26	4	1	11	8	60	3.3	0.5	7.5
2002—Charlotte	2	56	7	14	.500	1	6	.167	4	8	12	0	1	1	7	15	6.0	0.0	7.5
2003—Charlotte	2	32	2	7	.286	0	0	...	1	5	6	0	0	3	2	4	3.0	0.0	2.0
Totals	12	255	34	67	.507	11	20	.550	15	29	44	4	2	15	17	79	3.7	0.3	6.6

WNBA ALL-STAR GAME RECORD

Season Team	Min.	FGM	FGA	Pct.	FTM	FTA	Pct.	REBOUNDS Off.	Def.	Tot.	Ast.	PF	Dq.	St.	Blk.	TO	Pts.
2002—Charlotte	17	3	5	.600	3	4	.750	1	3	4	1	1	0	0	3	...	9
Totals	17	3	5	.600	3	4	.750	1	3	4	1	1	0	0	3	0	9

SWOOPES, SHERYL   F   COMETS

PERSONAL: Born March 25, 1971, in Brownfield, Texas ... 6-0/145 (1.83 m/66 kg). ... **Full name:** Sheryl Denise Swoopes.
HIGH SCHOOL: Brownfield (Brownfield, Texas).
COLLEGE: Texas Tech.
TRANSACTIONS/CAREER NOTES: Signed by WNBA and assigned to Houston, January 22, 1997.
MISCELLANEOUS: Member of WNBA Championship Team (1997, 1998, 1999, 2000).

COLLEGIATE RECORD

NOTES: Member of NCAA Division I championship team (1993). ... NCAA National Player of the Year (1993).

Season Team	G	Min.	FGM	FGA	Pct.	FTM	FTA	Pct.	Reb.	Ast.	Pts.	AVERAGES RPG	APG	PPG
91-92—Texas Tech	32	1027	265	527	.503	135	167	.808	285	152	690	8.9	4.8	21.6
92-93—Texas Tech	34	1153	365	652	.560	211	243	.868	312	139	973	9.2	4.1	28.6
Totals	66	2180	630	1179	.534	346	410	.844	597	291	1663	9.0	4.4	25.2

Three-point field goals: 1991-92, 25-for-61 (.410). 1992-93, 32-for-78 (.410). Totals, 57-for-139 (.410).

OLYMPICS

NOTES: Member of gold medal-winning U.S. Olympic Team (1996, 2000).

Season Team	G	Min.	FGM	FGA	Pct.	FTM	FTA	Pct.	Reb.	Ast.	Pts.	AVERAGES RPG	APG	PPG
1996—United States	8	...	40	66	.606	3	4	.750	28	31	104	3.5	3.9	13.0
2000—United States	8	232	46	89	.517	9	13	.692	37	24	107	4.6	3.0	13.4
Totals	24	232	126	221	.570	15	21	.714	93	86	315	3.9	3.6	13.1

Three-point field goals: 1996-97, 7-for-20 (.350). 1996-97, 7-for-20 (.350). 2000-01, 6-for-19 (.316). Totals, 20-for-59 (.339).

WNBA REGULAR-SEASON RECORD

NOTES: WNBA Most Valuable Player (2000, 2002). ... WNBA Defensive Player of the Year (2000, 2002, 2003). ... All-WNBA first team (1998, 1999, 2000, 2002). ... Led WNBA in scoring (20.8 ppg) and steals (2.81 spg) in 2000. ... All-WNBA second team (2003). ... Led WNBA in steals (2.48 spg) 2003.

Season Team	G	Min.	FGM	FGA	Pct.	FTM	FTA	Pct.	REBOUNDS Off.	Def.	Tot.	Ast.	St.	Blk.	TO	Pts.	AVERAGES RPG	APG	PPG
1997—Houston	9	129	25	53	.472	10	14	.714	6	9	15	7	7	4	4	64	1.7	0.8	7.1
1998—Houston	29	937	173	405	.427	71	86	.826	39	110	149	62	72	14	58	453	5.1	2.1	15.6
1999—Houston	32	1100	226	489	.462	100	122	.820	48	154	202	127	76	46	83	585	6.3	4.0	18.3
2000—Houston	31	1090	245	484	.506	119	145	.821	40	155	195	119	87	33	82	643	6.3	3.8	20.7
2001—Houston						Did not play—injured.													

Season Team	G	Min.	FGM	FGA	Pct.	FTM	FTA	Pct.	Off.	Def.	Tot.	Ast.	St.	Blk.	TO	Pts.	RPG	APG	PPG
2002—Houston	32	1154	221	509	.434	127	154	.825	30	128	158	107	88	23	87	592	4.9	3.3	18.5
2003—Houston	31	1084	175	434	.403	110	124	.887	32	111	143	121	77	26	73	484	4.6	3.9	15.6
Totals	164	5494	1065	2374	.449	537	645	.833	195	667	862	543	407	146	387	2821	5.3	3.3	17.2

Three-point field goals: 1997, 4-for-16 (.250). 1998, 36-for-100 (.360). 1999, 33-for-98 (.337). 2000, 34-for-91 (.374). 2002, 23-for-80 (.288). 2003, 24-for-79 (.304). Totals, 154-for-464 (.332).
Personal fouls/disqualifications: 1997, 5/0. 1998, 42/0. 1999, 57/0. 2000, 67/0. 2002, 50/0. 2003, 48/0. Totals, 269/0.

WNBA PLAYOFF RECORD

Season Team	G	Min.	FGM	FGA	Pct.	FTM	FTA	Pct.	REBOUNDS Off.	Def.	Tot.	Ast.	St.	Blk.	TO	Pts.	AVERAGES RPG	APG	PPG
1997—Houston	2	14	0	5	.000	0	0	...	1	2	3	0	0	1	0	0	1.5	0.0	0.0
1998—Houston	5	188	27	61	.443	14	15	.933	7	43	50	26	9	7	16	73	10.0	5.2	14.6
1999—Houston	6	216	29	81	.358	26	28	.929	7	15	22	7	14	3	12	88	3.7	1.2	14.7
2000—Houston	6	220	41	87	.471	23	29	.793	9	25	34	19	17	0	12	113	5.7	3.2	18.8
2002—Houston	3	127	25	63	.397	20	25	.800	10	12	22	17	12	2	8	73	7.3	5.7	24.3
2003—Houston	3	110	20	46	.435	15	16	.938	2	17	19	13	4	2	5	56	6.3	4.3	18.7
Totals	25	875	142	343	.414	98	113	.867	36	114	150	82	56	15	53	403	6.0	3.3	16.1

Three-point field goals: 1997, 0-for-2. 1998, 5-for-18 (.278). 1999, 4-for-13 (.308). 2000, 8-for-17 (.471). 2002, 3-for-9 (.333). 2003, 1-for-10 (.100). Totals, 21-for-69 (.304).
Personal fouls/disqualifications: 1997, 1/0. 1998, 10/0. 1999, 9/0. 2000, 11/0. 2002, 7/0. 2003, 8/0. Totals, 46/0.

WNBA ALL-STAR GAME RECORD

Season Team	Min.	FGM	FGA	Pct.	FTM	FTA	Pct.	REBOUNDS Off.	Def.	Tot.	Ast.	PF	Dq.	St.	Blk.	TO	Pts.
1999—Houston	19	4	7	.571	0	0	...	1	7	8	0	2	0	3	1	...	8
2000—Houston	21	3	7	.429	0	0	...	1	5	6	3	1	0	0	0	...	6
2002—Houston	23	4	12	.333	3	4	.750	5	1	6	3	1	0	2	0	...	11
2003—Houston	21	1	4	.250	2	4	.500	0	4	4	4	1	0	1	0	...	4
Totals	84	12	30	.400	5	8	.625	7	17	24	10	5	0	6	1	8	29

Three-point field goals: 2000, 0-for-1. 2002, 0-for-1. 2003, 0-for-1. Totals, 0-for-3.

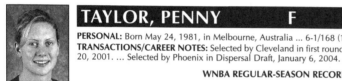

TAYLOR, PENNY   F   MERCURY   T

PERSONAL: Born May 24, 1981, in Melbourne, Australia ... 6-1/168 (1.85 m/76 kg).
TRANSACTIONS/CAREER NOTES: Selected by Cleveland in first round (11th round) of WNBA Draft, April 20, 2001. ... Selected by Phoenix in Dispersal Draft, January 6, 2004.

WNBA REGULAR-SEASON RECORD

Season Team	G	Min.	FGM	FGA	Pct.	FTM	FTA	Pct.	REBOUNDS Off.	Def.	Tot.	Ast.	St.	Blk.	TO	Pts.	AVERAGES RPG	APG	PPG
2001—Cleveland	32	561	86	225	.382	36	46	.783	36	76	112	44	35	11	38	230	3.5	1.4	7.2
2002—Cleveland	30	908	133	320	.416	87	102	.853	51	107	158	68	37	11	58	391	5.3	2.3	13.0
2003—Cleveland	34	898	143	340	.421	78	95	.821	44	104	148	80	38	10	60	398	4.4	2.4	11.7
Totals	96	2367	362	885	.409	201	243	.827	131	287	418	192	110	32	156	1019	4.4	2.0	10.6

Three-point field goals: 2001, 22-for-73 (.301). 2002, 38-for-111 (.342). 2003, 34-for-99 (.343). Totals, 94-for-283 (.332).
Personal fouls/disqualifications: 2001, 46/0. 2002, 66/0. 2003, 53/0. Totals, 165/0.

WNBA PLAYOFF RECORD

Season Team	G	Min.	FGM	FGA	Pct.	FTM	FTA	Pct.	REBOUNDS Off.	Def.	Tot.	Ast.	St.	Blk.	TO	Pts.	AVERAGES RPG	APG	PPG
2001—Cleveland	3	59	8	25	.320	3	4	.750	2	7	9	3	6	1	5	21	3.0	1.0	7.0
2003—Cleveland	3	99	16	36	.444	10	12	.833	1	12	13	3	6	1	6	45	4.3	1.0	15.0
Totals	6	158	24	61	.393	13	16	.813	3	19	22	6	12	2	11	66	3.7	1.0	11.0

Three-point field goals: 2001, 2-for-11 (.182). 2003, 3-for-10 (.300). Totals, 5-for-21 (.238).
Personal fouls/disqualifications: 2001, 4/0. 2003, 10/0. Totals, 14/0.

WNBA ALL-STAR GAME RECORD

Season Team	Min.	FGM	FGA	Pct.	FTM	FTA	Pct.	REBOUNDS Off.	Def.	Tot.	Ast.	PF	Dq.	St.	Blk.	TO	Pts.
2002—Cleveland	17	4	8	.500	1	1	1.000	1	2	3	0	0	0	2	0	...	9
Totals	17	4	8	.500	1	1	1.000	1	2	3	0	0	0	2	0	0	9

Three-point field goals: 2002, 0-for-2. Totals, 0-for-2 (.000).

TEASLEY, NIKKI   G   SPARKS

PERSONAL: Born March 22, 1979, in Washington, D.C. ... 6-0/165 (1.83 m/75 kg). ... **Full name:** Michelle Nicole Teasley.
HIGH SCHOOL: St. John's at Prospect Hall (Md.).
COLLEGE: North Carolina.
TRANSACTIONS/CAREER NOTES: Selected by Portland in first round (fifth overall) of WNBA Draft, April 19, 2002. ... Traded by Portland with G Sophia Witherspoon to Los Angeles for G Ukari Figgs and G Gergana Slavtcheva, April 19, 2002.
MISCELLANEOUS: Member of WNBA Championship Team (2002).

COLLEGIATE RECORD

Season Team	G	Min.	FGM	FGA	Pct.	FTM	FTA	Pct.	Reb.	Ast.	Pts.	RPG	APG	PPG
97-98—North Carolina..........	30	896	131	316	.415	74	96	.771	104	166	387	3.5	5.5	12.9
98-99—North Carolina..........	36	1189	193	467	.413	112	163	.687	169	211	555	4.7	5.9	15.4
99-00—North Carolina..........	26	858	131	336	.390	66	81	.815	104	162	379	4.0	6.2	14.6
00-01—North Carolina..........						Did not play.								
01-02—North Carolina..........	33	1062	146	398	.367	132	153	.863	145	189	501	4.4	5.7	15.2
Totals	125	4005	601	1517	.396	384	493	.779	522	728	1822	4.2	5.8	14.6

Three-point field goals: 1997-98, 51-for-142 (.359). 1998-99, 57-for-182 (.313). 1999-00, 51-for-161 (.317). 2001-02, 77-for-209 (.368). Totals, 236-for-694 (.340).

WNBA REGULAR-SEASON RECORD

NOTES: All-WNBA second team (2003).

Season Team	G	Min.	FGM	FGA	Pct.	FTM	FTA	Pct.	Off.	Def.	Tot.	Ast.	St.	Blk.	TO	Pts.	RPG	APG	PPG
2002—Los Angeles....	32	882	67	166	.404	30	40	.750	17	67	84	140	25	9	68	204	2.6	4.4	6.4
2003—Los Angeles....	34	1189	112	288	.389	98	112	.875	30	145	175	214	39	15	108	392	5.1	6.3	11.5
Totals.................	66	2071	179	454	.394	128	152	.842	47	212	259	354	64	24	176	596	3.9	5.4	9.0

Three-point field goals: 2002, 40-for-100 (.400). 2003, 70-for-165 (.424). Totals, 110-for-265 (.415).
Personal fouls/disqualifications: 2002, 63/1. 2003, 68/0. Totals, 131/1.

WNBA PLAYOFF RECORD

Season Team	G	Min.	FGM	FGA	Pct.	FTM	FTA	Pct.	Off.	Def.	Tot.	Ast.	St.	Blk.	TO	Pts.	RPG	APG	PPG
2002—Los Angeles....	6	184	14	42	.333	16	19	.842	3	10	13	47	9	1	22	49	2.2	7.8	8.2
2003—Los Angeles....	9	312	22	67	.328	16	20	.800	11	29	40	71	12	0	27	70	4.4	7.9	7.8
Totals.................	15	496	36	109	.330	32	39	.821	14	39	53	118	21	1	49	119	3.5	7.9	7.9

Three-point field goals: 2002, 5-for-22 (.227). 2003, 10-for-45 (.222). Totals, 15-for-67 (.224).
Personal fouls/disqualifications: 2002, 22/1. 2003, 23/0. Totals, 45/1.

WNBA ALL-STAR GAME RECORD

NOTES: WNBA All-Star Most Valuable Player (2003).

Season Team	Min.	FGM	FGA	Pct.	FTM	FTA	Pct.	Off.	Def.	Tot.	Ast.	PF	Dq.	St.	Blk.	TO	Pts.
2003—Los Angeles	24	2	6	.333	4	4	1.000	0	6	6	6	0	0	5	0	...	10
Totals.................	24	2	6	.333	4	4	1.000	0	6	6	6	0	0	5	0	0	10

Three-point field goals: 2003, 2-for-5 (.400). Totals, 2-for-5 (.400).

THOMAS, LATOYA   F   SILVER STARS

PERSONAL: Born July 6, 1981, in Greenville, Miss. ... 6-2/170 (1.88 m/77 kg). ... Full name: LaToya Monique Thomas.
HIGH SCHOOL: Greenville (Miss.).
COLLEGE: Mississippi State.
TRANSACTIONS/CAREER NOTES: Selected by Cleveland in first round (first overall) of WNBA Draft, April 25, 2003. ... Selected by San Antinio (third overall) in the 2004 Dispersal Draft, January 6, 2004.

COLLEGIATE RECORD

NOTES: Kodak All-America First Team (2002, 2001, 2000). ... AP All-America First Team (2002). ... SEC Player of the Year (2003). ... All-SEC First Team (2003, 2002, 2001, 2000). ... AP All-America Second Team (2001). ... SEC Freshman of the Year (2000). ... Led SEC in scoring as a freshman (21.0 ppg), sophomore (24.3 ppg) and junior (24.6 ppg). ... MSU's all-time career scoring leader (2,981). ... Broke her own single-season scoring records (763 points/24.6 ppg) as a junior.

Season Team	G	Min.	FGM	FGA	Pct.	FTM	FTA	Pct.	Reb.	Ast.	Pts.	RPG	APG	PPG
99-00—Mississippi State........	32	967	260	456	.570	142	181	.785	...	50	672	7.9	1.6	21.0
00-01—Mississippi State........	31	978	276	504	.548	195	265	.736	...	42	752	8.5	1.4	24.3
01-02—Mississippi State........	31	1085	286	502	.570	190	245	.776	...	62	763	9.9	2.0	24.6
02-03—Mississippi State........	31	1066	297	562	.528	182	223	.816	...	49	794	9.1	1.6	25.6
Totals	125	4096	1119	2024	.553	709	914	.776	0	203	2981	0.0	1.6	23.8

Three-point field goals: 1999-00, 10-for-35 (.286). 2000-01, 5-for-25 (.200). 2001-02, 1-for-8 (.125). 2002-03, 18-for-42 (.429). Totals, 34-for-110 (.309).

WNBA REGULAR-SEASON RECORD

Season Team	G	Min.	FGM	FGA	Pct.	FTM	FTA	Pct.	Off.	Def.	Tot.	Ast.	St.	Blk.	TO	Pts.	RPG	APG	PPG
2003—Cleveland......	32	852	137	296	.463	71	90	.789	63	101	164	37	28	13	42	345	5.1	1.2	10.8
Totals.................	32	852	137	296	.463	71	90	.789	63	101	164	37	28	13	42	345	5.1	1.2	10.8

Three-point field goals: 2003, 0-for-6. Totals, 0-for-6.
Personal fouls/disqualifications: 2003, 62/1. Totals, 62/1.

WNBA PLAYOFF RECORD

Season Team	G	Min.	FGM	FGA	Pct.	FTM	FTA	Pct.	Off.	Def.	Tot.	Ast.	St.	Blk.	TO	Pts.	RPG	APG	PPG
2003—Cleveland......	3	100	14	32	.438	13	17	.765	6	17	23	4	1	4	6	41	7.7	1.3	13.7
Totals.................	3	100	14	32	.438	13	17	.765	6	17	23	4	1	4	6	41	7.7	1.3	13.7

Three-point field goals: 2003, 0-for-2. Totals, 0-for-2.
Personal fouls/disqualifications: 2003, 11/0. Totals, 11/0.

THOMAS, STACEY   F   SHOCK

PERSONAL: Born August 29, 1978, in Flint, Mich. ... 5-10/154 (1.78 m/70 kg). ... Full name: Stacey Latrice Thomas.
HIGH SCHOOL: Flint Southwestern Academy (Flint, Mich.).
COLLEGE: Michigan.
TRANSACTIONS/CAREER NOTES: Selected by Portland in second round (23rd overall) of WNBA Draft, April 25, 2000. ... Became an unrestricted free agent when the Portland Fire ceased operation during the 2002-03 offseason. ... Signed by Seattle. ... Waived by Seattle, May 20, 2003. ... Signed by Phoenix, May 27, 2003. ... Traded by Phoenix to Detroit for Tamara Moore, July 31, 2003.
MISCELLANEOUS: Member of WNBA Championship Team (2003).

COLLEGIATE RECORD

NOTES: All-Big Ten first team (coaches: 2000; media: 2000). ... All-Big Ten second team (coaches: 1998, 1999; media: 1999). ... Big Ten All-Freshman team (1997). ... Big Ten Defensive Player of Year. ... Big Ten Freshman of Year (1997). ... Holds Big Ten Conference career steals record (372). ... Kodak/District 6 All-America (2000). ... Led Big Ten in steals 1998 (3.1 spg) 1999 (3.67 spg). ... Women's Basketball Journal Defensive All-America (2000).

Season Team	G	Min.	FGM	FGA	Pct.	FTM	FTA	Pct.	Reb.	Ast.	Pts.	AVERAGES		
												RPG	APG	PPG
96-97—Michigan	26	...	140	275	.509	54	104	.519	171	50	336	6.6	1.9	12.9
97-98—Michigan	29	...	131	303	.432	72	121	.595	213	53	338	7.3	1.8	11.7
98-99—Michigan	30	...	189	421	.449	59	95	.621	235	56	446	7.8	1.9	14.9
99-00—Michigan	30	...	162	425	.381	77	130	.592	232	64	436	7.7	2.1	14.5
Totals	115	...	622	1424	.437	262	450	.582	851	223	1556	7.4	1.9	13.5

Three-point field goals: 1996-97, 2-for-12 (.167). 1997-98, 4-for-23 (.174). 1998-99, 9-for-28 (.321). 1999-00, 35-for-124 (.282). Totals, 50-for-187 (.267).

WNBA REGULAR-SEASON RECORD

Season Team	G	Min.	FGM	FGA	Pct.	FTM	FTA	Pct.	REBOUNDS			Ast.	St.	Blk.	TO	Pts.	AVERAGES		
									Off.	Def.	Tot.						RPG	APG	PPG
2000—Portland	32	863	58	163	.356	44	74	.595	48	78	126	101	54	15	68	163	3.9	3.2	5.1
2001—Portland	32	413	22	60	.367	15	35	.429	31	39	70	41	30	10	40	59	2.2	1.3	1.8
2002—Portland	32	621	51	148	.345	31	61	.508	34	60	94	67	42	12	36	143	2.9	2.1	4.5
2003—Pho-Detroit	30	269	20	62	.323	14	27	.519	15	28	43	15	20	9	16	61	1.4	0.5	2.0
Totals	126	2166	151	433	.349	104	197	.528	128	205	333	224	146	46	160	426	2.6	1.8	3.4

Three-point field goals: 2000, 3-for-12 (.250). 2001, 0-for-7. 2002, 10-for-39 (.256). 2003, 7-for-27 (.259). Totals, 20-for-85 (.235).
Personal fouls/disqualifications: 2000, 93/1. 2001, 57/0. 2002, 62/0. 2003, 24/0. Totals, 236/1.

WNBA PLAYOFF RECORD

Season Team	G	Min.	FGM	FGA	Pct.	FTM	FTA	Pct.	REBOUNDS			Ast.	St.	Blk.	TO	Pts.	AVERAGES		
									Off.	Def.	Tot.						RPG	APG	PPG
2003—Detroit	4	13	0	1	.000	0	0	...	0	3	3	0	1	0	1	0	0.8	0.0	0.0
Totals	4	13	0	1	.000	0	0	...	0	3	3	0	1	0	1	0	0.8	0.0	0.0

THOMPSON, ALICIA   F   STORM

PERSONAL: Born June 30, 1976, in Big Lake, Texas ... 6-1/180 (1.85 m/82 kg).
HIGH SCHOOL: Reagan County (Big Lake, Texas).
COLLEGE: Texas Tech.
TRANSACTIONS/CAREER NOTES: Selected by New York in first round (ninth overall) of WNBA Draft, April 29, 1998. ... Waived by New York, June 7, 1999. ... Assigned to Indiana, May 2, 2000. ... Waived by Indiana, May 21, 2003. ... Signed as a free agent by Seattle, February 10, 2004.
NOTES: Associated Press All-American first team (1998). ... Kodak All-America (1998).

COLLEGIATE RECORD

Season Team	G	Min.	FGM	FGA	Pct.	FTM	FTA	Pct.	Reb.	Ast.	Pts.	AVERAGES		
												RPG	APG	PPG
94-95—Texas Tech	35	...	76	137	.555	43	78	.551	104	15	195	3.0	0.4	5.6
95-96—Texas Tech	32	...	226	482	.469	99	154	.643	295	77	556	9.2	2.4	17.4
96-97—Texas Tech	29	...	264	546	.484	143	204	.701	279	41	686	9.6	1.4	23.7
97-98—Texas Tech	31	...	299	551	.543	117	168	.696	275	62	719	8.9	2.0	23.2
Totals	127	...	865	1716	.504	402	604	.666	953	195	2156	7.5	1.5	17.0

Three-point field goals: 1995-96, 5-for-14 (.357). 1996-97, 15-for-43 (.349). 1997-98, 4-for-24 (.167). Totals, 24-for-81 (.296).

WNBA REGULAR-SEASON RECORD

Season Team	G	Min.	FGM	FGA	Pct.	FTM	FTA	Pct.	REBOUNDS			Ast.	St.	Blk.	TO	Pts.	AVERAGES		
									Off.	Def.	Tot.						RPG	APG	PPG
1998—New York	19	126	9	39	.231	12	19	.632	7	17	24	4	1	2	8	31	1.3	0.2	1.6
2000—Indiana	31	792	131	255	.514	30	42	.714	48	109	157	41	24	4	53	310	5.1	1.3	10.0
2001—Indiana	22	381	76	174	.437	17	23	.739	21	42	63	25	9	7	22	186	2.9	1.1	8.5
2002—Indiana	18	314	39	109	.358	12	17	.706	12	30	42	14	7	2	18	97	2.3	0.8	5.4
Totals	90	1613	255	577	.442	71	101	.703	88	198	286	84	41	15	101	624	3.2	0.9	6.9

Three-point field goals: 1998, 1-for-1. 2000, 18-for-40 (.450). 2001, 17-for-43 (.395). 2002, 7-for-29 (.241). Totals, 43-for-113 (.381).
Personal fouls/disqualifications: 1998, 12/0. 2000, 81/4. 2001, 24/0. 2002, 20/0. Totals, 141/4.

WNBA PLAYOFF RECORD

Season Team	G	Min.	FGM	FGA	Pct.	FTM	FTA	Pct.	REBOUNDS			Ast.	St.	Blk.	TO	Pts.	AVERAGES		
									Off.	Def.	Tot.						RPG	APG	PPG
2002—Indiana	1	2	1	1	1.000	0	0	...	0	0	0	0	0	0	0	2	0.0	0.0	2.0
Totals	1	2	1	1	1.000	0	0	...	0	0	0	0	0	0	0	2	0.0	0.0	2.0

THOMPSON, TINA   F   COMETS

PERSONAL: Born February 10, 1975, in Los Angeles, Calif. ... 6-2/178 (1.88 m/81 kg). ... Full name: Tina Marie Thompson.
HIGH SCHOOL: Morningside (Inglewood, Calif.).
COLLEGE: U.S.C..
TRANSACTIONS/CAREER NOTES: Selected by Houston in first round (first overall) of WNBA Draft, April 28, 1997.
MISCELLANEOUS: Member of WNBA Championship Team (1997, 1998, 1999, 2000).

COLLEGIATE RECORD

NOTES: Associated Press All-America second team (1997).

Season Team	G	Min.	FGM	FGA	Pct.	FTM	FTA	Pct.	Reb.	Ast.	Pts.	RPG	APG	PPG
93-94—Southern Cal	30	...	163	327	.498	91	142	.641	316	25	427	10.5	0.8	14.2
94-95—Southern Cal	28	...	193	372	.519	152	208	.731	294	24	545	10.5	0.9	19.5
95-96—Southern Cal	27	...	229	452	.507	141	190	.742	252	42	623	9.3	1.6	23.1
96-97—Southern Cal	29	...	222	445	.499	168	215	.781	306	59	653	10.6	2.0	22.5
Totals	114	...	807	1596	.506	552	755	.731	1168	150	2248	10.2	1.3	19.7

Three-point field goals: 1993-94, 10-for-28 (.357). 1994-95, 7-for-34 (.206). 1995-96, 24-for-76 (.316). 1996-97, 41-for-121 (.339). Totals, 82-for-259 (.317).

WNBA REGULAR-SEASON RECORD

HONORS: All-WNBA first team (1997, 1998). ... All-WNBA second team (1999, 2000, 2001, 2002).

Season Team	G	Min.	FGM	FGA	Pct.	FTM	FTA	Pct.	Off.	Def.	Tot.	Ast.	St.	Blk.	TO	Pts.	RPG	APG	PPG
1997—Houston	28	885	133	318	.418	67	80	.838	67	117	184	32	21	28	62	370	6.6	1.1	13.2
1998—Houston	27	874	121	289	.419	63	74	.851	65	127	192	24	31	25	47	342	7.1	0.9	12.7
1999—Houston	32	1074	142	339	.419	68	87	.782	67	139	206	28	31	31	72	391	6.4	0.9	12.2
2000—Houston	32	1087	191	407	.469	103	123	.837	68	177	245	48	47	25	84	540	7.7	1.5	16.9
2001—Houston	30	1102	199	528	.377	137	163	.840	84	149	233	58	29	22	87	579	7.8	1.9	19.3
2002—Houston	29	1052	176	408	.431	93	113	.823	67	150	217	62	25	20	92	485	7.5	2.1	16.7
2003—Houston	28	974	176	426	.413	81	104	.779	39	126	165	47	18	23	69	472	5.9	1.7	16.9
Totals	206	7048	1138	2715	.419	612	744	.823	457	985	1442	299	202	174	513	3179	7.0	1.5	15.4

Three-point field goals: 1997, 37-for-100 (.370). 1998, 37-for-103 (.359). 1999, 39-for-111 (.351). 2000, 55-for-132 (.417). 2001, 44-for-150 (.293). 2002, 40-for-108 (.370). 2003, 39-for-114 (.342). Totals, 291-for-818 (.356).
Personal fouls/disqualifications: 1997, 107/1. 1998, 89/0. 1999, 95/0. 2000, 88/0. 2001, 74/0. 2002, 76/0. 2003, 65/0. Totals, 594/1.

WNBA PLAYOFF RECORD

Season Team	G	Min.	FGM	FGA	Pct.	FTM	FTA	Pct.	Off.	Def.	Tot.	Ast.	St.	Blk.	TO	Pts.	RPG	APG	PPG
1997—Houston	2	74	9	21	.429	6	10	.600	8	10	18	3	2	1	6	26	9.0	1.5	13.0
1998—Houston	5	186	20	49	.408	11	12	.917	12	34	46	6	7	4	8	58	9.2	1.2	11.6
1999—Houston	6	208	21	57	.368	16	21	.762	6	24	30	4	5	7	13	67	5.0	0.7	11.2
2000—Houston	6	233	25	62	.403	17	18	.944	17	31	48	10	5	5	10	76	8.0	1.7	12.7
2001—Houston	2	68	11	20	.550	4	5	.800	4	8	12	7	1	0	10	29	6.0	3.5	14.5
2002—Houston	3	128	16	44	.364	7	10	.700	9	15	24	4	6	3	2	43	8.0	1.3	14.3
2003—Houston	3	106	18	46	.391	6	7	.857	3	11	14	5	2	6	6	45	4.7	1.7	15.0
Totals	27	1003	120	299	.401	67	83	.807	59	133	192	39	28	26	55	344	7.1	1.4	12.7

Three-point field goals: 1997, 2-for-5 (.400). 1998, 7-for-20 (.350). 1999, 9-for-24 (.375). 2000, 9-for-23 (.391). 2001, 3-for-5 (.600). 2002, 4-for-12 (.333). 2003, 3-for-13 (.231). Totals, 37-for-102 (.363).
Personal fouls/disqualifications: 1997, 5/0. 1998, 19/0. 1999, 24/1. 2000, 19/0. 2001, 5/0. 2002, 12/0. 2003, 9/0. Totals, 93/1.

WNBA ALL-STAR GAME RECORD

NOTES: WNBA All-Star Most Valuable Player (2000).

Season Team	Min.	FGM	FGA	Pct.	FTM	FTA	Pct.	Off.	Def.	Tot.	Ast.	PF	Dq.	St.	Blk.	TO	Pts.
1999—Houston	14	4	8	.500	0	0	...	0	5	5	0	0	0	0	0	...	8
2000—Houston	23	5	14	.357	2	2	1.000	6	5	11	1	1	0	3	1	...	13
2001—Houston	19	2	12	.167	0	0	...	1	2	3	0	5	0	3	0	...	4
2002—Houston	28	7	16	.438	5	6	.833	3	4	7	0	2	0	2	1	...	20
Totals	84	18	50	.360	7	8	.875	10	16	26	1	8	0	8	2	11	45

Three-point field goals: 2000, 1-for-4 (.250). 2001, 0-for-2. 2002, 1-for-3 (.333). Totals, 2-for-9 (.222).

THORN, ERIN   G   LIBERTY

PERSONAL: Born May 19, 1981, in Orem, Utah. ... 5-10 (1.78 m/ kg).
HIGH SCHOOL: Mountain View (Orem, Utah).
COLLEGE: Brigham Young.
TRANSACTIONS/CAREER NOTES: Selected by New York in second round (17th overall) of WNBA Draft, April 25, 2003.

COLLEGIATE RECORD

NOTES: Mountain West Conference MVP (2002). ... MWC All-Conference First Team (2003, 2002, 2001). ... MWC All-Conference Second Team (2000). ... MWC Freshman of the Year (2000). ... Set a BYU single-game record with nine three-pointers (December 14, 2001).

Season Team	G	Min.	FGM	FGA	Pct.	FTM	FTA	Pct.	Reb.	Ast.	Pts.	RPG	APG	PPG
												AVERAGES		
99-00—Brigham Young	31	995	135	321	.421	48	59	.814	...	114	409	3.5	3.7	13.2
00-01—Brigham Young	32	1044	173	415	.417	57	67	.851	...	101	496	4.5	3.2	15.5
01-02—Brigham Young	33	1107	199	454	.438	66	79	.835	...	114	572	4.0	3.5	17.3
02-03—Brigham Young	31	1084	199	447	.445	87	95	.916	...	176	584	4.2	5.7	18.8
Totals	127	4230	706	1637	.431	258	300	.860	0	505	2061	0.0	4.0	16.2

Three-point field goals: 1999-00, 91-for-210 (.433). 2000-01, 93-for-234 (.397). 2001-02, 108-for-264 (.409). 2002-03, 99-for-241 (.411). Totals, 391-for-949 (.412).

WNBA REGULAR-SEASON RECORD

Season Team	G	Min.	FGM	FGA	Pct.	FTM	FTA	Pct.	Off.	Def.	Tot.	Ast.	St.	Blk.	TO	Pts.	RPG	APG	PPG
									REBOUNDS								**AVERAGES**		
2003—New York	23	181	13	42	.310	10	10	1.000	3	8	11	16	4	1	13	44	0.5	0.7	1.9
Totals.................	23	181	13	42	.310	10	10	1.000	3	8	11	16	4	1	13	44	0.5	0.7	1.9

Three-point field goals: 2003, 8-for-33 (.242). Totals, 8-for-33 (.242).
Personal fouls/disqualifications: 2003, 8/0. Totals, 8/0.

TUVIC, SLOBODANKA C   MERCURY

PERSONAL: Born September 19, 1977, in Yugoslavia ... 6-4/194 (1.93 m/88 kg).
TRANSACTIONS/CAREER NOTES: Signed by the WNBA and added by Phoenix, April 30, 2001.
MISCELLANEOUS: Member of Yugoslavian National Team.

WNBA REGULAR-SEASON RECORD

Season Team	G	Min.	FGM	FGA	Pct.	FTM	FTA	Pct.	Off.	Def.	Tot.	Ast.	St.	Blk.	TO	Pts.	RPG	APG	PPG
									REBOUNDS								**AVERAGES**		
2001—Phoenix........	30	325	13	42	.310	28	59	.475	18	45	63	17	16	17	28	54	2.1	0.6	1.8
2002—Phoenix........	26	320	30	77	.390	25	32	.781	11	52	63	11	9	9	31	86	2.4	0.4	3.3
2003—Phoenix........	17	365	45	116	.388	37	46	.804	31	36	67	12	10	15	32	127	3.9	0.7	7.5
Totals.................	73	1010	88	235	.374	90	137	.657	60	133	193	40	35	41	91	267	2.6	0.5	3.7

Three-point field goals: 2002, 1-for-6 (.167). 2003, 0-for-4. Totals, 1-for-10 (.100).
Personal fouls/disqualifications: 2002, 53/0. 2003, 61/2. Totals, 163/2.

UDOKA, MFON   F   COMETS

PERSONAL: Born June 6, 1976 in Portland, Ore. ... 6-0/187 (1.83 m/85 kg).
HIGH SCHOOL: Benson (Portland).
COLLEGE: DePaul.
TRANSACTIONS/CAREER NOTES: Signed by the WNBA and assigned to Detroit on May 8, 1998. ... Signed by Houston Comets as free agent May 1, 2003.

COLLEGIATE RECORD

Notes: All-Conference USA First Team (1997, 1996).

Season Team	G	Min.	FGM	FGA	Pct.	FTM	FTA	Pct.	Reb.	Ast.	Pts.	RPG	APG	PPG
												AVERAGES		
94-95—DePaul........................	25		73	146	.580	46	83	.554	161	15	192	6.4	0.6	7.7
95-96—DePaul........................	30		145	263	.551	89	144	.618	266	24	379	8.9	0.8	12.6
96-97—DePaul........................	28		206	382	.539	94	171	.550	339	38	506	12.1	1.3	18.1
97-98—DePaul........................	24		168	326	.515	141	230	.613	281	45	482	11.7	1.8	20.1
Totals	107		592	1117	.530	370	628	.596	1047	122	1559	9.8	1.1	14.5

Three-point field goals: 1994-05, 0-for-1. 1995-96, 0-for-0. 1996-97, 0-for-0. 1997-98, 5-for-27 (.185). Totals, 5-for-28 (.178).

WNBA REGULAR-SEASON RECORD

Season Team	G	Min.	FGM	FGA	Pct.	FTM	FTA	Pct.	Off.	Def.	Tot.	Ast.	St.	Blk.	TO	Pts.	RPG	APG	PPG
									REBOUNDS								**AVERAGES**		
1998—Detroit	3	25	1	6	.120	2	4	.500	1	2	3	0	0	0	1	4	1.0	—	1.3
2003—Houston	25	251	32	64	.500	16	23	.696	22	29	51	4	4	2	21	80	2.0	0.2	3.2
Totals.................	25	251	32	64	.500	16	23	.696	22	29	51	4	4	2	21	80	2.0	0.2	3.2

Three-point field goals: 2003, 0-for-1. Totals, 0-for-1.
Personal fouls/disqualifications: 2003, 38/0. Totals, 38/0.

WNBA PLAYOFF RECORD

Season Team	G	Min.	FGM	FGA	Pct.	FTM	FTA	Pct.	Off.	Def.	Tot.	Ast.	St.	Blk.	TO	Pts.	RPG	APG	PPG
									REBOUNDS								**AVERAGES**		
2003—Houston	1	6	0	0	...	1	2	.500	0	1	1	0	0	0	2	1	1.0	0.0	1.0
Totals.................	1	6	0	0	...	1	2	.500	0	1	1	0	0	0	2	1	1.0	0.0	1.0

UJHELYI, PETRA   F/C   MYSTICS

PERSONAL: Born December 17, 1980, in Budapest, Hungary. ... 6-4/200 (1.93 m/91 kg).
HIGH SCHOOL: Varosmajori Budapest (Budapest, Hungary).
COLLEGE: South Carolina.
TRANSACTIONS/CAREER NOTES: Selected by Phoenix in second round (16th overall) of WNBA Draft, April 25, 2003. ... Traded along with Telisha Quarles by Phoenix to Detroit in exchange for Edwina Brown and Lenae Williams, April 28, 2003. ... Waived by Detroit, April 22, 2004. ... Signed by Washington as a free agent, April 25, 2004.

U

MISCELLANEOUS: Hungarian Youth Player of the Year (1998, 1997). … Led the 2000 Hungarian Junior National Team to a 25-4 record. … Led her Club Team to two Hungarian Championships. … Parents and older brother competed on Hungarian National Teams. … Member of WNBA Championship Team (2003).

COLLEGIATE RECORD

NOTES: Finished as the SEC's regular season leading rebounder (9.3), … As a senior broke the USC record for defensive rebounds in a season (198). … During her sophomore year she was named to the Torneo de Cancun Basquetbol All-Tournament Team.

Season Team	G	Min.	FGM	FGA	Pct.	FTM	FTA	Pct.	Reb.	Ast.	Pts.	RPG	APG	PPG
												AVERAGES		
99-00—South Carolina	28	732	70	179	.391	33	44	.750	…	56	174	6.4	2.0	6.2
00-01—South Carolina	28	651	96	207	.464	44	81	.543	…	42	236	6.3	1.5	8.4
01-02—South Carolina	32	830	93	215	.433	32	66	.485	…	64	218	5.9	2.0	6.8
02-03—South Carolina	31	1067	155	343	.452	47	89	.528	…	102	362	9.3	3.3	11.7
Totals	119	3280	414	944	.439	156	280	.557	0	264	990	0.0	2.2	8.3

Three-point field goals: 1999-00, 1-for-8 (.125). 2000-01, 0-for-2. 2001-02, 0-for-6. 2002-03, 5-for-17 (.294). Totals, 6-for-33 (.182).

WNBA REGULAR-SEASON RECORD

Season Team	G	Min.	FGM	FGA	Pct.	FTM	FTA	Pct.	Off.	Def.	Tot.	Ast.	St.	Blk.	TO	Pts.	RPG	APG	PPG
									REBOUNDS								AVERAGES		
2003—Detroit	14	68	2	8	.250	0	3	.000	3	9	12	3	0	1	10	4	0.9	0.2	0.3
Totals	14	68	2	8	.250	0	3	.000	3	9	12	3	0	1	10	4	0.9	0.2	0.3

VAN GORP, MICHELE   C   LYNX

PERSONAL: Born May 10, 1977, in Warren, Mich. … 6-6/187 (1.98 m/85 kg). … **Full name:** Michele Marie Van Gorp.

HIGH SCHOOL: Chippewa Valley (Clinton Township, Mich.).

COLLEGE: Duke.

TRANSACTIONS/CAREER NOTES: Selected by New York in the second round (18th overall) in the WNBA Draft, May 4, 1999. … Acquired by Portland from New York in exchange for selecting Sophia Witherspoon and Coquese Washington in the WNBA Expansion Draft, December 15, 1999. … Traded by Portland with G/F Lynn Pride to Minnesota for F Kristin Folkl and the 12th pick in the 2001 WNBA Draft, February 20, 2001.

COLLEGIATE RECORD

NOTES: Member of NCAA Division I championship team (1999). … Kodak All-America first team (1999).

Season Team	G	Min.	FGM	FGA	Pct.	FTM	FTA	Pct.	Reb.	Ast.	Pts.	RPG	APG	PPG
												AVERAGES		
94-95—Purdue	23	…	23	49	.469	9	15	.600	46	5	55	2.0	0.2	2.4
95-96—Purdue	31	…	97	160	.606	32	47	.681	113	15	226	3.6	0.5	7.3
97-98—Duke	32	…	131	233	.562	65	95	.684	130	23	333	4.1	0.7	10.4
98-99—Duke	36	…	258	416	.620	92	153	.601	197	40	610	5.5	1.1	16.9
Totals	122	…	509	858	.593	198	310	.639	486	83	1224	4.0	0.7	10.0

Three-point field goals: 1997-98, 6-for-19 (.316). 1998-99, 2-for-8 (.250). Totals, 8-for-27 (.296).

WNBA REGULAR-SEASON RECORD

Season Team	G	Min.	FGM	FGA	Pct.	FTM	FTA	Pct.	Off.	Def.	Tot.	Ast.	St.	Blk.	TO	Pts.	RPG	APG	PPG
									REBOUNDS								AVERAGES		
1999—New York	21	117	8	24	.333	4	5	.800	5	12	17	7	1	3	3	20	0.8	0.3	1.0
2000—Portland	28	199	25	50	.500	19	35	.543	16	26	42	5	3	4	30	69	1.5	0.2	2.5
2001—Minnesota	22	243	15	40	.375	11	20	.550	15	19	34	12	3	6	18	41	1.5	0.5	1.9
2002—Minnesota	22	352	41	90	.456	16	22	.727	29	35	64	14	6	11	20	100	2.9	0.6	4.5
2003—Minnesota	31	528	70	162	.432	35	52	.673	32	75	107	17	10	20	56	175	3.5	0.5	5.6
Totals	124	1439	159	366	.434	85	134	.634	97	167	264	55	23	44	127	405	2.1	0.4	3.3

Three-point field goals: 2001, 0-for-1. 2002, 2-for-7 (.286). 2003, 0-for-1. Totals, 2-for-9 (.222).
Personal fouls/disqualifications: 2001, 36/0. 2002, 53/2. 2003, 87/2. Totals, 236/4.

WNBA PLAYOFF RECORD

Season Team	G	Min.	FGM	FGA	Pct.	FTM	FTA	Pct.	Off.	Def.	Tot.	Ast.	St.	Blk.	TO	Pts.	RPG	APG	PPG
									REBOUNDS								AVERAGES		
2003—Minnesota	3	31	2	7	.286	5	8	.625	0	1	1	3	1	3	4	9	0.3	1.0	3.0
Totals	3	31	2	7	.286	5	8	.625	0	1	1	3	1	3	4	9	0.3	1.0	3.0

VODICHKOVA, KAMILA   F/C   STORM

PERSONAL: Born December 19, 1972, in Czech Republic … 6-4/190 (1.93 m/86 kg). … **Full name:** Kamila Vodichkova.

TRANSACTIONS/CAREER NOTES: Selected by Seattle in first round (ninth overall) of WNBA Draft, April 25, 2000.

MISCELLANEOUS: Member of Czech Republic National Team.

WNBA REGULAR-SEASON RECORD

Season Team	G	Min.	FGM	FGA	Pct.	FTM	FTA	Pct.	Off.	Def.	Tot.	Ast.	St.	Blk.	TO	Pts.	RPG	APG	PPG
									REBOUNDS								AVERAGES		
2000—Seattle	23	489	68	171	.398	60	78	.769	28	69	97	22	13	12	57	200	4.2	1.0	8.7
2001—Seattle	29	405	51	122	.418	38	44	.864	25	46	71	23	16	7	34	150	2.4	0.8	5.2

2002—Seattle	32	817	114	245	.465	54	67	.806	61	115	176	47	36	18	55	295	5.5	1.5	9.2
2003—Seattle	28	709	101	213	.474	82	101	.812	55	88	143	31	20	21	53	284	5.1	1.1	10.1
Totals	112	2420	334	751	.445	234	290	.807	169	318	487	123	85	58	199	929	4.3	1.1	8.3

Three-point field goals: 2000, 4-for-20 (.200). 2001, 10-for-25 (.400). 2002, 13-for-38 (.342). 2003, 0-for-5. Totals, 27-for-88 (.307).
Personal fouls/disqualifications: 2000, 63/0. 2001, 56/0. 2002, 96/1. 2003, 101/4. Totals, 316/5.

WNBA PLAYOFF RECORD

								REBOUNDS								AVERAGES		
Season Team	G	Min.	FGM	FGA	Pct.	FTM	FTA	Pct.	Off.	Def.	Tot.	Ast.	St.	Blk.	TO	Pts.	RPG	APG PPG
2002—Seattle	2	61	7	16	.438	10	11	.909	2	8	10	3	2	0	2	25	5.0	1.5 12.5
Totals	2	61	7	16	.438	10	11	.909	2	8	10	3	2	0	2	25	5.0	1.5 12.5

Three-point field goals: 2002, 1-for-2 (.500). Totals, 1-for-2 (.500).
Personal fouls/disqualifications: 2002, 3/0. Totals, 3/0.

WALKER, AYANA F SHOCK

PERSONAL: Born September 10, 1979, in Houston, Texas ... 6-3/143 (1.91 m/65 kg). ... **Full name:** Ayana D'Nay Walker.
HIGH SCHOOL: Westbury (Houston).
COLLEGE: Louisiana Tech.
TRANSACTIONS/CAREER NOTES: Selected by Detroit in second round (20th overall) of WNBA Draft, April 19, 2002.
MISCELLANEOUS: USA Basketball Female Athlete of the Year (2001). ... Member of gold-medal winning USA Basketball Women's National Team (2001). ... Set USA single-game record with 19 rebounds in gold-medal game. ... Member of WNBA Championship Team (2003).

COLLEGIATE RECORD

											AVERAGES		
Season Team	G	Min.	FGM	FGA	Pct.	FTM	FTA	Pct.	Reb.	Ast.	Pts.	RPG	APG	PPG
98-99—Louisiana Tech	33	524	70	141	.496	14	39	.359	123	9	154	3.7	0.3	4.7
99-00—Louisiana Tech	33	786	139	263	.529	54	75	.720	234	28	332	7.1	0.8	10.1
00-01—Louisiana Tech	36	1148	241	507	.475	94	135	.696	305	64	577	8.5	1.8	16.0
01-02—Louisiana Tech	29	824	162	364	.445	67	98	.684	266	46	391	9.2	1.6	13.5
Totals	131	3282	612	1275	.480	229	347	.660	928	147	1454	7.1	1.1	11.1

Three-point field goals: 1998-99, 0-for-1. 1999-00, 0-for-1. 2000-01, 1-for-4 (.250). 2001-02, 0-for-1. Totals, 1-for-7 (.143).

WNBA REGULAR-SEASON RECORD

								REBOUNDS								AVERAGES		
Season Team	G	Min.	FGM	FGA	Pct.	FTM	FTA	Pct.	Off.	Def.	Tot.	Ast.	St.	Blk.	TO	Pts.	RPG	APG PPG
2002—Detroit	32	548	63	167	.377	34	49	.694	56	62	118	17	12	34	29	162	3.7	0.5 5.1
2003—Detroit	34	271	24	70	.343	8	21	.381	34	37	71	10	10	11	19	56	2.1	0.3 1.6
Totals	66	819	87	237	.367	42	70	.600	90	99	189	27	22	45	48	218	2.9	0.4 3.3

Three-point field goals: 2002, 2-for-9 (.222). Totals, 2-for-9 (.222).
Personal fouls/disqualifications: 2002, 56/0. Totals, 89/0.

WNBA PLAYOFF RECORD

								REBOUNDS								AVERAGES		
Season Team	G	Min.	FGM	FGA	Pct.	FTM	FTA	Pct.	Off.	Def.	Tot.	Ast.	St.	Blk.	TO	Pts.	RPG	APG PPG
2003—Detroit	4	24	1	5	.200	3	3	1.000	3	3	6	0	4	1	1	5	1.5	0.0 1.3
Totals	4	24	1	5	.200	3	3	1.000	3	3	6	0	4	1	1	5	1.5	0.0 1.3

WALKER, DEMYA F MONARCHS

PERSONAL: Born November 28, 1977, in Mount Holly, N.J. ... 6-4/168 (1.93 m/76 kg). ... **Full name:** DeMya Chakheia Walker.
HIGH SCHOOL: Rancocas Valley Regional (Mount Holly, N.J.).
COLLEGE: Virginia.
TRANSACTIONS/CAREER NOTES: Signed by WNBA and assigned to Portland, May 2, 2000. ... Selected by Sacramento as the fifth overall pick in the 2003 WNBA Dispersal Draft on April 24, 2003.

COLLEGIATE RECORD

NOTES: ACC All-Conference First Team (1998-99). ... ACC All-Tournament Second Team (1998-99). ... First in ACC in blocked shots (1998-99). ... Only ACC player to be named a finalist for Naismith Player of the Year Award (1998-99). ... Women's Basketball Journal Defensive All-America Second Team (1998-99).

											AVERAGES		
Season Team	G	Min.	FGM	FGA	Pct.	FTM	FTA	Pct.	Reb.	Ast.	Pts.	RPG	APG	PPG
95-96—Virginia	33	...	106	203	.522	38	73	.521	209	19	250	6.3	0.6	7.6
96-97—Virginia	31	...	165	276	.598	96	132	.727	232	44	426	7.5	1.4	13.7
97-98—Virginia	29	...	190	344	.552	91	144	.632	245	55	472	8.4	1.9	16.3
98-99—Virginia	29	...	168	306	.549	95	144	.660	246	80	435	8.5	2.8	15.0
Totals	122	...	629	1129	.557	320	493	.649	932	198	1583	7.6	1.6	13.0

Three-point field goals: 1995-96, 0-for-1. 1996-97, 0-for-1. 1997-98, 1-for-7 (.143). 1998-99, 4-for-14 (.286). Totals, 5-for-23 (.217).

W

WNBA REGULAR-SEASON RECORD

								REBOUNDS								AVERAGES		
Season Team	G	Min.	FGM	FGA	Pct.	FTM	FTA	Pct.	Off.	Def.	Tot.	Ast.	St.	Blk.	TO	Pts.	RPG APG PPG	
2000—Portland	30	311	35	88	.398	22	47	.468	29	18	47	19	17	7	35	92	1.6 0.6 3.1	
2001—Portland	21	297	44	100	.440	23	40	.575	29	29	58	10	7	12	35	113	2.8 0.5 5.4	
2002—Portland	31	848	139	287	.484	59	95	.621	55	99	154	51	26	33	90	339	5.0 1.6 10.9	
2003—Sacramento	34	740	111	242	.459	83	143	.580	61	88	149	47	25	23	69	307	4.4 1.4 9.0	
Totals................	116	2196	329	717	.459	187	325	.575	174	234	408	127	75	75	229	851	3.5 1.1 7.3	

Three-point field goals: 2000, 0-for-2. 2001, 2-for-3 (.667). 2002, 2-for-12 (.167). 2003, 2-for-15 (.133). Totals, 6-for-32 (.188).
Personal fouls/disqualifications: 2000, 69/1. 2001, 51/0. 2002, 97/1. 2003, 95/0. Totals, 312/2.

WNBA PLAYOFF RECORD

								REBOUNDS								AVERAGES		
Season Team	G	Min.	FGM	FGA	Pct.	FTM	FTA	Pct.	Off.	Def.	Tot.	Ast.	St.	Blk.	TO	Pts.	RPG APG PPG	
2003—Sacramento	6	170	24	55	.436	11	20	.550	14	13	27	10	1	3	21	59	4.5 1.7 9.8	
Totals................	6	170	24	55	.436	11	20	.550	14	13	27	10	1	3	21	59	4.5 1.7 9.8	

WALSETH, MAREN   F   STORM

PERSONAL: Born October 28, 1978, in Minneapolis, Minn. ... 6-2/184 (1.88 m/83 kg). ... **Full name:** Maren Satrom Walseth.
HIGH SCHOOL: Thomas Jefferson (Bloomington, Minn.).
COLLEGE: Penn State.
TRANSACTIONS/CAREER NOTES: Selected by Sacramento in third round (46th overall) of WNBA Draft, April 20, 2001. ... Waived on June 15, 2001. ... Aded by Washington on April 25, 2002.

COLLEGIATE RECORD

											AVERAGES		
Season Team	G	Min.	FGM	FGA	Pct.	FTM	FTA	Pct.	Reb.	Ast.	Pts.	RPG APG PPG	
97-98—Penn State................	34	526	81	180	.450	54	102	.529	114	21	216	3.4 0.6 6.4	
98-99—Penn State................	30	478	84	159	.528	71	104	.683	114	22	239	3.8 0.7 8.0	
99-00—Penn State................	35	1018	193	380	.508	96	142	.676	203	72	482	5.8 2.1 13.8	
00-01—Penn State................	29	907	142	279	.509	107	153	.699	214	85	391	7.4 2.9 13.5	
Totals	128	2929	500	998	.501	328	501	.655	645	200	1328	5.0 1.6 10.4	

Three-point field goals: 1998-99, 0-for-1. 1999-000, 0-for-1. 2000-01, 0-for-2. Totals, 0-for-4.

WNBA REGULAR-SEASON RECORD

								REBOUNDS								AVERAGES		
Season Team	G	Min.	FGM	FGA	Pct.	FTM	FTA	Pct.	Off.	Def.	Tot.	Ast.	St.	Blk.	TO	Pts.	RPG APG PPG	
2001—Sacramento....	4	8	1	2	.500	2	2	1.000	2	0	2	0	0	0	2	4	0.5 0.0 1.0	
2002—Washington ...	18	104	6	25	.240	0	2	.000	7	14	21	7	2	0	9	13	1.2 0.4 0.7	
Totals................	22	112	7	27	.259	2	4	.500	9	14	23	7	2	0	11	17	1.0 0.3 0.8	

Three-point field goals: 2002, 1-for-7 (.143). Totals, 1-for-7 (.143).
Personal fouls/disqualifications: 2002, 8/0.

WNBA PLAYOFF RECORD

								REBOUNDS								AVERAGES		
Season Team	G	Min.	FGM	FGA	Pct.	FTM	FTA	Pct.	Off.	Def.	Tot.	Ast.	St.	Blk.	TO	Pts.	RPG APG PPG	
2002—Washington ...	1	7	0	2	.000	0	0	...	0	0	0	1	0	1	1	0	0.0 1.0 0.0	
Totals................	1	7	0	2	.000	0	0	...	0	0	0	1	0	1	1	0	0.0 1.0 0.0	

Personal fouls/disqualifications: 2002, 1/0. Totals, 1/0.

WASHINGTON, COQUESE G

PERSONAL: Born January 17, 1971, in Flint, Mich. ... 5-6/138 (1.68 m/63 kg). ... **Full name:** Coquese Makebra Washington.
HIGH SCHOOL: Flint (Flint, Mich.).
COLLEGE: Notre Dame.
TRANSACTIONS/CAREER NOTES: Signed by the WNBA and assigned to the New York Liberty, May 8, 1998. ... Selected by Portland in the fourth round (13th overall) of the WNBA Expansion Draft, December 15, 1999. ... Traded by Portland to Houston for Mila Nikolich, January 28, 2000. ... Traded by Houston to Indiana for G Rita Williams, July 20, 2002.
MISCELLANEOUS: Member of WNBA Championship Team (2000).

COLLEGIATE RECORD

											AVERAGES		
Season Team	G	Min.	FGM	FGA	Pct.	FTM	FTA	Pct.	Reb.	Ast.	Pts.	RPG APG PPG	
89-90—Notre Dame..............	29	...	85	105	.810	17	31	.548	62	114	198	2.1 3.9 6.8	
90-91—Notre Dame..............	32	...	120	250	.480	30	40	.750	123	179	294	3.8 5.6 9.2	
91-92—Notre Dame..............	25	...	67	179	.374	37	50	.740	94	141	185	3.8 5.6 7.4	
92-93—Notre Dame..............	27	...	106	273	.388	26	33	.788	104	120	271	3.9 4.4 10.0	
Totals	113	...	378	807	.468	110	154	.714	383	554	948	3.4 4.9 8.4	

Three-point field goals: 1989-90, 11-for-25 (.440). 1990-91, 24-for-61 (.393). 1991-92, 14-for-50 (.280). 1992-93, 33-for-95 (.347). Totals, 82-for-231 (.355)

WNBA REGULAR-SEASON RECORD

								REBOUNDS								AVERAGES		
Season Team	G	Min.	FGM	FGA	Pct.	FTM	FTA	Pct.	Off.	Def.	Tot.	Ast.	St.	Blk.	TO	Pts.	RPG APG PPG	
1998—New York......	28	226	15	51	.294	18	26	.692	5	21	26	44	17	0	37	53	0.9 1.6 1.9	
1999—New York......	19	77	5	18	.278	2	2	1.000	1	6	7	15	9	0	13	12	0.4 0.8 0.6	

W

Season Team	G	Min.	FGM	FGA	Pct.	FTM	FTA	Pct.	Off.	Def.	Tot.	Ast.	St.	Blk.	TO	Pts.	RPG	APG	PPG
2000—Houston	25	236	12	33	.364	16	20	.800	3	16	19	24	16	0	19	43	0.8	1.0	1.7
2001—Houston	32	1013	63	177	.356	14	22	.636	20	98	118	122	69	9	57	169	3.7	3.8	5.3
2002—Hou.-Ind.	32	674	43	120	.358	16	22	.727	14	60	74	79	36	2	44	124	2.3	2.5	3.9
2003—Indiana	20	348	19	67	.284	11	13	.846	2	27	29	48	14	2	30	63	1.5	2.4	3.2
Totals	156	2574	157	466	.337	77	105	.733	45	228	273	332	161	13	200	464	1.8	2.1	3.0

Three-point field goals: 1998, 5-for-21 (.238). 1999, 0-for-5. 2000, 3-for-15 (.200). 2001, 29-for-81 (.358). 2002, 22-for-52 (.423). 2003, 14-for-48 (.292). Totals, 73-for-222 (.329).
Personal fouls/disqualifications: 1998, 31/0. 1999, 15/0. 2000, 19/0. 2001, 63/1. 2002, 60/1. 2003, 32/0. Totals, 220/2.

WNBA PLAYOFF RECORD

Season Team	G	Min.	FGM	FGA	Pct.	FTM	FTA	Pct.	Off.	Def.	Tot.	Ast.	St.	Blk.	TO	Pts.	RPG	APG	PPG
2000—Houston	6	92	3	9	.333	5	6	.833	4	7	11	6	5	1	8	14	1.8	1.0	2.3
2001—Houston	2	74	3	17	.176	0	0	...	2	7	9	5	2	0	2	7	4.5	2.5	3.5
2002—Indiana	3	110	9	27	.333	1	1	1.000	1	5	6	14	3	0	6	25	2.0	4.7	8.3
Totals	11	276	15	53	.283	6	7	.857	7	19	26	25	10	1	16	46	2.4	2.3	4.2

Three-point field goals: 2000, 3-for-7 (.429). 2001, 1-for-10 (.100). 2002, 6-for-16 (.375). Totals, 10-for-33 (.303).
Personal fouls/disqualifications: 2000, 4/0. 2001, 5/0. 2002, 10/0. Totals, 19/0.

WAUTERS, ANN   C   LIBERTY

PERSONAL: Born October 12, 1980, in Sint-Niklaas, Belgium ... 6-4/193 (1.93 m/88 kg).
HIGH SCHOOL: Heilige Familie (Sint-Niklaas, Belgium).
TRANSACTIONS/CAREER NOTES: Selected by Cleveland in first round (first overall) of WNBA Draft, April 25, 2000. ... Selected by New York with the fourth overall pick in the 2004 Dispersal Draft, January 6, 2004.

WNBA REGULAR-SEASON RECORD

Season Team	G	Min.	FGM	FGA	Pct.	FTM	FTA	Pct.	Off.	Def.	Tot.	Ast.	St.	Blk.	TO	Pts.	RPG	APG	PPG
2000—Cleveland	32	598	78	149	.523	43	58	.741	47	82	129	37	21	24	63	199	4.0	1.2	6.2
2001—Cleveland	24	622	87	153	.569	60	75	.800	35	79	114	35	17	13	50	234	4.8	1.5	9.8
2002—Cleveland	28	802	120	217	.553	74	87	.851	45	95	140	39	16	21	59	314	5.0	1.4	11.2
Totals	84	2022	285	519	.549	177	220	.805	127	256	383	111	54	58	172	747	4.6	1.3	8.9

Three-point field goals: 2000, 0-for-2. 2001, 0-for-2. 2002, 0-for-1. Totals, 0-for-5.
Personal fouls/disqualifications: 2000, 75/0. 2001, 55/0. 2002, 74/0. Totals, 204/0.

WNBA PLAYOFF RECORD

Season Team	G	Min.	FGM	FGA	Pct.	FTM	FTA	Pct.	Off.	Def.	Tot.	Ast.	St.	Blk.	TO	Pts.	RPG	APG	PPG
2000—Cleveland	6	107	13	27	.481	2	6	.333	5	13	18	5	3	3	8	28	3.0	0.8	4.7
2001—Cleveland	3	86	13	19	.684	8	9	.889	6	4	10	2	2	3	4	34	3.3	0.7	11.3
Totals	9	193	26	46	.565	10	15	.667	11	17	28	7	5	6	12	62	3.1	0.8	6.9

Three-point field goals: 2000, 0-for-2. Totals, 0-for-2.
Personal fouls/disqualifications: 2000, 7/0. Totals, 17/0.

W

WEATHERSPOON, TERESA   G   SPARKS

PERSONAL: Born December 8, 1965, in Jasper, Texas ... 5-8/161 (1.73 m/73 kg). ... **Full name:** Teresa Gaye Weatherspoon.
HIGH SCHOOL: West Sabine (Pineland, Texas).
COLLEGE: Louisiana Tech.
TRANSACTIONS/CAREER NOTES: Signed by the WNBA and assigned to the New York Liberty, January 22, 1997. ... Signed by Los Angeles as an unrestricted free agent, February 4, 2004.

COLLEGIATE RECORD

NOTES: Member of NCAA Division I championship team (1988). ... Wade Trophy Recipient (1988). ... Kodak All-America first team (1987, 1988).

Season Team	G	Min.	FGM	FGA	Pct.	FTM	FTA	Pct.	Reb.	Ast.	Pts.	RPG	APG	PPG
84-85—Louisiana Tech	33	...	72	140	.514	51	100	.510	127	238	195	3.8	7.2	5.9
85-86—Louisiana Tech	32	...	110	226	.487	61	112	.545	125	253	281	3.9	7.9	8.8
86-87—Louisiana Tech	33	...	122	234	.521	67	95	.705	137	269	311	4.2	8.2	9.4
87-88—Louisiana Tech	33	...	119	249	.478	57	86	.663	144	198	300	4.4	6.0	9.1
Totals	131	...	423	849	.498	236	393	.601	533	958	1087	4.1	7.3	8.3

OLYMPICS

NOTES: Member of gold medal-winning U.S. Olympic Team (1988), and bronze medal-winning U.S. Olympic Team (1992).

Season Team	G	Min.	FGM	FGA	Pct.	FTM	FTA	Pct.	Reb.	Ast.	Pts.	RPG	APG	PPG
1988—United States	5	...	5	13	.385	6	8	.750	12	9	16	2.4	1.8	3.2
1992—United States	5	...	2	10	.200	7	8	.875	1	5	11	0.2	1.0	2.2
Totals	10	...	7	23	.304	13	16	.813	13	14	27	1.3	1.4	2.7

WNBA REGULAR-SEASON RECORD

HONORS: WNBA Defensive Player of the Year (1997, 1998). ... All-WNBA second team (1997, 1998, 1999, 2000).
NOTES: Led WNBA in steals in 1997 (3.04 spg) and 1998 (3.33 spg). ... Led WNBA in assists in 1997 (6.1 apg).

Season Team	G	Min.	FGM	FGA	Pct.	FTM	FTA	Pct.	REBOUNDS Off.	Def.	Tot.	Ast.	St.	Blk.	TO	Pts.	AVERAGES RPG	APG	PPG
1997—New York	28	924	64	137	.467	65	100	.650	25	91	116	172	85	2	94	196	4.1	6.1	7.0
1998—New York	30	1002	73	188	.388	42	69	.609	20	100	120	191	100	0	96	204	4.0	6.4	6.8
1999—New York	32	1086	80	190	.421	38	56	.679	22	82	104	205	78	3	80	229	3.3	6.4	7.2
2000—New York	32	1078	67	153	.438	60	81	.741	16	93	109	205	65	5	86	205	3.4	6.4	6.4
2001—New York	32	974	72	167	.431	53	79	.671	29	89	118	203	55	4	81	207	3.7	6.3	6.5
2002—New York	32	954	39	114	.342	28	54	.519	23	63	86	181	42	3	78	108	2.7	5.7	3.4
2003—New York	34	824	37	96	.385	24	32	.750	19	78	97	149	28	5	62	98	2.9	4.4	2.9
Totals	220	6842	432	1045	.413	310	471	.658	154	596	750	1306	453	22	577	1247	3.4	5.9	5.7

Three-point field goals: 1997, 3-for-35 (.086). 1998, 16-for-49 (.327). 1999, 31-for-82 (.378). 2000, 11-for-44 (.250). 2001, 10-for-26 (.385). 2002, 2-for-20 (.100). 2003, 0-for-4. Totals, 73-for-260 (.281).
Personal fouls/disqualifications: 1997, 72/0. 1998, 85/0. 1999, 91/1. 2000, 85/0. 2001, 83/1. 2002, 88/2. 2003, 60/0. Totals, 564/4.

WNBA PLAYOFF RECORD

Season Team	G	Min.	FGM	FGA	Pct.	FTM	FTA	Pct.	REBOUNDS Off.	Def.	Tot.	Ast.	St.	Blk.	TO	Pts.	AVERAGES RPG	APG	PPG
1997—New York	2	75	5	10	.500	0	2	.000	1	2	3	10	4	0	12	10	1.5	5.0	5.0
1999—New York	6	203	19	42	.452	6	8	.750	4	17	21	45	6	0	12	51	3.5	7.5	8.5
2000—New York	7	253	12	34	.353	7	11	.636	2	17	19	49	19	0	20	32	2.7	7.0	4.6
2001—New York	6	198	8	38	.211	4	4	1.000	7	15	22	28	7	0	5	23	3.7	4.7	3.8
2002—New York	8	241	19	40	.475	15	18	.833	8	27	35	53	8	0	14	53	4.4	6.6	6.6
Totals	29	970	63	164	.384	32	43	.744	22	78	100	185	44	0	63	169	3.4	6.4	5.8

Three-point field goals: 1997, 0-for-2. 1999, 7-for-19 (.368). 2000, 1-for-5 (.200). 2001, 3-for-11 (.273). 2002, 0-for-2. Totals, 11-for-39 (.282).
Personal fouls/disqualifications: 1997, 6/0. 1999, 23/0. 2000, 20/1. 2001, 16/0. 2002, 18/0. Totals, 83/1.

WNBA ALL-STAR GAME RECORD

Season Team	Min.	FGM	FGA	Pct.	FTM	FTA	Pct.	REBOUNDS Off.	Def.	Tot.	Ast.	PF	Dq.	St.	Blk.	TO	Pts.
1999—New York	17	1	6	.167	0	0	...	0	2	2	4	2	0	1	0	...	3
2000—New York	20	1	4	.250	0	0	...	1	2	3	3	3	0	3	0	...	2
2001—New York	15	0	1	.000	0	0	...	0	1	1	2	0	0	3	0	...	0
2002—New York	21	2	3	.667	0	0	...	0	2	2	2	1	0	2	1	...	4
2003—New York	16	0	1	.000	0	2	.000	1	2	3	2	0	0	0	0	...	0
Totals	89	4	15	.267	0	2	.000	2	9	11	13	6	0	9	1	17	9

Three-point field goals: 1999, 1-for-2 (.500). 2000, 0-for-1. 2002, 0-for-1. Totals, 1-for-4 (.250).

WHITE, STEPHANIE   G/F   FEVER

PERSONAL: Born June 20, 1977 in Danville, Ill. ... 5-9/155 (1.75 m/70 kg). **Full name:** Stephanie Joanne White McCarty.
HIGH SCHOOL: Seeger HS (West Lebanon, Ind.).
COLLEGE: Purdue.
TRANSACTIONS/CAREER NOTES: Selected by Charlotte in second round (21st overall) of WNBA Draft, May 4, 1999. ... Selected by Miami in second round (6th overall) in 2000 WNBA Expansion Draft on December 15, 1999. ... Traded to Indiana for G Sandy Brondello and Indiana first-round pick (10th overall) in the 2000 WNBA Draft.

WNBA REGULAR-SEASON RECORD

Season Team	G	Min.	FGM	FGA	Pct.	FTM	FTA	Pct.	REBOUNDS Off.	Def.	Tot.	Ast.	St.	Blk.	TO	Pts.	AVERAGES RPG	APG	PPG
2003—Indiana	28	577	60	173	.347	45	48	.938	14	27	41	58	34	6	37	194	1.5	2.1	6.9
Totals	28	577	60	173	.347	45	48	.938	14	27	41	58	34	6	37	194	1.5	2.1	6.9

Three-point field goals: 2003, 29-for-84 (.345). Totals, 29-for-84 (.345).
Personal fouls/disqualifications: 2003, 60/0. Totals, 60/0.

WHITMORE, TAMIKA   F   SPARKS

PERSONAL: Born June 5, 1977, in Tupelo, Miss. ... 6-2/190 (1.88 m/86 kg). ... **Full name:** Tamika Whitmore.
HIGH SCHOOL: Tupelo (Tupelo, Miss.).
COLLEGE: Memphis.
TRANSACTIONS/CAREER NOTES: Selected by New York in the third round (30th overall) of the 1999 WNBA Draft, May 4, 1999. ... Signed by Los Angeles as a restricted free agent, May 3, 2004.

COLLEGIATE RECORD

NOTES: Led NCAA in scoring in 1999 (26.3 ppg).

Season Team	G	Min.	FGM	FGA	Pct.	FTM	FTA	Pct.	Reb.	Ast.	Pts.	AVERAGES RPG	APG	PPG
95-96—Memphis	30	...	119	206	.578	68	101	.673	152	25	312	5.1	0.8	10.4
96-97—Memphis	29	...	230	381	.604	116	162	.716	244	24	579	8.4	0.8	20.0
97-98—Memphis	29	...	300	464	.647	151	212	.712	288	39	754	9.9	1.3	26.0
98-99—Memphis	32	...	325	556	.585	163	218	.748	268	37	843	8.4	1.2	26.3
Totals	120	...	974	1607	.606	498	693	.719	952	125	2488	7.9	1.0	20.7

Three-point field goals: 1995-96, 6-for-21 (.286). 1996-97, 3-for-17 (.176). 1997-98, 3-for-12 (.250). 1998-99, 30-for-64 (.469). Totals, 42-for-114 (.368).

W

WNBA REGULAR-SEASON RECORD

Season Team	G	Min.	FGM	FGA	Pct.	FTM	FTA	Pct.	REBOUNDS Off.	Def.	Tot.	Ast.	St.	Blk.	TO	Pts.	AVERAGES RPG	APG	PPG
1999—New York	27	573	80	184	.435	53	78	.679	43	53	96	18	16	6	56	214	3.6	0.7	7.9
2000—New York	32	689	109	253	.431	59	84	.702	34	71	105	20	17	17	53	277	3.3	0.6	8.7
2001—New York	32	752	96	222	.432	33	58	.569	29	68	97	19	17	10	33	226	3.0	0.6	7.1
2002—New York	32	977	148	310	.477	110	150	.733	43	98	141	23	27	43	49	406	4.4	0.7	12.7
2003—New York	33	823	110	242	.455	50	76	.658	38	84	122	25	35	22	57	271	3.7	0.8	8.2
Totals	156	3814	543	1211	.448	305	446	.684	187	374	561	105	112	98	248	1394	3.6	0.7	8.9

Three-point field goals: 1999, 1-for-8 (.125). 2000, 0-for-3. 2001, 1-for-2 (.500). 2002, 0-for-1. 2003, 1-for-3 (.333). Totals, 3-for-17 (.176).
Personal fouls/disqualifications: 1999, 78/1. 2000, 102/1. 2001, 70/0. 2002, 102/1. 2003, 100/1. Totals, 452/4.

WNBA PLAYOFF RECORD

Season Team	G	Min.	FGM	FGA	Pct.	FTM	FTA	Pct.	REBOUNDS Off.	Def.	Tot.	Ast.	St.	Blk.	TO	Pts.	AVERAGES RPG	APG	PPG
1999—New York	6	114	15	31	.484	5	14	.357	5	5	10	3	4	2	10	35	1.7	0.5	5.8
2000—New York	7	196	31	65	.477	18	24	.750	9	18	27	6	3	9	15	81	3.9	0.9	11.6
2001—New York	6	152	18	44	.409	6	10	.600	10	12	22	4	4	4	7	42	3.7	0.7	7.0
2002—New York	8	271	51	93	.548	26	37	.703	8	28	36	10	3	4	9	129	4.5	1.3	16.1
Totals	27	733	115	233	.494	55	85	.647	32	63	95	23	14	19	41	287	3.5	0.9	10.6

Three-point field goals: 2000, 1-for-2 (.500). 2001, 0-for-1. 2002, 1-for-3 (.333). Totals, 2-for-6 (.333).
Personal fouls/disqualifications: 2000, 22/0. 2001, 13/0. 2002, 20/0. Totals, 69/0.

WILLIAMS, ADRIAN   F/C   MERCURY

PERSONAL: Born February 15, 1977, in Fresno, Calif. ... 6-4/170 (1.93 m/77 kg).
HIGH SCHOOL: Clovis West (Fresno, Calif.).
COLLEGE: U.S.C..
TRANSACTIONS/CAREER NOTES: Selected by Phoenix in second round (21st overall) of WNBA Draft, April 25, 2000.

COLLEGIATE RECORD

NOTES: All-Pac-10 first team (1999). ... All-Pac-10 honorable mention (1998).

Season Team	G	Min.	FGM	FGA	Pct.	FTM	FTA	Pct.	Reb.	Ast.	Pts.	AVERAGES RPG	APG	PPG
95-96—Southern Cal	27	...	107	219	.489	45	80	.563	157	11	260	5.8	0.4	9.6
96-97—Southern Cal	29	...	88	220	.400	55	89	.618	161	23	235	5.6	0.8	8.1
97-98—Southern Cal	27	...	139	324	.429	71	134	.530	185	22	350	6.9	0.8	13.0
98-99—Southern Cal	23	...	125	334	.374	87	139	.626	191	35	340	8.3	1.5	14.8
Totals	106	...	459	1097	.418	258	442	.584	694	91	1185	6.5	0.9	11.2

Three-point field goals: 1995-96, 1-for-2 (.500). 1996-97, 4-for-24 (.167). 1997-98, 1-for-3 (.333). 1998-99, 3-for-19 (.158). Totals, 9-for-48 (.188).

WNBA REGULAR-SEASON RECORD

Season Team	G	Min.	FGM	FGA	Pct.	FTM	FTA	Pct.	REBOUNDS Off.	Def.	Tot.	Ast.	St.	Blk.	TO	Pts.	AVERAGES RPG	APG	PPG
2000—Phoenix	28	351	29	72	.403	20	38	.526	24	47	71	16	14	4	29	78	2.5	0.6	2.8
2001—Phoenix	25	375	38	113	.336	20	28	.714	21	54	75	11	15	5	34	96	3.0	0.4	3.8
2002—Phoenix	32	878	79	169	.467	42	60	.700	64	156	220	35	48	29	63	200	6.9	1.1	6.3
2003—Phoenix	34	985	141	351	.402	52	85	.612	68	184	252	31	57	19	73	334	7.4	0.9	9.8
Totals	119	2589	287	705	.407	134	211	.635	177	441	618	93	134	57	199	708	5.2	0.8	5.9

Three-point field goals: 2003, 0-for-1. Totals, 0-for-1.
Personal fouls/disqualifications: 2003, 95/1. Totals, 268/1.

WNBA PLAYOFF RECORD

Season Team	G	Min.	FGM	FGA	Pct.	FTM	FTA	Pct.	REBOUNDS Off.	Def.	Tot.	Ast.	St.	Blk.	TO	Pts.	AVERAGES RPG	APG	PPG
2000—Phoenix	2	30	2	4	.500	1	2	.500	1	3	4	1	0	2	1	5	2.0	0.5	2.5
Totals	2	30	2	4	.500	1	2	.500	1	3	4	1	0	2	1	5	2.0	0.5	2.5

WNBA ALL-STAR GAME RECORD

Season Team	Min.	FGM	FGA	Pct.	FTM	FTA	Pct.	REBOUNDS Off.	Def.	Tot.	Ast.	PF	Dq.	St.	Blk.	TO	Pts.
2003—Phoenix	19	4	6	.667	1	2	.500	1	5	6	0	1	0	2	0	...	9
Totals	19	4	6	.667	1	2	.500	1	5	6	0	1	0	2	0	1	9

WILLIAMS, NATALIE   F   FEVER

PERSONAL: Born November 30, 1970, in Long Beach, Calif. ... 6-2/210 (1.88 m/95 kg). ... **Full name:** Natalie Jean Williams.
HIGH SCHOOL: Taylorsville (Salt Lake City, Utah).
COLLEGE: UCLa..
TRANSACTIONS/CAREER NOTES: Selected by Utah in the first round (third overall) of the 1999 WNBA Draft, May 4, 1999. ... Traded by San Antonio with Coretta Brown to Indiana in exchange for Sylvia Crawley and Gwen Jackson, May 1, 2003.

NOTES: Kodak All-America first team (1994).

Season Team	G	Min.	FGM	FGA	Pct.	FTM	FTA	Pct.	Reb.	Ast.	Pts.	AVERAGES RPG	APG	PPG
90-91—UCLA	19	...	104	208	.500	61	91	.670	195	14	269	10.3	0.7	14.2
91-92—UCLA	23	...	197	352	.560	101	160	.631	318	29	495	13.8	1.3	21.5
92-93—UCLA	23	...	201	425	.473	86	115	.748	310	107	488	13.5	4.7	21.2
93-94—UCLA	24	...	243	426	.570	75	145	.517	314	31	561	13.1	1.3	23.4
Totals	89	...	745	1411	.528	323	511	.632	1137	181	1813	12.8	2.0	20.4

ABL REGULAR-SEASON RECORD

Notes: ABL Most Valuable Player (1998).

Season Team	G	Min.	FGM	FGA	Pct.	FTM	FTA	Pct.	Reb.	Ast.	Pts.	AVERAGES RPG	APG	PPG
96-97—Portland	32	...	215	412	.522	125	186	.672	400	50	555	12.5	1.6	17.3
97-98—Portland	44	...	351	633	.555	261	359	.727	508	84	964	11.5	1.9	21.9
98-99—Portland	13	...	94	162	.580	70	95	.737	129	29	258	9.9	2.2	19.8
Totals	89	...	660	1207	.547	456	640	.713	1037	163	1777	11.7	1.8	20.0

Three-point field goals: 1997-98, 1-for-5 (.200).

WNBA REGULAR-SEASON RECORD

HONORS: All-WNBA first team (1999, 2000, 2001).
NOTES: Led WNBA in rebounding in 2000 (11.6 rpg).

Season Team	G	Min.	FGM	FGA	Pct.	FTM	FTA	Pct.	REBOUNDS Off.	Def.	Tot.	Ast.	St.	Blk.	TO	Pts.	AVERAGES RPG	APG	PPG
1999—Utah	28	954	180	347	.519	144	191	.754	109	148	257	25	38	22	68	504	9.2	0.9	18.0
2000—Utah	29	1039	179	365	.490	182	228	.798	132	204	336	51	35	18	79	543	11.6	1.8	18.7
2001—Utah	31	1064	171	349	.490	97	133	.729	111	197	308	55	41	10	70	439	9.9	1.8	14.2
2002—Utah	31	1008	124	285	.435	98	132	.742	105	150	255	38	38	16	72	351	8.2	1.2	11.3
2003—Indiana	34	1054	176	363	.485	105	148	.709	109	146	255	46	43	21	70	457	7.5	1.4	13.4
Totals	153	5119	830	1709	.486	626	832	.752	566	845	1411	215	195	87	359	2294	9.2	1.4	15.0

Three-point field goals: 1999, 0-for-2. 2000, 3-for-5 (.600). 2001, 0-for-4. 2002, 5-for-12 (.417). 2003, 0-for-1. Totals, 8-for-24 (.333).
Personal fouls/disqualifications: 1999, 108/2. 2000, 124/3. 2001, 128/4. 2002, 122/4. 2003, 138/2. Totals, 620/15.

WNBA PLAYOFF RECORD

Season Team	G	Min.	FGM	FGA	Pct.	FTM	FTA	Pct.	REBOUNDS Off.	Def.	Tot.	Ast.	St.	Blk.	TO	Pts.	AVERAGES RPG	APG	PPG
2001—Utah	2	57	8	16	.500	5	6	.833	7	9	16	0	3	1	5	21	8.0	0.0	10.5
2002—Utah	5	186	25	47	.532	19	28	.679	21	25	46	7	5	7	8	70	9.2	1.4	14.0
Totals	7	243	33	63	.524	24	34	.706	28	34	62	7	8	8	13	91	8.9	1.0	13.0

Three-point field goals: 2002, 1-for-4 (.250). Totals, 1-for-4 (.250).
Personal fouls/disqualifications: 2002, 16/1. Totals, 26/2.

WNBA ALL-STAR GAME RECORD

NOTES: Winner of America Online NBA All-Star 2ball with Jeff Hornacek, Utah Jazz, at All-Star 2000 in Oakland.

Season Team	Min.	FGM	FGA	Pct.	FTM	FTA	Pct.	REBOUNDS Off.	Def.	Tot.	Ast.	PF	Dq.	St.	Blk.	TO	Pts.
1999—Utah	21	3	4	.750	8	10	.800	4	4	8	3	0	0	1	0	...	14
2000—Utah	17	2	6	.333	1	2	.500	4	6	10	0	3	0	1	0	...	5
2003—Indiana	22	3	5	.600	0	0	...	7	4	11	1	1	0	3	0	...	6
Totals	60	8	15	.533	9	12	.750	15	14	29	4	4	0	5	0	2	25

OLYMPICS

NOTES: Member of gold medal-winning U.S. Olympic Team (2000). ... USA Basketball's Female Athlete of the Year (1999).

Season Team	G	Min.	FGM	FGA	Pct.	FTM	FTA	Pct.	Reb.	Ast.	Pts.	AVERAGES RPG	APG	PPG
2000—United States	8	121	22	39	.564	17	25	.680	47	8	61	5.9	1.0	7.6
Totals	8	121	22	39	.564	17	25	.680	47	8	61	5.9	1.0	7.6

WILLIAMS, RITA　　　　G　　　　STORM

PERSONAL: Born January 14, 1976, in Norwalk, Conn. ... 5-6/135 (1.68 m/61 kg). ... **Full name:** Rita Williams.
COLLEGE: Connecticut.
TRANSACTIONS/CAREER NOTES: Selected by the Washington Mystics in the second round (13th overall) of the 1998 WNBA Draft, April 29, 1998. ... Selected by the Indiana Fever in the fifth round (17th overall) of the WNBA Expansion Draft, December 15, 1999. ... Traded by Indiana to Houston for G Coquese Washington, July 20, 2002. ... Traded by Houston to Seattle for a third-round selection in the 2004 WNBA Draft, May 21, 2003.

COLLEGIATE RECORD

Season Team	G	Min.	FGM	FGA	Pct.	FTM	FTA	Pct.	Reb.	Ast.	Pts.	AVERAGES RPG	APG	PPG
95-96—Connecticut	30	...	24	63	.381	27	52	.519	48	24	79	1.6	0.8	2.6
96-97—Connecticut	34	...	79	223	.354	74	134	.552	125	113	244	3.7	3.3	7.2
97-98—Connecticut	37	...	111	272	.408	101	150	.673	123	149	376	3.3	4.0	10.2
Totals	101	...	214	558	.384	202	336	.601	296	286	699	2.9	2.8	6.9

Three-point field goals: 1995-96, 4-for-19 (.211). 1996-97, 12-for-60 (.200). 1997-98, 53-for-150 (.353). Totals, 69-for-229 (.301).

Season Team	G	Min.	FGM	FGA	Pct.	FTM	FTA	Pct.	REBOUNDS Off.	Def.	Tot.	Ast.	St.	Blk.	TO	Pts.	AVERAGES RPG	APG	PPG
1998—Washington...	30	712	41	127	.323	38	60	.633	13	55	68	69	63	2	69	132	2.3	2.3	4.4
1999—Washington...	31	312	31	62	.500	23	36	.639	7	30	37	30	21	1	26	104	1.2	1.0	3.4
2000—Indiana.........	32	1014	112	274	.409	79	108	.731	22	73	95	101	76	3	69	352	3.0	3.2	11.0
2001—Indiana.........	32	1042	115	293	.392	109	130	.838	25	79	104	114	72	11	100	380	3.3	3.6	11.9
2002—Ind.a-Hou.......	29	569	44	146	.301	32	44	.727	10	33	43	50	32	2	39	139	1.5	1.7	4.8
2003—Seattle	32	381	28	75	.373	11	15	.733	3	19	22	41	14	0	27	78	0.7	1.3	2.4
Totals.................	186	4030	371	977	.380	292	393	.743	80	289	369	405	278	19	330	1185	2.0	2.2	6.4

Three-point field goals: 1998, 12-for-55 (.218). 1999, 19-for-34 (.559). 2000, 49-for-131 (.374). 2001, 41-for-109 (.376). 2002, 19-for-73 (.260). 2003, 11-for-43 (.256). Totals, 151-for-445 (.339).
Personal fouls/disqualifications: 1998, 51/0. 1999, 41/0. 2000, 69/1. 2001, 71/0. 2002, 45/0. 2003, 34/0. Totals, 311/1.

WNBA PLAYOFF RECORD

Season Team	G	Min.	FGM	FGA	Pct.	FTM	FTA	Pct.	REBOUNDS Off.	Def.	Tot.	Ast.	St.	Blk.	TO	Pts.	AVERAGES RPG	APG	PPG
2002—Houston	3	69	8	25	.320	0	0	...	3	3	6	7	3	0	1	20	2.0	2.3	6.7
Totals.................	3	69	8	25	.320	0	0	...	3	3	6	7	3	0	1	20	2.0	2.3	6.7

Three-point field goals: 2002, 4-for-14 (.286). Totals, 4-for-14 (.286).
Personal fouls/disqualifications: 2002, 5/0. Totals, 5/0.

WNBA ALL-STAR GAME RECORD

Season Team	Min.	FGM	FGA	Pct.	FTM	FTA	Pct.	REBOUNDS Off.	Def.	Tot.	Ast.	PF	Dq.	St.	Blk.	TO	Pts.
2001—Indiana	9	0	2	.000	0	0	...	0	0	0	1	0	0	0	0	...	0
Totals.................	9	0	2	.000	0	0	...	0	0	0	1	0	0	0	0	0	0

Three-point field goals: 2001, 0-for-2. Totals, 0-for-2.

WILLIAMS, SHAQUALA G   SPARKS

PERSONAL: Born April 14, 1980, in Portland, Ore. ... 5-6 (1.68 m/ kg). ... **Full name:** Shaquala Marie Williams.
HIGH SCHOOL: Reynolds (Portland, Ore.).
COLLEGE: Oregon.
TRANSACTIONS/CAREER NOTES: Selected by Cleveland in third round (30th overall) of WNBA Draft, April 25, 2003. ... Traded by Cleveland to Los Angeles for the third-round pick in the 2004 WNBA Draft, May 21, 2003.

COLLEGIATE RECORD

Season Team	G	Min.	FGM	FGA	Pct.	FTM	FTA	Pct.	Reb.	Ast.	Pts.	AVERAGES RPG	APG	PPG
98-99—Oregon	31	805	105	364	.288	69	87	.793	...	89	315	2.9	2.9	10.2
99-00—Oregon	31	1084	189	461	.410	118	145	.814	...	134	549	3.4	4.3	17.7
00-01—Oregon						Did not play—injured.								
01-02—Oregon	35	1130	206	486	.424	108	119	.908	...	137	572	2.9	3.9	16.3
02-03—Oregon	4	121	13	39	.333	13	16	.813	...	9	42	0.8	2.3	10.5
Totals	101	3140	513	1350	.380	308	367	.839	0	369	1478	0.0	3.7	14.6

Three-point field goals: 1998-99, 36-for-117 (.308). 1999-00, 53-for-170 (.312). 2001-02, 52-for-169 (.308). 2002-03, 3-for-10 (.300). Totals, 144-for-466 (.309).

WNBA REGULAR-SEASON RECORD

Season Team	G	Min.	FGM	FGA	Pct.	FTM	FTA	Pct.	REBOUNDS Off.	Def.	Tot.	Ast.	St.	Blk.	TO	Pts.	AVERAGES RPG	APG	PPG
2003—Los Angeles	25	229	19	53	.358	10	14	.714	11	21	32	19	6	0	7	49	1.3	0.8	2.0
Totals.................	25	229	19	53	.358	10	14	.714	11	21	32	19	6	0	7	49	1.3	0.8	2.0

Three-point field goals: 2003, 1-for-16 (.063). Totals, 1-for-16 (.063).
Personal fouls/disqualifications: 2003, 25/0. Totals, 25/0.

WNBA PLAYOFF RECORD

Season Team	G	Min.	FGM	FGA	Pct.	FTM	FTA	Pct.	REBOUNDS Off.	Def.	Tot.	Ast.	St.	Blk.	TO	Pts.	AVERAGES RPG	APG	PPG
2003—Los Angeles	4	13	0	0	...	0	0	...	0	0	0	0	0	0	0	0	0.0	0.0	0.0
Totals.................	4	13	0	0	...	0	0	...	0	0	0	0	0	0	0	0	0.0	0.0	0.0

WILLIAMS, TAMIKA   F   LYNX

PERSONAL: Born April 12, 1980, in Dayton, Ohio ... 6-2/205 (1.88 m/93 kg). ... **Full name:** Tamika Maria Williams.
HIGH SCHOOL: Chaminade-Julienne (Dayton, Ohio).
COLLEGE: Connecticut.
TRANSACTIONS/CAREER NOTES: Selected by Minnesota in first round (sixth overall) of WNBA Draft, April 19, 2002.

COLLEGIATE RECORD

NOTES: Member of NCAA Division I Championship Team (2002, 2000).

Season Team	G	Min.	FGM	FGA	Pct.	FTM	FTA	Pct.	Reb.	Ast.	Pts.	AVERAGES RPG	APG	PPG
98-99—Connecticut	33	738	173	263	.658	98	151	.649	226	27	444	6.8	0.8	13.5
99-00—Connecticut	31	509	115	161	.714	51	71	.718	111	24	281	3.6	0.8	9.1
00-01—Connecticut	33	656	132	174	.759	60	97	.619	186	25	324	5.6	0.8	9.8
01-02—Connecticut	35	766	140	199	.704	73	112	.652	240	44	353	6.9	1.3	10.1
Totals	132	2669	560	797	.703	282	431	.654	763	120	1402	5.8	0.9	10.6

W

Three-point field goals: 1998-99, 0-for-2. 2000-01, 0-for-1. Totals, 0-for-3.

WNBA REGULAR-SEASON RECORD

NOTES: Led the WNBA in field goal percentage (.668) in 2003.

									REBOUNDS							AVERAGES		
Season Team	G	Min.	FGM	FGA	Pct.	FTM	FTA	Pct.	Off.	Def.	Tot.	Ast.	St.	Blk.	TO	Pts.	RPG	APG	PPG
2002—Minnesota	31	1023	124	221	.561	63	108	.583	96	133	229	51	44	13	74	314	7.4	1.6	10.1
2003—Minnesota	34	1121	129	193	.668	45	93	.484	92	117	209	44	34	10	58	303	6.1	1.3	8.9
Totals.................	65	2144	253	414	.611	108	201	.537	188	250	438	95	78	23	132	617	6.7	1.5	9.5

Three-point field goals: 2002, 3-for-11 (.273). 2003, 0-for-2. Totals, 3-for-13 (.231).
Personal fouls/disqualifications: 2002, 57/0. 2003, 78/0. Totals, 135/0.

WNBA PLAYOFF RECORD

									REBOUNDS							AVERAGES		
Season Team	G	Min.	FGM	FGA	Pct.	FTM	FTA	Pct.	Off.	Def.	Tot.	Ast.	St.	Blk.	TO	Pts.	RPG	APG	PPG
2003—Minnesota	3	116	17	28	.607	16	24	.667	12	10	22	3	7	1	4	50	7.3	1.0	16.7
Totals.................	3	116	17	28	.607	16	24	.667	12	10	22	3	7	1	4	50	7.3	1.0	16.7

WITHERSPOON, SOPHIA   G   STING

PERSONAL: Born July 6, 1969, in Fort Pierce, Fla. ... 5-10/145 (1.78 m/66 kg).
HIGH SCHOOL: Fort Pierce Central (Fort Pierce, Fla.).
COLLEGE: Florida.
TRANSACTIONS/CAREER NOTES: Selected by New York in the second round (11th overall) of the WNBA Draft, April 28, 1997. ... Selected by Portland in the second round (fifth overall) of the WNBA Expansion Draft, December 15, 1999. ... Traded by Portland with G Nikki Teasley to Los Angeles for G Ukari Figgs and G Gergana Slavtcheva, April 19, 2002. ... Signed by Charlotte as an unrestricted free agent, April 5, 2004.
MISCELLANEOUS: Member of WNBA Championship Team (2002).

COLLEGIATE RECORD

												AVERAGES		
Season Team	G	Min.	FGM	FGA	Pct.	FTM	FTA	Pct.	Reb.	Ast.	Pts.	RPG	APG	PPG
88-89—Florida	29	...	176	423	.416	69	111	.622	164	62	436	5.7	2.1	15.0
89-90—Florida	28	...	161	396	.407	78	132	.591	122	62	424	4.4	2.2	15.1
90-91—Florida	28	...	155	353	.439	121	166	.729	159	54	461	5.7	1.9	16.5
Totals	85	...	492	1172	.420	268	409	.655	445	178	1321	5.2	2.1	15.5

Three-point field goals: 1988-89, 5-for-9 (.556). 1989-90, 8-for-25 (.320). 1990-91, 30-for-79 (.380). Totals, 43-for-113 (.381).

WNBA REGULAR-SEASON RECORD

									REBOUNDS							AVERAGES		
Season Team	G	Min.	FGM	FGA	Pct.	FTM	FTA	Pct.	Off.	Def.	Tot.	Ast.	St.	Blk.	TO	Pts.	RPG	APG	PPG
1997—New York......	28	867	140	345	.406	83	111	.748	30	54	84	64	49	7	77	407	3.0	2.3	14.5
1998—New York......	30	898	144	359	.401	92	117	.786	33	58	91	57	40	4	73	413	3.0	1.9	13.8
1999—New York......	32	581	97	245	.396	49	69	.710	20	27	47	37	33	2	48	271	1.5	1.2	8.5
2000—Portland	32	1061	175	456	.384	128	147	.871	23	82	105	68	38	8	88	538	3.3	2.1	16.8
2001—Portland	31	862	113	358	.316	90	106	.849	20	54	74	54	30	8	72	373	2.4	1.7	12.0
2002—Los Angeles ..	31	358	49	118	.415	35	46	.761	9	20	29	19	13	2	22	161	0.9	0.9	5.2
2003—Los Angeles...	23	235	17	53	.321	12	14	.857	6	13	19	4	7	0	7	56	0.8	0.2	2.4
Totals.................	207	4862	735	1934	.380	489	610	.802	141	308	449	313	210	31	387	2219	2.2	1.5	10.7

Three-point field goals: 1997, 44-for-126 (.349). 1998, 33-for-96 (.344). 1999, 28-for-78 (.359). 2000, 60-for-163 (.368). 2001, 57-for-182 (.313). 2002, 28-for-67 (.418). 2003, 10-for-29 (.345). Totals, 260-for-741 (.351).
Personal fouls/disqualifications: 1997, 62/0. 1998, 54/0. 1999, 54/0. 2000, 72/1. 2001, 59/0. 2002, 27/0. 2003, 17/0. Totals, 345/1.

WNBA PLAYOFF RECORD

									REBOUNDS							AVERAGES		
Season Team	G	Min.	FGM	FGA	Pct.	FTM	FTA	Pct.	Off.	Def.	Tot.	Ast.	St.	Blk.	TO	Pts.	RPG	APG	PPG
1997—New York......	2	65	5	18	.278	0	0	...	2	8	10	5	3	2	5	12	5.0	2.5	6.0
1999—New York......	6	86	17	38	.447	7	11	.636	7	6	13	2	4	0	8	45	2.2	0.3	7.5
2002—Los Angeles ..	6	39	5	14	.357	4	4	1.000	1	4	5	2	1	0	1	18	0.8	0.3	3.0
2003—Los Angeles...	5	14	1	5	.200	3	4	.750	0	2	2	0	1	0	2	5	0.4	0.0	1.0
Totals.................	19	204	28	75	.373	14	19	.737	10	20	30	9	9	2	16	80	1.6	0.5	4.2

Three-point field goals: 1997, 2-for-5 (.400). 1999, 4-for-10 (.400). 2002, 4-for-11 (.364). 2003, 0-for-3. Totals, 10-for-29 (.345).
Personal fouls/disqualifications: 1997, 7/0. 1999, 13/0. 2002, 3/0. 2003, 1/0. Totals, 24/0.

WOLTERS, KARA   C   STING

PERSONAL: Born August 15, 1975, in Holliston, Mass. ... 6-7/227 (2.01 m/103 kg). ... Full name: Kara Elizabeth Wolters.
HIGH SCHOOL: Holliston (Holliston, Mass.).
COLLEGE: Connecticut.
TRANSACTIONS/CAREER NOTES: Selected by Houston in the third round (36th overall) of the WNBA Draft, May 4, 1999. ... Selected by Indiana in the fourth round (16th overall) of the WNBA Expansion Draft, December 15, 1999. ... Traded by Indiana to Sacramento for the 14th pick in the 2001 WNBA Draft, April 11, 2000.
MISCELLANEOUS: Member of WNBA Championship Team (1999).

W

COLLEGIATE RECORD

NOTES: Member of NCAA Divison I championship team (1995). ... Kodak All-America first team (1997).

Season Team	G	Min.	FGM	FGA	Pct.	FTM	FTA	Pct.	Reb.	Ast.	Pts.	RPG	APG	PPG
93-94—Connecticut	33	...	168	264	.636	29	57	.509	159	9	365	4.8	0.3	11.1
94-95—Connecticut	33	...	222	354	.627	59	89	.663	204	38	503	6.2	1.2	15.2
95-96—Connecticut	37	...	306	486	.630	82	142	.577	291	37	694	7.9	1.0	18.8
96-97—Connecticut	34	...	251	403	.623	77	135	.570	273	46	579	8.0	1.4	17.0
Totals	137	...	947	1507	.628	247	423	.584	927	130	2141	6.8	0.9	15.6

ABL REGULAR-SEASON RECORD

Season Team	G	Min.	FGM	FGA	Pct.	FTM	FTA	Pct.	Reb.	Ast.	Pts.	RPG	APG	PPG
97-98—New England	44	...	169	316	.535	91	134	.679	228	36	430	5.2	0.8	9.8
98-99—New England	13	...	59	101	.584	25	29	.862	69	5	143	5.3	0.4	11.0
Totals	57	...	228	417	.547	116	163	.712	297	41	573	5.2	0.7	10.1

Three-point field goals: 1997-98, 1-for-2 (.500). 1998-99, 0-for-1. Totals, 1-for-3 (.333).

WNBA REGULAR-SEASON RECORD

Season Team	G	Min.	FGM	FGA	Pct.	FTM	FTA	Pct.	Off.	Def.	Tot.	Ast.	St.	Blk.	TO	Pts.	RPG	APG	PPG
1999—Houston	10	41	3	13	.231	10	12	.833	5	7	12	2	1	0	3	16	1.2	0.2	1.6
2000—Indiana	31	793	148	264	.561	74	100	.740	46	118	164	39	12	49	73	370	5.3	1.3	11.9
2001—Sacramento	31	378	63	134	.470	25	31	.806	21	53	74	17	4	25	33	151	2.4	0.5	4.9
2002—Sacramento	14	78	9	28	.321	6	10	.600	8	15	23	3	0	3	6	24	1.6	0.2	1.7
Totals	86	1290	223	439	.508	115	153	.752	80	193	273	61	17	77	115	561	3.2	0.7	6.5

Personal fouls/disqualifications: 1999, 11/0. 2000, 99/2. 2001, 55/0. 2002, 18/0. Totals, 183/2.

WNBA PLAYOFF RECORD

Season Team	G	Min.	FGM	FGA	Pct.	FTM	FTA	Pct.	Off.	Def.	Tot.	Ast.	St.	Blk.	TO	Pts.	RPG	APG	PPG
1999—Houston	2	5	1	1	1.000	2	2	1.000	1	0	1	0	0	0	1	4	0.5	0.0	2.0
2001—Sacramento	4	37	5	14	.357	0	0	...	1	3	4	1	2	2	1	10	1.0	0.3	2.5
Totals	6	42	6	15	.400	2	2	1.000	2	3	5	1	2	2	2	14	0.8	0.2	2.3

Personal fouls/disqualifications: 2000, 0/0. 2001, 10/0. Totals, 10/0.

OLYMPICS

NOTES: Member of gold medal-winning U.S. Olympic Team (2000).

Season Team	G	Min.	FGM	FGA	Pct.	FTM	FTA	Pct.	Reb.	Ast.	Pts.	RPG	APG	PPG
2000—United States	6	38	5	12	.417	0	3	.000	12	0	10	2.0	0.0	1.7
Totals	6	38	5	12	.417	0	3	.000	12	0	10	2.0	0.0	1.7

WYCKOFF, BROOKE   F   SUN

W

PERSONAL: Born March 30, 1980, in Lake Forest, Ill. ... 6-1/183 (1.85 m/83 kg). ... Full name: Brooke Elizabeth Wyckoff.

HIGH SCHOOL: Lakota (West Chester, Ohio).

COLLEGE: Florida State.

TRANSACTIONS/CAREER NOTES: Selected by Orlando in second round (26th overall) of WNBA Draft, April 20, 2001.

COLLEGIATE RECORD

Season Team	G	Min.	FGM	FGA	Pct.	FTM	FTA	Pct.	Reb.	Ast.	Pts.	RPG	APG	PPG
97-98—Florida State	27	...	96	204	.471	70	113	.619	216	53	268	8.0	2.0	9.9
98-99—Florida State	27	...	136	314	.433	93	140	.664	214	40	370	7.9	1.5	13.7
99-00—Florida State	24	...	92	225	.409	59	79	.747	170	61	259	7.1	2.5	10.8
00-01—Florida State	31	...	161	362	.445	98	125	.784	204	75	453	6.6	2.4	14.6
Totals	109	...	485	1105	.439	320	457	.700	804	229	1350	7.4	2.1	12.4

Three-point field goals: 1997-98, 6-for-25 (.240). 1998-99, 5-for-18 (.278). 1999-00, 16-for-54 (.296). 2000-01, 33-for-100 (.330). Totals, 60-for-197 (.305).

WNBA REGULAR-SEASON RECORD

Season Team	G	Min.	FGM	FGA	Pct.	FTM	FTA	Pct.	Off.	Def.	Tot.	Ast.	St.	Blk.	TO	Pts.	RPG	APG	PPG
2001—Orlando	32	648	41	125	.328	20	28	.714	48	74	122	37	26	15	50	108	3.8	1.2	3.4
2002—Orlando	32	514	31	95	.326	5	7	.714	28	62	90	32	19	18	30	81	2.8	1.0	2.5
2003—Connecticut	34	755	55	142	.387	26	36	.722	48	98	146	35	33	19	39	156	4.3	1.0	4.6
Totals	98	1917	127	362	.351	51	71	.718	124	234	358	104	78	52	119	345	3.7	1.1	3.5

Three-point field goals: 2001, 6-for-37 (.162). 2002, 14-for-50 (.280). 2003, 20-for-70 (.286). Totals, 40-for-157 (.255).
Personal fouls/disqualifications: 2001, 91/2. 2002, 71/1. 2003, 109/1. Totals, 271/4.

WNBA PLAYOFF RECORD

Season Team	G	Min.	FGM	FGA	Pct.	FTM	FTA	Pct.	Off.	Def.	Tot.	Ast.	St.	Blk.	TO	Pts.	RPG	APG	PPG
2003—Connecticut	4	89	7	16	.438	3	4	.750	3	9	12	5	2	1	2	18	3.0	1.3	4.5
Totals	4	89	7	16	.438	3	4	.750	3	9	12	5	2	1	2	18	3.0	1.3	4.5

Three-point field goals: 2003, 1-for-6 (.167). Totals, 1-for-6 (.167).
Personal fouls/disqualifications: 2003, 11/0. Totals, 11/0.

YAMASAKI, LINDSEY   G/F   LIBERTY

PERSONAL: Born June 2, 1980, in Oregon City, Ore. ... 6-1/190 (1.85 m/86 kg). ... **Full name**: Lindsey Brooke Yamasaki.
HIGH SCHOOL: Oregon City (Ore.).
COLLEGE: Stanford.
TRANSACTIONS/CAREER NOTES: Selected by Miami in second round (29th overall) of WNBA Draft, April 19, 2002.

COLLEGIATE RECORD

Season Team	G	Min.	FGM	FGA	Pct.	FTM	FTA	Pct.	Reb.	Ast.	Pts.	AVERAGES RPG	APG	PPG
98-99—Stanford	30	935	153	386	.396	49	68	.721	176	78	420	5.9	2.6	14.0
99-00—Stanford	23	344	58	127	.457	23	30	.767	71	20	153	3.1	0.9	6.7
00-01—Stanford	30	728	124	284	.437	74	90	.822	132	69	373	4.4	2.3	12.4
01-02—Stanford	32	915	208	430	.484	73	102	.716	152	83	551	4.8	2.6	17.2
Totals	115	2922	543	1227	.443	219	290	.755	531	250	1497	4.6	2.2	13.0

Three-point field goals: 1998-99, 65-for-167 (.389). 1999-00, 14-for-44 (.318). 2000-01, 51-for-120 (.425). 2001-02, 62-for-162 (.383). Totals, 192-for-493 (.389).

WNBA REGULAR-SEASON RECORD

Season Team	G	Min.	FGM	FGA	Pct.	FTM	FTA	Pct.	REBOUNDS Off.	Def.	Tot.	Ast.	St.	Blk.	TO	Pts.	AVERAGES RPG	APG	PPG
2002—Miami	15	147	19	43	.442	5	10	.500	3	12	15	9	4	1	10	52	1.0	0.6	3.5
2003—New York	24	148	6	27	.222	0	0	...	1	11	12	9	4	0	5	16	0.5	0.4	0.7
Totals	39	295	25	70	.357	5	10	.500	4	23	27	18	8	1	15	68	0.7	0.5	1.7

Three-point field goals: 2002, 9-for-17 (.529). 2003, 4-for-14 (.286). Totals, 13-for-31 (.419).
Personal fouls/disqualifications: 2002, 20/0. 2003, 19/1. Totals, 39/1.

YILMAZ, NEVRIYE   C

PERSONAL: Born June 16, 1980 ... 6-4/190 (1.93 m/86 kg).
TRANSACTIONS/CAREER NOTES: Signed by Phoenix as a free agent, May 2003. ... Waived by Phoenix, July 15, 2003.

WNBA REGULAR-SEASON RECORD

Season Team	G	Min.	FGM	FGA	Pct.	FTM	FTA	Pct.	REBOUNDS Off.	Def.	Tot.	Ast.	St.	Blk.	TO	Pts.	AVERAGES RPG	APG	PPG
2003—Phoenix	5	34	7	15	.467	0	2	.000	3	0	3	2	0	0	4	14	0.6	0.4	2.8
Totals	5	34	7	15	.467	0	2	.000	3	0	3	2	0	0	4	14	0.6	0.4	2.8

ZIRKOVA, ZUZANA   G   MYSTICS

PERSONAL: Born June 6, 1980, in Bojnica, Slovak Republic. ... 5-9 (1.75 m/ kg).
TRANSACTIONS/CAREER NOTES: Selected by Washington in second round (21st overall) of WNBA Draft, April 25, 2003.
MISCELLANEOUS: Member of the Slovak National team that was: runner-up in the 1998 European championship for juniors; finished 4th in the 1999 European Championships; and qualified for the 2001 European Championships.

OLYMPICS

NOTES: Member of Slovakian team that finished 7th with a 3-4 record at the 2000 Olympics.

Season Team	G	Min.	FGM	FGA	Pct.	FTM	FTA	Pct.	Reb.	Ast.	Pts.	AVERAGES RPG	APG	PPG
2000—Slovakia	7	221	29	69	.420	9	12	.750	23	12	75	3.3	1.7	10.7
Totals	7	221	29	69	.420	9	12	.750	23	12	75	3.3	1.7	10.7

Three-point field goals: 2000-01, 8-for-21 (.381).

ITALIAN LEAGUE RECORD

Season Team	G	Min.	FGM	FGA	Pct.	FTM	FTA	Pct.	Reb.	Ast.	Pts.	AVERAGES RPG	APG	PPG
01-02—Gysevringa Sopron	17	...	...	...	...	...	...	...	44	51	231	2.6	3.0	13.6
02-03—Gambrinus Brno	17	...	...	...	...	...	...	...	54	49	226	3.2	2.9	13.3

WNBA REGULAR-SEASON RECORD

Season Team	G	Min.	FGM	FGA	Pct.	FTM	FTA	Pct.	REBOUNDS Off.	Def.	Tot.	Ast.	St.	Blk.	TO	Pts.	AVERAGES RPG	APG	PPG
2003—Washington	6	30	2	4	.500	6	6	1.000	0	2	2	1	0	0	2	11	0.3	0.2	1.8
Totals	6	30	2	4	.500	6	6	1.000	0	2	2	1	0	0	2	11	0.3	0.2	1.8

Three-point field goals: 2003, 1-for-2 (.500). Totals, 1-for-2 (.500).
Personal fouls/disqualifications: 2003, 3/0. Totals, 3/0.

Y
Z

WNBA REGULAR SEASON SINGLE-GAME HIGHS

(Includes 2003 Season)

Player	FGM	FGA	FTM	FTA	REB	AST	STL	BLK	PTS
Abrosimova, Svetlana	10	23	12	18	15	9	5	2	27
Adams, Jordan	4	10	2	2	10	2	1	1	13
Anderson, Chantelle	4	6	2	3	3	2	3	1	8
Andrade, Mery	8	12	9	10	8	7	5	3	18
Arcain, Janeth	12	22	10	10	9	9	6	2	29
Aziz, Leigh	2	4	1	2	3	1	0	1	4
Baranova, Elena	9	18	10	11	17	8	6	6	26
Barnes, Adia	9	13	5	6	10	5	6	3	24
Berthieu, Lucienne	5	8	5	9	7	1	1	1	15
Bevilaqua, Tully	4	8	9	12	8	8	6	2	14
Bird, Sue	11	20	11	12	8	12	5	1	33
Black, Debbie	6	15	6	8	9	11	7	1	15
Blue, Octavia	5	9	6	8	7	2	3	1	13
Bolton, Ruthie	12	24	13	14	12	7	6	1	34
Bowie, Tamara	0	0	0	0	0	0	0	0	0
Brondello, Sandy	13	28	9	12	10	8	5	2	33
Brown, Coretta	8	14	5	6	5	5	3	1	26
Brown, Edwina	7	14	9	9	9	8	5	2	19
Brown, Kiesha	3	6	2	2	4	4	2	1	9
Brown, Rushia	9	15	8	11	11	5	7	3	24
Brumfield, Marla	6	8	4	4	4	4	4	1	14
Buescher, Erin	6	12	5	7	11	4	3	4	16
Burgess, Annie	5	11	6	6	7	11	5	1	15
Burras, Alisa	10	16	5	8	11	3	2	2	22
Burse, Janell	9	17	6	7	12	4	4	5	21
Campbell, Edna	10	21	8	12	7	8	3	3	22
Canty, Dominique	8	22	10	14	11	8	5	2	22
Cash, Swin	11	18	15	21	15	6	5	4	26
Castro Marques, Iziane	5	11	3	6	4	2	2	1	12
Catchings, Tamika	13	22	14	16	16	10	9	4	32
Christensen, Kayte	6	9	10	16	12	2	3	3	16
Coleman, Courtney	2	3	4	7	6	1	2	1	6
Cooper, Cynthia	15	28	22	24	8	10	8	2	44
Crawley, Sylvia	11	20	6	10	15	5	3	5	25
Crockrom, Danielle	3	6	4	5	5	1	0	1	6
Curry, Edniesha	3	5	2	3	2	3	4	0	8
Dales-Schuman, Stacey	8	15	11	12	7	8	4	2	26
Darling, Helen	6	12	8	8	6	8	4	3	18
DeForge, Anna	9	24	7	8	9	7	4	2	24
Dillard, Tai	4	7	2	2	5	3	2	1	9
Dixon, Tamecka	11	23	11	12	9	8	5	3	28
Donaphin, Bethany	0	0	0	0	0	0	0	0	0
Douglas, Katie	11	18	7	8	12	5	5	3	28
Dydek, Margo	13	25	10	11	16	7	3	10	27

Player	FGM	FGA	FTM	FTA	REB	AST	STL	BLK	PTS
Edwards, Simone	8	15	8	8	14	3	3	4	19
Edwards, Teresa	6	10	5	6	8	8	6	2	15
Enis, Shalonda	9	15	7	10	15	5	4	2	29
Farris, Barbara	6	13	8	10	10	3	2	2	14
Feaster, Allison	9	17	11	14	11	6	4	2	24
Ferdinand, Marie	11	20	11	14	7	7	5	2	27
Figgs, Ukari	6	17	7	8	8	9	4	1	22
Fijalkowski, Isabelle	10	16	8	11	12	6	3	3	25
Ford, Cheryl	8	14	8	12	21	5	3	4	20
Frett, La'Keshia	7	14	5	8	13	8	2	3	18
Frohlich, Linda	5	10	3	4	6	2	2	2	12
Gibson, Kelley	4	6	4	6	6	3	2	3	13
Gillom, Jennifer	13	27	12	15	15	5	5	3	36
Goodson, Adrienne	12	21	11	13	11	6	5	2	30
Gortman, Shaunzinski	5	11	2	3	6	2	3	2	14
Griffith, Yolanda	13	22	13	19	20	5	8	6	31
Grooms, Lady	7	13	8	12	8	6	3	2	16
Grubin, Gordana	8	19	9	10	7	8	5	1	23
Hammon, Becky	12	16	11	12	6	6	3	1	33
Harrison, Lisa	10	15	12	13	12	5	4	2	22
Harrower, Kristi	5	9	12	12	6	9	3	1	20
Hicks, Jessie	7	13	8	11	8	5	4	4	18
Holdsclaw, Chamique	12	27	13	17	24	7	8	4	34
Holland-Corn, Kedra	10	22	9	12	9	7	6	2	28
Hope, Kym	0	1	2	2	2	0	0	0	2
Ivey, Niele	5	9	6	6	6	7	4	1	14
Jackson, Deanna	11	14	7	8	6	5	2	3	30
Jackson, Gwen	7	20	5	8	14	3	3	2	16
Jackson, Lauren	17	29	14	16	20	5	5	8	34
Jackson, Tamicha	9	21	8	10	7	9	6	1	21
Johns Kimbrough, Pollyanna	7	10	7	8	12	5	3	2	16
Johnson, Chandra	1	2	2	2	4	1	0	1	4
Johnson, LaTonya	6	11	7	8	7	4	3	2	19
Johnson, Shannon	12	22	12	15	11	12	6	2	35
Johnson, Tiffani	6	11	7	7	15	4	2	3	14
Johnson, Vickie	12	19	8	10	12	8	5	2	27
Jones, Asjha	8	18	6	7	12	5	3	3	21
Jones, Merlakia	11	21	10	10	12	6	6	2	27
Jung, Sun-Min	5	10	2	2	5	1	2	0	10
Lambert, Sheila	5	8	8	8	5	3	1	0	14
Lassiter, Amanda	7	13	4	8	13	7	4	3	16
Lawson, Kara	7	13	5	6	11	4	3	1	24
Lennox, Betty	11	22	8	10	12	8	5	2	31
Leslie, Lisa	14	24	15	19	21	8	6	7	32
Lewis, Takeisha	2	2	5	8	7	1	1	0	7
Lewis, Tynesha	5	9	3	4	8	4	3	2	13
Luz, Helen	6	13	6	6	5	6	5	2	15
Mabika, Mwadi	11	28	11	11	12	9	6	3	32

Player	FGM	FGA	FTM	FTA	REB	AST	STL	BLK	PTS
Maiga, Tanty	2	7	2	4	7	2	4	1	6
Mallory, Sonja	2	4	2	2	4	0	1	3	4
Massaline, LaTonya	5	10	3	4	7	3	2	1	15
McCain, Brandi	3	6	4	4	5	5	2	1	9
McCray, Nikki	11	23	12	16	9	9	5	2	30
McCrimmon, Nicky	5	10	2	4	4	7	4	2	12
McCulley, Danielle	7	13	7	8	7	3	3	3	17
McKiver, Teana	7	9	3	4	9	1	2	2	15
McWilliams-Franklin, Taj	11	23	10	14	15	6	5	5	28
Melvin, Chasity	12	17	9	12	12	7	3	4	30
Miller, Coco	10	21	7	9	8	7	5	2	23
Miller, Kelly	8	14	4	6	7	5	4	1	23
Mills, Tausha	6	13	9	10	12	2	2	2	17
Milton-Jones, DeLisha	10	19	10	12	14	6	5	5	23
Moore, Tamara	7	13	8	8	7	7	3	2	22
Ndiaye-Diatta, Astou	11	23	5	7	12	5	3	4	27
Nolan, Deanna	10	19	6	8	9	6	5	3	27
Nygaard, Vanessa	7	14	6	6	11	5	3	1	18
Page, Murriel	9	16	7	10	15	7	4	4	20
Palmer, Wendy	14	31	12	18	15	5	7	3	32
Pavlickova, Michaela	1	2	1	2	2	1	1	1	2
Penicheiro, Ticha	9	17	12	15	14	16	10	3	27
Penn, Jocelyn	6	12	2	4	9	2	3	1	13
Pettis, Bridget	10	19	11	13	9	7	6	2	27
Phillips, Tari	13	21	8	12	16	6	5	3	30
Pierson, Plenette	11	17	12	19	6	5	3	2	26
Powell, Elaine	8	15	8	10	9	8	5	3	20
Pride, Lynn	6	11	6	8	8	5	6	4	13
Quick, LaQuanda	8	17	3	4	6	3	2	2	22
Ragland, Felicia	7	14	4	5	8	6	3	1	19
Randall, Semeka	10	21	8	13	10	6	4	1	28
Rasmussen, Kristen	8	11	11	12	9	6	4	3	19
Redd, Jamie	10	17	9	10	6	5	3	1	24
Riley, Ruth	7	14	8	10	11	5	3	5	19
Rizzotti, Jennifer	5	10	8	10	6	14	4	1	16
Robinson, Crystal	10	19	9	12	7	6	5	3	27
Sales, Nykesha	11	21	13	16	10	7	6	2	31
Sam, Sheri	12	26	7	10	10	8	6	2	27
Sanford, Nakia	5	6	3	7	4	1	1	1	10
Saunders, Jaynetta	5	14	5	6	9	3	2	3	12
Schumacher, Kelly	7	10	6	7	9	3	3	4	22
Schweitzer, Georgia	7	14	4	4	8	6	4	3	17
Scott-Richardson, Olympia	11	17	9	14	17	5	4	3	31
Sharp, K.B.	4	7	6	6	3	3	3	0	14
Slavtcheva, Gergana	0	2	0	0	0	1	0	0	0
Smith, Aiysha	5	11	4	4	7	2	2	3	10
Smith, Katie	13	23	18	19	10	8	4	2	46
Smith, Tangela	14	23	10	12	13	5	3	6	28

Player	FGM	FGA	FTM	FTA	REB	AST	STL	BLK	PTS
Smith-Taylor, Charlotte	7	14	6	10	11	6	3	4	17
Snow, Michelle	8	15	6	11	16	3	4	8	19
Staley, Dawn	10	17	10	12	9	13	6	1	23
Starbird, Kate	8	13	7	8	7	4	5	2	21
Stinson, Andrea	12	23	11	14	12	10	6	5	33
Stocks, Tamara	1	2	1	2	2	0	0	0	3
Suber, Tora	5	14	5	8	8	9	3	1	14
Sutton-Brown, Tammy	10	15	10	10	11	2	3	5	22
Swoopes, Sheryl	13	29	14	15	15	10	7	4	33
Taylor, Penny	11	23	11	13	11	6	5	2	33
Teasley, Nikki	8	20	10	10	11	13	3	2	23
Thomas, LaToya	10	16	9	9	13	5	3	3	23
Thomas, Stacey	6	13	7	8	8	9	7	4	14
Thompson, Alicia	10	18	5	6	15	6	3	2	22
Thompson, Tina	13	27	14	16	14	6	4	4	31
Thorn, Erin	4	7	2	2	3	3	1	1	12
Tuvic, Slobodanka	5	11	7	10	8	4	4	3	17
Udoka, Mfon	5	10	5	6	9	1	1	1	12
Ujhelyi, Petra	1	2	0	2	5	2	0	1	2
Van Gorp, Michele	8	13	5	6	10	4	1	3	18
Vodichkova, Kamila	10	15	9	10	12	4	3	4	22
Walker, Ayana	6	12	5	7	11	2	4	5	16
Walker, DeMya	9	16	7	12	14	5	4	4	21
Walseth, Maren	2	4	2	2	4	2	2	0	4
Wauters, Ann	9	13	8	10	10	5	3	4	20
Weatherspoon, Teresa	7	13	8	10	11	13	8	2	19
White, Stephanie	7	15	10	11	8	8	5	3	20
Whitmore, Tamika	11	16	10	11	13	3	4	5	28
Wideman, Jamila	4	9	5	6	5	8	4	1	16
Williams, Adrian	9	18	8	8	16	4	5	5	20
Williams, Lenae	3	10	0	4	3	1	1	0	8
Williams, Natalie	11	22	12	16	20	6	4	5	31
Williams, Rita	7	16	13	14	9	10	8	2	21
Williams, Shaquala	5	9	3	4	5	5	2	0	13
Williams, Tamika	9	15	6	8	12	5	6	2	19
Witherspoon, Sophia	12	20	11	12	8	7	5	3	31
Wolters, Kara	8	14	8	9	10	4	2	5	24
Wyckoff, Brooke	7	10	3	4	12	5	3	3	17
Yamasaki, Lindsey	5	8	2	4	4	3	2	1	12

WNBA POSTSEASON SINGLE-GAME HIGHS

(Includes 2003 Season)

Player	FGM	FGA	FTM	FTA	REB	AST	STL	BLK	PTS
Abrosimova, Svetlana	3	11	6	6	2	2	2	1	10
Adams, Jordan	0	0	0	0	0	0	0	0	0
Anderson, Chantelle	1	2	1	2	2	0	0	1	3
Andrade, Mery	3	8	2	4	5	4	2	3	7
Arcain, Janeth	9	19	6	6	10	4	3	1	18

Player	FGM	FGA	FTM	FTA	REB	AST	STL	BLK	PTS
Baranova, Elena	6	12	4	5	7	3	1	2	18
Barnes, Adia	2	5	0	0	5	2	2	0	5
Berthieu, Lucienne	2	6	0	0	2	1	1	1	4
Bird, Sue	6	13	4	4	0	8	3	0	17
Black, Debbie	3	8	0	0	8	5	3	1	6
Blue, Octavia	0	1	0	0	0	1	0	0	0
Bolton, Ruthie	9	19	6	7	5	4	3	0	23
Brondello, Sandy	6	14	4	4	5	5	2	1	18
Brown, Kiesha	2	3	0	0	1	1	2	0	4
Brown, Rushia	6	8	8	10	9	4	3	2	18
Brumfield, Marla	1	2	1	2	0	1	1	0	3
Buescher, Erin	4	5	2	3	4	1	0	1	11
Burgess, Annie	3	7	3	4	5	8	1	0	9
Burse, Janell	2	6	2	3	6	1	3	1	6
Campbell, Edna	6	10	2	3	3	6	2	1	15
Canty, Dominique	2	6	3	6	5	4	1	0	6
Cash, Swin	8	15	10	13	12	9	1	2	26
Catchings, Tamika	11	19	5	5	14	4	3	1	29
Coleman, Courtney	0	0	0	0	0	0	0	0	0
Cooper, Cynthia	11	24	13	15	7	12	4	2	31
Crockrom, Danielle	1	2	0	0	0	0	0	0	2
Dales-Schuman, Stacey	4	11	2	2	4	6	1	0	12
Darling, Helen	5	14	4	6	5	10	5	1	15
Dixon, Tamecka	8	15	6	6	6	8	6	2	19
Douglas, Katie	5	10	2	3	5	5	2	1	13
Dydek, Margo	5	13	6	7	13	4	1	5	16
Edwards, Simone	1	4	1	2	2	0	0	0	3
Edwards, Teresa	3	10	2	2	5	9	2	1	8
Enis, Shalonda	5	10	4	4	9	3	1	1	12
Farris, Barbara	3	9	3	4	6	3	1	0	6
Feaster, Allison	6	12	4	4	12	4	3	3	15
Ferdinand, Marie	8	17	11	14	6	4	5	0	22
Figgs, Ukari	4	9	4	4	7	10	2	2	12
Fijalkowski, Isabelle	6	14	8	9	11	2	1	2	20
Ford, Cheryl	6	14	5	7	15	2	2	3	17
Frett, La'Keshia	4	9	3	4	7	4	1	2	11
Frohlich, Linda	0	2	1	2	2	1	1	0	1
Gibson, Kelley	3	6	0	0	3	0	1	0	7
Gillom, Jennifer	10	20	6	6	10	2	2	4	27
Goodson, Adrienne	8	19	3	6	10	3	5	1	20
Gortman, Shaunzinski	0	0	0	0	0	0	0	0	0
Griffith, Yolanda	11	18	18	24	17	3	2	3	30
Grooms, Lady	3	7	3	4	5	1	1	0	7
Grubin, Gordana	5	14	1	2	5	9	3	0	13
Hammon, Becky	7	11	5	7	5	4	4	0	19
Harrison, Lisa	7	9	2	2	9	5	3	0	16
Harrower, Kristi	5	6	1	2	5	3	1	1	12
Hicks, Jessie	2	4	0	0	4	1	0	1	4

Player	FGM	FGA	FTM	FTA	REB	AST	STL	BLK	PTS
Holdsclaw, Chamique	9	20	8	10	13	6	5	2	26
Holland-Corn, Kedra	6	11	9	10	5	5	4	1	17
Ivey, Niele	0	1	0	0	1	1	1	0	0
Jackson, Deanna	2	8	4	6	5	1	1	0	6
Jackson, Lauren	8	17	3	5	5	2	2	3	19
Johns Kimbrough, Pollyanna	3	3	1	2	2	2	1	2	7
Johnson, LaTonya	4	8	2	2	2	1	0	1	9
Johnson, Shannon	5	12	6	10	9	8	3	1	16
Johnson, Tiffani	6	10	3	4	12	2	2	4	13
Johnson, Vickie	8	16	8	8	8	10	6	1	22
Jones, Asjha	3	6	1	2	4	1	0	1	6
Jones, Merlakia	8	24	3	3	12	7	3	1	19
Lambert, Sheila	1	3	0	0	1	1	0	0	3
Lassiter, Amanda	7	12	2	2	6	2	2	2	17
Lawson, Kara	4	10	3	4	8	5	1	1	12
Lennox, Betty	6	9	1	2	3	2	3	0	14
Leslie, Lisa	15	22	10	12	18	6	4	7	35
Lewis, Takeisha	0	0	0	0	0	0	0	0	0
Lewis, Tynesha	3	5	3	4	2	3	0	1	9
Luz, Helen	6	7	0	0	1	3	2	0	16
Mabika, Mwadi	11	20	6	10	11	6	6	3	29
Maiga, Tanty	1	2	0	0	2	1	0	0	2
Massaline, LaTonya	4	6	2	3	2	2	2	0	11
McCray, Nikki	7	13	3	5	4	11	1	0	15
McCrimmon, Nicky	2	5	3	4	3	4	2	0	7
McKiver, Teana	0	2	0	0	1	0	0	1	0
McWilliams-Franklin, Taj	8	17	6	6	13	2	3	2	20
Melvin, Chasity	6	16	11	14	10	4	2	2	21
Miller, Coco	8	13	4	6	5	3	1	0	21
Miller, Kelly	3	6	0	2	2	1	0	0	6
Mills, Tausha	3	5	3	6	3	0	0	0	9
Milton-Jones, DeLisha	8	18	6	6	10	5	4	5	20
Ndiaye-Diatta, Astou	4	5	1	2	6	1	1	0	8
Nolan, Deanna	10	17	6	6	7	4	3	1	26
Nygaard, Vanessa	1	2	0	0	2	0	1	1	3
Page, Murriel	6	8	6	6	5	2	1	3	17
Palmer, Wendy	5	11	2	3	9	2	1	1	13
Pavlickova, Michaela	0	0	0	0	0	0	0	0	0
Penicheiro, Ticha	7	12	4	4	6	10	2	2	19
Pettis, Bridget	9	17	8	9	11	5	3	1	27
Phillips, Tari	11	19	7	8	15	3	3	3	24
Powell, Elaine	3	10	3	4	8	9	2	1	9
Pride, Lynn	1	2	1	1	5	1	2	1	3
Ragland, Felicia	3	8	0	0	5	1	0	0	7
Randall, Semeka	4	8	2	3	3	2	1	0	8
Rasmussen, Kristen	0	4	1	2	3	0	1	0	1
Riley, Ruth	11	19	5	10	9	5	2	4	27
Rizzotti, Jennifer	3	5	0	0	2	6	0	0	9

Player	FGM	FGA	FTM	FTA	REB	AST	STL	BLK	PTS
Robinson, Crystal	7	15	5	5	6	3	3	2	21
Sales, Nykesha	7	15	10	10	5	4	4	2	22
Sam, Sheri	6	11	4	5	8	5	5	0	17
Schumacher, Kelly	6	9	3	5	4	2	0	1	17
Schweitzer, Georgia	0	0	0	0	0	0	0	0	0
Scott-Richardson, Olympia	5	6	3	3	14	3	1	1	10
Smith, Katie	8	16	4	5	5	4	1	0	23
Smith, Tangela	8	17	7	10	10	3	3	2	17
Smith-Taylor, Charlotte	4	11	3	4	9	4	3	2	10
Snow, Michelle	7	14	3	4	15	3	3	2	16
Staley, Dawn	6	16	6	8	5	9	3	2	18
Starbird, Kate	1	5	2	2	2	1	1	1	3
Stinson, Andrea	10	19	8	8	14	8	5	1	27
Suber, Tora	6	12	2	3	1	5	4	0	15
Sutton-Brown, Tammy	6	9	3	4	8	1	1	4	12
Swoopes, Sheryl	11	22	9	10	13	7	6	2	31
Taylor, Penny	7	13	5	6	5	2	5	1	17
Teasley, Nikki	5	14	6	6	8	11	3	1	13
Thomas, LaToya	7	15	9	11	9	2	1	2	17
Thomas, Stacey	0	1	0	0	1	0	1	0	0
Thompson, Alicia	1	1	0	0	0	0	0	0	2
Thompson, Tina	8	18	6	8	14	5	4	3	21
Udoka, Mfon	0	0	1	2	1	0	0	0	1
Van Gorp, Michele	1	4	3	4	1	1	1	2	5
Vodichkova, Kamila	6	12	6	6	5	2	2	0	17
Walker, Ayana	1	3	2	2	3	0	2	1	3
Walker, DeMya	6	11	6	9	6	4	1	1	16
Walseth, Maren	0	2	0	0	0	1	0	1	0
Wauters, Ann	5	8	4	5	5	2	2	2	12
Weatherspoon, Teresa	8	12	3	4	7	12	4	0	19
Whitmore, Tamika	10	15	7	9	8	2	1	2	24
Williams, Adrian	1	2	1	2	2	1	0	2	3
Williams, Natalie	11	16	9	14	12	3	2	3	25
Williams, Rita	4	10	0	0	3	3	1	0	9
Williams, Shaquala	0	0	0	0	0	0	0	0	0
Williams, Tamika	7	12	9	13	9	3	5	1	17
Witherspoon, Sophia	7	13	3	4	7	3	3	2	18
Wolters, Kara	3	5	2	2	1	1	1	2	6
Wyckoff, Brooke	3	6	2	2	6	2	1	1	9

BATTH, ERIN F/C SILVER STARS

PERSONAL: Born October 22, 1978, in Atlanta, Ga. ... 6-4/189. (1.93 m/86 kg). ... **Full name:** Erin Leigh Batth.
HIGH SCHOOL: Lassiter (Marietta, Ga.).
COLLEGE: Clemson.
TRANSACTIONS/CAREER NOTES: Selected by Cleveland in fourth round (59th overall) of WNBA Draft, April 20, 2001. ... Waived by Cleveland, May 22, 2001. ... Signed by San Antonio, April 16, 2004.

COLLEGIATE RECORD

Season Team	G	Min.	FGM	FGA	Pct.	FTM	FTA	Pct.	Reb.	Ast.	Pts.	RPG	APG	PPG
97-98—Clemson	33	355	41	108	.380	28	57	.491	96	16	113	2.9	0.5	3.4
98-99—Clemson	27	567	81	205	.395	44	71	.620	136	20	206	5.0	0.7	7.6
99-00—Clemson	31	822	112	297	.377	62	97	.639	230	33	289	7.4	1.1	9.3
00-01—Clemson	30	827	137	334	.410	89	128	.695	260	40	364	8.7	1.3	12.1
Totals	121	2571	371	944	.393	223	353	.632	722	109	972	6.0	0.9	8.0

Three-point field goals: 1997-98, 3-for-8 (.375). 1998-99, -for-4. 1999-0, 3-for-11 (.273). 190-1, 1-for-1. Totals, 7-for-24 (.292)

BEARD, ALANA G/F MYSTICS

PERSONAL: Born May 14, 1982, in Shreveport, La. ... 5-11/160. (1.80 m/73 kg). ... **Full name:** Alana Monique Beard.
HIGH SCHOOL: Southwood HS (Shreveport, La.).
COLLEGE: Duke.
TRANSACTIONS/CAREER NOTES: Selected by Washington (second overall) in first round (second overall) in the WNBA Draft, April 17, 2004.
MISCELLANEOUS: Member of the 2003 USA Championship for Young Women Team that captured the gold medal in Sibenik, Croatia. Member of the bronze medalist 2001 USA Junior World Championship Team. ... Earned a gold medal as a member of the 2000 USA Basketball Women's Junior World Championship Qualifying Team.

COLLEGIATE RECORD

NOTES: Notes: USBWA Player of the Year (2004). ... AP Player of the Year (2004). ... Wade Trophy Player of the Year (2004). ... AP All-America First team (2004, 2003, 2002). ... USBWA All-America (2004, 2003, 2002). ... Kodak All-America (2004, 2003, 2002). ... ACC Player of the Year (2004, 2003, 2002). ... All-ACC First team (2004, 2003, 2002, 2001). ... All-ACC Defensive team (2004, 2003, 2002). ... NCAA Final Four All-Tournament Team (2003). ... ACC All-Tournament Team (2004, 2003, 2002, 2001). ... USBWA, Sports Illustrated for Women, Sports Illustrated, CBS Sportsline and Women's Basketball Journal National Freshman of the Year (2001). ... ACC Freshman of the Year (2001). ... Duke's all-time leading scorer (2,687).

Season Team	G	Min.	FGM	FGA	Pct.	FTM	FTA	Pct.	Reb.	Ast.	Pts.	RPG	APG	PPG
00-01—Duke	30	893	194	379	.512	111	141	.787	136	113	509	4.5	3.8	17.0
01-02—Duke	35	1164	275	481	.572	119	158	.753	213	154	694	6.1	4.4	19.8
02-03—Duke	37	1161	294	558	.527	201	259	.776	256	110	813	6.9	3.0	22.0
03-04—Duke	34	1067	242	488	.496	151	194	.778	184	132	671	5.4	3.9	19.7
Totals	136	4285	1005	1906	.527	582	752	.774	789	509	2687	5.8	3.7	19.8

Three-point field goals: 190-1, 10-for-51 (.196). 191-2, 25-for-66 (.379). 192-3, 24-for-85 (.282). 193-4, 36-for-115 (.313). Totals, 95-for-317 (.300)

BENNINGFIELD, JENNI F STING

PERSONAL: Born October 6, 1981, in Louisville, KY ... 6-3/185. (1.91 m/84 kg). ... **Full name:** Jennifer Ann Benningfield.
HIGH SCHOOL: Assumption HS [Louisville, KY].
COLLEGE: Vanderbilt.
MISCELLANEOUS: Won a silver medal as a member of the 2003 USA Pan American Games Team.
TRANSACTIONS/CAREER NOTES: Selected by Charlotte in second round (22nd overall) in the WNBA Draft, April 17, 2004.

COLLEGIATE RECORD

NOTES: AP All-America honorable mention (2003). ... All-SEC Second Team (2004, 2003). ... Won two SEC Tournament Championships (2004, 2002). ... SEC All-Academic Team (2003).

Season Team	G	Min.	FGM	FGA	Pct.	FTM	FTA	Pct.	Reb.	Ast.	Pts.	RPG	APG	PPG
00-01—Vanderbilt	34	1070	113	266	.425	37	53	.698	241	107	319	7.1	3.1	9.4
01-02—Vanderbilt	37	885	80	195	.410	19	27	.704	162	83	221	4.4	2.2	6.0
02-03—Vanderbilt	32	992	212	381	.556	79	113	.699	253	91	528	7.9	2.8	16.5
03-04—Vanderbilt	33	842	165	340	.485	93	138	.674	195	48	433	5.9	1.5	13.1
Totals	136	3789	570	1182	.482	228	331	.689	851	329	1501	6.3	2.4	11.0

Three-point field goals: 190-1, 56-for-139 (.403). 191-2, 42-for-102 (.412). 192-3, 25-for-66 (.379). 193-4, 10-for-34 (.294). Totals, 133-for-341 (.390)

BIBRZYCKA, AGNIESZKA G/F SILVER STARS

PERSONAL: Born October 21, 1982, in Mikolow, Poland ... 6-2. (1.88 m/ kg).
TRANSACTIONS/CAREER NOTES: Signed by San Antonio as a free agent February 19, 2004.

POLISH INTERNATIONAL LEAGUE

Notes: Women's European Player of the Year (2003) ...

BJORKLUND, TERA   C   STING

PERSONAL: Born June 29, 1982 in St. Peter, Minn. ... 6-4/175 (1.93 m/79 kg). ... **Full name:** Tera Tracie Bjorklund.
HIGH SCHOOL: Sibley East HS (Arlington, Minn.)
COLLEGE: Colorado

COLLEGIATE RECORD

Season Team	G	Min.	FGM	FGA	Pct.	FTM	FTA	Pct.	Reb.	Ast.	Pts.	AVERAGES RPG	APG	PPG
00-01—Colorado	31	461	93	198	.495	103	126	.817	112	13	299	3.6	0.4	9.6
01-02—Colorado	34	672	155	302	.513	115	146	.788	163	43	425	4.8	1.3	12.5
02-03—Colorado	32	1004	229	425	.539	134	173	.775	217	84	592	6.8	2.6	18.5
03-04—Colorado	30	1018	211	359	.588	120	162	.741	236	67	542	7.9	2.2	18.1
Totals	127	3155	693	1284	.540	472	607	.778	728	207	1858	5.7	1.6	14.6

BOWIE, TAMARA   F   MYSTICS

PERSONAL: Born June 3, 1981, in Lansing, Mich. ... 6-0/165. (1.83 m/75 kg). ... **Full name:** Tamara Sanceri Bowie.
HIGH SCHOOL: Sexton (Lansing, Mich.).
COLLEGE: Ball State.
TRANSACTIONS/CAREER NOTES: Selected by Washington in third round (36th overall) of WNBA Draft, April 25, 2003.

COLLEGIATE RECORD

NOTES: Mid-America Conference Player of the Year (2003, 2001). ... All-MAC First Team (2001, 2002, 2003). ... MAC All-Freshman Team (2000). ... Led the MAC in scoring (18.6 ppg) and field-goal percentage (.591) as a sophomore.

Season Team	G	Min.	FGM	FGA	Pct.	FTM	FTA	Pct.	Reb.	Ast.	Pts.	AVERAGES RPG	APG	PPG
99-00—Ball State	29	719	159	315	.505	85	126	.675	...	41	431	7.4	1.4	14.9
00-01—Ball State	28	728	195	334	.584	1018	138	7.377	...	39	512	8.4	1.4	18.3
01-02—Ball State	32	879	215	391	.550	70	101	.693	...	48	530	7.2	1.5	16.6
02-03—Ball State	30	918	237	425	.558	116	145	.800	...	78	618	8.4	2.6	20.6
Totals	119	3244	806	1465	.550	1289	510	2.527	0	206	2091	0.0	1.7	17.6

Three-point field goals: 1999-0, 28-for-74 (.378). 190-1, 14-for-47 (.298). 191-2, 30-for-93 (.323). 192-3, 28-for-59 (.475). Totals, 100-for-273 (.366).

BROUSSARD, CHANIVIA   F

PERSONAL: Born February 14, 1981, in Miami, Fla. ... 6-0/185. (1.83 m/84 kg). ... **Full name:** Chanivia Shantreall Broussard.
HIGH SCHOOL: Miami Northwestern HS (Miami, Fla.).
COLLEGE: Miami (Fla.).

COLLEGIATE RECORD

NOTES: All-Big East Third Team (2004). ... Miami's sixth all-time leading scorer (1,482). ... Ranks third on Miami's all-time career blocked shot list (132). ... Also ninth on Miami's all-time career rebounds list (583).

Season Team	G	Min.	FGM	FGA	Pct.	FTM	FTA	Pct.	Reb.	Ast.	Pts.	AVERAGES RPG	APG	PPG
00-01—Miami (Fla.)	27	591	158	369	.428	36	74	.486	152	22	356	5.6	0.8	13.2
01-02—Miami (Fla.)	29	670	173	407	.425	54	85	.635	124	27	413	4.3	0.9	14.2
02-03—Miami (Fla.)	29	489	115	263	.437	35	69	.507	126	31	273	4.3	1.1	9.4
03-04—Miami (Fla.)	29	815	175	359	.487	87	127	.685	181	48	440	6.2	1.7	15.2
Totals	114	2565	621	1398	.444	212	355	.597	583	128	1482	5.1	1.1	13.0

Three-point field goals: 190-1, 4-for-15 (.267). 191-2, 13-for-51 (.255). 192-3, 8-for-31 (.258). 193-4, 3-for-15 (.200). Totals, 28-for-112 (.250)

BROWN, JUANA   G   SILVER STARS

PERSONAL: Born April 29, 1979, in Memphis, Tenn. ... 5-10/151. (1.78 m/68 kg). ... **Full name:** Juana Dremice Brown.
HIGH SCHOOL: Harding Academy (Memphis, Tenn.).
COLLEGE: North Carolina.
TRANSACTIONS/CAREER NOTES: Selected by Seattle in fourth round (49th overall) of WNBA Draft, April 20, 2001. ... Waived by Seattle, May 21, 2001. ... Signed by San Antonio as a free agent April 16, 2004.

COLLEGIATE RECORD

Season Team	G	Min.	FGM	FGA	Pct.	FTM	FTA	Pct.	Reb.	Ast.	Pts.	AVERAGES RPG	APG	PPG
97-98—North Carolina	32	907	109	274	.398	47	64	.734	77	11	154	2.4	0.3	4.8
98-99—North Carolina	35	1072	190	434	.438	67	109	.615	281	30	500	8.0	0.9	14.3
99-00—North Carolina	30	967	116	340	.341	38	53	.717	285	41	581	9.5	1.4	19.4
00-01—North Carolina	27	937	141	343	.411	41	57	.719	126	92	372	4.7	3.4	13.8
Totals	124	3883	556	1391	.400	193	283	.682	769	174	1607	6.2	1.4	13.0

Three-point field goals: 1997-98, 17-for-77 (.221). 1998-99, 64-for-160 (.400). 1999-0, 38-for-136 (.279). 190-1, 49-for-133 (.368). Totals, 168-for-506 (.332)

BRUNGO, JESSICA   F   SUN

PERSONAL: Born April 16, 1982, in Plainview, N.Y. ... 6-1/165. (1.85 m/75 kg). ... **Full name:** Jessica Kathryn Brungo.
HIGH SCHOOL: North Allegheny HS (Allison Park, Pa.).
COLLEGE: Penn State.
TRANSACTIONS/CAREER NOTES: Selected by Connecticut in second round (16th overall) of WNBA Draft, April 17, 2004.

COLLEGIATE RECORD

NOTES: All-Big Ten honorable mention, coaches and media (2004). ... All-Big Ten Second Team, coaches (2003). ... All-Big Ten honorable mention, media (2003). ... All-Academic Big Ten (2004, 2003, 2002).

Season Team	G	Min.	FGM	FGA	Pct.	FTM	FTA	Pct.	Reb.	Ast.	Pts.	RPG	APG	PPG
00-01—Penn State	29	415	60	143	.420	20	28	.714	86	28	167	3.0	1.0	5.8
01-02—Penn State	35	675	95	227	.419	30	37	.811	142	42	233	4.1	1.2	6.7
02-03—Penn State	35	1058	162	332	.488	38	47	.809	219	90	400	6.3	2.6	11.4
03-04—Penn State	34	1083	128	330	.388	47	56	.839	202	57	343	5.9	1.7	10.1
Totals	133	3231	445	1032	.431	135	168	.804	649	217	1143	4.9	1.6	8.6

Three-point field goals: 190-1, 27-for-62 (.435). 191-2, 13-for-52 (.250). 192-3, 38-for-113 (.336). 193-4, 39-for-135 (.289). Totals, 117-for-362 (.323)

BRUNSON, REBEKKAH F   MONARCHS

PERSONAL: Born December 11, 1981, in Washington, D.C. ... 6-3/175. (1.91 m/79 kg). ... **Full name:** Rebekkah Wright Brunson.
HIGH SCHOOL: Oxon Hill HS (Oxon Hill, Md.).
COLLEGE: Georgetown.
MISCELLANEOUS: A silver medalist with the USA Team at the Pan American Games in Santo Domingo, Dominican Republic.
TRANSACTIONS/CAREER NOTES: Selected by Sacramento in first round (10th overall) of WNBA Draft, April 17, 2004.

COLLEGIATE RECORD

NOTES: AP All-America honorable mention (2004). ... Big East Defensive Player of the Year (2004). ... All-Big East First Team (2004, 2003). ... All-Big East honorable mention (2002, 2001). ... Big East Rookie of the Year (2001). ... Georgetown's all-time leading rebounder (1,093). ... Georgetown's single season rebound record holder with 336 (2004). ... Ranked first and second in blocked shots for one season at Georgetown (51 in 2003, 50 in 2004).

Season Team	G	Min.	FGM	FGA	Pct.	FTM	FTA	Pct.	Reb.	Ast.	Pts.	RPG	APG	PPG
00-01—Georgetown	32	1022	192	377	.509	90	160	.563	293	23	474	9.2	0.7	14.8
01-02—Georgetown	18	567	102	212	.481	67	100	.670	153	11	272	8.5	0.6	15.1
02-03—Georgetown	29	985	170	367	.463	134	200	.670	311	44	481	10.7	1.5	16.6
03-04—Georgetown	28	1020	206	425	.485	121	199	.608	336	35	535	12.0	1.3	19.1
Totals	107	3594	670	1381	.485	412	659	.625	1093	113	1762	10.2	1.1	16.5

Three-point field goals: 191-2, 1-for-12 (.083). 192-3, 7-for-16 (.438). 193-4, 2-for-11 (.182). Totals, 10-for-39 (.256)

BULGER, KATE   G   LYNX

PERSONAL: Born March 27, 1982 in Pittsburgh ... 5-11/155 (1.80 m/70 kg). ... **Full name:** Katherine Bernice Bulger
High School: (Pittsburgh, Penn.)
College: West Virginia
TRANSACTIONS/CAREER NOTES: Selected by Minnesota in the third round (38th overall) of the 2004 draft.

COLLEGIATE RECORD

Notes: All-Big East Second Team (2004, 2002)...All-Big East Third Team (2003)...Big East all-rookie team (2001)...West Virginia's career three-point percentage leader (.416)...West Virginia's single season three-point field goals made leader (92).

Season Team	G	Min.	FGM	FGA	Pct.	FTM	FTA	Pct.	Reb.	Ast.	Pts.	RPG	APG	PPG
00-01—W. Virginia	27	938	149	352	.423	36	50	.720	94	63	390	3.5	2.3	14.4
01-02—W. Virginia	28	1043	164	406	.404	28	37	.757	100	58	432	3.6	2.1	15.4
02-03—W. Virginia	28	966	165	391	.422	36	45	.800	111	34	443	4.0	1.2	15.8
03-04—W. Virginia	32	1066	170	428	.397	35	46	.761	151	41	467	4.7	1.3	14.6
Totals	115	4013	648	1577	.411	135	178	.758	456	196	1732	4.0	1.7	15.1

Three-point field goals: 2000-01, 56-for-136 (.412). 2001-02, 76-for-189 (.402). 2002-03, 77-for-164 (.470). 2003-04, 92-for-234 (.393). Totals, 301-for-723 (.416).

ROOKIES & NEWCOMERS

BUTTS, TASHA   F   LYNX

PERSONAL: Born March 10, 1982, in Milledgeville, Ga. ... 5-11/155. (1.80 m/70 kg). ... **Full name:** LaTasha Rena Butts

HIGH SCHOOL: Baldwin County HS (Milledgeville, Ga.).

COLLEGE: Tennessee.

MISCELLANEOUS: USA Today and Gatorade high school Georgia Women's Basketball Player of the Year in 2000. High school Parade Magazine and Street & Smith All-American.

TRANSACTIONS/CAREER NOTES: Selected by Minnesota in second round (20th overall) of WNBA Draft, April 17, 2004.

COLLEGIATE RECORD

NOTES: All-SEC Second Team, coaches (2004) ... All-SEC Third Team, AP (2004).

Season Team	G	Min.	FGM	FGA	Pct.	FTM	FTA	Pct.	Reb.	Ast.	Pts.	AVERAGES RPG	APG	PPG
00-01—Tennessee	34	379	53	124	.427	36	47	.766	67	27	160	2.0	0.8	4.7
01-02—Tennessee	34	459	47	160	.294	35	47	.745	101	37	147	3.0	1.1	4.3
02-03—Tennessee	38	784	72	203	.355	66	83	.795	183	87	238	4.8	2.3	6.3
03-04—Tennessee	34	986	106	260	.408	112	137	.818	189	99	363	5.6	2.9	10.7
Totals	140	2608	278	747	.372	249	314	.793	540	250	908	3.9	1.8	6.5

Three-point field goals: 190-1, 18-for-48 (.375). 191-2, 18-for-60 (.300). 192-3, 28-for-81 (.346). 193-4, 39-for-101 (.386). Totals, 103-for-290 (.355).

CARTER, AMISHA   F   LIBERTY

PERSONAL: Born June 21, 1982, in Oakland, Calif. ... 6-2/179. (1.88 m/81 kg).

HIGH SCHOOL: McClymond HS (Oakland, Calif.).

COLLEGE: Louisiana Tech.

TRANSACTIONS/CAREER NOTES: Selected by New York in second round (17th overall) of WNBA Draft, April 17, 2004.

COLLEGIATE RECORD

NOTES: AP All-America honorable mention (2004). ... WAC Player of the Year (2004). ... All-WAC First Team (2004). ... WAC All-Defensive Team (2004). ... Louisiana Sports Writers Association All-Louisiana Honorable Mention (2003). ... NJCAA Honorable Mention All-American (2002). ... Region V First Team (2002). ... NJCAA All-Tournament Team (2001).

Season Team	G	Min.	FGM	FGA	Pct.	FTM	FTA	Pct.	Reb.	Ast.	Pts.	AVERAGES RPG	APG	PPG
02-03—Louisiana Tech	33	553	71	159	.447	57	89	.640	163	21	199	4.9	0.6	6.0
03-04—Louisiana Tech	32	931	195	386	.505	152	231	.658	344	25	542	10.8	0.8	16.9
Totals	65	1484	266	545	.488	209	320	.653	507	46	741	7.8	0.7	11.4

Three-point field goals: 193-4, -for-1.

CHONES, KAAYLA   C   MYSTICS

PERSONAL: Born January 11, 1981, in Pepper Pike, Ohio ... 6-3/180. (1.91 m/82 kg).

HIGH SCHOOL: Eastlake North HS (Pepper Pike, Ohio).

COLLEGE: North Carolina State.

MISCELLANEOUS: Father Jim Chones was a first-round draft pick in the 1972 ABA Draft (New York Nets). He also played for the Carolina Cougars (ABA) and the NBA's Cleveland Cavaliers, Los Angeles Lakers and Washington Bullets (now Wizards) ... Sister Kareeda played at Marquette.

TRANSACTIONS/CAREER NOTES: Selected by Washington in second round (15th overall) of WNBA Draft, April 17, 2004.

COLLEGIATE RECORD

MISCELLANEOUS: Father Jim Chones was a first-round draft pick in the 1972 ABA Draft (New York Nets). He also played for the Carolina Cougars (ABA) and the NBA's Cleveland Cavaliers, Los Angeles Lakers and Washington Bullets (now Wizards) ... Sister Kareeda played at Marquette.

Season Team	G	Min.	FGM	FGA	Pct.	FTM	FTA	Pct.	Reb.	Ast.	Pts.	AVERAGES RPG	APG	PPG
99-00—North Carolina State	29	792	129	229	.563	72	128	.563	228	23	330	7.9	0.8	11.4
01-02—North Carolina State	29	749	139	243	.572	79	125	.632	204	23	357	7.0	0.8	12.3
02-03—North Carolina State	28	823	142	269	.528	103	168	.613	217	47	387	7.8	1.7	13.8
03-04—North Carolina State	32	992	180	353	.510	104	161	.646	245	39	464	7.7	1.2	14.5
Totals	118	3356	590	1094	.539	358	582	.615	894	132	1538	7.6	1.1	13.0

CHRISTON, SHAMEKA   G/F   LIBERTY

PERSONAL: Born February 15, 1982, in Hot Springs, Ark. ... 6-1/175. (1.85 m/79 kg). ... **Full name:** Shameka Delynn Christon.
HIGH SCHOOL: Hot Springs HS (Hot Springs, Ark.).
COLLEGE: Arkansas.
MISCELLANEOUS: Member of the 2002 USA World Championship gold medal team for Young Women. Also won a bronze with the 2001 USA Junior World Championship team.
TRANSACTIONS/CAREER NOTES: Selected by New York in first round (fifth overall) of WNBA Draft, April 17, 2004.

COLLEGIATE RECORD

NOTES: AP All-America Third Team (2004). ... SEC Player of the Year (2004). ... All-SEC First Team (2004). ... All-SEC Second Team (2003). ... All-SEC Tournament Team (2003). ... SEC All-Freshman Team (2001). ... Second on Arkansas' all-time scoring list (1,951). ... Holds the Arkansas team record for most points scored in SEC play for one season (224).

Season Team	G	Min.	FGM	FGA	Pct.	FTM	FTA	Pct.	Reb.	Ast.	Pts.	AVERAGES RPG	APG	PPG
00-01—Arkansas	32	765	117	289	.405	56	72	.778	132	20	327	4.1	0.6	10.2
01-02—Arkansas	31	976	197	418	.471	92	133	.692	193	25	517	6.2	0.8	16.7
02-03—Arkansas	32	1052	193	434	.445	81	117	.692	194	47	496	6.1	1.5	15.5
03-04—Arkansas	28	931	219	500	.438	126	166	.759	195	49	611	7.0	1.8	21.8
Totals	123	3724	726	1641	.442	355	488	.727	714	141	1951	5.8	1.1	15.9

Three-point field goals: 190-1, 37-for-113 (.327). 191-2, 31-for-104 (.298). 192-3, 29-for-81 (.358). 193-4, 47-for-129 (.364). Totals, 144-for-427 (.337)

COKER, MONIQUE   F/C   SPARKS

PERSONAL: Born November 28, 1982, in Bronx, N.Y. ... 6-2/180. (1.88 m/82 kg).
HIGH SCHOOL: Monsignor Scanlan HS (Bronx, N.Y.).
COLLEGE: Old Dominion.
NOTES: All-CAA First Team (2004). ... All-CAA Second Team (2003). ... CAA All-Rookie Team (2001). ... CAA All-Tournament Team (2004, 2003, 2002, 2001). ... CAA Tournament MVP (2001).
TRANSACTIONS/CAREER NOTES: Signed by Los Angeles April 23, 2004.

COLLEGIATE RECORD

Season Team	G	Min.	FGM	FGA	Pct.	FTM	FTA	Pct.	Reb.	Ast.	Pts.	AVERAGES RPG	APG	PPG
00-01—Old Dominion	30	594	110	206	.534	41	94	.436	180	27	261	6.0	0.9	8.7
01-02—Old Dominion	34	818	131	255	.514	72	109	.661	188	29	334	5.5	0.9	9.8
02-03—Old Dominion	32	897	121	255	.475	87	123	.707	278	67	337	8.7	2.1	10.5
03-04—Old Dominion	32	990	174	355	.490	119	178	.669	305	68	477	9.5	2.1	14.9
Totals	128	3299	536	1071	.500	319	504	.633	951	191	1409	7.4	1.5	11.0

Three-point field goals: 190-1, -for-2. 191-2, -for-1. 192-3, 8-for-21 (.381). 193-4, 10-for-31 (.323). Totals, 18-for-55 (.327)

CONLON, MARIA   G   SPARKS

PERSONAL: Born November 20, 1982 ... 5-9. (1.75 m/ kg). ... **Full name:** Maria Ann Conlon.
HIGH SCHOOL: Seymour HS (Derby, Conn.).
COLLEGE: Connecticut.
TRANSACTIONS/CAREER NOTES: Signed by Los Angeles April 23, 2004.

COLLEGIATE RECORD

Season Team	G	Min.	FGM	FGA	Pct.	FTM	FTA	Pct.	Reb.	Ast.	Pts.	AVERAGES RPG	APG	PPG
00-01—Connecticut	23	164	26	61	.426	12	19	.632	18	13	83	0.8	0.6	3.6
01-02—Connecticut	39	691	54	165	.327	14	18	.778	78	72	161	2.0	1.8	4.1
02-03—Connecticut	38	1128	86	215	.400	36	48	.750	95	130	262	2.5	3.4	6.9
03-04—Connecticut	35	988	68	174	.391	14	21	.667	102	100	208	2.9	2.9	5.9
Totals	135	2971	234	615	.380	76	106	.717	293	315	714	2.2	2.3	5.3

Three-point field goals: 190-1, 19-for-45 (.422). 191-2, 39-for-118 (.331). 192-3, 54-for-148 (.365). 193-4, 58-for-141 (.411). Totals, 170-for-452 (.376).

CRONIN, KATIE   G   LIBERTY

PERSONAL: Born September 8, 1977 ... 6-0/155. (1.83 m/70 kg).
COLLEGE: Colorado State.

COLLEGIATE RECORD

NOTES: AP All-American honorable mention (1999). ... All-WAC First Team (1999, 1998, 1997). ... Kodak All-American honorable mention (1998). ... All-WAC honorable mention (1996).

Season Team	G	Min	FGM	FGA	Pct.	FTM	FTA	Pct	Off	Def	Tot	Ast	St	TO	Blk	Pts	AVERAGES RPG	APG	PPG
98-99—Colorado St.	36	1081	185	392	.472	108	136	.794	—	—	259	98	64	102	20	532	7.2	2.7	14.8
97-98—Colorado St.	30	983	158	395	.476	113	150	.763	—	—	247	95	58	107	18	545	8.2	3.2	18.2
96-97—Colorado St.	28	879	167	384	.435	71	87	.816	—	—	161	54	58	99	13	451	5.7	1.9	16.1
95-96—Colorado St.	31	900	137	299	.458	52	76	.684	—	—	190	51	52	76	10	353	6.1	1.6	11.4
Totals	125	3843	677	1470	.461	344	449	.768	—	—	857	299	232	384	61	1881	6.9	2.4	15.0

Three-point field goals: 1995-96, 27-for-75 (.360). 1996-97, 46-for-136 (.338). 1997-98, 56-for-146 (.384). 1998-99, 54-for-153 (.353). Totals, 183-for-510 (.359).

DALLAS, CINDY   F   SILVER STARS

PERSONAL: Born January 17, 1980, in Pittsburg, Pa. ... 6-2. (1.88 m/ kg). ... **Full name:** Cynthia Marie Dallas.
HIGH SCHOOL: Schenley HS (Pittsburg, Pa.).
COLLEGE: Illinois.
TRANSACTIONS/CAREER NOTES: Selected by San Antonio in second round (21st overall) of WNBA Draft, April 17, 2004.

COLLEGIATE RECORD

NOTES: All-Big Ten honorable mention (2004). ... Holds Illinois' all-time rebounding record (1014). ... Ranks sixth in the Big Ten in career rebounds. ... First player in Big Ten history to lead the conference in rebounding in back-to-back years (2004, 2003). ... Missed most of the 1989-99 and 1999-2000 seasons with torn anterior cruciate ligaments.

Season Team	G	Min.	FGM	FGA	Pct.	FTM	FTA	Pct.	Reb.	Ast.	Pts.	AVERAGES RPG	APG	PPG
98-99—Illinois	3	43	9	16	.563	8	11	.727	13	1	26	4.3	0.3	8.7
99-00—Illinois	1	5	1	1	1.000	2	2	1.000	1	0	4	1.0	0.0	4.0
00-01—Illinois	32	661	90	178	.506	35	49	.714	186	20	215	5.8	0.6	6.7
01-02—Illinois	29	903	164	308	.532	75	115	.652	272	32	403	9.4	1.1	13.9
02-03—Illinois	29	899	119	254	.469	120	170	.706	278	44	358	9.6	1.5	12.3
03-04—Illinois	26	884	130	264	.492	80	122	.656	264	34	340	10.2	1.3	13.1
Totals	120	3395	513	1021	.502	320	469	.682	1014	131	1346	8.5	1.1	11.2

Three-point field goals: 192-3, -for-3. 193-4, -for-3. Totals, 0-for-6 (.000)

FRIERSON, TRINA   F   STORM

PERSONAL: Born October 13, 1980, in Vicksburg, Mich. ... 6-2/186. (1.88 m/84 kg). ... **Full name:** Catrina Nicole Frierson.
HIGH SCHOOL: Vicksburg HS (Vicksburg, Mich.).
COLLEGE: Louisiana Tech.
MISCELLANEOUS: Street & Smith's high school honorable mention All-American team. First team all-state high school (1998, 1997).
TRANSACTIONS/CAREER NOTES: Selected by Seattle in second round (19th overall) of WNBA Draft, April 17, 2004.

COLLEGIATE RECORD

NOTES: AP All-America honorable mention (2004) ... All-WAC First Team (2004, 2003) ... WAC All-Tournament Team (2004, 2003).

Season Team	G	Min.	FGM	FGA	Pct.	FTM	FTA	Pct.	Reb.	Ast.	Pts.	AVERAGES RPG	APG	PPG
99-00—Louisiana Tech	32	592	132	272	.485	71	97	.732	148	11	336	4.6	0.3	10.5
01-02—Louisiana Tech	30	471	94	205	.459	44	61	.721	147	23	233	4.9	0.8	7.8
02-03—Louisiana Tech	34	894	210	397	.529	90	119	.756	249	21	510	7.3	0.6	15.0
03-04—Louisiana Tech	31	883	215	423	.508	70	99	.707	217	24	502	7.0	0.8	16.2
Totals	127	2840	651	1297	.502	275	376	.731	761	79	1581	6.0	0.6	12.4

Three-point field goals: 1999-0, 1-for-5 (.200). 191-2, 1-for-4 (.250). 192-3, -for-1. 193-4, 2-for-9 (.222). Totals, 4-for-19 (.211)

FUTRELL, CANDACE   G   SUN

PERSONAL: Born July 10, 1982, in Altoona, Pa. ... 5-10/154. (1.78 m/70 kg).
HIGH SCHOOL: Altoona HS (Altoona, Pa.).
COLLEGE: Duquesne.
TRANSACTIONS/CAREER NOTES: Selected by Connecticut in third round (29th overall) of WNBA Draft, April 17, 2004.

COLLEGIATE RECORD

NOTES: Atlantic 10 Co-Player of the Year (2004). ... All-Atlantic 10 First Team (2004). ... All-Atlantic 10 Third Team (2003). ... All-Atlantic 10 Second Team (2002). ... Atlantic 10's Most Improved Player (2002).

Season Team	G	Min.	FGM	FGA	Pct.	FTM	FTA	Pct.	Reb.	Ast.	Pts.	AVERAGES RPG	APG	PPG
00-01—Duquesne	29	483	36	119	.303	37	48	.771	78	11	119	2.7	0.4	4.1
01-02—Duquesne	29	982	172	395	.435	121	153	.791	143	83	518	4.9	2.9	17.9
02-03—Duquesne	21	680	151	369	.409	62	82	.756	78	53	410	3.7	2.5	19.5
03-04—Duquesne	29	1019	214	580	.369	119	151	.788	202	66	621	7.0	2.3	21.4
Totals	108	3164	573	1463	.392	339	434	.781	501	213	1668	4.6	2.0	15.4

Three-point field goals: 190-1, 10-for-45 (.222). 191-2, 53-for-145 (.366). 192-3, 46-for-124 (.371). 193-4, 74-for-209 (.354). Totals, 183-for-523 (.350)

GREAR, CHELSEA   F/G   MONARCHS

PERSONAL: Born December 11, 1979 in Houston, Texas ... 5-10. (1.78 m/ kg).
HIGH SCHOOL: Lutheran North HS (Houston, Texas).
COLLEGE: New Mexico.
TRANSACTIONS/CAREER NOTES: Signed by New York as a free agent, April 2004

COLLEGIATE RECORD

Season Team	G	Min	FGM	FGA	Pct.	FTM	FTA	Pct	Off	Def	Tot	Ast	St	TO	Blk	Pts	AVERAGES RPG	APG	PPG
99-00—New Mexico	25	237	20	65	.308	14	25	.560			56	7	18		5	54	2.2	0.3	2.2
00-01—New Mexico	35	759	87	219	.397	34	54	.629			196	39	40		11	213	5.6	1.1	6.1
01-02—New Mexico	31	852	108	216	.500	63	90	.700			206	32	48		15	295	6.6	1.0	9.5
02-03—New Mexico	32	933	133	268	.496	59	86	.686			221	46	46		8	348	6.7	1.4	10.5
Totals	124	2781	348	768	.453	170	255	.666			679	124	152		39	910	5.5	1.0	7.3

Three-point field goals: 1999-2000, 0-for-3 (.000). 2000-01, 5-for-32 (.156). 2001-02, 16-for-43 (.372). 2002-03, 23-for-54 (.426). Totals, 44-for-132 (.333).

HAYDEN, VANESSA   C   LYNX

PERSONAL: Born June 5, 1982, in Orlando, FL ... 6-4/224. (1.93 m/102 kg). ... **Full name:** Vanessa L'asonya Hayden.
HIGH SCHOOL: Boone HS (Orlando, Fla.)
COLLEGE: Florida.
MISCELLANEOUS: USA Today high school All-America player (2000) ... High school Gatorade Player of the Year for the State of Florida (2000).
TRANSACTIONS/CAREER NOTES: Selected by Minnesota in first round (seventh overall) of WNBA Draft, April 17, 2004.

COLLEGIATE RECORD

NOTES: AP All-America Second Team (2004). ... AP All-America honorable mention (2003, 2002). ... SEC Defensive Player of the Year (2004). ... All-SEC First Team (2004, 2002). ... SEC All-Freshman Team (2001). ... Led the nation in blocked shots per game in 2002 (4.3 bpg). ... Florida's all-time blocked shots leader (357).

Season Team	G	Min.	FGM	FGA	Pct.	FTM	FTA	Pct.	Reb.	Ast.	Pts.	RPG	APG	PPG
00-01—Florida	30	554	129	247	.522	54	115	.470	275	17	312	9.2	0.6	10.4
01-02—Florida	29	799	200	395	.506	96	156	.615	343	41	496	11.8	1.4	17.1
02-03—Florida	18	390	81	184	.440	35	58	.603	170	15	197	9.4	0.8	10.9
03-04—Florida	30	823	235	450	.522	101	171	.591	317	38	571	10.6	1.3	19.0
Totals	107	2566	645	1276	.505	286	500	.572	1105	111	1576	10.3	1.0	14.7

(AVERAGES columns: RPG, APG, PPG)

HELM, SELIA   C   SPARKS

PERSONAL: Born January 19, 1982, in Bowling Green, Ky. ... 6-3. (1.91 m/ kg). ... **Full name:** Selia Lauren Helm.
HIGH SCHOOL: Warren Central HS (Bowling Green, Ky.).
COLLEGE: Kentucky.
TRANSACTIONS/CAREER NOTES: Signed by Los Angeles April 23, 2004.

COLLEGIATE RECORD

NOTES: All-SEC Second Team (2002) ... All-SEC Freshman team (2001).

Season Team	G	Min.	FGM	FGA	Pct.	FTM	FTA	Pct.	Reb.	Ast.	Pts.	RPG	APG	PPG
00-01—Kentucky	24	555	115	246	.467	62	72	.861	112	7	14	4.7	0.3	0.6
01-02—Kentucky	29	882	198	388	.510	92	115	.800	194	17	492	6.7	0.6	17.0
02-03—Kentucky	27	716	122	251	.486	58	79	.734	176	27	309	6.5	1.0	11.4
03-04—Kentucky	27	746	153	301	.508	76	99	.768	184	18	385	6.8	0.7	14.3
Totals	107	2899	588	1186	.496	288	365	.789	666	69	1200	6.2	0.6	11.2

Three-point field goals: 190-1, 2-for-7 (.286). 191-2, 4-for-11 (.364). 192-3, 7-for-18 (.389). 193-4, 3-for-15 (.200). Totals, 16-for-51 (.314)

HODGES, DONEEKA   G   SPARKS

PERSONAL: Born July 19, 1982, in New Orleans, La. ... 5-9/160. (1.75 m/73 kg). ... **Full name:** Doneeka Danyell Hodges.
HIGH SCHOOL: O.P. Walker HS (New Orleans, La.).
COLLEGE: Louisiana State.
MISCELLANEOUS: Three-time high school All-New Orleans Metro Team. Twin sister Roneeka played at LSU for the last three seasons and is now at Florida State.
TRANSACTIONS/CAREER NOTES: Selected by Los Angeles in second round (25th overall) of WNBA Draft, April 17, 2004.

COLLEGIATE RECORD

NOTES: All-SEC Second Team (2004, 2002). ... Third Team All-Louisiana (2003). ... Womenscollegehoops.com Classic MVP (2002). ... Ranks second in LSU history for three-point field goals made (178).

Season Team	G	Min.	FGM	FGA	Pct.	FTM	FTA	Pct.	Reb.	Ast.	Pts.	RPG	APG	PPG
00-01—Louisiana State	30	631	100	214	.467	40	53	.755	124	40	253	4.1	1.3	8.4
01-02—Louisiana State	30	1106	157	373	.421	92	119	.773	134	106	459	4.5	3.5	15.3
02-03—Louisiana State	34	974	125	306	.408	25	34	.735	81	89	323	2.4	2.6	9.5
03-04—Louisiana State	35	1112	184	458	.402	56	73	.767	129	113	489	3.7	3.2	14.0
Totals	129	3823	566	1351	.419	213	279	.763	468	348	1524	3.6	2.7	11.8

Three-point field goals: 190-1, 13-for-34 (.382). 191-2, 53-for-139 (.381). 192-3, 48-for-134 (.358). 193-4, 64-for-193 (.332). Totals, 178-for-500 (.356)

HOFFMAN, EBONY   C   FEVER

PERSONAL: Born August 27, 1982, in Los Angeles, CA ... 6-2/210. (1.88 m/95 kg). ... **Full name:** Ebony Vernice Hoffman.
HIGH SCHOOL: Narbonne HS (Harbor City, Calif.).
COLLEGE: USC.
MISCELLANEOUS: Member of the gold medal-winning 2000 USA Junior World Championship Qualifying Team.

506

ROOKIES & NEWCOMERS

TRANSACTIONS/CAREER NOTES: Selected by Indiana in first round (ninth overall) of WNBA Draft, April 17, 2004.

COLLEGIATE RECORD

NOTES: All-Pac-10 First Team (2004, 2003, 2002). ... Pac-10 All Freshman Team (2001). ... First Pac-10 player to ever tally more than 1,500 career points, 1,000 rebounds and 245 steals.

Season Team	G	Min.	FGM	FGA	Pct.	FTM	FTA	Pct.	Reb.	Ast.	Pts.	AVERAGES RPG	APG	PPG
00-01—Southern California	28	768	128	285	.449	91	120	.758	223	58	350	8.0	2.1	12.5
01-02—Southern California	28	815	159	352	.452	84	111	.757	250	44	416	8.9	1.6	14.9
02-03—Southern California	31	952	177	384	.461	127	167	.760	303	70	504	9.8	2.3	16.3
03-04—Southern California	28	820	149	343	.434	97	141	.688	227	53	417	8.1	1.9	14.9
Totals	115	3355	613	1364	.449	399	539	.740	1003	225	1687	8.7	2.0	14.7

Three-point field goals: 190-1, 3-for-14 (.214). 191-2, 14-for-44 (.318). 192-3, 23-for-56 (.411). 193-4, 22-for-59 (.373). Totals, 62-for-173 (.358).

JACOBS, AMBER   G   LYNX

PERSONAL: Born June 29, 1982, in Elkhart, IN ... 5-8/147. (1.73 m/67 kg).
HIGH SCHOOL: Abington Heights HS (Clark Summit, Pa.).
COLLEGE: Boston College.
MISCELLANEOUS: Alternate for the USA Basketball World Championships for Young Women team (2003)
TRANSACTIONS/CAREER NOTES: Selected by Minnesota in third round (33rd overall) of WNBA Draft, April 17, 2004.

COLLEGIATE RECORD

NOTES: AP All-America honorable mention (2004). ... All-Big East Second Team (2004). ... Big East All-Tournament Team (2004). ... All-Big East honorable mention (2003). ... Big East All-Academic (2003). ... Big East All-Rookie Team (2001).

Season Team	G	Min.	FGM	FGA	Pct.	FTM	FTA	Pct.	Reb.	Ast.	Pts.	AVERAGES RPG	APG	PPG
00-01—Boston College..........	29	1015	123	289	.426	55	72	.764	54	109	333	1.9	3.8	11.5
01-02—Boston College..........	31	936	140	321	.436	40	56	.714	79	110	368	2.5	3.5	11.9
02-03—Boston College..........	31	970	131	318	.412	62	68	.912	71	112	374	2.3	3.6	12.1
03-04—Boston College..........	32	1053	150	310	.484	116	137	.847	93	138	469	2.9	4.3	14.7
Totals	123	3974	544	1238	.439	273	333	.820	297	469	1544	2.4	3.8	12.6

Three-point field goals: 190-1, 32-for-103 (.311). 191-2, 48-for-139 (.345). 192-3, 50-for-127 (.394). 193-4, 53-for-133 (.398). Totals, 183-for-502 (.365)

JOENS, CATHY   G/F   LIBERTY

PERSONAL: Born February 12, 1981, in Irvin Calif. ... 5-11/165. (1.80 m/75 kg).
HIGH SCHOOL: Calvery Chapel.
COLLEGE: George Washington.
TRANSACTIONS/CAREER NOTES: Selected by New York in third round (30th overall) of WNBA Draft, April 17, 2004.

COLLEGIATE RECORD

NOTES: AP All-America honorable mention (2004). ... Atlantic 10 Co-Player of the Year (2004). ... Atlantic 10 Player of the Year (2003). ... Atlantic 10 Student-Athlete of the Year (2004). ... Atlantic 10 First Team (2004, 2003, 2002). ... Set George Washington's record for most three-pointers made in a season with 95 (2004).

Season Team	G	Min.	FGM	FGA	Pct.	FTM	FTA	Pct.	Reb.	Ast.	Pts.	AVERAGES RPG	APG	PPG
99-00—George Washington ...	31	506	73	192	.380	36	49	.735	112	29	211	3.6	0.9	6.8
01-02—George Washington ...	30	919	161	379	.425	65	84	.774	117	87	459	3.9	2.9	15.3
02-03—George Washington ...	31	1030	189	418	.452	69	92	.750	149	96	540	4.8	3.1	17.4
03-04—George Washington ...	30	1051	198	442	.448	89	109	.817	184	96	581	6.1	3.2	19.4
Totals	122	3506	621	1431	.434	259	334	.775	562	308	1791	4.6	2.5	14.7

Three-point field goals: 1999-0, 29-for-95 (.305). 191-2, 72-for-175 (.411). 192-3, 92-for-214 (.430). 193-4, 95-for-213 (.446). Totals, 288-for-697 (.413)

JONES, CHANDI   G/F   SHOCK

PERSONAL: Born March 25, 1982, in Wharton, Texas ... 5-11/154. (1.80 m/70 kg). ... **Full name:** Chandi Montrease Jones.
HIGH SCHOOL: Bay City HS (Bay City, Texas).
COLLEGE: Houston.
MISCELLANEOUS: Member of the 2000 USA Junior World Championship Qualifying Team that captured the gold medal.
TRANSACTIONS/CAREER NOTES: Selected by Phoenix in first round (eighth overall) of WNBA Draft, April 17, 2004.

COLLEGIATE RECORD

NOTES: Kodak All-America Team (2004). ... AP All-America Second Team (2004). ... USBWA All-America Second Team (2004). ... AP All-America honorable mention (2003, 2002). ... Conference USA Player of the Year (2004, 2003, 2002). ... All-Conference USA First Team (2004, 2003, 2002, 2001). ... Conference USA Tournament MVP (2004). ... Conference USA All-Tournament Team (2004, 2002). ... Conference USA Freshman of the Year (2001). ... Houston's all-time leading scorer (2,692).

Season Team	G	Min.	FGM	FGA	Pct.	FTM	FTA	Pct.	Reb.	Ast.	Pts.	RPG	APG	PPG
												AVERAGES		
00-01—Houston	20	674	156	346	.451	99	138	.717	113	49	429	5.7	2.5	21.5
01-02—Houston	34	1221	277	604	.459	165	240	.688	196	91	766	5.8	2.7	22.5
02-03—Houston	28	1020	275	563	.488	168	233	.721	228	68	770	8.1	2.4	27.5
03-04—Houston	32	1139	255	607	.420	146	198	.737	177	77	727	5.5	2.4	22.7
Totals	114	4054	963	2120	.454	578	809	.714	714	285	2692	6.3	2.5	23.6

Three-point field goals: 190-1, 18-for-71 (.254). 191-2, 47-for-142 (.331). 192-3, 52-for-141 (.369). 193-4, 71-for-194 (.366). Totals, 188-for-548 (.343)

KING, VALERIE   G   MONARCHS

PERSONAL: Born February 23, 1982, in Columbus, OH ... 5-10/152. (1.78 m/69 kg). ... **Full name:** Valerie Lynne King.
HIGH SCHOOL: Washington Court House HS (Washington Court House, Ohio).
COLLEGE: Cincinnati.
MISCELLANEOUS: In high school, was named Division II All Southeast Player of the Year and was selected as MVP of the North/South All-Star game.

COLLEGIATE RECORD

NOTES: All-Conference USA Second Team (2004). ... All-Conference USA First Team (2003, 2002). ... Conference USA All-Tournament Team (2004, 2003, 2002, 2001). ... Conference USA Tournament MVP (2001). ... Recorded a Cincinnati and Conference USA scoring record of 46 points against Charleston Southern (11/25/03). ... Holds the career record for three-point field goals made (338) for Cincinnati and Conference USA. ... Broke her own Conference USA Tournament record with seven three-pointers against Houston (March 5, 2004).

Season Team	G	Min.	FGM	FGA	Pct.	FTM	FTA	Pct.	Reb.	Ast.	Pts.	RPG	APG	PPG
												AVERAGES		
00-01—Cincinnati	32	988	167	423	.395	124	145	.855	73	55	520	2.3	1.7	16.3
01-02—Cincinnati	32	1053	196	459	.427	141	158	.892	73	50	634	2.3	1.6	19.8
02-03—Cincinnati	31	1127	163	416	.392	89	102	.873	88	47	507	2.8	1.5	16.4
03-04—Cincinnati	31	1032	163	409	.399	86	103	.835	72	39	495	2.3	1.3	16.0
Totals	126	4200	689	1707	.404	440	508	.866	306	191	2156	2.4	1.5	17.1

Three-point field goals: 190-1, 62-for-168 (.369). 191-2, 101-for-235 (.430). 192-3, 92-for-245 (.376). 193-4, 83-for-199 (.417). Totals, 338-for-847 (.399)

KOSTAKI, ANASTASIA   G/F   SUN

PERSONAL: Born March 26, 1978, in Athens, Greece ... 5-7/137. (1.70 m/62 kg).
TRANSACTIONS/CAREER NOTES: Signed by Connecticut as a free agent, March 26, 2004.

PROFESSIONAL STATISTICS

Season Team	G	Min	FGM	FGA	Pct.	FTM	FTA	Pct	Off	Def	Tot	Ast	St	TO	Blk	Pts	RPG	APG	PPG
																	AVERAGES		
2002	18	—	80	182	.430	122	155	.780	—	—	74	87	—	—	—	327	4.1	4.8	18.2
2003	23	—	63	146	.430	85	108	.790	—	—	75	108	—	—	—	286	3.3	4.7	12.4
Totals	41	—	143	328	.436	207	263	.787	—	—	149	195	—	—	—	613	3.6	4.7	14.9

Three-point field goals: 2002, 15-for-53 (.280). 2003, 25-for-85 (.300). Totals, 40-for-138 (.290).

EUROPEAN LEAGUE

Season Team	G	Min	FGM	FGA	Pct.	FTM	FTA	Pct	Off	Def	Tot	Ast	St	TO	Blk	Pts	RPG	APG	PPG
																	AVERAGES		
2001	8	—	31	67	.460	20	38	.530	—	—	33	22	—	—	—	109	4.1	2.7	13.6
2002	2	—	11	16	.690	13	17	.770	—	—	6	6	—	—	—	41	3.0	3.0	20.5
Totals	10	—	42	83	.506	33	55	.600	—	—	39	28	—	—	—	150	3.9	2.8	15.0

Three-point field goals: 2001, 9-for-38 (.237). 2002, 2-for-10 (.200). Totals, 11-for-48 (.229).

KUBLINA, IEVA   F/C   FEVER

PERSONAL: Born July 8, 1982, in Riga, Latvia ... 6-4/190. (1.93 m/86 kg).
HIGH SCHOOL: Trinity Episcopal HS (Richmond, Va.).
COLLEGE: Virginia Tech.
MISCELLANEOUS: Member of the Latvian National Team that participated in the World Championship for Young Women. Was selected to the all-tournament team at the qualifying rounds for the European Championships (April 2000).
TRANSACTIONS/CAREER NOTES: Selected by Indiana in third round (31st overall) of WNBA Draft, April 17, 2004.

COLLEGIATE RECORD

NOTES: All-Big East Second Team (2004). ... All-Big East First Team (2003). ... All-Big East Tournament Team (2003). ... Big East Conference Most Improved Player (2002). ... Most Valuable Player of the 2003 Lady Luck Classic (2003). ... Virginia Tech's all-time blocked shots leader (256).

Season Team	G	Min.	FGM	FGA	Pct.	FTM	FTA	Pct.	Reb.	Ast.	Pts.	RPG	APG	PPG
00-01—Virginia Tech	31	642	87	199	.437	55	85	.647	154	15	242	5.0	0.5	7.8
01-02—Virginia Tech	32	976	198	419	.473	82	107	.766	249	30	498	7.8	0.9	15.6
02-03—Virginia Tech	32	1046	173	383	.452	112	140	.800	238	44	481	7.4	1.4	15.0
03-04—Virginia Tech	31	999	155	374	.414	95	115	.826	204	26	426	6.6	0.8	13.7
Totals	126	3663	613	1375	.446	344	447	.770	845	115	1647	6.7	0.9	13.1

Three-point field goals: 190-1, 13-for-38 (.342). 191-2, 20-for-53 (.377). 192-3, 23-for-65 (.354). 193-4, 21-for-78 (.269). Totals, 77-for-234 (.329).

MACFARLANE, KATIE　　F　　SUN

PERSONAL: Born January 16, 1982 in Clarence, N.Y. ... 6-0/ 168 (1.83 m/ 76 kg). **Full name:** Katie Ann Macfarlane
High School: Clarence High (Clarence, NY)
TRANSACTIONS/CAREER NOTES: Signed by Connecticut as a free agent, April 27, 2004.
College: Army

COLLEGIATE RECORD

Season Team	G	Min.	FGM	FGA	Pct.	FTM	FTA	Pct.	Reb.	Ast.	Pts.	RPG	APG	PPG
00-01—Army	29	693	117	232	.504	103	136	.757	236	20	340	8.1	0.7	11.7
01-02—Army	29	943	187	375	.499	148	197	.751	295	50	532	10.2	1.7	18.3
02-03—Army	31	1017	209	410	.510	125	173	.732	330	49	549	10.6	1.6	17.7
03-04—Army	28	930	193	361	.535	122	184	.663	282	36	520	10.1	1.3	18.6
Totals	117	3583	706	1378	.512	498	690	.722	1143	155	1941	9.8	1.3	16.6

Three-point field goals: 2000-01, 3-for-7 (.429). 2001-02, 10-for-35 (.289). 2002-03, 6-for-36 (.244). 2003-04, 12-for-39 (.308). Total, 31-for-117 (.265).

MARTINEZ, NURIA　　C　　MONARCHS

PERSONAL: Born February 29, 1984 ... 5-9. (1.75 m/ kg).
TRANSACTIONS/CAREER NOTES: Selected by Sacramento in third round (36th overall) of WNBA Draft, April 17, 2004.

SPANISH LEAGUE

Season,Team	G	Min	FGM	FGA	Pct.	FTM	FTA	Pct	Off	Def	Tot	Ast	St	TO	Blk	Pts	RPG	APG	PPG
00-01	25	407	45	105	.429	37	51	.725	31	13	44	30	33	22	2	148	1.8	1.2	5.9
01-02	32	515	63	131	.481	28	51	.490	39	12	51	34	58	34	5	196	1.6	1.1	6.1
02-03	34	726	97	202	.480	37	57	.649	52	10	62	66	73	52	5	276	1.8	1.9	8.1
03-04	26	943	108	264	.409	110	155	.710	65	19	84	91	82	106	9	380	3.2	4.1	14.6
Totals	117	2591	313	702	.446	212	314	.675	187	54	241	221	246	214	21	1000	2.6	1.9	8.5

Three-point field goals: 2000-01, 21-for-52 (.404). 2001-02, 22-for-55 (.400). 2002-03, 35-for-89 (.393). 2003-04, 19-for-73 (.260). Totals, 97-for-269 (.361).

MAZZANTE, KELLY　　G　　STING

PERSONAL: Born February 2, 1982, in Williamsport, PA ... 5-11/162. (1.80 m/73 kg). ... **Full name:** Kelly Anne Mazzante.
HIGH SCHOOL: Montoursville HS [Montoursville, PA].
COLLEGE: Penn State.
MISCELLANEOUS: Member of the 2002 USA World Championship for Young Women Qualifying Team that captured the gold medal.
TRANSACTIONS/CAREER NOTES: Selected by Charlotte in second round (18th overall) of WNBA Draft, April 17, 2004.

COLLEGIATE RECORD

NOTES: AP All-America First Team (2004, 2003). ... Kodak All-America Team (2004, 2003, 2002). ... USBWA All-America Team (2004, 2003, 2002). ... AP All-America Second Team (2002). ... CoSIDA Academic All-America of the Year (2004). ... Big Ten Player of the Year (2004, 2003). ... First Team All-Big Ten (2004, 2003, 2002, 2001). ... Big Ten Freshman of the Year (2001). ... Big Ten All-Freshman Team (2001). ... Academic All-American First Team (2004). ... Academic All-American Second Team (2002). ... Academic All-American Third Team (2001). ... Big Ten All-Tournament Team (2004, 2002) ... Ranks ninth all-time in career points in NCAA Division I (2,919). ... Big Ten and Penn State's all-time leading scorer (2,919). ... Holds Penn State's single season scoring record with 872 points (2002).

Season Team	G	Min.	FGM	FGA	Pct.	FTM	FTA	Pct.	Reb.	Ast.	Pts.	RPG	APG	PPG
00-01—Penn State	29	881	203	434	.468	58	76	.763	123	47	529	4.2	1.6	18.2
01-02—Penn State	35	1205	313	716	.437	144	177	.814	138	59	872	3.9	1.7	24.9
02-03—Penn State	35	1262	292	647	.451	155	184	.842	161	76	837	4.6	2.2	23.9
03-04—Penn State	34	1181	243	606	.401	103	125	.824	141	55	681	4.1	1.6	20.0
Totals	133	4529	1051	2403	.437	460	562	.819	563	237	2919	4.2	1.8	21.9

Three-point field goals: 190-1, 65-for-176 (.369). 191-2, 102-for-278 (.367). 192-3, 98-for-284 (.345). 193-4, 92-for-281 (.327). Totals, 357-for-1019 (.350)

MCDIVITT, APRIL   G   LIBERTY

PERSONAL: Born December 9, 1980, in Connersville, Ind. ... 5-7. (1.70 m/ kg).
HIGH SCHOOL: Connersville HS (Ind.).
COLLEGE: Tennessee/California-Santa Barbara.

COLLEGIATE RECORD

NOTES: Sat out 2002-03 season due to NCAA Transfer Rules

Season Team	G	Min	FGM	FGA	Pct.	FTM	FTA	Pct	Off	Def	Tot	Ast	St	TO	Blk	Pts	RPG	APG	PPG
00-01—Tennessee	34	605	60	139	.432	27	34	.794	3	51	54	76	34	50	2	185	1.6	2.2	5.4
01-02—Tennessee	33	620	53	131	.405	27	39	.692	5	48	53	60	47	49	2	162	1.6	1.8	4.9
03-04—UC Santa Bar.	31	896	81	226	.358	42	67	.627	10	88	98	136	56	76	1	257	3.2	4.4	8.3
Totals	98	2121	194	496	.391	96	140	.686	18	187	205	272	137	175	5	604	2.1	2.8	6.2

Three-point field goals: 2000-01, 38-for-93 (.409). 2001-02, 29-for-72 (.403). 2003-04, 53-for-139 (.381).

MENDIOLA, GIULIANA   G   MONARCHS

PERSONAL: Born January 8, 1982 in Fountain Valley, Calif. ... 5-11/174 (1.80 m/79 kg). ... **Full name:** Giuliana Priscilla Mendiola
HIGH SCHOOL: El Toro HS (Lake Forrest, Calif.)
COLLEGE: Washington
MISCELLANEOUS: Orange County Register High School Player of the Year and Los Angeles Times Orange County Player of the Year for the 1999-2000 season. ... Selected as a high school honorable mention All-American by USA Today and Street & Smith during her senior year. ... Older sister Gioconda played guard on the Washington Huskies basketball team.

COLLEGIATE RECORD

NOTES: AP All-America honorable mention (2004, 2003). ... Kodak All-America honorable mention (2003). ... All-Pac-10 First Team (2004, 2003, 2002). ... Pac-10 Player of the Year (2003). ... Pac-10 All-Tournament Team (2004). ... MVP of the Seattle Times Husky Classic (2004). ... Washington's all-time leader in total assists (600). ... Pac-10 All-Academic honorable mention (2003, 2002). ... Pac-10 All-Freshman Team (2001). ... All-Pac-10 honorable mention (2001).

Season Team	G	Min	FGM	FGA	Pct.	FTM	FTA	Pct	Off	Def	Tot	Ast	St	TO	Blk	Pts	RPG	APG	PPG
00-01—Washington..	32	963	126	281	.448	63	87	.724	79	123	202	126	35	86	2	357	6.3	3.9	11.2
01-02—Washington..	31	975	136	289	.471	89	112	.795	75	95	170	152	34	73	2	388	5.5	4.9	12.5
02-03—Washington..	30	968	195	359	.543	87	103	.845	75	121	196	162	51	101	2	525	6.5	5.4	17.5
03-04—Washington..	31	1126	244	478	.510	125	152	.822	72	129	201	172	48	91	4	661	6.5	5.5	21.3
Totals	124	4032	701	1407	.498	364	454	.802	301	468	769	612	168	351	10	1931	6.2	4.9	15.6

Three-point field goals: 2000-01, 39-for-113 (.345). 2001-02, 27-for-82 (.329). 2002-03, 48-for-105 (.457). 2003-04, 48-for-121 (.397). Totals: 162-for-421 (.384).

NDIAYE, NDEYE   C   LIBERTY

PERSONAL: Born in Dakar, Senegal ... 6-3. (1.91 m/ kg).
HIGH SCHOOL: Yalla-Suur-En (Dakar, Senegal)
COLLEGE: Southern Nazarene.

COLLEGIATE RECORD

NOTES: NAIA National Tournament MVP (2004). ... NAIA All-American First Team (2004, 2003, 2002). ... NAIA All-National Tournament First Team (2004, 2002, 2001).

Season, Team	G	Min	FGM	FGA	Pct.	FTM	FTA	Pct	Off	Def	Tot	Ast	St	TO	Blk	Pts	RPG	APG	PPG
00-01—S. Nazarene.	38		191	419	.456	99	158	.627			290	36	35		55	482	7.6	0.9	12.7
01-02—S. Nazarene.	36		217	384	.565	137	188	.729			266	82	71		32	571	7.4	1.7	15.9
02-03—S. Nazarene.	37		222	395	.562	133	182	.731			280	57	66		66	577	7.6	1.5	15.6
03-04—S. Nazarene.	37		262	437	.600	121	155	.781			282	65	52		63	646	7.6	1.8	17.5
Totals	148		892	1635	.546	490	683	.717			1118	240	224		216	2276	7.6	1.5	15.4

Three-point field goals: 2000-01, 1-for-10 (.100). 2001-02, 0-for-2 (.000). 2002-03, 0-for-4 (.000). 2003-04, 1-for-2 (.500). Totals, 2-for-18 (.111).

NORD, SARA   G   MYSTICS

PERSONAL: Born February 21, 1982 (Louisville, Ky.) ... 5-5/145 (1.65 m/66 kg). **Full name:** Sara Mae Nord
High School: Jefferson HS (Jefferson, Ind.)
College: Louisville
TRANSACTIONS/CAREER NOTES: Signed by Washington as a free agent, April 27, 2004.
Miscellaneous: Named Miss Indiana Basketball and USA Today honorable mention All-America in her senior year in high school. Has a twin sister, Shannon, who plays softball at Louisville.

COLLEGIATE RECORD

NOTES: AP All-America honorable mention (2004). ...All-Conference USA First Team (2004, 2003, 2002, 2001). ...Led Conference USA in assists four consecutive years. ...Holds Louisville and Conference USA career assist record (846). ... Louisville all-time steals leader (299). ...Conference USA Scholar Athlete of the Year (2003).

Season Team	G	Min.	FGM	FGA	Pct.	FTM	FTA	Pct.	Reb.	Ast.	Pts.	AVERAGES		
												RPG	APG	PPG
00-01—Louisville....................	28	1042	138	340	.406	65	85	.765	130	216	288	4.6	7.7	13.9
01-02—Louisville....................	30	920	102	273	.374	61	70	.871	127	235	312	4.2	7.8	10.4
02-03—Louisville....................	29	993	143	352	.406	55	73	.753	123	199	405	4.2	6.8	14.0
03-04—Louisville....................	30	1144	175	425	.412	70	87	.805	122	196	518	4.1	6.5	17/3
Totals.................................	117	4099	558	1390	.401	251	315	.797	502	846	523	4.3	7.2	13.0

Three-point field goals: 2000-01, 47-for-132 (.356). 2001-02, 47-for-136 (.346). 2002-03, 64-for-178 (.360). 2003-04, 98-for-252 (.389). Totals, 256-for-698 (.366).

OHA, UGO   C   SUN

PERSONAL: Born July 18, 1982, in Houston, Texas ... 6-4/185. (1.93 m/84 kg).
HIGH SCHOOL: Hastings HS (Houston, Texas).
COLLEGE: George Washington.
TRANSACTIONS/CAREER NOTES: Selected by Connecticut in second round (24th overall) of WNBA Draft, April 17, 2004.

COLLEGIATE RECORD

NOTES: Atlantic 10 Defensive Player of the Year (2004, 2002). ... All-Atlantic 10 First Team (2002). ... Atlantic 10 All-Defensive Team (2004, 2003). ... All-Atlantic 10 Second Team (2003). ... All-Atlantic 10 Rookie Team (2001). ... Atlantic 10 and George Washington's all-time blocked shots leader (354).

Season Team	G	Min.	FGM	FGA	Pct.	FTM	FTA	Pct.	Reb.	Ast.	Pts.	AVERAGES		
												RPG	APG	PPG
00-01—George Washington ...	32	772	112	246	.455	69	113	.611	157	24	293	4.9	0.8	9.2
01-02—George Washington ...	30	951	150	337	.445	92	143	.643	204	26	392	6.8	0.9	13.1
02-03—George Washington ...	31	957	192	377	.509	93	147	.633	208	38	478	6.7	1.2	15.4
03-04—George Washington ...	30	920	160	326	.491	94	134	.701	213	24	414	7.1	0.8	13.8
Totals	123	3600	614	1286	.477	348	537	.648	782	112	1577	6.4	0.9	12.8

Three-point field goals: 191-2, -for-3. 192-3, 1-for-4 (.250). Totals, 1-for-7 (.143)

OHLDE, NICOLE   F/C   LYNX

PERSONAL: Born March 12, 1982, in Clay Center, Kan. ... 6-4/180. (1.93 m/82 kg). ... **Full name:** Nicole Katherine Ohlde.
HIGH SCHOOL: Center HS (Clay Center, Kan.)
COLLEGE: Kansas State.
MISCELLANEOUS: Two-time Gold medalist as a member of the USA Basketball World Championship for Young Women team (2003, 2002).
TRANSACTIONS/CAREER NOTES: Selected by Minnesota in first round (sixth overall) of WNBA Draft, April 17, 2004.

COLLEGIATE RECORD

NOTES: Kodak All-America (2004, 2003). ... AP All-America First Team (2004, 2003). ... USBWA All-America (2004, 2003). ... Big 12 Conference Player of the Year (2004, 2003). ... All-Big 12 First Team (2004, 2003, 2002). ... All-Big 12 Third Team (2001). ... Big 12 Freshman of the Year (2001). ... Academic All-Big 12 First Team (2004, 2003, 2002). ... Kansas State's all-time leading scorer (2161), rebounder (970) and shot-blocker (201).

Season Team	G	Min.	FGM	FGA	Pct.	FTM	FTA	Pct.	Reb.	Ast.	Pts.	AVERAGES		
												RPG	APG	PPG
00-01—Kansas State..............	27	827	191	381	.501	82	122	.672	220	45	464	8.1	1.7	17.2
01-02—Kansas State..............	34	1149	245	423	.579	120	184	.652	262	94	610	7.7	2.8	17.9
02-03—Kansas State..............	34	1169	243	424	.573	138	205	.673	306	109	625	9.0	3.2	18.4
03-04—Kansas State..............	31	958	203	356	.570	136	196	.694	207	119	542	6.7	3.8	17.5
Totals	126	4103	882	1584	.557	476	707	.673	995	367	2241	7.9	2.9	17.8

Three-point field goals: 190-1, -for-2. 191-2, -for-2. 192-3, 1-for-5 (.200). Totals, 1-for-9 (.111)

PERKINS, JIA   G   STING

PERSONAL: Born February 23, 1982 in Newburgh, N.Y. ... 5-9 (1.75 m)
High School: Granbury HS (Granbury, Texas)
College: Texas Tech
TRANSACTIONS/CAREER NOTES: Selected by Charlotte in the third round (35th overall) of the 2004 draft, June 17, 2004.

COLLEGIATE RECORD

Season Team	G	Min.	FGM	FGA	Pct.	FTM	FTA	Pct.	Reb.	Ast.	Pts.	AVERAGES		
												RPG	APG	PPG
00-01—Texas Tech 32		894	158	345	.458	95	118	.805	131	123	435	4.1	3.8	13.6
01-02—Texas Tech 32		1015	217	509	.426	62	80	.775	161	121	513	5.0	5.0	16.0
02-03—Texas Tech 35		1096	242	563	.430	71	91	.780	178	99	556	5.1	2.8	15.9
Totals 99		3005	617	1417	.435	228	289	.789	470	343	1504	4.7	3.5	15.2

Three-point field goals: 2000-01, 24-for-66 (.364). 2001-02, 17-for-73 (.233). 2002-03, 1-for-19 (.053). Totals, 42-for-158 (.265).

POINTER, TASHA G LIBERTY

PERSONAL: Born June 27, 1979, in Chicago, Ill. ... 5-6/159. (1.68 m/72 kg). ... **Full name:** Natasha Teresa Pointer.
HIGH SCHOOL: Whitney Young (Chicago).
COLLEGE: Rutgers.
TRANSACTIONS/CAREER NOTES: Selected by Portland in fourth round (52nd overall) of WNBA Draft, April 20, 2001. ... Waived by Portland, May 12, 2001 ... Signed by New York as a free agent, April 21, 2004.

COLLEGIATE RECORD

Season Team	G	Min.	FGM	FGA	Pct.	FTM	FTA	Pct.	Reb.	Ast.	Pts.	AVERAGES RPG	APG	PPG
97-98—Rutgers	32	1095	160	340	.471	113	177	.638	135	179	448	4.2	5.6	14.0
98-99—Rutgers	33	1137	117	261	.448	99	140	.707	118	226	341	3.6	6.8	10.3
99-00—Rutgers	32	1076	111	237	.468	73	107	.682	148	177	310	4.6	5.5	9.7
00-01—Rutgers	31	1131	137	292	.469	72	107	.673	186	257	357	6.0	8.3	11.5
Totals	128	4439	525	1130	.465	357	531	.672	587	839	1456	4.6	6.6	11.4

Three-point field goals: 1997-98, 15-for-73 (.205). 1998-99, 8-for-31 (.258). 1999-0, 15-for-41 (.366). 190-1, 11-for-53 (.208). Totals, 49-for-198 (.247)

POWELL, NICOLE G/F STING

PERSONAL: Born June 22, 1982, in Sierra Vista, AZ ... 6-1/172. (1.85 m/78 kg). ... **Full name:** Nicole Kristen Powell.
HIGH SCHOOL: Mountain Pointe HS [Phoenix, AZ].
COLLEGE: Stanford.
MISCELLANEOUS: Member of the USA Team that won silver medal in the Pan American Games (2003). Won a bronze medal with the FIBA Junior World Championships in the Czech Republic (2001) and won a gold medal at the Women's Junior World Championship Qualifying Tournament in Argentina.
TRANSACTIONS/CAREER NOTES: Selected by Charlotte in first round (third overall) of WNBA Draft, April 17, 2004.

COLLEGIATE RECORD

NOTES: Kodak All-America (2004, 2003, 2002). ... AP All-America First Team (2004). ... AP All-America Second Team (2003, 2002). ... USBWA All-America (2004). ... Pac-10 Player of the Year (2004, 2002). ... First Team All-Pac-10 (2004, 2003, 2002, 2001). ... Pac-10 Tournament MVP (2004, 2003, 2002). ... Pac-10 All-Tournament Team (2004, 2003, 2002, 2001). ... Set Stanford single-season record for rebounding (346) in 2004.

Season Team	G	Min.	FGM	FGA	Pct.	FTM	FTA	Pct.	Reb.	Ast.	Pts.	AVERAGES RPG	APG	PPG
00-01—Stanford	30	1009	154	356	.433	75	102	.735	255	142	422	8.5	4.7	14.1
01-02—Stanford	35	1128	195	398	.490	123	149	.826	327	220	581	9.3	6.3	16.6
02-03—Stanford	23	710	149	310	.481	98	112	.875	215	88	432	9.3	3.8	18.8
03-04—Stanford	31	1041	204	476	.429	161	188	.856	346	127	627	11.2	4.1	20.2
Totals	119	3888	702	1540	.456	457	551	.829	1143	577	2062	9.6	4.8	17.3

Three-point field goals: 190-1, 39-for-106 (.368). 191-2, 68-for-162 (.420). 192-3, 36-for-89 (.404). 193-4, 58-for-161 (.360). Totals, 201-for-518 (.388)

ROBINSON, ASHLEY C MERCURY

PERSONAL: Born August 12, 1982, in Dallas, Texas ... 6-4/180. (1.93 m/82 kg). ... **Full name:** Ashley Khristina Robinson.
HIGH SCHOOL: South Ground Prairie HS (Grand Prairie, Texas).
COLLEGE: Tennessee.
MISCELLANEOUS: Member of the 2000 USA Junior World Championships Qualifying Team that earned a gold medal.
TRANSACTIONS/CAREER NOTES: Selected by Phoenix in second round (14th overall) of WNBA Draft, April 17, 2004.

COLLEGIATE RECORD

NOTES: SEC All-Freshman Team (2001). ... All-SEC honorable mention, media (2001). ... Ranks third all-time at Tennessee in blocked shots (200).

Season Team	G	Min.	FGM	FGA	Pct.	FTM	FTA	Pct.	Reb.	Ast.	Pts.	AVERAGES RPG	APG	PPG
00-01—Tennessee	34	749	124	252	.492	53	103	.515	181	26	301	5.3	0.8	8.9
01-02—Tennessee	26	377	47	123	.382	27	51	.529	68	10	121	2.6	0.4	4.7
02-03—Tennessee	37	800	87	208	.418	40	102	.392	198	20	215	5.4	0.5	5.8
03-04—Tennessee	35	991	120	247	.486	42	106	.396	223	55	282	6.4	1.6	8.1
Totals	132	2917	378	830	.455	162	362	.448	670	111	919	5.1	0.8	7.0

Three-point field goals: 190-1, -for-6. 191-2, -for-1. 192-3, 1-for-6 (.167). Totals, 1-for-13 (.077)

SANCHEZ, ISABEL G SHOCK

PERSONAL: Born November 28, 1976 in Spain ... 5-10/152. (1.78 m/69 kg).
TRANSACTIONS/CAREER NOTES: Signed by Detroit as a free agent, March 22, 2004.

SPANISH LEAGUE

NOTES: Liga Femenina, Spain's Women's Basketball League champion in 2003 with UB - FC Barcelona.

Played for Ensino Lugo from 1997-2002. Played for UB-FC Barcelona from 2002-04.

Season Team	G	Min.	FGM	FGA	Pct.	FTM	FTA	Pct.	Reb.	Ast.	Pts.	AVERAGES		
												RPG	APG	PPG
97-98—Ensino Lugo	27	655	86	171	.502	72	105	.685	78	13	245	2.8	0.4	9.0
98-99—Ensino Lugo	29	953	135	243	.555	136	167	.814	124	42	418	4.2	1.4	14.4
99-00—Ensino Lugo	26	756	90	185	.486	94	125	.752	99	25	290	3.8	0.9	11.1
00-01—Ensino Lugo	31	1119	159	330	.481	139	176	.789	135	38	472	4.3	1.2	15.2
01-02—Ensino Lugo	28	990	148	309	.478	84	121	.694	119	27	412	4.2	0.9	14.7
02-03—Barcelona	34	1079	179	370	.483	113	142	.795	87	63	514	2.5	1.8	15.1
03-04—Barcelona	25	736	129	289	.446	89	107	.831	70	56	360	2.8	2.2	14.4
Totals...............	200	6288	926	1897	.488	727	943	.770	712	264	2711	3.5	1.3	13.5

Three-point field goals: 1997-98, 1-for-12 (.083). 1998-99, 12-for-32 (.375). 1999-2000, 16-for-39 (.410). 2000-01, 15-for-54 (.277). 2001-02, 32-for-79 (.405). 2002-03, 43-for-114 (.377). 2003-04, 13-for-69 (.194). Totals, 132-for-397 (.332).

SMITH, JENNIFER   C   SHOCK

PERSONAL: Born April 10, 1982, in Lansing, Mich. ... 6-3. (1.91 m/ kg). ... **Full name:** Jennifer Elaine Smith.
HIGH SCHOOL: DeWitt HS (Lansing, Mich.).
COLLEGE: Michigan.
TRANSACTIONS/CAREER NOTES: Selected by Detroit in third round (32nd overall) of WNBA Draft, April 17, 2004.

COLLEGIATE RECORD

NOTES: All-Big Ten First Team, media (2004). ... All-Big Ten Second Team, coaches (2004). ... All-Big Ten honorable mention, coaches (2003).

Season Team	G	Min.	FGM	FGA	Pct.	FTM	FTA	Pct.	Reb.	Ast.	Pts.	AVERAGES		
												RPG	APG	PPG
00-01—Michigan	31	659	111	201	.552	70	86	.814	143	23	292	4.6	0.7	9.4
01-02—Michigan	30	913	157	304	.516	97	122	.795	234	39	412	7.8	1.3	13.7
02-03—Michigan	24	665	132	244	.541	79	94	.840	155	17	351	6.5	0.7	14.6
03-04—Michigan	31	1084	213	446	.478	203	251	.809	220	25	642	7.1	0.8	20.7
Totals	116	3321	613	1195	.513	449	553	.812	752	104	1697	6.5	0.9	14.6

Three-point field goals: 190-1, -for-1. 191-2, 1-for-3 (.333). 192-3, 8-for-20 (.400). 193-4, 13-for-38 (.342). Totals, 22-for-62 (.355)

STEPHENS, STACY   C   COMETS

PERSONAL: Born January 21, 1982, in Sulphur Springs, Texas ... 6-4/205. (1.93 m/93 kg). ... **Full name:** Stacy Diane Stephens.
HIGH SCHOOL: Winnsboro HS (Winnsboro, Texas).
COLLEGE: Texas.
MISCELLANEOUS: Member of the 2002 USA World Championship for Young Women Qualifying Team that captured the gold medal. High School Parade and USA Today All-American (2000).
TRANSACTIONS/CAREER NOTES: Selected by Houston in third round (37th overall) of WNBA Draft, April 17, 2004.

COLLEGIATE RECORD

NOTES: AP All-America Second Team (2004, 2003). ... USBWA All-America (2004). ... All-Big 12 First Team (2004, 2003). ... All-Big 12 Second Team (2002). ... All-Big 12 honorable mention (2001). ... Big 12 Rookie of the Year (2001). ... Big 12 Tournament MVP (2003). ... Big 12 All-Tournament Team (2003). ... Big 12 All-Academic Team (2003). ... NCAA West Regional All-Tournament Team (2003).

Season Team	G	Min.	FGM	FGA	Pct.	FTM	FTA	Pct.	Reb.	Ast.	Pts.	AVERAGES		
												RPG	APG	PPG
00-01—Texas........................	33	864	152	318	.478	60	110	.545	311	22	364	9.4	0.7	11.0
01-02—Texas........................	31	898	162	315	.514	111	162	.685	303	24	435	9.8	0.8	14.0
02-03—Texas........................	35	1020	204	404	.505	96	145	.662	318	48	504	9.1	1.4	14.4
03-04—Texas........................	35	933	157	287	.547	91	142	.641	291	33	405	8.3	0.9	11.6
Totals	134	3715	675	1324	.510	358	559	.640	1223	127	1708	9.1	0.9	12.7

Three-point field goals: 191-2, -for-1.

STEPHERSON, BRIANNE   G   SUN

PERSONAL: Born February 23, 1980, in Malden, Mass. ... 5-8. (1.73 m/ kg).
HIGH SCHOOL: Masconomet Regional (Middletown, Mass.).
COLLEGE: Boston College.

COLLEGIATE RECORD

Season Team	G	Min.	FGM	FGA	Pct.	FTM	FTA	Pct.	Reb.	Ast.	Pts.	AVERAGES		
												RPG	APG	PPG
98-99—Boston College...........	27	938	81	202	.401	73	96	.760	...	112	247	3.7	4.1	9.1
99-00—Boston College...........	34	1119	115	281	.409	73	94	.777	...	130	316	3.3	3.8	9.3
00-01—Boston College...........	3	72	4	20	.200	1	2	.500	...	5	9	1.3	1.7	3.0

	G	Min.	FGM	FGA	Pct.	FTM	FTA	Pct.		Reb.	Ast.	Pts.	RPG	APG	PPG
01-02—Boston College...........	31	961	121	258	.469	59	82	.720	...	125	305	5.1	4.0	9.8
02-03—Boston College...........	31	949	90	237	.380	58	83	.699	...	162	238	3.3	5.2	7.7
Totals	126	4039	411	998	.412	264	357	.739	0	534	1115	0.0	4.2	8.8

Three-point field goals: 1998-99, 12-for-37 (.324). 1999-0, 13-for-50 (.260). 190-1, 0-for-3. 191-2, 4-for-14 (.286). 192-3, 0-for-5. Totals, 29-for-109 (.266)

SUTTON, CANDICE   C   SPARKS

PERSONAL: Born September 27, 1982, in Silver Springs, Md. ... 6-4/200. (1.93 m/91 kg). ... **Full name:** Candice Monique Sutton.
HIGH SCHOOL: Largo HS (Largo, Md.).
MISCELLANEOUS: Named Maryland high school Player of the Year by USA Today during senior year. Mother played basketball at NC State in the early 1970s. Cousin is Chris Gatling who played at Old Dominion and in the NBA for nine seasons.
COLLEGE: North Carolina.

COLLEGIATE RECORD

NOTES: All-ACC Third Team (2003). ... All-ACC First Team (2002). ... All-ACC Tournament Team (2003, 2002). ... All-ACC Freshman Team (2001). ... ACC All-Academic Team (2002, 2001). ... Ranks second on North Carolina's all-time blocked shots list (208). ... Seventh player in ACC history to record over 200 blocked shots in a career.

Season Team	G	Min.	FGM	FGA	Pct.	FTM	FTA	Pct.	Reb.	Ast.	Pts.	RPG	APG	PPG
00-01—North Carolina...........	28	609	113	233	.485	48	81	.593	157	18	272	5.6	0.6	9.7
01-02—North Carolina...........	34	869	174	373	.466	59	116	.509	211	20	407	6.2	0.6	12.0
02-03—North Carolina...........	34	837	148	300	.493	70	131	.534	193	27	366	5.7	0.8	10.8
03-04—North Carolina...........	30	783	107	208	.514	71	104	.683	194	16	285	6.5	0.5	9.5
Totals	126	3098	542	1114	.487	248	432	.574	755	81	1330	6.0	0.6	10.6

TAURASI, DIANA   G   MERCURY

PERSONAL: Born June 11, 1982, in Glendale, Calif. ... 5-11/172. (1.80 m/78 kg). ... **Full name:** Diana Lurena Taurasi.
HIGH SCHOOL: Don Lugo HS (Chino, Calif.).
COLLEGE: Connecticut
MISCELLANEOUS: Earned a bronze medal as a member of the 2001 USA Junior World Championship team. ... Earned a gold medal as a member of the 2000 USA Basketball Women's Junior World Championship Qualifying team. ... Three-time NCAA Champion at University of Connecticut.
TRANSACTIONS/CAREER NOTES: Selected by Phoenix in first round (first overall) of WNBA Draft, April 17, 2004.

COLLEGIATE RECORD

NOTES: Naismith Player of the Year (2004, 2003). ... AP Player of the Year (2003). ... USBWA Player of the Year (2003). ... Wade Trophy Player of the Year (2003). ... Honda Broderick Player of the Year (2003). ... Kodak All-America (2004, 2003, 2002). ... USBWA All-America (2004, 2003). ... AP All-America First Team (2004, 2003). ... AP All-America Second Team (2002). ... NCAA Final Four Most Oustanding Player (2004, 2003). ... East Regional Most Oustanding Player (2003). ... Big East Player of the Year (2004, 2003). ... Wade Trophy recipient (2003). ... All-Big East First Team (2004, 2003, 2002). ... 2003 Big East All-Tournament team (2003, 2002) .... AP Second Team All-America (2002). ... Big East Championship Most Outstanding Player (2001) .... Big East All-Rookie Team (2001).

Season Team	G	Min.	FGM	FGA	Pct.	FTM	FTA	Pct.	Reb.	Ast.	Pts.	RPG	APG	PPG
00-01—Connecticut	33	791	127	286	.444	36	41	.878	106	109	361	3.2	3.3	10.9
01-02—Connecticut	39	1131	200	405	.494	72	87	.828	158	208	564	4.1	5.3	14.5
02-03—Connecticut	37	1181	237	498	.476	119	146	.815	225	161	663	6.1	4.4	17.9
03-04—Connecticut	34	1078	191	415	.460	85	107	.794	133	167	550	3.9	4.9	16.2
Totals	143	4181	755	1604	.471	312	381	.819	622	645	2138	4.3	4.5	15.0

Three-point field goals: 190-1, 71-for-184 (.386). 191-2, 92-for-209 (.440). 192-3, 70-for-200 (.350). 193-4, 83-for-211 (.393). Totals, 316-for-804 (.393)

TAYLOR, LINDSAY   C   MERCURY

PERSONAL: Born May 20, 1981, in Poway, Calif. ... 6-8/200. (2.03 m/91 kg). ... **Full name:** Lindsay Corine Taylor.
HIGH SCHOOL: Chandler HS (Chandler, Ariz.).
COLLEGE: California-Santa Barbara.
MISCELLANEOUS: Won the silver medal as a member of the 2003 USA Pan American Games Team.
TRANSACTIONS/CAREER NOTES: Selected by Houston in second round (26th overall) of WNBA Draft, April 17, 2004.

COLLEGIATE RECORD

NOTES: AP All-America honorable mention (2003). ... All-Big West First Team (2004, 2003). ... Big West Player of the Year

(2003). ... All-Big West Second Team (2002, 2001). ... Big West Tournament MVP (2004, 2003, 2002). ... Big West Freshman of the Year (2001). ... Big West All-Tournament Team (2004, 2003, 2002, 2001). ... UC Santa Barbara's all-time leader in career points (1755), blocked shots (242) and field goal percentage (.558).

Season Team	G	Min.	FGM	FGA	Pct.	FTM	FTA	Pct.	Reb.	Ast.	Pts.	AVERAGES		
---	---	---	---	---	---	---	---	---	---	---	---	RPG	APG	PPG
00-01—Cal.-Santa Barbara	30	499	101	183	.552	115	152	.757	175	16	317	5.8	0.5	10.6
01-02—Cal.-Santa Barbara	29	687	131	238	.550	106	135	.785	204	16	371	7.0	0.6	12.8
02-03—Cal.-Santa Barbara	32	822	189	333	.568	136	186	.731	239	27	521	7.5	0.8	16.3
03-04—Cal.-Santa Barbara	34	843	216	387	.558	109	153	.712	248	44	546	7.3	1.3	16.1
Totals	125	2851	637	1141	.558	466	626	.744	866	103	1755	6.9	0.8	14.0

Three-point field goals: 190-1, -for-2. 191-2, 3-for-6 (.500). 192-3, 7-for-10 (.700). 193-4, 5-for-18 (.278). Totals, 15-for-36 (.417)

THOMAS, CHRISTI   F   SPARKS

PERSONAL: Born August 14, 1982, in Marietta, Ga. ... 6-3/185. (1.91 m/84 kg). ... **Full name:** Christi Michelle Thomas.
HIGH SCHOOL: Buford HS (Buford, Ga.).
COLLEGE: Georgia.
MISCELLANEOUS: Member of the 2003 USA World Championship for Young Women team that won gold medal in Sibenik, Croatia.
TRANSACTIONS/CAREER NOTES: Selected by Los Angeles in first round (12th overall) of WNBA Draft, April 17, 2004.

COLLEGIATE RECORD

NOTES: AP All-America honorable mention (2004). ... All-SEC First Team, coaches (2004). ... All-SEC Second Team, coaches (2003). ... All-SEC Second Team, media (2004, 2003). ... SEC All-Tournament Team (2004). ... All-Midwest Regional Team in NCAA Tournament (2003).

Season Team	G	Min.	FGM	FGA	Pct.	FTM	FTA	Pct.	Reb.	Ast.	Pts.	AVERAGES		
---	---	---	---	---	---	---	---	---	---	---	---	RPG	APG	PPG
00-01—Georgia......................	29	623	130	255	.510	75	121	.620	188	18	338	6.5	0.6	11.7
01-02—Georgia......................	30	664	122	237	.515	62	103	.602	187	27	311	6.2	0.9	10.4
02-03—Georgia......................	30	850	180	335	.537	111	156	.712	241	22	481	8.0	0.7	16.0
03-04—Georgia......................	35	935	173	321	.539	112	145	.772	290	28	463	8.3	0.8	13.2
Totals	124	3072	605	1148	.527	360	525	.686	906	95	1593	7.3	0.8	12.8

Three-point field goals: 190-1, 3-for-16 (.188). 191-2, 5-for-20 (.250). 192-3, 10-for-37 (.270). 193-4, 5-for-22 (.227). Totals, 23-for-95 (.242)

TILLIS, ICISS   C/F   SUN

PERSONAL: Born December 6, 1981, in Tulsa, OK ... 6-5/165. (1.96 m/75 kg). ... **Full name:** Iciss Rose Tillis.
HIGH SCHOOL: Cascia Hall Prep HS (Tulsa, Okla.).
COLLEGE: Duke.
MISCELLANEOUS: Member of the 2003 USA Pan American Games Team that captured a silver medal in Santo Domingo, Dominican Republic. Member of the 1998 USA World Youth Games Team that captured the bronze medal.
TRANSACTIONS/CAREER NOTES: Selected by Detroit in first round (11th overall) of WNBA Draft, April 17, 2004.

COLLEGIATE RECORD

NOTES: Kodak All-America (2003). ... AP All-America honorable mention (2004, 2003, 2002). ... All-ACC First Team (2004, 2003, 2002). ... ACC Tournament MVP (2004, 2003). ... ACC All-Tournament Team (2004, 2003, 2002). ... All-ACC Defensive Team (2002).

Season Team	G	Min.	FGM	FGA	Pct.	FTM	FTA	Pct.	Reb.	Ast.	Pts.	AVERAGES		
---	---	---	---	---	---	---	---	---	---	---	---	RPG	APG	PPG
00-01—Duke..........................	34	829	118	270	.437	29	40	.725	188	60	70	5.5	1.8	2.1
01-02—Duke..........................	34	1032	197	436	.452	62	91	.681	271	94	486	8.0	2.8	14.3
02-03—Duke..........................	37	1128	212	476	.445	64	80	.800	273	79	535	7.4	2.1	14.5
03-04—Duke..........................	32	897	146	355	.411	83	96	.865	214	68	61	6.7	2.1	1.9
Totals	137	3886	673	1537	.438	238	307	.775	946	301	1152	6.9	2.2	8.4

Three-point field goals: 190-1, 27-for-74 (.365). 191-2, 30-for-89 (.337). 192-3, 47-for-122 (.385). 193-4, 24-for-82 (.293). Totals, 128-for-367 (.349)

TURNER, LATOYA   C   SPARKS

PERSONAL: ... 6-3. (1.91 m/ kg).
HIGH SCHOOL: Warren Central HS (Bowling Green, Mich.)
COLLEGE: Ohio State.

COLLEGIATE RECORD

NOTES: Big Ten Freshman of the Year (2000).

Season Team............	G	Min.	FGM	FGA	Pct.	FTM	FTA	Pct.	Off.	Def.	Reb.	Ast.	St.	TO	Blk.	Pts.	AVERAGES		
---	---	---	---	---	---	---	---	---	---	---	---	---	---	---	---	---	RPG	APG	PPG
99-00—Ohio State ...	27	625	117	240	.488	70	108	.648	59	101	160	10	34	61	36	304	5.9	0.3	11.3
00-01—Ohio State ...	13	317	96	169	.568	40	64	.625	39	47	86	5	33	35	30	232	6.6	0.3	17.8

April 17, 2004.

	G	Min.	FGM	FGA	Pct.	FTM	FTA	Pct.			Reb.	Ast.			Pts.	RPG	APG	PPG
02-03—Ohio State .2	8	747	95	209	.455	55	72	.746	55	97	152	48	39	55	47	245	5.4	1.7	8.8
03-04—Ohio State ...	27	824	140	245	.571	56	100	.560	36	141	177	49	27	51	45	336	6.6	1.8	12.4
Totals	95	2513	448	863	.519	221	344	.642	189	386	575	112	133	202	158	1117	6.1	1.2	11.8

Three-point field goals: 1999-2000, 0-for-2 (.000). 2002-03, 0-for-1 (.000). Totals, 0-for-3 (.000).

UNRAU, EVAN F MYSTICS

PERSONAL: Born January 21, 1982, in Kearney, Neb. ... 6-1/165. (1.85 m/75 kg). ... **Full name:** Evan Elizabeth Unrau.
HIGH SCHOOL: Rocky Mountain HS (Fort Collins, Colo.).
COLLEGE: Missouri.
TRANSACTIONS/CAREER NOTES: Selected by Washington in third round (28th overall) of WNBA Draft, April 17, 2004.

COLLEGIATE RECORD

Season Team	G	Min.	FGM	FGA	Pct.	FTM	FTA	Pct.	Reb.	Ast.	Pts.	AVERAGES RPG	APG	PPG
00-01—Missouri	32	864	103	180	.572	60	103	.583	230	38	266	7.2	1.2	8.3
01-02—Missouri	26	819	126	257	.490	55	86	.640	210	50	323	8.1	1.9	12.4
02-03—Missouri	31	1059	185	389	.476	102	133	.767	238	63	497	7.7	2.0	16.0
03-04—Missouri	30	1069	170	388	.438	129	161	.801	267	93	511	8.9	3.1	17.0
Totals	119	3811	584	1214	.481	346	483	.716	945	244	1597	7.9	2.1	13.4

Three-point field goals: 190-1, -for-1. 191-2, 16-for-41 (.390). 192-3, 25-for-75 (.333). 193-4, 42-for-118 (.356). Totals, 83-for-235 (.353)

VALEK, ERIKA G MERCURY

PERSONAL: Born April 9, 1982, in Bucaramanga, Colombia ... 5-6/146. (1.68 m/66 kg). ... **Full name:** Erika Yaneth Valek.
HIGH SCHOOL: Coronado HS (Lubbock, Texas).
COLLEGE: Purdue.
MISCELLANEOUS: High school Parade All-American and USA Today All-American during senior season.
TRANSACTIONS/CAREER NOTES: Selected by Detroit in second round (23rd overall) of WNBA Draft, April 17, 2004.

COLLEGIATE RECORD

NOTES: All-Big Ten Second Team - coaches (2004). ... All-Big Ten honorable mention - media (2004). ... Frances Pomeroy Naismith Award winner as the best NCAA Division I basketball player 5-8 or under (2004). ... All-Big Ten First Team - coaches (2003). ... All-Big Ten Second Team - media (2003). ... NCAA East Regional All-Tournament Team (2003). ... Big Ten All-Tournament Team (2003).

Season	G	Min	FGM	FGA	Pct.	FTM	FTA	Pct	Off	Def	Tot	Ast	St	TO	Blk	Pts	AVERAGES RPG	APG	PPG
00-01	33	798	79	191	.414	35	51	.686	11	70	81	93	57	74	3	212	2.5	2.8	6.4
01-02	30	930	75	185	.405	50	63	.794	28	78	106	82	49	95	2	228	3.5	2.7	7.6
02-03	35	1179	177	402	.440	96	116	.828	21	113	134	171	91	106	6	490	3.8	4.8	14.0
03-04	33	1011	108	263	.411	46	60	.767	17	107	124	133	65	78	6	289	3.8	4.0	8.8
Totals	131	3918	439	1041	.421	227	290	.782	77	368	445	479	262	353	17	1219	3.4	3.6	9.3

Three-point field goals: 2000-01, 19-for-49 (.388). 2001-02, 28-for-74 (.378). 2002-03, 40-for-101 (.396). 2003-04, 27-for-74 (.365). Totals: 114-for-298 (.382).

VILLARROEL, MARIA G COMETS

PERSONAL: Born December 3, 1978, in Porlamar, Margarita, Venezuela ... 5-8/135. (1.73 m/61 kg). ... **Full name:** Ofelia Maria Villarroel.
COLLEGE: Oklahoma.
TRANSACTIONS/CAREER NOTES: Selected by Phoenix in third round (27th overall) of WNBA Draft, April 17, 2004.

COLLEGIATE RECORD

NOTES: Big-12 All-Tournament Team (2004). ... Ranked 14th in the NCAA in field goal percentage with 57.6% (2003). ... Hawaiian Airlines Rainbow All-Tournament Team (2003). ... Two-time National Junior College All-American (2001, 2000). ... Two-time Conference Player of the Year (2001, 2000).

Season Team	G	Min.	FGM	FGA	Pct.	FTM	FTA	Pct.	Reb.	Ast.	Pts.	AVERAGES RPG	APG	PPG
01-02—NE Okla. A&M JC	33	0	312	473	.660	131	166	.789	184	82	792	5.6	2.5	24.0
02-03—Oklahoma	32	936	175	304	.576	120	169	.710	161	61	480	5.0	1.9	15.0
03-04—Oklahoma	33	927	168	319	.527	118	155	.761	211	54	472	6.4	1.6	14.3
Totals	65	1863	343	623	.551	238	324	.735	372	115	952	5.7	1.8	14.6

Three-point field goals: 191-2, 37-for-77 (.481). 192-3, 10-for-37 (.270). 193-4, 18-for-52 (.346). Totals, 28-for-89 (.315)

WHALEN, LINDSAY G SUN

PERSONAL: Born May 9, 1982, in Hutchinson, MI ... 5-8/150. (1.73 m/68 kg). ... **Full name:** Lindsay Marie Whalen.
HIGH SCHOOL: Hutchinson HS [Hutchinson, MI].
COLLEGE: Minnesota.
MISCELLANEOUS: Member of the 2003 USA World Championship for Young Women Team that captured the gold medal in Sibenik, Croatia. Earned the gold medal as a member of the 2002 USA World

Championship for Young Women Qualifying Team.
TRANSACTIONS/CAREER NOTES: Selected by Connecticut in first round (fourth overall) of WNBA Draft, April 17, 2004.

COLLEGIATE RECORD
NOTES: Kodak All-America (2004, 2003). ... AP All-America Second Team (2004, 2003). ... USBWA All-American Team (2004, 2003). ... AP All-America Third Team (2002). ... Kodak All-America honorable mention (2002). ... Big Ten Player of the Year (2002). ... All-Big Ten First Team (2004, 2003, 2002).

Season Team	G	Min.	FGM	FGA	Pct.	FTM	FTA	Pct.	Reb.	Ast.	Pts.	AVERAGES RPG	APG	PPG
00-01—Minnesota....	25	895	149	313	.476	111	151	.735	29	71	100	82 42 115	2 425 4.0	3.3 17.0
01-02—Minnesota....	30	1016	245	437	.561	147	191	.770	45	121	166	159 81 131	7 667 5.5	5.3 22.2
02-03—Minnesota....	31	1019	225	412	.546	155	183	.847	28	127	155	192 60 132	1 639 5.0	6.2 20.6
03-04—Minnesota....	27	888	185	360	.514	144	173	.832	26	112	138	145 52 100	0 554 5.1	5.4 20.5
Totals	113	3818	804	1522	.528	557	698	.798	128	431	559	578 235 478	10 2285 4.9	5.1 20.2

Three-point field goals: 2000-01, 16-for-53 (.302). 2001-02, 30-for-86 (.349). 2002-03, 34-for-105 (.324). 2003-04, 40-for-100 (.400). Totals, 120-for-344 (.349).

WHITE, DETRINA   F   LIBERTY

PERSONAL: Born April 3, 1980, in Lafayette, La. ... 5-11. (1.80 m/ kg). ... **Full name:** DeTrina Mary White.
HIGH SCHOOL: Acadiana (Lafayette, La.).
COLLEGE: Louisiana State.
TRANSACTIONS/CAREER NOTES: Selected by Indiana in second round (20th overall) of WNBA Draft, April 25, 2003.
MISCELLANEOUS: Won Louisiana state titles in shot put, javelin and discus as a high school senior.

COLLEGIATE RECORD

Season Team	G	Min.	FGM	FGA	Pct.	FTM	FTA	Pct.	Reb.	Ast.	Pts.	AVERAGES RPG	APG	PPG
98-99—Louisiana State..........	30	844	159	256	.621	74	132	.561	...	31	392	8.2	1.0	13.1
99-00—Louisiana State..........	32	903	163	264	.617	57	110	.518	...	26	383	8.8	0.8	12.0
00-01—Louisiana State..........	20	517	78	128	.609	34	53	.642	...	19	190	7.5	1.0	9.5
01-02—Louisiana State..........								Did not play—injured..						
02-03—Louisiana State..........	25	532	84	144	.583	34	46	.739	...	19	202	6.4	0.8	8.1
Totals	107	2796	484	792	.611	199	341	.584	0	95	1167	0.0	0.9	10.9

WILLIAMS, TOCCARA   G   SILVER STARS

PERSONAL: Born January 11, 1982, in Hollywood, FL ... 5-9/145. (1.75 m/66 kg). ... **Full name:** Toccara Yashica Williams.
HIGH SCHOOL: South Broward HS [Hollywood, FL].
COLLEGE: Texas A&M.
TRANSACTIONS/CAREER NOTES: Selected by San Antonio in third round (34th overall) of WNBA Draft, April 17, 2004.

COLLEGIATE RECORD
NOTES: All-Big 12 First Team (2004) ... All-Big 12 Second Team (2003) ... All-Big 12 honorable mention (2002) ... Matched her own record for steals at Texas A&M in 2003 (117) ... Big 12's all-time steals leader (452) ... Led the NCAA in steals per game with 4.1 (2004).

Season Team	G	Min.	FGM	FGA	Pct.	FTM	FTA	Pct.	Reb.	Ast.	Pts.	AVERAGES RPG	APG	PPG
00-01—Texas A&M	28	1022	90	242	.372	46	76	.605	134	196	235	4.8	7.0	8.4
01-02—Texas A&M	29	1015	119	277	.430	65	106	.613	160	187	313	5.5	6.4	10.8
02-03—Texas A&M	27	978	117	286	.409	97	138	.703	138	149	333	5.1	5.5	12.3
03-04—Texas A&M	27	1016	152	440	.345	113	167	.677	150	192	421	5.6	7.1	15.6
Totals	111	4031	478	1245	.384	321	487	.659	582	724	1302	5.2	6.5	11.7

Three-point field goals: 190-1, 9-for-29 (.310). 191-2, 10-for-46 (.217). 192-3, 2-for-31 (.065). 193-4, 4-for-20 (.200). Totals, 25-for-126 (.198)

WILLINGHAM, LE'COE F   SUN

PERSONAL: Born February 10, 1981 in Augusta, Ga, ... 6-0/200 (1.83 m/91 kg).
High School: Hephzibah HS (Augusta, Ga.)
College: Auburn
TRANSACTIONS/CAREER NOTES: Signed by Connecticut as a free agent, April 27, 2004.

COLLEGIATE RECORD
NOTES: All-SEC First Team (2004, 2000). ... All-SEC Second Team (2002). ... All-SEC Freshman Team (2000). ... Redshirted 2000-01 season.

Season Team	G	Min.	FGM	FGA	Pct.	FTM	FTA	Pct.	Reb.	Ast.	Pts.	AVERAGES RPG	APG	PPG
99-00—Auburn 27		696	113	228	.496	79	108	.731	206	29	305	7.6	1.0	11.3
01-02—Auburn 29		893	134	272	.493	79	126	.627	235	31	348	8.1	1.0	12.0
02-03—Auburn 33		823	113	234	.483	71	100	.710	205	44	316	6.2	1.3	9.6

| 03-04—Auburn | 31 | 928 | 192 | 316 | .608 | 117 | 153 | .765 | 281 | 51 | 506 | 9.1 | 1.6 | 16.3 |
| Totals | 120 | 3340 | 552 | 1050 | .525 | 346 | 487 | .710 | 927 | 155 | 1475 | 7.7 | 1.3 | 12.3 |

Three-point field goals: 1999-2000, 0-for-3 (.000). 2001-02, 1-for-2 (.500). 2002-03, 19-for-60 (.317). 2003-04, 5-for-15 (.333). Totals, 25-for-80 (.312).

WRIGHT, SHEREKA   F   MERCURY

PERSONAL: Born September 21, 1981, in Fort Riley, Kan. ... 5-10/155. (1.78 m/70 kg). ... **Full name:** Shereka Monique Wright.
HIGH SCHOOL: Copperas Cove HS (Copperas Cove, Texas).
COLLEGE: Purdue.
MISCELLANEOUS: Member of the 2001 USA World University Games Team that captured the gold medal.
TRANSACTIONS/CAREER NOTES: Selected by Detroit in first round (13th overall) of WNBA Draft, April 17, 2004.

COLLEGIATE RECORD

NOTES: AP All-America Second Team (2004). ... USBWA All-America (2004). ... Kodak All-America honorable mention (2003). ... AP All-America Third Team (2003). ... First Team All-Big Ten (2004, 2003, 2002). ... Big Ten Tournament MVP (2004). ... Big Ten All-Freshman Team (2001).

Season Team	G	Min.	FGM	FGA	Pct.	FTM	FTA	Pct.	Reb.	Ast.	Pts.	AVERAGES RPG	APG	PPG
00-01—Purdue	38	900	111	244	.455	135	203	.665	177	67	377	4.7	1.8	9.9
01-02—Purdue	30	1075	176	363	.485	205	279	.735	199	58	569	6.6	1.9	19.0
02-03—Purdue	34	1134	199	426	.467	231	311	.743	215	91	643	6.3	2.7	18.9
03-04—Purdue	33	995	22	449	.049	205	278	.737	202	75	662	6.1	2.3	20.1
Totals	135	4104	508	1482	.343	776	1071	.725	793	291	2251	5.9	2.2	16.7

Three-point field goals: 190-1, 20-for-39 (.513). 191-2, 12-for-51 (.235). 192-3, 14-for-44 (.318). 193-4, 13-for-36 (.361). Totals, 59-for-170 (.347).

HEAD COACHES

ADAMS, MICHAEL   MYSTICS

PERSONAL: Born January 19, 1963, in Hartford, Conn.
HIGH SCHOOL: Hartford (Conn.) Public
COLLEGE: Boston College
TRANSACTIONS/CAREER NOTES: Selected by Sacramento Kings in third round (66th pick overall) of 1985 NBA Draft. ... Played in USBL with Springfield Fame (1985 and 1986). ... Waived by Kings (December 17, 1985). ... Played in CBA with Bay State Bombardiers (1985-85). ... Signed as free agent by Washington Bullets (May 13, 1986). ... Waived by Bullets (September 25, 1986). ... Re-signed by Bullets (September 29, 1986). ... Waived by Bullets (October 28, 1986). ... Re-signed by Bullets (November 21, 1986). ... Traded by Bullets with F Jay Vincent to Denver Nuggets for F Mark Alarie and G Darrell Walker (November 2, 1987). ... Traded by Nuggets with 1991 first-round draft choice and future considerations to Bullets for 1991 first-round draft choice (June 11, 1991). ... Traded by Bullets to Charlotte Hornets for 1996 and 1997 second-round draft choices (August 2, 1994). ... Rights renounced by Hornets (July 11, 1996).
CAREER NOTES: Assistant Coach with the Vancouver Grizzlies in 2000-01 where he coached for two seasons. He moved with the team to Memphis in 2001 but left after the 2001-02 season.

COLLEGIATE RECORD

Season Team	G	Min.	FGM	FGA	Pct.	FTM	FTA	Pct.	Reb.	Ast.	Pts.	AVERAGES RPG	APG	PPG
81-82 Boston Coll.	26	379	51	103	.495	36	61	.590	30	40	138	1.2	1.5	5.3
82-83 Boston Coll.	32	1075	195	405	.481	127	157	.809	86	170	517	2.7	5.3	16.2
83-84 Boston Coll.	30	1026	195	429	.455	130	172	.756	102	105	520	3.4	3.5	17.3
84-85 Boston Coll.	31	1044	193	413	.467	89	119	.748	102	160	475	3.3	5.2	15.3
Totals	119	3524	634	1350	.470	382	509	.750	320	475	1650	2.7	4.0	13.9

NBA REGULAR-SEASON RECORD

Season Team	G	Min.	FGM	FGA	Pct.	FTM	FTA	Pct.	REBOUNDS Off.	Def.	Tot.	Ast.	St.	Blk.	TO	Pts.	AVERAGES RPG	APG	PPG
85-86 Sacramento	18	139	16	44	.364	8	12	.667	2	4	6	22	9	1	11	40	0.3	1.2	2.2
86-87 Washington	63	1303	160	393	.407	105	124	.847	38	85	123	244	85	6	81	453	2.0	3.9	7.2
87-88 Denver	82	2778	416	927	.449	166	199	.834	40	183	223	503	168	16	144	1137	2.7	6.1	13.9
88-89 Denver	77	2787	468	1082	.433	322	393	.819	71	212	283	490	166	11	180	1424	3.7	6.4	18.5
89-90 Denver	79	2690	398	989	.402	267	314	.850	49	176	255	495	121	3	141	1221	2.8	6.3	15.5
90-91 Denver	66	2346	560	1421	.394	465	529	.879	58	198	256	693	147	6	240	1752	3.9	10.5	26.5
91-92 Washington	78	2795	485	1233	.393	313	360	.869	58	252	310	594	145	9	212	1408	4.0	7.6	18.1
92-93 Washington	70	2499	365	831	.439	237	277	.856	52	188	240	526	100	4	175	1035	3.4	7.5	14.8
93-94 Washington	70	2337	285	698	.408	224	270	.830	37	146	183	480	96	6	167	849	2.6	6.9	12.1
94-95 Charlotte	29	443	67	148	.453	25	30	.833	6	23	29	95	23	1	26	188	1.0	3.3	6.5
95-96 Charlotte	21	329	37	83	.446	26	35	.743	5	17	22	67	21	4	25	114	1.0	3.2	5.4
Totals	653	20446	3257	7849	.415	2158	2543	.849	416	1484	1900	4209	1081	67	1402	9621	2.9	6.4	14.7

Three-point field goals: 1985-86, 0-for-3. 1986-87, 28-for-102 (.275). 1987-88, 139-for-379 (.367). 1988-89, 166-for-466 (.356). 1989-90, 158-for-432 (.366). 1990-91, 167-for-564 (.296). 1991-92, 1256-for-386 (.324). 1992-93, 68-for-212 (.321). 1993-94, 55-for-191 (.288). 1994-95, 29-for-81 (.358). 1995-96, 14-for-41 (.341). Totals, 949-for-2857 (.332).
Personal fouls/disqualifications: 1985-86, 9/0, 1986-87, 88/0. 1987-88, 138/0. 1988-89, 149/0. 1989-90, 133/0. 1990-91, 162/1. 1991-92, 162/1. 1992-93, 146/0. 1993-94, 140/0. 1994-95, 41/0. 1995-96, 25/0. Totals, 1193/2.

NBA PLAYOFF RECORD

Season Team	G	Min.	FGM	FGA	Pct.	FTM	FTA	Pct.	REBOUNDS Off.	Def.	Tot.	Ast.	St.	Blk.	TO	Pts.	AVERAGES RPG	APG	PPG
86-87 Washington	3	82	8	25	.320	1	3	.333	0	7	7	10	7	0	5	19	2.3	3.3	6.3
87-88 Denver	11	406	47	130	.362	36	41	.878	9	27	36	64	18	2	23	147	3.3	5.8	13.4
88-89 Denver	2	75	15	36	.417	7	8	.875	5	12	17	9	3	0	8	39	2.0	6.0	13.0
89-90 Denver	3	105	13	34	.382	7	8	.875	0	6	6	18	4	0	8	39	2.0	6.0	13.0
94-95 Charlotte	1	11	2	5	.400	0	0	...	0	1	1	2	0	0	4	4	1.0	2.0	4.0
Totals	20	679	85	230	.370	51	60	.850	14	53	67	103	32	2	44	256	3.4	5.2	12.8

Three-point field goals: 1986-87, 2-for-9 (.222). 1987-88, 17-for-54 (.315). 1988-89, 10-for-22 (.455). 1989-90, 6-for-20 (.300). 1994-95, 0-for-2. Totals, 35-for-107 (.327).
Personal fouls/disqualifications: 1986-87, 6/0. 1987-88, 19/0. 1988-89, 10/0. Totals, 41/0.

NBA ALL-STAR GAME RECORD

Season Team	Min.	FGM	FGA	Pct.	FTM	FTA	Pct.	Off.	Def.	Tot.	Ast.	PF	St.	Blk.	TO	Pts.
1992 Washington	14	4	8	.500	0	0	...	1	0	1	1	1	4	0	1	9

NOTES: CBA Rookie of the Year (1986). ... CBA All-League second team (1986). ... CBA All-Defensive second team (1986).

CBA REGULAR-SEASON RECORD

Season Team	G	Min.	FGM	FGA	Pct.	FTM	FTA	Pct.	Reb.	Ast.	Pts.	AVERAGES RPG	APG	PPG
85-86 Bay State	38	1526	262	558	.470	125	164	.762	149	320	670	3.9	8.4	17.6

Three-point field goals: 1985-86, 21-for-71 (.296).

ADUBATO, RICHIE   LIBERTY

PERSONAL: Born November 23, 1937, in East Orange, N.J. ... Full Name: Richard Adam Adubato.
HIGH SCHOOL: East Orange (N.J.).
COLLEGE: William Paterson College (N.J.).

HEAD COACHING RECORD

BACKGROUND: Led the Liberty to the playoffs in each of his four seasons as head coach. ... Won three

Eastern Conference titles (1999, 2000, 2002) and guided the Liberty to the WNBA Championship Series. ... Spent six of his 19-year NBA coaching career at the helm of teams including Detroit, Dallas and Orlando. ... Prior to the NBA, spent 18 years as a high school and college coach in New Jersey, compiling an overall record of 290-85 (.771).

COLLEGIATE COACHING RECORD

Season Team	W	L	Pct.	Finish
72-73 —Upsala College	15	9	.625	—
73-74 —Upsala College	17	10	.630	—
74-75 —Upsala College	18	11	.621	—
75-76 —Upsala College	20	9	.690	—
76-77 —Upsala College	11	14	.440	—
77-78 —Upsala College	19	9	.679	—
Totals (6 years)	100	62	.617	

NBA COACHING RECORD

Season Team	W	L	Pct.	Finish	W	L	Pct.
79-80 —Detroit	12	58	.171	6th/Central Division	—	—	—
89-90 —Dallas	42	29	.592	3rd/Midwest Division	0	3	.000
90-91 —Dallas	28	54	.341	6th/Midwest Division	—	—	—
91-92 —Dallas	22	60	.268	5th/Midwest Division	—	—	—
96-97 —Orlando	21	12	.636	3rd/Atlantic Division	2	3	.400
Totals (5 years)	125	213	.370		2	6	.250

NOTES:
1990—Lost to Portland in Western Conference first round.
1997—Replaced Brian Hill as Orlando head coach (February 18), with record of 24-25 and club in third place. Lost to Miami in Eastern Conference first round.

WNBA COACHING RECORD

Season Team	W	L	Pct.	Finish	W	L	Pct.
1999 —New York	18	14	.563	1st/Eastern Conference	3	3	.500
2000 —New York	20	12	.625	1st/East	4	3	.571
2001 —New York	21	11	.656	2nd/East	3	3	.500
2002 —New York	18	14	.563	T1st/East	4	4	.500
2003 —New York	16	18	.471	T6th/East			
Totals (5 years)	93	69	.574		14	13	.519

NOTES:
1999—Defeated Charlotte, 2-1, in Eastern Conference Finals; lost to Houston, 2-1, in the Championship Series.
2000—Defeated Washington, 2-0, in first round; defeated Cleveland, 2-1, in Eastern Conference Finals; lost to Houston, 2-0, in WNBA Championship Series.
2001—Defeated Miami, 2-1, in first round; lost to Charlotte, 2-1, in Eastern Conference Finals.
2002—Defeated Indiana, 2-1, in first round; defeated Washington, 2-1, in Eastern Conferecen Finals; lost to Los Angeles, 2-0, in WNBA Finals.

BROWN, DEE   SILVER STARS

PERSONAL: Born November 29, 1968, in Jacksonville, FL ... Full Name: DeCovan Kadell Brown
HIGH SCHOOL: The Bolles School (Jacksonville, FL)
COLLEGE: Jacksonville
TRANSACTIONS/CAREER NOTES: Selected by Boston Celtics in first round (19th pick overall) of 1990 NBA Draft. ... Traded b Celtics with G Chauncey Billups, F John Thomas and F Roy Rogers to Toronto Raptors for G Kenny Anderson, C Zan Tabak and F Popeye Jones (February 18, 1998). ... Signed as free agent by Orlando Magic (August 3, 2000). ... Announced retirement (August 29, 2001). ... Signed by Magic to 10-day contract (March 12, 2002). ... Released by Magic (March 29, 2002).

COLLEGIATE RECORD

Season Team	G	Min.	FGM	FGA	Pct.	FTM	FTA	Pct.	Reb.	Ast.	Pts.	RPG	APG	PPG
86-87—Jacksonville	21	186	28	65	.431	13	22	.591	28	17	71	1.3	0.8	3.4
87-88—Jacksonville	28	764	108	239	.452	54	66	.818	125	56	282	4.5	2.0	10.1
88-89—Jacksonville	30	1133	219	447	.490	108	131	.824	228	112	589	7.6	3.7	19.6
89-90—Jacksonville	29	1052	231	466	.496	69	101	.683	192	151	561	6.6	5.2	19.3
Totals	108	3135	586	121 7	.482	244	320	.763	573	336	1503	5.3	3.1	13.9

Three-point field goals: 1986-87, 2-for-12 (.167). 1987-88, 12-for-45 (.267). 1988-89, 43-for-101 (.426). 1989-90, 30-for-80 (.375). Totals, 87-for-238 (.366).

NBA REGULAR-SEASON RECORD

HONORS: Slam Dunk championship winner (1991). ... NBA All-Rookie first team (1991).
NOTES: Led NBA with 135 three-point field goals made and 349 three-point field goals attempted (1999).

Season Team	G	Min.	FGM	FGA	Pct.	FTM	FTA	Pct.	Off.	Def.	Tot.	Ast.	St.	Blk.	TO	Pts.	RPG	APG	PPG
90-91—Boston	82	1945	284	612	.464	137	157	.873	41	141	182	344	83	14	137	712	2.2	4.2	8.7
91-92—Boston	31	883	149	350	.426	60	78	.769	15	64	79	164	33	7	59	363	2.5	5.3	11.7
92-93—Boston	80	2254	328	701	.468	192	242	.793	45	201	246	461	138	32	136	874	3.1	5.8	10.9
93-94—Boston	77	2867	490	1021	.480	182	219	.831	63	237	300	347	156	47	126	1192	3.9	4.5	15.5
94-95—Boston	79	2792	437	977	.447	236	277	.852	63	186	249	301	110	49	146	1236	3.2	3.8	15.6
95-96—Boston	65	1591	246	616	.399	135	158	.854	36	100	136	146	80	12	74	695	2.1	2.2	10.7
96-97—Boston	21	522	61	166	.367	18	22	.818	8	40	48	67	31	7	24	160	2.3	3.2	7.6
97-98—Bos.-Tor.	72	1719	246	562	.438	58	71	.817	24	128	152	154	82	23	73	658	2.1	2.1	9.1
98-99—Toronto	49	1377	187	495	.378	40	55	.727	15	88	103	143	56	8	80	549	2.1	2.9	11.2
99-00—Toronto	38	673	93	258	.360	11	16	.688	9	45	54	86	24	5	39	264	1.4	2.3	6.9
00-01—Orlando	7	155	16	44	.364	4	5	.800	0	11	11	12	4	0	7	48	1.6	1.7	6.9
Totals	601	16778	2537	5802	.437	1073	1300	.825	319	1241	1560	2225	797	204	901	6751	2.6	3.7	11.2

Three-point field goals: 1990-91, 7-for-34 (.206). 1991-92, 5-for-22 (.227). 1992-93, 26-for-82 (.317). 1993-94, 30-for-96 (.313). 1994-95, 126-for-327 (.385). 1995-96, 68-for-220 (.309). 1996-97, 20-for-65 (.308). 1997-98, 108-for-271 (.399). 1998-99, 135-for-349 (.387). 1999-00, 67-for-187 (.358). 1900-01, 12-for-32 (.375). Totals, 604-for-1685 (.358).

Personal fouls/disqualifications: 1990-91, 161/0. 1991-92, 74/0. 1992-93, 203/2. 1993-94, 207/3. 1994-95, 181/0. 1995-96, 119/0. 1996-97, 45/0. 1997-98, 123/1. 1998-99, 75/0. 1999-00, 62/1. 1900-01, 10/0. Totals, 1260/7.

NBA PLAYOFF RECORD

Season Team	G	Min.	FGM	FGA	Pct.	FTM	FTA	Pct.	Off.	Def.	Tot.	Ast.	St.	Blk.	TO	Pts.	RPG	APG	PPG
90-91—Boston 11	11	284	53	108	.491	28	34	.824	9	36	45	41	11	6	22	134	4.1	3.7	12.2
91-92—Boston 6	6	120	22	44	.500	4	6	.667	3	9	12	31	1	4	7	48	2.0	5.2	8.0
92-93—Boston 4	4	133	15	41	.366	14	141	.000	2	4	6	15	2	4	6	45	1.5	3.8	11.3
94-95—Boston 4	4	172	26	62	.419	14	16	.875	6	14	20	19	5	1	7	75	5.0	4.8	18.8
99-00—Toronto 3	3	19	0	4	.000	0	0	...	0	2	2	2	2	0	1	0	0.7	0.7	0.0
00-01—Orlando 3	3	54	6	13	.462	0	0	...	0	3	3	4	2	0	1	18	1.0	1.3	6.0
Totals 31	31	782	122	272	.449	60	70	.857	20	68	88	112	23	15	44	320	2.8	3.6	10.3

Three-point field goals: 1990-91, 0-for-5. 1991-92, 0-for-3. 1992-93, 1-for-7 (.143). 1994-95, 9-for-26 (.346). 1999-00, 0-for-3. 1900-01, 6-for-11 (.545). Totals, 16-for-55 (.291).

Personal fouls/disqualifications: 1990-91, 32/0. 1991-92, 16/2. 1992-93, 11/0. 1994-95, 13/1. 1999-00, 4/0. 1900-01, 3/0. Totals, 79/3.

WNBA COACHING RECORD

Season Team	W	L	Pct.	Finish	W	L	Pct.
2002 Orlando	16	16	.500	T4th/East	–	–	–

CHANCELLOR, VAN   COMETS

PERSONAL: Born September 17, 1943, in Louisville, Miss. ... Full Name: Winston Van Chancellor.
HIGH SCHOOL: Louisville (Miss.).
COLLEGE: Mississippi State (1965)..

HEAD COACHING RECORD

BACKGROUND: Head coach of the 2002 USA Basketball women's world championship team. ... Won WNBA Coach of the Year 1997, 1998, 1999. ... Led Comets to four consecutive championships (1997, 1998, 1999, 2000). ... Left Mississippi as the 16th all-time winningest women's college basketball coach. ... Led Mississippi to 14 NCAA Tournament appearances.

COLLEGIATE COACHING RECORD

Season Team	W	L	Pct.	Finish
78-79 —Mississippi	31	9	.775	—
79-80 —Mississippi	23	14	.622	—
80-81 —Mississippi	14	12	.538	—
81-82 —Mississippi	27	5	.844	—
82-83 —Mississippi	26	6	.813	—
83-84 —Mississippi	24	6	.800	—
84-85 —Mississippi	29	3	.906	—
85-86 —Mississippi	24	8	.750	—

Season Team	W	L	Pct.	Finish
86-87 —Mississippi	25	5	.833	—
87-88 —Mississippi	24	7	.774	—
88-89 —Mississippi	23	8	.742	—
89-90 —Mississippi	22	10	.688	—
90-91 —Mississippi	20	9	.690	—
91-92 —Mississippi	29	3	.906	—
92-93 —Mississippi	19	10	.655	—
93-94 —Mississippi	21	8	.724	—
94-95 —Mississippi	21	8	.724	—
95-96 —Mississippi	18	11	.621	—
96-97 —Mississippi	16	11	.593	—
Totals (19 years)	436	153	.740	

WNBA COACHING RECORD

Season Team	W	L	Pct.	Finish	W	L	Pct.
1997 —Houston...	18	10	.643	1st/East	2	0	1.000
1998 —Houston...	27	3	.900	1st/West	4	1	.800
1999 —Houston...	26	6	.813	1st/West	4	2	.667
2000 —Houston...	27	5	.844	2nd/West	6	0	1.000
2001 —Houston...	19	13	.594	T3rd/West	0	2	.000
2002 —Houston...	24	8	.750	2nd/West	1	2	.333
2003 —Houston...	20	14	.588	2nd/West	0	1	.000
Totals (7 years)	161	59	.731		17	8	.680

NOTES:

1997—Defeated Charlotte in semifinals; defeated New York in the WNBA Championship Game.
1998—Defeated Charlotte, 2-0, in semifinals; defeated Phoenix, 2-1, in the WNBA Championship Series.
1999—Defeated Los Angeles, 2-1, in conference finals; defeated New York, 2-1, in Championship Series.
2000—Defeated Sacramento, 2-0, in first round; defeated Los Angeles, 2-0, in Western Conference Finals; defeated New York, 2-0 in WNBA Championship.
2001—Lost to Los Angeles, 2-0, in first round.
2002—Lost to Utah, 2-1, in first round.
2003—Lost to Sacramento, 2-0, in first round.

COOPER, MICHAEL — SPARKS

PERSONAL: Born April 15, 1956, in Los Angeles. ... Full Name: Michael Jerome Cooper.
HIGH SCHOOL: Pasadena (Calif.).
COLLEGE: University of New Mexico (1978).
MISCELLANEOUS: Played 12 seasons with the Los Angeles Lakers, winning five NBA championships (1980, 1982, 1985, 1987, 1988). ... Compiled career averages of 8.9 ppg, 3.2 rpg and 4.2 apg. ... Five-time First Team All-Defense (1982, 1984, 1985, 1987, 1988). ... Named Defensive Player of the Year in 1987 ... Won J. Walter Kennedy Citizenship Award in 1986.

NBA REGULAR-SEASON RECORD

Season Team	G	Min.	FGM	FGA	Pct.	FTM	FTA	Pct.	Off.	Def.	Tot.	Ast.	St.	Blk.	TO	Pts.	RPG	APG	PPG
78-79—Los Angeles..	3	7	3	6	.500	0	0	...	0		0	0	1	0	...	6	0.0	0.0	2.0
79-80—Los Angeles..	82	1973	303	578	.524	111	143	.776	101	128	229	221	86	38	...	722	2.8	2.7	8.8
80-81—Los Angeles..	81	2625	321	654	.491	117	149	.785	121	215	336	332	133	78	...	763	4.1	4.1	9.4
81-82—Los Angeles..	76	2197	383	741	.517	139	171	.813	185	84	269	230	120	61	...	907	3.5	3.0	11.9
82-83—Los Angeles..	82	2148	266	497	.535	102	130	.785	82	192	274	315	115	50	...	639	3.3	3.8	7.8
83-84—Los Angeles..	82	2387	273	549	.497	155	185	.838	53	209	262	482	113	67	...	739	3.2	5.9	9.0
84-85—L.A. Lakers...	82	2189	276	593	.465	115	133	.865	56	199	255	429	93	49	...	702	3.1	5.2	8.6
85-86—L.A. Lakers...	82	2269	274	606	.452	147	170	.865	44	200	244	466	898	43	...	758	3.0	5.7	9.2
86-87—L.A. Lakers...	82	2253	322	736	.438	126	148	.851	58	196	254	373	78	43	...	859	3.1	4.5	10.5
87-88—L.A. Lakers...	61	1793	189	482	.392	97	113	.858	50	178	228	289	66	26	...	532	3.7	4.7	8.7
88-89—L.A. Lakers...	80	1943	213	494	.431	81	93	.871	33	158	191	314	72	32	...	587	2.4	3.9	7.3
89-90—L.A. Lakers...	80	1851	191	493	.387	83	94	.883	59	168	227	215	67	36	...	515	2.8	2.7	6.4
Totals.................	873	23635	3014	6429	.469	1273	1529	.833	842	...	2769	3666	1842	523	...	7729	3.2	4.2	8.9

Three-point field goals: 1979-80, 5-for-20 (.250). 1980-81, 4-for-19 (.211). 1981-82, 2-for-17 (.118). 1982-83, 5-for-21 (.238). 1983-84, 38-for-121 (.314). 1984-85, 35-for-123 (.285). 1985-86, 63-for-163 (.387). 1986-87, 89-for-231 (.385). 1987-88, 57-for-178 (.320). 1988-89, 80-for-210 (.381). 1989-90, 50-for-157 (.318). Totals, 428-for-1260 (.340).

Personal fouls/disqualifications: 1978-79, 1/0. 1979-80, 215/3. 1980-81, 249/4. 1981-82, 216/1. 1982-83, 208/. 1983-84, 267/3. 1984-85, 208/0. 1985-86, 238/2. 1986-87, 199/1. 1987-88, 136/1. 1988-89, 186/0. 1989-90, 206/1. Totals, 2329/16.

HEAD COACHING RECORD

BACKGROUND: Led Sparks to back-to-back WNBA Championships (2001, 2002). ... Named WNBA Coach of the Year (2000). ... Finished with all-time league-high 28-4 (.875) record in 2001 as Los Angeles topped the WNBA for second straight season.

WNBA COACHING RECORD

Season Team	W	L	Pct.	Finish	W	L	Pct.
2000 —Los Angeles	28	4	.875	1st/West	2	2	.500
2001 —Los Angeles	28	4	.875	1st/West	6	1	.857
2002 —Los Angeles	25	7	.781	1st/West	6	0	1.000
2003—Los Angeles	24	10	.706	1st/West	5	4	.555
Totals (4 years)	105	25	.808		19	7	.731

NOTES:
2000—Defeated Phoenix, 2-0, in first round; lost to Houston, 2-0, in Western Conference Playoffs.
2001—Defeated Houston, 2-0, in first round; defeated Sacramento, 2-1, in Western Conference Finals; defeated Charlotte, 2-0, in WNBA Finals.
2002—Defeated Seattle, 2-0, in first round; defeated Utah, 2-0, in Western Conference Finals; defeated New York, 2-0, in WNBA Finals.
2003—Defeated Minnesota, 2-1, in first round; defeated Sacramento, 2-1, in Western Conference Finals; lost to Detroit, 2-1, in WNBA Finals.

DONOVAN, ANNE — STORM

PERSONAL: Born November 1, 1961, in Ridgewood, N.J.
HIGH SCHOOL: Paramus Catholic (N.J.).
COLLEGE: Old Dominion (1983).
MISCELLANEOUS: Member of the gold medal-winning U.S. Olympic Teams in 1984 and 1988, as well the 1980 Olympic Team. ... One of only four male or female USA players to have been named to three Olympic squads. ... A member of 12 USA Basketball teams. ... Of a possible 11 medals, has won nine golds and two silvers. ... Inducted into the Naismith Memorial Basketball Hall of Fame in 1995. ... Inducted into the Women's Basketball Hall of Fame in 1999.

HEAD COACHING RECORD

BACKGROUND: Named Storm head coach on December 18, 2002, becoming the first coach in WNBA history to take the helm of three different teams — Indiana (2000), Charlotte (2001-02) and Seattle (2003-). ... Led Charlotte to the WNBA Finals in 2001 after beginning the season with a 1-10 record. ... Head coach of Philadelphia Rage of ABL (1998). ... Served as head coach at East Carolina for three seasons (1995-1998). ... Led Lady Pirates to Colonial Athletic Association Tournament championship game in 1997. ... Served as assistant coach for 1997 USA Women's World Championship Qualifying Team that earned a silver medal. ... One of the most accomplished players in college history, led Old Dominion University to a 37-1 record and the AIAW national title as a freshman. ... Named the Naismith and Champion Player of the Year in 1983 as well as an All-American in 1981, 1982 and 1983. ... Finished collegiate career as Lady Monarchs' all-time leading scorer (2,179), rebounder (1,976) and shot blocker (801). ... Holds 25 ODU records. ... Played professionally in Shizuoka, Japan (1984-88) and Modena, Italy (1989).

COLLEGIATE COACHING RECORD

Season Team	W	L	Pct.	Finish
95-96 —East Carolina	11	16	.407	—
96-97 —East Carolina	13	16	.448	—
97-98 —East Carolina	9	19	.321	—
Totals (3 years)	33	51	.393	

ABL COACHING RECORD

Season Team	W	L	Pct.	Finish
98-99 —Philadelphia	9	5	.643	—
Totals	9	5	.643	

WNBA COACHING RECORD

Season Team	W	L	Pct.	Finish	W	L	Pct.
2000—Indiana	9	23	.281	7th/East	—	—	—
2001—Charlotte	18	14	.563	4th/East	4	4	.500
2002—Charlotte	18	14	.563	T1st/East	0	2	.000
2003—Seattle	18	16	.529	T4th/West			
Totals (4 years)	63	67	.485		4	6	.400

NOTES:

2001—Defeated Cleveland, 2-1, in first round; defeated New York, 2-1, in Eastern Conference Finals; lost to Los Angeles, 2-0, in WNBA Finals.

2002—Lost to Washington, 2-0, in first round.

GRAF, CARRIE — MERCURY

PERSONAL: Born June 23, 1967, in Australia.
COLLEGE: RMIT in Melbourne, Australia

HEAD COACHING RECORD

BACKGROUND: Head Coach of the Canberra Capitals of Australia's WNBL (Women's National Basketball League) where she won the WNBL Championship in 2000 and 2002. She was also the head coach for the WNBL's Sydney Flames from 1993-96, where she won her first WNBL Championship in 1993. Was an assistant coach with Phoenix (1998, 1999, 2001 and 2003) as well as an assistant coach with the Seattle Storm in 2002.

AUSTRALIAN LEAGUE

Season Team	W	L	Pct.	W	L	Pct.
1993 Sydney Flames	17	1	.944	2	0	1.000
1994 Sydney Flames	14	4	.777	-	-	-
1995 Sydney Flames	16	2	.888	0	2	.000
1996 Sydney Flames	17	1	.944	1	1	.500
1999-00 Canberra Capitals	16	5	.762	2	1	.666
2000-01 Canberra Capitals	17	4	.809	1	1	.500
2001-02 Canberra Capitals	15	6	.714	2	0	1.000
2003-04 Canberra Capitals	13	8	.619	0	1	.000
Totals (8 seasons)	125	31	.801	8	6	.571

LACEY, TRUDI — STING

PERSONAL: Born December 12, 1958.
COLLEGE: North Carolina State.

COLLEGIATE COACHING RECORD

Season Team	W	L	Pct.
86-87—Francis Marion	30	6	.833
87-88—Francis Marion	23	6	.793
88-89—South Florida	14	13	.519
89-90—South Florida	10	17	.370
90-91—South Florida	12	16	.429
91-92—South Florida	13	15	.464
92-93—South Florida	10	17	.370
93-94—South Florida	14	13	.519
94-95—South Florida	7	19	.269
95-96—South Florida	6	21	.222
Totals (10 years)	139	143	.493

WNBA COACHING RECORD

Season Team	W	L	Pct.	Finish	W	L	Pct.
2003—Charlotte	18	16	.529	T2nd/East	0	2	.000
Totals (1 year)	18	16	.529		0	2	.000

NOTES:

2003—Lost to Connecticut, 2-0, in first round.

LAIMBEER, BILL   SHOCK

PERSONAL: Born May 19, 1957, in Boston. ... 6-11/260 (2,10/117,9). ... Full name: William Laimbeer Jr. ... Name pronounced lam-BEER.
HIGH SCHOOL: Palos Verdes (Calif.).
JUNIOR COLLEGE: Owens Technical (Ohio).
COLLEGE: Notre Dame.
TRANSACTIONS: Selected by Cleveland Cavaliers in third round (65th pick overall) of 1979 NBA Draft. ... Played in Italy (1979-80). ... Traded by Cavaliers with F Kenny Carr to Detroit Pistons for F Phil Hubbard, C Paul Mokeski and 1982 first- and second-round draft choices (February 16, 1982). ... Announced retirement (December 1, 1993).
CAREER NOTES: Special consultant, Detroit Shock, WNBA (April 18-June 19, 2002). ... Head coach, Detroit Shock (WNBA).
MISCELLANEOUS: Member of NBA championship team (1989, 1990). ... Detroit Pistons franchise all-time leading rebounder with 9,430 (1981-82 through 1993-94). ... Led Shock to championship (2003).

HEAD COACHING RECORD

BACKGROUND: Named WNBA Coach of the Year (2003) ... Led Shock to WNBA Championship (2003).

COLLEGIATE RECORD

Season Team	G	Min.	FGM	FGA	Pct.	FTM	FTA	Pct.	Reb.	Ast.	Pts.	RPG	APG	PPG
76-77—Owens Tech...............						Did not play.								
75-76—Notre Dame..............	10	190	32	65	.492	18	23	.783	79	10	82	7.9	1.0	8.2
77-78—Notre Dame..............	29	654	97	175	.554	42	62	.677	190	31	236	6.6	1.1	8.1
78-79—Notre Dame..............	30	614	78	145	.538	35	50	.700	164	30	191	5.5	1.0	6.4
Totals	69	1458	207	385	.538	95	135	.704	433	71	509	6.3	1.0	7.4

ITALIAN LEAGUE RECORD

Season Team	G	Min.	FGM	FGA	Pct.	FTM	FTA	Pct.	Reb.	Ast.	Pts.	RPG	APG	PPG
79-80—Brescia......................	29	...	258	465	.555	97	124	.782	363	...	613	12.5	...	21.1

NBA REGULAR-SEASON RECORD

Season Team	G	Min.	FGM	FGA	Pct.	FTM	FTA	Pct.	Off.	Def.	Tot.	Ast.	St.	Blk.	TO	Pts.	RPG	APG	PPG
80-81—Cleveland	81	2460	337	670	.503	117	153	.765	266	427	693	216	56	78	132	791	8.6	2.7	9.8
81-82—Clev.-Det.....	80	1829	265	536	.494	184	232	.793	234	383	617	100	39	64	121	718	7.7	1.3	9.0
82-83—Detroit	82	2871	436	877	.497	245	310	.790	282	711	993	263	51	118	176	1119	12.1	3.2	13.6
83-84—Detroit	82	2864	553	1044	.530	316	365	.866	329	674*1003	149	49	84	151	1422	12.2	1.8	17.3	
84-85—Detroit	82	2892	595	1177	.506	244	306	.797	295	718	1013	154	69	71	129	1438	12.4	1.9	17.5
85-86—Detroit	82	2891	545	1107	.492	266	319	.834	305	*770*1075	146	59	65	133	1360	*13.1	1.8	16.6	
86-87—Detroit	82	2854	506	1010	.501	245	274	.894	243	712	955	151	72	69	120	1263	11.6	1.8	15.4
87-88—Detroit	82	2897	455	923	.493	187	214	.874	165	667	832	199	66	78	136	1110	10.1	2.4	13.5
88-89—Detroit	81	2640	449	900	.499	178	212	.840	138	638	776	177	51	100	129	1106	9.6	2.2	13.7
89-90—Detroit	81	2675	380	785	.484	164	192	.854	166	614	780	171	57	84	98	981	9.6	2.1	12.1
90-91—Detroit	82	2668	372	778	.478	123	147	.837	173	564	737	157	38	56	98	904	9.0	1.9	11.0
91-92—Detroit	81	2234	342	727	.470	67	75	.893	104	347	451	160	51	54	102	783	5.6	2.0	9.7
92-93—Detroit	79	1933	292	574	.509	93	104	.894	110	309	419	127	46	40	59	687	5.3	1.6	8.7
93-94—Detroit	11	248	47	90	.522	11	13	.846	9	47	56	14	6	4	10	108	5.1	1.3	9.8
Totals................	1068	33956	5574	11198	.498	2440	2916	.837	2819	7581104002184	710	965	159413790	9.7	2.0	12.9		

Three-point field goals: 1981-82, 4-for-13 (.308). 1982-83, 2-for-13 (.154). 1983-84, 0-for-11. 1984-85, 4-for-18 (.222). 1985-86, 4-for-14 (.286). 1986-87, 6-for-21 (.286). 1987-88, 13-for-39 (.333). 1988-89, 30-for-86 (.349). 1989-90, 57-for-158 (.361). 1990-91, 37-for-125 (.296). 1991-92, 32-for-85 (.376). 1992-93, 10-for-27 (.370). 1993-94, 3-for-9 (.333). Totals, 202-for-619 (.326).
Personal fouls/disqualifications: 1980-81, 332/14. 1981-82, 296/5. 1982-83, 320/9. 1983-84, 273/4. 1984-85, 308/4. 1985-86, 291/4. 1986-87, 283/4. 1987-88, 284/6. 1988-89, 259/2. 1989-90, 278/4. 1990-91, 242/3. 1991-92, 225/0. 1992-93, 212/4. 1993-94, 30/0. Totals, 3633/63.

NBA PLAYOFF RECORD

NOTES: Shares NBA Finals single-game record for most points in an overtime period—9 (June 7, 1990, vs. Portland).

Season Team	G	Min.	FGM	FGA	Pct.	FTM	FTA	Pct.	Off.	Def.	Tot.	Ast.	St.	Blk.	TO	Pts.	RPG	APG	PPG
83-84—Detroit	5	165	29	51	.569	18	20	.900	14	48	62	12	4	3	12	76	12.4	2.4	15.2
84-85—Detroit	9	325	48	107	.449	36	51	.706	36	60	96	15	7	7	16	132	10.7	1.7	14.7
85-86—Detroit	4	168	34	68	.500	21	23	.913	20	36	56	1	2	3	8	90	14.0	0.3	22.5
86-87—Detroit	15	543	84	163	.515	15	24	.625	30	126	156	37	15	12	20	184	10.4	2.5	12.3
87-88—Detroit	23	779	114	250	.456	40	45	.889	43	178	221	44	18	19	30	273	9.6	1.9	11.9
88-89—Detroit	17	497	66	142	.465	25	31	.806	26	114	140	31	6	8	19	172	8.2	1.8	10.1
89-90—Detroit	20	667	91	199	.457	25	29	.862	41	170	211	28	23	18	16	222	10.6	1.4	11.1
90-91—Detroit	15	446	66	148	.446	27	31	.871	42	80	122	19	5	12	17	164	8.1	1.3	10.9
91-92—Detroit	5	145	17	46	.370	5	5	1.000	5	28	33	8	4	1	5	41	6.6	1.6	8.2
Totals................	113	3735	549	1174	.468	212	259	.819	257	840	1097	195	84	83	143	1354	9.7	1.7	12.0

Three-point field goals: 1984-85, 0-for-2. 1985-86, 1-for-1. 1986-87, 1-for-5 (.200). 1987-88, 5-for-17 (.294). 1988-89, 15-for-42 (.357). 1989-90, 15-for-43 (.349). 1990-91, 5-for-17 (.294). 1991-92, 2-for-10 (.200). Totals, 44-for-137 (.321).
Personal fouls/disqualifications: 1983-84, 23/2. 1984-85, 32/1. 1985-86, 19/1. 1986-87, 53/2. 1987-88, 77/2. 1988-89, 55/1. 1989-90, 77/3. 1990-91, 54/0. 1991-92, 18/1. Totals, 408/13.

HEAD COACHES

NBA ALL-STAR GAME RECORD

Season Team	Min.	FGM	FGA	Pct.	FTM	FTA	Pct.	REBOUNDS Off.	Def.	Tot.	Ast.	PF	Dq.	St.	Blk.	TO	Pts.
1983—Detroit..............	6	1	1	1.000	0	0	...	1	0	1	0	1	0	0	0	1	2
1984—Detroit..............	17	6	8	.750	1	1	1.000	1	4	5	0	3	0	1	2	0	13
1985—Detroit..............	11	2	4	.500	1	2	.500	1	2	3	1	1	0	0	0	0	5
1987—Detroit..............	11	4	7	.571	0	0	...	0	2	2	1	2	0	1	0	0	8
Totals.........................	45	13	20	.650	2	3	.667	3	8	11	2	7	0	2	2	1	28

WNBA COACHING RECORD

Season Team	W	L	Pct.	Finish	W	L	Pct.
2002—Detroit..	9	13	.409	8th/West	—	—	—
2003—Detroit..	25	9	.735	1st/East	6	2	.750
Totals (2 years)...	34	22	.607		6	2	.750

NOTES:
2003—Defeated Houston, 2-1, in first round; defeated Connecticut, 2-0, in Eastern Conference Finals; defeated Los Angeles, 2-1, in WNBA Finals.

McCONNELL SERIO, SUZIE　　LYNX

PERSONAL: Born July 29, 1966, in Pittsburgh, Pa. ... Full Name: Suzanne Theresa McConnell Serio.
HIGH SCHOOL: Seton LaSalle (Pittsburgh, Pa.).
COLLEGE: Penn State.
TRANSACTIONS/CAREER NOTES: Selected by Cleveland in second round (16th overall) of WNBA Draft, April 29, 1998.

COLLEGIATE RECORD
NOTES: Kodak All-America first team (1988). ... Naismith Award for small player of year (1988).

Season Team	G	Min.	FGM	FGA	Pct.	FTM	FTA	Pct.	Reb.	Ast.	Pts.	AVERAGES RPG	APG	PPG
84-85—Penn State.................	33	...	157	343	.458	101	136	.743	93	321	415	2.8	9.7	12.6
85-86—Penn State.................	32	...	148	335	.442	86	109	.789	94	338	382	2.9	10.6	11.9
86-87—Penn State.................	30	...	169	337	.501	68	94	.723	141	355	418	4.7	11.8	13.9
87-88—Penn State.................	33	...	255	511	.499	116	143	.811	165	293	682	5.0	8.9	20.7
Totals.................................	128	...	729	1526	.478	371	482	.770	493	1307	1897	3.9	10.2	14.8

Three-point field goals: 1986-87, 12-for-41 (.293). 1987-88, 56-for-140 (.400). Totals, 68-for-181 (.376).

OLYMPICS
NOTES: Member of gold medal-winning U.S. Olympic team (1988) and bronze medal-winning U.S. Olympic team (1992).

Season Team	G	Min.	FGM	FGA	Pct.	FTM	FTA	Pct.	Reb.	Ast.	Pts.	AVERAGES RPG	APG	PPG
1988—United States..............	5	...	13	25	.520	11	12	.917	4	11	42	0.8	2.2	8.4
1988—United States..............	5	...	13	25	.520	11	12	.917	4	11	42	0.8	2.2	8.4
1992—United States..............	5	...	14	39	.359	1	2	.500	5	18	34	1.0	3.6	6.8
1992—United States..............	5	...	14	39	.359	1	2	.500	5	18	34	1.0	3.6	6.8
Totals.................................	20	...	54	128	.422	24	28	.857	18	58	152	0.9	2.9	7.6

Three-point field goals: 1988-89, 5-for-7 (.714). 1988-89, 5-for-7 (.714). 1992-93, 5-for-19 (.263). 1992-93, 5-for-19 (.263). Totals, 20-for-52 (.385).

WNBA REGULAR-SEASON RECORD
HONORS: WNBA Newcomer of year (1998). ... WNBA Sportsmanship Award (1998, 2000). ... All-WNBA first team (1998).

Season Team	G	Min.	FGM	FGA	Pct.	FTM	FTA	Pct.	REBOUNDS Off.	Def.	Tot.	Ast.	St.	Blk.	TO	Pts.	AVERAGES RPG	APG	PPG
1998—Cleveland......	28	882	80	176	.455	51	70	.729	8	54	62	178	49	5	104	240	2.2	6.4	8.6
1999—Cleveland......	18	511	36	98	.367	16	19	.842	4	39	43	76	10	2	54	108	2.4	4.2	6.0
2000—Cleveland......	32	705	58	140	.414	19	25	.760	9	41	50	119	15	1	69	173	1.6	3.7	5.4
Totals.................	78	2098	174	414	.420	86	114	.754	21	134	155	373	74	8	227	521	2.0	4.8	6.7

Three-point field goals: 1998, 29-for-71 (.408). 1999, 20-for-60 (.333). 2000, 38-for-97 (.392). Totals, 87-for-228 (.382)
Personal fouls/disqualifications: 1998, 48/0. 1999, 31/0. 2000, 30/0. Totals, 109/0.

WNBA PLAYOFF RECORD

Season Team	G	Min.	FGM	FGA	Pct.	FTM	FTA	Pct.	REBOUNDS Off.	Def.	Tot.	Ast.	St.	Blk.	TO	Pts.	AVERAGES RPG	APG	PPG
1998—Cleveland......	3	99	7	14	.500	2	3	.667	3	4	7	15	8	1	9	19	2.3	5.0	6.3
2000—Cleveland......	6	147	14	45	.311	2	2	1.000	3	11	14	25	5	1	16	39	2.3	4.2	6.5
Totals.................	9	246	21	59	.356	4	5	.800	6	15	21	40	13	2	25	58	2.3	4.4	6.4

Three-point field goals: 1998, 3-for-7 (.429). 2000, 9-for-36 (.250). Totals, 12-for-43 (.279)
Personal fouls/disqualifications: 1998, 9/0. 2000, 5/0. Totals, 14/0.

WNBA COACHING RECORD

Season Team	W	L	Pct.	Finish	W	L	Pct.
2003—Minnesota...	18	16	.529	T4th/West	1	2	.333
Totals (1 year)...	63	67	.485				

THIBAULT, MIKE   SUN

PERSONAL: Born September 28, 1950, in St. Paul, Minn. ... Full Name: Michael Francis Thibault.
HIGH SCHOOL: Bellarmine College Prep (San Jose, Calif.).
COLLEGE: St. Martin's College (Lacey, Wash.).

HEAD COACHING RECORD

BACKGROUND: Named head coach of Connecticut Sun on March 7, 2003. ... A 34-year coaching veteran. ... Joined the NBA as a scount for the Los Angeles Lakers in 1978. ... Has worked in various capacities for a number of NBA teams, including as an assistant coach/director of scouting for the Los Angeles Lakers (1978-82)-winning NBA Championships in '80 and '82-and the Chicago Bulls (1982-86), and as an assistant coach for the Milwaukee Bucks (1998-2002). ... Named World Basketball League Coach of the Year in 1988 during his one-year tenure as head coach of the Calgary 88's (record unavailable).

CBA COACHING RECORD

Season Team	W	L	Pct.	Finish
89-90 —Omaha	29	27	.518	—
90-91 —Omaha	39	17	.696	—
91-92 —Omaha	37	19	.661	—
92-93 —Omaha	28	28	.500	—
93-94 —Omaha	30	26	.536	—
94-95 —Omaha	26	30	.464	—
95-96 —Omaha	28	28	.500	—
96-97 —Omaha	22	34	.393	—
Totals (8 years)	239	209	.533	

NOTES:
1993—Defeated Grand Rapids, 4-2, in CBA Finals.
1994—Lost to Quad City, 4-1, in CBA Finals.

WNBA COACHING RECORD

Season Team	W	L	Pct.	Finish	W	L	Pct.
2003—Connecticut	18	16	.529	T2nd/East	2	2	.500
Totals (1 year)	63	67	.485		2	2	.500

NOTES:
2003—Defeated Charlotte, 2-0, in first round; lost to Detroit, 2-0, in Eastern Conference Finals.

WHISENANT, JOHN   MONARCHS

PERSONAL: Born June 18, 1945, in Gore, Okla. ... Full Name: John H. Whisenant
HIGH SCHOOL: Gore High School (Gore, Okla.)
COLLEGE: New Mexico State

HEAD COACHING RECORD

BACKGROUND: Named head coach of Sacramento Monarchs on July 10, 2003. ... More than 30 years of basketball experience including his role as head coach (51-35 record) and vice president of basketball operations for the New Mexico Slam (IBL/CBA).

IBL/CBA COACHING RECORD

Season Team	W	L	Pct.
New Mexico Slam	39	23	.629
New Mexico Slam	12	12	.500
Totals (2 seasons)	51	35	.593

COLLEGE COACHING RECORD

Season Team	W	L	Pct.
1968 -1972 Arizona Western (Yuma)			
Totals (4 seasons)	97	30	.763

WNBA COACHING RECORD

Season Team	W	L	Pct.	W	L	Pct.
2003 Sacramento	12	4	.750	3	3	.500

Notes:
2003 – Defeated Houston, 2-1, in first round; lost to Los Angeles, 2-1, in Western Conference Finals.

WINTERS, BRIAN FEVER

PERSONAL: Born March 1, 1952, in Rockaway, N.Y. ... Full Name: Brian Joseph Winters.
HIGH SCHOOL: Archbishop Molloy (Queens, N.Y.)
COLLEGE: South Carolina.
TRANSACTIONS/CAREER NOTES: Selected by Los Angeles Lakers in first round (12th pick overall) of 1974 NBA Draft. ... Traded by Lakers with C Elmore Smith, F/C Dave Meyers and F/G Junior Bridgeman to Milwaukee Bucks for C Kareem Abdul-Jabbar and C Walt Wesley (June 16, 1975).

NBA COACHING RECORD

Season	Team		Regular Season					Playoffs		
			W	L	Pct.	Finish		W	L	Pct.
1995-96	Vancouver		15	67	.183	7th/Midwest Div		–	–	–
1997	Vancouver		8	35	.186					
2001-02	Golden State		13	46	.220	7th/Pacific Div.		–	–	–
	Totals (3 seasons)		36	148	.196					

COLLEGIATE RECORD

Season Team	G	Min.	FGM	FGA	Pct.	FTM	FTA	Pct.	Reb.	Ast.	Pts.	RPG	APG	PPG
70-71 S. Carolina	16	...	138	299	.462	92	108	.852	156	69	368	9.8	4.3	23.0
71-72 S. Carolina	29	692	90	175	.514	60	71	.845	82	55	240	2.8	1.9	8.3
72-73 S. Carolina	26	834	120	258	.465	59	81	.728	164	69	299	6.3	2.7	11.5
73-74 S. Carolina	27	1016	229	446	.513	82	100	.820	85	68	540	3.1	2.5	20.0
Totals	**82**	**2542**	**439**	**879**	**.499**	**201**	**252**	**.798**	**331**	**192**	**1079**	**4.0**	**2.3**	**13.2**

NBA REGULAR-SEASON RECORD

Season Team	G	Min.	FGM	FGA	Pct.	FTM	FTA	Pct.	Off.	Def.	Tot.	Ast.	St.	Blk.	TO	Pts.	RPG	APG	PPG
74-75 Los Angeles	68	1516	359	810	.443	76	92	.826	39	99	138	195	74	18	...	794	2.0	2.9	11.7
75-76 Milwaukee	78	2795	618	1333	.464	180	217	.830	66	183	249	366	124	25	...	1416	3.2	4.7	18.2
76-77 Milwaukee	78	2717	652	1308	.498	206	242	.847	64	173	337	114	29	...	1509	3.0	4.3	19.3
77-78 Milwaukee	80	2751	674	1457	.463	246	293	.840	87	163	250	393	124	27	236	1594	3.1	4.9	19.9
78-79 Milwaukee	79	2575	662	1343	.493	237	277	.856	48	129	177	383	83	40	257	1561	2.2	4.8	19.8
79-80 Milwaukee	80	2623	535	1116	.479	184	214	.860	48	175	233	362	101	28	186	1292	2.8	4.5	16.2
80-81 Milwaukee	69	1771	331	697	.475	119	137	.869	32	108	140	185	70	10	136	799	2.0	2.7	11.6
81-82 Milwaukee	61	1829	404	806	.501	123	156	.788	51	119	170	253	57	9	118	967	2.8	4.1	15.9
82-83 Milwaukee	57	1361	255	587	.434	73	85	.859	35	75	110	156	45	4	81	605	1.9	2.7	10.6
Totals	**650**	**19938**	**4490**	**9457**	**.475**	**1443**	**1713**	**.842**	**470**	**1218**	**1688**	**2630**	**792**	**190**	**1014**	**10537**	**2.6**	**4.0**	**16.2**

Three-point field goals: 1979-80, 38-for-102 (.373). 1980-81, 18-for-51 (.353). 1981-82, 36-for-93 (.387). 1982-83, 22-for-68 (.324). Totals, 114-for-314 (.363).

Personal fouls/disqualifications: 1974-75, 168/1. 1975-76, 240/0. 1976-77, 228/1. 1977-78, 139/4. 1978-79, 243/1. 1979-80, 208/0. 1980-81, 185/2. 1981-82, 187/1. 1982-82, 132/2. Totals, 1830/12.

NBA PLAYOFF RECORD

Season Team	G	Min.	FGM	FGA	Pct.	FTM	FTA	Pct.	Off.	Def.	Tot.	Ast.	St.	Blk.	TO	Pts.	RPG	APG	PPG
75-76 Milwaukee	3	126	39	62	.629	4	5	.800	3	4	7	15	5	2	...	82	2.3	5.0	27.3
76-77 Milwaukee	9	305	82	165	.497	20	27	.741	26	4	30	58	12	8	...	184	3.3	6.4	20.4
79-80 Milwaukee	7	268	46	100	.460	10	10	1.00	4	17	21	37	11	0	...	111	3.0	5.3	15.9
80-81 Milwaukee	7	181	28	61	.459	12	16	.750	4	19	23	22	10	1	...	70	3.3	3.1	10.0
81-82 Milwaukee	6	232	38	77	.494	20	24	.833	4	11	15	28	8	1	...	101	2.5	4.7	16.8
82-83 Milwaukee	9	240	36	84	.429	14	17	.824	7	15	22	32	6	4	...	89	2.4	3.6	9.9
Totals	**41**	**1352**	**269**	**549**	**.490**	**80**	**99**	**.808**	**48**	**70**	**118**	**192**	**52**	**16**	**123**	**637**	**2.9**	**4.7**	**15.5**

Three-point field goals: 1979-80. 9-for-21 (.429). 1980-81, 2-for-6 (.333). 1981-82, 5-for-10 (.500). 1982-83, 3-for-11 (.273). Totals, 19-for-48 (.396).

Personal fouls/disqualifications: 1975-76, 11/1. 1977-78, 20/0. 1979-80, 25/1. 1980-81, 22/1. 1981-82, 23/0. 1982-83, 22/0. Totals, 123/3.

NBA ALL-STAR GAME RECORD

Season Team	Min.	FGM	FGA	Pct.	FTM	FTA	Pct.	Off.	Def.	Tot.	Ast.	PF	St.	Blk.	TO	Pts.
1977 —Milwaukee	16	1	5	.200	0	0	...	0	2	2	1	2	1	0	...	2
1979 —Milwaukee	14	4	7	.571	0	0	...	2	2	4	1	2	0	0	...	8
Totals	**30**	**5**	**12**	**.417**	**0**	**0**	**...**	**2**	**4**	**6**	**2**	**4**	**1**	**0**	**10**	

HEAD COACHES